Investment Analysis & Portfolio Management

ELEVENTH EDITION

FRANK K. REILLY
University of Notre Dame

KEITH C. BROWN
University of Texas at Austin

SANFORD J. LEEDS
University of Texas at Austin

CENGAGE

Australia • Brazil • Canada • Mexico • Singapore • United Kingdom • United States

Investment Analysis & Portfolio Management, Eleventh Edition
Frank K. Reilly, Keith C. Brown, and Sanford J. Leeds

Executive Product Director: Mike Schenk

Sr. Product Team Manager: Joe Sabatino

Project Manager: Julie Dierig

Content Developer:
Erica Longenbach, MPS

Product Assistant: Renee Schnee

Sr. Marketing Manager: Nathan Anderson

Digital Content Specialist: Timothy Ross

Digital Production Project Manager:
Scott Fidler

Manufacturing Planner: Kevin Kluck

Intellectual Property Analyst: Ann Hoffman

Intellectual Property Project Manager:
Erika Mugavin

Sr. Art Director: Michelle Kunkler

Cover Image Credit: Revers / ShutterStock.com

Cover Designer: Whirligig Studio/Kristina Mose-Libon

Internal Designer: Lou Ann Thesing

Production Management, and Composition: Lumina Datamatics, Inc.

For product information and technology assistance, contact us at
Cengage Customer & Sales Support, 1-800-354-9706.

For permission to use material from this text or product,
submit all requests online at **www.cengage.com/permissions.**
Further permissions questions can be emailed to
permissionrequest@cengage.com.

Library of Congress Control Number: 2018930283

ISBN-13: 978-1-305-26299-7

Cengage
200 Pier 4 Boulevard
Boston, MA 02210
USA

Cengage is a leading provider of customized learning solutions with employees residing in nearly 40 different countries and sales in more than 125 countries around the world. Find your local representative at **www.cengage.com**.

To learn more about Cengage platforms and services, register or access your online learning solution, or purchase materials for your course, visit **www.cengage.com**.

Printed in the United States of America
Print Number: 06   Print Year: 2022

To my best friend & wife,
Therese,
and the greatest gifts and
sources of our happiness,
Frank K. III, Charlotte, and Lauren
Clarence R. II, Michelle, Sophie, and Cara
Therese B. and Denise Z.
Edgar B., Lisa, Kayleigh, Madison J. T., Francesca, and Alessandra
—F. K. R.

To Sheryl, Alexander, and Andrew, who make it all worthwhile
—K. C. B.

To Jenny, Jay, John, and Genet, who bring meaning and happiness to my life.
—S. J. L.

Brief Contents

Contents

PART 2 Developments in Investment Theory 123

PART 3 Valuation and Management of Common Stocks 249

The pleasure of authoring a textbook comes from writing about a subject that we enjoy and find exciting. As authors, we hope that we can pass on to the reader not only knowledge but also the excitement that we feel for the topic. In addition, writing about investments brings an added stimulant because the subject can affect the reader during his or her entire business career and beyond. We hope that what readers derive from this course will help them enjoy better lives through managing their financial resources properly.

The purpose of this book is to help you learn how to manage your money so you will derive the maximum benefit from what you earn. To accomplish this purpose, you need to learn about the many investment alternatives that are available today and, what is more important, to develop a way of analyzing and thinking about investments that will remain with you in the years ahead when new and different investment opportunities become available.

Because of its dual purpose, the book mixes description and theory. The descriptive material discusses available investment instruments and considers the purpose and operation of capital markets in the United States and around the world. The theoretical portion details how you should evaluate current investments and future opportunities to develop a portfolio of investments that will satisfy your risk–return objectives. We feel that this marriage of theory and practice in the exposition will serve you quite well in both your professional careers and personal lives as investors.

Preparing this 11th edition has been challenging for at least two reasons. First, we continue to experience rapid changes in the securities markets in terms of theory, new financial instruments, innovative trading practices, and the effects of significant macroeconomic disruptions and the numerous regulatory changes that inevitably follow. Second, capital markets are continuing to become very global in nature. Consequently, to ensure that you are prepared to function in a global environment, almost every chapter discusses how investment practice or theory is influenced by the globalization of investments and capital markets. This completely integrated treatment is meant to ensure that you develop a broad mindset on investments that will serve you well in the 21st century.

Intended Market

This text is addressed to both graduate and advanced undergraduate students who are looking for an in-depth discussion of investments and portfolio management. The presentation of the material is intended to be rigorous and empirical, without being overly quantitative. A proper discussion of the modern developments in investments and portfolio theory must be rigorous. The discussion of numerous empirical studies reflects the belief that it is essential for alternative investment theories to be exposed to the real world and be judged on the basis of how well they help us understand and explain reality.

Key Features of the 11th Edition

When planning the 11th edition of *Investment Analysis and Portfolio Management*, we wanted to retain its traditional strengths and capitalize on new developments in the investments area to make it the most comprehensive and accessible investments textbook available. To achieve that goal, we have made a number of modifications to this edition.

First and foremost, we have considerably streamlined our presentation of the material from previous editions. Most notably, we have been able to compress our treatment of these important topics into 18 chapters, compared to the 25 chapters contained in the 10th edition. Importantly, we have not removed any content that we consider vital to a thorough understanding of investment management; rather, we have condensed and rearranged our presentations in a more effective way. An example of this is the section on equity valuation and management, which previously spanned six separate chapters but now is contained in Chapters 8–11.

Second, the current edition maintains its unparalleled international coverage. Investing knows no borders, and although the total integration of domestic and global investment opportunities may seem to contradict the need for separate discussions of international issues, it in fact makes the need for specific information on non-U.S. markets, instruments, conventions, and techniques even more compelling.

Third, both technology and regulations have caused more significant changes during the past decade in the functioning and organization of global security markets than during the prior 50 years. Chapter 3 contains a detailed discussion of this evolution and the results for global markets, and Chapter 2 describes how specific security innovations and asset allocation practices have been affected by these changes.

Fourth, today's investing environment includes derivative securities not as exotic anomalies but as standard investment instruments. We felt that *Investment Analysis and Portfolio Management* must reflect that reality. Consequently, our three chapters on derivatives (Chapters 14–16) are written to provide the reader with an intuitive, clear discussion of the different instruments, their markets, valuation, trading strategies, and general use as risk management and return enhancement tools.

Finally, we have updated and expanded the set of questions and problems at the end of each chapter to provide more student practice on executing computations concerned with more sophisticated investment problems. These problems are also available in an interactive format through the online resource described below.

Major Content Changes in the 11th Edition

The text has been thoroughly updated for currency as well as condensed for the sake of brevity. In addition to these time-related revisions, we have also made the following specific changes to individual chapters:

Chapter 1 This introductory discussion has been revised and updated to reflect recent changes in financial market conditions that impact the investment setting.

Chapter 2 This chapter has been completely reworked to combine the discussions of the asset allocation process and the global security markets that had been spread over multiple chapters in previous editions. After establishing the importance of the asset allocation decision to all investors, we focus on the notion of global diversification and provide an updated study on the variety of investment instruments available for the use of global investors, including global index funds and country-specific exchange-traded funds (ETFs).

Chapter 3 Because of the continuing growth in trading volume handled by electronic communications networks (ECNs), this chapter continues to detail the significant changes in the market as well as the results of this new environment. This includes a discussion on the continuing changes on the NYSE during recent years. We also consider the rationale for the continuing consolidation of global exchanges across asset classes of stocks, bonds, and derivatives. In addition, we document recent mergers and discuss several proposed and failed mergers. Finally, we note that the corporate bond market continues to experience major changes in how and when trades are reported and the number of bond issues involved.

Chapter 4 This chapter contains a discussion of fundamental weighted stock and bond indexes that use sales and earnings to weight components rather than market value. Also included is an updated analysis of the relationship among indexes and the myriad ways that investors can actually commit their financial capital to capture the returns on various indexes.

Chapter 5 New studies that both support the efficient market hypothesis and provide new evidence of anomalies are examined in this chapter. There is also discussion of behavioral finance and how it explains many of the anomalies, as well as a consideration of technical analysis. Further, we discuss the implications of the recent changes in the cost of trading (considered in Chapter 3) on some of the empirical results of prior studies.

Chapter 6 The development of modern portfolio theory, starting with a discussion of the risk tolerance of the investor, has been considerably revised and updated in an effort to stress the conceptual nature of the portfolio formation process. An extensive example of global portfolio optimization has also been included. The chapter now concludes with an intuitive discussion of the transition from Markowitz portfolio analysis to capital market theory and the development of the capital market line (CML).

Chapter 7 This chapter has been extensively revised to consider the topic of how asset pricing models evolved conceptually and how they are used by investors in practice. We begin with an extensive discussion of the capital asset pricing model (CAPM) in a more intuitive way, including how this model represents a natural progression from modern portfolio theory. We then describe the theory and practice of using multifactor models of risk and expected return. The connection between the arbitrage pricing theory (APT) and empirical implementations of the APT continues to be stressed, both conceptually and with several revised examples using style classification data.

Chapter 8 This is the first of three entirely new chapters focusing on equity analysis and valuation. We begin with a discussion of how valuation theory is used in practice. We distinguish between valuing the equity portion of the firm (FCFE) and valuing the entire firm (FCFF). Importantly, we show how the sustainable growth formula can be used to estimate the percentage of earnings that can be considered to be free cash flow. In the section on relative valuation, we focus on fundamental multiples so that students will consider the underlying drivers of value.

Chapter 9 This chapter presents a study of the top-down approach to equity analysis and introduces new material designed to link monetary policy and interest rates to stock prices. Most importantly, we describe the importance of the real federal funds rate, the shape of the yield curve, and the risk premium for BBB bonds (versus Treasury bonds). Later in the chapter, we discuss how the Shiller P/E ratio (also known as the cyclically adjusted price–earnings [CAPE] ratio) is applied to the overall market.

Chapter 10 In this completely new chapter we discuss several topics that students need to understand if they intend to enter the asset management industry as a profession. We provide a detailed description of the IPO process, the difference between the buy-side and sell-side, and the importance of management's capital allocation function. The chapter ends with a discussion of how to design and deliver a persuasive stock pitch.

Chapter 11 This chapter contains an enhanced discussion of the relative merits of passive versus active management techniques for equity portfolio management, focusing on the important role of tracking error. Expanded material on forming risk factor–based equity portfolios has been introduced, along with additional analysis of other equity portfolio investment strategies, including fundamental and technical approaches, as well as a detailed description of equity style analysis.

Chapter 12 This is the first of two new chapters that describe the information, tools, and techniques necessary to analyze fixed-income securities and portfolios. We begin with a discussion of the myriad bond instruments available to global investors, including traditional fixed-coupon securities from sovereign and corporate issuers, securities issued by government-sponsored entities (GSEs), collateralized debt obligations (CDOs), and auction-rate securities. We then develop the intuition and mechanics for how bonds are valued under a variety of market conditions, as well as the relationship that must exist between bond prices and bond yields.

Chapter 13 We continue our development of the quantitative toolkit required of successful bond investors by developing the technical concepts of implied forward rates, duration, and convexity. In particular, we discuss the importance of the duration statistic as a measure of price volatility in terms of both designing and managing bond portfolios. The discussion at the end of the chapter on bond portfolio management strategies has been enhanced and revised to include comparisons of active and passive fixed-income strategies, as well as updated examples of how the bond immunization process functions.

Chapter 14 Expanded discussions of the fundamentals associated with using derivative securities (interpreting price quotations, basic payoff diagrams, basic strategies) are included in this chapter. We also provide updated examples of both basic and intermediate risk management applications using derivative positions, as well as new material on how these contracts trade in the marketplace.

Chapter 15 New and updated examples and applications are provided throughout the chapter, emphasizing the role that forward and futures contracts play in managing exposures to equity, fixed-income, and foreign exchange risk. Also included is an enhanced discussion of how futures and forward markets are structured and operate, as well as how swap contracts can be viewed as portfolios of forward agreements.

Chapter 16 Here we expand the discussion linking valuation and applications of call and put options in the context of investment management. The chapter contains both new and updated examples designed to illustrate how investors use options in practice as well as a discussion of the recent changes to options markets. We also include extensive discussions of two other ways that options can be structured into other financial arrangements: convertible bonds and credit default swaps.

Chapter 17 This chapter includes a revised and updated discussion of the organization and participants in the professional asset management industry. Of particular note is an extensive update of the structure and strategies employed by hedge funds as well as enhanced analysis of how private equity funds function. The discussion of ethics and regulation in the asset management industry that concludes the chapter has also been updated and expanded.

Chapter 18 An updated and considerably expanded application of the performance measurement techniques introduced throughout the chapter is provided, including new material regarding the calculation of both simple and risk-adjusted performance measures. The discussion emphasizes the two main questions of performance measurement, as well as how the concept of downside risk can be incorporated into the evaluation process and the examination of techniques that focus on the security holdings of a manager's portfolio rather than the returns that the portfolio generates.

Supplement Package

Preparation of the 11th edition provided the opportunity to enhance the supplement products offered to instructors and students who use *Investment Analysis and Portfolio*

Management. The result of this examination is a greatly improved package that provides more than just basic answers and solutions. We are indebted to the supplement writers who devoted their time, energy, and creativity to making this supplement package the best it has ever been.

Website

The text's Website, which can be accessed through http://login.cengage.com, includes up-to-date teaching and learning aids for instructors. The *Instructor's Manual, Test Bank,* and PowerPoint slides are available to instructors for download. If they choose to, instructors may post, on a *password-protected site only,* the PowerPoint presentation for their students.

Instructor's Manual

The *Instructor's Manual* contains a brief outline of each chapter's key concepts and equations, which can be easily copied and distributed to students as a reference tool.

Test Bank

The *Test Bank* includes an extensive set of new questions and problems and complete solutions to the testing material. The *Test Bank* is available through Cognero, an online, fully customizable version of the *Test Bank,* which provides instructors with all the tools they need to create, author/edit, and deliver multiple types of tests. Instructors can import questions directly from the *Test Bank,* create their own questions, or edit existing questions.

Solutions Manual

This manual contains all the answers to the end-of-chapter questions and solutions to end-of-chapter problems.

Lecture Presentation Software

A comprehensive set of PowerPoint slides is available. Corresponding with each chapter is a self-contained presentation that covers all the key concepts, equations, and examples within the chapter. The files can be used as is for an innovative, interactive class presentation. Instructors who have access to Microsoft PowerPoint can modify the slides in any way they wish, adding or deleting materials to match their needs.

MindTap: Empower Your Students

MindTap is a platform that propels students from memorization to mastery. It gives you complete control of your course, so you can provide engaging content, challenge every learner, and build student confidence. Customize interactive syllabi to emphasize priority topics, then add your own material or notes to the eBook as desired. This outcomes-driven application gives you the tools needed to empower students and boost both understanding and performance.

Access Everything You Need in One Place Cut down on prep with the preloaded and organized MindTap course materials. Teach more efficiently with interactive multimedia, assignments, quizzes, and more. Give your students the power to read, listen, and study on their phones, so they can learn on their terms.

Empower Students to Reach Their Potential Twelve distinct metrics give you actionable insights into student engagement. Identify topics troubling your entire class and instantly communicate with those struggling. Students can track their scores to stay motivated towards their goals. Together, you can be unstoppable.

Control Your Course—And Your Content Get the flexibility to reorder textbook chapters, add your own notes, and embed a variety of content including Open Educational Resources (OER).

Personalize course content to your students' needs. They can even read your notes, add their own, and highlight key text to aid their learning.

Get a Dedicated Team, Whenever You Need Them MindTap isn't just a tool; it's backed by a personalized team eager to support you. We can help set up your course and tailor it to your specific objectives, so you'll be ready to make an impact from day one. Know we'll be standing by to help you and your students until the final day of the term.

Acknowledgments

So many people have helped us in so many ways that we hesitate to list them, fearing that we may miss someone. Accepting this risk, we will begin with the University of Notre Dame and the University of Texas at Austin because of their direct support. We are fortunate to have had the following excellent reviewers for this edition as well as for earlier ones:

JOHN ALEXANDER
Clemson University

ROBERT ANGELL
East Carolina University

GEORGE ARAGON
Boston College

BRIAN BELT
University of Missouri-Kansas City

OMAR M. BENKATO
Ball State University

ARAND BHATTACHARYA
University of Cincinnati

CAROL BILLINGHAM
Central Michigan University

SUSAN BLOCK
University of California, Santa
Barbara

GERALD A. BLUM
Babson College

PAUL BOLSTER
Northeastern University

ROBERT E. BROOKS
University of Alabama

ROBERT J. BROWN
Harrisburg, Pennsylvania

BOLONG CAO
Ohio University

CHARLES Q. CAO
Pennsylvania State University

ATREYA CHAKRABORTY
University of Massachusetts
Boston

HSIU-LANG CHEN
University of Illinois at Chicago

DOSOUNG CHOI
Gachon University

ROBERT CLARK
Husson University

JOHN CLINEBELL
University of Northern Colorado

DONALD L. DAVIS
Golden Gate University

JAMES D'MELLO
Western Michigan University

EUGENE F. DRZYCIMSKI
University of Wisconsin–Oshkosh

WILLIAM DUKES
Texas Tech University

JOHN DUNKELBERG
Wake Forest University

ERIC EMORY
Sacred Heart University

THOMAS EYSSELL
University of Missouri–St. Louis

HEBER FARNSWORTH
Rice University

JAMES FELLER
Middle Tennessee State University

EURICO FERREIRA
Clemson University

MICHAEL FERRI
John Carroll University

GREG FILBECK
Penn State Behrend

JOSEPH E. FINNERTY
University of Illinois

HARRY FRIEDMAN
New York University

R. H. GILMER
University of Mississippi

STEVEN GOLDSTEIN
University of South Carolina

STEVEN GOLDSTEIN
Robinson-Humphrey

KESHAV GUPTA
Oklahoma State University

SALLY A. HAMILTON
Santa Clara University

ERIC HIGGINS
Kansas State University

RONALD HOFFMEISTER
Arizona State University

SHELLY HOWTON
Villanova University

RON HUTCHINS
Eastern Michigan University

A. JAMES IFFLANDER
Arizona State University

STAN JACOBS
Central Washington University

KWANG JUN
Michigan State University

JAROSLAW KOMARYNSKY
Northern Illinois University

MALEK LASHGARI
University of Hartford

DANNY LITT
UCLA

MILES LIVINGSTON
University of Florida

CHRISTOPHER MA
Texas Tech University

ANANTH MADHAVAN
University of California Berkeley

DAVINDER MALHOTRA
Thomas Jefferson University

STEVEN MANN
University of South Carolina

IQBAL MANSUR
Widener University

ANDRAS MAROSI
University of Alberta

LINDA MARTIN
Arizona State University

GEORGE MASON
University of Hartford

JOHN MATHYS
DePaul University

MICHAEL MCBAIN
Marquette University

DENNIS MCCONNELL
University of Maine

JEANETTE MEDEWITZ
University of Nebraska–Omaha

JACOB MICHAELSEN
University of California, Santa Cruz

NICHOLAS MICHAS
Northern Illinois University

THOMAS W. MILLER JR.
University of Missouri–Columbia

LALATENDU MISRA
University of Texas at San Antonio

MICHAEL MURRAY
LaCrosse, Wisconsin

JONATHAN OHN
Bloomsburg University

HENRY OPPENHEIMER
University of Rhode Island

JOHN PEAVY
Southern Methodist University

GEORGE PHILIPPATOS
University of Tennessee

GEORGE PINCHES
University of Missouri Kansas City

ROSE PRASAD
Central Michigan University

LAURIE PRATHER
University of Tennessee at
Chattanooga

GEORGE A. RACETTE
University of Oregon

MURLI RAJAN
University of Scranton

NARENDAR V. RAO
Northeastern Illinois University

STEVE RICH
Baylor University

BRUCE ROBIN
Old Dominion University

JAMES ROSENFELD
Emory University

STANLEY D. RYALS
Investment Counsel, Inc.

JIMMY SENTEZA
Drake University

SHEKAR SHETTY
University of South Dakota

FREDERIC SHIPLEY
DePaul University

DOUGLAS SOUTHARD
Virginia Polytechnic Institute

HAROLD STEVENSON
Arizona State University

LAWRENCE S. TAI
Loyola Marymount College

KISHORE TANDON
The City University of New York,
Baruch College

DRAGON TANG
University of Hong Kong

DONALD THOMPSON
Georgia State University

DAVID E. UPTON
Virginia Commonwealth University

E. THEODORE VEIT
Rollins College

PREMAL VORA
Penn State Harrisburg

BRUCE WARDREP
East Carolina University

RICHARD S. WARR
North Carolina State University

ROBERT WEIGAND
University of South Florida

RUSSELL R. WERMERS
University of Maryland

ROLF WUBBELS
New York University

ELEANOR XU
Seton Hall University

YEXIAO XU
The University of Texas at Dallas

HONG YAN
Shanghai Advanced Institute of
Finance

SHENG-PING YANG
Gustavas Adolphus College

We have received invaluable comments from academic associates, including Jim Gentry (University of Illinois), David Chapman (University of Virginia), Amy Lipton (St. Joseph's University), Donald Smith (Boston University), and David Wright (University of Wisconsin–Parkside). Our university colleagues have also been very helpful over the years: Rob Batallio and Mike Hemler (University of Notre Dame); and Laura Starks, William Way, and Ken Wiles (University of Texas). Finally, we were once again blessed with bright, dedicated research assistants, such as Aaron Lin and Vincent Ng (Notre Dame) as well as Adam Winegar (University of Texas).

We are convinced that professors who want to write a book that is academically respectable and relevant, as well as realistic, require help from the "real world." We have been fortunate to develop relationships with a number of individuals (including a growing number of former students) whom we consider our contacts with reality. The following individuals have graciously provided important insights and material:

BRENT ADAMS
Kyle Capital

JAMES F. ARENS
Trust Company of Oklahoma

RICK ASHCROFT
Robert W. Baird

BRIAN BARES
Bares Capital Management

CHAD BAUMLER
Nuance Investments

DAVID G. BOOTH
Dimensional Fund Advisors, Inc.

GARY BRINSON
Brinson Foundation

KEVIN CASEY
Casey Capital

STALEY CATES
Southeastern Asset Management

DWIGHT D. CHURCHILL
State Street Global Advisors

ABBY JOSEPH COHEN
Goldman, Sachs

ROBERT CONWAY
Goldman, Sachs

ROBERT J. DAVIS
Highland Capital

PHILIP DELANEY JR.
Northern Trust Bank

PAT DORSEY
Dorsey Asset Management

FRANK J. FABOZZI
Journal of Portfolio Management

PHILIP FERGUSON
Salient Partners

KENNETH FISHER
Fisher Investments

H. GIFFORD FONG
Gifford Fong Associates

MARTIN S. FRIDSON
Lehmann, Livian, Fridson Advisors

M. CHRISTOPHER GARMAN
Bank of America/Merrill Lynch

KHALID GHAYUR
GPS Funds

BEN GIELE
Gearpower Capital

WILLIAM J. HANK
Moore Financial Corporation

RICK HANS
Fred's Inc.

LEA B. HANSEN
Institute for Research of Public Policy

W. VAN HARLOW
Fidelity Investments

BRITT HARRIS
University of Texas Investment
Management Company

CRAIG HESTER
Luther King Capital Management

JOANNE HILL
CBOE Vest

BRANDON HOLCOMB
Goldman, Sachs

JOHN W. JORDAN II
The Jordan Company

ANDREW KALOTAY
Kalotay Associates

WARREN N. KOONTZ JR.
Jennison Associates

MARK KRITZMAN
Windham Capital Management

MARTIN LEIBOWITZ
Morgan Stanley

DOUGLAS R. LEMPEREUR
Franklin Templeton Investments

ROBERT LEVINE
Nomura Securities

GEORGE W. LONG
LIM Advisors Ltd.

SCOTT LUMMER
Savant Investment Group

JOHN MAGINN
Maginn Associates

SCOTT MALPASS
University of Notre Dame
Endowment

JACK MALVEY
BNY Mellon Investment
Management

DOMINIC MARSHALL
Pacific Ridge Capital Partners

TODD MARTIN
Timucuan Asset Management

JOSEPH MCALINDEN
McAlinden Research Partners

RICHARD MCCABE
Bank of America/Merrill Lynch

MICHAEL MCCOWIN
State of Wisconsin Investment Board

MARK MCMEANS
Brasada Capital

OLEG MELENTYEV
Bank of America/Merrill Lynch

KENNETH MEYER
Lincoln Capital Management

JANET T. MILLER
Rowland and Company

BRIAN MOORE
U.S. Gypsum Corp.

SALVATOR MUOIO
SM Investors, LP

DAVID NELMS
Discover Financial Services

GEORGE NOYES
Hanover Strategic Management

WILL O'HARA
University of Texas

IAN ROSSA O'REILLY
Canadian Foundation for
Advancement of Investor Rights

ROBERT PARRINO
University of Texas

PHILIP J. PURCELL III
Continental Investors

JACK PYCIK
Consultant

RON RYAN
Asset Liability Management

ROBERT F. SEMMENS JR.
Semmens Private Investments

MICHAEL SHEARN
Time Value of Money L.P.

BRIAN SINGER
William Blair & Co.

CLAY SINGLETON
Rollins College

FRED H. SPEECE JR.
Speece, Thorson Capital Group

JAMES STORK
Pinnacle Financial Group

WARREN TENNANT
Abu Dhabi Investment Authority

KEVIN TERHAAR
Stairway Partners

JOHN THORTON
Stephens Investment Management
Group

STEPHAN TOMPSETT
Andeavor

JOSE RAMON VALENTE
Econsult

WILLIAM M. WADDEN
Wadden Enterprises

RICHARD S. WILSON
Consultant

ARNOLD WOOD
Martingale Asset Management

BRUCE ZIMMERMAN
Private Investor

We continue to benefit from the help and consideration of the dedicated people who have been associated with the CFA Institute: Tom Bowman, Whit Broome, Jeff Diermeier, Bob Johnson, and Katie Sherrerd. Professor Reilly would also like to thank his assistant, Rachel Karnafel, who had the unenviable task of keeping his office and his life in some sort of order during this project.

As always, our greatest gratitude is to our families—past, present, and future. Our parents gave us life and helped us understand love and how to give it. Most important are our wives who provide love, understanding, and support throughout the day and night. We thank God for our children and grandchildren who ensure that our lives are full of love, laughs, and excitement.

Frank K. Reilly
Notre Dame, Indiana

Keith C. Brown
Austin, Texas

Sanford J. Leeds
Austin, Texas

December 2017

About the Authors

Frank K. Reilly is the Bernard J. Hank Professor of Finance and former dean of the Mendoza College of Business at the University of Notre Dame. Holding degrees from the University of Notre Dame (BBA), Northwestern University (MBA), and the University of Chicago (PhD), Professor Reilly has taught at the University of Illinois, the University of Kansas, and the University of Wyoming in addition to the University of Notre Dame. He has several years of experience as a senior securities analyst, as well as experience in stock and bond trading. A chartered financial analyst (CFA), he has been a member of the Council of Examiners, the Council on Education and Research, the grading committee, and was chairman of the board of trustees of the Institute of Charted Financial Analysts and chairman of the board of the Association of Investment Management and Research (AIMR; now the CFA Institute). Professor Reilly has been president of the Financial Management Association, the Midwest Business Administration Association, the Eastern Finance Association, the Academy of Financial Services, and the Midwest Finance Association. He is or has been on the board of directors of the First Interstate Bank of Wisconsin, Norwest Bank of Indiana, the Investment Analysts Society of Chicago, UBS Global Funds (chairman), Fort Dearborn Income Securities (chairman), Discover Bank, NIBCO, Inc., the International Board of Certified Financial Planners, Battery Park High Yield Bond Fund, Inc., Morgan Stanley Trust FSB, the CFA Institute Research Foundation (chairman), the Financial Analysts Seminar, the Board of Certified Safety Professionals, and the University Club at the University of Notre Dame.

As the author of more than 100 articles, monographs, and papers, his work has appeared in numerous publications including *Journal of Finance, Journal of Financial and Quantitative Analysis, Journal of Accounting Research, Financial Management, Financial Analysts Journal, Journal of Fixed Income,* and *Journal of Portfolio Management.* In addition to *Investment Analysis and Portfolio Management,* 10th ed., Professor Reilly is the coauthor of another textbook, *Investments,* 7th ed. (South-Western, 2006) with Edgar A. Norton. He is editor of *Readings and Issues in Investments, Ethics and the Investment Industry,* and *High Yield Bonds: Analysis and Risk Assessment.*

Professor Reilly was named on the list of *Outstanding Educators in America* and has received the University of Illinois Alumni Association Graduate Teaching Award, the Outstanding Educator Award from the MBA class at the University of Illinois, and the Outstanding Teacher Award from the MBA class and the senior class at Notre Dame. He also received from the CFA Institute both the C. Stewart Sheppard Award for his contribution to the educational mission of the Association and the Daniel J. Forrestal III Leadership Award for Professional Ethics and Standards of Investment Practice. He also received the Hortense Friedman Award for Excellence from the CFA Society of Chicago and a Lifetime Achievement Award from the Midwest Finance Association. He was part of the inaugural group selected as a fellow of the Financial Management Association International. He is or has been a member of the editorial boards of *Financial Management, The Financial Review, International Review of Economics and Finance, Journal of Financial Education, Quarterly Review of Economics and Finance,* and the *European Journal of Finance.* He is included in *Who's Who in Finance and Industry, Who's Who in America, Who's Who in American Education,* and *Who's Who in the World.*

Keith C. Brown holds the position of University Distinguished Teaching Professor of Finance and Fayez Sarofim Fellow at the McCombs School of Business, University of Texas. He received a BA in economics from San Diego State University, where he was a member of the Phi Beta Kappa, Phi Kappa Phi, and Omicron Delta Epsilon honor societies. He received his MS and PhD in financial economics from the Krannert Graduate School of Management at Purdue University. Since leaving school in 1981, he has specialized in teaching investment management, portfolio management and security analysis, capital markets, and derivatives courses at the undergraduate, MBA, and PhD levels, and he has received numerous awards for teaching innovation and excellence, including election to the university's prestigious Academy of Distinguished Teachers. In addition to his academic responsibilities, he has also served as president and chief executive officer of The MBA Investment Fund, LLC, a privately funded investment company managed by graduate students at the University of Texas.

Professor Brown has published more than 45 articles, monographs, chapters, and papers on topics ranging from asset pricing and investment strategy to financial risk management. His publications have appeared in such journals as *Journal of Finance, Journal of Financial Economics, Review of Financial Studies, Journal of Financial and Quantitative Analysis, Review of Economics and Statistics, Journal of Financial Markets, Financial Analysts Journal, Financial Management, Journal of Investment Management, Advances in Futures and Options Research, Journal of Fixed Income, Journal of Retirement, Journal of Applied Corporate Finance,* and *Journal of Portfolio Management.* In addition to coauthoring *Investment Analysis and Portfolio Management,* 11th edition, he is a coauthor of *Interest Rate and Currency Swaps: A Tutorial,* a textbook published through the CFA Institute. He received a Graham and Dodd Award from the Financial Analysts Federation as an author of one of the best articles published by *Financial Analysts Journal* in 1990, a Smith-Breeden Prize from the *Journal of Finance* in 1996, and a Harry M. Markowitz Special Distinction Award from *Journal of Investment Management* in 2016.

In August 1988, Professor Brown received the Chartered Financial Analyst designation from the CFA Institute, and he has served as a member of that organization's CFA Candidate Curriculum Committee and Education Committee and on the CFA Examination Grading staff. For five years, he was the research director of the Research Foundation of the CFA Institute, from which position he guided the development of the research portion of the organization's worldwide educational mission. For several years, he was also associate editor for *Financial Analysts Journal,* and he currently holds that position for *Journal of Investment Management* and *Journal of Behavioral Finance.* In other professional service, Professor Brown has been a regional director for the Financial Management Association and has served as the applied research track chairman for that organization's annual conference.

Professor Brown is the cofounder and senior partner of Fulcrum Financial Group, a portfolio management and investment advisory firm located in Austin, Texas, that currently oversees three fixed-income security portfolios. From May 1987 to August 1988, he was based in New York as a senior consultant to the Corporate Professional Development Department at Manufacturers Hanover Trust Company. He has lectured extensively throughout the world on investment and risk management topics in the executive development programs for such companies as Fidelity Investments, JP Morgan Chase, Commonfund, BMO Nesbitt Burns, Merrill Lynch, Chase Manhattan Bank, Chemical Bank, Lehman Brothers, Union Bank of Switzerland, Shearson, Chase Bank of Texas, The Beacon Group, Motorola, and Halliburton. He is an advisor to the boards of the Teachers Retirement System of Texas and the University of Texas Investment Management Company and has served on the Investment Committee of LBJ Family Wealth Advisors, Ltd.

Sanford J. Leeds is a distinguished senior lecturer at the McCombs School of Business, University of Texas. He graduated summa cum laude from the University of Alabama with a BS in investment analysis. He has an MBA from The University of Texas Graduate School of Business, where he received the Dean's Award for Academic Excellence. He also has a JD from the University of Virginia, where he was on the editorial board of *The Virginia Tax Review*.

Professor Leeds has been a member of the McCombs faculty for 16 years. For 13 of those years, Professor Leeds also served as president of The MBA Investment Fund, LLC, a privately funded investment company managed by graduate students at the McCombs School. During his time on the faculty, he has taught a wide variety of classes, including Investment Theory and Practice, Portfolio Management, Capital Markets, Macroeconomics, Corporate Finance, and Advanced Corporate Finance. He has received numerous teaching awards, including three school wide awards: the Joe D. Beasley Teaching Award (for teaching in the graduate program), the CBA Foundation Advisory Council Award for Teaching Innovation, and the Jim Nolen Award for Excellence in Graduate Teaching. He has received recognition from his students with the "Outstanding MBA Professor Award" (selected by the full-time MBA students in multiple years, the Evening MBA students, and the Dallas MBA students) and the "Outstanding MSF Professor Award" (in multiple years). In 2015, he was selected (at the university level) to be a Provost Teaching Fellow and then served on the steering committee of that organization. He currently serves as a Senior Provost Fellow.

Professor Leeds received the Chartered Financial Analyst designation in 1998. He has served the CFA Institute as a grader, as a member of the Candidate Curriculum Committee, and as an editor of a candidate reading section. He is also a member of the Texas State Bar.

Prior to joining the faculty, Professor Leeds worked as an attorney and then as a money manager. After starting his career at a large law firm, he left to become a prosecutor. Then he attended business school and was one of four managers at a firm that had $1.6 billion under management. In recent years, he has served on the investment committee of the Austin Community Foundation (a $100 million endowment) and has also been the vice-chair of The Girls' School of Austin. He is frequently a speaker at industry conferences, normally discussing the economy and the markets.

The Investment Background

The chapters in this section will provide a background for your study of investments by answering the following questions:

- Why do people invest?
- How do you measure the returns and risks for alternative investments?
- What factors should you consider when you make asset allocation decisions?
- What investments are available?
- How do securities markets function?
- How and why are securities markets in the United States and around the world changing?
- What are the major uses of security market indexes?
- How can you evaluate the market behavior of common stocks and bonds?
- What factors cause differences among stock and bond market indexes?

In the first chapter, we consider why an individual would invest, how to measure the rates of return and risk for alternative investments, and what factors determine an investor's required rate of return on an investment. The latter point will be important when we work to understand investor behavior, the markets for alternative securities, and the valuation of various investments.

Because the ultimate decision facing an investor is the makeup of his or her portfolio, Chapter 2 deals with the all-important asset allocation decision. As we will see, to minimize risk, investment theory asserts the need to diversify, which leads to a discussion of the specific steps in the portfolio management process and factors that influence the makeup of an investor's portfolio over his or her life cycle. We also begin our exploration of investments available for investors to select by making an overpowering case for investing globally rather than limiting choices to only U.S. securities. Building on this premise, we discuss several global investment instruments used in global markets. We conclude the chapter with a review of the historical returns and measures of risk for a number of different asset class groups.

In Chapter 3, we examine how markets work in general and then specifically focus on the purpose and function of primary and secondary bond and stock markets. During the past two decades, significant changes have occurred in the operation of the securities market, including a trend toward a global capital market, electronic trading markets, and substantial worldwide consolidation. After discussing these changes and the rapid development of new capital markets around the world, we speculate about how global markets will continue to consolidate and will increase available investment alternatives.

Investors, market analysts, and financial theorists generally gauge the behavior of securities markets by evaluating the return and risk implied by various market indexes and evaluate portfolio performance by comparing a portfolio's results to an appropriate benchmark. Because these indexes are used to make asset allocation decisions and then to evaluate portfolio performance, it is important to have a deep understanding of how they are constructed and the numerous alternatives available. Therefore, in Chapter 4, we examine and compare a number of stock market and bond market indexes available for the domestic and global markets.

This initial section provides the framework for you to understand various securities, how to allocate among alternative asset classes, the markets where these securities are bought and sold, the indexes that reflect their performance, and how you might manage a collection of investments in a portfolio using *index funds*, which are an investable form of the security index.

CHAPTER 1

The Investment Setting

After you read this chapter, you should be able to answer the following questions:

- Why do individuals invest?
- What is an investment?
- How do investors measure the rate of return on an investment?
- How do investors measure the risk related to alternative investments?
- What factors contribute to the rates of return that investors require on alternative investments?
- What macroeconomic and microeconomic factors contribute to changes in the required rates of return for investments?

This initial chapter discusses several topics that are basic to the subsequent chapters. We begin by defining the term *investment* and discussing the returns and risks related to investments. This leads to a presentation of how to measure the expected and historical rates of returns for an individual asset or a portfolio of assets. In addition, we consider how to measure risk not only for an individual investment but also for an investment that is part of a portfolio.

The third section of the chapter discusses the factors that determine the required rate of return for an individual investment. The factors discussed are those that contribute to an asset's *total* risk. Because most investors have a portfolio of investments, it is necessary to consider how to measure the risk of an asset when it is a part of a large portfolio of assets. The risk that prevails when an asset is part of a diversified portfolio is referred to as its *systematic risk*.

The final section deals with what causes *changes* in an asset's required rate of return over time. Notably, changes occur because of both macroeconomic events that affect all investment assets and microeconomic events that affect only the specific asset.

1.1 What Is an Investment?

For most of your life, you will be earning and spending money. Rarely, though, will your current money income exactly balance with your consumption desires. Sometimes, you may have more money than you want to spend; at other times, you may want to purchase more than you can afford based on your current income. These imbalances will lead you either to borrow or to save to maximize the long-run benefits from your income.

When current income exceeds current consumption desires, people tend to save the excess, and they can do any of several things with these savings. One possibility is to put the money under a mattress or bury it in the backyard until some future time when consumption desires exceed current income. When they retrieve their savings from the mattress or backyard, they have the same amount they saved.

Another possibility is that they can give up the immediate possession of these savings for a future larger amount of money that will be available for future consumption. This trade-off of *present* consumption for a higher level of *future* consumption is the reason for saving. What you do with the savings to make them increase over time is *investment*.[1]

Those who give up immediate possession of savings (that is, defer consumption) expect to receive in the future a greater amount than they gave up. Conversely, those who consume more than their current income (that is, borrow) must be willing to pay back in the future more than they borrowed.

The rate of exchange between *future consumption* (future dollars) and *current consumption* (current dollars) is the *pure rate of interest*. Both people's willingness to pay this difference for borrowed funds and their desire to receive a surplus on their savings (that is, some rate of return) give rise to an interest rate referred to as the *pure time value of money*. This interest rate is established in the capital market by a comparison of the supply of excess income available (savings) to be invested and the demand for excess consumption (borrowing) at a given time. If you can exchange $100 of certain income today for $104 of certain income one year from today, then the pure rate of exchange on a risk-free investment (that is, the time value of money) is said to be 4 percent $(104/100 - 1)$.

The investor who gives up $100 today expects to consume $104 of goods and services in the future. This assumes that the general price level in the economy stays the same. This price stability has rarely been the case during the past several decades, when inflation rates have varied from 1.1 percent in 1986 to as much as 13.3 percent in 1979, with a geometric average of 4.2 percent a year from 1970 to 2016. If investors expect a change in prices, they will require a higher rate of return to compensate for it. For example, if an investor expects a rise in prices (that is, he or she expects inflation) at an annual rate of 2 percent during the period of investment, he or she will increase the required interest rate by 2 percent. In our example, the investor would require $106 in the future to defer the $100 of consumption during an inflationary period (that is, a 6 percent *nominal*, risk-free interest rate will be required instead of 4 percent).

Further, if the future payment from the investment is not certain (the borrower may not be able to pay off the loan when it is due), the investor will demand an interest rate that exceeds the nominal risk-free interest rate. The uncertainty of the payments from an investment is the *investment risk*. The additional return added to the nominal, risk-free interest rate is called a *risk premium*. In our previous example, the investor would require more than $106 one year from today to compensate for the uncertainty. As an example, if the required amount were $110, $4 (4 percent) would be considered a risk premium.

1.1.1 Investment Defined

From our discussion, we can specify a formal definition of investment. Specifically, an **investment** is the current commitment of dollars for a period of time in order to derive future payments that will compensate the investor for (1) the time the funds are committed, (2) the expected rate of inflation during this time period, and (3) the uncertainty of the future payments. The "investor" can be an individual, a government, a pension fund, or a corporation. Similarly, this definition includes all types of investments, including investments by corporations in plant and equipment and investments by individuals in stocks, bonds, commodities, or real estate. This text emphasizes investments by individual investors. In all cases, the investor is trading a *known* dollar amount today for some *expected* future stream of payments that will be greater than the current dollar amount today.

---

[1] In contrast, when current income is less than current consumption desires, people borrow to make up the difference. Although we will discuss borrowing on several occasions, the major emphasis of this text is how to invest savings.

At this point, we have answered the questions about why people invest and what they want from their investments. They invest to earn a return from savings due to their deferred consumption. They want a rate of return that compensates them for the time period of the investment, the expected rate of inflation, and the uncertainty of the future cash flows. This return, the investor's **required rate of return**, is discussed throughout this book. A central question of this book is how investors select investments that will give them their required rates of return.

The next section describes how to measure the expected or historical rate of return on an investment and also how to quantify the uncertainty (risk) of expected returns. You need to understand these techniques for measuring the rate of return and the uncertainty of these returns to evaluate the suitability of a particular investment. Although our emphasis will be on financial assets, such as bonds and stocks, we will refer to other assets, such as art and antiques. Chapter 2 discusses the range of financial assets and also considers some nonfinancial assets.

1.2 MEASURES OF RETURN AND RISK

The purpose of this book is to help you understand how to choose among alternative investment assets. This selection process requires that you estimate and evaluate the expected risk–return trade-offs for the alternative investments available. Therefore, you must understand how to measure the rate of return and the risk involved in an investment accurately. To meet this need, in this section we examine ways to quantify return and risk. The presentation will consider how to measure both *historical* and *expected* rates of return and risk.

We consider historical measures of return and risk because this book and other publications provide numerous examples of historical average rates of return and risk measures for various assets, and understanding these presentations is important. In addition, these historical results are often used by investors to estimate the *expected* rates of return and risk for an asset class.

The first measure is the historical rate of return on an individual investment over the time period the investment is held (that is, its holding period). Next, we consider how to measure the *average* historical rate of return for an individual investment over a number of time periods. The third subsection considers the average rate of return for a *portfolio* of investments.

Given the measures of historical rates of return, we will present the traditional measures of risk for a historical time series of returns (that is, the variance and standard deviation of the returns over the time period examined).

Following the presentation of measures of historical rates of return and risk, we turn to estimating the *expected* rate of return for an investment. Obviously, such an estimate contains a great deal of uncertainty, and we present measures of this uncertainty or risk.

1.2.1 Measures of Historical Rates of Return

When you are evaluating alternative investments for inclusion in your portfolio, you will often be comparing investments with widely different prices or lives. As an example, you might want to compare a $10 stock that pays no dividends to a stock selling for $150 that pays dividends of $5 a year. To properly evaluate these two investments, you must accurately compare their historical rates of returns. A proper measurement of the rates of return is the purpose of this section.

When we invest, we defer current consumption in order to add to our wealth so that we can consume more in the future. Therefore, when we talk about a return on an investment, we are concerned with the *change in wealth* resulting from this investment. This change in wealth can be either due to cash inflows, such as interest or dividends, or caused by a change in the price of the asset (positive or negative).

If you commit $200 to an investment at the beginning of the year and you get back $220 at the end of the year, what is your return for the period? The period during which you own an investment is called its *holding period*, and the return for that period is the **holding period return (HPR)**. In this example, the HPR is 1.10, calculated as follows:

1.1

$$HPR = \frac{\text{Ending Value of Investment}}{\text{Beginning Value of Investment}}$$

$$= \frac{\$220}{\$200} = 1.10$$

This HPR value will always be zero or greater—that is, it can never be a negative value. A value greater than 1.0 reflects an increase in your wealth, which means that you received a positive rate of return during the period. A value less than 1.0 means that you suffered a decline in wealth, which indicates that you had a negative return during the period. An HPR of zero indicates that you lost all your money (wealth) invested in this asset.

Although HPR helps us express the change in value of an investment, investors generally evaluate returns in *percentage terms on an annual basis*. This conversion to annual percentage rates makes it easier to directly compare alternative investments that have markedly different characteristics. The first step in converting an HPR to an annual percentage rate is to derive a percentage return, referred to as the **holding period yield (HPY)**. The HPY is equal to the HPR minus 1.

1.2

$$HPY = HPR - 1$$

In our example:

$$HPY = 1.10 - 1 = 0.10$$
$$= 10\%$$

To derive an *annual* HPY, you compute an **annual HPR** and subtract 1. Annual HPR is found by:

1.3

$$\text{Annual HPR} = HPR^{1/n}$$

where:

$n = $ number of years the investment is held

Consider an investment that cost $250 and is worth $350 after being held for two years:

$$HPR = \frac{\text{Ending Value of Investment}}{\text{Beginning Value of Investment}} = \frac{\$350}{\$250}$$

$$= 1.40$$

$$\text{Annual HPR} = 1.40^{1/n}$$

$$= 1.40^{1/2}$$

$$= 1.1832$$

$$\text{Annual HPY} = 1.1832 - 1 = 0.1832$$

$$= 18.32\%$$

If you experience a decline in your wealth value, the computation is as follows:

$$HPR = \frac{\text{Ending Value}}{\text{Beginning Value}} = \frac{\$400}{\$500} = 0.80$$

$$HPY = 0.80 - 1.00 = -0.20 = -20\%$$

A multiple-year loss over two years would be computed as follows:

$$\text{HPR} = \frac{\text{Ending Value}}{\text{Beginning Value}} = \frac{\$750}{\$1,000} = 0.75$$

$$\text{Annual HPY} = (0.75)^{1/n} = 0.75^{1/2}$$

$$= 0.866$$

$$\text{Annual HPY} = 0.866 - 1.00 = -0.134 = -13.4\%$$

In contrast, consider an investment of $100 held for only six months that earned a return of $12:

$$\text{HPR} = \frac{\$112}{100} = 1.12 \; (n = 0.5)$$

$$\text{Annual HPR} = 1.12^{1/.5}$$

$$= 1.12^2$$

$$= 1.2544$$

$$\text{Annual HPY} = 1.2544 - 1 = 0.2544$$

$$= 25.44\%$$

Note that we made some implicit assumptions when converting the six-month HPY to an annual basis. This annualized holding period yield computation assumes a constant annual yield for each year. In the two-year investment, we assumed an 18.32 percent rate of return each year, compounded. In the partial year HPR that was annualized, we assumed that the return is compounded for the whole year. That is, we assumed that the rate of return earned during the first half of the year is likewise earned on the value at the end of the first six months. The 12 percent rate of return for the initial six months compounds to 25.44 percent for the full year.[2] Because of the uncertainty of being able to earn the same return in the future six months, institutions will typically *not* compound partial year results.

Remember one final point: The ending value of the investment can be the result of a positive or negative change in price for the investment alone (for example, a stock going from $20 a share to $22 a share), income from the investment alone, or a combination of price change and income. Ending value includes the value of everything related to the investment.

1.2.2 Computing Mean Historical Returns

Now that we have calculated the HPY for a single investment for a single year, we want to consider **mean rates of return** for a single investment and for a portfolio of investments. Over a number of years, a single investment will likely give high rates of return during some years and low rates of return, or possibly negative rates of return, during others. Your analysis should consider each of these returns, but you also want a summary figure that indicates this investment's typical experience, or the rate of return you might expect to receive if you owned this investment over an extended period of time. You can derive such a summary figure by computing the mean annual rate of return (its HPY) for this investment over some period of time.

Alternatively, you might want to evaluate a portfolio of investments that might include similar investments (for example, all stocks or all bonds) or a combination of investments (for example, stocks, bonds, and real estate). In this instance, you would calculate the mean rate of return for this portfolio of investments for an individual year or for a number of years.

---

[2]To check that you understand the calculations, determine the annual HPY for a three-year HPR of 1.50. (Answer: 14.47 percent.) Compute the annual HPY for a three-month HPR of 1.06. (Answer: 26.25 percent.)

Single Investment Given a set of annual rates of return (HPYs) for an individual investment, there are two summary measures of return performance. The first is the arithmetic mean return, the second is the geometric mean return. To find the **arithmetic mean (AM)**, the sum (Σ) of annual HPYs is divided by the number of years (n) as follows:

1.4
$$AM = \Sigma HPY/n$$

where:

ΣHPY = sum of annual holding period yields

An alternative computation, the **geometric mean (GM)**, is the nth root of the product of the HPRs for n years minus one.

1.5
$$GM = [\pi HPR]^{1/n} - 1$$

where:

π = product of the annual holding period returns as follows:

$$(HPR_1) \times (HPR_2) \dots (HPR_n)$$

To illustrate these alternatives, consider an investment with the following data:

Year	Beginning Value	Ending Value	HPR	HPY
1	100.0	115.0	1.15	0.15
2	115.0	138.0	1.20	0.20
3	138.0	110.4	0.80	−0.20

$$AM = [(0.15) + (0.20) + (-0.20)]/3$$
$$= 0.15/3$$
$$= 0.05 = 5\%$$
$$GM = [(1.15) \times (1.20) \times (0.80)]^{1/3} - 1$$
$$= (1.104)^{1/3} - 1$$
$$= 1.03353 - 1$$
$$= 0.03353 = 3.353\%$$

Investors are typically concerned with long-term performance when comparing alternative investments. GM is considered a superior measure of the long-term mean rate of return because it indicates *the compound annual rate of return* based on the ending value of the investment versus its beginning value.[3] Specifically, using the prior example, if we compounded 3.353 percent for three years, $(1.03353)^3$, we would get an ending wealth value of 1.104.

Although the arithmetic average provides a good indication of the expected rate of return for an investment during a future individual year, it is biased upward if you are attempting to measure an asset's long-term performance. This is obvious for a volatile security. Consider, for example, a security that increases in price from $50 to $100 during year 1 and drops back to $50 during year 2. The annual HPYs would be:

Year	Beginning Value	Ending Value	HPR	HPY
1	50	100	2.00	1.00
2	100	50	0.50	−0.50

---

[3]Note that the GM is the same whether you compute the geometric mean of the individual annual holding period yields or the annual HPY for a three-year period, comparing the ending value to the beginning value, as discussed earlier under annual HPY for a multiperiod case.

This would give an AM rate of return of:

$$[(1.00) + (-0.50)]/2 = .50/2$$
$$= 0.25 = 25\%$$

This investment brought no change in wealth and therefore no return, yet the AM rate of return is computed to be 25 percent.

The GM rate of return would be:

$$(2.00 \times 0.50)^{1/2} - 1 = (1.00)^{1/2} - 1$$
$$= 1.00 - 1 = 0\%$$

This answer of a 0 percent rate of return accurately measures the fact that there was no change in wealth from this investment over the two-year period.

When rates of return are the same for all years, the GM will be equal to the AM. If the rates of return vary over the years, the GM will always be lower than the AM. The difference between the two mean values will depend on the year-to-year changes in the rates of return. Larger annual changes in the rates of return—that is, more volatility—will result in a greater difference between the alternative mean values. We will point out examples of this in subsequent chapters.

An awareness of both methods of computing mean rates of return is important because most published accounts of long-run investment performance or descriptions of financial research will use both the AM and the GM as measures of average historical returns. We will also use both throughout this book with the understanding that the AM is best used as an expected value for an individual year, while the GM is the best measure of long-term performance since it measures the compound annual rate of return for the asset being measured.

A Portfolio of Investments The mean historical rate of return (HPY) for a portfolio of investments is measured as the weighted average of the HPYs for the individual investments in the portfolio, or the overall percent change in value of the original portfolio. The weights used in computing the averages are the relative *beginning* market values for each investment; this is referred to as *dollar-weighted* or *value-weighted* mean rate of return. This technique is demonstrated by the examples in Exhibit 1.1. As shown, the HPY is the same (9.5 percent) whether you compute the weighted average return using the beginning market value weights or if you compute the overall percent change in the total value of the portfolio.

Although the analysis of historical performance is useful, selecting investments for your portfolio requires you to predict the rates of return you *expect* to prevail. The next section

---

Exhibit 1.1 Computation of Holding Period Yield for a Portfolio

Investment	Number of Shares	Beginning Price	Beginning Market Value	Ending Price	Ending Market Value	HPR	HPY	Market Weight[a]	Weighted HPY
A	100,000	$10	$1,000,000	$12	$1,200,000	1.20	20%	0.05	0.01
B	200,000	20	4,000,000	21	4,200,000	1.05	5	0.20	0.01
C	500,000	30	15,000,000	33	16,500,000	1.10	10	0.75	0.075
Total			$20,000,000		$21,900,000				0.095

$$HPR = \frac{21,900,000}{20,000,000} = 1.095$$

$$HPY = 1.095 - 1 = 0.095$$

$$= 9.5\%$$

[a]Weights are based on beginning values.

discusses how you would derive such estimates of expected rates of return. We recognize the great uncertainty regarding these future expectations, and we will discuss how one measures this uncertainty, which is referred to as the risk of an investment.

1.2.3 Calculating Expected Rates of Return

Risk is the uncertainty that an investment will earn its expected rate of return. In the examples in the prior section, we examined *realized* historical rates of return. In contrast, an investor who is evaluating a future investment alternative expects or anticipates a certain rate of return. The investor might say that he or she *expects* the investment will provide a rate of return of 10 percent, but this is actually the investor's most likely estimate, also referred to as a *point estimate*. Pressed further, the investor would probably acknowledge the uncertainty of this point estimate return and admit the possibility that, under certain conditions, the annual rate of return on this investment might go as low as -10 percent or as high as 25 percent. The point is, the specification of a larger range of *possible* returns from an investment reflects the investor's uncertainty regarding what the *actual* return will be. Therefore, a larger range of possible returns implies that the investment is riskier.

An investor determines how certain the expected rate of return on an investment is by analyzing estimates of possible returns. To do this, the investor assigns probability values to all *possible* returns. These probability values range from zero, which means no chance of the return, to one, which indicates complete certainty that the investment will provide the specified rate of return. These probabilities are typically subjective estimates based on the historical performance of the investment or similar investments modified by the investor's expectations for the future. As an example, an investor may know that about 30 percent of the time the rate of return on this particular investment was 10 percent. Using this information along with future expectations regarding the economy, one can derive an estimate of what might happen in the future.

The *expected* return from an investment is defined as:

$$\text{Expected Return} = \sum_{i=1}^{n}(\text{Probability of Return}) \times (\text{Possible Return})$$

1.6
$$E(R_i) = [(P_1)(R_1) + (P_2)(R_2) + (P_3)(R_3) + \cdots + (P_nR_n)]$$

$$E(R_i) = \sum_{i=1}^{n}(P_i)(R_i)$$

Let us begin our analysis of the effect of risk with an example of perfect certainty wherein the investor is absolutely certain of a return of 5 percent. Exhibit 1.2 illustrates this situation.

Perfect certainty allows only one possible return, and the probability of receiving that return is 1.0. Few investments provide certain returns and would be considered risk-free investments. In the case of perfect certainty, there is only one value for P_iR_i:

$$E(R_i) = (1.0)(0.05) = 0.05 = 5\%$$

In an alternative scenario, suppose an investor believed an investment could provide several different rates of return depending on different possible economic conditions. As an example, in a strong economic environment with high corporate profits and little or no inflation, the investor might expect the rate of return on common stocks during the next year to reach as high as 20 percent. In contrast, if there is an economic decline with a higher-than-average rate of inflation, the investor might expect the rate of return on common stocks during the next year to be -20 percent. Finally, with no major change in the economic environment, the rate of return during the next year would probably approach the long-run average of 10 percent.

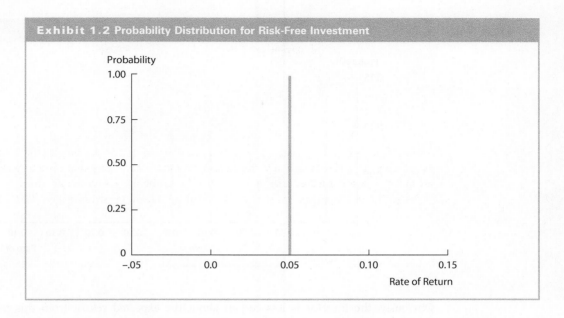

Exhibit 1.2 Probability Distribution for Risk-Free Investment

The investor might estimate probabilities for each of these economic scenarios based on past experience and the current outlook as follows:

Economic Conditions	Probability	Rate of Return
Strong economy, no inflation	0.15	0.20
Weak economy, above-average inflation	0.15	−0.20
No major change in economy	0.70	0.10

This set of potential outcomes can be visualized as shown in Exhibit 1.3.

The computation of the expected rate of return $[E(R_i)]$ is as follows:

$$E(R_i) = [(0.15)(0.20)] + [(0.15)(-0.20)] + [(0.70)(0.10)]$$

$$= 0.07$$

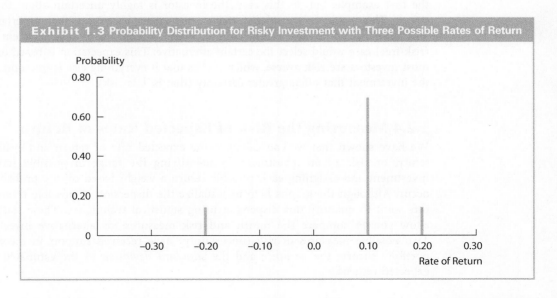

Exhibit 1.3 Probability Distribution for Risky Investment with Three Possible Rates of Return

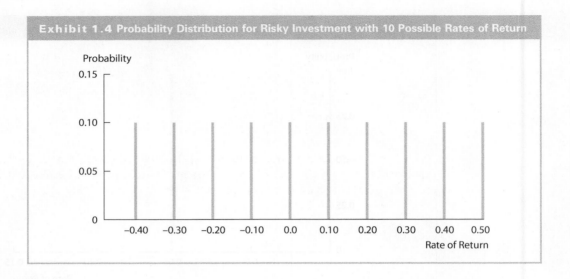

Exhibit 1.4 Probability Distribution for Risky Investment with 10 Possible Rates of Return

Obviously, the investor is less certain about the expected return from this investment than about the return from the prior investment with its single possible return.

A third example is an investment with 10 possible outcomes ranging from −40 percent to 50 percent with the same probability for each rate of return. A graph of this set of expectations would appear as shown in Exhibit 1.4.

In this case, there are numerous outcomes from a wide range of possibilities. The expected rate of return $[E(R_i)]$ for this investment would be:

$$
\begin{aligned}
E(R_i) &= (0.10)(-0.40) + (0.10)(-0.30) + (0.10)(-0.20) + (0.10)(-0.10) + (0.10)(0.0) \\
&\quad + (0.10)(0.10) + (0.10)(0.20) + (0.10)(0.30) + (0.10)(0.40) + (0.10)(0.50) \\
&= (-0.04) + (-0.03) + (-0.02) + (-0.01) + (0.00) + (0.01) + (0.02) + (0.03) \\
&\quad + (0.04) + (0.05) \\
&= 0.05
\end{aligned}
$$

The *expected* rate of return for this investment is the same as the certain return discussed in the first example; but, in this case, the investor is highly uncertain about the *actual* rate of return. This would be considered a risky investment because of that uncertainty. We would anticipate that an investor faced with the choice between this risky investment and the certain (risk-free) case would select the certain alternative. This expectation is based on the belief that most investors are **risk averse**, which means that if everything else is the same, they will select the investment that offers greater certainty (that is, less risk).

1.2.4 Measuring the Risk of Expected Rates of Return

We have shown that we can calculate the expected rate of return and evaluate the uncertainty, or risk, of an investment by identifying the range of possible returns from that investment and assigning each possible return a weight based on the probability that it will occur. Although the graphs help us visualize the dispersion of possible returns, most investors want to quantify this dispersion using statistical techniques. These statistical measures allow you to compare the return and risk measures for alternative investments directly. Two possible measures of risk (uncertainty) have received support in theoretical work on portfolio theory: the *variance* and the *standard deviation* of the estimated distribution of expected returns.

In this section, we demonstrate how variance and standard deviation measure the dispersion of possible rates of return around the expected rate of return. We will work with the examples discussed earlier. The formula for variance is as follows:

1.7

$$\text{Variance } (\sigma^2) = \sum_{i=1}^{n}(\text{Probability}) \times \left(\begin{array}{c}\text{Possible} \\ \text{Return}\end{array} - \begin{array}{c}\text{Expected} \\ \text{Return}\end{array}\right)^2$$

$$= \sum_{i=1}^{n}(P_i)[R_i - E(R_i)]^2$$

Variance The larger the **variance** for an expected rate of return, the greater the dispersion of expected returns and the greater the uncertainty, or risk, of the investment. The variance for the perfect-certainty (risk-free) example would be:

$$(\sigma^2) = \sum_{i=1}^{n}P_i[R_i - E(R_i)]^2$$

$$= 1.0\,(0.05 - 0.05)^2 = 1.0(0.0) = 0$$

Note that, in perfect certainty, there is *no variance of return* because there is no deviation from expectations and, therefore, *no risk* or *uncertainty*. The variance for the second example would be:

$$(\sigma^2) = \sum_{i=1}^{n}P_i[R_i - E(R_i)]^2$$

$$= [(0.15)(0.20 - 0.07)^2 + (0.15)(-0.20 - 0.07)^2 + (0.70)(0.10 - 0.07)^2]$$

$$= [0.010935 + 0.002535 + 0.00063]$$

$$= 0.0141$$

Standard Deviation The **standard deviation** is the square root of the variance:

1.8

$$\text{Standard Deviation} = \sqrt{\sum_{i=1}^{n}P_i[R_i - E(R_i)]^2}$$

For the second example, the standard deviation would be:

$$\sigma = \sqrt{0.0141}$$

$$= 0.11874 = 11.874\%$$

Therefore, when describing this investment example, you would contend that you expect a return of 7 percent, but the standard deviation of your expectations is 11.87 percent.

A Relative Measure of Risk In some cases, an unadjusted variance or standard deviation can be misleading. If conditions for two or more investment alternatives are not similar—that is, if there are major differences in the expected rates of return—it is necessary to use a measure of *relative variability* to indicate risk per unit of expected return. A widely used relative measure of risk is the **coefficient of variation (CV)**, calculated as follows:

1.9

$$\text{Coefficient of Variation}\,(CV) = \frac{\text{Standard Deviation of Returns}}{\text{Expected Rate of Return}}$$

$$= \frac{\sigma_i}{E(R)}$$

The CV for the preceding example would be:

$$CV = \frac{0.11874}{0.07000}$$
$$= 1.696$$

This measure of relative variability and risk is used by financial analysts to compare alternative investments with widely different rates of return and standard deviations of returns. As an illustration, consider the following two investments:

	Investment A	Investment B
Expected return	0.07	0.12
Standard deviation	0.05	0.07

Comparing absolute measures of risk, investment B appears to be riskier because it has a standard deviation of 7 percent versus 5 percent for investment A. In contrast, the CV figures show that investment B has less *relative* variability or lower risk per unit of expected return because it has a substantially higher expected rate of return:

$$CV_A = \frac{0.05}{0.07} = 0.714$$

$$CV_B = \frac{0.07}{0.12} = 0.583$$

1.2.5 Risk Measures for Historical Returns

To measure the risk for a series of historical rates of returns, we use the same measures as for expected returns (variance and standard deviation) except that we consider the historical holding period yields (HPYs) as follows:

1.10
$$\sigma^2 = \left[\sum_{i=1}^{n} [HPY_i - E(HPY)]^2 \right] \bigg/ n$$

where:

σ^2 = variance of the series
HPY_i = holding period yield during period i
$E(HPY)$ = expected value of the holding period yield that is equal to the arithmetic mean (AM) of the series
n = number of observations

The standard deviation is the square root of the variance. Both measures indicate how much the individual HPYs over time deviated from the expected value of the series. An example computation is contained in the appendix to this chapter. As is shown in subsequent chapters where we present historical rates of return for alternative asset classes, presenting the standard deviation as a measure of risk (uncertainty) for the series or asset class is fairly common.

1.3 DETERMINANTS OF REQUIRED RATES OF RETURN

In this section, we continue our discussion of factors that you must consider when selecting securities for an investment portfolio. You will recall that this selection process involves finding securities that provide a rate of return that compensates you for (1) the time value of money during the period of investment, (2) the expected rate of inflation during the period, and (3) the risk involved.

Exhibit 1.5 Promised Yields on Alternative Bonds

Type of Bond	2004	2005	2006	2007	2008	2009	2010
U.S. government 3-month Treasury bills	0.14%	3.16%	4.73%	4.48%	1.37%	0.15%	0.14%
U.S. government 10-year bonds	3.22	3.93	4.77	4.94	3.66	3.26	3.22
Aaa corporate bonds	4.94	5.24	5.59	5.56	5.63	5.31	4.94
Baa corporate bonds	6.04	6.06	6.48	6.47	7.44	7.29	6.04

Source: *Federal Reserve Bulletin,* various issues.

The summation of these three components is called the *required rate of return.* This is the minimum rate of return that you should accept from an investment to compensate you for deferring consumption. Because of the importance of the required rate of return to the total investment selection process, this section contains a discussion of the three components and what influences each of them.

The analysis and estimation of the required rate of return are complicated by the behavior of market rates over time. First, a wide range of rates is available for alternative investments at any point in time. Second, the rates of return on specific assets change dramatically over time. Third, the difference between the rates available (that is, the spread) on different assets changes over time.

The yield data in Exhibit 1.5 for alternative bonds demonstrate these three characteristics. First, even though all these securities have promised returns based upon bond contracts, the promised annual yields during any year differ substantially. As an example, during 2009 the average yields on alternative assets ranged from 0.15 percent on T-bills to 7.29 percent for Baa corporate bonds. Second, the changes in yields for a specific asset are shown by the three-month Treasury bill rate that went from 4.48 percent in 2007 to 0.15 percent in 2009. Third, an example of a change in the difference between yields over time (referred to as a spread) is shown by the Baa–Aaa spread.[4] The yield spread in 2007 was 91 basis points (6.47–5.56), but the spread in 2009 increased to 198 basis points (7.29–5.31). (A basis point is 0.01 percent.)

Because differences in yields result from the riskiness of each investment, you must include and understand the risk factors that affect the required rates of return. Because the required returns on all investments change over time, and because large differences separate individual investments, you need to be aware of the several components that determine the required rate of return, starting with the risk-free rate. In this chapter we consider the three components of the required rate of return and briefly discuss what affects these components. The presentation in Chapter 8 on valuation theory will discuss the factors that affect these components in greater detail.

1.3.1 The Real Risk-Free Rate

The **real risk-free rate (RRFR)** is the basic interest rate, assuming no inflation and no uncertainty about future flows. An investor in an inflation-free economy who knew with certainty what cash flows he or she would receive at what time would demand the RRFR on an investment. Earlier, we called this the *pure time value of money* because the only sacrifice the

---

[4]Bonds are rated by rating agencies based upon the credit risk of the securities, that is, the probability of default. Aaa is the top rating Moody's (a prominent rating service) gives to bonds with almost no probability of default. (Only U.S. Treasury bonds are considered to be of higher quality.) Baa is a lower rating Moody's gives to bonds of generally high quality that have some possibility of default under adverse economic conditions.

investor made was deferring the use of the money for a period of time. This RRFR of interest is the price charged for the risk-free exchange between current goods and future goods.

Two factors, one subjective and one objective, influence this exchange price. The subjective factor is the time preference of individuals for the consumption of income. When individuals give up $100 of consumption this year, how much consumption do they want a year from now to compensate for that sacrifice? The strength of the human desire for current consumption influences the rate of compensation required. Time preferences vary among individuals, and the market creates a composite rate that includes the preferences of all investors. This composite rate changes gradually over time because it is influenced by all the investors in the economy, whose changes in preferences may offset one another.

The objective factor that influences the RRFR is the set of investment opportunities available in the economy. The investment opportunities available are determined in turn by the *long-run real growth rate of the economy.* A rapidly growing economy produces more and better opportunities to invest funds and experience positive rates of return. A change in the economy's long-run real growth rate causes a change in all investment opportunities and a change in the required rates of return on all investments. Just as investors supplying capital should demand a higher rate of return when growth is higher, those looking to borrow funds to invest should be willing and able to pay a higher rate of return to use the funds for investment because of the higher growth rate and better opportunities. Thus, a *positive* relationship exists between the real growth rate in the economy and the RRFR.

1.3.2 Factors Influencing the Nominal Risk-Free Rate (NRFR)

Earlier, we observed that an investor would be willing to forgo current consumption in order to increase future consumption at a rate of exchange called the *risk-free rate of interest.* This rate of exchange was measured in real terms because we assume that investors want to increase the consumption of actual goods and services rather than consuming the same amount that had come to cost more money. Therefore, when we discuss rates of interest, we need to differentiate between *real* rates of interest that adjust for changes in the general price level, as opposed to *nominal* rates of interest that are stated in money terms. That is, nominal rates of interest that prevail in the market are determined by real rates of interest, *plus* factors that will affect the nominal rate of interest, such as the expected rate of inflation and the monetary environment.

Notably, the variables that determine the RRFR change only gradually because we are concerned with *long-run* real growth. Therefore, you might expect the required rate on a risk-free investment to be quite stable over time. As discussed in connection with Exhibit 1.5, rates on three-month T-bills were *not* stable over the period from 2004 to 2010. This is demonstrated with additional observations in Exhibit 1.6, which contains promised yields on T-bills for the period 1987–2016.

Investors view T-bills as a prime example of a default-free investment because the government has unlimited ability to derive income from taxes or to create money from which to pay interest. Therefore, one could expect that rates on T-bills should change only gradually. In fact, the data in Exhibit 1.6 show a highly erratic pattern. Specifically, yields increased from 4.64 percent in 1999 to 5.82 percent in 2000 before declining by over 80 percent in three years to 1.01 percent in 2003, followed by an increase to 4.73 percent in 2006, and concluding at 0.20 percent in 2016. Clearly, the *nominal* rate of interest on a default-free investment is *not* stable in the long run or the short run, even though the underlying determinants of the RRFR are quite stable because two other factors influence the nominal risk-free rate (NRFR): (1) the relative ease or tightness in the capital markets and (2) the expected rate of inflation.

Conditions in the Capital Market You will recall from prior courses in economics and finance that the purpose of capital markets is to bring together investors who want to invest

Exhibit 1.6 Three-Month Treasury Bill Yields and Rates of Inflation

Year	3-Month T-bills (%)	Rate of Inflation (%)	Year	3-Month T-bills (%)	Rate of Inflation (%)
1987	5.78	4.40	2002	1.61	2.49
1988	6.67	4.40	2003	1.01	1.87
1989	8.11	4.65	2004	1.37	3.26
1990	7.50	6.11	2005	3.16	3.42
1991	5.38	3.06	2006	4.73	2.54
1992	3.43	2.90	2007	4.48	4.08
1993	3.33	2.75	2008	1.37	0.09
1994	4.25	2.67	2009	0.15	2.72
1995	5.49	2.54	2010	0.14	1.50
1996	5.01	3.32	2011	0.04	2.96
1997	5.06	1.70	2012	0.06	1.74
1998	4.78	1.61	2013	0.02	1.51
1999	4.64	2.70	2014	0.02	0.76
2000	5.82	3.40	2015	0.02	0.73
2001	3.40	1.55	2016	0.20	2.07

Source: *Federal Reserve Bulletin*, various issues; *Economic Report of the President*, various issues.

savings with companies that need capital to expand or to governments that need to finance budget deficits. The cost of funds at any time (the interest rate) is the price that equates the current supply and demand for capital. Beyond this long-run equilibrium, there are short-run changes in the relative ease or tightness in the capital market caused by temporary disequilibrium in the supply and demand of capital.

As an example, disequilibrium could be caused by an unexpected change in monetary policy (for example, a change in the target federal funds rate) or fiscal policy (for example, a change in the federal deficit). Such changes will produce a change in the NRFR of interest, but the change should be short-lived because, in the longer run, the higher or lower interest rates will affect capital supply and demand. As an example, an increase in the federal deficit caused by an increase in government spending (easy fiscal policy) will increase the demand for capital and lead to an increase in interest rates. In turn, this increase in interest rates should cause an increase in savings and a decrease in the demand for capital by corporations or individuals. These changes in market conditions should bring rates back to the long-run equilibrium, which is based on the long-run growth rate of the economy.

Expected Rate of Inflation Previously, it was noted that if investors expect an increase in the inflation rate during the investment period, they will require the rate of return to include compensation for the expected rate of inflation. Assume that you require a 4 percent real rate of return on a risk-free investment, but you expect prices to increase by 3 percent during the investment period. In this case, you should increase your required rate of return by this expected rate of inflation to about 7 percent $[(1.04 \times 1.03) - 1]$. If you do not increase your required return, the \$104 you receive at the end of the year will represent a real return of about 1 percent, not 4 percent. Because prices have increased by 3 percent during the year, what previously cost \$100 now costs \$103, so you can consume only about 1 percent more at the end of the year $[(\$104/\$103) - 1]$. If you had required a 7.12 percent nominal return, your real consumption could have increased by 4 percent $[(\$107.12/\$103) - 1]$. Therefore, an investor's nominal required rate of return on a risk-free investment should be:

1.11 $$\text{NRFR} = [(1 + \text{RRFR}) \times (1 + \text{Expected Rate of Inflation})] - 1$$

Rearranging the formula, you can calculate the RRFR of return on an investment as follows:

1.12

$$RRFR = \left[\frac{(1 + \text{NRFR of Return})}{(1 + \text{Rate of Inflation})}\right] - 1$$

To see how this works, assume that the nominal return on U.S. government T-bills was 9 percent during a given year, when the rate of inflation was 5 percent. In this instance, the RRFR of return on these T-bills was 3.8 percent, as follows:

$$RRFR = [(1 + 0.09)/(1 + 0.05)] - 1$$
$$= 1.038 - 1$$
$$= 0.038 = 3.8\%$$

Clearly, the nominal rate of interest on a risk-free investment is not a good estimate of the RRFR because the nominal rate can change dramatically in the short run in reaction to temporary ease or tightness in the capital market or because of changes in the expected rate of inflation. As indicated in Exhibit 1.6, the significant changes in the average yield on T-bills typically were related to large changes in the rates of inflation.

The Common Effect All the factors discussed thus far regarding the required rate of return affect all investments equally. Whether the investment is in stocks, bonds, real estate, or machine tools, if the expected rate of inflation increases from 2 percent to 6 percent, the investor's required rate of return for *all* investments should increase by 4 percent. Similarly, if a decline in the expected real growth rate of the economy causes a decline in the RRFR of 1 percent, the required return on all investments should decline by 1 percent.

1.3.3 Risk Premium

A risk-free investment was defined as one for which the investor is certain of the amount and timing of the expected returns. The returns from most investments do not fit this pattern. An investor typically is not completely certain of the income to be received or when it will be received. Investments can range in uncertainty from basically risk-free securities, such as T-bills, to highly speculative investments, such as the common stock of small companies engaged in high-risk enterprises.

Most investors require higher rates of return on investments if they perceive that there is any uncertainty about the expected rate of return. This increase in the required rate of return over the NRFR is the **risk premium (RP)**. Although the required risk premium represents a composite of all uncertainty, it is possible to consider several fundamental sources of uncertainty. In this section, we identify and discuss briefly the major sources of uncertainty, including: (1) business risk, (2) financial risk (leverage), (3) liquidity risk, (4) exchange rate risk, and (5) country (political) risk.

Business risk is the uncertainty of income flows caused by the nature of a firm's business. The less certain the income flows of the firm, the less certain the income flows to the investor. Therefore, the investor will demand a risk premium that is based on the uncertainty caused by the basic business of the firm. As an example, a retail food company would typically experience stable sales and earnings growth over time and would have low business risk compared to a firm in the auto or airline industry, where sales and earnings fluctuate substantially over the business cycle, implying high business risk.

Financial risk is the uncertainty introduced by the method by which the firm finances its investments. If a firm uses only common stock to finance investments, it incurs only business risk. If a firm borrows money to finance investments, it must pay fixed financing charges (in the form of interest to creditors) prior to providing income to the common stockholders, so the uncertainty of returns to the equity investor increases. This increase in uncertainty because of fixed-cost financing is called *financial risk* or *financial leverage*, and it causes an increase in the stock's risk premium. For an extended discussion on this, see Brigham (2010).

Liquidity risk is the uncertainty introduced by the secondary market for an investment. When an investor acquires an asset, he or she expects that the investment will mature (as with a bond) or that it will be salable to someone else. In either case, the investor expects to be able to convert the security into cash and use the proceeds for current consumption or other investments. The more difficult it is to make this conversion to cash, the greater the liquidity risk. An investor must consider two questions when assessing the liquidity risk of an investment: How long will it take to convert the investment into cash? How certain is the price to be received? Similar uncertainty faces an investor who wants to acquire an asset: How long will it take to acquire the asset? How uncertain is the price to be paid?[5]

For example, a U.S. government Treasury bill has almost no liquidity risk because it can be bought or sold in seconds at a price almost identical to the quoted price. In contrast, examples of illiquid investments include a work of art, an antique, or a parcel of real estate in a remote area. Such investments may require a long time to find a buyer and the selling prices could vary substantially from expectations. Evaluating liquidity risk is critical when investing in foreign securities depending on the country and the liquidity of its stock and bond markets.

Exchange rate risk is the uncertainty of returns to an investor who acquires securities denominated in a currency different from his or her own. This risk is becoming greater as investors buy and sell assets from around the world, as opposed to only assets within their own countries. A U.S. investor who buys Japanese stock denominated in yen must consider not only the uncertainty of the return in yen but also any change in the exchange value of the yen relative to the U.S. dollar. That is, in addition to considering the foreign firm's business and financial risk and the security's liquidity risk, you must consider the additional uncertainty of the return on this Japanese stock when it is converted from yen to U.S. dollars.

As an example of exchange rate risk, assume that you buy 100 shares of Mitsubishi Electric at 1,050 yen when the exchange rate is 105 yen to the dollar. The dollar cost of this investment would be about $10.00 per share (1,050/105). A year later you sell the 100 shares at 1,200 yen when the exchange rate is 115 yen to the dollar. When you calculate the HPY in yen, you find the stock has increased in value by about 14 percent (1,200/1,050) − 1, but this is the HPY for a Japanese investor. A U.S. investor receives a much lower rate of return because during this period the yen has weakened relative to the dollar by about 9.5 percent (that is, it requires more yen to buy a dollar—115 versus 105). At the new exchange rate, the stock is worth $10.43 per share (1,200/115). Therefore, the return to you as a U.S. investor would be only about 4 percent ($10.43/$10.00) versus 14 percent for the Japanese investor. The difference in return for the Japanese investor and U.S. investor is caused by exchange rate risk—that is, the decline in the value of the yen relative to the dollar. Clearly, the exchange rate could have gone in the other direction, the dollar weakening against the yen—for example, assume the exchange rate declined from 105 yen to 95 yen to the dollar. In this case, as a U.S. investor, you would have experienced the 14 percent return measured in yen, as well as a currency gain from the exchange rate change that you should compute.[6]

The more volatile the exchange rate between two countries, the less certain you would be regarding the exchange rate, the greater the exchange rate risk, and the larger the exchange rate risk premium you would require. For an analysis of pricing this risk, see Jorion (1991).

---

[5]You will recall from prior courses that the overall capital market is composed of the primary market and the secondary market. Securities are initially sold in the primary market, and all subsequent transactions take place in the secondary market. These concepts are discussed in Chapter 3.

[6]At the new exchange rate, the value of the stock in dollars is $12.63 (1,200/95), which implies a dollar return of about 26 percent and a return of 14 percent in yen plus about 12 percent from the currency gain.

There can also be exchange rate risk for a U.S. firm that is extensively multinational in terms of sales and expenses. In this case, the firm's foreign earnings can be affected by changes in the exchange rate. As will be discussed, this risk can generally be hedged at a cost.

Country risk, also called *political risk*, is the uncertainty of returns caused by the possibility of a major change in the political or economic environment of a country. The United States is acknowledged to have the smallest country risk in the world because its political and economic systems are the most stable. During the spring of 2017, prevailing examples of political risk included the development of nuclear weapons in North Korea that threatened South Korea and Japan, chemical attacks in Syria against its own citizens and sanctioned by Russia, and Chinese attempts to colonize small islands in the South China Sea. In addition, deadly earthquakes in Japan have disturbed numerous global corporations and the currency markets. When you invest in countries that have unstable political or economic systems, you must add a country risk premium when determining their required rates of return.

When investing globally (which is emphasized throughout the book, based on a discussion in Chapter 2), investors must consider these additional uncertainties. How liquid are the secondary markets for stocks and bonds in the country? Are any of the country's securities traded on major stock exchanges in the United States, London, Tokyo, or Germany? What will happen to exchange rates during the investment period? What is the probability of a political or economic change that will adversely affect your rate of return? Exchange rate risk and country risk differ among countries. A good measure of exchange rate risk would be the absolute variability of a country's exchange rate relative to a composite exchange rate. The analysis of country risk is much more subjective and is generally based on the history and current political environment of the country.

This discussion of risk components can be considered a security's *fundamental risk* because it deals with the intrinsic factors that should affect a security's volatility of returns over time. In subsequent discussion, the standard deviation of returns for a security is referred to as a measure of the security's *total risk*, which considers only the individual stock—that is, the stock is not considered as part of a portfolio.

Risk Premium $= f$(Business Risk, Financial Risk, Liquidity Risk, Exchange Rate Risk, Country Risk)

1.3.4 Risk Premium and Portfolio Theory

An alternative view of risk has been derived from extensive work in portfolio theory and capital market theory by Markowitz (1952, 1959) and Sharpe (1964). These theories are dealt with in greater detail in Chapters 6 and 7, but their impact on a stock's risk premium should be mentioned briefly at this point. These prior works by Markowitz and Sharpe indicated that investors should use an *external market* measure of risk. Under a specified set of assumptions, all rational, profit-maximizing investors want to hold a completely diversified market portfolio of risky assets, and they borrow or lend to arrive at a risk level that is consistent with their risk preferences. Under these conditions, these authors showed that the relevant risk measure for an individual asset is its *comovement with the market portfolio*. This comovement, which is measured by an asset's covariance with the market portfolio, is referred to as an asset's **systematic risk**, which is the portion of an individual asset's total variance that is attributable to the variability of the total market portfolio. In addition, individual assets have variance that is unrelated to the market portfolio (the asset's nonmarket variance) that is due to the asset's unique features. This nonmarket variance is called *unsystematic risk*, and it is generally considered unimportant because it is eliminated in a large, diversified portfolio. Therefore, under these assumptions, *the risk premium for an individual earning asset is a function of the asset's* *systematic risk with the aggregate market portfolio of risky assets.* The measure of an asset's systematic risk is referred to as its *beta*:

$$\text{Risk Premium} = f(\text{Systematic Market Risk})$$

1.3.5 Fundamental Risk versus Systematic Risk

Some might expect a conflict between the market measure of risk (systematic risk) and the fundamental determinants of risk (business risk, and so on). A number of studies have examined the relationship between the market measure of risk (systematic risk) and accounting variables used to measure the fundamental risk factors, such as business risk, financial risk, and liquidity risk. The authors of these studies (especially Thompson, 1976) have generally concluded that *a significant relationship exists between the market measure of risk and the fundamental measures of risk.* Therefore, the two measures of risk can be complementary. This consistency seems reasonable because one might expect the market measure of risk to reflect the fundamental risk characteristics of the asset. For example, you might expect a firm that has high business risk and financial risk to have an above-average beta. At the same time, as we discuss in Chapters 6 and 7, a firm that has a high level of fundamental risk and a large standard deviation of returns can have a lower level of systematic risk simply because the variability of its earnings and its stock price is not related to the aggregate economy or the aggregate market; that is, a large component of its total risk is due to unique unsystematic risk. Therefore, one can specify the risk premium for an asset as either:

$$\text{Risk Premium} = f(\text{Business Risk, Financial Risk, Liquidity Risk, Exchange Rate Risk, Country Risk})$$

or

$$\text{Risk Premium} = f(\text{Systematic Market Risk})$$

1.3.6 Summary of Required Rate of Return

The overall required rate of return on alternative investments is determined by three variables: (1) the economy's RRFR, which is influenced by the investment opportunities in the economy (that is, the long-run real growth rate); (2) variables that influence the NRFR, which include short-run ease or tightness in the capital market and the expected rate of inflation. Notably, these variables, which determine the NRFR, are the same for all investments; and (3) the risk premium on the investment. In turn, this risk premium can be related to fundamental factors, including business risk, financial risk, liquidity risk, exchange rate risk, and country risk, or it can be a function of an asset's systematic market risk (beta).

Measures and Sources of Risk In this chapter, we have examined both measures and sources of risk arising from an investment. The *measures* of market risk for an investment are:

- Variance of rates of return
- Standard deviation of rates of return
- Coefficient of variation of rates of return (standard deviation/means)
- Covariance of returns with the market portfolio (beta)

The *sources* of fundamental risk are:

- Business risk
- Financial risk
- Liquidity risk
- Exchange rate risk
- Country risk

1.4 RELATIONSHIP BETWEEN RISK AND RETURN

Previously, we showed how to measure the risk and rates of return for alternative investments and we discussed what determines the rates of return that investors require. This section discusses the risk-return combinations that might be available at a point in time and illustrates the factors that cause *changes* in these combinations.

Exhibit 1.7 graphs the expected relationship between risk and return. It shows that investors increase their required rates of return as perceived risk (uncertainty) increases. The line that reflects the combination of risk and return available on alternative investments is referred to as the **security market line (SML)**. The SML reflects the risk-return combinations available for all risky assets in the capital market at a given time. Investors would select investments that are consistent with their risk preferences; some would consider only low-risk investments, whereas others welcome high-risk investments.

Beginning with an initial SML, three changes in the SML can occur. First, individual investments *can change positions on the SML* because of changes in the perceived risk of the investments. Second, *the slope of the SML can change* because of a change in the attitudes of investors toward risk; that is, investors can change the returns they require per unit of risk. Third, *the SML can experience a parallel shift* due to a change in the RRFR or the expected rate of inflation—that is, anything that can change in the NRFR. These three possibilities are discussed in this section.

1.4.1 Movements along the SML

Investors place alternative investments somewhere along the SML based on their perceptions of the risk of the investment. Obviously, if an investment's risk changes due to a change in one of its fundamental risk sources (business risk, financial risk and such), it will move along (up or down) the SML. For example, if a firm increases its financial risk by selling a large bond issue that increases its financial leverage, investors will perceive its common stock as riskier and the stock will move up the SML to a higher risk position implying that investors will require a higher rate of return. As the common stock becomes riskier, it changes its position on the SML. Any change in an asset that affects one or several of its fundamental risk factors or its market risk (that is, its beta) will cause the asset to move *along* the SML, as shown in Exhibit 1.8. Note that the SML does not change; only the positions of specific assets on the SML change.

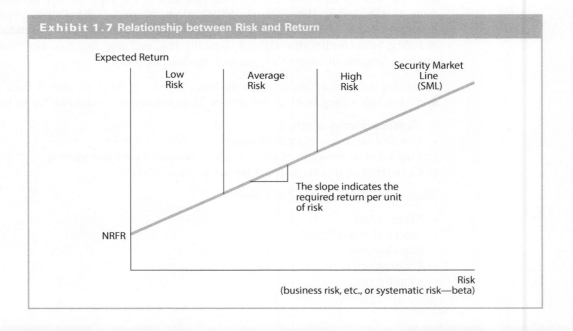

Exhibit 1.7 Relationship between Risk and Return

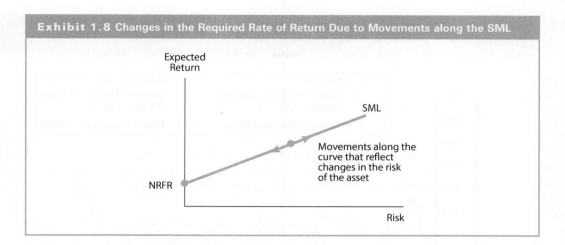

Exhibit 1.8 Changes in the Required Rate of Return Due to Movements along the SML

1.4.2 Changes in the Slope of the SML

The slope of the SML indicates the return per unit of risk required by all investors. Assuming a straight line, it is possible to select any point on the SML and compute a risk premium (RP) for an asset through the equation:

1.13
$$RP_i = E(R_i) - NRFR$$

where:

RP_i = risk premium for asset i
$E(R_i)$ = expected return for asset i
NRFR = nominal return on a risk-free asset

If a point on the SML is identified as the portfolio that contains all the risky assets in the market (referred to as the *market portfolio*), it is possible to compute a market RP as follows:

1.14
$$RP_m = E(R_m) - NRFR$$

where:

RP_m = risk premium on the market portfolio
$E(R_m)$ = expected return on the market portfolio
NRFR = nominal return on a risk-free asset

This market RP is *not constant* because the slope of the SML changes over time. Although we do not understand completely what causes these changes in the slope, we do know that there are changes in the *yield* differences between assets with different levels of risk even though the inherent risk differences are relatively constant.

These differences in yields are referred to as **yield spreads**, and these yield spreads change over time. As an example, if the yield on a portfolio of Aaa-rated bonds is 6.50 percent, and the yield on a portfolio of Baa-rated bonds is 8.00 percent, we would say that the yield spread is 1.50 percent. This 1.50 percent is referred to as a credit risk premium because the Baa-rated bond is considered to have higher credit risk—that is, it has a higher probability of default. This Baa–Aaa yield spread is *not* constant over time, as shown by the substantial volatility in the yield spreads shown in Exhibit 1.9.

Although the underlying business and financial risk characteristics for the portfolio of bonds in the Aaa-rated bond index and the Baa-rated bond index would probably not change dramatically over time, it is clear from the time-series plot in Exhibit 1.9 that the difference in yields (that is, the yield spread that reflects credit risk) has experienced increases of more than

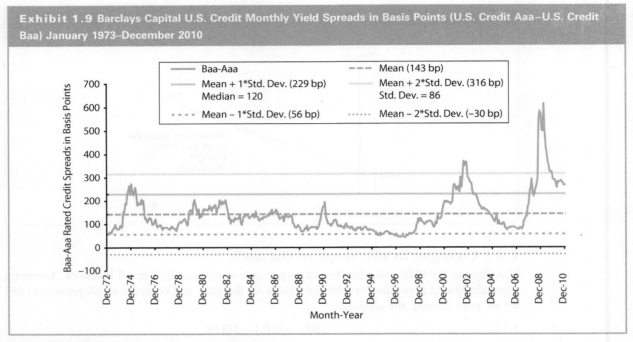

Exhibit 1.9 Barclays Capital U.S. Credit Monthly Yield Spreads in Basis Points (U.S. Credit Aaa–U.S. Credit Baa) January 1973–December 2010

Source: Barclays Capital data; computations by authors.

100 basis points (1 percent) in a short period of time (for example, increases in 1974–1975 and 1981–1983, an increase of over 200 basis points 2001–2002, an increase of over 500 basis points in 2008–2009, and subsequent dramatic declines in yield spread during 1975, 1983–1984, 2003–2004, and the second half of 2009). Such significant changes in the yield spread during a period when there is no major change in the fundamental risk characteristics of Baa bonds relative to Aaa bonds would imply a change in the market RP. Specifically, although the intrinsic financial risk characteristics of the bonds remain relatively constant, investors changed the yield spreads (that is, the credit risk premiums) they demand to accept this difference in financial risk.

This change in the RP implies a change in the slope of the SML. Such a change is shown in Exhibit 1.10. The exhibit assumes an increase in the market risk premium, which means an increase in the slope of the market line. Such a change in the slope of the SML (the market risk premium) will affect the required rate of return for all risky assets. Irrespective of where an investment is on the original SML, its required rate of return will increase by different amounts, although its intrinsic risk characteristics remain unchanged.

1.4.3 Changes in Capital Market Conditions or Expected Inflation

The graph in Exhibit 1.11 shows what happens to the SML when there are changes in one or more of the following factors: (1) expected real growth in the economy, (2) capital market conditions, or (3) the expected rate of inflation. For example, an increase in expected real growth, temporary tightness in the capital market, or an increase in the expected rate of inflation will cause the SML to experience a parallel shift upward as shown in

Exhibit 1.11. The parallel shift occurs because changes in one or more of expected real growth or changes in capital market conditions or a change in the expected rate of inflation affect the economy's nominal risk-free rate (NRFR) that impacts all investments, irrespective of their risk levels.

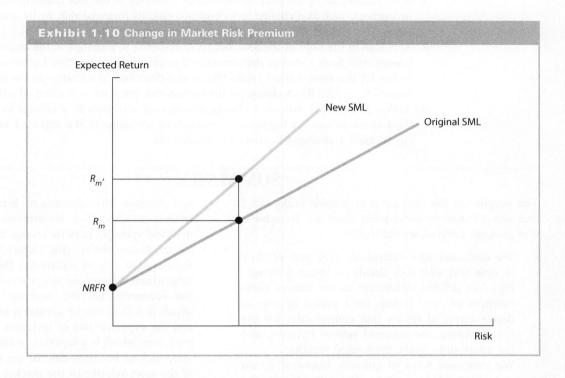

Exhibit 1.10 Change in Market Risk Premium

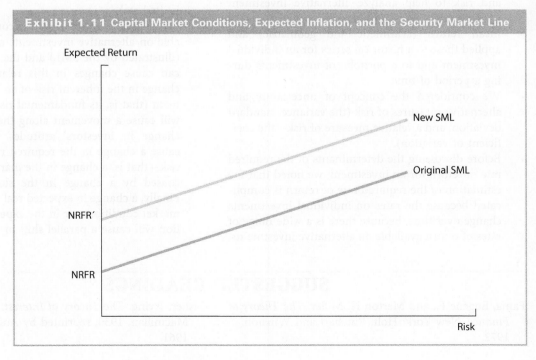

Exhibit 1.11 Capital Market Conditions, Expected Inflation, and the Security Market Line

1.4.4 Summary of Changes in the Required Rate of Return

The relationship between risk and the required rate of return for an investment can change in three ways:

1. A movement *along* the SML demonstrates a change in the risk characteristics of a specific investment, such as a change in its business risk, its financial risk, or its systematic risk (its beta). This change affects only the individual investment.
2. A change in the *slope* of the SML occurs in response to a change in the attitudes of investors toward risk. Such a change demonstrates that investors want either higher or lower rates of return for the same intrinsic risk. This is also described as a change in the market risk premium (R_m − NRFR). A change in the market risk premium will affect all risky investments.
3. A *shift* in the SML reflects a change in expected real growth, a change in market conditions (such as ease or tightness of money), or a change in the expected rate of inflation. Again, such a change will affect all investments.

SUMMARY

The purpose of this chapter is to provide background that can be used in subsequent chapters. To achieve that goal, we covered several topics:

- We discussed why individuals save part of their income and why they decide to invest their savings. We defined *investment* as the current commitment of these savings for a period of time to derive a rate of return that compensates for the time involved, the expected rate of inflation, and the uncertainty of the investment returns.
- We examined ways to quantify historical return and risk to help analyze alternative investment opportunities. We considered two measures of mean return (arithmetic and geometric) and applied these to a historical series for an individual investment and to a portfolio of investments during a period of time.
- We considered the concept of uncertainty and alternative measures of risk (the variance, standard deviation, and a relative measure of risk—the coefficient of variation).
- Before discussing the determinants of the required rate of return for an investment, we noted that the estimation of the required rate of return is complicated because the rates on individual investments change over time, because there is a wide range of rates of return available on alternative investments, and because the differences between required returns on alternative investments (for example, the yield spreads) likewise change over time.

- We examined the specific factors that determine the required rate of return: (1) the real risk-free rate, which is based on the real rate of growth in the economy, (2) the nominal risk-free rate, which is influenced by capital market conditions and the expected rate of inflation, and (3) a risk premium, which is a function of fundamental factors, such as business risk, or the systematic risk of the asset relative to the market portfolio (that is, its beta).
- We discussed the risk-return combinations available on alternative investments at a point in time (illustrated by the SML) and the three factors that can cause changes in this relationship. First, a change in the inherent risk of an individual investment (that is, its fundamental risk or market risk) will cause a movement along the SML. Second, a change in investors' attitudes toward risk will cause a change in the required return per unit of risk—that is, a change in the market risk premium caused by a change in the slope of the SML. Finally, a change in expected real growth, in capital market conditions, or in the expected rate of inflation will cause a parallel shift of the SML.

SUGGESTED READINGS

Fama, Eugene F., and Merton H. Miller. *The Theory of Finance*. New York: Holt, Rinehart and Winston, 1972.

Fisher, Irving. *The Theory of Interest*. New York: Macmillan, 1930, reprinted by Augustus M. Kelley, 1961.

QUESTIONS

1. Define *investment* and discuss the overall purpose people have for investing.
2. As a student, are you saving or borrowing? Why?
3. Divide a person's life from ages 20 to 70 into 10-year segments and discuss the likely saving or borrowing patterns during each period.
4. Discuss why you would expect the saving–borrowing pattern to differ by occupation (for example, for a doctor versus a plumber).
5. *The Wall Street Journal* reported that the yield on common stocks is about 2 percent, whereas a study at the University of Chicago contends that the annual rate of return on common stocks since 1926 has averaged about 10 percent. Reconcile these statements.
6. Some financial theorists consider the variance of the distribution of expected rates of return to be a good measure of uncertainty. Discuss the reasoning behind this measure of risk and its purpose.
7. Discuss the three components of an investor's required rate of return on an investment.
8. Discuss the two major factors that determine the market nominal risk-free rate (NRFR). Explain which of these factors would be more volatile over the business cycle.
9. Briefly discuss the five fundamental factors that influence the risk premium of an investment.
10. You own stock in the Gentry Company, and you read in the financial press that a recent bond offering has raised the firm's debt/equity ratio from 35 percent to 55 percent. Discuss the effect of this change on the variability of the firm's net income stream, other factors being constant. Discuss how this change would affect your required rate of return on the common stock of the Gentry Company.
11. Draw a properly labeled graph of the security market line (SML) and indicate where you would expect the following investments to fall along that line. Discuss your reasoning.
    a. Common stock of large firms
    b. U.S. government bonds
    c. U.K. government bonds
    d. Low-grade corporate bonds
    e. Common stock of a Japanese firm
12. Explain why you would change your nominal required rate of return if you expected the rate of inflation to go from 0 (no inflation) to 4 percent. Give an example of what would happen if you did not change your required rate of return under these conditions.
13. Assume the expected long-run growth rate of the economy increased by 1 percent and the expected rate of inflation increased by 4 percent. What would happen to the required rates of return on government bonds and common stocks? Show graphically how the effects of these changes would differ between these alternative investments.
14. You see in *The Wall Street Journal* that the yield spread between Baa corporate bonds and Aaa corporate bonds has gone from 350 basis points (3.5 percent) to 200 basis points (2 percent). Show graphically the effect of this change in yield spread on the SML and discuss its effect on the required rate of return for common stocks.
15. Give an example of a liquid investment and an illiquid investment. Discuss why you consider each of them to be liquid or illiquid.

PROBLEMS

1. On February 1, you bought 100 shares of stock in the Francesca Corporation for $34 a share and a year later you sold it for $39 a share. During the year, you received a cash dividend of $1.50 a share. Compute your HPR and HPY on this Francesca stock investment.

2. On August 15, you purchased 100 shares of stock in the Cara Cotton Company at $65 a share and a year later you sold it for $61 a share. During the year, you received dividends of $3 a share. Compute your HPR and HPY on your investment in Cara Cotton.

3. At the beginning of last year, you invested $4,000 in 80 shares of the Chang Corporation. During the year, Chang paid dividends of $5 per share. At the end of the year, you sold the 80 shares for $59 a share. Compute your total HPY on these shares and indicate how much was due to the price change and how much was due to the dividend income.

4. The rates of return computed in Problems 1, 2, and 3 are nominal rates of return. Assuming that the rate of inflation during the year was 4 percent, compute the real rates of return on these investments. Compute the real rates of return if the rate of inflation was 8 percent.

5. During the past five years, you owned two stocks that had the following annual rates of return:

Year	Stock T	Stock B
1	0.19	0.08
2	0.08	0.03
3	−0.12	−0.09
4	−0.03	0.02
5	0.15	0.04

a. Compute the arithmetic mean annual rate of return for each stock. Which stock is most desirable by this measure?

b. Compute the standard deviation of the annual rate of return for each stock. (Use the appendix to this chapter if necessary.) By this measure, which is the preferable stock?

c. Compute the coefficient of variation for each stock. (Use the appendix to this chapter if necessary.) By this relative measure of risk, which stock is preferable?

d. Compute the geometric mean rate of return for each stock. Discuss the difference between the arithmetic mean return and the geometric mean return for each stock. Discuss the differences in the mean returns relative to the standard deviation of the return for each stock.

6. You are considering acquiring shares of common stock in the Madison Beer Corporation. Your rate of return expectations are as follows:

Madison Beer Corp.

Possible Rate of Return	Probability
−0.10	0.30
0.00	0.10
0.10	0.30
0.25	0.30

Compute the expected return $[E(R_i)]$ on your investment in Madison Beer.

7. A stockbroker calls you and suggests that you invest in the Lauren Computer Company. After analyzing the firm's annual report and other material, you believe that the distribution of expected rates of return is as follows:

Lauren Computer Co.

Possible Rate of Return	Probability
−0.60	0.05
−0.30	0.20
−0.10	0.10
0.20	0.30
0.40	0.20
0.80	0.15

Compute the expected return $[E(R_i)]$ on Lauren Computer stock.

8. Without any formal computations, do you consider Madison Beer in Problem 6 or Lauren Computer in Problem 7 to present greater risk? Discuss your reasoning.

9. During the past year, you had a portfolio that contained U.S. government T-bills, long term government bonds, and common stocks. The rates of return on each of them were as follows:

U.S. government T-bills	5.50%
U.S. government long-term bonds	7.50
U.S. common stocks	11.60

During the year, the consumer price index, which measures the rate of inflation, went from 160 to 172 (1982 − 1984 = 100). Compute the rate of inflation during this year. Compute the real rates of return on each of the investments in your portfolio based on the inflation rate.

10. You read in *Business Week* that a panel of economists has estimated that the long-run real growth rate of the U.S. economy over the next five-year period will average 3 percent. In addition, a bank newsletter estimates that the average annual rate of inflation during this five-year period will be about 4 percent. What nominal rate of return would you expect on U.S. government T-bills during this period?

11. What would your required rate of return be on common stocks if you wanted a 5 percent risk premium to own common stocks given what you know from Problem 10? If common stock investors became more risk averse, what would happen to the required rate of return on common stocks? What would be the impact on stock prices?

12. Assume that the consensus required rate of return on common stocks is 14 percent. In addition, you read in *Fortune* that the expected rate of inflation is 5 percent and the estimated long-term real growth rate of the economy is 3 percent. What interest rate would you expect on U.S. government T-bills? What is the approximate risk premium for common stocks implied by these data?

Computation of Variance and Standard Deviation

Variance and standard deviation are measures of how actual values differ from the expected values (arithmetic mean) for a given series of values. In this case, we want to measure how rates of return differ from the arithmetic mean value of a series. There are other measures of dispersion, but variance and standard deviation are the best known because they are used in statistics and probability theory. Variance is defined as:

$$\text{Variance } (\sigma^2) = \sum_{i=1}^{n}(\text{Probability})(\text{Possible Return} - \text{Expected Return})^2$$

$$= \sum_{i=1}^{n}(P_i)[R_i - E(R_i)]^2$$

Consider the following example, as discussed in the chapter:

Probability of Possible Return (P_i)	Possible Return (R_i)	P_iR_i
0.15	0.20	0.03
0.15	−0.20	−0.03
0.70	0.07	0.10
		$\Sigma = 0.07$

This gives an expected return $[E(R_i)]$ of 7 percent. The dispersion of this distribution as measured by variance is:

Probability (P_i)	Return (R_i)	$R_i - E(R_i)$	$[R_i - E(R_i)]^2$	$P_i[R_i - E(R_i)]^2$
0.15	0.20	0.13	0.0169	0.002535
0.15	−0.20	−0.27	0.0729	0.010935
0.70	0.10	0.03	0.0009	0.000630
				$\Sigma = 0.014100$

The variance (σ^2) is equal to 0.0141. The standard deviation is equal to the square root of the variance:

$$\text{Standard Deviation } (\sigma^2) = \sqrt{\sum_{i=1}^{n} P_i[R_i - E(R_i)]^2}$$

Consequently, the standard deviation for the preceding example would be:

$$\sigma_i = \sqrt{0.0141} = 0.11874$$

In this example, the standard deviation is approximately 11.87 percent. Therefore, you could describe this distribution as having an expected value of 7 percent and a standard deviation of 11.87 percent.

In many instances, you might want to compute the variance or standard deviation for a historical series in order to evaluate the past performance of the investment. Assume that you are given the following information on annual rates of return (HPY) for common stocks listed on the New York Stock Exchange (NYSE):

Year	Annual Rate of Return
2018	0.07
2019	0.11
2020	−0.04
2021	0.12
2022	−0.06

In this case, we are not examining expected rates of return but actual returns. Therefore, we assume equal probabilities, and the expected value (in this case the mean value, R) of the series is the sum of the individual observations in the series divided by the number of observations, or 0.04 (0.20/5). The variances and standard deviations are:

Year	R_i	$R_i - \overline{R}$	$(R_i - \overline{R})^2$	
2018	0.07	0.03	0.0009	$\sigma^2 = 0.0286/5$
2019	0.11	0.07	0.0049	$= 0.00572$
2020	−0.04	−0.08	0.0064	
2021	0.12	0.08	0.0064	$\sigma = \sqrt{0.00572}$
2022	−0.06	−0.10	0.0110	$= 0.0756$
			$\Sigma = 0.0286$	$= 7.56\%$

We can interpret the performance of NYSE common stocks during this period of time by saying that the average rate of return was 4 percent and the standard deviation of annual rates of return was 7.56 percent.

Coefficient of Variation

In some instances, you might want to compare the dispersion of two different series. The variance and standard deviation are *absolute* measures of dispersion. That is, they can be influenced by the magnitude of the original numbers. To compare series with very different values, you need a *relative* measure of dispersion. A measure of relative dispersion is the coefficient of variation, which is defined as:

$$\text{Coefficient of Variation (CV)} = \frac{\text{Standard Deviation of Returns}}{\text{Expected Rate of Return}}$$

A larger value indicates greater dispersion relative to the arithmetic mean of the series. For the previous example, the CV would be:

$$CV_1 = \frac{0.0756}{0.0400} = 1.89$$

It is possible to compare this value to a similar figure having a markedly different distribution. As an example, assume you wanted to compare this investment to another investment that had an average rate of return of 10 percent and a standard deviation of 9 percent. The standard deviations alone tell you that the second series has greater dispersion (9 percent versus 7.56 percent) and might be considered to have higher risk. In fact, the *relative* dispersion for this second investment is much less.

$$CV_1 = \frac{0.0756}{0.0400} = 1.89$$

$$CV_2 = \frac{0.0900}{0.1000} = 0.90$$

Considering the relative dispersion and the total distribution, most investors would probably prefer the second investment.

Problems

1. Your rate of return expectations for the common stock of Gray Cloud Company during the next year are:

Gray Cloud Co.

Possible Rate of Return	Probability
−0.10	0.25
0.00	0.15
0.10	0.35
0.25	0.25

a. Compute the expected return $[E(R_i)]$ on this investment, the variance of this return (σ^2), and its standard deviation (σ).

b. Under what conditions can the standard deviation be used to measure the relative risk of two investments?

c. Under what conditions must the coefficient of variation be used to measure the relative risk of two investments?

2. Your rate of return expectations for the stock of Kayleigh Cosmetics Company during the next year are:

Kayleigh Cosmetics Co.

Possible Rate of Return	Probability
−0.60	0.15
−0.30	0.10
−0.10	0.05
0.20	0.40
0.40	0.20
0.80	0.10

a. Compute the expected return $[E(R_i)]$ on this stock, the variance (σ^2) of this return, and its standard deviation (σ).

b. On the basis of expected return $[E(R_i)]$ alone, discuss whether Gray Cloud or Kayleigh Cosmetics is preferable.

c. On the basis of standard deviation (σ) alone, discuss whether Gray Cloud or Kayleigh Cosmetics is preferable.

d. Compute the coefficients of variation (CVs) for Gray Cloud and Kayleigh Cosmetics and discuss which stock return series has the greater relative dispersion.

3. The following are annual rates of return for U.S. government T-bills and U.S. common stocks.

Year	U.S. Government T-Bills	U.S. Common Stock
2018	0.063	0.150
2019	0.081	0.043
2020	0.076	0.374
2021	0.090	0.192
2022	0.085	0.106

a. Compute the arithmetic mean rate of return and standard deviation of rates of return for the two series.

b. Discuss these two alternative investments in terms of their arithmetic average rates of return, their absolute risk, and their relative risk.

c. Compute the geometric mean rate of return for each of these investments. Compare the arithmetic mean return and geometric mean return for each investment and discuss the difference between mean returns as related to the standard deviation of each series.

CHAPTER **2**

Asset Allocation and Security Selection*

After you read this chapter, you should be able to answer the following questions:

- What is involved in the asset allocation process?
- What are the four steps in the portfolio management process?
- What is the role of asset allocation in investment planning?
- Why is a policy statement important to the planning process?
- What objectives and constraints should be detailed in a policy statement?
- How and why do investment goals change over a person's lifetime?
- Why should investors have a global perspective regarding their investments?
- What has happened to the relative size of U.S. and foreign stock and bond markets?
- What are the differences in the rates of return on U.S. and foreign securities markets?
- How can changes in currency exchange rates affect the returns that U.S. investors experience on foreign securities?
- What are the additional advantages to diversifying in international markets beyond domestic diversification?
- What alternative securities are available? What are their cash flow and risk properties?
- What are the historical return and risk characteristics of the major investment instruments?
- What is the relationship among the returns for foreign and domestic investment instruments?
- What is the implication of these relationships for portfolio diversification?

The previous chapter informed us that *risk drives return*. Therefore, the practice of investing funds and managing portfolios should focus primarily on managing risk rather than on managing returns.

This chapter examines some of the practical implications of risk management in the context of asset allocation. **Asset allocation** is the process of deciding how to distribute an investor's wealth among different countries and asset classes for investment purposes. An **asset class** is composed of securities that have similar characteristics, attributes, and risk–return relationships. A broad asset class, such as "bonds," can be divided into smaller asset classes, such as Treasury bonds, corporate bonds, and high-yield bonds. We will see that, in the long run, the highest compounded returns will most likely accrue to investors with larger exposures to risky assets. We will also see that although there are no shortcuts or guarantees to investment success, maintaining a disciplined approach to investing will increase the likelihood of investment success over time.

The asset allocation decision is not an isolated choice; rather, it is a component of a structured four-step portfolio management process that we present in this chapter. The first step in the process is to develop an investment policy statement that will guide all future decisions.

---

*The authors acknowledge comments from Professor Edgar Norton of Illinois State University on this chapter.

An asset allocation strategy depends on the investor's policy statement, which includes the investor's goals or objectives, constraints, and investment guidelines.

What we mean by an "investor" can range from an individual account to trustees overseeing a corporation's multibillion-dollar pension fund, a university endowment, or an insurance company portfolio. The point is that it is critical for an investor to develop a policy statement before making long-term investment decisions. Although most examples will be for an individual investor, the concepts we will introduce—investment objectives, constraints, benchmarks, and so on—apply to any investor, individual, or institution. We will review historical data to show the importance of the asset allocation decision and discuss the need for investor education, an important issue for companies who offer retirement or savings plans to their employees. The chapter concludes by examining asset allocation strategies across national borders to show the effects of regulations, market environment, and culture on investing patterns. Notably, what is appropriate for a U.S.-based investor is not necessarily appropriate for a non-U.S.-based investor.

2.1 INDIVIDUAL INVESTOR LIFE CYCLE

Financial plans and investment needs are different for each individual, and they change over a person's life cycle. How individuals structure their financial plan should be related to their age, financial status, future plans, risk aversion characteristics, and needs.

2.1.1 The Preliminaries

Before embarking on an investment program, we need to make sure other needs are satisfied. No serious investment plan should be started until a potential investor has a safety net to cover living expenses should the unexpected occur.

Insurance Life insurance should be a component of any financial plan. Life insurance protects loved ones against financial hardship should death occur before our financial goals are met. The death benefit paid by the insurance company can help pay medical bills and funeral expenses and provide cash that family members can use to maintain their lifestyle, retire debt, or invest for future needs (for example, children's education, spouse retirement). Therefore, one of the first steps in developing a financial plan is to purchase adequate life insurance coverage.

Insurance coverage also provides protection against other uncertainties. *Health* insurance helps to pay medical bills. *Disability* insurance provides continuing income should you become unable to work. *Automobile and home* (or rental) insurance provides protection against accidents and damage to cars or residences.

Although nobody ever expects to use his or her insurance coverage, a first step in a sound financial plan is to have adequate coverage "just in case." Lack of insurance coverage can ruin the best-planned investment program.

Cash Reserve Emergencies, job layoffs, and unforeseen expenses happen, and good investment opportunities emerge. It is important to have a cash reserve to help meet such events. In addition, a cash reserve reduces the likelihood of being forced to sell investments at inopportune times to cover unexpected expenses. Most experts recommend a cash reserve equal to about six months' living expenses. Calling it a "cash" reserve means the funds should be in investments you can easily convert to cash, with little chance of a loss in value, such as money market or short-term bond mutual funds.

Much like a financial plan, an investor's insurance and cash reserve needs will change over his or her life. For example, the need for disability insurance declines at retirement, while supplemental Medicare coverage or long-term-care insurance becomes more important.

2.1.2 Investment Strategies over an Investor's Lifetime

Assuming that basic insurance and cash reserve needs are met, individuals can start a serious investment program. Because of changes in their net worth and risk tolerance, individuals' investment strategies will change over their lifetime, and we will review various phases in the investment life cycle. Although each individual's needs and preferences are different, some general factors affect most investors over their life cycle.

The four life-cycle phases are shown in Exhibit 2.1 (the third and fourth phases—spending and gifting—are shown as concurrent) and described here.

Accumulation Phase Individuals in the early to middle years of their working careers are in the **accumulation phase**, wherein they are attempting to accumulate assets to satisfy fairly immediate needs (for example, a down payment for a house) or longer-term goals (children's college education, retirement). Typically, their net worth is small, and debt from car loans or their own past college loans may be heavy. As a result of their long investment time horizon and future earning ability, individuals in the accumulation phase are typically willing to make relatively high-risk investments in the hopes of making above-average nominal returns over time.

We will consistently emphasize the wisdom of investing early and regularly in one's life. Funds invested in early life cycle phases, with returns compounding over time, will reap significant financial benefits during later phases. Exhibit 2.2 shows growth from an initial $10,000 investment over 20, 30, and 40 years at assumed annual returns of 7 and 8 percent. A middle-aged person who invests $10,000 "when he or she can afford it" will only reap the benefits of compounding for about 20 years before retirement. In contrast, a person who begins saving at a younger age will reap the much higher benefits of funds invested for 30 or 40 years. Regularly investing as little as $2,000 a year reaps large benefits over time. As shown in Exhibit 2.2, a person who has invested a total of $90,000—an initial $10,000 investment followed by $2,000 annual investments over 40 years—will have over half a million dollars accumulated, assuming the 7 percent return. If the funds are invested more aggressively and earn the 8 percent return, the accumulation will be nearly three-quarters of a million dollars.

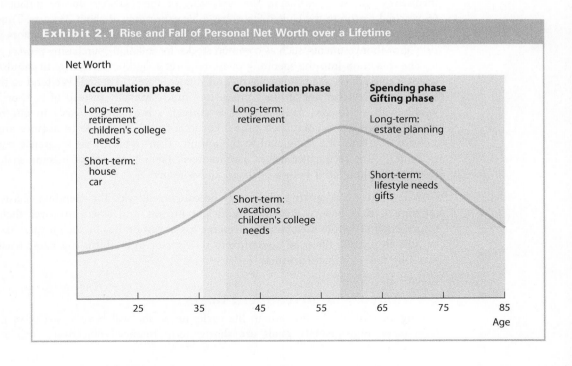

Exhibit 2.1 Rise and Fall of Personal Net Worth over a Lifetime

Exhibit 2.2 Benefits of Investing Early

		The Future Value of an Initial $10,000 Investment	The Future Value of Investing $2,000 Annually	The Future Value of the Initial Investment Plus the Annual Investment
Interest rate	7.0%			
20 years		$ 38,696.84	$ 81,990.98	$120,687.83
30 years		$ 76,122.55	$188,921.57	$265,044.12
40 years		$149,744.58	$399,270.22	$549,014.80
Interest rate	8.0%			
20 years		$ 46,609.57	$ 91,523.93	$138,133.50
30 years		$100,626.57	$226,566.42	$327,192.99
40 years		$217,245.21	$518,113.04	$735,358.25

Source: Calculations by authors.

Consolidation Phase Individuals in the **consolidation phase** are typically past the midpoint of their careers, have paid off much or all of their outstanding debts, and perhaps have paid, or have the assets to pay, their children's college bills. Earnings exceed expenses, and the excess can be invested for future retirement or estate planning needs. The typical investment horizon for this phase is still long (20 to 30 years), so moderately high-risk investments are attractive. Still, because individuals in this phase are concerned about capital preservation, they do not want to take abnormally high risks.

Spending Phase The **spending phase** typically begins when individuals retire. Living expenses are covered by Social Security income and income from prior investments, including employer pension plans. Because their earning years have concluded (although some retirees take part-time positions or do consulting work), they are very conscious of protecting their capital. Still, they must balance their desire to preserve the nominal value of their savings with the need to protect themselves against a decline in the *real* value of their savings due to inflation. The average 65-year-old person in the United States has a life expectancy of about 25 years. Thus, although the overall portfolio may be less risky than in the consolidation phase, these investors still need some risky growth investments, such as common stocks, for inflation (purchasing power) protection.

The transition into the spending phase requires a significant change in mindset; throughout our working life we are trying to save, and suddenly we can spend. We tend to think that if we spend less, say 4 percent of our accumulated funds annually instead of 5, 6, or 7 percent, our wealth will last longer. Although this is correct, a bear market early in our retirement can greatly reduce our accumulated funds. Fortunately, it is possible to acquire annuities, which transfer risk from the individual to the annuity firm (typically an insurance company). With an annuity, the recipient receives a guaranteed, lifelong stream of income that can be structured to continue until both a husband and wife die.

Gifting Phase The **gifting phase** may be concurrent with the spending phase. In this stage, individuals may believe they have sufficient income and assets to cover their current and future expenses while maintaining a reserve for uncertainties. In such a case, excess assets can be used to provide financial assistance to relatives or to establish charitable trusts as an estate planning tool to minimize estate taxes.

2.1.3 Life Cycle Investment Goals

During an individual's investment life cycle, he or she will have a variety of financial goals. **Near-term**, **high-priority goals** are shorter-term financial objectives, such as funds for a house down payment, a new car, or a vacation trip. Parents with teenage children may have a high-priority goal to accumulate funds for college expenses. Because these goals have short time horizons, high-risk investments are not considered suitable for achieving them.

Long-term, high-priority goals typically include financial independence, such as the ability to retire at a certain age. Because of their long-term nature, higher-risk investments can help meet these objectives.

Lower-priority goals involve desirable objectives but are not critical. Examples include a new car every few years, redecorating the home, or take a long, luxurious vacation. A well-developed policy statement considers these diverse goals over an investor's lifetime. The following sections detail the process for constructing an investment policy, creating a portfolio that is consistent with the investment policy, managing the portfolio, and monitoring its performance relative to its goals and objectives over time.

2.2 THE PORTFOLIO MANAGEMENT PROCESS*

The process of managing an investment portfolio never stops. Once the funds are initially invested according to the plan, the emphasis changes to evaluating the portfolio's performance and updating the portfolio based on changes in the economic environment and the investor's needs.

The first step in the portfolio management process, as shown in Exhibit 2.3, is for the investor to construct a **policy statement** that specifies the types of risks the investor is willing to take and his or her investment goals and constraints. All investment decisions should be consistent with the policy statement to ensure that these decisions are appropriate for the investor. Because investor needs, goals, and constraints change over time, the policy statement must be periodically reviewed and updated.

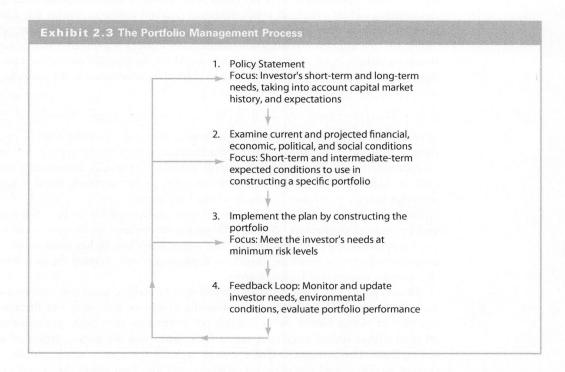

Exhibit 2.3 The Portfolio Management Process

1. Policy Statement
   Focus: Investor's short-term and long-term needs, taking into account capital market history, and expectations

2. Examine current and projected financial, economic, political, and social conditions
   Focus: Short-term and intermediate-term expected conditions to use in constructing a specific portfolio

3. Implement the plan by constructing the portfolio
   Focus: Meet the investor's needs at minimum risk levels

4. Feedback Loop: Monitor and update investor needs, environmental conditions, evaluate portfolio performance

*This section and the one that follows benefited from insights contained in Maginn, Tuttle, Pinto, and McLeavey (2007), especially Chapters 1 and 2.

The process of investing involves assessing the future and deriving strategies that meet the policy statement guidelines. In the second step, the portfolio manager studies current financial and economic conditions and forecasts future trends. The investor's needs, as reflected in the policy statement, and financial market expectations will jointly determine the **investment strategy**. Economies are dynamic and are affected by numerous industry struggles, politics, changing demographics, and social attitudes. Thus, the portfolio will require *constant* monitoring and updating to reflect changes in financial market expectations.

The third step of the portfolio management process is to **construct the portfolio**. Given the investor's policy statement and financial market forecasts as input, the advisors implement the investment strategy and determine how to allocate available funds across different countries, asset classes, and securities. This involves constructing a portfolio that will minimize the investor's risks while meeting the needs specified in the policy statement.

The fourth step in the portfolio management process is the **continual monitoring** of the investor's needs and capital market conditions and, when necessary, updating of the policy statement. In turn, the investment strategy is modified. The monitoring process involves evaluating a portfolio's performance compared to the expectations and the requirements listed in the policy statement. The evaluation of portfolio performance is discussed in Chapter 18. After completing the four steps, you will recognize that this is a *continuous* process in which it is essential to revisit all the steps to ensure that all the components remain valid.

2.3 THE NEED FOR A POLICY STATEMENT

Because a policy statement guides the investment process, it is an invaluable planning tool that will help an investor understand his or her needs better as well as assist an advisor or a portfolio manager in managing a client's funds. A policy statement does not guarantee success but does provide discipline for the investment process and reduce the possibility of making hasty, inappropriate decisions. There are two important reasons for constructing a policy statement: First, it helps the investor decide on realistic investment goals after learning about the financial markets and the risks of investing; second, it creates a standard by which to judge the performance of the portfolio manager.

2.3.1 Understanding and Articulating Realistic Investor Goals

When asked about their investment goal, people often say "to make a lot of money" or something similar. Such a goal has two drawbacks: First, it may not be appropriate for the investor, and second, it is too open-ended to provide guidance for specific investments and time frames. Such an objective is well suited for someone going to the racetrack, but it is inappropriate for someone investing in financial assets for the long term.

Writing a policy statement helps an investor understand his or her own needs, objectives, and investment constraints. Writing this statement requires an investor to learn about financial markets and the risks of investing that will prevent him or her from making inappropriate investment decisions based on unrealistic expectations and increase the possibility of satisfying the specific, measurable financial goals.

Thus, a policy statement helps an investor specify realistic goals and understand the risks and costs of investing. The market values of stocks, bonds, or real estate can fluctuate dramatically. A review of market history shows that it is not unusual for asset prices to decline by 10 percent to 20 percent over several months. A recent "bloodbath" was the market decline of over 30 percent during 2008. The problem is that investors typically focus on a single statistic, such as an 11 percent average annual rate of return on stocks, and they then expect the market to rise 11 percent every year. Such thinking ignores the risk of stock investing because, as discussed in Chapter 7, we know that there should be a strong positive relationship between risk and return.

One expert in the field recommends that investors should think about the following set of questions and explain their answers as part of the process of constructing a policy statement:

1. What are the real risks of an adverse financial outcome, especially in the short run?
2. What probable emotional reactions will I have to an adverse financial outcome?
3. How knowledgeable am I about investments and financial markets?
4. What other capital or income sources do I have? How important is this particular portfolio to my overall financial position?
5. What, if any, legal restrictions may affect my investment needs?
6. How would any unanticipated fluctuations in my portfolio value affect my investment policy?

Adapted from Charles D. Ellis, *Investment Policy: How to Win the Loser's Game* (Homewood, IL: Dow Jones-Irwin, 1985), 25–26. Reproduced with permission of the McGraw-Hill Companies.

In summary, constructing a policy statement is a process whereby investors articulate their realistic needs and goals and become familiar with financial markets and investing risks. Without this information, investors cannot adequately communicate their needs to a portfolio manager who needs this input to construct a portfolio that will satisfy clients' needs. Bypassing this step will likely lead to future aggravation, dissatisfaction, and disappointment.

2.3.2 Standards for Evaluating Portfolio Performance

A policy statement assists in judging the performance of a portfolio manager, which requires an objective standard; a policy statement provides such a standard. A portfolio's performance should be compared to guidelines specified in the policy statement, not based on the portfolio's overall return. For example, if an investor has a low tolerance for risky investments, the portfolio should not be expected to perform as well as the risky S&P 500 stock index. The point is that because risk drives returns, an investor's lower-risk investments, as specified in the investor's policy statement, will probably earn lower returns than the aggregate stock market.

A policy statement typically includes a **benchmark portfolio**, or comparison standard. Notably, both the client and the portfolio manager must agree that the benchmark portfolio reflects the risk preferences and appropriate return requirements of the client. The investment performance of the portfolio manager should be compared to this benchmark portfolio.

Because it sets an objective performance standard, the policy statement acts as a starting point for periodic portfolio review and client communication with managers. Managers should be judged by whether *they consistently followed the client's policy guidelines*. A portfolio manager who deviates from policy is not working in the best interests of the client.

Constructing a comprehensive policy statement is essential: The client must first understand his or her own needs before communicating them to the portfolio manager, and the manager must in turn implement the client's desires by following the investment guidelines. The policy statement should impose an investment discipline on the client and the portfolio manager.

2.3.3 Other Benefits

A sound policy statement protects the client against a portfolio manager's inappropriate investments or unethical behavior. Though legal recourse is a possibility against such action, writing a clear and unambiguous policy statement should reduce the possibility of such behavior.

It is important to recognize that managers can change. Because a portfolio manager may be promoted or dismissed or may take a better job, your funds may come under the management of an individual you do not know and who does not know you. To prevent costly delays during this transition, it is critical that you have a clearly written policy statement that will prevent delays in monitoring and rebalancing your portfolio and contribute to a seamless transition between money managers.

To summarize, a clearly written policy statement helps avoid numerous potential problems. Therefore, *the first step before beginning any investment program is to construct a comprehensive policy statement.*

Answering the following questions will help you evaluate a proposed policy statement:

1. Does the policy meet the specific needs and objectives of this particular investor?
2. Is the policy written so clearly that a competent stranger could use it to manage the portfolio in conformance with the client's needs? Given a manager transition, could the new manager use this policy statement to handle your portfolio in accordance with your needs?
3. Would the client have been able to remain committed to the policy during a variety of capital market experiences? Specifically, does the client fully understand investment risks and the need for a disciplined approach to the investment process?
4. Would the portfolio manager have been able to maintain the policy specified over the same period?
5. Would the policy, if implemented, have achieved the client's objectives and needs?

Adapted from Charles D. Ellis, *Investment Policy: How to Win the Loser's Game* (Homewood, IL: Dow Jones-Irwin, 1985), 62. Reproduced with permission of the McGraw-Hill Companies.

2.4 INPUT TO THE POLICY STATEMENT

Before an investor and advisor can construct a policy statement, they need to have an open and frank exchange of information regarding the client's investment objectives and constraints. To illustrate this framework, we discuss the investment objectives and constraints that may confront "typical" 25-year-old and 65-year-old investors.

2.4.1 Investment Objectives

The investor's **objectives** are his or her investment goals, expressed in terms of *both* risk and returns. (Goals should not be expressed only in terms of returns because such an approach can lead to inappropriate investment practices, such as high-risk strategies or excessive trading.)

A client should also become fully informed of investment risks associated with any specified goal, including the possibility of loss. *A careful analysis of the client's risk tolerance should precede any discussion of return objectives.* Investment firms survey clients to gauge their risk tolerance. Sometimes investment magazines or books contain tests that individuals can take to help them evaluate their risk tolerance. Subsequently, an advisor will use such test results to categorize a client's risk tolerance and suggest an initial asset allocation consistent with the client's risk tolerance and other factors noted below.

Risk tolerance is more than a function of an individual's psychological makeup; it is also affected by other factors, such as a person's current insurance coverage, cash reserves, family situation, and age. (Older persons generally have shorter investment time frames within which to make up any losses.) Risk tolerance is also influenced by one's current net worth and income expectations. All else being equal, individuals with higher incomes are generally willing to accept more risk because their incomes can help cover any shortfall. Likewise, individuals with larger portfolios can afford some risky investments, while the remaining assets provide a cushion against losses.

A person's return objective may be stated in terms of an absolute or a relative percentage return, but it may also be stated in terms of a general goal, such as capital preservation, current income, capital appreciation, or total return.

Capital preservation means that investors want to minimize their risk of loss, usually in real terms: They seek to maintain the purchasing power of their investment. In other words, the return needs to be no less than the rate of inflation. Generally, this is a strategy for strongly risk-averse investors or for funds needed in the short run, such as for next year's tuition payment or a down payment on a house.

Capital appreciation is an appropriate objective for investors who want the portfolio to grow in real terms over time to meet some future need. Under this strategy, growth mainly occurs through capital gains.

When **current income** is the return objective, investors want to generate income rather than capital gains. Retirees may favor this objective for part of their portfolio to help generate spendable funds.

The **total return** strategy is similar to that of capital appreciation; namely, the investors want the portfolio to grow over time to meet a future need. The total return strategy seeks to increase portfolio value by both capital gains and reinvesting current income.

Investment Objective: 25-Year-Old What is an appropriate investment objective for our typical 25-year-old investor? Assume that he holds a steady job, has adequate insurance coverage, and has enough money in the bank to provide a cash reserve. Also assume that his current long-term, high-priority investment goal is to build a retirement fund. Depending on his risk preferences, he can select a strategy carrying moderate to high amounts of risk because the income stream from his job will probably grow over time. Further, given his young age and income growth potential, a low-risk strategy, such as capital preservation or current income, is inappropriate for his retirement fund goal; a total return or capital appreciation objective would be most appropriate. Here's a possible objective statement:

> *Invest funds in a variety of moderate to higher-risk investments. The average risk of the equity portfolio should exceed that of a broad stock market index, such as the NYSE stock index. Foreign and domestic equity exposure should range from 80 percent to 95 percent of the total portfolio. Remaining funds should be invested in short- and intermediate-term notes and bonds.*

Investment Objective: 65-Year-Old Assume that our typical 65-year-old investor likewise has adequate insurance coverage and a cash reserve. Let's also assume she is retiring this year. This individual will want less risk exposure than the 25-year-old investor because her earning power from employment will soon be ending; she will not be able to recover any investment losses by saving more out of her paycheck. Depending on her income from Social Security and a pension plan, she may need some income from her retirement portfolio to meet current living expenses. Because she can expect to live an average of another 25 years, she will need protection against inflation. A risk-averse investor will choose a combination of current income and capital preservation strategies; a more risk-tolerant investor will choose a combination of current income and total return in an attempt to have principal growth outpace inflation. Here's an example of such an objective statement:

> *Invest in stock and bond investments to meet income needs (from bond income and stock dividends) and to provide for real growth (from equities). Fixed-income securities should comprise 55 to 65 percent of the total portfolio; of this, 5 to 10 percent should be invested in short-term securities for extra liquidity and safety. The remaining 35 to 45 percent of the portfolio should be invested in high-quality stocks whose risk is similar to that of the S&P 500 index.*

More detailed analyses for our 25-year-old and 65-year-old would include more specific risk tolerance assumptions, as well as clearly enumerate their investment goals, return objectives, the funds they have to invest at the present, as well as future funds they expect to invest, and the specific benchmark portfolios that will be used to evaluate the performance of their respective portfolio managers.

2.4.2 Investment Constraints

In addition to the risk and return objectives, other constraints include liquidity needs, an investment time horizon, tax factors, legal and regulatory constraints, and unique needs and preferences.

Liquidity Needs An asset is **liquid** if it can be quickly converted to cash at a price close to fair market value. Generally, liquid assets involve many traders who are interested in a fairly standardized product. Examples include Treasury bills that are very liquid in contrast to real estate and venture capital that are considered to be illiquid.

Investors may have liquidity needs that the investment plan must consider. For example, although an investor may have a primary long-term goal, several near-term goals may require available funds. Wealthy individuals with sizable tax obligations need adequate liquidity to pay their taxes without upsetting their investment plan. Some retirement plans may need funds for shorter-term purposes, such as buying a car or a house or making college tuition payments.

Our typical 25-year-old investor probably has little need for liquidity as he focuses on his long-term retirement fund goal. This constraint may change, however, if he faces a period of unemployment or if near-term goals, such as a house down payment, enter the picture. If changes occur, the investor needs to revise his policy statement and financial plans accordingly.

Our soon to be retired 65-year-old investor has a greater need for liquidity. Although she may receive regular checks from her pension plan and Social Security, they will probably not equal her working paycheck. She will need some of her portfolio in liquid securities to meet unexpected expenses, bills, or special needs such as trips.

Time Horizon Time horizon as an investment constraint briefly entered our earlier discussion of near-term and long-term high-priority goals. A close (but not perfect) relationship exists between an investor's time horizon, liquidity needs, and ability to handle risk. Investors with long investment horizons generally require less liquidity and can tolerate greater portfolio risk; they require less liquidity because the funds are not usually needed for many years and have greater risk tolerance because any shortfalls or losses can be overcome by subsequent earnings and returns.

Investors with shorter time horizons generally favor more liquid and less risky investments because losses are harder to overcome in a short time frame.

Because of life expectancies, our 25-year-old investor has a longer investment time horizon than our 65-year-old investor. But this does not mean the 65-year-old should only invest in short-term CDs because she needs the inflation protection that long-term investments such as common stock can provide. Still, because of the difference in the time horizons, the 25-year-old should have a greater proportion of his portfolio in equities, including small firms' stocks, as well as stocks of international and emerging market firms than the 65-year-old.

Tax Concerns Investment planning is complicated by taxes that can seriously become overwhelming if international investments are part of the portfolio. Taxable income from interest, dividends, or rents is taxable at the investor's marginal tax rate. The marginal tax rate is the proportion of the next one dollar in income paid as taxes.

A Note Regarding Taxes The impact of taxes on investment strategy and final results is clearly very significant. Unfortunately, a proper presentation on the numerous rules and regulations would be very long and complicated. In addition, the regulations are driven by politics more than financial and economic theory and, therefore, are constantly changing. As a result, the authors feel that such a presentation is beyond the scope of this book. Therefore, we must follow the lead of others and suggest that you contact your tax accountant for advice regarding tax regulations.

Legal and Regulatory Factors Both the investment process and the financial markets are highly regulated and subject to numerous laws. At times, these legal and regulatory factors constrain the investment strategies of individuals and institutions.

These legal rules and regulations are similar in many ways with the taxes noted previously. Therefore, we will *not* attempt to discuss these laws in detail but simply point out some major legal and regulatory factors that investors should consider.

An example of a regulation that would typically impact an investor is related to IRAs. Specifically, funds removed from a regular IRA, Roth IRA, or 401(k) plan before age 59½ are taxable and subject to an additional 10 percent withdrawal penalty. You may also be familiar with the tag line in many bank CD advertisements: "substantial interest penalty upon early withdrawal." Regulations and rules such as these may make such investments unattractive for investors with substantial liquidity needs in their portfolios.

Regulations can also constrain the investment choices available to someone in a fiduciary role. A *fiduciary*, or trustee, supervises an investment portfolio of a third party, such as a trust account or discretionary account.[1] Because the fiduciary must make investment decisions in accordance with the owner's wishes, a properly written policy statement assists this process. In addition, trustees of a trust account must meet the prudent-man standard, which means that they must invest and manage the funds as a prudent person would manage his or her own affairs. Notably, the prudent-man standard is based on the composition of the entire portfolio, not each individual asset.[2]

All investors must respect certain laws, such as insider trading prohibitions against the purchase and sale of securities on the basis of important non-public information. Typically, the people possessing such private (insider), information are the firm's managers, who have a fiduciary duty to their shareholders. Security transactions based on access to insider information violate the fiduciary trust the shareholders have placed with management because the managers seek personal financial gain from their privileged position.

For our typical 25-year-old investor, legal and regulatory matters will be of little concern, with the possible exception of insider trading laws and the penalties associated with early withdrawal of funds from tax-deferred retirement accounts. For a financial advisor to assist him in constructing a financial plan, that advisor would have to obey the regulations pertinent to a client–advisor relationship. Similar concerns confront our 65-year-old investor, who should seek legal and tax advice to ensure that her retirement plans and trust accounts are properly implemented.

Unique Needs and Preferences This category covers the unique concerns of each investor. For example, some investors may want to exclude certain investments solely on the basis of personal preference or for social consciousness reasons. For example, they may request that no firms that manufacture or sell tobacco, alcohol, pornography, or environmentally harmful products be included in their portfolio. Some mutual funds screen according to this type of social responsibility criterion.

Another personal constraint example is the time and expertise a person has for managing his or her portfolio. Busy executives may prefer to let a trusted advisor manage their investments. Retirees may have the time but believe they lack the expertise to manage their investments, so they also may seek professional advice.

In addition, a business owner with a large portion of her wealth—and emotion—tied up in her firm's stock may be reluctant to sell even when it may be financially prudent to do so and then reinvest the proceeds for diversification purposes. Further, if the stock is for a private company, it may be difficult to find a buyer unless shares are sold at a discount from their fair market value. Because each investor is unique, the implications of this final constraint differ for each person; there is no "typical" 25-year-old or 65-year-old investor. The point is that each individual must decide on and then communicate these specific needs and preferences in their policy statement.

---

[1]A discretionary account is one in which the fiduciary, many times a financial planner or stockbroker, has the authority to purchase and sell assets in the owner's portfolio without first receiving the owner's approval.

[2]As we will discuss in Chapter 7, it is sometimes wise to hold assets that are individually risky in the context of a well-diversified portfolio, even if the investor is strongly risk averse.

2.5 Constructing the Policy Statement

As we have seen, a policy statement allows an investor to communicate his or her objectives (risk and return) and constraints (liquidity, time horizon, tax, legal and regulatory, and unique needs and preferences). This helps give an advisor a better chance of implementing an investment strategy that will satisfy the investor. Even without an advisor, each investor needs to develop a financial plan to guide his or her investment strategy.

Constructing a policy statement is an investor's responsibility, but investment advisors often assist in the process. This section provides, for both investors and advisors, guidelines for good policy statement construction.

2.5.1 General Guidelines

In the process of constructing a policy statement, investors should think about the set of questions suggested previously on page 39.

When working with an investor to create a policy statement, an advisor should ensure that the policy statement satisfactorily answers the questions suggested previously, on page 40.

2.5.2 Some Common Mistakes

When constructing policy statements, participants in employer-sponsored retirement plans need to realize that in many such plans, 30 to 40 percent of their retirement funds may be invested in their employer's stock. Having so much money invested in one asset violates diversification principles and could be costly. To put this in context, most mutual funds are limited to no more than 5 percent of their assets in any one company's stock; a firm's pension plan can invest no more than 10 percent of its funds in its own stock. Unfortunately, individuals are doing what government regulations prevent many institutional investors from doing. Another problem may be that the average stock allocation in many retirement plans is lower than it should be—that is, investors tend to be too conservative.

A significant issue is stock trading. Numerous studies by Barber and Odean (1999, 2000, 2001) and Odean (1998, 1999) documented that individual investors typically trade stocks too often (driving up commissions), sell stocks with gains too early (prior to further price increases), and hold on to losers too long (as the price continues to fall). These costly mistakes are especially true for men and online traders.

Most investors neglect an important first step in achieving financial success: They do not plan for the future. Studies of retirement plans discussed by Ruffenach (2001) and Clements (1997a, 1997b, 1997c) indicate two significant problems: (1) Americans are not saving enough to finance their retirement years, and (2) they have not created an investing plan for their savings after they retire. Around 25 percent of workers have saved less than $50,000 for their retirement. Finally, about 60 percent of workers surveyed confessed that they were "behind schedule" in planning and saving for retirement.

2.6 The Importance of Asset Allocation

As noted, policy statements are intended to provide guidance for an overall investment strategy. Though a policy statement does not indicate which specific securities to buy or sell, it should provide guidelines as to the asset classes to include and a range of percentages of the investor's funds to invest in each class. How the investor divides funds into different asset classes is the process of *asset allocation*. Asset allocation is usually expressed in ranges that allow the investment manager some freedom, based on his or her reading of capital market trends, to invest toward the upper or lower ends of the ranges. For example, assume a policy statement requires that common stocks be 60 percent to 80 percent of the portfolio and that bonds be 20 percent to

40 percent of the portfolio's value. A manager bullish about stocks would increase the stock allocation toward the 80 percent upper end of the equity range and decrease bonds toward the 20 percent lower end of the bond range. Should she be optimistic about bonds or bearish on stocks, she could shift the allocation closer to 40 percent bonds and 60 percent equities.

A review of historical data and empirical studies provides strong support for the contention that the asset allocation decision is a critical component of the portfolio management process. In general, there are four decisions involved in constructing an investment strategy:

- What asset classes should be considered for investment?
- What policy weights should be assigned to each eligible asset class?
- What are the allowable allocation ranges based on policy weights?
- What specific securities or funds should be purchased for the portfolio?

The asset allocation decision involves the first three points and is a *very* important decision to an investor. Several studies by Ibbotson and Kaplan (2000); Brinson, Hood, and Beebower (1986); and Brinson, Singer, and Beebower (1991) have examined the effect of the normal policy weights on investment performance for both pension funds and mutual funds. All the studies found similar results: About 90 percent of a fund's returns over time can be explained by its target asset allocation policy. Exhibit 2.4 shows the relationship between returns on the target or policy portfolio allocation and actual returns on a sample mutual fund.

In contrast, some studies examined how much the asset allocation policy affects returns on a variety of funds with different target weights. Specifically, Ibbotson and Kaplan (2000) found

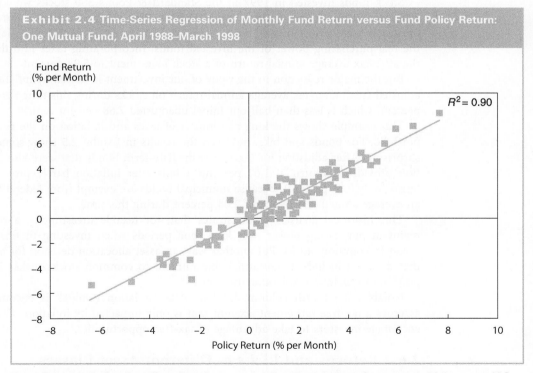

Exhibit 2.4 Time-Series Regression of Monthly Fund Return versus Fund Policy Return: One Mutual Fund, April 1988–March 1998

Note: The sample fund's policy allocations among the general asset classes were 52.4 percent U.S. large-cap stocks, 9.8 percent U.S. small-cap stocks, 3.2 percent non-U.S. stocks, 20.9 percent U.S. bonds, and 13.7 percent cash.

Source: Copyright © 2000, CFA Institute. Reproduced and republished from "Does Asset Allocation Policy Explain 40, 90 or 100 Percent of Performance?" in the *Financial Analysts Journal*, January/February 2000, with permission from CFA Institute. All Rights Reserved.

that, across a sample of funds, about 40 percent of the difference in fund returns is explained by differences in asset allocation policy. And what does asset allocation tell us about the *level* of a particular fund's returns? The studies by Brinson and colleagues (1986, 1991) and Ibbotson and Kaplan (2000) divided the policy return (what the fund return would have been had it been invested in indexes at the policy weights) by the actual fund return (which includes the effects of varying from the policy weights and security selection). Thus, a fund that was passively invested at the target weights would have a ratio value of 1.0, or 100 percent. A fund that employed market timing (for moving in and out of asset classes) and security selection would have a ratio less than 1.0 (or less than 100 percent); the manager's skill would result in a policy return less than the actual fund return. Because of market efficiency, fund managers practicing market timing and security selection, on average, have difficulty surpassing passively invested index returns after taking into account the expenses and fees of investing.

Thus, asset allocation is a very important decision (Brown, 2000). Across all funds, the asset allocation decision explains an average of 40 percent of the variation in fund returns. For a single fund, asset allocation explains 90 percent of the fund's variation in returns over time and slightly more than 100 percent of the average fund's level of return.

2.6.1 Investment Returns after Taxes and Inflation

Exhibit 2.5 indicates how an investment of $1 would have grown over the 1997–2016 period and, using fairly conservative assumptions, examines how investment returns are affected by taxes and inflation.

Stock funds invested in 1997 in the Standard & Poor's 500 stocks would have averaged a 7.68 percent annual return through 2016. Unfortunately, this return is unrealistic because if the funds were invested over time, taxes would have to be paid, and inflation would erode the real purchasing power of the invested funds. Incorporating taxes into the analysis lowers the after-tax average annual return of a stock investment to 5.98 percent.

But the major reduction in the value of our investment is caused by inflation. The inflation-adjusted (real) after-tax average annual return on stocks during this time period was only 2.87 percent, which is less than half our initial unadjusted 7.68 percent return!

This example shows the long-run impact of taxes and inflation on the real value of a stock portfolio. For bonds and bills, however, the results in Exhibit 2.5 show something even more surprising. After adjusting for taxes, intermediate-term bonds that were also adjusted for inflation provided a return of 1.64 percent; T-bills after inflation barely provided value in real terms (only 0.01 percent). Because municipal bonds are exempt from federal taxes, they earned an average annual real return of 2.04 percent during this time.

This historical analysis demonstrates that, for taxable investments, a reasonable way to maintain purchasing power over long time periods when investing in financial assets is to invest in common stocks. Put another way, an asset allocation decision for a taxable portfolio that does not include a substantial commitment to common stocks makes it difficult for the portfolio to maintain real value over time.[3]

Notably, the fourth column, labeled "After Inflation (Only)," is encouraging because it assumes a tax-free retirement account that is only impacted by inflation. These results should encourage investors to take advantage of tax-free opportunities.

2.6.2 Returns and Risks of Different Asset Classes

By focusing on returns, we have ignored its partner—risk. Assets with higher long-term returns have these returns to compensate for their risk. Exhibit 2.6 illustrates returns (unadjusted for

---

[3]Of course, other equity-oriented investments, such as venture capital or real estate, may also provide inflation protection after adjusting for portfolio costs and taxes. Future studies of the performance of Treasury inflation-protected securities (TIPs) will likely show their usefulness in protecting investors from inflation as well.

Exhibit 2.5 The Effect of Taxes and Inflation on Investment Returns: 1997–2016

	Before Taxes and Inflation	After Taxes	After Taxes and Inflation	After Inflation (Only)
Common stocks (S&P 500)	7.68%	5.98%	2.87%	5.44%
Inter-term Govt. Bonds	4.90%	3.67%	1.64%	2.72%
U.S. Treas. Bonds	2.13%	1.53%	−0.59%	0.01%
Municipal bonds	4.20%	4.20%	2.04%	2.04%

Legend:
- Common stocks (S&P 500)
- Inter-term Govt. Bonds
- U.S. Treas. Bonds
- Municipal bonds

Assumptions: 28 percent tax rate on income; 20 percent on price change. Compound inflation rate was 2.21 percent for full period.

Source: Computations by authors, using data indicated.

Exhibit 2.6 Summary Statistics of Annual Returns, 1997–2016, U.S. Securities

	Geometric Mean (%)	Arithmetic Mean (%)	Standard Deviation (%)
Large Company Stocks (S&P 500)	7.68	9.38	16.75
Small Company Stocks (Russell 2000)	10.52	11.61	19.90
Government Bonds (Barclays Capital)	7.16	7.69	5.55
Corporate Bonds (Barclays Capital)	7.29	7.82	6.19
High Yield Corp. Bonds (Barclays Capital)	8.50	9.05	15.43
30-day Treasury Bills (Fed. Reserve)	2.13	2.15	1.75
U.S. Inflation (Federal Reserve)	2.10	2.13	1.07

Source: Calculations by authors using data noted.

inflation, transaction costs and taxes) for several asset classes over time. As expected, the higher returns available from equities (both large cap and small cap) also include higher risk. This is precisely why investors need a policy statement and an understanding of capital markets as well as a disciplined approach to investing. Safe Treasury bills will sometimes outperform equities, and, because equities have higher risk (as indicated by the larger standard deviations), common stocks will sometimes experience significant losses. These are times when undisciplined and uneducated investors become frustrated, sell their stocks at a loss, and vow never to invest in equities again. During such times, disciplined investors stick to their investment plan and ideally hold on to their stocks and continue to purchase more at depressed prices because they expect the equity portion of the portfolio will experience a substantial increase in the future.

As noted earlier, the asset allocation decision is a major determinant of both the returns and the volatility of the portfolio. Exhibit 2.6 indicates that stocks are riskier than bonds or T-bills. Exhibit 2.7 shows that stocks have sometimes experienced returns lower than those of T-bills for extended periods of time. Still, the long-term results in Exhibit 2.6 show that sticking with an investment policy through difficult times provides attractive rates of return over long holding periods.[4]

As noted in Chapter 1, a popular measure of risk is the standard deviation of annual rates of return for an asset class. The results in Exhibit 2.6 indicate that stocks are relatively risky and T-bills are relatively safe. Another intriguing measure of risk is the probability of *not* meeting your investment return objective. Given this perspective, the results in Exhibit 2.7 show that if the investor has a long time horizon (that is, approaching 20 years), the risk of equities is small and that of T-bills is large because of their differences in *long-term* expected returns.

2.6.3 Asset Allocation Summary

A carefully constructed policy statement determines the types of assets that should be included in a portfolio, and the asset allocation decision dominates the portfolio's returns over time. Although seemingly risky, investors seeking capital appreciation, income, or even capital preservation over long time periods should stipulate a sizable allocation to the equity portion in their portfolio. As noted in this section, a strategy's risk depends on the investor's goals and time horizon. As demonstrated, investing in T-bills may actually be a riskier strategy than investing in common stocks due to the risk of *not meeting long-term investment return goals*, especially after considering the impact of inflation and taxes.

Thus far in this chapter we have been concerned with the *process* of asset allocation, mainly concerned with creating a policy statement that reflects the clients risk-return desires along with any constraints due to unique circumstances. Assuming that the client has articulated his or her general requirements, we now consider the array of financial assets available to implement the policy statement. We have introduced some well-known U.S. assets (stocks, bonds, and bills), but the rest of this chapter will consider a wide array of foreign and domestic financial instruments.

The point is, currently you have an array of investment choices that were unavailable a few decades ago. As discussed by Miller (1991), a combination of dynamic financial markets,

Exhibit 2.7 Higher Returns Offered by Equities over Long Time Periods: 1934–2015

Length of Holding Period (calendar years)	Percentage of Periods That Stock Returns Trailed T-Bill Returns*
1	34.10%
5	15.20%
10	8.40%
20	0.00
30	0.00

*Price change plus reinvested income

Source: Author calculations.

---

[4]The added benefits of diversification—combining different assets classes in the portfolio—may reduce overall risk without harming potential return. The important topic of diversification is discussed in Chapter 6.

technological advances, and new regulations have resulted in numerous new investment instruments and expanded trading opportunities. Improvements in communications and relaxation of international regulations have made it easier for investors to trade in both domestic and global markets. Today U.S. brokers can reach security exchanges in London, Tokyo, and other European and Asian cities as easily as those in New York, Chicago, and other U.S. cities. The deregulation of the brokerage industry and banking sector have made it possible for more financial institutions to compete for investor dollars. This has spawned investment vehicles with a variety of maturities, risk-return characteristics, and cash flow patterns that we will examine in this chapter.

As an investor, you need to understand the differences among investments so you can build a properly diversified **portfolio** that conforms to your objectives. That is, you should seek to acquire a group of investments with different patterns of returns over time. If chosen carefully, such portfolios minimize risk for a given level of return because low or negative rates of return on some investments during a period of time are offset by above-average returns on others. Your goal should be a balanced portfolio of investments with relatively stable rates of return. This text should help you understand and evaluate the risk-return characteristics of investment portfolios. An appreciation of alternative security types is the starting point for this analysis.

Because investors can choose securities from around the world, we initially consider reasons investors *should* include foreign securities in their portfolios. These reasons provide a compelling case for global investing.

We will also discuss securities in domestic and global markets, including their main features and cash flow patterns. You will see that the varying risk-return characteristics of alternative investments suit the preferences of different investors. We conclude the chapter with an analysis of the historical risk and return performance of several global investment instruments and examine the relationship among the returns for these securities. These results provide strong empirical support for global investing.

2.7 THE CASE FOR GLOBAL INVESTMENTS

Thirty years ago, the bulk of investments available to individual investors consisted of U.S. stocks and bonds. Now, however, your broker gives you access to a wide range of global securities. Currently, you can purchase stock in General Motors or Toyota, U.S. Treasury bonds or Japanese government bonds, a mutual fund that invests in U.S. biotechnology companies, a global growth stock fund, a German or Chinese stock fund, or options on a U.S. stock index.

This explosion of investment opportunities is due to the growth and development of numerous foreign financial markets, including those in Japan, the United Kingdom, and Germany, as well as emerging markets, such as China and India. U.S. investment firms have recognized this opportunity and established facilities in these countries aided by advances in telecommunications technology that allow constant contact with offices and financial markets around the world. In addition, foreign firms and investors undertook counterbalancing initiatives, including significant mergers of firms and security exchanges. Therefore, investors and investment firms can easily trade securities in markets around the world.

There are three interrelated reasons U.S. investors should think of constructing global investment portfolios:

1. When investors compare the absolute and relative sizes of U.S. and foreign markets for stocks and bonds, they see that ignoring foreign markets reduces their choices to less than 50 percent of available investment opportunities. Because more opportunities broaden your risk-return choices, it makes sense to evaluate the full range of foreign securities when building a portfolio.
2. The rates of return available on non-U.S. securities often have substantially exceeded those for U.S.-only securities. The higher returns on non-U.S. *equities* can be justified by the higher growth rates for these countries.

3. A major tenet of investment theory is that investors should diversify their portfolios. As discussed in detail in Chapter 6, the relevant factor when diversifying a portfolio is low correlation between asset returns over time. Therefore, diversification with foreign securities that have very low correlation with U.S. securities can substantially reduce portfolio risk.

In this section, we analyze these reasons to demonstrate the advantages to a U.S. investor of increasing the role of foreign financial markets.

2.7.1 Relative Size of U.S. Financial Markets

Prior to 1970, the securities traded in the U.S. stock and bond markets comprised about 65 percent of all the securities available in world capital markets. Therefore, a U.S. investor selecting securities strictly from U.S. markets had a fairly complete set of investments available. As a result, most U.S. investors probably believed that it was not worth the time and effort to expand their investment universe to include the limited investments available in foreign markets. That situation has changed dramatically over the past 45 plus years. Currently, investors who ignore foreign stock and bond markets limit their investment choices substantially.

Exhibit 2.8 shows the breakdown of securities available in world capital markets in 1969 and 2010. Not only has the overall value of all securities increased dramatically (from $2.3 trillion to $14 trillion), but the composition has also changed. Concentrating on proportions of bond and equity investments, the exhibit shows that in 1969 U.S. dollar bonds and U.S. equity securities made up 53 percent of the total value of all securities versus 28.4 percent for the total of nondollar bonds and equity. By 2010, U.S. bonds and equities accounted for 42.6 percent of the total securities market versus 47.2 percent for nondollar bonds and stocks. These data indicate that if you consider only the U.S. proportion of this combined stock and bond market, it has declined from 65 percent of the total in 1969 to about 47 percent in 2010.

The point is that the U.S. securities markets now include a substantially smaller proportion of the total world capital market, and this trend is expected to continue. The faster economic growth of many other countries compared to the United States (especially some emerging markets, such as China and India) will require foreign governments and individual companies to issue debt and equity securities to finance this growth. Therefore, U.S. investors should

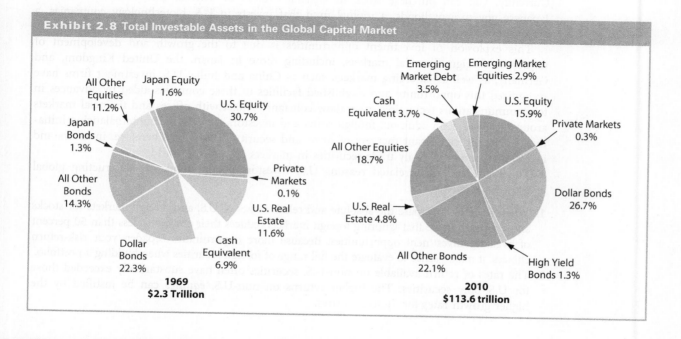

Exhibit 2.8 Total Investable Assets in the Global Capital Market

1969
$2.3 Trillion

2010
$113.6 trillion

consider investing in foreign securities because of the growing importance of these foreign securities in world capital markets. Put another way, *not* investing in foreign stocks and bonds means you are ignoring over 50 percent of the securities that are available to you. This approximate 50/50 breakdown is about the same for bonds alone, while U.S. stocks are only about 42 percent of global stocks.

2.7.2 Rates of Return on U.S. and Foreign Securities

An examination of the rates of return on U.S. and foreign securities not only demonstrates that many non-U.S. securities provide superior rates of return but also shows the impact of the exchange rate risk discussed in Chapter 1.

Global Bond-Market Returns Exhibit 2.9 contains annual rates of return for several major international bond markets for 1986–2010. The returns have been converted to U.S. dollar returns, so the exhibit shows mean annual returns and standard deviations that a U.S.-based investor would receive. As shown, the return performance (both geometric and arithmetic average) of the U.S. bond market ranked sixth out of the six countries. Part of the reason for the better performance in dollar terms of the non-U.S. markets is that the dollar generally weakened during this time frame, giving U.S. investors a boost to their returns on foreign securities. Put another way, U.S. investors who invested in these foreign bonds received the return on the bonds equal to that of local investors, but also received a return for holding the foreign currency that appreciated relative to the U.S. dollar during this period. An offsetting result is that U.S. bonds had the lowest standard deviation of the six countries.

Global Equity-Market Returns Exhibit 2.10 shows the annual returns in U.S. dollars for major equity markets yearly from 2007 through 2010. The United States' average rank in U.S. dollar returns in 2007–2010 was 17.5 out of 34 countries (and it was in the top 10 only once).

These results for equity and bond markets around the world indicate that investors who limit themselves to the U.S. market during many years may experience rates of return below those in some other countries.

2.7.3 Risk of Diversified Country Investments

Thus far, we have discussed the risk and return results for individual countries. In Chapter 1, we considered the idea of combining a number of assets into a portfolio and noted that investors should create diversified portfolios to reduce the variability of the returns over time. We discussed how proper diversification reduces the variability (our measure of risk) of the portfolio because alternative investments have different patterns of returns over time. Specifically, when the rates of return on some investments are negative or below average, potentially other investments in the portfolio will be experiencing above-average rates of return. Therefore, a properly diversified portfolio, should provide a more stable rate of return for the total

Exhibit 2.9 Global Government Bond Annual Rates of Return in U.S. Dollars: 1986–2010

	Geometric Mean	Arithmetic Mean	Standard Deviation
Canada	9.89	10.32	9.77
France	9.65	10.39	12.86
Germany	8.48	9.28	13.49
Japan	8.20	9.14	14.75
United Kingdom	9.09	9.84	13.28
Unites States	7.20	7.37	6.09

Source: Bank of America-Merrill Lynch.

Exhibit 2.10 Annual Equity Returns in U.S. Dollars

	Performance of Dow Jones Global Indexes							
	2010		**2009**		**2008**		**2007**	
	USD Returns	Rank	USD Returns	Rank	USD Returns	Rank	USD Returns	Rank
U.S.	**15.30%**	**13**	**25.70%**	**27**	**−38.60%**	**3**	**3.80%**	**27**
Australia	12.40%	17	70.90%	8	−54.50%	23	25.30%	14
Austria	NA		55.60%	15	−64.80%	30	1.60%	31
Belgium	4.70%	23	50.50%	17	−52.60%	18	5.60%	25
Brazil	5.70%	22	127.10%	2	−57.00%	28	71.10%	1
Canada	22.00%	12	56.90%	13	−49.10%	12	27.10%	12
Chile	49.60%	4	88.80%	4	−43.60%	7	23.00%	16
Denmark	26.60%	8	40.80%	21	−51.60%	15	17.60%	18
Finland	10.80%	19	17.50%	32	−56.40%	27	39.00%	4
France	−5.70%	26	28.60%	26	−45.50%	9	11.30%	22
Germany	7.10%	20	24.10%	29	−46.30%	10	30.50%	9
Greece	−46.50%	31	24.10%	29	−66.40%	32	29.80%	10
Hong Kong	14.20%	14	67.40%	10	−53.90%	22	44.50%	3
Iceland	57.20%	1	10.30%	33	−96.20%	34	13.10%	19
Indonesia	38.40%	5	129.30%	1	−63.00%	29	39.00%	4
Ireland	−11.00%	27	54.70%	16	−68.70%	33	−19.20%	34
Italy	−17.60%	29	23.20%	31	−52.50%	17	1.70%	30
Japan	13.80%	15	4.00%	34	−29.30%	1	−6.00%	33
Malaysia	35.90%	6	46.90%	19	−44.60%	8	44.60%	2
Mexico	26.40%	9	48.20%	18	−39.80%	4	10.80%	23
Netherlands	−0.30%	25	42.80%	20	−55.60%	25	12.00%	21
New Zealand	4.70%	23	38.80%	23	−52.40%	16	2.20%	29
Norway	13.40%	16	93.80%	3	−66.20%	31	26.80%	13
Philippines	55.90%	3	70.40%	9	−55.50%	24	36.70%	7
Portugal	−16.30%	28	35.40%	24	−53.80%	21	24.50%	15
Singapore	22.90%	11	74.00%	6	−53.10%	19	27.60%	11
South Africa	30.90%	7	56.00%	14	−42.80%	5	12.60%	20
South Korea	23.90%	10	65.30%	12	−55.60%	25	33.60%	8
Spain	−24.50%	30	32.60%	25	−43.40%	6	17.80%	17
Sweden	NA		65.50%	11	−53.20%	20	−3.10%	32
Switzerland	11.40%	18	25.10%	28	−31.00%	2	5.60%	25
Taiwan	NA		83.10%	5	−47.60%	11	6.50%	24
Thailand	56.70%	2	71.70%	7	−49.90%	13	39.00%	4
U.K.	7.00%	21	39.50%	22	−51.20%	14	3.80%	27

NA – not available (removed from sample)

Source: *The Wall Street Journal*, various issues, and author calculations.

portfolio (that is, it will have a lower standard deviation and therefore less risk). Although portfolio theory is discussed in detail in Chapter 6, we need to consider the concept at this point to fully understand the benefits of global investing.

To determine if two investments will contribute to diversifying a portfolio, it is necessary to compute the correlation coefficient between their rates of return over time. Correlation coefficients can range from +1.00 to −1.00. A correlation of +1.00 means that the rates of return for two investments move exactly together. Combining investments that move exactly together in a portfolio would not help diversify the portfolio because they have identical rate-of-return patterns over time. In contrast, a correlation coefficient of −1.00 means that the rates of return for two investments move exactly opposite to each other. When one investment is experiencing above-average rates of return, the other is suffering through similar below-average rates of return. Combining two investments with large negative correlation in a portfolio would be ideal for diversification because it would stabilize the rates of return over time, thereby reducing the standard deviation of the portfolio rates of return and the risk of the portfolio. Therefore, if you want to diversify your portfolio and reduce your risk, you want an investment that has either *low positive* correlation, *zero* correlation, or, ideally, *negative correlation* with the other investments in your portfolio. With this in mind, the following discussion considers the correlations of returns among U.S. bonds and stocks with the returns on foreign bonds and stocks.

Global Bond Portfolio Risk   Exhibit 2.11 lists the correlation coefficients between rates of return for bonds in the United States and bonds in major foreign markets in U.S. dollar terms from 1986 to 2016. For a U.S. investor, these important correlations averaged only 0.59.

These relatively low positive correlations among returns in U.S. dollars mean that U.S. investors can reduce risk through global diversification of their bond portfolios. A U.S. investor who added these non-U.S. bonds (especially Japanese bonds) would reduce the standard deviation of a well-diversified U.S. bond portfolio.

Why do these correlation coefficients for returns between U.S. bonds and foreign bonds differ? That is, why is the U.S.–Canada correlation 0.78, whereas the U.S.–Japan correlation is only 0.32? The answer is that the international trade patterns, economic growth, fiscal policies, and monetary policies of the countries differ. We do not have an integrated world economy but, rather, a collection of economies that are related to one another in different ways. As an example, the U.S. and Canadian economies are closely related because of their geographic proximity, similar domestic economic policies, and the extensive trade between them. Each is the other's largest trading partner. In contrast, the United States has less trade with Japan, and the fiscal and monetary policies of the two countries typically differ dramatically. For example, the U.S. economy was growing during much of the period between 1996 and 2010, while the Japanese economy experienced a prolonged recession.

The point is that macroeconomic differences cause the correlation of bond returns between the United States and each country to likewise differ, which makes it worthwhile to diversify with foreign bonds. The different correlations indicate which countries will provide the greatest reduction in the standard deviation (risk) of bond portfolio returns for a U.S. investor.

Also, *the correlation of returns between a single pair of countries changes over time* because the factors influencing the correlations—such as international trade, economic growth, fiscal policy, and monetary policy—change over time. A change in any of these variables will produce a change in how the economies are related and a change in the correlations between returns on bonds. For example, the correlation in U.S. dollar returns between U.S. and Japanese bonds was 0.07 in the late 1960s and 1970s; it was 0.35 in the 1980s and 0.25 in the 1990s but only about 0.30 in the 2000–2016 time frame.

Exhibit 2.12 shows what happens to the risk-return trade-off when we combine U.S. and foreign bonds. A comparison of a completely non-U.S. portfolio (100 percent foreign) and a

Exhibit 2.11 Correlation Coefficients Between U.S. Dollar Rates of Return on Bonds in the United States and in Major Foreign Markets: 1986–2016 (monthly data)

	Correlation Coefficient with U.S. Bonds
Canada	0.78
France	0.59
Germany	0.65
Japan	0.32
United Kingdom	0.62
Average	**0.59**

Source: Data from Barclays Capital; calculations by authors.

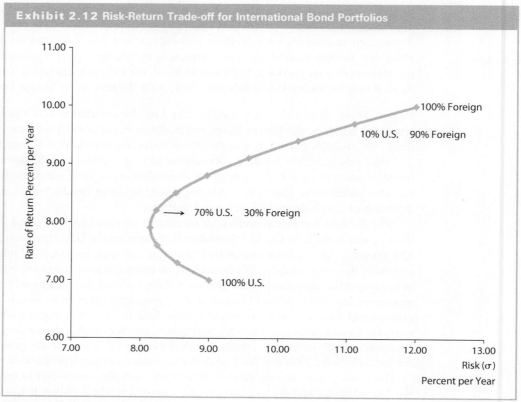

Exhibit 2.12 Risk-Return Trade-off for International Bond Portfolios

Source: Compiled by author.

100 percent U.S. portfolio indicates that the non-U.S. portfolio has both a higher rate of return and a higher standard deviation of returns than the U.S. portfolio. Combining the two portfolios in different proportions provides an interesting set of points.

As we will discuss in Chapter 9, the expected rate of return is a weighted average of the two portfolios. In contrast, the risk (standard deviation) of the combination is *not* a weighted average but also depends on the correlation between the two portfolios. In the example shown in Exhibit 2.12, the risk levels of the combined portfolios decline *below those of the individual portfolios.* Therefore, by adding foreign bonds that have low correlation with a portfolio of U.S. bonds, a U.S. investor is able to not only *increase* the expected rate of return but also *reduce* the risk compared to a total U.S. bond portfolio.

Global Equity Portfolio Risk The correlation of world equity markets resembles that for bonds. Exhibit 2.13 lists the correlation coefficients between monthly equity returns in U.S. dollars of each country and the U.S. market for the period from 1988 to 2010. Only 4 of the 11 correlations between U.S. dollar returns were over 0.70, and the average correlation was 0.65.

These relatively small positive correlations between U.S. stocks and foreign stocks have similar implications to those derived for bonds. Investors can reduce the overall risk of their stock portfolios by including foreign stocks.

Exhibit 2.14 demonstrates the impact of international equity diversification. These curves demonstrate that, as you increase the number of randomly selected securities in a portfolio, the standard deviation will decline due to the benefits of diversification *within your own country.* This is referred to as *domestic diversification.* After a certain number of securities (40 to 50), the domestic stock curve will flatten out at a risk level that reflects the basic market risk for the

Exhibit 2.13 Correlation Coefficient Between Common Stock Returns in the United States and in Foreign Markets (monthly return data: 1988–2010)

	Correlation Coefficient with U.S. Stocks
Australia	0.63
Canada	0.76
France	0.72
Germany	0.70
Italy	0.54
Japan	0.42
Netherlands	0.74
Spain	0.64
Sweden	0.68
Switzerland	0.61
United Kingdom	0.73
Average	**0.65**

Source: Calculations by authors using monthly data from MSCI.

Exhibit 2.14 Risk Reduction through Domestic and International Diversification

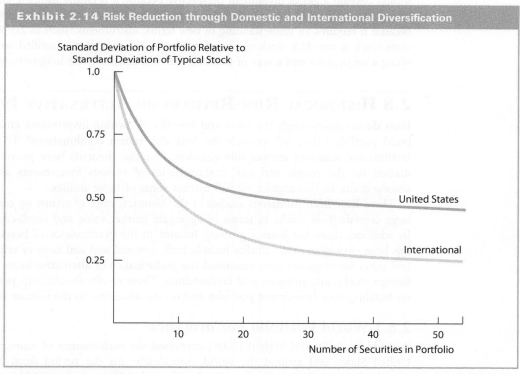

Source: Copyright 1974, CFA Institute. Reproduced and republished from "Why Not Diversify Internationally Rather Than Domestically?" in the *Financial Analysts Journal*, July/August 1974, with permission from CFA Institute. All rights reserved.

domestic economy (see Campbell, Lettau, Malkiel, and Xu [2001]). The lower curve illustrates the benefits of *international diversification*. This curve demonstrates that adding foreign securities to a U.S. portfolio to create a global portfolio enables an investor to experience lower overall risk because the non-U.S. securities are not correlated with our economy or our stock market, allowing the investor to eliminate some of the basic market risks of the U.S. economy.

To see how this works, consider, for example, the effect of inflation and interest rates on all U.S. securities. As discussed in Chapter 1, all U.S. securities will be affected by these variables. In contrast, a Japanese stock is mainly affected by what happens in the Japanese economy and will typically not be affected by changes in U.S. variables. Thus, adding Japanese, Australian, and Italian stocks to a U.S. stock portfolio reduces the portfolio risk because the *global* portfolio reflects only *worldwide* systematic factors.

Summary on Global Investing In this subsection, we have considered the relative size of the market for non-U.S. bonds and stocks and found that this non-U.S. market has grown in size and importance, becoming too big to ignore. We also examined the rates of return for foreign bond and stock investments and determined that their rates of return were often superior to those in the U.S. market. Finally, we discussed the importance of diversification in reducing the variability of portfolio returns over time, which reduces the risk of the portfolio. Successful diversification combines investments with low positive or negative correlations between rates of return, which is what we found between rates of return on U.S. and foreign bonds and stocks. Therefore, adding foreign stocks and bonds to a U.S. portfolio *will almost certainly reduce the risk of the portfolio and can possibly increase its average return.*

Given the several compelling reasons for adding foreign securities to a U.S. portfolio, investors should develop a global investment perspective because it is clearly justified, and this trend toward global investing will continue. Implementing a global investment perspective will not be easy because it requires an understanding of new terms, instruments (such as Eurobonds), and institutions (such as non-U.S. stock and bond markets). Still, the effort is justified because you are developing a set of skills and a way of thinking that will enhance your long-term investing results.

2.8 HISTORICAL RISK-RETURNS ON ALTERNATIVE INVESTMENTS

How do investors weigh the costs and benefits of owning investments and make decisions to build portfolios that will provide the best risk–return combinations? To help individual or institutional investors answer this question, financial theorists have provided extensive information on the return and risk characteristics of various investments and the correlations among them. In this section we will discuss some of these studies.

There have been numerous studies of the historical rates of return on common stocks (both large-capitalization stocks in terms of aggregate market value and small-capitalization stocks).[5] In addition, there has been a growing interest in the performance of bonds. Because inflation has been pervasive, many studies include both nominal and real rates of return on investments. Still other investigators have examined the performance of alternative assets such as real estate, foreign stocks, art, antiques, and commodities. These results should help you to make decisions on building your investment portfolio and on the allocation to the various asset classes.

2.8.1 World Portfolio Performance

A study by Reilly and Wright (2004) examined the performance of numerous assets from the United States and around the world. Specifically, for the period from 1980 to 2001, they examined the performance of stocks, bonds, cash (the equivalent of U.S. T-bills), real estate, and commodities from the world, United States, Europe, Pacific Basin, Japan, and the emerging markets. They computed annual returns, risk measures, and correlations among the returns for alternative assets. Exhibit 2.15 contains updated results through 2010.

---

[5]Small-capitalization stocks were broken out as a separate class of asset because several studies have shown that firms with relatively small capitalization (stock with low market value) have experienced rates of return and risk significantly different from those of stocks in general. Therefore, they were considered a unique asset class. We will discuss these studies in Chapter 5, which deals with the efficient markets hypothesis. The large-company stock returns are based upon the S&P Composite Index of 500 stocks—the S&P 500 (described in Chapter 4).

Exhibit 2.15 Summary Risk-Return Results for Alternative Capital Market Assets: 1980–2010

Index	Arithmetic Mean Annual Return	Geometric Mean Return	Standard Deviation Annual Return (Based on Arithmetic Mean Return)	Beta With S&P 500	Beta With Brinson GSMI
S&P 500	12.04%	10.80%	15.60%	1.00	1.33
Ibbotson Small Cap Index	14.30%	12.18%	20.33%	0.99	1.44
Wilshire 5000 Equal Weighted	19.12%	16.94%	20.83%	1.02	1.48
Wilshire 5000 S&P Cap Weighted	12.02%	10.78%	15.61%	1.00	1.33
Russell 1000	12.06%	10.75%	15.76%	1.01	1.35
Russell 1000 Value	12.50%	11.31%	15.04%	0.92	1.22
Russell 1000 Growth	11.49%	9.81%	17.91%	1.10	1.48
Russell 2000	12.36%	10.35%	19.94%	1.06	1.52
Russell 2000 Value	13.86%	12.31%	17.54%	0.91	1.29
Russell 2000 Growth	10.79%	8.00%	23.44%	1.21	1.75
Russell 3000	12.02%	10.70%	15.89%	1.01	1.37
Russell 3000 Value	12.56%	11.38%	15.04%	0.91	1.23
Russell 3000 Growth	11.35%	9.63%	18.12%	1.11	1.50
IFC Emerging Markets	14.16%	11.57%	22.98%	0.80	1.26
FTSE All World	8.45%	7.09%	15.98%	0.96	1.42
FTSE All World Developed	8.18%	6.83%	15.65%	0.95	1.39
FTSE All World Emerging	10.44%	7.47%	24.92%	1.15	1.83
MSCI EAFE	8.90%	7.26%	17.71%	0.73	1.34
MSCI Europe	12.51%	10.81%	17.80%	0.83	1.39
MSCI Pacifc Basin	10.08%	7.89%	21.13%	0.63	1.26
MSCI Japan	8.59%	6.13%	22.39%	0.54	1.15
Tokyo Stock Exchange Index	4.11%	2.15%	19.51%	0.50	0.88
M-S World Index	11.24%	10.00%	15.37%	0.86	1.34
Brinson GSMI	10.60%	10.01%	10.86%	0.64	1.00
LB Government Bond	8.30%	8.15%	5.51%	0.04	0.11
LB Corporate Bond	9.07%	8.82%	7.23%	0.14	0.28
LB Aggregate Bond	8.55%	8.39%	5.76%	0.08	0.17
High Yield Corporate Bond	10.43%	10.00%	9.24%	0.33	0.54
ML World Government Bond[1]	8.12%	7.88%	7.04%	0.03	0.18
ML World Government Bond ex U.S.[1]	9.06%	8.58%	9.84%	0.03	0.24
FTSE North American Equity REIT	13.30%	11.62%	17.49%	0.62	0.95
GS Commodities Index[2]	8.38%	6.39%	19.52%	0.18	0.35
Treasury Bill–30-Day	4.96%	4.95%	0.90%	0.00	0.00
Treasury Bill–6 month[3]	5.63%	5.62%	0.98%	0.00	0.00
Treasury Note–2 year[3]	6.80%	6.76%	3.11%	0.01	0.04
Inflation	3.40%	3.39%	1.22%	0.00	−0.01

[1]ML World Government Bond Index based on 1986–2010 only.

[2]GS Commodity Index based on 1983–2010 only.

[3]Treasury Bill–6 month and Treasury Note–2 year based on 1981–2010 only.

Source: Updated and modified, Frank K. Reilly and David J. Wright, "An Analysis of Risk-Adjusted Performance for Global Market Assets," *Journal of Portfolio Management* (Spring 2004).

Asset Return and Total Risk The results in Exhibit 2.15 generally confirm the expected relationship between annual rates of return and the total risk (standard deviation) of these securities. The riskier assets with higher standard deviations experienced higher returns. For example, the U.S. stock indexes had relatively high returns (10 to 17 percent) and large standard deviations (15 to 23 percent). It is not surprising that the highest-risk asset class (without commodities) was the two emerging market stock indexes with standard deviations of 22.98 and 24.92 percent, whereas risk-free U.S. cash equivalents (30-day T-bills) had low returns (4.96 percent) and the smallest standard deviation (0.90 percent).

Exhibit 2.16 Geometric Mean Return versus Brinson GSMI Beta for Alternative Capital Market Assets: 1980–2010

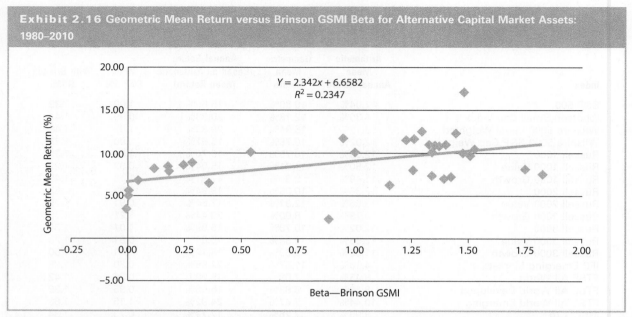

Source: Updated and modified results from Frank K. Reilly and David J. Wright, "An Analysis of Risk-Adjusted Performance for Global Market Assets," *Journal of Portfolio Management*, 30, no. 3 (Spring 2004): 63–77.

Return and Systematic Risk As shown in Exhibit 2.15, in addition to total risk (standard deviation), the authors also considered systematic risk, which is the volatility of an asset relative to a market portfolio of risky assets (this was discussed briefly in Chapter 1). One of the conclusions of the Reilly and Wright (2004) study was that the systematic risk measure (beta) did a better job of explaining the returns during the period than the total risk measure (standard deviation). In addition, the systematic risk measure (beta) that used the Brinson Global Security Market Index (GSMI) as a market proxy was somewhat better than the beta that used the S&P 500 Index.[6] Thus, Exhibit 2.16, which contains the scatter plot of geometric mean rate of return and GSMI systematic risk, indicates the expected positive risk-return relationship. The two outliers are the Tokyo Stock Exchange Index on the low side and the Wilshire 5000 equal-weighted index on the high side.

Correlations between Asset Returns Exhibit 2.17 contains a correlation matrix of selected U.S. and world assets. The first column shows that U.S. equities (as represented by the broad Wilshire 5000 capital weighted Index) have a reasonably high correlation with most developed countries but low correlation with emerging market stocks and Pacific Basin stocks (including Japan). Also, U.S. equities show almost zero correlation with world government bonds, and with the commodities index. Recall from our earlier discussion that you can use this information to build a diversified portfolio by combining assets with low positive or negative correlations.

The correlation of returns with inflation has implications regarding the ability of an asset class to be an inflation hedge: A good inflation hedge should have a *strong positive correlation with inflation*. As shown, most assets (including common stocks) have negative correlations with inflation, which implies that they are poor inflation hedges. The exceptions appear to be

---

[6]For a detailed analysis of the impact of different market benchmarks, including a detailed comparison of the S&P 500 Index versus the Brinson Global Security Market Index (GSMI), see Reilly and Akhtar (1995).

Exhibit 2.17 Correlations among Global Capital Market Asset Monthly Returns: 1980–2010							
	Wilshire 5000 Equal Weighted	Wilshire 5000 S&P Cap Weighted	IFC Emerging Markets	MSCI EAFE	M-S World	Brinson GSMI	Inflation
S&P 500	0.763	1.000	0.543	0.645	0.873	0.926	−0.046
Ibbotson Small Cap Index	0.935	0.759	0.533	0.544	0.695	0.771	−0.032
Wilshire 5000 Equal Weighted	1.000	0.763	0.561	0.546	0.702	0.770	−0.014
Wilshire 5000 S&P Cap Weighted	0.763	1.000	0.542	0.645	0.873	0.926	−0.046
Russell 1000	0.786	0.997	0.550	0.645	0.871	0.931	−0.049
Russell 1000 Growth	0.768	0.961	0.526	0.609	0.835	0.898	−0.049
Russell 2000	0.905	0.828	0.540	0.582	0.750	0.829	−0.059
Russell 2000 Value	0.860	0.806	0.511	0.568	0.728	0.801	−0.067
Russell 2000 Growth	0.891	0.807	0.535	0.562	0.731	0.810	−0.049
Russell 3000	0.809	0.993	0.556	0.647	0.871	0.934	−0.051
Russell 3000 Value	0.755	0.949	0.532	0.629	0.836	0.888	−0.047
Russell 3000 Growth	0.791	0.958	0.533	0.613	0.835	0.901	−0.049
IFC Emerging Market	0.561	0.542	1.000	0.569	0.608	0.594	0.004
FTSE All World	0.755	0.943	0.826	0.958	0.998	0.977	0.030
FTSE All World Developed	0.751	0.950	0.801	0.955	0.999	0.976	0.028
FTSE All World Emerging	0.714	0.722	0.985	0.796	0.801	0.804	0.042
MSCI EAFE	0.548	0.645	0.569	1.000	0.929	0.819	−0.072
MSCI Europe	0.595	0.726	0.574	0.884	0.888	0.851	−0.082
MSCI Pacific Basin	0.409	0.462	0.466	0.894	0.780	0.645	−0.020
MSCI Japan	0.329	0.377	0.368	0.835	0.702	0.558	−0.020
Tokyo Stock Exchange Index	0.376	0.399	0.411	0.685	0.622	0.492	0.017
M-S World Index	0.702	0.873	0.608	0.929	1.000	0.945	−0.059
Brinson GSMI	0.770	0.926	0.594	0.819	0.945	1.000	−0.078
LB Government Bond	−0.031	0.112	−0.148	0.072	0.088	0.223	−0.139
LB Corporate Bond	0.209	0.297	0.058	0.242	0.285	0.421	−0.140
LB Aggregate Bond	0.081	0.209	−0.054	0.158	0.189	0.327	−0.123
High Yield Corporate Bond	0.640	0.552	0.404	0.472	0.554	0.633	−0.012
ML World Government Bond[1]	−0.049	0.064	−0.034	0.364	0.255	0.278	−0.107
ML World Government Bond ex U.S.[1]	−0.043	0.041	−0.011	0.431	0.296	0.268	−0.074
FTSE North American Equity REIT	0.598	0.553	0.379	0.461	0.545	0.588	−0.003
GS Commodities Index[2]	0.155	0.145	0.206	0.228	0.212	0.196	0.200
Treasury Bill–30 Day	−0.041	0.027	−0.080	−0.036	−0.014	−0.006	0.411
Treasury Bill–6 Month[3]	−0.022	0.043	−0.078	−0.007	0.013	0.030	0.371
Treasury Note–2 Year[3]	−0.058	0.047	−0.152	0.035	0.037	0.151	−0.021
Inflation	−0.014	−0.046	0.004	−0.072	−0.059	−0.078	1.000

[1]ML World Government Bond Index based on 1986–2010 only.

[2]GS Commodity Index based on 1983–2010 only.

[3]Treasury Bill–6 month and Treasury Note–2 year based on 1981–2010 only.

Source: Updated and modified, Frank K. Reilly and David J. Wright, "An Analysis of Risk Adjusted Performance for Global Market Assets," *Journal of Portfolio Management*, 30, no. 3 (Spring 2004); 63–77.

commodities (0.20) and short-term government bonds (30-day and 6-month Treasury bills with 0.41 and 0.37 correlations).

2.8.2 Art and Antiques

Unlike financial securities, where transactions are reported daily, art and antique markets are fragmented and lack any formal transaction reporting system, which makes it difficult to gather data. The best-known series regarding the changing value of art and antiques was developed by Sotheby's, a major art auction firm. These value indexes covered 13 areas of art and antiques and a weighted aggregate series that combined the 13 areas.

Reilly (1992) examined these series for the period 1976 to 1991 and computed rates of return, measures of risk, and the correlations among the various art and antique series and compared them to stocks, bonds, and the rate of inflation.

There was a wide range of returns and risk, but a risk-return plot indicated a fairly consistent relationship between risk and return during this 16-year period. Notably, the art and antique results were very consistent with the bond and stock index results.

Analysis of the correlations among these assets using annual rates of return revealed several important relationships. First, the correlations among alternative antique and art categories vary substantially from above 0.90 to negative correlations. Second, the correlations between art/antiques and bonds were generally negative. Third, the correlations of art/antiques with stocks were typically small positive values. Finally, the correlation of art and antiques with the rate of inflation indicates that several of the categories were fairly good inflation hedges since they were positively correlated with inflation. Notably, they were clearly superior inflation hedges compared to long-term bonds and common stocks, as documented in Fama (1991) and Jaffe and Mandelker (1976). The reader should be aware that most art and antiques are quite *illiquid*, and the *transaction costs are very high* compared to those of financial assets.[7]

2.8.3 Real Estate

Similar to art and antiques, returns on real estate are difficult to derive because of the limited number of transactions and the lack of a national source of transaction data that allows one to accurately compute rates of return. In the study by Goetzmann and Ibbotson (1990), the authors gathered data on commercial real estate through real estate investment trusts (REITs) and commingled real estate funds (CREFs) and estimated returns on residential real estate from a series created by Case and Shiller (1987). Exhibit 2.18 contains real estate returns

Exhibit 2.18 Summary Statistics of Commercial and Residential Real Estate Series Compared to Stocks, Bonds, T-Bills, and Inflation

Series	Date	Geometric Mean	Arithmetic Mean	Standard Deviation
Annual Returns 1969–1987				
CREF (Comm.)	1969–87	10.8%	10.9%	2.6%
REIT (Comm.)	1972–87	14.2	15.7	15.4
C&S (Res.)	1970–86	8.5	8.6	3.0
S&P (Stocks)	1969–87	9.2	10.5	18.2
LTG (Bonds)	1969–87	7.7	8.4	13.2
TBILL (Bills)	1969–87	7.6	7.6	1.4
CPI (Infl.)	1969–87	6.4	6.4	1.8
Annual Returns over the Long Term				
I&S (Comm.)	1960–87	8.9%	9.1%	5.0%
CPIHOME (Res.)	1947–86	8.1	8.2	5.2
USDA (Farm)	1947–87	9.6	9.9	8.2
S&P (Stocks)	1947–87	11.4	12.6	16.3
LTG (Bonds)	1947–87	4.2	4.6	9.8
TBILL (Bills)	1947–87	4.9	4.7	3.3
CPI (Infl.)	1947–87	4.5	4.6	3.9

Source: William N. Goetzmann and Roger G. Ibbotson, "The Performance of Real Estate as an Asset Class," *Journal of Applied Corporate Finance*, 3, no. 1 (Spring 1990): 65–76.

---

[7]Unfortunately, it has not been possible to update these results because Sotheby's stopped computing and publishing the series in 1992.

Exhibit 2.19 Correlations of Annual Real Estate Returns with the Returns on Other Asset Classes

	I&S	CREF	CPI Home	C&S	Farm	S&P	20-Yr. Gvt.	1-Yr. Gvt.	Infl.
I&S	1								
CREF	0.79	1							
CPI Home	0.52	0.12	1						
C&S	0.26	0.16	0.82	1					
Farm	0.06	−0.06	0.51	0.49	1				
S&P	0.16	0.25	−0.13	−0.20	−0.10	1			
20-Yr. Gvt.	−0.04	0.01	−0.22	−0.54	−0.44	0.11	1		
1-Yr. Gvt.	0.53	0.42	0.13	−0.56	−0.32	−0.07	0.48	1	
Infl.	0.70	0.35	0.77	0.56	0.49	−0.02	−0.17	0.26	1

Note: Correlation coefficient for each pair of asset classes uses the maximum number of observations, that is, the minimum length of the two series in the pair.

Source: William N. Goetzmann and Roger G. Ibbotson, "The Performance of Real Estate as an Asset Class," *Journal of Applied Corporate Finance*, 3, no. 1 (Spring 1990): 65–76.

compared to various stock, bond, and inflation data. As shown, the two commercial real estate series reflected strikingly different results. The CREFs had lower returns and low volatility, while the REIT index had higher returns and risk. Notably, the REIT returns were higher than those of common stocks, but the risk measure for real estate was lower. (There was a small difference in the time period.) The residential real estate series reflected lower returns and low risk. All the longer-term results indicated that the real estate series experienced lower returns and much lower risk than common stock.

The correlations in Exhibit 2.19 among annual returns for the various asset groups indicate a relatively low positive correlation between commercial real estate and stocks. In contrast, there was negative correlation between stocks and residential and farm real estate. This negative relationship with real estate was also true for 20-year government bonds. Studies by Eichholtz (1996), Mull and Socnen (1997), and Quan and Titman (1997) that considered international commercial real estate and REITs indicated that the returns were correlated with stock prices, but they still provided significant diversification benefits.

These results imply that returns on real estate are equal to or slightly lower than returns on common stocks, but real estate possesses favorable risk and diversification results. Specifically, individual real estate assets had much lower standard deviations and either low positive or negative correlations with other asset classes in a portfolio context. Finally, all the real estate series had significant positive correlation with inflation, which implies strong potential as an inflation hedge.

SUMMARY

- In this chapter, we saw that investors need to prudently manage risk within the context of their investment goals and preferences. An individual's income, spending, and investing behavior will change over a person's lifetime.

- We reviewed the importance of developing an investment policy statement before implementing an investment plan. By forcing investors to examine their needs, risk tolerance, and familiarity with the capital markets, policy statements help investors correctly identify appropriate objectives and constraints. In addition, the policy statement provides a standard by which to evaluate the performance of the portfolio manager.

- We discussed the importance of the asset allocation decision in determining long-run portfolio investment returns and risks. Because the asset allocation decision follows setting the objectives and constraints, it is clear that the success of the investment program depends on the first step, the construction of the policy statement.

- Investors who want the broadest range of choices in investments must consider foreign stocks and bonds in addition to domestic financial assets. Many foreign securities offer investors higher risk-adjusted returns during individual years than do domestic securities. In addition, the low positive correlations between foreign and U.S. securities make them ideal for building a diversified portfolio.

- Exhibit 2.20 summarizes the risk and return characteristics of the investment alternatives described in this chapter. Some of the differences are due to unique factors that we discussed. Foreign stocks and bonds are considered riskier than domestic stocks and bonds because of the unavoidable uncertainty due to exchange rate risk and country risk. Such investments as art, antiques, coins, and stamps require heavy liquidity risk premiums. You should divide consideration of real estate

investments between your personal home, on which you do not expect as high a return because of non-monetary factors, and commercial real estate, which requires a much higher rate of return due to cash flow uncertainty and illiquidity.

- Studies on the historical rates of return for investment alternatives, as presented by Ibbotson and Brinson (1993) (including bonds, commodities, real estate, foreign securities, and art and antiques), point toward two generalizations:

1. A positive relationship typically holds between the rate of return earned on an asset and the variability of its historical rate of return or its systematic risk (beta). This is expected in a world of risk-averse investors who require higher rates of return to compensate for more uncertainty.

2. The correlation among rates of return for selected alternative investments can be quite low, especially for U.S. and foreign stocks and bonds and between these financial assets and real assets, such as art, antiques, and real estate. These correlations confirm the advantage of diversification among different global asset classes.

- In addition to describing many direct investments, such as stocks and bonds, there are also investment companies that allow investors to buy investments indirectly. These can be important to

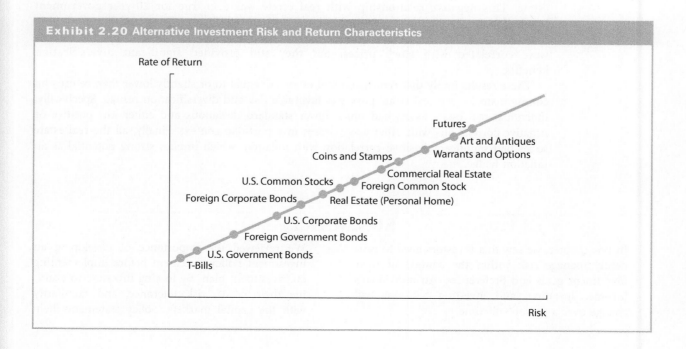

Exhibit 2.20 Alternative Investment Risk and Return Characteristics

investors who want to take advantage of professional management but also want instant diversification with a limited amount of funds. With $10,000, you may not be able to buy many individual stocks or bonds, but you could acquire shares in a mutual fund or an ETF, which would give you a share of a diversified portfolio that might contain

100 to 150 different U.S. and international stocks or bonds.

• Now that we know the range of domestic and foreign investment alternatives, it is important to learn about the markets in which they are bought and sold. That is the objective of the following chapter.

SUGGESTED READINGS

Bodie, Zvi, Dennis McLeavey, and Laurence Siegel, eds. *The Future of Life-Cycle Saving and Investing.* Charlottesville, VA: Research Foundation of CFA Institute, 2007.

Bodie, Zvi, Laurence B. Siegel, and Rodney N. Sullivan, eds. *The Future of Life-Cycle Saving and Investing: The Retirement Phase.* Charlottesville, VA: Research Foundation of CFA Institute, 2009.

Grabbe, J. Orlin. *International Financial Markets.* New York: Elsevier Science Publishing, 1986.

Ibbotson, R. S., M. A. Milevsky, P. Chen, and K. X. Zhu. *Lifetime Financial Advice: Human Capital Asset Allocation and Insurance.* Charlottesville, VA: The Research Foundation of the CFA Institute, 2007.

Lessard, Donald R. "International Diversification." In *The Financial Analyst's Handbook*, 2nd ed., ed. Sumner N. Levine. Homewood, IL: Dow Jones-Irwin, 1988.

Malvey, Jack. "Global Credit, Bond Portfolio Management." In *The Handbook of Fixed-Income Securities*, 8th ed., ed. Frank J. Fabozzi. New York: McGraw-Hill, 2012.

Milevsky, Mosha A., and Chris Robinson. "A Sustainable Spending Rate without Simulation," *Financial Analysts Journal* 61, no. 6 (November–December, 2005).

Miller, Janet T., ed. *Investment Counseling for Private Clients, III.* Charlottesville, VA: AIMR, 2001.

Ramanathan, Karthik. "International Bond Markets and Instruments." In *The Handbook of Fixed-Income Securities*, 8th ed., ed. Frank J. Fabozzi. New York: McGraw-Hill, 2012.

Ramanathan, Karthik, Frank Fabozzi and James Gerand. "International Bond Portfolio Management." In *The Handbook of Fixed-Income Securities*, 8th ed., ed. Frank J. Fabozzi. New York: McGraw-Hill, 2012.

Siegel, Laurence B., and Paul D. Kaplan. "Stocks, Bonds, Bills, and Inflation Around the World." In *Managing Institutional Assets*, ed. Frank J. Fabozzi. New York: Harper & Row, 1990.

Solnik, Bruno, and Dennis McLeavey. *International Investments*, 5th ed. Reading, MA: Addison-Wesley, 2004.

Thaler, Richard, and Schlomo Benartzi. "Save More Tomorrow; Using Behavioral Economics to Increase Employee Savings," *Journal of Political Economy*, 112, no. 1 (February 2004).

QUESTIONS

1. "Young people with little wealth should not invest money in risky assets such as the stock market, because they can't afford to lose what little money they have." Do you agree or disagree with this statement? Why?

2. Your healthy 63-year-old neighbor is about to retire and comes to you for advice. From talking with her, you find out she was planning on taking all the money out of her company's retirement plan and investing it in bond mutual funds and money market funds. What advice should you give her?

3. Discuss how an individual's investment strategy may change as he or she goes through the accumulation, consolidation, spending, and gifting phases of life.

4. Why is a policy statement important?

5. Your 45-year-old uncle is 20 years away from retirement; your 35-year-old older sister is about 30 years away from retirement. How might their investment policy statements differ?

6. What information is necessary before a financial planner can assist a person in constructing an investment policy statement?

7. Use the Internet to find the home pages for some financial-planning firms. What strategies do they emphasize? What do they say about their asset allocation strategy? What are their firms' emphases—for example, value investing, international diversification, principal preservation, retirement and estate planning?

8. Mr. Franklin is 70 years of age, is in excellent health, pursues a simple but active lifestyle, and has no children. He has interest in a private company for $90 million and has decided that a medical research foundation will receive half the proceeds now and will be the primary beneficiary of his estate upon his death. Mr. Franklin is committed to the foundation's well-being because he believes strongly that, through it, a cure will be found for the disease that killed his wife. He now realizes that an appropriate investment policy and asset allocations are required if his goals are to be met through investment of his considerable assets. Currently, the following assets are available for use in building an appropriate portfolio for him:

    > $45.0 million cash (from sale of the private company interest,
    >   net of a $45 million gift to the foundation)
    > $10.0 million stocks and bonds ($5 million each)
    > $ 9.0 million warehouse property (now fully leased)
    > $ 1.0 million value of his residence
    > _____
    > $65.0 million total available assets

    a. Formulate and justify an investment policy statement setting forth the appropriate guidelines within which future investment actions should take place. Your policy statement should encompass all relevant objective and constraint considerations.

    b. Recommend and justify a long-term asset allocation that is consistent with the investment policy statement you created in part (a). Briefly explain the key assumptions you made in generating your allocation.

9. What are the advantages of investing in the common stock rather than the corporate bonds of a company? Compare the certainty of returns for a bond with those for a common stock. Draw a line graph to demonstrate the pattern of returns you would envision for each of these assets over time.

10. Discuss three factors that should cause U.S. investors to consider including various global securities in their portfolios.

11. Discuss why international diversification reduces portfolio risk. Specifically, why would you *expect* low correlation in the rates of return for domestic and foreign securities?

12. Discuss why you would expect a *difference* in the correlation of returns between securities from the United States and from alternative countries (for example, Japan, Canada, South Africa).

13. Discuss whether you would expect any *change* in the correlations between U.S. stocks and the stocks for different countries. For example, discuss whether you would expect the correlation between U.S. and Japanese stock returns to change over time. If so, why?

14. When you invest in Japanese or German bonds, what major additional risks must you consider besides yield changes within the country?

15. Some investors believe that international investing introduces additional risks. Discuss these risks and how they can affect your return. Give an example.

16. What alternatives to direct investment in foreign stocks are available to investors?

17. You are a wealthy individual in a high tax bracket. Why might you consider investing in a municipal bond rather than a straight corporate bond, even though the promised yield on the municipal bond is lower?

18. You can acquire convertible bonds from a rapidly growing company or from a utility. Speculate on which convertible bond would have the lower yield and discuss the reason for this difference.

19. Compare the liquidity of an investment in raw land with that of an investment in common stock. Be specific as to why and how the liquidity differs. (Hint: Begin by defining *liquidity*.)

20. Discuss why financial analysts consider antiques and art to be illiquid investments. Why do they consider coins and stamps to be more liquid than antiques and art? What must an investor typically do to sell a collection of art and antiques? Briefly contrast this procedure to the sale of a portfolio of stocks listed on a national or international exchange.

21. You have a fairly large portfolio of U.S. stocks and bonds. You meet a financial planner at a social gathering who suggests that you diversify your portfolio by investing in emerging market stocks. Discuss whether the correlation results in Exhibit 2.16 support this suggestion.

22. The pension plan for the Sophie Corporation has historically invested in the stocks of only U.S.-domiciled companies. Recently, the fund has decided to add international exposure to the plan portfolio. Identify and briefly discuss *three* potential problems that the plan may confront in selecting international stocks that it did not face in choosing U.S. stocks.

23. Alessandra Capital has been experiencing increasing demand from its institutional clients for information and assistance related to international investment management. Recognizing that this is an area of growing importance, the firm has hired an experienced analyst/portfolio manager specializing in international equities and market strategy. His first assignment is to represent Alessandra Capital before a client company's investment committee to discuss the possibility of changing their present "U.S. securities only" investment approach to one including international investments. He is told that the committee wants a presentation that fully and objectively examines the basic, substantive considerations on which the committee should focus its attention, including both theory and evidence. The company's pension plan has no legal or other barriers to adoption of an international approach; no non-U.S. pension liabilities currently exist.

    Identify and briefly discuss *three* reasons for adding international securities to the pension portfolio and *three* risks associated with such an approach.

PROBLEMS

1. Suppose your first job pays you $28,000 annually. What percentage should your cash reserve contain? How much life insurance should you carry if you are unmarried? How much if you are married with two young children?

2. a. Someone in the 36 percent tax bracket can earn 9 percent annually on her investments in a tax-exempt IRA account. What will be the value of a one-time $10,000 investment in 5 years? 10 years? 20 years?

   b. Suppose the preceding 9 percent return is taxable rather than tax-deferred and the taxes are paid annually. What will be the after-tax value of her $10,000 investment after 5, 10, and 20 years?

3. a. Someone in the 15 percent tax bracket can earn 10 percent on his investments in a tax-exempt IRA account. What will be the value of a $10,000 investment in 5 years? 10 years? 20 years?

   b. Suppose the preceding 10 percent return is taxable rather than tax-deferred. What will be the after-tax value of his $10,000 investment after 5, 10, and 20 years?

4. Assume that the rate of inflation during all these periods was 3 percent a year. Compute the real value of the two tax-deferred portfolios in Problems 2a and 3a.

5. Using a source of international statistics, compare the percentage change in the following economic data for Japan, Germany, Canada, and the United States for a recent year. What were the differences, and which country or countries differed most from the United States?
   a. Aggregate output (GDP)
   b. Consumer price index
   c. Money supply growth

6. Using a recent edition of *Barron's*, examine the weekly percentage change in the stock price indexes for Japan, Germany, United Kingdom, and the United States. For each of three weeks, which foreign series moved most closely with the U.S. series? Which series diverged most from the U.S. series? Discuss these results as they relate to international diversification.

7. Using published sources (for example, *The Wall Street Journal, Barron's, Federal Reserve Bulletin*), look up the exchange rate for U.S. dollars with Japanese yen for each of the past 10 years (you can use an average for the year or a specific time period each year). Based on these exchange rates, compute and discuss the yearly exchange rate effect on an investment in Japanese stocks by a U.S. investor. Discuss the impact of this exchange rate effect on the risk of Japanese stocks for a U.S. investor.

8. The following information is available concerning the historical risk and return relationships in the U.S. capital markets:

U.S. CAPITAL MARKETS TOTAL ANNUAL RETURNS, 1990–2015

Investment Category	Arithmetic Mean	Geometric Mean	Standard Deviation of Return[a]
Common stocks	10.28%	8.81%	16.9%
Treasury bills	3.54	3.49	3.2
Long-term government bonds	5.10	4.91	6.4
Long-term corporate bonds	5.95	5.65	9.6
Real estate	9.49	9.44	4.5

[a]Based on arithmetic mean.

   a. Explain why the geometric and arithmetic mean returns are not equal and whether one or the other may be more useful for investment decision making.
   b. For the time period indicated, rank these investments on a relative basis using the coefficient of variation from most to least desirable. Explain your rationale.
   c. Assume the arithmetic mean returns in these series are normally distributed. Calculate the range of returns that an investor would have expected to achieve 95 percent of the time from holding common stocks.

9. You are given the following long-run annual rates of return for alternative investment instruments:

U.S. Government T-bills	3.50%
Large-cap common stock	11.75
Long-term corporate bonds	5.50
Long-term government bonds	4.90
Small-capitalization common stock	13.10

The annual rate of inflation during this period was 3 percent. Compute the real rate of return on these investment alternatives.

A. Covariance

Because most students have been exposed to the concepts of covariance and correlation, the following discussion is set forth in intuitive terms with examples. A detailed, rigorous treatment is contained in DeFusco, McLeavey, Pinto, and Runkle (2004).

Covariance is an absolute measure of the extent to which two sets of numbers move together over time, that is, how often they move up or down together. In this regard, *move together* means they are generally above their means or below their means at the same time. Covariance between i and j is defined as

$$COV_{ij} = \frac{\sum (i - \bar{i})(j - \bar{j})}{n}$$

If we define $(i - \bar{i})$ as i' and $(j - \bar{j})$ as j', then

$$COV_{ij} = \frac{\sum i'j'}{n}$$

Obviously, if both numbers are consistently above or below their individual means at the same time, their products will be positive, and the average will be a large positive value. In contrast, if the i value is below its mean when the j value is above its mean consistently or vice versa, their products will be large negative values, giving negative covariance.

Exhibit 2A.1 should make this clear. In this example, the two series generally moved together, so they showed positive covariance. As noted, this is an *absolute* measure of their relationship and, therefore, can range from $+\infty$ to $-\infty$. Note that the covariance of a variable with itself is its *variance*.

B. Correlation

To obtain a relative measure of a given relationship, we use the **correlation coefficient** (r_{ij}), which is a measure of the relationship:

$$r_{ij} = \frac{COV_{ij}}{\sigma_i \sigma_j}$$

You will recall from your introductory statistics course that

$$\sigma_i = \sqrt{\frac{\sum (i - \bar{i})^2}{N}}$$

Exhibit 2A.1 Calculation of Correlation Covariance

Observation	i	j	$i - \bar{i}$	$j - \bar{j}$	$i'\, j'$
1	3	8	−4	−4	16
2	6	10	−1	−2	2
3	8	14	+1	+2	2
4	5	12	−2	0	0
5	9	13	+2	+1	2
6	11	15	+4	+3	12
Σ	42	72			34
Mean	7	12			

$$COV_{ij} = \frac{34}{6} = +5.67$$

Exhibit 2A.2 Calculation of Correlation Coefficient

Observation	$i - \bar{i}$ [a]	$(i - \bar{i})^2$	$j - \bar{j}$ [a]	$(j - \bar{j})^2$
1	−4	16	−4	16
2	−1	1	−2	4
3	+4	1	+2	4
4	−2	4	0	0
5	+2	4	+1	1
6	+4	16	+3	9
		42		34

$$\sigma_i^2 = 42/6 = 7.00 \qquad \sigma_j^2 = 34/6 = 5.67$$

$$\sigma_i = \sqrt{7.00} = 2.65 \qquad \sigma_j = \sqrt{5.67} = 2.38$$

$$r_{ij} = COV_{ij}/\sigma_i\sigma_j = \frac{5.67}{(2.65)(2.38)} = \frac{5.67}{6.31} = 0.898$$

If the two series move completely together, then the covariance would equal $\sigma_i\sigma_j$ and

$$\frac{COV_{ij}}{\sigma_i\sigma_j} = 1.0$$

The correlation coefficient would equal unity in this case, and we would say the two series are perfectly correlated. Because we know that:

$$r_{ij} = \frac{COV_{ij}}{\sigma_i\sigma_j}$$

we also know that $COV_{ij} = r_{ij}\sigma_i\sigma_j$. This relationship may be useful when computing the standard deviation of a portfolio, because in many instances the relationship between two securities is stated in terms of the correlation coefficient rather than the covariance.

Continuing the example given in Exhibit 2A.1, the standard deviations are computed in Exhibit 2A.2, as is the correlation between i and j. As shown, the two standard deviations are rather large and similar but not exactly the same. Finally, when the positive covariance is normalized by the product of the two standard deviations, the results indicate a correlation coefficient of 0.898, which is obviously quite large and close to 1.00. This implies that these two series are highly related.

Problems

1. As a new analyst, you have calculated the following annual rates of return for the stocks of both Lauren Corporation and Kayleigh Industries.

Year	Lauren's Rate of Return	Kayleigh's Rate of Return
2015	5	5
2016	12	15
2017	−11	5
2018	10	7
2019	12	−10

Your manager suggests that because these companies produce similar products, you should continue your analysis by computing their covariance. Show all calculations.

2. You decide to go an extra step by calculating the coefficient of correlation using the data provided in Problem 1. Prepare a table showing your calculations and explain how to interpret the results. Would the combination of the common stock of Lauren and Kayleigh be good for diversification?

CHAPTER 3

Organization and Functioning of Securities Markets*

After you read this chapter, you should be able to answer the following questions:

- What is the purpose and function of a market?
- What characteristics determine the quality of a market?
- What is the difference between a primary and secondary capital market, and how do these two markets support each other?
- What are Rules 415 and 144A, and how do they affect corporate security underwriting?
- For secondary equity markets, what are the two basic trading systems?
- How are call markets typically used in U.S. markets?
- How are national exchanges around the world linked, and what is meant by "passing the book"?
- What are electronic communication networks (ECNs) and alternative trading systems (ATSs) and how do they differ from the primary listing markets?
- What are the major types of orders available to investors and market makers?
- What new trading systems on the NYSE and on NASDAQ have made it possible to handle the growth in U.S. trading volume?
- What are the three recent innovations that contribute to competition within the U.S. equity market?
- What are the factors causing a global consolidation of stock, bond, and derivative exchanges? What will this global market look like?

The stock market, the Dow Jones Industrials, and the bond market are part of our everyday experience. Each evening on television news broadcasts we find out how stocks and bonds fared; each morning daily newspapers discuss expectations for a market rally or decline. Yet most people have an imperfect understanding of how domestic and world capital markets actually function. To be a successful global investor you must know what global financial markets are available and how they operate.

In this chapter, we provide a detailed discussion of how major stock markets function, how they have been changing, and how they will probably change in the future.

We initially discuss securities markets and the characteristics of a good market. We describe two components of the capital markets: primary and secondary. Our main emphasis is on the secondary stock market including the national stock exchanges around the world and how these markets, separated by geography and by time zones, are linked into a 24-hour market. We also consider how alternative exchange markets have operated and how regulation national market system (Reg NMS) transformed the U.S. market structure. This transformation included the creation of

---

*The authors acknowledge very helpful comments on this chapter from Robert Battalio of the University of Notre Dame. He is not responsible for any errors or omissions that remain.

electronic communication networks (ECNs), most of which have become additional stock exchanges. It is also important to understand the emergence of alternative trading systems (ATSs) that include dark pools and the internalization of trading in numerous large and small broker-dealers. We discuss all of these changes in detail in the secondary equity market section and also consider the significant mergers of the several exchanges that have transformed how we buy and sell stocks in a global capital market. In the final section, we consider numerous recent changes in financial markets, including significant mergers, and future changes expected to have a profound effect on what global investments are available and how we buy and sell them and at what cost.

3.1 What Is a Market?

A **market** is the means through which buyers and sellers are brought together to aid in the transfer of goods and/or services. Several aspects of this general definition seem worthy of emphasis. First, a market need *not* have a physical location. It is only necessary that the buyers and sellers can communicate regarding the relevant aspects of the transaction.

Second, the market does not necessarily own the goods or services involved. The important criterion for a good market is the smooth, cheap transfer of goods and services. Those who establish and administer the market allow potential buyers and sellers to interact and enhance the experience by providing information and facilities to aid in the transfer of ownership.

Finally, a market can deal in any variety of goods and services. For any commodity or service with a diverse clientele, a market should evolve to aid in the transfer of that commodity or service. Both buyers and sellers benefit from the existence of a market.

3.1.1 Characteristics of a Good Market

Throughout this book, we will discuss markets for different investments such as stocks, bonds, options, and futures throughout the world. We will refer to these markets using various terms of quality such as *strong, active, liquid,* or *illiquid*. The point is, financial markets are not equal; some are active and liquid, others are relatively illiquid and inefficient in their operations. You should be aware of the following characteristics that determine the quality of a market.

One enters a market to buy or sell a good or service quickly at a price justified by the prevailing supply and demand. To determine the appropriate price, participants must have **timely and accurate information** on past transactions and prevailing buy and sell orders.

Another prime requirement is **liquidity**, the ability to buy or sell an asset quickly and at a price not substantially different from the prices for prior transactions, assuming no new information is available. An asset's likelihood of being sold quickly, sometimes referred to as its *marketability*, is a necessary, but not a sufficient, condition for liquidity. The expected price should also be fairly certain, based on the recent history of transaction prices and current bid-ask quotes. For a formal discussion of liquidity, see Handa and Schwartz (1996) and AIMR's articles on *Best Execution and Portfolio Performance* (Jost, 2001a).

A component of liquidity is **price continuity**, which means that prices do not change much from one transaction to the next unless substantial new information becomes available. In turn, a market with price continuity requires *depth* wherein there are numerous potential buyers and sellers willing to trade at prices above and below the current market price.[1]

---

[1]Notably, common stocks are currently sold in decimals (dollars and cents), which is a change from the pre-2000 period when stocks were priced in eighths and sixteenths. This change to decimals is discussed in the following subsection.

These buyers and sellers enter the market in response to changes in supply, demand, or both, and thereby prevent drastic price changes. In summary, liquidity requires marketability and price continuity, which, in turn, requires depth.

Another factor contributing to a good market is the **transaction cost**. Lower costs (as a percentage of the value of the trade) make for a more efficient market. An individual comparing the cost of a transaction between markets would choose a market that charges 2 percent of the value of the trade compared with one that charges 5 percent. Most microeconomic textbooks define an efficient market as one in which the cost of the transaction is minimal. This attribute is referred to as *internal efficiency*.[2]

Finally, a buyer or seller wants the prevailing market price to adequately reflect all the information available regarding supply and demand factors in the market. The point is, if new information enters the market, the price should change accordingly. Put another way, participants want prevailing market prices to reflect all available information about the asset. This attribute is referred to as **informational efficiency** and is discussed extensively in Chapter 5.

In summary, a good market for goods and services has the following characteristics:

1. Timely and accurate information on the price and volume of past transactions.
2. Liquidity, meaning an asset can be bought or sold quickly at a price close to the prices for previous transactions—that is, it has price continuity, which requires depth.
3. Low transaction costs, including the cost of reaching the market, the actual brokerage costs, and the cost of transferring the asset.
4. Prices that rapidly adjust to new information, so the prevailing price is fair since it reflects all available information regarding the asset.

3.1.2 Decimal Pricing

Prior to the initiation of changes in late 2000 that were completed in early 2001, common stocks in the United States were always quoted in fractions. Specifically, prior to 1997 they were quoted in eighths (e.g., $\frac{1}{8}, \frac{2}{8}, \ldots, \frac{7}{8}$), with each eighth equal to $0.125. This was modified in 1997, when the fractions for most stocks went to sixteenths (e.g., $\frac{1}{16}, \frac{2}{16}, \ldots, \frac{15}{16}$), each equal to $0.0625. Now U.S. equities are priced in decimals (cents), so the minimum spread can be in cents (e.g., $30.10 - $30.12).

The espoused reasons for the change to decimal pricing are threefold. First, investors can easily understand and compare prices. Second, decimal pricing reduces the minimum variation (e.g., the tick size) from a minimum of 6.25 cents (when prices are quoted in sixteenths) to 1 cent (when prices are in decimals). This allowed bid-ask spreads to fall from $0.0625 to $0.01. Third, the change made U.S. markets more competitive on a global basis since other countries were pricing on a comparable basis.

Decimalization has reduced spread size and transaction costs, which has led to a decline in transaction size and an increase in the number of transactions. For example, the number of transactions on the NYSE went from a daily average of 877,000 in 2000 to over 13 million during 2016, while the average trade size went from 1,187 shares in 2000 to about 250 shares in 2016.

3.1.3 Organization of the Securities Market

Before we discuss the specific operation of the securities market, we need to understand its overall organization. The principal distinction is between **primary markets**, where new securities are sold, and **secondary markets**, where outstanding securities are bought and sold.

---

[2]A subsequent discussion in this chapter on new innovations will make it clear that new technology and competition has resulted in a very internally efficient global equity market.

Each of these markets is further divided based on the economic unit that issued the security. We will consider these major segments of the securities market, with an emphasis on the individuals involved and the functions they perform.

3.2 PRIMARY CAPITAL MARKETS

The primary market is where new issues of bonds, preferred stock, or common stock are sold by government units, municipalities, or companies who want to acquire new capital. For a review of studies on the primary market, see Jensen and Smith (1986).

3.2.1 Government Bond Issues

U.S. government bond issues are subdivided into three segments based on their original maturities. **Treasury bills** are negotiable, non-interest-bearing securities with original maturities of one year or less. **Treasury notes** have original maturities of 2 to 10 years. Finally, **Treasury bonds** have original maturities of more than 10 years.

To sell bills, notes, and bonds, the Treasury relies on Federal Reserve System auctions. (The bidding process and pricing are discussed in Chapter 12.)

3.2.2 Municipal Bond Issues

New municipal bond issues are sold by one of three methods: competitive bid, negotiation, or private placement. **Competitive bid** sales typically involve sealed bids. The bond issue is sold to the bidding syndicate of underwriters that submits the bid with the lowest interest cost in accordance with the stipulations set forth by the issuer. **Negotiated sales** involve contractual arrangements between underwriters and issuers wherein the underwriter helps the issuer prepare the bond issue and set the price and has the exclusive right to sell the issue. **Private placements** involve the sale of a bond issue by the issuer directly to an investor or a small group of investors (usually institutions).

Note that two of the three methods require an *underwriting* function. Specifically, in a competitive bid or a negotiated transaction, the investment banker typically underwrites the issue, which means the investment firm purchases the entire issue at a specified price, relieving the issuer from the risk and responsibility of selling and distributing the bonds. Subsequently, the underwriter sells the issue to the investing public. For municipal bonds, this underwriting function is performed by both investment banking firms and commercial banks.

The underwriting function can involve three services: origination, risk-bearing, and distribution. Origination involves the design of the bond issue and initial planning. To fulfill the risk-bearing function, the underwriter acquires the total issue at a price dictated by the competitive bid or through negotiation and accepts the responsibility and risk of reselling it for more than the purchase price. Distribution involves selling it to investors with the help of a selling syndicate that includes other investment banking firms and/or commercial banks.

In a negotiated bid, the underwriter will carry out all three services. In a competitive bid, the issuer specifies the amount, maturities, coupons, and call features of the issue and the competing syndicates submit a bid for the entire issue that reflects the yields they estimate for the bonds. Finally, a private placement involves no risk-bearing, but an investment banker would typically assist in designing the characteristics of the issue and locating potential buyers.

3.2.3 Corporate Bond Issues

Corporate bond issues are typically sold through a negotiated arrangement with an investment banking firm that maintains a relationship with the issuing firm. In a global capital market there has been an explosion of new instruments, so that designing the characteristics and currency for the security is becoming more important because the corporate chief financial officer (CFO) may not be completely familiar with the many new instruments and the alternative capital markets around the world. Investment banking firms compete for underwriting business by creating new instruments that appeal to existing investors and by advising issuers regarding desirable countries and currencies. As a result, the expertise of the investment banker can help reduce the issuer's cost of new capital.

Once a stock or bond issue is specified, the underwriter will put together an underwriting syndicate of other major underwriters and a selling group of smaller firms for its distribution, as shown in Exhibit 3.1.

3.2.4 Corporate Stock Issues

In addition to issuing fixed-income securities, corporations can also issue equity securities—generally common stock. For corporations, new stock issues are typically divided into two groups: (1) seasoned equity issues and (2) initial public offerings (IPOs).

Seasoned equity issues are new shares offered by firms that already have stock outstanding. An example would be General Electric, which is a large, well-regarded firm that has had public stock trading on the NYSE for over 50 years. If General Electric needed additional capital, it could sell additional shares of its common stock to the public at a price very close to its current market price.

Initial public offerings (IPOs) involve a firm selling its common stock to the public for the first time. At the time of an IPO, there is no existing public market for the stock; that is, the company has been closely held. An example was an IPO by Polo Ralph Lauren, a leading manufacturer and distributor of men's clothing. The purpose of the offering was to get additional capital to expand its operations and to create a public market for future seasoned offerings.

New issues (seasoned or IPOs) are typically underwritten by investment bankers, who acquire the total issue from the company and sell the securities to interested investors. The lead underwriter gives advice to the corporation on the general characteristics of the issue, its

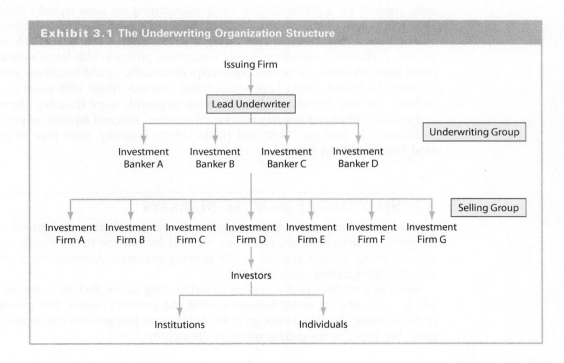

Exhibit 3.1 The Underwriting Organization Structure

pricing, the timing of the offering, and participates in a "road show" visiting potential institutional investors. The underwriter also accepts the risk of selling the new issue after acquiring it from the corporation. For further discussion, see Brealey and Myers (2010, Chapter 15).

Introduction of Rule 415   The typical practice of negotiated arrangements involving numerous investment banking firms in syndicates and selling groups has changed with the introduction of Rule 415, which allows large firms to register security issues and sell them piecemeal during the following two years. These issues are referred to as *shelf registrations* because, after they are registered, the issues lie on the shelf and can be taken down and sold on short notice whenever it suits the issuing firm. As an example, Apple Computer could register an issue of 5 million shares of common stock during 2018 and sell 1 million shares in early 2018, another million shares in late 2018, 2 million shares in early 2019, and the rest in late 2019.

Each offering can be made with little notice or paperwork by one underwriter or several. In fact, because relatively few shares may be involved, the lead underwriter often handles the whole deal without a syndicate or uses only one or two other firms. This arrangement has benefited large corporations because it provides great flexibility, reduces registration fees and expenses, and allows issuing firms to request competitive bids from several investment banking firms.

In contrast, some observers fear that shelf registrations do not allow investors enough time to examine the current status of the firm issuing the securities and reduce the participation of small underwriters. Shelf registrations are typically used for the sale of straight debentures rather than common stock or convertible issues. For further discussion of Rule 415, see Rogowski and Sorensen (1985).

3.2.5 Private Placements and Rule 144A

Rather than using a public sale through one of these arrangements, primary offerings can be sold privately. In such an arrangement, referred to as a *private placement*, the firm designs an issue with the assistance of an investment banker and sells it to a small group of institutions. The firm enjoys lower issuing costs because it does not need to prepare the extensive registration statement required for a public offering. Institutions buying the issue typically benefit because the issuing firm passes some of the cost savings on to the investor as a higher return.

The private placement market changed dramatically when Rule 144A was introduced because it allowed corporations to place securities privately with large, sophisticated institutional investors without extensive registration documents. In addition, these securities can subsequently be traded among large sophisticated investors (those with assets in excess of $100 million). The SEC introduced this innovation to provide more financing alternatives for U.S. and non-U.S. firms and possibly increase the number, size, and liquidity of private placements, as discussed by Milligan (1990) and Hanks (1990). Presently, more than 90 percent of high-yield bonds are 144A issues.

3.3 SECONDARY FINANCIAL MARKETS

In this section, we consider the importance of secondary markets and provide an overview of the global secondary markets for bonds, financial futures, and stocks. Finally, we discuss other primary listing markets and the rapidly growing electronic communication networks (ECNs) and alternative trading systems (ATSs).

Secondary markets permit trading in outstanding issues; that is, stocks or bonds already sold to the public are traded between current and potential owners. The proceeds from a sale in the secondary market do not go to the issuing unit (the government, municipality, or company) but rather to the current owner of the security.

3.3.1 Why Secondary Markets Are Important

Because the secondary market involves the trading of securities initially sold in the primary market, *it provides liquidity to the individuals who acquired these securities.* The point is, after acquiring securities in the primary market, investors may want to sell them again to acquire other securities, buy a house, or go on a vacation. The primary market benefits from this liquidity because investors would hesitate to acquire securities in the primary market if they thought they could not subsequently sell them in the secondary market. The point is, without an active secondary market, stock or bond issuers in the primary market would have to provide a higher rate of return to compensate investors for the substantial liquidity risk.

Secondary markets are also important to those selling seasoned securities because the prevailing market price of the securities (*price discovery*) is determined by transactions in the secondary market. As noted earlier, new issues of outstanding stocks or bonds to be sold in the primary market are based on prices and yields in the secondary market. Notably, the secondary market also affects market efficiency and price volatility, as discussed by Foster and Viswanathan (1993) and Jones, Kaul, and Lipson (1994). Even forthcoming IPOs are priced based on the prices and values of comparable stocks or bonds in the public secondary market.

3.3.2 Secondary Bond Markets

The secondary market for bonds distinguishes among those issued by the federal government, municipalities, or corporations.

Secondary Markets for U.S. Government and Municipal Bonds U.S. government bonds are traded by bond dealers that specialize in either Treasury bonds or agency bonds. Treasury issues are bought or sold through a set of 35 primary dealers, including large banks in New York and Chicago and some large investment banking firms like Goldman Sachs and Morgan Stanley. These institutions and other firms also make markets for government agency issues, but there is no formal set of dealers for agency securities.

The major market makers in the secondary municipal bond market are banks and investment firms. Banks are active in municipal bond trading and underwriting of general obligation bond issues since they invest heavily in these securities. Also, many large investment firms have municipal bond departments that underwrite and trade these issues.

Secondary Corporate Bond Markets Traditionally, most corporate bonds have been traded over the counter by dealers who buy and sell for their own accounts. The major bond dealers are the large investment banking firms that underwrite the issues: firms such as Goldman Sachs, JPMorgan, Barclay Capital, and Morgan Stanley. Because of the limited trading in corporate bonds compared to the active trading in government bonds, corporate bond dealers do not carry extensive inventories of specific issues. Instead, they hold a limited number of bonds desired by their clients, and when someone wants to do a trade, they work more like brokers than dealers.

Notably, there is a movement toward a widespread transaction-reporting service as with stocks, especially for large, actively traded bond issues. A firm pioneering in this area is Market Access, which currently accounts for about 15 percent of corporate bond trading. As discussed in Chapter 12, since 2005, dealers have been required to report trades within 15 minutes for transactions on 17,000 corporate bonds. Exhibit 3.2 is a daily table from *The Wall Street Journal* that provides data for a large set of secondary bond indexes that are similar to various stock indexes.

3.3.3 Financial Futures

In addition to the market for the bonds, a market has developed for futures contracts related to these bonds. These contracts allow the holder to buy or sell a specified amount of a given bond issue at a stipulated price. The two major futures exchanges are the Chicago Board of

Exhibit 3.2 Bond Benchmarks

Tracking Bond Benchmarks

Return on investment and spreads over Treasurys and/or yields paid to investors compared with 52-week highs and lows for different types of bonds

Total return close	YTD total return (%)	Index	Yield (%) Latest	Low	High
Broad Market Bloomberg Barclays					
1924.29	2.4	U.S. Aggregate	**2.520** 1.820	2.790	
U.S. Corporate Indexes Bloomberg Barclays					
2734.31	3.9	U.S. Corporate	**3.170** 2.750	3.520	
2591.70	2.8	Intermediate	**2.700** 2.190	3.010	
3744.64	6.6	Long term	**4.230** 3.960	4.710	
559.43	2.9	Double-A-rated	**2.620** 1.980	2.870	
703.55	4.4	Triple-B-rated	**3.470** 3.180	3.870	
High Yield Bonds Merrill Lynch					
407.50	4.9	High Yield Constrained	**5.630** 5.456	7.358	
405.40	5.4	Triple-C-rated	**10.203** 9.584	15.470	
2810.51	4.7	High Yield 100	**5.228** 5.050	6.491	
369.24	4.8	Global High Yield Constrained	**5.282** 5.129	6.948	
298.89	4.1	Europe High Yield Constrained	**2.591** 2.537	4.350	
U.S. Agency Bloomberg Barclays					
1633.26	1.8	U.S. Agency	**1.820** 1.150	1.960	
1462.54	1.1	10-20 years	**1.630** 0.960	1.750	
3320.18	6.3	20-plus years	**2.940** 2.390	3.460	
2424.84	3.5	Yankee	**2.740** 2.320	3.090	

Total return close	YTD total return (%)	Index	Yield (%) Latest	Low	High
Mortgage-Backed Bloomberg Barclays					
1969.30	1.5	Mortgage-Backed	**2.800** 1.930	3.120	
1940.54	1.1	Ginnie Mae (GNMA)	**2.760** 1.850	3.090	
1153.81	1.6	Fannie mae (FNMA)	**2.810** 1.950	3.120	
1776.68	1.6	Freddie Mac (FHLMC)	**2.830** 1.980	3.130	
514.81	3.2	Muni Master	**1.979** 1.307	2.516	
360.31	3.7	7-12 year	**1.992** 1.326	2.618	
400.13	3.7	12-22 year	**2.523** 1.610	3.047	
386.46	4.1	22-plus year	**2.995** 2.027	3.622	
Global Government J.P. Morgan†					
540.69	0.7	Global Government	**1.410** 0.750	1.560	
763.01	1.3	Canada	**1.800** 1.210	2.020	
366.23	-0.7	EMU§	**1.182** 0.512	1.363	
702.82	-0.5	France	**0.930** 0.270	1.210	
505.43	-1.8	Germany	**0.520** -0.100	0.520	
287.79	-0.1	Japan	**0.390** -0.120	0.460	
557.18	-0.6	Netherlands	**0.650** 0.020	0.680	
916.09	0.3	U.K.	**1.580** 0.960	1.790	
785.72	6.3	Emerging Markets**	**5.544** 5.134	6.290	

*Constrained indexes limit individual issuer concentrations to 2% the High yield 100 are the 100 largest bonds   †In local currency § Euro-zone bonds

**EMBI Global Index

Sources: Merrill Lynch; Bloomberg Barclays; J.P. Morgan

Source: Data from *The Wall Street Journal*, June 30, 2017, B8. All Rights Reserved Worldwide.

Trade (CBOT) and the Chicago Mercantile Exchange (CME) that merged during 2007. We discuss these futures contracts and the futures market in Chapter 14.

3.3.4 Secondary Equity Markets

Before 2000, the secondary equity markets in the United States and around the world were divided into three segments: national stock exchanges, regional stock exchanges, and over-the-counter (OTC) markets for stocks not on an exchange. Following our background discussions on alternative trading systems and call versus continuous markets, we will include a section on the dramatic regulatory transformation that has taken place in the U.S. equity market during the last 15 years.

Basic Trading Systems Although stock exchanges are similar because only qualified stocks can be traded by individuals who are members of the exchange, they can differ in their *trading systems.* There are two major trading systems, and an exchange can use one or a combination of them. One is a **pure auction market** (also referred to as an *order-driven market*), in which interested buyers and sellers submit bid-and-ask prices (buy and sell orders) for a given stock to a central location where the orders are matched by a broker who does not own the stock but acts as a facilitating agent. Participants also refer to this system as *price-driven* because shares of stock are sold to the investor with the highest bid price and bought from the seller with the lowest offering price. Advocates of an auction market argue at the extreme for a very centralized market that ideally will include all the buyers and sellers of the stock.

The other major trading system is a **dealer market** (also referred to as a *quote-driven* market) where individual dealers provide liquidity for investors by buying and selling the shares of stock for themselves. Ideally, this system involves numerous dealers competing against each other to provide the highest bid prices when you are selling and the lowest asking price when you are buying stock. This decentralized system derives its benefit from the competition among the dealers to provide the best price for the buyer and seller.

Call versus Continuous Markets Beyond the different trading systems for equities (brokers vs. dealers), the operation of exchanges can differ in terms of when and how the stocks are traded.

In **call markets**, the intent is to gather all the bids and asks for a stock at a point in time and derive a single price where the quantity demanded is as close as possible to the quantity supplied. Call markets are generally used during the early stages of development of an exchange when there are few stocks listed or a small number of active investor-traders. On a call market exchange, a designated market maker would call the roll of stocks and ask for interest in one stock at a time. After determining the available buy and sell orders, exchange officials would specify a single price that will satisfy *most* of the orders, and all orders are transacted at this designated price.

Call markets can also be used at the opening for stocks on any exchange if there is an overnight buildup of buy and/or sell orders, in which case the opening price can differ from the prior day's closing price. Also, a call market process is used if trading is suspended during the day because of some significant new information. In either case, the specialist or market maker would attempt to derive a new equilibrium price using a call-market approach that would reflect the imbalance and take care of most of the orders. For example, assume a stock has been trading at about $42 per share and some significant, new, positive information was released overnight or during the day. If it happened overnight it would affect the opening price; if it happened during the day, trading would be temporarily suspended and a call-market process would be used to determine a new equilibrium price. If the buy orders were three or four times as numerous as the sell orders, the new price based on the call market might be $44. For an analysis of price movements surrounding trading halts, see Hopewell and Schwartz (1978) and Fabozzi and Ma (1988). Several studies have shown that using the call-market mechanism contributes to a more orderly market and less volatility at openings and following trading halts.

In a **continuous market**, trades occur at any time the market is open wherein stocks are priced either by auction or by dealers. In a dealer market, dealers are willing to buy or sell for their own account at a specified bid-and-ask price. In an auction market, enough buyers and sellers are trading to allow the market to be continuous; that is, when one investor comes to buy stock, there is another investor available and willing to sell stock. A compromise between a pure dealer market and a pure auction market is a combination structure wherein the market trading system is basically an auction market, but there exists an intermediary who is willing to act as a dealer if the pure auction market does not have enough activity. These intermediaries who act as both brokers and dealers provide temporary liquidity to ensure the market will be liquid and continuous.

Notably, many continuous auction market exchanges (including the NYSE) also employ a call-market mechanism at the open and during trading suspensions.

3.3.5 Exchange Market-Makers

Earlier we discussed exchange "brokers" who bring buyers and sellers together for a transaction but never own the asset involved (real estate brokers are a popular example). We also discussed "dealers" who expedite transactions by buying and selling for their own account and make a living based on the bid-ask spread (the difference between what they paid for the asset [their bid price] and what they sell it for [the asking price]). As we will discuss subsequently, the NASDAQ market is composed of competing dealers who trade the stocks on that system. In contrast, the major market-makers on the NYSE are referred to as "specialists" or "designated market-makers (DMM)."

The specialist (DMM) is a member of the exchange who applies to the exchange to be assigned stocks to handle (generally 10–15). These DMMs have two major functions. First, they serve as brokers to match buy and sell orders and to handle special limit orders placed with other brokers; they transact when the market price reaches the limit price. The second major function is to act as a dealer to maintain a fair and orderly market by providing liquidity when the natural flow of orders is not adequate. The point is, a dealer must buy or sell for his or her own account when public supply or demand is not enough for a continuous liquid market.

3.4 CLASSIFICATION OF U.S. SECONDARY EQUITY MARKETS

In this section we consider the different secondary equity markets that currently exist in the United States, as listed in Exhibit 3.3.

3.4.1 Primary Listing Markets

Primary listing markets are formal exchanges or markets where a corporate stock is primarily or formally listed. Prior to the regulatory changes there were only two national exchanges—the NYSE and the NASDAQ markets that differ in how they trade securities (as will be discussed). We will also briefly discuss the American Stock Exchange (ASE) that no longer exists as an independent entity.

New York Stock Exchange (NYSE) The NYSE is the largest organized securities market in the United States. It was established in 1817 as the New York Stock and Exchange Board but dates its founding to when the famous Buttonwood Agreement was signed in May 1792 by 24 brokers.[3] The name was changed to the New York Stock Exchange in 1863.

At the end of 2016, approximately 2,850 companies had their common or preferred stock listed on the NYSE, with a total market value of more than $14 trillion. The average number of shares traded daily on the NYSE has increased substantially. Prior to the 1960s, the daily share trading volume averaged less than 3 million shares, compared with the 2016 average daily volume of about 3.5 billion shares. Notably, about half of this volume is attributable to high-frequency trading (HFT).

The NYSE has historically dominated the other exchanges in the United States in trading volume. Given its stringent listing requirements and its prestige, most of the largest and

---

[3]The NYSE considers the signing of this agreement the birth of the Exchange and celebrated its 200th birthday during 1992.

best-known U.S. companies are listed on the NYSE. Historically, about 55 percent of the trading volume for these listed stocks was on the NYSE, but this has changed dramatically beginning in 2004 when alternative trading venues were created as will be discussed in subsequent sections.

American Stock Exchange (AMEX) The AMEX originally traded unlisted shares at the corner of Wall and Hanover Streets in New York and was called the Outdoor Curb Market but changed its name to the New York Curb Market Association in 1910. In 1946, its volume in listed stocks finally outnumbered that in unlisted stocks. The current name was adopted in 1953.

The AMEX became a major stock options exchange in January 1975, including options on interest rates and stock indexes and subsequently added a number of exchange-traded funds (ETFs).

The AMEX and the NASDAQ merged in 1998, but in 2005 NASDAQ sold the AMEX back to its members (see Horowitz and Kelly, 2005). Finally the AMEX was acquired by the NYSE in 2007 and is currently referred to as the NYSE MKT AMEX.

Global Stock Exchanges The equity-market environment outside the United States is similar in that each country typically has one relatively large exchange that dominates the market. Examples include the Tokyo Stock Exchange, the London Stock Exchange, the Frankfurt Stock Exchange, and the Paris Bourse.

Notably, even emerging economies have stock exchanges because of the liquidity that secondary equity markets provide. There are several factors impacting these international exchange. First, there has been a trend toward consolidations that will provide more liquidity and greater economies of scale to support the technology required by investors. Second, many of the larger companies in these countries can qualify for listing on a U.S. exchange and have become dual-listed. About 20 percent of the stocks listed on the NYSE are non-U.S. firms. Third, these strong international exchanges have made possible a global equity market wherein stocks that have a global constituency can be traded around the world continuously, as discussed in the following section. Finally, there is intense competition between these exchanges, as discussed by Ewing and Ascarelli (2000) and Cherney and Beal (2000).

The Global 24-Hour Market The major markets in New York, London, and Tokyo, because of their relative size and importance, can be envisioned to represent the major segments of a worldwide 24-hour stock market wherein investment firms "pass the book" around the world. This means the major active market in securities moves around the globe as trading hours for these three markets (and other exchanges) begin and end.

As an example, consider the individual trading hours for each of the three exchanges, translated into a 24-hour eastern standard time (EST) clock:

	Local Time (24-hour notations)	24-hour EST
New York Stock Exchange (NYSE)	0930–1600	0930–1600
Tokyo Stock Exchange (TSE)	0900–1100	2300–0100
	1300–1500	0300–0500
London Stock Exchange (LSE)	0815–1615	0215–1015

Imagine trading starting in New York at 0930 and going until 1600 in the afternoon, being picked up by Tokyo late in the evening and going until 0500 in the morning, and continuing in London (with some overlap) until it begins in New York again (with some overlap) at 0930. Given this scenario, the U.S. trader asks, "What happened in Tokyo and what *is* happening in London?" The trader in Tokyo is concerned with what happened in New York, and subsequently the London traders are aware of what happened in New York and want to know what is happening in Tokyo. The point is, the markets operate almost continuously and are related in their response to economic events. Therefore, investors are not dealing with three or more separate and distinct exchanges, but with one interrelated world stock market because of the availability of sophisticated telecommunications. Paraphrasing a statement by O'Hara and Ye (2011), it is a single virtual market with multiple points of entry. Participants in this global market are the stocks of companies that have global markets for their products like Apple, General Electric, Coca-Cola, Johnson & Johnson, McDonald's, and similar international firms.

The NASDAQ Market[4]   This market system was historically known as the over-the-counter (OTC) market, which included stocks not formally listed on the two major exchanges (NYSE and AMEX). Subsequently it has been recognized as an equity market similar to the major exchanges with several minor differences. First, it is a dealer market, in contrast to a broker/ dealer (specialists) market as is the NYSE. Second, trading by dealers on NASDAQ takes place via computer communication rather than on a trading floor. Notably, as will be discussed, this is no longer a difference since electronic trading also dominates the NYSE. NASDAQ is similar to the other exchanges with a set of requirements for a stock to be traded on the NASDAQ National Market System (NMS).

NASDAQ is the largest U.S. secondary market in terms of the number of issues traded. As noted earlier, there are about 3,000 issues traded on the NYSE. In contrast, as of the end of 2015 there was a total of over 3,000 companies on the NASDAQ stock market. NAS-DAQ is also the most diverse secondary market component in terms of quality because it has multiple minimum requirements. Stocks that trade on the NASDAQ market range from small, unprofitable companies to large, extremely profitable firms such as Microsoft, Intel, and Apple.

In early 2017, an estimated 650 issues of NASDAQ were either foreign stocks or American Depository Receipts (ADRs). About 300 of these issues trade on both NASDAQ and a foreign exchange such as Toronto.

Although the NASDAQ market has the greatest number of issues, the NYSE has a larger total value of trading. In 2017 the approximate value of average daily equity trading on the NYSE was about $110 billion compared to about $80 billion on NASDAQ.

Listing Requirements for NASDAQ   Quotes and trading volume for the NASDAQ market are reported in two lists: a National Market System (NMS) list and a regular NASDAQ list. There are alternative standards for initial listing and continued listing on the NASDAQ NMS. The standards for the NMS listing are significant but not as onerous as for the NYSE. For stocks on NASDAQ the trading reports are similar to those on the NYSE.

3.4.2 The Significant Transition of the U.S. Equity Markets[5]

The prior discussion of the U.S. equity market is correct and relevant, but it does not reflect the dramatic changes over the past 25 years to financial institutions that have existed for over 225 years (recall that the NYSE Buttonwood Agreement was signed in 1792). While the significant transition started in 1994, there were some prior changes introduced by the SEC to bring about a national competitive securities market. The SEC mandated a consolidated tape in the mid-1970s that reported **centralized transactions** from the national exchanges and NASDAQ.

---

[4]NASDAQ is an acronym for National Association of Securities Dealers Automated Quotations. The system is discussed in detail in a later section. To be traded on the NMS, a firm must have a certain size and trading activity and at least four market makers.

[5]This section benefitted from the very informative essay by Daniel Mathisson titled "Man versus Machine: The Regulatory Changes that Led to the Modern Market," in Knight Capital Group (2010).

This was followed by **consolidated quotations** and then the introduction of the **Intermarket Trading System (ITS)** that linked the national exchanges as well as the CBOE. The ITS "allowed" trades to go to the best quotes, but unfortunately it was not required or automatic.

The Initial Setting The equity markets in the early 1990s were relatively busy, but the NYSE and its members dominated the prosperous listed stock market—a "seat" (membership) on the NYSE consistently sold for over $2 million in the early 2000s and had a peak price of $3.25 million in 2005. The NYSE had only one competitor—the NASDAQ OTC market that was basically an electronic dealer market.

The Transition Begins The U.S. equity market began to change in 1994 with the publication of a study by Christie and Schultz (1994) that documented the strong tendency for market quotes to be concentrated in quarters ($0, \frac{1}{4}, \frac{1}{2}, \frac{3}{4}$) even though price quotes could be in eighths ($\frac{1}{8}, \frac{3}{8}, \frac{5}{8}, \frac{7}{8}$). Christie and Schultz documented that the dealers apparently were colluding to maintain wide bid-ask spreads to ensure high profits. The reaction by the Justice Department and the SEC to these empirical findings was fast and dramatic.

In 1996 there were convictions for "anticompetitive behavior," and in early 1997 new order-handling rules were specified that required that electronic communications networks (ECNs) make their quotes available to the public markets. As a result, previously private quotes were made available to the total market including several small electronic trading markets. This legislation allowed existing and new ECNs to compete with the major exchanges and gain significant market share. As a result, significant competition developed among the ECNs on the basis of speed, price, and reliability. It also led to a battle for trading volume wherein ECNs began paying for order flow that involved rebates of commissions for limit orders. These rebate fees were revenue for traders and led to a significant increase in trading volume.

The Move to Decimal Pricing In June 1997 the first change in pricing increments occurred wherein prices went from being quoted in one-eighths (that had been used since the 1800s) to one-sixteenths. While this change caused a decline in spreads, there were still problems with a spread of six cents that led to civil violations by traders and NYSE specialists.

In 2000 the SEC required decimal pricing (pennies) by April 2001. The immediate impact was significantly smaller spreads—from six cents to possibly a penny—which caused many NASDAQ traders to leave the business. The NYSE responded by creating a new trading order entitled "Direct+" and an electronic order routing system that transformed how large orders were executed. Specifically, rather than "block trades" of 10,000 shares or, more, these innovations made it possible to do large trades using multiple small orders that could be executed without the information impounded in large trades. Quickly, firms developed computer programs (algorithms) to divide the large orders into small orders—these programs were really the initiation of **algorithmic trading**. This led to many competing ECNs creating "smart order routing" algorithms that selected where to send orders to minimize transaction costs and impact. As a result, the average size of trades declined dramatically from about 800 shares per trade in 2002 to about 200 shares in 2015, while the number of transactions exploded from 545 million in 2002 to more than 2 trillion in 2015. In turn, block trades (of 10,000 or more shares) that had accounted for almost 52 percent of the NYSE volume in 2000 declined to less than 10 percent in 2015.

The National Market System (NMS) The trend toward electronic trading accelerated when the SEC passed Regulation NMS in 2007, which contains four major components:

1. Rule 610—Access Rule: This rule provides standards for access to quotations for stock involved in the NMS. This rule provides complete access to all market prices for these stocks. Notably, it prohibits any trading system from discriminating against other participants in the market, as the major exchanges do, in limiting trading to their members. It also limits the fees that trading venues can charge for their quotations. As a result, quotations on the exchanges are available to all market participants.

2. **The Order Protection Rule.** This rule protects displayed quotations at the best bid or best offer (the national best bid and offer [NBBO]). Specifically, brokers or dealers who are internalizing trades must match or beat the prevailing NBBO.

3. **The Sub-Penny Rule.** This rule prevents exchanges, broker/dealers, or other traders from accepting orders priced in increments less than one cent for stocks priced over $1.00. Notably, transactions can be executed in sub-penny increments.

4. **Market Data Rules.** These rules govern revenue allocation between markets that contribute trade data to the consolidated tape.

Beyond the open, more competitive market allowed and encouraged by Regulation NMS, the trading environment has become more fragmented due to technology and the trading community responding to the unique preferences and needs of a diverse set of institutions and individuals of alternative clienteles. Specifically, total trading volume that previously was only divided among listed exchanges (the NYSE and the ASE) and the over-the-counter (OTC) market is now divided among a variety of trading venues best described as a decentralized electronic network that includes 13 exchanges and a vast off-exchange business where trading takes place in alternative trading systems (ATSs) that include electronic communication networks (ECNs); dark pools; and broker-dealer internalizations. We will describe each of these components in the following sub-sections. Exhibit 3.3 provides some structure to this discussion.

Stock Exchanges The new stock exchanges listed in Exhibit 3.3 are a sharp contrast to the historic exchanges that existed pre-1990 that depended on numerous individuals such as "specialists" (recently referred to as "designated market makers") and runners to provide liquidity

---

Exhibit 3.3 Breakdown of Trading Components Following Regulation National Market System

A. Exchanges

- New York Stock Exchange
  - NYSE
  - NYSE Arca
  - NYSE Mkt AMEX
- NASDAQ
  - NASDAX
  - Boston Stock Exchange
  - Pacific Stock Exchange

- CBOE Stock Exchange
  - Direct Edge (EDGX)
  - Direct Edge (EDGA)
  - BATS (BYX)
  - BZX
- Chicago Stock Exchange

B. Non-Exchanges (Dark Liquidity)

- Electronic Communication Networks (ECNs)
  - Lava Flow
- Dark Pools
  - Credit Suisse Crossfinder
  - Goldman Sachs Sigmax
  - Knight Link
  - An additional 12–15 firms

- Broker/dealer Internalizations (OTC)
  - Approximately 200 firms

Source: Adapted from: Rhodri Preece, "Dark Pools, Internalization and Equity Market Quality," CFA Institute, Charlottesville, VA, 2012.

using market orders (that would accept the current spread on a stock) or limit orders (where investors would specify a price and time period when they would buy or sell). Notably, the specialist would respond immediately to the market order or record the limit orders and fill them if and when market orders arrived to match them. Currently, virtually all of this is done electronically such that most exchanges are best described as electronic limit order book markets with numerous buyers and sellers trading based on a set of rules that give priority based on the time of arrival and price of orders. Notably, in this environment the liquidity is being provided by the numerous traders competing against one another with the use of computers rather than the individual specialist. Beyond the efficiencies and speed of transactions provided by these electronic exchanges, this system also allows pre-trade and post-trade transparency, that is, the full limit order book is always available as well as the results of all trades immediately after a transaction. The impact of this significant change came quickly. By the spring of 2007, the brokerage firms with people on the floor of the NYSE began laying off personnel while specialist firms consolidated and reduced employees on the floor.

Exhibit 3.4 shows the several exchanges and reflects the numerous mergers wherein there are currently three major exchange groups: the New York Stock Exchange, the NASDAQ Stock Exchange, and the CBOE Stock Exchanges. In addition to the registered exchanges there are several non-exchanges that provide what is referred to as "dark liquidity" since they do not provide pre and post-trade transparency as will be described.

Electronic Communication Networks (ECNs) ECNs were created shortly after Order Handling Rules to respond to the new regulations and were electronic trading markets structured as limit order book markets with pre and post trade transparency but were regulated as ATSs that involved less surveillance and oversight compared to registered exchanges. Given the similarities to exchanges almost all of them eventually applied to become registered exchanges or were acquired by the large exchanges and turned into registered exchanges. Therefore, there is currently only one significant ECN: Lava Flow.

Dark Pools[6] Dark pools are the ultimate response to pre-trade and post-trade transparency— the orders put into dark pool are *not* displayed to other market participants in order to reduce information leakage and minimize market impact costs. As such, they originally were a follow-on to **block traders** who dealt with large transactions (over 10,000 shares) off the exchanges because they were concerned that if the market became aware that an institution was buying or selling a large block of stock the market prices would move against the trade (if selling, prices would decline; if buying, prices would increase). Therefore, institutions would take the trade to a block trader—off the exchange—who would work to find other institutions who would buy or sell the stock. Dark pools do similar trades but also smaller trades with selected investors—the orders in the pool are not displayed to other market participants and are sold to anonymous buyers. Notably, the participants on both sides of the trade are generally in the pool by invitation; most pools contend that they do not allow high-frequency traders (HFTs) into the pools, though not everyone believes that. The advantage to participants beyond anonymity is better pricing (at the midpoint of bid-ask spread) and lower transaction fees. Similar to what transpired with block trades, with lower cost transactions, most block trades were broken up into 200 to 400 share transactions. As noted earlier, this caused the average size of trades to decline from an average of about 1,200 shares to about 250 shares while the number of transactions experienced a dramatic increase from about one million a day in 2000 to over 13 million a day in 2016.

In terms of regulation, dark pools are registered as ATSs. Finally, they do report their transactions on the composite tape and it is estimated that they are responsible for about 25 percent of trading volume.

---

[6]An interesting and insightful presentation on this topic is, Scott Patterson, *Dark Pools*, Crown Publishing Group, a division of Random House, Inc. New York, 2012.

Broker/Dealer Internalizations The final non-exchange activity is referred to as internalizations by individual broker/dealers which is quite common among about 200 firms. Internalization is when retail broker/dealers *internally* transact an order by buying or selling the stock against their own account on a consistent basis. Put another way, the firm is the counterparty to all transactions and uses its own capital. Again, it is considered "dark liquidity" because the brokers are acting as OTC market makers and are not required to display quotes prior to execution. These firms are also allowed to discriminate among their clients and decide from whom they will accept orders. This shows up when the firm decides which stocks to trade, for example, they will typically only accept orders for liquid securities, but can decide not to participate for illiquid stocks that they can direct to other public trading venues. Again, they generally report all trades to the consolidated tape, so there is post-trade information. Notably, internalization accounts for about 18% of total trading volume and almost 100% of all retail marketable order flow.

Beyond these components that make up the trading structure for common stocks, there are two trading practices that also influence the overall trading environments: algorithmic trading and high-frequency trading.

Algorithmic Trading (AT) Algorithmic trading is basically creating computer programs to make trading decisions. One of the earlier uses of AT was concerned with the routing of orders to alternative trading venues during the period when there were numerous ECNs. The algorithms were programmed to select the trading venue with the most liquid market or the one with the best current price for the buyer or seller. Using the algorithm the decision was made and implemented in seconds. Eventually the decisions became more sophisticated and complex including buying in one market and selling in another simultaneously for a small profit, or programming that would trade based on important company news (e.g., earning surprises or merger announcements) or macro-economic events such as Federal Reserve decisions or domestic or international political news. The point is, consider anything that will effect stock prices (which is just about everything) and someone can create an algorithm that will act on it in milliseconds in competition with other investors. Clearly, even the very best investors can benefit from a program that will trade faster and cheaper for small profits that will add up assuming numerous trades. This brings us to high frequency trading.

High-Frequency Trading (HFT) There have always been some individuals who "play the market" by constantly buying and selling stocks based on rapid reactions to company or macro-economic news as discussed in the AT section. It is hard to determine how many of these traders are successful since they generally do not divulge their records, but the fact is, prior to competitive commissions (in the 1970s) and the requirement to report prices in decimals, a major constraint of traders were "trading costs." The trader may have thought they were making money, but the real beneficiary of all the trading was the broker who got all the commissions.

As discussed, following legislation that allowed (required) competitive commissions and decimalization, the cost of trading experienced a significant decline—about 80–90 percent. This made it economically possible for many more individuals to get into trading, but also more professionals and even institutions who used AT to create programs that traded *thousands* of times a day for small profits that add up as noted earlier. The point is, if you have a trading idea that is profitable, a major constraint may be *how fast* can you implement the trade. In this scenario, it may be worth the cost of creating an AT that will implement your unique, profitable trades in milliseconds, thousands of times a day as a high frequency trader (HFT).

HFTs are both admired and detested. They are admired since they bring significant *liquidity* to the market, smaller bid-ask spreads, and substantially lower transaction costs which we know are very important attributes of a good market. The fact is, it is estimated that about 50 percent of all trading volume is attributable to HFTs. They are reviled because they bring added *volatility* to the market since their algorithms can cause significant shifts in the volume of trading and prices. Also, they contribute to a short term attitude toward investing when capital markets are meant to determine intrinsic value based on cash flows over very long horizons (decades into the future).

AT/HFT and the Flash Crash The negative side of AT/HFT is concerned with the potential for major trading problems or an algorithmic glitch or a "fat finger" event when an operator hits the wrong key and initiates a major blowout or crash. An example of such an event occurred on May 6, 2010, when the market experienced a "**flash crash**." Specifically, on the afternoon of May 6, when the major stock and futures indexes were already down over 4 percent for the day, prices suddenly declined a further 5 to 6 percent in a matter of minutes and this was followed by a very rapid recovery. The fact is, in a matter of minutes, an algorithmic trade by an investment firm in Kansas City caused numerous high-frequency traders to automatically withdraw from the market. In turn, this reduced the market's overall liquidity and caused numerous significant price declines—many of which were subsequently reversed. For a detailed discussion of what transpired, see an appendix in Harris (2015), a discussion in Fox, Glosten, and Rauterberg (2015), and Lewis (2014).

The Current Status Given the numerous developments discussed, it is useful to summarize what has changed, what has *not* changed, and what is likely to change in the future. Notably, the changes that have occurred, are the most obvious. The fact is, we now have a market that is generally more efficient because trading is easier, faster, and cheaper than it was 20 years ago. In the process, the NYSE has lost a lot of market power, the NASDAQ has grown in significance, and we have witnessed the creation of numerous exchanges that have reshaped our markets toward electronic trading.

What has not changed are the basic orders used to implement trading that will be described in the following section. What has started to change and will likely continue to change going forward is the basic makeup of our secondary equity market—that is, there have been numerous mergers over the past decade, for reasons discussed in the final section of the chapter.

3.5 ALTERNATIVE TYPES OF ORDERS AVAILABLE

It is important to understand the different types of orders available to investors, regardless of how the market is organized.

3.5.1 Market Orders

The most common type of order is a **market order**, an order to buy or sell a stock at the best current price. An investor who enters a market sell order indicates a willingness to sell immediately at the highest bid available at the time the order reaches a registered exchange, an ECN, or a dark pool. A market buy order indicates that the investor is willing to pay the lowest offering price available at the time of the order. Market orders provide *immediate liquidity* for an investor willing to accept the prevailing market price.

Assume you are interested in General Electric (GE) and you call your broker to find out the current "market" on the stock. The quotation machine indicates that the prevailing best market (NBBO) is 30 bid–30.05 ask. This means that the highest current bid is 30; that is, $30 is the most that anyone has offered to pay to buy GE stock. The lowest offer is 30.05, which is the lowest price anyone is willing to accept to sell the stock. If you placed a market buy order for 100 shares, you would buy 100 shares at $30.05 a share (the lowest ask price), for a total cost of $3,005 plus commission. If you submitted a market sell order for 100 shares, you would sell the shares at $30 each (the highest bid price) and receive $3,000 less commission.

3.5.2 Limit Orders

The individual placing a **limit order** specifies the buy or sell price. You might submit a limit–order bid to purchase 100 shares of Coca-Cola (KO) stock at $40 a share when the current market is 45 bid–45.10 ask, with the expectation that the stock will decline to $40 in the near future.

You must also indicate how long the limit order will be outstanding. Alternative time specifications are basically boundless. A limit order can be instantaneous ("fill or kill," meaning fill the order instantly or cancel it). In the world of algorithmic trading, this is a popular time specification for high-frequency traders. It can also be good for part of a day, a full day, several days, a week, or a month. It can also be open ended, or good until canceled (GTC).

Rather than wait for a given price on a stock, because KO is listed on the NYSE your broker will give the limit order to the exchange who will put it in the exchange's limit-order book. When and if the market price for KO reaches the limit-order price, the exchanges computer will execute the order and inform your broker.

3.5.3 Special Orders

In addition to these general orders, there are several special types of orders. A *stop loss order* is a conditional market order whereby the investor directs the sale of a stock if it drops to a given price. Assume you buy a stock at $50 and expect it to increase in value. If you are wrong, you want to limit your losses. To protect yourself, you could put in a stop loss order at $45. In this case, if the stock dropped to $45, your stop loss order would become a market sell order, and the stock would be sold at the prevailing market price. The stop loss order does not guarantee that you will get the $45; you can get a little bit more or a little bit less. Because of the possibility of market disruption caused by a large number of stop loss orders, exchanges have, on occasion, canceled all such orders on certain stocks and not allowed brokers to accept further stop loss orders on those issues.

A related stop loss tactic for an investor who has entered into a short sale is a *stop buy order*. Such an investor who wants to minimize his or her loss if the stock begins to increase in value would enter this conditional buy order at a price above the short-sale price. Assume you sold a stock short at $50, expecting it to decline to $40. To protect yourself from an increase, you could put in a stop buy order to purchase the stock (and close out your short sale) using a market buy order if it reached a price of $55. This conditional buy order would hopefully limit any loss on the short sale to approximately $5 a share.

3.5.4 Margin Transactions

When investors buy stock, they can pay for the stock with cash or borrow part of the cost, leveraging the transaction. Leverage is accomplished by buying on margin, which means the investor pays for the stock with some cash and borrows the rest through the broker, putting up the stock for collateral.

The dollar amount of margin credit extended by NYSE members has generally increased over time, but it is a fairly cyclical series that increases during rising markets and declines during falling markets. The interest rate charged on these loans by the investment firms is typically 1.50 percent above the rate charged by the bank making the loan. The bank rate, referred to as the *call money rate*, is generally about 1 percent below the prime rate. For example, in November 2017 the prime rate was 4.00 percent, and the call money rate was 2.75 percent.

Federal Reserve Board Regulations T and U determine the maximum proportion of any transaction that can be borrowed. This *margin requirement* (the proportion of total transaction value that must be paid in cash) has varied over time from 40 percent (allowing loans of 60 percent of the value) to 100 percent (allowing no borrowing). As of November 2017, the initial margin requirement specified by the Federal Reserve was 50 percent, although individual investment firms can require higher percents.

After the initial purchase, changes in the market price of the stock will cause changes in the *investor's equity*, which is equal to the market value of the collateral stock minus the amount borrowed. Obviously, if the stock price increases, the investor's equity as a proportion of the total market value of the stock increases; that is, the investor's margin will exceed the initial margin requirement.

Assume you acquired 200 shares of a $50 stock for a total cost of $10,000. A 50 percent initial margin requirement allowed you to borrow $5,000, making your initial equity $5,000. If the stock price increases by 20 percent to $60 a share, the total market value of your position is $12,000, and your equity is now $7,000 ($12,000 – $5,000), or 58 percent ($7,000/$12,000). In contrast, if the stock price declines by 20 percent to $40 a share, the total market value would be $8,000, and your investor's equity would be $3,000 ($8,000 – $5,000), or 37.5 percent ($3,000/$8,000).

This example demonstrates that buying on margin provides all the advantages and the disadvantages of leverage. Lower margin requirements (the proportion that must be paid in cash) allow you to borrow more, increasing the percentage of gain or loss on your investment when the stock price increases or decreases. The *leverage factor* equals 1/percent margin. Thus, as in the example, if the margin is 50 percent, the leverage factor is 2, that is, 1/0.50. Therefore, when the rate of return on the stock is plus or minus 10 percent, the return on *your* equity is plus or minus 20 percent. If the margin requirement declines to 33 percent, you can borrow more (67 percent), and the leverage factor is 3(1/0.33). As discussed by Ip/(2000), when you acquire stock or other investments on margin, you are increasing the financial risk of the investment beyond the risk inherent in the security itself. Therefore, you should increase your required rate of return accordingly.

The following example shows how borrowing by using margin affects the distribution of your returns *before commissions and interest* on the loan. If the stock increased by 20 percent, your return on the investment would be as follows:

1. The market value of the stock is $12,000, which leaves you with $7,000 after you pay off the loan.
2. The return on your $5,000 investment is 40 percent, as follows:

$$\frac{7,000}{5,000} - 1 = 1.40 - 1$$
$$= 0.40 = 40\%$$

In contrast, if the stock declined by 20 percent to $40 a share, your return would be as follows:

1. The market value of the stock is $8,000, which leaves you with $3,000 after you pay off the loan.
2. The negative return on your $5,000 investment is −40 percent, as follows:

$$\frac{3,000}{5,000} - 1 = 0.60 - 1$$
$$= -0.40 = -40\%$$

Notably, this symmetrical increase in gains and losses is only true prior to commissions and interest. For example, if we assume 4 percent interest on the borrowed funds (which would be $5,000 × 0.04 = $200), and a $100 commission on the transaction, the results would indicate a lower positive return and a larger negative return, as follows:

$$20\% \text{ increase}: \frac{\$12,000 - \$5,000 - \$200 - \$100}{5,000} - 1 = \frac{6,700}{5,000} - 1 = 0.34 = 34\%$$

$$20\% \text{ decline}: \frac{\$8,000 - \$5,000 - \$200 - \$100}{5,000} - 1 = \frac{2,700}{5,000} - 1 = -0.54 = -54\%$$

In addition to the initial margin requirement, another important concept is the **maintenance margin**, which is the required proportion of your equity to the total *value of the* stock after the initial transaction. The maintenance margin protects the broker if the stock price declines. At present, the minimum maintenance margin specified by the Federal Reserve is 25 percent, but, again, individual brokerage firms can dictate higher maintenance margins for their customers. If the stock price declines to the point where your investor's equity drops below 25 percent of the total value of the position, the account is considered undermargined, and you will receive a **margin call** to provide more equity. If you do not respond with the required funds in time, the stock will be sold to pay off the loan. The time allowed to meet a margin call varies between investment firms and is affected by market conditions. Under volatile market conditions, the time allowed to respond to a margin call can be shortened drastically (e.g., to one day).

Given a maintenance margin of 25 percent, when you buy on margin you must consider how far the stock price can fall before you receive a margin call. The computation for our example is as follows: If the price of the stock is P and you own 200 shares, the value of your position is $200P$ and the equity in your account is $(200P - \$5,000)$. The percentage margin is $(200P - 5,000)/200P$. To determine the price, P, that is equal to 25 percent (0.25), we use the following equation:

$$\frac{200P - 5,000}{200P} = 0.25$$
$$200P - \$5,000 = 50P$$
$$150P = \$5,000$$
$$P = \$33.33$$

Therefore, when the stock declines to $33.33, the equity value is exactly 25 percent; so if the stock declines from $50 to below $33.33, you will receive a margin call.

To continue the previous example, if the stock declines further to $30 a share, its total market value would be $6,000 and your equity would be $1,000, which is only about 17 percent of the total value ($1,000/$6,000). You would receive a margin call for approximately $667, which would give you equity of $1,667, or 25 percent of the total value of the account ($1,667/$6,667). If the stock declines further, you would receive additional margin calls.

3.5.5 Short Sales

Most investors purchase stock ("go long") expecting to derive their return from an increase in value. If you believe that a stock is overpriced, however, and want to take advantage of an expected decline in the price, you can sell the stock short. A **short sale** is the sale of stock that *you do not own* with the intent of purchasing it back later at a lower price. Specifically, you would *borrow* the stock from another investor through your broker and sell it in the market. Subsequently you would replace it by buying shares of the stock at a price lower (you hope) than the price at which you sold it (this is referred to as *covering your short position*). Although a short sale has no time limit, the lender of the shares can decide to sell the shares, in which case your broker must find another investor willing to lend the shares. For discussions of both good and bad experiences with short-selling, see Beard (2001).

Two technical points affect short sales.[7] The first technical point concerns dividends. The short seller must pay any dividends due to the investor who lent the stock. The purchaser of

---

[7]Prior to June 2007 there was a rule that short sales of individual stocks could only be made on "upticks," meaning the price of the short sale had to be higher than the last trade price. The SEC eliminated this rule in 2007.

the short-sale stock that you borrowed receives the dividend from the corporation, so the short seller must pay a similar dividend to the person who lent the stock.

Second, short sellers must post the same margin as an investor who had acquired stock. This margin can be in cash or any unrestricted securities owned by the short seller.

To illustrate this technique and demonstrate these technical points, consider the following example using Cara Corporation stock that is currently selling for $80 a share. You believe that the stock is overpriced and decide to sell 1,000 shares short at $80. Your broker borrows the Cara Corporation stock on your behalf, sells it at $80, and deposits the $80,000 (less commissions that we will ignore in this example) in your account. Although the $80,000 is in your account, you cannot withdraw it. In addition, you must post 50 percent margin ($40,000) as collateral. Your percent margin equals:

$$\text{Percent Margin} = \frac{\text{Value of Your Equity}}{\text{Value of Stock Owed}}$$

The value of your equity equals: the cash from the sale of stock ($80,000), plus the required margin deposited ($40,000), minus the value of the stock owed (1,000P). Therefore, the percent margin at the initiation is:

$$\text{Percent Margin} = \frac{\$80,000 + \$40,000 - \$80,000}{\$80,000}$$

$$= \frac{\$40,000}{\$80,000} = 0.50$$

Much as in the discussion of margin transactions, it is necessary to continue to compare the percent margin over time to the maintenance margin (assumed to be 25 percent). Notably, in the case of a short sale, a price decline is a positive event related to the percent margin. For example, if we assume that the price of Cara Corporation stock declines to $70, the percent margin would increase as follows:

$$\frac{\text{Your Equity}}{\text{Value of Stock Owed}} = \frac{\$80,000 + \$40,000 - \$70,000}{\$70,000}$$

$$= \frac{\$50,000}{\$70,000} = 0.71$$

Alternatively, if the stock price increases to $90 a share, the percent margin would experience a decline as follows:

$$\frac{\text{Your Equity}}{\text{Value of Stock Owed}} = \frac{\$80,000 + \$40,000 - \$90,000}{\$90,000}$$

$$= \frac{\$30,000}{\$90,000} = 0.33$$

As before, it is important to determine the stock price that would trigger a margin call, which is computed as follows:

$$\frac{\text{Your Equity}}{\text{Value of Stock Owed}} = \frac{\$120,000 - 1,000P}{1,000P} = 0.25$$

$$= \$120,000 - 1,000P = 250P$$

$$= 1,250P = 120,000$$

$$P = \$96$$

Therefore, if the stock price moves against your short sale and *increases* above $96, you will receive a margin call. Given this unlimited upside potential (which is a negative event for the short seller), most short sellers consistently enter stop-gain orders along with selling a stock short to limit this loss and possibly avoid a margin call; that is, they would put in a stop-gain order at some price below 96.

3.5.6 Exchange Merger Mania

While the basic purpose of security markets has not changed, and the alternative orders employed by investors and traders have been quite constant, a relatively recent phenomenon has been numerous mergers among exchanges both within countries and between countries. Equally important, it is envisioned that this phenomenon will continue into the future.

Why Merger Mania? There are two major reasons why exchange merger mania started and will continue. The first reason is caused by the trend suggested in Chapter 2—the trend toward portfolios that are diversified both between countries (globally) and among asset classes. Given this dual diversification, exchanges want to be able to service individual investors, but mainly institutional investors as they buy and sell different assets (e.g., stocks, bonds, and derivatives) in global markets. (The point is, the exchanges want to provide global one-stop investing.)

The second reason is the economics of high-technology trading. Earlier we discussed the trend toward electronic (computerized) trading venues that employ very sophisticated computers and highly trained personnel to develop the advanced algorithms that provide fast, efficient trading. Two facts dominate: (1) This equipment and the personnel to operate it are *very expensive*, and (2) there are significant *economies of scale* in the operation of these systems. This combination of high cost and required scale leads to the need for mergers within a country and across countries and asset classes so the exchange can afford the equipment *and* the staff to attain the scale required to have a desirable and profitable operation.

Some Past Mergers Following the creation of a number of ECNs in the 1990s, there were mergers of these entities into something like Archipelago (a registered stock exchange), which then acquired PCX Holdings, an electronic trader of options. In early 2006 the NYSE acquired Archipelago Holdings Co., a public company, and became a publicly traded entity, the NYSE Group, Inc. This was followed by a major merger in 2007 with Euronext NV, which itself was the product of several mergers of European exchanges including Lisbon and Oporto, Amsterdam, Brussels, and the Paris stock exchanges and Liffe, a derivatives exchange.

During this time, NASDAQ acquired the Instinet Group, an ECN, and became a public company that acquired the Philadelphia Stock Exchange and OMX, an ECN that became a registered exchange.

In the derivatives area, the Chicago Mercantile Exchange (CME) Holding went public in 2006, and subsequently the Chicago Board of Trade (CBOT) also went public. In late 2007 these two exchanges merged to create the largest derivatives exchange, and were subsequently joined by the New York Mercantile Exchange in 2008.

Another active participant has been the London Stock Exchange that acquired the Borsa Italiana in 2007.

The Present and Future As shown in Exhibit 3.3 the financial market landscape has become a few large holding companies that own global exchanges for stocks, bonds, and derivatives.

Because the two driving reasons for the merger mania are still true, we would envision continuing mergers within the major developed markets, but also in smaller, less developed sectors such as the Far East—for example, Singapore, China, India, Thailand, and Indonesia. Beyond mergers within these countries, someone will want to dominate regions such as Europe or Asia through mergers.

SUMMARY

- The securities market is divided into primary and secondary markets. While primary markets are important sources of new capital for the issuers of securities, the secondary markets provide the liquidity that is critical to the primary markets.
- The composition of the secondary bond market has experienced small changes over the past 30 years. In sharp contrast, the secondary, equity market has experienced significant change as demonstrated in Exhibit 3.3 and is continuing to evolve due to new technology and consolidation. In addition to a number of registered exchanges the secondary market includes an ECN, almost 20 firms that operate dark pools, and about 200 firms that internalize trading.

- The components of a good exchange market include several types of membership as well as various types of orders.
- It appears that changes, especially those due to these technological innovations, have only just begun. Therefore, investors need to understand how this market has evolved, its current structure and how it can develop in the future. As an investor, you will need to understand how to analyze securities to find the best securities for your portfolio, but also you need to know the best way to buy/sell the security, that is, how and where to complete the transaction. This chapter provides the background you need to make that trading decision.

SUGGESTED READINGS

Barclay, Michael, Terrence Hendershott, and D. Timothy McCormick, "Competition among Trading Venues: Information and Trading on Electronic Communications Networks," *Journal of Finance* 58, no. 6 (December 2003).

Fox, Merritt, Lawrence Glosten, and Gabriel Rauterberg, "The New Stock Market: Sense and Nonsense," *Duke Law Journal*, 65, no. 2 (November, 2015): 191–277.

Harris, Larry, "Trading and Electronic Markets: What Investment Professionals Need to Know." CFA Institute Research Foundation, 2015.

Hendershott, T.C., Jones, and A. Mankueld, "Does Algorithmic Trading Improve Liquidity?" *Journal of Finance*, 66, no. 1 (February, 2011): 1–33.

Larrymore, N. and A. Murphy, "Internalization and Market Quality: An Empirical Investigation," *Journal of Financial Research*, 32, no. 3 (Fall, 2009): 337–363.

Lewis, Michael, *Flash Boys*, W.W. Norton & Co., New York, 2014.

O'Hara, M. and M. Ye, "Is Market Fragmentation Harming Market Quality?" *Journal of Financial Economics*, 100, no. 3 (June, 2011) 459–474.

Preece, Rhodri, "Dark Pools, Internalization, and Equity Market Quality," CFA Institute, Charlottesville, VA, 2012.

Weaver, D., "Internalization and Market Quality in a Fragmented Market Structure," Working Paper, Rutgers Business School, (November, 2011).

QUESTIONS

1. Define *market* and briefly discuss the characteristics of a good market.
2. You own 100 shares of General Electric stock and you want to sell it because you need the money to make a down payment on a car. Assume there is absolutely no secondary market system in common stocks. How would you go about selling the stock? Discuss what you would have to do to find a buyer, how long it might take, and the price you might receive.
3. Define *liquidity* and discuss the factors that contribute to it. Give examples of a liquid asset and an illiquid asset, and discuss why they are considered liquid and illiquid.
4. Define a primary and secondary market for securities and discuss how they differ. Discuss how the primary market is dependent on the secondary market.

5. Give an example of an initial public offering (IPO) in the primary market. Give an example of a seasoned equity issue in the primary market. Discuss which would involve greater risk to the buyer.

6. Find an article about a recent primary offering in *The Wall Street Journal.* Based on the information in the article, indicate the characteristics of the security sold and the major underwriters. How much new capital did the firm derive from the offering?

7. Briefly explain the difference between a competitive-bid underwriting and a negotiated underwriting.

8. Which segment of the secondary stock market (NYSE or NASDAQ) is larger in terms of the number of issues? Which is larger in terms of the value of the issues traded?

9. Briefly define each of the following terms and give an example.
   a. Market order
   b. Limit order
   c. Short sale
   d. Stop loss order

10. Briefly discuss the two major functions for the NYSE specialist.

11. Briefly define each of the following terms.
   a. Dark pools
   b. Broker/Dealer internalization
   c. High Frequency Traders
   d. Algorithmic Trading

PROBLEMS

1. You have $40,000 to invest in Sophie Shoes, a stock selling for $80 a share. The initial margin requirement is 60 percent. Ignoring interest and commissions, show in detail the impact on your rate of return if the stock rises to $100 a share and if it declines to $40 a share, assuming (a) you pay cash for the stock, and (b) you buy the stock using maximum leverage.

2. Lauren has a margin account and deposits $50,000 into it. Assume the prevailing margin requirement is 40 percent, interest and commissions are ignored, and the Gentry Wine Corporation is selling at $35 per share.
   a. How many shares can Lauren purchase using the maximum allowable margin?
   b. What is Lauren's profit (loss) if the price of Gentry's stock
      i. rises to $45 and Lauren sells the stock?
      ii. falls to $25 and Lauren sells the stock?
   c. If the maintenance margin is 30 percent, to what price can Gentry Wine fall before Lauren will receive a margin call?

3. Assume that you buy 100 shares of Francesca Industries stock on 55 percent margin when the stock is selling at $20 a share. The broker charges a 5 percent annual interest rate, and commissions are 2 percent of the stock value on the purchase and sale. A year later you receive a $0.50 per share dividend and sell the stock for $27 a share. What is your rate of return on Francesca Industries?

4. You decide to sell short 100 shares of Charlotte Horse Farms when it is selling at its yearly high of $56. Your broker tells you that your margin requirement is 45 percent and that the commission on the purchase is $155. While you are short the stock, Charlotte pays a $2.50 per share dividend. At the end of one year, you buy 100 shares of Charlotte at $45 to close out your position and are charged a commission of $145 and 8 percent interest on the money borrowed. What is your rate of return on the investment?

5. You own 200 shares of Shamrock Enterprises that you bought at $25 a share. The stock is now selling for $45 a share.
   a. You put in a stop loss order at $40. Discuss your reasoning for this action.
   b. If the stock eventually declines in price to $30 a share, what would be your rate of return with and without the stop loss order (ignore commissions)?
6. Two years ago, you bought 300 shares of Kayleigh Milk Co. for $30 a share with a margin of 60 percent. Currently, the Kayleigh stock is selling for $45 a share. Assuming no dividends and ignoring commissions, compute (a) the annualized rate of return on this investment if you had paid cash, and (b) your annualized rate of return with the margin purchase.
7. The stock of the Madison Travel Co. is selling for $28 a share. You put in a limit buy order at $24 for one month. During the month the stock price declines to $20, then jumps to $36. Ignoring commissions, what would have been your rate of return on this investment? What would be your rate of return if you had put in a market order? What if your limit buy order was at $18?

CHAPTER 4

Security Market Indexes and Index Funds

After you read this chapter, you should be able to answer the following questions:

- What are some major uses of security market indexes?
- What major characteristics cause alternative indexes to differ?
- What are the major stock market indexes in the United States and globally, and what are their characteristics?
- Why are bond indexes more difficult to create and maintain than stock indexes?
- What are the major bond market indexes for the United States and the world?
- What are some of the composite stock–bond market indexes?
- Where can you get historical and current data for all these indexes?
- What is the relationship among many of these indexes during short run periods (monthly)?
- How can security market indexes be used to create investment portfolios and benchmark performance?
- What is the difference between an index mutual fund and an exchange-traded fund?

A fair statement regarding **security market indexes**—especially those outside the United States—is that everybody talks about them but few people understand them. Even those investors familiar with widely publicized stock market series, such as the Dow Jones Industrial Average (DJIA) or the S&P 500 Index, usually know little about indexes for the U.S. bond market or for non-U.S. stock markets such as Tokyo or London.

Although portfolios contain many different individual stocks, investors typically ask, "What happened to the market today?" The reason for this question is that if an investor owns more than a few stocks or bonds, it is cumbersome to follow each stock or bond individually to determine the composite performance of the portfolio. Also, there is an intuitive notion that most individual stocks or bonds move with the aggregate market. Therefore, if the overall market rose, an individual's portfolio probably also increased in value. To supply investors with a composite report on market performance, some financial publications or investment firms have created and maintain stock market and bond market indexes.

Initially in this chapter we discuss several important uses of security market indexes that provide an incentive for becoming familiar with these indexes. We also consider what characteristics cause various indexes to differ and why one index might be preferable for a given task given its characteristics. Subsequently we present the most well known U.S. and global stock market indexes. Then we consider bond market indexes that are important because the bond market continues to grow in size and importance, followed by consideration of composite stock market -bond market series. We conclude this presentation with an examination of the relationship among indexes and what factors impact high or low correlations.

With this background regarding indexes we transition to consider one of the fastest growing components in investments—passive investing. We consider the specific difference between active and passive management; why passive management has experienced significant growth, how to construct a passive index portfolio and how to evaluate the performance of a passive portfolio by measuring its tracking error.

4.1 Uses of Security Market Indexes

Security market indexes have at least five significant uses. A primary application is to use the index values to compute total returns and risk measures for an aggregate market or some component of a market over a specified time period. In turn, many investors use the computed return-risk results as a *benchmark* to judge the performance of individual portfolios. A basic assumption when evaluating portfolio performance is that any investor should be able to experience a risk-adjusted rate of return comparable to the market by randomly selecting a large number of stocks or bonds from the total market; hence, a superior portfolio manager should consistently do better than the market. Therefore, *an aggregate stock or bond market index can be used as a benchmark to judge the performance of professional money managers.*

An obvious use of indexes is to create an index portfolio. As we have discussed, it is difficult for most money managers to consistently outperform specified market indexes on a risk-adjusted basis over time.[1] Therefore, an obvious alternative is to invest in a portfolio that will emulate this market portfolio. This notion led to the creation of *index funds* and *exchange-traded funds* (ETFs) that would track the performance of the specified market series (index) over time. The original index funds were common-stock funds as discussed in Malkiel (2015) and Mossavar-Rahmani (2005). The development of comprehensive, well-specified bond market indexes and the inability of most bond portfolio managers to outperform these indexes have led to similar bond index funds, as noted by Hawthorne (1986). Securities analysts, portfolio managers, and academicians use security market indexes as proxies for the aggregate stock or bond market to examine the factors that influence aggregate security price movements and to compare the risk-adjusted performance of alternative asset classes (e.g., stocks vs. bonds vs. real estate). In addition, they examine the relative performance *within* asset classes such as large-cap stocks versus small-cap stocks.

"Technicians" are also interested in an aggregate market index because they believe past price changes can be used to predict future price movements. For example, to project future stock price movements, technicians would plot and analyze price and volume changes for a stock market series like the Dow Jones Industrial Average or the S&P 500 Index.

Finally, work in portfolio and capital market theory has implied that the relevant risk for an individual risky asset is its *systematic risk*, which is the relationship between the rates of return

---

[1]Throughout this chapter and the book, we will use *indicator series* and *indexes* interchangeably, although *indicator series* is the more correct specification because it refers to a broad class of series; one popular type of series is an index, but there can be other types and many different indexes.

for a risky asset and the rates of return for a market portfolio of risky assets.[2] Therefore, an aggregate market index is used as a proxy for the market portfolio of risky assets.

4.2 DIFFERENTIATING FACTORS IN CONSTRUCTING MARKET INDEXES

Because the indexes are intended to reflect the overall movements of a group of securities, we need to consider three factors that are important when constructing an index intended to represent a total population.

4.2.1 The Sample

The first factor is the sample used to construct an index. The size, the breadth, and the source of the sample are all important.

A small percentage of the total population will provide valid indications of the behavior of the total population *if* the sample is properly selected. In some cases, because of the economics of computers, virtually all the stocks on an exchange or market are included, with a few deletions of unusual securities. Where you do not include the total population, the sample should be *representative* of the total population; otherwise, its size will be meaningless. A large biased sample is no better than a small biased sample. The sample can be generated by completely random selection or by a nonrandom selection technique designed to incorporate the important characteristics of the desired population. Finally, the *source* of the sample is important if there are any differences between segments of the population, in which case samples from each segment are required.

4.2.2 Weighting Sample Members

The second factor is the weight given to each member in the sample. Four principal weighting schemes are used for security market indexes: (1) a price-weighted index, (2) a market-value weighted index, (3) an unweighted index, or what would be described as an equal-weighted index, and (4) a fundamental weighted index based on some operating variable like sales, earnings, or return on equity. We will discuss examples for each of these.

4.2.3 Computational Procedure

The final consideration is the computational procedure used. One alternative is to take a simple arithmetic mean of the various members in the index. Another is to compute an index and have all changes, whether in price or value, reported in terms of the basic index. Finally, some prefer using a geometric mean of the components rather than an arithmetic mean.

4.3 STOCK MARKET INDEXES

As mentioned previously, we hear a lot about what happens to the Dow Jones Industrial Average (DJIA) each day. You might also hear about other stock indexes, such as the S&P 500 Index, the NASDAQ composite, or even the Nikkei Average of Japanese stocks. If you listen carefully, you will realize that these indexes experience different percentage changes

[2]This concept and its justification are discussed in Chapters 6, 7, and 11. Subsequently, in Chapter 18, we consider the difficulty of finding an index that is an appropriate proxy for the theoretical market portfolio of risky assets.

(which is the way that the changes should be reported). Reasons for some differences in performance are obvious, such as the DJIA versus the Nikkei Average, but others are not. In this section, we briefly review how the major series differ in terms of the characteristics discussed in the prior section. This will help you understand why the alternative stock indexes *should* differ.

The discussion of the indexes is organized by the weighting of the sample of stocks. We begin with the price-weighted index because some of the most popular indexes are in this category. The next group is the widely used value-weighted indexes followed by the unweighted indexes, and finally the fundamental indexes.

4.3.1 Price-Weighted Index

A **price-weighted index** is an arithmetic mean of current stock prices, which means that index movements are influenced by the differential prices of the components.

Dow Jones Industrial Average   The best-known price-weighted index is also the oldest and certainly the most popular stock market index, the Dow Jones Industrial Average (DJIA). The DJIA is a price-weighted average of 30 large, well-known industrial stocks that are generally the leaders in their industry (blue chips). The DJIA is computed by totaling the current prices of the 30 stocks and dividing the sum by a divisor that has been adjusted to take account of stock splits and other investments (mainly changes in the sample over time).[3] The divisor is adjusted so the index value will be the same before and after the split or other changes. An adjustment of the divisor is demonstrated in Exhibit 4.1. The equation for the index is:

$$\text{DJIA}_t = \sum_{i=1}^{30} \frac{P_{it}}{D_\text{adj}}$$

where:

DJIA_t = value of the DJIA on day t
P_{it} = closing price of stock i on day t
D_adj = adjusted divisor on day t

In Exhibit 4.1, we employ three stocks to demonstrate the procedure used to derive a new divisor for the DJIA when a stock splits. When stocks split, the divisor becomes smaller, as shown. The cumulative effect of splits and other changes can be derived from the changes in the divisor that was originally 30.0, but as of June 29, 2017, it was 0.14602128057775.

Exhibit 4.1 Example of Change in DJIA Divisor When a Sample Stock Splits

Stock	Before Split	After Three-for-One Split by Stock A	
	Prices	Prices	
A	30	10	
B	20	20	
C	10	10	
	60 ÷ 3 = 20	40 ÷ X = 20	X = 2 (New Divisor)

[3]A complete list of all events that have caused a change in the divisor since the DJIA went to 30 stocks on October 1, 1928, is contained in Phyllis S. Pierce, ed., *The Business One Irwin Investor's Handbook* (Burr Ridge, IL: Dow Jones Books, annual).

Exhibit 4.2 Demonstration of the Impact of Differently Priced Shares on a Price-Weighted Index

| Stock | Period *T* | PERIOD *T* + 1 | |
		Case A	Case B
A	100	110	100
B	50	50	50
C	30	30	33
Sum	180	190	183
Divisor	3	3	3
Average	60	63.3	61
Percentage change		5.5	1.7

The adjusted divisor ensures that the new value for the index is the same as it would have been without the split or other change. In this example, the presplit index value was 20. Therefore, after the split, given the new sum of prices, the divisor is adjusted downward from 3 to 2 to maintain this value of 20. The divisor is also changed when there is a change in the sample makeup of the index.

Because the index is price weighted, a high-priced stock carries more weight than a low-priced stock. As shown in Exhibit 4.2, a 10 percent change in a $100 stock ($10) will cause a larger change in the index than a 10 percent change in a $30 stock ($3). For Case A, when the $100 stock increases by 10 percent, the average rises by 5.5 percent. For Case B, when the $30 stock increases by 10 percent, the average rises by only 1.7 percent.

The DJIA has been criticized on several counts. First, the sample used for the index is limited to 30 nonrandomly selected large, mature blue-chip stocks that cannot be representative of the thousands of U.S. stocks. As a result, the DJIA has not been as volatile as other stock market indexes, and its long-run returns are not comparable to other NYSE stock indexes.

In addition, because the DJIA is price weighted, when companies have a stock split, their prices decline and, therefore, the weight of the stock in the DJIA is reduced—even though the firm may be large and growing. Therefore, the weighting scheme causes a downward bias in the DJIA because high-growth stocks will have higher prices and because such stocks tend to split, these stocks of growing companies will consistently lose weight within the index. For a discussion of specific differences between indexes, see Ip (1998). Detailed reports of the Dow Jones averages are contained daily in *The Wall Street Journal* and weekly in *Barron's*.

Nikkei-Dow Jones Average Generally referred to as the Nikkei Stock Average Index, this is an arithmetic mean of prices for 225 stocks on the First Section of the Tokyo Stock Exchange (TSE) and shows stock price trends since the reopening of the TSE following World War II. Similar to the DJIA, it is a price-weighted index and is likewise criticized because the 225 stocks only comprise about 15 percent of all stocks on the First Section. It is reported daily in *The Wall Street Journal* and the *Financial Times* and weekly in *Barron's*.

4.3.2 Value-Weighted Index

A **value-weighted index** is generated by deriving the initial total market value of all stocks used in the index (Market Value = Number of Shares Outstanding (or freely floating shares) × Current Market Price). Prior to 2004, the tradition was to consider all outstanding shares. In mid-2004, Standard & Poor's began only considering "freely floating shares" that exclude shares held by insiders. This initial market value figure is established as the base and assigned an index value (typically the beginning index value is 100, but it can be set at 10 or 50). Subsequently, a new market value is computed for all securities in the index, and the current market value is compared to the initial "base" market value to determine the percentage change, which in turn is applied to the beginning index value:

$$\text{Index}_t = \frac{\sum P_t Q_t}{\sum P_b Q_b} \times \text{Beginning Index Value}$$

where:

Index_t = index value on day t
P_t = ending prices for stocks on day t
Q_t = number of outstanding or freely floating shares on day t
P_b = ending price for stocks on base day
Q_b = number of outstanding or freely floating shares on base day

The example for a three-stock index in Exhibit 4.3 indicates that there is an *automatic adjustment* for stock splits and other capital changes with a value-weighted index because the decrease in the stock price is offset by an increase in the number of shares outstanding. In a value-weighted index, the importance of individual stocks in the sample depends on the market value of the stocks. Therefore, a specified percentage change in the value of a large company has a greater impact than a comparable percentage change for a small company. As shown in Exhibit 4.4, if we assume that the only change is a 20 percent increase in the value of stock A, which has a beginning value of $10 million, the total ending index value would be $202 million, or an index value of 101. In contrast, if only stock C increases by 20 percent from $100 million, the ending total value will be $220 million or an index value of 110. The point is, price changes for large market value stocks in a value-weighted index will dominate changes in the index value over time. Therefore, it is important to be aware of the large-value stocks in the index.

Exhibit 4.3 Example of a Computation of a Value-Weighted Index

Stock	Share Price	Number of Shares	Market Value
December 31, 2018			
A	$10.00	1,000,000	$ 10,000,000
B	15.00	6,000,000	90,000,000
C	20.00	5,000,000	100,000,000
Total			$200,000,000
		Base Value Equal to an Index of 100	
December 31, 2019			
A	$12.00	1,000,000	$ 12,000,000
B	10.00	12,000,000[a]	120,000,000
C	20.00	5,500,000[b]	110,000,000
Total			$242,000,000

$$\text{New Index Value} = \frac{\text{Current Market Value}}{\text{Base Value}} \times \text{Beginning Index Value}$$

$$= \frac{\$242,000,000}{\$200,000,000} \times 100$$

$$= 1.21 \times 100$$

$$= 121$$

[a]Stock split two-for-one during the year.
[b]Company paid a 10 percent stock dividend during the year.

Exhibit 4.4 Demonstration of the Impact of Different Market Values on a Market-Value-Weighted Stock Index

| | DECEMBER 31, 2017 | | | DECEMBER 31, 2018 | | | |
| | | | | Case A | | Case B | |
Stock	Number of Shares	Price	Value	Price	Value	Price	Value
A	1,000,000	$10.00	$ 10,000,000	$12.00	$ 12,000,000	$10.00	$ 10,000,000
B	6,000,000	15.00	90,000,000	15.00	90,000,000	15.00	90,000,000
C	5,000,000	20.00	100,000,000	20.00	100,000,000	24.00	120,000,000
			$200,000,000		$202,000,000		$220,000,000
Index Value			100.00		101.00		110.00

4.3.3 Unweighted Index

In an **unweighted index**, all stocks carry equal weight regardless of their price or market value. A $20 stock is as important as a $40 stock, and the total market value of the company is unimportant. Such an index can be used by individuals who randomly select stock for their portfolio or invest the same dollar amount in each stock. One way to visualize an unweighted index is to assume that equal dollar amounts are invested in each stock in the portfolio (e.g., an equal $1,000 investment in each stock would work out to 50 shares of a $20 stock, 100 shares of a $10 stock, and 10 shares of a $100 stock). In fact, the actual movements in the index are typically based on *the arithmetic mean of the percent changes in price or value for the stocks in the index.* The use of percentage price changes means that the price level or the market value of the stock does not make a difference—each percentage change has equal weight.

Exhibit 4.5 demonstrates the computation of an equal weighted index using the average of the percent changes for each of the three stocks. There is also a comparison to the index value if market value weights are used. As shown, the equal weighting result gives a higher index value because of the large percent increase in value for the stock with the smallest market value (the small-cap stock). In contrast, the market value weighted index did not do as well because the large-cap stock (that has a large weight) experienced the poorest performance.

In contrast to computing an arithmetic mean of percentage changes, both *Value Line* and the *Financial Times* Ordinary Share Index compute a *geometric* mean of the holding period returns and derive the holding period yield from this calculation. Exhibit 4.6, which contains an example of an arithmetic and a geometric mean, demonstrates the downward bias of the geometric calculation. Specifically, the geometric mean of holding period yields (HPY) shows an average change of only 5.3 percent versus the actual change in wealth of 6 percent.

Exhibit 4.5 Computation of Index Value Assuming Equal Weights for Sample Stocks

| | DECEMBER 31, 2017 | | | DECEMBER 31, 2018 | | |
Stock	Number of Shares	Price	Value	Price	Value	Percent Change
X	2,000,000	$20	$ 40,000,000	$30	$ 60,000,000	50.0
Y	8,000,000	15	120,000,000	20	160,000,000	33.3
Z	10,000,000	30	300,000,000	33	330,000,000	10.0
			$460,000,000		$550,000,000	93.3/3 = 31.1

Equal Wtd. Index: $100 \times 1.311 = 131.100$

Market Value Wtd Index: $100 \times \dfrac{550,000,000}{460,000,000} = 119.565$

Exhibit 4.6 Example of an Arithmetic and Geometric Mean of Percentage Changes

	SHARE PRICE			
Stock	T	$T + 1$	HPR	HPY
X	10	12	1.20	0.20
Y	22	20	0.91	−0.09
Z	44	47	1.07	0.07

$$\Pi = 1.20 \times 0.91 \times 1.07 \qquad \sum(0.20) + (-0.09) + (0.07) = 0.18$$

$$= 1.168 \qquad\qquad\qquad 0.18/3 = 0.06$$

$$1.168^{1/3} = 1.0531 \qquad\qquad\qquad = 6\%$$

$$\text{Index Value } (T) \times 1.0531 = \text{Index Value } (T + 1)$$
$$\text{Index Value } (T) \times 1.06 = \text{Index Value } (T + 1)$$

4.3.4 Fundamental Weighted Index

As noted, one of the rationales for using market-value weighting is that the market value of a firm is an obvious measure of its economic importance. In contrast, some observers contend that this weighting scheme results in overweighting overvalued stocks over time and underweighting undervalued stocks. A prime example is what transpired during the technology boom in the 1998–2000 period when technology stocks exploded in price and, in retrospect, were clearly overvalued—selling for 60–70–100 times earnings. As a result, the high valuations caused the weight of the technology sector in the indexes to almost double, the result was an overweight in overvalued stocks. You can envision an opposite example for undervalued stocks.

In response to this implicit problem with market-value weighting, some observers have suggested other measures of a *company's economic footprint*. The leading advocates of an approach that weights firms based on company fundamentals are individuals involved with Research Affiliates, Inc. (Arnott, Hsu, and West, 2008). Their approach to creating a Fundamental Index is an example of employing some widely used fundamental factors.[4] Specifically, they proposed four broad fundamental measures of size: (1) sales, (2) profits (cash flow), (3) net assets (book value), and (4) distributions to shareholders (dividends). Given these variables for a large sample of firms, they created an index of 1,000 of the largest firms and computed the percent of each firm's sales, cash flow, book value, and dividends to the total for the sample and determined a company's relative size (weight) by averaging the weights of the four size metrics across the trailing five years (to avoid the impact of cyclicality). The authors contend that this index (entitled Research Associates Fundamental Index [RAFI]) is representative, but also ensures high liquidity, high quality, and low turnover.

As noted earlier, this is an example of such an index—other firms and authors can and have created indexes with single variables or a different set of fundamental variables to determine the weights.

4.3.5 Style Indexes

Financial service firms such as Dow Jones, Moody's, Standard & Poor's, and Russell are generally very fast in responding to changes in investment practices. One example is the growth in popularity of small-cap stocks following academic research in the 1980s that suggested that

---

[4]For further discussion of the justification and details on the variables and construction, see Arnott, Hsu, and West (2008).

over long-term periods, small-cap stocks outperformed large-cap stocks on a risk-adjusted basis. In response to this, Ibbotson Associates created the first small-cap stock index, and this was followed by small-cap indexes by Frank Russell Associates (the Russell 2000 Index), the Standard & Poor's 600, the Wilshire 1750, and the Dow Jones Small-Cap Index. For a comparative analysis of these indexes, see Reilly and Wright (2002). This led to sets of size indexes, including large-cap, mid-cap, small-cap, and micro-cap. These new size indexes can be used to evaluate the performance of money managers who concentrated in those size sectors.

The next innovation was for money managers to concentrate in *types* of stocks—that is, *growth* stocks or *value* stocks. As this money management innovation evolved, the financial services firms again responded by creating indexes of growth stocks and value stocks based on relative P/E, price–book value, price–cash flow ratios, and other metrics, such as return on equity (ROE) and revenue growth rates.

Eventually, these two factors (size and type) were combined into six major *style* categories:

Small-cap growth	Small-cap value
Mid-cap growth	Mid-cap value
Large-cap growth	Large-cap value

Currently, most money managers identify their investment style as one of these, and in turn consultants use these style categories to identify money managers.

The most recent style indexes are those created to track ethical funds referred to as *socially responsible investment* (*SRI*) funds. These SRI indexes are further broken down by country and include a global ethical stock index.

The best source for style stock indexes (both size and type of stock) is *Barron's*.

Exhibit 4.7 shows the stock market indexes from *The Wall Street Journal*, which contains values for many of the U.S. stock indexes we have discussed. Exhibit 4.8 shows a table for numerous international stock indexes contained in *The Wall Street Journal*.

4.3.6 Global Equity Indexes

As shown in Exhibits 4.8 and 4A.2 (the latter is in this chapter's appendix), there are stock market indexes available for most individual foreign markets. While these local indexes are closely followed within each country, a problem arises in comparing the results implied by these indexes for different countries because of a lack of consistency among them in terms of sample selection, weighting, or computational procedure. To solve these comparability problems, several investment data firms have computed a set of consistent country stock indexes. As a result, these indexes can be directly compared and combined to create various regional indexes (e.g., Pacific Basin). In the following sections, we describe the three major sets of global equity indexes.

FT/S&P-Actuaries World Indexes The FT/S&P-Actuaries World Indexes are jointly compiled by the Financial Times Limited, Goldman Sachs & Company, and Standard & Poor's (the "compilers") in conjunction with the Institute of Actuaries and the Faculty of Actuaries. Approximately 2,500 equity securities in 30 countries are included, covering at least 70 percent of the total value of all listed companies in each country. All securities included must allow direct holdings of shares by foreign nationals.

The indexes are market value weighted and have a base date of December 31, 1986 = 100. The index results are typically reported in U.S. dollars, but, on occasion, have been reported in U.K. pound sterling, Japanese yen, euros, and the local currency of the country. In addition to the individual countries and the world index, there are several geographic subgroups, subgroups by market value, and by industry sectors. These indexes are available daily in the *Financial Times*.

Exhibit 4.7 U.S. Major Stock Market Indexes

| | Latest Week | | | | | 52 Week | | | | %chg | |
	High	Low	Close	Net chg	% chg	Low	Close(●)	High	% chg	YFD	3-yr.ann.
Dow Jones											
Industrial Average	21506.21	21197.08	**21349.63**	−45.13	**−0.21**	17888.28		21528.99	**18.9**	8.0	**8.3**
Transportation Avg	9606 16	9383.67	**9563.73**	175.06	**1.86**	7557.62		9593.95	**26.5**	5.7	**5.3**
Utility Average	734.65	704.53	**706.91**	−18.36	**−2.53**	625.44		737.51	**−1.3**	7.2	**7.1**
Total Stock Market	25383.83	24931.22	**25124.96**	−132.15	**−0.52**	21498.96		25399.65	**15.9**	7.9	**6.9**
Barron's 400	651.38	639.61	**646.24**	0.77	**0.12**	514.60		650.48	**23.8**	7.4	**6.3**
Nasdaq Stock Market											
Nasdaq Composite	6303.45	6087.81	**6140.42**	−124.83	**−1.99**	4822.90		6321.76	**26.3**	14.1	**11.7**
Nasdaq 100	5845.15	5599.44	**5646.92**	−156.19	**−2.69**	4410.75		5885.3	**27.3**	16.1	**13.6**
Standard & Poor's											
500 Index	2450.42	2405.70	**2423.41**	−14.89	**−0.61**	2085.18		2453.46	**15.2**	8.2	**7.3**
MidCap 400	1760.30	1730.56	**1746.65**	2.70	**0.15**	1476.68		1769.34	**16.4**	5.2	**6.8**
SmallCap 600	862.34	846.92	**855.85**	2.68	**0.31**	700.06		866.07	**20.5**	2.1	**7.8**
Other Indexes											
Russell 2000	1428.03	1403.02	**1415.36**	0.58	**0.04**	1139.45		1425.98	**22.4**	4.3	**5.9**
NYSE Composite	11837.60	11683.31	**11761.70**	28.50	**0.24**	10289.35		11833.34	**11.8**	6.4	**2.3**
Value Line	525.84	517.70	**522.71**	1.94	**0.37**	453.96		529.13	**13.3**	3.3	**1.2**
NYSE Arca Biotech	4017.65	3842.77	**3859.60**	−157.26	**−3.91**	2834.14		4016.86	**24.5**	25.5	**11.6**
NYSE Arca Pharma	550.67	534.89	**536.30**	−12.62	**−2.30**	463.78		554.66	**0.9**	11.4	**0.8**
KBW Bank	97.09	91.46	**95.60**	4.06	**4.44**	62.34		99.33	**48.9**	4.1	**10.3**
PHLX§ Gold/Silver	83.80	79.96	**80.78**	−2.65	**−3.17**	73.03		112.86	**−21.2**	2.4	**−7.1**
PHLX§ Oil Service	132.65	127.39	**130.80**	−2.87	**2.24**	127.17		192.66	**−24.0**	−28.8	**−25.1**
PHLX§ Semiconductor	1099.41	1026.05	**1034.91**	−53.58	**−4.92**	672.51		1138.25	**−51.1**	14.2	**−17.6**
CBOE Volatility	15.16	9.68	**11.18**	1.16	**11.58**	9.75		22.51	**−24.3**	−20.4	**−1.1**

§Philadelphla Stock Exchange

Morgan Stanley Capital International (MSCI) Indexes The Morgan Stanley Capital International Indexes consist of three international, 22 national, and 38 international industry indexes. The indexes consider some 1,673 companies listed on stock exchanges in 22 countries, with a combined market capitalization that represents approximately 60 percent of the aggregate market value of the stock exchanges of these countries. All the indexes are market value weighted.

The following relative valuation information is available: (1) price-to-book value (*P/BV*) ratio, (2) price-to-cash earnings (earnings plus depreciation) (*P/CE*) ratio, (3) price-to-earnings (*P/E*) ratio, and (4) dividend yield (*YLD*). These ratios help in analyzing different valuation levels among countries and over time for specific countries.

Notably, the Morgan Stanley group index for Europe, Australia, and the Far East (EAFE) is the basis for futures and options contracts on the Chicago Mercantile Exchange and the Chicago Board Options Exchange.

Dow Jones Global Stock Market Indexes The Dow Jones Global Indexes is composed of more than 2,200 companies worldwide and organized into 120 industry groups. The index includes 35 countries representing more than 80 percent of the combined capitalization of these countries. In addition to the 35 individual countries shown in Exhibit 4.9, the countries

Exhibit 4.8 International Stock Market Indexes

Region/Country Index		Latest Week Close	% chg	52-Week Range Low	Close	High	YTD % chg
World	**The Global Dow**	2769.39	0.00	2284.45		2790.26	9.4
	DJ Global Index	359.68	−0.37	305.56		362.91	10.3
	DJ Global ex U.S.	240.94	−0.16	201.47		243.70	12.6
	Global Dow Euro	2286.32	−1.80	1942.86		2398.98	1.2
DJTSM	**Global**	3704.12	−0.34	3142.64		3735.77	10.2
	Global ex U.S.	2434.91	−0.16	2035.51		2462.44	12.7
	Developed ex U.S.	2367.72	−0.19	1986.18		2398.94	12.0
	Global Small-Cap	5055.79	0.02	4234.42		5086.94	9.4
	Global Large-Cap	3512.27	−0.40	2986.56		3545.24	10.4
Americas	**DJ Americas**	582.63	−0.40	502.62		588.47	7.8
Brazil	**Sao Paulo Bovespa**	62899.97	2.97	51842.27		69052.03	4.4
Canada	**S&P/TSX Comp**	15182.19	−0.90	14064.54		15922.37	−0.7
Mexico	**IPC All-Share**	49857.49	1.79	44364.17		49939.47	9.2
Chile	**Santlago IPSA**	3606.79	−0.40	3113.51		3782.66	11.9
Europe	**Stoxx Europe 600**	379.37	−2.13	318.76		396.45	5.0
	Stoxx Europe 50	3122.17	−2.18	2730.05		3276.11	3.7
Eurozone	**Euro Stoxx**	372.86	−2.61	295.77		392.06	6.5
	Euro Stoxx 50	3441.88	−2.87	2761.37		3658.79	4.6
Belgium	**Bel-20**	3793.62	−1.30	3236.01		4041.03	5.2
France	**CAC 40**	5120.68	−2.76	4085.30		5432.40	5.3
Germany	**DAX**	12325.12	−3.21	9373.26		12888.95	7.4
Israel	**Tel Avlv**	1433.63	−0.32	1378.66		1478.96	−2.5
Italy	**FTSE MIB**	20584.23	−1.20	15424		21788	7.0
Netherlands	**AEX**	507.15	−2.38	422.18		536.26	5.0
Spain	**IBEX 35**	10444.50	−1.75	7926.2		11135.4	11.7
Sweden	**SX All Share**	576.91	−2.92	459.48		596.72	7.9
Switzerland	**Swiss Market**	8906.89	−1.39	7593.20		9127.61	8.4
U.K.	**FTSE 100**	7312.72	−1.50	6463.59		7547.63	2.4
Asia-Pacific	**DJ Asia-Pacific TSM**	1624.81	−0.35	1359.38		1640.63	14.2
Australia	**S&P/ASX 200**	5721.50	0.10	5156.6		5956.5	1.0
China	**Shanghai Composite**	3192.43	1.09	2932.48		3288.97	2.9
Hong kong	**Hang Seng**	25764.58	0.37	20495.29		26063.06	17.1
India	**S&P BSE Sensex**	30921.61	−0.70	25765.14		31311.57	16.1
Japan	**Nikkel Stock Avg**	20033.43	−0.49	15106.98		20230.41	4.8
Singapore	**Straits Times**	3226.48	0.53	2787.27		3271.11	12.0
South Korea	**Kospi**	2391.79	0.55	1953.12		2395.66	18.0
Taiwan	**Weighted**	10395.07	0.17	8575.75		10513.96	12.3

Source: SIX Financial Information WSJ Market Data Group

Exhibit 4.9 Dow Jones Global Stock Market Indexes

Region/Country	DJ Global Indexes, Local Curr. 04/23/17	Wkly % Chg.	DJ Global Indexes, U.S.$ 04/23/17	Wkly % Chg.	DJ Global Indexes, U.S.$ on 12/31/16	Point Chg. From 12/31/16	% Chg. From 12/31/16
Americas			5866.04	0.24	5427.02	438.04	5.97
Brazil	91591225.27	— 0.98	10844.87	— 2.35	11028.00	— 183.13	— 1.66
Canada	5015.08	0.90	4370.02	0.77	4317.31	52.70	1.22
Chile	7843.25	— 1.39	4440.58	— 1.24	3918.60	521.99	13.32
Mexico	31335.08	— 0.37	5349.35	— 0.50	4352.19	997.16	22.91
U.S.	25257.11	0.26	25257.11	0.26	23276.73	1980.38	8.51
Latin America			5672.49	— 1.50	5820.64	452.85	8.29
Europe			1240.02	— 0.22	2349.82	390.19	13.69
Austria	3408.18	— 0.72	2973.20	— 1.71	2326.67	646.53	27.79
Belgium	6094.87	— 1.51	5319.72	— 1.50	4844.11	475.62	9.82
Denmark	10647.89	0.98	9488.39	0.98	7756.84	1731.55	22.32
Finland	14551.48	— 0.26	11353.42	— 0.25	9549.40	1604.03	18.69
France	3886.74	0.10	3438.68	0.11	2938.75	497.93	16.94
Germany	4035.97	— 0.23	3509.80	— 0.22	3034.14	475.65	15.68
Greece	439.04	1.54	253.22	1.56	198.77	54.45	27.39
Ireland	5401.39	— 0.51	5357.33	— 0.50	4668.61	688.72	14.75
Italy	2084.11	— 0.49	1493.75	— 0.47	1293.97	199.78	15.44
Netherlands	4925.83	0.27	4285.94	0.28	3586.49	699.45	19.50
Norway	4418.22	— 0.78	3130.18	— 0.54	3142.76	— 12.58	— 0.40
Portugal	1384.06	— 1.99	1033.11	— 1.97	911.62	121.49	13.33
Russia	1533.48	2.60	740.33	— 0.46	840.07	— 99.74	— 11.87
Spain	4303.54	— 1.10	2821.92	— 1.09	2335.44	488.48	20.83
Sweden	10795.45	0.40	6875.40	0.25	5931.68	943.72	15.91
Switzerland	6213.31	0.64	8623.33	1.08	7395.62	1227.52	16.60
United Kingdom	3297.95	— 0.53	2247.09	— 1.03	2085.69	161.19	7.73
South Africa	16922.06	1.81	3584.10	1.03	3308.21	275.89	8.34
Pacific Region			1630.44	0.42	1422.73	287.71	14.60
Australia	3529.73	— 1.07	3516.03	— 1.74	3339.07	176.96	5.30
China	2870.64	2.01	2853.64	2.02	2331.94	521.70	22.37
Hong Kong	5252.22	0.43	5237.08	0.44	4514.05	723.02	16.02
India	3445.20	— 0.61	2403.79	— 0.74	1926.97	476.62	24.74
Japan	999.92	0.96	1121.38	0.42	1013.18	108.21	10.68
Malaysia	3470.36	— 0.65	2201.49	— 0.95	1909.58	291.90	15.29
New Zealand	2337.36	0.10	3149.47	0.51	2791.92	357.55	12.61
Philippines	7727.40	— 0.59	3995.85	— 1.26	3557.60	438.25	12.32
Singapore	2185.56	— 0.10	2554.48	— 0.37	2200.00	354.48	16.11
South Korea	4643.22	0.91	3091.06	0.49	2461.43	629.64	25.58
Taiwan	2495.40	2.31	2115.74	2.14	1764.41	351.34	19.91
Thailand	2943.32	0.30	2045.14	0.35	1895.74	149.40	7.68
Euro Zone			2231.71	— 0.25	2766.10	485.81	16.83
Europe Developed (ex. U.K.).			2967.03	0.06	3402.82	584.27	16.58
Europe (Nordic)			6302.56	0.24	5437.03	685.52	15.92
Pacific (ex. Japan)			2837.68	0.42	2257.30	589.77	17.44
World (ex. US)			2438.71	0.10	2160.43	278.22	12.53
DOW JONES GLOBAL, TOTAL STOCK MARKET INDEX			2718.57	0.18	2280.23	258.47	10.61
GLOBAL DOW			2789.26	0.14	2531.51	237.75	9.39

Indexes based on 12/31/91 = 1000.   ©2017 Dow Jones & Co. Inc. All Rights Reserved.

Source: Data from *Barron's*, June 26, 2017, Page M 27. Copyright 2017, Dow Jones & Co. Inc. All rights reserved worldwide.

Exhibit 4.10 Correlations of Percentage Price Changes of Alternative World Stock Indexes, 12/31/91–12/31/16	
	U.S. Dollars
Financial Times/S&P–MSCI	.996
Financial Times/S&P–Dow Jones Global	.995
MSCI-Dow Jones Global	.993

are grouped into three major regions: Americas, Europe, and Pacific Region and some subregions. Finally, each country's index is calculated in its own currency as well as in U.S. dollars. The index for the individual countries is reported daily in *The Wall Street Journal* and the full presentations as shown in Exhibit 4.9 is published weekly in *Barron's*.

Comparison of World Stock Indexes As shown in Exhibit 4.10, the correlations between the three global stock series since December 31, 1991, when the DJ series became available, indicate that the results with the various world stock indexes are quite comparable.

A summary of the characteristics of the major price-weighted, market-value-weighted, and equal-weighted stock price indexes for the United States and major foreign countries is contained in Exhibit 4A.1 in the chapter appendix. As shown, the major differences are the number of stocks in alternative indexes, but more important is the *source* of the sample (e.g., stocks from the NYSE, NASDAQ, all U.S. stocks, or stocks from a foreign country such as the United Kingdom or Japan).

4.4 BOND MARKET INDEXES[5]

Investors know little about the growing number of bond market indexes currently available because these indexes are relatively new and not widely published. Still, knowledge regarding these indexes are important because of the growth of fixed-income money managers and mutual funds and the consequent need to have a reliable set of benchmarks to use in evaluating their performance. Also, because the performance of many fixed-income money managers has been unable to match that of the aggregate bond market, interest has been growing in bond index funds, which requires appropriate indexes to emulate.

Notably, it is more difficult to create and compute a bond market index than a stock market index for several reasons. First, the universe of bonds is much broader than that of stocks, ranging from U.S. Treasury securities to bonds in default. Second, the universe of bonds is changing constantly because of new issues, bond maturities, calls, and bond sinking funds. Third, the volatility of prices for individual bonds and bond portfolios changes because bond price volatility is affected by duration, which is likewise changing constantly because of changes in maturity, coupon, and market yield.[6] Finally, significant problems can arise in correctly pricing the individual bond issues in an index (especially corporate and mortgage bonds) compared to the current and continuous transactions prices available for most stocks used in stock indexes.

Our subsequent discussion contains the following three subsections: (1) U.S. investment-grade bond indexes, including Treasuries; (2) U.S. high-yield bond indexes; and (3) global government bond indexes. All of these indexes indicate total rates of return for the portfolio of bonds and are market value weighted. Exhibit 4.11 contains a summary of the characteristics for the indexes available for these three segments of the bond market.

---

[5]The discussion in this section draws heavily from Reilly and Wright (2012).

[6]This concept of duration is discussed in detail in Chapter 13.

Exhibit 4.11 Summary of Bond Market Indexes

Name of Index	Number of Issues	Maturity	Size of Issues	Weighting	Pricing	Reinvestment Assumption	Subindexes Available
Bloomberg Barclays	8,000	Over 1 Year	Over $250 million	Market value	Trader priced and model priced	No	Government, gov./corp., corporate mortgage-backed, asset-backed
Merrill Lynch	6,000	Over 1 Year	Over $50 million	Market value	Trader priced and model priced	In specific bonds	Government, gov./corp., corporate, mortgage
Ryan Treasury	300+	Over 1 Year	All Treasury	Market value and equal	Trader priced	In specific bonds	Treasury
U.S. High-Yield Bond Indexes							
C. S. First Boston	500+	All Maturities	Over $75 million	Market value	Trader Priced	Yes	Composite and by rating
Bloomberg Barclays	1,800	Over 1 Year	Over $100 million	Market value	Trader priced	No	Composite and by rating
Merrill Lynch	2,000	Over 1 Year	Over $25 million	Market value	Trader priced	Yes	Composite and by rating
Global Government Bond Indexes							
Bloomberg Barclays	1,200	Over 1 Year	Over $200 million	Market value	Trader Priced	Yes	Composite and 13 countries, local and U.S. dollars
Merrill Lynch	800	Over 1 Year	Over $50 million	Market value	Trader Priced	Yes	Composite and 9 countries, local and U.S. dollars
J. P. Morgan	700	Over 1 Year	Over $100 million	Market value	Trader priced	Yes in Index	Composite and 11 countries, local and U.S. dollars

Source: Created by the authors.

4.4.1 U.S. Investment-Grade Bond Indexes

As shown in Exhibit 4.11, three investment firms have created and maintain indexes for Treasury bonds and other bonds considered investment grade, that is, the bonds are rated BBB (or Baa) or higher. As demonstrated in a subsequent section, the relationship among the returns for these investment-grade bonds is strong (that is, correlations average about 0.95), regardless of the segment of the market.

4.4.2 High-Yield Bond Indexes

One of the fastest-growing segments of the U.S. bond market during the past 30 years has been the high-yield bond market, which includes bonds that are not investment grade—that is, they are rated Ba, B, Caa, Ca, and C. Because of this growth, three investment firms created indexes related to this market. A summary of the characteristics for these indexes is included in Exhibit 4.11. For an analysis of the alternative high-yield bond benchmarks, see Reilly and Wright (1994); for an overall analysis of this market, see Reilly, Wright, and Gentry (2009).

4.4.3 Global Government Bond Indexes

The global bond market has likewise experienced significant growth in size and importance during the past 15 years. Notably, this global bond segment is dominated by government (sovereign) bonds because most non-U.S. countries do not have a viable corporate bond market. Once again, three major investment firms have created indexes that reflect the performance for the global bond market. As shown in Exhibit 4.11, although the various indexes have similar computational characteristics, the total sample sizes and the number of countries included differ. Exhibit 4.12 is a table available daily in *The Wall Street Journal* that contains current results for a variety of domestic and global bond indexes.

4.5 COMPOSITE STOCK–BOND INDEXES

Beyond separate stock indexes and bond indexes for individual countries, a natural step is the development of a composite index that measures the performance of all securities in a given country. With a composite index investors can examine the benefits of diversifying with a combination of asset classes such as stocks and bonds in addition to diversifying within the asset classes of stocks or bonds. There are two such indexes available.

First, a market-value-weighted index called Merrill Lynch-Wilshire Capital Markets Index (ML-WCMI) measures the total return performance of the combined U.S. taxable fixed income and equity markets. It is basically a combination of the Merrill Lynch fixed-income indexes and the Dow Jones Total Stock Market common-stock index. As such, it tracks more than 10,000 U.S. stocks and bonds. As of late 2017, the relative weights are about 40 percent bonds and 60 percent stocks.

The second composite index is the Brinson Partner Global Security Market Index (GSMI), which contains U.S. stocks and bonds as well as non-U.S. equities and nondollar bonds. The specific breakdown as of July 2017 was:

	Percent (%)
J.P. Morgan Emerging Market Bond Index Global	2.0
Merrill Lynch U.S. High Yield Cash Pay Constrained	3.0
MSCI All Country World Stock Index (Not LU) (in USD)	65.0
Citigroup World Global Bond Index Non-U.S. (in USD)	15.0
Citigroup World Global Bond Index U.S. only (in USD)	15.0
Total	100.00

Exhibit 4.12 Listing of Bond Yields and Returns for Domestic and Global Indexes

Return on investment and spreads over Treasurys and/or yields paid to investors compared with 52-week highs and lows for different types of bonds

Total return close	YTD total return (%)	Index	Yield (%) Latest Low High	Total return close	YTD total return (%)	Index	Yield (%) Latest Low High
Broad Market Bloomberg Barclays				**Mortgage-Backed** Bloomberg Barclays			
1946.20	3.5	U.S. Aggregate	2.580 2.160 2.790	1991.29	2.5	Mortgage-Backed	2.820 2.330 3.120
U.S. Corporate Indexes Bloomberg Barclays				1957.25	2.0	Ginnie Mae (GNMA)	2.770 2.240 3.090
2786.99	5.9	U.S. Corporate	3.160 3.000 3.520	1168.21	2.7	Fannie Mae (FNMA)	2.830 2.360 3.120
2624.09	4.0	Intermediate	2.720 2.420 3.010	1798.88	2.8	Freddie Mac (FHLMC)	2.840 2.370 3.130
3871.22	10.1	Long term	4.100 4.100 4.170	523.70	5.0	Muni Master	1.935 1.689 2.516
568.62	4.4	Double-A-rated	2.650 2.350 2.870	366.51	5.5	7-12 year	1.937 1.688 2.618
719.83	6.5	Triple-B-rated	3.440 3.340 3.870	411.86	6.8	12-22 year	2.352 2.137 3.047
High Yield Bonds Merrill Lynch				398.09	7.3	22-plus year	2.787 2.609 3.622
417.16	7.4	High Yield Constrained	5.567 5.373 6.858	**Global Government** J.P. Morgan[†]			
418.34	8.8	Triple-C-rated	10.505 9.584 13.189	545.88	1.7	Global Government	1.380 1.110 1.560
2861.82	6.6	High Yield 100	5.251 4.948 6.448	759.18	0.8	Canada	1.960 1.470 2.190
378.90	7.6	Global High Yield Constrained	5.054 4.934 6.450	n.a	n.a	EMU§	n.a n.a. n.a
308.77	7.6	Europe High Yield Constrained	1.897 1.897 3.814	715.65	1.3	France	0.760 0.570 1.210
U.S. Agency Bloomberg Barclays				511.02	−0.7	Germany	0.410 0.210 0.620
1642.07	2.3	U.S. Agency	1.980 1.390 2.010	288.56	0.1	Japan	0.390 0.170 0.460
1467.08	1.4	10-20 years	1.830 1.210 1.840	564.08	−0.4	Netherlands	0.530 0.340 0.760
3382.19	8.2	20-plus years	2.880 2.730 3.460	922.61	1.0	U.K.	1.570 1.340 1.790
2463.06	5.0	Yankee	2.810 2.510 3.090	797.00	7.8	Emerging Markets**	5.618 5.279 6.290

*Constrained indexes limit individual issuer concentrations to 2% the High Yield 100 are the 100 largest bonds   [†]In local currency § Euro-zone bonds
**EMBI Global Index

Sources: Merrill Lynch: Bloomberg Barclays: J.P. Morgan

Source: Reprinted with permission of *The Wall Street Journal*, November 8, 2017, p. B11. Copyright 2017 by Dow Jones & Co. Inc. All Rights Reserved.

The index is balanced to the policy weights monthly.

Because the GSMI contains both U.S. and international stocks and bonds, it is clearly the most diversified benchmark available with a weighting scheme that approaches market values. As such, it is closest to the theoretically specified "market portfolio of risky assets" referred to in the CAPM literature. This index was used in Reilly and Akhtar (1995) to demonstrate the impact of alternative benchmarks when evaluating global portfolio performance and when calculating systematic risk (beta) measures.

4.6 COMPARISON OF INDEXES OVER TIME

We now look at price movements in the different indexes for monthly intervals.

4.6.1 Correlations between Monthly Equity Price Changes

Exhibit 4.13 contains a listing of the correlation coefficients of the monthly percentage of price changes for a set of U.S. and non-U.S. equity-market indexes with the Dow Jones Total Stock Market Index during the 36-year period from 1980 to 2016. The correlation differences are mainly attributable to the different sample of firms listed on the various stock exchanges. All of the indexes are market-value-weighted and include a large number of stocks. Therefore, the computational procedure is generally similar and the sample sizes are large or all-encompassing. Thus, the major difference between the indexes is the samples of stocks that are from different segments of the U.S. stock market or from different countries.

There is a high positive correlation (0.99) between the Dow Jones Total Stock Market Index and the several comprehensive U.S. equity indexes: the S&P 500, the Russell 3000 and Russell 1000 large cap index. In contrast, there are lower correlations with various style indexes such as the Russell 2000 Small-Cap index (0.850).

The correlations between the Dow Jones Total Stock Market Index and the several non-U.S. indexes are clearly lower ranging from 0.460 (Pacific Basin) to 0.740 (Europe). All of these results support the case for global investing. These diversification results were confirmed with the composite international series—with the MSCI EAFE (0.640) and the IFC Emerging Market (0.565) respectively. These results confirm the benefits of global diversification because, as will be discussed in Chapter 7, such low correlations would definitely reduce the variance of a pure U.S. stock portfolio.

4.6.2 Correlations between Monthly Bond Index Returns

The correlations with the monthly Bloomberg Barclays U.S. Aggregate bond return index in Exhibit 4.13 consider a variety of bond indexes. The correlations with the U.S. investment-grade bond indexes is about 0.93 confirming that although the *level* of interest rates differ due to the risk premium, the overriding determinate of rates of return for investment-grade bonds over time are Treasury interest rates.

In contrast, the correlations with high-yield bonds indicate a significantly weaker relationship (correlations about 0.51) caused by the strong equity characteristics of high-yield bonds as shown in Reilly, Wright, and Gentry (2009). Finally, the low and diverse relationships among U.S. investment-grade bonds and all world government bonds (0.58) and world government bonds without the United States (about 0.36) reflect different interest rate movements and exchange rate effects (these non-U.S. government results are presented in U.S. dollar terms). Again, these results support the benefits of global diversification of bond portfolios or stock portfolios.

Exhibit 4.13 Correlation Coefficients between Monthly Percentage Price Changes in Various Stock and Bond Indexes: 1980–2016

Stock Indexes	Dow Jones Total Stock Market	Bond Indexes	Bloomberg Barclays U.S. Aggregate Bond
S&P 500	0.990		
Russell 3000	0.993	BB Corporate Bds	0.931
Russell 1000	0.995	BB High Yield Bds	0.506
Russell 2000	0.850	ML World Govt Bds	0.580
MSCI EAFE	0.640	ML World Govt Bds w/o U.S.	0.359
MSCI Europe	0.740	Treasury Bill–30 day	0.195
MSCI Pacific Basin	0.460	Treasury Bill–6 months	0.520
IFC Emerging Mkts	0.565	Treasury Note–2 years	0.920
FTSE All World	0.940		
Brinson GSMI	0.926		

4.7 INVESTING IN SECURITY MARKET INDEXES

As discussed in the initial section of this chapter, there are several uses for these security market series. Beyond measuring the rates of return and risk for a number of asset classes, the two most significant uses are as a **benchmark** to measure the performance by portfolio managers and to create **index funds** and/or **exchange traded funds (ETFs)**. These two uses are closely related because when professional institutions measured performance using these market series they discovered that the vast majority of money managers could not match the risk-adjusted performance of the benchmarks. The results of these studies led to the conclusion (recommendation) that many investors should *not* attempt to beat the market (the market series) by engaging in active portfolio management that attempts to "beat the market" over time by selecting undervalued stocks. The alternative investment philosophy is prompted by the expression "if you can't beat them, join them." Specifically, if you can't beat the benchmark, you should buy (invest in) the benchmark.

Index Funds As we discuss in Chapter 17, mutual funds represent established security portfolios managed by professional investment companies (e.g., Fidelity, Vanguard, Putnam) in which investors can participate. The investment company decides how the fund is managed. For an indexed portfolio, the fund manager will typically attempt to replicate the composition of the particular index exactly, meaning that he or she will buy the exact securities comprising the index in their exact weights and then alter those positions anytime the index composition is changed. Since changes to most equity indexes occur sporadically, index funds tend to generate low trading and management expense ratios. A prominent example of an index fund is Vanguard's 500 Index Fund (VFINX), which is designed to mimic the S&P 500 Index. Exhibit 4.14 provides a descriptive overview of this fund and indicates that its historical return performance is virtually indistinguishable from that of the benchmark.

The advantage of index mutual funds is that they provide an inexpensive way for investors to acquire a diversified portfolio that emphasizes the desired market or industry within the context of a traditional money management product. The disadvantages of mutual funds are that investors can only liquidate their positions at the end of the trading day (i.e., no intraday trading), usually cannot short sell, and may have unwanted tax repercussions if the fund sells a portion of its holdings, thereby realizing capital gains.

Exchange-Traded Funds ETFs are a more recent development in the world of indexed investment products than index mutual funds. Essentially, ETFs are depository receipts that give investors a pro rata claim on the capital gains and cash flows of the securities that are held in deposit by the financial institution that issued the certificates. That is, a portfolio of securities is placed on deposit at a financial institution, which then issues a single type of certificate representing ownership of the underlying portfolio. In that way, ETFs are similar to the American depository receipts (ADRs) described in Chapter 2.

There are several notable example of ETFs, including (1) Standard & Poor's 500 Depository Receipts (SPDRs, or "spiders," as they are sometimes called), which are based on all the securities held in that index; (2) iShares, which recreate indexed positions in several global developed and emerging equity markets, including countries such as Australia, Mexico, Malaysia, the United Kingdom, France, Germany, Japan, and China; and (3) sector ETFs, which invest in baskets of stocks from specific industry sectors, including consumer services, industrial, technology, financial services, energy, utilities, and cyclicals/transportation. Exhibit 4.15 shows descriptive and return data for the SPDR Trust certificates. Note, however, that the returns to these shares do not track the index quite as closely as did the VFINX fund.

Exhibit 4.14 Details of the Vanguard 500 Index Trust Mutual Fund

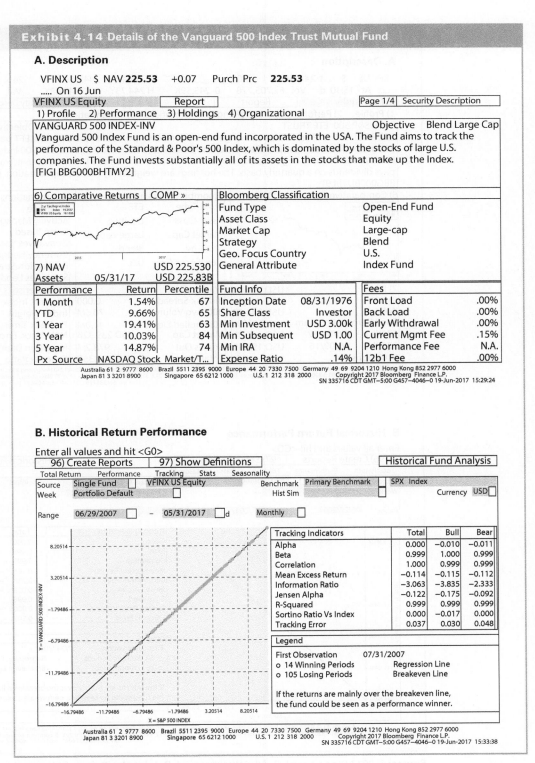

A. Description

VFINX US $ NAV **225.53**   +0.07   Purch Prc   **225.53**
..... On 16 Jun

VFINX US Equity	Report	Page 1/4 Security Description

1) Profile   2) Performance   3) Holdings   4) Organizational

VANGUARD 500 INDEX-INV   Objective   Blend Large Cap
Vanguard 500 Index Fund is an open-end fund incorporated in the USA. The Fund aims to track the performance of the Standard & Poor's 500 Index, which is dominated by the stocks of large U.S. companies. The Fund invests substantially all of its assets in the stocks that make up the Index. [FIGI BBG000BHTMY2]

6) Comparative Returns   COMP »

Bloomberg Classification	
Fund Type	Open-End Fund
Asset Class	Equity
Market Cap	Large-cap
Strategy	Blend
Geo. Focus Country	U.S.
General Attribute	Index Fund

7) NAV   USD 225.530
Assets   05/31/17   USD 225.83B

Performance	Return	Percentile	Fund Info		Fees	
1 Month	1.54%	67	Inception Date	08/31/1976	Front Load	.00%
YTD	9.66%	65	Share Class	Investor	Back Load	.00%
1 Year	19.41%	63	Min Investment	USD 3.00k	Early Withdrawal	.00%
3 Year	10.03%	84	Min Subsequent	USD 1.00	Current Mgmt Fee	.15%
5 Year	14.87%	74	Min IRA	N.A.	Performance Fee	N.A.
Px Source	NASDAQ Stock Market/T...		Expense Ratio	.14%	12b1 Fee	.00%

B. Historical Return Performance

Enter all values and hit <G0>

96) Create Reports	97) Show Definitions	Historical Fund Analysis

Total Return   Performance   Tracking   Stats   Seasonality

Source   Single Fund   VFINX US Equity   Benchmark   Primary Benchmark   SPX Index
Week   Portfolio Default   Hist Sim   Currency   USD

Range   06/29/2007   −   05/31/2017   d   Monthly

Tracking Indicators	Total	Bull	Bear
Alpha	0.000	−0.010	−0.011
Beta	0.999	1.000	0.999
Correlation	1.000	0.999	0.999
Mean Excess Return	−0.114	−0.115	−0.112
Information Ratio	−3.063	−3.835	−2.333
Jensen Alpha	−0.122	−0.175	−0.092
R-Squared	0.999	0.999	0.999
Sortino Ratio Vs Index	0.000	−0.017	0.000
Tracking Error	0.037	0.030	0.048

Legend

First Observation   07/31/2007
o 14 Winning Periods   Regression Line
o 105 Losing Periods   Breakeven Line

If the returns are mainly over the breakeven line, the fund could be seen as a performance winner.

Exhibit 4.15 Details of the SPDR Exchange-Traded Fund

A. Description

SPY US $ ↑ **244.66** +2.02		⌐⌐⌐	T244.64 / 244.64P	26 × 1071	
..... At 15:10 d Vol 62,705,728 0 243.59K			H 244.73Y	L 243.48Y	Val 15.315B

SPY US Equity	Report	Page 1/5	Security Description : ETF

1) Profile   2) Performance   3) Holdings   4) Allocations   5) Organizational

SPDR S&P 500 ETF TRUST   Objective   Large-cap

SPDR S&P 500 ETF Trust is an exchange-traded fund incorporated in the USA. The EFT tracks the S&P 500 Index. The Trust consists of a portfolio representing all 500 stocks in the S&P 500 Index. It holds predominantly large-cap U.S. stocks. This ETF is structured as a Unit Investment Trust and pays dividends on a quarterly basis. The holdings are weighted by market capitalization. [FIGI BBG000BDTBL9]

6) Comparative Returns I COMP »

Bloomberg Classification	
Fund Tybe	ETF
Asset Class	Equity
Market Cap	Large-cap
Strategy	Blend
Geo. Focus Co	U.S.

Appropriations	
Leverage	No
Actively Managed	No
Swap Based	No
Derivatives Based	No
Currency Hedged	No
Replication Strategy	Full
Securities Lending	No

1 yr Tot Ret vs Index
SPXT   Index 19.2618
SPY US Equity   20.107

7) Price		USD 244.66
8) NAV	06/16/17	USD 242.65
INAV		USD 244.67
Fund Percent Premium		−0.012%
52 Wk H	06/09/17	USD 245.01
52 Wk L	06/09/16	USD 198.65
9) Options		Yes

Trading Data	
Bid Ask Spread	0.000
30D Avg Volume	70.6M
10) Implied Liquidity	41.0M
Market Cap	USD 239.32B
Shares Out	978.2M
Total Assets	USD 237.35B

Characteristics	
11) Und. Index	SPXT
Index Weight	Market Cap
Px Track. Error	.380
NAV Track. Error	.024
Inception Date	01/22/93
Expense Ratio	.095%

Australia 61 2 9777 8600   Brazil 5511 2395 9000   Europe 44 20 7330 7500   Germany 49 69 9204 1210 Hong Kong 852 2977 6000
Japan 81 3 3201 8900   Singapore 65 6212 1000   U.S. 1 212 318 2000   Copyright 2017 Bloomberg Finance L.P.
SN 335716 CDT GMT−5:00 G457−4046−0 19-Jun-2017 15:29:48

B. Historical Return Performance

Enter all values and hit <GO>

96) Create Reports	97) Show Definitions	Historical Fund Analysis

Total Return   Performance   Tracking   Stats   Seasonality

Source	Single Fund	SPY US Equity	Benchmark Single Index	SPX Index	
Week	Portfolio Default		Hist Sim		Currency USD

Range   06/29/2007   -   05/31/2017   d   Monthly

Tracking Indicators	Total	Bull	Bear
Alpha	0.000	−0.018	−0.059
Beta	0.997	1.003	0.987
Correlation	0.999	0.998	0.998
Mean Excess Return	−0.106	−0.102	−0.114
Information Ratio	−0.210	−0.253	−0.173
Jensen Alpha	−0.099	−0.286	−0.570
R-Squared	0.998	0.997	0.997
Sortino Ratio Vs Index	0.000	−0.015	0.000
Tracking Error	0.507	0.404	0.661

Y = SPDR S&P 500 ETF TRUST
X = S&P 500 INDEX

Legend

First Observation   07/31/2007
o 54 Winning Periods   Regression Line
o 65 Losing Periods   Breakeven Line

If the returns are mainly over the breakeven line, the fund could be seen as a performance winner.

Australia 61 2 9777 8600   Brazil 5511 2395 9000   Europe 44 20 7330 7500   Germany 49 69 9204 1210 Hong Kong 852 2977 6000
Japan 81 3 3201 8900   Singapore 65 6212 1000   U.S. 1 212 318 2000   Copyright 2017 Bloomberg Finance L.P.
SN 335716 CDT GMT−5:00 G457−4046−0 19-Jun-2017 15:33:00

Source: © 2017 Bloomberg L.P. All rights reserved. Reprinted with permission.

A significant advantage of ETFs over index mutual funds is that they can be bought and sold (and short sold) like common stock through an organized exchange or in an over-the-counter market. Further, they are backed by a sponsoring organization (e.g., for SPDRs, the sponsor is PDR Services LLC, a limited liability company wholly owned by NYSE Euronext exchange where SPDR shares trade) that can alter the composition of the underlying portfolio to reflect changes in the composition of the index. Other advantages relative to index funds include an often smaller management fee, the ability for continuous trading while markets are open, and the ability to time capital gain tax realizations. ETF disadvantages include the brokerage commission and the inability to reinvest dividends, except on a quarterly basis.

SUMMARY

- Given the several uses of security market indexes, it is important to know how they are constructed and the differences between them. To determine how the market is doing, you need to be aware of what market you are dealing with so you can select the appropriate index. This choice is discussed in Merjos (1990).
- Indexes are also used as benchmarks to evaluate portfolio performance. In this case, you want the index (benchmark) to be consistent with your investing universe. For a bond portfolio, the index should likewise match your investment philosophy. Finally, if your portfolio contains both stocks and bonds, you must evaluate your performance against an appropriate combination of indexes.

- Investors need to examine numerous market indexes to evaluate the performance of their investments. The selection of the appropriate indexes for information or evaluation will depend on how knowledgeable you are about the various indexes. This chapter should help you understand what to look for and how to make the right decision regarding benchmarks.
- Passive equity portfolios attempt to track the returns of an established benchmark, such as the S&P 500, or one that meets the investor's needs. Index mutual funds and exchange-traded funds are popular ways for small investors to make passive investments.

SUGGESTED READINGS

Fisher, Lawrence, and James H. Lorie. *A Half Century of Returns on Stocks and Bonds*. Chicago: University of Chicago Graduate School of Business, 1977.

Ibbotson, Duff and Phelps. *Stocks, Bonds, Bills, and Inflation*. Hoboken, NJ: John Wiley and Sons, Inc. Annual.

Siegel, Laurence B. *Benchmarks and Investment Management*. The Research Foundation of AIMR, Charlottesville, VA, 2003.

QUESTIONS

1. Discuss briefly several uses of security market indexes.
2. What major factors must be considered when constructing a market index? Put another way, what characteristics differentiate indexes?
3. Explain how a market index is price weighted. In such a case, would you expect a $100 stock to be more important than a $25 stock? Give an example.
4. Explain how to compute a value-weighted index.
5. Explain how a price-weighted index and a value-weighted index adjust for stock splits.

6. Describe an unweighted price index and describe how you would construct such an index. Assume a 20 percent price change in GM ($40/share; 50 million shares outstanding) and Coors Brewing ($25/share and 15 million shares outstanding). Explain which stock's 20 percent change will have the greater impact on this index.

7. If you correlated percentage changes in the Dow Jones Total Stock Market Index with percentage changes in the NYSE composite and the NASDAQ composite index, would you expect a difference in the correlations? Why or why not?

8. There are high correlations between the monthly percentage price changes for the alternative NYSE indexes. Discuss the reason for this similarity: is it size of sample, source of sample, or method of computation?

9. Assume a correlation of 0.82 between the Nikkei and the TSE Composite Index. Examine the correlation between the MSCI Pacific Basin Index and the DJTSM in Exhibit 4.13. Explain why these relationships differ.

10. You learn that the Dow Jones Total Stock Market market-value-weighted index increased by 16 percent during a specified period, whereas a Dow Jones Total Stock Market equal-weighted index increased by 23 percent during the same period. Discuss what this difference in results implies.

11. Why is it contended that bond market indexes are more difficult to construct and maintain than stock market indexes?

12. Suppose the Dow Jones Total Stock Market market-value-weighted index increased by 5 percent, whereas the Merrill Lynch-Dow Jones Capital Markets Index increased by 15 percent during the same period. What does this difference in results imply?

13. Suppose the Russell 1000 increased by 8 percent during the past year, whereas the Russell 2000 increased by 15 percent. Discuss the implication of these results.

14. Based on what you know about the *Financial Times* (FT) World Index, the Morgan Stanley Capital International World Index, and the Dow Jones World Stock Index, what level of correlation would you expect between monthly rates of return? Discuss the reasons for your answer based on the factors that affect indexes.

15. How would you explain that the ML High-Yield Bond Index was more highly correlated with the NYSE composite stock index than the ML Aggregate Bond Index?

16. Assuming that the mandate to a portfolio manager was to invest in a broadly diversified portfolio of U.S. stocks, which two or three indexes should be considered as an appropriate benchmark? Why?

17. List two investment products that a manager following a passive investment strategy could use to make an investment in the Standard & Poor's 500 Index. Briefly discuss which product is likely to be the most accurate method for tracking the index.

PROBLEMS

1. You are given the following information regarding prices for a sample of stocks.

Stock	Number of Shares	PRICE	
		T	T+1
A	1,000,000	60	80
B	10,000,000	20	35
C	30,000,000	18	25

a. Construct a *price-weighted* index for these three stocks, and compute the percentage change in the index for the period from T to $T + 1$.

b. Construct a *value-weighted* index for these three stocks, and compute the percentage change in the index for the period from T to $T + 1$.

c. Briefly discuss the difference in the results for the two indexes.

2. a. Given the data in Problem 1, construct an equal-weighted index by assuming $1,000 is invested in each stock. What is the percentage change in wealth for this portfolio?

b. Compute the percentage of price change for each of the stocks in Problem 1. Compute the arithmetic mean of these percentage changes. Discuss how this answer compares to the answer in part (a).

c. Compute the geometric mean of the percentage changes in part (b). Discuss how this result compares to the answer in part (b).

3. For the past five trading days, on the basis of figures in *The Wall Street Journal*, compute the daily percentage price changes for the following stock indexes.

a. DJIA

b. S&P 500

c. NASDAQ Composite Index

d. FT-100 Share Index

e. Nikkei 225 Stock Price Average

f. Discuss the difference in results for parts (a) and (b), (a) and (c), (a) and (d), (a) and (e), and (d) and (e). What do these differences imply regarding diversifying within the United States versus diversifying between countries?

4.

Company	PRICE			SHARES		
	A	B	C	A	B	C
Day 1	12	23	52	500	350	250
Day 2	10	22	55	500	350	250
Day 3	14	46	52	500	175[a]	250
Day 4	13	47	25	500	175	500[b]
Day 5	12	45	26	500	175	500

[a]Split at close of day 2.
[b]Split at close of day 3.

a. Calculate a Dow Jones Industrial Average for days 1 through 5.

b. What effects have the splits had in determining the next day's index? (Hint: think of the relative weighting of each stock.)

c. From a copy of *The Wall Street Journal*, find the divisor that is currently being used in calculating the DJIA. (Normally this value can be found on pages C2 and C3.)

5. Utilizing the price and volume data in Problem 4,

a. Calculate a Standard & Poor's Index for days 1 through 5 using a beginning index value of 10.

b. Identify what effects the splits had in determining the next day's index. (Hint: think of the relative weighting of each stock.)

6. Based on the following stock price and shares outstanding information, compute the beginning and ending values for a price-weighted index and a market-value-weighted index.

	DECEMBER 31, 2017		DECEMBER 31, 2018	
	Price	Shares Outstanding Price	Price	Shares Outstanding
Stock K	20	100,000,000	32	100,000,000
Stock M	80	2,000,000	45	4,000,000[a]
Stock R	40	25,000,000	42	25,000,000

[a]Stock split two-for-one during the year.

   a. Compute the percentage change in the value of each index during the year.
   b. Explain the difference in results between the two indexes.
   c. Compute the percentage change for an unweighted index and discuss why these results differ from those of the other indexes.

7. Given the monthly returns that follow, how well did the passive portfolio track the S&P 500 benchmark? Find the R^2, alpha, and beta of the portfolio. Compute the average return differential with and without sign.

Month	Portfolio Return	S&P 500 Return
January	5.0%	5.2%
February	−2.3	−3.0
March	−1.8	−1.6
April	2.2	1.9
May	0.4	0.1
June	−0.8	−0.5
July	0.0	0.2
August	1.5	1.6
September	−0.3	−0.1
October	−3.7	−4.0
November	2.4	2.0
December	0.3	0.2

Stock Market Indexes

Exhibit 4A.1 Summary of Stock Market Indexes

Name of Index	Weighting	Number of Stocks	Source of Stocks
Dow Jones Industrial Average	Price	30	NYSE, NASDAQ
Nikkei-Dow Jones Average	Price	225	TSE
S&P 400 Industrial	Market value	400	NYSE, NASDAQ
S&P Transportation	Market value	20	NYSE, NASDAQ
S&P Utilities	Market value	40	NYSE, NASDAQ
S&P Financials	Market value	40	NYSE, NASDAQ
S&P 500 Composite	Market value	500	NYSE, NASDAQ
NYSE			
Industrial	Market value	1,601	NYSE
Utility	Market value	253	NYSE
Transportation	Market value	55	NYSE
Financial	Market value	909	NYSE
Composite	Market value	2,818	NYSE
NASDAQ			
Composite	Market value	5,575	NASDAQ
Industrial	Market value	3,394	NASDAQ
Banks	Market value	375	NASDAQ
Insurance	Market value	103	NASDAQ
Other finance	Market value	610	NASDAQ
Transportation	Market value	104	NASDAQ
Telecommunications	Market value	183	NASDAQ
Computer	Market value	685	NASDAQ
Biotech	Market value	121	NASDAQ
AMEX Market Value	Market value	900	AMEX
Dow Jones Total Stock Market Index	Market value	5,000	NYSE, AMEX, NASDAQ
Russell Indexes			
3000	Market value	3,000 largest in U.S.	NYSE, AMEX, NASDAQ
1000	Market value	1,000 largest of 3,000	NYSE, AMEX, NASDAQ
2000	Market value	2,000 smallest of 3,000	NYSE, AMEX, NASDAQ
Financial Times			
Actuaries Index			
All Share	Market value	700	LSE
FT100	Market value	100 largest	LSE
Small-Cap	Market value	250	LSE
Mid-cap	Market value	250	LSE
Combined	Market value	350	LSE
Tokyo Stock Exchange Price Index (TOPIX)	Market value	1,800	TSE
Value Line Averages	Equal (geometric mean)	1,499	NYSE, AMEX, NASDAQ
Industrials			
Utilities	Equal	177	NYSE, AMEX, NASDAQ
Rails	Equal	19	NYSE, AMEX, NASDAQ
Composite	Equal	1,695	NYSE, AMEX, NASDAQ
Financial Times Ordinary Share Index	Equal (geometric mean)	30	LSE
FT-Actuaries World Indexes	Market value	2,275	24 countries, 3 regions (returns in $, £, ¥, DM, and local currency)

Exhibit 4A.1 Summary of Stock Market Indexes *(Continued)*

Name of Index	Weighting	Number of Stocks	Source of Stocks
MSCI Indexes	Market value	1,375	19 countries, 3 international, 38 international industries (returns in $ and local currency)
Dow Jones World Stock Index	Market value	2,200	13 countries, 3 regions, 120 industry groups (returns in $, £, ¥, DM, and local currency)
Euromoney—First Boston Global Stock Index	Market value	—	17 countries (returns in $ and local currency)
Salomon-Russell World Equity Index	Market value	Russell 1000 and S-R PMI of 600 non-U.S. stocks	22 countries (returns in $ and local currency)

Exhibit 4A.2 Foreign Stock Market Indexes

Name of Index	Weighting	Number of Stocks	History of Index
ATX-index (Vienna)	Market value	All listed stocks	Base year 1967,1991 began including all stocks (Value = 100)
Swiss Market Index	Market value	18	Base year 1988, stocks selected from the Basle, Geneva, and Zurich Exchanges (Value = 1500)
Stockholm General Index	Market value	All listed stocks	Base year 1979, continuously updated (Value = 100)
Copenhagen Stock Exchange Share Price Index	Market value	All traded stocks	Share price is based on average price of the day
Oslo SE Composite Index (Sweden)	Market value	25	Base year 1972 (Value = 100)
Johannesburg Stock Exchange Actuaries Index	Market value	146	Base year 1959 (Value = 100)
Mexican Market Index	Market value	Variable number, based on capitalization and liquidity	Base year 1978, high dollar returns in recent years
Milan Stock Exchange MIB Market	Market value	Variable number, based on capitalization and liquidity	Change base at beginning of each year (Value = 1000)
Belgium BEL-20 Stock Index	Market value	20	Base year 1991 (Value = 1000)
Madrid General Stock Index	Market value	92	Change base at beginning of each year
Hang Seng Index (Hong Kong)	Market value	33	Started in 1969, accounts for 75 percent of total market
FT-Actuaries World Indexes	Market value	2,275	Base year 1986
FT-SE 100 Index (London)	Market value	100	Base year 1983 (Value = 1000)
CAC General Share Index (French)	Market value	212	Base year 1981 (Value = 100)
Singapore Straits Times Industrial Index	Unweighted	30	

Exhibit 4A.2 Foreign Stock Market Indexes *(Continued)*

Name of Index	Weighting	Number of Stocks	History of Index
German Stock Market Index (DAX)	Market value	30	Base year 1987 (Value = 1000)
Frankfurter Allgemeine Zeitung Index (FAZ) (German)	Market value	100	Base year 1958 (Value = 100)
Australian Stock Exchange Share Price Indexes	Market value	250	Introduced in 1979
Dublin ISEQ Index	Market value	All stocks traded	Base year 1988 (Value = 1000)
HEX Index (Helsinki)	Market value	Varies with different indexes	Base changes every day
Jakarta Stock Exchange (Indonesia)	Market value	All listed shares	Base year 1982 (Value = 100)
Taiwan Stock Exchange Index	Market value	All listed stocks	Base year 1966 (Value = 100)
TSE 300 Composite Index (Toronto)	Market value	300	Base year 1975 (Value = 1000)
KOSPI (Korean Composite Stock Price Index)	Market value (adjusted for cross-holdings)	All listed stocks	Base year 1980 (Value = 100)

Source: Compiled by authors.

Developments in Investment Theory

The chapters in Part 1 provided background on why individuals invest their funds and what they expect to derive from this activity. We also argued very strongly for a global investment program, described the major instruments and capital markets in a global investment environment, and showed the relationship among these instruments and markets. We now are ready to discuss how to analyze and value the various investment instruments available. In turn, valuation requires the estimation of expected returns (cash flows) and a determination of the risk involved in the securities. Before we can begin the analysis, we need to understand several major developments in investment theory that have influenced how we specify and measure risk in the valuation process. The purpose of the three chapters in Part 2 is to provide this background on risk and asset valuation.

Chapter 5 describes the concept of efficient capital markets, which hypothesizes that security prices reflect the effect of all information. This chapter considers why markets should be efficient, discusses how one goes about testing this hypothesis, and describes the results of numerous tests that both support the hypotheses and indicate the existence of anomalies that are inconsistent with the hypotheses. There is also a consideration of behavioral finance, which has experienced a growth in reputation because it provides a rationale for some of the results. We conclude the chapter with an extensive discussion of the implications of the results for those engaged in technical and fundamental analysis as well as portfolio management.

Chapter 6 provides an introduction to portfolio theory, which was developed by Harry Markowitz. This theory provided the first rigorous measure of the risk faced by investors and showed how one selects a collection of assets to diversify and reduce the risk of a portfolio. Markowitz also derived a risk measure for individual securities within the context of an efficient portfolio. We demonstrate how this "portfolio optimization" process can be useful to investors in many ways, such as helping them determine their appropriate asset allocation strategy. We conclude the chapter with an extension of portfolio theory—referred to as *capital market theory*—that led to the development of the *capital market line* (*CML*), which was the first formal equation connecting risk and expected return in an efficient market that could be used to value portfolio investments.

Following the development of the Markowitz portfolio model and the CML, William Sharpe and other academics created a general equilibrium asset pricing model that included an alternative risk measure for all risky assets. Chapter 7 contains a detailed description of these developments and an explanation of the relevant risk measure implied by this valuation model, referred to as the *capital asset pricing model* (*CAPM*). Although the CAPM has long been the preeminent theoretical explanation in finance for the connection between risk and expected return, the past several decades have seen the rise of several competing models. We conclude the chapter with an examination of the *arbitrage pricing theory* (*APT*), which was developed by Steve Ross in response to criticisms of the CAPM and suggests a linear relationship between a stock's expected return and several different systematic risk factors. This, in turn, has led to the development of several *multifactor models*, which attempt to link a stock's realized returns to market data on a collection of pre-specified variables believed to proxy for the APT risk factors. After explaining various approaches to estimate these risk proxies, we demonstrate how they are used by investors to both evaluate individual companies and assess the investment styles of money managers and mutual funds.

CHAPTER **5**

Efficient Capital Markets, Behavioral Finance, and Technical Analysis

After you read this chapter, you should be able to answer the following questions:

- What does it mean to say that capital markets are efficient?
- Why *should* capital markets be efficient?
- What factors contribute to an efficient market?
- Given the overall efficient market hypothesis (EMH), what are the three subhypotheses and what are the implications of each of them?
- For each set of tests, which results support the EMH and which results indicate an anomaly related to the hypothesis?
- What is behavioral finance and how does it relate to the EMH?
- What are the major findings of behavioral finance and what are the implications of these findings for the EMH?
- What are the implications of the efficient market hypothesis test results for the following?
  - Technical analysis
  - Fundamental analysis
  - Portfolio managers with superior analysts
  - Portfolio managers with inferior analysts
- What are the underlying assumptions of technical analysis?
- What assumptions differ between technical analysis and the EMH?
- What are the major advantages of technical analysis?
- What are the major challenges to technical analysis?
- What is the logic for the major contrary-opinion rules used by technicians?
- What rules are used by technicians who want to "follow the smart money"?
- What are the three price movements postulated in the Dow Theory?
- Why is trading volume important, and how do technicians use it?
- How do technicians use moving-average lines to detect changes in trends?
- What is the rationale behind a relative-strength line?

This chapter contains a range of topics that are related but are also inconsistent with one another. First, it looks at *market efficiency*, which argues for efficient markets wherein security prices reflect all the information about a security. *Behavioral finance* considers how various psychological traits affect how individuals act when investing. Advocates contend that the standard finance model of rational behavior and profit maximization is an incomplete model since it does not consider individual behavior that can result in the mispricing of securities compared to what is assumed by efficient markets. Finally, we consider *technical analysis*, which is very inconsistent with efficient markets because it assumes a gradual adjustment of security prices to new information such that past prices or events can predict future prices.

5.1 EFFICIENT CAPITAL MARKETS

An **efficient capital market** is one in which security prices adjust rapidly to the arrival of new information, which implies that the current prices of securities reflect all information about the security. Interesting and important academic research during the past 30 years has analyzed whether our capital markets are efficient because the results of this research have significant real-world implications for investors and portfolio managers. Capital market efficiency is also one of the most controversial areas in investment research. As noted, the controversy has been enhanced because of the rapidly expanding research in behavioral finance that has major implications related to efficient capital markets and has provided some reasons for many anomalies identified in efficient market research.

Because of its importance and controversy, you need to understand the meaning of the terms *efficient capital markets* and the *efficient market hypothesis* (*EMH*), and the results of studies that either support or contradict the hypothesis. Finally, you should be aware of the implications of these diverse results when you analyze alternative investments, estimate intrinsic value, and work to construct a portfolio.

This section contains three major subsections. The first discusses why we would expect capital markets to be efficient and the factors that contribute to an efficient market where security prices reflect available information.

The EMH has been divided into three subhypotheses to facilitate testing. The second subsection describes these three subhypotheses and the implications of each of them.

The third subsection contains a discussion of the results of numerous studies and reveals that a large body of evidence supports the EMH, but a growing number of studies do not support the hypotheses.

5.1.1 Why Should Capital Markets Be Efficient?

As noted earlier, in an efficient capital market, security prices adjust rapidly to new information, which implies that current security prices fully reflect all available information. This is referred to as an **informationally efficient market**. Although the idea of an efficient capital market is relatively straightforward, we need to consider *why* capital markets *should* be efficient. What set of assumptions imply an efficient capital market?

An important premise of an efficient market requires *a large number of independent profit-maximizing participants who analyze and value securities.*

A second assumption is that *new information regarding securities comes to the market in a random fashion*, and the timing of one announcement is generally independent of others.[1]

The third assumption is especially crucial: *The buy and sell decisions of all those profit-maximizing investors cause security prices to adjust rapidly to reflect the effect of new information.* Although the price adjustment may be imperfect, it is *unbiased*, which means that sometimes the market will overadjust and other times it will underadjust, but you cannot predict which will occur. Security prices adjust rapidly because the many profit-maximizing investors are competing against one another to profit from the new information.

The combined effect of (1) information coming in a random, independent, unpredictable fashion and (2) numerous competing investors adjusting stock prices rapidly to reflect this new information means that prices should be independent and random. This scenario implies that informationally efficient markets require some minimum amount of trading and that more trading by numerous competing investors should cause a faster price adjustment, making the market more efficient. We will return to this need for trading and investor attention when

---

[1]New information, by definition, must be information that was not known before and is not predictable. If it were predictable, it would have been impounded in the security price.

we discuss some anomalies of the EMH. Also recall the discussion in Chapter 3 regarding the significant increase in trading volume over the past decade and the lower cost of trading.

Finally, because security prices adjust to all new information, these security prices should reflect all information that is publicly available at any point in time, including the risk involved in owning the security. Therefore, *the expected returns implicit in the current price of the security should reflect its risk*, so investors who buy at these informationally efficient prices should receive a rate of return that is consistent with the security's risk.

5.1.2 Alternative Efficient Market Hypotheses

Most of the early work related to efficient capital markets was based on the *random walk hypothesis*, which contended that changes in stock prices occurred randomly. This early academic work contained extensive empirical analysis without much theory behind it. An article by Fama (1970) attempted to formalize the theory and organize the growing empirical evidence. Fama presented the efficient market theory in terms of a *fair game model*, contending that current market prices reflected all available information about a security and, therefore, the expected return based upon this price is consistent with its risk.

In his original article, Fama divided the overall efficient market hypothesis (EMH) and the empirical tests into three subhypotheses depending on the information set involved: (1) weak-form EMH, (2) semistrong-form EMH, and (3) strong-form EMH.

In the remainder of this subsection, we describe the three subhypotheses based on different information sets and the implications of each of them. Subsequently, we will briefly describe the tests of these hypotheses and summarize the test results.

Weak-Form Efficient Market Hypothesis The **weak-form EMH** assumes that current stock prices fully reflect *all security market information*, including the historical sequence of prices, rates of return, trading volume data, and other market-generated information, such as odd-lot transactions and transactions by market-makers. Because it assumes that current market prices already reflect all past returns and any other security market information, this hypothesis implies that past rates of return and other historical market data should have no relationship with future rates of return (that is, rates of return should be independent). Therefore, this hypothesis contends that you should gain little from using any trading rule which indicates that you should buy or sell a security based on past rates of return or any other past security market data.

Semistrong-Form Efficient Market Hypothesis The **semistrong-form EMH** asserts that security prices adjust rapidly to the release of *all public information*; that is, current security prices fully reflect all public information. The semistrong hypothesis encompasses the weak-form hypothesis, because all the market information considered by the weak-form hypothesis, such as stock prices, rates of return, and trading volume, is public. Notably, public information also includes all nonmarket information, such as earnings and dividend announcements, price-to-earnings (P/E) ratios, dividend-yield (D/P) ratios, price-book value (P/BV) ratios, stock splits, news about the economy, and political news. This hypothesis implies that investors who base their decisions on any important new information *after it is public* should not derive above-average risk-adjusted profits from their transactions, considering the cost of trading.

Strong-Form Efficient Market Hypothesis The **strong-form EMH** contends that stock prices fully reflect *all information from public and private sources*. This hypothesis assumes that no group of investors has monopolistic access to information relevant to the formation of prices, which implies that no group of investors should be able to consistently derive above-average risk-adjusted rates of return. The strong-form EMH encompasses both the weak-form EMH and the semistrong-form EMH. Further, the strong-form EMH extends the assumption of efficient markets to assume perfect markets, in which all information is cost-free and available to everyone at the same time.

5.1.3 Tests and Results of Efficient Market Hypotheses

Now that you understand the three components of the EMH and what each of them implies regarding the effect on security prices of different sets of information, we can consider the specific tests used to see whether the results support the hypotheses.

Like most hypotheses in finance and economics, the evidence on the EMH is mixed. Some studies have supported the hypotheses and indicate that capital markets are efficient. Results of other studies have revealed some **anomalies** related to these hypotheses, indicating results that do not support the hypotheses.

Weak-Form Hypothesis: Tests and Results Researchers have formulated two groups of tests of the weak-form EMH. The first category involves statistical tests of independence between rates of return. The second set of tests compares risk–return results for trading rules that make investment decisions based on past market information relative to the results from a simple buy-and-hold policy, which assumes that you buy stock at the beginning of a test period and hold it to the end.

Statistical Tests of Independence Recall that the EMH contends that security returns over time should be independent of one another because new information comes to the market in a random, independent fashion, and security prices adjust rapidly to this new information. Two major statistical tests have been employed to verify this independence.

First, **autocorrelation tests** of independence measure the significance of positive or negative correlation in returns over time. Does the rate of return on day t correlate with the rate of return on day $t - 1$, $t - 2$, or $t - 3$?[2] Those who believe that capital markets are efficient would expect insignificant correlations for all such comparisons.

The results of studies that examined the serial correlations among stock returns for relatively short time horizons including 1 day, 4 days, 9 days, and 16 days typically indicated insignificant correlation in stock returns over time. Some recent studies that considered portfolios of stocks of different market size have found that the autocorrelation is stronger for portfolios of small market size stocks. Therefore, although the initial results tend to support the hypothesis, some subsequent studies cast doubt on the hypothesis for portfolios of small firms, although these results could be offset by the higher transaction costs of small-cap stocks.

The second statistical test of independence is the **runs test**. Given a series of price changes, each price change is either designated a plus (+) if it is an increase in price or a minus (−) if it is a decrease in price. The result is a set of pluses and minuses, as follows: + + + − + − − + + − − + +. A run occurs when two consecutive changes are the same; two or more consecutive positive or negative price changes constitute one run. When the price changes in a different direction (for example, when a negative price change is followed by a positive price change), the run ends, and a new run may begin. To test for independence, you would compare the number of runs for a given series to the number in a table of expected values for the number of runs that should occur in a random series.

Studies that have examined stock price runs have confirmed the independence of stock price changes over time. The actual number of runs for stock price series consistently fell into the range expected for a random series, which would confirm the independence of stock price changes over time.

Although short-horizon stock returns (monthly, weekly, and daily) have generally supported the weak-form EMH, several studies that examined price changes for individual

---

[2]For a discussion of tests of time-series independence, see DeFusco, McLeavey, Pinto, and Runkle (2004), Chapter 10.

transactions on the NYSE found significant serial correlations. These studies indicated that the serial correlation meant that *momentum* could be used to generate excess risk-adjusted returns, but it was concluded that the substantial transaction costs wiped out the profits. In contrast, recent studies that considered the current substantially lower transaction cost as discussed in Chapter 3 indicate that return momentum may be a viable trading technique.

Tests of Trading Rules   The second group of tests of the weak-form EMH were developed in response to the assertion that some of the prior statistical tests of independence were too rigid to identify the intricate price patterns examined by technical analysts. As discussed later in this chapter, technical analysts do not expect a set number of positive or negative price changes as a signal of a move to a new equilibrium. They look for a general consistency in the price trends over time that might include both positive and negative changes. Therefore, technical analysts believed that their sophisticated trading rules could not be properly tested by rigid statistical tests. Hence, investigators attempted to examine alternative technical trading rules through simulation. Advocates of an efficient market would hypothesize that investors could not derive abnormal profits above a buy-and-hold policy using any trading rule that depended solely on past market information.

The trading-rule studies compared the risk–return results derived from trading-rule simulations, including transaction costs, to the results from a simple buy-and-hold policy. Three major pitfalls can negate the results of a trading-rule study:

1. The investigator should *use only publicly available data* when implementing the trading rule. As an example, the trading activities of some set of traders/investors for some period ending December 31 may not be publicly available until February 1. Therefore, you should not factor in information about the trading activity until the information is public.
2. When computing the returns from a trading rule, you should *include all transaction costs* involved in implementing the trading strategy because trading rules generally involve many more transactions than a simple buy-and-hold policy.
3. You must *adjust the results for risk* because a trading rule might simply select a portfolio of high-risk securities that should experience higher returns.

Researchers have encountered two operational problems in carrying out these tests of specific trading rules. First, some trading rules require too much subjective interpretation of data to simulate mechanically. Second, the almost infinite number of potential trading rules makes it impossible to test all of them. As a result, only the better-known technical trading rules that can be programmed into a computer have been examined.

Notably, the simulation studies have typically been restricted to relatively simple trading rules, which many technicians contend are rather naïve. In addition, many of the early studies employed readily available data from the NYSE, which is biased toward well-known, heavily traded stocks that certainly should trade in efficient markets. Recall that markets should be more efficient when there are numerous investors attempting to adjust stock prices to reflect new information, so market efficiency will be related to trading volume. Alternatively, for securities with relatively few stockholders and limited trading activity, the market could be inefficient simply because fewer investors would be analyzing the effect of any new information. Therefore, using only active, heavily traded stocks when testing a trading rule could bias the results toward finding efficiency.

Results of Simulations of Specific Trading Rules   One of the most popular trading techniques is the filter rule, wherein an investor trades a stock when the price change exceeds a filter value set for it. As an example, an investor using a 5 percent filter would identify a positive breakout if the stock were to rise 5 percent from some base, suggesting that the stock price would continue to rise. A technician would acquire the stock to take advantage of the expected increase. In contrast, a 5 percent decline from some peak price would be considered a negative breakout, and the technician would expect a further price decline and would sell any holdings of the stock and possibly even sell the stock short.

Studies of this trading rule have used a range of filters from 0.5 percent to 50 percent. The results indicated that small filters would yield above-average profits *before* taking account of trading commissions. However, small filters generate numerous trades and, therefore, substantial trading costs. When the pre-2000 trading costs were considered, all the trading profits turned to losses. It is possible that using recent lower trading costs (post-2011), the results could be different. Alternatively, trading using larger filters did not yield returns above those of a simple buy-and-hold policy.

Researchers have simulated other trading rules that used past market data other than stock prices. Trading rules have been devised that consider advanced-decline ratios, short sales, short positions, and specialist activities.[3] These simulation tests have generated mixed results. Early studies using higher commission fees suggested that these trading rules generally would not outperform a buy-and-hold policy on a risk-adjusted basis after commissions. In contrast, several recent studies have indicated support for specific trading rules. Therefore, evidence from simulations of specific trading rules indicates that most trading rules tested have not been able to beat a buy-and-hold policy. Therefore, the early test results generally support the weak-form EMH, but the results are clearly not unanimous, especially if one considers the current substantially lower commissions.

Semistrong-Form Hypothesis: Tests and Results Recall that the semistrong-form EMH asserts that security prices adjust rapidly to the release of all public information; that is, security prices fully reflect all public information. Studies that have tested the semistrong-form EMH can be divided into the following sets of studies:

1. *Studies to predict future rates of return using available public information beyond pure market information considered in the weak-form tests.* These studies can involve either *time-series analysis* of returns or the *cross-section distribution* of returns for individual stocks. Advocates of the EMH contend that it would not be possible to predict *future* returns using past returns or to predict the distribution of future returns (for example, the top quartile or decile of returns) using public information.

2. *Event studies that examine how fast stock prices adjust to specific significant economic events.* These studies test whether it is possible to invest in a security after the public announcement of a significant event (for example, earnings, stock splits, major economic events) and whether they can experience significant abnormal rates of return. Again, advocates of the EMH would expect security prices to adjust rapidly, such that it would not be possible for investors to experience superior risk-adjusted returns by investing after the public announcement and paying normal transaction costs.

Adjustment for Market Effects   For any of these tests, you need to adjust the security's rates of return for the rates of return of the overall market during the period considered. The point is that a 5 percent return in a stock during the period surrounding an announcement is meaningless until you know what the aggregate stock market did during the same period and how this stock normally acts under such conditions. If the market had experienced a 10 percent return during this announcement period, the 5 percent return for the stock may be lower than expected.

Early studies (pre-1980) generally recognized the need to make adjustments for market movements by assuming that the individual stocks should experience returns equal to the aggregate stock market. Thus, the market-adjustment process simply entailed subtracting the

---

[3]Many of these trading rules are discussed later in the chapter, when we consider technical analysis.

market return from the return for the individual security to derive its **abnormal rate of return**, as follows:

5.1
$$AR_{it} = R_{it} - R_{mt}$$

where:

AR_{it} = abnormal rate of return on security i during period t
R_{it} = rate of return on security i during period t
R_{mt} = rate of return on a market index during period t

In the example where the stock experienced a 5 percent increase while the market increased 10 percent, the stock's abnormal return would be minus 5 percent.

Recent authors have adjusted the rates of return for securities by an amount different from the market rate of return because they recognize that, based on work with the CAPM, all stocks do not change by the same amount as the market. That is, as will be discussed in Chapter 7, some stocks are more volatile than the market, and some are less volatile. Therefore, you must determine an **expected rate of return** for the stock based on the market rate of return *and* the stock's relationship with the market (its beta). As an example, suppose a stock is generally 20 percent more volatile than the market (that is, it has a beta of 1.20). In such a case, if the market experiences a 10 percent rate of return, you would expect this stock to experience a 12 percent rate of return. Therefore, you would determine the abnormal rate of return by computing the difference between the stock's actual rate of return and its *expected rate of return* as follows:

5.2
$$AR_{it} = R_{it} - E(R_{it})$$

where:

$E(R_{it})$ = expected rate of return for stock i during period t based on the market rate of return and the stock's normal relationship with the market (its beta)

Continuing with the example, if the stock that was expected to have a 12 percent return (based on a market return of 10 percent and a stock beta of 1.20) had only a 5 percent return, its abnormal rate of return during the period would be minus 7 percent. Over the normal long-run period, you would expect the abnormal returns for a stock to sum to zero. Specifically, during one period the returns may exceed expectations and the next period they may fall short of expectations.

Alternate Semistrong Tests   Given this understanding of the market adjustment, recall that there are two sets of tests of the semistrong-form EMH. The first set are referred to as **return prediction studies**. In these studies, investigators attempt to predict the time series of future rates of return for individual stocks or the aggregate market using public information. For example, is it possible to predict abnormal returns over time for the market based on public information such as changes in the aggregate dividend yield or the risk premium spread for bonds? Another example would be **event studies** that examine abnormal rates of return for a period immediately after an announcement of a significant economic event, such as a stock split or a proposed merger to determine whether an investor can derive above-average risk-adjusted rates of return by investing after the release of public information.

Another set of studies attempt to predict cross-sectional returns by examining public information regarding individual stocks that will allow investors to predict the cross-sectional distribution of future risk-adjusted rates of return. For example, they test whether it is possible to use variables such as the price-earnings ratio, market value size, the price/book-value ratio, the price–earnings/growth rate (PEG) ratio, or the dividend yield to predict which stocks will experience above-average (for example, top quartile) or below-average risk-adjusted rates of return in the future.

In both sets of tests, the emphasis is on the analysis of abnormal rates of return that deviate from long-term expectations.

Results of Return Prediction Studies The **time-series analysis** assumes that in an efficient market the best estimate of *future* rates of return will be the long-run *historical* rates of return. The tests attempt to determine whether any public information will provide superior estimates of returns for a short-run horizon (one to six months) or a long-run horizon (one to five years).

Risk Premium Proxies Return prediction studies have indicated limited success in predicting short-horizon returns but good success in the analysis of long-horizon returns. A prime example is dividend yield studies. After postulating that the aggregate dividend yield (*D/P*) was a proxy for the risk premium on stocks, they found a positive relationship between the *D/P* and future long-run stock market returns.

In addition, several studies have considered two variables related to interest rates: (1) a *default spread*, which is the difference between the yields on lower-grade and Aaa-rated long-term corporate bonds (this spread has been used in earlier chapters of this book as a proxy for a market risk premium), and (2) the *term structure spread*, which is the difference between the long-term Treasury bond yield and the yield on one-month Treasury bills. These variables have been used to predict stock returns and bond returns. Similar variables have been used for predicting returns for foreign common stocks.

The reasoning for these empirical results is as follows: When the two most significant variables—the dividend yield (D/P) and the bond default spread—are high, it implies that investors are requiring a high return on stocks and bonds. Notably, this occurs during poor economic environments when investors perceive an increase in risk for investments. As a result, investors will require a high rate of return (that is, a high-risk premium) that will cause a decline in prices for risky assets. Therefore, if you invest during this risk-averse period, your subsequent returns will be above normal. In contrast, when dividend yields and yield spreads are small, it implies that investors have reduced their risk premium, required rates of return, and the prices of assets increase; therefore, future returns will be below normal. The studies that support this expectation provide evidence against the EMH because they indicate you can use public information on dividend yields and yield spreads to predict future abnormal returns.

Quarterly Earnings Reports Studies that address quarterly reports are considered part of the times-series analysis. Specifically, these studies examine whether it is possible to predict future individual stock returns based on publicly available information on changes in quarterly earnings that differed from expectations.

The results generally indicated that there were abnormal stock returns during the 13 or 26 weeks *following* the announcement of a large *unanticipated* earnings change—referred to as an **earnings surprise**. These results indicate that an earnings surprise is *not* instantaneously reflected in security prices.

An extensive analysis by Rendleman, Jones, and Latané (1982) and a follow-up by Jones, Rendleman, and Latané (1985) using a large sample and daily data from 20 days before a quarterly earnings announcement to 90 days after the announcement indicated that 31 percent of the total response in stock returns came before the earnings announcement, 18 percent on the day of the announcement, and 51 percent *after* the announcement.

Several subsequent studies by Benesh and Peterson (1986), Bernard and Thomas (1989), and Baruch (1989) contended that the reason for the stock price drift was the *earnings revisions* that followed the earnings surprises and these revisions contributed to the positive correlations of prices.

In summary, these results indicate that the market does not adjust stock prices to reflect the release of quarterly earnings surprises as fast as expected by the semistrong EMH, which implies that earnings surprises and earnings revisions can be used to predict returns for individual stocks are evidence against the EMH.[4]

These results have also been enhanced by research that showed institutions are able to anticipate earning surprises. Also, some "calendar studies" questioned whether regularities in the rates of return during the calendar year would allow investors to predict returns on stocks. This research included numerous studies on "the January anomaly" and studies that consider other daily and weekly regularities.

The January Anomaly   Branch (1977) and Branch and Chang (1985) proposed a unique trading rule for those interested in taking advantage of tax selling. Investors (including institutions) tend to engage in tax selling toward the end of the year to establish losses on stocks that have declined. After the new year, the tendency is to reacquire these stocks or to buy similar stocks that look attractive. Such a scenario would produce downward pressure on stock prices in late November and December and positive pressure in early January. This seasonal pattern is inconsistent with the EMH since it should be eliminated by arbitrageurs who would buy in December and sell in early January.

A supporter of the hypothesis found that December trading volume was abnormally high for stocks that had declined during the previous year and that significant abnormal returns occurred during January for these stocks. It was concluded that, because of transaction costs, arbitrageurs must not be eliminating the January tax-selling anomaly. Subsequent analysis showed that most of the January effect was concentrated in the first week of trading, particularly on the first day of the year.

Several studies provided support for a January effect but were inconsistent with the tax-selling hypothesis because of what happened in foreign countries that did not have our tax laws. They found abnormal returns in January that could not be explained by tax laws. Also, the classic relationship between risk and return is strongest during January and there is a year-end trading volume bulge in late December and early January.

Another facet of the January effect (referred to as "the other January effect") is related to aggregate market returns. It is contended that stock market returns in January are a predictor of returns over the next 11 months of the year. Some studies have found strong support for this contention.

Other Calendar Effects   Several other "calendar" effects have been examined, including a monthly effect, a weekend/day-of-the-week effect, and an intraday effect. One study found that all the market's cumulative advance occurred during the first half of trading months.

An analysis of the weekend effect found that the mean return for Monday was significantly negative during five-year subperiods and a total period. In contrast, the average return for the other four days was positive.

A study decomposed the Monday effect that is typically measured from Friday close to Monday close into a *weekend effect* (from Friday close to Monday open), and a pure *Monday trading effect* (from Monday open to the Monday close). It was shown that the prior negative Monday effect actually occurs from the Friday close to the Monday open (it is really a weekend effect). After adjusting for this weekend effect, the pure Monday trading effect was positive. Subsequently, it was shown that the Monday effect was on average positive in January and negative for all other months.

Finally, for *large firms*, the negative Monday effect occurred before the market opened (it was a pure weekend effect), whereas for *smaller firms* most of the negative Monday effect occurred during the day on Monday (it was mainly a Monday trading effect).

---

[4]These academic studies, which have indicated the importance of earnings surprises, have led *The Wall Street Journal* to publish a section on earnings surprises in connection with regular quarterly earnings reports.

Predicting Cross-Sectional Returns   Assuming an efficient market, *all securities should have equal risk-adjusted returns* because security prices should reflect all public information that would influence the security's risk. Therefore, these studies attempt to determine if you can use public information to predict what stocks will enjoy above-average or below-average risk-adjusted returns.

These studies typically examine the usefulness of alternative measures of size or quality to rank stocks in terms of risk-adjusted returns. Note that all of these tests involve *a joint hypothesis* because they consider the efficiency of the market but also depend on the asset pricing model for the measure of risk used in the test. Specifically, if a test determines that it is possible to predict risk-adjusted returns, these results could occur because the market is not efficient, *or* they could be because the measure of risk is faulty and, therefore, the measures of risk-adjusted returns are wrong.

Price-Earnings Ratios   Numerous studies over time have examined the relationship between the historical **price-earnings (P/E) ratios** for stocks and the returns on the stocks. Some have suggested that low P/E stocks will outperform high P/E stocks because growth companies enjoy high P/E ratios, but the market tends to overestimate the growth potential and thus overvalues these growth companies, while undervaluing low-growth firms with low P/E ratios. A relationship between the historical P/E ratios and subsequent risk-adjusted market performance would constitute evidence against the semistrong EMH, because it implies that investors could use publicly available information regarding P/E ratios to predict future abnormal returns.

Risk-adjusted performance measures indicated that low P/E ratio stocks experienced superior risk-adjusted results relative to the market, whereas high P/E ratio stocks had significantly inferior risk-adjusted results.[5] These results are inconsistent with semistrong efficiency.

Peavy and Goodman (1983) examined P/E ratios with adjustments for firm size, industry effects, and infrequent trading and likewise found that the risk-adjusted returns for stocks in the lowest P/E ratio quintile were superior to those in the highest P/E ratio quintile.

Price-Earnings/Growth Rate (PEG) Ratios   During the past decade, there has been a significant increase in the use of the ratio of a stock's price-earnings ratio divided by the firm's expected growth rate of earnings (referred to as the PEG ratio) as a relative valuation tool, especially for stocks of growth companies with above-average P/E ratios. Advocates of the PEG ratio hypothesize an inverse relationship between the PEG ratio and subsequent rates of return—that is, they expect that stocks with relatively low PEG ratios (that is, less than one) will experience above-average rates of return while stocks with relatively high PEG ratios (that is, in excess of three or four) will have below-average rates of return. A study by Peters (1991) using quarterly rebalancing supported the hypothesis of an inverse relationship. These results would not support the EMH. A subsequent study by Reilly and Marshall (1999) assumed annual rebalancing and divided the sample on the basis of a risk measure (beta), market value size, and by expected growth rate. Except for stocks with low betas and very low expected growth rates, the results did not indicate an inverse relationship between the PEG ratio and subsequent rates of return.

In summary, the results related to using the PEG ratio to select stocks are mixed—several studies that assume either monthly or quarterly rebalancing indicate an anomaly because the authors use public information and derive above-average rates of return. In contrast, a study with more realistic annual rebalancing did not find a consistent relationship between the PEG ratio and subsequent rates of return.

The Size Effect   Banz (1981) examined the impact of size (measured by total market value) on the risk-adjusted rates of return. The risk-adjusted returns for extended periods (20 to

---

[5]Composite performance measures are discussed in Chapter 18.

35 years) indicated that the small firms consistently experienced significantly larger risk-adjusted returns than the larger firms. Reinganum (1981) contended that it was the size, not the P/E ratio, that caused the results discussed in the prior subsection, but this contention was disputed by Basu (1983).

Recall that abnormal returns may occur because the markets are inefficient or because the market model provides incorrect estimates of risk and expected returns. It was suggested that small firm risk was improperly measured because small firms are traded less frequently. An alternative risk measure technique confirmed that the small firms had much higher risk than previously measured, but the higher betas still did not account for the large difference in rates of return.

A study by Stoll and Whaley (1983) that examined the impact of transaction costs confirmed the size effect but also found that firms with small market value generally have low stock prices. Because transaction costs vary inversely with price per share, these costs must be considered when examining the small-firm effect. They found a significant difference in the percentage total transaction cost for large firms (2.71 percent) versus small firms (6.77 percent). This differential in transaction costs, assuming frequent trading, can have a significant impact on the results. Assuming daily transactions, the original small-firm effects are reversed. The point is, size-effect studies must consider realistic transaction costs and specify holding period assumptions. A study by Reinganum (1983) that considered both factors over long periods demonstrated that infrequent rebalancing (about once a year) is almost ideal; the results beat long-run buy-and-hold and avoid frequent rebalancing that causes excess costs. In summary, small firms outperformed large firms after considering higher risk and realistic transaction costs (assuming annual rebalancing).

Most studies on the size effect employed large databases and long time periods (over 50 years) to show that this phenomenon has existed for many years. In contrast, a study that examined the performance over various intervals of time concluded that *the small-firm effect is not stable.* During most periods, investigators found a negative relationship between size and return; but, during selected periods (such as 1967 to 1975), they found that large firms outperformed the small firms. Notably, this positive relationship (large firms outperformed) held during the following recent periods: 1984–1987; 1989–1990; 1995–1998; and during 2005–2009 on a risk-adjusted basis.[6] Reinganum (1992) acknowledges this instability but contends that the small-firm effect is still a long-run phenomenon.

In summary, firm size is a major efficient market anomaly. The two strongest explanations are higher risk measurements due to infrequent trading and the higher transaction costs. Depending on the frequency of trading, these two factors may account for much of the differential. Keim (1983) also related it to seasonality. These results indicate that the size effect must be considered in any event study that considers long time periods and contains a sample of firms with significantly different market values.

Neglected Firms and Trading Activity   Arbel and Strebel (1983) considered an additional influence beyond size: attention or neglect. They measured attention in terms of the number of analysts who regularly follow a stock and divided the stocks into three groups: (1) highly followed, (2) moderately followed, and (3) neglected. They confirmed the small-firm effect but also found a neglected-firm effect caused by the lack of information and limited institutional interest. The neglected-firm concept applied across size classes. Contrary results were reported by Beard and Sias (1997), who found no evidence of a neglected firm premium after controlling for capitalization.

---

[6]A sense of the significant difference in risk is provided by data from the Morningstar/Ibbotson SBBI data (2017) for the long-term period 1926–2016 that indicates a standard deviation for large-cap stocks at 19.9 percent versus 31.9 percent for small-cap stocks.

James and Edmister (1983) examined the impact of trading volume by considering the relationship between returns, market value, and trading activity. The results confirmed the relationship between size and rates of return, but the results indicated no significant difference between the mean returns of the highest and lowest trading activity portfolios.

Book Value–Market Value Ratio   This ratio relates the book value (*BV*) of a firm's equity to the market value (MV) of its equity. Rosenberg, Reid, and Lanstein (1985) found a significant positive relationship between current values for this ratio and future stock returns and contended that such a relationship between available public information on the BV/MV ratio and future returns was evidence against the EMH.[7]

Strong support for this ratio was provided by Fama and French (1992), who evaluated the joint effects of market beta, size, E/P ratio, leverage, and the BV/MV ratio (referred to as BE/ME) on a cross section of average returns. They analyzed the hypothesized positive relationship between beta and expected returns and found that this positive relationship held pre-1969 but disappeared during the period 1963 to 1990. In contrast, the negative relationship between size and average return was significant by itself and significant after inclusion of other variables.

In addition, they found a significant positive relationship between the BV/MV ratio and average return that persisted even when other variables are included. Most importantly, both size and the BV/MV ratio are significant when included together and they dominate other ratios. Specifically, although leverage and the *E/P* ratio were significant by themselves or with size, they become insignificant when *both* size and the BV/MV ratio are considered.

In summary, studies that have used publicly available ratios to predict the cross section of expected returns for stocks have provided substantial evidence in conflict with the semistrong-form EMH. Significant results were found for P/E ratios, market value size, and BV/MV ratios. Although the research by Fama and French indicated that the optimal combination appears to be size and the BV/MV ratio, a study by Jensen, Johnson, and Mercer (1997) indicated that this combination only works during periods of expansive monetary policy.

Results of Event Studies   Recall that the intent of event studies is to examine abnormal rates of return surrounding significant economic information. Those who advocate the EMH would expect returns to adjust quickly to announcements of new information such that investors cannot experience positive abnormal rates of return by acting after the announcement of an event. Because of space constraints, we can only summarize the results for some of the more popular events considered.

The discussion of results is organized by event or item of public information. Specifically, we will examine the price movements and profit potential surrounding stock splits, the sale of initial public offerings, exchange listings, unexpected world or economic events, and the announcements of significant accounting changes. Notably, the results for most of these studies have supported the semistrong-form EMH.

Stock Split Studies   Many investors believe that the prices of stocks that split will increase in value because the shares are priced lower, which increases demand for them. In contrast, advocates of efficient markets would not expect a change in value because the firm has simply issued additional stock and nothing fundamentally affecting the value of the firm has occurred.

The classic study by Fama, Fisher, Jensen, and Roll (1969), referred to hereafter as FFJR, hypothesized no significant price change following a stock split, because any relevant information (such as earnings growth) that caused the split would have already been discounted. The FFJR study analyzed abnormal price movements surrounding the time of the split and divided

---

[7]Many studies define this ratio as "book-to-market value" (BV/MV) because it implies a positive relationship, but most practitioners refer to it as the "price-to-book value" (P/B) ratio. Obviously, the concept is the same, but the sign changes.

the stock split sample into those stocks that did or did not raise their dividends. Both groups experienced positive abnormal price changes prior to the split. Stocks that split but did *not* increase their dividend experienced abnormal price *declines* following the split and within 12 months lost all their accumulated abnormal gains. In contrast, stocks that split and increased their dividend experienced no abnormal returns after the split.

These results support the semistrong EMH because they indicate that investors cannot gain from the information on a stock split after the public announcement. These results were confirmed by most (but not all) subsequent studies. In summary, most studies found no short-run or long-run positive impact on security returns because of a stock split, although the results are not unanimous.

Initial Public Offerings (IPOs)   During the past 30 years, a number of closely held companies have gone public by selling some of their common stock. Because of uncertainty about the appropriate offering price and the risk involved in underwriting such issues, it has been hypothesized that the underwriters would tend to underprice these new issues.

Given this general expectation of underpricing, the studies in this area have generally considered three sets of questions: (1) How great is the underpricing on average? Does the underpricing vary over time? If so, why? (2) What factors cause different amounts of underpricing for alternative issues? (3) How fast does the market price adjust for the underpricing?

As shown in Exhibit 5.1, the answer to the first question is an average underpricing of about 14 percent, but it varies over for the total period 1980–2016 and for various subperiods. The major variables that cause differential underpricing seem to be various risk measures, the size of the firm, the prestige of the underwriter, and the status of the company's accounting firm. On the question of direct interest to the EMH, results in Miller and Reilly (1987) and Ibbotson, Sindelar, and Ritter (1994) indicate that the price adjustment to the underpricing takes place within one day after the offering. Therefore, it appears that some underpricing occurs based on the original offering price, but the ones who benefit from this underpricing are basically the investors who receive allocations of the original issue. More specifically, institutional investors captured most (70 percent) of the short-term profits. This rapid adjustment of the initial underpricing would support the semistrong EMH. Finally, studies by Ritter (1991); Carter, Dark, and Singh (1998); and Loughran and Ritter (1995) that examined the long-run returns on IPOs indicate that investors who acquire the stock after the initial adjustment do *not* experience positive long-run abnormal returns.

Exhibit 5.1 Number of Offerings, Average First-Day Returns, and Gross Proceeds of Initial Public Offerings by Decade for the Period 1980–2016*

Year	Number of Offerings	Average First-Day Return[1]	Gross Proceeds ($ millions)[2]
1980–89	2,366	6.9	61,131
1990–99	4,192	21.0	294,890
2000–09	1,332	15.6	295,620
2010–16	874	15.5	211,455
1980–2016	**8,764**	**14.7**	**863,096**

*The period 2010–2016 is only seven years.
[1]First-day returns are computed as the percentage return from the offering price to the first closing market price.
[2]Gross proceeds exclude overallotment options but include the international tranche, if any. No adjustment for inflation has been made.
Source: Jay R. Ritter, "Number of Offerings, Average First-Day Returns, and Gross Products of Initial Public Offerings in 1980–2016" (University of Florida, January, 2017).

Exchange Listing   A significant economic event for a firm is the listing its stock on a national exchange, especially the NYSE. A listing is expected to increase the market liquidity of the stock and add to its prestige. An important question is: Can an investor derive abnormal returns from investing in the stock when a new listing is announced or around the time of the actual listing? The results regarding abnormal returns from such investing were mixed. All the studies agreed that (1) the stocks' prices increased before any listing announcements, and (2) stock prices consistently declined after the actual listing. The crucial question is: What happens between the announcement of the application for listing and the actual listing (a period of four to six weeks)? A study by McConnell and Sanger (1989) points toward profit opportunities immediately after the announcement that a firm is applying for listing and there is the possibility of excess returns (by selling short) from price declines after the actual listing. Finally, studies that have examined the impact of listing on the risk of the securities found no significant change in systematic risk or the firm's cost of equity.

In summary, because listing studies provide evidence of short-run profit opportunities for investors using public information, these studies would not support the semistrong-form EMH.

Unexpected World Events and Economic News   The results of studies that examined the response of security prices to world or economic news have supported the semistrong-form EMH. An analysis of the reaction of stock prices to unexpected world events, such as the Eisenhower heart attack, the Kennedy assassination, and major military events, found that prices adjusted to the news before the market opened or before it reopened after the announcement (generally, as with the World Trade Center attack, the Exchanges are closed immediately for various time periods—for example, one to four days). A study by Pierce and Roley (1985) that examined the response of stock prices to announcements about money supply, inflation, real economic activity, and the discount rate found an impact that did not persist beyond the announcement day. Finally, Jain (1988) did an analysis of an hourly response of stock returns and trading volume to surprise announcements and found that unexpected information about money supply impacted stock prices within one hour. For a review of studies that considered the impact of news on individual stocks, see Chan Wesley (2003).

Announcements of Accounting Changes   Numerous studies have analyzed the impact of announcements of accounting changes on stock prices. In efficient markets, security prices should react quickly and predictably to announcements of accounting changes that affect the economic value of the firm. An accounting change that affects reported earnings but has no economic significance should not affect stock prices. For example, when a firm changes its depreciation accounting method for reporting purposes from accelerated to straight line, the firm should experience an increase in reported earnings, but there is no economic consequence. An analysis of stock price movements surrounding a change in depreciation accounting supported the EMH because there were no positive price changes following the change. In fact, there were some negative price changes because firms making such an accounting change are typically performing poorly.

During periods of high inflation, many firms will change their inventory method from first-in, first-out (FIFO) to last-in, first-out (LIFO), which causes a decline in reported earnings but benefits the firm because it reduces the firm's taxable earnings and, therefore, tax expenses. Advocates of efficient markets would expect positive price changes because of the tax savings. Study results confirmed this expectation.

Therefore, studies such as those by Bernard and Thomas (1990) and Ou and Penman (1989) indicate that the securities markets react quite rapidly to accounting changes and adjust security prices as expected on the basis of changes in true value (that is, analysts pierce the accounting veil and value securities on the basis of relevant economic events).

Corporate Events   Corporate finance events such as mergers and acquisitions, spin-offs, reorganization, and various security offerings (common stock, straight bonds, convertible bonds) have been examined, relative to two general questions: (1) What is the market impact of these alternative events? (2) How fast does the market adjust the security prices?

Regarding the reaction to corporate events, the answer is very consistent—stock prices react as one would expect based on the underlying economic impact of the action. For example, the reaction to mergers is that the stock of the firm being acquired increases in line with the premium offered by the acquiring firm, whereas the stock of the acquiring firm typically declines because of the concern that they overpaid for the firm. On the question of speed of reaction, the evidence indicates fairly rapid adjustment—that is, the adjustment period declines as shorter interval data are analyzed (using daily data, most studies find that the price adjustment is completed in about three days). Studies related to financing decisions are reviewed by Smith (1986). Studies on corporate control that consider mergers and reorganizations are reviewed by Jensen and Warner (1988). Numerous corporate spin-offs have generated interesting stock performance as shown by Desai and Jain (1999) and Chemmanur and Yan (2004).

Summary on the Semistrong-Form EMH   Clearly, the evidence from tests of the semistrong EMH is mixed. The hypothesis receives almost unanimous support from the numerous event studies on a range of events including stock splits, initial public offerings, world events and economic news, accounting changes, and a variety of corporate finance events. About the only mixed results come from exchange listing studies.

In sharp contrast, the numerous studies on predicting rates of return over time or for a cross section of stocks presented evidence counter to semistrong efficiency. This included time-series studies on risk premiums, calendar patterns, and quarterly earnings surprises. Similarly, the results for cross-sectional predictors such as size, the *BV/MV* ratio (when there is expansive monetary policy), and P/E ratios also indicated anomalies counter to market efficiency.

Strong-Form Hypothesis: Tests and Results   The strong-form EMH contends that stock prices fully reflect *all information*, public and private. This implies that no group of investors has access to *private information* that will allow them to consistently experience above-average profits. This extremely rigid hypothesis requires not only that stock prices must adjust rapidly to new public information but also that no group has consistent access to private information.

Tests of the strong-form EMH have analyzed returns over time for different identifiable investment groups to determine whether any group consistently received above-average risk-adjusted returns. Such a group must have access to and act upon important private information or an ability to act on public information before other investors, which would indicate that security prices were not adjusting rapidly to *all* new information.

Investigators have tested this form of the EMH by analyzing the performance of three major groups of investors: (1) *corporate insiders*, (2) *security analysts* at Value Line and elsewhere, and (3) *professional money managers*.

Corporate Insider Trading   Corporate insiders are required to report monthly to the SEC on their transactions (purchases or sales) in the stock of the firm for which they are insiders. Insiders include major corporate officers, members of the board of directors, and owners of 10 percent or more of any equity class of securities. About six weeks after the reporting period, this insider trading information is made public by the SEC. These insider trading data have been used to identify how corporate insiders have traded and determine whether they bought on balance before abnormally good price movements and sold on balance before poor market periods for their stock. Studies by Chowdhury, Howe, and Lin (1993) and Pettit and Venkatesh (1995) indicated that corporate insiders consistently enjoyed above-average profits, based on selling prior to low returns and not selling before strong returns. This implies that many insiders had private information from which they derived above-average returns on their company stock.

In addition, an early study found that *public* investors who consistently traded with the insiders based on announced insider transactions would have enjoyed excess risk-adjusted returns (after commissions). Notably, a subsequent study concluded that the market had eliminated this inefficiency after considering total transaction costs.

Overall, these results provide mixed support for the EMH because several studies indicate that insiders experience abnormal profits. In contrast, pre-2006 studies indicate that noninsiders cannot use this information to generate excess returns. Notably, because of investor interest in these insider trading data as a result of academic research, *The Wall Street Journal* currently publishes a monthly column entitled "Inside Track" that discusses the largest insider transactions.

Security Analysts Several studies have attempted to identify a set of analysts who have the ability to select undervalued stocks. The analysis involves determining whether, after a public stock recommendation by an analyst, a significant abnormal return is available to investors who follow these recommendations. These studies and those that examine performance by money managers are more realistic and relevant than those that considered corporate insiders because these analysts and money managers are full-time investment professionals with no obvious advantage except emphasis and training. If anyone should be able to select undervalued stocks, it should be these "pros." We initially examine Value Line rankings and then recommendations by individual analysts.

The Value Line Enigma Value Line (VL) is a large well-known advisory service that publishes financial information on approximately 1,700 stocks. Included in its report is a timing rank, which indicates Value Line's expectation regarding a firm's common stock performance over the coming 12 months. A rank of 1 is the most favorable performance metric and 5 is the worst. This ranking system, initiated in April 1965, assigns numbers based on four factors:

1. An earnings and price rank of each security relative to all others
2. A price momentum factor
3. Year-to-year relative changes in quarterly earnings
4. A quarterly earnings "surprise" factor (actual quarterly earnings compared with VL estimated earnings)

The firms are ranked based on a composite score for each firm. The top and bottom 100 are ranked 1 and 5, respectively; the next 300 from the top and bottom are ranked 2 and 4; and the rest (approximately 900) are ranked 3. Rankings are assigned every week based on the latest data. Notably, all the data used to derive the four factors are public information.

Several years after the ranking was started, Value Line contended that the stocks rated 1 substantially outperformed the market and the stocks rated 5 seriously underperformed the market (the performance figures did not include dividend income but also did not charge commissions).

Early studies on the Value Line enigma indicated that there was information in the VL rankings (especially rank 1 or 5) and in changes in the rankings (especially going from 2 to 1). Evidence indicates that the market is fairly efficient, because the abnormal adjustments appear to be complete by Day + 2. A time series analysis indicates a faster adjustment to the rankings during recent years. Also, despite statistically significant price changes, some evidence indicates that it is not possible to derive abnormal returns from these announcements after considering pre-2006 transaction costs. As before, it would be informative to reconsider those results with current transaction costs. The strongest evidence regarding not being able to benefit from this information is that Value Line's Centurion Fund, which concentrates on investing in rank-1 stocks, has typically underperformed the market.

Analysts' Recommendations   There is evidence in favor of the existence of superior analysts who apparently possess private information. A study by Womack (1996) found that analysts appear to have both market timing and stock-picking ability, especially in connection with relatively rare sell recommendations. In contrast, Jegadeesh et al. (2004) found that consensus recommendations by a group of analysts who follow a stock do not contain incremental information for most stocks beyond available market signals (momentum and volume), but *changes* in consensus recommendations are useful. Alternatively, research by Ivkovic and Jegadeesh (2004) indicated that the most useful information consisted of upward earning revisions in the week prior to earnings announcements. A subsequent study examined the information content of analyst recommendations after the passage of Regulation Fair Disclosure (REGFD) and concluded that recommendation *changes* continue to be informative.

Performance of Professional Money Managers

The studies of professional money managers are more realistic than the analysis of insiders because money managers typically do not have monopolistic access to important new information but are highly trained professionals who work full time at investment management. Therefore, if any "normal" set of investors should be able to derive above-average profits, it should be this group because they conduct extensive management interviews and they may have the benefit of input from some superior analysts noted above.

Most studies on the performance of money managers have examined mutual funds because performance data are readily available for them. Regarding the performance by mutual funds, three articles in financial publications have discussed the performance of active fund managers compared to their benchmarks during various periods ending in December 2016 ("The Big Squeeze," 2017; Malkiel, 2017; Zweig, 2017). The Malkiel (2017) article noted that during the year 2016, 67 percent of large-cap managers and 85 percent of small-cap managers *underperformed* their S&P indexes. More damaging, over the 15-year period ending in 2016, 90 percent of active domestic managers *underperformed* their benchmark indexes, 89 percent of active international funds had *inferior* relative performance, and 89 percent of active emerging market funds *underperformed* their benchmarks.

The article by Zweig (2017) concentrated on the performance of active managers during declining markets over the 45 years from 1962 to 2016 because some observers speculate that although active managers do not appear to outperform during rising markets, they might protect investors during declining periods. He considered markets in 2007–2009, 2000–2002, and 1973–1974 and showed that in every "bear market," the declines in stock prices were almost equal for the aggregate stock market and the composite of actively managed mutual funds.

The article in *The Economist* ("The Big Squeeze," 2017) was primarily concerned with the current future consolidation of the fund-management industry that is in response to the generally inferior performance of the mutual funds relative to passive benchmarks. His evidence is similar to the results reported by Malkiel: Over the 15 years to the end of 2016, fewer than 8 percent of American equity funds managed to outperform their benchmarks.

Notably, all of these articles acknowledged that some funds were able to outperform their benchmarks, but this superior performance was sporadic, and individual managers were generally not able to outperform consistently. In addition, all the articles noted that the major reasons for the inferior performance were the added cost of active management including personnel (analysts); trading expenses, and the higher management fees.

These results support the strong-form EMH and suggest that investors should seriously consider investing in a diversified portfolio of passive index funds.

Now that it is possible to get performance data for pension plans and endowment funds, several studies have documented that the performances of pension plans likewise did not match that of the aggregate market. The performance by endowments is interesting.

Specifically, the results for a large sample of endowments confirm the inability to outperform the market. In contrast, the largest endowments in terms of size experienced superior risk-adjusted performance because of their ability and willingness to consider a wide variety of asset classes such as venture capital, private equity, unique hedge funds, real estate, and commodities on a global basis.

Conclusions Regarding the Strong-Form EMH   The tests of the strong-form EMH have generated mixed results. The result for corporate insiders did not support the hypothesis because these individuals apparently have monopolistic access to important information and use it to derive above-average returns.

Tests to determine whether there are any analysts with private information concentrated on the Value Line rankings and publications of analysts' recommendations. The results for Value Line rankings have changed over time and currently tend toward support for the EMH. Specifically, the adjustment to rankings and ranking changes is fairly rapid, and it appears that trading is not profitable after transaction costs. Alternatively, individual analysts' recommendations and changes in overall consensus estimates seem to contain significant information.

Finally, historical performance by professional money managers provided support for the strong-form EMH. Almost all recent money manager performance studies have indicated that these highly trained, full-time investors could not consistently outperform a simple buy-and-hold policy on a risk-adjusted basis. Because money managers are similar to most investors who do not have access to inside information, these recent results are more relevant to the hypothesis. Therefore, there is positive support for the strong-form EMH as applied to most investors.

5.2 Behavioral Finance[8]

Our discussion up to this point has dealt with standard finance theory and how to test within this theoretical context whether capital markets are informationally efficient. However, in the 1990s, a new branch of financial economics was added to the mix. **Behavioral finance** considers how various psychological traits affect how individuals or groups act as investors, analysts, and portfolio managers. As noted by Olsen (1998), behavioral finance advocates recognize that the standard finance model of rational behavior and profit maximization can be true within specific boundaries, but they assert that it is an *incomplete* model since it does not consider individual behavior. It is argued that some financial phenomena can be better explained using models where it is recognized that some investors are *not* fully rational or realize that it is *not* possible for arbitrageurs to offset all instances of mispricing (Barberis and Thaler, 2003). Specifically, according to Olsen (1998), behavioral finance

> *seeks to understand and predict systematic financial market implications of psychological decisions processes ... behavioral finance is focused on the implication of psychological and economic principles for the improvement of financial decision-making. (p. 11)*

In the preface for Wood (2010), the editor provides a helpful description of behavioral finance, alluding to a river with three tributaries that form the river of behavioral finance: (1) *psychology* that focuses on individual behavior, (2) *social psychology*, which is the study of how we behave and make decisions in the presence of others, and (3) *neurofinance*, which is the anatomy, mechanics, and functioning of the brain. It is contended that the goal of research in this area is to help us understand how and why we make choices.

---

[8]The discussion in this section was enhanced by two survey articles by Barberis and Thaler (2003) and by Hirschleifer (2001) and also by wonderful presentations at the CFA Research Foundation Workshop in Vancouver (May 2008), and finally a monograph from the Research Foundation of CFA Institute that contains a set of insightful articles edited by Arnold S. Wood (2010), titled *Behavioral Finance and Investment Management*.

While it is still being debated whether there is a unified theory of behavioral finance, the emphasis has been twofold. First, on identifying portfolio anomalies that can be explained by various psychological traits in individuals and, second, identifying groups or pinpointing instances when it is possible to experience above-normal rates of return by exploiting the biases of investors, analysts, or portfolio managers. Notably, this branch of Finance has been significantly enhanced by Richard Thaler being awarded the 2017 Nobel Prize in Financial Economics for his contributions in this area.

5.2.1 Explaining Biases

Over time it has been noted that investors have a number of biases that negatively affect their investment performance. Advocates of behavioral finance have been able to explain a number of these biases based on psychological characteristics. One major bias documented by Scott, Stumpp, and Xu (1999) is the propensity of investors to hold on to "losers" too long and sell "winners" too soon. Apparently, investors fear losses much more than they value gains—a tendency toward loss aversion. This aversion is explained by *prospect theory*, which contends that utility depends on deviations from moving reference points rather than absolute wealth.

There are two related biases that seriously impact analysis and investment decisions. The first is *belief perseverance*, which means that once people have formed an opinion (on a company or stock) they cling to it too tightly and for too long. As a result, they are reluctant to search for contradictory beliefs, and even when they find such evidence, they are very skeptical about it or even misinterpret such information. A related bias is *anchoring*, wherein individuals who are asked to estimate something, start with an initial arbitrary (casual) value and then adjust away from it. The problem is that the adjustment is often insufficient. Therefore, if your initial estimate is low, you may raise it with information, but it is likely you will not raise it enough and thus will still end up below the "best estimates."

Another bias documented by Solt and Statman (1989) for growth companies is *overconfidence* in forecasts, which causes analysts to overestimate the rates of growth and the duration of this growth for "growth" companies and overemphasize good news and ignore negative news for these firms. Analysts and many investors also suffer from *representativeness*, which causes them to believe that the stocks of growth companies will be "good" stocks. This bias is also referred to as *confirmation bias*, whereby investors look for information that supports prior opinions and decisions they have made. They also experience sample size neglect wherein they are prone to extrapolate the high growth results from a few past years (for example, four to six years) for long-term future periods. As a result, they will misvalue the stocks of these generally popular companies. Overconfidence is also related to *self-attribution bias* where people have a tendency to ascribe any success to their own talents while blaming any failure on "bad luck," which causes them to overestimate their talent (Gervais and Odean, 2001). Overconfidence is also nurtured by *hindsight bias*, which is a tendency after an event for an individual to believe that he or she predicted it, which causes people to think that they can predict better than they can.

A study by Brown (1999) examined the effect of *noise traders* (nonprofessionals with no special information) on the volatility of closed-end mutual funds. When there is a shift in sentiment, these traders move together, which increases the prices and the volatility of these securities during trading hours. Also, Clarke and Statman (1998) found that noise traders tend to follow newsletter writers, who in turn tend to "follow the herd." These writers and "the herd" are almost always wrong, which contributes to excess volatility.

Shefrin (2001) describes *escalation bias*, which causes investors to put more money into a failure that they feel responsible for rather than into a success. This leads to the relatively popular investor practice of "averaging down" on an investment that has declined in value since the initial purchase rather than consider selling the stock if it was a mistake. The thinking is that if it was a buy at $40, it is a screaming bargain at $30. Obviously, an alternative solution is to reevaluate the stock to see if some important bad news was missed in the initial valuation (therefore, sell it and accept the loss), or to confirm the initial valuation and acquire more of the "bargain." The difficult psychological factor noted by Shefrin (1999) is that you must seriously look for the bad news and consider the negative effects of this news on the valuation.

5.2.2 Fusion Investing

According to Charles Lee (2003), *fusion investing* is the integration of two elements of investment valuation—fundamental value and investor sentiment. In Robert Shiller's (1984) formal model, the market price of securities is the expected dividends discounted to infinity (its fundamental value) plus a term that indicates the demand from noise traders who reflect investor sentiment. It is contended that when noise traders are bullish, stock prices will be higher than normal or higher than what is justified by fundamentals. Under this combination pricing model of fusion investing, investors should engage in fundamental analysis but also should consider investor sentiment in terms of fads and fashions. During some periods, investor sentiment is rather muted and noise traders are inactive, so that fundamental valuation dominates market returns. In other periods, when investor sentiment is strong, noise traders are very active and market returns are more heavily impacted by investor sentiments. Both investors and analysts should be cognizant of these dual effects on the aggregate market, various economic sectors, and individual stocks.

Beyond advocating awareness of the dual components of fusion investing, results from other studies have documented that fundamental valuation may be the dominant factor but it takes much longer to assert itself—about three years. To derive some estimate of changing investor sentiment, Lee proposes several measures of investor sentiment, most notably analysts' recommendations, price momentum, and high trading turnover. Significant changes in these variables for a stock will indicate a movement from a glamour stock to a neglected stock or vice versa. The market price of a glamour stock will exceed its intrinsic value while a neglected stock will sell at a discount to its intrinsic value. This view of neglected stocks is similar to the expectation for these stocks in the semistrong studies.

5.3 IMPLICATIONS OF EFFICIENT CAPITAL MARKETS

Having reviewed the results of numerous studies related to different facets of the EMH, the important question is: What does this mean to individual investors, financial analysts, portfolio managers, and institutions? Overall, the results of many studies indicate that the capital markets are efficient as related to numerous sets of information. At the same time, research has uncovered a number of instances where the market fails to adjust prices rapidly to public information. Given these mixed results regarding efficient capital markets, we need to consider the implications of this contrasting evidence.

The following discussion considers the implications of both sets of evidence. Specifically given results that support the EMH, we consider what techniques will not work and what you should do if you cannot beat the market. In contrast, because of the evidence that fails to support the EMH, we discuss what information and psychological biases should be considered when attempting to derive superior investment results through active security valuation and portfolio management.[9]

5.3.1 Efficient Markets and Fundamental Analysis

As you know from our prior discussion, fundamental analysts believe that, at any time, there is a basic intrinsic value for the aggregate stock market, various industries, or individual

---

[9]Because the next section of the chapter contains a full presentation regarding technical analysis, we will defer the discussion of efficient markets and technical analysis to the end of the chapter.

securities and that these values depend on underlying economic factors. Therefore, investors should determine the intrinsic value of an investment asset by examining the variables that determine value such as future earnings or cash flows, interest rates, and risk variables. If the prevailing market price differs from the estimated intrinsic value by enough to cover transaction costs, you buy if the market price is substantially below intrinsic value and do not buy, or you sell, if the market price is above the intrinsic value. Fundamental analysts believe that, occasionally, market price and intrinsic value differ but eventually investors recognize the discrepancy and correct it.

An investor who can do a superior job of *estimating* intrinsic value can consistently make superior market timing (asset allocation) decisions or acquire undervalued securities and generate above-average returns. Fundamental analysis involves aggregate market analysis, industry analysis, company analysis, and portfolio management. The divergent results from the EMH research have important implications for all of these components.

Aggregate Market Analysis with Efficient Capital Markets Chapter 8 makes a strong case that intrinsic value analysis should begin with aggregate market analysis. Still, the EMH implies that if you examine only *past* economic events, it is unlikely that you will outperform a buy-and-hold policy because the market rapidly adjusts to known economic events. Evidence suggests that the market experiences long-run price movements; but, to take advantage of these movements in an efficient market, you must do a superior job of *estimating* the relevant variables that cause these long-run movements. Put another way, if you only use *historical* data to estimate future values and invest on the basis of these "old news" estimates, you will *not* experience superior, risk-adjusted returns.

Industry and Company Analysis with Efficient Capital Markets As we discuss in Chapter 9, the wide distribution of returns from different industries and from different companies in an industry clearly justifies industry and company analysis. Again, the EMH does not contradict the potential value of such analysis but implies that you need to (1) understand the relevant variables that affect rates of return, and (2) do a superior job of *estimating future* values for these relevant valuation variables. To demonstrate this, Malkiel and Cragg (1970) developed a model that did an excellent job of explaining past stock price movements using historical data. When this valuation model was employed to project *future* stock price changes using *past* company data, however, the results were consistently inferior to a buy-and-hold policy. This implies that, even with a good valuation model, you *cannot* select stocks that will provide superior future returns using only past data as inputs. The point is, most analysts are aware of the several well-specified valuation models, so the factor that differentiates superior from inferior analysts is the ability to *provide more accurate estimates* of the critical inputs to the valuation models *and be different from the consensus.*

A study by Benesh and Peterson (1986) showed that the crucial difference between the stocks that enjoyed the best and worst price performance during a given year was the relationship between expected earnings of professional analysts and actual earnings (that is, it was *earnings surprises*). Specifically, stock prices increased if actual earnings substantially exceeded expected earnings and stock prices fell if actual earnings were below expected levels. As suggested by Fogler (1993), if you can do a superior job of projecting earnings and your expectations *differ from the consensus* (that is, you project earnings surprises), you will have a superior stock selection record. To summarize this discussion, two factors are required to be a **superior analyst**: (1) You must be *correct* in your estimates, and (2) you must be *different* from the consensus. Remember, if you are only correct and not different, that assumes you were predicting the consensus and the consensus was correct, which implies no surprise and no abnormal price movement.

The quest to be a superior analyst holds some good news and some suggestions. The good news is that the strong-form tests that indicated the likely existence of superior analysts.

The rankings by Value Line contained information value, even though it might not be possible to profit from the work of these analysts after transaction costs. Also, the price adjustments to the publication of analyst recommendations also point to the existence of superior analysts. The point is, there are a limited number of superior analysts, and it is *not* easy to be among this select group. Most notably, to be a superior analyst, you must do a superior job of *estimating* the relevant valuation variables and *predicting earnings surprises*, which implies that *you differ from the consensus*, and you should consistently identify undervalued or overvalued securities.

The suggestions for the information that should be used in fundamental analysis are based on the studies that considered the cross section of future returns. Recall that these studies indicated that P/E ratios, market value, size, and the *BV/MV* ratios were able to differentiate future return patterns with size and the *BV/MV* ratio appearing to be the optimal combination. Therefore, these factors should be considered when selecting a universe or analyzing firms. In addition, the evidence suggests that neglected firms should be given extra consideration. Although these ratios and characteristics are useful in isolating superior stocks from a large sample, it is our suggestion that they are best used to derive a viable sample to analyze from the total universe (for example, select 200 stocks to analyze from a universe of 3,000). Then the 200 stocks should be rigorously valued using the techniques discussed in subsequent chapters.

How to Evaluate Analysts or Investors If you want to determine if an individual is a superior analyst or investor, you should examine the performance of numerous securities that this analyst or investor recommends over time in relation to the performance of a set of randomly selected stocks of the same risk class. The stock selections of a superior analyst or investor should *consistently* outperform the randomly selected stocks. The consistency requirement is crucial because you would expect a portfolio developed by random selection to outperform the market about half the time.

Conclusions about Fundamental Analysis A text on investments can indicate the relevant variables that you should analyze and describe the important analysis techniques, but actually estimating the future values for the relevant variables is as much an art and a product of hard work as it is a science. If the estimates could be done on the basis of some mechanical formula, you could program a computer to do it, and there would be no need for analysts. Therefore, the superior analyst or successful investor must understand what variables are relevant to the valuation process and have the ability and work ethic to do a superior job of *estimating* values for these important valuation variables. There is no magic formula for superior estimation. Many times it simply means digging deeper and wider in your analysis to derive a better understanding of the economy, the industry and the firm. Alternatively, one can be superior if he or she has the ability to interpret the impact or estimate the effect of some public information better than others due to this better understanding.

5.3.2 Efficient Markets and Portfolio Management

As noted, studies have indicated that the majority of professional money managers cannot beat a buy-and-hold policy on a risk-adjusted basis. One explanation for this generally inferior performance is that there are no superior analysts and the cost of research and trading forces the results of merely adequate analysis into the inferior category. Another explanation, which is favored by the authors and has some empirical support from the Value Line and analyst recommendation results, is that money management firms employ both superior and inferior analysts and the gains from the recommendations by the few superior analysts are offset by the costs and the poor results derived from the recommendations of the inferior analysts.

This raises the question: Should a portfolio be managed actively or passively? The following discussion indicates that the decision of how to manage the portfolio (actively or passively) depends on whether the manager (or an investor) has access to superior analysts. A portfolio manager with superior analysts can manage a portfolio actively by looking for undervalued or overvalued securities and trading accordingly. In contrast, without access to superior analysts, you should manage passively and assume that all securities are properly priced based on their levels of risk.

Portfolio Management with Superior Analysts A portfolio manager with access to superior analysts who have unique insights and analytical ability should follow their recommendations. The superior analysts should make investment recommendations for a certain proportion of the portfolio, and the portfolio manager should ensure that the risk preferences of the client are maintained.

Also, the superior analysts should be encouraged to concentrate their efforts in mid-cap and small-cap stocks that possess the liquidity required by institutional portfolio managers. But because these stocks typically do not receive the attention given the top-tier stocks, the markets for these neglected stocks may be less efficient than the market for large well-known stocks that are being analyzed by numerous analysts—for example, the number of analysts that follow top-tier stocks ranges from 25 to 40.

Recall that capital markets are expected to be efficient because many investors receive new information and analyze its effect on security values. If the analysts following a stock differ, one could conceive of differences in the efficiency of the markets. New information on top-tier stocks is well publicized and rigorously analyzed, so the price of these securities should adjust rapidly to reflect the new information. In contrast, mid-cap and small-cap stocks receive less publicity and fewer analysts follow these firms, so prices may differ from intrinsic value for one of two reasons. First, because of less publicity, there is less information available on these firms. Second, there are fewer analysts following these firms so the adjustment to the new information is slowed. Therefore, the possibility of finding temporarily undervalued securities among these neglected stocks is greater. Recall that these superior analysts should pay particular attention to the *BV/MV* ratio, to the size of stocks being analyzed, and to the monetary policy environment.

Portfolio Management without Superior Analysts A portfolio manager (or investor) who does not have access to superior analysts should proceed as follows. First, he or she should *measure the risk preferences* of his or her clients, then build a portfolio to match this risk level by investing a certain proportion of the portfolio in risky assets and the rest in a risk-free asset, as discussed in Chapter 7.

The risky asset portfolio must be *completely diversified* on a global basis so it moves consistently with the world market. In this context, proper diversification means eliminating all unsystematic (unique) variability. In our prior discussion, it was estimated that it required about 20 securities to gain most of the benefits (more than 90 percent) of a completely diversified portfolio. More than 100 stocks are required for complete diversification. To decide how many securities to actually include in your global portfolio, you must balance the added benefits of complete worldwide diversification against the costs of research for the additional stocks.

Finally, you should *minimize transaction costs*. Assuming that the portfolio is completely diversified and is structured for the desired risk level, excessive transaction costs that do not generate added returns will detract from your expected rate of return. Three factors are involved in minimizing total transaction costs:

1. *Minimize taxes.* Methods of accomplishing this objective vary, but it should receive prime consideration.
2. *Reduce trading turnover.* Trade only to sell overvalued stock out of the portfolio or add undervalued stock while maintaining a given risk level.
3. *When you trade, minimize liquidity costs by trading relatively liquid stocks.* To accomplish this, submit limit orders to buy or sell several stocks at prices that approximate the

market-makers quote. That is, you would put in limit orders to buy stock at the bid price or sell at the ask price. The stock bought or sold first is the most liquid one; all other orders should be withdrawn.

In summary, if you lack access to superior analysts, you should do the following:

1. Determine and quantify your risk preferences.
2. Construct the appropriate risk portfolio by dividing the total portfolio between risk-free assets and a risky asset portfolio.
3. Diversify completely on a global basis to eliminate all unsystematic risk.
4. Maintain the specified risk level by rebalancing when necessary.
5. Minimize total transaction costs.

The Rationale and Use of Index Funds and Exchange-Traded Funds As discussed, efficient capital markets and a lack of superior analysts imply that many portfolios should be managed *passively* to match the performance of the aggregate market, minimizing the costs of research and trading. In response to this demand, several institutions have introduced *index funds*, which are security portfolios designed to duplicate the composition, and performance, of a selected market index series.

Notably, this concept of stock-market index funds has been extended to other areas of investments and, as discussed by Gastineau (2001) and Kostovetsky (2003), has been enhanced by the introduction of exchange-traded funds (ETFs). Index bond funds attempt to emulate the bond-market indexes discussed in Chapter 4. Also, some index funds focus on specific segments of the market such as international bond-index funds, international stock-index funds that target specific countries, and index funds that target small-cap stocks in the United States and Japan. When financial planners want a given asset class in their portfolios, they often use index funds or ETFs to fulfill this need. Index funds or ETFs are less costly in terms of research and commissions, and, they generally provide the same or better performance than the majority of active portfolio managers. An innovation suggested by Arnott, Hsu, and West (2008) is to weight the stocks in an index fund based on fundamentals such as earnings, cash flow, and/or dividends rather than market values.

Insights from Behavioral Finance As noted earlier, the major contributions of behavioral finance researchers are explanations for some of the anomalies discovered by prior academic research. They also suggest opportunities to derive abnormal rates of return by acting on some of the deeply ingrained biases of investors. Clearly, their findings support the notion that the stocks of growth companies typically will not be growth stocks because analysts become overconfident in their ability to predict future growth rates and eventually derive valuations that either fully value or overvalue future growth. Behavioral finance research also supports the notion of contrary investing, confirming the notion of the herd mentality of analysts in stock recommendations or quarterly earning estimates and the recommendations by newsletter writers. Also, it is important to recall the loss aversion and escalation bias that causes investors to ignore bad news and hold losers too long and in some cases acquire additional shares of losers to average down the cost. Before averaging down, be sure you reevaluate the stock and consider all the potential bad news we tend to ignore. Finally, recognize that market prices are a combination of fundamental value and investor sentiment.

5.4 TECHNICAL ANALYSIS

Technical analysis is generally considered to be directly counter to the efficient market hypothesis (EMH). We consider it in the same chapter with efficient markets to ensure that the significant differences between these two concepts are clear. Put another way, we believe that it is not possible to understand either concept without a strong understanding of both of them. Beyond this joint understanding, we also believe that a strong understanding of technical analysis is important for a well-rounded investor simply because its use is so pervasive among investment professionals. The point is, as an investor or an investment professional, you will consistently be exposed to literature or presentations that use or imply technical terms or techniques—in many cases interspersed with fundamental analysis and conclusions. Therefore, you may or may not believe in technical analysis, but *you should understand it*—and helping you understand it is the purpose of this section.

> *The market reacted yesterday to the report of a large increase in the short interest on the NYSE.*
> *Although the market declined today, it was not considered bearish because of the light volume.*
> *The market declined today after three days of increases due to profit taking by investors.*
> *The market is benefiting from strong positive momentum.*
> *The fact that the vast majority of advisory services are quite bullish generally signals the end of a bull market or at least a correction.*

Statements such as these appear daily in the financial news, and each has as its rationale one of numerous technical trading rules. Technical analysts, technicians, or market analysts develop technical trading rules from observations of past price movements of the stock market and individual stocks. The philosophy behind technical analysis is in sharp contrast to the EMH that we discussed earlier in this chapter, which contends that past performance has no influence on future performance or market values. It also differs from the fundamental analysis we will discuss in future chapters, which involves making investment decisions based on the examination of the economy, an industry, and company variables that lead to an estimate of intrinsic value for an investment, which is then compared to its prevailing market price. In contrast to the efficient market hypothesis or fundamental analysis, **technical analysis**, according to the Market Technicians Association, is a method of evaluating securities by analyzing statistics generated by market activity. Whereas fundamental analysts use economic data that are usually separate from the stock or bond market, technical analysts use data *from the market itself*, such as prices and the volume of trading, because they contend that *the market is its own best predictor*. Therefore, technical analysis is an alternative method of making the investment decision and answering the questions What securities should an investor buy or sell? and When should these investments be made?

Technical analysts see no need to study the multitude of economic, industry, and company variables to arrive at an estimate of future value because they believe that past price and volume movements or some other market series will signal future price movements. Technicians also believe that a change in the price trend may predict a forthcoming change in some fundamental variables, such as earnings and risk, before the change is perceived by most fundamental analysts. Are technicians correct? Many investors using these techniques claim to have experienced superior rates of return on many investments. In addition, many newsletter writers base their recommendations on technical analysis. Finally, even the major investment firms that employ many fundamental analysts also employ technical (market) analysts to provide investment advice. Numerous investment professionals and individual investors believe in and use technical trading rules to make their investment decisions. Thus, we begin this section with an examination of the basic philosophy underlying technical analysis. Subsequently, we consider the advantages and potential problems with the technical approach. Finally, we present alternative technical trading rules.

5.4.1 Underlying Assumptions of Technical Analysis

Technical analysts base trading decisions on examinations of prior price and volume data to determine past market trends from which they predict future behavior for the market as a whole and for individual securities. Several assumptions lead to this view of price movements. Certain aspects of these assumptions are controversial, leading advocates of efficient markets to question their validity. We have italicized those aspects in the following list:

1. The market value of any good or service is determined solely by the interaction of supply and demand.
2. Supply and demand are governed by numerous rational and irrational factors. Included in these factors are economic variables considered by the fundamental analyst as well as opinions, moods, and guesses. The market weighs all these factors continually and automatically.
3. Disregarding minor fluctuations, *the prices for individual securities and the overall value of the market tend to move in trends, which persist for appreciable lengths of time.*
4. Prevailing trends change in reaction to shifts in supply and demand relationships. These shifts, no matter why they occur, *can be detected sooner or later in the action of the market itself.*

The first two assumptions are almost universally accepted by technicians and nontechnicians alike. Almost anyone who has had a basic course in economics would agree that, at any point in time, the price of a security (or any good or service) is determined by the interaction of supply and demand. In addition, most observers would acknowledge that supply and demand are governed by many variables. The only difference in opinion might concern the influence of the irrational factors. Certainly, everyone would agree that the market continually weighs all these factors.

In contrast, there is a significant difference of opinion regarding the assumption about the *speed of adjustment* of stock prices to changes in supply and demand. Technical analysts expect stock prices to move in trends that persist for long periods because they believe that new information does *not* come to the market at one point in time but rather enters the market *over a period of time*. This pattern of information access occurs because of different sources of information or because certain investors receive the information earlier than others. As various groups—ranging from insiders to well-informed professionals to the average investor—receive the information and buy or sell a security accordingly, its price moves *gradually* toward the new equilibrium. Therefore, technicians do not expect the price adjustment to be as abrupt as fundamental analysts and efficient market supporters do; rather, they expect a *gradual price adjustment* to reflect the gradual dissemination of information.

Exhibit 5.2 shows this process, wherein new information causes a decrease in the equilibrium price for a security but the price adjustment is not rapid. It occurs as a trend that persists until the stock reaches its new equilibrium. Technical analysts look for the beginning of a

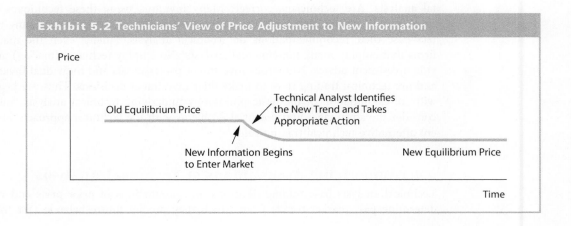

Exhibit 5.2 Technicians' View of Price Adjustment to New Information

movement from one equilibrium value to a new equilibrium value but do not attempt to predict the new equilibrium value. They attempt to create techniques that will identify the start of a change so that they can get on the bandwagon early and benefit from the move to the new equilibrium price by buying if the trend is up or selling if the trend is down. Obviously, with a rapid adjustment of prices to the new information (as expected by those who espouse an efficient market), the ride on the bandwagon would be so short that investors could not benefit.

5.5 ADVANTAGES OF TECHNICAL ANALYSIS

Although technicians understand the logic of fundamental analysis, they see several benefits in their approach. Most technical analysts admit that a fundamental analyst with good information, good analytical ability, and a keen sense of information's impact on the market should achieve above-average returns. However, this statement requires qualification. According to technical analysts, it is important to recognize that the fundamental analysts can experience superior returns *only* if they obtain new information before other investors and process it *correctly* and *quickly*. Technical analysts do not believe the majority of investors can consistently get new information before other investors and consistently process it correctly and quickly. Further, technicians attempt to take the emotion out of investing by applying rules that usually apply to almost every investment.

In addition, technical analysts claim that an advantage of their method is that *it is not heavily dependent on financial accounting statements*—the major source of information about the past performance of a firm or industry. As discussed in future chapters, the fundamental analyst evaluates such statements to help project future earning, cash flow and risk characteristics for industries and individual securities. The technician contends that there are several major problems with accounting statements:

1. They lack information needed by security analysts, such as information related to sales, earnings, and capital utilized by product line and customers.
2. According to GAAP (Generally Accepted Accounting Principles), corporations may choose among several procedures for reporting expenses, assets, or liabilities. Notably, these alternative procedures can produce vastly different values for expenses, income, return on assets, and return on equity, depending on whether the firm is conservative or aggressive. Hence, an investor can have trouble comparing the statements of two firms within the same industry, or firms across industries.
3. Many psychological factors and other nonquantifiable variables do not appear in financial statements. Examples include employee training and loyalty, customer goodwill, general investor attitude toward an industry, and political risk for an industry or a country.

Therefore, because technicians are suspicious of financial statements, they consider it advantageous not to depend on them. In contrast, most of the data used by technicians, such as security prices, volume of trading, and other trading information, are derived from the stock market itself.

Also, a fundamental analyst must process new information correctly and *quickly* to derive a new intrinsic value for the stock or bond before other investors. Technicians, on the other hand, only need to quickly recognize a movement to a new equilibrium value *for whatever reason*. Notably, technicians do not need to know about a specific event and determine the effect of the event on the value of the firm and its stock.

Finally, assume that a fundamental analyst determines that a given security is under- or overvalued before other investors. He or she still must determine *when* to make the purchase or sale. Ideally, the highest rate of return would come from making the transaction just before the change in market value occurs. For example, assume that based on your analysis in

February, you expect a firm to report substantially higher earnings in June. Although you could buy the stock in February, you would be better off waiting until about May to buy the stock so that your funds would not be tied up for an extra three months, but you may be reticent to wait that long. Because most technicians generally do not invest until the move to the new equilibrium is under way, they contend that they typically experience ideal timing.

5.6 CHALLENGES TO TECHNICAL ANALYSIS

Those who doubt the value of technical analysis for investment decisions question the usefulness of this technique in two areas. First, they challenge some of its basic assumptions. Second, they challenge some specific technical trading rules and their long-run usefulness.

5.6.1 Challenges to the Assumptions of Technical Analysis

The major challenge to technical analysis is based on the results of empirical tests of the efficient market hypothesis (EMH), discussed earlier in the chapter. Recall that for technical trading rules to generate superior risk-adjusted returns, the market would have to be slow to adjust prices to the arrival of new market information—that is, the weak-form efficient market hypothesis (EMH) that considered the two sets of tests. First was the statistical analysis of prices to determine if prices moved in trends or were a random walk. Second, we considered the analysis of specific trading rules to determine if their use could beat a buy-and-hold. Almost all the studies using statistical analysis found that prices do not move in trends based on statistical tests of autocorrelation and runs.

Regarding the analysis of specific trading rules, it was acknowledged that numerous technical trading rules cannot be tested, but the vast majority of the results for the trading rules support the EMH.

5.6.2 Challenges to Specific Trading Rules

An obvious challenge is that the past relationships between specific market variables and stock prices may not be repeated. As a result, a technique that previously worked might miss subsequent market turns. Because of this, most technicians follow several trading rules and seek a consensus of all of them to predict the future market pattern.

Critics contend that many price patterns become self-fulfilling prophecies. For example, assume that many analysts expect a stock selling at $40 a share to go to $50 or more if it breaks through its channel at $45. When it reaches $45, enough technicians will buy to cause the price to rise to $50, exactly as predicted. In fact, some technicians may place a limit order to buy the stock at such a breakout point. Under such conditions, the increase will probably be only temporary, and the price will return to its true equilibrium.

Another problem is that the success of a particular trading rule will encourage many investors to adopt it. This popularity and the resulting competition will eventually neutralize the technique. For example, suppose it becomes known that technicians who employ short-selling data have been enjoying high rates of return. As a result, other technicians will likely start using these data and thus accelerate the stock price pattern following changes in short selling. Hence, this profitable trading rule may no longer be profitable.

Further, as we will see when we examine specific trading rules, *most of them require a great deal of subjective judgment*. Two technical analysts looking at the same price pattern may arrive at widely different interpretations of what has happened and, therefore, will come to different investment decisions. This implies that the use of various techniques is neither completely mechanical nor obvious. Finally, we will see that with several trading rules, *the standard values that signal investment decisions can change over time*. Therefore, technical analysts adjust the specified values that trigger investment decisions to conform to the new environment or trading rules have been abandoned because they no longer work.

5.7 TECHNICAL TRADING RULES AND INDICATORS

To illustrate the specific technical trading rules, Exhibit 5.3 shows a typical stock price cycle that could be an example for the overall stock market or for an individual stock. The graph shows a peak and trough, along with a rising trend channel, a flat trend channel, a declining trend channel, and indications of when a technical analyst would ideally want to trade.

The graph begins with the end of a declining (bear) market that finishes in a **trough**, followed by an upward trend that breaks through the **declining trend channel**. Confirmation that the declining trend has reversed would be a buy signal. The technical analyst would typically buy stocks that showed this pattern.

The analyst would then expect the development of a **rising trend channel**. As long as the stock price stayed in this rising channel, the technician would hold the stock(s). Ideally, the technician wants to sell at the **peak** of the cycle but cannot identify a peak until after the trend changes.

If the stock (or the market) begins trading in a flat pattern, it will necessarily break out of its rising trend channel. At this point, some technical analysts would sell, but most would hold to see if the stock experiences a period of consolidation and then breaks out of the **flat trend channel** on the upside and begins rising again. Alternatively, if the stock were to break out of the channel on the downside, the technician would take this as a sell signal and would exit the stock and look for a declining trend channel. The next buy signal would come after the trough when the price breaks out of the declining channel and establishes a rising trend. We will consider strategies to detect these changes in trend and the importance of volume in this analysis shortly.

There are numerous technical trading rules and a range of interpretations for each of them. Most technical analysts watch many alternative rules and decide on a buy or sell decision based on a *consensus* of the signals because complete agreement of all the rules is rare. In the following discussion of several well-known techniques, we have divided the rules into four groups, based on the attitudes of technical analysts. The first group includes trading rules used by analysts who like to trade against the crowd using *contrary-opinion signals*. The second group attempts to emulate astute investors—that is, the *smart money*. The third group

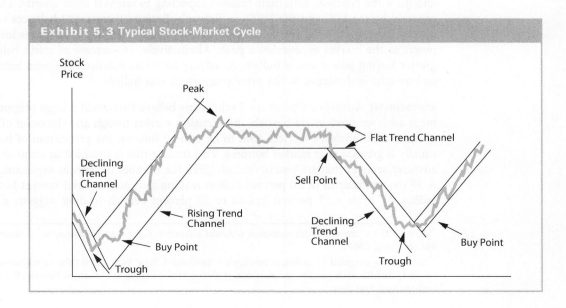

Exhibit 5.3 Typical Stock-Market Cycle

includes popular technical indicators that are not easily classified. Finally, the fourth group contains *pure price* and *volume techniques*, including the famous Dow Theory.

5.7.1 Contrary-Opinion Rules

Contrary-opinion rules are technical trading rules which assume that the majority of investors are wrong as the market approaches peaks and troughs. Therefore, the goal is to determine when the majority of investors is either strongly bullish or bearish and then trade in the opposite direction.

Mutual Fund Cash Positions   A mutual fund holds some cash in its portfolio for one of the following reasons: (1) It needs cash to liquidate shares submitted by fundholders; (2) new investments in the mutual fund have not been invested; (3) or the portfolio manager is bearish on the market and wants to increase the fund's defensive cash position.

Mutual funds' ratios of cash as a percentage of the total assets in their portfolios (the *cash ratio*, or *liquid asset ratio*) are reported in the press, including monthly figures in *Barron's*.[10] This percentage of cash historically varies from a low value of about 4 percent to a high point near 11 percent, although there has been a declining trend to the series.

Because technicians believe that mutual funds usually are wrong at peaks and troughs, they expect them to have a high percentage of cash near a market trough—when they should be fully invested to take advantage of the impending market rise. At market peaks, they expect mutual funds to be almost fully invested (with a low percentage of cash) when they should be selling stocks and realizing gains. Therefore, contrary-opinion technicians watch for the mutual fund cash position to approach one of the extremes and act contrary to the mutual funds. Specifically, they would buy when the cash ratio approaches 11 percent and sell when the cash ratio approaches 4 percent.

An alternative rationale for this buy–sell decision is that a high cash position is a bullish indicator because it reflects potential buying power. Regardless of the reasons, these technicians believe the large cash balance will eventually be invested and will cause stock prices to increase. Alternatively, a low cash ratio would indicate that the institutions have little potential buying power. As of July 2017, this ratio was at 6.5 percent, which would be a neutral signal.

Credit Balances in Brokerage Accounts   Credit balances result when investors sell stocks and leave the proceeds with their brokers, expecting to reinvest them shortly. The amounts are reported by the SEC and the NYSE in *Barron's*. Because these credit balances reflect potential purchasing power, a decline in these balances is bearish because it indicates lower purchasing power as the market approaches a peak. Alternatively, an increase of credit balances indicates greater buying power and is bullish. As of July 2017, the balances had been increasing for several months and relative to the prior year, which was bullish.

Investment Advisory Opinions   Technicians believe that when a large proportion of investment advisory services are bearish, this signals a market trough and the onset of a bull market. Because most advisory services tend to be trend followers, the proportion of bearish opinions usually is greatest near market bottoms. This trading rule is specified in terms of the percent of advisory services that are bearish/bullish given the number of services expressing an opinion.[11] A 35 percent bearish or 20 percent bullish reading indicates a major market bottom (a bullish indicator), while a 35 percent bullish or 20 percent bearish reading suggests a major market

---

[10]*Barron's* is a prime source for numerous technical indicators. For a readable discussion of relevant data and their use, see Zweig (1987).

[11]This ratio is compiled by Investors Intelligence, Larchmont, New York 10538. The technicians at B of A Merrill Lynch Global Research use this series as one of their investor sentiment indicators. Notably, the percentage signals have changed over time.

top (a bearish signal). As of July 2017, the percent bearish consensus index was 18 percent, which would be a bearish rating.

Chicago Board Options Exchange (CBOE) Put-Call Ratio Put options give the holder the right to sell stock at a specified price for a given time period and is used as a signal of a bearish attitude. A higher put-call ratio indicates that investors are bearish, which technicians consider a bullish indicator.

This ratio has historically fluctuated between 0.80 and 0.20 and was typically substantially less than 1 because investors tend to be bullish and avoid selling short or buying puts. Readings of 0.60 and above are considered bullish, while readings of 0.30 and below are bearish signals. As of July 2017, the ratio was about 0.65, implying that investors were quite bearish, which would be a strong bullish sign for contrary-opinion technicians.

Futures Traders Bullish on Stock-Index Futures Another relatively popular contrary-opinion measure is the percentage of speculators in stock-index futures who are bullish regarding stocks based on a survey of individual futures traders. It is considered a bearish sign when more than 70 percent of the speculators are bullish and a bullish sign when this ratio declines to 30 percent or lower.

Given the several contrary-opinion measures, technicians generally employ several of these series to provide a consensus regarding investors' sentiment.

5.7.2 Follow the Smart Money

Some technical analysts have created the following set of indicators that they believe indicate the behavior of smart, sophisticated investors.

Confidence Index Published by *Barron's*, the Confidence Index (CI) is the ratio of the *Barron's* average yield on the "Best Grade Bonds" to the average yield on the Dow Jones "Intermediate Grade Bonds" list.[12] This index measures the change in yield spread over time between high-grade and intermediate-grade bonds. Because the yields on high-grade bonds always should be lower than those on intermediate-grade bonds, this ratio should approach 100 as this spread gets smaller.

This ratio is considered a bullish indicator because during periods of high confidence, investors are willing to increase their investment in lower-quality bonds for the added yield, which causes a decrease in the yield spread between the intermediate-grade bonds and best-grade bonds. Therefore, this ratio of yields—the Confidence Index—will increase. In contrast, when investors are pessimistic, the yield spread will increase, and the Confidence Index will decline.

Unfortunately, this interpretation assumes that changes in the yield spread are caused almost exclusively by changes in investor demand for different-quality bonds. In fact, the yield differences have frequently changed because of changes in the supply of bonds. For example, a large issue of high-grade AT&T bonds could cause a temporary increase in yields on all high-grade bonds, which would reduce the yield spread and increase the Confidence Index without any change in investors' attitudes. Therefore, this change in supply would generate a false signal of a change in confidence. As of July 2017, the CI had been declining for several months and was down about 5 percent from its high point, which would indicate that the spread was increasing and would be mildly bearish.

T-Bill/Eurodollar Yield Spread A popular measure of investor attitude or confidence on a global basis is the spread between T-bill yields and Eurodollar rates measured as the ratio of

---

[12]Historical data for this index are contained in the *Dow Jones Investor's Handbook*, Princeton, New Jersey (Dow Jones Books, annual). Current figures appear in *Barron's*.

T-bill/Eurodollar yields. It is reasoned that, at times of international crisis, this spread widens as the smart money experiences a "flight to safety" and flows to safe-haven U.S. T-bills, which causes lower T-Bill yields and a decline in this ratio. It is contended that the stock market typically experiences a trough shortly thereafter.

Debit Balances in Brokerage Accounts (Margin Debt) Debit balances in brokerage accounts represent borrowing (margin debt) by knowledgeable investors from their brokers and indicate the attitude of sophisticated investors who engage in margin transactions. Therefore, an increase in debit balances implies buying by these smart investors and is a bullish sign, while a decline in debit balances would indicate selling and is a bearish indicator.

Monthly data on margin debt is reported in *Barron's*. Unfortunately, this index does not include borrowing by investors from other sources such as banks. Also, because it is an absolute value, technicians can only look for changes in the trend of aggregate borrowing—that is, increases are bullish, and declines are bearish. As of July 2017, these balances had been increasing for several weeks and were above the prior-year figures, which would be a bullish sign.

5.7.3 Momentum Indicators

The following are indicators of overall market momentum used to make aggregate market decisions.

Breadth of Market The breadth of market series measures the number of issues that have increased each day and the number of issues that have declined. It helps explain what caused a change of direction in a composite market index such as the S&P 500 Index. As we discussed in Chapter 4, most stock-market indexes are heavily influenced by the stocks of large firms because the indexes are value weighted. Therefore, a stock-market index can experience an overall increase while most individual issues are not increasing, which means that most stocks are not participating in the rising market. Such a divergence can be detected by examining the advance-decline figures for all stocks on the exchange, along with the overall market index.

The advance-decline index is typically a cumulative index of net advances or net declines. Specifically, each day major newspapers publish figures on the number of issues on the NYSE that advanced, declined, or were unchanged. The figures for a five-day sample from *Barron's* are shown in Exhibit 5.4. These figures, along with changes in the DJIA at the bottom of the table, indicate a strong market advance because the DJIA was increasing and the net advance figure was strong, indicating that the market increase was broadly based. Even the results on Day 3, when the market declined 15 points, were encouraging since it was a small overall decline and the individual stock issues were split just about 50–50, which points toward a fairly even environment.

Exhibit 5.4 Daily Advances and Declines on the New York Stock Exchange

Day	1	2	3	4	5
Issues traded	3,608	3,641	3,659	3,651	3,612
Advances	2,310	2,350	1,558	2,261	2,325
Declines	909	912	1,649	933	894
Unchanged	389	379	452	457	393
Net advances (advances minus declines)	+1,401	+1,438	−91	+1,328	+1,431
Cumulative net advances	+1,401	+2,839	+2,748	+4,076	+5,507
Changes in the DJIA	+40.47	+95.75	−15.25	+108.42	+140.63

Sources: New York Stock Exchange and *Barron's*.

Stocks above Their 200-Day Moving Average Technicians often compute moving averages of an index to determine its general trend. To examine the trend for individual stocks, the 200-day **moving average** of prices is fairly popular. From these moving-average indexes for numerous stocks, Media General Financial Services calculates how many stocks are currently trading above their 200-day moving-average index, and this is used as an indicator of general investor sentiment. The market is considered to be *overbought* and subject to a negative correction when more than 80 percent of the stocks are trading above their 200-day moving average. In contrast, if less than 20 percent of the stocks are selling above their 200-day moving average, the market is considered to be *oversold*, which means investors should expect a positive correction. As of July 2017, the percentage of stocks selling above their 200-day moving average was about 84 percent, which would be considered a bearish signal.

5.7.4 Stock Price and Volume Techniques

In the introduction to this section, we examined a hypothetical stock price chart that demonstrated market peaks and troughs along with rising and declining trend channels and breakouts from channels that signal new price trends or reversals of the price trends. While price patterns alone are important, most technical trading rules consider both stock price and corresponding volume movements.

Dow Theory Any discussion of technical analysis using price and volume data should begin with a consideration of the Dow Theory because it was among the earliest work on this topic and remains the basis for many technical indicators.[13] Dow described stock prices as moving in trends analogous to the movement of water. He postulated three types of price movements over time: (1) major trends that are like *tides* in the ocean, (2) intermediate trends that resemble *waves*, and (3) short-run movements that are like *ripples*. Followers of the Dow Theory attempt to detect the direction of the major price trend (tide), recognizing that intermediate movements (waves) may occasionally move in the opposite direction. They recognize that a major market advance does not go straight up, but rather includes small price declines as some investors decide to take profits.

Exhibit 5.5 shows the typical bullish pattern. The technician would look for every recovery to reach a new peak above the prior peak, and price rise should be accompanied by

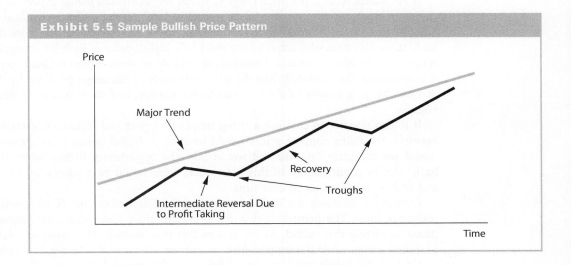

Exhibit 5.5 Sample Bullish Price Pattern

Price

Major Trend

Recovery

Troughs

Intermediate Reversal Due
to Profit Taking

Time

---

[13]A study that discusses and provides support for the Dow Theory is Glickstein and Wubbels (1983).

heavy trading volume. Alternatively, each profit-taking reversal that follows an increase to a new peak should have a trough above the prior trough, with relatively light trading volume during the profit-taking reversals. When this pattern of price and volume movements changes, the major trend may be entering a period of consolidation (a flat trend) or a major reversal.

Importance of Volume   As noted, technicians watch volume changes along with price movements as indicators of changes in supply and demand. A price movement in one direction means that the net effect on price is in that direction, but the price change alone does not indicate the breadth of the excess demand or supply. Therefore, the technician looks for a price increase on heavy volume relative to the stock's normal trading volume as an indication of bullish activity. Conversely, a price decline with heavy volume is considered bearish. A generally bullish pattern would be price increases accompanied by heavy volume and small price reversals occurring with light trading volume.

Technicians also use a ratio of upside-downside volume as an indicator of short-term momentum for the aggregate stock market. Each day the stock exchanges announce the volume of stocks that increased divided by the volume of trading in stocks that declined. These data are reported daily in *The Wall Street Journal* and weekly in *Barron's*. This ratio is an indicator of market momentum. Specifically, while values above 1.00 are generally bullish, technicians believe that an upside-downside volume value of 1.75 or more indicates an overbought position that is bearish. Alternatively, a value of 0.75 and lower supposedly reflects an oversold position and is considered bullish. The moving average value as of July 2017 was in the range 105–110, which was mildly positive but on balance neutral.

Support and Resistance Levels   A **support level** is the price range at which a technician would expect a substantial increase in the demand for a stock. Generally, a support level will develop after a stock has enjoyed a meaningful price increase and the stock experiences profit taking. Technicians reason that at some price below the recent peak, investors who did not buy during the first price increase (waiting for a small reversal) will get into the stock. When the price reaches this support price, demand surges, and price and volume begin to increase again.

A **resistance level** is the price range at which the technician would expect an increase in the supply of stock and a price reversal. A resistance level develops after a significant decline from a higher price level. After the decline, the stock begins to recover, but the prior decline in price leads some investors who acquired the stock at a higher price to look for an opportunity to sell it near their breakeven points. Therefore, the supply of stock owned by these nervous investors is *overhanging* the market. When the price rebounds to the target price set by these investors, this overhanging supply of stock comes to the market, and there is a price decline on heavy volume.

It is also possible to envision a rising trend of support and resistance levels for a stock. For example, the rising support prices would be a set of higher prices where investors over time would see the price increase and would take the opportunity to buy when there is a "pull back" due to profit taking. In this latter case, there would be a succession of higher support and higher resistance levels over time.

Exhibit 5.6 contains the daily stock prices for Caterpillar, Inc. (CAT), with support and resistance lines. The graphs show a rising pattern since Caterpillar experienced strong price increases during this period. At the end of this time period, the resistance level was at about $116 and rising, while the support level was about $102 and also rising. The bullish technician would look for future prices to rise in line with this channel. If prices fell significantly below the rising support line on strong volume, it would signal a possible trend reversal and would

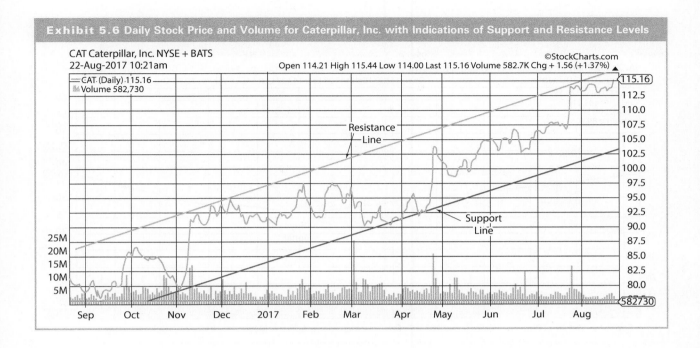

Exhibit 5.6 Daily Stock Price and Volume for Caterpillar, Inc. with Indications of Support and Resistance Levels

be considered a bearish signal. In contrast, an increase above the resistance price line, a "breakout," on strong volume would be considered a bullish signal.

Moving-Average Lines Earlier, we discussed how technicians use a moving average of past stock prices as an indicator of the overall trend and how they examine current prices relative to this trend for signals of a change. A 200-day moving average is a relatively popular measure of the long-term trend for individual stocks and the aggregate market. We add a 50-day moving-average price line (short-term trend) and consider large volume.

Exhibit 5.7 is a daily stock price chart for Jazz Pharmaceuticals, Inc. (JAZZ) for the year ending August 2017, with 50-day and 200-day moving-average (MA) lines. Two comparisons involving the MA lines are important. The first comparison is the specific prices to the shorter-run 50-day MA line. If the overall price trend of a stock has been down (which is the case for JAZZ in the early months), the moving-average price line generally is above current prices. If prices reverse and break through both the short 50-day moving average line and the long 200-day moving-average line *from below* with heavy trading volume, most technicians would consider this a *preliminary positive* change.

The second comparison is between the 50- and 200-day MA lines. Specifically, when these two lines cross, it confirms a significant change in the overall trend. Specifically, if the 50-day MA line crosses the 200-day MA line from above (referred to as a "death cross") on good volume (as shown in September), this would be a bearish indicator (sell signal) because it confirms an earlier reversal in trend from positive to negative when the price line crossed the 50-day moving average line. In contrast, when the 50-day line crosses the 200-day line from below (as it did in March), it confirms a change to a positive trend (a "golden cross") and would be a buy signal. These two crossings are shown in Exhibit 5.7 for Jazz Pharmaceuticals. The price line continued to increase after the buy signal to about $155 − $160, where it then fluctuated. Having bought the stock when the lines crossed in March, the investor benefitted from the subsequent increase, and the technician would look for the price to initially stop increasing—potentially declining and breaking through the 50-day MA line from above (as it

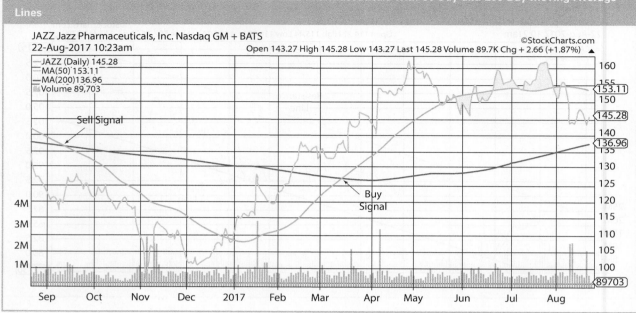

Exhibit 5.7 Stock Prices and Volume Chart for Jazz Pharmaceuticals with 50-Day and 200-Day Moving Average Lines

did in August) followed by a confirmation when the 50-day MA line would break below the 200-day MA line—and confirm a sell signal.

As noted, for a *bullish* trend, the 50-day MA line should be above the 200-day MA line. Notably, if this positive gap between the 50-day and 200-day lines gets too large (about 20 percent, which happens with a fast run-up in price), a technician might consider this an indication that the stock is temporarily overbought, which is bearish in the short run. In contrast, when the 50-day MA line is below the 200-day MA line, it would be a bearish environment. Similarly, if the gap gets too large on the downside (again, about 20 percent), it might be considered a signal of an oversold stock, which would be bullish for the short run.

Relative Strength Technicians believe that once a trend begins, it will continue until some major event causes a change in direction. They believe this is also true of *relative* performance. If an individual stock or an industry group is outperforming the market, technicians believe it will continue to do so.

Therefore, technicians compute weekly or monthly **relative-strength (RS) ratios** for individual stocks and industry groups. The RS ratio is equal to the price of a stock or an industry index divided by the value for some stock-market index such as the S&P 500.[14] If this ratio increases over time, it indicates that the stock for the firm is outperforming the overall stock market, and a technician would expect this superior performance to continue. Relative-strength ratios work during declining as well as rising markets. In a declining market, if a stock's price declines less than the market does, the stock's relative-strength ratio will continue to rise. Technicians believe that if this ratio is stable or increases during a bear market, the stock should do very well during the subsequent bull market.

Investment firms publish relative-strength charts for individual stocks relative to the market (for example, S&P Industrials Index). Using Walt Disney as an example, the discussion below

---

[14]In contrast to these indexes that are relative to market or industry ratios, there are ratios that are relative to the stock itself, which is fundamentally a momentum indicator. These ratios are not the same.

Exhibit 5.8 Stock Price and Volume Chart for Walt Disney Co. (DIS) with Indications of Outperformance and Underperformance Relative to the S&P 500 Index

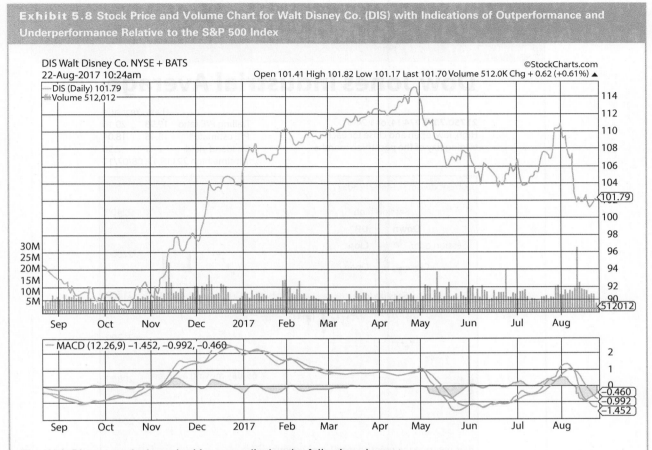

The Walt Disney stock charts in this report display the following elements:

1. A line chart of the daily close of the Walt Disney company stock price from August 2016 to July 2017, with the stock price indicated to the right
2. A relative-strength line (the dark line) of Walt Disney stock price compared with the S&P Industrials index
3. A 50-day moving average of Walt Disney relative strength line (the light line).

Source: http://finance.yahoo.com

the graph in Exhibit 5.8 describes how to read the charts. Finally, if you can collect the data for an industry index (for example, technology, pharmaceuticals), it is possible to examine the relative strength for the company versus its industry and the industry versus the market.

Bar Charts Technicians use charts that show daily, weekly, or monthly time series of stock prices. For a given interval, a technical analyst plots the high and low prices and connects the two points vertically to form a bar. Typically, he or she will also draw a small horizontal line across this vertical bar to indicate the closing price. Finally, almost all bar charts include the volume of trading at the bottom of the chart so that the technical analyst can relate the price and volume movements.

Candlestick Charts Candlestick charts are basically an extension of the bar charts discussed above. In addition to high, low, and closing prices for each trading day, they also include the opening and closing price and indicate the change from open to close by shading whether the market or individual stock went down (black shading) or up (white bar) for the day. Exhibit 5.9 shows the daily candlesticks for the Dow Jones Industrial Average as well as

Exhibit 5.9 A Typical Candlestick Chart Listing the Daily High, Low, Open, and Closing Prices for the Dow Jones Industrial Average and NYSE Volume for the Three Months Ending August 17, 2017

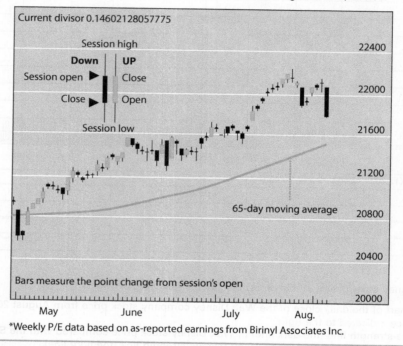

Dow Jones Industrial Average

21750.73 ▼274.14, or 1.24%
High, low, open and close for each
trading day of the past three months.

	Last	Year ago
Trailing P/E ratio	19.98	20.16
P/E estimate*	18.45	18.04
Dividend yield	2.37	2.56
All-time high 22118.42, 08/07/17		

*Weekly P/E data based on as-reported earnings from Birinyl Associates Inc.

Source: *The Wall Street Journal*, August 18, 2017, p. B7. Copyright 2017 by DOW JONES & CO.

additional fundamental information and insight regarding the stock market movements over a three-month period.

Multiple-Indicator Charts Thus far, we have presented charts that deal with only one trading technique, such as MA lines or RS rules. In the real world, it is fairly typical for technical charts to contain several indicators that can be used together—like the two MA lines (50- and 200-day) and the RS line—because they can provide added support to the analysis. Technicians include as many price and volume indicators as are reasonable on one chart and then, based on the performance of *several* technical indicators, arrive at a consensus about the future movement for the stock.

Point-and-Figure Charts Another popular graph is the point-and-figure chart. Unlike a bar chart, which typically includes all ending prices and volumes to show a trend, a point-and-figure chart includes only significant price changes, regardless of their timing. The technician determines what price interval to record as significant (one point, two points, and so on) and when to note price reversals.

Exhibit 5.10 Sample Point-and-Figure Chart

50								
48								
46				X				
44				X				
42		X	X	X				
40		X	X	X				
38			X	X				
36			X	X				
34			X	X				
32								
30								

To demonstrate how a technical analyst would use such a chart, suppose we want to chart a volatile stock that is currently selling for $40 a share. Because of its volatility, we believe that anything less than a two-point price change is not significant. Also, we consider anything less than a four-point reversal, meaning a movement in the opposite direction, quite minor. Therefore, we would set up a chart similar to the one in Exhibit 5.10, but our new chart would start at 40; it would also progress in two-point increments. If the stock moved to $42, we would place an X in the box above 40 and do nothing else until the stock rose to $44 or dropped to $38 (a four-point reversal from its high of $42). If it dropped to $38, we would move a column to the right, which indicates a reversal in direction, and begin again at 38 (fill in boxes at 42 and 40). If the stock price dropped to $34, we would enter an X at 36 and another at 34. If the stock then rose to $38 (another four-point reversal), we would move to the next column and begin at 38, going up (fill in 34 and 36). If the stock then went to $46, we would fill in more Xs as shown and wait for further increases or a reversal.

Depending on how fast the prices rise and fall, this process might take anywhere from two to six months. Given these figures, the technician would attempt to determine trends just as with the bar chart. As always, the technician would look for breakouts to either higher or lower price levels. A long horizontal movement with many reversals but no major trends up or down would be considered a *period of consolidation*, wherein the stock is moving from buyers to sellers and back again with no strong consensus about its direction. Once the stock breaks out and moves up or down after a period of consolidation, technical analysts anticipate a major move because previous trading set the stage for it. In other words, the longer the period of consolidation, the larger the expected subsequent move (up or down) when there is finally a breakout.

Point-and-figure charts provide a compact record of movements because they consider only significant price changes for the stock being analyzed. Therefore, some technicians contend that they are easier to work with and give more vivid pictures of price movements.

5.7.5 Efficient Markets and Technical Analysis

The assumptions of technical analysis directly oppose the notion of efficient markets. A basic premise of technical analysis is that stock prices move in trends that persist. Technicians believe that when new information comes to the market, it is not immediately available to everyone but is typically disseminated from the informed professional to the aggressive investing public and then to the great bulk of investors. Also, technicians contend that investors do not analyze information and act immediately. This process takes time. Therefore, they hypothesize that stock prices move to a new equilibrium after the release of new information in a gradual manner, which causes trends in stock price movements that persist.

Technical analysts believe that nimble traders can develop systems to detect the beginning of a movement to a new equilibrium (called a "breakout"). Hence, they hope to buy or sell the stock immediately after its breakout to take advantage of the subsequent, gradual price adjustment.

The belief in this pattern of price adjustment directly contradicts advocates of the EMH who believe that security prices adjust to new information very rapidly. These EMH advocates do not contend, however, that prices adjust perfectly, which implies a chance of overadjustment or underadjustment. Still, because it is uncertain whether the market will over- or under-adjust at any time, it is difficult to derive abnormal profits from adjustment errors.

If the capital market is weak-form efficient as indicated by most of the results, then prices fully reflect all relevant market information so technical trading systems that depend only on past trading data *cannot* have any value. By the time the information is public, the price adjustment has taken place. Therefore, a purchase or sale using a technical trading rule should not generate abnormal returns after taking account of risk and transaction costs. Still, recall the discussion in Chapter 3 regarding the dramatic decline in transaction costs due to the increase in trading volume and the significant new technology. Given this new environment, it is important to acknowledge that prior results that depended heavily on high transaction costs need to be reconsidered.

SUMMARY

- The efficiency of capital markets has implications for the investment analysis and management of your portfolio. Capital markets should be efficient because numerous rational, profit-maximizing investors react quickly to the release of new information. Assuming prices reflect new information, they are unbiased estimates of the securities' true, intrinsic value, and there should be a consistent relationship between the return on an investment and its risk.

- The voluminous research on the EMH has been divided into three segments. The weak-form EMH states that stock prices fully reflect *all market information*, so any trading rule that uses past market data to predict future returns should have no value. The results of most studies supported this hypothesis.

- The semistrong-form EMH asserts that security prices adjust rapidly to the release of *all public information*. The tests of this hypothesis either examine the opportunities to predict future rates of return or involve event studies that analyze whether investors could derive above-average returns from trading on the basis of public information. These test results were clearly mixed. On the one hand, the results for almost all the event studies related to economic events such as stock splits, initial public offerings, and accounting changes consistently supported the hypothesis. In contrast, several studies that examined

the ability to predict rates of return on the basis of unexpected quarterly earnings, P/E ratios, size, neglected stocks, and the BV/MV ratio generally did not support the hypothesis.

- Since the strong-form EMH states that security prices reflect all information, it implies that no group should be able to derive above-average returns consistently. Studies of corporate insiders did not support the strong-form hypothesis. An analysis of individual analysts using Value Line rankings or recommendations published in *The Wall Street Journal* gave mixed results. The results indicated that the specific Value Line rankings have significant information but it may not be possible to profit from it, whereas the analyst recommendations indicated the existence of private information. In contrast, the performance by professional money managers (of mutual funds and pension funds) supported the EMH because their risk-adjusted performance was typically inferior to passive benchmarks.

- During the past 15 years, significant research in behavioral finance by investigators has contended that the standard finance theory model is incomplete since it does not consider implications of psychological decisions made by individuals that help explain many anomalies and identify the existence of several biases. It is important to be aware of a number of these biases because they can lead to inferior performance by analysts and portfolio managers, and/or it is possible to exploit them for excess returns.

- Given the mixed results from numerous EMH studies, it is important to consider the implications of these results for analysts and portfolio managers. The EMH indicates that technical analysis should not be of value. In contrast, fundamental analysis is useful, but it is difficult to implement because it requires the ability *to correctly estimate future values* for relevant economic variables, and these superior projections need to differ from the consensus. Therefore, managers must constantly evaluate investment advice to determine whether it is superior.

- Without access to superior analytical advice, you should run your portfolio like an index fund or an ETF. In contrast, those with superior analytical ability should be allowed to make decisions, but they should concentrate their efforts on small-cap and micro-cap firms and neglected firms where there is a higher probability of discovering misvalued stocks. The analysis should concentrate on a firm's BV/MV ratio, its size, and the monetary environment.

- The section of this chapter on efficient markets contains some good news and some bad news. The good news is that the practice of investment analysis and portfolio management is not a lost art; it is a viable profession for those willing to extend the effort and able to accept the pressures. The bad news is that numerous bright, hardworking individuals with extensive resources make the game tough. In fact, those competitors have created a fairly efficient capital market wherein it is extremely difficult for most analysts and portfolio managers to consistently achieve superior results.

- Numerous investors believe in and use technical analysis. As a result, the large investment firms provide extensive support for technical analysis, and a large proportion of the discussion related to securities markets in the media is based on a technical view of the market.

- How they answer two main questions separate technical analysts and efficient market advocates. First, is the information dissemination process, does everybody get the information at about the same time? Second, how quickly do investors adjust security prices to reflect new information? From an early section of the chapter, we know the answers from efficient market advocates. In contrast, technical analysts believe that news takes time to travel from the insider and expert to the individual investor. They also believe that price adjustments are not instantaneous. As a result, they contend that security prices move in trends that persist and, therefore, investors can use past price trends and volume information along with other market indicators to determine future price trends.

- Technical trading rules fall into four general categories: contrary-opinion rules, follow-the-smart-money tactics, momentum indicators, and stock price and volume techniques. These techniques and trading rules can be applied to both domestic and foreign markets. They can also be used to analyze the bond market and currency exchange rates.

- Most technicians employ several indicators and attempt to derive a consensus to guide their decision to buy, sell, or do nothing.

SUGGESTED READINGS

Ariely, Dan. *Predictably Irrational: The Hidden Forces That Shape Our Decisions*. New York: Harper Collins, 2008.

Arnott, Robert D., Jason C. Hsu, and John M. West. *The Fundamental Index*. New York: Wiley, 2008.

Ball, Ray. "The Theory of Stock Market Efficiency: Accomplishments and Limitations," *Journal of Applied Corporate Finance* 8, no. 1 (Spring 1995).

Barberis, Nicholas, and Richard Thalen. "A Survey of Behavioral Finance." *Handbook of the Economics of Finance*, eds. G. M. Constantianides, M. Harris, and Rene Stulz. New York: Elsevier Science, 2003.

Bernard, Victor. "Capital Markets Research in Accounting during the 1980s: A Critical Review," in *The State of Accounting Research as We Enter the 1990s*, ed. Thomas J. Frecka. Urbana: University of Illinois Press, 1989.

Benning, Carl J. "Prediction Skills of Real-World Market Timers." *Journal of Portfolio Management* 23, no. 2 (Winter 1997).

Brown, David P., and Robert H. Jennings. "On Technical Analysis." *Review of Financial Studies* 2, no. 4 (October 1989).

Colby, Robert W., and Thomas A. Mayers. *The Encyclopedia of Technical Market Indicators*. Homewood, IL: Dow Jones–Irwin, 1988.

DeMark, Thomas R. *The New Science of Technical Analysis*. New York: Wiley, 1994.

Edwards, R. D., and John Magee, Jr. *Technical Analysis of Stock Trends*, 6th ed. Boston: New York Institute of Finance, 1992.

Fama, Eugene. "Market Efficiency, Long-Term Returns, and Behavioral Finance," *Journal of Financial Economics* 49, no. 3 (September 1998): 283–306.

Gervais, S., and T. Odean. "Learning to be Overconfident," *Review of Financial Studies* 14, no. 1 (2001): 1–27.

Hartford, Tim. *The Logic of Life*. New York: Random House, 2008.

Hirschleifer, David. "Investor Psychology and Asset Pricing," *Journal of Finance* 56, no. 4 (August 2001): 1533–1597.

Jagadeesh, Narasimhan. "Evidence of Predictable Behavior of Security Returns." *Journal of Finance* 45, no. 3 (July 1990).

Keim, Donald B., and Robert F. Stambaugh. "Predicting Returns in Stock and Bond Markets," *Journal of Financial Economics* 17, no. 2 (December 1986).

Koller, Tim, Marc Goedhart, and David Wessels. *Valuation: Measuring and Managing the Value of Companies*, 5th ed. New York: Wiley, 2010.

Lo, Andrew W., and A. Craig MacKinley. *A Non-Random Walk Down Wall Street*. Princeton, NJ: Princeton University Press, 1999.

Meyers, Thomas A. *The Technical Analysis Course*. Chicago: Probus, 1989.

Pring, Martin J. *Technical Analysis Explained*, 3rd ed. New York: McGraw-Hill, 1991.

Shaw, Alan R. "Market Timing and Technical Analysis." In *The Financial Analysts Handbook*, 2nd ed., ed. Sumner N. Levine. Homewood, IL: Dow Jones–Irwin, 1988.

Shefrin, Hersh. *A Behavioral Approach to Asset Pricing Theory*. Amsterdam: Elsevier-North Holland, 2005.

Shefrin, Hersh, and Meir Statman. "Behavioral Capital Asset Pricing Theory," *Journal of Financial and Quantitative Analysis* 30, no. 3 (September 1995).

Shermer, Michael. *The Mind of the Market*. New York: Times Books, 2008.

Wood, Arnold S., ed. *Behavioral Finance and Decision Theory in Investment Management*. Charlottesville, VA: CFA Research Foundation, AIMR, 1995.

Wood, Arnold S., ed. *Behavioral Finance and Investment Management*. Charlottesville, VA: The CFA Research Foundation of the CFA Institute, 2010.

Zweig, Martin E. *Winning on Wall Street*. New York: Warner Books, 1986.

INFORMATION FOR TECHNICAL ANALYST PROFESSIONALS

A. Market Technicians Association (MTA), Inc.

The Market Technicians Association (MTA) is the premier global organization for those interested in technical analysis. Members include technical analysts, portfolio managers, traders, investment advisors, market letter writers, and others involved in the technical aspects of equities, futures, options, fixed-income securities, currencies, international markets, derivatives, etc. Member benefits include:

- Weekly Education Web Series—technical analysis webcasts with leading analysts
- A knowledge base of technical analysis information, white papers, and videos
- A private social network for technical analysts and financial professionals in MyMTA
- Access to technical analysis blogs written by industry professionals
- Participation in the Chartered Market Technician (CMT) Program

- Local chapter meetings, regional seminars, and an annual symposium

Contact Information:

Market Technicians Association, Inc.
61 Broadway, Suite 514
New York, NY 10006
Phone: (646) 652-3300
Fax: (646) 652-3322
Web site: http://www.mta.org

B. Chartered Market Technician (CMT) Program

The Chartered Market Technician (CMT) Program is a certification process in which candidates are required to demonstrate proficiency in a broad range of technical analysis subjects. Administered by the Accreditation Committee of the Market Technicians Association (MTA), Inc., the program consists of three levels. CMT Level 1 and CMT Level

2 are multiple choice exams, while CMT Level 3 is in essay form.

The objectives of the CMT Program are:

- To guide candidates in mastering a professional body of knowledge and in developing analytical skills
- To promote and encourage the highest standards of education
- To grant the right to use the professional designation of Chartered Market Technician (CMT) to those members who successfully complete the program and agree to abide by the MTA Code of Ethics

In order to be granted your CMT designation, you must meet the following requirements:

- Successfully complete all three levels of the CMT Exam
- Obtain Member Status within the MTA
- Be gainfully employed in a professional analytical or investment management capacity for a minimum period of three years and be regularly engaged in this capacity at the time of successfully passing all three levels of the CMT Exam

The exams for all three levels are administered twice a year, once during the spring and again in the fall. The candidate will have five years from the date of registration in the CMT Program to complete all three levels of the CMT and will be sent a notice of expiration. Candidates may take only one exam per administration. Contact the Market Technicians Association for information on the CMT Program.

QUESTIONS

1. Discuss the rationale for expecting an efficient capital market. What factor would you look for to differentiate the market efficiency for two alternative stocks?
2. Define and discuss the weak-form EMH. Describe the two sets of tests used to examine the weak-form EMH.
3. Define and discuss the semistrong-form EMH. Describe the two sets of tests used to examine the semistrong-form EMH.
4. What is meant by the term *abnormal rate of return?*
5. Describe how you would compute the abnormal rate of return for a stock for a period surrounding an economic event. Give a brief example for a stock with a beta of 1.40.
6. Assume you want to test the EMH by comparing alternative trading rules to a buy-and-hold policy. Discuss the three common mistakes that can bias the results against the EMH.
7. Describe the results of a study that supported the semistrong-form EMH. Discuss the nature of the test and specifically why the results support the hypothesis.
8. Describe the results of a study that did *not* support the semistrong-form EMH. Discuss the nature of the test and specifically why the results did not support the hypothesis.
9. For many of the EMH tests, it is really a test of a "joint hypothesis." Discuss what is meant by this concept. What are the joint hypotheses being tested?
10. Define and discuss the strong-form EMH. Why do some observers contend that the strong-form hypothesis really requires a perfect market in addition to an efficient market? Be specific.
11. Discuss how you would test the strong-form EMH. Why are these tests relevant? Give a brief example.
12. Describe the results of a study that did *not* support the strong-form EMH. Discuss the test involved and specifically why the results reported did not support the hypothesis.
13. Describe the results of a study that *did* support the strong-form EMH. Discuss the test involved and specifically why these results support the hypothesis.
14. Describe the general goal of behavioral finance.
15. Why do the advocates of behavioral finance contend that the standard finance model theory is incomplete?
16. What does the EMH imply for the use of technical analysis?
17. What does the EMH imply for fundamental analysis? Discuss specifically what it does not imply.

18. In a world of efficient capital markets, what do you have to do to be a superior analyst? How would you test whether an analyst was superior?

19. What advice would you give to your superior analysts in terms of the set of firms to analyze and variables that should be considered in the analysis? Discuss your reasoning for this advice.

20. How should a portfolio manager without any superior analysts run his or her portfolio?

21. Describe the goals of an index fund. Discuss the contention that index funds are the ultimate answer in a world with efficient capital markets.

22. At a social gathering, you meet the portfolio manager for the trust department of a local bank. He confides to you that he has been following the recommendations of the department's six analysts for an extended period and has found that two are superior, two are average, and two are clearly inferior. What would you recommend that he do to run his portfolio?

23. a. Briefly explain the concept of the *efficient market hypothesis* (EMH) and each of its three forms—*weak*, *semistrong*, and *strong*—and briefly discuss the degree to which existing empirical evidence supports each of the three forms of the EMH.

    b. Briefly discuss the implications of the efficient market hypothesis for investment policy as it applies to:

    (i) Technical analysis in the form of charting
    (ii) Fundamental analysis

    c. Briefly explain *two* major roles or responsibilities of portfolio managers in an efficient market environment.

24. Technical analysts believe that one can use past price changes to predict future price changes. How do they justify this belief?

25. Technicians contend that stock prices move in trends that persist for long periods of time. What do technicians believe happens in the real world to cause these trends?

26. Briefly discuss the problems related to fundamental analysis that are considered advantages for technical analysis.

27. Discuss some disadvantages of technical analysis.

28. If the mutual fund cash position were to increase to close to 12 percent, would a technician consider this cash position bullish or bearish? Give two reasons for this opinion.

29. Assume a significant decline in credit balances at brokerage firms. Discuss why a technician would consider this bullish or bearish.

30. If the bearish sentiment index of advisory service opinions were to increase to 61 percent, discuss why a technician would consider this bullish or bearish.

31. Discuss why an increase in debit balances is considered bullish or bearish.

32. Describe the Dow Theory and its three components. Which component is most important? What is the reason for an intermediate reversal?

33. Describe a bearish price and volume pattern and discuss why it is considered bearish.

34. Discuss the logic behind the breadth of market index. How is it used to identify a peak in stock prices?

35. During a 10-day trading period, the cumulative net advance index goes from 1,572 to 1,053. During this same period of time, the DJIA goes from 11,200 to 12,100. As a technician, discuss what this set of events would mean to you.

36. Explain the reasoning behind a support level and a resistance level.

37. What is the purpose of computing a moving-average line for a stock? Describe a bullish pattern using a 50-day moving-average line and the stock volume of trading. Discuss why this pattern is considered bullish.

38. Assuming a stock price and volume chart that also contains a 50-day and a 200-day MA line, describe a bearish pattern with the two MA lines and discuss why it is bearish.

39. Explain how you would construct a relative-strength ratio for an individual stock or an industry group. What would it mean to say a stock experienced good relative strength during a bear market?

40. Discuss why most technicians follow several technical rules and attempt to derive a consensus.

PROBLEMS

1. Compute the abnormal rates of return for the following stocks during period t (ignore differential systematic risk):

Stock	R_{it}	R_{mt}
B	11.5%	4.0%
F	10.0	8.5
T	14.0	9.6
C	12.0	15.3
E	15.9	12.4

R_{it} = return for stock i during period t

R_{mt} = return for the aggregate market during period t

2. Compute the abnormal rates of return for the five stocks in Problem 1, assuming the following systematic risk measures (betas):

Stock	βi
B	0.95
F	1.25
T	1.45
C	0.70
E	−0.30

3. Compare the abnormal returns in Problems 1 and 2 and discuss the reason for the difference in each case.

4. Look up the daily trading volume for the following stocks during a recent five-day period:
- Merck
- Caterpillar
- Intel
- McDonald's
- General Electric

Randomly select five stocks from the NYSE and examine their daily trading volume for the same five days.

a. What are the average volumes for the two samples?

b. Would you expect this difference to have an impact on the efficiency of the markets for the two samples? Why or why not?

5. Select a stock on the NYSE and construct a daily high, low, and close bar chart for it that includes its volume of trading for 10 trading days.

6. Compute the relative-strength ratio for the stock in Problem 5 relative to the S&P 500 Index. Prepare a table that includes all the data and indicates the computations as follows:

	Closing Price		Relative-Strength Ratio
Day	Stock	S&P 500	Stock Price/S&P 500

7. Plot the relative-strength ratio computed in Problem 6 on your bar chart. Discuss whether the stock's relative strength is bullish or bearish.

8. Currently, Charlotte Art Importers is selling at $23 per share. Although you are somewhat dubious about technical analysis, you want to know how technicians who use point-and-figure charts would view this stock. You decide to note one-point movements and three-point reversals. You gather the following historical price information:

Date	Price	Date	Price	Date	Price
4/1	23½	4/18	33	5/3	27
4/4	28½	4/19	35⅜	5/4	26½
4/5	28	4/20	37	5/5	28
4/6	28	4/21	38½	5/6	28¼
4/7	29¾	4/22	36	5/9	28⅛
4/8	30½	4/25	35	5/10	28¼
4/11	30½	4/26	35¼	5/11	29⅛
4/12	32⅛	4/27	33⅛	5/12	30¼
4/13	32	4/28	32⅞	5/13	29⅞

   Plot the point-and-figure chart, using Xs for uptrends and Os for downtrends. How would a technician evaluate these movements? Discuss why you would expect a technician to buy, sell, or hold the stock based on this chart.

9. Assume the following daily closings for the Dow Jones Industrial Average:

Day	DJIA	Day	DJIA
1	23,010	7	23,220
2	23,100	8	23,130
3	23,165	9	23,250
4	23,080	10	23,315
5	23,070	11	23,240
6	23,150	12	23,310

   a. Calculate a four-day moving average for Days 4 through 12.
   b. Assume that the index on Day 13 closes at 23,300. Would this signal a buy or sell decision?

10. The cumulative advance-decline line reported in *Barron's* at the end of the month is 21,240. During the first week of the following month, the daily report for the *Exchange* is as follows:

Day	1	2	3	4	5
Issues traded	3,544	3,533	3,540	3,531	3,521
Advances	1,737	1,579	1,759	1,217	1,326
Declines	1,289	1,484	1,240	1,716	1,519
Unchanged	518	470	541	598	596

   a. Compute the daily net advance-decline line for each of the five days.
   b. Compute the cumulative advance-decline line for each day and the final value at the end of the week.

CHAPTER **6**

An Introduction to Portfolio Management

After you read this chapter, you should be able to answer the following questions:

- What do we mean by *risk aversion*, and what evidence indicates that investors are generally risk averse?
- What are the basic assumptions behind the Markowitz portfolio theory?
- What do we mean by *risk*, and what are some measures of risk used in investments?
- How do we compute the expected rate of return for a portfolio of assets?
- How do we compute the standard deviation of rates of return for an individual risky asset?
- What are the covariance and correlation statistics and what is the relationship between them?
- What is the formula for the standard deviation for a *portfolio* of risky assets, and how does it differ from the standard deviation of an individual risky asset?
- Given the formula for the standard deviation of a portfolio, how do we diversify a portfolio?
- What happens to the portfolio standard deviation when the correlation between the assets changes?
- What is the mean-variance efficient frontier of risky assets?
- What determines which portfolio an investor selects on the efficient frontier?
- How does capital market theory extend Markowitz portfolio theory with the addition of a risk-free asset?
- What is the capital market line (CML), and how does it enhance our understanding of the relationship between risk and expected return?
- What is the market portfolio, and what role does it play in the investment process implied by the CML?
- What is the difference between systematic and unsystematic risk, and how does that relate to the concept of diversification?
- Under what conditions does the CML recommend the use of leverage in forming an investor's preferred strategy?

One of the major advances in the investment field during the past few decades has been the recognition that you cannot create an optimal investment portfolio by simply combining numerous individual securities that have desirable risk–return characteristics. Specifically, it has been shown that an investor must consider the relationship *among* the investments to build the best portfolio to meet the investment objectives. In this chapter we explain portfolio theory in detail by introducing the basic portfolio risk formula for combining different assets. When you understand this formula and its implications, you will understand *why* and *how* you should diversify your portfolio.

6.1 SOME BACKGROUND ASSUMPTIONS

We begin by clarifying some general assumptions of portfolio theory. This includes not only what we mean by an *optimal portfolio* but also what we mean by the terms *risk aversion* and *risk*.

One basic assumption of portfolio theory is that investors want to maximize the returns from the total set of investments for a given level of risk. To understand such an assumption requires certain ground rules. First, your portfolio should *include all of your assets and liabilities*, not only your marketable securities but also less marketable investments such as real estate, art, and antiques. The full spectrum of investments must be considered because the returns from all these investments interact, and *this relationship among the returns for assets in the portfolio is important*. Hence, a good portfolio is *not* simply a collection of individually good investments.

6.1.1 Risk Aversion

Portfolio theory also assumes that investors are **risk averse**, meaning that, given a choice between two assets with equal rates of return, they will select the asset with the lower level of risk. Evidence that most investors are risk averse is that they purchase various types of insurance, including life insurance, car insurance, and health insurance. Buying insurance basically involves an outlay of a known dollar value to guard against an uncertain, possibly larger, outlay in the future. Further evidence of risk aversion is the difference in promised yield (the required rate of return) for different grades of bonds with different degrees of credit risk. Specifically, the promised yield on corporate bonds increases from AAA (the lowest risk class) to AA to A, and so on, indicating that investors require a higher rate of return to accept higher risk.

This does not imply that everybody is risk averse, or that investors are completely risk averse regarding all financial commitments. The fact is, not everybody buys insurance for everything. In addition, some individuals buy insurance related to some risks such as auto accidents or illness, but they also buy lottery tickets and gamble at race tracks or in casinos, where it is known that the expected returns are negative (which implies that participants are willing to pay for the excitement of the risk involved). This combination of risk preference and risk aversion can be explained by an attitude toward risk that depends on the amount of money involved. Researchers such as Friedman and Savage (1948) have speculated that this is the case for people who like to gamble for small amounts (in lotteries or slot machines) but buy insurance to protect themselves against large losses such as fire or accidents.

While recognizing such attitudes, we assume that most investors with a large investment portfolio are risk averse. Therefore, we expect a positive relationship between expected return and risk, which is consistent with the historical results shown in Chapter 2.

6.1.2 Definition of Risk

Although there is a difference in the specific definitions of *risk* and *uncertainty*, for our purposes and in most financial literature, the two terms are used interchangeably. For most investors, *risk* means *the uncertainty of future outcomes*. An alternative definition might be *the probability of an adverse outcome*. In our subsequent discussion of portfolio theory, we consider several measures of risk that are used when developing and applying the theory.

6.2 THE MARKOWITZ PORTFOLIO THEORY

In the early 1950s, the investment community talked about risk, but there was no specific measure for the term. To build a portfolio model, however, investors had to quantify their risk variable. The basic portfolio model was developed by Harry Markowitz (1952, 1959), who derived the expected rate of return for a portfolio of assets as well as a risk measure. Markowitz showed that the variance of the rate of return was a meaningful measure of portfolio risk under a reasonable set of assumptions. More important, he derived the formula for computing the variance of a portfolio. This portfolio variance formula not only indicated the importance of diversifying investments to reduce the total risk of a portfolio but also showed *how* to effectively diversify. The Markowitz model is based on several assumptions regarding investor behavior:

1. Investors consider each investment alternative as being represented by a probability distribution of potential returns over some holding period.
2. Investors maximize one-period expected utility, and their utility curves demonstrate diminishing marginal utility of wealth.
3. Investors estimate the risk of the portfolio on the basis of the variability of potential returns.
4. Investors base decisions solely on expected return and risk, so their utility curves are a function of expected return and the variance (or standard deviation) of returns only.
5. For a given risk level, investors prefer higher returns to lower returns. Similarly, for a given level of expected return, investors prefer less risk to more risk.

Under these assumptions, *a single asset or portfolio of assets is considered to be efficient if no other asset or portfolio of assets offers higher expected return with the same (or lower) risk or lower risk with the same (or higher) expected return.*

6.2.1 Alternative Measures of Risk

One of the best-known measures of risk is the *variance,* or *standard deviation of expected returns.*[1] It is a statistical measure of the dispersion of returns around the expected value whereby a larger variance or standard deviation indicates greater dispersion. The idea is that the more dispersed the potential returns, the greater the uncertainty of the potential outcomes.

Another measure of risk is the *range of returns.* It is assumed that a larger range of possible returns, from the lowest to the highest, means greater uncertainty regarding future expected returns.

Instead of using measures that analyze all deviations from expectations, some observers believe that investors should be concerned only with returns below some threshold level. These are sometimes called *downside risk* measures because they only consider potential returns that fall beneath that target rate. A measure that only considers deviations below the expected return is the *semi-variance.* Extensions of the semi-variance measure only computes return deviations *below zero* (that is, negative returns), or returns below the returns of some specific asset such as T-bills, the rate of inflation, or a benchmark. These measures of risk implicitly assume that investors want to *minimize the damage* (regret) from returns less than some target rate. Assuming that investors would welcome returns above some target rate, the returns above such a target rate are not considered when measuring risk.

Although there are numerous potential measures of risk, we will use the variance or standard deviation of returns because (1) this measure is somewhat intuitive, (2) it is widely recognized risk measure, and (3) it has been used in most of the theoretical asset pricing models.

6.2.2 Expected Rates of Return

We compute the expected rate of return for an *individual investment* as shown in Exhibit 6.1 and discussed in Chapter 1. The expected return for an individual risky asset with the set of potential returns and an assumption of the different probabilities used in the example would be 10.3 percent.

The expected rate of return for a *portfolio* of investments is simply the weighted average of the expected rates of return for the individual investments in the portfolio. The weights are the proportion of total value for the individual investment.

The expected rate of return for a hypothetical portfolio with four risky assets is shown in Exhibit 6.2. The expected return for this portfolio of investments would be 11.5 percent. The

---

[1]We consider the variance and standard deviation as one measure of risk because the standard deviation is the square root of the variance.

Exhibit 6.1 Computation of the Expected Return for an Individual Asset

Probability	Possible Rate of Return (%)	Expected Security Return (%)
0.35	0.08%	0.0280%
0.30	0.10	0.0300
0.20	0.12	0.0240
0.15	0.14	0.0210
		$E(R_i) = 0.1030$
		$= 10.3\%$

Exhibit 6.2 Computation of the Expected Return for a Portfolio of Risky Assets

Weight (w_i) (percentage of portfolio)	Expected Security Return (R_i)	Expected Portfolio Return ($w_i \times R_i$)
0.20	0.10	0.0200
0.30	0.11	0.0330
0.30	0.12	0.0360
0.20	0.13	0.0260
		$E(R_{\text{port}}) = 0.1150$
		$= 11.50\%$

effect of adding or dropping any investment from the portfolio would be easy to determine; we would use the new weights based on value and the expected returns for each of the investments. We can generalize this computation of the expected return for the Portfolio $E(R_{\text{port}})$ as follows:

6.1
$$E(R_{\text{port}}) = \sum_{i=1}^{n} w_i R_i$$

where:

w_i = weight of an individual asset in the portfolio, or the percent of the portfolio in Asset i

R_i = expected rate of return for Asset i

6.2.3 Variance (Standard Deviation) of Returns for an Individual Investment

The variance, or standard deviation, is a measure of the variation of possible rates of return R_i from the expected rate of return $E(R_i)$ as follows:

6.2
$$\text{Variance} = \sigma^2 = \sum_{i=1}^{n} [R_i - E(R_i)]^2 P_i$$

where:

P_i = probability of the possible rate of return R_i

6.3
$$\text{Standard Deviation} = \sigma = \sqrt{\sum_{i=1}^{n} [R_i - E(R_i)]^2 P_i}$$

Exhibit 6.3 Computation of the Variance for an Individual Risky Asset

Possible Rate of Return (R_i)	Expected Security Return $E(R_i)$	$R_i - E(R_i)$	$[R_i - E(R_i)]^2$	P_i	$[R_i - E(R_i)]^2 P_i$
0.08	0.103	−0.023	0.0005	0.35	0.000185
0.10	0.103	−0.003	0.0000	0.30	0.000003
0.12	0.103	0.017	0.0003	0.20	0.000058
0.14	0.103	0.037	0.0014	0.15	0.000205
					0.000451

Variance $= \sigma^2 = 0.000451$
Standard Deviation $= \sigma = 0.021237 = 2.1237\%$

The computation of the variance and standard deviation of returns for the individual risky asset in Exhibit 6.1 is set forth in Exhibit 6.3. Therefore, you would describe this asset as having an expected return of 10.3 percent and a standard deviation of 2.12 percent.

6.2.4 Variance (Standard Deviation) of Returns for a Portfolio

Two basic concepts in statistics, **covariance** and **correlation**, must be understood before we discuss the formula for the variance of the rate of return for a portfolio.

Covariance of Returns Covariance is a measure of the degree to which two variables move together relative to their individual mean values over time. In portfolio analysis, we usually are concerned with the covariance of *rates of return* rather than prices or some other variable.[2] A positive covariance means that the rates of return for two investments tend to move in the same direction relative to their individual means during the same time period. In contrast, a negative covariance indicates that the rates of return for two investments tend to move in opposite directions relative to their means during specified time intervals over time. The *magnitude* of the covariance depends on the variances of the individual return series, as well as on the relationship between the series.

Exhibit 6.4 contains the monthly rates of return values for U.S. stocks (measured using the Standard & Poor's 500 Stock Market Index) and U.S. bonds (measured by the Barclays Capital U.S. Aggregate Bond Index). Both indexes are total return indexes; that is, the stock index includes dividends paid, and the bond index includes accrued interest, as discussed in Chapter 4. Using end-of-month values for each index, we compute the percentage change in the index each month, which equals its monthly rates of return during 2016. Exhibits 6.5 and 6.6 contain a time-series plot of these monthly rates of return. Although the rates of return for the two assets moved together during some months, in other months they moved in opposite directions. The covariance statistic provides an *absolute* measure of how they moved together over time.

For two Assets, i and j, we define the covariance of rates of return as:

6.4
$$Cov_{ij} = E\{[R_i - E(R_i)][R_j - E(R_j)]\}$$

---

[2]Returns, of course, can be measured in a variety of ways, depending on the type of asset. You will recall that we defined returns (R_i) in Chapter 1 as:

$$R_i = \frac{EV - BV + CF}{BV}$$

where EV is ending value, BV is beginning value, and CF is the cash flow during the period.

Exhibit 6.4 Listing of Monthly Rates of Return for U.S. Stocks and Bonds During 2016

2016	S&P 500 Total Return Stock Market Index	Barclays Capital U.S. Aggregate Bond Index
Jan	−4.96	1.38
Feb	−0.14	0.71
Mar	6.78	0.92
Apr	0.39	0.38
May	1.79	0.03
Jun	0.26	1.80
Jul	3.68	0.63
Aug	0.14	−0.11
Sep	0.02	−0.06
Oct	−1.82	−0.76
Nov	3.70	−2.37
Dec	1.97	0.14
Mean $E(R)$	0.98	0.22

Source: Standard & Poor's and Barclays Capital.

When we apply this formula to the monthly rates of return for the S&P 500 Stock Market and the Treasury bond indexes during 2016, it becomes:

$$\frac{1}{11}\sum_{i=1}^{12}[R_i - \overline{R}_i][R_j - \overline{R}_j]$$

Exhibit 6.5 Time-Series Plot of the Monthly Returns for S&P 500 Total Return Stock Market Index, 2016

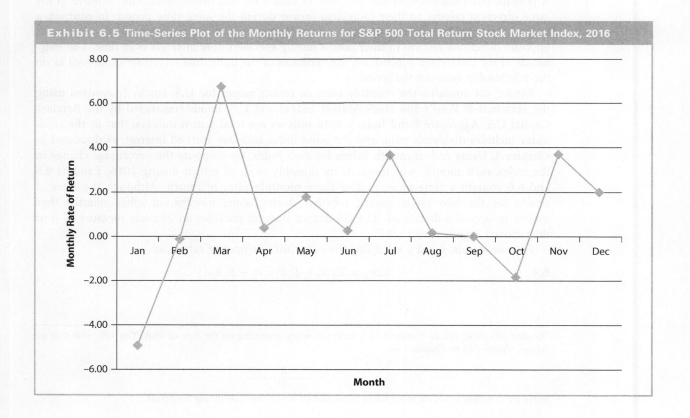

Exhibit 6.6 Time-Series Plot of the Monthly Returns for Barclays Capital U.S. Aggregate Bond Index, 2016

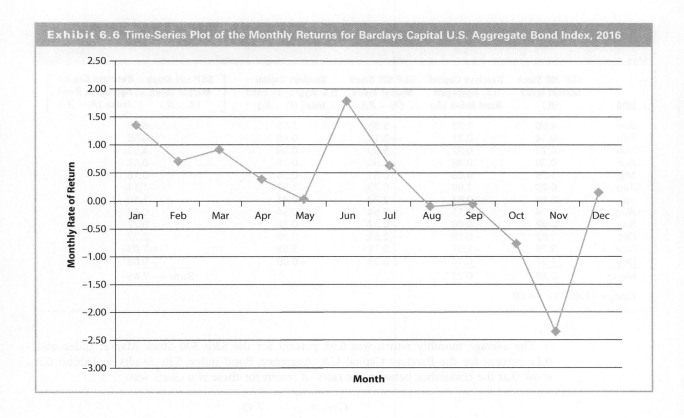

Note that when we apply formula in Equation 6.4 to actual sample data, we use the sample mean $(\overline{R})$ as an estimate of the expected return and divide the values by $(n-1)$ rather than by n to avoid statistical bias.

As can be seen, if the rates of return for one asset are above (below) its mean rate of return $(\overline{R})$ during a given period and the returns for the other asset are likewise above (below) its mean rate of return during this same period, then the *product* of these deviations from the mean is positive. If this happens consistently, the covariance of returns between these two assets will be a positive value. If, however, the rate of return for one of the securities is above its mean return, while the return on the other security is below its mean return, the product will be negative. If this contrary movement happens consistently, the covariance between the rates of return for the two assets will be a large negative value.

Exhibit 6.7 includes the monthly rates of return during 2016 contained in Exhibit 6.4. One might expect returns for these two asset indexes to have reasonably low covariance because of the differences in the nature of the assets themselves. The arithmetic means of the monthly returns were:

$$(\overline{R}_i) = \frac{1}{12} \sum_{i=1}^{12} R_{it} = 0.98 \; (stocks)$$

and:

$$(\overline{R}_j) = \frac{1}{12} \sum_{j=1}^{12} R_{jt} = 0.22 \; (bonds)$$

Exhibit 6.7 Computation of Covariance of Returns for the S&P 500 Stock Market Index and Barclays Capital Aggregate Bond Index, 2016

2016	S&P 500 Stock Market Index (R_i)	Barclays Capital U.S. Aggregate Bond Index (R_j)	S&P 500 Stock Market Index ($R_i - \bar{R}_i$)	Barclays Capital U.S. Aggregate Bond Index ($R_j - \bar{R}_j$)	S&P 500 Stock Market Index × ($R_i - \bar{R}_i$)	Barclays Capital Aggregate Bond Index ($R_j - \bar{R}_j$)
Jan	−4.96	1.38	−5.95	1.15		−6.85
Feb	−0.14	0.71	−1.12	0.49		−0.55
Mar	6.78	0.92	5.80	0.69		4.02
Apr	0.39	0.38	−0.60	0.16		−0.10
May	1.79	0.03	0.81	−0.20		−0.16
Jun	0.26	1.80	−0.73	1.57		−1.14
Jul	3.68	0.63	2.70	0.41		1.10
Aug	0.14	−0.11	−0.84	−0.34		0.28
Sep	0.02	−0.06	−0.97	−0.28		0.27
Oct	−1.82	−0.76	−2.81	−0.99		2.77
Nov	3.70	−2.37	2.71	−2.59		−7.03
Dec	1.97	0.14	0.99	−0.08		−0.08
Mean	0.98	0.22				Sum = −7.45

$Cov_{ij} = -7.45/11 = -0.68$

The average monthly return was 0.98 percent for the S&P 500 Stock Market Index and 0.22 percent for the Barclays Capital U.S. Aggregate Bond index. The results in Exhibit 6.7 show that the covariance between the rates of return for these two assets was:

$$Cov_{ij} = \frac{1}{11} \times -7.45$$
$$= -0.68$$

Interpretation of a number such as −0.68 is difficult; is that value high or low for a covariance statistic? We know the relationship between the two assets is clearly negative, but it is not possible to be a lot more specific. Exhibit 6.8 contains a scatterplot with paired values of R_{it} and R_{jt} plotted against each other. This plot demonstrates the linear nature and strength of the relationship. It is not surprising that the relationship during 2016 was a mildly negative value since during seven of the twelve months the two assets moved counter to each other as shown in Exhibit 6.7. As a result, the overall covariance was a definite negative value.

Covariance and Correlation Covariance is affected by the variability of the two individual return indexes. Therefore, a number such as −0.68 in our example might indicate a weak negative relationship if the two individual indexes were volatile, but would reflect a strong negative relationship if the two indexes were relatively stable. Obviously, we want to standardize this covariance measure by taking into consideration the variability of the two individual return indexes, as follows:

6.5
$$r_{ij} = \frac{Cov_{ij}}{\sigma_i \sigma_j}$$

where:

r_{ij} = correlation coefficient of returns
σ_i = standard deviation of R_{it}
σ_j = standard deviation of R_{jt}

Standardizing the covariance by the product of the individual standard deviations yields the correlation coefficient, r_{ij}, which can vary only in the range −1 to +1. A value of +1 indicates

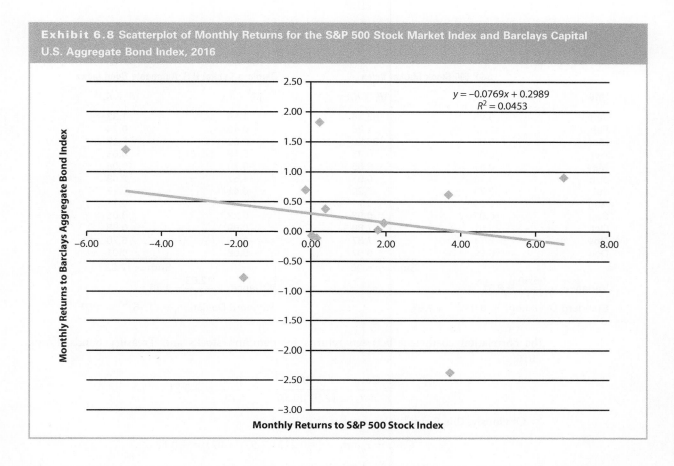

Exhibit 6.8 Scatterplot of Monthly Returns for the S&P 500 Stock Market Index and Barclays Capital U.S. Aggregate Bond Index, 2016

a perfect positive linear relationship between R_i and R_j, meaning the returns for the two assets move together in a completely linear manner. A value of -1 indicates a perfect negative relationship between the two return indexes, so that when one asset's rate of return is above its mean, the other asset's rate of return will be below its mean by a proportional amount.

To calculate this standardized measure of the relationship, we need to compute the standard deviation for the two individual return indexes. We already have the values for $(R_{it} - \overline{R}_i)$ and $(R_{jt} - \overline{R}_j)$ in Exhibit 6.7. We can square each of these values and sum them as shown in Exhibit 6.9 to calculate the variance of each return series; again, we divide by $(n - 1)$ to avoid statistical bias:

$$\sigma_i^2 = \frac{1}{11} \times 96.90 = 8.81$$

and:

$$\sigma_j^2 = \frac{1}{11} \times 12.63 = 1.15$$

The standard deviation for each index is the square root of the variance for each, as follows:

$$\sigma_i = \sqrt{8.81} = 2.97$$
$$\sigma_j = \sqrt{1.15} = 1.07$$

As expected, the stock index series is more volatile than the bond series. Thus, based on the covariance between the two indexes and the individual standard deviations, we can calculate

Exhibit 6.9 Computation of Standard Deviation of Monthly Returns for the S&P 500 Stock Market Index and Barclays Capital U.S. Aggregate Bond Index, 2016

2016	S&P 500 Stock Market Index		Barclays Capital U.S. Aggregate Bond Index	
	$(R_i - \overline{R}_i)$	$(R_i - \overline{R}_i)^2$	$(R_j - \overline{R}_j)$	$(R_j - \overline{R}_j)^2$
Jan	−5.95	35.36	1.15	1.33
Feb	−1.12	1.26	0.49	0.24
Mar	5.80	33.59	0.69	0.48
Apr	−0.60	0.35	0.16	0.03
May	0.81	0.65	−0.20	0.04
Jun	−0.73	0.53	1.57	2.48
Jul	2.70	7.29	0.41	0.17
Aug	−0.84	0.71	−0.34	0.11
Sep	−0.97	0.93	−0.28	0.08
Oct	−2.81	7.88	−0.99	0.98
Nov	2.71	7.37	−2.59	6.70
Dec	0.99	0.97	−0.08	0.01
		Sum = 96.90		Sum = 12.63

$\text{Variance}_i = \dfrac{96.90}{11} = 8.81$ $\text{Variance}_j = \dfrac{12.63}{11} = 1.15$

$\text{Standard Deviation}_i = (8.81)^{1/2} = 2.97$ $\text{Standard Deviation}_j = (1.15)^{1/2} = 1.07$

the correlation coefficient between returns for common stocks and Treasury bonds during 2016:

$$r_{ij} = \frac{Cov_{ij}}{\sigma_i \sigma_j} = \frac{-0.68}{(2.97)(1.07)} = \frac{-0.68}{3.18} = -0.213$$

Obviously, this formula also implies that:

$$Cov_{ij} = r_{ij}\sigma_i\sigma_j = (-0.213)(2.97)(1.07) = -0.68$$

As noted, a correlation of +1.0 indicates perfect positive correlation, and a value of −1.0 means that the returns moved in completely opposite directions. A value of zero means that the returns had no linear relationship, that is, they were uncorrelated statistically. That does *not* mean that they are independent. The value of $r_{ij} = -0.213$ is significantly different from zero. This significant negative correlation is not unusual for stocks versus bonds during a short time period such as one year.

6.2.5 Standard Deviation of a Portfolio

Portfolio Standard Deviation Formula Now that we have discussed the concepts of covariance and correlation, we can consider the formula for computing the standard deviation of returns for a *portfolio* of assets, our measure of risk for a portfolio. In Exhibit 6.2, we showed that the expected rate of return of the portfolio was the weighted average of the expected returns for the individual assets in the portfolio; the weights were the percentage of value of the portfolio. One might assume it is possible to derive the standard deviation of the portfolio in the same manner, that is, by computing the weighted average of the standard deviations for the individual assets. *This would be a mistake.* Markowitz (1959) derived the general formula for the standard deviation of a portfolio as follows:

6.6 $$\sigma_{\text{port}} = \sqrt{\sum_{i=1}^{n} w_i^2 \sigma_i^2 + \sum_{i=1}^{n}\sum_{\substack{j=1 \\ i \neq j}}^{n} w_i w_j Cov_{ij}} = \sqrt{\sum_{i=1}^{n} w_i^2 \sigma_i^2 + \sum_{i=1}^{n}\sum_{\substack{j=1 \\ i \neq j}}^{n} w_i w_j \sigma_i \sigma_j r_{ij}}$$

where:

σ_{port} = standard deviation of the portfolio

w_i = weights of an individual asset in the portfolio, where weights are determined by the proportion of value in the portfolio

σ_i^2 = variance of rates of return for Asset i

Cov_{ij} = covariance between the rates of return for Assets i and j, and $Cov_{ij} = \sigma_i \sigma_j r_{ij}$

This formula indicates that the standard deviation for a portfolio of assets is a function of the weighted average of the individual variances (where the weights are squared), *plus* the weighted covariances between all the assets in the portfolio. The very important point is that the standard deviation for a portfolio of assets encompasses not only the variances of the individual assets but *also* includes the covariances between all the pairs of individual assets in the portfolio. Further, it can be shown that, in a portfolio with a large number of securities, this formula reduces to the sum of the weighted covariances.

Impact of a New Security in a Portfolio   Although in most of the following discussion we will consider portfolios with only two assets (because it is possible to show the effect in two dimensions), we will also demonstrate the computations for a three-asset portfolio. Still, it is important at this point to consider what happens in a large portfolio with many assets. Specifically, what happens to the portfolio's standard deviation when we add a new security to such a portfolio? As shown by Equation 6.6, we see two effects. The first is the asset's own variance of returns, and the second is the covariance between the returns of this new asset and the returns of *every other asset that is already in the portfolio*. The relative weight of these numerous covariances is substantially greater than the asset's unique variance; the more assets in the portfolio, the more this is true. This means that the important factor to consider when adding an investment to a portfolio that contains a number of other investments is *not* the new security's own variance but *the average covariance of this asset with all other investments in the portfolio*.

Portfolio Standard Deviation Calculation   Because of the assumptions used in developing the Markowitz portfolio model, any asset or portfolio of assets can be described by two characteristics: the expected rate of return and the standard deviation of returns. Therefore, the following demonstrations can be applied to two *individual* assets, two *portfolios* of assets, or two *asset classes* with the indicated rate of return-standard deviation characteristics and correlation coefficients.

Equal Risk and Return—Changing Correlations   Consider first the case in which both assets have the same expected return and expected standard deviation of return. As an example, let's assume:

$$E(R_1) = 0.20, \; E(\sigma_1) = 0.10$$
$$E(R_2) = 0.20, \; E(\sigma_2) = 0.10$$

To show the effect of different covariances, we assume different levels of correlation between the two assets. We also assume that the two assets have equal weights in the portfolio ($w_1 = 0.50$; $w_2 = 0.50$). Therefore, the only value that changes in each example is the correlation between the returns for the two assets.

Now consider the following five correlation coefficients and the covariances they yield. Since $Cov_{ij} = r_{ij}\sigma_i\sigma_j$, the covariance will be equal to $r_{1,2}(0.10)(0.10)$ because the standard deviation of both assets is 0.10.

a. For $r_{1,2} = 1.00$, $Cov_{1,2} = (1.00)(0.10)(0.10) = 0.01$

b. For $r_{1,2} = 0.50$, $Cov_{1,2} = (0.50)(0.10)(0.10) = 0.005$

c. For $r_{1,2} = 0.00$, $Cov_{1,2} = (0.00)(0.10)(0.10) = 0.000$

d. For $r_{1,2} = -0.50,$ $Cov_{1,2} = (-0.50)(0.10)(0.10) = -0.005$
e. For $r_{1,2} = -1.00,$ $Cov_{1,2} = (-1.00)(0.10)(0.10) = -0.01$

Now let's see what happens to the standard deviation of the portfolio under these five conditions.

When we apply the general portfolio formula from Equation 6.6 to a two-asset portfolio, we get:

6.7
$$\sigma_{port} = \sqrt{w_1^2\sigma_1^2 + w_2^2\sigma_2^2 + 2w_1 w_2 r_{1,2}\sigma_1\sigma_2}$$

or:

$$\sigma_{port} = \sqrt{w_1^2\sigma_1^2 + w_2^2\sigma_2^2 + 2w_1 w_2 Cov_{1,2}}$$

Thus, in Case a:

$$
\begin{aligned}
\sigma_{port(a)} &= \sqrt{(0.5)^2(0.10)^2 + (0.5)^2(0.10)^2 + 2(0.5)(0.5)(0.01)} \\
&= \sqrt{(0.25)(0.01) + (0.25)(0.01) + 2(0.25)(0.01)} \\
&= \sqrt{(0.0025) + (0.0025) + (0.005)} \\
&= \sqrt{0.01} = 0.10
\end{aligned}
$$

In this case, where the returns for the two assets are perfectly positively correlated, the standard deviation for the portfolio is, in fact, the weighted average of the individual standard deviations. The important point is that we get no real benefit from combining two assets that are perfectly correlated; they are like owning the same asset twice because their returns move exactly together. Now consider Case b, where $r_{1,2}$ equals 0.50:

$$
\begin{aligned}
\sigma_{port(b)} &= \sqrt{(0.5)^2(0.10)^2 + (0.5)^2(0.10)^2 + 2(0.5)(0.5)(0.005)} \\
&= \sqrt{(0.0025) + (0.0025) + 2(0.25)(0.005)} \\
&= \sqrt{0.0075} = 0.0866
\end{aligned}
$$

The only term that changed from Case a is the last term, $Cov_{1,2}$, which changed from 0.01 to 0.005. As a result, the standard deviation of the portfolio declined by about 13 percent, from 0.10 to 0.0866. Note that *the expected return of the portfolio did not change* because it is simply the weighted average of the individual expected returns; it is equal to 0.20 in both cases.

This simple example demonstrates the concept of **diversification**, whereby the risk of the portfolio (8.66 percent) is lower than the risk of either of the assets held in the portfolio (10 percent each). This risk reduction benefit occurs to some degree any time the assets you combine in a portfolio are not perfectly positively correlated (that is, whenever $r_{i,j} < +1$). Diversification works in that case because there will be investment periods when a negative return to one asset will be offset by a positive return to the other, thereby reducing the variability of the overall portfolio return.

You should be able to confirm through your own calculations that the standard deviations for Portfolios c and d are 0.0707 and 0.050, respectively. The final case, where the correlation between the two assets is -1.00, indicates the ultimate benefits of diversification:

$$
\begin{aligned}
\sigma_{port(e)} &= \sqrt{(0.5)^2(0.10)^2 + (0.5)^2(0.10)^2 + 2(0.5)(0.5)(-0.01)} \\
&= \sqrt{(0.0050) + (-0.0050)} \\
&= \sqrt{0} = 0
\end{aligned}
$$

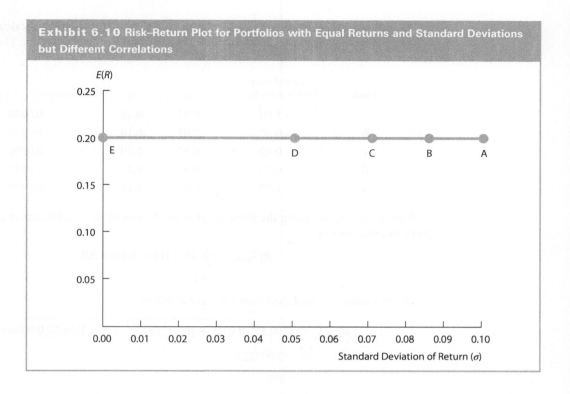

Exhibit 6.10 Risk–Return Plot for Portfolios with Equal Returns and Standard Deviations but Different Correlations

Here, the negative covariance term exactly offsets the individual variance terms, leaving an overall standard deviation of the portfolio of zero. *This would be a risk-free portfolio*, meaning that the average combined return for the two securities over time would be a constant value (that is, have no variability). Thus, a pair of completely negatively correlated assets provides the maximum benefits of diversification by completely eliminating variability from the portfolio.

The graph in Exhibit 6.10 shows the difference in the risk–return posture for our five cases. As noted, the only effect of the change in correlation is the change in the standard deviation of this two-asset portfolio. Combining assets that are not perfectly correlated does *not* affect the expected return of the portfolio, but it *does* reduce the risk of the portfolio (as measured by its standard deviation). When we eventually reach the ultimate combination of perfect negative correlation, risk is eliminated.

Combining Stocks with Different Returns and Risk   We have seen what happens when only the correlation coefficient (covariance) differs between the assets. We now consider two assets (or portfolios) with different expected rates of return and individual standard deviations.[3] We will show what happens when we vary the correlations between them. We will assume two assets with the following characteristics:

Asset	$E(R_i)$	w_i	σ_i^2	σ_i
1	0.10	0.50	0.0049	0.07
2	0.20	0.50	0.0100	0.10

---

[3]As noted, these could be two asset classes. For example, Asset 1 could be low-risk/low-return bonds, and Asset 2 could be higher-return/higher-risk stocks.

We will use the previous set of correlation coefficients, but we must recalculate the covariances because this time the standard deviations of the assets are different. The results are as follows:

Case	Correlation Coefficient $(r_{1,2})$	σ_1	σ_2	Covariance $(r_{1,2}\,\sigma_1\,\sigma_2)$
a	+1.00	0.07	0.10	0.0070
b	+0.50	0.07	0.10	0.0035
c	0.00	0.07	0.10	0.0000
d	−0.50	0.07	0.10	−0.0035
e	−1.00	0.07	0.10	−0.0070

Because we are assuming the same weights in all cases (0.50 − 0.50), the expected return in every instance will be:

$$E(R_{\text{port}}) = 0.50(0.10) + 0.50(0.20)$$
$$= 0.15$$

The portfolio standard deviation for Case a will be:

$$\sigma_{\text{port(a)}} = \sqrt{(0.5)^2(0.07)^2 + (0.5)^2(0.10)^2 + 2(0.5)(0.5)(0.0070)}$$
$$= \sqrt{0.007225}$$
$$= 0.085$$

Again, with perfect positive correlation, the portfolio standard deviation is the weighted average of the standard deviations of the individual assets:

$$(0.5)(0.07) + (0.5)(0.10) = 0.085$$

which means that there is no diversification benefit from combining the assets in the same portfolio.

For Cases b, c, d, and e, the portfolio standard deviations are as follows[4]:

$$\sigma_{\text{port(b)}} = \sqrt{(0.001225) + (0.0025) + (0.5)(0.0035)}$$
$$= \sqrt{0.005475}$$
$$= 0.07399$$
$$\sigma_{\text{port(c)}} = \sqrt{(0.001225) + (0.0025) + (0.5)(0.00)}$$
$$= 0.0610$$
$$\sigma_{\text{port(d)}} = \sqrt{(0.001225) + (0.0025) + (0.5)(-0.0035)}$$
$$= 0.0444$$
$$\sigma_{\text{port(e)}} = \sqrt{(0.003725) + (0.5)(-0.0070)}$$
$$= 0.015$$

---

[4]In all the following examples, we will skip some steps because you are now aware that only the last term changes. You are encouraged to work out the individual steps to ensure that you understand the computational procedure.

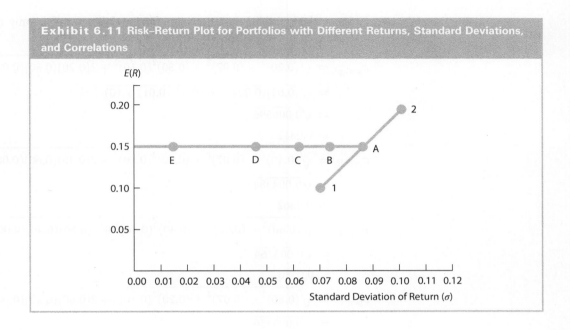

Exhibit 6.11 Risk–Return Plot for Portfolios with Different Returns, Standard Deviations, and Correlations

Note that, in this example, with perfect negative correlation, the portfolio standard deviation is not zero. This is because the different examples have equal weights, but the asset standard deviations are not equal.[5]

Exhibit 6.11 shows the results for the two individual assets and the portfolio of the two assets assuming the correlation coefficients vary as set forth in Cases a through e. As before, the expected return does not change because the investment weights are always equal at 0.50 each, so all the portfolios lie along the horizontal line at the return, $R = 0.15$.

Constant Correlation with Changing Weights   If we changed the weights of the two assets while holding the correlation coefficient constant, we would derive a set of combinations that trace an ellipse starting at Asset 2, going through the 0.50−0.50 point, and ending at Asset 1. We can demonstrate this with Case c, in which the correlation coefficient of zero eases the computations. We begin with 100 percent in Asset 2 (Case f) and change the weights as follows, ending with 100 percent in Asset 1 (Case l):

Case	w_1	w_2	$E(R_i)$
f	0.00	1.00	0.20
g	0.20	0.80	0.18
h	0.40	0.60	0.16
i	0.50	0.50	0.15
j	0.60	0.40	0.14
k	0.80	0.20	0.12
l	1.00	0.00	0.10

---

[5]The two appendixes to this chapter show proofs for equal weights with equal variances and solve for the appropriate weights to get zero standard deviation when standard deviations are not equal.

We already know the standard deviations (σ) for Portfolios f and l (only one asset) and Portfolio i. In Cases g, h, j, and k, the standard deviations are[6]:

$$\sigma_{\text{port(g)}} = \sqrt{(0.20)^2 + (0.07)^2 + (0.80)^2(0.10)^2 + 2(0.20)(0.80)(0.00)}$$

$$= \sqrt{(0.04)(0.0049) + (0.64)(0.01) + (0)}$$

$$= \sqrt{0.006596}$$

$$= 0.0812$$

$$\sigma_{\text{port(h)}} = \sqrt{(0.40)^2 + (0.07)^2 + (0.60)^2(0.10)^2 + 2(0.40)(0.60)(0.00)}$$

$$= \sqrt{0.004384}$$

$$= 0.0662$$

$$\sigma_{\text{port(j)}} = \sqrt{(0.60)^2 + (0.07)^2 + (0.40)^2(0.10)^2 + 2(0.60)(0.40)(0.00)}$$

$$= \sqrt{0.003364}$$

$$= 0.0580$$

$$\sigma_{\text{port(k)}} = \sqrt{(0.80)^2 + (0.07)^2 + (0.20)^2(0.10)^2 + 2(0.80)(0.20)(0.00)}$$

$$= \sqrt{0.003536}$$

$$= 0.0595$$

The various weights with a constant correlation yield the following risk–return combinations:

Case	w_1	w_2	$E(R_i)$	σ_{port}
f	0.00	1.00	0.20	0.1000
g	0.20	0.80	0.18	0.0812
h	0.40	0.60	0.16	0.0662
i	0.50	0.50	0.15	0.0610
j	0.60	0.40	0.14	0.0580
k	0.80	0.20	0.12	0.0595
l	1.00	0.00	0.10	0.0700

A graph of these combinations appears in Exhibit 6.12. We could derive a complete curve by simply varying the weighting by smaller increments.

A notable result is that with low, zero, or negative correlations, it is possible to derive portfolios that have *lower risk than either single asset*. In our set of examples where $r_{ij} = 0.00$, this occurs in Cases h, i, j, and k. As we saw earlier, this ability to reduce risk is the essence of diversification.

As shown in Exhibit 6.12, assuming the normal risk–return relationship where assets with higher risk (larger standard deviation of returns) provide high rates of return, it is possible for a conservative investor to experience *both* lower risk *and* higher return by diversifying into a higher risk-higher return asset, assuming that the correlation between the two assets is fairly low. Exhibit 6.12 shows that, in the case where we used the correlation of zero (0.00), the low-risk investor at Point L—who would receive a return of 10 percent and risk of 7 percent—could, by investing in Portfolio j, *increase* his or her return to 14 percent *and* experience a *decline* in risk to 5.8 percent by investing (diversifying) 40 percent of the portfolio in

---

[6]Again, you are encouraged to fill in the steps we skipped in the computations.

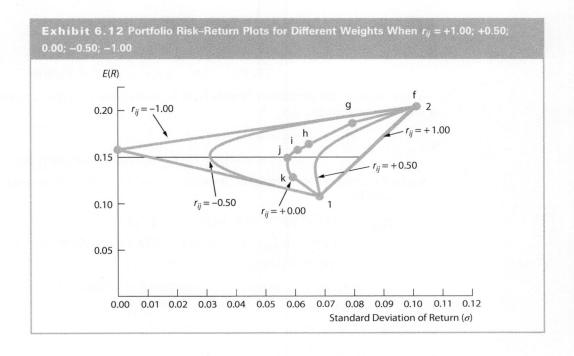

Exhibit 6.12 Portfolio Risk–Return Plots for Different Weights When $r_{ij} = +1.00; +0.50;$ 0.00; −0.50; −1.00

riskier Asset 2. As noted, *the benefits of diversification are critically dependent on the correlation between assets.* The exhibit shows that there is even some benefit when the correlation is 0.50.

Exhibit 6.12 also shows that the curvature in the graph depends on the correlation between the two assets or portfolios. With $r_{ij} = +1.00$, the combinations lie along a straight line between the two assets. When $r_{ij} = 0.50$, the curve is to the right of the $r_{ij} = 0.00$ curve; when $r_{ij} = -0.50$, the curve is to the left. Finally, when $r_{ij} = -1.00$, the graph would be two straight lines that would touch at the vertical line (zero risk) with some combination. As shown in Appendix 6B, it is possible to solve for the specified set of weights that would give a portfolio with zero risk. In this case, it is $w_1 = 0.412$ and $w_2 = 0.588$, which implies an $E(R)$ of 0.1588.

6.2.6 A Three-Asset Portfolio

A demonstration of what occurs with a three-asset portfolio is useful because it shows the dynamics of the portfolio formation process when assets are added. It also shows the rapid growth in the computations required, which is why we will stop at three!

In this example, we will combine three asset classes we have been discussing: stocks, bonds, and cash equivalents. We will assume the following characteristics:

Asset Classes	$E(R_i)$	σ_i	w_i
Stocks (S)	0.12	0.20	0.60
Bonds (B)	0.08	0.10	0.30
Cash equivalent (C)	0.04	0.03	0.10

The correlations are:

$$r_{S,B} = 0.25; r_{S,C} = -0.08; r_{B,C} = 0.15$$

Given the weights specified, the $E(R_{port})$ is:

$$E(R_{port}) = (0.60)(0.12) + (0.30)(0.08) + (0.10)(0.04)$$
$$= (0.072 + 0.024 + 0.004) = 0.100 = 10.00\%$$

When we apply the generalized formula from Equation 6.6 to the expected standard deviation of a three-asset portfolio, it is:

6.8
$$\sigma^2_{port} = (w_S^2\sigma_S^2 + w_B^2\sigma_B^2 + w_C^2\sigma_C^2)$$
$$+ (2w_S w_B \sigma_S \sigma_B \sigma_{S,B} + 2w_S w_C \sigma_S \sigma_C \sigma_{S,C} + 2w_B w_C \sigma_B \sigma_C \sigma_{B,C})$$

From the characteristics specified, the standard deviation of this three-asset-class portfolio (σ_{port}) would be:

$$\sigma^2_{port} = [(0.6)^2(0.20)^2 + (0.3)^2(0.10)^2 + (0.1)^2(0.3)^2]$$
$$+ \{[2(0.6)(0.3)(0.20)(0.10)(0.25)] + [2(0.6)(0.1)(0.20)(0.03)(-0.08)]$$
$$+ [2(0.3)(0.1)(0.10)(0.03)(0.15)]\}$$
$$= [0.015309 + (0.0018) + (-0.0000576) + (0.000027)]$$
$$= 0.0170784$$
$$\sigma_{port} = (0.0170784)^{1/2} = 0.1306 = 13.06\%$$

6.2.7 Estimation Issues

It is important to keep in mind that the results of this portfolio asset allocation depend on the accuracy of the statistical inputs. In the current instance, this means that for every asset (or asset class) being considered for inclusion in the portfolio, we must estimate its expected returns and standard deviation. We must also estimate the correlation coefficient among the entire set of assets. The number of correlation estimates can be significant—for example, for a portfolio of 100 securities, the number correlation estimates is 4,950 (that is, 99 + 98 + 97 + ...). The potential source of error that arises from these approximations is referred to as *estimation risk*.

We can reduce the number of correlation coefficients that must be estimated by assuming that stock returns can be described by the relationship of each stock to the same market index—that is, a single index market model, as follows:

6.9
$$R_i = a_i + b_i R_m + \varepsilon_i$$

where:

b_i = slope coefficient that relates the returns for Security i to the returns for the aggregate market index

R_m = returns for the aggregate market index

If all the securities are similarly related to the market and a slope coefficient b_i is derived for each one, it can be shown that the correlation coefficient between two securities i and j is:

6.10
$$r_{ij} = b_i b_j \frac{\sigma_m^2}{\sigma_i \sigma_j}$$

where:

σ_m^2 = variance of returns for the aggregate stock market

This reduces the number of estimates from 4,950 to 100—that is, once we have derived a slope estimate b_i for each security, we can compute the correlation estimates. Notably, this assumes that the single index market model provides a good estimate of security returns.

6.3 THE EFFICIENT FRONTIER

What is the optimal way for an investor to combine any collection of available assets into a portfolio? That is, how should an investor select the investment weights for all possible asset holdings in order to achieve his or her expected return goal in the best manner possible? Since we know investors are risk averse, the "best" (that is, optimal) portfolio can be defined as the one that is capable of producing the specific expected return objective while also minimizing risk. However, for each different expected return goal, there will be a different combination of assets that will represent the risk-minimizing portfolio, with larger expected return goals requiring portfolios having larger levels of risk. The set of risk-minimizing portfolios for each potential expected return goal is called the **efficient frontier**. Specifically, *the efficient frontier represents that set of portfolios that has the maximum rate of return for every given level of risk or the minimum risk for every level of return.*

An illustration of such a frontier is shown in Exhibit 6.13. Every portfolio that lies on the efficient frontier has either a higher rate of return for the same risk level or lower risk for an equal rate of return than some portfolio falling below the frontier. Thus, we would say that Portfolio A in Exhibit 6.13 *dominates* Portfolio C because it has an equal rate of return but substantially less risk. Similarly, Portfolio B dominates Portfolio C because it has equal risk but a higher expected rate of return. Because of the benefits of diversification among less-than-perfectly correlated assets, we would expect the efficient frontier to be made up of *portfolios* of investments rather than individual securities. Two possible exceptions arise at the end points, which represent the asset with the highest return and the asset with the lowest risk.

Calculating the set of investment weights, $\{w_i\}$, that define any given portfolio on the efficient frontier is not a straightforward process. Markowitz (1952, 1959) defined the basic problem that the investor needs to solve as:

Select $\{w_i\}$ so as to:

6.11
$$\text{Minimize } \sigma_{\text{port}} = \sqrt{\sum_{i=1}^{n} w_i^2 \sigma_i^2 + \sum_{\substack{i=1 \\ i \neq j}}^{n} \sum_{j=1}^{n} w_i w_j \sigma_i \sigma_j r_{ij}}$$

subject to the following conditions:

(i) $E(R_{\text{port}}) = \Sigma w_i \, E(R_i) = R^*$
(ii) $\Sigma w_i = 1.0$

The general method for solving the formula in Equation 6.11 is called a *constrained optimization* procedure because the task the investor faces is to select the investment weights that will "optimize" the objective (minimize portfolio risk) while also satisfying two restrictions (constraints) on the investment process: (i) the portfolio must produce an expected return at least as large as the return goal, R^*; and (ii) all of the investment weights must sum to 1.0. The approach to forming portfolios according to Equation 6.11 is often referred to as **mean-variance optimization** since it requires the investor to minimize portfolio risk for a given expected (mean) return goal.

6.3.1 The Efficient Frontier: An Example

An efficient frontier can be created for any set of assets by repeatedly solving the mean-variance optimization problem in Equation 6.11 for different levels of R^*. In principle, this can be accomplished for a portfolio of any size, such as a mutual fund containing hundreds of stocks. However, as a practical matter, the process works best when determining an

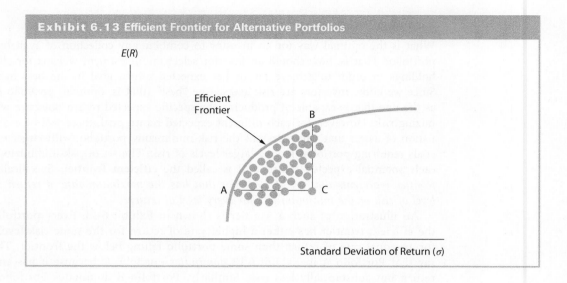

Exhibit 6.13 Efficient Frontier for Alternative Portfolios

investor's optimal *asset allocation* strategy, where the number of possible asset classes is smaller (for example, 3 to 12).

As an example of an actual efficient frontier, consider the expected returns, standard deviations, and correlations for five different asset classes—U.S. Bonds, Global (non-U.S.) Bonds, U.S. Stocks, Global Developed Market Stocks, Emerging Market Stocks—using historical return data over a 15-year period as of April 2016:

Asset Class:	E(R):	σ:
U.S. Bonds (USB)	2.11%	3.51%
Global Bonds (GB)	4.12%	8.47%
U.S. Stocks (USS)	8.08%	15.14%
Global DM Stocks (GS)	9.83%	17.61%
Emerging Market Stocks (EMS)	11.05%	23.00%

Correlations:

$$r_{usb,gb} = 0.52 \qquad r_{gb,gs} = 0.40$$
$$r_{usb,uss} = -0.05 \qquad r_{gb,ems} = 0.29$$
$$r_{usb,gs} = -0.03 \qquad r_{uss,gs} = 0.85$$
$$r_{usb,ems} = -0.05 \qquad r_{uss,ems} = 0.75$$
$$r_{gb,uss} = 0.17 \qquad r_{gs,ems} = 0.87$$

What would be the optimal asset allocation strategy using these five asset classes? As we have seen, the answer to that question depends on the investor's desired expected return. Exhibit 6.14 lists the optimal asset allocation portfolio weights and risk levels, generated as the solution to Equation 6.11, for five different return goals: 5 percent, 6 percent, 7 percent, 8 percent, and 9 percent. The entire efficient frontier based on these mean-variance optimal asset allocations is illustrated in Exhibit 6.15.

Notice from the optimal allocation weights shown in Exhibit 6.14 that investors who desire a higher return goal will have to take more overall risk, which means that their optimal allocation strategy will have to have a larger percentage invested in the riskier asset classes. For instance, moving from $R^* = 5$ percent to $R^* = 9$ percent would require reducing the total bond allocation from 63.2 percent $(= 48.0 + 15.2)$ to 11.7 percent $(= 0.0 + 11.7)$ and

Exhibit 6.14 Optimal Weights for a Five-Asset-Class Allocation Strategy, April 2016

Optimal Portfolio		Optimal Allocation Weights				
R*	σ_{port}	USB	GB	USS	GS	EMS
5%	6.8%	48.0%	15.2%	16.2%	17.9%	2.6%
6	8.8	26.4	25.6	21.3	22.7	3.9
7	10.9	4.9	36.0	26.5	27.5	5.2
8	13.1	0.0	26.7	22.0	44.7	6.6
9	15.5	0.0	11.7	14.7	65.5	8.1

Source: Author calculations.

Exhibit 6.15 Efficient Frontier for a Five-Asset-Class Allocation Strategy, April 2016

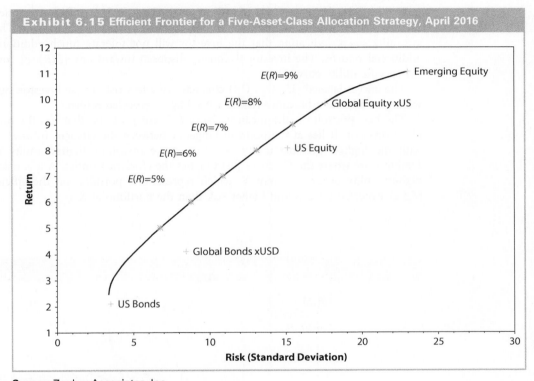

Source: Zephyr Associates, Inc.

shifting those funds to an increased overall stock allocation. The important point, though, is to recognize that for any given return goal, there is no way to combine these five asset classes to achieve a lower-risk allocation strategy than the mean-variance optimal weights shown here.

6.3.2 The Efficient Frontier and Investor Utility

Which specific portfolio on the efficient frontier should an investor select? This decision will depend on the investor's attitude on how much risk they are willing to take. So, as an investor, you will target a point along the efficient frontier based on your *utility function*, which reflects your attitude toward risk. No portfolio on the efficient frontier can dominate any other portfolio on the efficient frontier. All of these portfolios have different return and risk measures, with expected rates of return that increase with higher risk.

The curve in Exhibit 6.13 shows that the slope of the efficient frontier curve decreases steadily as we move upward. This implies that adding equal increments of risk as we move up the efficient frontier gives diminishing increments of expected return. To evaluate this situation, we calculate the slope of the efficient frontier as follows:

$$\frac{\Delta E(R_{\text{port}})}{\Delta E(\sigma_{\text{port}})}$$

An individual investor's utility curves specify the trade-offs he or she is willing to make between expected return and risk. In conjunction with the efficient frontier, these utility curves determine which *particular* portfolio on the efficient frontier best suits an individual investor. Two investors will choose the same portfolio from the efficient set only if their utility curves are identical.

Exhibit 6.16 shows two sets of utility curves along with an efficient frontier of investments. The curves labeled U_1, U_2, and U_3 are for a strongly risk-averse investor. These utility curves are quite steep, indicating that the investor will not tolerate much additional risk to obtain additional returns. The investor is equally disposed toward any $[E(R), \sigma]$ combinations along the specific utility curve U_1.

The curves labeled $(U_{3'}, U_{2'}, U_{1'})$ characterize a less risk-averse investor. Such an investor is willing to tolerate a bit more risk to get a higher expected return.

The best portfolio is the mean-variance efficient portfolio that has the highest utility for a given investor. It lies at the point of tangency between the efficient frontier and the U_1 curve with the highest possible utility. A conservative investor's highest utility is at Point X in Exhibit 6.16, where the U_2 curve just touches the efficient frontier. A less risk-averse investor's highest utility occurs at Point Y, which represents a portfolio on the efficient frontier with higher expected returns and higher risk than the portfolio at X.

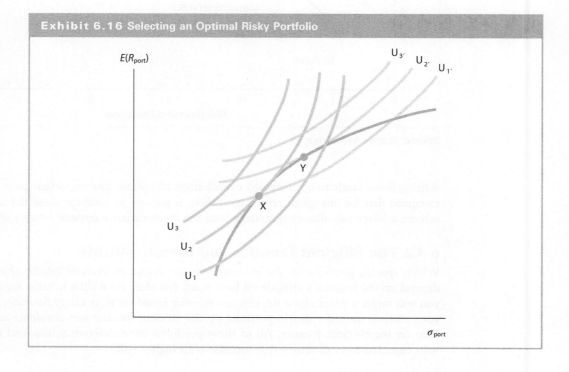

Exhibit 6.16 Selecting an Optimal Risky Portfolio

6.4 CAPITAL MARKET THEORY: AN OVERVIEW

Capital market theory builds directly on the portfolio theory we have just developed by extending the Markowitz efficient frontier into a model for valuing all risky assets. As we will see, capital market theory also has important implications for how portfolios are managed in practice. The development of this approach depends critically on the existence of a risk-free asset, which in turn will lead to the designation of the **market portfolio**, a collection of all available risky assets.

6.4.1 Background for Capital Market Theory

Because capital market theory builds on the Markowitz portfolio model, it requires the same assumptions, along with some additional ones:

1. All investors seek to invest in portfolios representing tangent points on the Markowitz efficient frontier. The exact location of this tangent point and, therefore, the specific portfolio selected will depend on the individual investor's risk–return utility function.

2. Investors can borrow or lend any amount of money at the risk-free rate of return (*RFR*). (Clearly, it is always possible to lend money at the nominal risk-free rate by buying risk-free securities such as government T-bills. It is not possible in practice for everyone to borrow at this level.)

3. All investors have homogeneous expectations; that is, they estimate identical probability distributions for future rates of return.

4. All investors have the same one-period time horizon, such as one month or one year. The model will be developed for a single hypothetical period, and its results could be affected by a different assumption since it requires investors to derive risk measures and risk-free assets that are consistent with their investment horizons.

5. All investments are infinitely divisible, so it is possible to buy or sell fractional shares of any asset or portfolio. This assumption allows us to discuss investment alternatives as continuous curves.

6. There are no taxes or transaction costs involved in buying or selling assets. This is a reasonable assumption in many instances. Neither pension funds nor charitable foundations have to pay taxes, and the transaction costs for most financial institutions are negligible on most investment instruments.

7. Either there is no inflation or any change in interest rates, or inflation is fully anticipated. This is a reasonable initial assumption, and it can be modified.

8. Capital markets are in equilibrium. This means that we begin with all investments properly priced in line with their risk levels.

Some of these assumptions may seem unrealistic, but keep in mind two things. First, as mentioned, relaxing them would have only a minor effect on the model and would not change its main implications or conclusions. Second, a theory should never be judged on the basis of its assumptions but rather on how well it explains and helps us predict behavior in the real world. If this theory and the model it implies help us explain the rates of return on a wide variety of risky assets, it is useful, even if some of its assumptions are unrealistic.

6.4.2 Developing the Capital Market Line

We have defined a **risky asset** as one for which future returns are uncertain, and we have measured this uncertainty by the standard deviation of expected returns. Because the expected return on a risk-free asset is entirely certain, the standard deviation of its expected return is zero ($\sigma_{\mathrm{RF}} = 0$). The rate of return earned on such an asset should be the risk-free rate of return (*RFR*), which, as we discussed in Chapter 1, should equal the expected long-run growth rate of the economy with an adjustment for short-run liquidity. We now show what happens when we introduce this risk-free asset into the risky world of the Markowitz portfolio model.

Covariance with a Risk-Free Asset Recall that the covariance between two sets of returns is:

$$Cov_{ij} = \sum_{i=1}^{n} [R_i - E(R_i)][R_j - E(R_j)]/n$$

Assume for the moment that Asset *i* in this formula is the risk-free asset. Because the returns for the risk-free asset are certain ($\sigma_{RF} = 0$), $R_i = E(R_i)$ during all periods. Thus, $R_i - E(R_i)$ will equal zero, and the product of this expression with any other expression will equal zero. Consequently, the covariance of the risk-free asset with any risky asset or portfolio of assets will always equal zero. Similarly, the correlation between any risky Asset *i*, and the risk-free asset, RF, would also be zero.

Combining a Risk-Free Asset with a Risky Portfolio What happens to the expected rate of return and the standard deviation of returns when you combine a risk-free asset with a portfolio of risky assets such as those that exist on the Markowitz efficient frontier?

Expected Return Like the expected return for a portfolio of two risky assets, the expected rate of return for a portfolio that combines a risk-free asset with a collection of risky assets (call it Portfolio M) is the weighted average of the two returns:

$$E(R_{port}) = w_{RF}(RFR) + (1 - w_{RF})E(R_M)$$

where:

w_{RF} = proportion of the portfolio invested in the risk-free asset

$E(R_M)$ = expected rate of return on risky Portfolio M

Standard Deviation Recall from Equation 6.6 that the variance for a two-asset portfolio is:

$$\sigma_{port}^2 = w_1^2 \sigma_1^2 + w_2^2 \sigma_2^2 + 2w_1 w_2 r_{1,2} \sigma_1 \sigma_2$$

Substituting the risk-free asset for Security 1, and the risky asset Portfolio M for Security 2, this formula would become:

$$\sigma_{port}^2 = w_{RF}^2 \sigma_{RF}^2 + (1 - w_{RF})^2 \sigma_M^2 + 2w_{RF}(1 - w_{RF})r_{RF,M}\sigma_{RF}\sigma_M$$

We know that the variance of the risk-free asset is zero, that is, $\sigma_{RF}^2 = 0$ so the correlation between the risk-free asset and any risky asset, M, is also zero. When you make these adjustments, the variance formula becomes:

$$\sigma_{port}^2 = (1 - w_{RF})^2 \sigma_M^2$$

and the standard deviation is:

$$\sigma_{port} = \sqrt{(1 - w_{RF})^2 \sigma_M^2}$$
$$= (1 - w_{RF})\sigma_M$$

Therefore, the standard deviation of a portfolio that combines the risk-free asset with risky assets is *the linear proportion of the standard deviation of the risky asset portfolio.*

The Risk–Return Combination   With these results, we can develop the risk–return relationship between $E(R_{port})$ and σ_{port} by using a few algebraic manipulations:

$$
\begin{aligned}
E(R_{port}) &= (w_{RF})(RFR) + (1 - w_{RF})E(R_M) + \{RFR - RFR\} \\
&= RFR - (1 - w_{RF})RFR + (1 - w_{RF})E(R_M) \\
&= RFR + (1 - w_{RF})[E(R_M) - RFR] \\
&= RFR + (1 - w_{RF})\{\sigma_M/\sigma_M\}[E(R_M) - RFR]
\end{aligned}
$$

so that:

6.12
$$
E(R_{port}) = RFR + \sigma_{port}\left[\frac{E(R_M) - RFR}{\sigma_M}\right]
$$

Equation 6.12 is the primary result of capital market theory. It can be interpreted as follows: Investors who allocate their money between a riskless security and the risky Portfolio M can expect a return equal to the risk-free rate plus compensation for the number of risk units (σ_{port}) they accept.

This outcome is consistent with the concept underlying all of investment theory that investors perform two functions in the capital markets for which they can expect to be rewarded. First, they allow someone else to use their money, for which they receive the risk-free rate of interest. Second, they bear the risk that the returns they have been promised in exchange for their invested capital will not be repaid. The term $[E(R_M) - RFR]/\sigma_M$ is the expected compensation per unit of risk taken, which is more commonly referred to as the investor's expected *risk premium* per unit of risk.

The Capital Market Line   The risk–return relationship shown in Equation 6.12 holds for every combination of the risk-free asset with *any* collection of risky assets. However, investors would obviously like to maximize their expected compensation for bearing risk (that is, they would like to maximize the risk premium they receive). Let us now assume that Portfolio M is the single collection of risky assets that happens to maximize this risk premium. With this assumption, Portfolio M is called the *market portfolio* and, by definition, it contains all risky assets held anywhere in the marketplace and receives the highest level of expected return (in excess of the risk-free rate) per unit of risk for any available portfolio of risky assets. Under these conditions, Equation 6.12 is called the **capital market line (CML)**.

Exhibit 6.17 shows the various possibilities when a risk-free asset is combined with alternative risky combinations of assets along the Markowitz efficient frontier. Each of the straight lines depicted represents mixtures of a risky portfolio with the riskless asset. For instance, the risk-free asset could be combined in various weights with Portfolio A, as shown by the straight line *RFR–A*. Any combination on this line would dominate portfolio possibilities that fall below it because it would have a higher expected return for the same level of risk. Similarly, any combination of the risk-free asset and Portfolio A is dominated by some mixture of the risk-free asset and Portfolio B.

You can continue to draw lines from *RFR* to portfolios on the efficient frontier with increasingly higher slopes until you reach the point of tangency at Portfolio M. The set of portfolio possibilities along line *RFR–M*—which is the CML—dominates *all* other feasible combinations that investors could form. For example, Point C could be established by investing half of your assets in the riskless security (that is, lending at *RFR*) and the other half in Portfolio M. Notice in Exhibit 6.17 that there is no way to invest your money and achieve a higher expected return for the same level of risk (σ_c). In this sense, *the CML represents a new efficient frontier* that combines the Markowitz efficient frontier of risky assets with the ability to invest in the risk-free security. The slope of the CML is $[E(R_M) - RFR]/\sigma_M$, which is the maximum risk premium compensation that investors can expect for each unit of risk they bear.

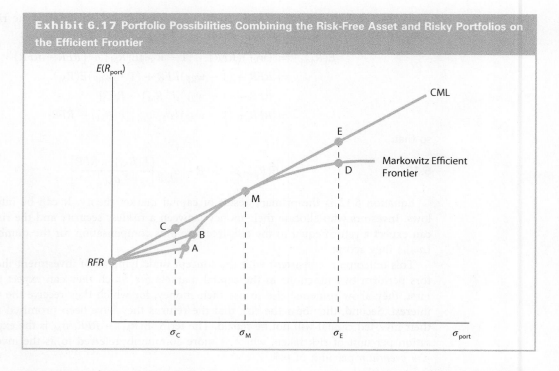

Exhibit 6.17 Portfolio Possibilities Combining the Risk-Free Asset and Risky Portfolios on the Efficient Frontier

Risk–Return Possibilities with Leverage   An investor may want to attain a higher expected return than is available at Point M—which represents a 100 percent allocation to Portfolio M—in exchange for accepting higher risk. One alternative would be to invest in one of the risky asset portfolios on the Markowitz frontier beyond Point M such as the portfolio at Point D. A second alternative is to add *leverage* to the portfolio by *borrowing* money at the risk-free rate and investing the proceeds in the risky asset portfolio at Point M; this is depicted as Point E. What effect would this have on the return and risk for your portfolio?

If you borrow an amount equal to 50 percent of your original wealth at the risk-free rate, w_{RF} will not be a positive fraction but, rather, a negative 50 percent ($w_{RF} = -0.50$). The effect on the expected return for your portfolio is:

$$E(R_{port}) = w_{RF}(RFR) + (1 - w_{RF})E(R_M)$$
$$= -0.50(RFR) + [1 - (-0.50)]E(R_M)$$
$$= -0.50(RFR) + 1.50E(R_M)$$

The return will increase in a *linear* fashion along the CML because the gross return increases by 50 percent, but you must pay interest at the *RFR* on the money borrowed. If $RFR = 0.06$ and $E(R_M) = 0.12$, the return on your leveraged portfolio would be:

$$E(R_{port}) = -0.50(0.06) + 1.5(0.12)$$
$$= -0.03 + 0.18$$
$$= 0.15$$

The effect on the standard deviation of the leveraged portfolio is similar:

$$\sigma_{port} = (1 - w_{RF})\sigma_M$$
$$= [1 - (-0.50)]\sigma_M = 1.50\sigma_M$$

where:

σ_M = standard deviation of Portfolio M

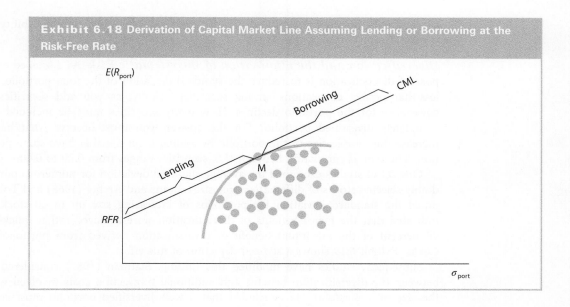

Exhibit 6.18 Derivation of Capital Market Line Assuming Lending or Borrowing at the Risk-Free Rate

Therefore, *both return and risk increase in a linear fashion along the CML.* This is shown in Exhibit 6.18.

Because the CML is a straight line, it implies that all the portfolios on the CML are perfectly positively correlated. This occurs because all portfolios on the CML combine the risky asset Portfolio M and the risk-free asset. You either invest part of your money in the risk-free asset (that is, you *lend* at the *RFR*) and the rest in the risky asset Portfolio M, or you *borrow* at the risk-free rate and invest these funds in the risky asset portfolio. In either case, all the variability comes from the risky asset M portfolio. The only difference between the alternative portfolios on the CML is the magnitude of that variability, which is caused by the proportion of the risky asset portfolio held in the total portfolio.

6.4.3 Risk, Diversification, and the Market Portfolio

The investment prescription that emerges from capital market theory is clear-cut: Investors should only invest their funds in two types of assets—the risk-free security and the risky collections of assets representing Portfolio M—with the weights of these two holdings determined by the investors' tolerance for risk. Because of the special place that the market Portfolio M holds for all investors, it must contain *all risky assets* that exist in the marketplace. This includes not just U.S. common stocks, but also non-U.S. stocks, U.S. and non-U.S. bonds, real estate, private equity, options and futures contracts, art, antiques, and so on. Further, these assets should be represented in Portfolio M in proportion to their relative market values.

Since the market portfolio contains all risky assets, it is a **completely diversified portfolio**, which means that all risk unique to individual assets in the portfolio has been diversified away. Unique risk—which is often called **unsystematic risk**—of any single asset is completely offset by the unique variability of all of the other holdings in the portfolio. This implies that only **systematic risk**, defined as the variability in all risky assets caused by marketwide variables, remains in Portfolio M. Systematic risk can be measured by the standard deviation of returns to the market portfolio, and it changes over time whenever there are changes in the underlying economic forces that affect the valuation of all risky assets, such as variability of money supply growth, interest rate volatility, and variability in industrial production or corporate earnings.[7]

Diversification and the Elimination of Unsystematic Risk As discussed earlier, the purpose of diversification is to reduce the standard deviation of the total portfolio. This assumes less-than-perfect correlations among securities. Ideally, as you add securities, the average covariance for the portfolio declines. How many securities must be included to arrive at a completely diversified portfolio? For the answer, you must observe what happens as you increase the sample size of the portfolio by adding securities that have some positive correlation. The typical correlation between U.S. securities ranges from 0.20 to 0.60.

One set of studies examined the average standard deviation for numerous portfolios of randomly selected stocks of different sample sizes. Evans and Archer (1968) and Tole (1982) computed the standard deviation for portfolios of increasing size up to 20 stocks. The results indicated that the major benefits of diversification were achieved rather quickly, with about 90 percent of the maximum benefit of diversification derived from portfolios of 12 to 18 stocks. Exhibit 6.19 shows a stylized depiction of this effect.

Subsequent studies have modified this finding. Statman (1987) considered the trade-off between the diversification benefits and additional transaction costs involved with increasing the size of a portfolio. He concluded that a well-diversified portfolio must contain at least 30–40 stocks. Campbell, Lettau, Malkiel, and Xu (2001) demonstrated that because the unique portion of an individual stock's total risk has been increasing in recent years, it now takes more stocks to diversify a portfolio. For instance, they showed that the level of diversification that was possible with only 20 stocks in the 1960s would require about 50 stocks by the late 1990s. Alexeev and Tapon (2014) confirmed this trend and demonstrated for five different developed markets that it might take as many as 70 stocks to diversify away extreme downside risk events.

The important point is that, by adding to a portfolio new stocks that are not perfectly correlated with stocks already held, you can reduce the overall standard deviation of the portfolio, which will eventually reach the level in the market portfolio. At that point, you will have

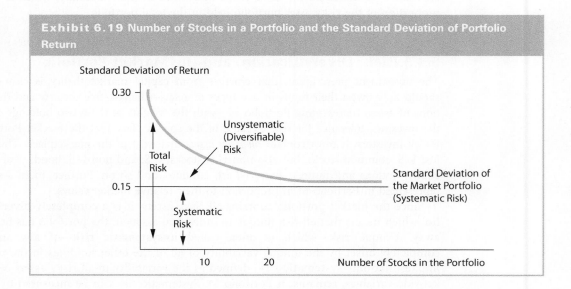

Exhibit 6.19 Number of Stocks in a Portfolio and the Standard Deviation of Portfolio Return

---

diversified away all unsystematic risk, but you still have market or systematic risk. You cannot eliminate the variability and uncertainty of macroeconomic factors that affect all risky assets. Further, you can attain a lower level of systematic risk by diversifying globally versus only diversifying within the United States because some of the systematic risk factors in the U.S. market (such as U.S. monetary policy) are not perfectly correlated with systematic risk variables in other countries, like Germany and Japan.

The CML and the Separation Theorem The CML leads all investors to invest in the same risky asset Portfolio M. Individual investors should only differ regarding their position on the CML, which depends on their risk preferences. In turn, how they get to a point on the CML is based on their *financing decisions*. If you are relatively risk averse, you will lend some part of your portfolio at the *RFR* by buying some risk-free securities and investing the remainder in the market portfolio of risky assets (for example, Point C in Exhibit 6.17). In contrast, if you prefer more risk, you might borrow funds at the *RFR* and invest everything (all of your capital plus what you borrowed) in the market portfolio (Point E in Exhibit 6.17). This financing decision provides more risk but greater expected returns than the market portfolio. Because portfolios on the CML dominate other portfolio possibilities, the CML becomes the new efficient frontier of portfolios, and investors decide where they want to be along this efficient frontier. Tobin (1958) called this division of the investment decision from the financing decision the **separation theorem**. Specifically, to be somewhere on the CML efficient frontier, you initially decide to invest in the market Portfolio M. This is your *investment* decision. Subsequently, based on your risk preferences, you make a separate *financing* decision either to borrow or to lend to attain your preferred risk position on the CML.

A Risk Measure for the CML In discussing the Markowitz portfolio model, we noted that the relevant risk to consider when adding a security to a portfolio is *its average covariance with all other assets in the portfolio*. Capital market theory now shows that *the only relevant portfolio is the market Portfolio M*. Together, this means that the only important consideration for any individual risky asset is its average covariance with all the risky assets in Portfolio M or *the asset's covariance with the market portfolio*. This covariance, then, is the relevant risk measure for an individual risky asset.

Because all individual risky assets are a part of the market portfolio, one can describe their rates of return in relation to the returns to Portfolio M using the following linear model:

6.13
$$R_{it} = a_i + b_i R_{Mt} + \varepsilon$$

where:

R_{it} = return for Asset i during period t
a_i = constant term for Asset i
b_i = slope coefficient for Asset i
R_{Mt} = return for Portfolio M during period t
ε = random error term

The variance of returns for a risky asset can similarly be described as:

6.14
$$\begin{aligned}
\text{Var}(R_{it}) &= \text{Var}(a_i + b_i R_{Mt} + \varepsilon) \\
&= \text{Var}(a_i) + \text{Var}(b_i R_{Mt}) + \text{Var}(\varepsilon) \\
&= 0 + \text{Var}(b_i R_{Mt}) + \text{Var}(\varepsilon)
\end{aligned}$$

Note that $\text{Var}(b_i R_{Mt})$ is the variance of return for an asset related to the variance of the market return, or the asset's *systematic variance or risk*. Also, $\text{Var}(\varepsilon)$ is the residual variance of return for the individual asset that is not related to the market portfolio. This residual variance is what we have referred to as the unsystematic or *unique risk* because it arises from the unique features of the asset. Therefore:

$$\text{Var}(R_{i,t}) = \text{Systematic Variance} + \text{Unsystematic Variance}$$

We know that a completely diversified portfolio has had all of its unsystematic variance eliminated. Therefore, only the systematic variance is relevant because it cannot be diversified away.

6.4.4 Investing with the CML: An Example

Suppose that after doing considerable research on current capital market conditions, you have estimated the investment characteristics for six different combinations of risky assets. Exhibit 6.20 lists your expected return and standard deviation forecasts for these portfolios. You have also established that each of these portfolios is completely diversified so that its volatility estimate represents systematic risk only. The risk-free rate at the time of your analysis is 4 percent.

Based on your forecasts for $E(R)$ and σ alone, none of these portfolios clearly dominates the others since higher levels of expected return always come at the cost of higher levels of risk. Which portfolio offers the best trade-off between risk and return? The last column in Exhibit 6.20 calculates the ratio of the expected risk premium $E(R) - RFR$ to volatility (σ) for each portfolio. As explained earlier, this ratio is the *amount of compensation that investors can expect for each unit of risk* they assume in a particular portfolio. For example, Portfolio 2 offers investors $0.429 (= [7 - 4]/7)$ units of compensation per unit of risk while the comparable ratio for Portfolio 6 is lower at $0.393 (= [15 - 4]/28)$, despite promising a much higher overall return.

By this measure, Portfolio 3 offers investors the best combination of risk and return. No other feasible collection of risky assets in this comparison can match the 0.500 units of expected risk premium per unit of risk. Consequently, Portfolio 3 should be considered as the market portfolio, Portfolio M. Capital market theory would recommend that you only consider two alternatives when investing your funds: (1) lending or borrowing in the riskless security at 4 percent, and (2) buying Portfolio 3.

Suppose now that given your risk tolerance you are willing to assume a standard deviation of 8.5 percent. How should you go about investing your money, according to the CML? First, using Equation 6.12, the return you can expect is:

$$4\% + (8.5\%)(0.500) = 8.25\%$$

As we have seen, there is no way for you to obtain a higher expected return under the current conditions without assuming more risk. Second, you can find the investment strategy necessary to achieve this return by solving:

$$8.25\% = w_{RF}(4\%) + (1 - w_{RF})(9\%)$$

or

$$w_{RF} = (9 - 8.25)/(9 - 4) = 0.15$$

Exhibit 6.20 Investment Characteristics for Portfolios of Risky Assets ($RFR = 4\%$)

Portfolio	Expected Return	Standard Deviation	$[E(R) - RFR]/\sigma$
1	5%	5%	0.200
2	7	7	0.429
3	9	10	0.500
4	11	15	0.467
5	13	21	0.429
6	15	28	0.393

This means that you would need to invest 15 percent of your funds in the riskless asset and the remaining 85 percent in Portfolio 3. Finally, notice that the expected risk premium per unit of risk for this position is 0.500 ($= [8.25 - 4]/8.5$), the same as Portfolio 3. In fact, all points along the CML will have the same risk–return trade-off as the market portfolio since this ratio is just the slope of the CML.

As a last extension, consider what would happen if you were willing to take on a risk level of $\sigma = 15$ percent. From Exhibit 6.20, you could realize an expected return of 11 percent if you placed 100 percent of funds in Portfolio 4. However, you can do better than this by following the investment prescription of the CML. Specifically, for a risk level of 15 percent, you can obtain an expected return of:

$$4\% + (15\%)(0.500) = 11.5\%$$

This expected outcome is greater than the expected return offered by a 100 percent investment in the market portfolio (that is, 9 percent), so you will have to use leverage to achieve it. Specifically, solving for the investment weights along the CML leaves $w_{RF} = (9 - 11.5)/(9 - 4) = -0.50$ and $(1 - w_{RF}) = 1.50$. Thus, for each dollar you currently have to invest, you will need to borrow an additional 50 cents and place all of these funds in Portfolio 3.

SUMMARY

- The basic portfolio model derives the expected rate of return for a portfolio of assets and a measure of risk, which is the standard deviation of potential rates of return. Markowitz showed that the expected rate of return of a portfolio is the weighted average of the expected return for the individual investments in the portfolio. The standard deviation of a portfolio is a function not only of the standard deviations for the individual investments but also of the covariance between the rates of return for all the pairs of assets in the portfolio. In a large portfolio, these covariances are the important factors.

- By changing the investment weights, or the amounts of a portfolio held in various assets, an investor can generate a curve of potential risk–return combinations. Correlation coefficients among assets are the critical factor to consider when selecting investments. Investors can maintain their rate of return while reducing the risk level of their portfolio by combining assets or portfolios that have low-positive or negative correlation.

- Assuming numerous assets and a multitude of combination curves, the efficient frontier is the envelope curve that encompasses all of the best combinations. It defines the set of portfolios that has the highest expected return for each given level of risk or, equivalently, the minimum risk for each given level of return. From this set of optimal portfolios, investors select the one that lies at the point of tangency between the efficient frontier and their highest utility curve. Because risk–return utility functions differ, the point of tangency and, therefore, the portfolio choice will differ among investors.

- Capital market theory expanded the concepts introduced by Markowitz portfolio theory by introducing the notion that investors could borrow or lend at the risk-free rate in addition to forming efficient portfolios of risky assets. This insight led to the development of the *capital market line* (*CML*), which can be viewed as a new efficient frontier that emanates from the risk-free rate and is tangent to the Markowitz efficient frontier. The point of tangency is called the market portfolio.

- The CML's main contribution is the relationship it specifies between the risk and expected return of a well-diversified portfolio. The CML makes it clear that the market portfolio is the single collection of risky assets that maximizes the ratio of expected risk premium to portfolio volatility. The investment prescription of the CML is that investors cannot do better, on average, than when they divide their investment funds between (1) the riskless asset and (2) the market portfolio.

SUGGESTED READINGS

Elton, Edwin J., Martin J. Gruber, Stephen J. Brown, and William N. Goetzmann. *Modern Portfolio Theory and Investment Analysis*, 9th ed. New York: Wiley, 2014.

Farrell, James L., Jr. *Portfolio Management: Theory and Application*, 2nd ed. New York: McGraw-Hill, 1997.

Maginn, John L., Donald L. Tuttle, Jerald E. Pinto, and Dennis W. Mcleavy, *Managing Investment Portfolios: A Dynamic Process*, 3rd ed. Hoboken, NJ: John Wiley & Sons, 2016.

QUESTIONS

1. Why do most investors hold diversified portfolios?
2. What is covariance, and why is it important in portfolio theory?
3. Why do most assets of the same type show positive covariances of returns with each other? Would you expect positive covariances of returns between *different* types of assets such as returns on Treasury bills, Apple common stock, and commercial real estate? Why or why not?
4. What is the relationship between covariance and the correlation coefficient?
5. Explain the shape of the Markowitz (that is, mean-variance) efficient frontier, specifically what causes it to be curved rather than a straight line.
6. Draw a properly labeled graph of the Markowitz efficient frontier. Describe the efficient frontier in exact terms. Discuss the concept of dominant portfolios, and show an example of one on your graph.
7. Assume you want to run a computer program to derive the efficient frontier for your feasible set of stocks. What information must you input to the program?
8. Why are investors' utility curves important in portfolio theory?
9. Explain how a given investor chooses an optimal portfolio. Will this choice always be a diversified portfolio, or could it be a single asset? Explain your answer.
10. Assume that you and a business associate develop an efficient frontier for a set of investments. Why might the two of you select different portfolios on the frontier?
11. Draw a hypothetical graph of an efficient frontier of U.S. common stocks. On the same graph, draw an efficient frontier assuming the inclusion of U.S. bonds as well. Finally, on the same graph, draw an efficient frontier that includes U.S. common stocks, U.S. bonds, and stocks and bonds from around the world. Discuss the differences in these frontiers.
12. Stocks K, L, and M each has the same expected return and standard deviation. The correlation coefficients between each pair of these stocks are:

    K and L correlation coefficient = +0.8
    K and M correlation coefficient = +0.2
    L and M correlation coefficient = −0.4

    Given these correlations, a portfolio constructed of which pair of stocks will have the lowest standard deviation? Explain.
13. What changes would you expect in the standard deviation for a portfolio of between four and 10 stocks, between 10 and 20 stocks, and between 50 and 100 stocks?
14. Draw a graph that shows what happens to the Markowitz efficient frontier when you combine a risk-free asset with alternative risky asset portfolios on the Markowitz efficient frontier. Explain why the line from the *RFR* that is tangent to the efficient frontier defines the dominant set of portfolio possibilities.
15. Explain how the capital market line (CML) allows an investor to achieve an expected return goal that is greater than that available to a 100 percent allocation to the market portfolio of risky assets, Portfolio M.

PROBLEMS

1. Considering the world economic outlook for the coming year and estimates of sales and earnings in the pharmaceutical industry, you expect the rate of return for Lauren Labs common stock to range between −20 percent and +40 percent with the following probabilities:

Probability	Possible Returns
0.10	−0.20
0.15	−0.05
0.20	0.10
0.25	0.15
0.20	0.20
0.10	0.40

Compute the expected rate of return $E(R_i)$ for Lauren Labs.

2. Given the following market values of stocks in your portfolio and their forecasted rates of return, what is the expected rate of return for your common stock portfolio?

Stock	Market Value ($ millions)	$E(R_i)$
Disney	$15,000	0.14
Starbucks	17,000	−0.14
Harley Davidson	32,000	0.18
Intel	23,000	0.16
Walgreens	7,000	0.12

3. The following are the monthly rates of return for Madison Cookies and for Sophie Electric during a six-month period.

Month	Madison Cookies	Sophie Electric
1	−0.04	0.07
2	0.06	−0.02
3	−0.07	−0.10
4	0.12	0.15
5	−0.02	−0.06
6	0.05	0.02

Compute the following:

a. Average monthly rate of return, $\bar{R}_i$, for each stock
b. Standard deviation of returns for each stock
c. Covariance between the rates of return
d. The correlation coefficient between the rates of return

What level of correlation would you have expected before performing your calculations? How did your expectations compare with the computed correlation? Would these two stocks be good choices for diversification? Why or why not?

4. You are considering two assets with the following characteristics:

$$E(R_1) = 0.15 \qquad \sigma_1 = 0.10 \qquad w_1 = 0.5$$
$$E(R_2) = 0.20 \qquad \sigma_2 = 0.20 \qquad w_2 = 0.5$$

Compute the mean and standard deviation of two portfolios if $r_{1,2} = 0.40$ and -0.60, respectively. Plot the two portfolios on a risk–return graph and briefly explain the results.

5. Given:

$$E(R_1) = 0.10$$
$$E(R_2) = 0.15$$
$$\sigma_1 = 0.03$$
$$\sigma_2 = 0.05$$

Calculate the expected returns and standard deviations of a two-stock portfolio in which Stock 1 has a weight of 60 percent under each of the following conditions:

a. $r_{1,2} = 1.00$
b. $r_{1,2} = 0.75$
c. $r_{1,2} = 0.25$
d. $r_{1,2} = 0.00$
e. $r_{1,2} = -0.25$
f. $r_{1,2} = -0.75$
g. $r_{1,2} = -1.00$

6. Given: $E(R_1) = 0.12$

$$E(R_2) = 0.16$$
$$E(\sigma_1) = 0.04$$
$$E(\sigma_2) = 0.06$$

Calculate the expected returns and expected standard deviations of a two-stock portfolio having a correlation coefficient of 0.70 under the following conditions:

a. $w_1 = 1.00$
b. $w_1 = 0.75$
c. $w_1 = 0.50$
d. $w_1 = 0.25$
e. $w_1 = 0.05$

Plot the results on a risk-return graph. Without calculations, draw what the curve would look like first if the correlation coefficient had been 0.00 and then if it had been -0.70.

7. The following are monthly percentage price changes for four market indexes:

Month	DJIA	S&P 500	Russell 2000	Nikkei
1	0.03	0.02	0.04	0.04
2	0.07	0.06	0.10	−0.02
3	−0.02	−0.01	−0.04	0.07
4	0.01	0.03	0.03	0.02
5	0.05	0.04	0.11	0.02
6	−0.06	−0.04	−0.08	0.06

Compute the following:

a. Average monthly rate of return for each index
b. Standard deviation for each index
c. Covariance between the rates of return for the following indexes:

DJIA–S&P 500
S&P 500–Russell 2000
S&P 500–Nikkei
Russell 2000–Nikkei

d. The correlation coefficients for the same four combinations
e. Using the answers from parts (a), (b), and (d), calculate the expected return and standard deviation of a portfolio consisting of equal parts of (1) the S&P and the Russell 2000 and (2) the S&P and the Nikkei. Discuss the two portfolios.

8. The standard deviation of Shamrock Corp. stock is 19 percent. The standard deviation of Cara Co. stock is 14 percent. The covariance between these two stocks is 100. What is the correlation between Shamrock and Cara stock?

9. As chief investment officer of a small endowment fund, you are considering expanding the fund's strategic asset allocation from just common stock (CS) and fixed-income (FI) to include private real estate partnerships (PR) as well:

Current Allocation: 60 percent of Asset CS, 40 percent of Asset FI
Proposed Allocation: 50 percent of Asset CS, 30 percent of Asset FI, 20 percent of Asset PR

You also consider the following historical data for the three risky asset classes (CS, FI, and PR) and the risk-free rate (*RFR*) over a recent investment period:

| | | | | r_{ij}: | |
Asset Class	E(R)	σ	CS	FI	PR
CS	8.6%	15.2%	1.0		
FI	5.6	8.6	0.2	1.0	
PR	7.1	11.7	0.6	0.1	1.0
RFR	3.1	—			

You have already determined that the expected return and standard deviation for the Current Allocation are: $E(R_{current}) = 7.40$ percent and $\sigma_{current} = 10.37$ percent

a. Calculate the expected return for the Proposed Allocation.
b. Calculate the standard deviation for the Proposed Allocation.
c. For *both* the Current and Proposed Allocations, calculate the expected risk premium per unit of risk (that is, $[E(R_p) - RFR]/\sigma$).
d. Using your calculations from part (c), explain which of these two portfolios is the most likely to fall on the Markowitz efficient frontier.

10. You are evaluating various investment opportunities currently available and you have calculated expected returns and standard deviations for five different well-diversified portfolios of risky assets:

Portfolio	Expected Return	Standard Deviation
Q	7.8%	10.5%
R	10.0	14.0
S	4.6	5.0
T	11.7	18.5
U	6.2	7.5

a. For each portfolio, calculate the risk premium per unit of risk that you expect to receive ($[E(R) - RFR]/\sigma$). Assume that the risk-free rate is 3.0 percent.
b. Using your computations in part (a), explain which of these five portfolios is most likely to be the market portfolio. Use your calculations to draw the capital market line (CML).
c. If you are only willing to make an investment with $\sigma = 7.0$ percent, is it possible for you to earn a return of 7.0 percent?

d. What is the minimum level of risk that would be necessary for an investment to earn 7.0 percent? What is the composition of the portfolio along the CML that will generate that expected return?

e. Suppose you are now willing to make an investment with $\sigma = 18.2$ percent. What would be the investment proportions in the riskless asset and the market portfolio for this portfolio? What is the expected return for this portfolio?

A. Proof That Minimum Portfolio Variance Occurs with Equal Investment Weights When Securities Have Equal Variance

When $\sigma_1 = \sigma_2$, we have:

$$\begin{aligned}
\sigma_{\text{port}}^2 &= w_1^2(\sigma_1)^2 + (1-w_1)^2(\sigma_1)^2 - 2w_1(1-w_1)r_{1,2}(\sigma_1)^2 \\
&= (\sigma_1)^2\left[w_1^2 + 1 - 2w_1 + w_1^2 + 2w_1r_{1,2} - 2w_1^2r_{1,2}\right] \\
&= (\sigma_1)^2\left[2w_1^2 + 1 - 2w_1 + 2w_1r_{1,2} - 2w_1^2r_{1,2}\right]
\end{aligned}$$

For this to be a minimum:

$$\frac{\partial(\sigma_{\text{port}}^2)}{\partial w_1} = 0 = (\sigma_1)^2[4w_1 \times 2 + 2r_{1,2} \times 4w_1r_{1,2}]$$

Since $(\sigma_1)^2 > 0$:

$$4w_1 - 2 + 2r_{1,2} - 4w_1r_{1,2} = 0$$
$$4w_1(1 - r_{1,2}) - 2(1 - r_{1,2}) = 0$$

from which:

$$w_1\frac{2(1-r_{1,2})}{4(1-r_{1,2})} = \frac{1}{2}$$

regardless of $r_{1,2}$. Thus, if $\sigma_1 = \sigma_2$, σ_{port}^2 will *always* be minimized by choosing $w_1 = w_2 = 1/2$, regardless of the value of $r_{1,2}$, except when $r_{1,2} = +1$ (in which case $\sigma_{\text{port}} = \sigma_1 = \sigma_2$). This can be verified by checking the second-order condition:

$$\frac{\partial(\sigma_{\text{port}}^2)}{\partial w_1^2} > 0$$

Problem

1. The general equation for the weight of the first security to achieve minimum variance (in a two-stock portfolio) is given by:

$$w_1 = \frac{(\sigma_2)^2 - r_{1,2}(\sigma_1)(\sigma_2)}{(\sigma_1)^2 + (\sigma_2)^2 - 2r_{1,2}(\sigma_1)(\sigma_2)}$$

1a. Show that $w_1 = 0.5$ when $\sigma_1 = \sigma_2$.

1b. What is the weight of Security 1 that gives minimum portfolio variance when $r_{1,2} = 0.5$, $\sigma_1 = 0.04$, and $\sigma_2 = 0.06$?

B. Derivation of Investment Weights That Will Give Zero Variance When Correlation Equals −1.00

$$\begin{aligned}
\sigma_{\text{port}}^2 &= w_1^2(\sigma_1)^2 + (1-w_1)^2(\sigma_2)^2 + 2w_1(1-w_1)r_{1,2}(\sigma_1)(\sigma_2) \\
&= w_1^2(\sigma_1)^2 + (\sigma_2)^2 + 2w_1(\sigma_2) - w_1^2(\sigma_2)^2 + 2w_1r_{1,2}(\sigma_1)(\sigma_2) - 2w_1^2r_{1,2}(\sigma_1)(\sigma_2)
\end{aligned}$$

If $r_{1,2} = -1$, this can be rearranged and expressed as:

$$\sigma^2_{\text{port}} = w_1^2[(\sigma_1)^2 + 2(\sigma_1)(\sigma_2) + (\sigma_2)^2] - 2w[(\sigma_2)^2 + (\sigma_1)(\sigma_2)] + (\sigma_2)^2$$
$$= \{w_1[(\sigma_1) + (\sigma_2) - (\sigma_2)]\}^2$$

We want to find the weight, w_1, which will reduce (σ^2_{port}) to *zero*; therefore:

$$w_1[(\sigma_1) + (\sigma_2)] - (\sigma_2) = 0$$

which yields:

$$w_1 = \frac{(\sigma_2)}{(\sigma_1) + (\sigma_2)}, \text{ and } w_2 = 1 - w_1 = \frac{(\sigma_1)}{(\sigma_1) + (\sigma_2)}$$

Problem

1. Given two assets with the following characteristics:

$$E(R_1) = 0.12 \;\; \sigma_1 = 0.04$$
$$E(R_2) = 0.16 \;\; \sigma_2 = 0.06$$

Assume that $r_{1,2} = -1.00$. What is the weight that would lead to a zero variance for the portfolio?

CHAPTER **7**

Asset Pricing Models

After you read this chapter, you should be able to answer the following questions:

- How does the capital asset pricing model (CAPM) extend the results of capital market theory?
- What special role does beta play in the CAPM, and how do investors calculate a security's characteristic line in practice?
- What is the security market line (SML), and what are the similarities and differences between the SML and the capital market line (CML)?
- How can the SML be used to evaluate whether securities are properly priced?
- What do the various empirical tests of the CAPM allow us to conclude, and does the selection of a proxy for the market portfolio matter?
- What is the arbitrage pricing theory (APT), and how is it similar to and different from the CAPM?
- How can the APT be used in the security valuation process?
- How do you test the APT by examining anomalies found with the CAPM?
- What are multifactor models, and how are they related to the APT?
- What are the two primary approaches used in defining common risk factors?
- What are the main macroeconomic variables used in practice as risk factors?
- What are the main security characteristic–oriented variables used in practice as risk factors?
- How are multifactor models used to estimate the expected risk premium of a security or portfolio?

Following the development of portfolio theory by Markowitz, two major theories have been derived for the valuation of risky assets. In this chapter, we first introduce the **capital asset pricing model (CAPM)**. The background on the CAPM is important at this point in the book because the risk measure it implies is a necessary input for much of our subsequent discussion. We then consider an alternative asset valuation model—the **arbitrage pricing theory (APT)**—which has led to the development of numerous other **multifactor models** of risk and expected return.

7.1 THE CAPITAL ASSET PRICING MODEL

The capital market theory described in Chapter 6 represented a major step forward in how investors should think about the investment process. The formula for the CML (Equation 6.12) offers a precise way of calculating the return that investors can expect for (1) providing their financial capital (RFR) and (2) bearing σ_{port} units of risk ($[E(R_M) - RFR]/\sigma_M$). This last term is especially significant because it expresses the expected risk premium prevailing in the marketplace.

Unfortunately, capital market theory is an incomplete explanation for the relationship that exists between risk and return. This is because the CML defined the risk an investor bears by the *total* volatility (σ) of the investment. However, since investors cannot expect to be compensated for any portion of risk that they could have diversified away (unsystematic risk), the

CML is based on the assumption that investors only hold *fully diversified portfolios*, for which total risk and systematic risk are the same thing. So, the CML cannot provide an explanation for the risk–return trade-off for *individual* risky assets because the standard deviation for these securities will contain a substantial amount of unique risk.

The capital asset pricing model (CAPM) extends capital market theory in a way that allows investors to evaluate the risk–return trade-off for both diversified portfolios *and* individual securities. To do this, the CAPM redefines the relevant measure of risk from total volatility to just the nondiversifiable portion of that total volatility (systematic risk). This new risk measure is called the **beta** coefficient, and it calculates the level of a security's systematic risk compared to that of the market portfolio. Using beta as the relevant measure of risk, the CAPM then redefines the expected risk premium per unit of risk in a commensurate fashion. This in turn leads once again to an expression of the expected return that can be decomposed into (1) the risk-free rate and (2) the expected risk premium.

7.1.1 A Conceptual Development of the CAPM

Sharpe (1964), along with Lintner (1965) and Mossin (1966), developed the CAPM in a formal way. In addition to the assumptions listed before, the CAPM requires others, such as that asset returns come from a normal probability distribution. Rather than provide a mathematical derivation of the CAPM, we will present a conceptual development of the model, emphasizing its role in the natural progression that began with the Markowitz portfolio theory.

Recall that the CML expresses the risk–return trade-off for fully diversified portfolios as follows:

$$E(R_{\text{port}}) = RFR + \sigma_{\text{port}} \left[\frac{E(R_{\text{M}}) - RFR}{\sigma_{\text{M}}} \right]$$

When trying to extend this expression to allow for the evaluation of any individual risky Asset i, the logical temptation is to simply replace the standard deviation of the portfolio (σ_{port}) with that of the single security (σ_i). However, this would overstate the relevant level of risk in the ith security because it does not take into account how much of that volatility the investor could diversify away by combining that asset with other holdings. One way to address this concern is to "shrink" the level of σ_i to include only the portion of risk in Security i that is systematically related to the risk in the market portfolio. This can be done by multiplying σ_i by the correlation coefficient between the returns to Security i and the market portfolio ($r_{i\text{M}}$). Inserting this product into the CML and adapting the notation for the ith individual asset leaves:

$$E(R_i) = RFR + (\sigma_i r_{i\text{M}}) \left[\frac{E(R_{\text{M}}) - RFR}{\sigma_{\text{M}}} \right]$$

This expression can be rearranged as:

$$E(R_i) = RFR + \left(\frac{\sigma_i r_{i\text{M}}}{\sigma_{\text{M}}} \right) [E(R_{\text{M}}) - RFR]$$

7.1
$$E(R_i) = RFR + \beta_i [E(R_{\text{M}}) - RFR]$$

Equation 7.1 is the CAPM. The CAPM redefines risk in terms of a security's beta (β_i), which captures the nondiversifiable portion of that stock's risk *relative to the market as a whole*. Because of this, beta can be thought of as *indexing* the asset's systematic risk to that of the market portfolio. This leads to a very convenient interpretation: A stock with a beta of 1.20 has a level of systematic risk that is 20 percent greater than the average for the entire market, while a stock with a beta of 0.70 is 30 percent less risky than the market. By definition, the market portfolio itself will always have a beta of 1.00.

Indexing the systematic risk of an individual security to the market has another nice feature as well. From Equation 7.1, it is clear that the CAPM once again expresses the expected return for an investment as the sum of the risk-free rate and the expected risk premium. However, rather than calculate a different risk premium for every separate security that exists, the CAPM states that only the overall **market risk premium** $(E(R_M) - RFR)$ matters and that this quantity can then be adapted to any risky asset by scaling it up or down according to that asset's riskiness relative to the market (β_i). As we will see, this substantially reduces the number of calculations that investors must make when evaluating potential investments for their portfolios.

7.1.2 The Security Market Line

The CAPM can also be illustrated in graphical form as the **security market line (SML)**. This is shown in Exhibit 7.1. Like the CML, the SML shows the trade-off between risk and expected return as a straight line intersecting the vertical axis (zero-risk point) at the risk-free rate. However, there are two important differences between the CML and the SML. First, the CML measures total risk by the standard deviation of the investment while the SML considers only the systematic component of an investment's volatility. Second, because of the first point, the CML can be applied only to portfolio holdings that are already fully diversified, whereas the SML can be applied to any individual asset or collection of assets.

Determining the Expected Rate of Return for a Risky Asset To demonstrate how you would compute expected or required rates of return with the CAPM, consider as an example the following stocks, assuming you have already computed betas:

Stock	Beta
A	0.70
B	1.00
C	1.15
D	1.40
E	−0.30

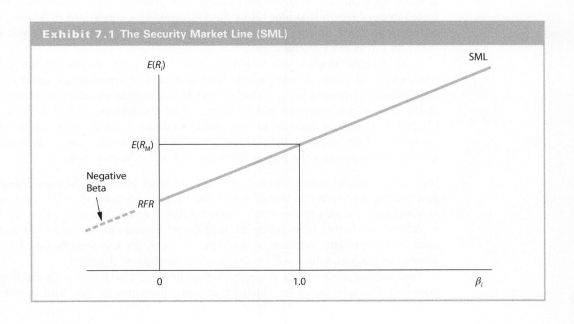

Exhibit 7.1 The Security Market Line (SML)

We expect the economy's *RFR* to be 5 percent (0.05) and the expected return on the market portfolio ($E(R_M)$) to be 9 percent (0.09). This implies a market risk premium of 4 percent (0.04). With these inputs, the SML would yield the following required rates of return for these five stocks:

$$E(R_i) = RFR + \beta_i[E(R_M) - RFR]$$
$$E(R_A) = 0.05 + 0.70(0.09 - 0.05)$$
$$= 0.078 = 7.80\%$$
$$E(R_B) = 0.05 + 1.00(0.09 - 0.05)$$
$$= 0.09 = 9.00\%$$
$$E(R_C) = 0.05 + 1.15(0.09 - 0.05)$$
$$= 0.096 = 9.60\%$$
$$E(R_D) = 0.05 + 1.40(0.09 - 0.05)$$
$$= 0.106 = 10.60\%$$
$$E(R_E) = 0.05 + (-0.30)(0.09 - 0.05)$$
$$= 0.05 - 0.012$$
$$= 0.038 = 3.80\%$$

Stock A has lower risk than the aggregate market, so you should not expect its return to be as high as the return on the market portfolio. You should expect Stock A to return 7.80 percent. Stock B has systematic risk equal to the market's (beta = 1.00), so its required rate of return should likewise be equal to the expected market return (9 percent). Stocks C and D have systematic risk greater than the market's, so they should provide returns consistent with their risk. Finally, Stock E has a *negative* beta (which is quite rare in practice), so its required rate of return, if such a stock could be found, would be below the *RFR* of 5 percent.

In equilibrium, *all* assets and *all* portfolios of assets should plot on the SML. That is, all assets should be priced so that their **estimated rates of return**, which are the actual holding period rates of return that you anticipate, are consistent with their levels of systematic risk. Any security with an estimated rate of return that plots above the SML would be considered undervalued because it implies that you forecast receiving a rate of return on the security that is above its *required* rate of return based on its systematic risk. In contrast, assets with estimated rates of return that plot below the SML would be considered overvalued. This position relative to the SML implies that your estimated rate of return is below what you should require based on the asset's systematic risk.

In an efficient market, you would not expect any assets to plot off the SML because, in equilibrium, all stocks should provide holding period returns that are equal to their required rates of return. Alternatively, a market that is not completely efficient may misprice certain assets because not everyone will be aware of all the relevant information. As discussed in Chapter 5, a superior investor has the ability to derive value estimates for assets that consistently outperform the consensus market evaluation. As a result, such an investor will earn better rates of return than the average investor on a risk-adjusted basis.

Identifying Undervalued and Overvalued Assets Now that we understand how to compute the rate of return one should expect for a risky asset using the SML, we can compare this *required* rate of return to the asset's *estimated* rate of return over a specific investment horizon to determine whether it would be an appropriate investment. To make this comparison, you need an independent estimate of the return outlook for the security based on fundamental analysis techniques, which will be discussed in subsequent chapters.

Assume that analysts at a major brokerage firm have been following the five stocks in the preceding example. Based on extensive analysis, they provide you with forecasted price and

Exhibit 7.2 Price, Dividend, and Rate of Return Estimates

Stock	Current Price (P_t)	Expected Price (P_{t+1})	Expected Dividend (D_{t+1})	Estimated Future Rate of Return (%)
A	25	26	1.00	8.00%
B	40	42	0.50	6.25
C	33	37	1.00	15.15
D	64	66	1.10	4.84
E	50	53	0.00	6.00

dividend information for the next year, as shown in Exhibit 7.2. Given these projections, you can compute an estimated rate of return for each stock by summing the expected capital gain ($[P_{t+1} - P_t]/P_t$) and the expected dividend yield (D_{t+1}/P_t). For example, the analysts' estimated future return for Stock A is 8.00 percent ($=[26 - 25]/25 + 1/25$).

Exhibit 7.3 summarizes the relationship between the required rate of return for each stock based on its systematic risk, as computed earlier, and its estimated rate of return. This difference between estimated return and expected return is sometimes referred to as a stock's expected *alpha* or its excess return. This alpha can be positive (the stock is undervalued) or negative (the stock is overvalued). If the alpha is zero (or nearly zero), the stock is on the SML and is properly valued in line with its systematic risk.

Plotting these estimated rates of return and stock betas on the SML gives Exhibit 7.4. Stock A is very close to being on the line, so it is considered properly valued because its estimated rate of return is almost equal to its required rate of return. Stocks B and D are considered overvalued because their estimated rates of return during the coming period are substantially less than what an investor should expect for the risk involved. As a result, they plot below the SML. In contrast, Stocks C and E are expected to provide rates of return greater than we would require based on their systematic risk. Therefore, both stocks plot above the SML, indicating that they are undervalued.

If you trusted these analysts to forecast estimated returns, you would take no action regarding Stock A, but you would buy Stocks C and E and sell Stocks B and D. You might even sell short Stocks B and D if you favored such aggressive tactics.

Calculating Systematic Risk   There are two ways that a stock's beta coefficient can be calculated in practice. First, given our conceptual discussion of the CAPM, a beta coefficient for Security i can be calculated directly from the following formula:

7.2
$$\sigma_i = \left(\frac{\sigma_i}{\sigma_M}\right)(r_{iM}) = \frac{\text{Cov}(R_i, R_M)}{\sigma_M^2}$$

where, in addition to the terms defined earlier, σ^2_M is the return variance for the market portfolio and $\text{Cov}(R_i, R_M)$ is the covariance between returns to the Security i and the market.

Exhibit 7.3 Comparison of Required Rate of Return to Estimated Rate of Return
($RFR = 5\%$; Market Risk Premium = 4%)

Stock	Beta	Required Return $E(R_i)$	Estimated Return	Estimated Return Minus $E(R_i)$	Evaluation
A	0.70	7.80	8.00	0.20	Properly valued
B	1.00	9.00	6.25	−2.75	Overvalued
C	1.15	9.60	15.15	5.55	Undervalued
D	1.40	10.60	4.84	−5.76	Overvalued
E	−0.30	3.80	6.00	2.20	Undervalued

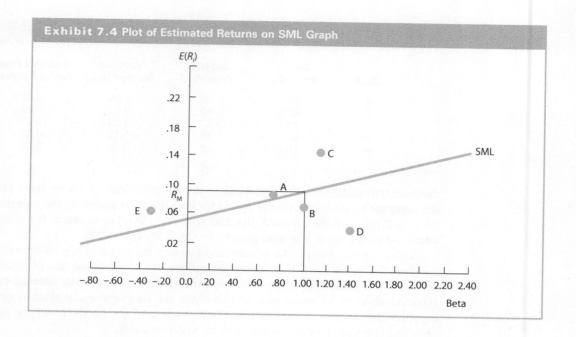

Exhibit 7.4 Plot of Estimated Returns on SML Graph

Alternatively, security betas can also be estimated as the slope coefficient in a regression equation between the returns to the security (R_{it}) over time and the returns (R_{Mt}) to the market portfolio:

7.3
$$R_{it} = a_i + \beta_i(R_{Mt}) + \varepsilon_{it}$$

where a_i is the intercept of the regression and ε_{it} is the random error term that accounts for Security i's unsystematic risk. Equation 7.3 is known as the security's **characteristic line** with the market portfolio.

Equations 7.2 and 7.3 will produce the same estimate of β_i for any given sample of security and market portfolio returns. However, the regression-based method in Equation 7.3 is often preferred because it is a formal estimation process, meaning that the statistical reliability of the estimate can be assessed (that is, a t-statistic on the β_i estimate can be evaluated).

The Impact of the Time Interval   In practice, the number of observations and the time interval used in the calculation of beta vary widely. For example, Morningstar derives characteristic lines for common stocks using monthly returns for the most recent five-year period (60 observations). Reuters Analytics calculates stock betas using daily returns over the prior two years (504 observations). Bloomberg uses two years of weekly returns (104 observations) in its basic calculations, although its system allows the user to select daily, weekly, monthly, quarterly, or annual returns over other time horizons. Because there is no theoretically correct time interval for this estimation, we must make a trade-off between enough observations to eliminate the impact of random rates of return and an excessive length of time, such as 10 or 20 years, over which the company in question may have changed dramatically. Remember that what you really want is the systematic risk for the period of your potential investment. In this process, you are analyzing historical data to help derive a reasonable estimate of the asset's future level of systematic risk.

Reilly and Wright (1988) analyzed the differential effects of return computation, market index, and the time interval and showed that the major cause of the differences in beta was the use of monthly versus weekly return intervals. Also, the shorter weekly interval caused a larger beta for large firms and a smaller beta for small firms.

The Effect of the Market Proxy   Another significant decision when computing an asset's characteristic line is which indicator series to use as a proxy for the market portfolio of all risky assets. Many investigators use the Standard & Poor's 500 Composite Index as a proxy for the market portfolio because the stocks in this index encompass a large proportion of the total market value of U.S. stocks. Still, this series is dominated by large-cap U.S. stocks, most of them listed on the NYSE. By contrast, the market portfolio of all risky assets should include U.S. stocks and bonds, non-U.S. stocks and bonds, real estate, coins, stamps, art, antiques, and any other marketable risky asset from around the world.[1]

Computing a Characteristic Line: An Example   The following example shows how you would estimate a characteristic line for Microsoft Corp (MSFT) using monthly return data from January 2016 to December 2016. Twelve monthly rates are typically not considered sufficient for statistical purposes, but they are adequate for demonstration purposes. We calculate betas for MSFT using two different proxies for the market portfolio: (1) the S&P 500 (SPX), an index of stocks mostly domiciled in the United States, and (2) the MSCI World Equity (MXWO) index, which represents a global portfolio of stocks.

Exhibit 7.5 lists monthly total returns for MSFT, SPX, and MXWO, which are computed using month-end closing prices and include dividend payments. Exhibit 7.6 shows a scatterplot of these return data for MSFT and SPX, while Exhibit 7.7 contains a similar display for MSFT and MXWO. During this period, there were some months when the MSFT returns diverged from the S&P 500 Index series. Nevertheless, the calculation in Exhibit 7.5 shows that the covariance between MSFT and SPX was positive and large (8.15). The covariance divided by the variance of SPX (8.07) equals MSFT's beta compared to the S&P 500. For this period, the beta was 1.01, indicating that MSFT was just slightly more risky than the aggregate market. The intercept for this characteristic line is 0.35, calculated as the average monthly return for MSFT (1.35) less the product of the average monthly return for SPX (0.99) and the beta coefficient. The fact that most of the observations plotted in Exhibit 7.6 are fairly close to the characteristic line is consistent with the correlation coefficient between MSFT and SPX of 0.49.

How does this analysis change if we use a different market proxy? Exhibit 7.5 also lists calculations for the MSFT beta using a global equity index as a market portfolio. Two things are notable when this substitution is made. First, the volatility of the MSCI World Index (9.29) was somewhat larger than the S&P 500 over this period. Second, the covariance between MSFT and MXWO (8.04) is virtually the same, although the overall correlation coefficient between the two is slightly lower (0.45) than between MSFT and SPX. Taken together, the higher volatility of the World Index has the greatest effect so the beta coefficient between MSFT and MXWO is 0.87, which is lower than when the S&P 500 was used as the market proxy. In fact, notice that the interpretation of the nature of MSFT's relative systematic risk changes with this new index. Rather than being 1 percent *more* risky than the domestic equity market, MSFT is now seen as being 13 percent *less* risky than the global index.

Beyond demonstrating the computations involved in the process, the important point illustrated in this example is that the proper selection of a proxy for the market portfolio is of vital importance when measuring risk. Reilly and Akhtar (1995) showed that beta differences of this magnitude are to be expected when comparing the stock of any company to both U.S. and world equity indexes.

Industry Characteristic Lines   Characteristic lines can also be calculated for entire portfolios of stocks, such as market or sector indexes. Exhibit 7.8 summarizes a set of computations

---

[1]Substantial discussion surrounds the market proxy used and its impact on the empirical results and usefulness of the CAPM. This concern is discussed further and demonstrated in the subsequent section on computing an asset's characteristic line. The effect of the market proxy is also considered later in this chapter and in Chapter 18, when we discuss the evaluation of portfolio performance.

Exhibit 7.5 Computation of Beta for JPMorgan Chase with Selected Indexes

Date	RETURN SPX	RETURN MSFT	RETURN MXWO	S&P 500 (SPX) (1) R_{SPX} − Avg. R_{SPX}	MSCI World (MXWO) (2) R_{MXWO} − Avg. R_{MXWO}	MSFT (3) R_{MSFT} − Avg. R_{MSFT}	(4)[a]	(5)[b]
Jan-16	−4.96	−0.70	−5.95	−5.95	−6.65	−2.05	12.16	13.61
Feb-16	−0.13	−6.99	−0.68	−1.12	−1.38	−8.34	9.31	11.54
Mar-16	6.78	8.55	6.86	5.79	6.16	7.21	41.74	44.35
Apr-16	0.39	−9.70	1.64	−0.60	0.94	−11.05	6.59	−10.34
May-16	1.80	7.03	0.65	0.81	−0.05	5.69	4.62	−0.31
Jun-16	0.26	−3.45	−1.07	−0.73	−1.77	−4.80	3.48	8.51
Jul-16	3.69	10.77	4.25	2.70	3.55	9.43	25.48	33.42
Aug-16	0.14	2.01	0.14	−0.85	−0.56	0.67	−0.56	−0.38
Sep-16	0.02	0.24	0.58	−0.97	−0.12	−1.11	1.07	0.14
Oct-16	−1.82	4.03	−1.91	−2.81	−2.61	2.69	−7.54	−7.02
Nov-16	3.70	1.23	1.51	2.71	0.81	−0.12	−0.31	−0.09
Dec-16	1.97	3.12	2.43	0.98	1.73	1.78	1.75	3.06
							Total = 97.79	96.49
Average	0.99	1.35	0.70					
Standard Deviation	2.84	5.80	3.05					

$\text{Cov}_{(MSFT,SPX)} = 97.79/12 = 8.15$ $\text{Var}_{(SPX)} = \text{StdDev}^2_{(SPX)} = (2.84)^2 = 8.07$ $\text{Beta}_{(MSFT,SPX)} = 8.15/8.07 = 1.01$ $\text{Intercept}_{(MSFT,SPX)} = 1.35 - (1.01 \times 0.99) = 0.35$

$\text{Cov}_{(MSFT,MXWO)} = 96.49/12 = 8.04$ $\text{Var}_{(MXWO)} = \text{StdDev}^2_{(MXWO)} = (3.05)^2 = 9.29$ $\text{Beta}_{(MSFT,MXWO)} = 8.04/9.29 = 0.87$ $\text{Intercept}_{(MSFT,MXWO)} = 1.35 - (0.87 \times 0.70) = 0.74$

$\text{Correlation Coeff.}_{(MSFT,SPX)} = 8.15/(2.84 \times 5.80) = 0.49$

$\text{Correlation Coeff.}_{(MSFT,MXWO)} = 8.04/(3.05 \times 5.80) = 0.45$

[a]Column 4 is equal to Column 1 multiplied by Column 3.
[b]Column 5 is equal to Column 2 multiplied by Column 3.

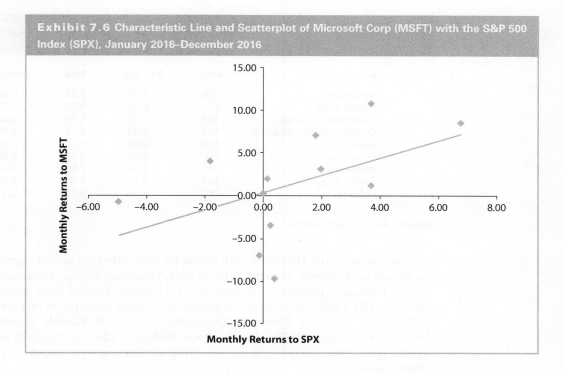

Exhibit 7.6 Characteristic Line and Scatterplot of Microsoft Corp (MSFT) with the S&P 500 Index (SPX), January 2016–December 2016

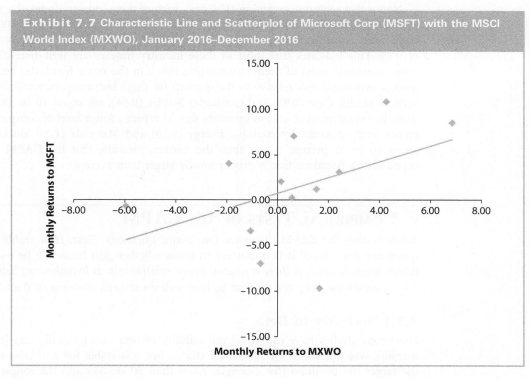

Exhibit 7.7 Characteristic Line and Scatterplot of Microsoft Corp (MSFT) with the MSCI World Index (MXWO), January 2016–December 2016

Exhibit 7.8 Characteristic Line Coefficients for Selected Industry Indexes with the S&P 500 Index (SPX), January 2014–December 2016

Industry	Index	Intercept	Beta	Correlation
Materials	IXB	−0.45	1.34	0.83
Health Care	IXV	0.14	0.92	0.78
Consumer Staples	IXR	0.20	0.64	0.64
Consumer Discretionary	IXY	−0.03	1.13	0.92
Energy	IXE	−0.93	1.10	0.60
Financials	IXM	0.20	1.12	0.80
Industrials	IXI	−0.06	1.06	0.91
Technology	IXT	0.29	1.08	0.88
Utilities	IXU	0.66	0.19	0.14

Source: Author calculations.

over the January 2014–December 2016 period for nine different industry segments comprising the overall stock market: Materials, Health Care, Consumer Staples, Consumer Discretionary, Energy, Financials, Industrials, Technology, and Utilities. Each of these industry segments is represented by a different index of companies that operate primarily in that area. For instance, leading firms such as Monsanto (Materials), Procter & Gamble (Consumer Staples), Amazon.com (Consumer Discretionary), and JPMorgan Chase (Financials) are divided into separate portfolios. Microsoft, from the previous example, is included in the Technology industry index.

Notice that with one exception (Utilities), each of these industry indexes is strongly correlated with the designated overall market portfolio (that is, the Standard & Poor's 500). The correlation coefficients range from 0.60 to 0.92, with six of the nine industries having coefficients in excess of 0.75. This indicates that most of these industry indexes are well-diversified portfolios that have eliminated most of their unsystematic risk. On the other hand, the beta coefficients (the level of systematic risk relative to the market) for these industries vary widely. Some industries, such as Health Care (0.92) and Consumer Staples (0.64), are about 10 to 35 percent less risky than the overall market, and so investors should expect a lower level of compensation from companies in these areas. By contrast, Energy (1.10) and Materials (1.34) stocks are, on average, about 10 to 35 percent riskier than the market, meaning that the CAPM would predict an expected risk premium that is proportionally larger than average.

7.2 EMPIRICAL TESTS OF THE CAPM

When testing the CAPM, there are two major questions. First, *How stable is the measure of systematic risk (beta)?* It is important to know whether past betas can be used as estimates of future betas. Second, *Is there a positive linear relationship as hypothesized between beta and the rate of return on risky assets?* That is, how well do returns conform to the SML?

7.2.1 Stability of Beta

Numerous studies have examined the stability of beta and generally concluded that the risk measure was *not* stable for individual stocks, but was stable for *portfolios* of stocks. Further, the larger the portfolio (for example, more than 50 stocks) and the longer the period (over 26 weeks), the more stable the beta estimate. Also, the betas tended to regress toward the mean. Specifically, high-beta portfolios tended to decline over time toward 1.00, whereas low-beta portfolios tended to increase over time toward unity.

7.2.2 Relationship between Systematic Risk and Return

The ultimate question regarding the CAPM is whether it is useful in explaining the return on risky assets. Specifically, is there a positive linear relationship between the systematic risk and the rates of return on these risky assets? Sharpe and Cooper (1972) found a positive relationship between return and risk, although it was not completely linear. Black, Jensen, and Scholes (1972) examined the risk and return for portfolios of stocks and found a positive linear relationship between monthly excess return and portfolio beta, although the intercept was higher than zero. Exhibit 7.9 contains charts from this study, which show that (1) most of the measured SMLs had a positive slope, (2) the slopes change between periods, (3) the intercepts are not zero, and (4) the intercepts change between periods.

Effect of a Zero-Beta Portfolio Black (1972) suggested that the existence of a risk-free asset is not necessary for the CAPM if there is a zero-beta portfolio available. The characteristic line using a zero-beta portfolio instead of *RFR* should have a higher intercept and a lower slope coefficient. Several studies have tested this model with its higher intercept and flatter slope and found conflicting results. Specifically, Gibbons (1982) and Shanken (1985) rejected the model, while Stambaugh (1982) supported the zero-beta CAPM.

Effect of Size, P/E, and Leverage Earlier, we discussed the size effect (the small-firm anomaly of Banz (1981)) and the P/E effect of Basu (1977) and showed that these variables have an inverse impact on returns after considering the CAPM. These results imply that size and P/E are additional risk factors that need to be considered along with beta. Specifically, expected returns are a positive function of beta, but investors also require higher returns from relatively small firms and for stocks with relatively low P/E ratios. Bhandari (1988) found that financial leverage also helps explain the cross section of average returns after both beta and size are considered. This suggests a multivariate CAPM with three risk variables: beta, size, and financial leverage.

Effect of Book-to-Market Value Fama and French (1992) evaluated the joint roles of market beta, size, E/P, financial leverage, and the book-to-market equity ratio in the cross section of average returns on the NYSE, AMEX, and NASDAQ stocks. They showed that the relationship between beta and the average rate of return disappears during the period 1963 to 1990, even when beta is used alone to explain average returns. In contrast, univariate tests between average returns and size, leverage, E/P, and book-to-market equity (BE/ME) indicate that all of these variables are significant and have the expected sign.

Fama and French concluded that size and book-to-market equity capture the cross-sectional variation in average stock returns associated with size, E/P, book-to-market equity, and leverage. Moreover, of the two variables, BE/ME appears to subsume E/P and leverage. Following these results, Fama and French (1993) suggested the use of a three-factor extension of the CAPM. Fama and French (1995) used this model to explain a number of the anomalies from prior studies.[2]

7.2.3 Additional Issues

Two additional practical issues that can affect the CAPM relationship are transaction costs and taxes.

Effect of Transaction Costs The CAPM assumes that there are no transaction costs, so investors will buy or sell mispriced securities until they plot on the SML. If there are transaction costs, investors will not correct all mispricing because in some instances the cost of

---

[2]This three-factor model by Fama and French is discussed further and demonstrated later in the chapter, when we consider multifactor models of risk and return.

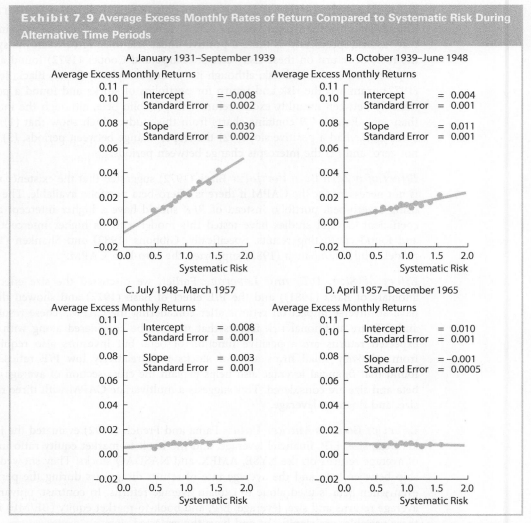

Exhibit 7.9 Average Excess Monthly Rates of Return Compared to Systematic Risk During Alternative Time Periods

A. January 1931–September 1939

Average Excess Monthly Returns

Intercept = −0.008
Standard Error = 0.002

Slope = 0.030
Standard Error = 0.002

Systematic Risk

B. October 1939–June 1948

Average Excess Monthly Returns

Intercept = 0.004
Standard Error = 0.001

Slope = 0.011
Standard Error = 0.001

Systematic Risk

C. July 1948–March 1957

Average Excess Monthly Returns

Intercept = 0.008
Standard Error = 0.001

Slope = 0.003
Standard Error = 0.001

Systematic Risk

D. April 1957–December 1965

Average Excess Monthly Returns

Intercept = 0.010
Standard Error = 0.001

Slope = −0.001
Standard Error = 0.0005

Systematic Risk

Source: Michael C. Jensen, ed., *Studies in the Theory of Capital Markets* (New York: Praeger Publishers, 1972): 96–97. Reprinted with permission.

buying and selling the mispriced security will exceed any potential excess return. Degennaro and Robotti (2007) demonstrated that transaction costs can reduce the slope of an asset pricing model.

Effect of Taxes   The expected returns in the CAPM are pretax returns. Clearly, though, tax rates differ between individuals and institutions. Because some investors have heavy tax burdens, Black and Scholes (1979) and Litzenberger and Ramaswamy (1979) argued that this could cause major differences in the SML among investors. Elton, Gruber, and Rentzler (1983), Miller and Scholes (1982), and Christie (1990) have examined the effect of the differential taxes on dividends versus capital gains, but the evidence is inconclusive.

7.2.4 Summary of Empirical Results for the CAPM

Most of the early evidence regarding the relationship between returns and systematic risk of portfolios supported the CAPM; there was evidence that the intercepts were generally higher than implied by the *RFR* that prevailed, which is either consistent with a zero-beta model or the existence of higher borrowing rates. To explain these unusual returns, additional variables were considered, and there is now extensive evidence that size, the P/E ratio, financial leverage, and the book-to-market value ratio have explanatory power regarding returns beyond beta.

In contrast to Fama and French, who measured beta with monthly returns, Kothari, Shanken, and Sloan (1995) measured beta with annual returns and found substantial compensation for beta risk. They suggested that the results obtained by Fama and French may have been time period specific. Further, when Jagannathan and Wang (1996) employed a conditional CAPM that allows for changes in betas and in the market risk premium, this model performed well in explaining the cross section of returns. Finally, when Reilly and Wright (2004) examined the performance of 31 different asset classes with betas computed using a broad market portfolio proxy, the risk–return relationship was significant and as expected by theory.

7.3 THE MARKET PORTFOLIO: THEORY VERSUS PRACTICE

Throughout our presentation of the CAPM, we noted that the market portfolio included *all* the risky assets in the economy. Although this concept is reasonable in theory, it is difficult to implement when testing or using the CAPM. The easy part is getting an index series for U.S. and foreign stocks and bonds. Because of the difficulty in deriving series that are available monthly in a timely fashion for numerous other assets, most studies have been limited to using a stock or bond series alone. In fact, the vast majority of studies have chosen an index limited to just U.S. stocks, which constitutes *a small fraction* of a truly global risky asset portfolio. It is then assumed that the particular series used as a proxy for the market portfolio was highly correlated with the true market portfolio.

Most researchers recognize this potential problem but assume that the deficiency is not serious. Roll (1977a, 1978, 1980, 1981), however, concluded that the use of these indexes as a proxy for the market portfolio had very serious implications for tests of the CAPM and especially for using the model when evaluating portfolio performance. He referred to this problem as a **benchmark error** because the practice is to compare the performance of a portfolio manager to the return of an unmanaged portfolio of equal risk—that is, the market portfolio adjusted for risk would be the benchmark. Roll's point is that, if the benchmark is incorrectly specified, you cannot measure the performance of a portfolio manager properly. A misspecified market portfolio can have two effects. First, the beta computed for investor portfolios would be wrong because the market portfolio used to compute the portfolio's systematic risk is inappropriate. Second, the SML derived would be wrong because it goes through the improperly specified M portfolio.

Exhibit 7.10 illustrates this second problem by showing that the intercept and slope of the SML will differ if (1) there is an error in selecting a proper risk-free asset and (2) if the market portfolio selected is not the correct mean-variance efficient portfolio. Obviously, it is very possible that under these conditions, a portfolio judged to be superior relative to the first SML (that is, the portfolio plotted above the measured SML) could be inferior relative to the true SML (that is, the portfolio would plot below the true SML).

Roll contends that a test of the CAPM requires an analysis of whether the proxy used to represent the market portfolio falls on the Markowitz efficient frontier and whether it is the true optimum market portfolio. Roll showed that if the proxy market portfolio (for example, the S&P 500 Index) is mean-variance efficient, it is mathematically possible to show a linear relationship between returns and betas derived with this portfolio.

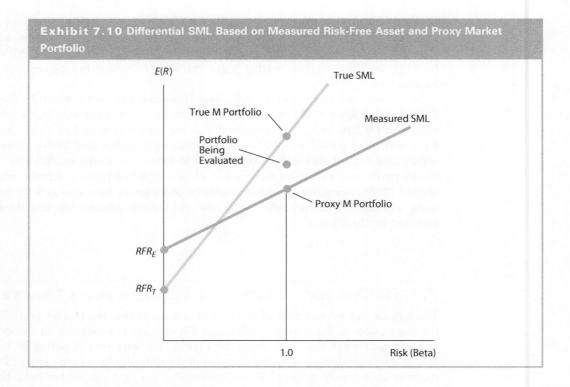

Exhibit 7.10 Differential SML Based on Measured Risk-Free Asset and Proxy Market Portfolio

A demonstration of the impact of the benchmark problem is provided in a study by Reilly and Akhtar (1995). They estimated the components of the SML using two different proxies for the market portfolio: (1) the S&P 500 Index and (2) the Brinson Partners Global Security Market Index (GSMI), which includes U.S. and non-U.S. stocks and bonds. As shown in Exhibit 7.11, there was a substantial difference in the SMLs implied by each of the market proxies. The display reports the average *RFR*, the market returns, and the slope of the SML during three time periods for the two indexes. Clearly, the slopes differ dramatically for the alternative indexes and over time, suggesting that the benchmark used does indeed make a difference.

In summary, an incorrect market proxy will affect both the beta risk measure and the position and slope of the SML that is used to evaluate portfolio performance. However, recognize that benchmark problems do not invalidate the CAPM as *a normative model of asset pricing*; they only indicate a problem in *measurement* when attempting to test the theory and when using this model for evaluating portfolio performance.

Exhibit 7.11 Components of Security Market Lines Using Alternative Market Proxies

	2000–2004			1989–1994			1983–1988		
	R_M	*RFR*	$(R_M - RFR)$	R_M	*RFR*	$(R_M - RFR)$	R_M	*RFR*	$(R_M - RFR)$
S&P 500	−2.01	3.05	−5.06	13.07	5.71	7.36	18.20	8.31	9.90
Brinson GSMI	3.02	3.05	−0.03	10.18	5.71	4.48	18.53	8.31	10.22

Source: Adapted from Frank K. Reilly and Rashid A. Akhtar, "The Benchmark Error Problem with Global Capital Markets," *Journal of Portfolio Management* 22, no. 1 (Fall 1995): 33–52. The updated results were provided by Frank K. Reilly.

7.4 ARBITRAGE PRICING THEORY

The preceding discussion highlights many of the ways in which the CAPM has contributed to the investment management field. In many respects, the CAPM has been one of the most frequently used financial economic theories ever developed. However, some of the empirical studies cited point out deficiencies in the model as an explanation of the link between risk and return.

One major challenge to the CAPM was the set of results suggesting that it is possible to use knowledge of certain firm or security characteristics to develop profitable trading strategies, even after adjusting for investment risk as measured by beta. For instance, Fama and French (1992) also demonstrated that "value" stocks (those with high book value-to-market price ratios) tend to produce larger risk-adjusted returns than "growth" stocks (those with low book-to-market ratios). In an efficient market, these return differentials should not occur, meaning that either (1) markets are not efficient over extended periods of time (investors have been ignoring profitable investment opportunities for decades), or (2) market prices are efficient, but there is something wrong with the way single-factor models such as the CAPM measure risk.

Given the implausibility of the first possibility, in the early 1970s financial economists began to consider the implications of the second. The academic community searched for an alternative asset pricing theory to the CAPM that was reasonably intuitive and allowed for multiple dimensions of investment risk. The result was the APT, which was developed by Ross (1976, 1977) in the mid-1970s and has three major assumptions:

1. Capital markets are perfectly competitive.
2. Investors always prefer more wealth to less wealth with certainty.
3. The process generating asset returns can be expressed as a linear function of a set of K risk factors (or indexes), and all unsystematic risk is diversified away.

Equally important, the following major assumptions—which were used in the development of the CAPM—are *not* required: (1) Investors possess quadratic utility functions, (2) Normally distributed security returns, and (3) a market portfolio that contains all risky assets and is mean-variance efficient. Obviously, if a model is simpler and can also explain differential security prices, it will be considered a superior theory to the CAPM.

Prior to discussing the empirical tests of the APT, we provide a brief review of the basics of the model. The theory assumes that the return-generating process can be represented as a K factor model of the form:

7.4
$$R_i = E(R_i) + b_{i1}\delta_1 + b_{i2}\delta_2 + \cdots + b_{ik}\delta_k + \varepsilon_i \text{ for } i = 1 \text{ to } n$$

where:

R_i = actual return on Asset i during a specified time period, $i = 1, 2, 3, \ldots n$

$E(R_i)$ = expected return for Asset i if all the risk factors have zero changes

b_{ij} = reaction in Asset i's returns to movements in a common risk factor j

δ_k = set of common factors or indexes with a zero mean that influences the returns on all assets

ε_i = unique effect on Asset i's return (a random error term that, by assumption, is completely diversifiable in large portfolios and has a mean of zero)

n = number of assets

The δ terms are the multiple risk factors that are expected to impact the returns to *all* assets. Examples of these factors might include inflation, growth in gross domestic product (GDP), major political upheavals, or changes in interest rates. The APT contends that there are many such factors that affect returns, in contrast to the CAPM, where the only relevant risk to measure is the covariance of the asset with the market portfolio (the asset's beta).

The b_{ij} terms determine how each asset reacts to the jth particular common factor. Although all assets may be affected by growth in GDP, the impact (reaction) to a factor will differ. For example, stocks of cyclical firms will have larger b_{ij} terms for the "growth in GDP" factor than noncyclical firms, such as grocery store chains. Likewise, all stocks are affected by changes in interest rates; however, some experience larger impacts. An interest-sensitive stock might have a b_j of 2.0 or more, whereas a stock that is relatively insensitive to interest rates has a b_j of 0.5. Note, however, that when we apply the theory, *the factors are not identified.* That is, when we discuss the empirical studies of the APT, the investigators will claim that they found two, three, or four factors that affect security returns, but *they will give no indication of what these factors represent.*

Similar to the CAPM model, the APT assumes that the unique effects (ε_i) are independent and will be diversified away in a large portfolio. The APT requires that in equilibrium the return on a zero-investment, zero-systematic-risk portfolio is zero when the unique effects are fully diversified. This assumption (and some mathematical manipulation) implies that the expected return on any Asset i can be expressed as:

7.5
$$E(R_i) = \lambda_0 + \lambda_1 b_{i1} + \lambda_2 b_{i2} + \cdots + \lambda_k b_{ik} \quad \text{(APT)}$$

where:

λ_0 = expected return on an asset with zero systematic risk

λ_j = risk premium related to the jth common risk factor

b_{ij} = pricing relationship between the risk premium and the asset; that is, how responsive Asset i is to the jth common factor. (These are called factor betas or factor loadings.)

Equation 7.5 represents the fundamental result of the APT. It is useful to compare the form of the APT's specification of the expected return-risk relationship with that of the CAPM in Equation 7.1. Exhibit 7.12 contrasts the relevant features of the two models. The ultimate difference between these two theories lies in the way systematic investment risk is defined: a single, market-wide risk factor for the CAPM versus a few (or several) factors in the APT that capture the nuances of that market-wide risk. However, both theories specify linear models based on the common belief that investors are compensated for performing two functions: committing capital and bearing risk. Finally, the equation for the APT suggests a relationship that is analogous to the security market line associated with the CAPM. However, instead of a line connecting risk and expected return, the APT implies a *security market plane* with $(K + 1)$ dimensions—K risk factors and one additional dimension for the security's expected return. Exhibit 7.13 illustrates this relationship for two risk factors ($K = 2$).

7.4.1 Using the APT

To illustrate how the APT model works, we will assume that there are two common factors: one related to unexpected changes in the level of inflation and another related to unanticipated changes

Exhibit 7.12 Comparing the Capital Asset Pricing Model (CAPM) and the Arbitrage Pricing Theory (APT)

	CAPM	APT
Form of Equation	Linear	Linear
Number of Risk Factors	1	$K (\geq 1)$
Factor Risk Premium	$[E(R_M) - RFR]$	$\{\lambda_j\}$
Factor Risk Sensitivity	β_i	$\{b_{ij}\}$
"Zero-Beta" Return	RFR	λ_0

Exhibit 7.13 The Relationship Between Expected Return and Two Common Risk Factors ($\lambda_0 = 4\%$, $\lambda_1 = 2\%$, $\lambda_2 = 3\%$)

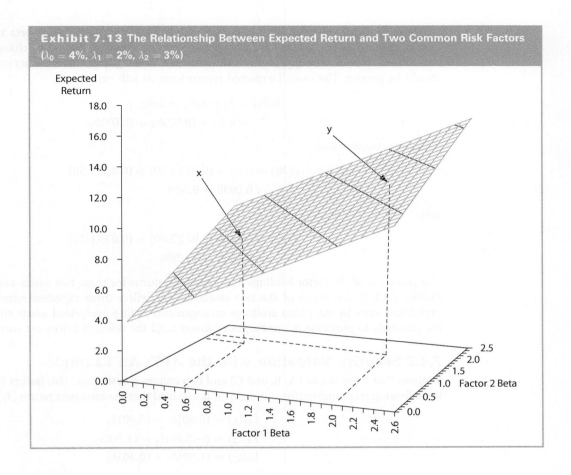

in the real level of GDP. If the risk premium related to GDP sensitivity is 0.03 and a stock that is sensitive to GDP has a b_j (where j represents the GDP factor) of 1.5, this means that this factor would cause the stock's expected return to increase by 4.5 percent ($= 1.5 \times 0.03$).

Consider the following example of two stocks and a two-factor model, with these risk factor definitions and sensitivities:

δ_1 = unanticipated changes in the rate of inflation. The risk premium related to this factor is 2 percent for every 1 percent change in the rate ($\lambda_1 = 0.02$).

δ_2 = unexpected changes in the growth rate of real GDP. The average risk premium related to this factor is 3 percent for every 1 percent change in the rate of growth ($\lambda_2 = 0.03$).

λ_0 = rate of return on a zero-systematic risk asset (zero-beta) is 4 percent ($\lambda_0 = 0.04$).

Assume also that there are two assets (x and y) that have the following sensitivities to these common risk factors:

b_{x1} = response of Asset x to changes in the inflation factor is 0.50

b_{x2} = response of Asset x to changes in the GDP factor is 1.50

b_{y1} = response of Asset y to changes in the inflation factor is 2.00

b_{y2} = response of Asset y to changes in the GDP factor is 1.75

These factor sensitivities can be interpreted in much the same way as beta in the CAPM; that is, the higher the level of b_{ij}, the greater the sensitivity of Asset i to changes in the jth risk factor. Thus, Asset y is a higher risk asset than Asset x, and, therefore, its expected return should be greater. The overall expected return formula will be:

$$E(R_i) = \lambda_0 + \lambda_1 b_{i1} + \lambda_2 b_{i2}$$
$$= 0.04 + (0.02)b_{i1} + (0.03)b_{i2}$$

So, for Assets x and y:

$$E(R_x) = 0.04 + (0.02)(0.50) + (0.03)(1.50)$$
$$= 0.0950 = 9.50\%$$

and:

$$E(R_y) = 0.04 + (0.02)(2.00) + (0.03)(1.75)$$
$$= 0.1325 = 13.25\%$$

The positions of the factor loadings and expected returns for these two assets are illustrated in Exhibit 7.13. If the prices of the two assets do not reflect these expected returns, we would expect investors to enter into arbitrage arrangements selling overpriced assets short and using the proceeds to purchase the underpriced assets until the relevant prices are corrected.

7.4.2 Security Valuation with the APT: An Example

Suppose that three stocks (A, B, and C) and two common systematic risk factors (1 and 2) have the following relationship (for simplicity, it is assumed that the zero-beta return $[\lambda_0]$ equals zero):

$$E(R_A) = (0.80)\lambda_1 + (0.90)\lambda_2$$
$$E(R_B) = (-0.20)\lambda_1 + (1.30)\lambda_2$$
$$E(R_C) = (1.80)\lambda_1 + (0.50)\lambda_2$$

If $\lambda_1 = 4$ percent and $\lambda_2 = 5$ percent, then the returns expected by the market over the next year can be expressed as:

$$E(R_A) = (0.80)(4\%) + (0.90)(5\%) = 7.7\%$$
$$E(R_B) = (-0.20)(4\%) + (1.30)(5\%) = 5.7\%$$
$$E(R_C) = (1.80)(4\%) + (0.50)(5\%) = 9.7\%$$

which, assuming that all three stocks are currently priced at $35 and do not pay a dividend, implies the following expected prices a year from now:

$$E(P_A) = \$35(1.077) = \$37.70$$
$$E(P_B) = \$35(1.057) = \$37.00$$
$$E(P_C) = \$35(1.097) = \$38.40$$

Now, suppose your own fundamental analysis suggests that in one year the actual prices of stocks A, B, and C will be $37.20, $37.80, and $38.50. How can you take advantage of what you consider to be a market mispricing?

According to your forecasts, Stock A will not reach a price level in one year consistent with investor return expectations. Accordingly, you conclude that at a current price of $35 a share, Stock A is *overvalued*. Similarly, Stock B is *undervalued* and Stock C is (slightly) *undervalued*. Consequently, any investment strategy designed to take advantage of these discrepancies will, at the very least, need to consider purchasing Stocks B and C while short selling Stock A.

The idea of *riskless arbitrage* is to assemble a portfolio that (1) requires no net wealth invested initially and (2) will bear no systematic or unsystematic risk but (3) still earns a profit. Letting w_i represent the percentage investment in Security i, the conditions that must be satisfied can be written formally as follows:

1. $\Sigma_i w_i = 0$ [no net wealth invested]
2. $\Sigma_i w_i b_{ij} = 0$ for all K factors no systematic risk] and w_i is "small" for all i [unsystematic risk is fully diversified]
3. $\Sigma_i w_i R_i > 0$ [the actual portfolio return is positive]

In this example, since Stock A is the only one that is overvalued, assume that it is the only one that actually is short sold. The proceeds from the short sale of Stock A can then be used to purchase the two undervalued securities, Stocks B and C. To illustrate this process, consider the following investment proportions:

$$w_A = -1.0$$
$$w_B = +0.5$$
$$w_C = +0.5$$

These investment weights imply the creation of a portfolio that is *short two shares of Stock A for each one share of Stock B and one share of Stock C held long*. Notice that this portfolio meets the net investment and risk mandates of an arbitrage-based trade:

Net Initial Investment:	
Short 2 shares of A:	+70
Purchase 1 share of B:	−35
Purchase 1 share of C:	−35
Net investment:	0

Net Exposure to Risk Factors:

	Factor 1	Factor 2
Weighted exposure from Stock A:	(−1.0)(0.8)	(−1.0)(0.9)
Weighted exposure from Stock B:	(0.5)(−0.2)	(0.5)(1.3)
Weighted exposure from Stock C:	(0.5)(1.8)	(0.5)(0.5)
Net risk exposure:	0	0

If in one year prices actually do rise to the levels that you initially "knew" they would, the net profit from covering the short position and selling the long holdings will be:
Net Profit:

$$[2(35) - 2(37.20)] + [37.80 - 35] + [38.50 - 35] = \$1.90$$

Thus, from a portfolio in which you invested no net wealth and assumed no net risk, you have realized a positive profit. This is the essence of arbitrage investing and is an example of the "long–short" trading strategies often employed by hedge funds.

Finally, if everyone else in the market today begins to believe the way you do about the future price levels of A, B, and C—but they do not revise their forecasts about the expected factor returns or factor betas for the individual stocks—then the current prices for the three stocks will be adjusted by arbitrage trading to:

$$P_A = (\$37.20) \div (1.077) = \$34.54$$
$$P_B = (\$37.80) \div (1.057) = \$35.76$$
$$P_C = (\$38.50) \div (1.097) = \$35.10$$

Thus, the price of Stock A will be bid down, while the prices of Stocks B and C will be bid up until arbitrage trading in the current market is no longer profitable.

7.4.3 Empirical Tests of the APT

Although the APT is newer than the CAPM by several years, it has also undergone considerable academic scrutiny. In discussing these empirical tests, remember the crucial earlier caveat that we do not know what the factors in the formal model actually represent. This becomes a major point in some discussions of test results.

Roll and Ross Study Roll and Ross (1980) produced one of the first large-scale empirical tests of the APT. Their methodology followed a two-step procedure:

1. Estimate expected returns and factor coefficients from time-series data on individual stock returns.
2. Use these estimates to test the basic cross-sectional pricing conclusion implied by the APT. Specifically, are the expected returns for these assets consistent with the common factors derived in step 1?

The authors tested the following pricing relationship:

H_0: There exist nonzero constants $(\lambda_0, \lambda_1, \dots \lambda_k)$ such that for any Asset i:

$$[E(R_i) - \lambda_0] = \lambda_1 b_{i1} + \lambda_2 b_{i2} + \cdots + \lambda_k b_{ik}$$

The specific b_i coefficients were estimated using the statistical technique *factor analysis*, which forms "portfolios" of the underlying assets (factors) based on the correlations in the underlying returns. Their database consisted of daily returns for the period from 1962 through 1972. Stocks were put into 42 portfolios of 30 stocks each (1,260 stocks) by alphabetical order.

Assuming a risk-free rate of 6 percent ($\lambda_0 = 0.06$), their analysis revealed the existence of at least three meaningful factors but probably not more than four. However, when they allowed the model to estimate the risk-free rate (λ_0), only two factors were consistently significant. Roll and Ross concluded that the evidence generally supported the APT but acknowledged that their tests were not conclusive.

Extensions of the Roll–Ross Tests Cho, Elton, and Gruber (1984) tested the APT by examining the number of factors in the return-generating process that were priced. They concluded that even when returns were generated by a two-factor model, two or three factors are required to explain the returns. Dhrymes, Friend, and Gultekin (1984) reexamined the methodology used in prior studies and found *no* relationship between the factor loadings for groups of 30 stocks and for a group of 240 stocks. Also, they could not identify the actual number of factors that characterize the return-generating process. When they applied the model to portfolios of different sizes, the number of factors changed from two to as many as nine.

Roll and Ross (1984) contended that the important consideration is whether the resulting estimates are *consistent* because it is not feasible to consider all of the stocks at once. When they tested for consistency, the APT was generally supported. Connor and Korajczyk (1993) developed a test that identifies the number of factors in a model that allows the unsystematic components of risk to be correlated across assets. Using this framework, they showed that between one and six priced factors exist for their sample of NYSE and ASE-listed stocks. Harding (2008) also showed the connection between systematic and unsystematic risk factors.

The APT and Stock Market Anomalies An alternative set of tests of the APT considers how well the theory explains pricing anomalies: the **small-firm effect** and the **January effect**.

APT Tests of the Small-Firm Effect Reinganum (1981) addressed the APT's ability to account for the differences in average returns between small firms and large firms, which could not be explained by the CAPM. His results were clearly inconsistent with the APT in that small-firm portfolios experienced positive and statistically significant average excess returns, whereas the large-firm portfolios had statistically significant negative average excess returns. Conversely, Chen (1983) compared the APT model to the CAPM using 180 stocks and 5 factors. He concluded that the CAPM was misspecified and that the missing price information was picked up by the APT.

APT Tests of the January Effect Gultekin and Gultekin (1987) tested the ability of the APT model to account for the so-called January effect, where returns in January are significantly larger than in any other month. They concluded that the APT model can explain the risk–return relationship only in January, meaning that the APT model does not explain this anomaly any better than the CAPM. On the other hand, Kramer (1994) showed that an empirical form of the APT accounts for the January seasonal effect in average stock returns while the CAPM cannot.

Is the APT Even Testable? Similar to Roll's critique of the CAPM, Shanken (1982) challenged whether it is possible for K factor models like the APT to be empirically verified at all. One problem is that if stock returns are not explained by such a model, it is not considered a rejection of the model; however, if the factors do explain returns, it is considered support. Also, equivalent sets of securities may conform to different factor structures, meaning that the APT may yield different empirical implications regarding the expected returns for a given set of securities. Unfortunately, this implies that the theory cannot explain differential returns between securities because it cannot identify the relevant factor structure that explains the differential returns. A number of subsequent papers, such as Brown and Weinstein (1983), Geweke and Zhou (1996), and Zhang (2009), have proposed new methodologies for testing the APT.

7.5 MULTIFACTOR MODELS AND RISK ESTIMATION

When it comes to putting theory into practice, one advantage of the CAPM framework is that the identity of the single risk factor—the excess return to the market portfolio—is well specified. The challenge in implementing the CAPM is to specify the market portfolio, which requires identifying the relevant investment universe. As we saw, this is not a trivial problem, as an improperly chosen proxy for the market portfolio (for example, using the S&P 500 Index to represent the market when evaluating a fixed-income portfolio) can lead to erroneous judgments. However, we also saw that once the returns to an acceptable surrogate for the market portfolio (R_M) are identified, the process for estimating the CAPM is straightforward.

In contrast, the primary practical problem associated with implementing the APT is that neither the identity nor the exact number of the underlying risk factors are developed by theory and therefore must be specified in an ad hoc manner. Said differently, before the APT can be used to value securities or measure investment performance, the investor must fill in a considerable amount of missing information about the fundamental relationship between risk and expected return.

The first attempts to implement a usable form of the APT relied on multivariate statistical techniques, such as factor analysis, wherein many periods of realized returns for a large number of securities are analyzed in order to detect recognizable patterns of behavior. A consistent finding of these studies is that there appear to be as many as three or four "priced" (that is, statistically significant) factors, although researchers were not able to establish that the same set of factors was generated by different subsets of their sample. Indeed, we also saw that the inability to identify the risk factors is a major limitation to the usefulness of the APT. Jones (2001) and Ludvigson and Ng (2007) provided some recent extensions along these lines.

A different approach to developing an empirical model that captures the essence of the APT relies on the direct specification of the form of the relationship to be estimated. That is, in a *multifactor model*, the investor chooses the exact number and identity of risk factors in the following equation:

7.6
$$R_{it} = a_i + [b_{i1}F_{1t} + b_{i2}F_{2t} + \ldots + b_{iK}F_{Kt}] + e_{it}$$

where F_{jt} is the period t return to the jth designated risk factor and R_{it} can be measured as either a nominal or excess return to Security i. The advantage of this approach is that the investor knows precisely how many and what things need to be estimated. The major disadvantage of a multifactor model is that it is developed with little theoretical guidance as to the true nature of the risk–return relationship. In this sense, developing a useful factor model is as much art form as theoretical exercise.

7.5.1 Multifactor Models in Practice

A wide variety of empirical factor specifications have been employed in practice. Each alternative model attempts to identify a set of economic influences that is simultaneously broad enough to capture the major nuances of investment risk but small enough to provide a workable solution to the investor. Two general approaches have been employed. First, risk factors can be viewed as *macroeconomic* in nature; that is, they attempt to capture variations in the underlying reasons an asset's returns might change over time (for example, changes in inflation or real GDP growth in the example discussed earlier). On the other hand, risk factors can also be viewed at a *microeconomic* level by focusing on relevant characteristics of the securities themselves, such as the size of the firm in question or some of its financial ratios. A few examples representative of both of these approaches are discussed in the following sections.

Macroeconomic-Based Risk Factor Models   One particularly influential model was developed by Chen, Roll, and Ross (1986), who hypothesized that security returns are governed by a set of broad economic influences in the following fashion:

7.7
$$R_{it} = a_i + [b_{i1}R_{Mt} + b_{i2}MP_t + b_{i3}DEI_t + b_{i4}UI_t + b_{i5}UPR_t + b_{i6}UTS_t] + e_{it}$$

where:

R_M = return on a value-weighted index of NYSE-listed stocks
MP = monthly growth rate in U.S. industrial production
DEI = change in inflation; measured by the U.S. consumer price index
UI = difference between actual and expected levels of inflation
UPR = unanticipated change in the bond credit spread (Baa yield – RFR)
UTS = unanticipated term structure shift (long-term less short-term RFR)

In estimating this model, the authors used a series of monthly returns for a large collection of stocks over the period 1958–1984. Exhibit 7.14 shows the factor sensitivities (along with the associated t-statistics in parentheses) that they established. Notice two things about these findings. First, the economic significance of the designated risk factors changed dramatically over time. For instance, the inflation factors (*DEI* and *UI*) appear to only be relevant during the 1968–1977 period. Second, the parameter on the market portfolio proxy is never significant, suggesting that it contributes little to the explanation beyond the information contained in the other macroeconomic risk factors.

Burmeister, Roll, and Ross (1994) analyzed the predictive ability of a model based on a different set of macroeconomic factors. Specifically, they define the following five risk exposures: (1) *confidence risk*, based on unanticipated changes in the willingness of investors to take on investment risk; (2) *time horizon risk*, which is the unanticipated changes in investors' desired time to receive payouts; (3) *inflation risk*, based on a combination of the unexpected components of short-term and long-term inflation rates; (4) *business cycle risk*, which represents unanticipated changes in the level of overall business activity; and (5) *market-timing risk*,

Period	Constant	R_M	MP	DEI	UI	UPR	UTS
1958–1984	10.71	−2.40	11.76	−0.12	−0.80	8.27	−5.91
	(2.76)	(−0.63)	(3.05)	(−1.60)	(−2.38)	(2.97)	(−1.88)
1958–1967	9.53	1.36	12.39	0.01	−0.21	5.20	−0.09
	(1.98)	(0.28)	(1.79)	(0.06)	(−0.42)	(1.82)	(−0.04)
1968–1977	8.58	−5.27	13.47	−0.26	−1.42	12.90	−11.71
	(1.17)	(−0.72)	(2.04)	(−3.24)	(−3.11)	(2.96)	(−2.30)
1978–1984	15.45	−3.68	8.40	−0.12	−0.74	6.06	−5.93
	(1.87)	(−0.49)	(1.43)	(−0.46)	(−0.87)	(0.78)	(−0.64)

Exhibit 7.14 Estimating a Multifactor Model with Macroeconomic Risk Factors

Source: Nai-fu Chen, Richard Roll, and Stephen A. Ross, "Economic Forces and the Stock Market," *Journal of Business* 59, no. 3 (April 1986).

defined as the part of the Standard & Poor's 500 total return that is not explained by the other four macroeconomic factors.

The authors compared the risk factor sensitivities from their model for several different individual stocks and stock portfolios. Panels A and B of Exhibit 7.15 show these factor beta estimates for a particular stock (Reebok International Ltd.) versus the S&P 500 Index and for a portfolio of small-cap firms versus a portfolio of large-cap firms. Also included in these graphs is the security's or portfolio's exposure to the BIRR composite risk index, which is designed to indicate which position has the most overall systematic risk. These comparisons highlight how a multifactor model can help investors distinguish the nature of the risk they are assuming when they hold with a particular position. For instance, notice that Reebok has greater exposures to all sources of risk than the S&P 500. Additionally, smaller firms are more exposed to business cycle and confidence risk than larger firms but less exposed to horizon risk.

Microeconomic-Based Risk Factor Models In contrast to macroeconomic-based explanations, it is also possible to specify risk in microeconomic terms using proxy variables that concentrate on certain characteristics of the underlying sample of securities. Typical of this *characteristic-based approach* to forming a multifactor model is the work of Fama and French (1993), who use the following functional form:

7.8
$$(R_{it} - RFR_t) = \alpha_i + b_{i1}(R_{Mt} - RFR_t) + b_{i2}SMB_t + b_{i3}HML_t + e_{it}$$

where, in addition to the excess return on a stock market portfolio, two other risk factor proxies are defined:

SMB (small minus big) = return to a portfolio of small-capitalization stocks less the return to a portfolio of large-capitalization stocks

HML (high minus low) = return to a portfolio of stocks with high ratios of book-to-market ratios less the return to a portfolio of low book-to-market ratio stocks

In this specification, *SMB* is designed to capture elements of risk associated with firm size, while *HML* is intended to distinguish risk differentials associated with "value" (high book-to-market) and "growth" (low book-to-market ratio) firms. As we saw earlier, these are two dimensions of a security—or portfolio of securities—that have consistently been shown to matter when evaluating investment performance. Also, notice that without *SMB* and *HML* this model reduces to the excess returns form of the single-index market model.

Fama and French examined the behavior of a broad sample of stocks grouped into portfolios by their price-to-earnings (P/E) ratios on a yearly basis over the period from July 1963 to December 1991. The results for both the single-index and multifactor versions of the model for the two extreme quintiles are shown in Exhibit 7.16 (*t*-statistics for the estimated

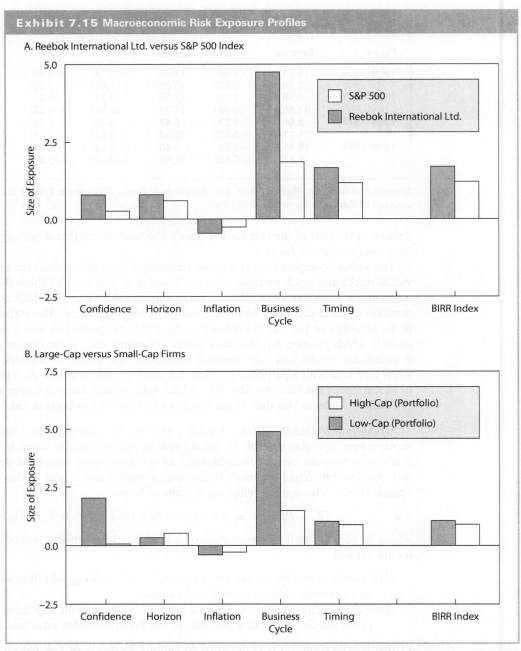

Exhibit 7.15 Macroeconomic Risk Exposure Profiles

A. Reebok International Ltd. versus S&P 500 Index

B. Large-Cap versus Small-Cap Firms

coefficients are listed parenthetically). Notice that while there are substantial differences between low and high P/E stocks (single-index betas of 0.94 versus 1.10), this gap is dramatically reduced in the multifactor specification (1.03 versus 0.99). This suggests that the market portfolio in a one-factor model serves as a proxy for some, but not all, of the additional risk dimensions provided by *SMB* and *HML*. Further, low P/E stocks tend to be positively correlated with the small-firm premium, but the reverse is not really true for high P/E stocks.

Exhibit 7.16 Estimating a Multifactor Model with Characteristic-Based Risk Factors

Portfolio	Constant	Market	SMB	HML	R^2
		(1) Single-Index Model			
Lowest P/E	0.46	0.94	—	—	0.78
	(3.69)	(34.73)			
Highest P/E	−0.20	1.10	—	—	0.91
	(−2.35)	(57.42)			
		(2) Multifactor Model			
Lowest P/E	0.08	1.03	0.24	0.67	0.91
	(1.01)	(51.56)	(8.34)	(19.62)	
Highest P/E	0.04	0.99	−0.01	−0.50	0.96
	(0.70)	(66.78)	(−0.55)	(−19.73)	

Source: Reprinted from Eugene F. Fama and Kenneth R. French, "Common Risk Factors in the Returns on Stocks and Bonds," *Journal of Financial Economics* 33, no. 1 (January 1993).

Finally, low P/E stocks also tend to have high book-to-market ratios, while high P/E stocks tend to have low book-to-market ratios (estimated *HML* parameters of 0.67 and −0.50, respectively). Not surprisingly, relative levels of P/E and book-to-market ratios are both commonly employed in practice to classify growth and value stocks.

Carhart (1997) directly extended the Fama–French three-factor model by including a fourth common risk factor to account for the tendency for firms with positive (negative) past returns to produce positive (negative) future returns. He called this additional risk dimension a *price momentum factor* and estimated it by taking the average return to a set of stocks with the best performance over the prior year minus the average return to stocks with the worst returns. In this fashion, Carhart defined the momentum factor—labeled here as *MOM*—in a fashion similar to *SMB* and *HML*. Formally, the model he proposed is:

7.9 $(R_{it} - RFR_t) = \alpha_i + b_{i1}(R_{Mt} - RFR_t) + b_{i2}SMB_t + b_{i3}HML_t + b_{i4}MOM_t + e_{it}$

He demonstrated that the typical factor sensitivity (factor beta) for the momentum variable is positive, and its inclusion into the Fama–French model increases explanatory power by as much as 15 percent. Equation 7.9 is often referred to as the four-factor Fama–French model.

Fama and French (2015) developed their own extension of the original three-factor model by adding two additional terms to account for *company quality*: a corporate profitability risk exposure and a corporate investment risk exposure. Specifically, they created a five-factor risk model by expanding their original specification in Equation 7.8 as follows:

7.10 $(R_{it} - RFR_t) = \alpha_i + b_{i1}(R_{Mt} - RFR_t) + b_{i2}SMB_t + b_{i3}HML_t + b_{i4}RMW_t + b_{i5}CMA_t + e_{it}$

where the new terms are defined:

RMW (robust minus weak) = return to a portfolio of high profitability stocks less the return to a portfolio of low profitability stocks

CMA (conservative minus aggressive) = return to a portfolio of stocks of low-investment firms (low total asset growth) less the return to a portfolio of stocks in companies with rapid growth in total assets

Blitz, Hanauer, Vidojevic, and van Vliet (2016) noted that Equation 7.10 does not include the momentum risk factor.

Extensions of Characteristic-Based Risk Factor Models Another type of security characteristic-based method for defining systematic risk exposures involves the use of index portfolios (for example, S&P 500, Wilshire 5000) as common factors. Intuitively, if the indexes themselves are designed to emphasize certain investment characteristics, they can act as proxies for the underlying exposure. Examples include the Russell 1000 Growth Index, which emphasizes large-cap stocks with low book-to-market ratios, or the EAFE (Europe, Australia, and the Far East) Index that selects a variety of companies that are domiciled outside the United States. Typical of this approach is the work of Elton, Gruber, and Blake (1996), who relied on four indexes: the S&P 500, the Barclays Capital aggregate bond index, the Prudential Bache index of the difference between large- and small-cap stocks, and the Prudential Bache index of the difference between value and growth stocks.

MSCI, a leading risk forecasting and investment consulting firm, provides a final example of the microeconomic approach to building a multifactor model. The model they employ for analyzing global equity markets (GEM) includes as risk factors several characteristic-based variables and several industry indexes.[3] Exhibit 7.17 provides a brief description of the characteristic-based factors representative of their approach to capturing investment style risk.

Exhibit 7.17 Construction of MSCI GEM2 Characteristic-Based Style Factors

GEM2L Style Factor	Purpose	Descriptor Components (Weight)
Volatility	Captures relative volatility	• Historical sigma (0.050) • Historical beta (0.500) • Cumulative range (0.150) • Daily standard deviation (0.300)
Momentum	Captures sustained relative performance	• 12-month relative strength (0.250) • 6-month relative strength (0.375) • Historical alpha (0.375)
Size	Differentiates between large- and small-cap companies	• Logarithm of market capitalization (1.000)
Value	Captures the extent to which a stock is priced inexpensively in the market	• Forecast earnings to price (0.450) • Earnings to price (0.100) • Book to price (0.200) • Dividend yield (0.100) • Cash earnings to price (0.150)
Growth	Captures stock's growth prospects	• 5-year earnings growth (0.150) • 5-year sales growth (0.150) • Analyst predicted 5-year earnings growth (0.700)
Size Non-Linearity	Captures deviations from linearity in the relationship between returns and logarithm of market	• Cube of logarithm of market capitalization (1.000)
Liquidity	Measures the relative trading activity of a firm's shares in the market	• Monthly share turnover (0.200) • Quarterly share turnover (0.350) • Annual share turnover (0.450)
Financial Leverage	Measures a firm's financial leverage	• Book leverage (0.400) • Market leverage (0.500) • Debt to assets (0.100)

Source: Kassam, Altaf, Abhishek Gupta, Saurabh Jain, and Roman Kouzmenko. "Introducing MSCI IndexMetrics: An Analytical Framework for Factor Investing." *MSCI Research Insight*, December 2013.

---

[3]A more complete description of the Barra approach to analyzing investment risk can be found in Grinold and Kahn (1994).

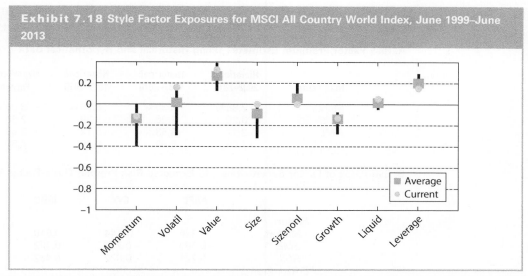

Exhibit 7.18 Style Factor Exposures for MSCI All Country World Index, June 1999–June 2013

Source: Kassam, Altaf, Abhishek Gupta, Saurabh Jain, and Roman Kouzmenko. "Introducing MSCI IndexMetrics: An Analytical Framework for Factor Investing." *MSCI Research Insight*, December 2013.

Exhibit 7.18 illustrates this for the MSCI All Country World Index (ACWI) over the period June 1999–June 2013. The display indicates that the ACWI portfolio emphasized value stocks over growth stocks (that is, positive Value factor exposure, negative Growth factor exposure) as well as stocks that tended to be highly levered (that is, positive Leverage factor exposure).

7.5.2 Estimating Risk in a Multifactor Setting: Examples

Estimating Expected Returns for Individual Stocks One direct way to employ a multi-factor risk model is to use it to estimate the expected return for an individual stock position. In order to do this, the following steps must be taken: (1) A specific set of K common risk factors (or their proxies) must be identified, (2) the risk premia (F_j) for the factors must be estimated, (3) the sensitivities (b_{ij}) of the ith stock to each of those K factors must be estimated, and (4) the expected returns can be calculated by combining the results of the previous steps.

As an example, we will use both the three-factor and four-factor versions of the Fama–French model discussed earlier. This addresses the first step by designating proxies for the four common risk factors: ($R_M - RFR$), *SMB*, *HML*, and *MOM*. The second step is often addressed in practice by using historical return data to calculate the average values for each of the risk factors. However, it is important to recognize that these averages can vary tremendously depending on the time period the investor selects. For these four factors, the first panel of Exhibit 7.19 lists the average annual factor risk premia over three different time frames: a 15-year period ending in December 2016, a 30-year period ending in December 2016, and an 83-year period ending in December 2016.[4] Notice that these data confirm that small stocks earned higher returns than large stocks, on average, and value stocks outperformed growth stocks (that is, positive risk premia for the *SMB* and *HML* factors).

To illustrate the final steps involved in estimating expected stock returns, risk factor sensitivities were estimated by using regression analysis for three different stocks with monthly return data over the period January 2012–December 2016. The three stocks were Apple Inc.

---

[4]The data in these calculations are available from Professor Kenneth French's Website, at http://mba.tuck.dartmouth.edu/pages/faculty/ken.french.

Exhibit 7.19 Estimates for Risk Factor Premia, Factor Sensitivities, and Expected Returns

A. Risk Factor Premium Estimates Using Historical and Hypothetical Data

Risk Factor	Historical: 2002–2016	Historical: 1987–2016	Historical: 1927–2016	Hypothetical Forecast
Market	7.85%	8.39%	8.36%	8.00%
SMB	3.29	1.06	3.29	2.50
HML	2.12	3.53	5.12	3.50
MOM	−1.09	5.96	9.26	4.50

B. Estimates of Factor Sensitivities and Expected Risk Premia: Three-Factor Model

	AAPL	CVX	ISBC
Factor:			
Market	1.326	1.144	0.610
SMB	−0.569	−0.227	0.402
HML	−0.721	0.922	0.482
E(Risk Prem):			
2002–2016	7.01%	10.18%	7.13%
Hypothetical	6.67	11.81	7.57

C. Estimates of Factor Sensitivities and Expected Risk Premia: Four-Factor Model

	AAPL	CVX	ISBC
Factor:			
Market	1.213	1.077	0.703
SMB	−0.572	−0.228	0.404
HML	−0.948	0.788	0.670
MOM	−0.317	−0.186	0.262
E(Risk Prem):			
2002–2016	5.98%	9.57%	7.98%
Hypothetical	3.53	9.96	10.16

(AAPL), a multinational personal computing developer; Chevron Corp. (CVX), an integrated energy firm; and Investors Bancorp (ISBC), a bank holding company. The estimated factor betas are listed in Panel B of Exhibit 7.19 for the three-factor model and in Panel C for the four-factor version of the equation.

These factor betas provide some interesting comparisons between the three stocks. First, the positive coefficients on the market factor indicate that all of these companies are positively correlated with general movements in the stock market. The coefficients on the SMB factor confirm that AAPL and CVX produce returns consistent with large-cap stocks (negative SMB exposures), while ISBC acts like a small-cap or mid-cap stock. Further, CVX and ISBC are more likely to be considered value stocks (positive HML exposures), while AAPL can be considered a growth-oriented stock. Finally, AAPL and CVX exhibited negative price momentum (negative MOM exposure in Panel C), while ISBC was a positive momentum stock over this period.

Whichever specific factor risk estimates are used, the expected return for any stock in excess of the risk-free rate (the stock's expected risk premium) can be calculated with either the three-factor or four-factor version of the formula:

7.11 $[E(R_i) - RFR] = b_{im}\lambda_m + b_{iSMB}\lambda_{SMB} + b_{iHML}\lambda_{HML} + b_{iMOM}\lambda_{MOM}$

In Panels B and C of Exhibit 7.19, these expected excess return calculations are summarized for all three stocks using two different factor risk premia estimates: (1) historical data from the

2002–2016 period and (2) a set of hypothetical forecasts. For example, the expected risk premium estimates for AAPL using the historical risk factor data are:

$$\text{Three-Factor:} [E(R) - RFR] = (1.326)(7.85) + (-0.569)(3.29) + (-0.721)(2.12)$$
$$= 7.01\%$$

$$\text{Four-Factor:} [E(R) - RFR] = (1.213)(7.85) + (-0.572)(3.29) + (-0.948)(2.12) + (-0.317)(-1.09)$$
$$= 5.98\%$$

The forecasts in Exhibit 7.19 appear to be reasonable. Also, the forecasted expected stock returns generated by the hypothetical factor estimates are uniformly lower than those produced by using historical data. Finally, the three-factor and four-factor models produce fairly comparable forecasts for the three stocks, although ignoring either the positive (ISBC) or negative (AAPL and CVX) *MOM* exposure does seem to matter.

Comparing Mutual Fund Risk Exposures To get a better sense of how risk factor sensitivity is estimated at the portfolio level, consider the returns produced by two popular mutual funds: Fidelity's Contrafund (FCNTX) and T. Rowe Price's Mid-Cap Value Fund (TRMCX). Morningstar Inc., an independent stock and mutual fund advisory service, classifies FCNTX's investment style into the "large-cap growth" category. This means that the typical equity holding of FCNTX is characterized as a large market capitalization firm whose P/E and book-to-market ratios exceed those of the average firm in the market. Exhibit 7.20 shows a sample page for FCNTX from Morningstar's public-access Website and shows graphically where the fund fits into the investment "style box" as of the reporting date in 2017. Conversely, as shown in Exhibit 7.21, Morningstar plots TRMCX into the "mid-cap value" category, meaning that the portfolio generally emphasizes smaller companies than does FCNTX as well as those that fall closer to the middle of the value-growth spectrum. So, assuming that Morningstar's classification system is meaningful, the two funds should differ in the relative sensitivities to both the *SMB* and the *HML* factors.

Using monthly returns over April 2014 to March 2017, the risk parameters for both funds were estimated relative to three different specifications: (1) a single-factor model using the Standard & Poor's 500 Index as proxy for the market portfolio, (2) a single-factor model using a broader composite index of the U.S. stock market as a market proxy, and (3) the Fama–French three-factor model using the U.S. market composite. The results of these estimations are summarized in Exhibit 7.22.

From both versions of the one-factor market model, it is apparent that FCNTX and TRMCX have similar levels of systematic market risk. In particular, the beta coefficients for TRMCX indicate slightly higher than average market risk regardless of how the market portfolio is estimated, but this exposure is always less that a market average level of 1.00. Additionally, notice that during April 2014–March 2017, the beta estimates for the two funds differ somewhat when the market portfolio is defined by the S&P 500 rather than the U.S. Composite Index (for example, 0.90 versus 0.86 for FCNTX).

The multifactor model gives a much better sense of how FCNTX's and TRMCX's risk exposures actually differ from each other. First, notice that including the *SMB* and *HML* factors does not seem to affect the systematic market exposures of the two funds in a dramatic way. For instance, the beta relative to the U.S. Composite Index for FCNTX is 0.86 in the single-index model, but increases only to 0.87 when estimated as part of the broader three-factor model. The comparable change in the market beta for TRMCX (from 0.93 to 0.89) is only slightly greater.

A second implication of the multifactor equation is how the funds should react to the *HML* variable. Consistent with its Morningstar style category, FCNTX is tilted toward holding growth-oriented stocks. The fund's *HML* sensitivity of −0.32 is statistically significant, which

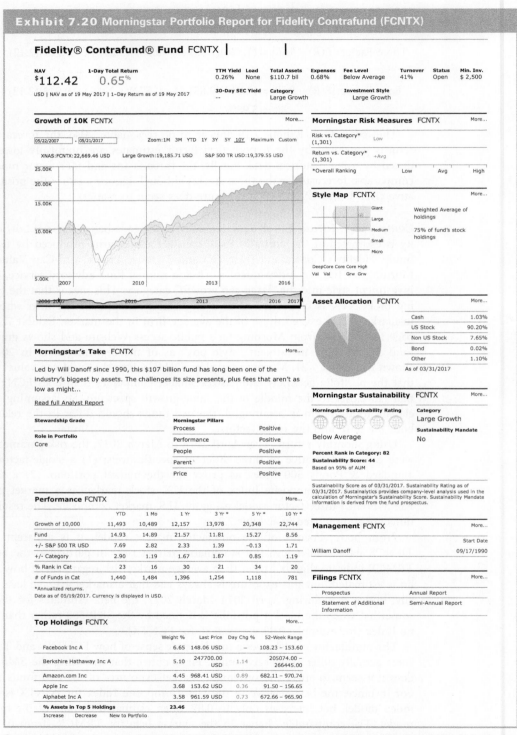

Exhibit 7.20 Morningstar Portfolio Report for Fidelity Contrafund (FCNTX)

Source: Morningstar.com, May 22, 2017. © 2017 Morningstar Inc. All Rights Reserved. The information contained herein: (1) is proprietary to Morningstar and/or its content providers; (2) may not be copied or distributed; and (3) is not warranted to be accurate, complete or timely. Neither Morningstar nor its content providers are responsible for any damages or losses arising from any use of this information. Past performance is no guarantee of future results.

Exhibit 7.21 Morningstar Portfolio Report for T. Rowe Price Mid-Cap Value (TRMCX) Fund

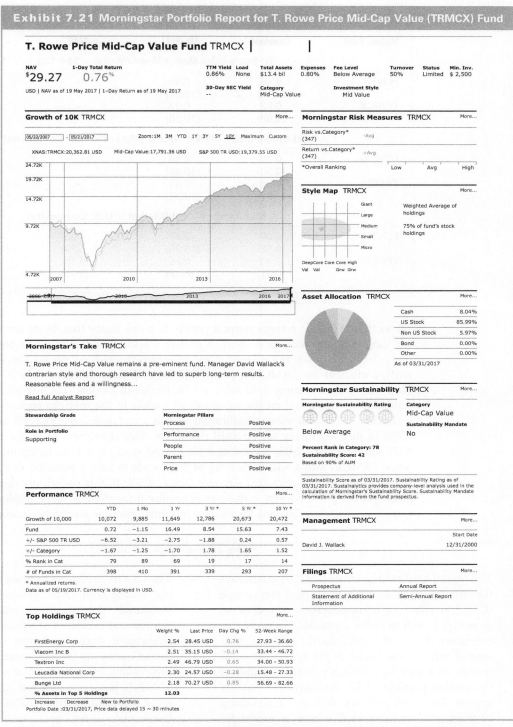

T. Rowe Price Mid-Cap Value Fund TRMCX

NAV	1-Day Total Return		TTM Yield	Load	Total Assets	Expenses	Fee Level	Turnover	Status	Min. Inv.
$29.27	**0.76**%		0.86%	None	$13.4 bil	0.80%	Below Average	50%	Limited	$ 2,500

USD | NAV as of 19 May 2017 | 1–Day Return as of 19 May 2017

30-Day SEC Yield --   **Category** Mid-Cap Value   **Investment Style** Mid Value

Growth of 10K TRMCX   More...

05/22/2007 - 05/21/2017   Zoom:1M 3M YTD 1Y 3Y 5Y 10Y Maximum Custom

XNAS:TRMCX:20,362.81 USD   Mid-Cap Value:17,791.36 USD   S&P 500 TR USD:19,379.55 USD

24.72K
19.72K
14.72K
9.72K
4.72K
2007   2010   2013   2016

2006 2017   2010   2013   2016 2017

Morningstar's Take TRMCX   More...

T. Rowe Price Mid-Cap Value remains a pre-eminent fund. Manager David Wallack's contrarian style and thorough research have led to superb long-term results. Reasonable fees and a willingness...

Read full Analyst Report

Stewardship Grade

Role in Portfolio
Supporting

Morningstar Pillars	
Process	Positive
Performance	Positive
People	Positive
Parent	Positive
Price	Positive

Performance TRMCX   More...

	YTD	1 Mo	1 Yr	3 Yr *	5 Yr *	10 Yr *
Growth of 10,000	10,072	9,885	11,649	12,786	20,673	20,472
Fund	0.72	−1.15	16.49	8.54	15.63	7.43
+/- S&P 500 TR USD	−6.52	−3.21	−2.75	−1.88	0.24	0.57
+/- Category	−1.67	−1.25	−1.70	1.78	1.65	1.52
% Rank in Cat	79	89	69	19	17	14
# of Funds in Cat	398	410	391	339	293	207

* Annualized returns.
Data as of 05/19/2017. Currency is displayed in USD.

Top Holdings TRMCX   More...

	Weight %	Last Price	Day Chg %	52-Week Range
FirstEnergy Corp	2.54	28.45 USD	0.76	27.93 - 36.60
Viacom Inc B	2.51	35.15 USD	−0.14	33.44 - 46.72
Textron Inc	2.49	46.79 USD	0.65	34.00 - 50.93
Leucadia National Corp	2.30	24.57 USD	−0.28	15.48 - 27.33
Bunge Ltd	2.18	70.27 USD	0.85	56.69 - 82.66
% Assets in Top 5 Holdings	12.03			

Increase   Decrease   New to Portfolio
Portfolio Date :03/31/2017, Price data delayed 15 ~ 30 minutes

Morningstar Risk Measures TRMCX   More...

| Risk vs.Category* (347) | -Avg |
| Return vs.Category* (347) | +Avg |

*Overall Ranking   Low   Avg   High

Style Map TRMCX   More...

Giant
Large
Medium
Small
Micro

Deep Core Core High
Val Val Grw Grw

Weighted Average of holdings

75% of fund's stock holdings

Asset Allocation TRMCX   More...

Cash	8.04%
US Stock	85.99%
Non US Stock	5.97%
Bond	0.00%
Other	0.00%

As of 03/31/2017

Morningstar Sustainability TRMCX   More...

Morningstar Sustainability Rating

Below Average

Category Mid-Cap Value

Sustainability Mandate No

Percent Rank in Category: 78
Sustainability Score: 42
Based on 90% of AUM

Sustainability Score as of 03/31/2017. Sustainability Rating as of 03/31/2017. Sustainalytics provides company-level analysis used in the calculation of Morningstar's Sustainability Score. Sustainability Mandate information is derived from the fund prospectus.

Management TRMCX   More...

	Start Date
David J. Wallack	12/31/2000

Filings TRMCX   More...

| Prospectus | Annual Report |
| Statement of Additional Information | Semi-Annual Report |

Exhibit 7.22 Risk Factor Estimates for FCNTX and TRMCX					
Mutual Fund	Constant	Market	*SMB*	*HML*	R^2
(1) Single-Index Market Model (Market = S&P 500)					
FCNTX	0.03	0.90	—	—	0.84
	(0.17)	(13.55)			
TRMCX	0.02	0.92	—	—	0.77
	(0.09)	(10.55)			
(2) Single-Index Market Model (Market = U.S. Composite)					
FCNTX	0.10	0.86	—	—	0.84
	(0.50)	(13.45)			
TRMCX	0.06	0.93	—	—	0.84
	(0.27)	(13.37)			
(3) Multifactor Model (Market = U.S. Composite)					
FCNTX	0.08	0.87	−0.05	−0.32	0.93
	(0.52)	(18.26)	(−0.95)	(−5.73)	
TRMCX	0.13	0.89	0.19	0.26	0.92
	(0.81)	(16.77)	(3.11)	(4.12)	

shows that FCNTX's returns move inversely to a risk factor that, by its construction, is implicitly long in value stocks and short in growth stocks. (Recall that a low book-to-market ratio, like a high P/E ratio, is a characteristic of a growth-oriented stock.) On the other hand, the *HML* coefficient for TRMCX is positive (0.26) and also significant, which is as expected for a fund that tends to mainly hold value stocks. Notice in Exhibit 7.21 that Morningstar places the fund in a style grid cell on the value side of middle in the mid-cap row.

Finally, the Morningstar classification system also implies that FCNTX and TRMCX should differ in their sensitivity to the *SMB* risk factor. This does seem to be the case: FCNTX has a *SMB* sensitivity of −0.05, suggesting a tilt toward stocks that have larger market capitalizations, while TRMCX, with a *SMB* sensitivity of 0.19, tends to hold a portfolio that emphasizes smaller stocks. However, the estimated size risk factor of TRMCX is statistically significant, which suggests that the portfolio may contain even smaller firms than its name implies. Nevertheless, the respective style classifications for these two mutual funds appear to be appropriate.

SUMMARY

- The *capital asset pricing model* (*CAPM*) generalizes the risk–return trade-off in the capital market line (CML) to allow for a consideration of individual securities as well as entire portfolios. To make this extension, the CAPM redefines the relevant measure of risk as beta, which is the systematic component of a security's volatility relative to that of the market portfolio. Like the CML, the *security market line* (*SML*) shows that the relationship between risk and expected return is a straight line with a positive slope. The SML provides investors with a tool for judging whether securities are undervalued or overvalued given their level of systematic (beta) risk.

- The CAPM has been subjected to extensive empirical testing with mixed findings. Early tests substantiated the positive relationship between returns and measures of systematic risk, although subsequent studies indicated that the single-beta model needed to be supplemented with additional dimensions of risk (for example, skewness, firm size, P/E, book value/market value). Another challenge confronting the CAPM in practice is the benchmark error problem that results from improperly specifying a proxy for the market portfolio.

- Ross devised an alternative asset pricing model— the *arbitrage pricing theory* (*APT*)—that makes fewer assumptions than the CAPM and does not specifically require the designation of a market portfolio. Instead, the APT posits that expected security returns are related in a linear fashion to multiple common risk factors. Unfortunately, the theory does not specify how many factors exist or what their identities might be. The results from the empirical tests of the APT have thus far been mixed.

• The APT is difficult to put into practice because the common risk factors are not identified in advance. Multifactor models of risk and return attempt to bridge this gap by selecting a set of variables that are thought to capture the essence of the systematic risk exposures that exist in the capital market. One general approach has been to use macroeconomic variables—such as unexpected inflation, unanticipated shifts in the yield curve, or unexpected changes in real GDP—as surrogates for the types of exposures that will have an impact on all securities.

• A second approach to implementing a multifactor model has focused on the characteristics of the securities themselves. Typical of this sort of microeconomic approach is the work of Fama and French, who originally posited that three risk factors should be employed: the excess returns to a broad market index, the return difference between portfolios of small and large-cap stocks, and the return difference between portfolios of value and growth-oriented stocks. One advantage of this specification is the flexibility to modify it in response to changing market conditions. For instance, the Fama–French model has been expanded to include factors accounting for stock return momentum and company quality.

• It is probably safe to assume that both the CAPM and APT will continue to be used to value capital assets. Coincident with their use will be further empirical tests of both theories, the ultimate goal being to determine which theory does the best job of explaining current returns and predicting future ones. Subsequent work in this area will seek to identify the set of factors that best captures the relevant dimension of investment risk as well as explore the intertemporal dynamics of the models (for example, factor betas and risk premia that change over time).

SUGGESTED READINGS

Fabozzi, Frank J., and Harry M. Markowitz. *The Theory and Practice of Investment Management*, 2nd ed. Hoboken, NJ: John Wiley & Sons, 2011.

Grinold, Richard C., and Ronald N. Kahn. *Active Portfolio Management*, 2nd ed. New York: McGraw-Hill, 2000.

Huberman, Gur, and Zhenyu Wang. "Arbitrage Pricing Theory." In Steven N. Durlauf and Lawrence E. Blume, eds. *The New Palgrave Dictionary of Economics*, 2nd ed. London: Palgrave Macmillan, 2008.

Sharpe, William F. *Investors and Markets: Portfolio Choices, Asset Prices, and Investment Advice*. Princeton, NJ: Princeton University Press, 2007.

QUESTIONS

1. The capital asset pricing model (CAPM) contends that there is systematic and unsystematic risk for an individual security. Which is the relevant risk variable and why is it relevant? Why is the other risk variable not relevant?

2. What are the similarities and differences between the CML and SML as models of the risk–return trade-off?

3. While the capital asset pricing model (CAPM) has been widely used to analyze securities and manage portfolios for the past 50 years, it has also been widely criticized as providing too simple a view of risk. Describe three problems in relation to the definition and estimation of the beta measure in the CAPM that would support this criticism.

4. You have recently been appointed chief investment officer of a major charitable foundation. Its large endowment fund is currently invested in a broadly diversified portfolio of stocks (60 percent) and bonds (40 percent). The foundation's board of trustees is a group

of prominent individuals whose knowledge of modern investment theory and practice is superficial. You decide a discussion of basic investment principles would be helpful.

a. Explain the concepts of *specific risk*, *systematic risk*, *variance*, *covariance*, *standard deviation*, and *beta* as they relate to investment management.

You believe that the addition of other asset classes to the endowment portfolio would improve the portfolio by reducing risk and enhancing return. You are aware that depressed conditions in U.S. real estate markets are providing opportunities for property acquisition at levels of expected return that are unusually high by historical standards. You believe that an investment in U.S. real estate would be both appropriate and timely, and have decided to recommend a 20 percent position be established with funds taken equally from stocks and bonds.

Preliminary discussions revealed that several trustees believe real estate is too risky to include in the portfolio. The board chairman, however, has scheduled a special meeting for further discussion of the matter and has asked you to provide background information that will clarify the risk issue.

To assist you, the following expectational data have been developed:

			CORRELATION MATRIX			
Asset Class	Return	Standard Deviation	U.S. Stocks	U.S. Bonds	U.S. Real Estate	U.S. T-Bills
U.S. Stocks	12.0%	21.0%	1.00			
U.S. Bonds	8.0	10.5	0.14	1.00		
U.S. Real Estate	12.0	9.0	−0.04	−0.03	1.00	
U.S. Treasury Bills	4.0	0.0	−0.05	−0.03	0.25	1.00

b. Explain the effect on *both* portfolio risk *and* return that would result from the addition of U.S. real estate. Include in your answer *two* reasons for any change you expect in portfolio risk. (Note: It is *not* necessary to compute expected risk and return.)

c. Your understanding of capital market theory causes you to doubt the validity of the expected return and risk for U.S. real estate. Justify your skepticism.

5. According to the CAPM, what assets are included in the market portfolio, and what are the relative weightings? In empirical studies of the CAPM, what are the typical proxies used for the market portfolio? Assuming that the empirical proxy for the market portfolio is not a good proxy, what factors related to the CAPM will be affected?

6. Both the capital asset pricing model (CAPM) and arbitrage pricing theory (APT) rely on the proposition that a no-risk, no-wealth investment should earn, on average, no return. Explain why this should be the case, being sure to describe briefly the similarities and differences between the CAPM and the APT. Also, using either of these theories, explain how superior investment performance can be established.

7. You are the lead manager of a large mutual fund. You have become aware that several equity analysts who have recently joined your management team are interested in understanding the differences between the capital asset pricing model (CAPM) and arbitrage pricing theory (APT). In particular, they are interested in how these two asset pricing models can help them perform better security analysis.

a. Explain what the CAPM and APT attempt to model. What are the main differences between these two asset pricing models?

b. Under what circumstances would the APT be preferred over the CAPM as a tool for selecting stocks for the fund portfolio?

8. The *small-firm effect* refers to the observed tendency for stock prices to behave in a manner that is contrary to normal expectations. Describe this effect and discuss whether it

represents sufficient information to conclude that the stock market does not operate efficiently. In formulating your response, consider (a) what it means for the stock market to be inefficient and (b) what role the measurement of risk plays in your conclusions about each effect.

9. Suppose you are considering the purchase of shares in the XYZ mutual fund. As part of your investment analysis, you regress XYZ's monthly returns for the past five years against the three factors specified in the Fama and French models. This procedure generates the following coefficient estimates: market factor = 1.2, SMB factor = −0.3, HML factor = 1.4. Explain what each of these coefficient values means. What types of stocks are XYZ likely to be holding?

10. It is widely believed that changes in certain macroeconomic variables may directly affect performance of an equity portfolio. As the chief investment officer of a hedge fund employing a global macro-oriented investment strategy, you often consider how various macroeconomic events might impact your security selection decisions and portfolio performance. Briefly explain how each of the following economic factors would affect portfolio risk and return: (a) industrial production, (b) inflation, (c) risk premia, (d) term structure, (e) aggregate consumption, and (f) oil prices.

11. Describe the intuition underlying (a) the macroeconomic approach to identifying risk factors and (b) the microeconomic (that is, characteristic-based) approach to identifying risk factors. Is it conceptually and practically possible for these two approaches to lead to the same estimate of expected return for any given security?

PROBLEMS

1. Assume that you expect the economy's rate of inflation to be 3 percent, giving an *RFR* of 6 percent and a market return (R_M) of 12 percent.
   a. Draw the SML under these assumptions.
   b. Subsequently, you expect the rate of inflation to increase from 3 percent to 6 percent. What effect would this have on the *RFR* and the R_M? Draw another SML on the graph from part (a).
   c. Draw an SML on the same graph to reflect an *RFR* of 9 percent and an R_M of 17 percent. How does this SML differ from that derived in part (b)? Explain what has transpired.

2. a. You expect an *RFR* of 10 percent and the market return (R_M) of 14 percent. Compute the expected return for the following stocks, and plot them on an SML graph.

Stock	Beta	$E(R_i)$
U	0.85	
N	1.25	
D	−0.20	

   b. You ask a stockbroker what the firm's research department expects for these three stocks. The broker responds with the following information:

Stock	Current Price	Expected Price	Expected Dividend
U	22	24	0.75
N	48	51	2.00
D	37	40	1.25

Plot your estimated returns on the graph from part (a) and indicate what actions you would take with regard to these stocks. Explain your decisions.

3. You are an analyst for a large public pension fund and you have been assigned the task of evaluating two different external portfolio managers (Y and Z). You consider the following historical average return, standard deviation, and CAPM beta estimates for these two managers over the past five years:

Portfolio	Actual Avg. Return	Standard Deviation	Beta
Manager Y	10.20%	12.00%	1.20
Manager Z	8.80	9.90	0.80

Additionally, your estimate for the risk premium for the market portfolio is 5.00 percent and the risk-free rate is currently 4.50 percent.

a. For both Manager Y and Manager Z, calculate the expected return using the CAPM. Express your answers to the nearest basis point (xx.xx percent).

b. Calculate each fund manager's average "alpha" (actual return minus expected return) over the five-year holding period. Show graphically where these alpha statistics would plot on the security market line (SML).

c. Explain whether you can conclude from the information in part (b) if (1) either manager outperformed the other on a risk-adjusted basis, and (2) either manager outperformed market expectations in general.

4. Based on five years of monthly data, you derive the following information for the companies listed:

Company	a_i (Intercept)	σ_i	r_{iM}
Intel	0.22	12.10%	0.72
Ford	0.10	14.60	0.33
Anheuser Busch	0.17	7.60	0.55
Merck	0.05	10.20	0.60
S&P 500	0.00	5.50	1.00

a. Compute the beta coefficient for each stock.

b. Assuming a risk-free rate of 8 percent and an expected return for the market portfolio of 15 percent, compute the expected (required) return for all the stocks and plot them on the SML.

c. Plot the following estimated returns for the next year on the SML and indicate which stocks are undervalued or overvalued.

- Intel—20 percent
- Ford—15 percent
- Anheuser Busch—19 percent
- Merck—10 percent

5. The following are the historic returns for the Chelle Computer Company:

Year	Chelle Computer	General Index
1	37	15
2	9	13
3	−11	14
4	8	−9
5	11	12
6	4	9

Based on this information, compute the following:

a. The correlation coefficient between Chelle Computer and the General Index.
b. The standard deviation for the company and the index.
c. The beta for the Chelle Computer Company.

6. As an equity analyst, you have developed the following return forecasts and risk estimates for two different stock mutual funds (Fund T and Fund U):

	Forecasted Return	CAPM Beta
Fund T	9.0%	1.20
Fund U	10.0	0.80

a. If the risk-free rate is 3.9 percent and the expected market risk premium ($E(R_M) -$ RFR) is 6.1 percent, calculate the expected return for each mutual fund according to the CAPM.
b. Using the estimated expected returns from part (a) along with your own return forecasts, demonstrate whether Fund T and Fund U are currently priced to fall directly on the security market line (SML), above the SML, or below the SML.
c. According to your analysis, are Funds T and U overvalued, undervalued, or properly valued?

7. Draw the security market line for each of the following conditions:
a. (1) $RFR = 0.08$; $R_M(\text{proxy}) = 0.12$
   (2) $R_z = 0.06$; $R_M(\text{true}) = 0.15$
b. Rader Tire has the following results for the last six periods. Calculate and compare the betas using each index.

RATES OF RETURN

Period	Rader Tire (%)	Proxy Specific Index (%)	True General Index (%)
1	29	12	15
2	12	10	13
3	−12	−9	−8
4	17	14	18
5	20	25	28
6	−5	−10	0

c. If the current period return for the market is 12 percent and for Rader Tire it is 11 percent, are superior results being obtained for either index beta?

8. Consider the following data for two risk factors (1 and 2) and two securities (J and L):

$\lambda_0 = 0.05$ $b_{J1} = 0.80$
$\lambda_1 = 0.02$ $b_{J2} = 1.40$
$\lambda_2 = 0.04$ $b_{L1} = 1.60$
         $b_{L2} = 2.25$

a. Compute the expected returns for both securities.
b. Suppose that Security J is currently priced at $22.50 while the price of Security L is $15.00. Further, it is expected that both securities will pay a dividend of $0.75 during the coming year. What is the expected price of each security one year from now?

9. Suppose that you have estimated the Fama–French three-factor and four-factor models for three different stocks: BCD, FGH, and JKL. Specifically, using return data from 2005 to 2009, the following equations were estimated:

Three-Factor Model:

BCD: $[E(R) - RFR] = (0.966)(\lambda_M) + (-0.018)(\lambda_{SMB}) + (-0.388)(\lambda_{HML})$

FGH: $[E(R) - RFR] = (1.042)(\lambda_M) + (-0.043)(\lambda_{SMB}) + (0.370)(\lambda_{HML})$

JKL: $[E(R) - RFR] = (1.178)(\lambda_M) + (0.526)(\lambda_{SMB}) + (0.517)(\lambda_{HML})$

Four-Factor Model:

BCD: $[E(R) - RFR] = (1.001)(\lambda_M) + (-0.012)(\lambda_{SMB}) + (-0.341)(\lambda_{HML}) + (0.073)(\lambda_{MOM})$

FGH: $[E(R) - RFR] = (1.122)(\lambda_M) + (-0.031)(\lambda_{SMB}) + (0.478)(\lambda_{HML}) + (0.166)(\lambda_{MOM})$

JKL: $[E(R) - RFR] = (1.041)(\lambda_M) + (0.505)(\lambda_{SMB}) + (0.335)(\lambda_{HML}) + (-0.283)(\lambda_{MOM})$

a. You have also estimated factor risk premia over a recent 15-year period as: $\lambda_M = 7.23$ percent, $\lambda_{SMB} = 2.00$ percent, $\lambda_{HML} = 4.41$ percent, and $\lambda_{MOM} = 4.91$ percent. Use these estimated risk premia along with the factor model estimated to confirm that the expected excess returns for the three stocks are 5.24 percent, 9.08 percent, and 11.86 percent (three-factor model) or 6.07 percent, 10.98 percent, and 8.63 percent (four-factor model), respectively.

b. Suppose that you have also estimated historical factor risk prices for two different time frames: (1) *30-year period:* ($\lambda_M = 7.11$ percent, $\lambda_{SMB} = 1.50$ percent, and $\lambda_{HML} = 5.28$ percent), and (2) *80-year period:* ($\lambda_M = 7.92$ percent, $\lambda_{SMB} = 3.61$ percent, and $\lambda_{HML} = 5.02$ percent). Calculate the expected excess returns for BCD, FGH, and JKL using both of these alternative sets of factor risk premia *in conjunction with the three-factor risk model.*

c. You now also consider historical estimates for the *MOM* risk factor over the two additional time frames: (1) $\lambda_{MOM} = 7.99$ percent (*30-year period*), and (2) $\lambda_{MOM} = 9.79$ percent (*80-year period*). Using this additional information, calculate the expected excess returns for BCD, FGH, and JKL *in conjunction with the four-factor risk model.*

d. Do all of the expected excess returns you calculated in part (a) and part (b) make sense? If not, identify which ones seem inconsistent with asset pricing theory and discuss why.

10. You have been assigned the task of estimating the expected returns for three different stocks: QRS, TUV, and WXY. Your preliminary analysis has established the historical risk premia associated with three risk factors that could potentially be included in your calculations: the excess return on a proxy for the market portfolio (MKT), and two variables capturing general macroeconomic exposures (MACRO1 and MACRO2). These values are: $\lambda_{MKT} = 7.5$ percent, $\lambda MACRO1 = -0.3$ percent, and $\lambda MACRO2 = 0.6$ percent. You have also estimated the following factor betas (loadings) for all three stocks with respect to each of these potential risk factors:

FACTOR LOADING

Stock	MKT	MACRO1	MACRO2
QRS	1.24	−0.42	0.00
TUV	0.91	0.54	0.23
WXY	1.03	−0.09	0.00

a. Calculate expected returns for the three stocks using just the MKT risk factor. Assume a risk-free rate of 4.5 percent.

b. Calculate the expected returns for the three stocks using all three risk factors and the same 4.5 percent risk-free rate.

c. Discuss the differences between the expected return estimates from the single-factor model and those from the multifactor model. Which estimates are most likely to be more useful in practice?

d. What sort of exposure might MACRO2 represent? Given the estimated factor betas, is it really reasonable to consider it a common (systematic) risk factor?

11. Consider the following information about two stocks (D and E) and two common risk factors (1 and 2):

Stock	b_{i1}	b_{i2}	$E(R_i)$
D	1.2	3.4	13.1%
E	2.6	2.6	15.4%

a. Assuming that the risk-free rate is 5.0 percent, calculate the levels of the factor risk premia that are consistent with the reported values for the factor betas and the expected returns for the two stocks.

b. You expect that in one year the prices for Stocks D and E will be $55 and $36, respectively. Also, neither stock is expected to pay a dividend over the next year. What should the price of each stock be today to be consistent with the expected return levels listed at the beginning of the problem?

c. Suppose now that the risk premium for Factor 1 that you calculated in part (a) suddenly increases by 0.25 percent (from x percent to $(x + 0.25)$ percent, where x is the value established in part (a)). What are the new expected returns for Stocks D and E?

d. If the increase in the Factor 1 risk premium in part (c) does not cause you to change your opinion about what the stock prices will be in one year, what adjustment will be necessary in the current (that is, today's) prices?

12. Suppose that three stocks (A, B, and C) and two common risk factors (1 and 2) have the following relationship:

$$E(R_A) = (1.1)\lambda_1 + (0.8)\lambda_2$$
$$E(R_B) = (0.7)\lambda_1 + (0.6)\lambda_2$$
$$E(R_C) = (0.3)\lambda_1 + (0.4)\lambda_2$$

a. If $\lambda_1 = 4$ percent and $\lambda_2 = 2$ percent, what are the prices expected next year for each of the stocks? Assume that all three stocks currently sell for $30 and will not pay a dividend in the next year.

b. Suppose that you know that next year the prices for Stocks A, B, and C will actually be $31.50, $35.00, and $30.50. Create and demonstrate a riskless, arbitrage investment to take advantage of these mispriced securities. What is the profit from your investment? You may assume that you can use the proceeds from any necessary short sale.

Problems 13 and 14 refer to the data contained in Exhibit 7.23, which lists 30 monthly excess returns to two different actively managed stock portfolios (A and B) and three different common risk factors (1, 2, and 3). (Note: You may find it useful to use a computer spreadsheet program such as Microsoft Excel to calculate your answers.)

13. a. Compute the average monthly return and monthly standard return deviation for each portfolio and all three risk factors. Also state these values on an annualized basis. (Hint: Monthly returns can be annualized by multiplying them by 12, while monthly standard deviations can be annualized by multiplying them by the square root of 12.)

b. Based on the return and standard deviation calculations for the two portfolios from part (a), is it clear whether one portfolio outperformed the other over this time period?

c. Calculate the correlation coefficients between each pair of the common risk factors (1 and 2, 1 and 3, and 2 and 3).

d. In theory, what should be the value of the correlation coefficient between the common risk factors? Explain why.

Exhibit 7.23 Monthly Excess Return Data for Two Portfolios and Three Risk Factors

Period	Portfolio A	Portfolio B	Factor 1	Factor 2	Factor 3
1	1.08%	0.00%	0.01%	−1.01%	−1.67%
2	7.58	6.62	6.89	0.29	−1.23
3	5.03	6.01	4.75	−1.45	1.92
4	1.16	0.36	0.66	0.41	0.22
5	−1.98	−1.58	−2.95	−3.62	4.29
6	4.26	2.39	2.86	−3.40	−1.54
7	−0.75	−2.47	−2.72	−4.51	−1.79
8	−15.49	−15.46	−16.11	−5.92	5.69
9	6.05	4.06	5.95	0.02	−3.76
10	7.70	6.75	7.11	−3.36	−2.85
11	7.76	5.52	5.86	1.36	−3.68
12	9.62	4.89	5.94	−0.31	−4.95
13	5.25	2.73	3.47	1.15	−6.16
14	−3.19	−0.55	−4.15	−5.59	1.66
15	5.40	2.59	3.32	−3.82	−3.04
16	2.39	7.26	4.47	2.89	2.80
17	−2.87	0.10	−2.39	3.46	3.08
18	6.52	3.66	4.72	3.42	−4.33
19	−3.37	−0.60	−3.45	2.01	0.70
20	−1.24	−4.06	−1.35	−1.16	−1.26
21	−1.48	0.15	−2.68	3.23	−3.18
22	6.01	5.29	5.80	−6.53	−3.19
23	2.05	2.28	3.20	7.71	−8.09
24	7.20	7.09	7.83	6.98	−9.05
25	−4.81	−2.79	−4.43	4.08	−0.16
26	1.00	−2.04	2.55	21.49	−12.03
27	9.05	5.25	5.13	−16.69	7.81
28	−4.31	−2.96	−6.24	−7.53	8.59
29	−3.36	−0.63	−4.27	−5.86	5.38
30	3.86	1.80	4.67	13.31	−8.78

e. How close do the estimates from part (b) come to satisfying this theoretical condition? What conceptual problem(s) is created by a deviation of the estimated factor correlation coefficients from their theoretical levels?

14. a. Using regression analysis, calculate the factor betas of each stock associated with each of the common risk factors. Which of these coefficients are statistically significant?

b. How well does the factor model explain the variation in portfolio returns? On what basis can you make an evaluation of this nature?

c. Suppose you are now told that the three factors in Exhibit 7.23 represent the risk exposures in the Fama–French characteristic-based model (excess market, *SMB*, and *HML*). Based on your regression results, which one of these factors is the most likely to be the market factor? Explain why.

d. Suppose it is further revealed that Factor 3 is the *HML* factor. Which of the two portfolios is most likely to be a growth-oriented fund and which is a value-oriented fund? Explain why.

Valuation and Management of Common Stocks

In Parts 1 and 2, you learned the purpose of investing and the importance of making appropriate asset allocation decisions. You also learned about the numerous investment instruments available on a global basis and the background regarding the institutional characteristics of the capital markets. In addition, you are now aware of the major developments in investment theory as they relate to efficient capital markets, portfolio theory, capital asset pricing, and multifactor valuation models. At this point, you are in a position to consider the theory and practice of estimating the value of stocks and to discuss various strategies for forming equity portfolios.

We begin this section with an introduction to the stock valuation process. In Chapter 8, we start by describing the dividend discount model and then transition into the *free cash flow to equity* (FCFE) model. After that, we discuss the two most common approaches to valuation: the *free cash flow to the firm* (FCFF) model and relative valuation methods, using tools such as price-earnings or price-book ratios. We start with this chapter on valuation because it is necessary to understand these ideas if you want to do any part of the *top-down* approach, where the investor values the aggregate economy and market, examines various industries, and concludes with the analysis of individual companies. In other words, you must understand valuation if you are going to value the market, an industry, or an individual stock.

In Chapter 9, we examine the top-down approach from a very practical perspective. We start with an analysis of the market. This can be done from a macroanalysis perspective (where we try to link the market to the economy) and a microanalysis perspective (where we try to value the cash flows of the market). After examining the overall market, we move on to the second step: the industry. An analyst has to examine how the industry is impacted by cyclical forces, structural changes in the economy, where the industry is in its life cycle, and the competitive forces that are driving the profitability of the industry. The final step of the top-down approach then requires the analyst to examine the individual security. In our discussion, we make important distinctions between growth companies and growth stocks, defensive companies and defensive stocks, and cyclical companies and stocks.

In Chapter 10, we provide considerable institutional detail on equity investing that will be valuable to anyone entering the field of asset management. We describe the initial public offering (IPO) process in detail and the different ways that the shares can be distributed to investors. We examine theories about why stock underpricing exists. This chapter also helps the aspiring analyst to understand the difference between the buy side and the sell side of the business. After that, we discuss how investors think about company management's capital allocation decision to either to either reinvest in their own business, to acquire another company, to distribute cash to debtholders, or to repurchase shares or pay dividends. We end the chapter with a particularly practical exercise for anyone who will interview with an asset management firm: We show how to structure a stock pitch and initiate further research that would be necessary to fully understand an investment.

Chapter 11 deals with equity portfolio management strategies. We begin with a general discussion of passive versus active management styles, including and introduction to the important concept of *tracking error* as a means of assessing how well an investor has replicated the benchmark portfolio. The overview of active equity portfolio management strategies includes a discussion of how one constructs a portfolio that reflects the client's risk–return objectives and constraints from three different perspectives: fundamental analysis (asset class and sector rotation, stock under- and overvaluation), technical analysis (overreaction, price momentum), and factor, attribute, and anomaly analysis (earnings momentum, firm size, low volatility). In this discussion, we pay special attention to the conceptual and practical differences between forming portfolios based on both value-oriented and growth-oriented investment styles. Notably, all of these approaches should consider global opportunities. We conclude Chapter 11 with a discussion of how the equity portfolio management decision fits into the investor's overall asset allocation strategy.

CHAPTER **8**
Equity Valuation

After you read this chapter, you should be able to answer the following questions:

- What does it mean to say that an investment is fairly priced versus overvalued versus undervalued?
- What is the difference between a constant-growth model, a no-growth model, and a multistage model?
- What is free cash flow?
- What is the intrinsic value of a business?
- What is the difference between a free cash flow to the firm (FCFF) model and a free cash flow to equity (FCFE) model? How are the cash flows different? How are the discount rates different?
- Should the FCFE model and the FCFF model result in the same value? What adjustments will allow this to happen?
- What is the difference between the free cash flow to equity model and the dividend discount model?
- What is the sustainable growth rate? How is the sustainable growth rate used to calculate the free cash flow that belongs to the equityholder?
- How can the FCFE model be applied to a bank stock?
- How do you calculate the present value of the growth opportunity? What does it represent?
- What is relative valuation?
- What are the underlying fundamentals that drive the price–earnings ratio? The price–sales ratio? The price–book ratio?
- What are the advantages and disadvantages of relative valuation?
- What is the purpose of ratio analysis?

8.1 IMPORTANT DISTINCTIONS

At the start of this book, we defined an *investment* as a commitment of funds for a period of time to derive a rate of return that would compensate the investor for the time during which the funds are invested, for the expected rate of inflation during the investment horizon, and for the uncertainty involved. In short, we defined an investment as committing funds in order to receive a fair rate of return for the risk that we assumed.

8.1.1 Fairly Valued, Overvalued, and Undervalued

We can be a bit more specific now and say that our earlier definition described a fair investment—one that gives us a return that matches the risk. But, in the real world, some investments are so expensive that we will not receive a fair return if we buy them. These investments are said to be **overvalued**. And occasionally, some investments are so cheap that they offer a rate of return that is a greater reward than the risk that the investor has taken. These investments are said to be **undervalued**.

As a simple example, imagine that you have identified your dream house and you believe that it will be worth $400,000 next year. You estimate that the risk of investing in real estate would require a 7 percent rate of return. This means that the house should be worth approximately $373,832 right now. This is $400,000 discounted at 7 percent for one year. We would consider that to be the fair price. If you can pay less than that, you should earn a return greater than the return justified by the risk. Of course, if you overpay, you'll earn a lower return than you should.

The purpose of this chapter is to study how investors determine whether a stock is fairly priced, overpriced, or underpriced. In other words, this is the study of **valuation**. Specifically, we will examine two approaches to valuation: (1) discounted cash flow (DCF) valuation and (2) relative valuation. These two methodologies will be described in just a short while.

8.1.2 Top-Down Approach versus Bottom-Up Approach

Before studying DCF and relative valuation, one other distinction is important. There are two different approaches to selecting, analyzing, and valuing a stock: the top-down approach and the bottom-up approach. The top-down approach (see Exhibit 8.1) does three studies in the examination of a security:

1. The overall market and economy
2. The industry
3. The individual company

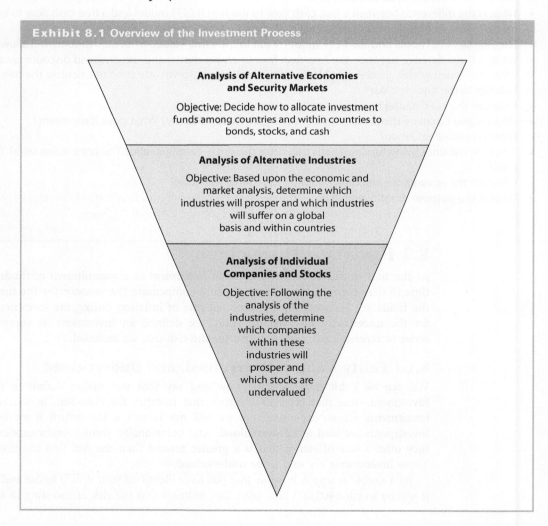

Exhibit 8.1 Overview of the Investment Process

Analysis of Alternative Economies and Security Markets

Objective: Decide how to allocate investment funds among countries and within countries to bonds, stocks, and cash

Analysis of Alternative Industries

Objective: Based upon the economic and market analysis, determine which industries will prosper and which industries will suffer on a global basis and within countries

Analysis of Individual Companies and Stocks

Objective: Following the analysis of the industries, determine which companies within these industries will prosper and which stocks are undervalued

Top-down analysts examine the value of an overall market (often studying the underlying economy) and determine which markets to invest in or to *overweight* (own more than the normal allocation or the allocation of an index). Within a specific market, the top-down analyst then searches for the best industries. Within the best industries, the analyst searches for the best companies (again looking for industries to overweight and individual companies to overweight). Of course, in the valuation process, the analyst may discover that the "best companies" are not the best investments because they may be overvalued. The analyst may also find that a company in a good (but not the best) industry offers the greatest potential for excess returns.

Those who employ the **bottom-up approach** start their search immediately at the company level. Of course, investors have various approaches. Some certainly start at the company level. Others may consider the market, economy, and industry but do it in a much less formal way than captured by the top-down approach. Obviously, different investors will place different amounts of weight on the importance of overall market and industry analysis.

The obvious argument in favor of the top-down approach is that it's difficult for most stocks to fare well in the face of a declining market or a hurting industry. Of course, bottom-up analysts would counter this by arguing that forecasting the overall market is difficult and this is evidenced by the poor record of market-timers. (Market-timers are investors who try to increase their allocation to an asset class when they are bullish and reduce their investment when they are bearish.)

In Chapter 9, we will discuss how an analyst can implement the top-down approach. If an analyst chooses to follow a bottom-up approach, she will likely still use some of the thoughts and analytical tools that are used in the top-down approach. Regardless of which approach is used, top-down or bottom-up, it is crucial for the analyst to understand valuation and that is what we're studying in this chapter.

Does the Three-Step Process Work? It is important to recognize that the results of several academic studies have supported the top-down technique. First, studies have indicated that most changes in an individual firm's *earnings* could be attributed to changes in aggregate corporate earnings and changes in earnings for the firm's industry, with the aggregate earnings changes being more important. Although the relative influence of the general economy and the industry on a firm's earnings varied among individual firms, the results consistently demonstrated that the economic environment had a significant effect on firm earnings.

Second, studies by Moore and Cullity (1988) and Siegel (1991) found a relationship between aggregate stock prices and various economic series, such as employment, income, and production. These results supported the view that a relationship exists between stock prices and economic expansions and contractions.

Third, an analysis of the relationship between *rates of return* for the aggregate stock market, alternative industries, and individual stocks showed that most of the changes in rates of return for individual stocks could be explained by changes in the rates of return for the aggregate stock market and the stock's industry. As shown by Meyers (1973), although the importance of the market effect tended to decline over time and the significance of the industry effect varied among industries, the combined market–industry effect on an individual stock's rate of return was still important.

These results from academic studies support the use of the three-step investment process. This investment decision approach is consistent with the discussion in Chapter 2, which contended that the most important decision is the asset allocation decision.[1] The asset allocation specifies (1) what proportion of your portfolio will be invested in various nations' economies,

---

[1]The classic studies that established the importance of asset allocation are Brinson, Hood, and Beebower (1986), followed by Brinson, Singer, and Beebower (1991). A subsequent well-regarded application of these concepts is contained in Cohen (1996).

(2) within each country, how you will divide your assets among stocks, bonds, or other assets, and (3) your industry selections, based on which industries are expected to prosper in the projected economic environment. We provide an example of global asset allocation in Chapter 11.

Now that we have described and justified the three-step process, our focus turns to the theory of valuation. The application of valuation theory allows the analyst to compute estimated intrinsic values for the market, for alternative industries, and for the stocks of individual firms. Finally, the analyst compares these estimated intrinsic values to current market prices and determines appropriate investment decisions.

8.2 An Introduction to Discounted Cash Flow and Relative Valuation

Imagine that you are going to buy a business when you graduate from school. There's a local bookstore that caters to your school, and the owners are looking to sell. The question that you have to answer is how much this bookstore is worth. The value can be calculated by using **discounted cash flow analysis** and **relative valuation**. We'll start with a simple example to understand the intuition.

The first way to think about valuing this business is to ask what cash you will receive from owning the business. In other words, if you run this business, hopefully it will be profitable and will grow. Some of these profits will need to be reinvested in the business in order to finance the growth. After reinvesting in the business, hopefully there will also be some cash left over that can be distributed to you. We'll refer to that as *free cash flow*—the cash flow that can be distributed to the providers of capital after operating a business and reinvesting in the short-term assets (net working capital) and the long-term assets (property, plant, and equipment). If we calculate the present value of those cash flows (also known as *discounting the cash flows*), the result will be the value that we ascribe to the business. This is known as the **intrinsic value**.

We can conduct this discounted cash flow analysis in several ways. One way is to calculate the cash flows that are left over for all of the providers of capital. In other words, after operating the business and reinvesting in the business, what cash remains? The providers of capital (stockholders, bondholders, and preferred stockholders) have claims on these cash flows. The cash flows must be discounted by using a rate that captures the riskiness of those cash flows. The discounted value of all of the cash flows will amount to the value of the entire firm. Then, that firm value is broken into pieces, assigning part of the total value to each of the capital providers. In other words, the firm value is comprised of the value of the debt, the value of any preferred stock, and the value of the equity. This is the standard discounted cash flow analysis. Sometimes, it's referred to as **free cash flow to the firm (FCFF)** valuation or weighted average cost of capital (WACC) analysis.

This discounted cash flow analysis could be done in a slightly different manner. Instead of calculating the free cash flow to the firm, the analyst could calculate the free cash flow that remains after operating the business, reinvesting in the short-term assets and the long-term assets, *and* also considering any cash that came in to the firm from debtholders or any cash that was used to pay the debtholders. In other words, if the debtholders have already been paid, anything that remains will belong to the shareholders. This is referred to as a **free cash flow to equity (FCFE)** model.

A special case of the free cash flow to the equity model is the *dividend discount model* (*DDM*). With this approach, the cash flows are the dividends that will be paid to shareholders. This really only works (in the real world) if a company pays out the vast majority of its free cash flow in the form of dividends. With that said, the dividend discount model is crucial. It is the basis of all valuation. When the dividend discount model is used correctly (as discussed below), it really becomes the free cash flow to equity model.

In addition to trying to discount the cash flows of the bookstore, there is a second methodology to valuing the business. The analyst could look at the value of other bookstores that have recently sold or have recently been appraised. Based on a comparison of the bookstore you are considering buying to ones with known values, the analyst could try to estimate how much it is worth. This is referred to as relative valuation or comparable analysis.

In the remainder of this chapter, we will examine how to value a company in much more detail. We will study the methodologies that we just described, looking at discounting cash flows and performing relative valuation. The approach will be very nuts-and-bolts. When you're done reading this chapter, you should know how to put together a DCF model and how to perform relative valuation analysis. Then, after studying valuation, the focus will be how to apply the top-down approach; Chapter 9 describes how to value an overall market and an industry.

Before delving into the nuts and bolts, one final comment is warranted. In order to care about this chapter, you must believe that valuation matters. Warren Buffett credited his mentor, Benjamin Graham (known as the father of value investing), as saying, "In the short run, the market is a voting machine—reflecting a voter-registration test that requires only money, not intelligence or emotional stability—but in the long run, the market is a weighing machine" (Berkshire Hathaway 1993 Annual Report). By this, he meant that stocks can become overvalued or undervalued in the short term as they move in and out of favor. But, over the long term, valuation matters. We share this belief.

8.2.1 The Foundations of Discounted Cash Flow Valuation

As mentioned above, the valuation of a financial asset requires two steps:

1. Identify the cash flows that the asset will generate.
2. Discount those cash flows to account for their riskiness.

This can be stated formulaically, where the value of a stock (or any other financial asset) is represented by the following equation:

8.1
$$V_0 = \sum_{t=1}^{\infty} \frac{CF_t}{(1+k)^t}$$

Equation 8.1 can be restated to emphasize the importance of growth and the discount rate:

8.2
$$P_0 = \sum_{t=1}^{\infty} \frac{CF_0(1+g)^t}{(1+k)^t} = CF_0 \sum_{t=1}^{\infty} \frac{(1+g)^t}{(1+k)^t}$$

Equation 8.1 simply states that the value is equal to the sum of the present value of each of the cash flows. The cash flow is represented by CF, and the discount rate is represented by k. Below, we will describe different approaches to valuing equity, where the cash flows and discount rates will vary based on the methodology used.

This approach is actually the same, regardless of whether the analyst is valuing stocks or bonds. Of course, it is easier to value bonds. The cash flows and their timing are known. Assuming that there is no default, the bondholder will receive periodic coupon payments and a $1,000 principal payment at maturity. Those cash flows are discounted at the yield to maturity, and the result is the value of the bond.

Valuing equity is more difficult. The cash flows are less certain. This is because the shareholders have a *residual interest*; in other words, the shareholders receive what's left over after the creditors have been paid. In addition, the timing of the cash flows is less certain.

The difficulty in valuing a stock does not make valuation any less important. In fact, it likely makes valuation even more important. Investors are likely to use very different inputs (for the cash flows, the growth rates, and the discount rates), and this will result in very different valuations. Differences in opinion can create opportunities for investors to earn excess returns or (unfortunately) inferior returns.

We will examine three approaches to discounted cash flow valuation: the free cash flow to equity (FCFE) approach, the dividend discount model (DDM) approach, and the free cash flow to the firm (FCFF) approach. The FCFE and DDM methods are used to estimate the intrinsic value of the equity of a firm. The FCFF method is used to value the entire firm (equity plus debt plus preferred stock). The various numerators and denominators can be seen in the following table:

	FCFE	DDM	FCFF
Cash flow (numerator)	Free cash flow to the equity	Dividends	Free cash flow to the firm
Owner of cash flow	Shareholders	Shareholders	All providers of capital (shareholders, bondholders, and preferred stockholders)
Discount rate (denominator)	Cost of equity	Cost of equity	Weighted average cost of capital
Resulting value	Value of equity	Value of equity	Value of entire firm; to calculate the value of the equity, you must subtract the value of the debt and preferred stock from the value of the firm

In this table, you may notice that the FCFE and DDM appear to be similar. As described above, DDM is actually a specialized case of FCFE. DDM may be used when all (or virtually all) of the available free cash flow for the equityholder is actually paid out in the form of a dividend. Assuming that the company does not distribute all of its free cash flow, the FCFE model provides a more accurate valuation. This will be discussed in more detail later.

When using the FCFE, DDM, and FCFF approaches, analysts often make some simplifying assumptions about how cash flows grow. These assumptions can be classified as:

- Constant growth
- No growth (growth equals zero)
- Two-stage or multistage growth

In the next three sections, these three assumptions (or models) are described.

8.2.2 The Constant Growth Model

Probably the most important growth assumption is the **constant growth model** (also known as the *Gordon growth model*). This approach treats cash flow as a growing perpetuity. In other words, the cash flow will grow at a constant rate forever. The equation for the constant growth dividend discount model is:

8.3
$$V_0 = D_1/(k - g)$$

This model assumes that k is greater than g. In other words, this model may be used assuming that a company is growing at a rate that is no higher than the economy's nominal growth rate. Since k includes a risk-free rate (and this should capture an economy's growth rate) and adds a risk premium, k will be larger than g as long as g is equal to or smaller than the economic growth rate (and the risk premium is positive). The derivation of the constant growth model can be seen in the appendix to this chapter.

For example, imagine that you are trying to value Brinker International, Inc. (ticker EAT), and you conclude that it will have $3.05 of cash flow next year that will be available for the shareholders. The cost of equity is 10 percent, and the expected growth rate in the future is 3.3 percent. The value of EAT would be:

$$V_0 = \$3.05/(.10 - .033) = \$45.60$$

At the current time, EAT is trading for $43. By using this approach, most analysts would think that EAT is relatively fairly valued.

There are many important takeaways from Equation 8.3:

- If the cash flow is larger (because the company has higher earnings or can pay out a larger percentage of earnings), the intrinsic value is greater.
- If the cash flow is less risky, it is discounted at a lower cost of equity (k), and the intrinsic value is greater.
- If the cash flow grows at a faster rate (g), the stock will be more valuable.
- This model assumes that a company is relatively mature and in a steady state. This model would not be appropriate, for example, for a very high-growth company if the growth rate is higher than the discount rate. In addition, a high-growth company's growth rate would not be expected to remain elevated into perpetuity.
- No analyst is actually expecting the company's growth rate to be constant forever. At the same time, few analysts truly believe that they can predict all of the variation over the long term. Instead, this growth rate reflects an average growth rate for the long term.
- As a general rule, the growth rate for a large company is capped at the growth rate of the economy. If a company grows in perpetuity at a rate faster than the economy's growth rate, the company will become a larger and larger percentage of the economy. At some point, this can become unrealistic.
- The highest economic growth rate that can be used in this equation (as described immediately above) is the *nominal growth rate*, not the real growth rate. Nominal numbers include inflation. Real numbers exclude inflation. This is a large point of confusion in practice, as many practitioners believe that the growth rate is capped by the real growth rate of the economy. Remember that all of the estimates involve nominal numbers: the cash flow is in nominal numbers (they include inflation) and the discount rate is also in nominal terms. In other words, if the capital asset pricing model is used, one component is the risk-free rate, which is a nominal number (not a real number). Real numbers should never be mixed with nominal numbers.

To have a real sense of valuation, it is important to understand how a growing perpetuity works from a mathematical perspective. In other words, it is important to understand the math behind the growing perpetuity equation and the three variables D_1, g, and k (and V_0, the value of the stock):

- The growth rate (g) describes how much the dividend increases each year. It also describes how much the value of the investment must grow each year. For example, in Exhibit 8.2, the stock is worth $15 currently. One year from now, it must be worth $15 \times 1.04 = \$15.60$. The value must grow 4 percent per year if it is going to generate a 4 percent larger dividend each year. The dividend in year 2 should be $\$1.50 \times 1.04 = \$1.56$.
- The required rate of return (k) describes the amount that the investment earns each year. As a result, if the stock is worth $15.60 at the end of the year and earns 14 percent the following year, this is $\$15.60 \times .14 = \$2.184$.
- The company cannot pay out the entire $2.184 ($k$). It must retain g to grow. g is the 4 percent of $15.60 or $.624. This is what allows the principal to grow at the growth rate so that the dividend can continue to increase at that rate. The amount that can be paid out is $k-g$. That is $14\% - 4\% = 10\%$ of $15.60 (and this explains the $1.56 dividend).

Exhibit 8.2 Understanding the Growing Perpetuity (Constant Growth) Formula

A company is expected to pay a dividend of $1.50 next year. That dividend should grow 4% per year in perpetuity. The cost of equity is 14%. What is the stock worth? How will the stock price grow over time?

$$V_0 = D_1/(k - g) = 1.50/(.14 - .04) = \textbf{\$15}$$

Now, let's look at how this works over time...

If you pay $15 and the investment earns 14%, this is $2.10 (i.e., $15 × 14%). But, the company is only going to pay out $1.50. This leaves 60 cents for the company to retain. The value of the stock at the end of year 1 should be $15.60.

The key idea is that your investment earns "r" (14% in this case). The company can pay out "$k-g$" (14%−4% in this case). The company has to retain g (4% in this example) so that it will grow. This is what allows the company to continue to grow its dividend payments.

This also reminds you that your total return is 14% (the "k") and it's a combination of the 10% dividend income ("$k-g$") and capital appreciation of 4% (g). So, the intrinsic value will increase 4% each year.

The constant growth dividend discount equation is widely used in practice. There are three uses that an analyst should consider:

1. **A general estimate of value.** While valuation is often presented as if it is a science, this may be misleading. Certainly, there are some mathematical facts that can't be ignored. At the same time, one reason that markets exist is that buyers and sellers have different opinions concerning the value of the company. An analyst will be helped to the extent that she can use the constant growth model to determine whether a stock is grossly undervalued (and should be examined further), relatively fairly priced, or grossly overvalued (and should be avoided or considered as a candidate for a short sale). Below this list of three uses, there is an example of calculating a general estimate of value.
2. **The basis for understanding fundamental multiples.** Later in this chapter, we will discuss relative valuation. We will use the constant growth dividend discount model to estimate a company's (or the overall market's) appropriate price–earnings ratio, as well as its price–sales ratio and price–book ratio.
3. **The terminal value of a model.** Analysts often build models that involve two or more stages of growth. Most frequently, the analyst will be projecting high growth in early years but will anticipate that growth will eventually stabilize. This will be described in greater detail in Section 8.2.4.

An Example of Using the Constant Growth Model to Estimate Value One way of investing is to focus on simply avoiding disasters. For example, let's go back to the tech bubble of the late 1990s. We will use Cisco, one of the high-flying tech stocks of the time. In 2000, CSCO had earnings per share of 53 cents. Let's imagine that Cisco was able to pay out all of its earnings. (This wasn't actually the case because Cisco had to retain some earnings to finance growth.)

At the time, CSCO likely had a cost of equity of at least 12 percent. Assume that CSCO was going to grow its earnings at 10 percent per year into perpetuity (which would be an extremely aggressive assumption because it imagines that the company would be growing significantly faster than the economy forever). Using these extreme assumptions (100 percent payout of earnings and 10 percent growth), the value of CSCO would have been:

$$V_0 = \$.53/(.12 - .10) = \$26.50$$

In 2000, the stock traded as high as $82. If an investor simply used the constant growth dividend discount model (and these overly optimistic assumptions), he could have avoided investing in a security that was greatly overvalued.

8.2.3 The No-Growth Model

In the no-growth model, the assumption is that a company's cash flows are not growing. The no-growth assumption can be seen as a special case of the constant growth assumption. If we start with Equation 8.3 and simply set the growth rate at zero, the result is the no-growth model.

8.3
$$V_0 = D_1/(k - g)$$

8.4
$$V_0 = D_1/k$$

As an example, imagine that an analyst believes that Target Corp. (TGT) will generate $4.74 of cash flow next year and that the cash flow will not grow. The analyst believes that TGT has a cost of equity of 9.0 percent. This would give TGT an intrinsic value of $4.74/9.0 percent = $52.67. This intrinsic value is similar to the current price of the stock. Of course, if the analyst believed that the cash flows will grow or that the appropriate discount rate is less than 9 percent, the stock would become more attractive.

In each of these models (constant growth, no-growth, and multistage growth), the goal is simply to forecast a company's future cash flows and discount them back to the present. The no-growth model treats the cash flows as a perpetuity; the payment goes on forever. As a result, the value of the stock is represented by $V_0 = D_1/k$.

Depending on which approach the analyst is using (FCFE, DDM, or FCFF), this equation is stating that the value of the stock (or the enterprise value, if using FCFF) is calculated by dividing next year's cash flow (the free cost to equity or the dividend or the free cash flow to the firm) by the discount rate (the cost of equity or the weighted average cost of capital). Remember that in the no-growth model, the cash flow is expected to be constant in the future.

As you think about the no-growth model, there are some important takeaways from this simple equation:

- The larger the cash flow, the greater the value of the firm or the equity. Hopefully, it is obvious that if an investor receives larger payments, an investment is worth more.
- A less risky cash flow requires a lower discount rate (lower cost of equity or WACC). A lower discount rate results in a greater value of the firm or the equity. This is important intuition: less risky cash flows (that the investor is more certain to receive) are discounted at a lower rate and they are worth more. An investor would pay more for a $100 cash flow that she was very likely to receive than for a $100 cash flow that she was less likely to receive.
- Realize that no one is predicting that the cash flow will stay exactly the same forever. Rather, this model is used when the best prediction is that this company does not have any growth opportunities.
- If a company doesn't grow and the overall economy does grow, the company will become a smaller part of the economy in real terms.

100 Percent Payout With the no-growth model, the assumption is that a company can pay out all of its earnings. It may seem strange to think of paying out 100 percent of earnings.

Consider a food delivery service with the following income statement:

Sales	$ 300,000
Cost of Goods Sold	−$ 120,000
Gross Profit	$ 180,000
Selling, Gen'l & Admin.	−$ 80,000
Earnings Before Interest and Taxes	$ 100,000
Interest	−$ 10,000
Earnings Before Taxes	$ 90,000
Taxes	−$ 30,000
Net Income	$ 60,000

This company has $15,000 of depreciation. This is part of the SG&A expense. This is not a cash flow. So, the company's cash flow from operations would = $60,000 + $15,000 = $75,000.

Then, the company would have to pay for capital expenditures. The no-growth model assumes that these are approximately the same amount as depreciation. This brings the Free Cash Flow back to $60,000. Free Cash Flow = $60,000 + $15,000 − $15,000 = $60,000. (Note that a no-growth company should not have any change in net working capital. In other words, you don't need more inventory, for example, if you're not growing.)

Even if a company isn't growing, the company has to replace its assets. Doesn't it need to retain some of its earnings? For example, imagine that an analyst is valuing a food delivery business that is not growing. The company has net income of $60,000 per year. Even though the company is not growing, it will still need to replace its two cars at some point.

The answer to this issue is that there is an important distinction between *earnings* and *cash flows*. In order to calculate net income, depreciation was subtracted. Depreciation is not a cash expense; it's an accounting entry. The cash was used when the company bought the cars (not when the company depreciated the cars). The result is that the cash flow generated by operating this business is greater than the net income. But the company will eventually have to replace the cars, and those capital expenditures should (approximately) equal the depreciation.

You can see an example of this in Exhibit 8.3. In Exhibit 8.3, the company's operations generated cash flow of $75,000 (the operating cash flow). To calculate free cash flow, capital expenditures must be subtracted. The normal assumption in a no-growth model is that capital expenditures and depreciation will be equal. As a result, after the $15,000 of capital expenditures is subtracted from the operating cash flow, we are left with $60,000 (the net income).

8.2.4 Multistage (or Two-Stage) Growth Assumption

Often times, it is not correct to assume that a company's cash flows will grow at a constant rate or won't grow at all. The company might be in a high-growth phase of its life cycle, and the analyst wants to model that high growth while also recognizing that the high growth will not continue forever. As a result, after the high-growth period, the model might return to a constant growth assumption. Or, it is possible that the analyst might model a high-growth period followed by a transitional period of slowing growth and then a period of constant (slower) growth. The idea is that a model will frequently have different growth rates for different time periods.

In addition to a high-growth firm that is expected to slow over time, it is also possible to have a company that is currently growing at a slow rate, but growth is expected to increase. The current slow growth may be the result of a slowdown in the overall economy or temporary issues that are unique to an industry or individual company.

Exhibit 8.4 The Two-Stage DDM (Using the Constant Growth DDM for the Terminal Value)

Here, we examine Cisco Systems (CSCO) in 2000 (the height of the technology bubble). Assume that CSCO had a 53 cent dividend in 2000 (even though 53 cents was actually CSCO's earnings). Imagine that you thought that CSCO would grow their dividends-per-share at 20% per year for five years and then growth would subside to 5% and that would be their long-term growth rate. We could build a two-stage model that would capture both the high growth and then the constant growth. The cost of equity is 12%.

	2001	2002	2003	2004	2005	2006
Dividend	$ 0.64	$0.76	$0.92	$1.10	$ 1.32	$1.38
Terminal Value					$19.78	
PV of Dividend	$ 0.57	$0.61	$0.65	$0.70	$ 0.75	
PV of Terminal Value					$11.22	
Value of Stock	**$14.50**					

For the first five years (2001–2005), we grew the 53 cent dividend by 20% per year. In 2006, growth slowed to 5%. The 2006 dividend was used to calculate the terminal value in 2005. Think of this as saying that the stock will be worth $19.78 in 2005. This is $1.38/ (.12 − .05). Then, all of the dividends and the terminal value were discounted to the present.

The two-stage model can also be considered formulaically, starting with Equation 8.2:

$$8.2 \qquad P_0 = \sum_{t=1}^{\infty} \frac{CF_0(1+g)^t}{(1+k)^t} = CF_0 \sum_{t=1}^{\infty} \frac{(1+g)^t}{(1+k)^t}$$

$$8.5 \qquad P_0 = \sum_{t=1}^{N} \frac{CF_0[\Pi(1+g_t)]}{(1+k_t)^t} + \left[\frac{CF_N(1+g_2)}{(k_L - g_2)} \right] (1+k_N)^{-N}$$

$$= \text{PV of Stage 1 ("Abnormal") Growth} + \text{PV of Stage 2 ("Constant") Growth}$$

The stage 1 growth in Equation 8.5 can be a constant rate or an irregular rate. The second stage would be a constant rate (which could also include a growth rate of zero, or the no-growth model).

Most analysts' models have two or more stages of growth. An example of this can be seen in Exhibit 8.4, where we have valued Cisco during the technology bubble. We assumed a very high growth rate (20 percent) that would eventually subside to a more stable rate (5 percent). The stable rate was used in the constant growth model to calculate the terminal value of the stock (that is, the value of the stock at the end of Year 5).

We will see another example of a two-stage model in Exhibit 8.7.

8.3 DISCOUNTED CASH FLOW

8.3.1 Method #1: The Dividend Discount Model

The simplest way to approach valuation is through the **dividend discount model (DDM)**. While most students have already seen this approach in an earlier class, it is important to review the key concepts. The DDM is the basis of all valuation. It can be used to develop the intuition that will be necessary to understand the FCFE model.

An analyst can apply the constant growth assumption, no-growth assumption, or a multi-stage growth assumption with the DDM. Below, there are some examples of the dividend discount model, with some crucial learning points. The key ideas to remember are:

- **The numerator is next year's dividend.** Sometimes, in the real world or in academic problems, the analyst will be told this explicitly. Other times, the analyst will know "the dividend that was just paid." This must be grown to next year's dividend. This is done by multiplying the dividend that was just paid by (1 + growth rate). Other times, an analyst may forecast "next year's earnings." To turn this into the dividend, the earnings must be multiplied by the payout ratio. Still other times, the analyst may start with "last year's earnings." To turn this into next year's dividend, last year's earnings must be grown to this year's earnings and then multiplied by the payout ratio.

- **The discount rate in the denominator is the cost of equity.** Most frequently, this will be calculated using the capital asset pricing model:

8.6 $\text{Cost of Equity} = k = \text{Risk-Free Rate} + \text{Beta}\,(\text{Risk Premium})$

Constant Growth Examples Imagine that an analyst is valuing a company that is expected to pay a dividend of $1.05 next year. The dividend is expected to grow 5 percent per year, and the cost of equity is 15 percent. Using Equation 8.3, the value would equal $1.05/(.15 − .05) = $10.50.

It's important to realize that the numerator could have been described in many other ways. The analyst could have been told that next year's earnings will be $1.50 and the payout ratio would be 70 percent. Be careful: Sometimes you are told the percentage of earnings that can be paid out (the *payout ratio*), while other times you are told that the percentage of earnings that must be retained (known as the *retention ratio* or *plowback ratio*). This example could have either been stated as a 70 percent payout ratio or a 30 percent retention ratio (or plowback ratio). The payout ratio plus the retention ratio must always add up to 100 percent.

Another way of framing this question would be to say that last year's dividend was $1.00 per share and that dividends are expected to grow 5 percent per year. Alternatively, you could have been told that last year's earnings were $1.43 and that earnings are expected to grow 5 percent per year forever, and the payout ratio is 70 percent.

The discount rate of 15 percent could be described in many ways. Most simplistically, you could be told that the cost of equity is 15 percent. Or, you could be told that the risk-free rate is 7.8 percent, the beta is 1.2, and the market risk premium is 6 percent. This would result in a calculation of 7.8% + 1.2(6%) = 15%.

Another way that the 15 percent cost of equity could be described is to be told that the risk-free rate is 7.8 percent, the expected return from the market is 13.8 percent, and the beta is 1.2. This would lead to a cost of equity calculation of 7.8% + 1.2(13.8% − 7.8%) = 15%. In this way of describing the data, you are told the expected return from the market (13.8 percent) and the risk-free rate (7.8 percent), and you use those two numbers to calculate the risk premium of 6 percent.

No-Growth Examples Imagine that you're looking at a company that will earn $1.50 next year and has no growth opportunities. The company has a cost of equity of 15 percent. Using Equation 8.3, the value of the equity would equal $1.50/15% = $10. It's important to remember that if a company has no growth opportunities, the correct assumption is that the company will be able to pay out 100 percent of the earnings. This is why (with the no-growth assumption) the earnings equal the dividend.

The numerator could have been described in other ways. You could have been told that next year's dividend will be $1.50, and there will be no growth opportunities. Or, you could have been told that the earnings (or dividend) for the year that just ended were $1.50, and the company has no growth opportunities in the future.

Present Value of the Growth Opportunity (PVGO), Using Both the Constant Growth Model and the No-Growth Model Examine the constant growth and no-growth examples that we just looked at. In both examples, the company is expected to earn $1.50 next year.

When we assumed that the company has to plow back 30 percent of its earnings in order to grow 5 percent per year, the value of the stock was $10.50. If the company had no growth opportunities, the entire $1.50 could be paid out as a dividend, and the stock was worth $10.

These two examples can be used to show an important concept: the **present value of the growth opportunity (PVGO)**. The PVGO represents the portion of a stock's intrinsic value that is attributable to the company's growth. When an analyst is valuing a stock that is expected to have some growth, it is important to know how much of the intrinsic value is derived from growth. (We'll discuss why it's important to know this in just a moment.) In order to calculate the PVGO, we will use the constant growth model and no-growth model.

If you consider the company that is expected to earn $1.50 next year and will retain 30 percent of its earnings, we have already seen that this stock should be worth $10.50. In order to calculate the value of the growth, we can ask how much the stock would be worth if the company did not grow. If the company did not grow, the company could pay out all of its earnings. This means that the stock would be worth $10. This was the no-growth calculation that was done above. This means that the value of the growth is $10.50 − $10.00 = 50 cents. In other words, approximately 5 percent of the stock's value comes from growth.

It is important to recognize one common error that is often made when calculating the PVGO. In this example, a common error would have been to assume that next year's $1.05 dividend doesn't grow and to calculate the no-growth value of this growing company as $1.05/.15 = $7. Obviously, this is incorrect because it assumes that the company has to retain some of its earnings, even though the company is not growing. The correct assumption is that 100 percent of the $1.50 of earnings can be paid out (with the no-growth assumption).

It is also interesting to think about why the 5 percent growth in this example adds only 5 percent to the value of this stock. The answer is based on the idea that value is created when a firm earns more than its cost of capital. In this case, we know that the firm has a cost of equity of 15 percent. Given the analyst's assumptions of 5 percent growth and that the company has to plowback 30 percent of its earnings, we can use the **sustainable growth rate equation** to back out the company's return on equity assumption. The sustainable growth rate equation will be discussed in detail later in this chapter. But, right now, think of this equation as describing how fast a company can grow if they generate a certain amount of additional equity (the ROE) and retain some percentage of it (the plowback ratio).

8.7   Sustainable Growth Rate (g) = Return on Equity × RR

RR is the *retention rate*. This is the percentage of earnings that are plowed back into the company. As a result, it is also sometimes referred to as the *plowback ratio*.

Using Equation 8.7, we can say that 5% = ROE × 30%. This means that the return on equity is 16.67 percent. Since the company earns more on its equity (16.67 percent) than the cost of equity (15 percent), the growth creates value. But the spread between the ROE and the cost of equity is small, and this is why the 5 percent growth assumption has not created even more value.

In sum, the PVGO is calculated in three steps:

1. **Calculate the intrinsic value of the stock.** This is frequently done using the constant growth DDM. But, it could be done using a two-stage model or any other way.
2. **Calculate the no-growth value of the stock.** This assumes that the company could pay out 100 percent of its Year 1 earnings. In other words, if the company is not going to grow, the company does not need to retain any earnings. We often think about this no-growth value as the value of the *assets-in-place*.
3. **Calculate the PVGO by subtracting the no-growth value from the intrinsic value.** For example, if a stock has an intrinsic value of $15, but it would be worth $10 if the company never grows again, the value of the growth is $5.

PVGO as a Risk Factor   For an analyst, it's very important to understand how much of a model's value comes from assets-in-place and how much comes from future growth. Let's imagine two stocks. Your models value both stocks at $20. But stock A has $20 of assets in place and no growth opportunity. Stock B has $12 of assets-in-place and $8 of value that is attributable to future growth.

Next, imagine that both companies miss their earnings estimates by 1 cent. How will the stocks react? The market is likely to ignore Company A's earnings miss. It simply doesn't matter (unless the market thinks that future earnings will be significantly impaired). Over the long term, we still expect the dividend to continue. In short, some analysts may view the no-growth model (based on a truly sustainable dividend) as something close to a price floor.

The stock price of Company B, on the other hand, may plummet, if the company misses its earnings estimate by 1 cent. Analysts may infer that Company B is less likely to meet the lofty growth expectations that are responsible for such a significant portion of Company B's stock price. In sum, the PVGO calculation is crucial in helping analysts understand the significance of growth in his valuation—and this may be thought of as a risk factor.

PVGO Can Be Negative   Too often, students leave business school with the impression that growth is always valuable. Unfortunately, this is not correct.

Imagine a bank that attracts deposits by paying 7 percent interest, and the bank loans this money to borrowers at a 2 percent interest rate. This bank could grow its business. But, at some point, the bank would become insolvent. It's not profitable to pay 7 percent for money and to loan it out at 2 percent. This is a really important point: Value is created by earning more on capital than the capital costs. Applying this to the dividend discount model, this means that growth is valuable if the return on equity is greater than the cost of equity.

For example, imagine that a company is going to earn $2 per share next year, and it should be able to pay out 25 percent of those earnings in the form of a dividend. (The remaining 75 percent of earnings needs to be retained in order to finance growth.) The company is expected to grow 4 percent per year and has a cost of equity of 12 percent. To calculate the present value of the growth opportunity:

Step 1: Calculate the intrinsic value of the stock:

$$V_0 = (\$2 \times .25)/(.12 - .04) = \$6.25$$

Step 2: Calculate the no-growth value of the stock:

$$V_0 = \$2/.12 = \$16.67$$

Step 3: Calculate the present value of the growth opportunity:

$$PVGO = \$6.25 - \$16.67 = -10.42$$

In this example, growth is destroying value. Again, using Equation 8.7, the sustainable growth rate equation, the ROE can be calculated. Growth = ROE × RR, so 4% = ROE × 75%. Therefore, ROE = 5.33%. This company is earning 5.33 percent on capital that costs 12 percent. It is destroying value.

Two-Stage DDM   In addition to the constant growth assumption and the no-growth assumption, an analyst may assume two or three stages of growth or even irregular growth for some time period. Earlier, we saw an example of this in Exhibit 8.4. As another example, let's imagine that an analyst expects a company to pay a $1 dividend next year and that this dividend will grow 10 percent per year for two more years. After Year 3, the dividend will grow 4 percent per year. The cost of equity is 14 percent. The value of the stock can be calculated by discounting:

1. The value of the dividends in Years 1–3. These dividends will be $1.00, $1.10, and $1.21. They must be discounted at 14 percent for one year, two years, and three years, respectively. The present value of these three dividends is $2.54.

Exhibit 8.5 Two-Stage Dividend Discount Model				
	1	**2**	**3**	**4**
Dividend	$ 1.00	$1.10	$ 1.21	$1.258
Terminal Value			$12.58	
PV of CFs	$ 0.88	$0.85	$ 9.31	
Total Value	**$11.03**			

2. The value of the dividends in years 4 through perpetuity. Dividend 4 will equal (dividend 3) × (1 + growth rate) = $1.21 × 1.04 = $1.258. Since we know dividend four, we can calculate the value of the stock at the end of Year 3. $V_3 = \$1.258/(.14 - .04) = \$12.58$. This was simply the constant growth model. This $12.58 must be discounted for three years at 14 percent. The value of this is $\$12.58/(1.14)^3 = \$8.49$

3. Adding the present value of the dividends plus the present value of the terminal value equals $2.54 + $8.49 = $11.03.

This example can be seen in Exhibit 8.5.

Again, the analyst could examine how much of this $11.03 comes from growth. If the company never grew again, it could pay out all of next year's $1 of earnings. This would make the no-growth value equal to $1/.14 = $7.14. This means that the PVGO = $11.03 − $7.14 = $3.89.

8.3.2 Method #2: Free Cash Flow to Equity—The Improved DDM

Many students learn about the dividend discount model and get frustrated. They try to apply it and find that it often predicts values that are far below market prices. Almost all stocks look grossly overvalued.

There is one simple issue that you must understand in order to make the dividend discount model useful in all situations. Instead of using actual dividends paid, what you are actually valuing is the amount of dividends that *could* be paid. This is the free cash flow to equity (FCFE).

To begin, FCFE is defined (measured) as follows:

Net Income

    + Depreciation expense
       − Capital expenditures
       − Change in working capital
       − Principal debt repayments
    + New debt issues

The goal is to determine the free cash flow that is available to the stockholders after payments to all other capital suppliers and after providing for the continued growth of the firm. This model is a more general version of the dividend discount model.

Imagine that you are the sole shareholder in a company. After running the business, reinvesting in the business (investing in more long-term assets as well as investing in net working capital), making any interest payments, and possibly making principal payments (or borrowing more), there is $10 million remaining. The company could send you a $10 million dividend check. If the company planned on doing that, it would be easy for you to apply the dividend discount model and obtain an accurate valuation.

But what happens if the company doesn't pay any dividend? It retains all $10 million. If the dividend is zero, does that mean that the company is worthless? Obviously, the company is not worthless. As the sole shareholder, you are still $10 million better off. Instead of receiving a $10 million dividend check, you are the owner of a company that is holding $10 million for you.

The key takeaway is that we are valuing the $10 million of free cash flow that belongs to the equityholder—whether it is paid to the shareholder in the form of a dividend or the company holds the money for the shareholder. The actual amount that a company pays out is not relevant in the valuation. Whether the dividend check is for $10 million, $6 million, or $2 million or there is no dividend check does not matter. As the sole shareholder, you will be $10 million better off.

Remember that there are many different reasons that management might decide to retain earnings rather than pay them out. It may be that they hold cash to avoid the risk that they would have to issue more debt or equity in an economic downturn or that they expect to acquire another company in the future (and don't want to issue more equity). Tax reasons may explain a company's dividend policy. Or, it could be that the company doesn't pay out all of its free cash flow in the form of dividends because it prefers to have smooth dividends and not ever have a situation in which it has to cut dividends (if cash flow drops one year).

The bottom line is that it's very rare for a company to pay out all of its free cash flow in the form of dividend. So, if you are valuing a company and using the dividends that are actually paid, you're not capturing all of the free cash flow and your valuation will be inaccurate.

As a result, the question becomes how to calculate how much free cash flow belongs to the equityholders. There is one simple trick. We will review this trick and then we will apply the free cash flow to equity methodology.

The trick involves the sustainable growth rate equation. As described earlier, this equation says that growth reflects the return on equity and the percentage of earnings that are plowed back (or retained). In other words:

8.7   Sustainable Growth Rate (g) = Return on Equity × Retention Rate

Remember that the retention rate (RR) is the percentage of earnings that are retained or plowed back. This allows us to represent the sustainable growth rate equation as:

$$g = \text{ROE} \times \text{RR}$$

As an example of the sustainable growth rate, consider a company has an ROE of 10 percent. This means that a company is generating 10 percent more equity. If the company retains 60 percent of these earnings, the company can grow 6 percent. This is simply 10% × 60% = 6%.

The sustainable growth rate equation makes two assumptions:

1. **The firm will keep the capital structure the same.** This means that the debt has to increase by the same percentage amount as the equity.
2. **The firm is not becoming any more or less efficient.** This means that the firm needs the asset turnover ratio (Sales/Assets) to stay constant.

It is very important to understand this equation and how the assumptions work. An example of how the sustainable growth rate is traditionally used can be seen in Exhibit 8.6. In this example, the company is generating 10 percent more equity; this is what the return on equity represents. But, since the firm is only retaining 60 percent of its earnings, this means that the equity will grow 6 percent. Since we assume that the firm wants its capital structure to remain constant, this means the firm will issue 6 percent more debt. With 6 percent more capital, the firm will have a 6 percent increase in assets that can be used to generate 6 percent more growth.

In reality, analysts rarely use the sustainable growth rate equation in this "traditional" way. They do not estimate growth by asking how much capital the firm will have. That may be the case if a company were capital constrained. But, if you gave an extra billion dollars to a yo-yo manufacturer, this wouldn't ensure that the company could sell more yo-yos.

Analysts are in the business of making forecasts. They forecast how fast a company will grow. They understand past growth and examine how demand for the company's good or

Exhibit 8.6 Sustainable Growth Rate Formula, Traditional Use

Consider a firm with $300 of assets that is financed 2/3 with equity and 1/3 with debt and has a 10% ROE. The firm plows back 60% of earnings. Using the SGR formula, how fast can this company grow?

Assets	$300	Debt	$100
		Equity	$200

Assets	$318	Debt	$106
		Equity	$212

SGR = 10% × 60% = **6%**

This is our starting point: $300 of assets, financed with 1/3 debt and 2/3 equity.

$ROE = \text{Net Income}_1/\text{Equity}_0$

$10\% = \text{NI}_1/\$200$

NI_1 must equal $20

If the firm plows back 60% of earnings, this will equal $12. It is a 6% increase. Assuming that capital structure will stay the same, debt must also increase 6%.

Assuming asset turnover is stable, sales and assets will also grow 6%.

service will change in the future. They look at the overall economy, relevant demographics, the competition, the consumers, any supply issues for input, and so on. These factors are described in Chapter 9.

Analysts also estimate how efficient and profitable the company will be, as well as how the capital structure may change. These estimates are all captured in the estimate for the return on equity.

8.8
$$\frac{\text{Net Income}}{\text{Common Equity}} = \frac{\text{Net Income}}{\text{Net Sales}} \times \frac{\text{Net Sales}}{\text{Total Assets}} \times \frac{\text{Total Assets}}{\text{Common Equity}}$$
$$= \text{Profit Margin} \times \text{Total Asset Turnover} \times \text{Financial Leverage}$$

Once an analyst has forecasted the growth and the ROE, the sustainable growth rate equation can be used in a different way. Instead of using the equation to solve for growth, the equation can be used to solve for the plowback (also known as the retention rate). In other words, we can solve for the percentage of earnings that need to be retained in order to support the level of growth that the analyst is forecasting. All remaining cash is free cash flow that belongs to the equityholder and should be valued. This use of the sustainable growth rate equation is an incredibly powerful tool.

For example, in Exhibit 8.7, the firm is expected to grow 6 percent. Since we assume that the firm is not becoming any more or less efficient, this means that the company's assets will need to increase by 6 percent. It also means that we want the firm's debt and equity to increase 6 percent (because we're assuming that the capital structure will remain constant). Since the firm is generating 10 percent more equity (the ROE) but only needs 6 percent more equity, this means the firm only needs to retain 60 percent of this additional equity (the earnings). If the firm retains 60 percent of its earnings, this means that the firm can pay out 40 percent of its earnings.

It is crucial that you understand Exhibit 8.7. Since free cash flow is the key to valuation, the sustainable growth rate equation and intuition are incredibly important. This intuition has solved the main problem associated with the dividend discount model—where you did not know anything other than the actual dividend.

Now that we understand how to calculate the free cash flow to equity, we can apply these ideas. In order to use the FCFE model, an analyst needs to make the following forecasts:

1. Sales growth
2. Profit margin

Exhibit 8.7 Sustainable Growth Rate Formula, Calculating FCFE

Consider a firm with $300 of assets that is financed 2/3 with equity and 1/3 with debt and has a 10% ROE. You are forecasting that the firm will grow 6%. Using the SGR formula, what percentage of earnings must be plowed back? How much FCFE exists?

Assets	$300	Debt	$100
		Equity	$200

This is our starting point: $300 of assets, financed with 1/3 debt and 2/3 equity.

$$ROE = \text{Net Income}_1 / \text{Equity}_0$$

$$10\% = NI_1 / \$200$$

NI_1 must equal $20

Assets	$318	Debt	$106
		Equity	$212

If the firm is growing 6% and efficiency is constant, assets should also grow 6%. Assuming that capital structure will stay the same, debt and equity must also increase 6%. This means that $12 of earnings must be retained and **$8 will be FCFE**.

$$6\% = 10\% \times RR$$

Plowback must equal 60%

3. Return on equity
4. Cost of equity

Think about this: If you have four estimates, you can value a stock. But realize that in the real world, a lot goes into these four estimates! Right now, we just want to understand valuation.

As an example, we will value CSCO at the end of 2016. We will proceed by identifying the four forecasts we need to make.

1. **Sales growth.** At the end of 2016, CSCO had sales per share of $9.78. Sales are expected to grow by approximately 4 percent per year for the next five years. After that, we are forecasting slightly lower growth (3.75 percent) into perpetuity. This growth rate is more consistent with our current forecast of the long-term nominal growth rate of the economy.
2. **Profit margin.** The company's profit margin is approximately 24 percent. Profit margin represents the net income divided by the sales. In other words, for every dollar of sales, CSCO generates 24 cents of net income.
3. **Return on equity.** You expect that CSCO will have a return on equity of 20 percent.
4. **Cost of equity.** You have estimated CSCO's cost of equity as 9.5 percent.

In Exhibit 8.8, you can see the valuation. Let's walk through the steps in calculating this value.

Exhibit 8.8 Cisco Valuation, End of 2016

Year	2017	2018	2019	2020	2021	2022
Sales	$ 10.17	$ 10.58	$ 11.00	$ 11.44	$ 11.90	$ 12.35
EPS	$ 2.44	$ 2.54	$ 2.64	$ 2.75	$ 2.86	$ 2.96
FCFE	$ 1.95	$ 2.03	$ 2.11	$ 2.20	$ 2.28	$ 2.41
Terminal Value					$ 41.87	
PV of Cash Flow	$ 1.78	$ 1.69	$ 1.61	$ 1.53	$ 28.05	
Value of Stock	$ 34.66					

We'll start with the sales line. You were told that sales for the year that just ended were $9.78. We're estimating that sales will grow 4 percent per year. As a result, next year's sales should be $10.17. (This is $9.78 × 1.04; in other words, we grew this past year's sales at the 4 percent growth rate.) This growth rate continues throughout the first five years. After Year 5, growth slows slightly to 3.75 percent. We used that slower growth rate to calculate sales in 2022. The 2022 sales number is going to help us to calculate our terminal value (as of the end of 2021).

After calculating sales, we forecast earnings. We do this by multiplying the profit margin by our sales number. Next year's earnings should be $2.44. (This is $10.17 × 24%; in other words, for every dollar of sales, the company has 24 cents of earnings.)

The next step is probably the most important: We need to calculate how much of those earnings actually reflect free cash flow to equityholders. The FCFE is what we are valuing. We are going to do this for the next five years and then we will do this again for Year 6 (2022) for the terminal value. We need to do a second calculation for the terminal value because estimates have changed.

In order to calculate the FCFE, we are going to use the sustainable growth rate equation (as described above). Remember that this equation states that growth equals the return on equity multiplied by the retention rate. We have estimated growth (for the next five years) to be 4 percent. We have also estimated that Cisco will have an ROE of 20 percent. From here, we can calculate how much of earnings must be plowed back and how much can be paid out as free cash flow.

An ROE of 20 percent means that Cisco is generating 20 percent more equity each year. But, if the company is only growing at 4 percent per year, and assuming that the company wants to maintain its capital structure (that is, keep their debt-to-equity ratio constant), it will only need 4 percent more equity (and 4 percent more debt). So, using the sustainable growth rate equation, we can solve for the retention rate. This means 4% = 20% × RR. The retention rate must equal 20 percent. This means that we have to plow back 20 percent of earnings, and we can pay out 80 percent of earnings. So, in Year 1, the free cash flow to the equityholder is 80 percent of the $2.44 of earnings. This comes out to $1.95. We'll also apply that 80 percent payout to Years 2 through 5 (2018–2021).

Now that we have the FCFE for the first five years, we need to calculate the terminal value. Think of this as the intrinsic value of the stock at the end of Year 5. We will calculate this value using the continuous growth model. We'll need the free cash flow in the terminal year (2022) in order to calculate the terminal value.

In order to calculate the free cash flow in 2022, we grow the prior year's sales by 3.75 percent (the sustainable growth rate). Then we apply the 24 percent profit margin to these sales to reach earnings per share of $2.96. Since the growth rate has changed (from 4 percent to 3.75 percent), we must recalculate the payout by using the SGR equation, 3.75% = 20% × RR. The retention rate now equals 19 percent, and that means we can pay out 81 percent of earnings. Notice that the change in growth rate was slight, and the result was that the payout ratio also changed by only a slight amount (80 percent to 81 percent). This allows us to calculate the FCFE for the terminal year as $2.41.

In order to calculate the terminal value, we use $FCFE_6/(k - g)$, or $2.41/(9.5% − 3.75%)$. The result is $41.87. Again, this is the *terminal value*. Think of this as our estimate for what the stock will be worth in five years.

Now that we have all of our cash flows and the terminal value, all we need to do is discount them and sum them. We discount them by using the cost of equity. Again, since we have cash flows that belong to the equityholders, we discount them at the cost of equity (in order to arrive at the value of the equity). We discount $1.95 at 9.5 percent for one year, $2.03 at 9.5 percent for two years, and so on. Be careful with Year 5: We are discounting both the $2.28 cash flow and the $41.87 terminal value. We discount their combined value ($44.15) for five years. When we add all of these values together, the intrinsic value of the stock is $34.66.

At the end of 2016, CSCO was trading at $30.22. So, this valuation shows CSCO to be slightly undervalued by the market.

You should also notice that this model would be considered to be a *two-stage model*. We estimated that growth would be 4 percent in the next five years and 3.75 percent thereafter. This change is slight. We did not change the profit margins or the ROE from the first period to the sustainable (perpetuity) period. So, while this is technically a two-stage model, the two stages are not that different.

Returning to DDM and PVGO

Let's return to some concepts that we studied earlier in the chapter: the continuous growth model and the PVGO. Returning to our constant growth equation from the dividend discount model, we know that the value of the stock is next year's cash flow divided by the difference between the cost of equity minus the growth rate. This gives us a value of $1.95/(9.5\% - 4\%) = \$35.51$. Again, this is very similar to the FCFE model. The only difference is that the FCFE model assumes that growth will slow to 3.75 percent. In the continuous growth model that we just calculated, we assumed 4 percent growth in perpetuity.

Let's also apply the concept of PVGO. Our FCFE model calculated a value of $34.66. What would CSCO be worth if the company never grew again? We would assume that CSCO would be able to pay out all of its earnings if it never grew again after Year 1. This means the value would be $2.44/.095 = \$25.68$. Since we believe the company is worth $34.66 but it would be worth only $25.68 if it never grew again, the PVGO is $8.98. This is almost 25 percent of the intrinsic value comes from our estimate of future growth. One other interesting thing to think about is that in June 2016 (right after the Brexit vote), CSCO's stock was trading for less than $28. An investor would have been able to buy the stock at a significant discount to intrinsic value—hardly paying for the expected growth.

It is crucial that an investor have basic intuition about valuation. By quickly valuing a company like this, an investor may save himself the problem that many new investors encounter. They work for weeks in researching a company, and when they finally build a model, they conclude that the stock is grossly overvalued. By doing a quick valuation, you may quickly conclude that a stock is not worth looking at.

Framing Your Research

Another way of using this valuation is that it helps you to frame your research. Ultimately, you are researching in order to simply understand:

1. Do you expect that CSCO can continue to grow at 4 percent into the future?
2. Do you expect profit margins of 24 percent to be attainable over the long term?
3. Can CSCO continue to earn an ROE of 20 percent?
4. Will a 9.5 percent return justify the risk that you are taking by investing in Cisco?

To the extent that you are confident in these forecasts, you will feel more comfortable buying the stock when it is selling for less than intrinsic value. Analysts spend their days trying to make these forecasts and then monitor them, deciding whether or not anything has changed.

What if the Stock Is Trading at Intrinsic Value?

Before we move on, look at one more important piece of intuition. Our FCFE model came out to a value of $34.66. Imagine that the current stock price is also $34.66. Then, let's imagine even further that all of your forecasts about this stock turn out to be exactly correct. In other words, the company will grow 4 percent per year for the next five years, and then growth will slow to 3.75 percent. The profit margin will continue at 24 percent, and the ROE will be 20 percent. If this were the case, what would be your long-term rate of return on this investment?

In our experience, most students guess that you would earn zero over the long term. The reason that most students make this guess is that you paid $34.66 for something that is worth $34.66. You bought something that was priced fairly. But, that's not the answer! You would earn 9.5 percent per year—your cost of equity. In effect, you would be compensated appropriately for the risk you are assuming. Remember that when we came up with a value of $34.66, we did this by discounting future cash flows by 9.5 percent. Another way of thinking about this is to realize that our model shows the stock being worth $34.66 today, and this assumes that you'll receive cash flows for the next five years (the FCFE in the next five years) and that you'll be able to sell the stock for $41.87 (the terminal value) in Year 5. Hopefully, it now looks like a return greater than zero.

Of course, if you pay less than fair value (that is, you buy the stock for less than $34.66), you will earn more than 9.5 percent. And finally, if the stock is worth $34.66 and you pay more than that amount for the stock, you will earn less than 9.5 percent.

FCFE for a Bank   There's one last topic that should be discussed before we move on to the next approach to valuation. We should apply the FCFE model to a bank stock. The reason for specifically looking at a bank stock is that financial stocks look different. Their income statements look different; they don't have revenue followed by cost of goods sold. In addition, their balance sheets have two main assets: loans and securities. Remember that from a bank's perspective, loans are assets; they are investments for the bank.

Many students don't ever try to value a bank because they don't know how to model banks. So, we want to show you two simple adjustments to the FCFE model that you need to make in order to value a bank.

Remember that in order to use the FCFE model, we need to make the following forecasts:

1. Sales growth
2. Profit margin
3. Return on equity
4. Cost of equity

If we're going to do this for banks, we need to change the first two forecasts so that it looks like this:

1. Asset growth
2. Return on asset
3. Return on equity
4. Cost of equity

The intuition is that banks don't have stated revenue. The way that banks attempt to earn profits is that they invest in securities and make loans (which are similar to investments). As a result, we examine the assets that a bank has (its loans and investments) and how profitable those assets will be (return on assets). By multiplying the assets by the ROA, we can estimate the earnings.

You can see an example of a bank valuation in Exhibit 8.9. We made several assumptions for U.S. Bancorp (USB) over the coming years. We assumed that assets per year (for the year that just ended) were $272.19 and would grow 3.64 percent over the next five years. After that, the bank will grow its assets at 3 percent per year for the sustainable future. We assumed an ROE of 13 percent over the next five years, slowing to 12.5 percent. Finally, we assumed a cost of equity of 9 percent. The result of the model was a valuation of $45.47. The stock was trading at about $51.50 at the start of 2017.

Exhibit 8.9 U.S. Bancorp Valuation, End of 2016

Year	2017	2018	2019	2020	2021	2022
Assets	$282.09	$292.36	$302.99	$314.02	$325.44	$335.21
EPS	$ 3.67	$ 3.80	$ 3.94	$ 4.08	$ 4.23	$ 4.19
FCFE	$ 2.64	$ 2.74	$ 2.84	$ 2.94	$ 3.05	$ 3.18
Terminal Value					$ 53.07	
PV of Cash Flow	$ 2.42	$ 2.30	$ 2.19	$ 2.08	$ 36.47	
Value of Stock	$ 45.47					

Again, it's important to remember that the FCFE model that we did for USB is really the same thing that we did for CSCO. The only difference is that we estimated asset growth and we turned assets into earnings per share by multiplying assets per share by the ROA.

8.3.3 Method #3: Discounted Cash Flow (FCFF)

Finally, we've arrived at the third way to execute discounted cash flow analysis, the free cash flow to the firm (FCFF) approach. It's important to realize that this method is often referred to by the generic term of discounted cash flow (DCF) or the weighted average cost of capital (WACC) approach. In other words, when an analyst says that she did a DCF analysis, FCFF is likely what she is referring to.

Valuation is important. It's our belief that every student should leave business school understanding how to value a stock. We're not just referring to students who want to be investors. We're also referring to any student who wants to manage any business. The goal of management is to maximize shareholder value. It's hard to understand how someone can maximize shareholder value if they don't understand how to measure it. In studying the FCFF methodology, we are studying the most common method of measuring value.

The FCFF method is different from the FCFE method that we just studied. The FCFE method forecast cash flows that belong to the equityholders. These cash flows were discounted using the cost of equity. The resulting value was the value of the equity.

The FCFF uses different cash flows, a different discount rate, and results in a different value:

1. The *free cash flow* in the FCFF model is the cash flow that is available to distribute to *all providers of capital* (shareholders *and* debtholders) after estimating the cash flow generated from running the business and reinvesting in the business (that is, investing in long-term assets and net working capital). The key difference is that the FCFE uses cash flow after the debtholders were already paid. The FCFF does not subtract payments to debtholders; instead, the cash flow that is left over is what can be distributed to shareholders and debtholders. (In other words, the debtholder has not been paid yet and we are calculating the amount of cash that is available to pay them and the shareholders.) The equation for the FCFF is:

$$\text{EBIT}(1 - \text{Tax Rate}) + \text{Depreciation Expense} - \text{Capital Expenditures}$$
$$- \text{Change in Working Capital} - \text{Change in Other Assets}$$

2. Since the cash flows in the FCFF model belong to all providers of capital, the *discount rate* must incorporate *all the different costs of capital*. In other words, the discount rate must include the cost of equity, the cost of debt, and the cost of preferred stock (if the firm has issued preferred stock). This discount rate is known as the weighted average cost of capital (WACC) and will be discussed later.

3. The resulting value of this calculation is the *value of the firm*. In other words, if you discount the cash flows that are available to all the providers of capital, you are going to calculate a value that belongs to all the providers of capital. We can loosely refer to this value as the calculated *enterprise value*.

Steps in Calculating Free Cash Flow to the Firm In order to understand how to put together a model, we will approach this as a simple series of steps. Then, we will show an FCFF valuation and review the key concepts. In the steps described below, we assume that we're going to forecast and discount five years of cash flows and we also calculate the terminal value at the end of Year 5:

1. **Forecast the sales.** Analysts often forecast somewhere between 3 and 10 years of sales and then use a terminal year forecast. It is most common to forecast 5 years. Reasons used to

defend this are that the analyst is trying to capture an entire business cycle and is trying to avoid making specific forecasts that are too far out in time.

2. **Forecast the operating profits.** By operating profits, we are referring to the earnings before interest and taxes (EBIT). You can think about *operating profits* as how profitable the operations are before considering the capital structure (which impacts interest expense) and taxes (which are also impacted by capital structure because interest is deductible). Realize that when the analyst forecasts operating profits, this is going to force her to think about gross margins as well as selling, general, and administrative expenses (SG&A).

3. **Forecast the taxes as a percentage of the operating profit.** Multiply the *effective tax rate* (the average tax rate that the firm pays) by the EBIT (the operating profit). This may strike you as odd because you know that you normally subtract interest from EBIT and then calculate taxes (and subtracting interest lowers the tax bill). But remember, if you subtracted interest, that would mean that you have already paid the debtholders. Instead, we are trying to calculate how much cash is available for the debtholders (and equity-holders). Subtracting interest is only done if you are trying to calculate the FCFE, not the FCFF.

4. **Calculate the net operating profit after taxes (NOPAT).** This is simply the EBIT minus the taxes that would be paid on that amount of EBIT. Again, you might recognize that the taxes you calculate in this step are higher than they would have been if you had deducted interest before calculating taxes. In other words, we did not capture the fact that the taxable income should have been lowered by deducting interest. (The benefit of the deductibility of interest will be captured later. When we calculate the discount rate [the WACC], we will use the after-tax cost of debt. This lower rate results in a higher value.)

5. **Add back depreciation.** We add back depreciation because we are calculating the free cash flow. Depreciation is not a cash flow. It's an accounting entry to lower the book value of assets. We capture the cash flow when the plant and equipment was purchased, not when it is depreciated. After adding depreciation back to NOPAT, this is often referred to as *operating cash flow.* It represents the cash generated by the day-to-day business.

6. **Subtract the capital expenditures.** This is a difficult number for analysts to estimate. Capital expenditures are often done in a stair-step fashion, but that is not something that an outside investor can easily forecast. The best way to estimate capital expenditures is to examine the relationship between net PP&E (property, plant, and equipment) and revenue. You are effectively trying to calculate how much PP&E is needed in order to generate a dollar of revenue. Of course, after understanding this relationship, the analyst will need to determine whether the company is becoming more or less efficient. You can see an example of this in Exhibit 8.10. In this exhibit, the assumption is that property, plant, and equipment is approximately 13.5 percent as large as revenue. As a result, if an analyst creates a model with revenue growing $100, the PP&E should grow $13.50.

7. **Subtract the investment in additional net working capital (NWC).** NWC represents current assets minus current liabilities. You can think of this as your net investment in short-term assets. The most significant short-term assets are cash, accounts receivable, and inventory. The most significant short-term liability is accounts payable. The simplest approach is very similar to how we projected capital expenditures. Examine the historic relationship between NWC and revenue. Ask if there is anything that you expect to change going forward. There is one extra subtlety when using this methodology: the cash that you use in calculating the NWC is only the cash needed for operations; you should exclude the *excess cash.* Obviously, as an outside analyst, it's very difficult to determine how much cash is needed to run a business and how much is simply extra. (This topic is described below during the discussion of enterprise value.) In Exhibit 8.11, you can see an

Exhibit 8.10 Estimating Capital Expenditures

Imagine that we're building a model and trying to estimate the FCFF for Boeing (BA). Further, imagine that you're forecasting growth of 4% per year in revenue. How much capital expenditures should you forecast?

Below, you will see BA's revenue and net PP&E for the past seven years. You'll also see the Net PP&E/Sales. In effect, this tells us how many cents of PP&E BA has for every dollar of revenue.

	2010	2011	2012	2013	2014	2015	2016
Sales	64306	68375	81698	86623	90762	96114	94571
PP&E	8931	9313	9660	10224	11007	12076	12807
PP&E/Sales	13.9%	13.6%	11.8%	11.8%	12.1%	12.6%	13.5%

After analyzing the company, you will need to make an estimate concerning BA's future efficiency (asset intensity). You may end up assuming that BA needs 13.5 cents of PP&E for every dollar of sales. Or, you may find that they recently did some cap ex and this number is temporarily inflated and 12.5 cents is more of an average. Or, you may find that something will significantly change in the future and have a totally different estimate. Assuming you decide that BA will need to do 12.5 cents of net cap ex (cap ex minus depreciation), here's what those cash flows will look like (based on the change in sales for the year multiplied by 12.5 cents of net PP&E):

	2017	2018	2019	2020	2021
Sales	98354	102288	106380	110635	115060
Net Cap Ex	−473	−492	−511	−532	−553

Exhibit 8.11 Estimating Net Working Capital (Boeing)

Similar to estimating Capital Expenditures, a starting point is to study how NWC has changed with sales. Below, you will see the current assets as a percentage of sales, the current liabilities as a percentage of sales and the NWC. To arrive at NWC as a percentage of sales, we added the current assets and then subtracted the current liabilities.

	2010	2011	2012	2013	2014	2015	2016
Cash/Sales	8.3%	14.7%	12.7%	10.5%	12.9%	11.8%	9.3%
Receivables/Sales	8.4%	8.5%	6.9%	7.6%	8.5%	8.3%	8.3%
Inventories/Sales	37.8%	47.2%	46.2%	49.5%	51.5%	49.2%	45.7%
A/P/Safes	12.0%	12.3%	11.5%	11.0%	11.8%	11.2%	11.8%
Total NWC	42.6%	58.0%	54.2%	56.6%	61.2%	58.0%	51.4%

From here, we'll likely read the 10-k and talk with management. Receivables and A/P seem relatively stable. Cash appears high and probably represents a lot of excess cash (that is not needed to run the business). The large increase in inventory likely has a story behind it. This is what an analyst would need to understand. If we concluded that cash was 5%, receivables 8%, inventories 44%, and A/P 11.5%, the NWC would equal to 45.5% of sales. So, for every dollar that you project sales to increase, you would project NWC to increase by 45.5 cents. This is a very high number because of the nature of Boeing's business.

example of how to estimate NWC as a percentage of sales. Also, realize that it is possible that NWC can be an inflow of cash.

8. **Calculate the free cash flow to the firm.** This is the operating cash flow less the capital expenditures less the additional investment in net working capital. This is what is left over and can be distributed to the providers of capital after running the business, reinvesting in the long-term assets (capital expenditures) and the net short-term assets (net working capital).

> ### Exhibit 8.12 Calculating the Weighted Average Cost of Capital (WACC)
>
> Assume that a company has a market cap of $200 billion and debt of $40 billion. The stock has a beta of 1.05. The risk free rate is 2.50% and the risk premium is 6%. The average cost of debt is 5% and the tax rate is 35%. Calculate the WACC.
>
> Cost of Equity = risk free rate + Beta(risk premium) = 2.50% + 1.05(6%) = **8.80%**
>
> After-Tax Cost of Debt = Yield-to-Maturity(1 − Tax Rate) = 5%(1 − .35) = **3.25%**
>
> WACC = (200/240)(8.80%) + (40/240)(3.25%) = **7.875%**
>
> Two issues to note:
>
> 1. We use market values (not book values). These market values serve as the weight that we assign to each cost of capital.
> 2. We use the after tax cost of debt. Remember, when we calculated the FCFF, we used after-tax cash flows. As a result, the discount rate should be after-taxes. Debt is the only source of capital that has tax consequences. Using the after-tax rate is how we capture the value of the tax shield (the deductibility of interest).

9. **Calculate the weighted average cost of capital (the discount rate).** This is the rate that captures the cost of all of the different sources of capital. You can see an example in Exhibit 8.12. In this exhibit, you will notice that the analyst uses the market weights of the source of capital. In addition, the after-tax cost of debt is used. Since we didn't subtract interest before calculating the tax bill (in step 3), we missed the tax-shield that interest provides. By using the after-tax cost of debt (that is, a lower cost of debt), this is how the analyst captures the value of the tax shield.

10. **Calculate the terminal value at the end of Year 5.** Think of this as what the entire firm will be worth at the end of Year 5. Do this by estimating the FCFF in Year 6 and dividing it by the difference between the WACC minus the growth rate. In other words, Terminal Value = $FCFF_6/(WACC - g)$. This is just an application of the constant growth model that we studied earlier.

11. **Discount all of the free cash flow back to the present.** The appropriate discount rate is the WACC. Remember, in Year 5, you are discounting the sum of the terminal value and the FCFF from Year 5.

12. **Sum the present values.** When you add all of the present values together, you have the preliminary value of the entire firm: the debt plus the equity plus the preferred stock (if there is any preferred stock outstanding). But, you're not quite done. There are some adjustments you need to make in order to reach the enterprise value. Those adjustments are discussed next.

13. **Add the value of any nonoperating assets.** Think of a nonoperating asset as any asset that is not captured by the cash flow analysis that you performed. For example, imagine that the firm has recently acquired some real estate but they have not used it yet. That real estate is not resulting in any cash flows, so the DCF did not capture its value. This means that your model missed this part of the value.

14. **Add the value of any excess cash.** Excess cash is any cash that is not required in order to run the business. For example, a chain of retail stores needs to have cash on hand for their cash registers and to buy inventory. The cash that they need in order to run the business is part of net working capital. But the company may hold more cash than it needs. This is just another form of nonoperating asset. It is always difficult to know how much cash is needed to run the business. One approach is to look at the amount of cash that a firm held as a percentage of revenue for each of the past ten years. Throw out the lowest percentage (as a possible outlier) and use the second lowest number. This could be a good

estimate of the amount of cash that is required to run the business. Of course, if the company has been holding excess cash for a long period of time, this might not be a good answer. You might also look at comparable companies and calculate how much cash they need as a percentage (of sales) by using this same methodology with them. Then, apply this percentage to the company that you are valuing. After adding the nonoperating assets and the excess cash, you have your estimate of the enterprise value.

15. **Subtract the value of debt.** Most practitioners simply subtract the value of the debt on the balance sheet. Later in this chapter, we'll discuss an alternative approach.

16. **Subtract any other debt that was not captured by the DCF analysis.** A classic example of this would be an unfunded or underfunded pension liability. An underfunded pension liability occurs when the amount of assets in a company's pension fund is less than the present value that is required to pay off the firm's pension obligations. From a theoretical perspective, think of this as a debt because the firm could issue debt to become fully funded.

17. **Calculate the value of the equity on a per share basis.** After starting with the present value from the DCF, adding any nonoperating assets and excess cash, and subtracting debt, you will be left with the value of the equity. Divide this by the diluted shares outstanding and you will have the value of a share of stock.

For an example of moving from the present value of the cash flows in your DCF to equity value, see Exhibit 8.13. In this exhibit, you can capture the two biggest pieces of intuition. First, we are trying to capture the value of any assets that are not reflected in the discounted cash flow model, such as any asset that is not used in operations yet or any excess cash (since we don't include interest income in the calculation of free cash flow). Second, the analyst must capture any debt that is not as explicit as bonds or loans.

Putting Together the FCFF Model   Now that we've discussed the steps in calculating the FCFF model, we can put together a model. Earlier in this chapter, we made some simple assumptions about Cisco. Next, we will display a few more assumptions (consistent with the original example) so that we have enough information to calculate a FCFF model. We will do this a bit differently in that we will use firm numbers as opposed to "per share" numbers that we used in the FCFE model.

Exhibit 8.13 Adjusting the Present Value of the Cash Flows

Imagine that you perform a FCFF analysis. After discounting the cash flows, they add up to $100 billion. You want to value the equity. You know that the firm has $3 billion of excess cash (more cash than is needed to run the business), a $1 billion nonoperating asset (a group of buildings and real estate that are not yet being used), and a pension plan that is underfunded by $2.5 billion (i.e., the fund has $3.5 billion of assets and the present value of the obligation is $6 billion). The firm also has $20 billion of debt. The firm has 2 billion shares outstanding. What is the value per share?

Present Value of Cash Flows	$ 100
Add:	
Excess Cash	$ 3
Nonoperating Assets	$ 1
Less:	
Unfunded Pension	−$ 2.5
Debt	−$ 20
Equity Value	$ 81.5
Shares Outstanding	2
Equity Value Per Share	$ 40.75

Here are the assumptions that we will use:

Sales for the year that just ended: $48.9 billion
Sales growth for next five years: 4 percent
Sales growth after Year 5: 3.75 percent
Operating margins = 33 percent
Tax rate = 22 percent
Net margins = 24 percent
Debt = $25 billion
Pre-tax cost of debt = 4.54 percent
Number of shares outstanding = 5 billion
Book value of equity: $61.05 billion
Book value of assets: $86.05
ROA (calculated as $NOPAT_1/Equity_0$): 15.21 percent
Percentage of NOPAT that must be reinvested (calculated as growth rate/ROA):
Reinvestment rate Years 1–5: 26.29 percent
Reinvestment rate after Year 5: 24.65 percent
Market value of equity: $150 billion
Market value of debt: $25 billion
Cost of Equity = 9.5 percent
$WACC = (6/7)(9.5\%) + (1/7)(4.54\%)(1 - .22) = 8.65\%$

Given these assumptions, we can use the FCFF model to value CSCO, as shown in Exhibit 8.14. It's important to notice how Exhibit 8.14 is different from a FCFE model. The FCFE model would have subtracted interest so that the debtholders were paid and any remaining cash flow was for shareholders. It would have also considered any capital that was provided by borrowing in order to finance the assets (or any capital that was returned to debtholders). The result of the FCFF calculation in the exhibit is the value of the entire firm. In order to reach the equity value, the debt must be subtracted.

Why Didn't the FCFF Model Value Equal the FCFE Model Value? If you ask most "finance people" whether the equity value derived from the FCFF model will be the same as the FCFE valuation, you'll usually hear one of two answers:

Exhibit 8.14 Free Cash Flow to the Firm (CSCO)

	2017	2018	2019	2020	2021	2022
Sales	$ 50.86	$ 52.89	$55.01	$ 57.21	$ 59.49	$ 61.73
EBIT	$ 16.78	$ 17.45	$18.15	$ 18.88	$ 19.63	$ 20.37
Taxes	–$ 3.69	–$ 3.84	–$ 3.99	–$ 4.15	–$ 4.32	–$ 4.48
NOPAT	$ 13.09	$ 13.61	$14.16	$ 14.72	$ 15.31	$ 15.89
Reinvestment	–$ 3.44	–$ 3.58	–$ 3.72	–$ 3.87	–$ 4.03	–$ 3.92
FCFF	$ 9.65	$ 10.03	$10.44	$ 10.85	$ 11.29	$ 11.97
Terminal Value					$244.38	
PV	$ 8.88	$ 8.50	$ 8.14	$ 7.79	$168.87	
EV	$202.17					
Less: Debt	–$ 25.00					
Equity Value	$177.17					
Shares Outstanding	2 billion					
Intrinsic Value	**$ 35.43**					

1. The values will be similar but will just be different by a few dollars per share.
2. If you make the same assumptions, the values should be the same.

There is some truth to both of these answers. You have already seen the reality of the first answer: The values are slightly different. The FCFE came out to $34.66. The FCFF resulted in a value of $35.43. The difference is small. Yet, even though the difference is small, it still is bothersome that they are not the same.

So, now we will discuss the assumption that you need to make in order for the FCFF to have the same value as the FCFE. This "second approach" to the FCFF model is important to understand because reaching the identical answer (as the FCFE) should convince you that this second approach is the "correct" approach, even though it is not used in practice. But, in order to accept this explanation, you will need to accept that valuation is based on a set of assumptions.

Here is the idea: When you build a DCF model, you are effectively saying, "If all my assumptions are true, this is the value of this stock." One of the assumptions is the basis of the weighted average cost of capital. In our example, we assumed that six-sevenths of our capital came from equity and one-seventh came from debt. These were the weights used when we calculated the WACC. In this case, the DCF was based on the assumption that "if six-sevenths of these cash flows belong to the equityholders and one-seventh belong to the debtholders, this is the value of the firm."

The result of these assumptions means that when we calculated the enterprise value (the discounted cash flows), we then have to assign values based on the weights used in the WACC. In other words, if our WACC was based on the weights described above, we should take the enterprise value and say that six-sevenths belong to the equityholders and one-seventh belong to the debtholders. You can see this in Exhibit 8.15. The only difference in this model (compared to Exhibit 8.14) is that instead of using the actual amount of debt, we used the amount of debt that was consistent with the WACC. Since we said that one-seventh of our capital was provided by debt, we multiplied one-seventh by the enterprise value to obtain the value of the debt.

The approach that we're describing is generally not used in practice. Practitioners simply deduct the existing debt and claim that the remainder is the equity value. That is what we did above in Exhibit 8.14. Most would argue against the method that we're describing in Exhibit 8.15, asking why you would deduct a theoretical amount of debt when you know the actual amount of debt. The answer is that you have to accept that a DCF model is a theoretical exercise. It is not a scale that weighs an object and gives us a definitive answer. This second approach, although generally not used in practice, is the correct methodology.

Exhibit 8.15 Free Cash Flow to the Firm, Improved Methodology

	2017	2018	2019	2020	2021	2022
Sales	$ 50.86	$ 52.89	$55.01	$ 57.21	$ 59.49	$ 61.73
EBIT	$ 16.78	$ 17.45	$18.15	$ 18.88	$ 19.63	$ 20.37
Taxes	−$ 3.69	−$ 3.84	−$ 3.99	−$ 4.15	−$ 4.32	−$ 4.48
NOPAT	$ 13.09	$ 13.61	$14.16	$ 14.72	$ 15.31	$ 15.89
Reinvestment	−$ 3.44	−$ 3.58	−$ 3.72	−$ 3.87	−$ 4.03	−$ 3.92
FCFF	$ 9.65	$ 10.03	$10.44	$ 10.85	$ 11.29	$ 11.97
Terminal Value					$244.38	
PV	$ 8.88	$ 8.50	$ 8.14	$ 7.79	$168.87	
EV	$202.17					
Less: Debt	**−$ 28.88**					
Equity Value	$173.29					
Shares Outstanding	2 billion					
Intrinsic Value	**$ 34.66**					

Let's use one final example to drive this point home. Imagine that we are valuing a firm that currently has equity with a market value of $2 billion and debt that has a value of $1 billion. As a result, when we calculate the WACC, we will use the two-thirds equity and one-third debt as the weights. Next, imagine that when you calculate the enterprise value, the result is $5 billion. Most practitioners would deduct $1 billion and tell you that the equity is worth $4 billion. We are telling you that two-thirds of the $5 billion is the value of the equity and one-third is the value of the debt. Remember that by assigning a weight of one-third to the debt, you were creating a lower WACC. Since debt is cheaper than equity, this low WACC results in a higher enterprise value. It isn't fair to have this low discount rate that creates this (theoretical) high value and for you to simply subtract the low amount of debt.

8.4 RELATIVE VALUATION

While discounted cash flow analysis attempts to calculate the intrinsic value of a company, relative valuation attempts to value a company by comparing it to similar companies or the overall market or the stock's own trading history. DCF is often described as the best way to determine absolute value while relative valuation describes what others seem willing to pay.

When analysts use multiples, they are typically used in one of the following ways:

1. Comparing multiples to *comparable companies* (that is, is the stock expensive or cheap relative to peer companies).
2. Comparing a stock multiple to the *market multiple* (that is, is the stock expensive or cheap relative to the market). This is particularly valuable in normalizing multiples. In other words, if interest rates are low, stock multiples tend to be higher. This approach effectively strips out the fact that market multiples are high or low and simply looks at whether this stock is trading at a high or low multiple relative to the market.
3. Comparing a stock's multiple to its *historic multiple* (that is, is the stock expensive relative to how it has traded historically). Be careful if using this approach. As companies mature, their growth rate slows and multiples contract.
4. Comparing a stock's multiple to *recent transactions* (that is, what would the stock be worth if it were acquired).

As we proceed in this chapter, we will discuss relative valuation as if we are comparing a company with comparable firms. But the analysis would be similar if we were comparing a company's multiple to how it traded in the past or how it historically traded relative to the overall market, or what it was worth based on recent transactions.

There are three steps involved in performing relative valuation analysis:

1. Find comparable companies.
2. Determine the appropriate multiple to use.
3. Apply the multiple.

Below, we will examine each of these steps. Then, we will address the advantages and disadvantages of multiples. But before we discuss the steps in valuation, two other distinctions are significant: equity multiples versus enterprise value multiples and trailing multiples versus forward multiples.

Enterprise multiples are an attempt to value the entire firm. They are often based on a metric such as EBITDA (earnings before interest, taxes, depreciation, and amortization). The goal is to avoid the influence of capital structure that occurs when we use equity multiples. **Equity multiples** are simply trying to value the equity portion of the firm.

Trailing multiples use an underlying fundamental metric from the year that just ended. For example, imagine we are looking at a company's price–earnings multiple. The stock is trading for $25 per share. The earnings for the year that just ended were $2 per share. Earnings are expected to be $2.50 next year. A trailing P/E multiple would be 12.5 times earnings. This is $25 divided by $2. A **forward multiple** would use the expected earnings for the next year. This would result in a P/E of 10 ($25 divided by $2.50).

Proponents of trailing multiples argue that we know the amount of earnings for the past year. Forward earnings are uncertain. Advocates for forward multiples will tell you that stocks are priced based on future expectations, not what has happened in the past. Cynical professors (who write textbooks) will also point out that forward multiples usually make stocks sound cheaper (assuming next year's earnings are expected to increase) and the sell side would prefer to call clients and market cheap stocks.

8.4.1 Implementing Relative Valuation

There are three steps to follow when implementing relative valuation analysis.

Step 1: Find Comparable Companies Finding comparable companies is extremely difficult. Obviously, analysts typically search for companies in the same (or a very similar) industry. That's the easy part. But, that would be like buying a house and thinking that all houses in the same neighborhood should sell for $300 per square foot. Some houses are smaller (smaller houses typically sell for a greater per-square foot value in the same neighborhood), have more land, are better maintained, have nicer appliances, and so on. So, the buyer has to know how the houses or businesses differ. The buyer or analyst really wants to find the few houses (or businesses) that are truly comparable to the one that he is considering.

When trying to find comparable businesses within an industry, the analyst can think about factors that make the business similar or different. The most common approach is to ask how they are different from a **business risk** perspective and **financial risk** perspective.

Business risk analysis searches for differences between companies regarding growth rates, expected term of high growth, products, market share, cyclicality, distributions, cost structures, and management experience. Financial risk often assesses differences in leverage, size, potential liabilities, interest coverage, and beta.

While it is always easiest to start the search for comparable companies by simply finding a list of companies in the same industry and searching for similar market capitalizations, there's another source that may help your search. Each year, public companies issue a proxy statement before their annual shareholder meeting. In the proxy statement, the company will describe how they set compensation. In that discussion, they will disclose companies that they view as peer companies. While many of these companies will be very different, you may glean some insight from these disclosures.

Step 2: Determine the Appropriate Multiple Once you determine comparable companies to consider, you must determine which multiple to use. There are two common ways to do this. The first approach is simply to understand what multiples other analysts use. While this may seem like "cheating," it's always important to know how other analysts think about a stock. The second approach is to try to determine what underlying metric seems to move a stock. In other words, you might try to regress a stock's performance against sales, or earnings, or book value. If stock prices seem highly correlated with earnings, use a price–earnings multiple. If a stock's price seems to be more correlated with sales or book value, use the price–sales multiple or the price–book value multiple.

Step 3: Apply the Multiple As expressed above, it is incorrect to simply compare multiples and decide that one stock should be purchased because it is trading at a lower multiple. An analyst must understand the fundamentals that drive multiples.

Below, we will review one way to think about multiples. This is often referred to as **fundamental multiples**. It is a way of assessing what multiple a stock should be assigned. In other words, should a stock trade at eight times earnings or 12 times earnings? What factors impact this multiple?

We will analyze fundamental multiples using price–earnings, price–sales, and price–book value.

Price–Earnings The P/E ratio is the most frequently cited multiple. Imagine that you have two companies, both with $2 of earnings per share. Yet, one of the stocks trades for $20 and the other trades for $30. It may seem like $2 is worth $2. So, why would the market value the earnings differently? In other words, why does one stock trade at 10 times earnings while the other trades at 15 times earnings?

The best way to think about this is to approach this from the constant growth dividend discount model. We simply rearrange this so that P/E is on one side. You can see this below:

$$P_0 = \frac{D_1}{k - g}$$

$$P_0 = \frac{E_0 \times (1 + \text{growth rate}) \times \text{Payout Ratio}}{k - g}$$

8.9 Trailing P/E Multiple:

$$\frac{P}{E_0} = \frac{(1 + \text{growth rate}) \times \text{Payout Ratio}}{k - g}$$

8.10 Forward P/E Multiple:

$$\frac{P}{E_1} = \frac{\text{Payout Ratio}}{k - g}$$

The conclusion is that investors should pay more for a dollar of earnings if:

1. **Those earnings will grow at a higher rate.** Investors would be willing to pay more for $2 of earnings if these earnings will grow quickly and the company will generate $4 of earnings in a few years, as opposed to $2 of earnings that will turn into $2.25 of earnings in a few years.

2. **The company is more efficient.** In other words, if the company has a higher return on equity (that is, the company generates a lot more equity each year), it can pay out a higher percentage of its earnings in the form of dividends. Or, said differently, the company will have more free cash flow that is available for the equityholders.

3. **The cash flows are lower risk.** Investors should be willing to pay more for a dollar of earnings if those earnings are more certain.

This is all just another way of saying that the price–earnings multiple should be higher if growth (g) is higher, the payout ratio is higher, or the cost of equity (r) is lower.

Price–Sales The price–sales multiple is also frequently used, most commonly when a company doesn't have earnings. If a company doesn't have earnings, it's impossible to use the price–earnings multiple. The thought process behind using the price–sales multiple is that the company will eventually become profitable or will be acquired by a company that can earn profits from those sales.

Before we examine the metrics behind the price–sales multiple, we want to point out one comment that is often made about a price–sales multiple. Some people will argue that equity multiples (where we're trying to value the stock as opposed to the enterprise value) should be based on an underlying fundamental that belongs to equityholders (such as earnings or book value). In other words, earnings belong to the shareholders because the debtholders have already been paid. Book value is the equityholders' stake on the balance sheet.

It is true that an enterprise value requires an underlying metric that belongs to both the shareholders AND the debtholders. In other words, analysts use EBIT or EBITDA or could use sales. All of those metrics are calculated before debtholders are paid, so the debtholders (and shareholders) have a claim on those metrics. But, it is not true that equity multiples can only be based on a metric that solely belongs to equityholders. In other words, while analysts may use EV/sales (because sales belong to both shareholders and debtholders), it is also possible to use price–sales (P/S). The profit margin (which we will see has an impact on the multiple) will capture the fact that one firm has debt and another doesn't. The cost of equity will also be impacted by the debt.

Again, we can examine the price–sales multiple by using the constant growth dividend discount model. We want to manipulate this equation in order to have price–sales on one side. In order to do this, we needed to start with sales in the numerator (rather than dividends), multiply this by profit margin (in order to have the earnings), and multiply these earnings by payout ratio (to reach the dividend):

$$P_0 = \frac{D_1}{k - g}$$

$$P_0 = \frac{S_0 \times (1 + \text{growth rate}) \times \text{Profit Margin} \times \text{Payout Ratio}}{k - g}$$

8.11 Trailing P/S Multiple:

$$\frac{P}{S_0} = \frac{(1 + \text{growth rate}) \times \text{Profit Margin} \times \text{Payout Ratio}}{k - g}$$

8.12 Forward P/S Multiple:

$$\frac{P}{S_1} = \frac{\text{Profit Margin} \times \text{Payout Ratio}}{k - g}$$

Based on this analysis, we can conclude that investors should be willing to pay more for a dollar of sales if a company:

1. **Has a higher profit margin.** Investors will pay more for a dollar of sales if those sales will turn into a greater amount of earnings.
2. **Is more efficient.** A company with a higher ROE can afford to pay out more in the form of dividends for every dollar of earnings. In other words, for a given level of earnings, this company has a larger amount of free cash flow available for the equityholders.
3. **Has less risky cash flows.** In other words, the company has a lower cost of equity.
4. **Has higher growth.** Investors will pay more for a dollar of sales that will grow at a higher rate.

Price–Book   The price–book multiple is often used to assess financial stocks. The reason for this is that the book value has greater significance for a financial stock than for other types of companies. If you examine a bank's balance sheet (for example), the assets and liabilities are closer to market value than the assets and liabilities of many other industries. In addition, the most important assets for a bank are on the balance sheet: loans and securities. Compare that to industrial companies that may have depreciated assets or technology companies that usually do not have their most important assets (people, patents, etc.) listed on their balance sheet.

Again, we can use the constant growth dividend discount model to understand the important fundamentals that drive the price–book value multiple. This can be seen below. You can see that the goal was to reach price–book on one side of the equation. This requires us to start with book value in the numerator (rather than dividend). So, with book value multiplied by return on equity multiplied by payout ratio, we started with the equivalent of the dividend:

$$P_0 = \frac{D_1}{k - g}$$

$$P_0 = \frac{BV_0 \times \text{ROE} \times \text{Payout Ratio}}{k - g}$$

8.13 Trailing P/B Multiple:

$$\frac{P}{BV_0} = \frac{\text{ROE} \times \text{Payout Ratio}}{k - g}$$

Note that analysts normally only talk about the trailing price–book multiple. They don't normally talk about a forward price–book multiple, even though they may use a forward price–earnings or price–sales multiple. The reason for this is that analysts will always forecast next year's sales and next year's earnings. But, analysts rarely forecast next year's book value.

The conclusion is that investors will pay more for a dollar of book value if a company:

1. *Generates a higher return on equity*—in other words, if every dollar of capital results in more earnings, the book value is worth more
2. *Is less risky*—meaning that the cost of equity is lower
3. *Is expected to grow* its book value at a faster rate

How to Remember Fundamental Multiples   We have broken down the price–earnings, price–sales, and price–book multiples to understand how underlying fundamentals should drive these multiples. If you find yourself memorizing the math that was used to prove this, you are doing yourself a disservice. You should understand the intuition.

To do this simple math, you always start with the constant growth dividend discount model. Then, in the numerator, you need to replace next year's dividend. In replacing next year's dividend, you start with whatever metric you are trying to use. In other words, if you're doing this for the price–earnings multiple, you ask how to start with earnings and eventually reach dividends. If you are trying to do this for the price–sales multiple, you replace next year's dividend and start with sales. Finally, with price–book multiple, you replace next year's dividend with book value. Ask how you move from that underlying metric (earnings, sales, or book value) to dividend and you should be able to reason out the math.

These fundamental multiples are intended to make an important point: a multiple is not some mystical number. Multiples are based upon the underlying fundamentals. Most importantly, when an analyst makes an argument based on relative valuation, it is crucial that the underlying fundamental is also used in the argument. In other words, showing that a company has a lower price–earnings multiple than peer companies is not all that interesting. But, it becomes interesting if you show that a company is selling at a lower price–earnings multiple and will grow as fast as or faster than peer companies.

8.4.2 Relative Valuation with CSCO

We are going to make a series of assumptions in order to perform a relative valuation analysis for Cisco (CSCO). For purposes of this simplified exercise, we will use Juniper Networks as Cisco's primary competitor. In reality, Juniper is Cisco's main competitor in Internet routing. Cisco has other competitors, such as Hewlett Packard and Aruba and several others in various markets. But we will simply use Juniper in our example. We will perform this analysis in order to answer the question concerning which of these two stocks is more attractive.

	Cisco	Juniper
Market capitalization	$171 billion	$10.7 billion
Debt	$35 billion	$2.13 billion
Expected growth	4.6%	4.6%
Expected ROE	21%	19%
Expected profit margin	25%	13%
Potential payout ratio	78%	76%
Cost of equity (CAPM)	8.9%	9.5%

It's important to analyze the nature of the businesses and whether the companies are truly similar. The easiest thing to notice is that Cisco is substantially larger than Juniper, with a market cap of $170 billion versus $10 billion. The size difference likely makes Cisco less volatile (resulting in a lower cost of equity and a higher multiple). Intuitively, we might expect the smaller company (Juniper) to have higher growth expectations, but both companies are expected to grow at similar rates.

It's interesting to notice that the companies look similar from several perspectives. Their debt-to-equity ratio looks relatively similar on a book-value basis as well as a market-value basis. They have relatively similar returns on equity, despite the fact that they have very different profit margins. As already mentioned, the capital structures are similar. It turns out that Juniper has a higher asset turnover (Sales/Assets) than Cisco, and this brings their returns on equity closer together.

From a fundamental perspective, Cisco should trade at approximately 18.1 times forward earnings. This can be calculated using Equation 8.10. Cisco's forward price–earnings ratio could be calculated as . $78/(.089 - .046) = 18.14$. Similarly, Juniper should trade at 15.5 times forward earnings. This is calculated as . $76/(.095 - .046) = 15.51$. Cisco is currently trading at 14.25 times forward earnings while Juniper is trading at 16 times forward earnings. From this perspective, Cisco appears cheap relative to its fundamental value, while Juniper is trading just above its fundamental multiple.

Looking at the fundamental trailing price–book multiple, Cisco should trade at approximately 3.8 times book value. This can be calculated using Equation 8.13. Cisco's trailing price–book could be calculated as $(.21 \times .78)/(.089 - .046) = 3.81$. Juniper should trade at approximately 2.95 times trailing earnings. This can be calculated as $(.19 \times .76)/(.095 - .046) = 2.95$. Cisco is currently trading at 2.71 times book value and appears cheap. Juniper also appears cheap, as it is trading at 2.16 times book value.

Finally, Cisco should trade at approximately 4.5 times next year's sales. This can be calculated using Equation 8.12 as $(.25 \times .78)/(.089 - .046) = 4.53$. Juniper's forward price–sales should be $(.13 \times .76)/(.095 - .046) = 2.02$. This multiple makes Cisco appear cheap, as the company is selling at 3.54 times next year's sales. Juniper is trading at fair value using this multiple, as their forward price–sales multiple is 2.01.

	Fundamental	Actual	Conclusion
Cisco			
Forward P/E	18.1	14.25	Cheap
Trailing P/B	3.8	2.71	Cheap
Forward P/S	4.5	3.54	Cheap
Juniper			
Forward P/E	15.5	16	Fairly priced
Trailing P/B	2.95	2.16	Cheap
Forward P/S	2.02	2.01	Fairly priced

The overall conclusion of this analysis is that Cisco appears to be cheaper than Juniper on a relative basis. Of course, the analyst would need to study their assumptions and both companies' accounting in order to gain confidence in their analysis. The analyst could also try to perform relative valuation where he would compare Cisco to the overall market.

8.4.3 Advantages of Multiples

Proponents of multiples will make many arguments in favor of this type of analysis. First of all, multiples can be easy to use. You don't have to build a model or make a series of assumptions. Of course, while multiples (used incorrectly) can be much easier to use, you are implicitly making a series of assumptions. For example, by applying the multiple that the market has assigned to another company, you are assuming that this other company is priced fairly. You are also assuming that they are using similar accounting, that they have similar prospects, and that they have similar risk levels. The real difference between multiples and DCF is that the DCF requires you to make explicit assumptions. Using multiples results in assumptions being implicitly made.

Second, for a money manager with a mandate to be fully invested, absolute value (intrinsic value) may not matter. Relative value is what matters. In other words, it may be that all stocks are overvalued. You may be searching for the stock that is the least overvalued.

Another argument that investors make is that relative value also incorporates sentiment—something that is not valued in a DCF. In addition, it's important to realize that multiples are widely used on both the buy side and the sell side. Finally, multiples are a great way to confirm the value that you have calculated with your discounted cash flow analysis.

8.4.4 Disadvantages of Multiples

Critics of multiples will make counterarguments concerning some of the very same issues that proponents had used in support of multiples. While multiples are simple to use, they are difficult to use correctly. You must find truly comparable companies and that's difficult. You must make adjustments when using multiples. In other words, since comparable companies will never be exactly the same, you must make adjustments for accounting policies, future prospects, and risk. Using multiples to purchase a security because it is "less overvalued" than some other securities is not a valid investment strategy.

Even if you use multiples correctly, when you find that the stock you are analyzing is cheaper than some others, you are making a significant assumption when you conclude that the one stock is incorrectly priced. It is possible that the other stocks may be mispriced.

8.5 Ratio Analysis

Ratio analysis is often presented to students as an "end" rather than a means to an end. In other words, many people see ratio analysis as something you do—similar to building a financial model. But, that's not how you should think about it. You should think about it as a tool.

The best analogy is to think about ratio analysis in the same way that you would think about blood tests at the doctor. Usually, there is a wide range of results that would be absolutely fine. If a number is outside of that range, the first thing you should do is to make sure that the result is correct. Assuming that it's correct, it could signal something that you should further investigate. Or, it could be that you are fine, but you just have some results that are different than most other people.

Even though the blood tests are not the end result, they are still a very valuable tool for your doctor. They help her to understand your overall health and the result may explain issues that you have described. Sometimes, the blood tests show issues that you are not aware of yet. All of these same ideas are true about ratios. They may corroborate stories you have heard from management. Or, they may alert you to issues that management has not told you about.

As you analyze a company, you should think about performing ratio analysis in order to help you to make better estimates for your discounted cash flow model and to better understand the business. Ratio analysis may also help you to ask better questions as you discuss the company with management or others.

As an analyst performs ratio analysis, he hopes to determine whether earnings represent cash flows and whether those cash flows will recur. In fact, when Dechev, Graham, Harvey, and Rajgopal (2016) surveyed 375 CFOs, they found that the CFOs believe that high quality earnings are:

- Sustainable
- Useful in helping analysts to predict future earnings
- Backed by cash flows
- The result of consistent reporting choices through time
- Reflective of minimal use of long-term estimates

Based on these characteristics of high-quality earnings, we will describe the top 10 ratios and pieces of financial data that we would consider in analyzing a company.

8.5.1 Growth Rate of Sales

A company can grow its earnings by growing revenue or cutting expenses. But, at some point, expenses can't be cut any further. Sales growth provides an analyst with information about demand for the company's product and the company's pricing power. It's important to understand whether the sales growth rate is changing, how it compares to peer companies and how it compares to the overall economy's growth rate (GDP). It is also important to understand if sales are growing organically or through acquisition. With respect to organic growth, is this due to greater sales volume, or a price change or a change in product mix? Finally, analysts also search for economic indicators that are correlated with the revenue growth of the company that they are studying and use this relationship to help predict the future.

8.5.2 Gross Margins

The gross margin is defined as:

8.14   Gross Profit/Sales

The analyst uses this ratio to understand whether revenue or cost of goods sold is growing at a faster rate and how gross margins compare to peer companies. Again, it is the analyst's job to understand the basis of any changes. The analyst will study the company's pricing power and the pricing power of suppliers. Also, some costs may be fixed and economies (or diseconomies) of scale may explain changes. Changes in the product mix must also be investigated.

8.5.3 Operating Margins

Operating margins are defined as:

8.15   Operating Profit/Sales

(Note: Operating profit is also described as EBIT, or earnings before interest and taxes.)

Again, the analyst wants to understand any changes in margins and how these margins (and changes) compare to the competition. It is important to understand what is included in the Selling, General & Administrative (SG&A) expense as well as any changes in depreciation methodologies. The analyst may try to understand how much of the SG&A expense is fixed as opposed to variable.

8.5.4 Net Margins

Net margins are defined as:

8.16   Net Income/Sales

In examining net margins, the analyst is capturing changes in gross margins, operating margins, interest expense, and taxes. The analyst will search for changes in the amount of debt, changes in interest rates, and changes in effective tax rates (as well as reasons for these changes).

8.5.5 Accounts Receivable Turnover

Accounts receivable turnover is defined as:

8.17   Sales/Average Accounts Receivable

Analysts review this ratio because it can serve as a warning if a company has changed its credit policies in order to meet sales goals. In other words, if accounts receivable are growing relative to sales, the company may be pushing excess product out to customers with the promise that customers can pay later. Of course, if there's too much product in the pipeline, eventually orders will drop and the company will miss its sales growth target.

8.5.6 Inventory Turnover

Inventory turnover is defined as:

8.18   Cost of Goods Sold/Average Inventory

Analysts review this ratio because it could be a warning sign if inventories are growing too quickly. It may serve as evidence that the company is having difficulty selling its product. This could lead to lower margins in the future or a write-off. Of course, it could also reflect optimism, as a company may build inventories in order to meet higher expected future sales.

8.5.7 Net PP&E Turnover

Net PP&E turnover is defined as:

8.19   Sales/Net PP&E

Analysts examine this ratio to understand how long-term assets are growing with sales. If this ratio is growing, the analyst will try to determine whether the company is becoming more efficient or if the company is not doing necessary capital expenditures. It is also possible that the company may have started to outsource some production. If this ratio is shrinking, the analyst wants to understand whether the company is becoming less efficient. It may also be that the company is capitalizing expenses in order to keep them from the income statement or the company may be depreciating assets too slowly.

8.5.8 Debt as a Percentage of Long-Term Capital

This ratio is defined as:

8.20   Debt/Long-Term Capital

In this ratio, debt should include interest-bearing debt. Long-term capital should include interest-bearing debt and equity (including preferred stock).

Debt can be a low-cost source of capital until the company has too much debt. At that point, the cost of debt can increase or it can become difficult to refinance. A company with too much debt is said to have financial risk. Financial risk increases the sensitivity of a stock's performance to changes in the economy. The analyst will examine changes in the capital structure and how the company's capital structure compares to peer companies.

8.5.9 Changes in Reserve Accounts

Analysts always watch for significant changes in reserve accounts, such as allowances for bad debts (whether the allowance is for accounts receivables or loans that a bank made). Reserves are a great tool to manage earnings. Management may "under-reserve" in order to meet earnings expectations or they may "over-reserve" in order to smooth future earnings (sometimes referred to as "cookie jar accounting"). It is crucial to understand that reserves must match the underlying fundamentals of the business and the business cycle.

8.5.10 Operating Earnings/GAAP Earnings

Analysts know that companies usually want to report the highest earnings possible. Many companies will try to present non-GAAP earnings where they strip out certain expenses. Most frequently, they will strip out the expense of granting options to management. In addition, companies often discuss operating earnings in which they strip out one-time losses (or gains) and other non-recurring expenses. While this makes some intuitive sense, the analyst has to be aware of companies that seem to have recurring "non-recurring" expenses! In other words, it is easy to appear profitable if all expenses are considered non-recurring or if a company writes down its assets so that future expenses are low.

Finally, analysts examine much more in financial statements than just ratios. For example, analysts will try to understand the strategy as it is discussed in the Management's Discussion and Analysis (MD&A). Analysts will also examine the proxy statement in order to understand the compensation structure. They will try to understand how forthcoming management is in the financial reports as well as the earnings conference call. But, ratios certainly do play a part in all of this analysis.

8.6 THE QUALITY OF FINANCIAL STATEMENTS

Analysts sometimes speak of the quality of a firm's earnings or the quality of a firm's balance sheet. In general, quality financial statements are a good reflection of reality; accounting tricks and one-time changes are not used to make the firm appear stronger than it really is. Some factors that lead to lower-quality financial statements were mentioned previously when we discussed ratio analysis. Other quality influences are discussed here and in Palepu, Healy, and Bernard (2012).

8.6.1 Balance Sheet

A high-quality balance sheet typically has limited use of debt or leverage. Therefore, the potential of financial distress resulting from excessive debt is quite low. Little use of debt also implies the firm has unused borrowing capacity, which implies that the firm can draw on that unused capacity to make profitable investments.

A quality balance sheet contains assets with market values greater than their book value. The capability of management and the existence of intangible assets—such as goodwill, trademarks, or patents—will make the market value of the firm's assets exceed their book values. In general, as a result of inflation and historical cost accounting, we might expect the market value of assets to exceed their book values. Overpriced assets on the books occur when a firm has outdated, technologically inferior assets; obsolete inventory; and nonperforming assets such as a bank that has not written off nonperforming loans.

The presence of off-balance-sheet liabilities also harms the quality of a balance sheet, but this is offset by capitalizing operating leases, which are quite prevalent in some industries. Such liabilities may include joint ventures and loan commitments or guarantees to subsidiaries, which are discussed in Stickney, Brown, and Wahlen (2007, Chapter 6) and need to be noted and discussed by the analyst.

8.6.2 Income Statement

High-quality earnings are *repeatable* earnings. For example, they arise from sales to customers who are expected to do repeat business with the firm and reflected in costs that are not artificially low as a result of unusual and short-lived input price reductions. One-time and *nonrecurring* items—such as accounting changes, mergers, and asset sales—are often ignored when examining earnings. But again, this should be done judiciously. Unexpected exchange rate fluctuations that work in the firm's favor to raise revenues or reduce costs should also be viewed as nonrecurring. High-quality earnings result from the use of conservative accounting principles that do not result in overstated revenues and understated costs. The closer the earnings are to cash earnings, the higher the quality of the income statement. An example would be a firm that sells furniture on credit by allowing customers to make monthly payments. A higher-quality income statement will recognize revenue using the "installment" principle; that is, as the cash is collected each month, in turn, annual sales will reflect only the cash collected from sales during the year. A lower-quality income statement will recognize 100 percent of the revenue at the time of sale, even though payments may stretch well into next year. There is a detailed discussion of income items in Stickney, Brown, and Wahlen (2007, Chapter 5).

8.6.3 Footnotes

A word to the wise: *Read the footnotes!* They have come to include many pages in most annual reports—the 2016 Cisco report had more than forty pages of footnotes. The purpose of the footnotes is to provide information on how the firm handles balance sheet and income items. While the footnotes may not reveal everything you should know (for example, Enron), if you do not read them you cannot hope to be informed. The fact is, many analysts recommend that you should read an annual report *backward*, that is, you would read the footnotes first!

8.7 Moving on to Chapter 9

The purpose of this chapter is to help you to develop a sense of valuation. This chapter is crucial to your future in investing. It's also important as you move on to Chapter 9. In Chapter 9, we will examine the top-down approach to investing. We will not repeat all of the ideas that we've discussed about valuation. We will add on to these ideas and describe some valuation issues that are specific to the overall market or to industry analysis. But, you should make sure that you understand valuation before you move on.

SUMMARY

- As an investor, you want to select investments that will provide a rate of return that compensates you for the time your capital is invested, the expected rate of inflation, and the risk involved. To help you find these investments, this chapter considers the theory of valuation by which you derive the value of an investment using your required rate of return. We consider the two investment decision processes, which are the top-down three-step approach and the bottom-up stock-picking approach. Although either process can provide abnormal positive returns if the analyst is superior, we feel that a preferable approach is the top-down approach, in which you initially consider the aggregate economy and market, then examine alternative global industries, and finally analyze individual firms and their stocks.

- The valuation of common stock is more complex than valuing bonds because a stock's cash flows are

unknown and do not have a fixed life. In this chapter, we suggest two alternative approaches (the present value of cash flows and the relative valuation approach) and several techniques for each of these approaches. Notably, these are *not* competitive approaches, and we suggest that both approaches be used. Although we suggest using several different valuation models, the investment decision rule is always the same: If the estimated intrinsic value of the investment is greater than the market price, you should buy the investment or hold it if you own it; if the estimated intrinsic value of an investment is less than its market price, you should not invest in it and if you own it, you should sell it.

- We conclude with a review of ratios and factors that we believe are important to consider when attempting to estimate the intrinsic value of a stock.

SUGGESTED READINGS

Arzac, Enrique. *Valuations for Mergers, Buyouts, and Restructuring*, 2nd ed. New York: Wiley, 2007.

Damodaran, Aswath. *Damodaran on Valuation*, 2nd ed. New York: Wiley, 2008.

Damodaran, Aswath. *Investment Valuation*, 3rd ed. New York: Wiley, 2012.

Dechev, I., J. Graham, C. R. Harvey, and S. Rajgopal. 2016. "The Misrepresentation of Earnings." *Financial Analysts Journal* 72(1): 22–35.

English, James. *Applied Equity Analysis*. New York: McGraw-Hill, 2001.

Fridson, Martin, and Fernando Alvarez. *Financial Statement Analysis*, 4th ed. New York: Wiley, 2011.

Helfert, Erich A. *Techniques of Financial Analysis*, 11th ed. New York: McGraw-Hill, 2002.

Higgins, Robert C. *Analysis for Financial Management*, 11th ed. New York: McGraw-Hill Irwin, 2015.

Kelleher, Jim. *Equity Valuation for Analysts & Investors*. New York: McGraw-Hill, 2010.

Koller, Tim, and McKinsey & Co. *Valuation: Measuring and Managing the Value of Companies*, 6th ed. New York: Wiley, 2015.

Palepu, Krishna, Paul Healy, and Victor Bernard. *Business Analysis and Valuation*, 5th ed. Cincinnati, OH: South-Western Publishing, 2012.

Thomas, Rawley, and Benton E. Gup. *The Valuation Handbook*. New York: Wiley, 2009.

Valentine, James. *Best Practices for Equity Research Analysts*. New York: McGraw-Hill, 2011.

QUESTIONS

1. What does it mean to say that an investment is fairly priced versus overvalued versus undervalued?
2. What is the difference between the top-down and the bottom-up approaches to selecting stocks?
3. What is the difference between the free cash flow to the firm (FCFF) model and the free cash flow to equity model (FCFE)? How are the discount rates different?
4. What is the difference between free cash flow to equity and net income?

5. In the constant growth model, should you use a nominal growth rate or a real growth rate? Why?

6. Can the present value of the growth opportunity be negative? Why would this happen?

7. If a stock's price is the same as its intrinsic value, what will the investor's rate of return be?

8. Should the FCFE model and the FCFF model result in the same value? What adjustments will allow this to happen?

9. What would explain why two different companies have different P/E ratios? Price–sales ratios? Price–book ratios?

10. What the advantages and disadvantages of relative valuation?

PROBLEMS

1. The Baron Basketball Company (BBC) earned $10 a share last year and paid a dividend of $7 a share. Next year, you expect BBC to earn $11 and continue its payout ratio. Assume that you expect to sell the stock for $132 a year from now.
   a. If you require 12 percent on this stock, how much would you be willing to pay for it?
   b. If you expect a selling price of $110 and require an 8 percent return on this investment, how much would you pay for the BBC stock?

2. The Clipper Sailboat Company is expected to earn $3 per share next year. The company will have a return on equity of 15 percent and the company will grow 5 percent in the future. The company has a cost of equity of 12 percent. Given that information, answer the following questions.
   a. What is the value of the company's stock?
   b. What is the present value of the growth opportunity?
   c. Assume that the growth rate is only 3 percent. What would the appropriate P/E multiple be for this stock?

3. The Shamrock Dogfood Company (SDC) has consistently paid out 40 percent of its earnings in dividends. The company's return on equity is 16 percent.
   a. What would you estimate as its dividend growth rate?
   b. If you found out that the company was only growing at 2 percent, how much could the company afford to pay out?

4. You have been reading about the Madison Computer Company (MCC), which currently retains 90 percent of its earnings ($5 a share this year). It earns an ROE of almost 30 percent.
   a. Assuming a required rate of return of 14 percent, how much would you pay for MCC on the basis of the earnings multiplier model? Discuss your answer.
   b. What would you pay for Madison Computer if its retention rate were 60 percent and its ROE were 19 percent? Show your work.

5. Gentry Can Company's (GCC's) latest annual dividend of $1.25 a share was paid yesterday and maintained its historic 7 percent annual rate of growth. You plan to purchase the stock today because you believe that the dividend growth rate will increase to 8 percent for the next three years and the selling price of the stock will be $40 per share at the end of that time.
   a. How much should you be willing to pay for the GCC stock if you require a 12 percent return?
   b. What is the maximum price you should be willing to pay for the GCC stock if you believe that the 8 percent growth rate can be maintained indefinitely and you require a 12 percent return?
   c. If the 8 percent rate of growth is achieved, what will the price be at the end of Year 3, assuming the conditions in part (b)?

6. A company earned $5 per share in the year that just ended. The company has no more growth opportunities. The company has a 12 percent return on equity and a 12 percent cost of equity. What is the stock worth today?
   a. What if the company was expected to earn $5.50 next year and then never grow again? Assuming that their return on equity and cost of equity didn't change, what would the stock be worth today?

7. The current risk-free rate is 3 percent and the market risk premium is 5 percent. You are trying to value ABC company and it has an equity beta of .9. The company earned $2.50 in the year that just ended. You expect the company's earnings to grow 4 percent per year. The company has an ROE of 12 percent.
   a. What is the value of the stock?
   b. What is the present value of the growth opportunity?

8. A company had $18 of sales per share for the year that just ended. You expect the company to grow their sales at 6.5 percent for the next five years. After that, you expect the company to grow 3.5 percent in perpetuity. The company has a 14 percent ROE and you expect that to continue forever. The company's net margins are 6 percent and the cost of equity is 11 percent. Use the free cash flow to equity model to value this stock.

9. You are valuing a bank. The bank currently has assets of $300 per share. Five years from now (that is, at the end of five years), you expect their assets per share to be $450. After Year 5, you expect their assets per share to grow at 3 percent per year forever. The bank has an ROA of 1.2 percent and an ROE of 12.5 percent. The bank's cost of equity is 11.5 percent. What is the value of the bank's stock?

10. You are building a free cash flow to the firm model. You expect sales to grow from $1 billion for the year that just ended to $2 billion five years from now. Assume that the company will not become any more or less efficient in the future. Use the following information to calculate the value of the equity on a per-share basis.
    a. Assume that the company currently has $300 million of net PP&E.
    b. The company currently has $100 million of net working capital.
    c. The company has operating margins of 10 percent and has an effective tax rate of 28 percent.
    d. The company has a weighted average cost of capital of 9 percent. This is based on a capital structure of two-thirds equity and one-third debt.

11. Assume a company has a payout ratio of 45 percent, a profit margin of 4 percent, a cost of equity of 10 percent and a growth rate of 2.5 percent.
    a. What is the forward price–sales multiple?
    b. What is the trailing price–sales multiple?

12. Assume that a company has an ROE of 16 percent, a growth rate of 4 percent, and a payout ratio of 75 percent. The company also has a cost of equity of 13 percent. What is the trailing price–book multiple?

Derivation of Constant-Growth Dividend Discount Model (DDM)

The basic model is:

$$P_0 = \frac{D_1}{(1+k)^1} + \frac{D_2}{(1+k)^2} + \frac{D_3}{(1+k)^3} + \cdots + \frac{D_n}{(1+k)^n}$$

where:

P_0 = current price

D_i = expected dividend in Period i

k = required rate of return on Asset j

If growth rate (g) is constant:

$$P_0 = \frac{D_0(1+g)^1}{(1+k)^1} + \frac{D_0(1+g)^2}{(1+k)^2} + \cdots + \frac{D_0(1+g)^n}{(1+k)^n}$$

This can be written as:

$$P_0 = D_0 \left[\frac{(1+g)}{(1+k)} + \frac{(1+g)^2}{(1+k)^2} + \frac{(1+g)^3}{(1+k)^3} + \cdots + \frac{(1+g)^n}{(1+k)^n} \right]$$

Multiply both sides of the equation by $\frac{(1+k)}{(1+g)}$:

$$\left[\frac{(1+k)}{(1+g)} \right] P_0 = D_0 \left[1 + \frac{(1+g)}{(1+k)} + \frac{(1+g)^2}{(1+k)^2} + \cdots + \frac{(1+g)^{n-1}}{(1+k)^{n-1}} \right]$$

Subtract the previous equation from this equation:

$$\left[\frac{(1+k)}{(1+g)} - 1 \right] P_0 = D_0 \left[1 - \frac{(1+g)^n}{(1+k)^n} \right]$$

$$\left[\frac{(1+k) - (1+g)}{(1+g)} \right] P_0 = D_0 \left[1 - \frac{(1+g)^n}{(1+k)^n} \right]$$

Assuming $k > g$, as $n \to \infty$, the term in brackets on the right side of the equation goes to 1, leaving:

$$\left[\frac{(1+k) - (1+g)}{(1+g)} \right] P_0 = D_0$$

This simplifies to:

$$\left[\frac{(1+k-1+g)}{(1+g)} \right] P_0 = D_0$$

which equals:

$$\left[\frac{(k-g)}{(1+g)} \right] P_0 = D_0$$

This equals:

$$(k - g)P_0 = D_0(1 + g)$$
$$D_0(1 + g) = D_1$$

so:

$$(k - g)P_0 = D_1$$
$$P_0 = \frac{D_1}{k - g}$$

Remember, this model assumes:

- A constant growth rate
- An infinite time period
- The required return on the investment (k) is greater than the expected growth rate (g).

CHAPTER 9

The Top-Down Approach to Market, Industry, and Company Analysis

After you read this chapter, you should be able to answer the following questions:

- What is the relationship between stock prices and the economy (as represented by GDP)?
- What methodologies can be used to value the overall market?
- What are leading economic indicators? What are coincident indicators? What are lagging indicators?
- How do interest rates impact stock prices?
- What arguments support the importance of performing industry analysis?
- How do the business cycle, structural issues, the industry life cycle, and competitive forces impact an industry?
- What's the difference between a growth company and a growth stock?
- How do competitive strategies and SWOT analysis help company analysis?
- What is the growth duration model?

While the focus of Chapter 8 was to examine equity valuation, we opened that chapter with a discussion of the top-down approach. The top-down approach does three studies in the examination of a security:

1. The overall market and economy
2. The industry
3. The individual company

In this chapter, our goal is to explain how to think about applying the top-down approach in practice. We will proceed from top to bottom, meaning that we will start by examining how to think about whether the overall market is overvalued or undervalued. Next, we will examine how analysts think about an industry. Finally, within an industry, the analyst must select an individual security.

We should mention a few ideas before we get started:

- We will use U.S. markets when studying these topics. Rest assured that these approaches are just as useful in other markets. Of course, in different markets, there will be different amounts of data available.
- In this chapter, we will spend more time on the first two parts of top-down analysis (the overall market and the industry) than on the final component (the individual company). This is because we examined the valuation of the individual company in Chapter 8.
- The goal of this chapter is to help you learn what analysts are thinking about as they view the overall market, an industry, and an individual stock. But, at the end of the day, the best analyst is the one who can most accurately estimate inputs (such as cash flows, growth, and the cost of capital). In other words, in an investments class, we can teach you how to value a company. Making the best estimates requires experience. In addition, pay attention when you take a strategy class because the information taught there is incredibly important for analysts.

- Remember that a good company might not be a good investment. A high-quality company may grow at a relatively high and steady rate, it may have little competition, and it may have success in keeping costs low. But, if the price of that stock is too high, this successful company might not be a good investment.

In this chapter, we will proceed in top-down order. We will examine how analysts value the overall market, industries, and individual stocks.

9.1 Introduction to Market Analysis

The first stage of top-down analysis is to examine the attractiveness of a particular market. We will study this subject by describing how an analyst can assess whether the S&P 500 is an attractive investment. Remember that the S&P 500 is a market cap–weighted index that measures the value of large-cap U.S. companies. At any given time, companies within the S&P 500 account for approximately 80 percent of the value of all U.S. equities.

It's crucial to understand that stock prices reflect investors' expectations of what is going on in the economy. More specifically, stock prices reflect investors' expectations of future economic events. We will see later that the stock market turns down before the economy is actually in recession and starts to recover before the economy is actually growing again. In other words, the stock market leads or precedes the economy.

To see the importance of the economy from a really big-picture perspective, examine the Exhibits 9.1 and 9.2. Exhibit 9.1 shows that as the economy grows, profits grow. This should make some intuitive sense. As the value of goods and services produced in this country increases (GDP), companies increase their income. Similarly, Exhibit 9.2 shows that as companies earn more money, they are worth more. Simply put, economic growth leads to greater profits, and greater profits lead to higher stock prices. In Exhibit 9.2, you should notice the technology bubble, where stock prices were very high, despite the fact that profits were not.

The observation that stock prices are a reflection of the economy allows us to take two complementary approaches to viewing the overall market: the *macroanalysis approach* and

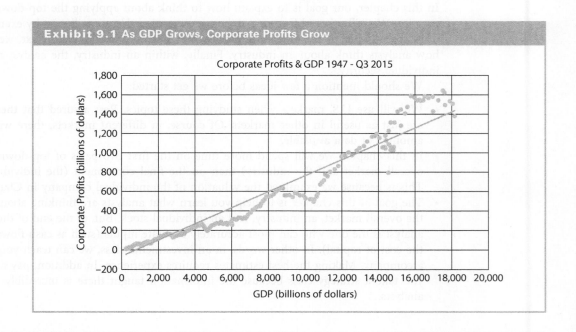

Exhibit 9.1 As GDP Grows, Corporate Profits Grow

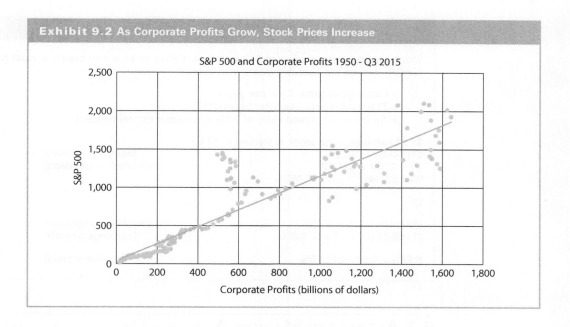

Exhibit 9.2 As Corporate Profits Grow, Stock Prices Increase

S&P 500 and Corporate Profits 1950 - Q3 2015

the *microvaluation approach*. In the macroanalysis approach, we will attempt to directly tie the value of stocks to the economy. In the microvaluation approach, we will try to value the market by discounting cash flows and by using relative valuation. These two approaches can also be applied to our examination of industries and individual companies.

It's important to realize that both approaches are driven by the economy. It is obvious that the macroanalysis approach is directly tied to the economy. With respect to the microvaluation approach, the cash flows, growth rate, and risk are also significantly impacted by the economy.

To give a better (and very important) view of the relationship between the economy and the microvaluation approach, let's think about another way to estimate returns. Returns from the overall market (or an individual stock) can be thought of as a combination of *three factors*: earnings growth, multiple expansion (or contraction), and dividend yield. A mathematical example of this can be seen in Exhibit 9.3. This is a particularly important idea: You can estimate returns for the market, an industry, or an individual company by estimating the earnings growth, multiple expansion (or contraction), and dividend yield. For example, if a company's multiple does not change, the investor will earn the growth rate plus the dividend yield. In Exhibit 9.3, the 6.5 percent earnings growth plus the 2.5 percent dividend yield would have added up to 9 percent. From there, the question is whether the multiple will expand or contract. In Exhibit 9.3, the multiple expanded 2.7 percent per year. The result of the 9 percent return and 2.7 percent resulted in an 11.88 percent annualized return (due to compounding).

As you think about those three components, realize that earnings growth and dividend yield will be impacted by GDP growth. Multiple expansion (or contraction) will be driven by sentiment about the economy and market and interest rates.

Finally, many investors think of macroanalysis and microvaluation as the two (sequential) components of studying the value of the aggregate stock market rather than alternative approaches. In other words, many investors examine that economy (the macroanalysis) and then attempt to value the market (microvaluation). While we examine these two approaches sequentially, we do not mean to imply that they need to stand alone.

Exhibit 9.3 Stock Returns

Stocks are currently trading at 14X earnings. Calculate your compound annual growth rate (CAGR) if, over the next five years, you expect:

> ➤ Earnings to grow 6.5% per year
> ➤ The market multiple to expand to 16
> ➤ An annual dividend yield of 2.5% (dividends not reinvested)

$1 of earnings — so stock is trading at $14

$\$1(1.065)^5 = \$1.37$	(earnings growth)
$16 \times \$1.37 = \$21.92$	(multiple expansion)
$(\$21.92/14)^{(1/5)} - 1 = 9.383\%$	

Or

$(16/14)^{(1/5)} - 1 = 2.7\%$	(multiple expansion)
$(1.065)(1.027) - 1 = 9.383\%$	(earnings growth)
$9.38\% + 2.5\% = \mathbf{11.88\%}$	(dividend yield)

9.2 Aggregate Market Analysis (Macroanalysis)

As mentioned above (and shown graphically), economic growth leads to higher stock prices. It may seem that this leads to an easy conclusion: Study GDP growth, and this should allow us to predict stock prices. Unfortunately, there are three problems with this approach:

1. Preliminary GDP data is released approximately one month after each quarter ends. This means that it is not timely.
2. The preliminary GDP data will be revised. Often times, the revisions are meaningful.
3. The stock market moves ahead of the economy. In other words, investors are anticipating future cash flows. (In fact, in just a moment, you will read that the stock market is seen as a leading economic indicator.) As a result, it's hard to identify stocks (which move ahead of the economy) by examining old economic data that may need to be revised significantly.

There are two possible reasons stock prices lead the economy. One is that stock prices reflect expectations of earnings, dividends, and interest rates. As investors attempt to estimate these future variables, their stock price decisions reflect expectations for future economic activity, not past or current activity. A second possible reason is that the stock market reacts to various leading indicator series, the most important being corporate earnings, corporate profit margins, and interest rates. Because these series tend to lead the economy, when investors adjust stock prices to reflect these leading economic series, expectations for stock prices become a leading series as well.

Since the actual GDP data will not provide a solution to the analysts' need to anticipate future stock prices, analysts need to look for other measures of the economy. In this section, we will examine three common approaches:

1. The leading, coincident, and lagging economic indicators
2. Sentiment indicators
3. Interest rates

Recognize the focus of these three approaches: We are going to be looking at economic series that are moving ahead of stock prices (or at least at the same time as stock prices). To the extent that we look at any data that is less timely, such as data that moves at the same time as the economy (*coincident indicators*) or after the economy (*lagging indicators*), the reason for this is simply to confirm existing data and beliefs.

9.2.1 Leading, Coincident, and Lagging Indicators

The cyclical indicator approach to monitoring and forecasting the economy is built on the belief that the aggregate economy experiences periods of expansion and contraction that can be identified by the movements in specific economic series. The Conference Board has grouped these series into three major categories, based on their relationship to the business cycle.

Leading Indicators   The first category, *leading indicators*, includes economic series that usually reach peaks or troughs before corresponding peaks or troughs in aggregate economic activity. The group currently includes the 10 series shown in Exhibit 9.4 with their factor weights. You may notice an oddity in this exhibit: Even though the economy is becoming more service based, manufacturing and the production of goods still seem very important. The production of goods tends to be more volatile than services and therefore has a larger impact on the state of economic growth.

In Exhibit 9.5, you can see that the index of leading economic indicators turns down before a recession and turns back up before the economy is out of recession. (Note that the shaded area represents the time period in which the economy is in recession.) The fact that this indicator anticipates the moves in the economy is what makes it so valuable.

The second category, coincident indicators, includes four economic time series that have peaks or troughs that roughly coincide with the peaks and troughs in the business cycle. The series included in this category can be seen in Exhibit 9.6 with their factor weights. You will notice that this series is dominated by jobs and income. In other words, when the economy is doing well, people are employed and receiving income that they can use for consumption.

In Exhibit 9.7, you can see that the index of coincident economic indicators turns down at (roughly) the same time as the recession starts and turns back up as the recession ends. This indicator helps analysts confirm that the economy is actually entering a recession or finishing a recession.

The third category, lagging indicators, includes seven series that experience their peaks and troughs after those of the aggregate economy. In Exhibit 9.8, you can see the seven components and their factor weights.

In Exhibit 9.9, you can see that the index of lagging economic indicators turns down after the recession has already started and turns back up after the recession has already ended. This indicator helps analysts confirm that the economy is actually in recession or that the recession is actually over. You should notice in this exhibit that the lagging indicators are dominated by

Exhibit 9.4 Leading Economic Indicators

Leading Economic Index	Factor
1. Average weekly hours, manufacturing	.2774
2. ISM new orders index	.1587
3. Average consumer expectations for business conditions	.1447
4. Interest rate spread, 10-year UST less Fed funds rate	.1123
5. Manufacturing new orders, consumer goods and materials	.0821
6. Leading Credit Index™	.0818
7. Manufacturers' new orders, nondef cap goods excl. aircraft	.0405
8. Stock prices, 500 common stocks	.0397
9. Average weekly initial claims for unemployment insurance	.0330
10. Building permits, new private housing units	.0298

Source: Copyright The Conference Board 2017.

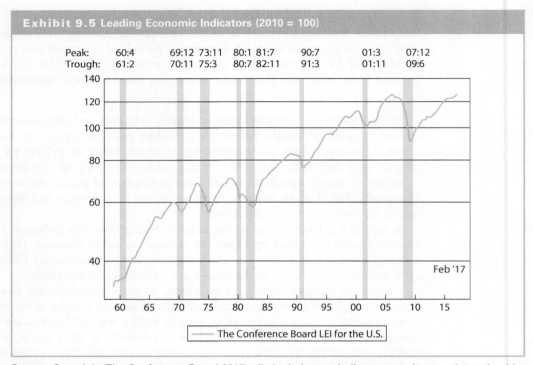

Exhibit 9.5 Leading Economic Indicators (2010 = 100)

| Peak: | 60:4 | 69:12 73:11 | 80:1 81:7 | 90:7 | 01:3 | 07:12 |
| Trough: | 61:2 | 70:11 75:3 | 80:7 82:11 | 91:3 | 01:11 | 09:6 |

The Conference Board LEI for the U.S.

Source: Copyright The Conference Board 2017; all shaded areas indicate recessions as determined by The National Bureau of Economic Research.

interest rates and loans. Lending slows in a recession and usually does not pick up again until the recovery is well under way.

Some analysts also use a ratio of these composite series, contending that the ratio of the composite coincident series divided by the composite lagging series (known as the C/L ratio) acts like a leading series, in some instances even moving prior to the composite leading series. The rationale for expecting this leading relationship for this ratio is that the coincident series should turn before the lagging series, and the ratio of the two series will be quite sensitive to such changes. As a result, this ratio series is expected to lead both of the individual composite series, especially at turning points. The C/L ratio can be seen in Exhibit 9.10. As shown in the chart, this indicator seems to precede recessions by a fair amount of time, but it also delivers some false signals.

Although movements for this ratio series are generally parallel to those of the leading series, its real value comes when this ratio series diverges from the composite leading indicator series because this divergence signals a change in the normal relationship between the indicator series. For example, if the leading indicator series has been rising for a period of time, we

Exhibit 9.6 Coincident Economic Indicators

Coincident Economic Index

1. Employees on nonagricultural payrolls	0.5295
2. Personal income less transfer payments	0.2050
3. Industrial production	0.1461
4. Manufacturing and trade sales	0.1194

Source: Copyright The Conference Board 2017.

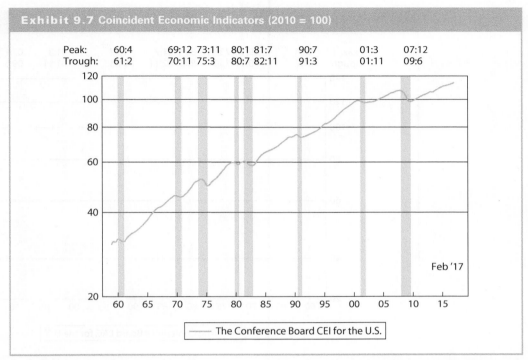

Exhibit 9.7 Coincident Economic Indicators (2010 = 100)

Peak:	60:4	69:12	73:11	80:1	81:7	90:7	01:3	07:12
Trough:	61:2	70:11	75:3	80:7	82:11	91:3	01:11	09:6

Feb '17

——— The Conference Board CEI for the U.S.

Source: Copyright The Conference Board 2017; all shaded areas indicate recessions as determined by The National Bureau of Economic Research.

would expect both the coincident and the lagging series also to be rising, but the coincident series should be rising faster than the lagging series, so the ratio of the coincident to the lagging series should likewise be rising. In contrast, assume that the composite leading indicator series is rising but the coincident to lagging series ratio is flattening out or declining. This change in trend in the ratio series could occur because the coincident series is not rising as fast as the lagging indicator series or because the coincident series has turned down. Either scenario would indicate a possible end to an economic expansion or at least a less-robust expansion.

There are no perfect indicators. The Conference Board acknowledges the following limitations that are also discussed in Koenig and Emery (1991):

1. **False signals.** A series that is moving in one direction may suddenly reverse and nullify a prior signal or hesitate, which is difficult to interpret. High variability in a series causes this problem.

Exhibit 9.8 Lagging Economic Indicators

Lagging Economic Index	Factor
1. Average prime rate	.2993
2. Consumer price index for services	.2071
3. Consumer installment credit outstanding to personal income ratio	.1847
4. Inventories to sales ratio, manufacturing, and trade	.1256
5. Commercial and industrial loans	.0961
6. Labor cost per unit of output, manufacturing	.0501
7. Average duration of unemployment	.0371

Source: Copyright The Conference Board 2017.

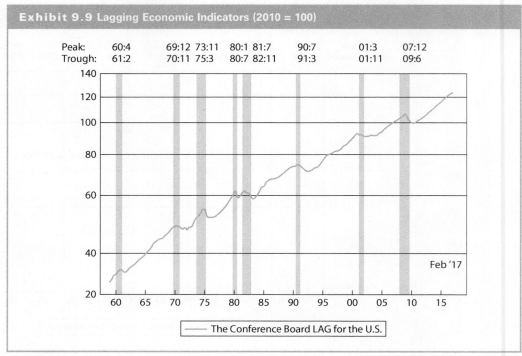

Exhibit 9.9 Lagging Economic Indicators (2010 = 100)

| Peak: | 60:4 | | 69:12 | 73:11 | 80:1 | 81:7 | 90:7 | | 01:3 | 07:12 |
| Trough: | 61:2 | | 70:11 | 75:3 | 80:7 | 82:11 | 91:3 | | 01:11 | 09:6 |

The Conference Board LAG for the U.S.

Source: Copyright The Conference Board 2017; all shaded areas indicate recessions as determined by The National Bureau of Economic Research.

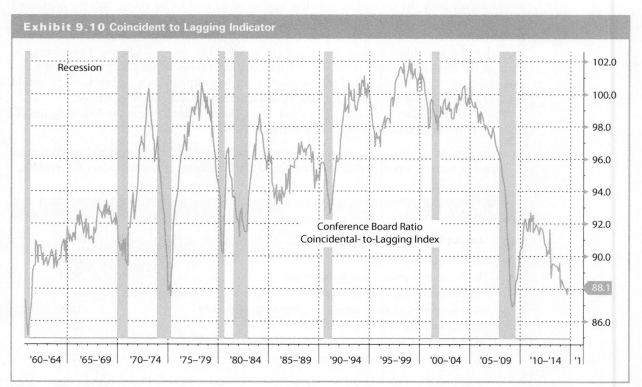

Exhibit 9.10 Coincident to Lagging Indicator

Recession

Conference Board Ratio
Coincidental- to-Lagging Index

Source: Zerohedge.com.

2. **Timeliness of the data and revisions.** Some data series take time to be reported, but a bigger problem is revisions in data, especially if a revision changes the direction implied by the original data.
3. **Economic sectors not represented.** Examples include the service sector, import–export data, and many international series.

9.2.2 Sentiment and Expectations Surveys

Consumer expectations are considered relevant as the economy approaches cyclical turning points. The intuition is that consumers must have confidence in order to spend. Consumer spending accounts for approximately 70 percent of gross domestic product.

Two widely followed surveys of consumer expectations are reported monthly. The University of Michigan Consumer Sentiment Index and the Conference Board Consumer Confidence Index both query a sample of households on their expectations. Although the two indexes deviate from month to month, over longer time periods, they track each other fairly closely. Both indexes are meant to be leading indicators of the economy. Exhibit 9.11 shows a chart of the University of Michigan Consumer Sentiment survey. Notice that expectations tend to lead or coincide with changes in the economy.

9.2.3 Interest Rates

In addition to the leading economic indicator series and sentiment indicators, the final approach to tracking the economy is to follow interest rates. Specifically, we will discuss:

1. The real federal funds rate
2. The yield curve (the term spread)
3. The risk premium between Treasury bonds and BBB bonds
4. The Fed model

Before discussing these four indicators, we want to mention something that you might wonder about. In prior editions of this book, as well as most other economics and finance books, you will find discussions of money supply (M1, M2, M3). You'll notice that we are no longer mentioning this. Previously, the money supply was what the Fed attempted to control,

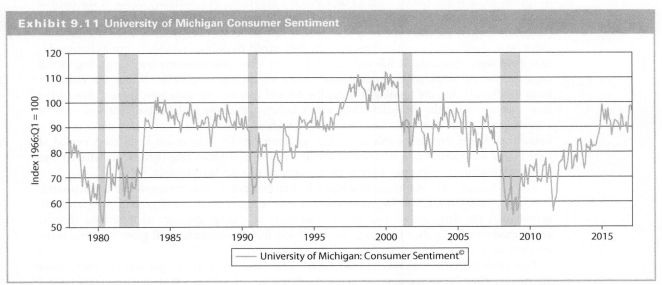

Exhibit 9.11 University of Michigan Consumer Sentiment

University of Michigan: Consumer Sentiment©

Source: University of Michigan, University of Michigan: Consumer Sentiment© [UMCSENT], retrieved from FRED, Federal Reserve Bank of St. Louis; https://fred.stlouisfed.org/series/UMCSENT, March 25, 2017.

how the Fed communicated about the economy, and what analysts watched. In recent years, the Fed has moved away from setting (and discussing) policy in terms of money supply. The Fed has found that it is much more direct to think of policy in terms of setting the federal funds rate (commonly referred to as "the Fed funds rate").

Further evidence that this change has occurred can be seen by noticing that The Conference Board has removed money supply measures from its leading economic series indicator. It still includes an indicator that tries to capture the shape of the yield curve (discussed later in this chapter). The Conference Board replaced M2 with its own (trademarked) Leading Credit Index.

The Real Federal Funds Rate Given that we no longer look at money supply, the first interest rate that analysts should review is the federal funds rate. This rate is set by the Fed's Federal Open Market Committee (FOMC). The FOMC meets every six weeks (and can meet more frequently if there is an emergency) to set policy. This rate is actually a target that the FOMC sets for what banks will charge each other when one bank makes overnight loans to another bank. More technically, this is the rate that is charged when these banks loan excess reserves to each other. But, for our purpose (as investment analysts), we can simply think of the federal funds rate as the rate set by the Fed on short-term (overnight) loans.

Analysts want to know the level of the federal funds rate and whether it is intended to stimulate the economy or restrict the economy. The first thing to realize is that we should think about the federal funds rate in *real terms* rather than *nominal terms*. For example, imagine that the federal funds rate is 6 percent. If inflation is 1 percent, the real rate is 5 percent, and this would be considered to be expensive money. On the other hand, if the federal funds rate is 6 percent and inflation is 5 percent, the real rate is 1 percent, and this would be considered to be cheaper money. During the 10 years since the financial crisis started, the real rate has actually been negative for most of this time. This can be seen in Exhibit 9.12. This policy was considered to be very accommodative policy (in other words, designed to stimulate growth).

In order to truly understand whether Fed policy is stimulative or restrictive, we have to go even further than just thinking about the real federal funds rate. We need to have an understanding of the natural rate. The *natural rate*, which is also known as the *neutral rate*, is the rate that would be neither stimulative nor restrictive if the economy were operating at the Fed's dual mandate—for the economy to be operating at full capacity (full employment) and for prices to be stable (considered to be 2 percent inflation). We normally think of the natural rate in real terms, consistent with how we think of the real federal funds rate.

Unfortunately, we can't solve for the neutral rate or know exactly what it is. We can only estimate it. Again, we are estimating the rate that would be neither restrictive nor accommodative if we were operating at full capacity. But, even when the economy isn't operating at full capacity, we ask what is the neutral rate given our current conditions. When the economy faces headwinds that are holding it back, the neutral rate can be quite low. In fact, during the slow recovery after the financial crisis, many believed that the real neutral rate was zero or even negative. (The economy faced headwinds such as homeowners who owed more on their house than the house was worth and a U.S. government that shut down for a short period of time.) This low natural rate means that the low real federal funds rate (which we believed was so accommodative) might not have been as aggressive as we had thought.

For an analyst, it's important to know whether Fed policy is accommodative or restrictive. If policy is accommodative, we know that the Fed is trying to increase growth. We normally believe that the direction of Fed policy is unlikely to change quickly. As described shortly, accommodative Fed policy increases the likelihood that the economy will grow and that earnings will increase.

Low rates help the economy in many ways. Low rates make mortgages and car loans more affordable. They lower the cost of capital for firms, and this means that more projects have a positive net present value. Lower rates often result in a country's currency depreciating, and this

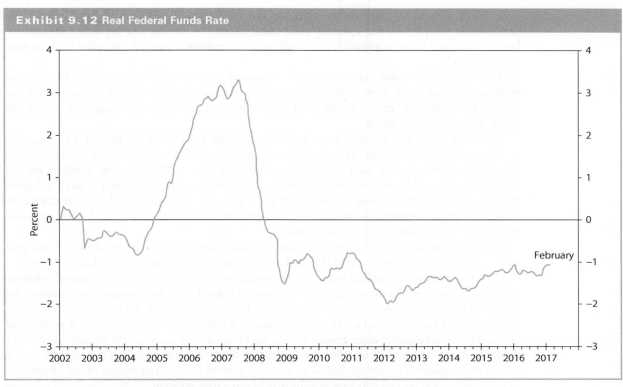

Exhibit 9.12 Real Federal Funds Rate

Source: Bureau of Economic analysis & Board of governors via Haver Analytics

helps growth by making it easier to export and by making imports more expensive (which benefits domestic producers). Most important to equity analysts, if a low federal funds rate results in lower long-term rates, this can make stocks more attractive. In addition to stocks being more attractive relative to low-yielding bonds, the value of a stock is the present value of future cash flows. Low rates mean that the present value of those distant cash flows is greater.

Low rates result in higher stock prices for all the reasons described above. Low rates result in increased demand by consumers and businesses. They help exporters and domestic producers that compete with imports. Low rates simply make stocks more attractive to investors. If investors have a choice between a 2 percent yield on a U.S. Treasury bond or a stock with a 2 percent dividend yield, investors will often move money from bonds to stocks, pushing stock prices up. Obviously, when the Fed is raising rates, all these factors can work in reverse and make stocks less attractive.

A significant driver of interest rates is inflation. Yet one of the very uncertain factors in looking at the economy is the impact that inflation will have on stocks. Typically, inflation results in higher interest rates. Based on the prior discussion, you would think that this would make stocks worth less. But, there's another side to this: If there is inflation, this means the company's cash flows should also increase. So, shouldn't stock prices rise, or at the very least, shouldn't the higher cash flows offset the higher discount rates?

Part of the question concerning the impact of inflation is whether a particular company can pass cost increases on to the customer or whether the company's costs will rise at a faster rate. But, regardless of whether an individual company can pass on higher costs to customers, there is probably a bigger reason to worry that high, unexpected inflation will be a hindrance to stock prices. If inflation is higher than the Fed wants, we expect that the Fed will raise the federal funds rate until inflation drops back to an allowable level. This means that the Fed will be trying to slow the economy, which is not beneficial to stock prices.

The Yield Curve In addition to watching Fed policy, analysts watch the yield curve. As described in Chapter 12, the Treasury yield curve charts the interest rate for different maturity bonds. The yield curve is probably the single most important economic indicator that an analyst can watch.

The shape of the yield curve is crucial. A *normal yield curve* is one in which longer-term yields are greater than short-term yields. A *flat yield curve* occurs when long-term rates are similar to short-term rates. An *inverted yield curve* occurs when the long-term yields are lower than short-term yields.

The yield curve has inverted prior to every recession since 1970. In Exhibit 9.13, you can see the yield on the 10-year Treasury bond minus the yield on the two-year Treasury note. When this difference is at zero, it indicates a flat yield curve. When the line is below zero, it means that the yield curve is inverted (because the yield on the two-year Treasury is higher than the yield on the 10-year Treasury). A flat yield curve indicates a 50 percent chance of recession (approximately one year later). Evidence shows that the likelihood of a recession increases with the severity of the inversion.

Of course, the question is whether it makes intuitive sense that an inverted yield curve predicts a recession. We would argue that it does. We can tell this story in two different ways.

First, we can roughly think of yields as representing a real rate of return plus expected inflation. (In addition, we typically expect that there is some additional yield that compensates investors for the risk of buying longer-term bonds.) To the extent that long-term yields are lower, it reflects expectations of lower real yields and lower inflation. Since real returns are correlated with real growth and inflation tends to be higher when growth is high, the inverted yield curve simply reflects the market's expectation of lower growth. In other words, you can think of this as a leading indicator because it reflects expectations of the future. Just as we saw with surveys (in the prior section of this chapter) to gauge expectations, we can also look at market prices to gauge inflation.

Another way of telling the first story of why an inverted yield curve predicts recessions is to again start with the idea that long-term rates reflect current short-term rates and expected short-term rates in the future. But now, we can consider why the market expects slower growth in the future (which causes the inversion). To start, the reason that the short end of the yield curve increases is that the Fed raises short-term rates in response to rising inflation. In effect, the FOMC raises rates to slow the economy (to eliminate inflation). Unfortunately, when the Fed raises rates, this often pushes us into recession, and then the Fed eventually

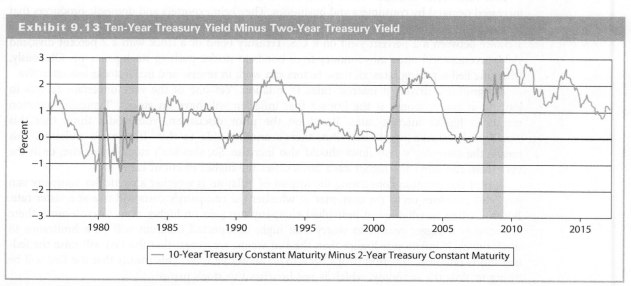

Exhibit 9.13 Ten-Year Treasury Yield Minus Two-Year Treasury Yield

— 10-Year Treasury Constant Maturity Minus 2-Year Treasury Constant Maturity

Source: Federal Reserve bank of St. Louis

has to lower rates. In sum, if the yield curve inverts, it is usually because the Fed has raised short-term rates, and the expectation is that the Fed will eventually have to lower rates significantly, and even the term premium that longer-term investors require will not be enough to keep the yield curve normal.

Finally, the second way of telling the story is slightly different. Rather than explaining why the yield curve inverts, this story simply says that an inverted yield curve can cause a recession (regardless of why the yield curve arrived at that shape). You must understand that banks are intermediaries that borrow significant funds in the short-term market and loan funds out in the longer-term market. They profit from the spread of a normal yield curve. In other words, they borrow short-term at low rates and make longer-term loans at higher rates. When the yield curve inverts, it is no longer profitable to lend because banks have to pay more for short-term funds, and they can charge less for longer-term loans. So, this second explanation is that an inverted yield curve results in less bank lending, and the decrease in the availability of credit slows economic growth.

Risk Premium In addition to the real federal funds rate and the yield curve, analysts also examine the **risk premium** on bonds. Most commonly, we look at the difference between BBB corporate bonds and the yield on U.S. Treasury bonds. A larger spread indicates fear in the markets. It indicates that investors are requiring additional compensation for taking risk.

When investors require higher compensation to own risky bonds, they also require additional compensation to own stocks (which are even riskier). In a perfect world, investors would want to invest new money in stocks when the risk premium is the largest and sell stocks when the risk premium is the smallest. Of course, this is just another way of saying that you want to buy when everyone else is selling and you want to sell when everyone else is buying.

Exhibit 9.14 shows the risk premium. During the Great Recession, the risk premium increased significantly. Riskier bonds had a greater chance of downgrade and/or default due to a weak economy. As a result, investors required higher yields. As mentioned earlier, if investors perceive a company's debt to be riskier, they must also perceive the equity to be

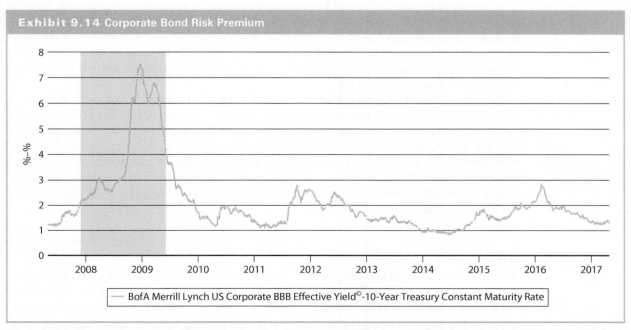

Exhibit 9.14 Corporate Bond Risk Premium

BofA Merrill Lynch US Corporate BBB Effective Yield©-10-Year Treasury Constant Maturity Rate

Source: BofA Merrill Lynch, BofA Merrill Lynch US Corporate BBB Effective Yield© [BAMLC0A4CBBBEY], retrieved from FRED, Federal Reserve Bank of St. Louis; https://fred.stlouisfed.org/series/BAMLC0A4CBBBEY, April 30, 2017.

riskier. This caused investors to demand greater compensation for stocks, and that meant lower prices. As the perceived risk dissipated, the bond risk premium decreased, and stock prices increased.

The Fed Model   The final idea that we want to discuss as part of interest rates and stocks is known as "the Fed model." The Fed model came from Alan Greenspan's Monetary Report to Congress in the summer of 1997. In this report, he showed a simple valuation model that indicated stocks were overvalued. A well-known market strategist and economist, Ed Yardeni, frequently spoke about this and is credited with dubbing it "the Fed model."

The Fed model says that the S&P 500 should be worth next year's earnings divided by the yield on the 10-year Treasury bond. For a long period of time, the correlation between this model's predicted value for the S&P 500 and actual stock prices was very high. It makes intuitive sense that higher earnings and lower interest rates would make stocks worth more.

The reason that we want to discuss the Fed model is that it is widely referenced in market publications, and it is important for you to realize that it is meaningless. Think about the equation. It's the equation for a perpetuity (rather than a growing perpetuity). That doesn't make sense. In addition, the numerator is earnings. Earnings are not cash flows; earnings cannot be distributed to investors. Finally, earnings are certainly not risk free, so this violates the basic concept that we discount cash flows at a rate that reflects the riskiness of those cash flows.

If you think about the constant growth dividend discount model, you can get an understanding of why the Fed model worked for so long and why it no longer works. Back in the early 1990s, the 10-year Treasury yielded closer to 6 percent (or higher). This made the denominator twice as big as it should have been if we had simply taken the cost of capital minus the growth rate. In addition, the numerator happened to be twice as big as it should have been (because earnings were approximately twice as large as the free cash flow that belonged to equityholders). Since the numerator and denominator were both twice as large as they should have been, the model worked! (As an aside, that's an important lesson: When you make one mistake, try to make a second mistake that will offset the first mistake!)

In recent years, the Fed model has indicated that stocks are grossly undervalued. You can see this in Exhibit 9.15. Think about why that is. The numerator is still two times too large—because it uses earnings rather than free cash flow. The denominator, however, is no longer two times too large. Interest rates are low and are a better reflection of the cost of equity minus the growth rate ($k - g$). So now, the numerator is still two times too big, and the denominator is no longer too big.

We believe that it's important for you to understand this model, even though it is wrong. As mentioned earlier, the model is frequently cited by market participants to indicate that stocks are undervalued. In addition, the model is an important reminder of valuation and how we should discount cash flows. Finally, it is important to realize that even if this model were correct, it is incorrect to use it to simply make a comment about stocks. At best, it is a relative valuation model. In other words, if the model shows that stocks are undervalued, the model can return to fair value by stock prices increasing *or* bond yields increasing (pushing the model's predicted fair value down).

9.3 MICROVALUATION ANALYSIS

After analyzing the health of the economy and the trajectory of the business cycle, the analyst's goal is to calculate an actual estimate of the value of the market. We will think about doing this in two ways: a free cash flow to the equityholder (FCFE) model and relative valuation. In addition, as part of valuation, we will examine Robert Shiller's *cyclically adjusted price–earnings (CAPE)* ratio.

Exhibit 9.15 Fed Model Valuation

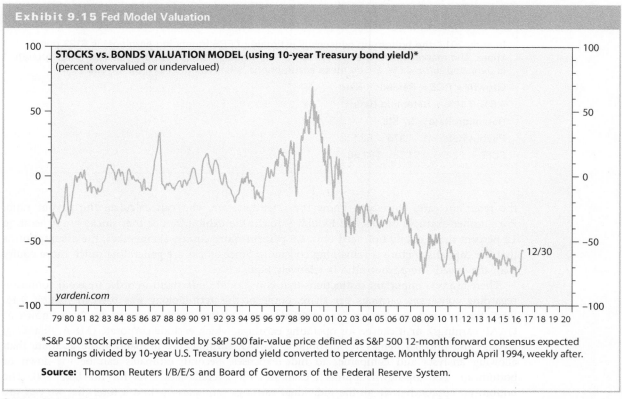

STOCKS vs. BONDS VALUATION MODEL (using 10-year Treasury bond yield)*
(percent overvalued or undervalued)

12/30

yardeni.com

*S&P 500 stock price index divided by S&P 500 fair-value price defined as S&P 500 12-month forward consensus expected earnings divided by 10-year U.S. Treasury bond yield converted to percentage. Monthly through April 1994, weekly after.

Source: Thomson Reuters I/B/E/S and Board of Governors of the Federal Reserve System.

Source: Yardeni.com

9.3.1 FCFE to Value the Market

As discussed in Chapter 8, we can think of the FCFE model as an improved version of the dividend discount model that students traditionally learn. In most cases, we should not value a company based on the actual dividend payments that are made. Many companies pay much smaller dividends than they could afford to pay. We should value a company based on the amount of cash flow that could be distributed to shareholders after running the business; reinvesting in property, plant, and equipment (capital expenditures); investing in short-term assets (net working capital); and measuring any cash flows to (or from) debtholders.

As also seen in Chapter 8, we could use a two-stage FCFE model or a constant growth model. In this chapter, we will simply think about market valuation by using a constant growth model. While we sometimes value the overall market by thinking that there will be a few years of particularly high growth or particularly low growth, the majority of valuation is captured by the constant growth model. This certainly makes sense in valuing a mature economy (such as the United States).

In order to use the FCFE model, you will need an estimate of next year's cash flows (including the growth rate) and the discount rate. We'll review each of these two components.

Cash Flows Estimating the cash flows can be done in several ways. The simplest way, which is far from perfect, is to use the reported consensus estimate for earnings per share. From there, you need to turn it into FCFE. Your model hinges upon your assumption of growth, the discount rate, and the return on equity. Remember from Chapter 8 that you will turn earnings into FCFE by using the sustainable growth rate (Growth = ROE × Retention Rate). The way you use this equation is by using your growth and ROE assumption and solving for

> **Exhibit 9.16** Using Consensus Estimate of EPS to Calculate FCFE
>
> In early 2017, the bottom-up consensus estimate of EPS (operating earnings) is $132 per share. The market's ROE is expected to be 12% while the long-term expected earnings growth is expected to be 4.5%. Given these assumptions, what will the FCFE be for this year?
>
> Growth = ROE × Retention Rate
>
> 4.5% = 12% × Retention Rate
>
> Retention Rate = 37.5%
>
> Payout Rate = 1 − .375 = 62.5%
>
> FCFE = 62.5% × $132 = **$82.50**

the retention rate. Once you know the retention rate, you can calculate the payout ratio. For another example of this, see Exhibit 9.16. In the exhibit, notice that stocks are generating 12 percent more equity but need only 4.5 percent more equity. (Remember, the assumption is that the capital structure is remaining constant.) Since stocks are generating much more equity than they need, the payout ratio is relatively high.

There are two important distinctions that you should understand in order to avoid confusion regarding consensus earnings per share. Some of this terminology was used in Exhibit 9.16. First, the estimate can be for "as reported" earnings for ongoing operations (also known as GAAP earnings), or it can be for operating earnings, which exclude corporate (M&A, financing, layoffs) and unusual items. In our opinion, GAAP earnings are probably more accurate than allowing analysts and companies to hide expenses. Second, estimates can be top-down or bottom-up. The top-down approach examines the overall sales level for the S&P 500. The bottom-up approach rolls all the individual earnings estimates up into a total that we can use for the index.

Brokerage firms tend to use the operating earnings estimates rather than the GAAP earnings. The operating earnings are higher since they exclude certain items. These higher earnings make the market's price/earnings multiple appear to be lower (cheaper).

A second way to use the consensus estimate for earnings per share for the S&P 500 is to calculate the amount that you reasonably expect the actual earnings per share to be based on the consensus. Here, we're describing the reality that consensus estimates are normally far too high and are reduced as we move closer to the earnings announcement dates. The analyst can develop a curve to forecast how earnings estimates will be reduced and what factors will drive estimates to be reduced more or less. To the extent that you can estimate that earnings will be higher or lower than the true consensus, you may be able to profit.

Finally, we arrive at the hardest (and best) way to estimate the earnings per share (that you can use to turn into FCFE). An analyst can build a model organically. Again, much of this will be related to macroeconomic factors. The analyst will start with the sales per share (for the entire S&P 500) for the year that just ended and will estimate each of the following:

1. Growth rate of sales
2. Operating margin
3. Interest expense
4. Tax rate

A simple example of this can be seen in Exhibit 9.17. As you examine Exhibit 9.17, it is important to recognize the difficulty in making broad-market estimates for factors such as operating margins. But, assuming that the analyst does this, she can use this estimate of earnings per share to move to FCFE by using the methodology shown in Exhibit 9.16. The following sections discuss the four estimates listed above.

Exhibit 9.17 Calculating "As Reported" Earnings per Share

Given the following information, estimate the S&P 500's EPS:
S&P 500 Estimated Sales: $1,200

Operating Margin = 14%

Interest Margin (as a percentage of sales) = 2.5%

Tax rate = 23.91%

_____SOLUTION:_____

Operating Profit = $168	($1,200 × 14%)
Interest Expense = $30	($1,200 × 2.5%)
Earnings Before Taxes = $138	($168 − $30)
Taxes = $33	($138 × 23.91%)
NetIncome = $105	($138 − $33)

Growth Rate of Sales per Share   It's easy to start with sales per share for the year that just ended. This number is widely available; probably the easiest place to locate it is on Standard & Poor's Website. Then, you need to estimate growth of sales. A reasonable approach would be to compare the historic growth rate of GDP to the historic growth rate of the sales per share of the S&P 500. Once you establish that relationship, you can estimate the economic growth for the future.

There are a few things to know as you estimate the future growth rate of GDP. First, you are really not trying to guess next quarter's GDP or even next year's GDP. You are trying to estimate the long-term growth rate. (This might be slightly different if you're doing a two-stage model.) Second, remember that the real long-term growth rate is dependent upon two factors: growth in the labor force and productivity. Once you estimate these numbers, you need to add expected inflation because you build models using nominal numbers, not real numbers. In the United States, the labor force is expected to grow approximately 0.5 percent to 0.8 percent over the next 10 to 20 years. Productivity is very difficult to predict. But, if we experience 1 percent productivity growth, the real growth rate will be 1.75 percent. If you add in the Fed's 2 percent desired inflation rate, nominal growth will be 3.75 percent.

Operating Margin   To move from sales per share to operating profit, you must multiply the sales per share by the operating margin. Obviously, this is a difficult number to estimate, whether you are doing this for a particular stock or for the overall market. It's best to start by looking at the current operating margin and the trend. Then, consider economic factors that impact the operating margin and how they are changing. Research indicates that the four most significant factors are:

1. Capacity utilization
2. Unit labor costs
3. Rate of inflation
4. Foreign competition

There's little question that the first two factors, capacity utilization and unit labor costs, are the most important. Increasing capacity utilization results in a decrease in per-unit fixed cost (increasing margins). (Of course, there can be diseconomies of scale at very high levels of capacity utilization as companies have to use marginal labor or old equipment.) Unit labor costs are impacted by wages per hour and productivity. You can think of this simply as the increase in wages per hour minus the change in productivity. Obviously, when unit labor costs shrink, this means higher margins.

The impact of the rate of inflation depends upon how much costs increase and how they can be passed on to customers. Foreign competition matters because selling in foreign markets can be extremely competitive (lower margins), and for domestic companies selling in their home country, competing with foreign imports can result in lower margins.

It's also important to understand why margins increase after a recession. Utilization increases, helping margins. Unit labor costs tend to improve because there is increased productivity (producing more with the same amount of labor that was underutilized during recession), and wages are subdued because of an excess supply of labor.

Of course, as the business cycle peaks, operating margins will drop. This is because companies are operating at full capacity, so utilization will eventually decrease. Inflation leads to wage increases, and productivity growth is low. When you think about the difficulty in estimating each of these factors and how they interact, it may be best to simply try to estimate the direction of future operating margins.

Interest Expense   Next, interest expense must be deducted from operating profit. Interest expense depends on two factors: the amount of debt and the interest rate. The best way to estimate debt is to think about growth, the trend in asset turnover (sales divided by assets), and any changes in the trend in financial leverage. With respect to interest rates, you can estimate that by observing changes in the yield curve.

Tax Rate   Finally, to estimate the tax rate, you should consider the current tax rate and any political action that is being considered. In addition, you must weigh the trend in where goods are produced and sold (due to the difference in tax rates in different jurisdictions).

The Discount Rate   After calculating the cash flows, you need a discount rate. Since we are discounting cash flows that belong to the equityholder, we need to use the cost of equity for the overall market. Using the capital asset pricing model, you need the risk free rate and the risk premium. (Remember that the market beta is 1, so that doesn't need to be estimated.) Below, we discuss the issue with the risk free rate and risk premium.

A bond is considered to be risk free if it has no **default risk** and no **interest rate risk** (including the elimination of **reinvestment rate risk**). To eliminate the default risk, we look at Treasury bonds. Eliminating interest rate risk implies that we should use a short-term instrument (such as a Treasury bill) or a zero-coupon bond (which eliminates reinvestment rate risk). But the risk-free rate that should be used should also match the duration of the cash flows that are being discounted. As a result, most practitioners use the yield on the 10-year U.S. Treasury bond as the risk-free rate.

Finally, we need the risk premium. This is often a great source of confusion, and it is important that you understand this controversy. Imagine a situation in which the market has been rallying and has had several years of great performance. If you measured the risk premium historically, it would be very high (because stocks had outperformed bonds by a significant amount). If you discounted cash flows at high rates, stocks would appear to be significantly overvalued. But, if you thought about how much compensation you expect to earn for owning stocks going forward, the amount would likely be small. Of course, if you discounted cash flows at low rates, this would justify high valuations. So, what is the right thing to do? In other words, is the risk premium large or small?

The key is to understand terminology.[1] If you are thinking about the *historic risk premium*, this measures past performance, and the number will be high. If you are thinking about the *expected risk premium* (the amount of extra compensation that you expect to receive, given that you are buying at an expensive time), the number will be low. But what you are really looking for is the *required risk premium*—the compensation that will justify the risk

---

[1]For a detailed discussion of this topic, see Doole, Renelleau, and Sevilla (2009), citing Fernández (2006).

Exhibit 9.18 Implied Risk Premium

You know that the S&P 500 is at 2,000. Next year's EPS = $128. The ROE is 16.6%. The risk-free rate is 2.5%. Expected growth = 6%. What risk premium is being implied by the market?

$P = DIV_1/(r - g)$

Let $x = (r - g)$

$2{,}000 = (\$128)(.6386)/(x)$

$2{,}000 = \$81.73/x$

$x = .041$

So $r - g = 4.1\%$

We know $g = 6\%$, so $r = 10.1\%$

$r = rf + B(rp)$

$r = 2.5\% + 1(7.6\%)$

Risk Premium = **7.6%**

Need to Calculate the Payout Ratio

G = ROE × Plowback (plowback represented as b)

$6\% = 16.6\% \times b$

B = 36.14%

So, you can pay out 63.86%

Note: This is a relatively high risk premium; it could be that the market is pricing in that profitability will decrease in the future.

---

of investing in equities as opposed to investing in risk-free bonds. It is likely that your required risk premium will be relatively high due to the risk of investing when valuations are extended.

There is one final way to think about the risk premium, and that is the *implied risk premium.* This is the risk premium that is implied by current market prices. In other words, you must make some assumptions and back out the risk premium that is priced into stock prices. An example of how to do this can be seen in Exhibit 9.18. In this exhibit, we start with a constant growth dividend discount model. In the numerator, we use earnings and the payout ratio (obtained again by using the idea that growth equals the return on equity multiplied by the retention rate). In the denominator, we estimate growth and then back out the discount rate that is required in order to justify current stock prices. Once we have the discount rate, we know the risk-free rate, so we can calculate the implied risk premium. Interestingly, the average risk premium priced into U.S. stocks over the past 25 years is in the area of 4 percent.

Finally, it is important to recognize that it is incredibly difficult to build this estimated value for the overall market. Probably the easiest thing to do is to estimate the long-term growth rate of sales. But estimating operating margins, interest rates, changes in the trend of capital structure, tax rate, and ROE is very difficult to do with a meaningful sense of confidence. This is why you see more investors look at the overall market by using a multiplier approach. That is what we'll look at next

9.3.2 Multiplier Approach

In addition to using a discounted cash flow approach to value the market, an analyst can also use a multiplier approach. In fact, this is more common. In this chapter, as well as Chapter 8, we have already examined most of what you need to know in order to use the multiplier approach. But here we review the key concepts.

P/E Multiple In order to use a price–earnings multiple approach, an analyst needs to estimate two variables: the *earnings per share* and the *multiplier*. Earlier in this chapter, where we examined using the FCFE methodology, we saw how to estimate the earnings per share. In Chapter 8, we studied fundamental multiples. In order to estimate the multiplier, an analyst needs to estimate:

1. The growth rate
2. The cost of capital
3. The return on equity

Earlier in this chapter, we examined the growth rate and the cost of capital. In Chapter 8, we examined the return on equity. You can see all of this applied in Exhibit 9.19. Again, we are using a constant growth model and trying to calculate how much free cash flow will be available for shareholders.

In addition to calculating the fundamental multiple, as shown in Exhibit 9.19, there is another approach to deciding on the multiple. An analyst can start with the current multiple and estimate how the variables are going to change. Of course, if you take this approach, you are effectively saying that the starting multiple is the correct starting point.

While we have studied the basics before, there are a few other ideas that an analyst should be aware of:

1. Multiples tend to be very volatile and are sensitive to small changes in the spread between k and g.
2. When using the constant growth model, you should be using long-term estimates.
3. The free cash flow to the equity represents the amount of cash that can be paid out. It doesn't matter if the cash is or is not paid out.
4. It is always beneficial to calculate a range of multiples, assuming that your inputs may not be correct.

This same approach can be used with other multiples, such as price–book, price–sales, and price–cash flow.

9.3.3 Shiller P/E Ratio

Another methodology for valuing the overall market is the Shiller P/E ratio, also known as the cyclically adjusted price–earnings (CAPE) multiple. (Note that while Robert Shiller has

---

Exhibit 9.19 Using a P/E Multiple to Estimate the Value of the S&P 500

Use the following information to estimate the value of the S&P 500:

- Next Year's Estimated EPS = $132
- Earnings Growth Rate = 4%
- 10-Year UST = 2.5%
- Equity Risk Premium = 6%
- ROE = 11%

_____SOLUTION:_____

Cost of Equity = 2.5% + 6% = 8.5% (Remember: beta of the market = 1)

G = ROE × RR, so 4% = 11% × RR   RR = 36%, so payout = 64%

Estimated Value of S&P 500 = $132(.64)/(8.5% − 4%) = 1,877

Since the S&P 500 is trading above 2,000, this would imply that stocks are overvalued.

Of course, if the risk premium is lowered to 5%, the estimated value would be well over 2,000 and the market would be seen as fairly valued.

popularized this approach, the original idea is attributed to Benjamin Graham.) In this approach, the numerator is the same: It is the value of the S&P 500. The denominator, however, is different. Instead of simply using the past year's earnings (or next year's earnings, if you are using a forward multiple), you are using the average earnings for the past 10 years. You do not simply average the past 10 years of earnings. You inflate past earnings to the current year (and then average them). Past earnings are brought to today's dollars ("inflating" them) by using the inflation rate for each year that has passed since their occurrence.

The idea of the CAPE multiple is that one-year's earnings are highly volatile and probably mean-reverting. By averaging several years, we are able to get a better feel for the earnings power of a company or an overall market. We are reducing the impact of years that really amount to earnings anomalies—particularly during a peak or recession. In addition, it is important to realize that, just as with all other valuation methodologies, this is not a timing mechanism. Most investors believe that valuation matters in the long term but not necessarily in the short term. As you will see in Exhibit 9.20, this valuation measure seems to have some power to forecast the long-time horizon. In other words, if you invest when the Shiller P/E ratio is at a high level (the market is expensive), your long-term returns are low.

The Shiller P/E ratio is interesting, but it is not without critics. This methodology can be wrong for long periods of time. Again, this is similar to all other valuation methodologies. This approach also ignores factors that may impact multiples, most notably interest rates. Certainly, investors expect higher multiples when rates are low. In addition, the risk premium certainly changes over time, and that impacts multiples. Finally, accounting standards change over time. As a result, it is difficult to compare earnings and multiples over time.

Asness (2012) probably provides the best take on how to use this approach. He suggests that this model should be given some small weight when trading on tactical allocation. It is probably most valuable in helping to set reasonable expectations. In other words, if you enter the market when prices are high, you are unlikely to get very high returns over the long term.

9.3.4 Macrovaluation and Microvaluation of World Markets

As mentioned earlier, we have used the S&P 500 to study the valuation of the market, and we have also used economic indicators focused on the U.S. economy. Obviously, each market is different—for example, economies are growing at different rates, different economic data may exist for each country, risks are different, accounting standards are different, and different types of companies may inhabit the public markets.

Exhibit 9.20 Shiller P/E Ratio and 10-Year Performance

Results for S&P 500 from Different Starting Shiller P/Es 1926–2012

Starting P/E		Avg. Real 10 Yr Return	Worst Real 10 Yr Return	Best Real 10 Yr Return	Standard Deviation
Low	High				
5.2	9.6	10.3%	4.8%	17.5%	2.5%
9.6	10.8	10.4%	3.8%	17.0%	3.5%
10.8	11.9	10.4%	2.8%	15.1%	3.3%
11.9	13.8	9.1%	1.2%	14.3%	3.8%
13.8	15.7	8.0%	−0.9%	15.1%	4.6%
15.7	17.3	5.6%	−2.3%	15.1%	5.0%
17.3	18.9	5.3%	−3.9%	13.8%	5.1%
18.9	21.1	3.9%	−3.2%	9.9%	3.9%
21.1	**25.1**	**0.9%**	**−4.4%**	**8.3%**	**3.8%**
25.1	46.1	0.5%	−6.1%	6.3%	3.6%

Source: "An Old Friend: The Stock Market's Shiller P/E," by Clifford S. Asness (2012).

Given the fact that differences exist, it is crucial to keep in mind three important factors. First, the basic valuation model and concepts apply globally. Specifically, value is still based on the discounted value of future cash flows whether you are in New York, London, Moscow, or Beijing. Also, the ultimate decision is still based on the relationship between estimated intrinsic value and the market price.

Second, while the models and concepts are the same, the input values can and will vary dramatically across countries, which means values will differ and opportunities will differ; for example, when stocks appear overpriced in the United States, they may be undervalued in Japan or Australia, which provides an opportunity to adjust your global asset allocations.

Third, the valuation of nondomestic markets will almost certainly be more onerous because of several additional variables or constraints that must be considered. The most obvious is that you must estimate a value in the local currency and also estimate potential changes in the value of the foreign currency relative to the U.S. dollar. The difficulty of estimating these changes or attempting to hedge this currency risk (if it is possible) becomes an added risk factor discussed in Chapter 1—exchange rate risk.

It is also necessary to consider country or political risk, which can be very significant in many countries. This risk generally *cannot* be hedged away. Notably, until recently, investors in U.S. stocks generally did not think about this risk even during elections. Until the 2016 presidential election, the only change had been terrorist risk since the September 11, 2001, event—a risk that is present around the world. The point is, country risk must be evaluated and estimated when investing.

As a result of the two added risk factors—exchange rate risk and country risk—the required rate of return on foreign securities will generally be higher than for domestic stock. Notably, these added risks can be offset by higher growth expectations, such as in China and India. As always, it is the individual who identifies the best estimates of these critical valuation variables (k and g) who will be the superior analyst.

Another added burden relates to different accounting conventions in alternative countries. Therefore, you must understand how firms in a country account for various items and how this impacts cash flows and so forth. The good news is that the adoption of International Financial Reporting Standards (IFRS) in many countries should substantially reduce this problem. (For a recent discussion of the SEC's plans for incorporating IFRS into the U.S. reporting system, see Securities and Exchange Commission, 2011.)

In summary, as money management becomes more global and industry analysis requires global constituents, you will need to evaluate stock markets and industries around the globe, and you should keep these added factors in mind.

9.4 Introduction to Industry Analysis: Why Industry Analysis Matters

The second step of top-down analysis is industry analysis. Once an analyst has decided to make an allocation to a particular market, she must decide which industries are worthy of investment. Our discussion of industry analysis will start with a brief argument that industry analysis is worthwhile. After making that argument, we will examine four considerations in analyzing an industry:

1. How the business cycle impacts industries
2. Structural issues that impact industries
3. The life cycle of the industry
4. The competitive forces within an industry (Porter analysis)

After discussing these issues, we will briefly address discounted cash flow analysis and relative valuation. We will not repeat what we have already discussed. Rather, we will mention a few differences when implementing these valuation techniques for an industry.

Exhibit 9.21

10 Best Performing Industries		10 Worst Performing Industries	
Industry Name	Percent Change (over time selected)	Industry Name	Percent Change (over time selected)
WSJ U.S. Audio/Video Equipment Inde…	3,006.94%	WSJ U.S. Alcoholic Beverages/Drinks…	−99.80%
WSJ U.S. Home Electronics/Appliance…	1,161.57%	WSJ U.S. Beverages/Drinks Index	−99.75%
WSJ U.S. Mining Support Services In…	1,114.20%	WSJ U.S. Food/Beverages/Tobacco Ind…	−98.19%
WSJ U.S. Shell companies Index	948.48%	Dow Jones U.S. Coal Index	−71.33%
WSJ U.S. Alternative Fuel Index	322.04%	Dow Jones U.S. Nonferrous Metals In…	−71.11%
WSJ U.S. Watch/Clocks/Parts Index	237.17%	WSJ U.S. Consumer Goods Index	−59.48%
WSJ U.S. Passenger Transport, Other…	156.04%	WSJ U.S. Semiconductors Index	−58.08%
WSJ U.S. Banking/Credit Index	130.42%	Dow Jones U.S. Mining Index	−51.33%
WSJ U.S. Tourism Index	88.33%	Dow Jones U.S. Platinum & Precious…	−49.23%
WSJ U.S. Fishing Index	83.97%	Dow Jones U.S. Industrial Metals In…	−48.35%

Source: Marketwatch.com one-year returns March 31, 2017.

Let us start by simply making the case that industry analysis matters. The simplest argument is that profit-seeking firms have determined that it matters, as evidenced by the fact that investment firms often assign analysts to cover a particular industry. At the very least, this serves as evidence of the belief that specific industry knowledge helps to create value.

Of course, the question is why analysts are assigned to cover specific industries. In other words, why is this valuable? Most importantly, there is significant variance in the performance among industries during any given time period. See Exhibit 9.21 for an example of this. In that exhibit, you will see a sub-industry that increased 3,000 percent and another one that decreased by almost 50 percent. Hand-in-hand with the idea of performance variation is the belief that different industries have different levels of risk and different risk factors. By studying a specific industry, the goal is to isolate unique investment opportunities and to identify trends early in their life so that the investor can find an advantageous risk–return trade-off.

Of course, not all investment firms are set up to allow for industry specialization among analysts. One argument against industry analysis is that industry performance does not seem to persist. In other words, an industry's good performance or its outperformance versus the overall market does not predict future performance or outperformance. In addition, the anti-specialization forces will argue that there is wide dispersion among companies within an industry. (The proponents of industry analysis will respond by arguing that this is why the third step of the top-down approach is needed.) After identifying an industry, an analyst must decide which stocks should be selected. But it should be easier to find a superior company in a good industry than in a flawed industry.

Interestingly, while returns vary among industries and even for stocks within an industry, and risk varies among industries, it does seem that an industry's overall risk can be relatively stable over time. This indicates that a deep understanding of this risk can be particularly worthwhile.

Finally, it's important to realize that the same argument that can be made for a macroanalysis of the overall market can be made for an industry. Security markets reflect the economy, even though markets may move ahead of the economy. The same macroeconomic factors (for example, interest rates, growth, earnings) that drive the market can also impact an industry. In addition, we will see additional forces that impact an industry (such as structural impacts, the life cycle of the industry, and the competitive forces within an industry).

9.5 INDUSTRY ANALYSIS

Armed with the idea that industry analysis matters, let's move on to the macroanalysis of industries. Again, we will examine four components:

1. Cyclical impacts
2. Structural impacts
3. The life cycle of the industry
4. The competitive forces within an industry (Porter analysis)

9.5.1 The Business Cycle and Industry Sectors

The **business cycle** refers to the period of time from which an economy's output of goods and services peaks, contracts (in a recession), recovers from the prior expansion to reach the prior peak (recovery), and then grows further (expansion). Different industries tend to perform well or poorly in different parts of the business cycle.

Some investors try to engage in **sector rotation**, where they monitor economic trends and attempt to move their investments from one sector (or industry within a sector) to another sector (or industry) as economic trends change. Obviously, this is easier said than done.

Below, we will describe some common beliefs about sectors. But it is very important to realize that every business cycle is different, and industries constantly change. As a result, it just cannot be so easy that we formulaically follow a path of simply rotating from one sector to another. With that said, it's important to have the institutional knowledge of what investors typically expect.

We will start by describing some common beliefs about sectors:

- Toward the end of a recession, *financial stocks* often recover first as their earnings rise in anticipation of improvement of loan performance and the generation of new loans (as the economy starts to recover). Of course, this did not happen in 2009, and it serves as great evidence that every cycle is different. Aside from basic banks, brokerage firms turn up because there is a belief that the assets under management will increase and that trading will increase with recovery. Investment banks rally because more mergers and acquisitions occur during a recovery and expansion.
- *Consumer durable goods* do well as the economy recovers. These are companies that produce cars, computers, refrigerators, lawn tractors, and other long-lasting items. They rally with consumer confidence. In addition, the Fed has typically lowered interest rates during the recession, and the low rates allow consumers to finance their purchases. Of course, consumers will only make these large purchases if they are confident about their employment situation (which will improve during the recovery). Many of these purchases also result from the uptick in home purchases that follows the lower interest rates.
- *Capital goods* tend to do well as the economy moves past recovery and into expansion. Companies see their profits recover and demand pick up again. As a result, companies plan to meet increased demand and also attempt to become more productive. The capital goods producers include heavy equipment manufacturers, machine tool makers, and airplane manufacturers. It's important to realize that this was another sector that didn't recover as quickly as expected after the financial crisis. Companies were reluctant to spend on more machinery because they were pessimistic about demand.
- *Cyclical companies* tend to move in anticipation of the business cycle, turning up in anticipation of recovery and turning down at signs of economic weakness. Cyclical companies often have a high degree of operating leverage. This means that these companies have a large amount of fixed costs. As sales increase, earnings can increase at a startling rate. Of course, when sales drop, earnings can also decrease at a startling rate.

- *Consumer staples* tend to outperform during an economic slowdown. These are goods and services that consumers purchase regardless of the state of the economy. For example, mainstream grocery stores, soft drinks, and tobacco all tend to experience relatively stable sales. Investors value that stability in times of uncertainty.

As mentioned earlier, sector rotation is difficult. Each business cycle is different, and industries change. In addition, we don't always know (in real time) exactly where we are in the business cycle.

Since using the business cycle to engage in sector rotation is difficult, an alternative approach to sector rotation is to simply ask what variables drive performance. Again, this is not an exhaustive list, but it may help gain some basic institutional knowledge:

- High inflation often benefits basic *material stocks*. High inflation represents demand outstripping supply. It usually occurs during periods of high growth and extreme optimism. This creates demand for basic materials and pushes these stocks higher.
- High inflation often means more uncertainty about future prices and costs. Companies that have *high operating leverage* may do well, as their costs are fixed. In addition, companies that have a significant amount of *fixed-rate debt* may also do well.
- High interest rates (which tend to be highly correlated with high inflation) tend to hurt *housing* and *construction*. Obviously, they are helped by low interest rates.
- A weak dollar tends to help U.S. *exporters* and U.S. companies with *significant foreign operations*. These companies, operating overseas, can translate their earnings back into higher earnings (because the foreign currency has appreciated).
- A weak dollar also helps domestic companies that face competition from imports. The weak dollar raises the cost of imports and makes the local companies more competitive.
- Low growth tends to help the few *technology companies* that can deliver high growth (in a low-growth environment). Demand for cutting-edge technology can have greater resistance to slow growth.
- High energy costs tend to hurt *transportation companies*.

9.5.2 Structural Economic Changes Impact the Industry (Noncyclical Factors)

As an analyst studies an industry, he has to search for major changes in the economy and how it functions. Four categories of changes are demographics, lifestyles, technology, and politics and regulation.

Demographics **Demographics** are crucial to both the demand side (consumption) and the supply side (particularly labor). When we examine demographics, we look at population growth, age distribution, changing ethnic mix, the geographical distribution of people, and changes in income distribution.

Recently, Cohn and Caumont (2016) provided some examples of key demographic trends that could impact U.S. industries, including:

- Americans are more racially and ethnically diverse. By 2055, the United States will not have a single racial majority. In addition, approximately 14 percent of the country's population is foreign born.
- Asia is replacing Latin America (including Mexico) as the largest source of new immigrants.
- The electorate has become the most diverse ever.
- There are more millennials (young adults born after 1980) than baby boomers (born 1946–1964).
- The percentage of Americans living in the middle class is shrinking. The percentage of adults who are classified as upper income or lower income has increased.
- The entire world population is aging.

Lifestyles **Lifestyles** deal with how people live, work, form households, consume, enjoy leisure, and educate themselves. Examples of important lifestyle issues include divorce rates, dual-career families, population shifts from cities, and computer-based education and entertainment.

Again, Cohn and Caumont (2016) have identified some recent changes in lifestyles, including:

- Single mothers are the primary provider in approximately 25 percent of all households.
- Only 69 percent of children live with two parents.
- The share of American adults who have never been married is at record highs.
- Divorce, remarriage, and cohabitation are on the rise.
- A growing number of Americans have no religious affiliation.
- On a worldwide basis, Christians remain the largest religious group, but Islam will grow faster than any other major religion because Muslims are younger and have more children than any other religious group. By 2050, Muslims will nearly equal the number of Christians (although this will not be the case in the United States).
- A growing percentage of Americans are leaving college with student debt.

Technology **Technology** can affect numerous industry factors, including a product or service and how it is produced and delivered. Obviously, new technology can completely change an industry. Simple examples include the impact of Amazon on the retail industry or the impact of Uber on the local transportation business. Changes in technologies have spurred capital spending in technological equipment as a way for firms to gain competitive advantages. Technology has also allowed outsourcing and has impacted the ability to work from home while also widening exposure to markets.

Examples of technological changes include automation/artificial intelligence, big data, autonomous cars, mobile payments, 3D printing, drones, and smart home technology.

Politics and Regulation **Politics and regulations** can have a tremendous impact on industries. Political change reflects social values, and the result is that today's social trend may be tomorrow's law, regulation, or tax. Examples of laws and regulations that impact industries include the minimum wage, the Affordable Care Act, NAFTA, FDA regulation, and the Keystone Pipeline.

9.5.3 Industry Life Cycle

When predicting industry sales and profitability, insight can be gained from viewing the industry over time and dividing its development into stages similar to those that humans progress through. As you analyze an industry, it is important to ask how long the industry will remain in a particular stage of the life cycle. Exhibit 9.22 shows the five stages of the life cycle, the analogy to the human life cycle, and events that occur during each phase of the life cycle. A graphical depiction of the industry life cycle can be seen in Exhibit 9.23.

9.5.4 Industry Competition

Industry competition has a tremendous impact on profitability. Michael Porter's concept of *competitive strategy* is described as the search by a firm for a favorable competitive position in an industry. To create a profitable competitive strategy, a firm must first examine the basic competitive structure of its industry because the potential profitability of a firm is heavily influenced by the profitability of its industry.

Porter believes that the competitive environment of an industry (the intensity of competition among the firms in that industry) determines the ability of the firms to sustain above-average rates of return on invested capital. As shown in Exhibit 9.24, he suggests that five

Exhibit 9.22 Events During the Life Cycle

Life Cycle	Human	Important Takeaways
Pioneering Development	Birth	Market for product or service is small Modest sales growth Negative profits (major development costs)
Rapid Accelerating Growth	Adolescence	Market develops and becomes substantial Sales grow at increasing rate Limited competition (high margins] Profits explode
Mature Growth	Adulthood	Sales growth no longer accelerating Growth may be higher than GDP High margins attract competitors Profit margins begin to decline
Stabilization/Market Maturity	Middle Age	Growth declines to GDP growth rate Profit margins vary by industry Controlling costs becomes more important Competition and low margins brings returns on capital down to cost of capital
Deceleration of Growth/Decline	Old Age	Sales growth declines due to shifts in demand or substitutes Profit margins squeezed Low profits or losses Low returns on capital

Exhibit 9.23 Life Cycle of an Industry

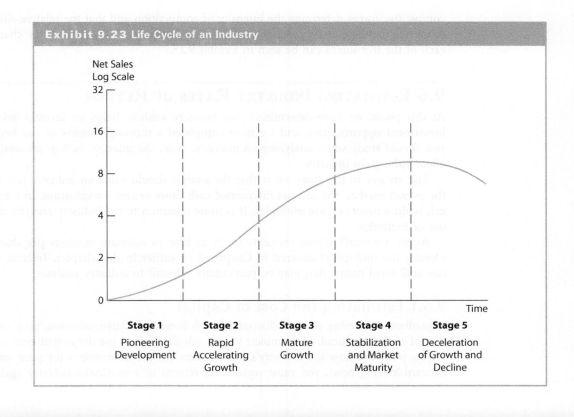

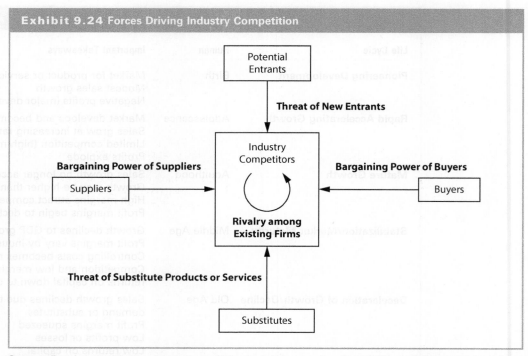

Exhibit 9.24 Forces Driving Industry Competition

competitive forces determine the intensity of competition and that the relative effect of each of these five factors can vary dramatically among industries. Some of the key characteristics of each of the five forces can be seen in Exhibit 9.25.

9.6 ESTIMATING INDUSTRY RATES OF RETURN

At this point, we have determined that industry analysis helps an investor select profitable investment opportunities, and we have completed a thorough review of the key factors that you should study when analyzing an industry. Now, the question is *how an analyst should go about valuing an industry.*

The answer to this question is that the analyst should value an industry just as she values the overall market. She can use discounted cash flows or relative valuation. In other words, she can build a model or use multiples. It is more common to see industry analysis done with the use of multiples.

Again, we won't repeat concepts (such as how to estimate earnings per share or how to identify the multiplier) covered in Chapter 8 or earlier in this chapter. Instead, we'll make a few additional points that may be particularly relevant to industry analysis.

9.6.1 Estimating the Cost of Capital

Regardless of whether you use discounted cash flows or relative valuation, your estimate of the cost of capital is crucial. The simplest way to calculate k is to use the capital asset pricing model. If you want to know the industry's historic beta (to get information for your estimate of the forward-looking beta), you must regress the returns of a particular industry against a market

---

Exhibit 9.25 Characteristics of Each of the Five Forces

Rivalry among Existing Firms   **Increases if:**

Equal size companies
Slow growth
High fixed costs
Exit barriers

Threat of New Entrants   **Increases with low barriers to entry:**

High profit margins (low prices vs. costs)
Small financial resources needed to compete
No economies of scale
Distribution channel that is easy to build
Low switching costs
No government licensing requirements
Unlimited access to materials

Threat of Substitute Products   **Increases if:**

Large profit potential
Substitutes that are close in price or function More
commodity-like product or service

Bargaining Power of Buyers   **Increases if:**
Buyer accounts for large percentage of your sales
Buyer has knowledge of seller's profits
Product accounts for large percentage of buyer's cost
Many sellers

Bargaining Power of Suppliers   **Increases if:**

Fewer suppliers
Seller industry is more concentrated than buyer
industry
Supplier supplies critical input
Supplier sells to several industries
Few substitutes

---

index (such as the S&P 500). This is much easier to do now as many industries have very liquid exchange-traded funds (ETFs). If these don't exist, you can put together a composite index by calculating individual stock betas and weighting them to calculate an industry beta.

If you decide to not use the capital asset pricing model, you can estimate the cost of capital by considering all of the significant risks: business risk, financial risk, liquidity risk, exchange rate risk, and country risk. The factors that determine each of these risks are described in Exhibit 9.26.

Exhibit 9.26 Factors Driving Equity Risk

Business Risk	Sales volatility Operating leverage
Financial Risk	Use of debt Be careful when a firm has significant operating leases
Liquidity Risk	Number of shareholders Number of shares and market value of shares Number of shares traded Institutional interest in shares
Exchange Rate Risk	Uncertainty of earnings due to changes in exchange Rate How are sales distributed across countries
Country Risk	Amount of foreign sales and production Stability of political system/economy

9.6.2 Sales Growth Estimates

At the industry level, sales growth estimates can be aided by knowledge of three approaches:

1. **Time series analysis:** Overlaying industry sales with the business cycle and estimating changes
2. **Input/output analysis:** Identifying suppliers and customers; looking for long-run sales outlooks for supplies and customers
3. **Industry–economy relationship:** Identifying the economic variable that has the most significant influence on industry demand

9.6.3 Other Considerations

The following are a few ideas specific to industry analysis:

- It can be very difficult to apply regression and time-series analysis. As analysts, we're always looking forward. This type of quantitative analysis may ignore certain unique factors, such as price wars, labor negotiations, building plans, foreign competition, or changes in competitive structure.
- The industry tax rate may be vastly different from the overall market tax rate.
- Relative valuation often involves comparing the industry multiple to the market multiple. It is particularly important to study the relationship between the underlying fundamental variables of the industry and the market. As always, try to understand how they're changing and how you expect them to change in the future.
- Always understand the underlying fundamentals that drive a multiple. The price–earnings ratio is driven by the growth of the earnings, the riskiness of the earnings, and the ROE (which impacts the plowback). The price–book ratio should reflect a firm's ability to earn a high return on equity. The price–cash flows ratio is driven by the growth rate and the stability of those cash flows. The price–sales multiple is driven by the profit margin, sales growth, and the risk of the sales growth.
- It's always important to ask yourself why the market views an industry in a particular way. What is the market missing? What will change?

9.7 GLOBAL INDUSTRY ANALYSIS

Because so many firms are active in foreign markets and because the proportion of foreign sales is growing for many firms, it is necessary to consider the effects of foreign firms on industry returns. To see why this is so, consider the auto industry. Besides Ford and General Motors, the auto industry for a global investor includes numerous firms from Japan, Germany, Italy, and Korea, among others. Thus, we must extend our analysis to include global factors.

While space does not permit an example, the following major factors need to be analyzed in this context:

- The macroenvironment in the major producing and consuming countries for an industry. This will impact demand from these countries.
- An overall analysis of the significant global companies in the industry, the products they produce, and how successful they are in terms of the DuPont three-component analysis.
- Regarding company analysis, what are the accounting differences by country, and how do these differences impact the relative valuation ratios? Because of accounting differences, it is typically not possible to directly compare many ratios across countries but only to examine them over time within a country. This problem should be reduced as the use of international accounting standards grows.

- What is the effect of currency exchange rate trends for the major countries? Significant currency changes can affect the demand for U.S. products from specific countries and also impact costs, assuming that U.S. firms receive inputs from foreign firms.

Global industry analysis is growing in importance, as documented by Cavaglia, Brightman, and Aked (2000). Specifically, prior research showed that country factors dominated industry factors in terms of explaining equity returns, but the Cavaglia et al. study presented evidence that industry factors have been growing in importance and currently dominate country factors. In summary, it is important to carry out industry analysis on a global scale.

9.8 COMPANY ANALYSIS

At this point, an analyst has made two decisions about her investment in equity markets. First, after analyzing the economy and stock markets for several countries, she has decided what percentage of her portfolio should be invested in common stocks and her allocation to alternative countries (that is, overweight, market weight, or underweight). Second, after analyzing various industries, she has identified the ones that appear to offer above-average risk-adjusted performance over her investment horizon. The final questions in the fundamental analysis procedure are: (1) Which are the best companies within these desirable industries?; (2) What is the intrinsic value of the firm's stock?; and (3) How does the intrinsic value compare with the market value?

In this section of our top-down approach, we will examine:

1. The difference between company analysis and stock valuation
2. Company analysis
3. Valuation

Again, we will make an effort not to repeat the same valuation material that you have read in Chapter 8 or earlier in this chapter (about analyzing an industry). When we discuss valuation, we will simply discuss a few additional ideas. But again, it's crucial that you understand the valuation concepts from Chapter 8.

It is important to remember that the common stocks of good companies are not necessarily good investments. An analyst must understand a company's strengths and weaknesses, calculate the intrinsic value of the company, and then compare that intrinsic value to the market value. The stock of a great company can be priced so high that it should not be acquired. The stock of a less impressive company may be priced so cheaply that it should be purchased. This issue is particularly important with growth stocks, which we will address next.

9.8.1 Growth Companies and Growth Stocks

Practitioners commonly describe **growth companies** as those that consistently grow sales and earnings at a rate that is faster than the overall economy. In contrast, financial theorists such as Solomon (1963) and Miller and Modigliani (1961) define a growth company as a firm with the management ability and the opportunities to consistently make investments that yield rates of return greater than the firm's required rate of return. For example, if a firm has a weighted average cost of capital of 10 percent and can earn 15 percent on investments, the firm's sales and earnings should grow faster than those of firms facing similar risk and the overall economy. One other requirement is that these firms should be retaining a significant amount of their earnings in order to invest in these high-return opportunities.

Growth stocks are *not* necessarily shares in growth companies. A **growth stock** is a stock with a higher expected rate of return than other stocks in the market with similar risk characteristics. The stock achieves this expected superior risk-adjusted rate of return because the market has undervalued it compared to other stocks. In the language introduced in Chapter 8 and used subsequently, an *undervalued stock* has an intrinsic value (estimated by alternative valuation models) that is greater than its current market price. Although the stock market adjusts stock prices relatively quickly and accurately to reflect new information, available information is not always perfect or complete. Therefore, imperfect or incomplete information may cause a given stock to be undervalued or overvalued at a point in time.[2]

If the stock is undervalued, its price should eventually increase to reflect its true fundamental (intrinsic) value when the correct information becomes available. During this period of price adjustment, the stock's realized return will exceed the required return for a stock with its risk, and during this period of adjustment, it will be a growth stock. Growth stocks are not necessarily limited to growth companies. A future growth stock can be the stock of any type of company; the stock need only be undervalued by the market.

The fact is, if investors recognize a growth company and discount its future earnings stream properly, the current market price of the growth company's stock will reflect its future earnings stream. Those who acquire the stock of a growth company at this correct market price will receive a rate of return consistent with the risk of the stock, even when the superior earnings growth is attained. In many instances, overeager investors tend to overestimate the expected growth rate of earnings and cash flows for the growth company and, therefore, inflate the price of a growth company's stock. Investors who pay the inflated stock price (compared to its true intrinsic value) will earn a rate of return *below* the risk-adjusted required rate of return, despite the fact that the growth company experiences above-average growth of sales and earnings. Studies by Solt and Statman (1989), Shefrin and Statman (1995), Clayman (1987), and Chan and Lakonishok (2004) have examined the stock price performance for samples of growth companies and found that their stocks performed poorly—that is, the stocks of growth companies have generally *not* been growth stocks.

9.8.2 Defensive Companies and Stocks

Defensive companies are those whose future earnings are likely to withstand an economic downturn. One would expect them to have relatively low business risk and not excessive financial risk. Typical examples are fast food chains and grocery stores—firms that supply basic consumer necessities.

There are two closely related concepts of a **defensive stock**. First, a defensive stock's rate of return is not expected to decline during an overall market decline, or it is expected to decline less than the overall market. Second, our CAPM discussion indicated that an asset's relevant risk is its covariance with the market portfolio of risky assets—that is, an asset's systematic risk. A stock with low or negative systematic risk (a small positive or negative beta) may be considered a defensive stock according to this theory because its returns are unlikely to be harmed significantly in a bear market.

9.8.3 Cyclical Companies and Stocks

A **cyclical company's** sales and earnings will be heavily influenced by aggregate business activity. Examples would be firms in the steel, auto, or heavy machinery industries. Such companies will outperform other firms during economic expansions and seriously underperform during economic contractions. This volatile earnings pattern is typically a function of the firm's business risk (including sales volatility and operating leverage) and can be compounded by financial risk.

---

[2]An analyst is more likely to find such stocks outside the top tier of companies that are scrutinized by numerous analysts; in other words, look for neglected stocks. Recent research also suggests that opportunities may exist in complex stocks that are difficult to understand.

A **cyclical stock** will experience changes in its rates of return greater than changes in overall market rates of return. In terms of the CAPM, these would be stocks that have high betas. The stock of a cyclical company, however, is not necessarily cyclical. A cyclical stock is the stock of any company that has returns that are more volatile than the overall market—that is, high-beta stocks that have high correlation with the aggregate market and greater volatility. To be clear, a cyclical company does not have to be a cyclical stock, but it is likely to be a cyclical stock.

9.8.4 Speculative Companies and Stocks

A **speculative company** is one whose assets involve great risk but that also has a possibility of great gain. A good example of a speculative firm is one involved in oil exploration.

A **speculative stock** possesses a high probability of low or negative rates of return and a low probability of normal or high rates of return. Specifically, a speculative stock is one that is overpriced, leading to a high probability that during the future period when the market adjusts the stock price to its true value, it will experience either low or possibly negative rates of return. Such an expectation might be the case for an excellent growth company whose stock is selling at an extremely high price/earnings ratio—that is, it is substantially *overvalued*.

9.8.5 Value versus Growth Investing

Some analysts also divide stocks into growth stocks and value stocks. As we have discussed, growth stocks are companies that will experience above-average risk-adjusted rates of return because the stocks are undervalued. If the analyst does a good job in identifying such companies, investors in these stocks will reap the benefits of seeing their stock prices rise after other investors identify their earnings growth potential. **Value stocks** are those that appear to be undervalued for reasons other than earnings growth potential. Value stocks are usually identified by analysts as having low price–earnings or price–book value ratios. Notably, in these comparisons between growth and value stocks, the specification of a growth stock is *not* consistent with our preceding discussion. In these discussions, a growth stock is generally specified as a stock of a company that is experiencing rapid growth of sales and earnings (for example, Google, Apple, Facebook). As a result of this company performance, the stock typically has a high P/E and price–book value ratio. Unfortunately, the specification does not consider the critical comparison we advocate between intrinsic value and market price. Therefore, these specifications will not be used in subsequent discussions of valuation.

The major point of this section is that you must initially examine a company in detail to determine its fundamental characteristics and subsequently use this information to derive an estimate of the intrinsic value of its stock. When you compare this intrinsic value of the stock to its current market price, you decide whether you should acquire it—that is, will it be a growth stock that provides a rate of return greater than what is consistent with its risk?

9.9 Connecting Industry Analysis to Company Analysis

As we have moved from the second step of top-down analysis (industry analysis) to the third step (company analysis), it's important to realize that this analysis should all be linked together. In step 2, you identified industries that would be aided by the economic trends that you expect as well as the structural influences (such as social trends, technology, political issues, regulatory issues, demographic changes, lifestyle issues, etc.). Now, in step 3, you must search for companies that will be favorably influenced by these economic and structural factors. In addition to being favorably influenced by these factors, the company must have an attractive valuation.

As we move on to company analysis, we will look at two tools: the firm's competitive strategy (as described by Michael Porter) and SWOT analysis. After that, we will discuss valuation and some models to help think about growth.

9.9.1 Firm Competitive Strategies

In describing competition within industries, we discussed the five competitive forces that could affect the competitive structure and profit potential of an industry. After you have determined the competitive structure of an industry, you should attempt to identify the specific competitive strategy employed by each firm in the industry.

A company's competitive strategy can either be *defensive* or *offensive*. A **defensive competitive strategy** involves positioning the firm to deflect the effect of the competitive forces in the industry. Examples may include investing in fixed assets and technology to lower production costs or creating a strong brand image with increased advertising expenditures.

An **offensive competitive strategy** is one in which the firm attempts to use its strengths to affect the competitive forces in the industry. For example, Walmart used its buying power to obtain price concessions from its suppliers. This cost advantage, coupled with a superior delivery system to its stores, allowed Walmart to grow against larger competitors and eventually become the leading U.S. retailer.

As an investor, you must understand the alternative competitive strategies available, determine each firm's strategy, judge whether the firm's strategy is reasonable for its industry, and, finally, evaluate how successful the firm is in implementing its strategy.

In the following sections, we discuss analyzing a firm's competitive position and strategy. The analyst must decide whether the firm's management is correctly positioning the firm to take advantage of industry and economic conditions. The analyst's opinion about management's decisions should ultimately be reflected in the analyst's estimates of the firm's growth of cash flow and earnings.

Porter (1980a, 1985) suggests two major competitive strategies: low-cost leadership and differentiation. These two competitive strategies dictate how a firm has decided to cope with the five competitive conditions that define an industry's environment. The strategies available and the ways of implementing them differ within each industry.

Low-Cost Strategy The firm that pursues the low-cost strategy is determined to become *the* low-cost producer and, hence, the cost leader in its industry. Cost advantages vary by industry and might include economies of scale, proprietary technology, or preferential access to raw materials. In order to benefit from cost leadership, the firm must command prices near the industry average, which means it must differentiate itself about as well as other firms. If the firm discounts price too much, it could erode the superior rates of return available because of its low cost. During the past decade, Walmart was considered a low-cost source. The firm achieved this by volume purchasing of merchandise and lower-cost operations. As a result, the firm had lower prices but still enjoyed higher profit margins and returns on capital than many of its competitors.

Differentiation Strategy With the differentiation strategy, a firm seeks to identify itself as unique in its industry in an area that is important to buyers. Again, the possibilities for differentiation vary widely by industry. A company can attempt to differentiate itself based on its distribution system (selling in stores, by mail order, over the Internet, or door to door) or some unique marketing approach. A firm employing the differentiation strategy will enjoy above-average rates of return only if the price premium attributable to its differentiation exceeds the extra cost of being unique. Therefore, when you analyze a firm using this strategy, you must determine whether the differentiating factor is truly unique, whether it is sustainable, what is its cost, and whether the price premium derived from the unique strategy is greater than its cost (is the firm experiencing above-average rates of return?).

Focusing a Strategy   Whichever strategy it selects, a firm must determine where it will focus this strategy. Specifically, a firm must select segments in the industry and tailor its strategy to serve these specific groups. For example, a low-cost strategy would typically exploit cost advantages for certain segments of the industry, such as being the low-cost producer for the expensive segment of the market. Similarly, a differentiation focus would target the special needs of buyers in specific segments. For example, in the athletic shoe market, companies have attempted to develop shoes for unique sport segments, such as tennis, basketball, aerobics, or walkers and hikers, rather than offering only shoes for runners. Athletic shoe firms thought that participants in these alternative activities needed shoes with characteristics different from those desired by joggers. Equally important, they believed that these athletes would be willing to pay a premium for these special shoes. Again, you must ascertain if special possibilities exist, if they are being served by another firm, and if they can be priced to generate abnormal returns to the firm. Exhibit 9.27 details some of Porter's ideas for the skills, resources, and company organizational requirements needed to successfully develop a cost leadership or a differentiation strategy.

Given this knowledge, the analyst must determine which strategy the firm is pursuing and its success. Also, can the strategy be sustained? Further, the analyst should evaluate a firm's competitive strategy over time because strategies need to change as an industry evolves; different strategies work during different phases of an industry's life cycle. For example, differentiation strategies may work for firms in an industry during the early growth stages. Subsequently, when the industry is in the mature stage, firms may try to lower their costs and become a cost leader.

Through the analysis process, the analyst identifies what the company does well, what it doesn't do well, and where the firm is vulnerable to the five competitive forces. Some call this process developing a company's "story." This evaluation enables the analyst to determine the outlook and risks facing the firm. In summary, understanding the industry's competitive forces and the firm's strategy for dealing with this competitive environment is the key to

Exhibit 9.27 Skills, Resources, and Organizational Requirements Needed to Successfully Apply Cost Leadership and Differentiation Strategies

Generic Strategy	Commonly Required Skills and Resources	Common Organizational Requirements
Overall cost leadership	Sustained capital investment and access to capital Process engineering skills Intense supervision of labor Products designed for ease in manufacture Low-cost distribution system	Tight cost control Frequent, detailed control reports Structured organization and responsibilities Incentives based on meeting strict quantitative targets
Differentiation	Strong marketing abilities Product engineering Creative flair Strong capability in basic research Corporate reputation for quality or technological leadership Long tradition in the industry or unique combination of skills drawn from other businesses Strong cooperation from channels	Strong coordination among functions in R&D, product development and marketing Subjective measurement and incentives instead of quantitative measures Amenities to attract highly skilled labor, scientists, or creative people

Source: Adapted from *Competitive Strategy: Techniques for Analyzing Industries and Competitors* by Michael E. Porter.

understanding how a company makes money and deriving an accurate and unique estimate of the firm's long-run cash flows and its risks.

9.9.2 SWOT Analysis

Another framework for examining and understanding a firm's competitive position and its strategy is a company SWOT analysis.

SWOT analysis involves an examination of a firm's strengths, weaknesses, opportunities, and threats. It should help you evaluate a firm's strategies to exploit its competitive advantages or defend against its weaknesses. Strengths and weaknesses involve identifying the firm's *internal* abilities or lack thereof. Opportunities and threats include *external* situations, such as competitive forces, discovery and development of new technologies, government regulations, and domestic and international economic trends.

The *strengths* of a company give the firm a comparative advantage in the marketplace. Perceived strengths can include good customer service, high-quality products, strong brand image, customer loyalty, innovative R&D, market leadership, or strong financial resources. To remain strengths, they must continue to be developed, maintained, and defended through prudent capital investment policies.

Weaknesses result when competitors have potentially exploitable advantages over the firm. Once weaknesses are identified, the firm can select strategies to mitigate or correct the weaknesses. For example, a firm that is only a domestic producer in a global market can make investments that will allow it to export or produce its product overseas. Another example would be a firm with poor financial resources that would form joint ventures with financially stronger firms.

Opportunities, or environmental factors that favor the firm, can include a growing market for the firm's products (domestic and international), shrinking competition, favorable exchange rate shifts, identification of new markets or products, and new marketing or distribution channels (for example, the Web).

Threats are environmental factors that can hinder the firm in achieving its goals. Examples include a slowing domestic economy (or sluggish overseas economies for exporters), additional government regulation, an increase in industry competition, threats of entry, buyers or suppliers seeking to increase their bargaining power, and new technology that can make the industry's product obsolete. By recognizing and understanding opportunities and threats, an investor can make informed decisions about how the firm can exploit opportunities and mitigate threats.

9.10 CALCULATING INTRINSIC VALUE

After analyzing the company from qualitative and quantitative perspectives, the analyst must calculate the stock's intrinsic value. Of course, the methodologies are the same as those discussed in Chapter 8. Most analysts will create a discounted cash flow model (using either dividends, FCFE, or FCFF) and will also use relative valuation.

9.10.1 Some Additional Insights on Valuation—For Individual Companies

As our goal is not to repeat what we have already discussed in Chapter 8 as well as earlier in this chapter, here are a few additional concepts to consider with respect to your valuation:

- Blindly using historic growth rates or margins is incorrect. Historic rates are interesting and help us understand a company. But your model must be forward-looking. You must identify what you believe will change and why. Your story (or pitch) should be consistent with your model.

- When examining the sales of a company, always study how the sales mix is changing. This will also impact margins.
- The growth rate of a company is going to be influenced by where the industry is in its life cycle, structural changes, industry competition, and economic trends. Obviously, it's crucial to examine the customers (buyers) and try to understand how their demand will change and why.
- When looking at historic growth, always try to distinguish between *organic growth* and acquired growth. Increasing revenue by selling more units or charging a higher price is organic. If sales increase because the company bought more sales (that is, bought another company), that had a cost and is not indicative of future growth.
- Remember what your cost of equity represents. It represents the return that the investor requires in order to receive fair compensation for his investment. Historical risk premia are interesting but not definitive. When estimating the risk premium, you are asking how much return is needed in order to justify the risk of investing in stocks rather than a risk-free asset. Likewise, historical betas are helpful. But you are trying to figure out if the company's business risk or financial risk has changed. You can think of the business risk as being represented by the unlevered beta. Financial risk is impacted by the amount of debt a company has.
- When estimating the profit margin of a specific company, be sure to understand the competitive strategy (low cost or differentiation). Study the firm's internal performance. Study the firm's relationship with its industry.
- Realize that it is important for you to have quarterly estimates for the next year. This way, when the company announces its earnings, you will know whether your analysis is correct.
- When doing relative valuation, compare the company to its historic multiple, competitors in the industry, an overall industry multiple, and the market multiple. Always ask whether the multiple is trading at a discount or premium, how that should change, and what will make that change. Always compare the company's underlying fundamentals (such as profit margin, ROE, growth, and cost of capital) to those of the peer companies (or industry or market).

9.10.2 Analyzing Growth Companies

As discussed earlier, growth companies have the ability to continue to reinvest significant amounts of capital and earn rates of return that are greater than their cost of capital. In order for a stock to be a growth stock, where the price compounds at a rate of return greater than required by the market, the growth company must be undervalued. In reality, there are few successful growth companies, and only some of them will be undervalued such that they will be growth stocks. Those few true growth companies that are growth stocks will create tremendous wealth.

In many of the models that financial analysts build, the underlying assumption is that growth will be constant. While this may be an adequate assumption for the market, an industry, or a mature company, it is questionable for a true growth company. The opportunity to earn a return on capital that is greater than the cost of capital is usually a temporary state. Other companies will see these excess returns, enter the industry, increase the supply, and eventually drive product prices down until the rates of return on capital invested are consistent with the risk involved.

Returns that are greater than the cost of capital are referred to as *pure profits* (or *excess profits*). Excess profits are possible only in a noncompetitive market. Since we know that some firms have derived excess profits for a number of years, these excess returns are probably not due to temporary disequilibrium but rather are due to some noncompetitive factors that exist, such as patents or copyrights that provide monopoly rights to a process or a manuscript for a specified period. During this period of protection from competition, the firm can derive above-normal returns. Also, a firm could possess strategies, discussed by Porter, that provide added profits (for example, a unique marketing technique or other organizational characteristics). Finally, there may be significant barriers to entry, such as capital requirements.

In a purely competitive economy, true growth companies would not exist because competition would not allow continuing excess return investments. The fact is that our economy is not perfectly competitive (although this typically is the best model to use) because a number of frictions restrict competition. Therefore, it is possible for temporary true growth companies to exist in our economy. The significant question is *how long can these growth companies earn these excess profits?*

The key to truly understanding a growth company is to think about the definition that we've used: A growth company is a company that has the opportunity to reinvest significant amounts of capital at rates of return that are higher than the firm's cost of capital. This means that the analyst must consider three issues:

1. The amount of capital invested in growth investments
2. The relative rate of return earned on funds retained
3. The time period for these growth companies

It is important to realize that if you use the constant growth model and you are modeling a company that is earning more than its cost of capital, you are making some strong assumptions:

- Earnings and dividends are growing at a constant rate.
- The firm is investing larger and larger dollar amounts in projects that generate returns greater than their cost of capital.
- The firm can do this for an infinite amount of time.

These are very aggressive assumptions and must be questioned by an analyst. A valuable approach is to examine how long the superior growth can continue or, alternatively, the extent and length of the superior growth. In order to do this, we will use the **growth duration model**.

The purpose of the growth duration model is to help you evaluate the high P/E ratio for the stock of a growth company by relating its P/E ratio to the firm's rate of growth and duration of growth. As discussed earlier, a stock's P/E ratio is a function of three factors:

1. The firm's expected rate of growth of earnings per share
2. The stock's required rate of return
3. The firm's dividend payout ratio

The growth duration model is based on two assumptions:

1. Equal risk between the firms that you're analyzing
2. No significant differences in the payout ratios

In effect, we have told you that three factors (growth, risk, and payout) determine P/E ratios and if you assume that two of them are the same (between the firms that you're comparing), only the third factor matters. This factor that matters (growth) must consider both the rate of growth and how long this growth can be sustained (the duration of the expected growth rate). Remember that no company can grow indefinitely at a rate substantially above normal; a large company would become a huge portion of the economy.

If we assume that a growth stock and a nongrowth stock have similar risk and dividend payouts, the market should value the two stocks in direct proportion to their earnings in year T (that is, they will have the same P/E ratio), where T is the time when the growth company will begin to grow at the same rate as the market (that is, the nongrowth stock). Put another way, T is the number of years the growth stock is expected to grow at the high rate. In other words, current prices should be in direct proportion to the expected future earnings ratio that will prevail in year T.

This relationship implies that the P/E ratios of the two stocks are in direct proportion to the ratio of composite growth rates raised to the Tth power. Allowing g to represent the high-growth company and a to represent the market or slower growth company, you can solve for T by using the following equation:

9.1
$$\ln\left(\frac{P_g(0)/E_g(0)}{P_a(0)/E_a(0)}\right) \approx T \, \ln\left(\frac{(1 + G_g + D_g)}{(1 + G_a + D_a)}\right)$$

The growth duration model answers the question of *how long the earnings of the growth stock must grow at this expected high rate, relative to the nongrowth stock, to justify its prevailing above-average P/E ratio.* You must then determine whether this implied growth duration estimate is reasonable in terms of the company's potential.

Consider an example. The stock of a high-growth company is selling for $43 a share with expected per-share earnings of $2.38 (that is, its future earnings multiple is about 18 times). The expected EPS growth rate for the company is estimated to be about 10 percent a year, and its dividend yield has been 1 percent and is expected to remain at this level. In contrast, the S&P 500 Index has a future P/E ratio of about 16, an average dividend yield of 2 percent, and an expected growth rate of 6 percent. Therefore, the comparison is as follows:

	S&P 500	High-Growth Co.
P/E ratio	16.00	18.00
Expected growth rate	0.06	0.10
Dividend yield	0.02	0.01

Inserting these values into Equation 9.1 yields the following:

$$\ln\left(\frac{18.00}{16.00}\right) = T \, \ln\left(\frac{(1 + 0.10 + 0.01)}{(1 + 0.06 + 0.02)}\right)$$

$$\ln(1.125) = T \, \ln\left(\frac{1.11}{1.08}\right)$$

$$\ln(1.125) = T \, \ln(1.028)$$

$$T = \frac{\ln(1.125)}{\ln(1.028)} \times (\text{log base } 10)$$

$$= \frac{0.0511482}{0.01199311}$$

$$= 4.26 \text{ years}$$

These results indicate that the market is implicitly assuming that High-Growth Co. can continue to grow at this composite rate (11 percent) for about 4.3 more years, after which it is assumed that the company will grow at the same total rate (8 percent) as the aggregate market (that is, the S&P 500). *You must now ask whether this superior growth rate can be sustained by the company for at least this period.* If the implied growth duration is greater than you believe is reasonable, you would advise against buying the company's stock. If the implied duration is below your expectations (for example, you believe the company can sustain this growth rate differential for six or seven years), you would recommend buying the stock.

It is important to recognize that you can compare a company to a market series (such as the S&P 500 or a sector) as we just did or you can directly compare two firms. For an inter-company analysis, you should compare firms in the same industry because the equal risk assumptions of this model are probably more reasonable. An example of this type of analysis can be seen in Exhibit 9.28.

Exhibit 9.28 Growth Duration Analysis

Consider the following example from the computer software industry:

	Company A	Company B
P/E ratios	31.00	25.00
Expected annual growth rate	0.1700	0.1200
Dividend yield	0.0100	0.0150
Growth rate plus dividend yield	0.1800	0.1350
Estimate of T^a	5.53 years	

[a]Readers should check to see that they get the same answer.

Source: These results imply that the market expects Company A to grow at an annual total rate of 18 percent for about 5.5 years, after which it will grow at Company B's rate of 13.5 percent. If you believe the implied duration for growth at 18 percent is too long, you will prefer Company B; if you believe the estimated duration is reasonable or low, you will recommend Company A.

An Alternative Use of T Instead of solving for T and then deciding whether the figure derived is reasonable, you can use this formulation to compute a reasonable P/E ratio for a security relative to the aggregate market (or another stock) if the implicit assumptions are reasonable for the stock involved. Again, using High-Growth Co. from our earlier example, you estimate its expected composite growth to be 11 percent a year compared to the expected total market growth of 8 percent.

Further, you believe that High-Growth Co. can continue to grow at this above-normal rate for about five years. Using Equation 9.1, this becomes:

$$\ln(X) = 5 \times \ln \frac{1.11}{1.08}$$
$$= 5 \times \ln(1.028)$$
$$= 5 \times 0.011993$$
$$= 0.059965$$

To determine what the P/E ratio for High-Growth Co. should be given these assumptions, you must derive the antilog of 0.059965, which is approximately 1.148. Therefore, assuming the market multiple is 16, the earnings multiple for High-Growth Co. should be about 1.148 times the market P/E ratio, or about 18.4 times.

Alternatively, if you estimate that High-Growth Co. can maintain a lower growth rate of 9 percent for a longer period (for example, 10 years), you would derive the antilog for 0.07961 (10 × 0.007961). The answer is 1.203, which implies a P/E ratio of about 19.22 times for the stock. Notably, both of these estimates are above the current forward P/E for High-Growth Co. of 18 times.

Factors to Consider When using the growth duration technique, remember the following factors: First, the technique assumes equal risk, which may be acceptable when comparing two large, well-established firms in the same industry (for example, Merck and Pfizer) to each other. It is also reasonable to compare a large conglomerate, like General Electric, with a beta close to 1.0, to the market. In the case of a company with a beta below 1.0, the result is conservative (if comparing it to the market), meaning that the duration would be slightly lower for the company than the estimated years. It is probably *not* a valid assumption when comparing a small growth company with a high beta to the aggregate market. In this case, the growth duration generated would be an underestimate of what is required.

Second, which growth estimate should be used? We prefer to use the *expected* rate of growth based on the factors that affect g (that is, the retention rate and the components of ROE).

Third, the growth duration technique assumes that stocks with higher P/E ratios have the higher growth rates. However, there are cases in which the stock with the higher P/E ratio does not have a higher expected growth rate or the stock with a higher expected growth rate has a lower P/E ratio. Either of the cases generates a useless negative-growth duration value. Inconsistency between the expected growth and the P/E ratio could be attributed to one of four factors:

1. There is a major difference in the risk involved (the low P/E high-growth company is much riskier).
2. Growth rate estimates are inaccurate. You may want to reexamine your growth rate estimate for the firm with the higher P/E ratio; that is, could it be higher, or should the growth estimate for the low P/E stock be lower?
3. The stock with a low P/E ratio relative to its expected growth rate is undervalued. (Before you accept this possibility, consider the first two factors.)
4. The stock with a high P/E and a low expected growth rate is overvalued. (Before this is accepted, consider both its risk and your estimated growth rate.)

The growth duration concept is valid, *given the assumptions made*, and can help you evaluate growth investments. It is not universally valid, though, because its answers are only as good as the data inputs (expected growth rates) and the applicability of the assumptions. The answer must be evaluated based on the analyst's knowledge.

The technique probably is most useful for helping spot overvalued growth companies with very high multiples. In such a case, the technique will highlight that the company must continue to grow at some very high rate for an extended period of time to justify its high P/E ratio (for example, duration of 15 to 20 years). Also, it can help you decide between two growth companies in the same industry by comparing each to the market, to the industry, or directly to each other. Such a comparison has provided interesting insights wherein the new firms in an industry were growing faster than the large competitor, but their P/E ratios were *substantially* higher and implied that these new firms had to maintain this large growth rate superiority for over *10 years* to justify the much higher P/E ratio.

9.11 Lessons from Some Legends

We'll close this chapter with some lessons from three investing legends, Peter Lynch, Warren Buffett, and Howard Marks.

9.11.1 Some Lessons from Lynch

Peter Lynch, the former portfolio manager of Fidelity Investments' highly successful Magellan Fund, looks for the following favorable attributes when he analyzes firms:

1. The firm's product is not faddish; it is one that consumers will continue to purchase over time.
2. The company has a *sustainable* comparative competitive advantage over its rivals.
3. The firm's industry or product has market stability. Therefore, it has little need to innovate or create product improvements or fear that it may lose a technological advantage. Market stability means less potential for entry.
4. The firm can benefit from cost reductions (for example, a computer manufacturer that uses technology provided by suppliers to deliver a faster and less-expensive product).
5. The firm buys back its shares or management purchases shares, which indicates that its insiders are putting their money into the firm.

9.11.2 Tenets of Warren Buffett

The following tenets of Warren Buffet are from Robert Hagstrom (2001). The parenthetical comments are based on discussions in Hagstrom's book and Berkshire Hathaway annual report letters.

Business Tenets

- Is the business simple and understandable?
  (Knowing this makes it easier to estimate future cash flows with a high degree of confidence.)
- Does the business have a consistent operating history?
  (Again, cash flow estimates can be made with more confidence.)
- Does the business have favorable long-term prospects?
  (Does the business have a franchise product or service that is needed or desired, has no close substitute, and is not regulated? This implies that the firm has pricing flexibility.)

Management Tenets

- Is management rational?
  (Is the allocation of capital to projects that provide returns above the cost of capital? If not, does management pay capital to stockholders through dividends or the repurchase of stock?)
- Is management candid with its shareholders?
  (Does management tell owners everything you would want to know?)
- Does management resist the institutional imperative?
  (Does management not attempt to imitate the behavior of other managers?)

Financial Tenets

- Focus on return on equity, not earnings per share.
  (Look for strong ROE with little or no debt.)
- Calculate owner earnings.
  (Owner earnings are basically equal to free cash flow after capital expenditures.)
- Look for a company with relatively high sustainable profit margins for its industry.
- Make sure the company has created at least one dollar of market value for every dollar retained.

Market Tenets

- What is the intrinsic value of the business?
  (Value is equal to future free cash flows discounted at a government bond rate. Using this low discount rate is considered appropriate because Warren Buffett is very confident of his cash flow estimates due to his deep understanding of the business based on extensive analysis. This confidence implies low risk.)
- Can the business be purchased at a significant discount to its fundamental intrinsic value?

9.11.3 Tenets of Howard Marks

Howard Marks is the co-chair of Oaktree Capital Management. Marks is a well-known investor who also periodically writes memos that are a must-read for investors. He recently used many of the ideas from his memos to write the book *The Most Important Thing*. The following list contains some of the many important ideas from his book:

- To succeed, you must engage in second-level thinking. You must understand how the price reflects consensus opinion, what are the range of possible outcomes, how your view is different, and the likelihood that you're right.
- An investor must have an accurate sense of intrinsic value. Without this, all you have is hope.

- There are times when some investors are forced to sell (for example, due to margin calls). This is when other investors have true opportunities.
- Risk is the risk of permanent capital loss. This risk is greatest when prices are high relative to intrinsic value.
- Risk is greatest when other investors say that there is no risk.
- Almost everything in business is cyclical. The great opportunities occur when other investors forget this.
- The market is a pendulum that swings between fear and greed. A great investor recognizes this. But it's difficult to know how far it swings.
- The way to avoid trouble is to avoid greed, fear, envy, dismissal of logic, following the herd, and ego.
- To be a successful investor, you must understand intrinsic value, be able to act when prices deviate from value, understand past cycles, understand how bad behavior can hurt you, and remember the idea that when things seem too good to be true, they are.
- A great investor must be able to buy when other investors are despondent and selling.
- You should keep a list of potential investments. This list should include estimates of intrinsic value, the margin of safety, and an understanding of risk.
- You must exercise patience. Again, the key to doing this is to have a strong sense of value.
- You have to understand what you know and what you don't know.
- You should always have context about where we are right now. In other words, are investors optimistic or pessimistic? How are valuations?

SUMMARY

In earlier chapters, we emphasized the importance of analyzing the aggregate markets before any industry or company analysis. You must assess the economic and security market outlooks and their implications regarding the bond, stock, and cash components of your portfolio. Then you proceed to consider the best industry or company.

- Two techniques are used to make the market decision: (1) the macroeconomic technique, which is based on the relationship between the aggregate economy and the stock market; and (2) the microeconomic technique, which determines future market values by applying the two valuation approaches discussed in Chapter 8 to the aggregate stock market.
- The economy and the stock market have a strong, consistent relationship, but the stock market generally turns before the economy does. Therefore, the best macroeconomic projection techniques use economic series that likewise lead the economy, and possibly the stock market. The Conference Board leading indicator series (which includes stock prices) is one possibility. We also discussed sentiment indicators and the importance of interest rates. More specifically, with respect to interest rates, we discussed three indicators that

many market participants watch: the yield curve, the real federal funds rate, and the bond risk premium.

- Our microanalysis of the U.S. equity market considered both approaches to equity valuation—the present value of cash flow techniques and the relative valuation ratio techniques. The relative valuation approach included a discussion of how to estimate factors such as growth, operating margins, interest, and taxes. We also introduced the Shiller P/E ratio (also known as the cyclically adjusted price–earnings ratio).
- After studying the aggregate market, the next step in the top-down approach is to study industries. Several studies examined industry performance and risk and found wide dispersion in the performance of alternative industries during specified time periods, implying that industry analysis can help identify superior investments. They also showed inconsistent industry performance over time, implying that looking at only past performance of an industry has little value in projecting future performance. Also, the performance by firms within industries typically is not very consistent, so you must analyze the individual companies in an industry following the industry analysis.

- The analysis of industry risk indicated wide dispersion in the measures of risk for different industries but strong consistency in the risk measure over time for individual industries. These results imply that risk analysis and measurement are useful and necessary. The good news is that past risk measures are useful when estimating future risk.
- Specific to industry analysis, we examined how the business cycle impacts industries, structural issues that impact industries, the life cycle of the industry, and the competitive forces within an industry (often referred to as Porter analysis).
- In the final step of the top-down approach, we focused on company analysis. We discussed the idea that a growth company may not be a growth stock as well as the difference between defensive stocks and cyclical stocks. We also examined the strategic alternatives available to firms in response

to different competitive pressures in their industries. The alternative corporate strategies include low-cost leadership or differentiation, which if properly implemented, should help the company attain above-average rates of return. In addition, we discussed applying SWOT analysis to a firm. This strategic analysis of the firm's goals, objectives, and strategy should put you in a position to properly estimate the intrinsic value of the stock.

- This chapter does not repeat the valuation lessons from Chapter 8. Rather, we discuss additional insights concerning the valuation process with respect to growth rates, margins, and the cost of capital. In addition, we provide insight as to a growth duration model in order to help the analyst understand how long a company must grow at a high rate in order to justify an above-market multiple.

SUGGESTED READINGS

Dorsey, Pat. *The Little Book That Builds Wealth*. New Jersey: Wiley, 2008.

English, James. *Applied Equity Analysis*. New York: McGraw-Hill, 2001.

Grant, Robert M. *Contemporary Strategy Analysis*, 9th ed. West Sussex, MA: Wiley, 2016.

Palepu, Krishna, Paul Healy, and Victor Bernard. *Business Analysis and Valuation*, 5th ed. Cincinnati, OH: South-Western Publishing, 2012.

Porter, Michael E. *Competitive Strategy*. New York: Simon & Schuster, 1998.

Porter, Michael E. "How to Conduct an Industry Analysis." In *The Financial Analysts Handbook*, 2nd ed., ed. Sumner N. Levine. Homewood, IL: Dow Jones-Irwin, 1988.

Valentine, James. *Best Practices for Equity Research Analysts*. New York: McGraw-Hill, 2011.

Watson, David. *Business Models*. Hampshire, UK: Harriman-House, 2005.

QUESTIONS

1. If stock returns are related to economic growth, why can't you simply track the GDP data that has been released in order to make investment decisions?
2. Why does the real federal funds rate matter to stock prices? How do low rates impact stock prices?
3. Why does an inverted yield curve serve as a predictor of a recession?
4. What four factors impact operating margins for the overall market?
5. When calculating the cost of equity, should you use a historic risk premium, an expected risk premium, or a required risk premium?
6. When performing industry analysis, what are the four categories of structural (noncyclical) economic changes that an analyst should review?
7. What are the five forces that determine the competitive structure of an industry?
8. What's the difference between a growth company and a growth stock? What is a defensive stock? A cyclical stock?
9. What is the difference between a low cost strategy and a differentiation strategy?
10. What are the assumptions that underlie the growth duration model?

PROBLEMS

1. Use the St. Louis Fed database ("FRED") to calculate the real GDP growth rate from the end of 2010 through 2017 and the nominal GDP growth rate for the different time periods. Also, use that information to calculate the inflation rate that explains the difference between the nominal and real growth rate. Calculate this inflation rate on an annual basis.

2. There has been considerable growth in recent years in the use of economic analysis in investment management. Further significant expansion may lie ahead as financial analysts develop greater skills in economic analysis and these analyses are integrated more into the investment decision-making process. The following questions address the use of economic analysis in the investment decision-making process:
   a. (1) Differentiate among leading, lagging, and coincident indicators of economic activity and give an example of each.
      (2) Indicate whether the leading indicators are useful for achieving above-average investment results. Briefly justify your conclusion.
   b. Interest rate projections are used in investment management for a variety of purposes. Identify three significant reasons interest rate forecasts may be important in reaching investment conclusions.
   c. Assume that you are a fundamental research analyst following the automobile industry for a large brokerage firm. Identify and briefly explain the relevance of three major economic time series, economic indicators, or economic data items that would be significant to automotive industry and company research.

3. Currently, the dividend–payout ratio (D/E) for the aggregate market is 55 percent, the required return (k) is 9 percent, and the expected growth rate for dividends (g) is 4 percent.
   a. Compute the current earnings multiplier.
   b. You expect the D/E payout ratio to decline to 40 percent, but you assume there will be no other changes. What will be the P/E?

4. As an analyst for Charlotte and Chelle Capital, you are forecasting the market P/E ratio using the dividend discount model. Because the economy has been expanding for nine years, you expect the dividend–payout ratio will be at its low of 40 percent and that long-term government bond rates will rise to 7 percent. Because investors are becoming less risk averse, the equity risk premium will decline to 3 percent. As a result, investors will require a 10 percent return, and the return on equity will be 12 percent.
   a. What is the expected growth rate?
   b. What is your expectation of the market P/E ratio?
   c. What will be the value for the market index if the expectation is for earnings per share of $115?

5. You are given the following estimated per share data related to the S&P 500 Index for the year 2018:

Sales	$1,950.00
Depreciation	98.00
Interest expense	58.00

You are also informed that the estimated operating profit (EBIT) margin is 12 percent and the tax rate is 32 percent.
   a. Compute the estimated EPS for 2018.
   b. Assume that a member of the research committee for your firm feels that it is important to consider a range of operating profit margin (OPM) estimates. Therefore, you

are asked to derive both optimistic and pessimistic EPS estimates using 11 and 13 percent for the OPM and holding everything else constant.

6. Given the three EPS estimates in the Problem 5, you are also given the following estimates related to the market earnings multiple:

	Pessimistic	Consensus	Optimistic
D/E	0.65	0.55	0.45
Nominal RFR	0.10	0.09	0.08
Risk premium	0.05	0.04	0.03
ROE	0.11	0.13	0.15

a. Based on the three EPS and P/E estimates, compute the high, low, and consensus intrinsic market value for the S&P 500 Index in 2018.

b. Assuming that the S&P 500 Index at the beginning of the year was priced at 2,050, compute your estimated rate of return under the three scenarios from part (a). Assuming that your required rate of return is equal to the consensus, how would you weight the S&P 500 Index in your global portfolio?

7. You are analyzing the U.S. equity market based upon the S&P 500 Index and using the present value of free cash flow to equity technique. Your inputs are as follows:

Beginning FCFE: $80
k = 0.09

Growth Rate:

Years 1–3:	9%
4–6:	8%
7 and beyond:	7%

a. Assuming that the current value for the S&P 500 Index is 2,050, would you underweight, overweight, or market weight the U.S. equity market?

b. Assuming that there is a 1 percent increase in the rate of inflation, what would be the market's value, and how would you weight the U.S. market? State your assumptions.

8. Given Cara's beta of 1.75 and a risk-free rate of 7 percent, what is the expected rate of return for Cara, assuming:
a. a 15 percent market return?
b. a 10 percent market return?

9. What is the implied growth duration of Kayleigh Industries, given the following:

	S&P 500	Kayleigh Industries
P/E ratios	16.00	20.00
Expected growth	0.06	0.14
Dividend yield	0.04	0.02

10. Lauren Entertainment, Inc., has an 18 percent annual growth rate compared to the market rate of 8 percent. If the market multiple is 18, determine P/E ratios for Lauren Entertainment, Inc., assuming that its beta is 1.0 and you feel it can maintain its superior growth rate for the next:
a. 10 years.
b. 5 years.

11. You are given the following information about two computer software firms and the S&P 500 Index:

	Company A	Company B	S&P 500
P/E ratio	30.00	27.00	18.00
Expected annual growth rate	0.18	0.15	0.07
Dividend yield	0.00	0.01	0.02

   a. Compute the growth duration of each company stock relative to the S&P 500.
   b. Compute the growth duration of Company A relative to Company B.
   c. Given these growth durations, what determines your investment decision?

12. The constant-growth dividend discount model can be used both for the valuation of companies and for the estimation of the long-term total return of a stock.

$$\text{Assume}: \$20 = \text{price of a stock today}$$
$$8\% = \text{expected growth rate of dividends}$$
$$\$0.50 = \text{annual dividend one year forward}$$

   a. Using *only* the preceding data, compute the expected long-term total return on the stock using the constant-growth dividend discount model.
   b. Briefly discuss *three* disadvantages of the constant-growth dividend discount model in its application to investment analysis.
   c. Identify *three* alternative methods to the dividend discount model for the valuation of companies.

13. Assume that the 10-year U.S. Treasury is yielding 4.5 percent. Next year's earnings for the S&P 500 are expected to be $130. Use the Fed model to estimate the value of the S&P 500. If the S&P 500 is trading at 2,200, is the market overvalued or undervalued, and by how much?

14. Use the St. Louis Fed database (FRED) to create a chart for 2005–2017 that captures the risk premium. Create a chart that subtracts the 10-year U.S. Treasury yield from the yield on BBB-rated corporate bonds.

15. Use the St. Louis Fed database (FRED) to create a chart for 2005–2017 that captures the real federal funds rate. Create a chart that subtracts the PCE (chain-type price index) from the federal funds rate.

16. Go to the Richmond Federal Reserve Bank Website and find its charts for national economic data. Examine the yield curve. Is it normal, inverted, or flat?

CHAPTER **10**

The Practice of Fundamental Investing

After you read this chapter, you should be able to answer the following questions:

- What should an investor know about the management of an initial public offering?
- Why does underpricing occur in the IPO market?
- Why are there many more bookbuilt offerings as opposed to auctions?
- What does a sell-side analyst do? What does a buy-side analyst do?
- How do investors analyze the capital allocation of management? Where are the seven places that a company's management can allocate capital?
- When should a company pay a dividend as opposed to repurchase shares?
- What are the three main corporate governance issues that analysts think about?
- What are the key elements of a stock pitch?

In the prior two chapters, we studied equity valuation and the top-down approach to security analysis. These are necessary building blocks for the fundamental analyst. The purpose of this chapter is to go deeper. We will address five topics that traditional fundamental investors face on a regular basis and need to understand in order to effectively manage portfolios.

The chapter starts with a detailed discussion of **initial public offerings**. While most students may have some familiarity with the process of how a company "goes public," there is a significant amount for an investor to know. Among other things, we will describe the reasons to take a company public, the IPO process, the three main players, the difference between a bookbuilt offering and an auction, and how newly public stocks perform.

After studying IPOs, we will discuss the difference between the **buy-side** and the **sell-side**. You will already have much greater insight about the buy-side and the sell-side after thinking about the IPO process.

We will then discuss **capital allocation**, or the investment decisions that management makes. For many fundamental investors, this is the single most important factor in their security selection process. After that, we'll discuss **corporate governance** and management compensation, tools used to align the interests of shareholders and management and to ensure that they approach capital allocation in the right way. While many investors conduct rigorous analysis on capital allocation, our discussions with investors lead us to believe that corporate governance is an issue that they sometimes neglect. As long as there are no glaring problems, it is not at the top of most investors' lists of concern.

Finally, the chapter ends with a simple discussion of a **stock pitch**. We will take a short article from the financial news and show you how to turn it into a stock pitch. This will help you understand how market participants talk about stocks, and it will be particularly useful to anyone seeking employment in the asset management field.

10.1 Initial Public Offerings

IPOs and the process of going public were briefly discussed in Chapter 4. In this chapter, our goal is to deliver a much more detailed examination of the topic in order to equip the future analyst with a deeper understanding of the process and incentives.

10.1.1 Why Go Public

When a company **goes public**, it is selling shares to public investors. You might wonder why the owners of a private company would make this decision, which we will see can be very expensive. It turns out that there are many reasons—and an analyst needs to understand them.

First, the most obvious reason is that a company might need more capital in order to finance growth. In exchange for receiving shares of common stock, new investors contribute capital that can be used to acquire other companies, expand the existing business, conduct research and development, or retire debt (among other things). Of course, many companies go public even though they already have easy access to capital in private markets. As a result, there must be other factors that potentially encourage owners to take a company public.

It is very possible that the original investors and the management team would like **liquidity**. In other words, they want to be able to easily sell their shares at a fair value without having to search for buyers. While there is a cost to going public (which we'll discuss later), a public company should be worth more than the same company if it were private. This is due to the liquid nature of the shares. In other words, investors would pay more for stock that they can easily sell than they would pay for stock that can be sold only if the owner searches and finds a potential buyer.

Of course, being a public company has additional benefits. It's much easier to use public stock as currency to acquire other companies. In addition, publicly traded stock can be valuable compensation that is useful in attracting the best personnel. Being public also brings a certain level of prestige. Finally, publicly traded stock provides valuable signaling information concerning the health of the company, as well as how the market values decisions made by management.

Unfortunately, being a public company also has some disadvantages. Management has to answer to outside shareholders, and this has the potential to result in management having a shorter-term focus. Management will spend significant time meeting with analysts to discuss the company and earnings. Management may have to disclose more of its strategy than they prefer. There are also direct costs, such as those associated with Sarbanes-Oxley compliance; in fact, a 2016 survey by Protiviti found that the annual compliance costs were more than $1.1 million for the average public company.

10.1.2 The IPO Process

When a firm decides to go public, it hires an investment bank to lead the company through the process. The investment bank can do the offering as a **firm commitment** or a **best efforts offering**. In a firm commitment underwriting, the bank actually purchases the shares from the company and has the risk of reselling the shares to the ultimate investors. In effect, the investment bank has the risk that there will be no market for the offering, and the bank could be left with the shares. A best efforts offering, on the other hand, only commits the investment bank to use its best efforts to find buyers for the shares. If the bank cannot find buyers, the bank does not need to buy the remaining shares.

Based on the description of a firm commitment underwriting, it may sound as if the investment bank is taking a very significant risk in agreeing to this type of offering. In reality, this is not the case; the firm commitment is not as risky as it may appear. (The reason is that the actual contract to buy the shares is not signed until the night before the shares are distributed. At that point, the investment bank already has investors lined up to buy the shares.) With all that said, it is reasonable to assume that lower-quality companies may only convince a bank to do a best efforts offering. High-quality companies would only hire a bank that would agree to do a firm commitment offering. Throughout the rest of this chapter, our focus will be on firm commitment offerings.

The investment bank that is conducting a firm commitment offering is often referred to as the underwriter. The underwriter helps the firm hire additional professional staff, including a legal team and an audit team. These professional groups work together to prepare a **registration statement** (which is also known as SEC Form S-1 and commonly referred to simply as an **S-1**).

The most significant part of the S-1 is known as the **prospectus**. The prospectus is a document that helps potential investors understand the company. It contains information about the business, a discussion of past performance and management's plans, financial information, how the company will use the proceeds from the offering, the dividend policy, management compensation, and critical accounting issues.

The prospectus is available for potential investors to review as they decide whether to invest in the company. This **preliminary prospectus** is often referred to as a **red herring** because of the warning on its cover that is printed in red ink. In Exhibit 10.1, you can see the cover of the Snap, Inc. (ticker SNAP)prospectus, as well as the warning. The warning states that this prospectus is not an offer to sell the securities and that information contained in the prospectus may change. Most importantly, the IPO has not been priced yet, so there could be no agreement to buy or sell the stock. While a price will not be set at this point, there will be a range of prices that is being targeted. Normally, this is a $2 range, such as $18 to $20. There is no guarantee that the offering will happen within this price range. The actual price will be set later.

After filing the S-1, the underwriter takes the issuing company's management to the large money centers around the country (and possibly around the world) to meet with potential investors. This is referred to as the **road show**. During the road show, management makes presentations so that investors better understand the business. In general, these investors are institutions, such as mutual funds and hedge funds. The investment bankers receive **indications of interest** from the investors. An investor gives an indication of interest by telling the underwriter how many shares he or she is willing to purchase at particular prices. At the same time that the road show is occurring, the SEC is reviewing the registration statement and usually asking for additional information from the issuing firm (the company that is going public).

Normally, the SEC is eventually satisfied that the issuing company has fairly disclosed all necessary information, and the SEC deems the offering **effective**, which means the offering can be sold to the public. It's important to realize that this is not an indication that the SEC believes that the offering is an attractive value. Rather, the securities laws are often referred to as a **disclosure statute**, meaning that the SEC simply ensures that the issuing firm has disclosed all necessary information so that an investor can fairly make an informed decision.

Once the offering has been deemed effective, the investment bank and the issuing firm (the company that is going public) have a **pricing meeting**. Based on the feedback received during the road show, they set a price for the stock. At that point, the contract between the issuing

Exhibit 10.1 Snap Inc. Prospectus

UNITED STATES
SECURITIES AND EXCHANGE COMMISSION
WASHINGTON, D.C. 20549

FORM S-1
REGISTRATION STATEMENT
UNDER
THE SECURITIES ACT OF 1933

Snap Inc.
(Exact Name of Registrant as Specified in Its Charter)

Delaware	**7370**	**45-5452795**
(State or Other Jurisdiction of Incorporation or Organization)	(Primary Standard Industrial Classification Code Number)	(I.R.S. Employer Identification Number)

63 Market Street

Venice, California 90291

(310) 399-3339

(Address, Including Zip Code, and Telephone Number, Including
Area Code, of Registrant's Principal Executive Offices)

Evan Spiegel
Chief Executive Officer
Snap Inc.
63 Market Street
Venice, California 90291
(310) 399-3339
(Name, address, Including zip code, and telephone number,
including area code, of agent for service)

The information in this preliminary prospectus is not complete and may be changed. These securities may not be sold until the registration statement feild with the Securities and Exchange Commission is effective. This preliminary prospectus is not an offer to sell nor does it seek an offer to buy these securities in any jurisdiction where the offer or sale is not permitted.

PROSPECTUS (Subject to Completion)
Dated February 2, 2017

firm and the underwriter is signed. Pursuant to this contract, the underwriter is obligated to purchase the shares from the issuing company. The shares will be distributed to the investors the following day.

It's important to realize that a successful offering is **oversubscribed**. This means that there is demand for more shares than are available at that price. If there weren't enough demand, the bank would have advised the issuer to either lower the price or pull the offering (meaning that the offering would have been withdrawn, and the company would not have gone public). Most successful offerings are several times oversubscribed. Part of the reason for this is that investors know that most offerings are underpriced (as will be discussed later).

Earlier, we stated that a firm commitment offering sounds very risky, but in reality, the risk is not as great as it may appear. The risk is not great because the investment bank has indications of interest from potential investors and knows how much demand exists for the stock. So, when the bank agrees to buy the stock, the bank has a very short holding period before distributing the stock to the initial investors the following morning. Once the shares are distributed to the initial investors, trading in the secondary market can begin.

We also mentioned earlier that it is expensive to do an initial public offering. In addition to spending on legal fees, audit fees, exchange listing fees, and printing fees, management also spends a significant amount of time focused on the offering, as opposed to being focused on the company's business. Furthermore, a fee is paid to the underwriter. For most offerings in the United States, the fee is 7 percent of the offering proceeds. In other words, if shares are sold for $15 to investors, the bank receives $1.05 per share, and the issuing firm receives the remaining $13.95. This $1.05 is often referred to as the **gross spread**, or the **underwriting spread**.

10.1.3 Underpricing

After shares are distributed to investors, trading can begin in the secondary market. In other words, initial investors may sell their shares to other investors. Normally, but not always, the stock ends its first day of trading at a price that is higher than the IPO price. From 1980 to 2016, the average IPO in the United States closed 18 percent higher than the IPO price. In other words, if a stock went public at $15, on average, it closed at $17.70. This 18 percent gain is referred to as **underpricing**. Another way of thinking about this is that the market seems to value this stock at $17.70, so it was underpriced when it was sold for $15 in the IPO. This $2.70 per share is money that the issuing firm left on the table because we assume that the issuing firm could have sold the stock for somewhere closer to $17.70. Exhibit 10.2 shows IPO underpricing since 1980. This data is kept by Jay Ritter, a researcher at the University of Florida.

It is important to recognize a few important points about underpricing. First, the 18 percent average underpricing is skewed higher by the technology bubble in the late 1990s. Notice that the underpricing during 1999–2000 was above 50 percent! With that time frame excluded, the average underpricing would be closer to 12 to 15 percent. Second, you should repress your dream of simply investing in all IPOs and not working for a living. While that would certainly be nice, you will not have access to all IPOs. In fact, most individual investors will never have direct access to any IPOs that are worth participating in. These IPOs are allocated to institutional investors and to very high net worth individuals. As a general rule, if a broker calls you and invites you to participate in an IPO, this means that the institutions do not want the stock (and you shouldn't want it either!). You might think that even if you cannot participate in the initial public offering of $15, you could buy the stock during the first day (before it reaches the average price of $17.70 in the example we've been using). In reality, when the secondary market trading starts, the stock's first trade will often be at $17.70 (or possibly higher). In other words, the stock will not trade continuously from $15 up to $17.70. The primary investors (who received the IPO allocation) bought at $15 and will reap these gains. Finally, Ritter (2011) cites studies of the U.S., European, and Japanese markets to argue that the single best predictor of underpricing is whether the IPO offer price is above or below the midpoint of the initial price range in the preliminary prospectus.

It should strike you as strange that underpricing is so significant. Leaving 18 percent of the value on the table is a lot. Intuitively, think about working hard to build a company, hiring an

Exhibit 10.2 Underpricing from 1980 to 2016

| Year | Number of IPOs | Mean First-Day Return | | Aggregat Amount Left on the Table | Aggregate Proceeds |
		Equal-Weighted	Proceeds-Weighted		
1980	71	14.3%	20.0%	$0.18 billion	$0.91 billion
1981	192	5.9%	5.7%	$0.13 billion	$2.31 billion
1982	77	11.0%	13.3%	$0.13 billion	$1.00 billion
1983	451	9.9%	9.4%	$0.84 billion	$8.89 billion
1984	172	3.6%	2.5%	$0.05 billion	$2.06 billion
1985	187	6.4%	5.3%	$0.23 billion	$4.31 billion
1986	393	6.1%	5.1%	$0.68 billion	$13.40 billion
1987	285	5.6%	5.7%	$0.66 billion	$11.68 billion
1988	102	5.7%	3.5%	$0.13 billion	$3.72 billion
1989	113	8.2%	4.7%	$0.24 billion	$5.20 billion
1990	110	10.8%	8.1%	$0.34 billion	$4.27 billion
1991	286	11.9%	9.7%	$1.50 billion	$15.35 billion
1992	412	10.3%	8.0%	$1.82 billion	$22.69 billion
1993	509	12.7%	11.2%	$3.50 billion	$31.35 billion
1994	403	9.8%	8.5%	$1.46 billion	$17.25 billion
1995	461	21.2%	17.5%	$4.90 billion	$27.95 billion
1996	677	17.2%	16.1%	$6.76 billion	$42.05 billion
1997	474	14.0%	14.4%	$4.56 billion	$31.76 billion
1998	281	21.9%	15.6%	$5.25 billion	$33.65 billion
1999	477	71.1%	57.1%	$37.11 billion	$64.95 billion
2000	381	56.3%	46.0%	$29.83 billion	$64.86 billion
2001	79	14.2%	8.7%	$2.97 billion	$34.24 billion
2002	66	9.1%	5.1%	$1.13 billion	$22.03 billion
2003	63	11.7%	10.4%	$9.96 billion	$9.54 billion
2004	173	12.3%	12.4%	$3.86 billion	$31.19 billion
2005	159	10.3%	9.3%	$2.64 billion	$28.23 billion
2006	157	12.1%	13.0%	$3.95 billion	$30.48 billion
2007	159	14.0%	13.9%	$4.95 billion	$35.66 billion
2008	21	5.7%	24.8%	$5.63 billion	$22.76 billion
2009	41	9.8%	11.1%	$1.46 billion	$13.17 billion
2010	91	9.4%	6.2%	$1.84 billion	$29.82 billion
2011	81	13.9%	13.0%	$3.51 billion	$26.97 billion
2012	93	17.8%	8.9%	$2.77 billion	$31.11 billion
2013	157	21.1%	20.5%	$7.94 billion	$38.75 billion
2014	206	15.5%	12.8%	$5.40 billion	$42.20 billion
2015	115	18.7%	18.7%	$4.06 billion	$21.72 billion
2016	74	14.6%	14.4%	$1.75 billion	$12.12 billion
1980-1989	2,043	7.3%	6.1%	$3.27 billion	$53.47 billion
1990-1998	3,613	14.8%	13.3%	$30.09 billion	$226.36 billion
1999-2000	858	64.5%	51.6%	$66.94 billion	$129.81 billion
2001-2016	1,735	14.0%	12.8%	$54.84 billion	$430.00 billion
1980-2016	**8,249**	**17.9%**	**18.5%**	**$155.14 billion**	**$839.65 billion**

Source: Jay R. Ritter, "initial Public Offerings: Updated Statistics," March 29, 2017, available at https://site.warrington.ufl.edu/ritter/ipo-data/.

investment bank to take your company public, and then finding out that the stock price closed almost 20 percent higher on the first day (meaning that you received almost 20 percent less than you could have received). Below, we'll discuss theories to help explain this underpricing. But, before we do, you have to understand one other significant issue: What happens if the offering isn't so successful? In other words, what happens if the stock starts to trade below the IPO price? You need to understand this in order to understand some of the theories explaining underpricing.

10.1.4 Market Stabilization

Of course, not every IPO increases in price. Sometimes a new issue declines in value. During the early trading in the secondary market, the SEC allows the investment bank to help stabilize the price. The investment bank stabilizes the price by purchasing shares in the open market. "Market stabilization" is simply an exception to the SEC's prohibitions against market manipulation. Of course, it should surprise you to think that the investment bank would be willing to risk its capital to buy a stock that is dropping in price. There must be an explanation for this, and there is: It's the overallotment option. When you understand the overallotment option, you will see that the investment bank is not really risking its capital.

Most offerings have an **overallotment option** (also known as the **green shoe option**). The overallotment gives the investment bank the right to buy 15 percent more shares within the next 30 days. The overallotment option is crucial in the bank's management of the offering. Imagine that the company is going public by selling 50 million shares. As a result of the overallotment option, the investment bank has the right to buy an additional 7.5 million shares (an extra 15 percent).

In this example, the bank will fill orders from clients for 57.5 million shares, even though the bank has bought only 50 million shares. Of course, by filling orders for 57.5 million shares (rather than just 50 million shares), investors are receiving larger allocations than they would have otherwise received. Or, more investors are having their orders filled (meaning that banks are keeping their customers happy).

How does a bank fill orders for 57.5 million shares when the bank has only 50 million shares? The bank is short 7.5 million shares. As discussed in Chapter 4, a short sale involves the sale of shares that you don't own. In this situation, it is the bank that has sold shares that it does not own.

Next, imagine that the stock increases in value (above the $15 offer price). The bank has sold shares to clients for $15 but doesn't have 7.5 million of those shares. It may seem as if the bank is at great risk if the stock goes up. Of course, this is not the case. If the stock jumped to $40, for example, it would not be a problem for the bank. The bank could exercise its overallotment option. The bank has the right to buy those 7.5 million shares from the issuing company for $13.95. This is the $15 offer price, but the bank is able to buy the shares at a 7 percent discount. In doing this, the bank makes an extra $1.05 per share profit on 7.5 million shares. The bank normally has this option for 30 days.

Now, let's imagine that an offering has problems, and the stock price immediately drops to $12 in the secondary market. Remember that the bank is short 7.5 million shares (the bank has sold shares that it does not have). In this situation, the bank will not exercise its option. There is no reason for the bank to pay $13.95 for shares that it could buy in the open market for $12. The bank will pay $12 for 7.5 million shares that it sold for $15. Remember, the purchase of such a large percentage of the offering is intended to help stabilize the offering. The key takeaway is that the overallotment option helps the bank to manage the offering. It's also important to realize that the underwriter's obligation to stabilize the market reduces the risk for investors and increases their willingness to bid. In effect, market stabilization may increase investors' participation in an offering. It also helps counteract the selling pressure that may result from investors quickly flipping (selling) their allocations.

10.1.5 Reasons for Underpricing

When an investor leaves 15 percent on the table (through underpricing) and also pays a 7 percent spread, an IPO becomes a very expensive venture. To be clear, it is important to realize that the costs we just described do not amount to 22 percent of the value of the equity of the entire company. The reason for this is that not all shares have been distributed in the IPO. The post-IPO float often averages around 30 percent of the shares. In other words, 70 percent of the stock is held by insiders, including management and original investors (which may be venture capital firms). The issuer is paying 22 percent (in this example) of 30 percent of the equity. In other words, this cost amounts to approximately 6.6 percent of the equity. So, why does this underpricing occur?

To be clear, we do not know why underpricing occurs, particularly at such a significant level. But, we have theories that may help explain underpricing. As we discuss some of these theories, realize that the point is not to identify a single correct theory and to conclude that every other theory is wrong. Rather, the goal should be to use these theories to help understand how the markets work and how incentives affect the various parties. It is also important to realize that if you look at some of these theories too long, they can blur into each other.

One possible explanation for underpricing is that it is a way to compensate institutional investors for providing pricing information. These investors have devoted time and resources to researching the issuing company, attending the road show, and providing feedback. They do this because they know that they will be compensated in the form of an allocation of an underpriced security.

It is easy to wonder why investors do not always indicate that a stock is worth even less than the investor truly believes. The investor doesn't lie because she believes that the size of her allocation will be based on her bid. In addition, she fears being excluded from future offerings if she always bids too low. If investors bid high, on the other hand, the underwriter does not penalize the group by raising the offering price as much as it could, given the positive information. This type of behavior by the underwriter results in trust from the investors. The conclusion of all this is that in addition to providing compensation for information from investors, underpricing encourages the institutional investor to tell the truth about the value of the stock.

A second possible theory is similar and involves the winner's curse. The **winner's curse** is the idea that anyone who wins an auction must have bid too much (greater than the intrinsic value). To the extent that this scares investors, they may not provide indications of interest or they may systematically offer prices that are too low. To the extent that the investor trusts the banker to systematically underprice the security based on the best available information, the investor will again provide an accurate assessment of the value.

A third possibility is that bankers believe that the issuing company's managers estimate their personal wealth based on the midpoint of the initial range. As a result, the initial range is set at a low level, knowing that the managers will feel much more pain if the range is adjusted down than they would feel joy if it were adjusted higher. This is based on prospect theory and was suggested by Ritter (2011; citing Loughran and Ritter, 2002; and Kahneman and Tversky, 1979).

A fourth possibility is that bankers set prices low in order to minimize their litigation risk and/or to protect their reputational capital. If a stock trades below the initial offering price, the banker knows that the bank will likely be a defendant in a lawsuit. Whether that suit is meritorious or frivolous, it has costs. In addition, the banker also knows that competitors will use this failed offering against the bank when competing for future business. When the initial price is set low, there is less risk of the price dropping (in the aftermarket) below the offering price, which effectively lowers the bank's litigation risk and the risk to its reputation.

Finally, a fifth possibility provides the most cynical explanation. There is some evidence that investment banks receive "kickbacks" from allocating cheap IPOs to some clients. In other words, banks may allocate cheap IPOs to a hedge fund, which is expected to return some of those profits through additional commissions (either additional trading or higher commissions on trades). To the extent that this is true, a bank may have an incentive to underprice the security in order to create a larger pool of profits, some of which the bank will receive back in the form of later commissions. In the fourth and fifth explanation, it may be that banks use their market power in order to demand underpricing as opposed to charging a higher direct fee (which seems to be a consistent spread of 7 percent).

10.1.6 Bookbuilt Offering versus Auction

The offering that we have described in this chapter is referred to as a "bookbuilt" offering. You can think of the underwriters "building a book" of offers to buy the stock. As described earlier, bookbuilt offerings normally result in underpricing, where the issuing company leaves money on the table.

It would seem as if there could be a different approach to conducting an offering—and there is. An offering could be run as an auction. In an auction, investors can bid for shares at particular prices.

There are many ways to run an auction, but we will discuss the two most common ways. Imagine that a company is going public and is selling 10 million shares. It receives unique bids from different investors at the following schedule:

Price ($)	Number of Shares (millions)
16	3
15	5
14	6
13	4
12	8
11	2

It is easy to look at this auction table and to think that the investors who bid $16 would all have their orders filled at $16, and the investors who bid $15 would have their orders filled at $15. At that point, the company has sold 8 million shares and still needs to sell 2 million more. The company could fill one-third of the orders at $14 on a pro rata basis. In other words, an investor who put in a bid for 600 shares would receive 200 shares at a price of $14.

This is not exactly how auctions normally work! Normally, the orders are filled in the way we just described, but all the winning bidders receive the auction clearing price of $14. In other words, even the investors who bid $16 and $15 pay only $14 (the same as the investors who bid $14 and had only one-third of their orders filled). The reason to fill all orders at the clearing price is that it removes the fear of overbidding. It also means that when trading starts in the secondary market, there are not some investors who are already in a losing position (and may sell if the stock price returns to their cost). The downside is that it may encourage the uninformed retail investor to bid high in order to "free ride" on the research of institutional investors. This may result in a higher market clearing price and make the offering less attractive to institutional investors.

The auction we just described has some benefits. First, it is open to more bidders than just the large institutional investors. Second, and more importantly, shares are placed in the hands of the investors who value them the most. This should mean that underpricing is minimized.

There's a second way to conduct this auction, referred to as a **dirty auction**. In a dirty auction, the issuing company could agree to sell the shares at a price below the clearing price. For example, even if $14 is the price at which 10 million shares could be sold, the stock may be issued at $13. There are bids for 18 million shares at $13 or higher. Since there are 10 million shares that have to be split between investors who placed orders for 18 million shares, every bid could be filled at 10/18 or 5/9. In other words, if you bid for 900 shares, you will receive 500 shares.

This second approach seems to violate the idea of placing the shares in the hands of the investors who value them the most. Instead, investors who bid $16 received only 5/9 of their order size. Surprisingly, there is some merit to this approach. This approach leaves demand in the aftermarket (the secondary market) as trading begins. If an investor bid $16 in the auction, she should still be willing to pay this amount in the secondary market. In addition, if bidders do not believe that their entire order will be filled, they may bid for more shares than they want (even though they do not know what percentage of their order will be filled). In sum, a dirty offering can result in an offering being oversubscribed (which couldn't happen with a normal auction) and can also result in underpricing.

All this begs the question: If an auction can bring in more potential investors and can reduce the amount of underpricing, why isn't it more widely used? In fact, in the past 20 years, only approximately 20 IPOs have used this approach.

Reasons That Auctions Are Not More Popular There are many possible reasons that auctions have not caught on. For the large investment banks, auctions are less profitable, and there is little question that they are opposed to them. First, the gross spread is lower. Second, and likely more importantly, the bank loses discretion over the allocation (that is, which institutions should receive shares) because the shares are awarded to the highest bidder. This eliminates the bank's ability to demand other revenue, such as additional commissions on other trading activity, from clients. In addition, while we have very few data points, a greater percentage of auction offerings have dropped in value, and this makes it easier for traditional banks to market bookbuilt offerings.

From investors' perspective, an auction IPO may be less attractive. An auction allows uninformed retail investors to bid, which could eliminate some of the underpricing. While this is a widely repeated theory, it may be difficult to believe in practice. While retail investors have placed the vast majority of bids in auctions, the number of shares they receive is a very low percentage. In other words, there are many retail bids, but they are for a small number of shares. It is more likely that institutional investors simply do not feel confident that underpricing will occur, and this makes the offering less attractive. Of course, if institutional investors don't participate, underpricing is actually more likely to occur.

Ultimately, the company issuing the security drives the decision as to whether to hire a bank to conduct a bookbuilt offering or an auction. Since the majority of bankers are promoting bookbuilt offerings, this decision may be based on relationships. It may also be related to a desire to signal the high quality of the offering (by being associated with a high-quality investment bank). Or, it could simply be the fear of the unknown, since there have not been many auctions.

Alternatively, an issuing company may accept a bookbuilt offering because the company's management sees underpricing as a necessary expense in exchange for the services received. The issuing company may be paying for the bankers to help create demand for the offering, for the stabilization that occurs due to the overallotment option (but does not occur in an auction), and for the analyst coverage that the bank will provide after the offering. (The importance of sell-side research is discussed in Section 10.2.) In effect, the large size of the underpricing may reflect payment for a group of bundled services, and the size of the underpayment may reflect the amount of services that will be received.

10.1.7 Longer-Term Performance of IPOs

If you measure performance from the first-day closing price (that is, after the underpricing has been remedied), IPOs seem to have a poor performance record. Many studies indicate that these newly public stocks underperform the market over the next three years. In Exhibit 10.3, Ritter shows that IPOs underperform by approximately 3.3 percent per year after the first day's close. Alternatively, Ritter (2011) cites Eckbo, Masulis, and Norli (2007) and Lyandres, Sun, and Zhang (2008) to suggest that this underperformance may simply result from these stocks largely being small-cap growth stocks with a high investment factor. In other words, these stocks may have efficient returns based on a factor model that includes those particular factors.

Exhibit 10.3 Returns on IPOs During the Five Years After Issuing for IPOs from 1980 to 2015

This table shows that IPOs have underperformed other firms of the same size (market cap) by an average of 3.3% per year during the five years after issuing, not including the first-day return. The underperformance relative to other firms of the same size and book-to-market ratio has averaged 2.1% per year. Returns are through Dec. 30, 2016.

	First Six Months	Second Six Months	First Year	Second Year	Third Year	Fourth Year	Fifth Year	Geometric Mean Years 1–5
IPO firms	6.5%	0.6%	7.4%	6.2%	11.6%	18.7%	10.3%	10.8%
Size-matched	5.6%	5.9%	11.9%	14.5%	15.0%	16.1%	12.9%	14.1%
Difference	0.9%	−5.3%	−4.5%	−8.3%	−3.4%	2.6%	−2.6%	−3.3%
No of IPOs	8,175	8,154	8,175	8,030	7,260	6,277	5,442	
IPO firms	6.5%	0.6%	7.4%	6.2%	11.5%	18.7%	10.1%	10.7%
Size & BM-Matched	3.9%	4.5%	8.6%	13.3%	11.6%	18.0%	12.6%	12.8%
Difference	2.6%	−3.9%	−1.2%	−7.1%	−0.1%	0.8%	−2.5%	−2.1%
No. of IPOs	8,171	8,134	8,173	8,018	7,236	6,252	5,430	

Source: Jay R. Ritter, "Initial Public Offerings: Updated Statistics," March 29, 2017, available at https://site.warrington.ufl.edu/ritter/ipo-data/.

10.2 BUY-SIDE ANALYSTS AND SELL-SIDE ANALYSTS

An important distinction in the financial markets is the buy-side versus the sell-side. The **sell-side** refers to firms that facilitate securities transactions. These are the investment banks and brokerage firms. The **buy-side** refers to firms that actually invest in securities. Examples include mutual funds, hedge funds, trust companies, pension funds, and endowments.

10.2.1 Sell-Side Analysts

We referred to sell-side analysts in Section 10.1 (about IPOs). These analysts typically cover the stocks within a particular industry and produce reports that are intended to help the buy-side reach investment decisions. The buy-side analysts use the research from the sell-side if the sell-side analyst is particularly knowledgeable about the industry (and individual companies within the industry), if they have access to management of the companies that they research, and if they have a track record of accurate forecasts. Below, you will see some important concepts about the sell-side. An excellent analysis of the sell-side can be found in Brown, Call, Clement, and Sharp (2015).

How Does the Sell-Side Make Forecasts? Sell-side analysts use their industry knowledge and communications with management, vendors, and customers to make earnings forecasts. Earnings forecasts are often the basis of the analyst's recommendation to buy or sell a stock.

What Companies Does the Sell-Side Cover? Sell-side analysts cover stocks that their clients demand coverage on and also companies that have investment banking relationships or prospective relationships with the firm.

Why Does a Sell-Side Analyst Want to Be Known as the Best Analyst Within an Industry? Each year, institutions survey the buy-side investors and ask them to vote on the best analyst in each industry. If an analyst is seen as influential within an industry, it is easier for the investment bankers in the firm to win banking business. This means that influential analysts can demand more compensation because they help bring in more investment banking business. In addition, if a sell-side analyst is seen as influential, management (of the companies the analyst covers) is likely to be more accessible to them.

How Does the Sell-Side Get Paid? Different models exist for a sell-side firm to receive compensation for the research it provides to the buy-side. One model is for the buy-side to pay a fixed amount for research. Another model is for the buy-side to direct trades to the sell-side firm that provided valuable services (including research).

Why Is It Difficult to Be a Sell-Side Analyst? Sell-side analysts are in a very difficult position. The buy-side demands accurate information from them. At the same time, there is evidence that some companies will not provide access to sell-side analysts who make negative statements about the company. In effect, these sell-side analysts need access to management in order to make the accurate recommendations that the buy-side values. But, in order to have access to management, the sell-side analyst can only make positive comments about the company, and this lowers the sell-side analyst's value to the buy-side. In addition, it is difficult to generate investment banking business if the firm's analyst is making negative comments about the company. Again, the result is that analysts may be biased as being too positive. Since the buy-side tends to believe that the sell-side is highly biased toward making positive comments, any negative comments by an analyst may be seen as particularly credible.

What Kind of Pressure Does Management Put on the Sell-Side? Management (of the companies being covered) may put significant pressure on analysts. There can be pressure to understand management's view of the company and recent events. In addition, there can be pressure on the analyst to produce an earnings forecast that the company will be able to beat. In other words, management doesn't want the analyst to set earnings expectations at a level that is so high that the company's actual earnings will disappoint investors. Koh, Matsumoto, and Rajgopal (2008) found that earnings management decreased after the Enron scandal but that expectations management increased.

What Does the Buy-Side Value Most About the Sell-Side? Ultimately, the buy-side places particular value on the sell-side's access to management. The sell-side can set up meetings for the buy-side and can invite the buy-side to conferences in which management is present. Of course, if management is unhappy with the sell-side, this access is lost. The result is that the sell-side analyst may be beholden to the management of the companies that the analyst covers. This makes the sell-side analyst's research less valuable.

10.2.2 Buy-Side Analysts

Buy-side analysts provide information and recommendations to their firm's portfolio manager(s). The information is designed to help the firm earn superior risk-adjusted returns. While there is a fair amount of academic research about sell-side analysts and their research, we have significantly less information about buy-side analysts because they don't release their reports. Their analysis is used internally to make decisions. Their client is internal (the portfolio manager). This is significantly different from the sell-side. Below, we'll examine some of what we do know. An excellent analysis of the buy-side can be found in Brown et al. (2016).

Does the Buy-Side Use Sell-Side Research? The buy-side analyst reads sell-side research. Despite the conflicts of interest discussed earlier, sell-side research has great value. As a general rule, the buy-side values the information contained in the sell-side's report (and access to management) more than it values the sell-side analyst's actual buy or sell recommendation. Overall, the buy-side has great respect for the information and knowledge of the sell-side.

In General, Does a Sell-Side Analyst or a Buy-Side Analyst Cover More Stocks? In general, buy-side analysts tend to have broader coverage than sell-side analysts. This indicates that the sell-side is expected to know every detail about the few stocks that an individual analyst covers.

Do Analysts Move from the Sell-Side to the Buy-Side? Some buy-side analysts have sell-side experience, but it's important to realize that this can be a difficult transition because there are many sell-side analysts who would like to make it. Note that it is uncommon to see a buy-side analyst move over and become a sell-side analyst.

What Are the Primary Reasons a Buy-Side Analyst Talks to a Sell-Side Analyst? Buy-side analysts communicate frequently with sell-side analysts. According to Brown et al. (2016), the reasons for this communication include:

- The buy-side needs a meeting with a management team that the sell-side follows closely.
- The sell-side pays for expensive data that the buy-side may not have access to.
- Some buy-side analysts like to talk to one bullish sell-side analyst and one bearish sell-side analyst prior to making an investment.
- A sell-side analyst can help a buy-side analyst quickly learn about an industry or a company.

How Does the Sell-Side Help the Buy-Side Understand What's Going On with the Buy-Side? Interestingly, the buy-side often views the sell-side as a hub of information. As a general rule, buy-side analysts tend to be somewhat secretive. In other words, they don't like to share their positions with others. More importantly, they don't want to tip others off to moves that they anticipate making. At the same time, buy-side analysts want to know what others on the buy-side are thinking and doing. They often hope to gather that information by talking to the sell-side. Since the sell-side talks to most investors and executes many trades, they have this insight.

The secretive nature of the buy-side also makes these analysts more reluctant to ask questions on an earnings call (which occurs each quarter, when earnings are announced). They fear tipping off their competitors. This adds to the importance of private meetings. Brown et al. (2016) argue that the buy-side also believes that management will be more honest with the buy-side in a private meeting because the buy-side's research is not published.

What Does a Buy-Side Analyst Do? Ultimately, buy-side analysts play a role similar to that of a government intelligence officer. They gather information and determine what information is credible and what is not. Most importantly, they have to predict the future with very imperfect information. Analysts read everything they can get their hands on—including popular press articles, industry articles, financial reports issued by the company, and sell-side reports. They also speak with everyone that they can. They try to interview management, they speak with lower-level employees, they speak with competitors (who have no fear of saying what they really think about the competition), and they speak to vendors and customers. An ambitious analyst may walk the floor of a trade show and try to learn how customers make decisions and what issues are important to them.

How Are Buy-Side Analysts Compensated? Buy-side analysts are typically compensated for the quality of their recommendations. Firms attempt to identify two variables: (1) Was the analyst's recommendation valuable?; and (2) was the analyst able to convince the portfolio manager to act on her recommendation? In other words, it is not enough to be right if the firm didn't profit from the recommendation. This is why the ability to "pitch" an idea is so important to an analyst. She must learn how to make a compelling argument. We will discuss this later in the chapter.

10.2.3 Financial Analyst Forecasting Literature

Ramnath, Rock, and Shane (2008) have provided a taxonomy of research conducted about analysts. The paper provides valuable insights that can help analysts and students learn about the industry. Here, we will simply summarize some of their key ideas.

Sell-Side Research Clearly Matters Three ways we know this are that sell-side reports can move the market, investors reference the research, and we have evidence that the buy-side reads it.

Analysts Obtain Much Value from Segment Reports Obviously, it's easier to value and understand a piece of a business than it is to value a conglomerate. Candid disclosures by management in the MD&A (Management Discussion and Analysis) section of the 10-Q and 10-K reports are very valuable to analysts.

Sell-Side Analysts Tend to Rely On Multiples (for Valuation) More Than Discounted Cash Flow This means their earnings forecasts are particularly important. To the extent that an analyst is better than the competition at forecasting earnings, the hope is that this translates into better recommendations.

Forecast Accuracy Seems to Improve with Experience and Decrease When an Analyst Follows Too Many Industries and Firms With that said, it is very difficult to measure the accuracy of earnings forecasts and recommendations. Analysts frequently leave out different expenses when calculating earnings, and recommendations can be for different time horizons.

As an Investor, It Is Particularly Interesting When There Is a Wide Dispersion of Analyst Forecasts Such dispersion reflects significant differences in opinion. When one analyst is willing to make a forecast that is far removed from the consensus opinion, we are forced to ponder whether the analyst has useful private information.

10.2.4 Snap Inc. IPO and Analysts

The buy-side, as well as sophisticated individual investors, must decipher valuable sell-side analyst insights from comments that simply reflect a conflict of interest. In other words, investors must identify when an analyst truly believes in a stock that he is recommending versus touting a stock to please a company that has just provided investment banking revenue to the analyst's firm.

In the first quarter of 2017, Snap Inc. went public (ticker SNAP). Snap Inc. is responsible for the video and messaging application Snapchat. Many commentators viewed SNAP as an expensive company with weak corporate governance (which we'll discuss later in this chapter).

The first 11 sell-side analysts to issue SNAP rated it as a sell or a hold. But, this did not include analysts from the banks that were part of the syndicate that brought SNAP public. Those analysts normally wait 25 days after issuance before releasing their research. Once the 25th day arrived, analysts from the underwriting firms issued bullish reports, highlighting the potential of the company. The onslaught of mostly positive reports pushed the stock price higher in late March. Unfortunately for investors, SNAP released earnings as a public company for the first time in early May 2017. The earnings (or lack thereof) were very disappointing, and the stock price dropped more than 20 percent as a result.

The conclusion is that the market clearly considers the knowledge that the sell-side analysts possess. Their recommendations influence stock prices. But, at the same time, a sophisticated investor has to recognize the inherent conflicts of interest that exist. Sell-side analysts are paid in some part with revenue that is generated by investment banking, and this requires the analyst to tout these companies.

Finally, the buy-side certainly appreciates the access to management that the sell-side can arrange. However, it is difficult for the sell-side to arrange access to management if the sell-side analyst has a negative view of the company. The result is that sell-side reports are bullishly biased. In fact, reporters Serena Ng and Thomas Gryta from *The Wall Street Journal* (2017) used FactSet data to determine that only 6 percent of 11,000 analyst ratings were "sell" ratings. Therefore, while the conflict of interest may appear obvious when research is issued by analysts 25 days after an IPO, sophisticated investors are aware that this conflict always exists.

10.3 CAPITAL ALLOCATION

Capital allocation is the description of how management uses resources to create value on behalf of shareholders. When investors study the capital allocation practices of management, they are really analyzing how managers fulfill their overriding responsibility to create value by selecting the best projects and financing them as inexpensively as possible.

Another way to think about capital allocation is to think about the corporate manager as being similar to an equity portfolio manager. The equity portfolio manager is judged on whether she creates excess risk-adjusted returns. She does this by deciding which markets to enter, which industries to overweight, and which stocks to own and which to sell. If the equity manager doesn't have any attractive investments, she should return capital to her investors. Ultimately, the corporate manager does exactly the same thing, deciding which projects will make his portfolio more attractive and returning capital if he does not have any attractive choices. Another similarity between corporate managers and equity portfolio managers is that they cannot take the same actions as everyone else and expect to have different results.

To understand how significant capital allocation is, imagine an unlevered (that is no debt) company with $1 billion of assets, a 15 percent return on equity, and a 100 percent retention ratio. If this company could continue this high return on equity for 10 years, its capital would grow from $1 billion to $4 billion. An investor is trusting this manager to make a tremendous number of decisions about how to invest all this capital. While 15 percent ROE for 10 years may be an extreme example, the point is that when you invest in a firm, you are trusting a management team to invest a large amount of capital. You must assess the team's capital allocation decisions.

When investors meet with managers, one of the most important things the investors try to understand is how the managers think about value. Interestingly, an investor is likely to hear many different answers from management when questioned about value. Some managers simply discuss growth, despite the fact that not all growth is valuable. Others discuss earnings per share, which may not reflect true value creation. But, value creation really refers to the increase in the intrinsic value of the stock; it is about earning more than the firm's capital costs.

Over time, companies obtain the majority of their capital by retaining earnings. While this implies that companies generate their capital by being profitable, it also means that managers do not have to explain their plans to the capital markets. The result can be a lack of checks and balances on the capital allocation process. This also creates opportunities for investors who can distinguish the great capital allocators from the worst.

10.3.1 The Seven Places That Capital Can Be Allocated

There are seven primary ways to allocate capital:

1. Engage in mergers and acquisitions
2. Reinvest in the existing business through capital expenditures
3. Pay dividends
4. Invest in research and development
5. Repurchase shares
6. Increase the working capital of the business
7. Return cash to debtholders

It's important to recognize that different types of allocation are better at different times. For example, repurchasing shares may be a great way to create value when shares are cheap, but it will destroy value when shares are expensive.

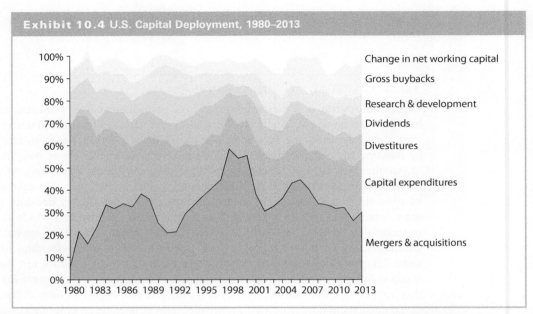

Note: Data for R&D, capital expenditures, buybacks, and dividends exclude financial companies and regulated utilities; data for mergers & acquisitions and divestitures include all industries.

Source: Credit Suisse HOLT, Thomson Reuters DataStream.

It is also important to realize that more capital is allocated to mergers and acquisitions, for example, than to net working capital. In Exhibit 10.4, you can see how capital was allocated from 1980 to 2013. You'll notice that this chart includes divestitures and does not include returning cash to debtholders. On our list of seven uses of capital, we have not included divestitures. While this is an important part of the capital allocation decision, it is a *source* of capital as opposed to a *use* of capital. Again, this is similar to the equity manager's decision to sell a stock; it is crucial, but we would not include the sell decision while discussing how the equity manager allocates his capital. The chart in Exhibit 10.4 does not include returning cash to debtholders because companies have had a net inflow of capital from debtholders as opposed to returning capital to debtholders. Regardless, this is one possible option for capital allocation, and we will briefly discuss when it makes sense. Below, we will discuss each of these seven uses of capital. For the reader who desires more detail, Callahan and Mauboussin (2014) provide an excellent analysis of capital allocation.

Mergers and Acquisitions Mergers and acquisitions tend to be somewhat cyclical. It is easier to acquire another company when your company is doing well (because your stock can be used as currency) or when interest rates are low (because the acquirer can borrow money and pay cash). Remember, if investors are willing to pay a high price for your stock, the company's cost of equity is low.

As an investor, there are several issues to examine when studying an acquisition. The three most important issues are (1) the purpose of the acquisition, (2) the method of payment, and (3) the price paid.

When considering the purpose of a transaction, it is important to consider whether the goal is simply to increase scale (and reduce costs), to extend the business by growing into related (but slightly different) lines of business, or to move into completely different areas of business. As a general rule, acquiring companies seem to have more success in meeting goals related to cost cutting than in generating new revenue. Promises of synergies often go unfulfilled. (Always be careful when a banker or consultant says that "one plus one can equal three." If you listen more carefully, what the person really means is that "one plus one can equal a fee.")

With respect to the form of payment, an acquiring company can use cash or stock. When a company uses its own stock to acquire another company, it may be a signal that management thinks the company stock is overvalued. (Certainly, you would hope that management would not use an undervalued currency to pay for an acquisition.) Another way of thinking about using stock in an acquisition is that it is similar to selling stock and using the cash to buy the target company. In effect, management is saying that they can create value by selling their expensive stock and buying this cheaper company.

On average, markets respond better when the acquirer uses cash. This may be a signal that the acquirer does not see its own stock as overvalued and, therefore, doesn't want to use it as currency. Alternatively, it could be a sign that the acquirer has generated a significant amount of cash and a reminder of the company's profitability. Another possibility is that the firm has taken on cheap debt to fund the acquisition, and this could be a signal that the debt providers believe in the transaction and that management is not concerned by the burden of servicing the debt.

Of course, the most important issue is the amount paid for an acquisition. When a company acquires another public company, it typically pays a significant premium above the previous market price. If you believe that markets are at least relatively efficient, it is difficult to believe that managers can pay 20 percent or 30 percent above the market price and still create value. Callahan and Mauboussin (2014) support the view that the majority of the gains from a transaction accrue to the selling shareholders. This also helps explain why a more attractive M&A strategy may be to acquire smaller private companies. It is possible that these companies can be acquired at a significantly lower price.

Capital Expenditures Capital expenditures represent investment in the existing business. Analysts often try to distinguish between maintenance capital expenditures (replacing depreciated or inefficient assets) and growth capital expenditures (investments designed to generate revenue growth). Unless management can accurately provide the analyst with this information, the analyst will normally assume that depreciation is a good estimate of the amount of maintenance capital expenditures that must be done. Any additional capital expenditures are designed to generate growth.

In a low-growth economy, it is difficult to know how much growth capital expenditures will occur. As discussed in Chapter 9, growth is a combination of the increase in the labor force and the increase in productivity. In the United States, annual real growth is expected to be in the 1.8 percent range over the next 20 years, and inflation will bring that up to 3.8 percent in nominal terms. This low expected growth rate does not encourage companies to invest heavily. Of course, if companies don't make significant investments, productivity doesn't increase, and growth can be even slower.

Another complexity with capital expenditures is that many industries seem to be changing and becoming less capital intensive. For example, the personal transportation industry is being impacted by Uber, and there may be less demand for taxis. Similarly, Airbnb might be reducing the need for more hotels. The idea is that industry patterns and the behavior of individual companies may be impacted by changing trends, and this may make these companies more difficult to analyze.

To a large extent, investors don't worry about capital expenditures in the same way that they worry when companies do acquisitions. The reason for this is that companies are not paying a premium when they do capital expenditures. In addition, investors tend to assume that these investments will earn returns similar to historic returns. Most importantly, management understands the business, and these expenditures do not disrupt the business as an acquisition can.

Ultimately, an analyst wants to try to distinguish between expenditures that create value as opposed to those that are simply used to build empires. Empire building can create complexity and result in higher compensation for management, but it is not associated with creating value for shareholders. Analysts sometimes calculate an incremental return on capital to measure the value that management has created with recent investments. It's important to be careful when doing this and to also include any capital that the company has written down in a restructuring effort.

Finally, recognize that recent research has included the amount of asset growth as a factor in a five-factor model. Fama and French (2015) found that high asset growth is associated with low stock returns. (This topic was also briefly covered in Chapter 7.)

Dividends Dividends are cash payments made directly to all shareholders. Investors often look at dividends and share repurchases together when examining a firm's payout policy.

Dividends can be thought of as the firm's last alternative. In other words, if a firm cannot create value by reinvesting in the business or buying another company or doing research and development or buying their own stock or paying back debt, it can distribute cash to shareholders. In reality, though, not many firms seem to think of dividends as their last alternative. Many firms pay dividends on a regular basis, and dividends are rarely cut.

The companies that do seem to use dividends as their last alternative usually declare a dividend to be a **special dividend**. By referring to a payment as a special dividend, the company signals to the market that this dividend is a one-time event, and investors should not expect it to continue. As an example, Costco paid special dividends of $7 per share in 2012, $5 per share in 2015, and $7 per share in 2017.

Some investors are attracted to companies that pay dividends. One simple reason is just preferences or a clientele effect. In other words, some investors want the income that is generated from dividends (and prefer this to selling shares and creating their own dividend). A second reason that some investors like dividends is that they believe that dividends reduce the **agency conflict** (between shareholders and management) by removing free cash flow from the hands of management. A third reasons is a **signaling effect**. Investors may see dividends as sending a signal that management expects future cash flows to be high or that management will be more disciplined, or that the board of directors is controlling the empire-building tendencies of management, or that dividends will help keep leverage high.

Of course, there are also some taxpayers who dislike dividends. Dividends result in double-taxation being forced upon the shareholder. In addition, if an investor has not owned the stock for a long period of time, the tax rate that is imposed on the dividend can be high. Furthermore, investors really don't like to see a company pay a dividends and then enter the capital markets and issue more equity (which is expensive).

It is important to recognize the dates related to a dividend. The **declaration date** is the date that a dividend is announced by the board of directors. The **date of record** is the date on which the transfer agent "closes the book" and looks at who is the shareholder. In other words, shares are trading hands constantly throughout the day, but the transfer agent must take a snapshot at one point in time in order to determine who will receive the dividend. This is the end of the day on the date of record.

The **ex-dividend date** is the day on which the stock starts trading without the right to the dividend. Holding all else equal, investors expect the stock price to fall by the value of the dividend (on an after-tax basis for the marginal investor) when the stock starts trading ex-dividend. In other words, ignoring taxes, if investors were willing to pay $100 for a stock that is planning on paying a $2 dividend, they see the ongoing business as being worth $98 and the dividend as being worth $2 (ignoring taxes). The ex-dividend day is two trading days before the date of record. This is because equities settle three days after the trade date (T + 3). So, you need to own the stock three days earlier in order to be on the transfer agent's books as the shareholder who will receive the dividend. The dividend is distributed on the **payment date**.

Investors often examine the percentage of earnings that are paid out as dividend (the payout ratio). More significantly, investors should examine the percentage of the free cash flow that is paid out. This ratio may help the investor form a belief as to the stability of the dividend.

Research and Development   The eventual success of research and development is usually impossible to assess ex ante. R&D conducted by a firm is expensed, while R&D that is acquired (in the form of another firm) is capitalized. An analyst can examine the trend in the amount spent on R&D, the addressable market that the R&D is focused on, and the historical success of the company's efforts.

Share Repurchases   The repurchase of shares may be the most interesting (and misunderstood) category within capital allocation. Callahan and Mauboussin (2014) indicate that companies tend to conduct share repurchases with residual cash. In other words, when a company has cash left over, it is often used to repurchase shares. Not surprisingly, in strong economic times, companies often have significant residual cash. This is frequently the time when share prices are the highest. So, when prices are the highest, this is when companies often do the most repurchases.

In reality, investors want management to avoid repurchases when the stock is expensive. Buying back expensive shares can be thought of as a gift to the exiting shareholders at the expense of the remaining shareholders. Long-term investors want management to purchase shares when they are cheap.

Analyzing management's repurchase behavior is one of the easiest ways to understand management's view on capital allocation. Many managers repurchase shares systematically. In other words, they assume that the market is relatively efficient. Their view is that sometimes they may overpay and sometimes they may underpay. But, at the end of the day, the stock is usually fairly priced.

Other managers believe that they understand the value of their company, and they repurchase shares opportunistically. This means they have a model or some metric to value their own company, and when the stock is undervalued, they act on it. If they are correct, this creates value for the remaining shareholders.

It's important for an analyst to realize that share repurchases do not always create value. That is like thinking that if you go out and buy a house, you have increased your net worth. As many people who bought houses in 2007 can tell you, that is not always the case. You will create an immediate increase in your net worth if you are able to purchase a home for less than it is worth. If you overpay, you have lowered your net worth (destroyed value).

Finally, there are two other issues to consider when examining repurchases. Sometimes, repurchases are announced but not executed. In other words, companies sometimes attempt to send a positive signal about the value of the stock, yet they never actually repurchase the shares. Other times, repurchases are executed, but the company's share count never decreases. This is because the repurchased shares are issued to management as a result of option grants (employee compensation).

Net Working   Capital Allocations to net working capital are generally the least analyzed decision with respect to capital allocation. It's important for an analyst to exclude excess cash and to not mistakenly think that a company is investing significant amounts in net working capital when, in reality, the company is simply accumulating cash. As discussed in Chapter 8, an analyst should examine unusual increases in inventory or accounts receivable.

Returning Cash to Debtholders   As a general rule, debt is a low-cost source of capital. For an unlevered firm, taking on some debt lowers the weighted average cost of capital. The tax shield that the debt provides (that is, the deductibility of interest) is greater than the risk of bankruptcy caused by the small amount of debt. At some point, however, the amount of debt can be so large that the increased risk of bankruptcy can outweigh the benefit of the tax shield.

At that point, the weighted average cost of capital is higher than if the company had the optimal level of debt. In this situation, it would be value-creating to return capital to the debtholders and reduce the amount of debt outstanding.

10.3.2 Dividends versus Repurchases

At this point, it's important to understand the impact that dividends and repurchases can have on a stock's price. Let's imagine a stock with 1,000 shares outstanding, with shares being worth $50 and trading for $50. In other words, the stock is trading for its intrinsic value. The company has $2 of earnings per share, meaning that the stock has a P/E ratio of 25. The market capitalization is $50,000 (1,000 shares multiplied by the $50 price).

The company decides to use $5,000 to pay a dividend. The value of the company should drop from $50,000 to $45,000. This is because investors now have $5,000 of cash and $45,000 worth of stock. The P/E ratio is now 22.5 because the stock price is $45, and the earnings per share is still $2.

Alternatively, imagine that that company is overvalued according to your model. While you believe the stock has an intrinsic value of $50, it is trading for $100. If this is the way that the market values the company, we would imagine that the stock would be worth $95 after the dividend is paid (where shareholders will receive $5 of dividends for each share that they own).

This same thing would happen if the shares were undervalued. In other words, if the stock were trading at $25 even though you believe it is worth $50, you would expect that a $5 dividend would be valued in that way by the market, and the stock would drop to $20 when it starts trading ex-dividend.

The point of reviewing these examples is to show that a dividend should be seen as relatively neutral. In other words, we assume that a $5 dividend is valued as $5 in any of the three cases. The dividend does not impact the earnings per share, but it results in a lower stock price and a lower P/E ratio in all three cases.

Now, let's examine how a share repurchase is different. Starting with the case where the stock is trading at intrinsic value, we'll see that it is not much different. If the company uses $5,000 to repurchase $50 shares, the share count will drop by 100. Now, the $45,000 company will be divided by 900 shares, and the share price will still be $50. This means that existing shareholders continue to have their $50 stock. Exiting shareholders also received $50 per share when they sold their shares to the company. The earnings per share have increased. The EPS is now $2.22—the $2,000 of earnings divided by 900 shares. This means that the P/E ratio is 22.5.

If, on the other hand, shares are overvalued, things turn out very differently. If the company uses $5,000 to repurchase shares that are trading for $100, it will repurchase 50 shares. The exiting shareholders (who sold their shares back to the company) received $100. But, according to your model, this $50,000 company is now worth $45,000. When $45,000 is divided by the remaining 950 shares, the stock price has dropped to $47.37. In effect, the remaining shareholders have subsidized the exiting shareholders. In this situation, the earnings per share have increased from $2 to $2.105 ($2,000 divided by 950 shares).

Finally, if the company is able to repurchase shares at a price below intrinsic value, the remaining shareholders win. If the company uses $5,000 to repurchase $25 shares, it will repurchase 200 shares. According to your model, the $50,000 company will become a $45,000 company. But, there are only 800 shares outstanding, and the intrinsic value should increase to $56.25 ($45,000/800 shares). The exiting shareholders sold at a low price, and this benefits the remaining shareholders.

Management should be running the company for the benefit of the remaining shareholders. This means that management should repurchase shares when they are trading below intrinsic value and pay a dividend when the shares are trading above intrinsic value. When the stock is trading at intrinsic value, management should be indifferent between a repurchase and a dividend (although taxable investors may prefer a share repurchase). Finally, investors should also be aware that earnings per share increases that result from share repurchases are different from increases that occur because companies have increased revenue or cut expenses.

10.3.3 What Do Investors Want to See?

Ultimately, investors want to see management engaged in a process that truly indicates value creation. In other words, investors want to see management start with a clean chalkboard each year and assess the capital allocation decision with a fresh eye. Investors want to see that management understands valuation and behaves opportunistically, purchasing shares when cheap, using their equity as currency when expensive, and acquiring targets as a first-mover in the industry, as opposed to reacting defensively to acquisitions accomplished by competitors. As discussed later, investors want to see that compensation is structured in a way that incents management to think about the long-term value creation, as opposed to short-term goals.

10.4 CORPORATE GOVERNANCE

Corporate governance refers to the rules, policies, and procedures that are used to direct and control a company. From an investor's perspective, corporate governance refers to the tools used to align the interest of management with the interest of shareholders. In other words, corporate governance is designed to minimize the agency conflict.

Corporate governance includes many issues, such as the corporate charter and bylaws, the board of directors, board committees, and compensation of top management. As mentioned earlier in this chapter, corporate governance is an issue that investors sometimes ignore or discount. With that said, a growing percentage of institutional investors are integrating **environmental, social, and governance (ESG)** factors into their investment decisions. With respect to governance factors, ESG investors often examine issues such as the composition of the board of directors, having a non-CEO board chairperson, and how the board oversees strategy. ESG investors believe that companies with high ESG scores will have lower volatility, lower costs of capital, and greater transparency.

Investors who ignore governance issues do so at their own peril. These are issues that are easy to ignore until there is a problem. As an example, when SNAP went public in early 2017, it issued shares with no voting rights. That offering was oversubscribed, as the lack of voting power did not seem to scare investors away. In the future, investors will see whether this becomes an issue.

Despite some investors' willingness to overlook corporate governance issues, we will discuss the three most important governance issues below:

1. The board of directors
2. Anti-takeover provisions
3. Compensation of management

10.4.1 The Board of Directors

In an influential Harvard Business Review article (1979), William W. Wommack stated that the most important purpose of the board of directors is to approve or disapprove of management's proposals concerning the future direction of the company. With that said, management and investors often have contrasting views of the purpose of the board. Management sometimes views the board as something similar to a consulting firm. In other words, management may see the board as a group of experienced businesspeople who can offer advice when needed. Investors, on the other hand, rely on the board to oversee management. This is more similar to a regulatory function, designed to prevent any actions that conflict with the best interests of shareholders.

The key issues that investors seem to care about with respect to a board are the separation of the CEO and board chair positions, the size of the board, the independence of the board, how the board is compensated, and how the board responds to shareholder proposals.

CEO/Chair of the Board   As a general rule, investors prefer the board chair to be someone other than the CEO. To the extent that an investor believes that the job of the board is to oversee management, investors do not want to see management in charge of the board. A board led by a non-CEO chair may be more likely to replace a poorly performing CEO.

Board Size   With respect to the size of the board, there is not a magic number. But, it is important that a board not be too large. Boards that are too large may cause directors to feel as if their voices are not important. It would be easy for a member of a large board to feel as if a red flag that he has spotted must not be important because no one else has raised the issue. Of course, a board must not be so small that it doesn't include a diverse set of experiences and knowledge. On average, companies within the S&P 500 have approximately nine board members, but there is significant variation.

Board Independence   The independence of board members is particularly important to investors. The idea of independence is far greater than any legal definition. Investors want directors who will voice their opinion, who are not beholden to the CEO or board chair, and who have enough experience that their opinion carries weight on the board. A classic example of investor unhappiness with the independence of a board occurred when Michael Eisner ran Disney. While 12 of the 16 board members were legally defined as independent, the board included "his personal lawyer, his children's former elementary-school principal, an architect who has done work for Disney and three former Disney executives" (Orwall & Lublin, 1997). Investors worry that board members like these would never take a stand contrary to the CEO or would ever voice an opinion that management's compensation is too high.

Board Compensation   Serving as a board member can be lucrative. According to a 2017 *Wall Street Journal* article by Renee Lightner and Theo Francis, approximately half of the companies in the S&P 500 provide compensation greater than $250,000 per year to board members. It is rare for compensation to be below $150,000. It is possible for compensation to be significantly higher than $250,000. Some companies require directors to hold stock in the company, and frequently this stock is offered as part of the compensation. Obviously, the intent is to align the directors' interests with those of the shareholders. At the same time, compensating directors with stock can result in directors overlooking bad acts and may defeat the purpose of the board.

Responses to Shareholder Proposals   Finally, investors watch how boards respond to shareholder proposals, particularly recommendations from large activist investors. These issues can be particularly complicated. Sometimes, activist investors can have valid ideas that may benefit the long-term value of the company. Other times, activist investors may be promoting ideas that will simply impact the short term. In any case, investors hope to see a thoughtful response from management.

10.4.2 Anti-Takeover Provisions

Corporations can use many tools in order to prevent takeovers. A non-exhaustive list includes poison pills, requiring a supermajority of shareholder votes to approve selling the firm, selling the most profitable part of the company, and staggered boards (so that it takes several years for an opponent to gain control of the board). We will focus solely on poison pills in order to develop the key intuition about these provisions.

When we entered the 21st century, more than half of the companies in the S&P 500 had poison pills—that is, plans designed to thwart takeovers. Today, fewer than 5 percent of S&P 500 companies have these plans.

A typical poison pill plan might work like this: If any person or entity (whom we'll call "Mr. Big") becomes an owner of 15 percent or more of the company's stock, all investors other than Mr. Big can buy an additional share for 1 cent. Imagine a company with 100 shares outstanding. If Mr. Big buys 15 shares, the poison pill is triggered. Now, the owners of the 85 remaining shares each get to buy an additional share for virtually no cost. The result is that there are now 185 shares outstanding (the 85 shares plus the new 85 shares plus Mr. Big's 15 shares). Remember that the poison pill gave the right to everyone other than the party that owns 15 percent or more. The effect of the plan is to dilute the large owner. Mr. Big bought 15 percent of the stock but now owns only 8.11 percent of it (15 out of 185 shares).

Poison pills were very unpopular with institutional investors. The fear was that poison pills deterred takeovers and helped entrench managers. In reality, it's uncertain that this was the case. It's also possible that poison pills allowed management to negotiate for a higher selling price. In other words, a company would be willing to rescind its poison pill plan if it received a particular price. Of course, we'll never know how many offers never happened because of the existence of a poison pill.

In sum, while poison pills are very unpopular with institutional investors, the evidence is not clear as to whether poison pills destroyed or created value for shareholders. Possibly the best approach to determine whether a poison pill was shareholder-friendly or not was to look at other evidence to understand whether management acted in shareholders' best interest. One of the best ways to do this is to look at compensation—which we'll do next.

10.4.3 Compensation

CEO compensation (as well as the compensation of other top managers) is a highly controversial subject. Many investors disagree about whether top managers are overpaid and whether compensation is related to performance. For an investor, it's important to understand some key ideas about the goals of compensation, the level of compensation, how compensation is set, and where to find information.

Compensation is often used to try to remedy the **principal–agent conflict**. In other words, management may not act in the best interest of shareholders. According to Callahan and Mauboussin (2014), conflicts tend to occur in three areas:

1. Management may derive benefits from controlling resources that don't create value for shareholders (this may lead to empire building to generate higher compensation).
2. Management has most of their wealth in this one company, so they may take too little risk (while the diversified investor wants them to take more risk).
3. Compensation is often short-term focused, which can result in management focusing on earnings per share rather than long-term value maximization.

According to Gressle and O'Byrne (2013), executive compensation has three goals:

1. It provides strong incentives to create shareholder value (and address the three issues described above).
2. It helps retain key talent (particularly in periods of poor performance attributable to market and industry factors).
3. It limits compensation cost to levels that maximize the wealth of shareholders.

In other words, the goal is to align management's interest with the shareholders, to keep management from leaving in bad times, and to refrain from giving too much of shareholder profits to management. This is a difficult balancing act.

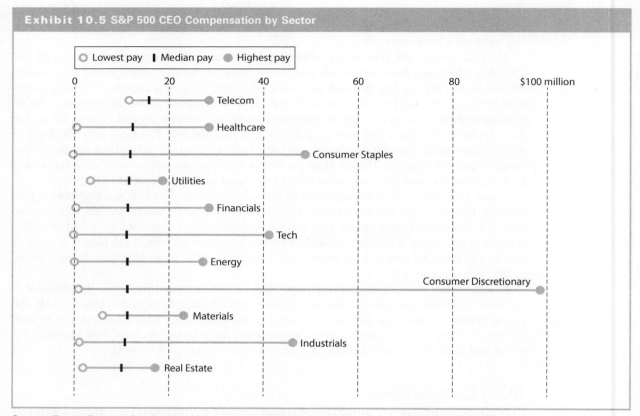

Exhibit 10.5 S&P 500 CEO Compensation by Sector

Source: Top to Bottom: Pay for 500 CEOs, by Theo Francis and Jieqian Zhang, May 31, 2017, WSJ.

Level of Compensation The three goals of executive compensation just mentioned have resulted in compensation that many people consider to be very high. At public companies with market capitalizations greater than $1 billion, the average pay package in 2015 proxy statements (for the 2014 fiscal year) for the 200 highest CEOs was $22.6 million (a 9 percent gain over the previous year), and the median was $17.6 million. An examination of a broader universe (the CEOs of the 500 companies in the S&P 500) based on the 2016 proxy statements showed that the median income had increased to $11.7 million (from $10.8 million in 2015). The salary range and median salary for each S&P 500 sector can be seen in Exhibit 10.5.

While the average person sees CEO salaries as being very high, Kaplan (2013) argues that the market for top executives is competitive, and compensation of other professionals is growing even faster. Other investors, who believe that CEO compensation is exorbitant, complain that the variability in compensation is not significant. In other words, CEOs benefit from a rising stock market (that they are not responsible for) and strong corporate performance but are not hurt by a declining market. They also argue that compensation is being set by a group that the CEO may have had a hand in selecting. As a result of these conflicting opinions, it is important to consider how this compensation is set.

How Compensation Is Set Compensation for the top executives at public companies is set by a compensation committee, a subset of the board of directors. New York Stock Exchange rules require the compensation committee to be composed completely of independent directors, while NASDAQ requires at least two independent directors.

Typically, the compensation committee hires a compensation consultant. The consultant selects peer companies based on factors such as industry, market capitalization, and revenue.

For example, the criteria used to identify Cisco's peers in 2016 were major information technology companies with a market capitalization greater than $30 billion and revenue greater than $10 billion.

Financial targets are set for management. For example, in fiscal year 2016, Cisco's managers reached 102 percent of their target when company performance included revenue growth of 0 percent, operating income growth of 7 percent, operating cash flow growth of 8 percent, and earnings per share growth of 7 percent. In effect, higher margins with no revenue growth were sufficient to surpass management's goals. To be clear, even if the company had not met its goals, the performance rating would have simply been a lower percentage of the goal.

The problem with hiring consultants and examining peer companies is that it would be very unusual for a board to not believe that their CEO is in the top half of the peer group. As a result, any CEO who is currently compensated in the bottom 50 percent will need to be move up to the top 50 percent, which obviously pushes others down into the bottom 50 percent. As a result, salaries of top management increase at high rates. Mishel and Davis (2015) argue that CEO compensation rose 90 times faster than the typical worker's wages between 1978 and 2014.

Many commentators suggest that compensation should be awarded for industry outperformance. At first blush, that seems as if it makes intuitive sense. Unfortunately, it can lead to behavior that is detrimental to the health of the industry as firms may try to injure each other. It may be better to require a firm to earn its cost of capital and then award management some percentage of the excess (economic) profits. This can be done on a long-term basis, where the audit committee measures the long-term profit that has been earned.

Where to Find Compensation Information   The level of compensation of the top five earners within each public company can be found in the company's proxy statement. This includes disclosure about the amounts of compensation, the breakdown of the types of compensation, the financial goals that management is being judged against, and the peer companies. These disclosures can often fill 10 to 20 pages. The summary table describing the total compensation for Cisco's top executives can be seen in Exhibit 10.6.

It is important to recognize that many investors tend to simply think that aligning compensation to share price will align management to shareholders. But, Callahan and Mauboussin (2014) argue that a stock's performance is, at best, "a rough measure of corporate performance." Stock prices are impacted by many factors outside management's control, as evidenced by the technology bubble in the late 1990s and the financial crisis of 2008–2009.

Ultimately, compensation is very important because it may be the easiest item that analysts can use to assess whether management is worried about shareholders or simply worried about themselves. Analysts examine several issues when considering CEO compensation. First, what percentage of a company's earnings are going to top management? Second, is the compensation at risk, meaning does it drop significantly when the company does poorly? Third, does the compensation reward long-term behavior or short-term stock performance? Fourth, and most importantly, is the compensation system designed to reward value creation or a goal that can lead to gaming the system while possibly destroying value (such as earnings per share or growth)?

Finally, while investors can continue to argue about the merits of compensation structure, there's little denying that some things have improved over the past 20 years. For example, as described above, there is a requirement that the majority of the compensation committee must be independent directors. Companies seem to be feeling more pressure to link compensation to performance. The benchmarks that are used to establish corporate performance are established before the fact rather than simply created to explain compensation after the fact. Repricing options seems to be going away. Many companies are tying stock awards to multiple-year stock performance, and officers are often prohibited from hedging their stock and option awards. With that said, CEO compensation has increased much faster than the wages of the other corporate employees.

Exhibit 10.6 Cisco Compensation

Name and Principal Position (1)	Fiscal Year (1)	Salary ($) (2)	Bonus ($)	Stock Awards ($) (3)	Option Awards ($)	Non-Equity Incentive Plan Compensation ($) (4)	All Other Compensation ($) (5)	Total ($)
Charles H. Robbins Chief Executive Office	2016	1,172,115	—	10,277,074	—	4,486,725	98,657	16,034,571
Kelly A. Kramer Executive Vice President and Chief Financial Officer	2016 2015	749,135 632,866	500,000(6) 500,000(6)	5,974,708 5,871,542	— —	1,821,771 1,438,245	11,925 30,055	9,057,539 8,472,708
John T. Chambers Executive Chairman	2016 2015 2014	1,019,231 1,100,000 1,100,000	— — —	8,828,446 14,509,424 12,876,709	— — —	4,000,000 2,500,000 —	12,098 11,700 11,475	9,859,775 19,621,124 16,488,184
Pankaj Patel Former Executive Vice President and Chief Development Officer, Global Engineering	2016 2015 2014	749,135 700,000 700,000	700,000 700,000 —	6,163,251 10,333,425 6,622,059	— — —	1,518,143 1,909,950 1,239,875	67,500 67,500 67,500	8,498,029 13,010,875 8,629,434
Chris Dedicoat Executive Vice President, Worldwide Sales and Field Operations	2016	691,490(7)	—	5,279,794	—	1,476,144	386,820(7)	7,834,248

10.5 CREATING A STOCK PITCH

Pitching stocks is a crucial skill in both asset management and investment banking. Analysts who work for stock funds research a stock and pitch their idea to a portfolio manager. Investment bankers pitch their ideas to corporate clients (concerning companies to buy). The purpose of this section of the chapter is to provide you with a framework for what a stock pitch looks like.

The most important idea to remember is that a stock pitch is an argument. The goal of the stock pitch is to convince an investor to buy a stock or to sell a stock short. Written pitches can take different forms. Some are slide decks and others are written reports with charts embedded.

Normally, a pitch includes the following:

- **Background information about the company**—This includes what the company does, market capitalization, stock price (noting if it is near its high or low), revenue, growth rates, and so on.
- **Merits**—Usually you want to pitch a few key reasons an investor should buy (or sell short) a stock. It is crucial that the merits be forward looking and represent a viewpoint that is not already priced into the stock. Normally, valuation (the idea that a stock is cheap) is not listed as a merit. The valuation will be shown in the next section of the pitch, and it is assumed that the analyst believes the stock is cheap if she is recommending it.
- **Model and multiples**—You need to show a discounted cash flow analysis and a relative valuation analysis. It helps to also show a scenario analysis, where some of the assumptions (for example, the growth rate, the discount rate) have been changed.
- **Risks**—It's important to recognize that all stocks have some risks. The fact that a stock is trading at a particular price means that there are an equal number of buyers and sellers at that price.

In order to give you an example of a pitch, we have taken a stock that was pitched in *Barron's* and turned it into a short two-minute pitch. A "two-minute pitch" is how you would pitch a stock if you were being interviewed and asked if there were any stocks that you're interested in right now.

It's important to note that this pitch is being done simply to show how to argue about a stock. It is based on a *Barron's* article, not our research. Using an article from *Barron's* is not intended to say that this is the appropriate level of research. Rather, this is just the starting point from which you could research more. Given that, read the *Barron's* article about Air Lease in this chapter's **appendix** and then read the pitch below. The pitch below does not include the development of a valuation model.

10.5.1 Air Lease Pitch

Background Information Air Lease (ticker AL) is a $3.5 billion market cap company that buys planes from Boeing, Airbus, and Embraer and then leases them to 86 airlines in 54 countries. Many of these airlines are smaller companies. These smaller airlines are often growing the fastest, but they don't have access to cheap financing, and they don't buy enough planes to have bargaining power with manufacturers. Air Lease effectively handles these negotiations and financing, allowing the airlines to focus on operations without having the debt on their balance sheet. Currently, Air Lease's fleet includes 243 planes.

Air Lease has grown revenue 21 percent per year over the past four years, from $660 million in 2012 to $1.42 billion in 2016. The vast majority of this revenue (94 percent) is from leasing (renting) planes, and the remaining 6 percent of revenue is from buying and selling jets. The company's biggest markets are Asia (43 percent) and Europe (28 percent), but Air Lease also does significant business in Central and South America, the Middle East, Africa, Australia, and the United States.

Recently, Air Lease stock has been trading near $35. This is approximately 10 times projected earnings. It trades at a slight premium (that is, higher multiple) than its competitors, but this makes sense because Air Lease has a younger, more desirable fleet than the competition. The average age of the company's planes is only 3.7 years. The Air Lease fleet is mainly (approximately 80 percent) narrow-body planes, the workhorse of the airline industry. These good assets serve as collateral and allow Air Lease to borrow at attractive rates.

Air Lease is trading at book value, despite the fact that it has the highest ROE (12 percent) and lowest leverage in its sector. With an ROE greater than its cost of equity (approximately 9 to 10 percent), the stock should be trading at a higher price-to-book multiple.

It's also worth noting that Air Lease was founded by Steven Udvar-Házy, a legend in the industry who pioneered aircraft leasing in 1973. He has run another company that was acquired by AIG and eventually merged into AerCap Holdings (AER). He is currently the executive chair of Air Lease and owns 5.2 percent of the stock.

Merits There are three reasons to buy this stock: growth in the travel industry, Air Lease's access to planes (which will help ensure growth), and the mispricing that has resulted from a first quarter earnings miss and a misunderstanding of Air Lease's susceptibility to higher interest rates. Below, we will review each of these three merits.

First, and most importantly, air travel is expanding rapidly. There were 25 million international tourists in the 1950s. In 2016, there were 1.2 billion. The global middle class is expected to increase by 3 billion people by 2031. In China alone, the percentage of passport holders is expected to increase from 4 percent today to 12 percent of the population by 2025. In sum, in 2015, only 6 percent of the world's 7 billion people flew in a plane. This will increase significantly with the rising world middle class.

Second, Air Lease has access to planes. The backlog for aircraft manufacturers has increased from 6,913 planes in 2009 to 13,467 in 2015. There are 233 airlines and leasing companies vying for that backlog. Air Lease is an expert in this field and has 300 planes on order. In addition, Air Lease has already reached lease agreements for 91 percent of the planes that will be delivered through 2019 and 72 percent of the deliveries through 2020.

Third, the market has mispriced Air Lease for two reasons: The company missed first quarter earnings, and the market fears that higher interest rates will hurt the company. Air Lease missed first quarter earnings because manufacturer delays caused 40 percent of Q1 deliveries to arrive during the final two weeks of the quarter—so they weren't leased for as much of the quarter as expected. As described earlier, this is a company that is going to grow its fleet, and that will take earnings per share from $3.48 in 2017 to $4.16 in 2018.

In addition, the fear that higher interest rates will cause Air Lease significant problems is misguided. Approximately 85 percent of the company's debt is fixed rate. In addition, while this debt will eventually result in higher rates, Air Lease's contracts with its lessees allow Air Lease to increase lease rates if interest rates rise after the contract is signed. The Q1 earnings as well as the beliefs about interest rates have created an opportunity to purchase this stock.

Valuation Normally, at this point, you would discuss how you value the company and what you believe it's worth.

Risks Air Lease would certainly be hurt by any factors that would reduce air travel. The two most obvious reasons would be a global recession and an outbreak of terrorism. Of course, these events would hurt most companies. In addition, Air Lease's leadership has managed through past terrorist attacks (such as 9/11) and other issues that affected air travel (such as the SARS outbreak).

10.5.2 A Few Closing Points Concerning Stock Pitches

When you're doing a stock pitch, always remember that you are making an argument. The tone of the pitch should convince the audience to buy the stock; it isn't a book report or a news report. In addition, in the finance industry, participants love numbers. Make assertions and back them up with numbers. While we did not include a model in this example, it's always important to describe your estimate of intrinsic value and also what the company would be worth if the risks actually occurred. Finally, recognize that risks are real. Be careful when explaining mitigating factors. In other words, a pitch walks a fine line (and we may have crossed that line with the Air Lease pitch) when risks are all mitigated. The reality is that Air Lease's management has managed through financial crises, terrorist attacks, and other horrible events. But, that doesn't mean Air Lease is risk free. As an investor, you risk appearing naïve if you try to present a stock as having little risk.

SUMMARY

This chapter focuses on five topics that sophisticated investors should understand: (1) initial public offerings, (2) the role of buy-side analysts versus sell-side analysts, (3) capital allocation by management, (4) the most important corporate governance issues that investors consider, and (5) how to pitch a stock.

When a private company goes public, the shares of the company are sold to the public. The company may need capital, the owners may want more liquidity, or the company may want to have publicly traded stock that can be used to attract employees or to use as currency to acquire other companies.

Most IPOs end their first day of trading at a price that is higher than the IPO offering price. This occurs because of underpricing, which may be a way to compensate institutional investors for their efforts in helping price the stock. Another possible reason for underpricing is that investors would fear overbidding (the winner's curse) if IPOs weren't systematically underpriced. Alternatively, IPOs may be underpriced in order to avoid disappointing the management of the issuing company. Or, it's possible that a low price helps reduce the chance of a disappointing offering that results in a lawsuit against the investment bank. Finally, underpricing results in greater profits for the investors, and this may create a larger pool of profits that the underwriter can try to seek (in the form of future commissions) from the investors.

Some investors believe that auctions are the best solution to underpricing. Auctions attempt to place shares in the hands of those investors who value them the most. But, auctions have not been popular, which may indicate that issuing firms are balancing underpricing against several benefits they receive from the underwriter (such as market stabilization and analyst coverage).

Sell-side analysts write research about public stocks, such as recent IPOs. These analysts tend to know a tremendous amount about the companies they cover. Buy-side analysts research stocks in order to make recommendations internally, to their portfolio managers. Buy-side analysts have respect for sell-side research but tend to be unimpressed with the ultimate recommendations of the sell-side because the sell-side tends to be overly bullish. The buy-side also places great value on the sell-side's access to management.

Investors often spend significant time studying how management allocates capital. In other words, how do managers use the resources that they have access to? Their main options are to acquire other companies, do capital expenditures (reinvesting in their own business), conduct R&D, invest in net working capital, pay dividends, repurchase shares, or pay off debt.

Investors also examine the tools and policies which help ensure that management acts in the best interest of shareholders. Most importantly, investors examine the quality and independence of the board of directors, whether the company discourages other companies from attempting to acquire it, and how top management is compensated.

As a result of all this research about a company, it is possible to create a stock pitch. With a stock pitch, an analyst makes an argument about why a stock should be purchased. Normally, a stock pitch discusses background facts about the company, the merits (a few arguments as to why the stock should be purchased), the valuation, and any risks that exist.

SUGGESTED READINGS

Brown, Lawrence D., Andrew C. Call, Michael B. Clement, and Nathan Y. Sharp, "Inside the 'Black Box' of Sell-Side Financial Analysts." *Journal of Accounting Research* 53, no. 1 (March 2015).

Brown, Lawrence D., Andrew C. Call, Michael B. Clement, and Nathan Y. Sharp, "The Activities of Buy-Side Analysts and the Determinants of the Stock Recommendations." *Journal of Accounting and Economics* 62, no. 1 (August 2016).

Callahan, Dan, and Michael J. Mauboussin, "Capital Allocation: Evidence, Analytical Methods, and Assessment Guidance." *Journal of Applied Corporate Finance* 26, no. 4 (Fall 2014).

Chen, Zhaohui, Alan D. Morrison, and William J. Wilhelm, Jr., "Another Look at Bookbuilding, Auctions, and the Future of the IPO Process." *Journal of Applied Corporate Finance* 26, no. 2 (Spring 2014).

Chew, Don, and John McCormack, "Capital Deployment Roundtable: A Discussion of Corporate Investment and Payout Policy." *Journal of Applied Corporate Finance* 26, no. 4 (Fall 2014).

Gressle, Mark, and Stephen F. O'Byrne, "How 'Competitive Pay' Undermines Pay for Performance (and What Companies Can Do to Avoid That)." *Journal of Applied Corporate Finance* 25, no. 2 (Spring 2013).

Kaplan, Steven N. "CEO Pay and Corporate Governance in the U. S.: Perceptions, Facts, and Challenges." *Journal of Applied Corporate Finance* 25, no. 2 (Spring 2013).

Mauboussin, Michael J. "Share Repurchases from All Angles." *Legg Mason Perspectives* (June 2012).

Ramnath, Sundaresh, Steve Rock, and Philip Shane, "The Financial Analyst Forecasting Literature: A Taxonomy with Suggestions for Further Research." *International Journal of Forecasting* 24 (2008).

Ritter, Jay R. "Equilibrium in the Initial Public Offering Market." *Annual Review of Financial Economics* 3 (2011).

QUESTIONS

1. What are possible explanations for underpricing?
2. How does market stabilization work with an IPO?
3. How does a dirty auction work?
4. What would make a sell-side firm pay great compensation to an analyst? In other words, what factors would push the analyst's compensation higher?
5. When should a company repurchase shares as opposed to pay a dividend?
6. What are the four important dates surrounding a dividend?
7. When would you prefer that management engage in capital expenditures as opposed to purchasing another company?
8. If a company announces that it has instituted a poison pill, is this good news or bad news? Why?
9. What arguments would you make to say that CEOs are overpaid? What arguments would you make to say that CEO compensation is fair?
10. Find an article about a stock and turn it into a stock pitch. Describe what additional information you would want to know.

PROBLEMS

1. A company is going public at $16 and will use the ticker XYZ. The underwriters will charge a 7 percent spread. The company is issuing 20 million shares, and insiders will continue to hold an additional 40 million shares that will not be part of the IPO. The company will also pay $1 million of audit fees, $2 million of legal fees, and $500,000 of printing fees. The stock closes the first day at $19. Answer the following questions:
   a. At the end of the first day, what is the market capitalization of the company?
   b. What are the total costs of the offering? Include underpricing in this calculation.

2. What are the total costs of going public for XYZ from Problem 1 as a percentage of the total pre-cost equity value? In calculating the pre-cost equity value, use the closing price of the stock at the end of the first day as the pre-cost equity value.

3. The company in Problem 1 grants a 15 percent overallotment option to the underwriter. The underwriter issues shares that are backed by the entire overallotment option but has not yet exercised the option.

   a. Explain what will happen if the price of the stock increases to $22. Describe the underwriter profits from the overallotment option in your explanation.

   b. Explain what will happen if the price of the stock decreases to $11.50. Describe the underwriter profits from the overallotment option in your explanation.

4. A company goes public by using an auction. The bids are contained in the table below. The firm wants to sell 10 million shares.

Price ($)	Number of Shares (millions)
20	2.5
19	7
18	4
17	5
16	8
15	6

   In a traditional offering, describe which bidders would receive shares, the price they would pay, and how much of their orders would be filled.

5. Assume that the auction in Problem 4 is conducted as a dirty auction, and the clearing price is $17. Describe which bidders would receive shares, the price they would pay, and how much of their orders would be filled.

6. On Thursday, May 18, the board of directors of ABC declares a 30-cent-per-share dividend to shareholders of record as of Tuesday, June 13. The dividend will be paid on Wednesday, June 28.

   a. What is the declaration date?
   b. What is the date of record?
   c. What is the ex-dividend date?
   d. What is the payment date?

7. A stock is currently trading for $35. The company has a price–earnings multiple of 10. There are 100 million shares outstanding. Your model indicates that the stock is actually worth $45. The company announces that it will use $300 million to repurchase shares.

   a. After the repurchase, what is the value of the stock, according to your model?
   b. After the repurchase, what is the actual price–earnings multiple of the stock?
   c. If the company had used the $300 million to pay a cash dividend instead of doing a repurchase, how would the value of the stock have changed, according to your model?
   d. If the company had used the $300 million to pay a cash dividend instead of doing a repurchase, what would be the actual price–earnings multiple after the dividend?

8. A stock is currently trading for $35. The company has a price–earnings multiple of 10. There are 100 million shares outstanding. Your model indicates that the stock is actually worth $25. The company announces that it will use $300 million to repurchase shares.

   a. After the repurchase, what is the value of the stock, according to your model?
   b. After the repurchase, what is the actual price–earnings multiple of the stock?

    c. If the company had used the $300 million to pay a cash dividend instead of doing a repurchase, how would the value of the stock have changed, according to your model?

    d. If the company had used the $300 million to pay a cash dividend instead of doing a repurchase, what would be the actual price–earnings multiple after the dividend?

9. A company is going public with an offering price of $20 per share. The gross spread is 7 percent. The company plans on issuing 10 million shares. How much money will the company raise in the offering?

10. A company goes public with an offering price of $18. There is a 7 percent underwriting spread. There is also a 15 percent overallotment option. The company is selling 25 million shares. The underwriter fills orders for 28.75 million shares but has not exercised the overallotment option. The stock rises to $20. How much would it cost the underwriter to cover the short position? If the underwriter used all its profits from the short position to purchase shares, how many shares would it purchase (include the shares that must be purchased to cover the short position)?

11. Use an article from *Barron's* to write a stock pitch. Examine the compensation for the CEO by using the firm's most recent proxy statement.

FEATURE

Why Air Lease Should Soon Be Flying High

Air Lease has been buffeted by fears of rising rates. But its virtues should propel the stock up over 30%.

By KOPIN TAN

Updated May 13, 2017 12:23 a.m. ET

Globally, middle classes are growing and filling airplanes and airports with new travelers. Thats bullish for aviation leasing companies. *Rawpixel Ltd/Alamy*

To travel the world is one of lifes persistent romances, and lately it seems everyone wants to do it. The throngs of international tourists have grown from 25 million in the 1950 s to 1.2 billion last year, says the World Economic Forum, and their ranksand airports and airplanes will only get more crowded as the global middle class expands by three billion people by 2031. In China alone, a small projected uptick in the percentage of passport holders, from 4% of the population to 12% by 2025, will disgorge millions into tourist meccas from Tuscany to Tokyo.

A long-term travel boom is good news for Air Lease (ticker: AL), which buys planes from Boeing (BA), Airbus (AIR.France), and Embraer (ERJ), and leases them to 86 airlines in 54 countries. Because smaller airlines in emerging marketswhere growth often is fastestlack easy access to cheap financing, and because they dont order enough planes to have bargaining power with manufacturers, they often turn to leasing companies like Air Lease. It also lets airlines focus on operations and keep hefty assets off their balance sheets. Today, 42% of the worlds commercial jets are leased, from zero in the 1960 s.

With airlines operating at record capacity, and with ugly publicity about the fallout from overbooking, youd think shares of Air Lease would be soaring. Yet the Los Angeles companys shares have been more turbulent than its results. Revenue is climbing steadily, from $660 million in 2012 to $1.05 billion in 2014 to $1.42 billion last year. But shares have fluctuated between $23 and $42 since 2014. They were recently at $34.91, just 10 times projected 2017 profit, and trading at book value, near the low end of their range since a 2011 initial public offering.

The 13 analysts who cover Air Lease think shares are worth $46.42 on average, or 33% higher. But the company is often misunderstoodand unjustly shunned. Its a growth stock with a value price tag, and that unnerves investors from both camps. Because Air Lease borrows to fund purchases, investors fret about its debt as interest rates rise, even though tepid economic growth should keep rates lower longer.

A WORLDWIDE RECESSION or a fresh outbreak of terrorism would hurt travel, but how many companies in todays pricey stock market are immune to such events? Air Leases management has navigated crises from the 9/11 attacks to the SARS outbreak, and has the experience to buy more planes when prices fall and sell as the cycle peaks. By the time Alitalia filed for bankruptcy protection, for instance, Air Lease had trimmed its exposure to just four planes, which it stands ready to repossess and lease to new customers.

The Plane Truth

Air Lease trades at a small premium to its peers but sports a younger, more desirable fleet and less leverage-and is still modestly priced compared with many other stocks.

Company/Ticker	Recent Price	Market Value (bil)	12-Month Change	Earnings per share		2017 E P/E	%LT Debt to Capital
				2017 E	2018 E		
Air Lease/AL	$34.91	$3.7	16%	$3.48	$4.16	10.0	72.0%
AerCap Holdings/AER	45.03	7.9	12	6.12	6.90	7.4	76.4
Aircastle/AYR	21.75	1.7	1	2.41	2.47	9.0	69.7
FLY Leasing/FLY	12.59	0.4	5	1.64	2.17	7.7	81.0

Note: E = Estimate
Source: Thomson Reuters

Chris Retzler, portfolio manager at Needham Asset Management, calls Air Lease an asset managerbut of airplanes, adding it helps that the management team is at the forefront of where aviation is headed. Air Lease may have started life only in 2010, but it was founded by Steven Udvar-Hazy, who pioneered aircraft leasing in 1973 and had run another company that was eventually acquired by American International Group and then merged into AerCap Holdings (AER), another leasing company. Today, Udvar-Hazywho is to aircraft leasing what Bill Gates is to softwareis executive chairman of Air Leases board and owns 5.2% of the stock, which should give management extra incentive to lift shares to cruising altitude.

What elevates Air Lease above its peers? It has one of the industrys youngest fleetsits 243 planes are an average age of 3.7 years oldwhich lets it borrow at cheaper rates even as it charges customers more. It has more than 300 planes on order, and has already snagged long-term leases for 91% of planes scheduled to be delivered through 2019 and 72% of deliveries through 2020, which gives it a predictable stream of future revenue. Its ratio of fixed- to floating-rate debt stands at a prudent 85% to 15%, and a BBB credit rating keeps average borrowing costs at 3.48%. RBC analyst Jason Arnold rates Air Lease his top pick, given its sizable and growing fleet of new and in-favor aircraft, and the highest return-on-equity and lowest leverage in the sector.

The Bottom Line

Air Lease stock trades at $35, just 10 times 2017 earnings, largely on fears of rising interest rates. But with its young fleet and robust order book, its shares should be worth $46. or 33% higher.

While Air Lease earned some 6% of its revenue in 2016 from buying and selling jets, the 94% it earned from rental income is geographically diversifiedwith 28% from Europe, 21 % from China, 22% from the rest of Asia, 8% from Central and South America, 7.5% from the Middle East and Africa, and the rest from North America and Australia.

In early May, it reported first-quarter profits that missed forecasts, but manufacturer delays had caused 40% of its first-quarter deliveries to arrive only in the quarters final two weeks. Analysts have trimmed estimates but still expect Air Lease to earn $3.48 a share in fiscal 2017 and $4.16 in 2018, up from $3.44 in 2016.

Air Leases interest-rate risk also isnt as big as feared, argues David Swartz of investment firm Pacific West Land, who has shared his views of air-leasing stocks on SumZero.com, a social network for fund managers and professional investors. Contract clauses let Air Lease boost lease rates if interest rates rise after the contract was signed. As CEO John Plueger once pointed out, airlines need leasing companies in good times to deliver more planes, while in bad times airlines need leasing companies for their balance sheets.

Air Lease recently sold 19 older jets into an entity it created called Thunderbolt, which was then securitized. This lets Air Lease collect servicing fees and maintain a young fleet. While the industry worries about a possible glut in wide- body jets, 80% of Air Leases fleet are narrowbody, single-aisle planes considered the industrys workhorses.

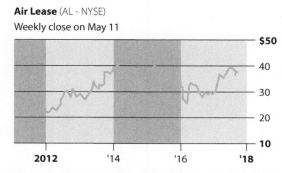

Air Lease (AL - NYSE)

Weekly close on May 11

Source: Why Air Lease Should Soon Be Flying High Air Lease has been buffeted by fears of rising rates. But its virtues should propel the stock up over 30%. May 13, 2017.

A 2016 Deloitte study showed that only 6% of the planets seven billion people flew on an airplane in 2015, which shows how vast and untapped the market remains. Aircraft makers backlog ballooned from 6,913 planes in 2009 to a record 13,467 by 2015. With 233 airlines and leasing companies vying for that backlog, and possible economic turbulence ahead, investors should climb on board only with a seasoned expert like Air Lease.

CHAPTER **11**

Equity Portfolio Management Strategies

After you read this chapter, you should be able to answer the following questions:

- What are the two generic equity portfolio management styles?
- What are three techniques for constructing a passive index portfolio?
- How does the goal of a passive equity portfolio manager differ from the goal of an active manager?
- What is a portfolio's tracking error and how is it useful in the construction of a passive equity investment?
- What is the difference between an index mutual fund and an exchange-traded fund?
- What are the three themes that active equity portfolio managers can use?
- How does factor investing differ from fundamental approaches to active management?
- What is active share and how can the measure help identify an investor as being active or passive?
- What stock characteristics do momentum-oriented investors look for?
- How can an investor measure the tax efficiency of an actively managed portfolio?
- What stock characteristics differentiate value-oriented and growth-oriented investment styles?
- What is style analysis and what does it indicate about a manager's investment performance?
- What techniques do active managers use in an attempt to outperform their benchmarks?
- What are the differences between the integrated, strategic, tactical, and insured approaches to asset allocation?

Recent chapters have reviewed how to analyze industries and companies, how to estimate a stock's intrinsic value, and how technical analysis can assist in stock picking. Some equity portfolios are constructed one stock at a time. Research staffs analyze the economy, industries, and companies; evaluate firms' strategies and competitive advantages; and recommend individual stocks for purchase or for sale.

Other equity portfolios are constructed using quantitative methods. Computers analyze relationships between stocks and market sectors to identify undervalued stocks. Quantitative screens and factor models are used to construct portfolios of stocks with such attributes as low P/E ratios, low price–book ratios, small capitalization, or high dividend yield; those neglected by analysts; or stocks whose returns are strongly correlated with economic variables, such as interest rates.

Managers of equity portfolios can also increase an investor's wealth through their sector and asset allocation decisions. For example, a manager using *tactical* asset allocation might split his funds into two index portfolios—one containing stocks and the other containing bonds—and then shift the allocation between these portfolios depending on which asset class he believes will perform the best during the coming period. Similarly, *insured* asset allocation attempts to limit investment losses by shifting funds between an existing equity portfolio and a risk-free security depending on changing market conditions.

11.1 PASSIVE VERSUS ACTIVE MANAGEMENT

Equity portfolio management strategies can be placed into either a passive or an active category. One way to distinguish between these strategies is to decompose the total actual return that the portfolio manager attempts to produce:

11.1

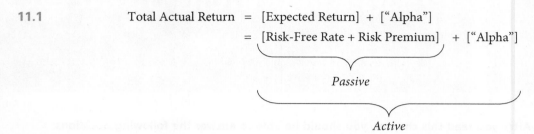

Passive portfolio managers just try to capture the expected return consistent with the risk level of their portfolios. In contrast, active managers attempt to "beat the market" by forming portfolios capable of producing actual returns that exceed risk-adjusted expected returns. The difference between the actual and expected return is often called the portfolio's *alpha*, and it represents the amount of value that the active manager has added (if positive) or subtracted (if negative) to the investment process.

Passive equity portfolio management typically holds stocks so the portfolio's returns will track those of a benchmark index over time. This approach to investing is generally referred to as *indexing*, and there is no attempt on the manager's part to generate alpha. While indexing is often thought to be a long-term buy-and-hold strategy, occasional rebalancing of the portfolio is necessary as the composition of the benchmark changes and cash distributions must be reinvested. However, since the purpose is to mimic an index, the passive managers are judged by how well they track the target—that is, minimize the deviation between stock portfolio and index returns.

Conversely, *active equity portfolio management* is an attempt by the manager to outperform an equity benchmark on a risk-adjusted basis. The active manager can employ any of several specific investment strategies to do this, but, broadly speaking, there are two main ways to try to add alpha: *tactical adjustments* (for example, equity style or sector timing) or *security selection* (stock-picking) skills. So-called hybrid investment strategies that may appear to fall into the middle ground between the passive and active categories (for example, enhanced indexing) are really just more modest variations of an active approach to equity portfolio management. Further, *hedge funds* are actively managed portfolios that often pursue a "pure alpha" (or absolute return) strategy in which the manager seeks to isolate the alpha component of return; these strategies are discussed in Chapter 17.

When deciding to follow either an active or a passive strategy (or some combination of the two), an investor must assess the trade-off between the low-cost but less-exciting alternative of indexing versus the potentially more lucrative alternative of active investing, which almost certainly will have higher management fees and trading costs. Sharpe (1991) argued that these higher expenses will *always* make active management the inferior alternative. Sorensen, Miller, and Samak (1998) noted that the critical factor in this evaluation is the stock-picking skill of the portfolio manager and showed that the optimal allocation to indexing declines as managerial skill increases. Alford, Jones, and Winkelmann (2003) support this position by arguing that a disciplined approach to active management—which they term *structured portfolio management*—is likely to be the most effective method for investors. Harlow and Brown (2006) showed that the active versus passive management decision for many investors comes down to their ability to identify superior managers in advance. Finally, Pastor, Stambaugh, and Taylor (2015) have shown that the active investment management industry has become more skilled over time.

Exhibit 11.1 Active and Passive Investment in U.S. Equity and Fixed-Income Markets

Strategy	2016 ($ billions)	2008 ($ billions)	% Change
Active equity	$2,332.9	$1,281.7	82.0%
Passive equity	2,153.4	789.1	172.9
Active fixed-income	3,029.4	1,706.0	77.6
Passive fixed-income	639.4	211.2	202.7

Source: *Pensions & Investments Money Manager Directory*, May 29, 2017, and May 30, 2009.

Exhibit 11.1 reports the amount of money in the U.S. equity and fixed-income markets using active and passive strategies for two recent years. The data are compiled from a survey of almost 1,000 professional managers on behalf of their clients. The main conclusion is that both active and passive funds play a prominent role with investors. Further, while active management strategies control the largest percentage of investor wealth, passively managed investment products are growing in importance at a much more rapid pace.

11.2 AN OVERVIEW OF PASSIVE EQUITY PORTFOLIO MANAGEMENT STRATEGIES

Passive equity portfolio management attempts to design a set of stock holdings that *replicates* the performance of a specific benchmark. A passive manager earns a fee by constructing a portfolio that closely tracks the returns to a particular equity index meeting the client's needs and objectives. If the manager tries to outperform the benchmark, he or she clearly violates the passive premise of the portfolio.

Chapter 4 contained a summary of many of the different market indexes that a passive manager can attempt to replicate. Domestic equity indexes include the S&P 500, the NASDAQ Composite Index, and the Wilshire 5000. Benchmarks also exist for various sectors of the stock market, such as those for small capitalization stocks (Russell 2000), for value- or growth-oriented stocks (Russell Growth Index and the Russell Value Index), for numerous developed world regions (such as the EAFE Index), and for collections of smaller countries (emerging markets). Khorana, Nelling, and Trester (1998) have noted that as passive investing has grown in popularity, money managers have created an index fund for virtually every broad market category.

In Chapter 5, we presented several reasons for investing in a passive equity portfolio. Consistent evidence indicates that stock markets throughout the world are often fairly efficient. For many active managers, the annual costs of trying to beat the market (1 to 2 percent of the portfolio's assets) are difficult to overcome. However, passive strategies are also not costless to employ. Because of cash flows into and out of an index fund, as well as events that change the composition of the benchmark itself (for example, mergers, bankruptcies, index rebalancing), the passive manager will need to buy and sell securities over time. These transactions mean that the passive portfolio will inevitably underperform its index over time, even if the manager minimizes turnover in the portfolio for every other reason. The extent of this underperformance can range from 0.05 to 0.25 percent in developed stock markets to 3 percent for portfolios mimicking less liquid indexes (for example, emerging markets).

11.2.1 Index Portfolio Construction Techniques

There are three basic techniques for constructing a passive index portfolio: full replication, sampling, and quadratic optimization. The most obvious technique is **full replication**, wherein all the securities in the index are purchased in proportion to their weights in the index. This technique helps ensure close tracking, but the need to buy many securities will increase transaction costs that will detract from performance. In addition, the reinvestment of dividends will also result in high trading expenses when many firms pay small dividends at different times in the year.

The second technique, **sampling**, addresses the problem of having to buy numerous stock issues. With sampling, a portfolio manager would only need to buy a representative sample of stocks comprising the benchmark index. Stocks with larger index weights are purchased according to their weight in the index; smaller issues are purchased so their aggregate characteristics (such as beta, industry designation, dividend yield) approximate the underlying benchmark. With fewer stocks to purchase, larger positions can be taken in the issues acquired, which should lead to proportionately lower transaction costs. The disadvantage of sampling is that portfolio returns will almost certainly not track the returns for the benchmark index as closely as with full replication.

Rather than obtaining a sample based on industry or security characteristics, **quadratic optimization** (or programming) techniques can be used to construct a passive portfolio. Historical information on price changes and correlations between securities are input to a computer program that determines the composition of a portfolio that will minimize return deviations from the benchmark. A problem with this technique is that it relies on historical price changes and correlations, and if these change over time, the portfolio may experience very large differences from the benchmark.

Sometimes customized passive portfolios, called **completeness funds**, are constructed to complement active portfolios that do not cover the entire market. For example, a large pension fund may allocate some of its holdings to active managers expected to outperform the market. Many times, these active portfolios are overweighted in certain market sectors or stock types. In this case, the pension fund sponsor may want the remaining funds to be invested passively to "fill the holes" left vacant by the active managers.

For example, suppose a pension fund hires three active managers to invest part of its money. One manager emphasizes small-capitalization U.S. stocks, the second invests only in Pacific Rim countries, and the third invests in U.S. stocks with low P/E ratios. To ensure adequate diversification, the pension fund may want to passively invest the remaining assets in a completeness fund that will have a customized benchmark that includes large- and mid-capitalization U.S. stocks, U.S. stocks with normal to high P/E ratios, and international stocks outside the Pacific Rim.

Still other passive portfolios and benchmarks exist for investors with certain unique needs and preferences. Some investors may want their funds to be invested only in stocks that pay dividends or in a company that produces a product or service that the investor deems socially responsible. Dialynas and Murata (2006) shows that benchmarks can be produced that reflect these desired attributes and passive portfolios can be constructed to track the performance of the customized benchmark over time so that investors' special needs can be satisfied.

11.2.2 Tracking Error and Index Portfolio Construction

If the goal of forming a passive portfolio is to replicate a particular equity index, the success of such a fund lies not in the absolute returns it produces but in how closely its returns match those of the benchmark. That is, the goal of the passive manager should be to minimize the portfolio's return volatility relative to the index. Said differently, the manager should try to minimize **tracking error**.

As Ammann and Zimmermann (2001) note, tracking error can be defined as the extent to which return fluctuations in the managed portfolio are *not correlated* with return fluctuations in the benchmark. A flexible and straightforward way of measuring tracking error can be developed as follows. Let:

$$w_i = \text{investment weight of Asset } i \text{ in the managed portfolio}$$
$$R_{it} = \text{return to Asset } i \text{ in Period } t$$
$$R_{bt} = \text{return to the benchmark portfolio in Period } t$$

so that the Period t return to managed portfolio is:

$$R_{pt} = \sum_{i=1}^{N} w_i R_{it}$$

where:

$N =$ number of assets in the managed portfolio

With these definitions, the Period t *return differential* between the managed portfolio and the benchmark is:

11.2
$$\Delta_t = \sum_{i=1}^{N} w_i R_{it} - R_{bt} = R_{pt} - R_{bt}$$

Given the returns to the managed portfolio and the benchmark, Δ is a function of the N investment weights that the manager selects. Also, not all of the assets in the benchmark need be included in the managed portfolio (that is, $w = 0$ for some assets).

For a sample of T return observations, the variance of Δ can be calculated as follows:

11.3
$$\sigma_\Delta^2 = \frac{\sum_{t=1}^{T} (\Delta_t - \overline{\Delta})^2}{(T-1)}$$

Finally, the standard deviation of the return differential is:

$$\sigma_\Delta = \sqrt{\sigma_\Delta^2} = \text{periodic tracking error}$$

so that *annualized tracking error* (*TE*) can be calculated as:

11.4
$$TE = \sigma_\Delta \sqrt{P}$$

where P is the number of return periods in a year (for example, $P = 12$ for monthly returns, $P = 252$ for daily returns).

Suppose an investor has formed a portfolio designed to track a particular benchmark. Over the past eight quarters, the returns to this portfolio, as well as the index returns and the return difference between the two, were:

Period	Manager	Index	Difference (Δ)
1	2.3%	2.7%	−0.4%
2	−3.6	−4.6	1.0
3	11.2	10.1	1.1
4	1.2	2.2	−1.0
5	1.5	0.4	1.1
6	3.2	2.8	0.4
7	8.9	8.1	0.8
8	−0.8	0.6	−1.4

The periodic average and standard deviation of the manager's return differential ("delta") relative to the benchmark are:

$$\text{Average } \Delta = [-0.4 + 1.0 + \cdots + 0.8 - 1.4] \div 8 = 0.2\%$$

$$\sigma = \sqrt{(-0.4 - 0.2)^2 + (1.0 - 0.2)^2 + \cdots + (-1.4 - 0.2)^2} \div \sqrt{(8-1)} = 1.0\%$$

Thus, the manager's annualized tracking error for this two-year period is 2.0 percent ($=1.0$ percent $\times \sqrt{4}$).

Generally speaking, there is an inverse relationship between a passive portfolio's tracking error relative to its index and the time and expense necessary to create and maintain the portfolio. For example, full replication of the S&P 500 would have virtually no tracking error but would involve positions in 500 different stocks and require frequent rebalancing. As smaller samples are used, the expense of forming the managed portfolio would decline, but the potential tracking error is likely to increase. Thus, the art of being a manager of a passive equity portfolio lies in balancing the costs (larger tracking error) and the benefits (easier management, lower trading commissions) of using smaller samples. Exhibit 11.2 estimates the tracking error that occurs from such sampling.

Alford, Jones, and Winkelmann (2003) have also shown that tracking error can be a useful way to categorize a fund's investment style. They argue that money managers can be classified using the following chart with regard to the tracking errors of their portfolios compared to the relevant benchmark:

Investment Style	Tracking Error Range
Passive	Less than 1.0% (0.5% or lower is normal)
Structured	Between 1.0% and 3.0%
Active	Over 3.0% (5.0% to 15.0% is normal)

Source: Andrew Alford, Robert Jones, Kurt Winkelmann, "A Spectrum Approach to Active Risk Budgeting," *Journal of Portfolio Management* 30, no. 1 (September 2003): 49–60.

They also document that structured portfolio managers, who can be viewed as active managers with the tightest controls on the permissible level of their tracking errors, tend to produce superior risk-adjusted returns to those active managers whose investment mandates allow them to stray further from their indexes.

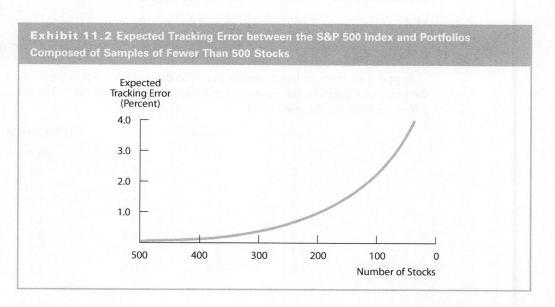

Exhibit 11.2 Expected Tracking Error between the S&P 500 Index and Portfolios Composed of Samples of Fewer Than 500 Stocks

11.2.3 Methods of Index Portfolio Investing

Although investors can construct their own passive investment portfolios that mimic a particular equity index, in Chapter 4 we discussed at least two prepackaged ways of accomplishing this goal that are typically more convenient and less expensive. These are (1) buying shares in an *index mutual fund* or (2) buying shares in an *exchange-traded fund* (ETF).

Index Funds As we will see in more detail later on in the book (Chapter 17), mutual funds represent established security portfolios managed by professional investment companies (for example, Fidelity, Vanguard, Putnam) in which investors can participate. The investment company is responsible for deciding how the fund is managed. For an indexed portfolio, the fund manager will typically attempt to replicate the composition of the particular index exactly, meaning that he or she will buy the exact securities comprising the index in their exact weights and then alter those positions anytime the composition of the index itself is changed. Since changes to most equity indexes occur sporadically, index funds tend to generate low trading and management expense ratios. A prominent example of an index fund is Vanguard's 500 Index Fund (VFINX), which is designed to mimic the S&P 500 index. Panel A of Exhibit 11.3 provides a descriptive overview of this fund and indicates that its historical return performance is virtually indistinguishable from that of the benchmark, with of a tracking error of 0.037 percent.

The advantage of index mutual funds is that they provide an inexpensive way for investors to acquire a diversified portfolio that emphasizes the desired market or industry. In the case of VFINX, the annual expense ratio is just 0.14 percent, substantially lower than the 1.0 percent expense ratio a typical actively managed fund might charge. As with any mutual fund, the disadvantages are that investors can only liquidate their positions at the end of the trading day (that is, no intraday trading), usually cannot short sell, and may have unwanted tax repercussions if the fund has an unforeseen need to sell a portion of its holdings, thereby realizing capital gains.

Exchange-Traded Funds ETFs are a more recent development in the world of indexed investment products than index mutual funds. Essentially, ETFs are depository receipts that give investors a pro rata claim on the capital gains and cash flows of the securities that are held in deposit by the financial institution that issued the certificates. That is, a portfolio of securities is placed on deposit at a financial institution or into a unit trust, which then issues a single type of certificate representing ownership of the underlying portfolio. In that way, ETFs are similar to the American depository receipts (ADRs) described in Chapter 2.

There are several notable example of ETFs, including (1) Standard & Poor's 500 Depository Receipts (SPDRs, or "spiders," as they are sometimes called), which are based on a basket of all the securities held in that index; (2) iShares, which recreate indexed positions in several global developed and emerging equity markets; and (3) sector ETFs, which invest in baskets of stocks from specific industry sectors, including consumer services, industrial, technology, financial services, energy, utilities, and cyclicals/transportation. Exhibit 11.4 shows descriptive and return data for the SPDR Trust certificates. Notice that the expense ratio of this EFT (that is, 0.95 percent) is even lower than that for the index mutual fund. However, with a tracking error of 0.507 percent, the returns to these shares do not track the index quite as closely as did the VFINX fund.

A significant advantage of ETFs over index mutual funds is that they can be bought and sold (and short sold) like common stock through an organized exchange or in an over-the-counter market. Further, they are backed by a sponsoring organization (for example, for SPDRs, the sponsor is PDR Services LLC, a limited liability company wholly owned by Intercontinental Exchange Inc.) that can alter the composition of the underlying portfolio to reflect changes in the composition of the index. Other advantages relative to index funds

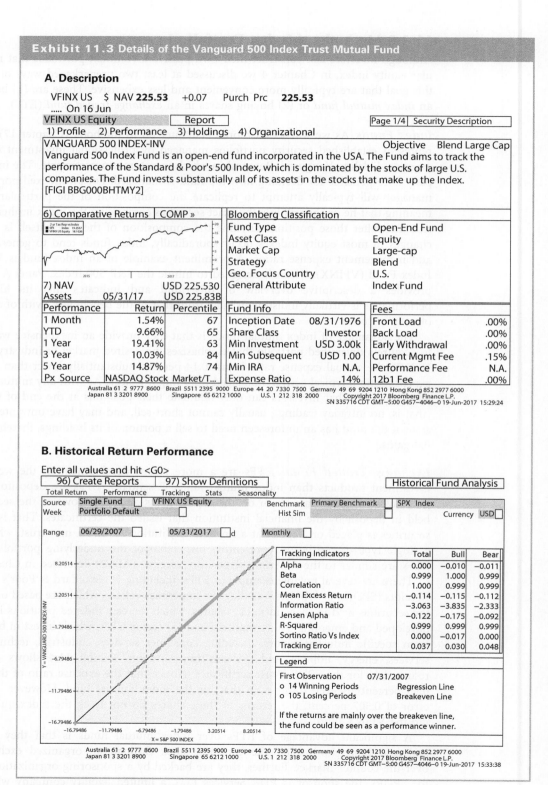

Exhibit 11.3 Details of the Vanguard 500 Index Trust Mutual Fund

A. Description

VFINX US $ NAV **225.53**   +0.07   Purch Prc   **225.53**
..... On 16 Jun

VFINX US Equity	Report		Page 1/4 Security Description
1) Profile   2) Performance   3) Holdings   4) Organizational

VANGUARD 500 INDEX-INV   Objective   Blend Large Cap
Vanguard 500 Index Fund is an open-end fund incorporated in the USA. The Fund aims to track the performance of the Standard & Poor's 500 Index, which is dominated by the stocks of large U.S. companies. The Fund invests substantially all of its assets in the stocks that make up the Index.
[FIGI BBG000BHTMY2]

6) Comparative Returns	COMP »		Bloomberg Classification	
			Fund Type	Open-End Fund
			Asset Class	Equity
			Market Cap	Large-cap
			Strategy	Blend
			Geo. Focus Country	U.S.
7) NAV		USD 225.530	General Attribute	Index Fund
Assets	05/31/17	USD 225.83B		

Performance	Return	Percentile	Fund Info		Fees	
1 Month	1.54%	67	Inception Date	08/31/1976	Front Load	.00%
YTD	9.66%	65	Share Class	Investor	Back Load	.00%
1 Year	19.41%	63	Min Investment	USD 3.00k	Early Withdrawal	.00%
3 Year	10.03%	84	Min Subsequent	USD 1.00	Current Mgmt Fee	.15%
5 Year	14.87%	74	Min IRA	N.A.	Performance Fee	N.A.
Px Source	NASDAQ Stock Market/T...		Expense Ratio	.14%	12b1 Fee	.00%

B. Historical Return Performance

Enter all values and hit <G0>

96) Create Reports	97) Show Definitions		Historical Fund Analysis
Total Return Performance Tracking Stats Seasonality			

| Source | Single Fund | VFINX US Equity | Benchmark | Primary Benchmark | SPX Index | |
| Week | Portfolio Default | | Hist Sim | | | Currency   USD |

Range   06/29/2007   –   05/31/2017   d   Monthly

Tracking Indicators	Total	Bull	Bear
Alpha	0.000	−0.010	−0.011
Beta	0.999	1.000	0.999
Correlation	1.000	0.999	0.999
Mean Excess Return	−0.114	−0.115	−0.112
Information Ratio	−3.063	−3.835	−2.333
Jensen Alpha	−0.122	−0.175	−0.092
R-Squared	0.999	0.999	0.999
Sortino Ratio Vs Index	0.000	−0.017	0.000
Tracking Error	0.037	0.030	0.048

Legend
First Observation   07/31/2007
o 14 Winning Periods   Regression Line
o 105 Losing Periods   Breakeven Line
If the returns are mainly over the breakeven line, the fund could be seen as a performance winner.

Y = VANGUARD 500 INDEX-INV
X = S&P 500 INDEX

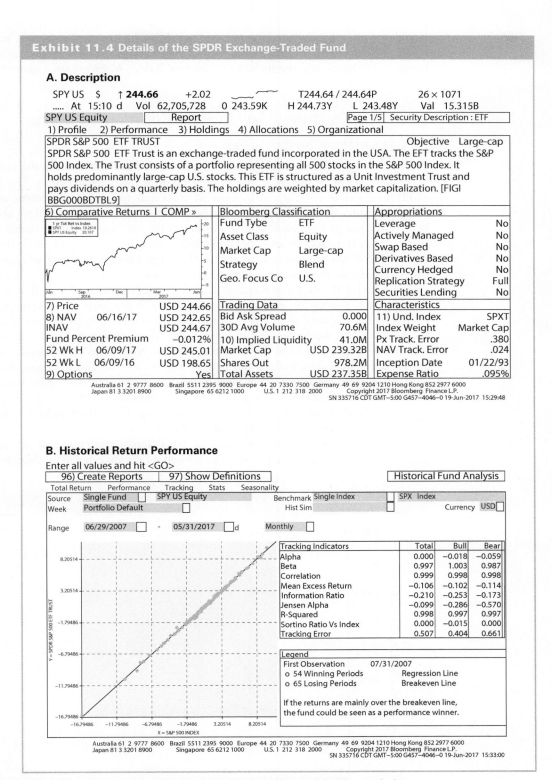

Exhibit 11.4 Details of the SPDR Exchange-Traded Fund

A. Description

SPY US $ ↑ **244.66**   +2.02   T244.64 / 244.64P   26 × 1071
..... At 15:10 d   Vol 62,705,728   0 243.59K   H 244.73Y   L 243.48Y   Val 15.315B

SPY US Equity	Report			Page 1/5 Security Description : ETF

1) Profile   2) Performance   3) Holdings   4) Allocations   5) Organizational

SPDR S&P 500 ETF TRUST   Objective   Large-cap
SPDR S&P 500 ETF Trust is an exchange-traded fund incorporated in the USA. The EFT tracks the S&P 500 Index. The Trust consists of a portfolio representing all 500 stocks in the S&P 500 Index. It holds predominantly large-cap U.S. stocks. This ETF is structured as a Unit Investment Trust and pays dividends on a quarterly basis. The holdings are weighted by market capitalization. [FIGI BBG000BDTBL9]

6) Comparative Returns I COMP »	Bloomberg Classification		Appropriations	
	Fund Tybe	ETF	Leverage	No
	Asset Class	Equity	Actively Managed	No
	Market Cap	Large-cap	Swap Based	No
	Strategy	Blend	Derivatives Based	No
	Geo. Focus Co	U.S.	Currency Hedged	No
			Replication Strategy	Full
			Securities Lending	No

1 yr Tot Ret vs Index
SPXT   Index 19.2618
SPY US Equity   20.107

7) Price	USD 244.66	Trading Data		Characteristics	
8) NAV 06/16/17	USD 242.65	Bid Ask Spread	0.000	11) Und. Index	SPXT
INAV	USD 244.67	30D Avg Volume	70.6M	Index Weight	Market Cap
Fund Percent Premium	−0.012%	10) Implied Liquidity	41.0M	Px Track. Error	.380
52 Wk H 06/09/17	USD 245.01	Market Cap	USD 239.32B	NAV Track. Error	.024
52 Wk L 06/09/16	USD 198.65	Shares Out	978.2M	Inception Date	01/22/93
9) Options	Yes	Total Assets	USD 237.35B	Expense Ratio	.095%

Australia 61 2 9777 8600   Brazil 5511 2395 9000 Europe 44 20 7330 7500 Germany 49 69 9204 1210 Hong Kong 852 2977 6000
Japan 81 3 3201 8900   Singapore 65 6212 1000   U.S. 1 212 318 2000   Copyright 2017 Bloomberg Finance L.P.
SN 335716 CDT GMT−5:00 G457−4046−0 19-Jun-2017 15:29:48

B. Historical Return Performance

Enter all values and hit <GO>

96) Create Reports	97) Show Definitions		Historical Fund Analysis

Total Return   Performance   Tracking   Stats   Seasonality

Source	Single Fund	☐	SPY US Equity	Benchmark	Single Index		SPX Index	
Week	Portfolio Default	☐		Hist Sim			Currency USD☐	

Range   06/29/2007 ☐ - 05/31/2017 ☐ d   Monthly ☐

Tracking Indicators	Total	Bull	Bear
Alpha	0.000	−0.018	−0.059
Beta	0.997	1.003	0.987
Correlation	0.999	0.998	0.998
Mean Excess Return	−0.106	−0.102	−0.114
Information Ratio	−0.210	−0.253	−0.173
Jensen Alpha	−0.099	−0.286	−0.570
R-Squared	0.998	0.997	0.997
Sortino Ratio Vs Index	0.000	−0.015	0.000
Tracking Error	0.507	0.404	0.661

Y = SPDR S&P 500 ETF TRUST
X = S&P 500 INDEX

Legend
First Observation   07/31/2007
o 54 Winning Periods   Regression Line
o 65 Losing Periods   Breakeven Line

If the returns are mainly over the breakeven line, the fund could be seen as a performance winner.

Australia 61 2 9777 8600   Brazil 5511 2395 9000 Europe 44 20 7330 7500 Germany 49 69 9204 1210 Hong Kong 852 2977 6000
Japan 81 3 3201 8900   Singapore 65 6212 1000   U.S. 1 212 318 2000   Copyright 2017 Bloomberg Finance L.P.
SN 335716 CDT GMT−5:00 G457−4046−0 19-Jun-2017 15:33:00

Source: © 2017 Bloomberg L.P. All rights reserved. Reprinted with permission.

include an often smaller management fee, the ability for continuous trading while markets are open, and the ability to time capital gain tax realizations. ETF disadvantages include the brokerage commission and the inability to reinvest dividends, except on a quarterly basis.

11.3 AN OVERVIEW OF ACTIVE EQUITY PORTFOLIO MANAGEMENT STRATEGIES

The goal of active equity management is to earn a return that exceeds the return of a passive benchmark portfolio, net of transaction costs, on a risk-adjusted basis. The job of an active equity manager is not easy. If transaction costs and fees total 1.5 percent of the portfolio's assets annually, the portfolio has to earn a return 1.5 percentage points above the passive benchmark just to keep pace with it. Further, if the manager's strategy involves overweighting specific market sectors in anticipation of price increases, the risk of the active portfolio may exceed that of the passive benchmark, so the active portfolio's return will have to exceed the benchmark by an even wider margin to compensate.

Exhibit 11.5 shows the percentage of U.S.-domiciled mutual funds that were able to produce annual returns in excess of the S&P 500 Index over a 15-year period ending in 2016. For the majority of this period, the average fund manager was not able to outperform the broad index; the percentage of active funds whose return exceeded that of the index was less than 50 percent in 12 of the 15 years. However, the display also indicates that the percentage of active managers beating the market was never zero and averaged almost 36 percent, which is notable given that there were more than 3,200 domestic equity funds by the end of 2016. Indeed, evidence provided by Brown and Goetzmann (1995) and Chen, Jegadeesh, and Wermers (2000) shows that fund managers possess significant stock-picking skills that can translate into superior and persistent investment returns.

Exhibit 11.6 offers a broad overview of the different strategies that investment managers might adopt in forming their portfolios, as well as the investment philosophy that underlies

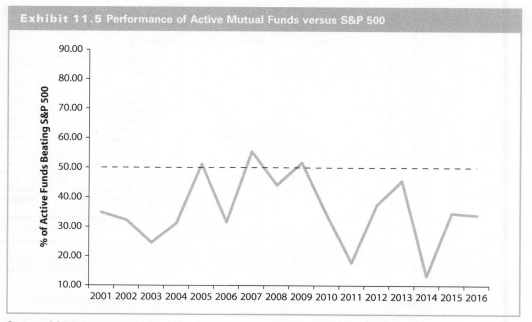

Exhibit 11.5 Performance of Active Mutual Funds versus S&P 500

Source: S&P Dow Jones Indices LLC, *SPIVA U.S. Scorecard, 2016*; author calculations.

Exhibit 11.6 Equity Portfolio Investment Philosophies and Strategies

Passive Management Strategies

1. Efficient Markets Hypothesis
   Buy and hold
   Indexing

Active Management Strategies

2. Fundamental Analysis
   "Top down" (e.g., asset class rotation, sector rotation)
   "Bottom up" (e.g., stock undervaluation/overvaluation)

3. Technical Analysis
   Contrarian (e.g., overreaction)
   Continuation (e.g., price momentum)

4. Factors, Attributes, and Anomalies
   Security characteristic factors (e.g., P/E, P/B, earnings momentum, firm size)
   Investment style factors (e.g., value, growth, volatility, company quality)
   Calendar effects (e.g., weekend, January)
   Information effects (e.g., neglect)

---

each strategy. The passive strategies we just considered are based (at least implicitly) on the notion that capital markets are efficient, and so equity portfolios should be invested to mimic broad indexes and should not be traded actively. The realm of active management, however, is one in which managers are effectively betting against markets being perfectly efficient. For convenience, Exhibit 11.6 characterizes these bets as falling into three general categories: (1) fundamental, (2) technical, and (3) factors, security attributes, and market anomalies.

11.3.1 Fundamental Strategies

As we saw in Chapter 9, the top-down investment process begins with an analysis of broad country and asset class allocations and progresses down through sector allocation decisions to the bottom level, where individual securities are selected. Alternatively, a bottom-up process simply emphasizes the selection of securities without any initial market or sector analysis. Active equity management based on fundamental analysis can start from either direction, depending on what the manager thinks is mispriced relative to his or her valuation models. Generally, active fundamental managers use three generic themes. First, they can try to time the equity market by shifting funds into and out of stocks, bonds, and T-bills depending on broad market forecasts. Second, they can shift funds among different equity sectors and industries (for example, financial stocks, technology stocks, consumer cyclicals) or among investment styles (for example, large capitalization, small capitalization, value, growth) to catch the next hot concept before the rest of the market. Third, equity managers can look at individual issues in an attempt to find undervalued stocks.

An asset class rotation strategy shifts funds in and out of the stock market depending on the manager's perception of how the stock market is valued compared to the various alternative asset classes. Formally, such a strategy is called **tactical asset allocation** and will be described in more detail later in the chapter. A **sector rotation strategy** positions the portfolio to take advantage of the market's next move. Often this means emphasizing or overweighting (relative to the benchmark portfolio) certain economic sectors or industries in response to the next expected phase of the business cycle. Exhibit 11.7 suggests how sector rotators may position their portfolios to take advantage of stock market trends during the economic cycle.

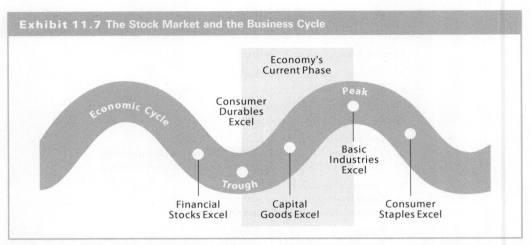

Exhibit 11.7 The Stock Market and the Business Cycle

In general, asset and sector rotation strategies can be extremely profitable but also very risky for a manager to follow. This is shown in Exhibit 11.8, which lists the annual returns in each of several asset and sector classes from 1997 to 2016. The chart documents the tremendous volatility that existed during this period. For instance, bonds, which comprised the best performing asset class in 2011, made up the worst class in the preceding two years *and* in the following two years. Conversely, large-cap growth stocks were one of the best places to invest for the first three years (1997–1999), but this period was followed by years when this sector performed quite poorly. The message from this display is clear: While there are impressive gains to be made by correctly timing the hottest (or the coldest) market sectors, a manager must be right substantially more than he or she is wrong. Because this is an extremely difficult thing to do consistently, many investors choose to interpret Exhibit 11.8 as ultimately extolling the virtue of asset and sector class diversification.

A fundamental stock picker operating on a bottom-up basis will form a portfolio of equities that can be purchased at a substantial discount to what his or her valuation model indicates they are worth. As we discussed in Chapter 8, these valuation models might be based on absolute judgments about the future of the company (that is, discounted cash flow) or relative assessments of how attractive the stock is compared with shares in otherwise similar firms (that is, relative price multiples). In either case, it is usually true that the active manager will find stock picking to be a more reliable, although less profitable, way to invest than market timing.

An interesting trend in fundamental equity management has been the development of the so-called **130/30 strategy**. Funds based on this approach are allowed to take long positions up to 130 percent of the portfolio's original capital and have short positions up to 30 percent. Relative to "long only" portfolios, these *enhanced active* funds let managers exploit their expertise in two ways. First, as Jacobs and Levy (2007) note, the use of the short positions creates the leverage needed to extend the long holdings beyond the original capital limit, potentially increasing both risk and expected returns compared to the fund's benchmark. Second, 130/30 strategies enable managers to make full use of their fundamental research to buy stocks they identify as undervalued as well as short those that are overvalued. Thus, these strategies expand the ways in which investors can capture available alpha opportunities.

11.3.2 Technical Strategies

Earlier, we discussed the role that technical analysis plays in the stock evaluation process. As we saw, assessing past stock price trends for what they imply about future price movements

Exhibit 11.8 Asset and Sector Class Return Performance: 1997-2016

1997	1998	1999	2000	2001	2002	2003	2004	2005	2006	2007	2008	2009	2010	2011	2012	2013	2014	2015	2016
LV 35.2%	LG 38.7%	SG 43.1%	SV 22.8%	SV 14.0%	B 10.1%	SG 48.5%	SV 22.2%	F 13.8%	F 26.6%	LG 11.8%	B 7.0%	LG 37.2%	SG 28.9%	B 7.9%	SV 17.9%	SG 43.2%	LV 13.3%	LG 5.6%	SV 31.2%
L 32.9%	L 27.0%	LG 33.2%	B 11.6%	B 8.4%	SV -11.4%	S 47.3%	F 20.3%	LV 7.1%	SV 23.7%	F 11.6%	SV -28.9	SG 34.5%	S 26.6%	LG 2.6%	F 17.6%	S 38.6%	L 13.1%	L 0.9%	S 21.0%
SV 31.8%	F 20.3%	F 27.4%	LV 7.0%	S 2.5%	F -15.3%	SV 46.0%	S 18.3%	L 6.3%	LV 22.4%	SG 7.1%	S -33.8%	F 31.6%	SV 24.2%	L 1.5%	LV 17.3%	SV 34.2%	LG 12.9%	B 0.5%	LV 17.0%
LG 30.5%	LV 15.6%	S 21.3%	S -3.0%	LV -5.6%	LV -15.5%	F 38.3%	LV 16.5%	LG 5.3%	S 18.4%	B 7.2%	LV -36.8%	L 28.5%	LG 16.5%	LV 0.4%	L 16.3%	LG 33.2%	B 5.9%	F -0.1%	L 11.9%
S 22.4%	B 8.7%	L 20.9%	L -7.8%	SG -9.2%	S -20.5%	LV 30.0%	SG 14.3%	SV 4.8%	L 15.5%	L 5.8%	L -37.6%	S 27.2%	L 15.8%	SG -2.9%	S 16.3%	L 32.8%	SG 5.6%	SG -1.3%	SG 11.2%
SG 12.9%	SG 1.2%	LV 7.3%	F -13.7%	L -12.5%	L -21.7%	L 29.9%	L 11.4%	S 4.6%	SG 13.4%	LV -0.1%	LG -38.4%	SV 20.6%	LV 15.2%	S -4.2%	LG 15.2%	LV 32.2%	S 4.8%	LV -3.8%	LG 7.0%
B 9.6%	S -2.5%	SV -1.5%	SG -22.4%	LG -20.4%	LG -27.9%	LG 29.7%	LG 6.3%	SG 4.2%	LG 9.1%	S -1.6%	SG -38.5%	LV 19.7%	F 8.0%	SV -5.5%	SG 14.6%	F 23.0%	SV 4.1%	S -4.3%	B 2.7%
F 2.2%	SV -6.5%	B -0.8%	LG -22.4%	F -20.8%	SG -30.3%	B 4.2%	B 4.5%	B 2.6%	B 4.3%	SV -9.8%	F -41.9%	B 5.1%	B 6.3%	F -11.3%	B 4.2%	B -2.0%	F -4.2%	SV -7.4%	F 1.5%

Legend:
L = Large stocks	(Russell 1000 Index)	
LG = Large growth stocks	(Russell 1000 Growth Index)	
LV = Large value stocks	(Russell 1000 Value Index)	
S = Small stocks	(Russell 2000 Index)	
SG = Small growth stocks	(Russell 2000 Growth Index)	
SV = Small value stocks	(Russell 2000 Value Index)	
F = Foreign stocks	(MSCI EAFE Index)	
B = Bonds	(Citigroup Broad Investment-Grade Bond Index)	

Source: Frank Russell Company.

was one of the primary tools of this analytical approach. Active managers can form equity portfolios on the basis of past stock price trends by assuming that one of two things will happen: (1) Past stock price trends will continue in the same direction, or (2) they will reverse themselves.

A **contrarian** investment strategy is based on the belief that the best time to buy (sell) a stock is when the majority of other investors are the most bearish (bullish) about it. The contrarian investor will attempt to always purchase the stock when it is near its lowest price and sell it (or even short sell it) when it nears its peak. The belief is that stock returns are *mean reverting*, indicating that, over time, stocks will be priced so as to produce returns consistent with their risk-adjusted expected (or, mean) returns.

DeBondt and Thaler (1985) demonstrated the potential benefits of forming active portfolios based on this notion. They showed that investing on an *overreaction hypothesis* could provide consistently superior returns. Exhibit 11.9 summarizes their experiment in which they measured returns to a portfolio of stocks that had had the worst market performance over the prior three years ("losers") and a portfolio of stocks with the best past performance ("winners"). If investors overreacted to either bad news or good news about companies, as DeBondt and Thaler contended, we should see subsequent abnormal returns move in the opposite direction. The cumulative abnormal returns (CARs) shown in the display appear to support this notion, although the evidence is stronger for losers than for winners.

At the other extreme, active portfolios can also be formed on the assumption that recent trends in past prices will continue. A **price momentum** strategy, as it is more commonly called, assumes that stocks that have been hot will stay hot, while cold stocks will also remain so. Although there may well be sound economic reasons for these trends to continue (for example, company revenues and earnings that continue to grow faster than expected), it may also be the case that investors periodically *underreact* to the arrival of new information. Thus, a pure price momentum strategy focuses on the trend of past prices alone and makes purchase and sale decisions accordingly.

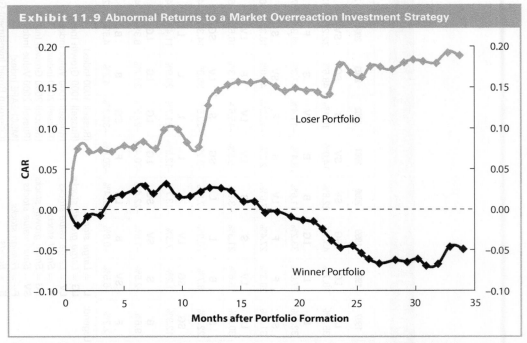

Exhibit 11.9 Abnormal Returns to a Market Overreaction Investment Strategy

Source: Werner F. M. DeBondt and Richard Thaler, "Does the Stock Market Overreact?" *Journal of Finance* 40, no. 3 (July 1985): 793–805. Data from Blackwell Publishing.

Exhibit 11.10 Performance of Momentum and Value Stock Portfolios in Global Markets

Market		P1 (Low)	P2	P3 (High)	P3 – P1	Factor Portfolio
A. Price Momentum–Based Portfolios						
U.S. stocks: 1972.1–2011.7	Avg. return	8.8%	9.7%	14.2%	5.4%	7.7%
	Std. dev.	18.6%	14.8%	18.5%	16.4%	17.0%
U.K. stocks: 1972.1–2011.7	Avg. return	9.2	13.8	15.2	6.0	7.2
	Std. dev.	24.9	22.7	23.7	15.9	15.0
Europe stocks: 1974.1–2011.7	Avg. return	9.2	13.3	17.3	8.1	9.8
	Std. dev.	20.6	17.5	19.0	14.7	13.1
Japan stocks: 1974.1–2011.7	Avg. return	8.4	9.9	10.1	1.7	2.2
	Std. dev.	23.5	20.6	23.1	18.6	16.5
B. Value-Based Portfolios						
U.S. stocks: 1972.1–2011.7	Avg. return	9.5%	10.6%	13.2%	3.7%	3.9%
	Std. dev.	17.9%	15.4%	15.9%	12.8%	14.8%
U.K. stocks: 1972.1–2011.7	Avg. return	10.8	12.5	15.3	4.5	5.5
	Std. dev.	18.6	19.7	20.3	13.4	14.4
Europe stocks: 1974.1–2011.7	Avg. return	11.8	14.6	16.7	4.8	5.2
	Std. dev.	18.3	18.0	19.8	11.5	9.7
Japan stocks: 1974.1–2011.7	Avg. return	2.6	8.2	14.2	12.0	10.2
	Std. dev.	23.6	22.1	21.8	15.3	13.2

Source: Clifford S. Asness, Tobias J. Moskowitz, and Lasse Heje Pedersen, "Value and Momentum Everywhere," *Journal of Finance* 53, no. 6 (June 2013): 929–985. Reprinted with permission of Blackwell Publishing.

Asness, Moskowitz, and Pedersen (2013) investigated the profitability of this approach in four different global markets: United States, United Kingdom, Europe, and Japan. Using four decades of data, they divided all of the stocks traded in these markets into three different portfolios based on their past 12-month price movements and then calculated returns over the following year. Panel A of Exhibit 11.10 shows these average returns and standard deviations for every portfolio in each market, from the ones with the worst past price trends (P1) to the best price trends (P3). In all four markets, the data strongly justify the price momentum strategy in that the portfolios with the highest (lowest) level of price momentum generated the highest (lowest) subsequent returns, as indicated by the consistently positive (P3–P1) return differentials. Notice also that the high-momentum portfolios had either similar or lower levels of volatility than the low-momentum portfolios. Finally, the last column (labeled "Factor Portfolio") shows that a momentum-based hedge fund that was long in the best-trend stocks and short in the worst-trend positions would also have been quite profitable.

11.3.3 Factors, Attributes, and Anomalies

A portfolio strategy that has become increasingly popular in recent years is **factor investing**. The main idea underlying a factor-based investment strategy is for the manager to form portfolios that emphasize certain characteristics of a collection of securities—such as firm size, relative valuation, low return volatility, momentum, or company quality—that are believed to produce higher risk-adjusted returns than those in a traditional benchmark that is weighted by the market capitalization of the stocks in the index. The risk premia associated with these characteristic-oriented portfolios—or factors, as they are called—allow the investor to earn superior returns with better diversification than holding a traditional passive index fund.[1]

---

[1] For an excellent and thorough overview of factor investing, see Ang (2014).

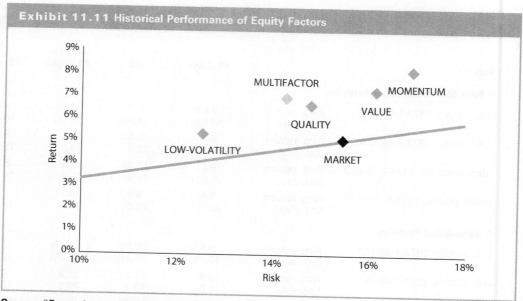

Exhibit 11.11 Historical Performance of Equity Factors

Source: "Factor Investing: Made Simple Guide." Pension and Lifetime Savings Association, May 2017. Based on David Blitz, "Factor Investing Revisited," *Journal of Index Investing* 6, no. 2 (Fall 2015): 7–17.

This idea is illustrated in Exhibit 11.11, which is based on the analysis of Blitz (2015). Recall from our discussion of multifactor models of risk and expected return in Chapter 7 that many of these factor-oriented portfolios (for example, firm size, relative value, momentum, company quality) also appear as risk factors in expanded versions of the CAPM. So, a factor-based approach to investing can be viewed as one that overweights or underweights the various systematic risk exposures in the risk model in an attempt to outperform a conventional market portfolio benchmark over time. The adjustment of these systematic risk exposures as market conditions fluctuate is what makes factor investing an active portfolio strategy and is why it is sometimes called a **smart beta** approach to investing.

Two characteristics that are often used as the basis for forming factor portfolios are the total capitalization of the firm's outstanding equity (firm size) and the relative valuation of the firm, as indicated by its various financial ratios (for example, P/E, P/B). Over time, firms with smaller market capitalizations often produce bigger risk-adjusted returns than those with large market capitalizations. Also, over time, firms with lower P/E and P/B ratios produce bigger risk-adjusted returns than those with higher levels of those ratios. In fact, we saw in Chapter 7 that low and high levels of these ratios are used in practice to define value and growth stocks, respectively.

Another reason these firm-specific attributes may be important in a factor-based approach to investing is that the term *sector* considered earlier in the context of rotation strategies also can be defined by different stock attributes. Because the market seems to favor some attributes more than others, sector rotation may involve overweighting stocks with certain characteristics, such as small- or large-capitalization stocks or stocks classified more generally as value or growth stocks. For example, Panel A of Exhibit 11.12 shows the difference in returns to portfolios invested in small- and large-cap stocks on a monthly basis from 1991 to 2016. The graph shows the large-cap portfolio return minus the small-cap return, so any net return above the horizontal axis indicates a period when the former outperformed the latter. Notice the consistent firm size rotation and spread in returns that occurred in this period; in given months, both large- and small-cap stocks outperformed the other by over 30 percent. Keep in mind, however, that small-cap stocks are almost always riskier than large-cap stocks. This is shown in Panel B of Exhibit 11.12 as the difference in the standard deviations of the large- and small-cap portfolios.

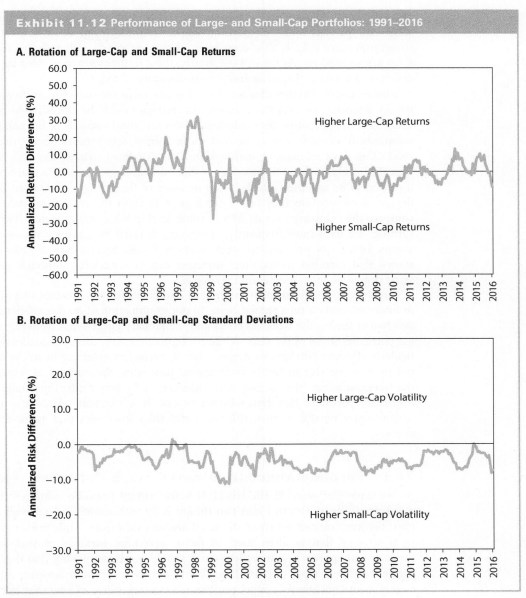

Exhibit 11.12 Performance of Large- and Small-Cap Portfolios: 1991–2016

A. Rotation of Large-Cap and Small-Cap Returns

B. Rotation of Large-Cap and Small-Cap Standard Deviations

Source: Rolling 12-month returns to Russell 1000 and Russell 2000 Indexes.

Similar analysis reveals the potential benefits of forming active global portfolios around financial ratios, such as P/B. In addition to their analysis of momentum factor investing, Asness et al. (2013) also examined the performance of investment portfolios based on a relative value factor for the U.S., U.K., Europe, and Japan. Over their 40-year sample period, they divided stocks in each market into three portfolios based on P/B ratios, with stocks having the lowest levels of this ratio (P3) being labeled *value stocks* and those having the highest P/B ratios (P1) being called *growth stocks*. They also computed the returns to a value factor portfolio that consisted of long positions in value stocks and short positions in growth stocks. Panel B of Exhibit 11.10 indicates that there was a significant return premium over time for investing in the value factor. In the U.S., U.K., and European markets, both the annual return difference between low and high P/B stocks (P3–P1) as well as the return to the value factor portfolio averaged between 3.7 percent and 5.5 percent, while the comparable figures for Japan were 12.0 percent and 10.2 percent, respectively However, those low-ratio portfolios were sometimes more volatile than their high-ratio counterparts, although this finding was not uniform across markets. As we will see shortly, these findings are important for understanding the differences between the value and growth investment styles.

Momentum is another characteristic that can form the basis for an investable factor portfolio. As discussed above, price momentum strategies could be either based on pure price trend analysis or supported by the underlying economic fundamentals of the company. An **earnings momentum** strategy is a somewhat more formal active portfolio approach that purchases stocks that have accelerating earnings and sells (or short sells) stocks with disappointing earnings. The notion behind this strategy is that, ultimately, a company's share price will follow the direction of its earnings, which is one measure of the firm's economic success. In judging the degree of momentum in a firm's earnings, it is often the case in practice that investors will compare the company's actual EPS to some level of what was expected. Two types of expected earnings are used most frequently: (1) those generated by a statistical model and (2) the consensus forecast of professional stock analysts. Chan, Jegadeesh, and Lakonishok (1999) have shown that earnings momentum strategies can be successful, although generally not to the same degree as price momentum strategies.

Finally, active investment strategies can also be based on anomalies that are believed to occur in financial markets on a regular basis. In our examination of market efficiency in Chapter 5, we saw two of these—the weekend effect and the January effect—that would involve investing during particular times of the year. While conceptually viable, these anomalies do not produce particularly effective portfolio strategies. That is, managers investing in stocks only in January are not likely to be able to justify their annual fees, while the number of transactions implied by the weekend effect (that is, buy every Monday, sell every Friday) generally makes for a cost-ineffective portfolio. However, whether or not these calendar-related anomalies produce successful active portfolios, they still are useful rules for trades that an investor plans to make anyway.

11.3.4 Forming Momentum-Based Stock Portfolios: Two Examples

As we have just seen, in the world of active equity portfolio management, the concept of momentum investing can mean two things: *price momentum* and *earnings momentum*. However, the justifications for these strategies are very different—while price momentum is a technical strategy that is often used in factor investing, earnings momentum is ultimately a fundamental approach to investing—so it should not be surprising that they can lead to forming very different types of portfolios. That is, a price momentum investor might be attracted to a stock with consistently strong, positive returns, regardless of why they occurred. In contrast, the earnings momentum investor is likely to be attracted to stocks for companies that generate earnings in excess of market expectations, even if the past returns have been negative.

To examine these differences in more specific terms, we performed two separate computer screenings of the stocks in the Standard & Poor's 500 Index during a recent period. In the first, the stocks were ranked from highest to lowest in terms of their returns over the past six months, the characteristic likely to be appealing to a price momentum investor. In the second screen, the stocks were ranked from highest to lowest by their *earnings surprise* (the percentage difference between the firm's actual earnings and the consensus forecast of professional stock analysts) over the prior year, which is what an earnings momentum investor would be interested in knowing. Financial data for 10 of the top-ranked stocks from each screening are shown in Exhibit 11.13.

The stocks most likely to be included in a price momentum–based portfolio all share the feature that they have had strong positive price increases over the prior six-month and

Exhibit 11.13 Financial Data for 20 Selected Momentum-Oriented Stocks from the Standard & Poor's 500 Index

Company	Ticker	Current EPS	Forecast Next Year EPS	Current P/E	3-Month Total Return	6-Month Total Return	12-Month Total Return	1-Year EPS Surprise [Act–Est]	Est PEG
			Price Momentum Stocks:						
NVIDIA CORP	NVDA	$2.60	$3.92	41.26	−2.33%	65.34%	213.26%	4.12%	3.45
UNITED RENTALS	URI	6.04	10.18	19.99	11.81	59.92	96.14	4.43	0.86
CSX CORP	CSX	1.80	2.37	25.60	26.28	56.96	82.30	−0.72	2.58
BANK OF AMERICA	BAC	1.46	2.10	15.78	2.38	49.61	71.85	−1.62	1.10
NETFLIX	NFLX	0.42	2.39	337.71	12.94	47.84	42.42	17.77	2.66
GOLDMAN SACHS GROUP	GS	16.95	21.65	13.68	−3.51	41.24	52.56	6.24	0.96
SOUTHWEST AIRLINES	LUV	3.73	4.62	14.03	3.99	41.17	18.93	1.60	1.45
ROYAL CARIBBEAN CRUISES	RCL	5.98	8.05	16.61	18.52	40.41	38.58	0.18	0.78
BOEING	BA	10.37	10.15	17.09	13.30	36.72	37.84	1.64	1.38
PRUDENTIAL FINANCIAL	PRU	8.33	11.08	12.66	0.01	33.14	49.55	1.20	1.19
Average:		5.77	7.65	51.44	8.34	47.23	70.34	3.48	1.64
			Earnings Momentum Stocks:						
MICRON TECHNOLOGY	MU	$0.77	$3.44	34.28	13.80%	51.43%	148.54%	93.55%	0.84
VORNADO REALTY TRUST	VNO	1.65	2.38	61.80	0.05	−0.10	15.14	90.59	7.48
HALLIBURTON	HAL	−0.05	2.86	N/A	−9.05	19.61	44.06	55.56	1.54
CROWN CASTLE INTERNATIONAL	CCI	1.20	1.49	77.78	7.73	−0.17	13.05	41.38	3.48
LEVEL 3 COMMUNICATIONS	LVLT	1.43	1.78	39.10	−1.27	17.90	9.30	23.00	4.82
UNDER ARMOUR	UAA	0.60	0.52	31.49	−35.20	−51.89	−55.67	17.94	2.28
NUCOR CORP	NUE	2.33	4.14	26.30	0.24	27.24	37.01	14.53	1.78
EXTRA SPACE STORAGE	EXR	2.90	2.74	26.03	2.07	−3.62	−12.04	14.03	3.79
L BRANDS	LB	3.74	3.47	12.84	−27.18	−34.85	−41.59	10.22	1.71
EXXON MOBIL	XOM	2.36	4.70	34.63	−8.93	−0.13	1.22	9.45	1.47
Average:		1.69	2.75	38.25	−5.77	2.54	15.90	37.02	2.92

Source: Author calculations.

one-year periods. However, there appear to be few other similarities between these securities. In particular, the earnings surprise component is actually negative for two of the stocks listed, even though the average earnings per share for these companies is forecast to rise from $5.77 to $7.65. Thus, the price momentum investor is making a bet on the *continuation* of past price trends, perhaps for reasons that have more to do with the psychology of other investors than with the underlying economic position of the companies themselves.

On the other hand, the earnings momentum manager will be attracted to stocks for companies that consistently produce earnings that surpass analyst expectations. The 10 positions shown at the bottom of Exhibit 11.13 all have demonstrated that ability over the past year. In addition, 7 of these stocks have a forecast future level of earnings that is higher than current earnings. However, a few of these stocks have also experienced negligible or negative returns at some point over the prior 12 months, which could mean that the stock disappointed investors in some other way in the past. Despite this, the belief of the earnings momentum investor is that firms whose fundamental economic position allows them to beat expectations will eventually see their stock prices increase to reflect that performance. Thus, the trading strategy in an earnings momentum portfolio is simple: Buy (and hold) stocks with positive earnings momentum and sell those stocks when that momentum deteriorates or turns negative.

Two final points should be mentioned. First, notice that no stock was ranked at the top of both the price momentum and the earnings momentum screens. This supports the earlier observation that these two active strategies tend to produce different collections of stocks. Second, the stocks listed in Exhibit 11.13 were selected in a purely mechanical manner, without any additional insight from a professional money manager who might override the computer screen for any of several reasons. For instance, an earnings momentum manager following a "growth at a reasonable price" (GARP) discipline might be more attracted to positive earnings surprise stocks that also sell at lower PEG ratios (MU and XOM in Exhibit 11.13) than to those that appear to be more expensive by that measure (VNO and LVLT in Exhibit 11.13).

11.3.5 Tax Efficiency and Active Equity Management

The primary intention for an actively managed equity portfolio is to produce a return that exceeds that of its passive benchmark. Of course, to accomplish that goal the active manager must form a portfolio that differs from the index itself, which usually requires trading stocks on a frequent basis. Compared to a passively managed portfolio, there are two potential costs associated with these additional stock trades. First, the active fund will incur additional transaction costs, which will reduce the net return to the portfolio. Second, selling stocks that have appreciated in price will create a capital gain on which investors may have to pay taxes.

While the negative effect on returns due to high transaction fees are shared by all investors, the tax consequences of active equity management are a concern only for those investors who hold their portfolio in a taxable account. Many investors—pension funds, university endowment funds, or individuals with tax-deferred retirement plans—do not have to worry about paying additional taxes on the trades of an active portfolio manager. Reichenstein (2006) as well as Horan and Adler (2009) note that many other investors—particularly individuals not investing through a retirement plan—do need to worry about the **tax efficiency** of the active portfolio because this is an expense that they will ultimately bear.

The fund's **portfolio turnover** is an indirect measure of the amount of trading that could lead to a higher tax bill for a taxable investor. The portfolio turnover ratio is typically measured as the total dollar value of the securities sold from the portfolio in a year divided by the average dollar value of the assets managed by the fund. For instance, an active manager that sold $75 million worth of stocks in a year from a portfolio that averaged $100 million in assets under management would have a turnover ratio of 75 percent. In essence, the manager has replaced three out of every four stocks in the portfolio at some point during the year. While the turnover ratio is a good indicator of overall trading activity, it does not necessarily indicate that the majority of those trades generated capital gains that in turn created taxable events. Many of those trades might have been transacted at losses that actually *offset* the gains created by other sales.

A more direct measure of how well portfolio managers balance the capital gains and losses resulting from their trades is the **tax cost ratio**. As developed by Morningstar, Inc., a leading provider of investment analysis in the mutual fund industry, this statistic compares a fund's pretax return (PTR) with this same return adjusted for taxes (TAR), assuming that investors pay taxes on net short-term and long-term capital gains at the highest rate:

11.5 $$\text{Tax Cost Ratio} = [1 - \{(1 + \text{TAR})/(1 + \text{PTR})\}] \times 100$$

Ptak (2002) explains that the tax cost ratio represents the percentage of an investor's assets that are lost to taxes on a yearly basis due to the trading strategy employed by the fund manager. Notice that even if there is high turnover in a portfolio, TAR need not be significantly below PTR if the manager was able to "harvest" enough capital losses to balance out the capital gains associated by other trades.

For example, Exhibit 11.14 lists tax efficiency statistics for both a passive mutual fund (the Vanguard 500 Index Fund we saw earlier) and an active mutual fund (JPMorgan U.S. Dynamic Plus Fund). Compared to the index fund, the active fund had both a higher **expense ratio** (which includes all management, operating, and administrative fees as a percentage of the funds assets) and a higher turnover ratio (116 percent versus 4 percent). Thus, JPSAX was clearly a more expensive fund to investors with substantially more stock trading than VFINX. Perhaps because of those additional expenses, it underperformed the benchmark fund on a pretax basis over the one-year period (15.15 percent versus 17.32 percent) and five-year period (10.70 percent versus 14.57 percent) shown. However, once the tax efficiency of the trades in the two funds is considered, the story gets even worse. Specifically, notice that there is very little difference between the pretax and tax-adjusted returns for VFINX, meaning that what little trading there was in the index fund was fairly balanced in the creation of capital gains and losses. This leads to a five-year tax cost ratio for VFINX of just 0.59 percent ($= [1-(1.1457/1.1525)] \times 100$). Conversely, the trades in JPSAX were far less tax efficient; its five-year tax cost ratio was 2.71 percent, meaning that taxable investors in

Exhibit 11.14 Tax Efficiency of Passive and Active Stock Funds: An Example

	Vanguard 500 Index Fund (VFINX)	JPMorgan U.S. Dynamic Plus Fund (JPSAX)
Management Approach	*Passive*	*Active*
Expense Ratio	0.14%	1.20%
Portfolio Turnover	4%	116%
5-yr: Avg. Pretax Return	15.25%	13.78%
Tax-Adjusted Return	14.57%	10.70%
Tax Cost Ratio	0.59%	2.71%
1-yr: Avg. Pretax Return	17.32%	15.15%
Tax-Adjusted Return	16.55%	6.45%
Tax Cost Ratio	0.66%	7.56%

the fund saw their positions reduced by over 270 basis points per year due to taxes. This tax efficiency gap was even more dramatic for the one-year period in 2016.

11.3.6 Active Share and Measuring the Level of Active Management

As we have seen, a portfolio's tracking error statistic can be used to characterize whether the portfolio manager's investment style was passive or active in nature. The tracking error measure does this in an indirect way by looking at the difference in the returns a manager's portfolio produced compared to those of the benchmark index, with returns closer to those of the benchmark more likely to indicate an index fund. A more direct way to assess how active a manager's strategy is would be to look directly at the portfolio's holdings compared to those in the benchmark. Cremers and Petajisto (2009) have suggested calculating the portfolio's **active share** measure as:

11.6
$$\text{Active Share} = \text{AS} = \frac{1}{2} \sum_{i=1}^{N} |w_{p,i} - w_{b,i}|$$

where $[w_{p,i}, w_{b,i}]$ represent the investment weight of the ith security in the managed portfolio (p) and benchmark index (b), respectively. Generally speaking, the larger the value of the statistic in Equation 11.6, the bigger the absolute deviation of the portfolio's holdings from the index and so the more likely it is that the manager is an active investor.

As an example of the active share calculation, consider the composition of two different fund managers and the benchmark index that they both use. We assume that both portfolios and the index are all based on the same investable universe of five securities. We also assume for simplicity that the index is equally weighted (that is, $w_{b,i} = 20$ percent for each security). The investment weights for the two managers and the index are shown as:

	% Security Investment Weight:		
Security	Benchmark Index	Fund 1	Fund 2
1	20%	25%	55%
2	20	15	0
3	20	25	40
4	20	15	0
5	20	20	5

Using these investment weights, the active share measures for Fund 1 and Fund 2 are:

$$\text{AS}_1 = \frac{1}{2}\left(|25 - 20| + |15 - 20| + |25 - 20| + |15 - 20| + |20 - 20|\right) = 10\%$$

and:

$$\text{AS}_2 = \frac{1}{2}\left(|55 - 20| + |0 - 20| + |40 - 20| + |0 - 20| + |5 - 20|\right) = 55\%$$

The active share statistic can be interpreted as the percentage of security holdings in the manager's portfolio that differ from those in the benchmark index. In this example, Fund 1 is considered more passive (indexed) because its security holdings come closer to matching the benchmark, both in number of holdings and the investment weights of those holdings. Fund 2 is more concentrated than the benchmark (fewer holdings, bigger investment positions) and is therefore more likely to be considered an actively managed portfolio. Finally, notice that any portfolio that matches the index composition exactly (same investment weights for all holdings) would have an active share score of 0 percent.

Exhibit 11.15 shows where a variety of active and passive portfolios would plot according to both their tracking error and active share scores. Under this depiction, the passively managed

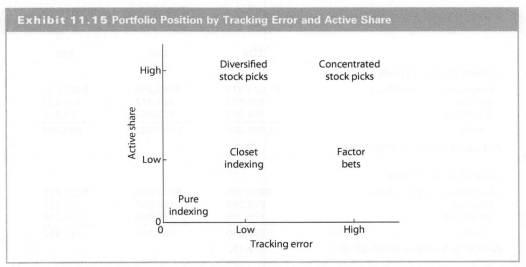

Exhibit 11.15 Portfolio Position by Tracking Error and Active Share

Source: K. J. Martijn Cremers and Antti Petajisto, "How Active Is Your Fund Manager? A New Measure That Predicts Performance," *Review of Financial Studies* 22, no. 9 (September 2009): 3329–3365. Reprinted with permission of Oxford University Press.

Fund 1 would likely be characterized as a closet (or enhanced) index portfolio whereas the actively managed Fund 2 would fall toward the Concentrated Stock Picks category. Cremers and Petajisto (2009) document that active share scores for mutual funds have been declining over time; the percentage of funds with an AS score of less than 60 percent was just 1.5 percent in 1980 but had risen to almost 45 percent of the sample three decades later. Also, Petajisto (2013) reports that while the average active fund has underperformed its index (produced a lower net-of-expenses return) by about 0.4 percent annually, the most active stock-picking managers—those with an AS score in excess of 90 percent—do beat their benchmarks by an average of more than 1.25 percent per year after fees and expenses.

11.4 VALUE VERSUS GROWTH INVESTING: A CLOSER LOOK

An important development in active equity management during the past several years has been the creation of portfolio strategies based on value- and growth-oriented investment styles. In addition to serving as a primary source of exposure in a factor-based investment strategy, it is now common for money management firms to define themselves as "value stock managers" or "growth stock managers" when selling their services to clients. Exhibit 11.16 indicates how pervasive these styles have become. Using the classifications of Morningstar, Inc., the amount of money invested in growth- and value-oriented funds exceeds $2.5 trillion. The chart also shows that the capital committed to growth fund products has increased recently by more than for value funds, with large-cap and multi-cap portfolios being responsible for much of this expansion.

The distinction between value and growth investing can be best appreciated by considering the thought process of a representative manager for each style.[2] In Chapter 8, we saw that the price–earnings ratio for any company can be expressed as:

11.7
$$P/E\ Ratio = \frac{(Current\ Price\ per\ Share)}{(Earnings\ per\ Share)}$$

---

[2]This motivation is based on a lucid overview of value- and growth-oriented investment styles that can be found in Christopherson and Williams (1995).

Exhibit 11.16 Total Net Assets Held by Growth and Value Mutual Funds ($ billions)

	2016	2012	2009	2006
Growth-Oriented Funds				
Large-cap and multi-cap	$1,024.976	$763.248	$660.634	$793.397
Mid-cap	186.763	161.472	128.430	157.827
Small-cap	158.867	115.862	94.830	114.522
Total	1,370.606	1,040.582	883.894	1,065.746
Annual % Increase (2006–2016)	2.6%			
Value-Oriented Funds				
Large-cap and multi-cap	$901.296	$646.929	$557.711	$767.631
Mid-cap	224.280	152.990	121.027	155.866
Small-cap	171.304	133.265	104.214	130.100
Total	1,296.880	933.184	782.952	1,053.597
Annual % Increase (2006–2016)	2.1%			

Source: Investment Company Institute and author calculations.

where the earnings per share (EPS) measure can be based on either current or forecast firm performance. Value and growth managers will focus on different aspects of this equation when evaluating stocks. Specifically, a growth-oriented investor will:

- Focus on the EPS component (the denominator) of the P/E ratio and its economic determinants
- Look for companies that he or she expects to exhibit rapid EPS growth in the future
- Often implicitly assume that the P/E ratio will remain constant over the near term, meaning that the stock price will rise as forecast earnings growth is realized.

On the other hand, a value-oriented investor will:

- Focus on the price component (the numerator) of the P/E ratio; he or she must be convinced that the price of the stock is "cheap" by some means of comparison
- Not care a great deal about current earnings or the fundamental drivers of earnings growth
- Often implicitly assume that the P/E ratio is below its natural level and that the market will soon "correct" this situation by increasing the stock price with little or no change in earnings

In summary, a growth investor focuses on the current and future economic "story" of a company, with less regard for share valuation. The value investor focuses on share price in anticipation of a market correction and, possibly, improving company fundamentals.

The conceptual difference between value and growth investing may be reasonably straightforward, but classifying individual stocks into the appropriate style is not always simple in practice. Since detailed company valuations are time-consuming to produce, most analysts rely on more easily obtained financial indicators—such as P/E and P/B ratios, dividend yields, and EPS growth rates—to define both individual equity holdings and style benchmark portfolios. Exhibit 11.17 shows one approach for classifying firms according to style and market capitalization. Notice that value stocks are relatively cheap (for example, low P/B, high yield) and have modest growth opportunities (for example, regulated firms), while growth stocks tend to be more expensive, reflecting their superior earnings potential (for example, technology firms).

To get a better feel for the types of portfolios these two investment styles might produce, Exhibit 11.18 lists representative samples of the top holdings for the Harbor Capital

Exhibit 11.17 Characteristics of Growth and Value Stocks

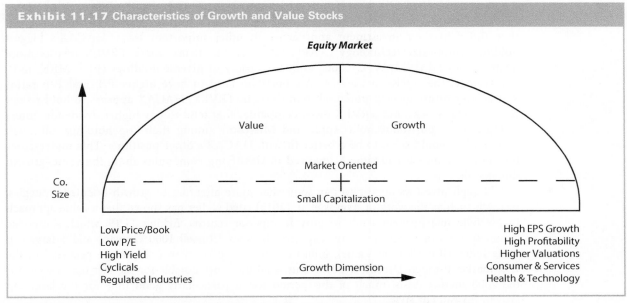

Source: Copyright © Frank Russell Company. Data from Frank Russell Company, Tacoma, WA.

Exhibit 11.18 Top Stock Holdings of Growth and Value Mutual Funds

A. Harbor Capital Appreciation Fund (HACAX)

Company	Ticker	Market Cap ($ billions)	P/E	P/BV	Est Growth EPS (%)	Div. Yld. (%)	Beta
Apple	AAPL	752.8	16.90	5.60	10.41	1.75	1.21
Amazon.com	AMZN	461.4	181.20	21.28	67.55	0.00	1.15
Facebook	FB	434.1	39.62	6.95	30.73	0.00	1.09
Microsoft	MSFT	540.9	32.36	7.76	10.48	2.23	1.12
Alibaba	BABA	345.0	57.76	2.30	18.86	0.00	1.33
Netflix	NFLX	65.4	199.80	22.00	54.05	0.00	1.55
Alphabet	GOOGL	657.0	32.43	4.58	18.74	0.00	1.26
Adobe Systems	ADBE	68.1	52.57	8.98	17.44	0.00	1.04
Celgene	CELG	94.2	27.14	12.37	20.44	0.00	1.24
Allergan	AGN	78.8	14.59	1.12	13.26	1.19	0.84
Median:		*389.6*	*36.03*	*7.36*	*18.80*	*0.00*	*1.18*

B. T. Rowe Price Value Fund (TRVLX)

Company	Ticker	Market Cap ($ billions)	P/E	P/BV	Est. Growth EPS (%)	Div. Yld. (%)	Beta
JP Morgan Chase	JPM	307.2	13.41	1.34	10.42	2.31	1.20
Tyson Foods	TSN	24.2	12.76	2.27	7.40	1.45	0.64
Microsoft	MSFT	540.9	32.36	7.76	10.48	2.23	1.12
Wells Fargo	WFC	269.2	13.48	1.53	11.44	2.82	1.16
PG&E	PCG	35.3	17.34	1.92	3.70	3.07	0.58
Medtronic	MDT	120.0	24.98	2.39	6.33	1.96	0.83
Apple	AAPL	752.8	16.90	5.60	10.41	1.75	1.21
Pfizer	PFE	195.8	17.91	3.35	5.01	3.90	0.82
Merck	MRK	172.8	20.35	4.35	5.55	2.98	0.90
Johnson & Johnson	JNJ	358.4	20.99	5.10	6.42	2.53	0.77
Median:		*195.8*	*17.91*	*3.35*	*6.42*	*2.53*	*0.83*

Source: Author calculations.

Appreciation (HACAX) growth-oriented mutual fund and the T. Rowe Price Value (TRVLX) mutual fund as of June 15, 2017. Both funds feature large-cap companies, but they differ in their investment approaches in other important ways. HACAX's biggest holdings emphasize technology (AAPL, GOOGL, FB) firms, while TRVLX invests more on the financial (JPM, WFC) side, among a variety of diverse holdings (PFE, MRK, JNJ). On average, the stocks in the HACAX portfolio tend to have higher P/E and P/B ratios and greater future growth potential than those in TRVLX. HACAX appears to hold riskier (higher beta) stocks, but TRVLX owns companies that tend to pay higher dividends. Interestingly, both portfolios hold Apple and Microsoft among their top holdings, although these stocks would seem to be a better fit with HACAX's other positions. This underscores the room for investor judgment involved in classifying companies along the value–growth dimension.

Although investors appear to pay somewhat more attention to growth-oriented strategies, research such as the work of Asness et al. (2013) cited earlier has shown that a value approach to portfolio management tends to provide superior returns. Exhibit 11.19, which shows the cumulative performance of a large-cap growth index (Russell 1000 Growth) and a large-cap value index (Russell 1000 Value), indicates that this performance advantage persisted in the U.S. market through December 2016. This is all the more notable for the fact that, except for the 2008 market crisis, much of this period was a particularly good time for the large-cap growth investment style.

It is tempting to conclude that value is unambiguously superior to growth as an investment style. However, although value investing produces higher average returns than growth

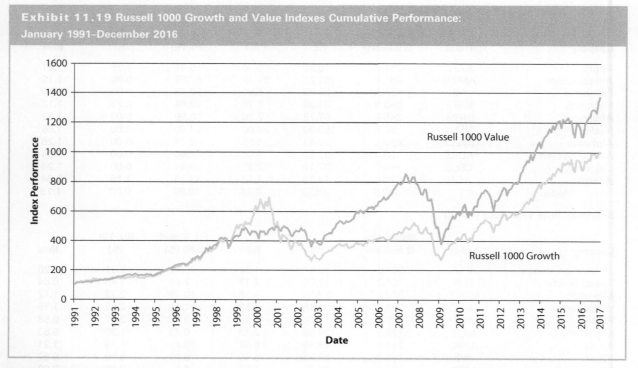

Exhibit 11.19 Russell 1000 Growth and Value Indexes Cumulative Performance: January 1991–December 2016

Note: January 1991 = 100.
Source: Frank Russell Company.

investing, this does not occur with much consistency from one investment period to another. Panel A of Exhibit 11.20 shows that there are significant differences in the value–growth return spread (based on the rolling annual performance of the Russell 1000 Value and Growth Indexes) over time. The spread ranged from over 50 percent in favor of value investing to more than 30 percent to the advantage of the growth style. Knewston, Sias, and Whidbee (2010) show how investors can benefit from timing this style rotation. Conversely, Panel B indicates that the spread between value and growth return standard deviations, while itself volatile, is generally negative, meaning that the growth strategy is usually riskier than the value approach.

Exhibit 11.20 Performance of Value and Growth Portfolios: 1991–2016

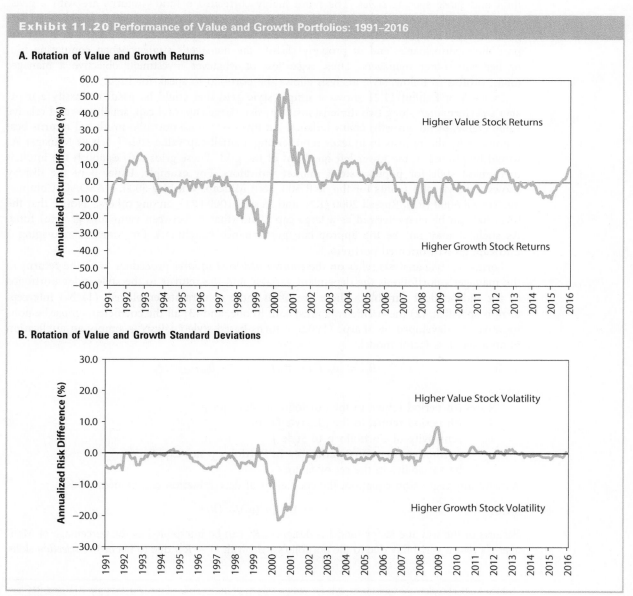

A. Rotation of Value and Growth Returns

B. Rotation of Value and Growth Standard Deviations

Source: Rolling 12-month returns to Russell 1000 Value and Growth Indexes.

11.5 An Overview of Style Analysis

As we have seen, there are many equity investment styles, including forming portfolios around stock characteristic factors such as market capitalization, leverage, industry sector, relative valuation, and growth potential. **Style analysis** attempts to explain the variability in the observed returns to a security portfolio in terms of the movements in the returns to a series of benchmark portfolios capturing the essence of a particular security characteristic. Effectively, style analysis determines the combination of long positions in a collection of passive indexes that best mimics the past performance of a security portfolio.

The process compares the past returns to a manager's portfolio with those to a series of indexes representing different investment styles to determine the relationship between the fund and those specific styles. The more highly correlated a fund's returns are with a given style index, the greater the weighting that style is given in the statistical assessment. The goals of style analysis are to better understand the underlying influences responsible for the portfolio's performance and to properly classify the manager's strategy when comparing him or her with other managers. Thus, regardless of whatever investment objective a manager might profess to follow, style analysis allows the portfolio to speak for itself.

Panel A of Exhibit 11.21 shows a simple **style grid** that could be used to classify a manager's performance along two dimensions: firm size (large cap, mid cap, small cap) and relative value (value, blend, growth) characteristics. An investor whose portfolio produced returns best mimicked by the returns to indexes representing a small-cap value style (such as Manager A) would be plotted in the lower left quadrant of the grid. These grids also establish the implicit investment style for popular stock market indicators. For example, Panel B of the display shows the style plot points for the S&P 500, S&P Midcap, Wilshire 5000, NASDAQ Composite, Russell 3000 (R3), Russell 2000 (R2), and Russell 1000 (R1), among others.[3] Notice that the S&P 500 can be characterized as a large-cap blend (that is, between value and growth) fund. As such, it may not be the appropriate performance benchmark for someone managing a mid-cap, growth-oriented portfolio.

Formally, style analysis relies on the *constrained least squares* procedure, with the returns to the manager's portfolio as the dependent variable and the returns to the style index portfolios as the independent variables. There are often three constraints employed: (1) No intercept term is specified, (2) the coefficients must sum to one, and (3) all the coefficients must be nonnegative. As developed by Sharpe (1992), returns-based style analysis is simply an application of an asset class factor model:

11.8
$$R_{pt} = [b_{p1}F_{1t} + b_{p2}F_{2t} + \dots + b_{pn}F_{nt}] + e_{pt}$$

where:

R_{pt} = tth period return to the portfolio of Manager p
F_{jt} = tth period return to the jth style factor
b_{pj} = sensitivity of Portfolio p to Style j
e_{pt} = portion of the return variability in Portfolio p not explained by variability in the set of factors

As with any regression equation, the coefficient of determination can be defined as:

11.9
$$R^2 = 1 - [\sigma^2(e_p)/\sigma^2(R_p)]$$

Because of the way the factor model is designed, R^2 can be interpreted as the percentage of Manager p's return variability due to the portfolio's *style*, with $(1 - R^2)$ due to his or her *selection* skills.

---

[3]Exhibit 11.21 also plots the investment style for various subsets of the Russell indexes. For example, R1V and R1G are, respectively, the value and growth components of the Russell 1000. They are created by ranking the 1,000 companies in the index by their price–book ratios and assigning those with the lowest (highest) ratios to the value (growth) subindex.

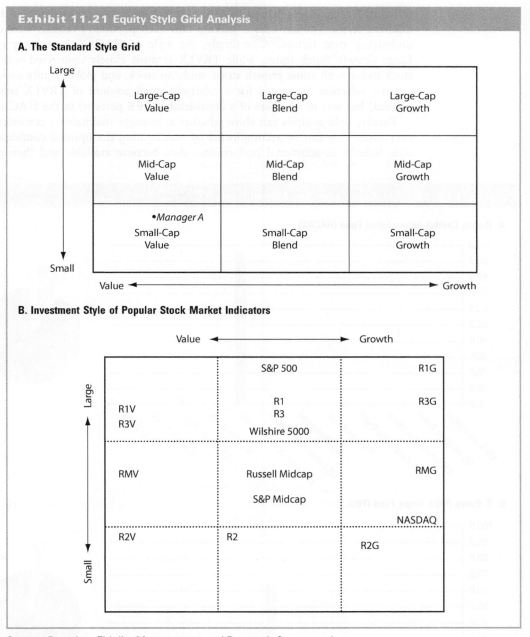

Exhibit 11.21 Equity Style Grid Analysis

A. The Standard Style Grid

	Value ◄──────────────────► Growth		
Large	Large-Cap Value	Large-Cap Blend	Large-Cap Growth
	Mid-Cap Value	Mid-Cap Blend	Mid-Cap Growth
	•*Manager A* Small-Cap Value	Small-Cap Blend	Small-Cap Growth
Small			

B. Investment Style of Popular Stock Market Indicators

Value ◄──────────────────► Growth

Large

	S&P 500	R1G
R1V R3V	R1 R3 Wilshire 5000	R3G
RMV	Russell Midcap S&P Midcap	RMG
		NASDAQ
R2V	R2	R2G

Small

Source: Based on Fidelity Management and Research Company data.

The benchmark portfolios selected as style analysis factors should be consistent with the manager's pronounced style. A different set of indexes might be specified for a domestic equity fund than for a global bond fund. Also, an effective benchmark portfolio should be easy to measure, have an investable proxy, and be as uncorrelated as possible with other style indexes.

To illustrate how this process can be implemented, the investment styles of the two mutual funds we considered earlier—Harbor Capital Appreciation Fund and T. Rowe Price Value Fund—were analyzed over a five-year interval ending in June 2017. Both portfolios performed well during the period, generating average annual returns that exceeded their respective benchmarks. However, Exhibit 11.22 shows that the managers of these portfolios followed very different styles. The bar charts indicate how each portfolio's returns were correlated with the underlying style factors. Accordingly, the style of HACAX is strongly related to the U.S. Large Growth Stock Index, while TRVLX is most closely connected with a large-cap value stock index, with some growth stock, mid-cap stock, and global equity exposure as well. Also, security selection accounted for a relatively small amount of TRVLX return variability (3.4 percent) but was much more of a consideration (9.6 percent) in the HACAX portfolio.

Finally, style analysis can show whether a manager maintains a consistent investment style over time. This can be accomplished by reestimating the optimal combination of mimicking style indexes as additional performance data become available and then overlaying the plot

Exhibit 11.22 Style Analysis for Two Mutual Funds

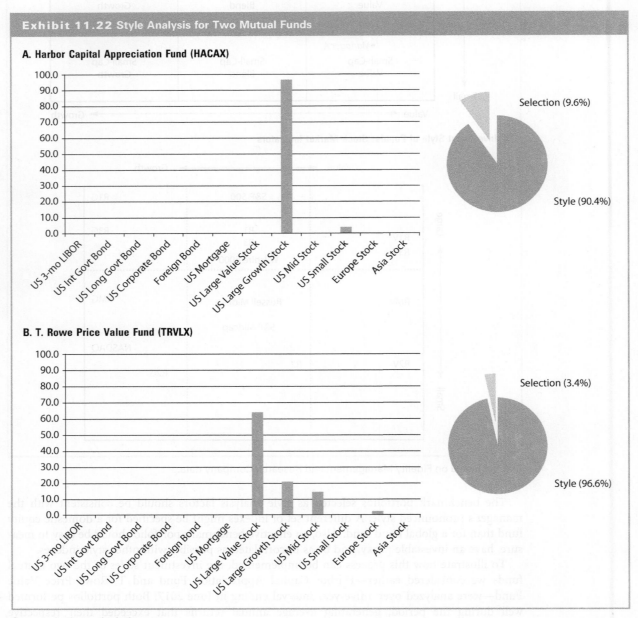

A. Harbor Capital Appreciation Fund (HACAX)

Selection (9.6%)

Style (90.4%)

B. T. Rowe Price Value Fund (TRVLX)

Selection (3.4%)

Style (96.6%)

Source: Author calculations.

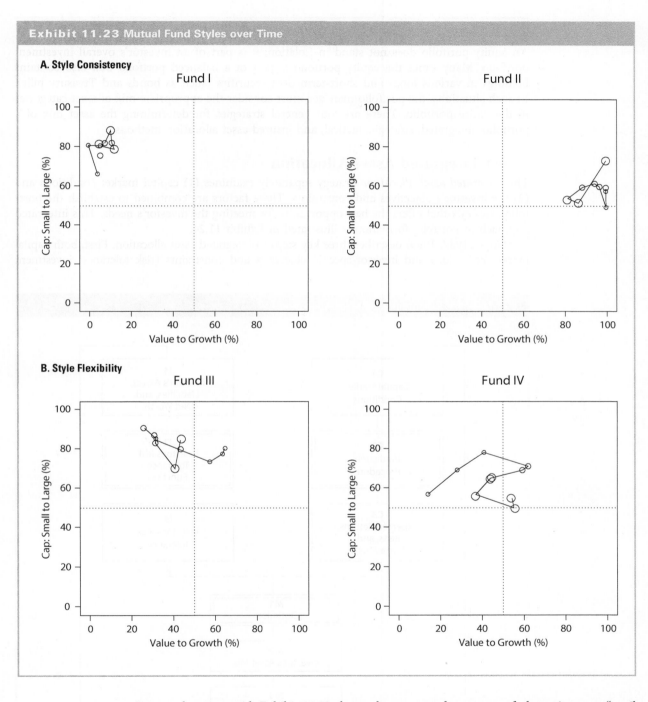

Exhibit 11.23 Mutual Fund Styles over Time

A. Style Consistency

Fund I

Fund II

B. Style Flexibility

Fund III

Fund IV

points on the same grid. Exhibit 11.23 shows the connected sequence of plot points—or "snail trails," as they are sometimes called—for four different mutual funds managed by a leading investment company. Two of these funds (I and II) have well-defined style mandates and have been able to achieve relatively stable investment policies. The other two (III and IV) have exhibited considerable *style drift*, which in both cases is due to their flexible investment missions. Of course, an investor needs to be cautious about a manager whose portfolio exhibits unintentional style drift.

11.6 ASSET ALLOCATION STRATEGIES

An equity portfolio does not stand in isolation; it is part of an investor's overall investment portfolio. Many times the equity portfolio is part of a balanced portfolio that also contains holdings in various long- and short-term debt securities (such as bonds and Treasury bills). In such situations, the portfolio manager must consider the appropriate mix of asset categories in the entire portfolio. There are four general strategies for determining the asset mix of a portfolio: integrated, strategic, tactical, and insured asset allocation methods.

11.6.1 Integrated Asset Allocation

The *integrated asset allocation* strategy separately examines (1) capital market conditions and (2) the investor's objectives and constraints. These factors are combined to establish the portfolio asset mix that offers the best opportunity for meeting the investor's needs. This integrated approach to portfolio formation is illustrated in Exhibit 11.24.

Sharpe (1987, 1990) describes three key steps to integrated asset allocation. First, both capital market conditions and investor-specific objectives and constraints (risk tolerance, investment

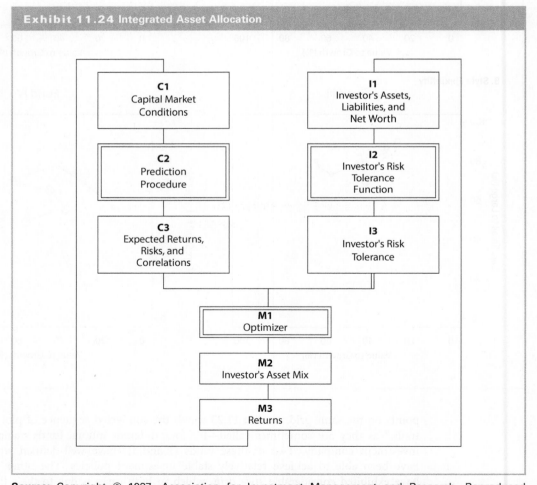

Exhibit 11.24 Integrated Asset Allocation

C1 Capital Market Conditions		**I1** Investor's Assets, Liabilities, and Net Worth
C2 Prediction Procedure		**I2** Investor's Risk Tolerance Function
C3 Expected Returns, Risks, and Correlations		**I3** Investor's Risk Tolerance

M1 Optimizer

M2 Investor's Asset Mix

M3 Returns

horizon, tax status) are established before the asset mix is determined. These processes are summarized in boxes C2 and I2, respectively, with the outcomes of those processes in boxes C3 and I3. An example of C3 might be the Markowitz efficient frontier containing portfolios of optimal variance–expected return combinations; the end product of I3 might be captured in an investment policy statement.

The second step in the integrated asset allocation process combines the information from the first step to select the single best portfolio for the investor in question. This is captured by the optimizer box in M1, with the resulting asset mix being shown in M2. One simple way of seeing how M1 might work is to calculate the *expected utility* (*EU*) of each prospective asset mix using the following formula:

11.10
$$EU_{pk} = ER_p - \left(\frac{\sigma_p^2}{RT_k}\right) = ER_p - (\text{Risk Penalty})$$

where ER_p and σ_p^2 are the expected return and variance for Portfolio p (which come from C3) and RT_k is the risk-tolerance factor for Investor k (which comes from I3). The risk-tolerance factor is intended to capture the essence of an investor's attitude toward risk bearing. Notice that the higher this number, the more risk tolerant the investor is and the less Portfolio p has its expected return "penalized" by its risk level. The optimal asset mix for any particular investor is then the one that generates the highest level of expected utility.

As an example, Panel A of Exhibit 11.25 shows the expected returns and variances for three different potential asset mixes (C3), while Panel B lists risk-tolerance factors for two investors (I3). Panel C shows the expected utility calculations that combine this information (M2). For instance, the expected utility generated by Portfolio A for Investor 1 is 5.6 ($= 7 - 7/5$), which is the largest value of the three potential allocations and therefore his optimal asset mix. By contrast, Investor 2 is more tolerant of risk and finds that Portfolio 3, which generates an expected utility level of 8.5 ($= 9 - 20/40$), is her optimal allocation. Notice that the risk-tolerance factor effectively

Exhibit 11.25 Optimal Portfolio Selection: An Example

A. Prospective Efficient Portfolios (C3)

Portfolio	ASSET MIX		*ER*	σ^2
	Stock	**Bond**		
A	20%	80%	7%	7%
B	50	50	8	3
C	80	20	9	20

B. Risk-Tolerance Factors (I3)

Investor	*RT*	
1	5	(i.e., *less* tolerant)
2	40	(i.e., *more* tolerant)

C. Expected Utility Results (M2)

Investor	A	B	C
Investor #1 *EU*	5.6	5.4	5.0
Investor #2 *EU*	6.8	7.8	8.5

deflates the risk penalty, allowing more risk-tolerant investors to pursue more volatile portfolios with higher expected returns.

The third stage of the integrated allocation process occurs after enough time has passed that the optimal portfolio's actual performance can be compared with the manager's original expectations. This evaluation process is represented by Box M3 in Exhibit 11.24. Following this assessment, the manager can make adjustments to the portfolio by including new information into the optimization process. Modifications to the initial asset mix can result from either a fundamental change in capital market conditions (increased inflation) or a change in the investor's circumstances (increased risk tolerance). It is this feedback loop that makes portfolio management a *dynamic* process.

11.6.2 Strategic Asset Allocation

Strategic asset allocation is used to determine the long-term policy asset weights in a portfolio. Typically, long-term average asset returns, risk, and covariances are used as estimates of future capital market results. Efficient frontiers are generated using this historical information, and the investor decides which asset mix is appropriate for his or her needs during the planning horizon. This results in a *constant-mix* asset allocation with periodic rebalancing to adjust the portfolio asset weights.

One way to think of the strategic allocation process is as being equivalent to the integrated asset allocation process shown in Exhibit 11.24 but without the feedback loops. That is, the manager will determine the long-term asset allocation that is best suited for a particular investor by optimizing information from both the capital market and that investor. However, once this asset mix is established, the manager does not attempt to adjust the allocation according to temporary changes in market and investor circumstances.

As an example, Brown, Garlappi, and Tiu (2010) examined the asset allocation patterns of college and university endowment funds in the United States and Canada. Exhibit 11.26 shows both the average actual and strategic (or, target) investment proportions for their fund sample in 2005. As investors with a very long-term focus, it is appropriate that university endowment funds place a lot of their assets in riskier asset classes, such as public and private equity.

Exhibit 11.26 Strategic and Tactical Asset Allocations for University Endowment Funds (2005 Year-End Data, 709 Funds)

Asset Class	Actual Allocation	Strategic Allocation	Tactical Adjustment
U.S. Equity	45.7%	44.7%	+1.0%
Non-U.S. Equity	12.7	12.8	−0.1
U.S. Fixed Income	20.5	21.5	−1.0
Non-U.S. Fixed Income	0.9	1.0	−0.1
Real Estate-Public	1.2	1.3	−0.1
Real Estate-Private	2.0	2.2	−0.2
Hedge Funds	8.9	9.0	−0.1
Private Equity-Venture Capital	0.8	1.5	−0.7
Private Equity-Buyout	1.6	2.5	−0.9
Natural Resources	1.0	1.2	−0.2
Cash	3.4	1.6	+1.8
Other	1.4	0.8	+0.6

Source: Adapted from Keith C. Brown, Lorenzo Garlappi, and Cristian Tiu, "Asset Allocation and Portfolio Performance: Evidence from University Endowment Funds," *Journal of Financial Markets* 13, no. 2 (May 2010): 268–294.

Altogether, these strategic equity allocations account for more than 61 percent of the capital commitment for the average endowment. Conversely, less risky investments in fixed-income and cash only accounted for less than 25 percent of the average asset allocation.

11.6.3 Tactical Asset Allocation

Unlike an investor's strategic allocation, which is set with a long-term focus and modified infrequently, *tactical asset allocation* frequently adjusts the asset class mix in the portfolio to take advantage of changing market conditions. With tactical asset allocation, these adjustments are driven solely by perceived changes in the relative values of the various asset classes; the investor's risk tolerance and investment constraints are assumed to be constant over time. In Exhibit 11.24, this is equivalent to an integrated approach to asset allocation that removes the feedback loop involving investor-specific information (I2).

Tactical asset allocation is often based on the premise of *mean reversion*: whatever a security's return has been in the recent past, it will eventually revert to its long-term average (mean) value. This assessment is usually done on a comparative basis. For instance, suppose that the ratio of stock and bond returns is normally 1.2, reflecting the greater degree of risk in the equity market. If stock returns were suddenly double those of bond returns, the tactical investor might determine that bonds were now undervalued relative to stock and therefore overweight the fixed-income component of the portfolio.

Notice that tactical asset allocation is an inherently *contrarian* method of investing. The investor adopting this approach will always be buying the asset class that is currently out of favor—on a relative basis, at least—and selling the asset class with the highest market value. DuBois (1992) notes that how frequently the investor chooses to adjust the asset class mix in the portfolio will depend on several factors, such as the general level of volatility in the capital markets, relative equity and fixed-income risk premia, and changes in the macroeconomic environment.

The endowment fund example in Exhibit 11.26 also shows the tactical adjustments made by managers. These adjustments can be measured as the difference between the actual and strategic (planned) allocation proportions and are listed in the last column. Notice that endowment fund managers went from being *overweighted* in the U.S. equity category by +1.0 percent, although they were collectively *underweighted* in the private equity classes by −1.6 percent. These tactical adjustments in private equity were probably not intentional but likely due to managers not being able to invest all of the money they had planned, which would also explain the overweight position in their cash accounts. Private equity investments will be discussed in Chapter 17.

11.6.4 Insured Asset Allocation

Insured asset allocation likewise results in frequent adjustments in the portfolio allocation, assuming that expected market returns and risks are constant over time, while the investor's objectives and constraints change as his or her wealth position changes. For example, rising portfolio values increase the investor's wealth and consequently his or her ability to handle risk, which means the investor can increase his or her exposure to risky assets. Declines in the portfolio's value lower wealth, consequently decreasing his or her ability to handle risk, which means the portfolio's exposure to risky assets must decline. Often, insured asset allocation involves only two assets, such as common stocks and T-bills. As stock prices rise, the asset allocation increases the stock component. As stock prices fall, the stock component of the mix falls while the T-bill component increases. This is opposite of what would happen under tactical asset allocation. Insured asset allocation is like the integrated approach without the capital market feedback loop (C2 in Exhibit 11.24).

SUMMARY

- Passive equity portfolios attempt to track the returns of an established benchmark index, such as the S&P 500, or one that meets the investor's needs. Active portfolios attempt to add value relative to their benchmark by market timing and/or by seeking to buy undervalued stocks. Index mutual funds and exchange-traded funds are popular ways for small investors to make passive investments.

- Tracking error, which is defined as the standard deviation of the difference between the returns to a managed fund and a benchmark, is a convenient way to categorize various management styles. Portfolios with tracking errors of less than 1 percent are generally considered to be passive, while active equity strategies often have tracking errors in excess of 5 percent. Active share, which examines a portfolio's security holdings relative to those held in a benchmark index, is another popular way to establish how actively managed a fund may be.

- There are several methods for constructing and managing a passive portfolio, including full replication of a benchmark or sampling. Several active management approaches exist, including factor investing in security characteristic portfolios, such as price and earnings momentum strategies. Value- and growth-oriented strategies have become particularly popular in recent years, and style analysis helps the investor determine the exact investment style the manager is using. Investors should also consider the tax efficiency of an actively managed portfolio.

- Since equity portfolios typically are used with other assets in an investor's overall portfolio, we reviewed several common asset allocation strategies, including integrated asset allocation, strategic asset allocation, tactical asset allocation, and insured asset allocation. The basic difference between these strategies is whether they rely on current market expectations or long-run projections, as well as whether the investor's objectives and constraints remain constant or change with market conditions.

SUGGESTED READINGS

Ang, Andrew. *Asset Management: A Systematic Approach to Factor Investing.* New York: Oxford University Press, 2014.

Bernstein, Richard. *Style Investing: Unique Insight into Equity Management.* New York: Wiley, 1995.

Dreman, David M. *Contrarian Investment Strategies: The Psychological Edge.* New York: Free Press, 2012.

Kinlaw, William, Mark P. Kritzman, and David Turlington. *A Practitioner's Guide to Asset Allocation.* Hoboken, NJ: John Wiley, 2017.

Malkiel, Burton G., and Charles D. Ellis. *The Elements of Investing.* Hoboken, NJ: John Wiley, 2010.

Sharpe, William F. "Expected Utility Asset Allocation," *Financial Analysts Journal* 63, no. 5 (September/October 2007): 18–30.

QUESTIONS

1. Why have passive portfolio management strategies increased in use over time?

2. What is meant by an *indexing portfolio strategy*, and what is the justification for this strategy? How might it differ from another passive portfolio?

3. Briefly describe four techniques considered active equity portfolio management strategies.

4. List two investment products that a manager following a passive investment strategy could use to make an investment in the Standard & Poor's 500 Index. Briefly discuss which product is likely to be the most accurate method for tracking the index.

5. Discuss three strategies active managers can use to add value to their portfolios relative to a benchmark index. What is the difference between a fundamental approach to active management and a factor-based approach?

6. How do trading costs and market efficiencies affect the active manager? How may an active manager try to overcome these obstacles to success?

7. Discuss how the four asset allocation strategies differ from one another.

8. There has been a long-standing debate regarding the existence of a "value–growth" anomaly in financial economic research. Previous studies have shown that value stocks (low price–book ratios) have higher returns than growth stocks (high price–book ratios) in the United States and markets around the world, even after adjusting for a marketwide risk factor. What are some possible explanations for why value stocks might outperform growth stocks on a risk-adjusted basis? Is this value-growth "anomaly" consistent with the existence of an efficient stock market?

9. Describe the difference between a price momentum strategy and an earnings momentum strategy. Under what conditions would you expect the two approaches to produce similar portfolios?

10. Because of inflationary expectations, you expect natural resource stocks, such as mining companies and oil firms, to perform well over the next three to six months. As an active portfolio manager, describe the various methods available to take advantage of this forecast.

PROBLEMS

1. Given the monthly returns that follow, how well did the passive portfolio track the S&P 500 benchmark? Find the R^2, alpha, and beta of the portfolio. Compute the average return differential with and without sign.

Month	Portfolio Return	S&P 500 Return
January	5.0%	5.2%
February	−2.3	−3.0
March	−1.8	−1.6
April	2.2	1.9
May	0.4	0.1
June	−0.8	−0.5
July	0.0	0.2
August	1.5	1.6
September	−0.3	−0.1
October	−3.7	−4.0
November	2.4	2.0
December	0.3	0.2

2. Beth Stewart is an investment analyst for the U.S.-based Empire Pension Fund. Empire is considering the addition of two recently established U.S. large-capitalization equity mutual funds to its asset mix. Stewart utilizes return-based-style analysis to compare the performance of the Foreman Fund and the Copeland Fund for the past year.

	S&P 500 Index	Foreman Fund	Copeland Fund
R^2	—	68.5%	99.4%
Annual Return (gross)*	6.8%	9.2%	7.0%
Portfolio Turnover	—	45%	15%

*Management fees and administrative charges have not been deducted

Based on this data, Stewart concludes that Foreman is an actively managed fund, that Copeland is an index fund, and that Foreman outperformed Copeland for the year.

A colleague tells Stewart that her conclusions may not be accurate and makes the following statements:

- Even though Foreman has a low R^2 with the S&P 500 Index, Foreman may not be an actively managed fund.
- Copeland may be an actively managed fund even though Copeland has low portfolio turnover.
- Foreman may not have had superior risk-adjusted performance compared with Copeland for the year.

For each of these three statements, describe one circumstance in which the statement could be correct.

3. Consider the following trading and performance data for four different equity mutual funds:

	Fund W	Fund X	Fund Y	Fund Z
Assets under Management, Avg. for Past 12 months (mil)	$289.4	$653.7	$1,298.4	$5,567.3
Security Sales, Past 12 months (mil)	$37.2	$569.3	$1,453.8	$437.1
Expense Ratio	0.33%	0.71%	1.13%	0.21%
Pretax Return, 3-year avg.	9.98%	10.65%	10.12%	9.83%
Tax-adjusted Return, 3-year avg.	9.43%	8.87%	9.34%	9.54%

a. Calculate the portfolio turnover ratio for each fund.
b. Which two funds are most likely to be actively managed and which two are most likely passive funds? Explain.
c. Calculate the tax cost ratio for each fund.
d. Which funds were the most and least tax efficient in the operations? Why?

4. Global Advisers Company (GAC) is an SEC-registered investment counseling firm involved solely in managing international securities portfolios. After much research on the developing economy and capital markets of the country of Otunia, GAC has decided to include an investment in the Otunia stock market in its Emerging Market Commingled Fund. However, GAC has not yet decided whether to invest actively or by indexing. Your opinion on the active versus indexing decision has been solicited. A summary of the research findings follows.

Otunia's economy is fairly well diversified across agricultural and natural resources, manufacturing (both consumer and durable goods), and a growing finance sector. Transaction costs in securities markets are relatively large in Otunia because of high commissions and government "stamp taxes" on securities trades. Accounting standards and disclosure regulations are quite detailed, resulting in wide public availability of reliable information about companies' financial performance.

Capital flows into and out of Otunia and foreign ownership of Otunia securities are strictly regulated by an agency of the national government. The settlement procedures under these ownership rules often cause long delays in settling trades made by nonresidents. Senior finance officials in the government are working to deregulate capital flows and foreign ownership, but GAC's political consultant believes that isolationist sentiment may prevent much real progress in the short run.

a. Briefly discuss four aspects of the Otunia environment that favor investing actively and four aspects that favor indexing.
b. Recommend whether GAC should invest in Otunia actively or by indexing, and justify your recommendation based on the factors identified in part (a).

5. Betty Black's investment club wants to buy the stock of either NewSoft Inc. or Capital Corp. In this connection, Black has prepared the following table. You have been asked to

help her interpret the data, based on your forecast for a healthy economy and a strong market over the next 12 months.

	NewSoft Inc.	Capital Corp.	S&P 500 Index
Current price	$30	$32	n/a
Industry	Computer Software	Capital Goods	n/a
P/E ratio (current)	25×	14×	16×
P/E ratio (5-year avg.)	27×	16×	16×
P/B ratio (current)	10×	3×	3×
P/B ratio (5-year avg.)	12×	4×	2×
Beta	1.5	1.1	1.0
Dividend yield	0.3%	2.7%	2.8%

NewSoft's shares have higher price–earnings (P/E) and price–book (P/B) ratios than those of Capital Corp. Identify and briefly discuss three reasons why the disparity in ratios may not indicate that NewSoft's shares are overvalued relative to the shares of Capital Corp. Answer the question in terms of the two ratios, and assume that there have been no extraordinary events affecting either company.

6. As the chief investment officer for a money management firm specializing in taxable individual investors, you are trying to establish a strategic asset allocation for two different clients. You have established that Ms. A has a risk-tolerance factor of 8, while Mr. B has a risk-tolerance factor of 27. The characteristics for four model portfolios follow:

ASSET MIX

Portfolio	Stock	Bond	ER	σ^2
1	5%	95%	8%	5%
2	25	75	9	10
3	70	30	10	16
4	90	10	11	25

a. Calculate the expected utility of each prospective portfolio for each of the two clients.
b. Which portfolio represents the optimal strategic allocation for Ms. A? Which portfolio is optimal for Mr. B? Explain why there is a difference in these two outcomes.
c. For Ms. A, what level of risk tolerance would leave her indifferent between having Portfolio 1 or Portfolio 2 as her strategic allocation? Demonstrate.

7. Consider the annual returns produced by two different active equity portfolio managers (A and B) as well as those to the stock index with which they are both compared:

Period	Manager A	Manager B	Index
1	12.8%	13.9%	11.8%
2	−2.1	−4.2	−2.2
3	15.6	13.5	18.9
4	0.8	2.9	−0.5
5	−7.9	−5.9	−3.9
6	23.2	26.3	21.7
7	−10.4	−11.2	−13.2
8	5.6	5.5	5.3
9	2.3	4.2	2.4
10	19.0	18.8	19.7

a. Did either manager outperform the index, based on the average annual return differential that he or she produced relative to the benchmark? Demonstrate.

b. Calculate the tracking error for each manager relative to the index. Which manager did a better job of limiting his or her client's unsystematic risk exposure? Explain.

8. Shown below are the investment weights for the securities held in four different portfolios: three mutual funds and the benchmark index that each of those funds uses.

Security	Benchmark Index	Fund X	Fund Y	Fund Z
1	10%	12%	40%	11%
2	10	13	0	9
3	10	8	5	9
4	10	15	0	9
5	10	7	0	11
6	10	10	0	11
7	10	5	30	9
8	10	14	0	11
9	10	6	0	11
10	10	10	25	9

% Security Investment Weight:

a. Calculate the active share (AS) measure for Fund X, Fund Y, and Fund Z relative to the benchmark index.

b. Using these active share calculations, indicate which fund is the most likely to be considered: (i) a passive index fund, (ii) a closet (or enhanced) index fund, and (iii) an actively managed concentrated stock-picking fund. Explain the reason for your classification.

9. Each month for the past several years, you have collected the monthly returns to an index of large-cap value stocks and an index of large-cap growth stocks. For the last two years, for both of the indexes you have converted these monthly returns into a series of *rolling average annualized returns* by taking an average of the previous 12 monthly returns and multiplying that average by 12. These rolling average annualized returns are shown below for each index over the past 24 months.

Month	Value Index Annualized Return (%)	Growth Index Annualized Return (%)
1	8.97%	9.50%
2	17.38	17.48
3	28.11	26.81
4	16.19	12.92
5	16.66	14.60
6	16.72	14.90
7	19.43	13.21
8	16.88	9.68
9	17.88	10.14
10	20.41	12.42
11	28.86	20.69
12	23.02	16.09
13	27.38	20.05
14	21.43	15.65
15	20.76	18.25
16	25.62	25.59

Month	Value Index Annualized Return (%)	Growth Index Annualized Return (%)
17	28.46	26.74
18	28.92	29.62
19	18.87	22.49
20	21.75	26.38
21	20.18	21.63
22	19.62	19.51
23	18.48	20.76
24	21.97	24.59

a. For both the value and growth indexes, calculate the arithmetic mean of the 24 monthly average annualized returns. Which index appears to have outperformed the other over this period? Explain.

b. For each month in this sample period, compute the difference in annualized returns between the value index and the growth index ($R_{value} - R_{growth}$). Calculate the average of this return differential series and compare it to your answers from part (a).

c. Plot the return differential series on a graph similar to Panel A of Exhibit 11.20.

d. The average return differential from part (b) is one way of calculating the *risk premium* associated with a value investment factor. Interpret this risk premium statistic and explain how it can be seen as the average annualized return earned by a hedge fund following a strategy to go long in value stocks and short in growth stocks.

e. Compute the percentage of the months in the two-year sample period when the rolling average annualized return to the growth index was actually larger than that for the value index. What, if anything, does this tell you about the reliability of the value risk premium over time?

For most investors, bonds receive limited attention and very little respect. This is surprising considering that the total market value of the bond market in the United States and in most other countries is substantially larger than the market value of the stock market. For example, by 2017, the aggregate value of the global bond market exceeded $100 trillion, while the comparable value of the global stock market was about $65 trillion. Despite the size factor, bonds have a reputation for producing low, unexciting returns. Although this may have been true 40 or 50 years ago, it certainly has not been true during the past 30 years. Specifically, the average annual compound rate of return on government/corporate bonds for the period 1987–2016 was about 8.5 percent versus roughly 12.0 percent for common stocks. These rates of return along with corresponding standard deviations (10 percent for bonds versus 19 percent for stocks) and the low correlation between stocks and bonds (about 0.05) indicate that there are substantial opportunities in bonds for individual and institutional investors to enhance their risk–return performance.

The chapters in this section are intended to provide (1) a basic understanding of bonds and the bond markets around the world, (2) background on analyzing returns and risks in the bond market, (3) insights regarding the valuation of bonds, including numerous new fixed-income securities with very unusual cash flow characteristics, and (4) an understanding of either active or passive bond portfolio management.

Chapter 12 describes the global bond market in terms of country participation and the makeup of the bond market in major countries. Also, we examine characteristics of bonds in alternative categories, such as government, corporate, and municipal. We also discuss the many new corporate bond instruments developed in the United States, such as asset-backed securities, zero-coupon bonds, high-yield bonds, and inflation protection securities. While the use of these securities globally has generally been limited to the large developed markets, it is certain that they will eventually be used around the world. Finally, we provide a thorough examination of yield curves and the role they play in the bond valuation process, including a detailed discussion of how one values a fixed-income security using a single discount rate or using series of spot rates. We conclude the chapter by considering alternative yield measures for a bond, including those that contain embedded prepayment (call) features.

Chapter 13 extends the investor's bond toolkit by considering several other techniques and measures that are useful in the evaluation of these instruments. Specifically, we consider what characteristics influence the volatility of bond returns, including the very important concept of bond duration, which is a measure of bond price volatility with respect to interest rate changes in the market. We also consider the notion of bond convexity and the impact it has on bond price volatility. We finish with an extended discussion of how an investor can use these analytical concepts to create and manage a bond portfolio. We consider three major categories of portfolio strategies: *passive* management strategies, which include either a simple buy-and-hold strategy or indexing to one of the major benchmarks; *active* management strategies, which involve structuring the characteristics of a portfolio to respond to a forecasted market condition; and *matched funding* strategies, which include constructing dedicated portfolios, constructing classical or contingent immunization portfolios, or horizon matching.

The fact that two fairly long chapters are devoted to the study of bonds attests to the importance of the topic and the extensive research done in this area. During the past 25 years, there have been more developments related to the valuation and portfolio management of bonds than of stocks. This growth of the fixed-income sector does not detract from the importance of equities but certainly enhances the significance of fixed-income securities. Finally, readers should keep in mind that this growth in size, sophistication, and specialization of the bond market implies numerous and varied career opportunities in the bond area, including trading these securities, valuation, credit analysis, and domestic and global portfolio management.

CHAPTER **12**

Bond Fundamentals
and Valuation

After you read this chapter, you should be able to answer the following questions:

- What are some of the basic features of bonds that affect their risk, return, and value?
- What is the current country structure of the world bond market, and how has the makeup of the global bond market changed in recent years?
- What are the major components of the world bond market?
- What are bond ratings, and what is their purpose? What is the difference between investment-grade bonds and high-yield (junk) bonds?
- What are the characteristics of bonds in the major bond categories, such as governments, agencies, municipalities, and corporates, and how are their prices quoted?
- What are the important characteristics of corporate bond issues developed in the United States over the past decades, such as mortgage-backed securities, other asset-backed securities, zero-coupon bonds, and high-yield bonds?
- What is a yield curve, and how is its shape determined?
- What is the difference between the par and spot yield curves?
- How do you determine the value of a bond based on the discounted cash flow formula?
- How does bond valuation change when you are between two coupon dates?
- How do you compute the following yields on bonds: current yield, yield to maturity, yield to call, and compound realized (horizon) yield?

The global bond market is large and diverse and represents an important investment opportunity. This chapter is concerned with publicly issued, long-term, nonconvertible debt obligations of public and private issuers in the United States and other major global markets. An understanding of bonds is helpful in an efficient market because the existence of U.S. and foreign bonds increases the universe of investments available for the creation of a diversified portfolio.

We begin by reviewing some basic features of bonds and examine the structure of the world bond market, including an in-depth discussion of the major fixed-income investments. We also discuss the notion of what a bond yield curve represents and discuss how the information that it contains is essential to understanding how bonds are valued in practice.

We then apply the valuation principles that were introduced in Chapter 8 to the valuation of bonds. This includes a demonstration of how one would value bonds using the traditional single yield to maturity rate or using multiple spot rates. We will also come to understand the several measures of yields for bonds with are important to help us understand how and why bond values change over time.

12.1 BASIC FEATURES OF A BOND

Public bonds are long-term, fixed-obligation debt securities packaged in convenient, affordable denominations for sale to individuals and financial institutions. They differ from other debt, such as individual mortgages and privately placed debt obligations, in that they are sold to the public rather than channeled directly to a single lender. Bond issues are considered fixed-income securities because they impose fixed financial obligations on the issuers. Specifically, the issuer of a bond agrees to:

1. Pay a fixed amount of *interest periodically* to the holder
2. Repay a fixed amount of *principal* at the date of maturity

Normally, interest on bonds is paid every six months, although some bond issues pay in intervals as short as a month or as long as a year. The principal is due at maturity and is often called the *par* (or *face*) *value*. A bond has a specified term to maturity, which defines the life of the issue. The public debt market typically is divided into three time segments based on an issue's original maturity:

1. Short-term issues with maturities of 1 year or less. The market for these instruments is commonly known as the **money market**.
2. Intermediate-term issues with maturities in excess of 1 year but less than 10 years. These instruments are known as **notes**.
3. Long-term obligations with maturities in excess of 10 years, called *bonds*.

The lives of debt obligations decline steadily as the issues progress toward maturity. This change in maturity is important because a major determinant of the price volatility of bonds is the remaining life (maturity) of the issue.

12.1.1 Bond Characteristics

A bond can be characterized by its (1) intrinsic features, (2) type, (3) indenture provisions, or (4) features that affect its cash flows or its maturity.

Intrinsic Features The coupon, maturity, principal value, and the type of ownership are important intrinsic features of a bond. The **coupon** of a bond indicates the income that the bond investor will receive over the life (or holding period) of the issue. This is known as *interest income*, or *coupon income*.

The **term to maturity** specifies the date or the number of years before a bond matures (or expires). There are two different types of maturity. The most common is a **term bond**, which has a single maturity date. Alternatively, a **serial obligation bond** issue has a series of maturity dates, perhaps 20 or 25. Each maturity, although a subset of the total issue, is really a small bond issue with generally a different coupon. Municipalities issue most serial bonds.

The **principal**, or **par value**, of an issue represents the original value of the obligation. This is generally stated in $1,000 increments from $1,000 to $25,000 or more. Principal value is *not* the same as the bond's market value. The market prices of many issues rise above or fall below their principal values because of differences between their coupons and the prevailing market rate of interest, which is known as the bond's *yield to maturity*.

Finally, bonds differ in terms of ownership. With a **bearer bond**, the person physically holding the security is the owner, so the issuer keeps no record of ownership. Interest from a bearer bond is obtained by clipping coupons attached to the bonds and sending them to the issuer for payment. In contrast, the issuers of **registered bonds** maintain ownership records and pay the interest directly to the current owner of record.

Types of Issues In contrast to common stock, companies can have many different bond issues outstanding at the same time. **Secured (senior) bonds** are backed by a legal claim on some specified property of the issuer in the case of default. For example, mortgage bonds can be secured by real estate assets; equipment trust certificates, which are used by railroads and airlines, provide a senior claim on the firm's equipment.

Unsecured bonds (debentures) are backed only by the promise of the issuer to pay interest and principal on a timely basis. As such, they are secured by the general credit of the issuer. **Subordinate (junior) debentures** possess a claim on income and assets that is subordinated to other debentures. Income issues are the most junior type because interest on them is paid only if it is earned. Although income bonds are unusual in the corporate sector, they are very popular municipal issues, where they are referred to as **revenue bonds**.

Indenture Provisions The *indenture* is the contract between the issuer and the bondholder specifying the issuer's legal requirements. A trustee (usually a bank) acting on behalf of the bondholders ensures that all the indenture provisions are met, including the timely payment of interest and principal. All the factors that dictate a bond's features, its type, and its maturity are set forth in the indenture.

Features Affecting a Bond's Maturity There are three alternative call option features that can affect the life (maturity) of a bond. One extreme is a *freely callable* provision that allows the issuer to retire the bond at any time with a typical notification period of 30 to 60 days. The other extreme is a *noncallable* provision wherein the issuer cannot retire the bond prior to its maturity.[1] Between these is a *deferred call* provision, in which the issue cannot be called for a certain period of time after its issue (for example, 5 to 10 years). At the end of the deferred call period, the issue becomes freely callable. Callable bonds have a **call premium**, which is the amount above par value that the issuer must pay to the bondholder for prematurely retiring the bond.

A *nonrefunding provision* prohibits a call and premature retirement of an issue from the proceeds of a lower-coupon **refunding bond**. This is meant to protect the bondholder from a typical refunding, but it is not foolproof. An issue with a nonrefunding provision can be called and retired prior to maturity using other sources of funds, such as excess cash from operations, the sale of assets, or proceeds from a sale of common stock.

Another important indenture provision that can affect a bond's maturity is the **sinking fund**, which specifies that a bond must be paid off systematically over its life rather than only at maturity. The size of the sinking fund can be a percentage of a given issue, a percentage of the total debt outstanding, or a fixed sum stated on a dollar basis. Similar to a call feature, sinking fund payments may commence shortly after the date of issue or may be deferred for 5 or 10 years. The amount that must be repaid before maturity from a sinking fund can range from a small portion to 100 percent. Like a call, the sinking fund feature typically carries a nominal premium but is generally smaller than the straight call premium (for example, 1 percent). For example, a bond issue with a 20-year maturity might have a sinking fund that requires that 5 percent of the issue be retired every year beginning in year 10. The effect of this is that by year 20, half of the issue has been retired and the rest is paid off at maturity. Sinking-fund provisions have a small effect on comparative yields at the time of issue but have little subsequent impact on price behavior.

---

[1]The main issuer of noncallable bonds between 1985 and 2017 was the U.S. Treasury. Corporate long-term bonds typically have contained some form of call provision, except during periods of relatively low interest rates (for example, 1994–2001; 2010–2011) when the probability of exercising the option was very low.

12.2 THE GLOBAL BOND MARKET STRUCTURE[2]

The market for fixed-income securities is substantially larger than the listed equity exchanges (for example, NYSE Euronext) because corporations tend to raise a lot of capital by issuing bonds. Corporations issue less common or preferred stock because firms derive most of their equity financing from internally generated funds (retained earnings). Also, although the equity market involves just corporations, the bond market in most countries has four noncorporate sectors: the pure government sector (for example, the Treasury in the United States), government agencies (for example, GNMA), state and local government bonds (municipals), and international bonds (for example, Yankees and Eurobonds in the United States).

The size of the global bond market and the distribution among countries can be gleaned from Exhibit 12.1, which lists the dollar value of debt outstanding and the percentage distribution for the major currencies in the years 2010 and 2016. There has been consistent overall growth, at a rate of 5 to 10 percent a year. Also, the currency trends are significant. Specifically, the U.S. dollar market went from 43 percent of the total world bond market in 2010 to more than 50 percent in 2016. A significant change in 1999 was the creation of the Eurozone sector, which includes a large part of Europe (for example, Germany, Italy, France) with the significant exception of the United Kingdom. Notably, this euro currency sector has held at about 20 to 25 percent over the past decade.

12.2.1 Participating Issuers

There are five different categories of bonds for each currency: (1) sovereign bonds (for example, the U.S. Treasury), (2) quasi- and foreign governments (including agency bonds), (3) securitized and collateralized bonds from governments or corporations, (4) directly issued corporate bonds, and (5) high-yield and emerging market bonds. Exhibit 12.2 shows the division of bonds among these five categories for three large currency markets and the Eurozone during 2016.

Sovereigns On a percentage basis, the market for government securities is the largest sector, particularly in Japan. It involves a variety of debt instruments issued to meet the growing needs of the federal government.

Quasi-governments (Agencies) and Foreign Governments Agency issues have become a notable segment in the U.S. dollar, yen, and pound sterling markets (over 6 percent) but are a larger

Exhibit 12.1 Estimated Total Face Value and Percentage of Total for Significant Markets

	2016 (estimated)		2010 (estimated)	
Currency	$ Millions	%	$ Millions	%
U.S. dollar	22,365,696	52.1%	16,207,960	43.4%
Euro	9,385,707	21.8%	9,462,897	25.3%
Japanese yen	6,965,857	16.2%	7,254,856	19.4%
Pound sterling	1,870,967	4.4%	1,849,483	4.9%
Canadian dollar	1,139,448	2.7%	1,078,130	2.9%
Australian dollar	571,360	1.3%	441,174	1.2%
All other	660,045	1.5%	1,075,660	2.9%
Total	**42,959,080**	**100.0%**	**37,370,160**	**100.0%**

Source: Estimated by authors based on data from Bank of America Merrill Lynch Global Research.

---

[2]For additional discussion of global bond markets, see Ramanathan (2012) and Malvey (2012).

Exhibit 12.2 Estimated Makeup of Bonds Outstanding by Currency: December 31, 2016

	2016 (estimated)	
	Total Value ($ millions)	% of Total
A. U.S. Dollars		
Sovereign	9,204,000	37.8%
Quasi- and foreign govt.	1,738,947	7.1%
Securitized/collateralized	6,279,011	25.8%
Corporate	6,000,946	24.7%
High-yield/emerging mkt.	1,112,310	4.6%
Total	24,335,213	100.0%
B. Euros		
Sovereign	6,212,364	56.8%
Quasi- and foreign govt.	1,528,451	14.0%
Securitized/collateralized	909,152	8.3%
Corporate	1,927,615	17.6%
High-yield/emerging mkt.	354,645	3.3%
Total	10,932,228	100.0%
C. Japanese Yen		
Sovereign	6,970,922	90.9%
Quasi- and foreign govt.	526,527	6.9%
Securitized/collateralized	1,760	0.0%
Corporate	164,010	2.1%
High-yield/emerging mkt.	8,074	0.1%
Total	7,671,293	100.0%
D. Pound Sterling		
Sovereign	1,668,971	67.3%
Quasi- and foreign govt.	143,326	5.8%
Securitized/collateralized	107,343	4.3%
Corporate	438,964	17.7%
High-yield/emerging mkt	120,672	4.9%
Total	2,479,276	100.0%

Sources: Estimated by authors based on historical data from Bank of America Merrill Lynch Global Research; euro totals based on year-end data for 2015.

proportion in the Eurozone (about 14 percent). These agencies represent political subdivisions of the government, although the securities are *not* typically direct obligations of the government. The U.S. agency market has two types of issuers: government-sponsored enterprises and federal agencies. The proceeds of agency bond issues are used to finance many legislative programs. Foreign government issues are typically not denominated in its own currency (for example, a Japanese government issue denominated in dollars and sold in the United States).

Securitized/Collateralized Issues These can be either government agencies or corporate issues that are backed by cash flow from a portfolio of other assets, such as mortgages or car loans. Collateralized securities can include several different issues and structured cash flows. As shown in Exhibit 12.2, this has become a major sector in the United States and is fairly strong in the Eurozone countries.

Corporations The major nongovernmental issuer of debt is the corporate sector. The importance of this sector differs dramatically among countries. It is a slow-growth component in Japan but a significant part of the U.S. dollar, euro, and pound sterling markets. The market for corporate bonds is commonly subdivided into several segments: industrials, public utilities, transportation, and financial issues.

High-Yield/Emerging Market This section includes both high-yield bonds (noninvestment grade) from corporations in developed countries, and government or corporate issues from emerging market countries such as China and India, where the bonds can be either investment grade or high yield (noninvestment grade). Notably, the only markets where this sector is significant are those for the U.S. dollar and the pound sterling.

12.2.2 Participating Investors

Numerous individual and institutional investors with diverse investment objectives participate in the bond market. Individual investors are a minor portion because of the market's complexity and the high minimum denominations of most issues. Institutional investors typically account for 90 to 95 percent of the trading, although different segments of the market are more institutionalized than others. For example, institutions are involved heavily in the agency market, but they are somewhat less active in the corporate sector.

A variety of institutions invest in the bond market. Life insurance companies invest in corporate bonds and, to a lesser extent, in Treasury and agency securities. Commercial banks invest in municipal bonds and government and agency issues. Property and liability insurance companies concentrate on municipal bonds and Treasuries. Private and government pension funds are heavily committed to corporates but also invest in Treasuries and agencies. Finally, fixed-income mutual funds have experienced significant growth, and their demand spans the full spectrum of the market as they develop bond funds that meet the needs of a variety of investors.

Alternative institutions tend to favor different sectors of the bond market based on two factors: (1) the tax code applicable to the institution and (2) the nature of the institution's liability structure. For example, pension funds and endowments are virtually tax-free institutions with long-term commitments, so they often prefer high-yielding, long-term government or corporate bonds.

12.2.3 Bond Ratings

The primary risk that a bondholder faces is that the borrower will not be able to pay the promised coupons and principal refunding. When this occurs, the borrower is said to be in *default* on the loan. To assess the possibility of default, nearly all bonds are rated by professional analysts for the creditworthiness of the issuer. The exceptions, such as very small issues and bonds from certain industries, are known as *nonrated bonds*. There are three major rating agencies: (1) Fitch Investors Service, (2) Moody's, and (3) Standard & Poor's (S&P).

Bond ratings provide the fundamental analysis for thousands of issues. The rating agencies analyze the issuing organization and the specific issue to determine the probability of default. The primary question in bond credit analysis is whether the firm can service its debt in a timely manner over the life of a given issue. Consequently, the rating agencies consider expectations over the life of the issue, along with the historical and current financial position of the company.

Gentry, Whitford, and Newbold (1988) examined the relationship between bond ratings and issue quality as indicated by financial variables. The results clearly demonstrated that bond ratings were positively related to profitability, size, and cash flow coverage, and they were inversely related to financial leverage and earnings instability. May (2010) demonstrated that rating changes can have a significant impact on the bond's price and the time the rating adjustment is announced.

The original ratings assigned to bonds have an impact on their marketability and effective yield. Generally, the three agencies' ratings agree in their assessments. When they do not, the issue is said to have a *split rating*.[3] Seasoned issues are regularly reviewed to ensure that

---

[3]Split ratings are discussed in Billingsley, Lamy, Marr, and Thompson (1985) and Liu and Moore (1987). Studies that consider shopping for ratings, the acquisition of indicative ratings, and ratings bias are Mathis, McAndrews, and Rochet (2009) and Skreta and Veldkamp (2009).

the assigned rating is still valid. If it is not, revisions are made either upward or downward. Revisions are usually done in increments of one rating grade. The ratings are based on both the company and the issue. After an evaluation of the creditworthiness of the total company is completed, a company rating is assigned to the firm's most senior unsecured issue. All junior bonds receive lower ratings based on indenture specifications. Also, an issue could receive a higher rating because of credit-enhancement devices, such as the attachment of bank letters of credit, surety, or indemnification provisions from insurance companies.

The agencies assign letter ratings depicting what they view as the risk of default of an obligation. The letter ratings range from AAA (Aaa) to D. Exhibit 12.3 describes the various ratings assigned by the major services. Except for slight variations in designations, the meaning and interpretation are basically the same. The agencies modify the ratings with + and − signs for Fitch and S&P or with numbers (1-2-3) for Moody's. As an example, an A+ (A1) bond is at the top of the A-rated group, while A− (A3) is at the bottom of the A category.

Exhibit 12.3 Description of Bond Ratings

	Fitch	Moody's	Standard & Poor's	Definition
High grade	AAA	Aaa	AAA	The highest rating assigned to a debt instrument, indicating an extremely strong capacity to pay principal and interest. Bonds in this category are often referred to as *gilt-edge securities.*
	AA	Aa	AA	High-quality bonds by all standards with a strong capacity to pay principal and interest. These bonds are rated lower primarily because the margins of protection are not as strong as those for Aaa and AAA bonds.
Medium grade	A	A	A	These bonds possess many favorable investment attributes, but elements may suggest a susceptibility to impairment given adverse economic changes.
	BBB	Baa	BBB	Bonds that are regarded as having adequate capacity to pay principal and interest, but they do not have certain protective elements, in the event of adverse economic conditions that could lead to a weakened capacity for payment.
Speculative	BB	Ba	BB	These bonds are considered to have only moderate protection of principal and interest payments during both good and bad times.
	B	B	B	Bonds that generally lack characteristics of other desirable investments. Assurance of interest and principal payments over any long period of time may be small.
Default	CCC	Caa	CCC	Poor-quality issues that may be in default or in danger of default.
	CC	Ca	CC	Highly speculative issues that are often in default or possess other marked shortcomings.
	C			The lowest-rated class of bonds. These issues can be regarded as extremely poor in investment quality.
		C	C	Rating given to income bonds on which no interest is being paid.
	DDD, DD, D		D	Issues in default with principal or interest payments in arrears. Such bonds are extremely speculative and should be valued only on the basis of their value in liquidation or reorganization.

Sources: *Bond Guide* (Standard & Poor's); *Bond Record* (Mergent/Moody's); and *Rating Register* (Fitch Investors Service, Inc.).

The top four ratings—AAA (or Aaa), AA (or Aa), A, and BBB (or Baa)—are generally considered to be *investment-grade* securities. The next level of securities, known as speculative bonds, includes the BB- and B-rated obligations. The C categories are generally either income obligations or revenue bonds. In the case of D-rated obligations, the issues are in outright default, and the ratings indicate the bonds' relative salvage values. Bonds rated below investment grade are also referred to as *high-yield*, or "junk," bonds.

12.3 SURVEY OF BOND ISSUES

In this section, we provide a detailed discussion of the instruments available from the major bond issuers.

12.3.1 Domestic Government Bonds

United States As shown in Exhibit 12.2, a significant portion of the U.S. dollar fixed-income market is U.S. Treasury obligations. The U.S. government, backed by the full faith and credit of the U.S. Treasury, issues Treasury bills (T-bills), which mature in less than 1 year, and two forms of long-term obligations: government notes, which have maturities of 10 years or less, and Treasury bonds, with maturities of 10 to 30 years. Current Treasury obligations come in denominations of $1,000 and $10,000. The interest income from the U.S. government securities is subject to federal income tax but exempt from state and local levies. These bonds are popular because of their risk-free credit quality, substantial liquidity, and noncallable feature.

Short-term T-bills differ from notes and bonds in that they are sold at a discount from par to provide the desired yield. The return is the difference between the purchase price and the face value at maturity. In contrast, government notes and bonds pay semiannual coupons through their maturity dates.

Exhibit 12.4 illustrates the quote system for Treasury bonds, notes, and bills on July 5, 2017. The tenth entry in the left-hand column is a 3 percent obligation, due in May 2047. The ask quote is listed as 102-28, which corresponds to a bond yield to maturity of 2.856 percent. Government bonds are traded in 32nds (and fractions thereof) of a point, so the figure to the right of the hyphen indicates the number of 32nds in the quote. In this case, the ask price is actually 102-28/32, or 102.875 percent of par. These quotes also are notable in terms of the bid–ask spread, which typically is one 32nd or less. This small spread reflects the outstanding liquidity and low transaction costs for Treasury securities. By contrast, short-term bills are quoted on a *discount yield* basis rather than on a price basis. So, for the bill that matures on June 21, 2018 (a one-year bill shown as the fourth entry), the ask discount rate of 1.205 percent would be the basis for the amount the investor would subtract from the bill's face value of 100 (as a percentage of par) to determine the current price.

Treasury Inflation-Protected Securities (TIPS)[4] The Treasury began issuing these inflation-indexed bonds in January 1997 to appeal to investors who wanted a *real* default-free rate of return. To ensure the investors receive the promised yield in real terms, the bond principal and interest payments are indexed to the *consumer price index*. Because the actual level of inflation is generally not known immediately, the index value used has a built-in three-month lag. For example, for a bond issued on June 30, 2011, the beginning base index value used would be the CPI value as of March 30, 2011. Following the issuance of a TIPS bond, its principal value is adjusted every six months to reflect the inflation since the base period. In turn, the interest payment is computed based on this adjusted principal—that is, the interest payments equal the original coupon times the adjusted principal. Exhibit 12.5 demonstrates a

---

[4]This section draws from excellent discussions by Shen (1998), Kothari and Shanken (2004), and Brynjolfsson (2012).

Exhibit 12.4 Sample Quotes for Treasury Bonds, Notes, and Bills

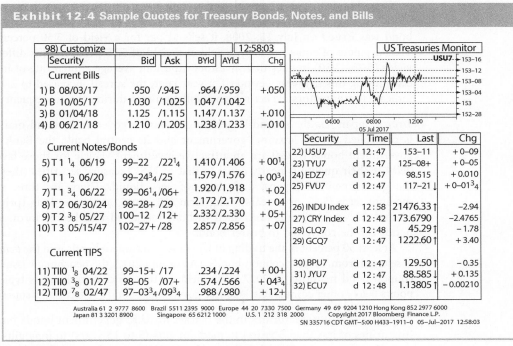

Security	Bid	Ask	BYld	AYld	Chg
Current Bills					
1) B 08/03/17	.950	/.945	.964	/.959	+.050
2) B 10/05/17	1.030	/1.025	1.047	/1.042	—
3) B 01/04/18	1.125	/1.115	1.147	/1.137	+.010
4) B 06/21/18	1.210	/1.205	1.238	/1.233	−.010
Current Notes/Bonds					
5) T 1 $\frac{1}{4}$ 06/19	99–22	/22$^1_4$	1.410	/1.406	+ 00$^1_4$
6) T 1 $\frac{1}{2}$ 06/20	99–24$^3_4$	/25	1.579	/1.576	+ 00$^3_4$
7) T 1 $\frac{3}{4}$ 06/22	99–06$^1_4$	/06+	1.920	/1.918	+ 02
8) T 2 06/30/24	98–28+	/29	2.172	/2.170	+ 04
9) T 2 $\frac{3}{8}$ 05/27	100–12	/12+	2.332	/2.330	+ 05+
10) T 3 05/15/47	102–27+	/28	2.857	/2.856	+ 07
Current TIPS					
11) TII0 $\frac{1}{8}$ 04/22	99–15+	/17	.234	/.224	+ 00+
12) TII0 $\frac{3}{8}$ 01/27	98–05	/07+	.574	/.566	+ 04$^3_4$
12) TII0 $\frac{7}{8}$ 02/47	97–03$^3_4$	/09$^3_4$	.988	/.980	+ 12+

Security		Time	Last	Chg
22) USU7	d	12:47	153–11	+ 0–09
23) TYU7	d	12:47	125–08+	+ 0–05
24) EDZ7	d	12:47	98.515	+ 0.010
25) FVU7	d	12:47	117–21 ↓	+ 0–01$^3_4$
26) INDU Index		12:58	21476.33 ↑	−2.94
27) CRY Index	d	12:42	173.6790	−2.4765
28) CLQ7	d	12:48	45.29 ↑	− 1.78
29) GCQ7	d	12:47	1222.60 ↑	+ 3.40
30) BPU7	d	12:47	129.50 ↑	− 0.35
31) JYU7	d	12:47	88.585 ↓	+ 0.135
32) ECU7	d	12:48	1.13805 ↑	− 0.00210

Australia 61 2 9777 8600 Brazil 5511 2395 9000 Europe 44 20 7330 7500 Germany 49 69 9204 1210 Hong Kong 852 2977 6000
Japan 81 3 3201 8900   Singapore 65 6212 1000   U.S. 1 212 318 2000   Copyright 2017 Bloomberg Finance L.P.
SN 335716 CDT GMT–5:00 H433–1911–0 05–Jul–2017 12:58:03

Exhibit 12.5 Principal and Interest Payment for a Representative Treasury Inflation-Protected Security (TIPS)

Par Value—$1,000
Issued on July 15, 2008
Maturity on July 15, 2013
Coupon—3.50%
Original CPI Value—185.00

Date	Index Value[a]	Rate of Inflation	Accrued Principal	Interest Payment[b]
7/15/08	185.00	—	$1,000.00	—
1/15/09	187.78	0.015	1,015.00	$17.76
7/15/09	190.59	0.015	1,030.22	18.03
1/15/10	193.83	0.017	1,047.74	18.34
7/15/10	197.51	0.019	1,067.65	18.68
1/15/11	201.46	0.020	1,089.00	19.06
7/15/11	205.49	0.020	1,110.78	19.44
1/15/12	209.19	0.018	1,130.77	19.79
7/15/12	212.96	0.018	1,151.13	20.14
1/15/13	217.22	0.020	1,174.15	20.55
7/15/13	222.65	0.025	1,203.50	21.06

[a]The CPI value is for the period three months prior to the date.
[b]Semiannual interest payment equals 0.0175 (accrued principal).

representative example of how a TIPS issue works. Both the interest payments and the principal payments are adjusted over time to reflect the prevailing inflation, thereby ensuring that the investor receives a *real* rate of return on these bonds of 3.50 percent.

These bonds can also be used to derive the prevailing market estimate of the expected rate of inflation during the remaining time to maturity. For example, if we assume that when this bond was issued on July 15, 2008, it sells at par for a yield of 3.50 percent, while a nominal Treasury note of equal maturity is sold at a yield of 5.75 percent. This differential in promised yields (5.75−3.50) implies that investors expect an average annual rate of inflation of 2.25 percent during this five-year period. If, a year later, the spread increased to 2.45 percent, it would indicate that investors expect a higher inflation rate during the subsequent four years.

Japan Japan has the second-largest single country government bond market in the world. It is controlled by the Japanese government and its central bank, the Bank of Japan. Japanese government bonds (JGBs) are an attractive investment vehicle for those favoring Japanese yen because their quality is nearly equal to that of U.S. Treasury securities (they are guaranteed by the government of Japan), and they are very liquid. There are three maturity segments: medium-term (2, 3, or 4 years), long-term (10 years), and super-long (private placements for 15 and 20 years). Bonds are issued in both registered and bearer form, although registered bonds can be converted to bearer bonds.

At least 50 percent of the trading in Japanese government bonds is in the *benchmark issue*, which is selected from 10-year coupon bonds. (As of mid-2017, the benchmark issue was a 0.10 percent coupon bond maturing in 2027.) The yield on this benchmark bond is typically about 30 basis points below other comparable Japanese government bonds, reflecting its superior marketability.

United Kingdom Maturities in the market for U.K. government bonds range from short gilts (maturities of less than 5 years) to medium gilts (5 to 15 years) to long gilts (15 years and longer). Government bonds either have a fixed redemption date or a range of dates with redemption at the option of the government after appropriate notice. These issues are extremely liquid and are highly rated because they are guaranteed by the British government. All gilts are quoted and traded on the London Stock Exchange and pay interest semiannually.

Gilts are issued through the Bank of England (the British central bank) using the tender method, whereby prospective purchasers tender offering prices at which they hope to be allotted bonds. If the issue is oversubscribed, allotments are made first to those submitting the highest tenders.

Eurozone The combined value of the euro sovereign bond market is actually larger in U.S. dollar terms than the Japanese market because it includes several significant markets, including Germany, France, and Italy. Because the Eurozone includes numerous countries that were previously economically independent, the issuing process for alternative countries differs dramatically except that all of the bonds are denominated in euros.

12.3.2 Government Agency Issues

In addition to pure government bonds, the federal government in each country can establish agencies that have the authority to issue their own bonds. In the United States, agency securities are obligations issued by the government through either a specific agency or a government-sponsored enterprise (GSE). Six government-sponsored enterprises and more than two dozen federal agencies issue bonds. Exhibit 12.6 lists the most popular government-sponsored and federal agencies and their purposes; see Cabana and Fabozzi (2012) for more details.

Agency issues usually pay interest semiannually, and the minimum denominations vary between $1,000 and $10,000. These obligations are not direct Treasury issues, yet they carry the full faith and credit of the U.S. government. Moreover, some of the issues are subject to state and local income tax, whereas others are exempt.[5]

---

[5]Federal National Mortgage Association (Fannie Mae) debentures, for example, are subject to state and local income tax, whereas interest income from Federal Home Loan Bank bonds is exempt. In fact, a few issues are exempt from federal income tax as well (for example, public housing bonds).

Exhibit 12.6 Government Agencies and Government-Sponsored Enterprises (GSEs)

Agency	Purpose
Federal National Mortgage Association (Fannie Mae)	Promote liquid secondary market for residential mortgages
Federal Home Loan Mortgage Corporation (Freddie Mac)	Promote liquid secondary market for residential mortgages
Government National Mortgage Association (Ginnie Mae)	Promote liquid secondary market for residential mortgages
Federal Home Loan Banks	Supply credit for residential mortgages
Farm Credit Banks	Supply credit to agricultural sector
Farm Credit System Financial Assistance Corporation	Finance recapitalization of Farm Credit System institutions
Federal Agricultural Mortgage Corporation (Farmer Mac)	Promote liquid secondary market for agricultural and rural housing loans
Student Loan Marketing Association (Sallie Mae)	Increase availability of student loans
Financing Corporation	Finance recapitalization of Federal Savings and Loan Insurance Corporation
Resolution Funding Corporation	Finance recapitalization of savings and loan industry
Tennessee Valley Authority	Promote development of Tennessee River and adjacent areas

Sources: Farmer Mac, Freddie Mac, and *Statistical Supplement to the Federal Reserve Bulletin*, Table 1.44.

One agency issue that offers particularly attractive investment opportunities is GNMA ("Ginnie Mae") pass-through certificates, which are obligations of the Government National Mortgage Association. These bonds represent an undivided interest in a pool of federally insured mortgages. The bondholders receive monthly payments from Ginnie Mae that include both principal and interest because the agency "passes through" mortgage payments made by the original borrower (the mortgagee) to Ginnie Mae.

The coupons on these pass-through securities are related to the interest charged on the pool of mortgages. The portion of the cash flow that represents the repayment of the principal is tax free, but the interest income is subject to federal, state, and local taxes. The issues have minimum denominations of $25,000 with maturities of 25 to 30 years but an average life of only 12 years because, as mortgages in the pool are paid off, payments and prepayments are passed through to the investor. Therefore, the monthly payment is not fixed because the rate of prepayment can vary dramatically over time when interest rates change.

In addition, two other entities have also acquired mortgages and created mortgage-backed securities—the Federal National Mortgage Association (Fannie Mae) and the Federal Home Loan Mortgage Corporation (Freddie Mac). Fannie and Freddie were publicly traded corporations regulated by the government, and the bonds they issued to fund the purchase of mortgages have historically sold at yields that are typically very close to Treasury issues. However, the lending practices of these two GSEs came under scrutiny during 2006–2007 because they were issuing large amounts of debt at low yields and then using the funds to acquire mortgages that paid higher rates for the benefit of their stockholders. When the subprime mortgages they purchased experienced high default rates, they suffered substantial losses that seriously eroded their capital.

12.3.3 Municipal Bonds

Municipal bonds are issued by states, counties, cities, and other political subdivisions. Again, the size of the municipal bond market varies substantially among countries. It is about

9 percent of the total U.S. market, compared to less than 3 percent in Japan, and it is nonexistent in the United Kingdom.

Municipalities in the United States issue two distinct types of bonds: general obligation bonds and revenue issues. **General obligation bonds (GOs)** are essentially backed by the full faith and credit of the issuer and its entire taxing power. Revenue bonds, in turn, are serviced by the income generated from specific revenue-producing projects of the municipality, such as bridges, toll roads, hospitals, municipal coliseums, and waterworks. Revenue bonds generally provide higher returns than GOs because of the higher default risk that occurs if a municipality fails to generate sufficient income from a project designated to service its obligations.

GO municipal bonds tend to be issued on a serial basis so that the issuer's cash flow requirements remain steady over the life of the obligation. Therefore, the principal portion of the total debt service requirement generally begins at a fairly low level and builds up over the life of the obligation. In contrast, most municipal revenue bonds are term issues, so the principal value is not due until the final maturity date.

As Feldstein, Fabozzi, Grant, and Ratner (2012) note, the most important feature of municipal obligations is that the interest payments are exempt from federal income tax and from taxes for some states in which the bond was issued. Consequently, their attractiveness varies with the investor's tax bracket. You can convert the tax-free yield of a municipal to an equivalent taxable yield (ETY) as follows:

12.1
$$ETY = \frac{i}{1 - t}$$

where:

ETY = equivalent taxable yield
i = yield of the municipal obligations
t = marginal tax rate of the investor

For an investor in the 35 percent marginal tax bracket, a 5 percent yield on a municipal bond selling close to its par value is equivalent to a 7.69 percent fully taxable yield:

$$ETY = \frac{0.05}{(1 - 0.35)} = 0.0769$$

Although the interest payment on municipal bonds is tax-free, any capital gains are not, which is why the ETY formula is correct only for a bond selling close to par.

A significant feature of the U.S. municipal bond market is *municipal bond insurance*, wherein an insurance company will guarantee to make principal and interest payments in the event that the issuer of a bond defaults. The insurance is placed on the bond at date of issue and is *irrevocable* over the life of the issue. The issuer purchases the insurance for the benefit of the investor, and the municipality benefits from lower interest costs due to an increase in the rating on the bond (often to AAA) and the increased marketability as more institutions are able to invest. The companies that provide municipal bond insurances are known as financial guarantors, or "monolines," and they include National Public Finance (formerly Municipal Bond Insurance Association [MBIA]) and Assured Guaranty Corp. (AGC).

12.3.4 Corporate Bonds

Again, the importance of corporate bonds varies across countries. The dollar value of corporate bonds in the United States is substantial and growing as a percentage of long-term capital. The pure corporate sector in Japan is small and declining, and the ex-bank corporate sector in the Eurozone and United Kingdom are over 17 percent of those respective markets.

U.S. Corporate Bond Market The important sectors that define the U.S. corporate bond market include utilities, industrials, rail and transportation, and financial issues. This market is very diverse and includes debentures, first-mortgage issues, convertible obligations, bonds with warrants, subordinated debentures, income bonds (similar to municipal revenue bonds), collateral trust bonds backed by financial assets, equipment trust certificates, and a variety of asset-backed securities (ABS), including mortgage-backed securities (MBS).

Most bonds have semiannual fixed interest payments, sinking funds, and a single maturity date. Maturities range from 25 to 40 years, with public utilities generally on the longer end and industrial companies preferring the 25- to 30-year range. Corporate bonds often provide for deferred calls after 5 to 10 years. The deferment period varies directly with the level of market yields. During periods of higher interest rates, bond issues typically will carry a 7- to 10-year deferment, while during periods of lower interest rates, the deferment periods decline.

On the other hand, corporate notes—with maturities of five to seven years—are generally non-callable. Notes become popular when interest rates are high because issuing firms prefer to avoid long-term obligations with large interest costs. In contrast, during periods of low interest rates, such as 2001–2004, and 2008–2017, many corporate issues did not include a call provision because corporations did not want to pay the higher yield required for an option they were not likely to use.

Exhibit 12.7 lists quotes for the most actively traded investment-grade bonds on July 3, 2017. Consider the highlighted securities, which were issued by two financial services companies, Wells Fargo and JPMorgan Chase, respectively. The Wells Fargo bond pays a stated coupon of 3.000 percent annually (or 1.500 percent every six months) and matures in a little over nine years. Notice that prices for corporate bonds are quoted in decimal form—in this case, the last traded price was 97.3700 percent of par value. As we will show later in the chapter, this value translates into a promised yield to maturity of 3.330977 percent, which makes it a bond that trades at a *discount*. By contrast, the JPMorgan bond matures in a little over 10 years and has a coupon rate of 4.250 percent. On this date, the bond traded a *premium* to par (104.43700 percent of face value) with a quoted yield of 3.724010 percent.

Other types of corporate bonds include mortgage bonds, equipment trust certificates, and collateral trust bonds, which differ from debentures primarily in the specific nature of the collateral that is pledged to protect the investor.

As Crawford (2012) notes, **collateralized mortgage obligations (CMOs)** were developed in the early 1980s to offset some of the problems with the traditional mortgage pass-throughs. The main innovation of the CMO instrument is the segmentation of irregular mortgage cash flows to create short-term, medium-term, and long-term securities that appeal to a wider range of investors. These bonds are also very high-rated securities (AAA) because of the structure and quality of the collateral. The credit risk of the collateral is minimal because most CMOs are backed by mortgages guaranteed by a federal agency (GNMA) or by the FHLMC. Those mortgages not backed by agencies carry private insurance from one of the GSEs or *overcollateralize* the issue, which also enhances credit quality.

Another rapidly expanding segment of the securities market is that for **asset-backed securities (ABS)**, which involve securitizing other types of debt besides residential mortgages. This is an important concept because it substantially increases the liquidity of these individual debt instruments, whether they be car loans, credit card debt, student loans, or home equity loans. This general class of securities was introduced in 1983. As of 2017, there was almost $1.25 trillion of asset-backed securities outstanding. **Certificates for automobile receivables (CARs)** are securities collateralized by loans made to individuals to finance the purchase of cars. These auto loans can either be direct loans from a lending institution or indirect loans that are originated by an auto dealer and sold to the ultimate lender. **Credit card–backed securities** are the fastest-growing segment of the ABS market and differ from mortgage-backed and car loan-backed securities in that the principal payments from credit card receivables are not paid to the investor but are retained by the trustee to reinvest in additional receivables.

Exhibit 12.7 Investment-Grade Corporate Bond Price and Yield Quotation

Issuer Name	Symbol	Coupon	Maturity	Moody's®/ S&P	High	Low	Last	Change	Yield%
VORNADO RLTY L P	VNO.AA	5.000%	01/15/2022	Baa2/BBB	108.35500	108.27200	108.35500	−0.445000	2.907035
VERIZON COMMUNICATIONS INC	VZ4050437	5.150%	09/15/2023	Baa1/BBB+	111.19800	110.79400	110.86500	−0.420000	3.200034
CREDIT SUISSE GROUP FDG GUERNSEY LTD	CS4248911	4.875%	05/15/2045	Baa2/	110.57900	109.60000	109.60000	−0.910000	4.281349
CENTERPOINT ENERGY RES CORP DEL	CNP.HQ	4.500%	01/15/2021	Baa2/A−	105.54900	105.54900	105.54900	0.804000	2.717130
ABBVIE INC	ABBV4362386	3.200%	05/14/2026	Baa2/A−	100.04200	98.93900	99.03800	−0.182000	3.325983
WELLS FARGO & COMPANY	WFC4416762	3.000%	10/23/2026	A2/A	97.64200	97.37000	97.37000	−0.028000	3.330977
BURLINGTON NORTHN SANTA FE LLC	BRK4463979	4.125%	06/15/2047	A3/A	104.94300	104.88900	104.94300	−0.473000	3.842002
CENTERPOINT ENERGY RES CORP	CNP.HI	6.000%	05/15/2018	Baa2/A−	103.60700	103.60700	103.60700	0.112000	1.731363
TEVA PHARMACEUTICAL FIN NETH III B V	TEVA4384554	4.100%	10/01/2046	Baa2/	92.30300	91.29600	91.29600	−2.704000	4.647019
JPMORGAN CHASE & CO	JPM4292068	4.250%	10/01/2027	Baa1/BBB+	104.53700	103.94500	104.43700	0.051000	3.724010

Source: Data from Financial Industry Regulatory Authority TRACE Market Aggregate Information, July 3, 2017.

Closely related to asset-backed securities are **collateralized debt obligations (CDOs)**. In contrast to most ABSs that are backed by one specific type of asset (mortgages, car loans, and so on), a CDO is generally backed by a diversified pool of several assets including investment-grade or high-yield bonds, domestic bank loans, emerging market bonds, residential mortgages (some subprime) and commercial mortgages, and even other CDOs. The CDO is typically structured into tranches similar to the CMOs, but the tranches differ by credit quality, from those rated AAA to BBB or lower. Therefore, investors can benefit from higher returns as they select their desired credit risk based on the ratings assigned.

These securities created significant problems for investors, beginning with the 2006 real estate "boom" when mortgage loans made to individuals with very low credit scores were put into CDOs. In 2007 and 2008, a high proportion of these subprime loans defaulted, which reduced the value of the CDOs tranches that held them. Even the highly rated tranches that were protected by credit enhancement techniques were not easily tradable. As a result, there were significant price declines in a short period of time (for example, from par value to 65 percent of par).

12.3.5 Nontraditional Bond Coupon Structures

Two other important bond structures involve variations on how the periodic coupon payments are made: **variable-rate (or floating-rate) notes** and **zero-coupon bonds**.

Introduced in the United States in the mid-1970s, *variable-rate notes* became popular during periods of high interest rates, often caused by high levels of inflation. As discussed by Fabozzi and Mann (2012), the typical variable-rate note possesses two unique features. First, after the bond's issue date, the coupon rate is allowed to adjust ("float"), so that every six months it changes to follow some index rate (for example, London Interbank Offer Rate [LIBOR]). Second, after the first year or two, the notes are redeemable at par, at the *holder's* option, usually at six-month intervals.

Such instruments represent a long-term commitment on the part of the borrower but also provide the lender with all the characteristics of a short-term obligation. They typically are available to investors in minimum denominations of $1,000. However, although the six-month redemption feature provides periodic cash flow, the variable rates can cause these issues to experience wide swings in the amount of those semiannual coupons.

In contrast to a bond with a periodic coupon payment that varies with market conditions, the *zero-coupon* (or pure discount) *bond* promises to pay a stipulated principal amount at a future maturity date, but no interim interest payments. Therefore, the price of the bond is simply the present value of the principal payment at the maturity date using the applicable discount rate. The return on the bond is the difference between what the investor pays for the bond at the time of purchase and the principal payment at maturity.

Consider a zero-coupon, $1,000 par value bond with a 20-year maturity. As we will demonstrate shortly, if the required rate of return is 8 percent and we assume semiannual discounting, the initial selling price for this bond would be $208.29. From the time of purchase to maturity, the investor would not receive any cash flow from the issuer. However, the investor must pay taxes on the implied interest on the bond, although no cash is actually received. Because of this feature, these bonds are primarily in investment accounts not subject to taxes, such as pensions, IRAs, or Keogh accounts. Also, because the investor will not receive any payments from the borrower until maturity, the securities are most often created by government issuers rather than corporations having greater credit risk.

A modified form of zero-coupon bond is the original issue discount (OID) bond, where the coupon is set substantially below the prevailing market rate—for example, a 3 percent coupon on a bond when market yields are 8 percent. As a result, the bond is issued at a deep discount from par value. Again, taxes must be paid on the implied 8 percent return rather than the

3 percent coupon rate, so the cash flow disadvantage of zero-coupon bonds, though lessened, remains. Smith (2011) discusses the development of the market for these bonds.

12.3.6 High-Yield Bonds

A segment of the corporate market that has grown in size, importance, and controversy is **high-yield bonds**, also referred to as *speculative-grade bonds* or *junk bonds*. These are corporate bonds that have been assigned a noninvestment grade bond rating, that is, they have a rating below BBB or Baa. The term *high-yield* (*HY*) was coined as an indication of the returns available for these bonds relative to Treasury bonds and investment-grade corporate bonds. However, the *junk bond* designation also indicates the low credit quality of these issues.

The high-yield segment of the corporate bond market has existed as long as there have been rating agencies. Prior to 1980, however, most HY bonds were referred to as *fallen angels*. This means that these bonds were originally issued as investment-grade securities, but because of adverse changes in the firm over time, they were downgraded to ratings of BB or below. The market changed in the early 1980s, when the investment firm Drexel Burnham Lambert began aggressively underwriting new-issue HY bonds for two groups of clients: (1) small firms that did not have the financial strength to receive an investment-grade rating and (2) large and small firms that issued HY bonds in connection with leveraged buyouts (LBOs). The primary investors in these newly issued high-yield bonds were mutual funds, insurance companies, and pension funds, all of which were attracted by the potential for a new source of high risk-adjusted returns.

The high-yield bond market exploded in size with this new influx of activity. Exhibit 12.8 contains global issuance statistics for the period 1997–2016. Notably, large junk bond issues have become more common over the past two decades, with the average size of an issue currently exceeding $650 million. The distribution of credit ratings in this market as of December 2016 was BBB (44.2 percent), BB (41.8 percent), and CCC/Unrated (14.0 percent). Also, high-yield issues have become a significant percentage of the total new-issue bond market.

Exhibit 12.8 High-Yield Bond Issue Volume: 1997–2016

Year	Total Global Issuance ($ millions)	Number of Issues	Average Issue Size ($ millions)
1997	212,715	963	220.89
1998	255,097	1112	229.40
1999	291,835	1180	247.32
2000	363,776	1466	248.14
2001	402,644	1529	263.34
2002	551,658	1998	276.10
2003	640,560	2191	292.36
2004	673,550	2162	311.54
2005	740,931	2132	347.53
2006	787,248	2077	379.03
2007	843,053	2008	419.85
2008	843,857	1963	429.88
2009	1,023,813	2238	457.47
2010	1,201,563	2494	481.78
2011	1,393,802	2824	493.56
2012	1,630,426	3098	526.28
2013	1,936,918	3489	555.15
2014	2,076,242	3660	567.28
2015	2,144,787	3653	587.13
2016	2,052,079	3145	652.49

Source: Bank of America Merrill Lynch Global Research.

As of mid-year 2017, total outstanding high-yield debt constituted about 20 percent of all corporate debt in the United States.[6]

Exhibit 12.9 shows price and yield quotes for the most actively traded high-yield bonds on July 3, 2017. As with the investment-grade corporate bonds discussed earlier, junk bond prices are quoted on a decimal basis. For instance, the highlighted bond for Petrobras, the Brazilian petrochemical company, pays a coupon of 7.375 percent and matures in about 9.5 years. Given its last quoted price of 107.5000 percent of par value, this bond has a yield to maturity of 6.314982 percent. Notice that this yield for the B1-rated Petrobras bond is substantially higher than the yields for either Wells Fargo (A2-rated) or JPMorgan Chase (Baa1-rated) from Exhibit 12.7, even though all three bonds mature at roughly the same time. This higher credit spread is the investor's additional expected compensation for holding a riskier bond.

12.3.7 International Bonds

Each country's international bond market has two components: foreign bonds and Eurobonds. *Foreign bonds* are issues sold primarily in one country and currency by a borrower of a different nationality. An example would be U.S. dollar–denominated bonds sold in the United States by a Japanese firm. (These are called *Yankee bonds.*) *Eurobonds* are bonds underwritten by international bond syndicates and sold in several national markets. An example would be Eurodollar bonds, which are securities denominated in U.S. dollars and sold to investors outside the United States.

United States The Eurodollar bond market in the United States has become much larger than the Yankee bond market. However, because the Eurodollar bond market is heavily affected by changes in the value of the U.S. dollar, it experiences slower growth during periods when the dollar is weak.

Yankee bonds are issued by foreign firms that register with the SEC and borrow U.S. dollars. These bonds are traded in the United States and pay interest semiannually. Historically, the majority of Yankee bonds have been issued by Canadian corporations and typically have shorter maturities and longer call protection than U.S. domestic issues. These features increase their appeal to investors.

The Eurodollar bond market is dominated by foreign investors, with the center of trading in London. Eurodollar bonds pay interest annually. The Eurodollar bond market currently comprises almost 40 percent of the total Eurobond market.

Japan Historically, the Japanese yen international bond market was dominated by foreign bonds (called *Samurai bonds*) with the balance in Euroyen bonds. After the issuance requirements for Euroyen bonds were liberalized in the mid-1980s, the ratio of issuance swung heavily in favor of Euroyen bonds.

Samurai bonds are yen-denominated bonds sold by non-Japanese issuers and mainly sold in Japan. The market is fairly small and has limited liquidity. Notably, the market has experienced slow growth in terms of yen but substantial growth in U.S. dollar terms because of changes in the exchange rate.

United Kingdom *Bulldog bonds* are sterling-denominated bonds issued by non-English firms and sold in London. Conversely, Eurosterling bonds are traded in markets outside London. Similar to the experience in other countries, the U.K. international bond market has become dominated by Eurosterling bonds. The procedure for issuing Eurosterling bonds is similar to that of Eurodollar bonds.

---

[6]The development of the high-yield debt market has had a positive impact on the capital-raising ability of the economy; see Perry and Taggart (1988). Additional discussions on the characteristics of this market are contained in Fridson (1994), Fabozzi (1990), and Reilly, Wright, and Gentry (2009).

Exhibit 12.9 High-Yield Corporate Bond Price and Yield Quotation

Issuer Name	Symbol	Coupon	Maturity	Moody's/S&P	High	Low	Last	Change	Yield%
PETROBRAS GLOBAL FIN B V	PBR4443368	7.375%	01/17/2027	B1/	107.50000	105.95000	107.50000	1.000000	6.314982
CNH INDL CAP LLC	CNHI4308049	4.375%	11/06/2020	Ba1/BBB-	105.12500	104.92500	105.12500	0.000000	2.752977
FRONTIER COMMUNICATIONS CORP	FTR3684517	8.500%	04/15/2020	B2/B+	105.75000	103.75000	105.75000	0.038000	4.990006
SPRINT CORP	SFTBF4176280	7.875%	09/15/2023	B3/B	115.25000	113.81900	115.20000	0.200000	4.011455
ZEBRA TECHNOLOGIES CORP	ZBRA4300294	7.250%	10/15/2022	B2/B+	106.50000	106.25000	106.25000	-0.156000	5.814697
PETROBRAS GLOBAL FIN B V	PBR4106372	6.250%	03/17/2024	B1/	103.87500	101.95000	102.37500	0.425000	7.378025
PETROBRAS GLOBAL FIN B V	PBR4106363	7.250%	03/17/2044	B1/	100.74000	98.40000	98.50000	-0.625000	4.364957
BECTON DICKINSON & CO	BDX4499468	4.669%	06/06/2047	Ba1/BBB+	105.06000	104.29000	105.06000	1.252000	4.364957
FIRSTENERGY CORP	FE4509020	3.900%	07/15/2027	Baa3/BB+	100.76800	100.08600	100.13600	-0.308000	3.882967
ROYAL BK SCOTLAND GROUP PLC	BNPQF4127992	5.125%	05/28/2024	Ba1/	105.20200	105.10300	105.10300	-0.081000	4.262513

Source: Data from Financial Industry Regulatory Authority TRACE Market Aggregate Information, July 3, 2017.

Eurozone The growth of Eurobonds issued by nonresidents has been impressive in recent years. This growth confirmed the popularity of the Euro markets among foreign issuers, including issuers domiciled in the United States.

12.4 BOND YIELD CURVES

From our discussion of the features and characteristics that define the vast array of available fixed-income securities, it is clear that the bond's *yield to maturity* is perhaps the most important statistic for an investor to consider. In fact, the yield to maturity can be viewed as the expected return to the bond, meaning that it is an expression of how the investor anticipates being compensated for owning the security. So, how are yields determined, and how should they be interpreted? This is the topic to which we now turn.

12.4.1 The Determinants of Bond Yields

Consider the average interest rates (yields) associated with the long-term (30-year) government bonds from four different global regions—United States, United Kingdom, Eurozone, Japan—on three different dates:

	June 2007	June 2012	June 2017
United States	5.242%	2.736%	2.739%
United Kingdom	4.859	3.093	1.678
Eurozone	4.794	2.276	1.066
Japan	2.500	1.857	0.805

Notice that throughout the world, yields fell sharply from June 2007 (which was a time just prior to the global financial crisis) to June 2017. However, it is also apparent that the nature of this rate decline differed across the different areas of the world. As a bond investor, you should understand why there are differences in country yields and why interest rates within each country changed.

At the most basic level, the factors causing interest rates (*i*) to rise or fall are described by the following model:

12.2
$$i = \text{RFR} + I + \text{RP}$$

where:

RFR = real risk-free rate of interest
I = expected rate of inflation
RP = risk premium

This relationship should be familiar, based on our presentations in Chapters 1 and 7. It is a simple but complete statement of interest rate behavior. The more difficult task is estimating the *future* behavior of some of the variables that impact the RFR, *I*, and the RP, such as real economic growth, expected inflation, and economic uncertainty. In this regard, interest rates, like stock prices, are extremely difficult to forecast with any degree of accuracy, as discussed by Fabozzi and Mann (2012). Alternatively, we can visualize the source of interest rate changes in terms of the economic conditions and issue characteristics as follows:

12.3
$$i = f(\text{Economic Factors} + \text{Issue Characteristics})$$
$$= (\text{RFR} + I) + \text{RP}$$

This rearranged version of the previous equation helps isolate the factors that determine interest rates; this is discussed in Van Horne (2001).

Effect of Economic Factors The real risk-free rate of interest (RFR) is the economic cost of money—that is, the opportunity cost necessary to compensate individuals for forgoing consumption. It is determined by the real growth rate of the economy with short-run effects due to easing or tightening in the capital market.

The expected rate of inflation is the other economic influence on interest rates. We add the expected level of inflation (I) to the real risk-free rate (RFR) to specify the nominal RFR, which is an observable rate like the current yield on government T-bills. Given the historical stability of the real RFR, the wide swings over time in nominal risk-free interest rates usually occur because of the volatility of expected inflation. Besides the unique country and exchange rate risk that we discuss in the section on risk premia, differences in the rates of inflation between countries have a major impact on their level of interest rates.

One way to estimate the nominal RFR is to begin with the real growth rate of the economy, adjust for short-run capital market conditions, and then add a forecast of the expected rate of inflation. Another approach to estimating changes in the nominal rate is the macroeconomic view, where the supply and demand for loanable funds are the fundamental economic determinants of i. As the supply of loanable funds increases, the level of interest rates declines, other things being equal. Federal Reserve monetary policies have a significant impact on the supply of money, as we have seen since 2008. The savings patterns of U.S. and non-U.S. investors also affect the supply of funds. Non-U.S. investors have become a strong influence on the supply of U.S. loanable funds available during recent years.

Interest rates increase when the demand for loanable funds increases, all else the same. The demand for loanable funds is affected by the capital and operating needs of the U.S. government, federal agencies, state and local governments, corporations, institutions, and individuals. Federal and state budget deficits increase the demand for loanable funds. Likewise, the level of consumer demand for funds to buy houses and capital goods will affect rates, as will corporate demand for funds to pursue investment opportunities. The sum of all of this activity determines the aggregate demand and supply of loanable funds and the level of the nominal RFR.

The Impact of Bond Characteristics The economic forces that determine the nominal RFR affect all securities, whereas issue characteristics that are unique to individual securities, market sectors, or countries will influence the bond's risk premium (RP). Thus, the differences in the yields of corporate and Treasury bonds are generally not caused by economic factors but, rather, by different issue characteristics that affect the risk premium. Bond investors separate the risk premium into four components:

1. The quality of the issue as determined by its risk of default relative to other bonds
2. The term to maturity of the issue, which can affect price volatility
3. Indenture provisions, including collateral, call features, and sinking-fund provisions
4. Foreign bond risk, including exchange rate risk and country risk

Of the four factors, quality and maturity have the greatest impact on the risk premium for domestic bonds, while exchange rate risk and country risk are important considerations for non-U.S. bonds.

The credit quality of a bond reflects the ability of the issuer to service its outstanding debt, which is largely captured in the default ratings. As a result, bonds with different ratings have different yields. For example, AAA-rated obligations possess lower risk of default than BBB obligations, so they have a lower required yield. In fact, the credit quality component is so important in determining the overall yield that the bond's risk premium is often referred to as its *credit spread*.

The risk premium differences between bonds of different quality levels change dramatically over time, depending on prevailing economic conditions. When the economy experiences a recession or a period of economic uncertainty, the desire for safety increases (that is, there is a "flight to quality"), and investors sell lower-quality debt and bid up prices of higher-rated bonds, which increases the difference in yield. The U.S. market has experienced dramatic short-run risk premium explosions on several occasions, as follows: in August 1998, in response to defaults on Russian bonds; in 2001, following the terrorist attacks; and especially during the significant credit crisis in 2008–2009.

Term to maturity also influences the risk premium because it affects the price volatility of the bond. Shortly, we will describe the typical positive relationship between the term to maturity of a bond issue and its yield.

As we have seen, indenture provisions include the collateral pledged for a bond, its callability, and its sinking-fund provisions. Collateral gives protection to the investor if the issuer defaults on the bond because the investor has a specific claim on some assets in case of liquidation. Call features indicate when an issuer can buy back the bond prior to its maturity. Obviously, an investor will charge the issuer for including the call option, and the cost of the option (which is a higher required yield) will increase with the level of interest rates. Therefore, more protection against having the bond called reduces the risk premium. The value of call protection increases during periods of high interest rates. Marshall and Yawitz (1980) and Booth, Gounopoulos, and Skinner (2014) note that when you buy a bond with a high coupon, you want protection from having it called away when rates decline.

As discussed by Kalotay (1981, 1982b), a sinking fund reduces the investor's risk and causes a lower yield for several reasons. First, a sinking fund requires the issuer to reduce systematically the outstanding amount of debt. Second, purchases of the bond by the issuer to satisfy sinking fund requirements provide price support for the bond. Finally, sinking fund provisions require that the issuer retire a bond before its stated maturity, which reduces the issue's average maturity.

Finally, we know that foreign currency exchange rates change over time and that this increases the risk of global investing. Exchange rates vary among countries because trade balances and rates of inflation differ. Volatile trade balances and inflation rates make exchange rates more volatile, which adds to the uncertainty of future exchange rates and increases the exchange rate risk premium. In addition, when investors are unsure about the political or economic environment in a country, they will increase the required risk premium to reflect this country risk.

12.4.2 Yield Curves and the Term Structure of Interest Rates

The **term structure of interest rates** (or the *yield curve*, as it is more popularly known) relates the term to maturity to the yield to maturity for a sample of bonds at *a given point in time*.[7] Thus, it represents a cross section of yields for a category of bonds that are comparable in all respects but maturity. Specifically, the quality of the issues should be constant, and ideally you should have issues with similar coupons and call features within a single industry category. You can construct different yield curves for Treasuries, government agencies, prime-grade municipals, utilities and corporates with different ratings, and so on. The accuracy of the yield curve will depend on the comparability of the bonds in the sample.

As an example, Exhibit 12.10 shows yield curves for a sample of U.S. Treasury obligations. It is based on yield to maturity information for a set of comparable Treasury issues, all of which pay semiannual coupons for maturities beyond one year. These promised yields were plotted on the graph, and a yield curve was drawn that represents the general pattern of

[7]For a discussion of the theory and empirical evidence, see Sundaresan (2009).

Exhibit 12.10 Yield Curve for U.S. Treasury Bonds at Different Times

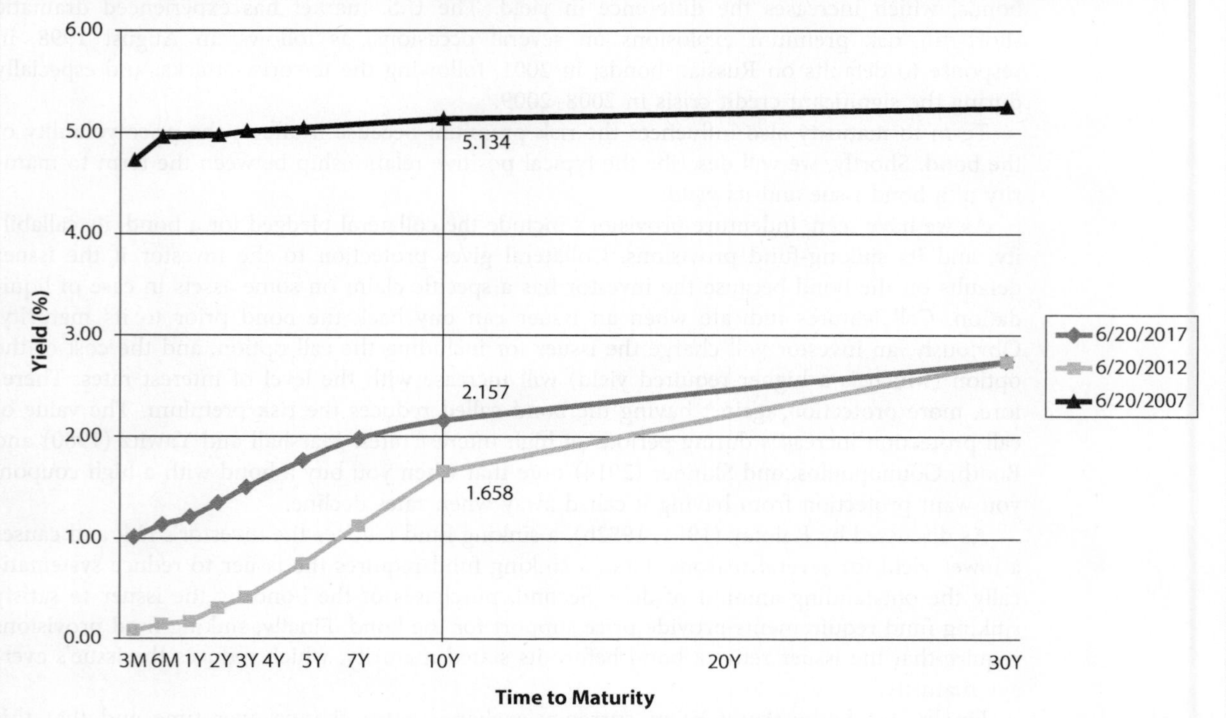

Source: Resource Center, U.S. Department of the Treasury

those rates. These data show the Treasury yield curve at three different points in time to demonstrate the changes in the level and shape of the yield curve over time.

Of course, not all yield curves will have the same shape as those in Exhibit 12.10. Although individual yield curves are static, their behavior over time is quite fluid. As shown, the yield curve was relatively flat during June 2007. Subsequently, by June 2012, rates had fallen (for example, the 10-year T-bond yield declined from 5.134 percent to 1.658 percent), and the entire curve had a strong positive slope due to significant reductions in short-term rates by the Federal Reserve. In June 2017, the slope was still very positive but at a somewhat higher level, particularly for the shorter-maturity securities. The point is that the shape of the yield curve can undergo dramatic alterations, following one of the four patterns shown in Exhibit 12.11. The rising (upward-sloping) yield curve is the most common and tends to prevail when interest rates are at low or moderate levels. A declining yield curve tends to occur when rates are relatively high. The flat yield curve rarely exists for any period of time. The humped yield curve prevails when extremely high rates are expected to decline to more normal levels. Note that the slope of the yield curve tends to level off after about 10 years.

12.4.3 Par versus Spot Yield Curves

An important consideration when evaluating yield curves is that the bonds that are being evaluated have exactly the same characteristics except for their maturity dates. Two bonds that may have the same credit quality might still be expected to offer different yields from one another if they have dramatically different cash flow patterns. For instance, consider the

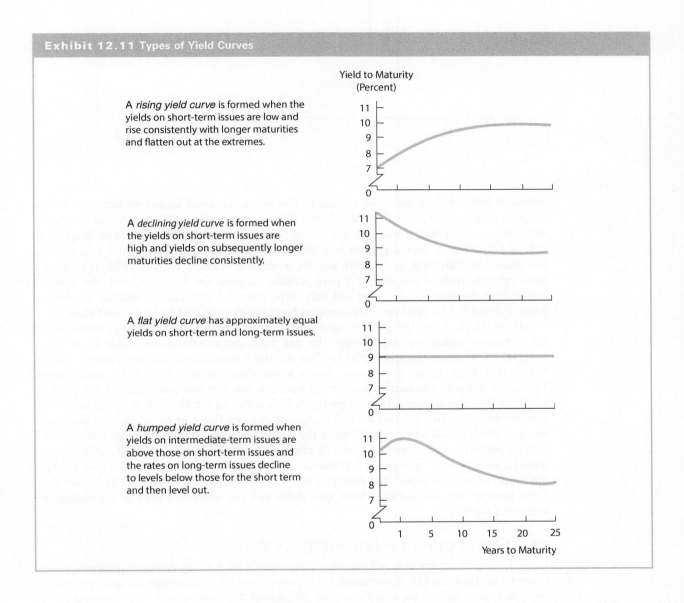

Exhibit 12.11 Types of Yield Curves

A *rising yield curve* is formed when the yields on short-term issues are low and rise consistently with longer maturities and flatten out at the extremes.

A *declining yield curve* is formed when the yields on short-term issues are high and yields on subsequently longer maturities decline consistently.

A *flat yield curve* has approximately equal yields on short-term and long-term issues.

A *humped yield curve* is formed when yields on intermediate-term issues are above those on short-term issues and the rates on long-term issues decline to levels below those for the short term and then level out.

following schematic illustration of the cash flow patterns associated with two different bonds from the same issuer, both with a five-year maturity date:

Coupon (Par) Bond:

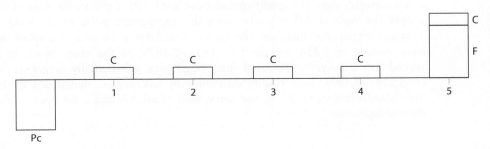

Zero-Coupon (Spot) Bond:

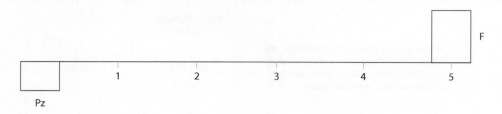

Although both of these securities mature in five years, the bond shown on top pays several coupons (assumed to annual, for simplicity) before repaying the principal in year 5. So, the investor's expected return over the life of the bond will involve all five of these coupons as well as any potential capital gain or loss from the difference in the initial price (P_c) and the face value (F). This yield to maturity statistic is sometimes called the **par yield** (i) because a bond can only trade at par value if it pays periodic coupons. On the other hand, the expected return from the zero-coupon bond will only come from the appreciation between the current price (P_z) and F. The yield on a zero-coupon bond is often referred to as the **spot yield** (z).

Exhibit 12.12 shows the par and spot yield curves for coupon-bearing and zero-coupon U.S. Treasury securities, respectively. The par yield curve reflects the yields to maturity attached to the most recently issued (or "on the run"), semiannual coupon Treasury bonds. Notice that these values are almost always lower than the spot yield for a zero-coupon Treasury bond with the same maturity (for example, the five-year par yield is 1.792 percent, while the five-year spot rate is 1.861 percent). This is due to the fact that the yield curves are upward sloping in this case. As we will discuss shortly, the five-year par yield is an average of the spot yields for all of the cash flows in the coupon-bearing bond up through maturity (the coupon payments in 6 months, 1 year, 18 months, and so on). So, since 1.792 percent represents an average of 10 spot yields that start at slightly higher than 1 percent, the spot yield for the longer-term cash flows (for example, the year 5 payment) will have to be higher than 1.792 percent. We will see how both spot yields and par yields are used in calculating the value of a bond.

12.4.4 Yield Curves for Credit-Risky Bonds

As we have seen, an investor will expect a higher return for lending money to a corporate borrower rather than the U.S. government for the simple reason that the corporation's promise to repay is riskier. Earlier, we called this yield differential the *credit spread*, and it represents the risk premium associated with the possibility that the corporate issuer will be unable to pay back what it has promised to the investor.

Exhibit 12.13 illustrates seven different par yield curves—for the U.S. Treasury and six separate classes of corporate borrowers differing by the bond default rating. The bond rating categories shown in the figure are AAA, AA, and A as well as BBB, BB, and B. For any given maturity date, the credit spread associated with a particular class of corporate bond is simply the vertical difference between the appropriate point on its yield and that on the Treasury curve. For instance, the credit spread for a 10-year, AA-rated bond is about 82 basis points, or 0.824 percent ($= 2.981 - 2.157$). At the same point in time, the credit spread for a 10-year, BB-rated junk bond was substantially larger at 307 basis points ($= 5.228 - 2.157$). This sizable difference in risk premia demanded by investors reflects the considerable variation in the perception of an AA and a BB borrower's ability to meet their obligations.

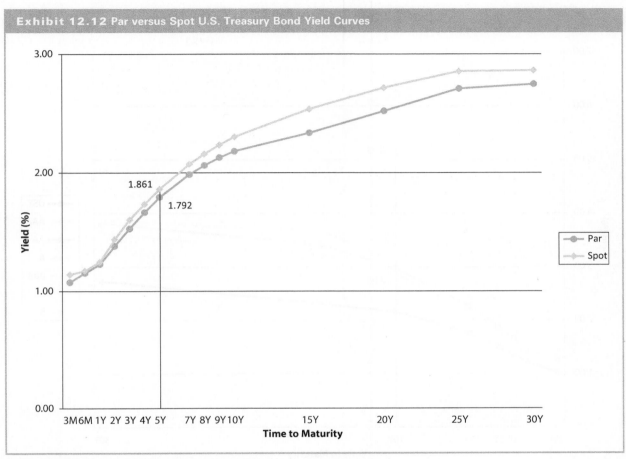

Exhibit 12.12 Par versus Spot U.S. Treasury Bond Yield Curves

Source: Resource Center, U.S. Department of the Treasury; June 20, 2017

Exhibit 12.13 shows some other interesting patterns as well. Notice that corporate bond rating categories produce credit spreads that are consistent with finance theory. That is, for each maturity, it is the case that the more highly rated bond (with less perceived default risk) has the lower yield to maturity. However, in many cases, there is very little difference between the yields for two different bond rating classes, as seen for the AAA and AA categories. Finally, there is a large increase in the credit spread between the BBB and BB categories, particularly for longer-term bonds. This should not be surprising given our earlier discussion that the BB rating category is the first rating that falls below the investment grade designation.

12.4.5 Determining the Shape of the Term Structure

Why does the term structure assume different shapes? Three major theories attempt to address this question: the expectations hypothesis, the liquidity preference hypothesis, and the segmented market hypothesis.

Expectations Hypothesis According to this theory, the shape of the yield curve results from the interest rate expectations of market participants. More specifically, it holds that *any long-term interest rate simply represents the geometric mean of current and future one-year interest rates expected to prevail over the life of the issue.* In essence, the term structure

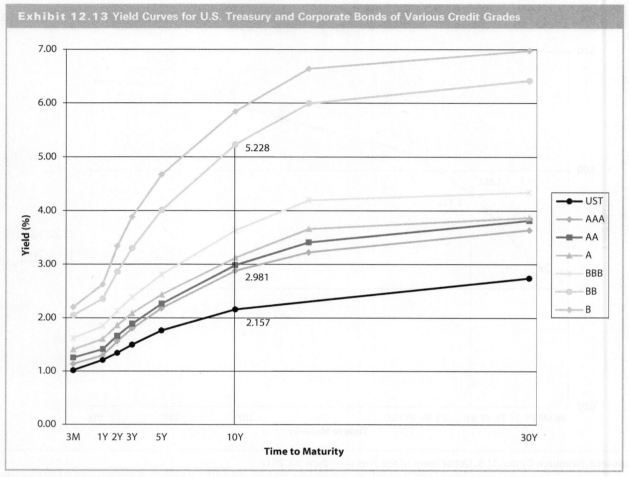

Exhibit 12.13 Yield Curves for U.S. Treasury and Corporate Bonds of Various Credit Grades

Sources: Resource Center, U.S. Department of the Treasury; June 20, 2017; author calculations.

involves a series of intermediate and long-term interest rates, each of which reflects the geometric average of current and expected one-year interest rates. Under such conditions, the equilibrium long-term yield is the rate the long-term bond investor would expect to earn through successive investments in short-term bonds over the term to maturity of the long-term bond.

The expectations theory can potentially explain any shape of yield curve. Expectations for rising short-term rates in the future cause a rising yield curve; expectations for falling short-term rates in the future will cause long-term rates to lie below current short-term rates, and the yield curve will decline. Similar explanations account for flat and humped yield curves. The evidence is fairly substantial and convincing that the expectations hypothesis is a workable explanation of the term structure. Because of the supporting evidence, its relative simplicity, and the intuitive appeal of the theory, the expectations hypothesis of the term structure of interest rates is rather widely accepted.

It is also possible to present a scenario wherein investor actions will *cause* a predicted yield curve to occur. For instance, the theory predicts a declining yield curve when interest rates are expected to fall in the future. If this is indeed what investors expect, long-term bonds would be considered attractive investments now for the opportunity to lock in prevailing higher yields. Thus, investor transactions will reinforce the declining shape of the yield curve as they bid up the prices of long-maturity bonds (forcing yields to decline) while short-term bond issues are sold (so prices decline and yields rise). At the same time, there is confirming action by suppliers of bonds in that government or corporate issuers will avoid selling long bonds at the current high rates, waiting until the rates decline. This will continue until equilibrium occurs or expectations change.

Liquidity Preference (Term Premium) Hypothesis The theory of liquidity preference holds that long-term securities should provide higher returns than short-term obligations because investors are willing to accept lower yields for short-maturity obligations to avoid the higher price volatility of long-maturity bonds. Another way to interpret the liquidity preference hypothesis is to say that lenders prefer short-term, more liquid loans, and to induce them to invest in more volatile long-term bonds, it is necessary to offer higher yields. Taken in isolation, this theory argues that the yield curve should generally slope upward and that any other shape should be viewed as a temporary aberration.

Liquidity preference is generally considered to be an extension of the expectations hypothesis because the term premium inherent in the yields for longer maturity bonds should be added to the *expected* future rate to arrive at long-term yields. Specifically, the liquidity (or term) premium (L) compensates the investor in long-term bonds for the added volatility inherent in long-term bonds compared to short-maturity securities. The liquidity preference theory has been found to possess some strong empirical support by Cagan (1969) and McCulloch (1975). As a matter of historical fact, the yield curve does show an upward bias, which implies that some combination of the expectations theory and the liquidity preference (term premium) theory will more accurately explain the shape of the yield curve than either of them alone.

Segmented Market Hypothesis A third theory for the shape of the yield curve is the segmented market hypothesis, which enjoys wide acceptance among market practitioners despite little empirical support. Also known as the *preferred habitat theory*, it asserts that different institutional investors have different maturity needs that lead them to confine their security selections to specific maturity segments. That is, investors supposedly focus on either short-, intermediate-, or long-term securities. This theory contends that the shape of the yield curve ultimately is a function of these unique investment preferences of major financial institutions.

The segmented market theory contends that the business environment, along with legal and regulatory limitations, tends to direct each type of financial institution to allocate its resources to particular types of bonds with specific maturity characteristics. In its strongest form, the segmented market theory holds that the maturity preferences of investors and borrowers are so strong that investors never purchase securities outside their preferred maturity range to take advantage of yield differentials. As a result, the short- and long-maturity portions of the bond market are effectively segmented, and yields for a segment depend on supply and demand conditions *within* that maturity segment. Depending on the particular nature of those segmented market conditions, any yield curve shape is possible.

12.5 Bond Valuation

From our discussion of stock valuation in Chapter 8, we saw that the most basic way to think about the value of any investment security is as the sum of the present values of all of the future cash flows the investor can expect to receive by owning that security.

This was the *discounted cash flow* approach to valuation, and we will use that same model to calculate the value of a fixed-income security. In fact, compared to equities, there are two features of a typical bond that make the discounted cash flow model easier to apply: (1) The promised periodic cash flows associated with a bond (the coupon payments) are fixed in amount and known to the investor at Date 0, and (2) the bond matures at a certain future date, which means there are a finite number of cash flows involved in the calculation. Further, since most bonds are designed to repay the whole principal amount at maturity (so the security is *nonamortizing*), the entire pattern and timing of the future cash flows is known to investors in advance. So, the only remaining practical challenge the investor faces when valuing a typical bond is to select the appropriate interest rate to use in the discounting process.

12.5.1 Par versus Spot Bond Valuation

Earlier in the chapter we saw that yield curves can be defined in two ways, depending on the cash flow pattern of the bond. First, for zero-coupon bonds, which paid no periodic cash flows prior to maturity Date N, the spot yield was labeled as z_N. Second, for bonds that paid periodic coupons until maturity, the par yield (i_N) was the single discount rate that would be applied to every cash flow (that is, coupon payments and principal) associated with the bond. This par yield is often referred to as the bond's *yield to maturity*.

This distinction between spot and par yields means that there are two ways we can think about calculating the discounted value of any particular set of future bond cash flows. Letting c_t be the Date t coupon payment and F_N be the face value of the bond that is repaid to the investor at maturity, we can calculate either:

12.4
$$P_0 = \sum_{t=1}^{N} \frac{c_t}{(1 + Z_t)^t} + \frac{F_N}{(1 + Z_N)^N} \quad \text{(Spot Yield Valuation)}$$

or:

12.5
$$P_0 = \sum_{t=1}^{N} \frac{c_t}{(1 + i_N)^t} + \frac{F_N}{(1 + i_N)^N} \quad \text{(Yield to Maturity Valuation)}$$

Of course, for the same set of cash flows attached to the same bond, Equation 12.4 and Equation 12.5 must generate the same value, P_0. This means that there must be a predictable relationship between the set of N different spot rates and the single yield to maturity for that security.

As an example, we can consider a bond that matures in five years and, for simplicity, makes annual coupon payments of 7 percent of the face value. These cash flows (based on a principal of 100), along with the spot rates applicable for each payment date, are shown as:

Payment Date	Cash Flow	Spot Rate (z_t)
1	7	5.10%
2	7	5.30%
3	7	5.50%
4	7	6.10%
5	107	6.63%

The present value of the bond under these conditions would be:

$$P_0 = \frac{7}{(1+.051)^1} + \frac{7}{(1+.053)^2} + \frac{7}{(1+.055)^3} + \frac{7}{(1+.061)^4} + \frac{107}{(1+.0663)^5}$$
$$= 6.66 + 6.31 + 5.96 + 5.53 + 77.62 = \$102.08.$$

To value this bond using the yield to maturity method in Equation 12.5, we need to find the single discount rate that could be used to calculate the present value of all of the cash flows and reach the same current value of 102.08. That is, we want to find the yield to maturity, i, such that:

$$P_0 = \frac{7}{(1+i)^1} + \frac{7}{(1+i)^2} + \frac{7}{(1+i)^3} + \frac{7}{(1+i)^4} + \frac{107}{(1+i)^5}$$
$$= 102.08$$

In this case, whether computed by trial and error or a more formal iteration method, the yield to maturity can be shown to be $i = 6.50$ percent. So, the second way to calculate the value of this bond is:

$$P_0 = \frac{7}{(1+.065)^1} + \frac{7}{(1+.065)^2} + \frac{7}{(1+.065)^3} + \frac{7}{(1+.065)^4} + \frac{107}{(1+.065)^5}$$
$$= 6.57 + 6.17 + 5.80 + 5.44 + 78.10 = \$102.08.$$

Generally, most investors prefer to value bonds using the yield to maturity method because they are only interested in what the entire security is worth today and not the exact present values of each separate cash flow payment. Notice that the yield to maturity must be an average of the underlying spot rates, meaning in this case that the five-year par yield (6.50 percent) had to fall between the lowest (5.10 percent) and the highest (6.63 percent) of the spot rates. However, this yield is not a simple average of the spot rates; it will have to take into account both the timing and relative size of all of the payments.

12.5.2 Bond Valuation and Yields with Semiannual Coupons

Many bonds, particularly those issued by the U.S. government or U.S.-based corporations, make coupon payments on a semiannual basis, even though a bond's coupon rate will usually be quoted on an annualized basis. For instance, the issuer of a bond with a stated coupon rate of 5 percent would actually make payments of 2.5 percent of the bond's face value every six months. The valuation formula in Equation 12.5 can be adjusted for this convention by converting all of the relevant variables to a *periodic basis*. So, the formula for valuing a bond making semiannual payments becomes:[8]

12.6
$$P_0 = \sum_{t=1}^{2n} \frac{C/2}{(1+i/2)^t} + \frac{F}{(1+i/2)^{2n}}$$

where:

$C =$ stated annual coupon rate
$i =$ yield to maturity, stated on an annualized basis
$n =$ maturity date of the bond, stated in years

The value computed indicates what an investor would be willing to pay for this bond to realize a rate of return that takes into account expectations regarding the RFR, the expected rate of

---

[8]Almost all bonds following conventions in the U.S. markets pay interest semiannually, so it is appropriate to use semiannual compounding wherein you cut the annual coupon rate and yield to maturity in half and double the number of years to maturity.

inflation, and the risk of the bond. This valuation technique assumes holding the bond to its maturity. In this case, the number of periods ($2n$) would be double the number of years to the maturity of the bond and the cash flows include all the periodic interest payments and the payment of the bond's par value at maturity.

We can demonstrate this formula by using an 8 percent coupon bond that matures in 20 years with a par value of $1,000. An investor who holds this bond to maturity will receive $40 every 6 months (one-half of the $80 coupon) for 20 years (40 periods) and $1,000 at the maturity. If we assume a yield to maturity for this bond of 10 percent (the market's required rate of return on the bond), the bond's value using Equation 12.6 would be established as:

$$P_0 = \sum_{t=1}^{40} \frac{80/2}{(1 + .10/2)^t} + \frac{1000}{(1 + .10/2)^{40}}$$

The first term is the present value of an annuity of $40 every 6 months for 40 periods at the six-month (periodic) discount rate of 5 percent, while the second term is the present value of $1,000 to be received in 40 periods at 5 percent per period. This can be summarized as follows:

Present value of 40 interest payments of $40:	$686.36
Present value of principal payment of $1,000:	142.05
Total value of bond at 10 percent annual yield:	$828.41

As expected, the bond will be value at a discount (82.841 percent) to its par value because the market's required rate of return of 10 percent is greater than the bond's 8 percent coupon rate.

Alternatively, if the market's required rate was 6 percent, the value would be computed as the present value of the annuity at 3 percent for 40 periods and the present value of the principal at 3 percent for 40 periods, as follows:

Present value of 40 interest payments of $40:	$924.59
Present value of principal payment $1,000:	306.56
Total value of bond at 6% annual yield:	$1,231.15

Because the bond's discount rate is lower than its coupon, the bond would sell at a premium (123.115 percent) above par value.

The Yield Model Instead of determining the value of a bond in dollar terms, investors often price bonds in terms of their **yields**—the promised rates of return on bonds under certain assumptions. Thus far, we have used cash flows and our required rate of return to compute an estimated value for the bond. To compute an expected yield, we use the observed current market price (MP_0) and the promised cash flows to *compute the expected yield on the bond.* We can do this using the same discounted cash flow model just described. The difference is that in Equation 12.6, it was assumed that we knew the appropriate discount rate (the required rate of return), and we computed the estimated value of the bond. In this case, we still use Equation 12.6, but it is assumed that we know the price of the bond and we compute the discount rate (yield) that will give us the current market price (MP_0):

$$MP_0 = \sum_{t=1}^{2n} \frac{C/2}{(1 + i/2)^t} + \frac{F}{(1 + i/2)^{2n}}$$

where the variables are the same as previously, except:

> i = annualized rate that will cause the sum of the discounted expected cash flows to equal the current market price of the bond

This i value gives the expected ("promised") yield of the bond assuming you pay the price MP_0. Two additional assumptions are necessary to make i an expected return that the investor will actually realize: (1) the bond is held through its maturity date and (2) all interim cash flows are reinvested at the same rate i until maturity.

As an example of the promised yield calculation using the same 8 percent coupon, 20-year bond, if you observed a market price of $907.992, the expected yield of the security would be established by solving for i in the following equation:

$$907.992 = \sum_{t=1}^{40} \frac{40}{(1 + i/2)^t} + \frac{1000}{(1 + i/2)^{40}}$$

In this case, your expected return from buying this bond and holding it until it matures will be higher than the 8 percent stated coupon rate because in addition to those semiannual payments, you will also get a capital gain of $92.008 $(= 1000 - 907.992)$ over the life of the security. Taken together, these two components of compensation give the investor an expected return of 4.50 percent per period $(= i/2)$, 9.00 percent annually $(= i)$.

These approaches to pricing bonds and making investment decisions are similar to the two alternative approaches by which firms make investment decisions. We referred to one approach as the *discounted cash flow* (*DCF*) method in Chapter 8. On the other hand, when you use the net present value (NPV) approach, you compute the present value of the net cash flows from the proposed investment at your cost of capital and subtract the present value cost of the investment to get the NPV of the project. If positive, you consider accepting the investment; if it is negative, you reject it. This is basically the way we compared the intrinsic value of an equity investment to its market price.

The second approach is to compute the **internal rate of return (IRR)** on a proposed investment project. The IRR is the discount rate that equates the present value of cash outflows for an investment with the present value of its cash inflows. You compare this discount rate, or IRR (which is also the estimated rate of return on the project), to your cost of capital, and accept any investment proposal with an IRR equal to or greater than your cost of capital. We do the same thing when we price bonds on the basis of yield. If the promised yield on the bond is equal to or exceeds your required rate of return on the bond, you should invest in it; if the estimated yield is less than your required rate of return on the bond, you should not invest in it.

12.5.3 Relationship between Bond Yields, Coupon Rates, and Bond Prices

When you know the basic characteristics of a bond in terms of its coupon rate, maturity, and par value, the only factor that determines its value (or market price) is the market discount rate—its required rate of return. As shown in the previous example of an 8 percent, 20-year bond, as we increase the required rate, the price declines. We can demonstrate the specific relationship between the price of a bond and its yield by computing the bond's price at a range of yields, as listed in Exhibit 12.14. A graph of this relationship is shown in Exhibit 12.15.

Besides demonstrating that the price for a fixed-coupon bond moves in the opposite direction to changes in yield to maturity, the graph shows three other important points:

1. When the yield to maturity is *less than* the coupon rate, the bond will be priced at a **premium** to its par value.
2. When the yield to maturity is *greater than* the coupon rate, the bond will be priced at a **discount** to its par value.

Exhibit 12.14 Price–Yield Relationship for a 20-Year, 8 Percent Coupon Bond ($1,000 Par Value)

Required Yield to Maturity	Price of Bond
2%	$1,985.04
4	1,547.11
6	1,231.15
8	1,000.00
10	828.41
12	699.07
14	600.05
16	523.02

3. The price–yield relationship is not a straight line; rather, it is *convex*. As yields decline, the price increases at an increasing rate; and, as yields increase, the price declines at a declining rate. This concept of a convex price–yield trade-off is referred to as *convexity* and will be discussed in the next chapter.

Bond Characteristics and Price Change Magnitude   Exhibit 12.15 illustrates the crucial fact that a bond's value is inversely related to its yield to maturity. All bonds with a fixed

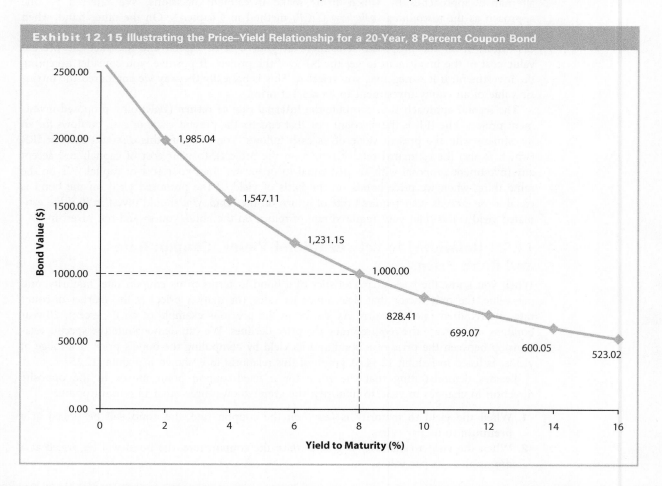

Exhibit 12.15 Illustrating the Price–Yield Relationship for a 20-Year, 8 Percent Coupon Bond

coupon rate and no embedded options (such as a call feature) will demonstrate this negative *direction effect*. However, the magnitude of the value change (expressed in percentage terms) in response to a given yield change will depend on the other characteristics of the security, such as the coupon rate and time to maturity. These *magnitude effects* can be summarized by two additional facts:

4. For two bonds with the same maturity, the one with the *lower coupon rate* will experience the *greater percentage price change* for a given shift in yields.

5. Generally, for two bonds with the same coupon rate, the one with the *longer maturity* will experience the *greater percentage price change* for a given shift in yields.

As an example of these concepts, consider three bonds paying semiannual coupons and have the same credit rating and same face value of $1,000. The securities differ only by their coupon rates and maturities, as shown below:

Bond	Coupon Rate	Maturity	Value at $i = 7\%$	Value at $i = 6\%$	% Price Change
1	4%	10 years	$786.81	$851.23	+8.19%
2	8	10	1,071.06	1,148.78	+7.26
3	8	5	1,041.58	1,085.30	+4.20

Assuming a yield curve that is flat for all maturities, the bonds are valued under two conditions: an initial yield of $i = 7$ percent and, after a 100 basis point decline in yields, at $i = 6$ percent. The two next-to-last columns of the chart show that all three bonds increase in value when rates decrease; this is the direction effect described above. However, Bond 1, which had the lowest coupon rate and longest maturity, saw its value increase by the most at 8.19 percent ($= 851.23/786.81-1$). On the other hand, Bond 3, which had the highest coupon rate and shortest maturity, increased in value by only 4.20 percent, the smallest percentage change for any of the three securities. These illustrate the combined magnitude effect that the coupon and maturity characteristics have on bond values.

12.5.4 Bond Valuation between Coupon Dates

The bond valuation formulas in Equation 12.6 assume that every future cash flow is exactly the same amount of time away from the previous one (for example, six months for a semiannual coupon bond). So, these formulas only calculate accurate measures when the bond is being valued on an interest payment (coupon) date. Of course, the specific sequence of payment dates for each cash flow in the valuation formulas could be adjusted manually to make them accurate, but the investor would have to make these adjustments every day.

An important issue that also has to be considered when valuing a bond between coupon dates is the notion of **accrued interest**. The basic idea of accrued interest is that since a bond represents a loan, whoever owns the bond on a particular day is entitled to receive the interest payment for that day. Thus, if a new investor buys a bond from its current owner, say, exactly three months after the last semiannual payment date—and three months before the next coupon date—the two parties would each be entitled to half of the next coupon payment. (The bond market convention is that coupon payments are made at the end of the lending period.)

The practical significance of this is that when an investor acquires a bond from an existing owner between coupon dates, she will actually have to pay an amount that represents two things: (1) the actual value of the bond itself, which is the discounted value of the remaining future cash flows, and (2) the interest that has accrued since the last coupon date. This latter term is necessary because the new bond investor will receive from the issuer the entire amount of the next coupon when it is paid, meaning she will need to "cash out" the bond seller for the accrued interest to which he is entitled at the time of the transaction. The actual amount of the accrued interest (AI) payment is determined as:

12.7 $$AI = (\text{Coupon Payment}) \times \frac{(\text{Days Since Last Coupon Payment})}{(\text{Total Days in Coupon Period})}$$

Notice from Equation 12.7 that interest accrues on a straight-line basis, meaning that each day an investor is the lender of record deserves the same amount of interest.[9]

To see how this valuation process works in practice, consider an investor who wants to buy a bond of Oracle Corporation, a multinational computer technology company, on June 29, 2017. Exhibit 12.16 shows details of this instrument, which makes semiannual interest payments with a stated annual coupon rate of 2.500 percent (or 1.250 percent every six months) and matures on October 15, 2022. Since this bond was issued in October 2012, the investor will need to buy this bond in the secondary market, rather than from Oracle Corp. directly. Panel B of Exhibit 12.16 indicates that the bond price and yield to maturity on the trade settlement date were 101.258 (expressed as a percentage of the bond's par value) and 2.246313 percent, respectively.

Exhibit 12.17 summarizes how this Oracle 2.500 percent of 2022 bond would be valued on this particular day. Notice from Panel A that the trade date of June 29 falls between the last coupon date (April 15) and the next one (October 15). Using the "30/360" day count convention, 74 days of the 180 total days in the payment period have already passed, meaning that the seller of this bond deserves accrued interest of about 41 percent (=74/180) of the next coupon payment. With this information, the value of the bond on the settlement date is calculated using the three-step procedure illustrated in Panel B of Exhibit 12.17:

1. Use Equation 12.6 to calculate what this bond would have been worth on the *previous* coupon date (April 15, 2017) using today's yield to maturity of 2.246313 percent. This amount (101.3057) is a hypothetical value since the actual bond yield on April 15 was almost certainly different than the one prevailing on the valuation date.

2. Compute the present value of the 101.3057 in step 1 by compounding this amount from April 15 to June 29 using the semiannual-adjusted trade date yield of 2.246313 percent in the calculation. The resulting amount (101.7719) is called the **total invoice price** (or "dirty" price) as it represents both the present value of the bond and the accrued interest that the buyer will have to pay to the seller on June 29, 2017.

3. To calculate just what the bond itself is worth, the accrued interest is subtracted from the total invoice price. This amount (101.2580) is called the **flat price** (or "clean" price) of the bond.

As shown in Panel B of Exhibit 12.16, it is common for bond prices to be quoted using the flat price value (for example, 101.258 in this example). However, as indicated in the lower-right portion of the display, the total amount that the investor will have to pay to buy this bond between coupon dates will exceed that flat price by the amount of the accrued interest.

---

[9]There are two *day count conventions* used in determining accrued interest. The "Actual/Actual" convention, which is used for Treasury bonds, counts the actual number of days that have passed between the last coupon date and the bond trade date and next coupon date, respectively. The "30/360" convention, which is used by most corporate bonds, approximates the actual number of days by assuming that each month has 30 days—whether February or August—so a full year has 360 days. For more on these conventions, see Fabozzi and Mann (2012, Chapter 6).

Exhibit 12.16 Oracle Corporation 2.50 Percent of 2022 Bond on June 29, 2017

A. Bond Characteristics

Company:	Oracle Corporation	*Bond Rating:*	
Ticker Symbol:	ORCL	Moody's	A1
Bond CUSIP:	68389XAP0	S&P	AA–
		Fitch	A+
Issue Date:	October 18, 2012	Composite	A+
Maturity Date:	October 15, 2022		
Issue Amount:	USD 2,500 million	*Day Count Convention:*	30/360
Coupon Rate:	2.500%	*Call Provision:*	Make Whole (+12.5 bp)
Coupon Frequency:	Semiannual		
Coupon Dates:	April 15, October 15	*Trade Settlement Date:*	June 29, 2017

B. Bond Yield & Value

YA
Bond Matures on a SATURDAY
ORCL 2 1/2 10/15/22 Corp | Settings | Yield and Spread Analysis
101.115/101.258 | 2.275/2.246 | BMRK @ 17:45 | 95) Buy | 96) Sell
1) Yield & Spread 2) Graphs 3) Pricing 4) Description 5) Custom

ORCL 2 1/2 10/15/22 (68389XAP0)				Risk	Workout	OAS
Spread	48.98 bp	vs	5y T 1 3/4 05/31/22			
Price	101.258		99-31 18:43:45	◉ M.Dur ○ Dur	4.915	4.945
Yield	2.246313	Wst	1.756548 S/A	Risk	5.002	5.032
Wkout	10/15/2022	@ 100.00	Consensus Yld 6 6	Convexity	0.276	0.279
Settle	06/29/17		06/27/17	DV 01 on 1MM	500	503
				Benchmark Risk	4.699	4.724
				Risk Hedge	1,064 M	1,065 M
				Proceeds Hedge	1,017 M	

Spreads		Yield Calculations		Invoice	
11) G-Sprd	45.0	Street Convention	2.246313	Face	1,000 M
12) I-Sprd	39.6	Equiv 1 /Yr	2.258927	Principal	1,012,580.00
13) Basis	2.8	Mmkt (Act/ 360)		Accrued (74 Days)	5,138.89
14) Z-Sprd	40.0	True Yield	2.244011	Total (USD)	1,017,718.89
15) ASW	39.6	Current Yield	2.469		
16) OAS	45.3				
After Tax (Inc 43.400 % CG 23.800 %)			1.223695		

Australia 61 2 9777 8600 Brazil 5511 2395 9000 Europe 44 20 7330 7500 Germany 49 69 9204 1210 Hong Kong 852 2977 6000
Japan 81 3 3201 8900 Singapore 65 6212 1000 U.S. 1 212 318 2000
SN 335716 CDT GMT–5:00 H698–3396–2 26–Jun–2017 18:43:49

Source: Data from

12.5.5 Computing Other Bond Yield Measures

The preceding discussion highlights that, when calculating the value of a bond, the two most useful yield statistics are (1) the *coupon rate* and (2) the *yield to maturity*. Three additional yield measures associated with a bond are often computed as well: (3) the *current yield*, (4) the *yield to call*, and (5) the *realized (or horizon) yield*.

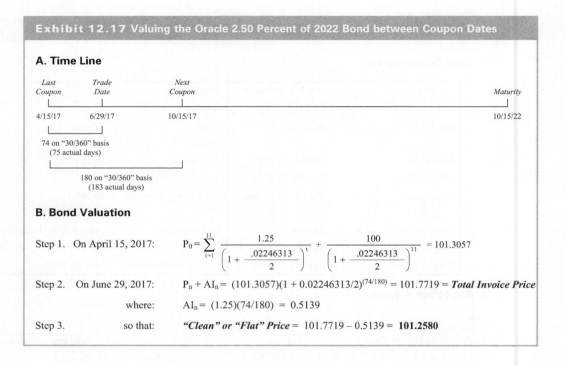

Exhibit 12.17 Valuing the Oracle 2.50 Percent of 2022 Bond between Coupon Dates

A. Time Line

Last Coupon	Trade Date	Next Coupon		Maturity
4/15/17	6/29/17	10/15/17		10/15/22

74 on "30/360" basis
(75 actual days)

180 on "30/360" basis
(183 actual days)

B. Bond Valuation

Step 1.   On April 15, 2017:

$$P_0 = \sum_{t=1}^{11} \frac{1.25}{\left(1 + \frac{.02246313}{2}\right)^t} + \frac{100}{\left(1 + \frac{.02246313}{2}\right)^{11}} = 101.3057$$

Step 2.   On June 29, 2017:

$$P_n + AI_n = (101.3057)(1 + 0.02246313/2)^{(74/180)} = 101.7719 = \textbf{\textit{Total Invoice Price}}$$

where: $AI_n = (1.25)(74/180) = 0.5139$

Step 3.   so that: **_"Clean" or "Flat" Price_** $= 101.7719 - 0.5139 = \textbf{101.2580}$

Current Yield   Recall that the bond's coupon rate expresses the annual coupon payment as a fraction of the face value of the bond. The face value is used in that calculation specifically because it will not change during the life of the bond, meaning the coupon rate will remain the same as well. However, a better measure of how much of the investor's return comes in the form of annual cash payments would be to take the ratio of the bond's annual coupon and its current price. That is what the current yield (CY) does:

12.8

$$CY = \frac{C}{MP_0}$$

where C is once again the fixed annual coupon and MP_0 is the bond's current market price. For the Oracle Corporation bond considered earlier, the coupon rate was 2.500 percent, but its current yield would be $CY = 2.469$ percent ($= 2.50/101.258$). This is shown in the lower left side of Panel B in Exhibit 12.16.

   The current yield measure is to bonds what dividend yield is to stock. Because this yield measures the current income from the bond as a percentage of its price, it is important to income-oriented investors (for example, retirees) who want current cash flow from their investment portfolios. Current yield is not as useful for investors who are interested in total return because it is a partial measure that excludes the capital gain or loss component.

Yield to Call   Although investors use the promised yield to maturity (*YTM*) to value most bonds, they must estimate the return on certain callable bonds with a different measure: the promised **yield to call (YTC)**. Whenever a bond with a call feature sells for a price at a premium to par value and also equal to or greater than its call price, a bond investor should consider valuing the bond in terms of YTC rather than YTM. This is because the marketplace uses the lowest, most conservative yield measure in pricing a bond. As discussed in Leibowitz and Homer (2013), when bonds are trading at or above a specified **crossover price**, which is approximately the bond's call price plus a small premium that increases with time to call, the yield to call will provide the lowest yield measure. The crossover price is important because at this price the *YTM* and the *YTC* are equal. When the bond rises to this level, it would be profitable for the issuer to call the bond and refinance it by selling a new bond at this prevailing market interest rate.[10] Therefore, the *YTC* measures the promised rate of return the investor will receive from holding this bond until it is retired at the first available call date.

Yield to call is calculated using a variation of Equation 12.6. To compute the *YTC* by the discounted cash flow method, we would adjust the semiannual present value equation to give:

12.9
$$MP_0 = \sum_{t=1}^{2ncall} \frac{C/2}{(1 + i/2)^t} + \frac{P_{call}}{(1 + i/2)^{2ncall}}$$

where:

$ncall$ = number of years to first call date
P_{call} = call price of the bond

We solve for i in Equation 12.9 by using the same computational process used to determine YTM. As before, YTC is a promised yield but one that now assumes that you hold the bond until the first call date.

If an issue has multiple call dates at different prices, it will be necessary to compute which of these scenarios provides the *lowest* yield—this is referred to as the **yield to worst**. Investors must consider computing the *YTC* for their bonds after a period when numerous high-coupon par bonds have been issued. Following such a period, interest rates will likely decline, bond prices will rise, and the high-coupon bonds will subsequently have a strong probability of being called.

Realized (Horizon) Yield The final measure of bond yield, **realized yield**, or **horizon yield**, measures the expected rate of return of a bond that you anticipate selling prior to its maturity. So, instead of assuming that the bond is held until it matures—as in the case of YTM—the horizon yield assumes that the investor has a holding period (*hp*, expressed in years) that is less than *n*. Making the appropriate adjustment to the discounted cash flow valuation equation leaves:

12.10
$$MP_0 = \sum_{t=1}^{2hp} \frac{C/2}{(1 + i/2)^t} + \frac{P_{hp}}{(1 + i/2)^{2hp}}$$

where:

P_{hp} = anticipated selling price of the bond at the end of the investment horizon

Notice that investors can also use this technique to compute the actual return they realized during a holding period after selling a bond.

Although it is a very useful measure, the horizon yield does require additional estimates not needed for the other yield measures. First, the investor must estimate the expected future selling price of the bond at the end of the holding period. Second, this measure requires an estimate of the specific reinvestment rate for the coupon flows prior to selling the bond. From Equation 12.10, note that the coupon flows are implicitly discounted at the computed horizon yield. In many cases, however, this is an inappropriate assumption because available market rates might be very different.

---

[10]An extensive literature on the refunding of bond issues includes studies by Kalotay (1982a) and Finnerty (1983).

SUMMARY

- We considered the basic features of bonds: interest, principal, and maturity. Each bond has unique intrinsic characteristics and can be differentiated by type of issue and indenture provisions. Major benefits to bond investors include predictable returns for nominal risk, the potential for capital gains, certain tax advantages, and possibly additional returns from active trading of bonds. Active bond investors must consider market liquidity, investment risks, and interest rate behavior.

- The global bond market includes numerous countries. The non-U.S. markets have experienced strong relative growth, whereas the U.S. market has continued to constitute a stable half of the world bond market. The four major bond markets (the United States, Japan, Eurozone, and the United Kingdom) have a different makeup in terms of the proportion of governments, agencies, municipals, corporates, and international issues. It is important to recognize that the various market sectors are unique in terms of liquidity, yield spreads, tax implications, and operating features.

- To gauge default risk, most bond investors rely on credit agency ratings. For additional information on the bond market, prevailing economic conditions, and intrinsic bond features, individual and institutional investors rely on a host of readily available publications. Extensive up-to-date quotes are generally available on Treasury bonds and notes, as well as for corporate bonds. Although, trading and price information for corporates has been historically difficult to find, this changed dramatically beginning in 2004.

- The yield curve (or the term structure of interest rates) shows the relationship between the yields on a set of comparable bonds and the term to maturity. Yield curves exhibit four basic patterns. Three theories attempt to explain the shape of the yield curve: the expectations hypothesis, the liquidity preference (term premium) hypothesis, and the segmented market (preferred habitat) hypothesis. The fundamental determinants of interest rates are a real risk-free rate, the expected rate of inflation, and a risk premium.

- The value of a bond equals the sum of the discounted value of all future cash flows accruing to the investor. The discount rates used in the valuation process can either date specific (spot rates) or a single rate covering the entire payment structure (par yield). There are five yield measures that investors need to consider when valuing bonds: coupon rate, current yield, promised yield to maturity, promised yield to call, and realized (horizon) yield. The promised YTM and promised YTC equations include the coupon reinvestment assumption. For the realized (horizon) yield computation, the investor must estimate the reinvestment rate and the future selling price for the bond.

SUGGESTED READINGS

Bagaria, Rajay. *High Yield Debt: An Insider's Guide to the Marketplace*. West Sussex, UK: John Wiley & Sons, 2016.

Fabozzi, Frank J., and Steven V. Mann. *The Handbook of Fixed Income Securities*, 8th ed. New York: McGraw-Hill, 2012.

Hu, Joseph C. *Asset Securitization: Theory and Practice*. Hoboken, NJ: John Wiley & Sons, 2011.

Smith, Donald J. *Bond Math*. Hoboken, NJ: John Wiley & Sons, 2011.

Sundaresan, Suresh. *Fixed-Income Markets and Their Derivatives*, 3rd ed. San Diego, CA: Academic Press, 2009.

QUESTIONS

1. Identify the three most important determinants of the value of a bond. Describe the effect of each.
2. Explain the differences in the taxation of income from municipal bonds, from U.S. Treasury bonds, and from corporate bonds.
3. Explain the difference between calling a bond and a bond refunding.
4. What is the purpose of bond ratings? What types of risk associated with a bond investment are these ratings designed to measure?

5. Based on the data in Exhibit 12.2, discuss the makeup of the Japanese bond market and how and why it differs from the U.S. bond market.
6. Discuss the difference between a foreign bond (for example, a Samurai) and a Eurobond (for example, a Euroyen issue).
7. Why does the discounted cash flow valuation equation appear to be more useful for the bond investor than for the common stock investor?
8. What are the important assumptions you have to make when calculating the promised yield to maturity? How do these differ from the assumptions you have to make when calculating promised yield to call?
9. a. Define the variables included in the following model:

$$i = (RFR, I, RP)$$

 b. Assume that the firm whose bonds you are considering is not expected to generate positive earnings this year. Discuss which factor in the model might be affected by this information.
10. a. Explain what is meant by the *term structure of interest rates*. Explain the theoretical basis of an upward-sloping yield curve.
 b. Explain the economic circumstances under which you would expect to see an inverted yield curve.
 c. Define *"real" rate of interest*.
 d. Over the past several years, fairly wide yield spreads between AAA-rated corporates and Treasuries have occasionally prevailed. Discuss the possible reasons for this.
11. The asset-backed securities (ABS) market has grown in the past few years partly as a result of credit enhancements to ABS. Discuss how the credit rating of an ABS issue can be higher than the credit quality of the assets in the underlying portfolio upon which the security is based.

PROBLEMS

1. What would be the initial offering price for the following bonds (assume semiannual compounding):
 a. A 15-year zero-coupon bond with a yield to maturity (YTM) of 12 percent?
 b. A 20-year zero-coupon bond with a YTM of 10 percent?
2. An 8.4 percent coupon bond issued by the state of Indiana sells for $1,000. What coupon rate on a corporate bond selling at its $1,000 par value would produce the same after-tax return to the investor as the municipal bond if the investor is in:
 a. the 15 percent marginal tax bracket?
 b. the 25 percent marginal tax bracket?
 c. the 35 percent marginal tax bracket?
3. An investor in the 28 percent tax bracket is trying to decide which of two bonds to purchase. One is a corporate bond carrying an 8 percent coupon and selling at par. The other is a municipal bond with a 5½ percent coupon, and it, too, sells at par. Assuming all other relevant factors are equal, which bond should the investor select?
4. The Shamrock Corporation has just issued a $1,000 par value zero-coupon bond with an 8 percent yield to maturity, due to mature 15 years from today. (Assume semiannual compounding.)
 a. What is the market price of the bond?
 b. If interest rates remain constant, what will be the price of the bond in three years?
 c. If interest rates rise to 10 percent, what will be the price of the bond in three years?

5. Complete the information requested for each of the following $1,000 face value, zero-coupon bonds, assuming semiannual compounding.

Bond	Maturity (Years)	Yield (%)	Value ($)
A	20	12	?
B	?	8	601
C	9	?	350

6. Four years ago, your firm issued $1,000 par, 25-year bonds, with a 7 percent coupon rate and a 10 percent call premium.
   a. If these bonds are now called, what is the *actual* yield to call for the investors who originally purchased them at par?
   b. If the current interest rate on the bond is 5 percent and the bonds were not callable, at what price would each bond sell?

7. Assume that you purchased an 8 percent, 20-year, $1,000 par, semiannual payment bond priced at $1,012.50 when it has 12 years remaining until maturity. Compute:
   a. Its promised yield to maturity
   b. Its yield to call if the bond is callable in three years with an 8 percent premium

8. Bonds of Francesca Corporation with a par value of $1,000 sell for $960, mature in five years, and have a 7 percent annual coupon rate paid semiannually. Calculate:
   a. Current yield
   b. Yield to maturity, to the nearest basis point (that is, x.xx percent)
   c. Horizon yield (or realized return) for an investor with a three-year holding period and a reinvestment rate of 6 percent over the period. At the end of three years, the 7 percent coupon bonds with two years remaining will sell to yield 7 percent.

9. Consider price quotes and characteristics for two different bonds:

	Bond A	Bond B
Coupon Payment	Annual	Annual
Maturity	3 years	3 years
Coupon Rate	10%	6%
Yield to Maturity	10.65%	10.75%
Price	98.40	88.34

At the same time, you observe the spot rates for the next three years:

Term	Spot (Zero-Coupon) Rates
1 year	5%
2 years	8%
3 years	11%

Demonstrate whether the price for either of these bonds is consistent with the quoted spot rates. Under these conditions, recommend whether Bond A or Bond B appears to be the better purchase.

10. It is April 2, 2018, and you are considering purchasing an investment-grade corporate bond that has a $1,000 face value and matures on June 4, 2022. The bond's stated coupon rate is 4.60 percent, and it pays on a semiannual basis (that is, on June 4 and December 4). The bond dealer's current ask yield to maturity is 3.80 percent. (Note: Between the

last coupon date and today, there are 118 "30/360" days. Between last coupon date and the next coupon date, there are 180 "30/360" days.)

a. Calculate the total amount (invoice price) you would have to pay for this bond if you purchased the issue to settle today.

b. Separate this total invoice amount into (i) the bond's current "flat" (without accrued interest) price and (ii) the accrued interest.

13
Bond Analysis and Portfolio Management Strategies

After you read this chapter, you should be able to answer the following questions:

- What are implied forward rates, and how do you calculate these rates from a spot yield curve?
- What is meant by the duration of a bond, how do you compute it, and what factors affect it?
- What is modified duration, and what is the relationship between a bond's modified duration and its price volatility?
- What is the convexity for a bond, how do you compute it, and what factors affect it?
- What happens to the duration and convexity of bonds that have embedded call options?
- What are the static yield spread and the option-adjusted spread?
- What are the five major classes of bond portfolio management strategies?
- How is the investment style box defined for fixed-income portfolios?
- What are the two main types of passive bond portfolio management strategies?
- How do active bond portfolio strategies differ from one another in terms of scope, scalability, and risk-adjusted return potential?
- What is meant by core-plus bond portfolio management?
- How does bond immunization work and how does that strategy differ from a cash-matching approach to managing a bond portfolio?
- What is meant by a contingent immunization approach to bond portfolio management?

Prior to the 1970s, it was not uncommon for institutional investors, such as pension plans or endowment funds, to have most of their assets allocated passively to fixed-income security portfolios. However, with the dramatic change in yields—and the volatility of those yield movements—that resulted from monetary policies of the past several decades, there has been renewed interest in exploring additional techniques for managing those bond positions. This has required investors to become more sophisticated users of analytical tools to evaluate how bond values can be impacted by changing market conditions as well as more knowledgeable about the various strategic alternatives available to them.

Having considered the important topic of how bonds are valued, we begin this chapter by expanding the investor's "toolkit" to include several other useful measures. For example, we will discuss *implied forward rates* as a way to help the bondholder make choices between two bonds maturing at different times. Also, we will look at two critical statistics called *duration* and *convexity* that give the investor a very precise indication of how a bond's value will be affected when interest rates change in the marketplace. Finally, we will consider how *embedded options* (for example, a call feature) can impact the price of the bond in certain circumstances.

Following this analytical development, we shift attention to an examination of the most widely used bond portfolio management strategies. After a brief discussion of how bonds have performed as an asset class in recent years and how to define fixed-income investment styles, we will see that these strategies can be classified into one of five broad approaches: passive management, active management, core-plus management, matched-funding management, and contingent and structured active management. We describe these approaches in more detail and give examples of how each is used in practice.

13.1 BOND ANALYSIS TOOLS

As we saw in Chapter 12, a primary concern for a bond portfolio manager is to be able to value bonds accurately, whether that value is expressed in dollar terms or as a yield to maturity. However, the bond valuation formula is not the only analytical technique an investor needs to know. In this section, we discuss some other computational tools essential to managing bond portfolios.

13.1.1 Implied Forward Rates

Suppose a bond portfolio manager would like to invest some uncommitted funds for the next two years. She is considering two potential strategies: (1) Buy a single two-year zero-coupon bond or (2) buy a one-year zero-coupon bond and replace it with another one-year zero-coupon bond when the first instrument matures. At the current time, the zero-coupon (spot) yield curve offers to the following returns: $z_1 = 5.00$ percent and $z_2 = 5.50$ percent. Which strategy should she choose?

To answer that question definitively, the manager would have to know now what next year's one-year bond rate will be, which she clearly does not. However, she can calculate what that yield would have to be next year to leave her indifferent between the two schemes. Letting r represent this rate, she can solve the following equation for how much a $1 investment would be worth at the end of Year 2:

$$(1 + .055)^2 = (1 + .05) \times (1 + r)$$

so:

$$r = \frac{(1.055)^2}{(1.05)} - 1 = 6.00\%$$

This means that the investor will earn the same return if she invests (1) at 5.5 percent per year compounded annually for two years or (2) at 5 percent for the first year and then rolls the cash flow from the maturing bond into a second one-year security yielding 6 percent. In this case, $r = 6$ percent represents the *breakeven yield*, or the **implied forward rate**.

To put more structure around this concept, we now will express this implied forward rate—which calculates the breakeven yield on a one-year bond investment between Year 1 and Year 2—as follows:

$$_2r_1 = \frac{(1 + z_2)^2}{(1 + z_1)} - 1$$

This can be interpreted as the one-year implied rate, one year forward. Recognize that it is not an actual forward rate reflected in a bond forward or future contract. We will discuss the relationship between implied forward rates and actual forward rates in Chapter 15.

It is possible to use the spot yield curve to calculate the implied forward rate for any investment horizon starting at any time in the future. For example, the implied forward rate for an N-year bond that would begin at the end of Year T would be computed:

$$(1 + z_{T+N})^{T+N} = (1 + z_T)^T \times (1 + {}_{T+N}r_T)^N$$

or:

13.1
$$_{T+N}r_T = \sqrt[N]{\frac{(1 + z_{T+N})^{T+N}}{(1 + z_T)^T}} - 1$$

This rate $({}_{T+N}r_T)$ would be referred to as the N-year forward rate, T years forward. Extending the previous example, suppose that a three-year zero-coupon bond available today is priced to yield $z_3 = 5.8$ percent. Then, the two-year implied forward rate, one year forward would be calculated as:

$$_3r_1 = \sqrt[3-1]{\frac{(1 + .058)^3}{(1 + .05)^1}} - 1 = 6.20\%$$

Summarizing these computations gives us the following *implied forward rate curve* based on today's observable spot yield curve:

Maturity (yrs)	Spot Rates Today (%)	Implied Forward Rates One Year Later (%)
1	5.00%	6.00%
2	5.50	6.20
3	5.80	—

Notice that by the expectations hypothesis discussed in Chapter 12, an upward-sloping yield curve today implies that interest rates will rise in the future.

13.1.2 Bond Duration

A bond's **duration** measure is often considered the second most important statistic used to evaluate a bond, after the yield to maturity. This is because, in its various forms, duration can be interpreted as a measure of the bond's price volatility (interest rate sensitivity).

Calculating Bond Duration The notion of bond duration was first developed by Frederick R. Macaulay (1938) about 80 years ago. **Macaulay duration**, as the most basic form of the statistic is called, calculates a *weighted average of the payment dates* associated with an N-period bond:

13.2
$$D = \frac{\sum_{t=1}^{N} \frac{CF_t \times t}{(1 + i)^t}}{\sum_{t=1}^{N} \frac{CF_t}{(1 + i)^t}} = \frac{\sum_{t=1}^{N} \frac{CF_t \times t}{(1 + i)^t}}{P_0}$$

where:

CF_t = cash flow (that is, coupon or principal) paid on Date t
  t = date on which payment is made
  i = yield to maturity of the bond, stated on a periodic basis.

By its design, the duration statistic in Equation 13.2 is measured in a unit of time, not dollars. The weights associated with each payment date are the present value of that period's cash flow scaled by the overall present value (P_0) of the bond.

Exhibit 13.1 Computation of Macaulay Duration (Assuming an 8 Percent Yield)

BOND A

(1) Year	(2) Cash Flow	(3) PV at 8%	(4) PV of Flow	(5) PV as % of Price	(6) (1) × (5)
1	$40	0.9259	$37.04	0.0506	0.0506
2	40	0.8573	34.29	0.0469	0.0937
3	40	0.7938	31.75	0.0434	0.1302
4	40	0.7350	29.40	0.0402	0.1608
5	40	0.6806	27.22	0.0372	0.1861
6	40	0.6302	25.21	0.0345	0.2067
7	40	0.5835	23.34	0.0319	0.2233
8	40	0.5403	21.61	0.0295	0.2363
9	40	0.5002	20.01	0.0274	0.2462
10	1,040	0.4632	481.72	0.6585	6.5845
Sum			$731.60	1.0000	8.1184

D = 8.118 years

BOND B

(1) Year	(2) Cash Flow	(3) PV at 8%	(4) PV of Flow	(5) PV as % of Price	(6) (1) × (5)
1	$80	0.9259	$74.07	0.0741	0.0741
2	80	0.8573	68.59	0.0686	0.1372
3	80	0.7938	63.51	0.0635	0.1905
4	80	0.7350	58.80	0.0588	0.2352
5	80	0.6806	54.45	0.0544	0.2722
6	80	0.6302	50.41	0.0504	0.3025
7	80	0.5835	46.68	0.0467	0.3268
8	80	0.5403	43.22	0.0432	0.3458
9	80	0.5002	40.02	0.0400	0.3602
10	1,080	0.4632	500.25	0.5002	5.0025
Sum			$1,000.00	1.0000	7.2469

D = 7.247 years

To illustrate this process, consider the following two bonds:

	Bond A	Bond B
Face value	$1,000	$1,000
Maturity	10 yrs	10 yrs
Coupon	4%	8%

Here we assume that the yield to maturity for both bonds is 8 percent and that both bonds pay annual coupons.[1] The Macaulay duration computations for Bond A and Bond B are summarized in Exhibit 13.1. (A closed-form equation to calculate D directly is demonstrated in the appendix at the end of the chapter.)

The key point to recognize from these calculations is that both of these bonds have durations that are shorter than their 10-year maturity: $D_A = 8.118$ years and $D_B = 7.247$ years. This is because the maturity date is when the last cash flow (principal and final coupon) is paid, but each bond pays nine other cash flows before then. So, an average of all ten payment dates would have to be less than 10.00 years. Notice also that the bond with the *higher coupon rate* (Bond B) had a *lower duration* because, on a percentage basis, more of the total cash flow

---

[1]We assume annual interest payments to simplify the notation and reduce the number of calculations necessary. In practice, you would assume semiannual payments that would lead to a slightly shorter duration since you receive payments earlier.

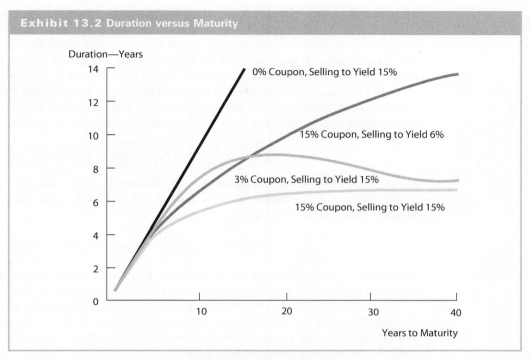

Exhibit 13.2 Duration versus Maturity

was paid sooner, thereby reducing the weighted average payment date. Finally, recognize that only a zero-coupon bond will have a duration statistic equal to its maturity because all of its future cash flow is paid on a single date. These relationships between maturity, coupon rates, and duration are illustrated in Exhibit 13.2.

Measuring Bond Price Volatility An extremely useful property of the duration statistic comes from its interpretation as the bond's *price elasticity coefficient* with respect to yield changes:

13.3
$$D \approx -\frac{\dfrac{\Delta P}{P}}{\dfrac{\Delta\left(1 + \dfrac{i}{m}\right)}{\left(1 + \dfrac{i}{m}\right)}}$$

where:

m = frequency of periodic payments per year ($m = 1$ for annual, $m = 2$ for semiannual, $m = 12$ for monthly)

$\Delta P/P$ = change in price divided by original price (the percentage change in price)

$\Delta(1 + i/m)/(1 + i/m)$ = percentage change in (one plus) the original annualized yield to maturity, adjusted to a periodic basis

Equation 13.3 is usually rewritten to "predict" what the change in a bond's price will be for a small change in the yield to maturity, given its current duration:

13.4
$$\frac{\Delta P}{P} \approx -(D) \times \left[\frac{\Delta\left(1 + \dfrac{i}{m}\right)}{\left(1 + \dfrac{i}{m}\right)}\right]$$

In words, Equation 13.4 states that the percentage change in the price of a bond can be approximated by multiplying the opposite of the Macaulay duration statistic by the percentage change in (one plus) the periodic yield to maturity. Hopewell and Kaufman (1973) noted that this approximation is quite accurate for relatively small changes in interest rates, which is the reason why bond investors are interested in calculating duration in the first place.

As an example, consider what would happen to the price of Bond B in the previous example if its yield to maturity suddenly fell by 50 basis points, from 8.00 percent to 7.50 percent. Since this bond makes annual coupon payments ($m = 1$), the predicted change in the bond's price would be:

$$\frac{\Delta P_B}{P_B} \approx -(7.247) \times \frac{-.005}{(1 + .08)} = 0.0336$$

or, an increase in price of 3.36 percent for this decrease in yields. Also, the same yield decrease would have a slightly different effect on Bond A, which had the same ten-year maturity but a longer duration of $D_A = 8.118$:

$$\frac{\Delta P_A}{P_A} \approx -(8.118) \times \frac{-.005}{(1 + .08)} = 0.0376, \text{ or } 3.76 \text{ percent}$$

This outcome underscores the important point that bonds having *longer durations* will have their *prices affected to a greater extent* by any given change in interest rates.

The bond price change prediction formula in Equation 13.4 contains three components on the right-hand side: (1) the Macaulay duration of the bond, D; (2) the prevailing bond yield, i; and (3) the forecasted change in the bond yield, Δi. It is often computationally convenient to combine the first two components as follows:

$$\text{Mod } D = \frac{D}{\left(1 + \dfrac{i}{m}\right)}$$

When the Macaulay duration statistic is adjusted in this fashion it is called the **modified duration**, or Mod D. The advantage of this modification is that Equation 13.4 can be simplified to:

13.5
$$\frac{\Delta P}{P} \approx -(\text{Mod } D) \times \left[\Delta\left(1 + \frac{i}{m}\right)\right]$$

which allows the investor to focus on just the forecasted rate change. For Bond B in the last example, Mod $D_B = (7.247)/(1.08) = 6.710$, so the predicted price change for the change in yield from 8.00 percent to 7.50 percent would be $-(6.710) \times (-0.005) = 3.36\%$.

Another adaption of the basic duration statistic that is widely used in practice is the **basis point value (BPV)** of the bond. The BPV is a measure of the bond's *dollar* price change for a one basis point change in yields (for example, from 8.00 percent to 7.99 percent). It is calculated by altering Equation 13.5 to focus on just the dollar price change (ΔP) and assuming $\Delta i = 0.0001$, or 0.01 percent:

13.6
$$\Delta P \approx -(\text{Mod } D) \times (-0.0001) \times (P) = \text{BPV}$$

In the case of Bond B, which was originally priced at its par value of $1,000.00 when the yield was 8.00 percent, the basis point value of the instrument would be:

$$\text{BPV} = -(6.710) \times (-0.0001) \times (1,000.00) = \$0.6710$$

This means that the investor can expect the bond's price to change by about 67 cents (per $1,000 of face value) for every basis point movement in yields. So, a 50 basis point decline in yields (that is, from 8.00 percent to 7.50 percent) would lead to an approximate increase in the bond's price of $33.55 (=50 × $0.671), which is about 3.36 percent of the original price.

Duration of a Portfolio Bond investors are seldom concerned with the effect that interest rate changes might have on just a single bond holding. Rather, they are concerned with the impact that a yield curve shift would have on their entire portfolio. Extending the basic idea, the duration of a bond portfolio is simply the weighted average of the payment dates for all of the cash flows across the entire collection of bonds. This can be estimated by taking a weighted average of the duration statistics for each of the bonds, with the investment weight of each position (that is, w_j is the percentage of capital allocated to Bond j) in the averaging process:

$$D_{port} = \sum_{j=1}^{N} w_j \times D_j$$

To demonstrate this calculation, suppose an investor holds a portfolio of three bonds, with the dollar allocations and security characteristics shown as follows:

Face Value ($ millions)	Coupon (%)	Maturity (yrs)	Yield (%)	Market Value ($ millions)	Duration
$40	8.00%	10	8.00%	$40.000	7.247
23	3.50	3	4.00	$22.681	2.899
37	6.50	6	5.75	$38.375	5.173
				$101.056	

With these inputs, the duration of the entire portfolio would be:

$$D_{port} = \left(\frac{40.000}{101.056}\right)(7.247) + \left(\frac{22.681}{101.056}\right)(2.899) + \left(\frac{38.375}{101.056}\right)(5.173)$$

$$= 5.484$$

So, from a price volatility standpoint, this three-bond bond portfolio will act like a single asset having a current market value of $101 million and a duration of just under 5.5 years.

13.1.3 Bond Convexity

In Chapter 12, we saw that the trade-off between a bond's price and its yield to maturity was not a straight line but a curved (that is, convex) function. (See Exhibit 12.15 to review this concept.) The reason that the duration-based prediction formula in Equation 13.5 is an approximation of the actual price change that would occur for a given yield change is that it does not take this curvature into account. That is, by only focusing on the ModD statistic, the formula misses the bond's **convexity** property. Essentially, Equation 13.5 attempts to estimate movements along a curved line with a straight (tangent) line. This is illustrated in Exhibit 13.3.

An important thing to recognize in this display is that the duration-based approximation of the price–yield relationship is always conservative in the sense that it *overestimates* the *price decline* following a yield increase and it *underestimates* the *price increase* induced by a yield decrease. So, the convexity property of a noncallable bond is a good thing for the investor in that it will "add back" to the value of the instrument relative to if the duration effect alone is considered. More formally, Exhibit 13.3 also indicates that modified duration of the bond is related to the first differential of the price–yield relationship with respect to yield:

$$\text{Mod } D = \frac{\frac{dP}{di}}{P}$$

whereas convexity is related to the second derivative of this relationship:

$$\text{Convexity} = \frac{\frac{d^2P}{di^2}}{P}$$

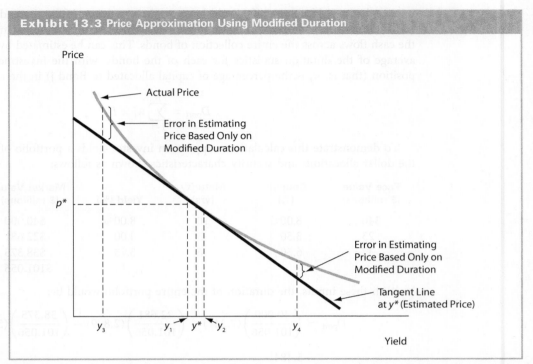

Exhibit 13.3 Price Approximation Using Modified Duration

Source: Frank J. Fabozzi, Gerald W. Buetow, Robert R. Johnson, and Brian J. Henderson "Measuring Interest-Rate Risk," in the *Handbook of Fixed Income Securities*, 8th ed. (New York: McGraw-Hill, 2012). Reproduced with permission from The McGraw-Hill Companies.

Extending this interpretation, modified duration approximates how the bond's price will change as interest rates changes, while convexity (the second derivative) approximates how modified duration (the first derivative) will change with yield curve shifts.

Using the previous notation, the convexity statistic can be computed with the following formula:

13.7 $$\text{Convexity} = \left\{ \frac{1}{(1+i)^2} \left[\sum_{t=1}^{N} \frac{\text{CF}_t}{(1+i)^t} \times (t^2 + t) \right] \right\} \div P$$

For Bond B in the previous example, which had a 10-year maturity and made annual coupon payments of 8 percent, this convexity calculation is demonstrated in Exhibit 13.4, assuming once again that the initial yield to maturity is also 8 percent. In this case, the convexity of this bond is shown to be 60.53. There are several things to notice about the convexity formula in Equation 13.7. First, for a noncallable bond, the convexity statistic will always be positive. Second, for two bonds with the same maturity, the one with the *lower coupon rate* will have the *larger convexity*. Third, for two bonds with the same coupon rate, the one with the *longer maturity* will have the *larger convexity*. Finally, the degree of convexity for a bond changes inversely with its yield, meaning convexity will be larger at lower interest rates.

Convexity can be used to make the price change approximation formula in Equations 13.5 and 13.6 more precise by accounting for the curvature in the actual price–yield relationship that duration misses. Specifically, assuming for simplicity that the bond pays annual cash flows ($m = 1$), the formula for predicting the dollar price change in the bond can be further modified by adding a second term involving the convexity statistic:

13.8 $$\Delta P \approx \left\{ -(\text{Mod } D) \times [\Delta i] \times P \right\} + \left\{ (0.5) \times (\text{Convexity}) \times [\Delta i]^2 \times P \right\}$$

Exhibit 13.4 Computation of Convexity (Assuming an 8 Percent Yield)

(1) Year (t)	(2) CF	(3) PV @ 8%	(4) PV(CF)	(5) $t^2 + t$	(4) × (5)
1	80	0.9259	$ 74.07	2	148.15
2	80	0.8573	68.59	6	411.52
3	80	0.7938	63.51	12	762.08
4	80	0.7350	58.80	20	1176.05
5	80	0.6806	54.45	30	1633.40
6	80	0.6302	50.41	42	2117.37
7	80	0.5835	46.68	56	2614.04
8	80	0.5403	43.22	72	3111.95
9	80	0.5002	40.02	90	3601.79
10	1080	0.4632	500.25	110	55027.39
			$ 1000.00		70603.73

So:

$$\text{Convexity} = \frac{(70603.73/(1.08)^2)}{1000.00} = \frac{60531.32}{1000.00} = \mathbf{60.53}$$

To see how this improvement might work, consider again the 10-year, 8 percent coupon bond as its yield to maturity declines by 50 basis points from 8.00 percent to 7.50 percent. As summarized in Exhibit 13.5, the actual change in the bond's value given this yield decrease will be $34.32 ($= 1,034.32 - 1000.00$), or 3.43 percent of the original price. We saw earlier that approximating this price change with the modified duration term alone will understate the true effect—here the predicted price change would be just $33.55 ($= -(6.710) \times (-0.005) \times (1000.00)$), or 3.36 percent. However, adding a second term to this prediction to account for the bond's convexity will increase the forecast by $0.76 ($= (0.5) \times (60.53) \times (-0.005)^2 \times (1000.00)$), bringing the total predicted price change to virtually the same amount as the actual effect.

Exhibit 13.5 Analysis of Bond Price Change Considering Duration and Convexity (Original Yield of 8 Percent)

Bond Characteristics:

Maturity:	10 years	Macaulay Duration:	7.247
Coupon Rate:	8.00%	Modified Duration:	6.710
Coupon Frequency:	Annual	Convexity:	60.53
Par Value:	$1,000.00		

Bond Valuation:

Price at $i = 8.00\%$	$1,000.00
Price at $i = 7.50\%$	$1,034.32

		Dollar Change	% Change
Actual Price Change:			
$= (1034.32 - 1000.00)$		**$34.32**	**3.43%**
Approximate Price Change:			
Duration Effect: $= -(6.710) \times (-0.005) \times (1000.00)$		$33.55	3.36%
Convexity Effect: $= (0.5) \times (60.53) \times (-0.005)^2 \times (1000.00)$		$0.76	0.07%
Total:		**$34.31**	**3.43%**

13.1.4 Bonds with Embedded Options

So far, the discussion regarding duration and convexity has involved option-free bonds. A callable bond is different because it provides the issuer with an option to refinance the bond by paying it off with funds from a new issue sold at a lower yield. Alternatively, a putable bond gives the investor the option to sell the bond back to the issuer at a fixed price, which is likely to occur when market yields rise. These are examples of bonds containing an *embedded option* feature.

The challenge involved with trying to calculate the modified duration and convexity statistics for a bond with an embedded option is that exercising the option feature—whether an issuer calls the bond or an investor puts the bond—will shorten the effective maturity of the security. So, would a bond with a 20-year maturity that could be called next year have a duration more like a regular 20-year bond or like a 1-year bond? To concentrate on the callable bond example, recognize that from the investor's standpoint, owning a callable bond is equivalent to holding a prepackaged portfolio consisting of (1) a long position in a noncallable bond, and (ii) a short position in a call option. Therefore, the value of a callable bond is:

$$\text{Callable bond value} = (\text{Noncallable bond value}) - (\text{Call option value})$$

From this perspective, anything that increases the value of the call feature, such as a decrease in market interest rates that make the issuer more likely to refinance, will reduce the value of the bond. Accordingly, as Fabozzi, Kalotay, and Dorigan (2012) discuss, the *option-adjusted duration* of the callable bond can be thought of as:

$$\text{Option-adjusted duration} = (\text{Duration of noncallable bond}) - (\text{Duration of call option})$$

Intuitively, we see that when market yields are substantially above a bond's coupon rate, the probability of the bond being called is very small (that is, the call option has very little value), and the option-adjusted duration will approach the duration to maturity. In contrast, if interest rates decline to levels substantially below the coupon rate, the probability of the bond being called at the first opportunity is very high (that is, the call option will probably be exercised), and the option-adjusted duration will approach the duration to the first call date. Typically, the bond's option-adjusted duration will be somewhere between these two extremes, depending on the level of interest rates relative to the bond's coupon rate.

To consider the convexity effect of an embedded option, Exhibit 13.6 shows what happens to the price of a callable bond versus the value of a noncallable bond when interest rates change. Starting from yield y* (which is close to the par value yield), if interest *rates increase*, the value of the call option declines because it is unlikely the issuer will want to call the issue.[2] Therefore, the call option has very little value, and the price of the callable bond will be similar to the price of a noncallable bond. In contrast, when interest rates *decline below y*,* there is an increase in the probability that the issuer will exercise the call option and so the value of the call option increases. As a result, the value of the callable bond will deviate from the value of the noncallable bond in that its price will initially not increase as fast as that of the noncallable bond and eventually will not increase at all. This is shown in curve *a–b*.

The noncallable bond is said to have *positive convexity* because as yields declined, the price of the bond increased at a *faster* rate. With the callable bond, however, when rates decline, the price increases at a *slower* rate and ultimately does not change at all. This pattern of price–yield change for a callable bond when yields decline is referred to as *negative convexity*. Of course, this negative convexity price pattern is one of the risks of owning a callable bond.

---

[2] In both Exhibits 13.3 and 13.6, the bond's yield to maturity is represented by the symbol y instead of by the symbol i that is used throughout the rest of this text. The two symbols are frequently used interchangeably in practice when expressing bond yields.

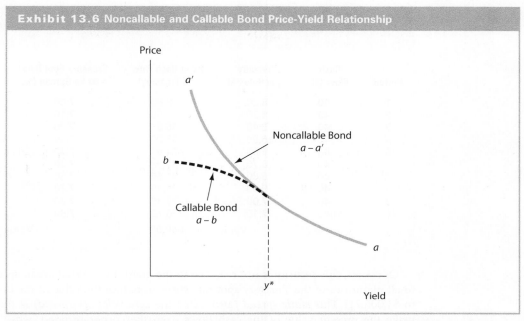

Exhibit 13.6 Noncallable and Callable Bond Price-Yield Relationship

Source: Frank J. Fabozzi, Gerald W. Buetow, Robert R. Johnson, and Brian J. Henderson "Measuring Interest-Rate Risk," in the *Handbook of Fixed-Income Securities*, 8th ed. (New York: McGraw-Hill, 2012). Reproduced with permission from The McGraw-Hill Companies.

13.1.5 Yield Spread Analysis

As we saw in Chapter 12, the yield spread for a corporate bond represents the risk premium an investor expects to receive by holding the bond to maturity. We now consider in more detail how to calculate those spreads relative to a prevailing term structure of Treasury spot yields. Specifically, we discuss two different spread concepts: (1) **static yield spreads** that take account of the total term structure and (2) **option-adjusted spreads (OAS)**, which also consider alternative estimates of interest rate volatility.

Static Yield Spreads The traditional yield spread compares the yields between two bonds with similar coupons and equal maturities as follows:

6%, 20-Year AA-Rated Corporate Bond	6.20%
6%, 20-Year Treasury Bond	5.10%
Yield Spread	1.10%, or 110 bp

However, this approach considers only a single point in the term structure rather than the entire shape of the curve and it also does not account for possibility that the corporate bond might have an embedded option that could alter future cash flow patterns. The static yield spread addresses the first concern.

To see how this process works, consider a corporate bond with a five-year maturity that pays semiannual coupons at the stated coupon rate of 8 percent. At present, this bond sells at a price of $1,006.71 relative to its face value of $1,000.00. The 10 payment dates and cash flows are shown in the first two columns of Exhibit 13.7. The third column indicates the Treasury spot yields that currently prevail on each of those payment dates. If we discount this bond's flows using the hypothetical Treasury spot rate curve, the price would be $1,040.03, which is what this bond would be worth if it were a Treasury bond. This calculation is summarized in fourth column of the exhibit.

Exhibit 13.7 Calculation of the Static Spread for a Five-Year, 8 Percent Coupon Corporate Bond

Period	Cash Flow ($)	Treasury Spot Rate (%)	PV of Cash Flow (as Treasury)	Treasury Spot Rate + 80 bp Spread (%)	PV of Cash Flow (as corporate)
1	40	6.20	38.80	7.00	38.65
2	40	6.30	37.59	7.10	37.30
3	40	6.40	36.39	7.20	35.97
4	40	6.50	35.20	7.30	34.66
5	40	6.60	34.01	7.40	33.36
6	40	6.70	32.82	7.50	32.07
7	40	6.80	31.65	7.60	30.81
8	40	6.90	30.49	7.70	29.57
9	40	7.00	29.35	7.80	28.35
10	1040	7.10	733.72	7.90	705.97
			Value = $ 1,040.03		Value = $ 1,006.71

Of course, this security is not risk-free so the question is: What credit spread must be added to all maturities of the Treasury spot rate curve to reduce the value of the bond from $1,040.03 to $1,006.71? This *static spread* (also called the *zero-volatility spread*) is the number that will make the present value of the cash flows from the corporate bond, when discounted at the Treasury spot rate plus this static spread, equal to the corporate bond's market price. As shown in the final two columns of Exhibit 13.7, using a spread of 80 basis points (or 0.80 percent) generates a present value of $1,006.71. This is the static spread for the bond.

Option-Adjusted Spread Although static spreads account for the relevant portion of the entire spot yield curve, they do not consider the impact that yield changes can have on expected cash flows when a bond has embedded options. Including this interest rate volatility factor is the essential point of option-adjusted spread (OAS) analysis, which has a goal similar to static spread calculation but allows for a *change in the term structure* over time based on alternative volatility estimates.

The *OAS* concept is best understood by a presentation of the steps involved in its estimation for a specific bond:

1. Based on the prevailing Treasury spot rate curve, calculate implied forward rates to help select a probability distribution for short-term Treasury spot rates. The significant estimate is *the volatility of interest rates* (the standard deviation of yields)—in other words, how much will the forward rates change each period?
2. Using the probability distribution specified in step 1 and Monte Carlo simulation, randomly generate a large number (for example, 1,000) of possible interest rate paths.
3. For bonds with embedded options (such as callable bonds), develop rules for determining when the option will be exercised (for example, at what interest rate level and point in the future will the issue be called?)
4. For each interest rate path from step 2, determine the cash flows from the bond, given (a) the features of the bond (its call provision), and (b) the rules established in step 3 for calling the bond.
5. For an assumed spread relative to the Treasury spot rates along a path, calculate a present value for all paths created in step 2.
6. Calculate the *average* present value of the bond for all the interest rate paths.
7. Compare the average present value calculated in step 6 to the market price of the bond. If they are equal, the assumed spread used in step 5 is the option-adjusted spread. If they are not, try another spread and repeat steps 5, 6, and 7.

To summarize, the option-adjusted spread is the average spread over the Treasury spot rate curve based on the potential interest rate paths that might be realized in the future. Therefore, the OAS is the spread *after* taking account of the compensation required for the embedded option making it comparable to a spread for an option-free bond. For example, a nominal credit spread of 300 basis points for a callable corporate bond may look desirable relative to a noncallable corporate bond with a spread of only 125 basis points. However, the OAS for this callable bond might be only 130 basis points, which implies that the required yield for the embedded call option is 170 basis points. It is the OAS of 130 basis points that needs to be compared to the 1.25 percent spread for the noncallable bond.

13.2 AN OVERVIEW OF BOND PORTFOLIO MANAGEMENT: PERFORMANCE, STYLE, AND STRATEGY

The volatile pattern of interest rates prevailing during recent decades has provided increasingly attractive returns to bond investors of all types. Active bond portfolio managers have found the frequent opportunities to realize capital gains that resulted from those rate shifts to be especially attractive. However, despite the favorable economic climate that has prevailed for most of the last thirty years, it is still the case that fixed-income portfolios generally produce both less return and less volatility than other asset classes (for example, domestic equity, foreign equity, real estate). Exhibit 13.8 summarizes the average annual returns and standard deviations for several performance indexes over the 25-year period ending in 2016, a time horizon that saw two major downturns in equity markets. Bond portfolios—as represented by

Exhibit 13.8 Risk–Return Comparison between Bond Portfolios and Other Asset Classes

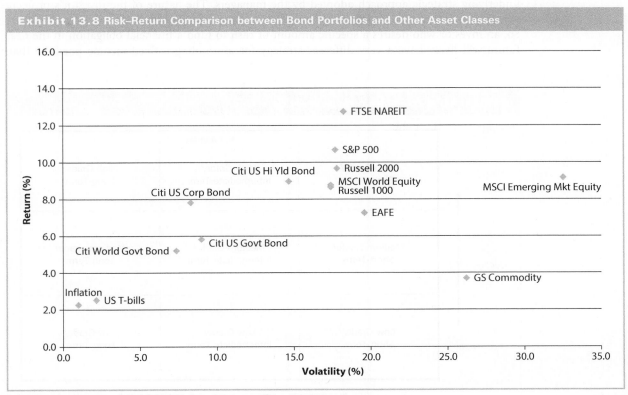

Source: Author calculations.

the Citigroup U.S. Government Bond, World Government Bond, and U.S. Corporate Bond indexes—fall at the lower end of the risk-return spectrum, making them a conservative choice within an investor's overall asset allocation strategy. On the other hand, the U.S. High Yield Bond Index exhibited risk and return dynamics that made it more comparable to many of the equity indexes. Finally, notice that the negative historical correlation between fixed-income and equity securities—only −0.10 in this time period—has made bond portfolios an excellent tool for diversifying risk as well.

In Chapter 11, we saw that it can be useful to classify the investment style of equity portfolios along two dimensions: market capitalization and relative valuation (that is, value versus growth). Similarly, the investment style of a bond portfolio can be summarized by its two most important characteristics: *credit quality* and *interest rate sensitivity*. Exhibit 13.9 shows how the 3×3 style grid can be adjusted to these dimensions. The average credit quality of the portfolio is classified as *high grade* (government, agency, AAA-rated or AA-rated corporate bonds), *medium grade* (A-rated or BBB-rated), or *low grade* (below BBB-rated). Since duration effectively measures a bond's price sensitivity to interest rate changes, the second dimension of the bond portfolio's investment style is separated into *short term* (duration less than 3.0 years), *intermediate term* (duration between 3.0 and 6.5 years), or *long term* (duration more than 6.5 years). For example, the Barclays Capital U.S. Aggregate Bond Index, a widely used benchmark, is purposely constructed to mimic the profile of the investment grade fixed-income security market in the United States, which typically consists of 70 percent to 80 percent government, agency, or AAA-rated bonds. The BCA Index is structured to maintain an average duration of between 4.0 and 6.0 years. Thus, it plots in the upper middle cell of the style grid in Exhibit 13.9 and is classified as a high-grade/intermediate-term portfolio.

Just as the inherent investment style of two bond portfolios can vary widely, so too can the underlying strategic approach adopted by the managers. The nature of the investor's problem usually dictates how the manager will think about designing a portfolio to solve that problem. So, an investor who desires a specific amount of cash to fund a financial obligation in the near future will likely have a very different strategy for assembling a fixed-income portfolio than

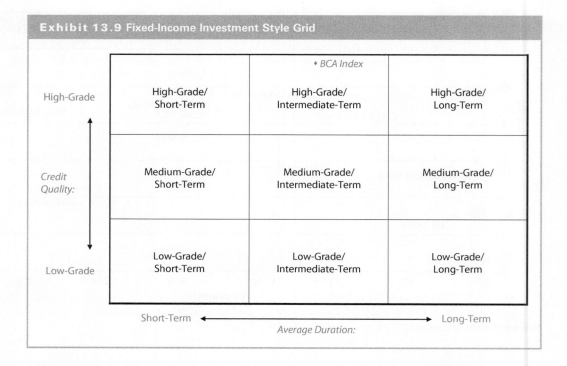

Exhibit 13.9 Fixed-Income Investment Style Grid

	Short-Term	Intermediate-Term	Long-Term
High-Grade	High-Grade/ Short-Term	High-Grade/ Intermediate-Term *(• BCA Index)*	High-Grade/ Long-Term
Credit Quality:	Medium-Grade/ Short-Term	Medium-Grade/ Intermediate-Term	Medium-Grade/ Long-Term
Low-Grade	Low-Grade/ Short-Term	Low-Grade/ Intermediate-Term	Low-Grade/ Long-Term

Short-Term ⟷ Long-Term

Average Duration:

Exhibit 13.10 Bond Portfolio Investment Strategies

1. Passive Management Strategies
   a. Buy and hold
   b. Indexing
2. Active Management Strategies
   a. Interest rate anticipation
   b. Valuation analysis
   c. Credit analysis
   d. Yield spread analysis
   e. Sector/country analysis
   f. Prepayment/option analysis
   g. Other (e.g., liquidity, currency, anomaly capture)
3. Core-Plus Management Strategies
   a. Enhanced indexing
   b. Active/passive "plus" sectors
4. Matched-Funding Strategies
   a. Dedicated: exact cash match
   b. Dedicated: optimal cash match
   c. Classical immunization
   d. Horizon matching
5. Contingent and Structured Strategies
   a. Contingent immunization
   b. Structured management

someone whose goal is to maximize capital gains resulting from an anticipated shift in interest rates. Exhibit 13.10, which is based in part on Leibowitz (1986a), indicates that bond portfolio strategies can be divided into the five broad groups mentioned earlier.

Prior to the 1970s, only the first two strategic approaches—passive and active—were widely available, and most bond portfolios were managed on a buy-and-hold basis with the intention of producing a steady stream of cash flow for the investor. The early 1970s saw a growing level of curiosity with alternative active bond portfolio management approaches, while the late 1970s and early 1980s were characterized by record-breaking inflation and interest rates as well as extremely volatile yields across all spectrums of the bond market. This led to the introduction of many new financial instruments in response to the increase in rate volatility (for example, adjustable-rate bonds and mortgages). Since the mid-1980s, matched-funding techniques, core-plus strategies, and contingent bond management approaches have been developed to meet the increased needs of institutional investors, such as pension funds and insurance companies. Finally, beginning in the mid-1990s and continuing today, it has become increasingly common to see bonds combined with positions in derivative securities in the management of sophisticated fixed-income portfolios.

13.3 PASSIVE MANAGEMENT STRATEGIES

Two specific passive portfolio management strategies exist. First, in a **buy-and-hold** strategy, a manager selects a portfolio of bonds based on the objectives and constraints of the client with the intent of holding these bonds through maturity. In the second passive strategy—**indexing**—the objective is to construct a portfolio of bonds matched as closely as possible to the performance of a specified bond index, such as the Barclays U.S. Aggregate Bond Index described earlier.

13.3.1 Buy-and-Hold Strategy

The simplest fixed-income portfolio management strategy is to buy and hold. This approach involves finding securities with the desired levels of credit quality, coupon rate, term to maturity or duration, and other important indenture provisions, such as call and sinking fund features. Buy-and-hold investors do not consider active trading a viable alternative but look for a bond issue whose maturity/duration characteristics approximate their investment horizon in order to reduce price and reinvestment risk. Many successful bond investors and institutional portfolio managers follow a modified buy-and-hold strategy wherein they invest in an issue with the intention of holding it to maturity, but still look for opportunities to trade into a more desirable position should the occasion arise.

Recognize that there is an important fundamental difference between managing a bond portfolio and a stock portfolio on a buy-and-hold basis. Since bonds eventually mature with the passing of time whereas stock shares do not, the bond manager is faced with the need to periodically reinvest the funds from a matured issue. Fixed-income portfolio managers often address this concern by forming a **bond ladder**, in which they divide their investment funds evenly into instruments that mature at regular intervals. For instance, a manager with an intermediate-term investment focus, instead of investing all of her funds in a five-year zero-coupon security—which would become a four-year security after one year had passed—could follow a laddered approach and buy equal amounts of bonds maturing in annual intervals between one and nine years. The idea would then be to hold each bond to maturity, but to reinvest the proceeds from a maturing bond into a new instrument with a maturity at the far end of the ladder (that is, reinvest a maturing bond in a new nine-year issue). In this way, the desired duration target for the portfolio can be maintained over time without having to continually adjust the investment weights for the remaining positions.

13.3.2 Indexing Strategy

As with stock index funds, when designing a bond portfolio to mimic a hypothetical index, managers can follow two different paths: *full replication* or *stratified sampling*. While it is quite common when constructing stock index funds to fully replicate the underlying index, the bond index fund manager often follows a sampling approach. One reason for this is that bond indexes often contain several thousand specific issues and are adjusted frequently, making them both impractical and expensive to replicate precisely in practice. The goal of the stratified sampling approach is to create a bond portfolio that matches the important characteristics of the underlying index—such as credit quality, maturity/duration, or average yield—while maintaining a portfolio that is more cost effective to manage. To the extent that the manager is not able to match these characteristics over time, the tracking error of the indexed portfolio will typically increase.

When initiating an indexing strategy, the selection of an appropriate market index is clearly a very important decision, chiefly because it directly influences the client's risk–return results. Consequently, it is important for investors to be acquainted with the main characteristics (maturity/duration, credit quality) of their selected index. Reilly and Wright (1997, 2012) have examined many aspects of the major bond indexes, such as their risk-return characteristics and the correlations between them over time. Also, Volpert (2012) and Dialynas and Murata (2006) discuss how the characteristics of indexes affect their performance in different interest rate environments. Finally, recognize that the aggregate bond market and the indexes change over time, as described by Mossavar-Rahmani (1991). Reilly, Kao, and Wright (1992) show that the market experienced significant shifts in composition, maturity, and duration since 1975, which significantly impacted the tracking error performance of indexed portfolios.

13.3.3 Bond Indexing in Practice: An Example

To see how two actual managers have responded to the challenge of forming a bond portfolio designed to track one of the leading indexes, we consider the several aspects of the Vanguard Total Bond Market Index Fund (ticker: VBMFX) and the iShares Core U.S. Aggregate (ticker: AGG) exchange-traded fund over a recent investment period. Both of these portfolios were created to mimic the performance of the Bloomberg Barclays U.S. Aggregate Bond Index (ticker: LBUSTRUU) and represent the two methods widely used in practice to create indexed portfolios for retail investors (that is, index mutual funds and ETFs).

Exhibit 13.11 summarizes the most important characteristics for these funds as well as for the underlying index. It is interesting to contrast the approaches these managers have adopted to replicate the index, which contains over 9,300 separate bond issues and would be difficult to recreate exactly. The manager of VBMFX actually holds more positions than the index (over 17,000 names), whereas AGG's manager follows a stratified sampling method that tries to mimic the index by holding only about 6,200 distinct security positions. Not surprisingly, AGG also has a substantially higher portfolio turnover statistic than VBMFX—242 percent versus 61 percent—which results from trying to keep the ETF's portfolio composition aligned with that of the larger index.

This difference in index replication approaches also leads to slight differences in the relevant investment characteristics of the portfolios. Generally speaking, the index mutual fund is closer to the index in terms of average duration (LBUSTRUU: 6.0, VBMFX: 6.1, AGG: 5.8), but both of the managed funds deviate from the index in terms of credit quality, as measured by the percentage of the portfolio carrying a rating of AAA or higher (LBUSTRUU: 70.9, VBMFX: 69.3, AGG: 72.1). These slight discrepancies lead to modest tracking error statistics produced by each manager, with VBMFX and AGG having annualized values of 0.27 percent and 0.37 percent, respectively. Finally, the ETF's expense ratio is significantly lower

Exhibit 13.11 Indexed Bond Investing: Index Fund versus ETF, July 2017

	Bloomberg Barclays U.S. Aggregate Bond Index (LBUSTRUU)	Vanguard Total Bond Market Index Fund (VBMFX)	iShares Core U.S. Aggregate ETF (AGG)
Style Classification (credit grade/duration)	High Grade/ Intermediate Term	High Grade/ Intermediate Term	High Grade/ Intermediate Term
No. of holdings	9,348	17,319	6,202
Annual turnover (%)	—	61	242
Annual yield (%)	2.5	2.4	2.4
Avg. duration (yrs)	6.0	6.1	5.8
Avg. maturity (yrs)	8.2	8.4	8.0
Credit quality (% of port.):			
Govt/agency/AAA	70.9	69.3	72.1
AA	4.8	4.0	3.5
A	10.6	11.7	10.6
BBB	13.8	15.0	13.8
Other/not rated	0.0	0.0	0.0
Tracking error (%/yr): (7/14–6/17)	—	0.27	0.37
Expense ratio (%)	—	0.16	0.05

Source: Prepared by the authors using data from Morningstar, Inc., and Fidelity Investments.

(5 versus 16 basis points), but both are much smaller than what would be typical for an actively managed bond portfolio.

13.4 ACTIVE MANAGEMENT STRATEGIES

As we have seen with active equity portfolio management, the active fixed-income manager attempts to form a portfolio of securities that will outperform her designated benchmark over time. That is, she will attempt to hold a collection of bonds that produce superior risk-adjusted returns (alpha) compared to the index used to measure investment performance. Of course, to beat a benchmark, the active manager must form a portfolio that differs from the index in a meaningful way. Thus, active bond management strategies are closely tied to the manager's view of what factors or market conditions will be the source of the incremental alpha returns she seeks.

Layard-Liesching (2001) analyzed the investment attributes of several potential sources of alpha for the active bond portfolio manager, all of which depend on some structural barrier that prevents the bond market from being fully efficient. These characteristics are summarized in Exhibit 13.12, which compares each active strategy on four dimensions: (1) scalability: how large a position can be taken, (2) sustainability: how far into the future the strategy can be successfully employed, (3) risk-adjusted performance: how profitable the strategy can be, and (4) extreme values: how exposed the strategy is to the chance of a large loss. For instance, in the interest rate anticipation category, duration-based active bets—in which the manager alters the average duration level of the active portfolio on a forecast of yield curve shifts—are highly scalable since they can be implemented with virtually any securities available in the market. However, they also offer the lowest chance of sustainable performance as well as the worst risk-adjusted returns. By contrast, credit risk bets—where the manager holds bonds he thinks have a substantially different default potential than priced in by the market—are a much more sustainable and reliable source of potential alpha. Finally, while valuation analysis offers the

Exhibit 13.12 Characteristics of Active Bond Portfolio Strategies

Source	Scalability	Sustainability	Risk-Adjusted Performance*	Extreme Values
Interest rate Anticipation:				
Duration	High	Very weak	1	Yes
Yield curve Shape	Low	Very weak	3	No
Valuation Analysis:				
Security Selection	Low	Medium	5	No
Anomaly Capture	Low	Weak	7	Yes
Credit risk	High	Strong	8	Yes
Yield spread Analysis:				
Optionality	Medium	Medium	7	Yes
Prepayment	Medium	Medium	6	Yes
Liquidity	Low	Strong	3	Yes
Global & tactical:				
Sector Allocation	High	Strong	6	No
Country Allocation	High	Strong	5	No
Currency	High	Medium	2	Yes

*1 = Low, 10 = High

Note: This list is subjective; investors should make their own assessment of these criteria.

Source: Adapted from Ronald Layard-Liesching, "Exploiting Opportunities in Global Bond Markets," in *Core-Plus Bond Management* (Charlottesville, VA: AIMR), 2001.

active manager reasonable alpha potential, it is a less scalable strategy since it relies on identifying pricing errors in specific bond issues.

In the remainder of this section, we will explore two of the most popular active bond strategies—interest rate anticipation and credit risk—in more detail, as well as describe bond swaps as a means to implement a specific active strategic view.

13.4.1 Interest Rate Anticipation

Interest rate anticipation is perhaps the riskiest active management strategy because it involves relying on uncertain forecasts of future interest rates. The idea is to preserve capital when an increase in interest rates is anticipated and achieve attractive capital gains when yields are expected to decline. Such objectives are usually achieved by altering portfolio duration (reducing duration when interest rates are expected to increase and increasing duration when a decline in yields is anticipated). Thus, the risk in the strategy is largely tied to these duration adjustments. When portfolio duration is shortened, substantial income could be sacrificed and the opportunity for capital gains could be lost if interest rates decline rather than rise. Similarly, an investor sacrifices current income by shifting from high-coupon short bonds to longer-duration bonds in anticipation of a rate decline. Further, the portfolio is purposely exposed to greater price volatility that could work against the portfolio if an unexpected increase in yields occurs. Note that the portfolio adjustments prompted by an anticipated rate increase involve less risk of an absolute capital loss. When you reduce portfolio maturity, the worst that can happen is that interest income is reduced or capital gains are forgone (opportunity cost).

Once interest rate expectations have been determined, the strategic process becomes a technical matter. Assume that you expect an increase in interest rates and want to preserve your capital by reducing the duration of your portfolio. A popular choice would be short-term obligations, such as Treasury bills. Although your primary concern is to preserve capital, you would nevertheless look for the best return possible given the maturity constraint. Liquidity also is important because, after interest rates increase, yields may experience a period of stability before they decline, and you would want to shift positions quickly to benefit the change.

To illustrate this process, suppose that the yield curve for U.S. Treasury bonds is currently flat across all maturities at 4.75 percent. You have observed the following "paired" transaction by an active bond portfolio manager:

Bond	Transaction	Type	Maturity (yrs)	Coupon Rate (%)	Modified Duration
1	Buy	U.S. govt.	7	8	5.438
2	Sell	U.S. govt.	13	0	12.698

What does this trade suggest about the manager's view as to how the yield curve is likely to change in the future? First, by switching out of a long-maturity, zero-coupon bond into an intermediate-maturity, high-coupon bond, the manager has significantly shortened the modified duration of the position and, presumably, of the entire portfolio. Thus, this trade is consistent with a view that the yields will rise in the future (the yield curve will shift up). Exhibit 13.13 shows two potential situations for how this might happen. In Scenario #1, the manager forecasts that all rates will shift up by 50 basis points, keeping the yield curve flat. In Scenario #2, all future yields increase but rates on longer-term securities increase by more, so the shape of the curve moves from flat to upward sloping. In either case, the manager will benefit from replacing a bond with a single cash flow paid out more than a decade in the future to one with a much shorter maturity that also makes payments every six months. Of course, the trade will be the most profitable (in present value terms) under Scenario #2, since the 7-year bond will be subjected to a smaller yield increase than the 13-year security. Finally, notice that by using one Treasury security to replace another, the manager has not introduced any credit risk into the portfolio.

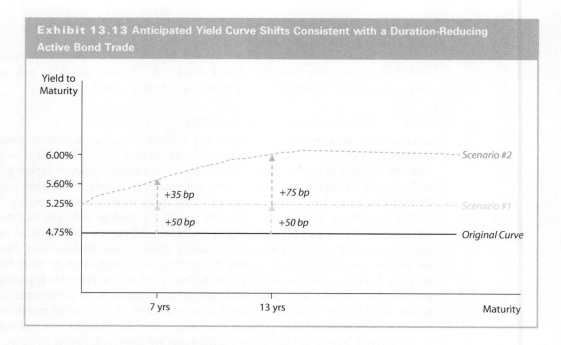

Exhibit 13.13 Anticipated Yield Curve Shifts Consistent with a Duration-Reducing Active Bond Trade

An alternative way to shorten maturities is to use a *cushion bond*—a high-yielding, long-term obligation that carries a coupon substantially above the current market rate and that, due to its current call feature and call price, has a market price lower than what it should be given current market yields. An example would be a 10-year bond with a 12 percent coupon, currently callable at 110. If current market rates are 8 percent, this bond (if it were noncallable) would have a price of about 127; because of its call price, however, it will stay close to 110, and its yield will be about 10 percent rather than 8 percent. As described by Leibowitz and Homer (2013), bond portfolio managers look for cushion bonds when they expect a modest increase in rates because such issues provide attractive current income *and* protection against capital loss.

A totally different posture is assumed by investors who anticipate a rate decline. The significant risk involved in restructuring a portfolio to take advantage of a decline in interest rates is balanced by the potential for substantial capital gains. When you expect lower interest rates, you should increase the duration of the portfolio because the longer the duration, the greater the positive price volatility. Because interest rate sensitivity is critical, it is important to note that the higher the quality of the bond, the more sensitive it is to interest rate changes. Therefore, high-grade securities should be used, such as Treasuries, agencies, or corporates rated AAA through BBB. Finally, you should concentrate on noncallable issues or those with strong call protection because of the substantial call risk when yields decline.

13.4.2 Credit Analysis

A **credit analysis** strategy involves detailed analysis of the bond issuer to determine expected changes in its default risk. This involves attempting to project changes in the credit ratings assigned to bonds by the various rating agencies. These rating changes are affected by internal changes in the borrower (changes in important financial ratios) and by changes in the external environment (changes in the firm's industry and the economy). During periods of strong economic expansion, even financially weak firms may survive and prosper. In contrast, during severe economic contractions, normally strong firms may find it very difficult to meet financial obligations. Therefore, historically there has been a strong cyclical pattern to rating changes: typically, downgrades increase during economic contractions and decline during economic expansions.

To use credit analysis as a bond management strategy, it is necessary to predict rating changes prior to the announcement by the rating agencies. This can be quite challenging because the market adjusts rather quickly to bond rating changes. You want to acquire bond issues expected to experience a rating upgrade and sell or avoid those bond issues expected to be downgraded.

Credit Analysis of High-Yield (Junk) Bonds A good opportunity for credit analysis involves high-yield (junk) bonds. The yield differential between junk bonds that are rated below BBB and Treasury securities ranges from about 250 basis points to over 1,500 basis points. Notably, this yield differential has varied substantially over time, as shown by a time-series plot in Exhibit 13.14. Specifically, the average yield spread ranged from less than 300 basis points in 1985, 1997, and 2014 to a high of almost 1,550 basis points during late 2008.

Although spreads have changed, Mody and Taylor (2003) showed that the average credit quality of high-yield bonds also changed over time, as indicated by interest coverage changes over the business cycle. Also, the credit quality of bonds *within* rating categories changed over the business cycle, as demonstrated by Reilly, Wright, and Gentry (2009). These credit quality changes make analysis of high-yield bonds more important, but it also becomes more difficult to select bonds that will survive. Given the spread in promised yields, Vine (2001) notes that if a portfolio manager can avoid bonds with a high probability of default or downgrade, high-yield bonds will provide substantial risk-adjusted returns.

Exhibit 13.15 lists the cumulative average default rates for bonds with different ratings and for various time periods after issue. Over 10 years—the holding period often used in practice for comparative purposes—the default rate for BBB investment-grade bonds is only 3.76 percent, but the default rate increases to over 13 percent for BB-rated bonds, to over 25 percent for B-rated bonds, and to over 51 percent for CCC-rated bonds. These default rates do not

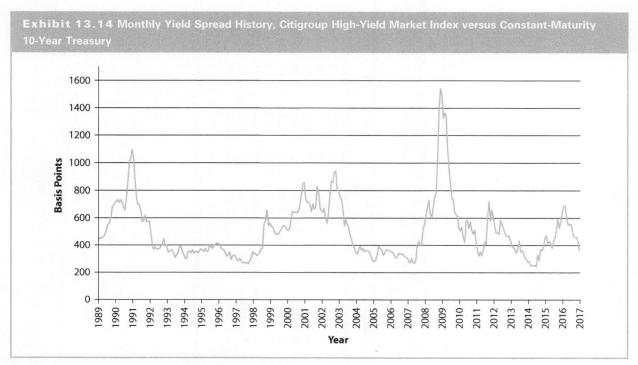

Exhibit 13.14 Monthly Yield Spread History, Citigroup High-Yield Market Index versus Constant-Maturity 10-Year Treasury

Source: Author calculations from Federal Reserve Board and index data.

Exhibit 13.15 Cumulative Average Default Rates for Corporate Bonds: 1981–2016 (%)

Rating	1	2	3	4	5	6	7	8	9	10	11	12	13	14	15
															—Time horizon (years)—
AAA	0.00	0.03	0.13	0.24	0.35	0.46	0.52	0.60	0.66	**0.72**	0.75	0.78	0.81	0.88	0.94
AA	0.02	0.06	0.13	0.23	0.33	0.44	0.54	0.62	0.69	**0.77**	0.85	0.91	0.98	1.05	1.11
A	0.06	0.15	0.25	0.38	0.53	0.69	0.88	1.05	1.23	**1.41**	1.57	1.73	1.89	2.03	2.20
BBB	0.18	0.51	0.88	1.33	1.78	2.24	2.63	3.01	3.39	**3.76**	4.16	4.48	4.79	5.10	5.43
BB	0.72	2.24	4.02	5.80	7.45	8.97	10.26	11.41	12.42	**13.33**	14.06	14.71	15.29	15.80	16.34
B	3.76	8.56	12.66	15.87	18.32	20.32	21.96	23.23	24.37	**25.43**	26.34	27.03	27.64	28.21	28.80
CCC/C	26.78	35.88	40.96	44.06	46.42	47.38	48.56	49.52	50.38	**51.03**	51.55	52.10	52.81	53.37	53.37
Investment grade	0.10	0.27	0.46	0.71	0.96	1.21	1.45	1.67	1.89	2.11	2.33	2.51	2.69	2.86	3.05
Speculative grade	3.83	7.48	10.63	13.20	15.29	17.01	18.45	19.65	20.71	21.67	22.47	23.13	23.73	24.27	24.80
All rated	1.52	2.99	4.27	5.35	6.25	7.02	7.67	8.22	8.72	9.18	9.58	9.91	10.22	10.50	10.78

Source: Adapted from *2016 Annual Global Corporate Default Study and Rating Transitions* (New York: Standard & Poor's, April 13, 2017): pp. 61–62. Reprinted with permission.

mean that investors should avoid high-yield bonds, but they do indicate that extensive credit analysis is a critical component for success within this risky sector of the fixed-income market.

Credit Analysis Models The credit analysis of high-yield bonds can use statistical or fundamental analysis that recognizes some of the unique characteristics of these bonds. Altman and Nammacher (1987) suggest that a modified *Z-score model* designed to predict the probability of bankruptcy within two years can also be used to predict changes in credit quality for these high-yield bonds. The Z-score model combines traditional financial measures with a multivariate technique known as *multiple discriminant analysis* to derive a set of weights for the specified variables. The result is an overall credit score (Z) for each firm. The model is of the form:

13.9
$$Z = a_0 + a_1X_1 + a_2X_2 + a_3X_3 + \cdots + a_nX_n$$

where:

$\qquad Z$ = overall credit score
$X_1 \ldots X_n$ = explanatory variables (for example, financial ratios and market measures)
$\quad a_0 \ldots a_n$ = weightings or coefficients

The specific model used in the analysis included seven financial measures:

X_1 = profitability: earnings before interest and taxes (EBIT)/total assets (TA)
X_2 = stability of profitability measure: the standard error of estimate of EBIT/TA
$\qquad$ (normalized for 10 years)
X_3 = debt service capabilities (interest coverage): EBIT/interest charges
X_4 = cumulative profitability: retained earnings/total assets
X_5 = liquidity: current assets/current liabilities
X_6 = capitalization levels: market value of equity/total capital (five-year average)
X_7 = size: total tangible assets (normalized)

As an example of this process, Exhibit 13.16 illustrates the Z-score calculations for two companies as of July 2017: Ford Motors (Baa2 rating), a multinational automobile manufacturer, and Kronos Worldwide (B1), a specialty chemical producer. Z-scores typically range from −5.0 to +20.0, with higher scores (above +3.0) indicating that bankruptcy over the next two years is unlikely, while lower scores (below +1.8) suggest an increased potential for business failure. In this case, Kronos's Z-score shows that it is in stronger financial condition than Ford (+2.26 versus +1.02), despite having the lower bond credit rating. It is important to note, however, that these scores are best interpreted as they change over time, rather than as a single observation. The charts at the bottom of each panel of Exhibit 13.16 show that both companies' Z-scores have improved since the stock market crisis in late 2008.[3] Active bond managers following a credit analysis strategy might use this as a tool to help predict rating upgrades and downgrades before they occur.

In contrast to using a model that provides a composite credit score, many analysts simply adapt their basic corporate bond analysis techniques to the unique needs of high-yield bonds, which have characteristics of common stock as shown by Reilly and Wright (1994). Fridson, Fabozzi, and Cohen (2012) suggest that the analysis of high-yield bonds is the same as for any bond with the following expansions:

1. What is the firm's *competitive position* in terms of cost and pricing?
2. What is the firm's *cash flow* relative to cash requirements for interest, research, growth, and periods of economic decline? Also, what is the firm's *borrowing capacity* that can serve as a safety net and provide flexibility?

---

[3]Exhibit 13.16 also reports a *double prime Z-score* for each company, which is just a modification of the Z-score that uses fewer of the financial measures described earlier.

Exhibit 13.16 Altman's *Z*-Score Analysis

A. Ford Motor

Ford Motor Co - F US Equity		Altman's Z-Score Model
Financial Data Input		
Fiscal Period	2016 A	User Input
Tangible Assets	237,753	237753.00
Working Capital	18,180	18180.00
Retained Earnings	15,634	15634.00
Earnings Before Int & Taxes	4,116	4116.00
Market Value of Equity	48,201.16	48201.16
Total Liabilities	208,668	208668.00
Sales to Tangible Assets	0.64	0.64
Total Shareholders' Equity	29,283	29283.00
Financial Health Assessment and Outlook		
Altman's Z-score	1.02	1.02
Altman's Double Prime Z-score	0.98	0.98
Z-score History		

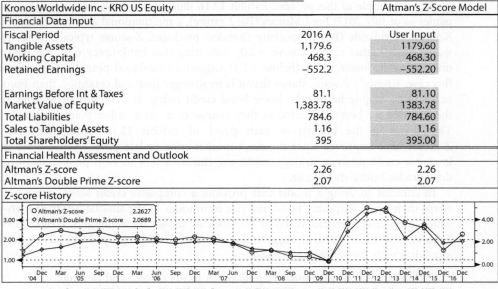

| | O Altman's Z-score | 1.018 |
| | ◇ Altman's Double Prime Z-score | 0.9797 |

Australia   61 2 9777 8600   Brazil   5511 2395 9000   Europe 44 20 7330 7500   Germany 49 69 9204 1210   Hong Kong 852 2977 6000
Japan 81 3 3201 8900   Singapore   65 6212 1000   U.S. 1 212 318 2000   Copyright 2017 Bloomberg Finance L.P.
SN 335716 CDT   GMT-5:00 G564-3716-0 19-Jul-2017 12:09:08

B. Kronos Worldwide

Kronos Worldwide Inc - KRO US Equity		Altman's Z-Score Model
Financial Data Input		
Fiscal Period	2016 A	User Input
Tangible Assets	1,179.6	1179.60
Working Capital	468.3	468.30
Retained Earnings	−552.2	−552.20
Earnings Before Int & Taxes	81.1	81.10
Market Value of Equity	1,383.78	1383.78
Total Liabilities	784.6	784.60
Sales to Tangible Assets	1.16	1.16
Total Shareholders' Equity	395	395.00
Financial Health Assessment and Outlook		
Altman's Z-score	2.26	2.26
Altman's Double Prime Z-score	2.07	2.07
Z-score History		

| O Altman's Z-score | 2.2627 |
| ◇ Altman's Double Prime Z-score | 2.0689 |

Australia   61 2 9777 8600   Brazil   5511 2395 9000   Europe 44 20 7330 7500   Germany 49 69 9204 1210   Hong Kong 852 2977 6000
Japan 81 3 3201 8900   Singapore   65 6212 1000   U.S. 1 212 318 2000   Copyright 2017 Bloomberg Finance L.P.
SN 335716 CDT   GMT-5:00 G564-3716-0 19-Jul-2017 12:09:34

3. What is the *liquidity value of the firm's assets?* Are these assets available for liquidation (are there any claims against them)?
4. How good is the *total management team?* Is the management team committed to and capable of operating in the high-risk environment of this firm?
5. What is the firm's *financial leverage* on an absolute basis and on a market-adjusted basis (using market value of equity and debt)?

In addition to the potentially higher financial risks, Sondhi (1995) points out an increase in business risk may exist if the firm sells off some operations that have favorable risk characteristics, such as a division that has low correlation of earnings with other units of the firm. Further, a change in management operating philosophy could have a negative impact on earnings. Asset divestiture plans often are a major element of a leveraged buyout and so it is important to examine the liquidity of the assets, their estimated selling values, and the timing of these programs. Finally, it is necessary to constantly monitor the firm's refinancing flexibility.

13.4.3 Implementing an Active Bond Transaction

Once a bond manager has decided on the specifics of an active strategy, the next step is to create a portfolio (or alter an existing one) to take advantage of that view. A popular approach for implementing these adjustments involves the use of **bond swaps**, which entail liquidating a current position and simultaneously buying a different issue with similar attributes but better return potential. These trades can be executed to increase current yield, to increase yield to maturity, to take advantage of shifts in interest rates or yield spreads, to improve the quality of a portfolio, or for tax purposes. All swaps have one basic purpose: portfolio improvement. In fact, Boyd and Mercer (2010) demonstrate that these trades lead to a substantial improvement in risk-adjusted performance relative to standard bond benchmarks.

Most bond swaps involve several different types of risk. One obvious risk is that interest rates may move up over the holding period and cause you to incur a loss. Alternatively, yield spreads may fail to respond as anticipated. Possibly the new bond may not be a true substitute and so, even if your expectations and interest rate formulations are correct, the swap may be unsatisfactory. Finally, if the work-out time is longer than anticipated, the realized yield might be less than expected.

As an example of this sort of transaction, the *pure yield pickup swap* involves trading out of a low-coupon bond into a comparable higher-coupon bond to realize an instantaneous increase in current yield and yield to maturity. An example would be an investor who currently holds a 30-year, AA-rated 10 percent issue that is trading at an 11.50 percent yield. Assume that a comparable 30-year, AA-rated obligation bearing a 12 percent coupon priced to yield 12 percent becomes available. The investor would report (and realize) some book loss if the original issue was bought at par but is able to improve current yield and yield to maturity simultaneously if the new obligation is held to maturity, as shown in Exhibit 13.17.

The investor need not predict rate changes, and the swap is not based on any imbalance in yield spreads. The object simply is to seek higher yields. Quality and maturity stay the same as do all other factors *except coupon.* The major risk is that future reinvestment rates may be lower than anticipated, meaning the total terminal value of the investment may not be as high as expected. This reinvestment risk can be evaluated by analyzing the results with a number of alternative scenarios to determine the minimum reinvestment rate that would make the swap viable.

13.4.4 Active Global Bond Investing: An Example

An active approach to global fixed-income management must consider three interrelated factors: (1) the local economy in each country that includes the effect of domestic and international demand, (2) the impact of this total demand and domestic monetary policy on

---

Exhibit 13.17 A Pure Yield Pickup Swap

Pure yield pickup swap: A bond swap involving a switch—from a low-coupon bond to a higher-coupon bond of similar quality and maturity—in order to pick up a higher current yield and a better yield to maturity.

Example: Currently hold: 30-year, 10.0% coupon priced at 874.12 to yield 11.5%

Swap candidate: 30-year, AA 12% coupon priced at $1,000 to yield 12.0%

	Current Bond	Candidate Bond
Dollar investment	$874.12	$1,000.00[a]
Coupon	100.00	120.00
i on one coupon (12.0% for 6 months)	3.000	3.600
Principal value at year end	874.66	1,000.00
Total accrued	977.66	1,123.60
Realized compound yield	11.514%	12.0%

Value of swap: 48.6 basis points in one year (assuming a 12.0% reinvestment rate)

The rewards for a pure yield pickup swap are automatic and instantaneous in that both a higher-coupon yield and a higher yield to maturity are realized from the swap. Other advantages include:

1. No specific work-out period needed because the investor is assumed to hold the new bond to maturity
2. No need for interest rate speculation
3. No need to analyze prices for overvaluation or undervaluation

A major disadvantage of the pure yield pickup swap is the book loss involved in the swap. In this example, if the current bond were bought at par, the book loss would be $125.88 ($1,000 − 874.12). Other risks involved in the pure yield pickup swap include:

1. Increased risk of call in the event interest rates decline
2. Greater reinvestment risk with higher-coupon bonds

[a]Obviously, the investor can invest $874.12—the amount obtained from the sale of the bond currently held—and still obtain a realized compound yield of 12.0%. Swap evaluation procedure is patterned after a technique suggested by Sidney Homer and Martin L. Leibowitz.

Source: Adapted from Sidney Homer and Martin L. Leibowitz, *Inside the Yield Book* (Englewood Cliffs, NJ: Prentice Hall, 1972).

---

inflation and interest rates, and (3) the effect of the economy, inflation, and interest rates on the exchange rates among countries.[4] Based on the evaluation of these factors, a portfolio manager must decide on the relative weight for each country and, possibly, the allocation within each country among government, municipal, and corporate bonds. In the example that follows, most portfolio recommendations concentrate on the country allocation and do not become more specific except in the case of the United States.

Exhibit 13.18 is from UBS Global Asset Management, a global institutional asset manager. The table's "Benchmark" column indicates what the asset allocation would be if UBS had no opinion regarding the expected bond market performance in the alternative countries. In most cases, the normal allocation is based on the country's relative market value. Specifically, the normal allocation is 20.1 percent for the United States, 29.0 percent for Japan, and the remaining 50.9 percent for the other countries, including 40.0 percent for the combined EMU countries. Clearly, UBS *does* have an opinion regarding these countries (as shown in its implied *market strategy*, which equals the benchmark percentage plus or minus the over/underweight percentage). For example, at this point in time, it overweighted the EMU block of countries bond markets with a market strategy allocation of 42.9 percent (versus the benchmark allocation of 40.0 percent) and underweighted the U.K. bond market with a market strategy

---

[4]For a detailed discussion of the benefits of international bond investing, see Malvey (2012) and Nemerever (2010).

Exhibit 13.18 UBS Global Bond Portfolio Strategy

Market Allocation

	GLOBAL		GLOBAL (Ex-US)	
	Benchmark	Over/Under Weight	Benchmark	Over/Under Weight
North America	22.0%	−0.3%	2.4%	0.0%
Canada	1.9	0.0	2.4	0.0
US	20.1	−0.3	0.0	0.0
EMU	40.0	2.9	50.1	3.5
Other Europe (Ex-UK)	3.3	−2.4	4.2	−3.1
Denmark	0.8	−0.8	1.0	−1.0
Norway	0.2	−0.2	0.3	−0.3
Poland	0.6	−0.6	0.7	−0.7
Sweden	0.9	0.0	1.1	0.0
Switzerland	0.8	−0.8	1.0	−1.0
UK	5.0	−2.0	6.2	−2.2
Japan	29.0	0.0	36.3	0.0
Australia	0.3	2.0	0.4	2.0
Singapore	0.2	−0.2	0.3	−0.3
	100.0%		100.0%	

	Europe (EMU)	
	Benchmark	Over/Under Weight
Austria	3.6%	6.7%
Belgium	7.0	−3.3
Finland	1.5	5.6
France	20.7	1.2
Germany	23.0	18.2
Greece	4.6	−4.6
Ireland	1.0	−1.0
Italy	22.7	−11.5
Netherlands	5.6	−0.8
Portugal	1.8	−1.9
Spain	8.5	−8.5
	100.0%	

Currency Allocation

	GLOBAL		GLOBAL (Ex-US)	
	Benchmark	Over/Under Weight	Benchmark	Over/Under Weight
North America	22.0%	0.0%	2.4%	0.0%
Canada	1.9	0.0	2.4	0.0
US	20.1	0.0	0.0	0.0
EMU	40.0	0.0	50.1	0.0
Other Europe (Ex-UK)	3.3	0.0	4.2	0.0
Denmark	0.8	0.0	1.0	0.0
Norway	0.2	0.0	0.3	0.0
Poland	0.6	0.0	0.7	0.0
Sweden	0.9	0.0	1.1	0.0
Switzerland	0.8	0.0	1.0	0.0
UK	5.0	−4.0	6.2	−4.0
Japan	29.0	2.0	36.3	2.0
Australia	0.3	0.0	0.4	0.0
Singapore	0.2	2.0	0.3	2.0
	100.0%		100.0%	

Totals may not add to 100% due to rounding.

Source: UBS Global Asset Management, *Quarterly Investment Strategy*, March 31, 2005 (Chicago, IL: UBS Global Asset Management).

allocation of only 3 percent (versus the benchmark of 5 percent). Another country over-weighted was Australia, while several were underweighted, including Denmark, Norway, Poland, and Switzerland. In addition, UBS does a specific currency allocation between countries, which would be based on the normal policy weight unless the firm had an opinion on currencies. Again, UBS has an opinion: It heavily underweighted the U.K. pound and over-weighted the currencies of Japan and Singapore.

13.5 CORE-PLUS MANAGEMENT STRATEGIES

Beyond a pure passive strategy or any of the active management strategies we have just seen, there has been increased interest recently among professional bond investors in a management approach that combines the two styles. **Core-plus** bond portfolio management places a significant part (70 to 80 percent) of the available funds in a passively managed portfolio of high-grade securities that broadly reflects the overall bond market; this is the "core" of the strategy. The remainder of the funds are managed actively in the "plus" portion of the portfolio, using the manager's selection skills to offer a higher probability of achieving positive abnormal returns.

The core portion of a portfolio following this combination approach is effectively managed as an index fund based on the belief that the designated core sectors of the bond market are efficient. Examples of market sectors that are often included in this definition include the U.S. broad market sector or the U.S. government/corporate sector, both of which have been dominated historically by issues that carry a credit rating of AAA or higher. (The difference between these two core sectors is that the former includes the rapidly growing markets for mortgage-backed and asset-backed bonds.) The plus sectors included in the portfolio consist of those segments of the global bond market that are regarded as being less efficient and therefore more likely to be sources of alpha in the managed portfolio. This would include high-yield bonds, non-U.S. bonds from developed countries, and emerging market debt.

A core-plus approach to bond management can also be considered a form of **enhanced indexing**, depending on how much of the portfolio is placed in the core portion and how actively the plus sectors are managed. As Davidson (2001) points out, the core-plus bond manager attempts to combine a substantial beta investment—that is, the funds invested to mimic the systematic risk exposure of the benchmark index—with the alpha potential associated with selecting bonds from the actively managed sectors. Thus, an important feature of a potential security position coming from the plus sectors is that it has the possibility of delivering high risk-adjusted returns over time that are not driven by systematic movements in the general bond market. High-yield bonds are a good example of a plus sector since they tend to have very high standard deviations that make them equivalent to equity investments in many respects, but have very low correlations (0.30 or lower) with the investment-grade bond sector.

Relative to a passive index strategy, a core-plus approach to managing a bond portfolio offers three potential advantages: (1) higher returns from exploiting market inefficiencies outside the traditional core sectors, (2) increased opportunities for exploiting the manager's security selection skills, and (3) the ability to alter the composition of the fixed-income asset class in a manner consistent with the insights and views of the manager. The incremental risk that the core-plus approach introduces into the passive portfolio can be particularly significant in no-growth or declining-growth economic scenarios, since much of the plus investing is likely to be in lower credit-grade instruments whose market values will be most affected under those circumstances. Further, there are other risks associated with investments in the plus sectors—such as prepayment and liquidity risks—that are not as prevalent in the core portion of the portfolio.

Hersey (2001) analyzed the composition and investment mandates for a broad sample of core and core-plus portfolios managed by leading U.S.-based fixed-income investment organizations.

Exhibit 13.19 Characteristics of Core and Core-Plus Investments

A. Typical Portfolio Composition

Sector	Core	Core-Plus	Barclays U.S. Aggregate
Treasury/Agency	22%	19%	42%
Mortgage backed	37	36	36
Asset backed	10	8	1
Investment grade Corporate	27	21	21
High yield	1	7	N/A
Eurodollar	1	5	N/A
Other	2	3	N/A

Note: N/A = not applicable

B. Investment Mandates

Characteristic	Core	Core-Plus
Benchmark excess return target	35–70 bp	100–125 bp
Tracking error	75–100 bp	125–150 bp
Consensus benchmark	Barclays U.S. Aggregate	Barclays U.S. Aggregate
Nonbenchmark exposures	0% (5% common)	15–40%
Management-fee differential	—	About a 10% premium over core

Note: bp = basis points

Source: Adapted from Brian E. Hersey, "Core-Plus: Prospects and Implications," in *Core-Plus Bond Management* (Charlottesville, VA: AIMR), 2001.

Exhibit 13.19 summarizes these findings. While both core and core-plus managers are given some investment latitude relative to the index—the Barclays U.S. Aggregate was the benchmark for the majority of these managers—the plus sectors were given substantially more. For instance, while core portfolios are allowed to hold an average of 5 percent of its positions in non-benchmark exposures, core-plus managers can maintain 15 to 40 percent. Although the index contained no high-yield positions, the typical core-plus portfolio invested 7 percent in this bond market segment. Both core and core-plus portfolios also contained larger allocations in asset-backed bonds than the index. However, it is also important to note that core-plus managers face strict constraints on their ability to take on additional risk in the pursuit of these abnormal returns. Panel B of Exhibit 13.19 shows that core-plus portfolios are expected to produce excess returns of 100 to 125 basis points while maintaining tracking errors that do not exceed 1.50 percent.

13.6 MATCHED-FUNDING MANAGEMENT STRATEGIES

The goal for many participants in the bond market is simply to increase the wealth of their overall portfolios while providing risk diversification benefits across asset classes. For these investors, the passive, active, and core-plus strategies are all potentially appropriate management styles. Other investors, however, face a more precise investment problem in which a specific set of liabilities needs to be met. For instance, life insurance companies have a series of future cash flow payments they are obligated to make, which they can predict in advance with a reasonable degree of accuracy given their actuarial forecasts. Defined-benefit pension funds can also predict fairly precisely the future retirement benefits they will be required to pay to their constituents. For investors in these situations, bond portfolios should take into account the nature of the liabilities that those assets are intended to fund.

Matched-funding strategies are a form of **asset-liability management** whereby the characteristics of the bonds held in the portfolio are coordinated with those of the liabilities the investor is obligated to pay. These matching techniques can range from an attempt to exactly match the levels and timing of the required cash payments to more general approaches that focus on other investment characteristics, such as setting the average duration or investment horizon of the bond portfolio equal to that of the underlying liabilities. An important assumption underlying all matched-funding techniques is that the investor's liabilities are predictable with some degree of precision. As long as the fixed-income manager knows the obligations he faces, he can create a portfolio specifically designed to meet those needs in an optimal way.

13.6.1 Dedicated Portfolios

Dedication refers to bond portfolio management techniques that are used to service a prescribed set of liabilities. We will discuss two alternatives. Using a **pure cash-matched dedicated portfolio** is the most conservative strategy. The objective of pure cash matching is to develop a portfolio of bonds that will provide a stream of payments from coupons and principal payments that exactly match the specified liability schedules. An example of typical liability stream for a pension system is shown in Exhibit 13.20. The goal is to build a portfolio that will generate sufficient funds in advance of each scheduled payment. One alternative is to find a number of zero-coupon Treasury securities that will exactly match each liability. Such an exact cash-match portfolio is referred to as a *total passive* portfolio because it is designed so that any prior receipts would not be reinvested (that is, it assumes a zero reinvestment rate).

Dedication with reinvestment is similar to the pure cash-matched technique except that it allows that the bond cash flows do not have to exactly match the liability stream. Any inflows that precede liability claims can be reinvested at some reasonably conservative rate. This assumption lets the portfolio manager consider a wider set of bonds that may have higher

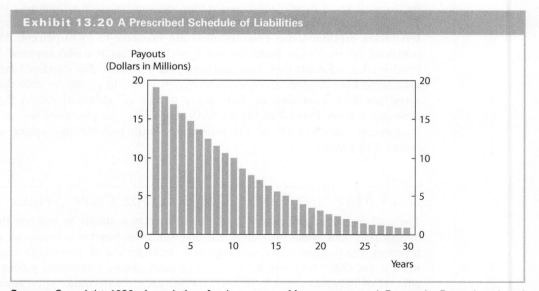

Exhibit 13.20 A Prescribed Schedule of Liabilities

return characteristics. In addition, the assumption of reinvestment within each period and between periods also will generate a higher return for the asset portfolio. As a result, the net cost of the portfolio will be lower with almost equal safety, assuming the reinvestment rate assumption is conservative. An example would be to assume a reinvestment rate of 4 percent in an environment where market interest rates are currently ranging from 5 to 7 percent.

Potential problems exist with both of these approaches to a dedicated portfolio. When selecting potential bonds for these portfolios, it is critical to be aware of call/prepayment possibilities with specific bonds or mortgage-backed securities. These prepayment possibilities become very important following periods of historically high rates. A good example is the period 1982–1986, when interest rates went from over 18 percent to under 8 percent. Because of this substantial change in rates, many dedicated portfolios were negatively affected when numerous bonds were called that were not expected to be refinanced under normal conditions. Obviously, the reinvestment of these proceeds at the lower rates caused many dedicated portfolios to be underfunded. Also, while quality is always a concern, it is probably not necessary to invest only in Treasury bonds if the portfolio is diversified across industries and sectors. A diversified portfolio of AA- or A-rated corporate bonds can provide a current and total annual return substantially above Treasuries, which can have a significant impact on the net cost of funding a liability stream.

13.6.2 Immunization Strategies

Instead of using a dedicated portfolio technique, a portfolio manager may decide that the optimal strategy is to *immunize* a portfolio against interest rate changes. Immunization techniques attempt to derive a specified rate of return (generally quite close to the current market yield) during a given investment horizon, regardless of what happens to the future level of interest rates.

Components of Interest Rate Risk A major problem encountered in bond portfolio management is deriving a given rate of return to satisfy an ending-wealth requirement at a future specific date—that is, the **investment horizon**. If the term structure of interest rates was flat and market rates never changed between the time of purchase and the horizon date when funds were required, you could acquire a bond with a term to maturity equal to the desired investment horizon, and the ending wealth from the bond would equal the expected wealth position implied by the promised yield to maturity. For example, assume you acquire a 10-year, $1 million bond with an 8 percent coupon at its par value. If the yield curve was flat with no changes, your wealth position at the end of your 10-year investment horizon (assuming semiannual compounding) would be:

$$\$1,000,000 \times (1.04)^{20} = \$2,191,123$$

You can get the same answer by taking the $40,000 interest payment every six months and compounding it semiannually to the end of the period at 4 percent and adding the $1,000,000 principal at maturity. Unfortunately, in the real world, the term structure of interest rates typically is not flat and the level of interest rates is constantly changing. Consequently, the bond portfolio manager faces **interest rate risk** between the time of investment and the future target date. Interest rate risk is the uncertainty regarding the ending-wealth value of the portfolio due to changes in market interest rates between the time of purchase and the investor's horizon date. This involves two components: **price risk** and **coupon reinvestment risk**.

Price risk occurs because if interest rates change before the horizon date and the bond is sold before maturity, the realized market price for the bond will differ from the *expected* price, assuming no change in rates. If rates increased after the time of purchase, the realized price for the bond in the secondary market would be below expectations, whereas if rates declined, the realized price for the bond would be above expectations. Because you do not know whether interest rates will increase or decrease, you are uncertain about the bond's future selling price.

Coupon reinvestment risk arises because the yield to maturity computation implicitly assumes that all coupon cash flows are reinvested at the promised yield to maturity. If, after the purchase of the bond, interest rates decline, the coupon cash flows will be reinvested at rates below the initial promised yield, and the ending wealth will be below expectations. If interest rates increase, the coupon cash flows will be reinvested at higher rates and the ending wealth will be above expectations.

Classical Immunization and Interest Rate Risk Fisher and Weil (1971) and Bierwag and Kaufman (1977) show that (1) price risk and reinvestment risk are affected inversely by a change in market rates, and (2) duration is the point in time when these two risks are of equal magnitude and offset each other. An increase in interest rates will cause an ending price below expectations, but the reinvestment rate for interim cash flows will be above expectations. A decline in market interest rates will cause the reverse situation. Clearly, a bond portfolio manager with a specific target date (investment horizon) will attempt to eliminate these two components of interest rate risk. The process intended to eliminate interest rate risk is referred to as **immunization** and was discussed by Redington (1952).

Fisher and Weil (1971) described immunization as follows:

A portfolio of investments in bonds is immunized for a holding period if its value at the end of the holding period, regardless of the course of interest rates during the holding period, must be at least as large as it would have been had the interest-rate function been constant throughout the holding period. [p. 411].

Source: Fisher, Lawrence, and Roman L. Weil. 1971. "Coping with the Risk of Interest-Rate Fluctuations: Returns to Bondholders from Naïve and Optimal Strategies." *Journal of Business 44*, no. 4 (October): 408–431.

They showed that it is possible to immunize a bond portfolio if you can assume that any change in interest rates will be the same for all maturities (that is, there is a parallel shift of the yield curve). Given this assumption, Fisher and Weil proved that *a portfolio of bonds is immunized from interest rate risk if the duration of the portfolio is always equal to the desired investment horizon.*

The authors simulated the effects of applying the immunization concept (a duration-matched strategy) compared to a naive portfolio strategy, where the portfolio's maturity was equal to the investment horizon. In a perfectly immunized portfolio, the actual ending wealth should equal the expected ending wealth implied by the promised yield. The duration-matched strategy results were consistently closer to the promised yield, but the results were not perfect because the basic assumption about rates always changing by the same amount did not always hold.

The Mechanics of Bond Immunization: A Simple Illustration[5] Suppose that an investor has a liability that she needs to pay off in exactly three years. Thus, her desired investment horizon is three years, which can also be considered as the duration of the liability she faces. Suppose also that the yield curve is currently flat at 10 percent but that it declines to 8 percent as soon as her initial investment is made. She considers four alternative bond investments to fund this liability:

(A) Purchase a 10-year bond paying a 9 percent annual coupon and sell it in three years
(B) Purchase three consecutive one-year "pure discount" (zero-coupon) bonds
(C) Purchase a three-year pure discount bond
(D) Purchase a four-year bond paying a 34.85 percent annual coupon and sell it in three years

---

[5]The authors gratefully acknowledge Professor Robert Radcliffe's contribution to this example.

Under these assumptions, the promised yield for each of these prospective investments is 10 percent at the time she makes her initial decision. So, the relevant question to consider is: What are the realized yields (RY) for all four positions at the end of her three-year investment horizon?

For *Bond A*, the initial investment (per $1,000 of face value) is:

$$P_0 = \sum_{t=1}^{10} \frac{90}{(1+.10)^t} + \frac{1000}{(1+.10)^{10}} = \$938.55$$

Since this position will not have matured by Year 3, it will have to be sold at the prevailing market rate (assumed to then be 8 percent). Also, she will be able to reinvest the coupons she receives prior to her planning horizon. Thus, the ending-wealth in this position is the combination of:

(1) Sale of bond:

$$P_3 = \sum_{t=1}^{7} \frac{90}{(1+.08)^t} + \frac{1000}{(1+.08)^7} = \$1052.06, \text{ and}$$

(2) Reinvested coupon payments:

$$90(1+.08)^2 + 90(1+.08) + 90 = \$292.18$$

or $1344.24. This means the investor's realized yield in Bond A would be:

$$RY_A = \sqrt[3]{\frac{1344.24}{938.55}} - 1 = 12.72\%$$

For *Bond B*, assume for simplicity that the bondholder invests $1,000 initially at 10 percent and then reinvests the total annual proceeds for two more years at 8 percent:

Year 1: $(1000.00)(1+.10) = \$1100.00$
Year 2: $(1100.00)(1+.08) = \$1188.00$
Year 3: $(1188.00)(1+.08) = \$1283.04$

Thus, her realized yield from this "rollover" strategy would be:

$$RY_B = \sqrt[3]{\frac{1283.04}{1000.00}} - 1 = 8.66\%$$

The initial purchase price of *Bond C* (per $1,000 face value) is:

$$P_0 = (1000) \div (1+.10)^3 = \$751.31$$

So, the realized yield would be:

$$RY_c = \sqrt[3]{\frac{1000.00}{751.31}} - 1 = 10.00\%$$

Finally, *Bond D* is similar to Bond A in that it must be sold prior to maturity and its coupons must be reinvested. The initial price for this security is:

$$P_0 = \sum_{t=1}^{4} \frac{348.50}{(1+.10)^t} + \frac{1000}{(1+.10)^4} = \$1787.71$$

The ending-wealth level in Year 3 combines:

(1) Sale of bond:

$$P_3 = (1000 + 348.50) \div (1+.08) = \$1248.61, \text{ and}$$

(2) Coupon payments:

$$348.50(1 + .08)^2 + 348.50(1 + .08) + 348.50 = \$1131.37$$

or $2379.98 and, thus, the realized yield would be:

$$RY_D = \sqrt[3]{\frac{2379.98}{1787.71}} - 1 = 10.00\%$$

Notice that only for Bonds C and D does the yield to maturity at the time of the original investment decision (that is, the *promised* or *expected* return) equal the *actual* rate of return over the three-year investment horizon. To see why this is the case, it is easy to confirm that the duration statistics for each of these bonds are:

> Bond A: 6.89 years
> Bond B: 1.00 year (per bond)
> Bond C: 3.00 years
> Bond D: 3.00 years

Because the investor's planning horizon is three years, the only bonds that produce the expected yield of 10 percent are the two that have durations of three years. Put another way, by investing in a bond that pays out the "average" cash flow at precisely the time it is desired, it is possible to completely offset interest rate risk. If yields fall (rise) after purchase, the bond price will rise (fall) by exactly enough to offset the decline (increase) in income from reinvested coupons. Once again, this is *immunization*.

On the other hand, when the investor tries to fund a three-year liability with a longer-duration bond (that is, Bond A), she has to sell the bond to get her cash out of the position. This results in a situation where the price risk component dominates the reinvestment risk component (that is, *net price risk*). This produces a higher actual return than she is promised (12.72 percent versus 10 percent) because rates in the market have fallen, which benefits the bond's price more than it hurts coupon reinvestment potential. Conversely, when she tries to fund the three-year liability with a series of shorter-duration positions (that is, Bond B), she receives her cash back sooner than she needs it and therefore faces a *net reinvestment risk* problem, which in this case leads to a lower realized yield. The important point here is that with either Bond A or Bond B, the investor faces uncertainty over the ultimate outcome of her investment.

In summary, given that bond risk caused by changing interest rates can be split into price risk and reinvestment risk, the following general statements can be made:

> If *duration* > *investment horizon*, the investor faces *net price risk* (Bond A).
> If *duration* < *investment horizon*, the investor faces *net reinvestment risk* (Bond B).
> If *duration* = *investment horizon*, the investor is *immunized* (Bonds C and D).

Finally, it should be noted that setting the duration of an asset equal to the duration of the liability (that is, investment horizon) will just immunize an investment against the *next* interest rate movement. However, the position will remain immunized to subsequent yield changes as long as it is rebalanced promptly.

Application of Classical Immunization Stonewall Insurance Ltd. (a pseudonym for a real company) is a property and casualty insurance firm that operates as an offshore subsidiary of a construction firm based in the United States. Stonewall's primary function is to provide worker's compensation insurance benefits to the employees of the parent firm. Although the construction firm has an excellent safety record, there are nevertheless occasional worksite accidents that require payment of compensation benefits. These payments can last from a few months to several years; the parent firm conservatively plans for payments to continue an average of 3.50 to 4.50 years. Thus, the firm considers this to be the duration range of the potential liabilities (planning horizon) the company faces.

The uncertainty of both the size and length of the benefit claims makes the implementation of a cash-matched portfolio impractical. Their solution to this asset-liability management problem is to construct a bond portfolio that has a duration statistic (expressed in modified form) of around 4.00 years. Details of the specific securities they held as of June 2017 are shown in Exhibit 13.21. The portfolio holds 31 separate positions—mostly corporate bonds— with an aggregate market value of $28.6 million and an average credit grade of A1 (Moody's) and A+ (Standard & Poor's). More importantly, the portfolio has been assembled to have a modified duration of 3.99 years, which closely matches the target horizon period implied by their projected liabilities. Thus, the position is effectively immunized; an unexpected increase or decrease in interest rates at this point in time would have approximately equal and offsetting effects on the value of both Stonewall's assets and liabilities, leaving the firm's net worth unaffected by the rate movement.

This example also helps highlight some practical challenges an investor faces when designing an immunization strategy. First, because certain segments of the fixed-income market can be illiquid, there sometimes is a problem acquiring the bonds identified as the optimal positions for the portfolio. So, it may not be possible to find a combination of bonds that exactly produces the desired duration target. Second, except for the special case of a zero-coupon bond, an immunized portfolio will require frequent rebalancing. Even if market rates do not change, after a year has passed (June 2018), the modified duration of the bond portfolio will be substantially lower than 3.99 years. Of course, since the target investment horizon would still be 4.00 years, this decay in portfolio duration would leave the firm in a position of net reinvestment risk and therefore adversely exposed to a subsequent downward movement in the yield curve. Thus, to remain immunized over time, the bond manager for Stonewall will periodically need to rebalance the portfolio to maintain the original duration target.

Finally, the manager of an immunized bond portfolio should also pay attention to the convexity statistic of the position. Specifically, the manager should attempt to construct a bond portfolio that has *greater convexity* than the firm's liabilities. When the convexity of the assets exceeds that of the liabilities at a time when the durations are matched, the *actual* decline in value for an upward rate movement will be less severe for the assets than for the liabilities. Kritzman (1992) demonstrates that for two portfolios with the same duration, the one with cash flows that are more spread out (less concentrated around the duration date) will have greater convexity. Thus, the bond ladder approach adopted by Stonewall's managers (for example, maturity dates ranging from 2019 to 2026) is likely to produce a more successful outcome than a portfolio that concentrated its cash flow payments around June 2021 (the current date plus 4.00 years). In summary, it is important to recognize that classical immunization is generally *not* a passive strategy because it is subject to all of these practical issues that demand the attention of the manager.

13.6.3 Horizon Matching

Horizon matching is a combination of two of the techniques just discussed: cash-matching dedication and immunization. As shown in Exhibit 13.22, the liability stream is divided into two segments. In the first segment, the portfolio is constructed to provide a cash match for the liabilities during this horizon period (for example, the first 5 years). The second segment is the remaining liability stream following the end of the horizon period—in the example, it is the 25 years following 2018. During this second time period, the liabilities are covered by a duration-matched strategy based on immunization principles. As a result, Leibowitz (1986b)

Exhibit 13.21 Immunized Bond Portfolio of Stonewall Insurance Ltd., June 2017

Category	Sector	Issuer	Ticker Symbol	CUSIP	Maturity	Coupon	Call Date (Price)	Par Value (000s)	Bid Yield	Bid Price	Total Bond Value	Accrued Interest	Total Pos. Value	% of Ttl Position	Mod. Dur.	Convex	Moody Rating	S&P Rating
Agency: 12.62%	—	Federal Home Loan Bank	FHLB	3133XAS1	8/15/2019	5.125%	Not Callable	1000	1.494%	107.5748	$1,075,748.20	1.908	$1,094,824.59	3.825%	1.997	5.137	Aaa	AAA
		Federal Home Loan Bank	FHLB	3133MDYF4	2/15/2021	6.000%	Not Callable	1000	1.774%	114.7822	$1,147,821.66	2.233	$1,170,154.99	4.089%	3.247	12.900	Aaa	AAA
		Federal Farm Credit Bank	FFCB	31331H2S5	9/12/2025	6.890%	Not Callable	1000	2.478%	132.5629	$1,325,628.65	2.048	$1,346,107.26	4.703%	6.492	51.656	Aaa	AAA
Corporate: 87.38%	Aerospace:	Boeing	BA	097023BR5	6/15/2026	2.250%	MW (+10)	1000	2.652%	96.8118	$968,118.47	0.088	$968,993.47	3.386%	8.035	72.622	A2	A
	Basic Materials:	Dupont	DD	263534CK3	2/15/2023	2.800%	MW (+12.5)	750	2.583%	101.1281	$758,461.05	1.042	$766,277.72	2.677%	5.129	30.295	A3	A-
		Air Products & Chemicals	APD	009158AR7	11/3/2021	3.000%	MW (+12.5)	500	2.107%	103.6871	$518,435.58	0.467	$520,768.91	1.820%	4.051	19.051	A2	A
	Conglomerates:	Emerson Electric	EMR	291011BG8	6/1/2025	3.150%	MW (+15)	584	2.639%	103.6302	$605,200.59	0.245	$606,631.39	2.120%	6.983	55.841	A2	A
		General Dynamics	GD	369550AR9	7/15/2021	3.875%	MW (+25)	1000	2.019%	107.1727	$1,071,727.02	1.765	$1,089,379.80	3.806%	3.695	16.257	A2	A+
	Consumer-Products:	Procter & Gamble	PG	742718EG0	11/1/2019	1.900%	MW (+7.5)	500	1.669%	100.5269	$502,634.28	0.306	$504,164.84	1.762%	2.273	6.363	Aa3	AA-
		Anheuser Busch	ABIBB	035231BB3	2/15/2021	4.375%	MW (+20)	500	2.236%	107.4114	$537,057.02	1.628	$545,199.38	1.905%	3.317	13.242	A3	A-
	Consumer-Restaurants:	McDonald's	MCD	58013MEQ3	5/29/2019	1.875%	MW (+15)	1000	1.847%	100.0519	$1,000,518.92	0.156	$1,002,081.42	3.501%	1.872	4.462	Baa1	BBB+
	Consumer-Retail:	Costco	COST	22160KAK1	5/18/2022	2.300%	MW (+10)	1000	2.264%	100.1645	$1,001,644.98	0.262	$1,004,264.42	3.509%	4.586	24.015	A1	A+
		Target	TGT	239753BC9	7/1/2020	9.875%	Not Callable	500	2.622%	120.8312	$604,155.78	4.883	$628,568.97	2.196%	2.568	8.563	A2	A
		Wal-Mart Stores	WMT	931142CP6	2/1/2019	4.125%	Not Callable	1000	1.667%	103.8372	$1,038,372.04	1.696	$1,055,330.38	3.687%	1.518	3.121	Aa2	AA
	Energy:	Exxon Mobil	XOM	30231GAP72	3/1/2019	1.708%	MW (+12.5)	1000	1.580%	100.2097	$1,002,096.63	0.560	$1,007,695.08	3.521%	1.634	3.509	Aaa	AA+
		Baker Hughes	BHI	057224BC0	8/15/2021	3.200%	MW (+15)	1000	2.326%	103.4192	$1,034,192.21	1.191	$1,046,103.32	3.655%	3.816	17.125	Baa1	A
	Financial-Diversified:	General Electric Capital	GE	36164NFG5	11/15/2025	3.373%	MW (+20)	1000	2.791%	104.3189	$1,043,189.12	0.412	$1,047,311.68	3.659%	7.264	60.866	A1	AA-
	Financial-Global:	HSBC Bank	HSBC	404280AN9	3/30/2022	4.000%	Not Callable	1000	2.737%	105.5896	$1,055,895.70	0.989	$1,065,784.59	3.724%	4.289	21.616	A1	A+
		Goldman Sachs	GS	38148FAB5	10/23/2019	2.550%	Not Callable	500	2.128%	100.9474	$504,737.22	0.468	$507,074.72	1.772%	2.231	6.169	A3	BBB+
		JPMorgan	JPM	46625HHS2	7/22/2020	4.400%	Not Callable	500	2.226%	106.4031	$532,015.47	1.919	$541,609.91	1.892%	2.823	9.770	A3	A-
	Financial-Commercial:	Comerica Bank	CMA	200339DW6	6/2/2020	2.500%	Not Callable	1000	2.403%	100.2715	$1,002,714.56	0.188	$1,004,589.56	3.510%	2.800	9.381	A3	A
		Wells Fargo	WFC	94974BGM6	7/22/2020	2.600%	Not Callable	500	2.152%	101.3207	$506,603.53	1.134	$512,272.98	1.790%	2.902	10.119	A2	A
	Healthcare:	AstraZeneca	AZN	046353AK4	11/16/2020	2.375%	MW (+15)	1000	2.092%	100.9179	$1,009,178.99	0.284	$1,012,015.79	3.536%	3.227	12.250	A3	A-
		Bristol-Myers Squibb	BMY	110122AW8	11/1/2023	3.250%	MW (+15)	1000	2.484%	104.4649	$1,044,648.62	0.524	$1,049,884.73	3.668%	5.696	37.290	A2	A+
		Merck	MRK	589331AT4	9/15/2022	2.400%	MW (+12.5)	1000	2.122%	101.3637	$1,013,636.97	0.693	$1,020,570.31	3.566%	4.848	26.882	A1	AA
	Industrial Equipment:	Caterpillar	CAT	149123BF7	7/15/2017	6.625%	MW (+10)	1000	3.673%	100.1275	$1,001,274.58	3.018	$1,031,455.13	3.604%	0.044	0.023	A3	A
	Manufacturing-Tools:	Snap-On	SNA	833034AH4	9/1/2021	6.125%	MW (+37.55)	1000	2.144%	115.8039	$1,158,038.55	2.008	$1,178,114.94	4.116%	3.678	16.415	A2	A-
	Technology:	Intl. Business Machines	IBM	459200HP9	8/1/2023	3.375%	MW (+12.5)	1000	2.549%	104.6298	$1,046,297.68	1.388	$1,060,172.68	3.704%	5.428	34.237	A1	A+
		Oracle	ORCL	68389XAP0	10/15/2022	2.500%	MW (+12.5)	1000	2.246%	101.2580	$1,012,579.98	0.514	$1,017,718.87	3.556%	4.915	27.602	A1	A+
	Telecommunications:	Nippon TT	NTT	EJ623396	2/26/2020	2.150%	Not Callable	1000	2.140%	100.0245	$1,000,244.69	0.735	$1,007,590.53	3.521%	2.552	7.913	Aa3	AA-
		Indiana Bell	T	45461AL2	8/15/2026	7.300%	Not Callable	1000	4.829%	118.0592	$1,180,591.59	2.717	$1,207,763.81	4.220%	6.710	57.187	A3	A

Portfolio Summary

Number of Bond Issues	31
Total Portfolio Market Value	$28,620,476.16
Total Portfolio Par Value	$26,834,000.00
Wght. Avg. Bond Yield to Maturity	2.374%
Wght. Avg. Bond Coupon	3.907%
Portfolio Modified Duration	3.992
Portfolio Convexity	23.203
Wght. Avg. Moody's Rating	A1
Wght. Avg. S&P Rating	A+

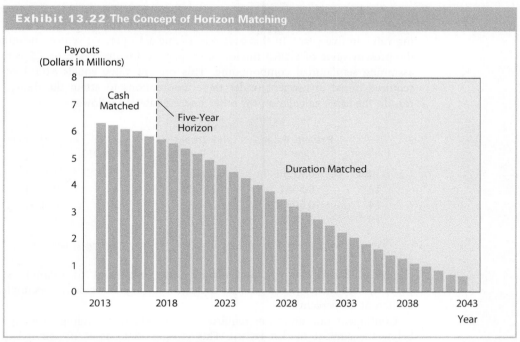

Exhibit 13.22 The Concept of Horizon Matching

Payouts (Dollars in Millions)

Cash Matched

Five-Year Horizon

Duration Matched

Source: "Horizon Matching: A New Generalized Approach for Developing Minimum Cost Dedicated Portfolios." Copyright 1983 Salomon Brothers Inc. This chart was prepared for Salomon Brothers Inc. by Martin Leibowitz, a former Managing Director; Thomas E. Klaffky, Managing Director; Steven Mandel, a former Managing Director; and Alfred Weinberger, a former Director. Although the information in this chart has been obtained from sources that Salomon Brothers Inc. believed to be reliable, SSB does not guarantee their accuracy, and such information may be incomplete or condensed. All figures included in this chart constitute SSB's judgment as of the original publication date. Reprinted with permission from Salomon Smith Barney.

contends that the client receives the certainty of cash matching during the early years and the cost saving and flexibility of duration-matched flows thereafter.

The combination technique also helps alleviate one of the problems with classical immunization: the potential for nonparallel shifts in the yield curve. Most of the problems related to nonparallel shifts are concentrated in the short end of the yield curve because this is where the most severe curve reshaping typically occurs. Because the near-term horizon is cash-matched, however, these irregular rate changes are not of concern. Leibowitz, Klaffky, Mandel, and Weinberger (1983) also point out that it also is possible to consider *rolling out* the cash-matched segment over time. Specifically, after the first year, the portfolio manager would restructure the portfolio to provide a cash match during the original Year 6, which would still have a five-year horizon. They note that the cost of rolling out depends on future rate movements.

13.7 CONTINGENT AND STRUCTURED MANAGEMENT STRATEGIES

Contingent procedures for managing bond portfolios are a form of what has come to be called structured active management. The specific contingent procedure we discuss here is *contingent immunization*, which Leibowitz and Weinberger (1982, 1983) describe as a strategy that allows the bond manager flexibility to actively manage the portfolio subject to an overriding constraint that the portfolio remains immunized at some predetermined yield level.

Consider an example of this process. Assume that your desired terminal wealth value is $206.3 million, and we want to determine how much you must invest today to attain that ending value in five years. In this case, we assume a 15 percent return, meaning that we compute the present value of $206.3 million at 15 percent for five years, or 7.5 percent for 10 periods, assuming semiannual compounding. This present value equals $100.1 million, which is the required initial investment under these assumptions to attain the desired ending value. We can do the same calculation for other interest rates as follows:

Percent	Present Value Factor[a]	Required Investment ($ millions)	Percent	Present Value Factor[a]	Required Investment ($ millions)
10%	0.6139	$126.65	16%	0.4632	$95.56
12	0.5584	115.20	18	0.4224	87.14
14	0.5083	104.87	20	0.3855	79.54
15	0.4852	100.10			

[a]Present value for 10 periods (5 years) at one-half the annual percentage rate.

Clearly, at lower yields, you need a larger initial investment (for example, $126.65 million at 10 percent), and this required amount declines with higher yields (for example, it is less than $80 million at 20 percent).

Contingent immunization requires that the client be willing to accept a potential return below the current market return. This is referred to as a *cushion spread*, or the difference between the current market return and some floor rate. This cushion spread in required yield provides flexibility for the portfolio manager to engage in active portfolio strategies. For example, if current market rates are 15 percent, the client might be willing to accept a floor rate of 14 percent. If we assume the client initiated the fund with $100.10 million, the acceptance of this lower rate will mean that the portfolio manager does not have the same ending-asset requirements. Specifically, at 14 percent the required ending-wealth value would be $196.72 million (7 percent per period for 10 periods) compared to the $206.3 million at 15 percent. Because of this lower floor rate (and lower ending-wealth value), it is possible to experience some declines in the value of the portfolio while attempting to do better than the market through active management strategies.

Exhibit 13.23 shows the value of assets that are required at the beginning, assuming a 14 percent required return and the implied ending-wealth value of $196.90 million. Assuming current market rates of 15 percent, the required value of assets at the beginning would be $95.54 million, which is the present value of $196.90 million at 15 percent for five years. The difference between the client's initial fund of $100.10 million and the required assets of $95.54 million is the dollar cushion available to the portfolio manager to manage actively. So, the manager effectively now has a $4.56 million (=100.10 − 95.54) "side fund" with which to pursue active management strategies in an attempt to add alpha to the overall portfolio.

With this side fund, the portfolio manager can engage in strategies to increase the ending-wealth value of the portfolio above that required at 14 percent. As an example, suppose the portfolio manager believes that market rates will decline and therefore acquires 30-year bonds that have a modified duration greater than the 5-year investment horizon. If rates decline as expected, the value of the long-duration portfolio will experience a rapid increase above the initial value. In contrast, if rates increase, the value of the portfolio will decline rapidly. In this case, depending on how high rates go, the value of the portfolio could decline to a value below that needed to reach the desired ending-wealth value of $196.90 million.

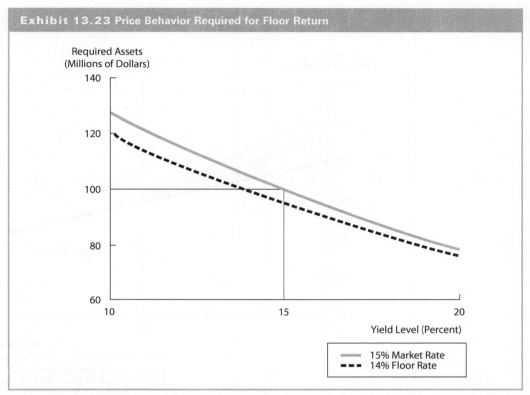

Exhibit 13.23 Price Behavior Required for Floor Return

Exhibit 13.24 shows what happens to the value of this portfolio if we assume an instantaneous yield change when the fund is established. Specifically, if rates decline from 15 percent, the portfolio of long-duration, 30-year bonds would experience a large increase in value and develop a *safety margin*—a portfolio value above the required value. In contrast, if rates increase, the value of the portfolio will decline until it reaches the asset value required at 14 percent. When the value of the portfolio reaches this point of minimum return (referred to as a *trigger point*), it is necessary to stop active portfolio management and use classical immunization with the remaining assets to ensure that you attain the desired terminal wealth value (that is, $196.90 million).

The concept of *potential return* is also helpful in understanding the objective of contingent immunization. This is the return the portfolio would achieve over the entire investment horizon if, at any point, the assets on hand were immunized at the prevailing market rate. Exhibit 13.25 contains the various potential rates of return based on dollar asset values shown in Exhibit 13.24. If the portfolio were immediately immunized when market rates were 15 percent, its potential return would naturally be 15 percent. Alternatively, if yields declined instantaneously to 10 percent, the portfolio's asset value would increase to $147 million, which if immunized at the market rate of 10 percent over the remaining five-year period, would grow to a total value of $239.45 million (= $147 million × 1.6289, which is the compound growth factor for 5 percent and 10 periods). This ending value of

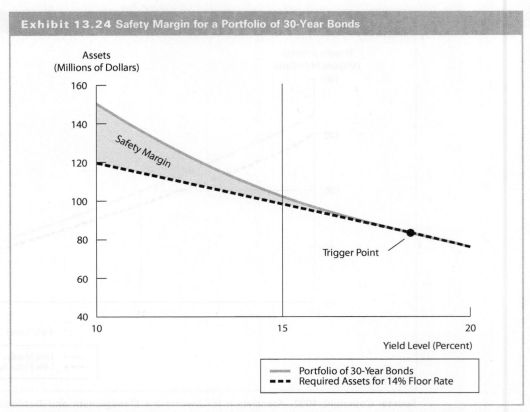

Exhibit 13.24 Safety Margin for a Portfolio of 30-Year Bonds

Legend:
- Portfolio of 30-Year Bonds
- Required Assets for 14% Floor Rate

$239.45 million represents an 18.23 percent realized (horizon) yield on the original $100.10 million portfolio.

In contrast, if interest rates increase, the value of the portfolio will decline substantially and the potential return will decline. For example, if market rates rise by 200 basis points to 17 percent, the asset value of the 30-year bond portfolio will decline to $88 million. If this portfolio of $88 million was then immunized for the remaining 5 years at the prevailing market rate of 17 percent, the terminal value would be $198.97 million. This ending value implies a potential return of 14.22 percent for the total period.

As Exhibit 13.24 shows, if interest rates rose to 18.50 percent, the 30-year bonds would decline to a value of $81.2 million (or, the trigger point) and the portfolio would have to be immunized. If this occurred, the value of the immunized portfolio would grow to $196.7 million (= $81.2 × 2.4222, which is the compound value factor for 9.25 percent for 10 periods). This ending value implies that a potential return for the portfolio of exactly 14 percent, the floor rate in the contingent immunization process. With proper monitoring, the investor will always know the trigger point at which the portfolio must be immunized to guarantee receiving no less than the minimum specified rate.

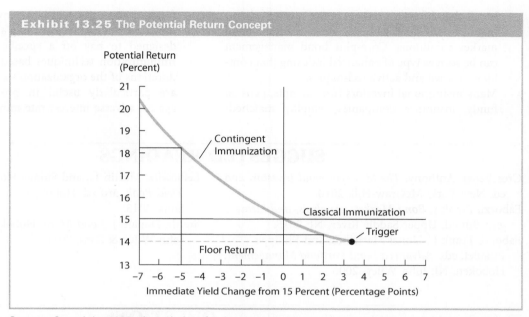

Exhibit 13.25 The Potential Return Concept

Source: Copyright 1982, Association for Investment Management and Research. Reproduced and republished from "Contingent Immunization—Part I: Risk Control Procedures" from the November/December 1982 issue of the *Financial Analysts Journal*, with permission from the CFA Institute. All Rights Reserved.

SUMMARY

- The analytical toolkit used by a bond portfolio manager extends well beyond basic valuation skills. In particular, it is important for a manager to understand how the overall value of her portfolio will change when there is a shift in the prevailing yield curve. The duration statistic, in both its original and modified forms, provides an estimate of how bond prices respond to changes in interest rates. Because modified duration provides a straight-line estimate of the curvilinear price–yield function, it was also important to consider the convexity of a bond for large changes in yields. Notably, an embedded call option feature on a bond can have a significant impact on its duration (the call feature can shorten it dramatically) and on its convexity. (The call feature can change the convexity from a positive value to a negative value.)

- A portfolio manager must also pay attention to implied forward rates, which can be viewed as breakeven rates when evaluating maturity choice investment strategies, and yield spreads for bonds with embedded options. To take account of the spread across the total term structure of interest rates, we demonstrated the static spread. In order to consider the impact of interest rate volatility on the embedded options, we described the steps to estimate the option-adjusted spread (OAS) for these bonds.

- During the past few decades, there has been a significant increase in the number and variety of bond portfolio strategies employed by individual investors and professional managers. These strategies, which range from being quite simple to quite complex to implement, can be classified into five separate categories: passive management techniques, active management techniques, core-plus management techniques, matched-funding techniques, and contingent and structured techniques.

- The most common passive approach to managing a bond portfolio is indexing, which constructs a portfolio that mimics the contents of a particular bond index. Conversely, active bond management strategies attempt to exceed the risk–return performance produced by a bond index over time. The active manager does this by assembling a collection of bonds that differs from those in the benchmark in a manner consistent with his view of future bond market conditions. Core-plus bond management can be seen as type of enhanced indexing that combines passive and active techniques.

- Many institutional investors (for example, pension funds, insurance companies) employ matched-

funding strategies when the investment problem they confront involves forming a portfolio of assets designed to pay off a specific set of liabilities. Immunization techniques based on matching the durations of the organization's assets and liabilities are particularly useful in providing protection against adverse interest rate movements.

SUGGESTED READINGS

Creschenzi, Anthony. *The Strategic Bond Investor*, 2nd ed. New York: McGraw-Hill, 2010.

Fabozzi, Frank J. *Bond Markets, Analysis, and Strategies*, 9th ed. Upper Saddle River, NJ: 2015.

Fabozzi, Frank J., Lionel Martellini, and Philippe Priaulet, eds. *Advanced Bond Portfolio Management*. Hoboken, NJ: John Wiley, 2006.

Leibowitz, Martin L., and Sidney Homer. *Inside the Yield Book*, 3rd ed. Hoboken, NJ: John Wiley & Sons, 2013.

Smith, Donald J. *Bond Math*. Hoboken, NJ: John Wiley & Sons, 2011.

QUESTIONS

1. You expect interest rates to decline over the next six months.
   a. Given your interest rate outlook, state what kinds of bonds you want in your portfolio in terms of duration and explain your reasoning for this choice.
   b. You must make a choice between the following three sets of noncallable bonds. For each set, select the bond that would be best for your portfolio, given your interest rate outlook and the consequent strategy set forth in part (a). In each case, briefly discuss why you selected the bond.

		Maturity (yrs)	Coupon (%)	Yield to Maturity (%)
Set 1:	Bond A	15	10%	10%
	Bond B	15	6	8
Set 2:	Bond C	15	6	10
	Bond D	10	8	10
Set 3:	Bond E	12	12	12
	Bond F	15	12	8

2. At the present time, you expect a decline in interest rates and must choose between two portfolios of bonds with the following characteristics:

	Portfolio A	Portfolio B
Average maturity	10.5 yrs	10.0 yrs
Average YTM	7%	10%
Modified duration	5.7 yrs	4.9 yrs
Convexity	125.18	40.30
Call features	Noncallable	Deferred call features that range from 1 to 3 years

Select one of the portfolios and discuss three factors that would justify your selection.

3. The Francesca Finance Corporation has issued a bond with the following characteristics:

   Maturity—25 years
   Coupon—9 percent
   Yield to maturity—9 percent
   Callable—after 3 years @ 109
   Duration to maturity—8.2 years
   Duration to first call—2.1 years

   a. Discuss the concept of call-adjusted duration, and indicate the approximate value (range) for it at the present time.
   b. Assuming interest rates increase substantially (that is, to 13 percent), discuss what will happen to the call-adjusted duration and the reason for the change.
   c. Assuming interest rates decline substantially (that is, they decline to 4 percent), discuss what will happen to the bond's call-adjusted duration and the reason for the change.
   d. Discuss the concept of negative convexity as it relates to this bond.

4. a. Explain the impact on *both* bond duration and convexity of adding a call feature to a proposed bond issue.
   Assume that a portfolio of corporate bonds is managed to maintain targets for modified duration and convexity.
   b. Explain how the portfolio could include *both* callable and noncallable bonds while maintaining the targets.
   c. Describe *one* advantage and *one* disadvantage of including callable bonds in this portfolio.

5. On May 30, 2018, Alessandra Burke is considering purchasing one of the newly issued 10-year AAA corporate bonds shown in the following exhibit. Alessandra notes that the yield curve is currently flat and assumes that the yield curve shifts in an instantaneous and parallel manner.

   Bond Characteristics

Description	Coupon	Price	Callable	Call Price
Sophie due May 30, 2028	6.00%	100.00	Noncallable	Not applicable
Celeste due May 30, 2028	6.20%	100.00	Currently callable	102.00

   a. Contrast the effect on the price of *both* bonds if yields decline more than 100 basis points. (No calculation is required).
   b. State and explain under which *two* interest rate forecasts Alessandra would prefer the Celeste bond over the Sophie bond.
   c. State the directional price change, if any, assuming interest rate volatility increases, for *each* of the following:

   (1) The Sophie bond
   (2) The Celeste bond

6. Bond index mutual funds and exchange-traded funds (ETFs) using bonds have become increasingly popular in recent years.
   a. Would it be more or less difficult to construct a bond index mutual fund than an equity index mutual fund? Give three reasons to support your argument.
   b. Would it be more or less difficult to maintain a bond index ETF than an equity index ETF? Give three reasons to support your argument.

7. After determining the appropriate asset allocation to meet Lucinda Kennedy's needs, Richard Bulloch, CFA, invests a portion of Kennedy's assets in two fixed-income investment funds:

Trinity Index Fund: A passively managed portfolio of global bonds designed to track the Barclays Global Aggregate Bond (LGAB) Index using a pure bond indexing strategy. The management fee is 15 basis points annually.

Montego Global Bond Fund: An actively managed portfolio of global bonds designed to outperform the LGAB net of fees. The management fee is 50 basis points annually.

Six months after investing in these funds, Kennedy and Bulloch review the following performance data:

Total Returns on Index and Funds
Index or Fund Six-Month Return
LGAB Index 3.21%
Trinity Index Fund* 3.66%
Montego Global Bond Fund* 3.02%
*Net of Fees

Kennedy makes the following statements regarding her fixed-income investments:

a. "The Trinity Index Fund is being managed well."
b. "I expected that, as an active manager, Montego would outperform the index; therefore, the fund should be sold."

Determine whether you agree or disagree with *each* of Kennedy's statements. Justify your response with *one* reason for *each* statement.

8. As a hedge fund specializing in locating attractively priced fixed-income instruments, Millennium Cerberus Fund is now reviewing its overall bond allocation strategy following the recent "liquidity squeeze" in the financial markets.

   a. Consider three classes of traditional fixed-income vehicles: Treasury bonds, high-grade corporate bonds, and low-grade corporate bonds. In "normal" market conditions, would you expect the liquidity of all these bond classes to be the same? What would you expect to happen to the liquidity of these bond classes during a credit crisis, such as the one we experienced in 2008?

   b. As an analyst for the fund, you note that the correlation of the rate of return between Treasury bills and high-grade corporate bonds is high (0.95), whereas the correlation between Treasury bills and high-yield (junk) bonds is relatively low (0.52). What are the reasons for the difference in correlations? How would such a disparity affect your bond portfolio allocation?

   c. "The duration of junk bonds is typically shorter than that of high-grade corporate bonds." Briefly defend or refute the validity of this statement and support your position.

9. As a bond portfolio manager, you try to read all of the written analysis you can regarding the current conditions of the financial markets. The following is an extract of a bond strategy briefing note issued by an investment bank:

   The recent fire sale puts excessive selling pressure on high-grade corporate bonds. The fear of systemic risk over the banking system and of the increasing default risk in junk bonds provides an unprecedented opportunity under which yield spreads have widened to extremely attractive levels. We recommend that our clients reduce their portfolio weights in U.S. Treasuries and increase their positions in AA- and A-rated bonds with coupon rates between 7–9% as part of its core strategic reallocation.

   After reading the analysis and recommendation, you note that the current 30-year U.S. Treasury bond yield is about 5 percent. Also, you agree that the yield spreads have widened to attractive levels and interest rates will fall further by as much as 100 basis points in the next 12 months.

a. Explain why the investment bank's bond portfolio reallocation recommendation would not work, given your view of the market.

b. How can you modify the recommendation in the briefing note in view of the reservations you expressed in part (a)?

10. You begin with an investment horizon of four years and a portfolio with a duration of four years with a market interest rate of 10 percent. A year later, what is your investment horizon? Assuming no change in interest rates, what is the duration of your portfolio relative to your investment horizon? What does this imply about your ability to immunize your portfolio?

11. During the past several years, there has been substantial growth in the dollar amount of portfolios managed using *immunization* and *dedication* techniques. Assume that a client wants to know the basic differences between (1) classical immunization, (2) contingent immunization, (3) cash-matched dedication, and (4) duration-matched dedication.

a. Briefly describe each of these four techniques.

b. Briefly discuss the ongoing investment action you would have to carry out if managing an *immunized portfolio*.

c. Briefly discuss three of the major considerations involved with creating a *cash-matched dedicated* portfolio.

d. Describe two parameters that should be specified when using *contingent immunization*.

e. Select one of the four alternative techniques that you believe requires the least degree of active management and justify your selection.

12. Robert Devlin and Neil Parish are portfolio managers at the Broward Investment Group. At their regular Monday strategy meeting, the topic of adding international bonds to one of their portfolios came up. The portfolio, an ERISA-qualified pension account for a U.S. client, was currently 90 percent invested in U.S. Treasury bonds and 10 percent invested in 10-year Canadian government bonds.

Devlin suggested buying a position in 10-year German government bonds, while Parish argued for a position in 10-year Australian government bonds.

a. Briefly discuss the *three* major issues that Devlin and Parish should address in their analyses of the return prospects for German and Australian bonds relative to those of U.S. bonds.

Having made no changes to the original portfolio, Devlin and Parish hold a subsequent strategy meeting and decide to add positions in the government bonds of Japan, the United Kingdom, France, Germany, and Australia.

b. Identify and discuss *two* reasons for adding a broader mix of international bonds to the pension portfolio.

PROBLEMS

1. Calculate the Macaulay duration of an 8 percent, $1,000 par bond that matures in three years if the bond's YTM is 10 percent and interest is paid semiannually.

a. Calculate this bond's modified duration.

b. Assuming the bond's YTM goes from 10 percent to 9.5 percent, calculate an estimate of the price change.

2. A bond for the Chelle Corporation has the following characteristics:

Maturity—12 years
Coupon—10 percent
Yield to maturity—9.50 percent
Macaulay duration—5.7 years
Convexity—48
Noncallable

a. Calculate the approximate price change for this bond using only its duration, assuming its yield to maturity increased by 150 basis points. Discuss (without calculations) the impact when you include the convexity effect.

b. Calculate the approximate price change for this bond, using only duration, if its yield to maturity declined by 300 basis points.

c. Calculate the approximate price change for this bond using both duration and convexity in the computation, once again assuming that its yield to maturity declined by 300 basis points.

d. Discuss (without calculations) what would happen to your estimate of the price change if this was a callable bond.

3. The Clarence Corporation has issued bonds that pay semiannually with the following characteristics:

Coupon	Yield to Maturity	Maturity	Macaulay Duration
8%	8%	15 years	10 years

a. Calculate modified duration using the information provided.

b. Explain why modified duration is a better measure than maturity when calculating the bond's sensitivity to changes in interest rates.

c. Identify the direction of change in modified duration if:

(1) The coupon of the bond were 4 percent, not 8 percent.
(2) The maturity of the bond were 7 years, not 15 years

d. Define *convexity* and explain how modified duration *and* convexity are used to approximate the bond's percentage change in price, given a large change in interest rates.

4. The following table shows yields to maturity on U.S. Treasury securities as of January 1, 2018:

Term to Maturity (yrs)	Yield to Maturity (%)
1	3.50%
2	4.50
3	5.00
4	5.50
5	6.00
10	6.60

a. Based on the data in the table, calculate the implied forward one-year rate of interest at January 1, 2021.

b. Describe the conditions under which the calculated forward rate would be an unbiased estimate of the one-year spot rate of interest at January 1, 2021.
Assume that one year earlier, at January 1, 2017, the prevailing term structure for U.S. Treasury securities was such that the implied forward one-year rate of interest at January 1, 2021, was significantly higher than the corresponding rate implied by the term structure at January 1, 2018.

c. On the basis of the pure expectations theory of the term structure, briefly discuss two factors that could account for such a decline in the implied forward rate.

d. Briefly describe how the information conveyed by this observed decrease in the implied forward rate for 2021 could be used in making a yield forecast.

5. Consider the characteristics of two annual pay bonds from the same issuer with the same priority in the event of default:

	Bond A	Bond B
Coupons	Annual	Annual
Maturity	3 yrs	3 yrs
Coupon rate	10%	6%
Yield to maturity	10.65%	10.75%
Price	98.40	88.34

You also observe the following spot interest rates from the current yield curve:

Term (yrs)	Spot Rates (zero coupon, %)
1	5%
2	8
3	11

Neither bond's price is consistent with the spot rates. Using the information in these displays, recommend *either* Bond A or Bond B for purchase. Justify your choice.

6. The following are the current coupon yields to maturity and spot rates of interest for six U.S. Treasury securities. Assume that all securities pay interest annually.

Yields to Maturity and Spot Rates of Interest

Term to Maturity (yrs)	Current Coupon Yield to Maturity (%)	Spot Rate of Interest (%)
1-yr Treasury	5.25%	5.25%
2-yr Treasury	5.75	5.79
3-yr Treasury	6.15	6.19
5-yr Treasury	6.45	6.51
10-yr Treasury	6.95	7.10
30-yr Treasury	7.25	7.67

Compute the 2-year implied forward rate three years from now, given the information provided in the preceding table. State the assumption underlying the calculation of the implied forward rate.

7. The par yield curve for U.S. Treasury bonds is currently flat across all maturities at 5.50 percent. You have observed following "paired" transaction by your bond portfolio manager:

Bond	Transaction	Type	Credit Spread (bp)	Maturity (yrs)	Coupon Rate (%)	Modified Duration
G	Buy	U.S. Govt.	—	15	0%	14.599
H	Sell	Corporate	100	7	8	5.386

Briefly discuss what this paired trade suggests to you about the manager's implied view as to (1) the general direction of future interest rate movement, (2) the future shape of the par yield curve, and (3) the future level of corporate bond credit spreads.

8. Compute the Macaulay duration under the following conditions:
   a. A bond with a four-year term to maturity, a 10 percent coupon (annual payments), and a market yield of 8 percent.
   b. A bond with a four-year term to maturity, a 10 percent coupon (annual payments), and a market yield of 12 percent.

c. Compare your answers to parts (a) and (b), and discuss the implications of this for classical immunization.

9. Evaluate the following pure-yield pickup swap: You currently hold a 20-year, AA-rated, 9.0 percent coupon bond priced to yield 11.0 percent. As a swap candidate, you are considering a 20-year, AA-rated, 11 percent coupon bond priced to yield 11.5 percent. (Assume reinvestment at 11.5 percent.)

	Current Bond	Candidate Bond
Dollar investment	_____	_____
Coupon	_____	_____
i on one coupon	_____	_____
Principal value at year end	_____	_____
Total accrued	_____	_____
Realized compound yield	_____	_____

Value of swap: _____ basis points in one year

10. A university endowment fund has sought your advice on its fixed-income portfolio strategy. The characteristics of the portfolio's current holdings are listed below:

Bond	Credit Rating	Maturity (yrs)	Coupon Rate (%)	Modified Duration	Convexity	Market Value of Position
A	U.S. Govt.	3	0%	2.727	9.9	$30,000
B	A1	10	8	6.404	56.1	30,000
C	Aa2	5	12	3.704	18.7	30,000
D	Agency	7	10	4.868	32.1	30,000
E	Aa3	12	0	10.909	128.9	30,000
						$150,000

a. Calculate the modified duration for this portfolio (Mod D_p).
b. Suppose you learn that the implied sensitivity (modified duration) of the endowment's liabilities is about 6.50 years. Identify whether the bond portfolio is (1) immunized against interest rate risk, (2) exposed to net price risk, or (3) exposed to net reinvestment risk. Briefly explain what will happen to the net position of the endowment fund if in the future there is a significant parallel upward shift in the yield curve.
c. Briefly describe how you could increase the convexity of the portfolio while keeping the modified duration at the same level.
d. Your current active view for the fixed-income market over the coming months is that Treasury yields will decline and corporate credit spreads will also decrease. Briefly discuss how you could restructure the existing portfolio to take advantage of this view.

11. A major requirement in managing a fixed-income portfolio using a contingent immunization policy is monitoring the relationship between the current market value of the portfolio and the required value of the floor portfolio. This difference is defined as the *margin of error*. In this regard, assume a $300 million portfolio with a time horizon of five years. The available market rate at the initiation of the portfolio is 12 percent, but the client is willing to accept 10 percent as a floor rate to allow use of active management strategies.

The current market values and current market rates at the end of Years 1, 2, and 3 are as follows:

End of Year	Market Value ($ millions)	Market Yield	Required Floor Portfolio ($ millions)	Margin of Error ($ millions)
1	$340.9	10%		
2	405.5	8		
3	395.2	12		

Assuming semiannual compounding:

a. Calculate the required ending-wealth value for this portfolio.

b. Calculate the value of the required floor portfolios at the end of Years 1, 2, and 3.

c. Compute the margin of error at the end of Years 1, 2, and 3.

d. Indicate the action that a portfolio manager utilizing a *contingent immunization* policy would take if the margin of error at the end of any year had been zero or negative.

12. Mike Smith, CFA, an analyst with Blue River Investments, is considering buying a Montrose Cable Company Corporate bond. He has collected the balance sheet and income statement information for Montrose, as shown in Exhibit 13.26. He has also calculated the three ratios shown in Exhibit 13.27, which indicate that the bond is currently rated "A," according to the firm's internal bond-rating criteria shown in Exhibit 13.28.

Exhibit 13.26 Montrose Cable Company: Year Ended March 31, 1999 ($ thousands)

Balance Sheet

Current assets	$ 4,735
Fixed assets	43,225
Total assets	$47,960
Current liabilities	$ 4,500
Long-term debt	10,000
Total liabilities	$14,500
Shareholder's equity	33,460
Total liabilities and shareholder's equity	$47,960

Income Statement

Revenue	$18,500
Operating and administrative expenses	14,050
Operating income	$ 4,450
Depreciation and amortization	1,675
Interest expense	942
Income before income taxes	$ 1,833
Taxes	641
Net income	$ 1,192

Exhibit 13.27 Selected Ratios and Credit Yield Premium Data for Montrose

EBITDA/interest expense	4.72
Long-term debt/equity	0.30
Current assets/current liabilities	1.05
Credit yield premium over U.S. Treasuries	55 bp

Exhibit 13.28 Blue River Investments: Internal Bond-Rating Criteria and Credit Yield Premium Data

Bond Rating	Interest Coverage (EBITDA/interest expense)	Leverage (long-term debt/equity)	Current Ratio (current assets/current liabilities)	Credit Yield Premium over U.S. Treasuries (in basis points)
AA	5.00 to 6.00	0.25 to 0.30	1.15 to 1.25	30 bp
A	4.00 to 5.00	0.30 to 0.40	1.00 to 1.15	50 bp
BBB	3.00 to 4.00	0.40 to 0.50	0.90 to 1.00	100 bp
BB	2.00 to 3.00	0.50 to 0.60	0.75 to 0.90	125 bp

Exhibit 13.29 Montrose Off-Balance-Sheet Items

- Montrose has guaranteed the long-term debt (principal only) of an unconsolidated affiliate. This obligation has a present value of $995,000.
- Montrose has sold $500,000 of accounts receivable with recourse at a yield of 8%.
- Montrose is a lessee in a new noncancelable operating leasing agreement to finance transmission equipment. The discounted present value of the lease payments is $6,144,000, using an interest rate of 10%. The annual payment will be $1,000,000.

Smith has decided to consider some off-balance-sheet items in his credit analysis, as shown in Exhibit 13.29. Specifically, Smith wishes to evaluate the impact of each of the off-balance-sheet items on each of the ratios found in Exhibit 13.27.

a. Calculate the combined effect of the *three* off-balance-sheet items in Exhibit 13.29 on *each* of the following *three* financial ratios shown in Exhibit 13.27.

(1) EBITDA/interest expense
(2) Long-term debt/equity
(3) Current assets/current liabilities

The bond is currently trading at a credit premium of 55 basis points. Using the internal bond-rating criteria in Exhibit 13.28, Smith wants to evaluate whether or not the credit yield premium incorporates the effect of the off-balance-sheet items.

b. State and justify whether or not the current credit yield premium compensates Smith for the credit risk of the bond, based on the internal bond-rating criteria found in Exhibit 13.28.

Closed-Form Equation for Calculating Macaulay Duration

To calculate the duration statistic, it helps to think of a bond that pays a fixed coupon for a finite maturity as being just a portfolio of zero coupon cash flows. Duration is then the weighted average of the payment (maturity) dates of those zero coupon cash flows, or its *zero-coupon-equivalent maturity*.

Consider a nonamortizing, 5-year bond with a face value of $1,000 making annual coupon payments of $120 (or 12 percent). Assuming a yield to maturity of 10 percent, this bond will trade at a premium and its weighted average payment date (duration) is 4.0740 years, as shown in Exhibit 13A.1. The duration of 4.0740 years is the weighted average maturity of that portfolio, where the weights are the respective shares of market value (for example, the 1-year zero coupon cash flow is 10.14 percent of the value of the portfolio; the 5-year zero is 64.64 percent).

This 5-year coupon bond with a duration of 4.0740 years is equivalent in terms of price risk to a zero coupon bond having a maturity of 4.0740 years. When the interest rate increases by 1 percent above its original level (that is, $[\Delta(1+i) \div (1+i)] = 0.01$), the price of this bond will decline by about 4.074 percent.

The Macaulay duration can also be calculated with the following formula:

13.A1
$$D = \frac{1 + \dfrac{i}{m}}{\dfrac{i}{m}} - \frac{1 + \dfrac{i}{m} + \left[(m \times N)\left(\dfrac{C}{F} - \dfrac{i}{m}\right)\right]}{\dfrac{C}{F}\left[\left(1 + \dfrac{i}{m}\right)^{m \times N} - 1\right] + \dfrac{i}{m}}$$

where:

- C = periodic coupon payment
- F = face value at maturity
- N = number of years until maturity
- m = payments per year
- i = annual yield to maturity

In the preceding numerical example, $i = 0.10$, $m = 1$, $N = 5$, $C/F = 0.12$, and $Y/n = 0.10$. The bond's duration can therefore be solved as:

$$D = \frac{1 + 0.10}{0.10} - \frac{1 + 0.10 + 5(0.12 - 0.10)}{(0.12)[(1 + 0.10)^5 - 1] + 0.10} = 4.0740$$

As a second example, what is the duration of a 30-year Treasury bond with a 7.625 percent coupon and a stated yield to maturity of 7.72 percent? Recall that T-bonds pay semiannual

Exhibit 13A.1 A Duration Calculation

Year	Cash Flow	PV at 10%	PV ÷ Price	Year × (PV ÷ Price)
1	$ 120	$ 109.09	0.1014	0.1014
2	120	99.17	0.0922	0.1844
3	120	90.16	0.0838	0.2514
4	120	81.96	0.0762	0.3047
5	$1,120	695.43	0.6464	3.2321
		Price = $1,075.82		Duration = 4.0740 years

interest and so the appropriate definitions of the variables are $C/F = 0.38125$, $N = 30$, $m = 2$, and $i/m = 0.0386$. So, by Equation 13A.1:

$$D = \frac{1 + 0.0386}{0.0386} - \frac{1 + 0.0386 + 60(0.038125 + 0.0386)}{(0.038125)[1 + 0.0386)^{60} - 1] + 0.0386} = 24.18$$

or 12.09 years.

Derivative Security Analysis

In recent years, it has been difficult to read the financial press without encountering at least a passing reference to an economic scandal attributed to trading in derivative securities. Procter & Gamble's ill-fated swap transactions and the equity index futures trades that brought down Barings Bank give the casual reader the impression that derivatives are highly volatile instruments used only by investors interested in placing speculative "bets." Of course, nothing could be further from the truth. Although it is true that the companies in these examples either miscalculated or misunderstood the nature of their investment positions, the vast majority of derivative transactions are used by individuals and institutions seeking to reduce the risk exposures generated by their other business ventures.

Derivatives, in their many forms, have become a vital part of modern security markets, trailing only stocks and bonds in terms of importance. Unlike with stocks and bonds, however, their widespread use is a relatively recent phenomenon, and misconceptions still exist about how derivatives work and the proper way for investors to trade them. The chapters in this section address this concern by providing the investor with a framework for understanding how derivatives are valued and used in practice. Chapter 14 begins this process by detailing the mechanics of the two basic forms of derivative contract—*forwards* and *options*. After providing an initial description of these instruments and the markets in which they trade, we present the fundamental principles that determine their prices. The chapter concludes with several specific examples of how investors use derivatives to adjust the risk–return characteristics of their stock and bond portfolios.

Chapter 15 analyzes forward, futures, and swap contracts—the most prevalent form of derivative instruments. The similarities and differences between forward and futures contracts are described, with particular emphasis on the creation of (and subsequent adjustments to) margin accounts and the concept of basis risk. In addition, the calculation of the optimal hedge ratio and the arbitrage-free approach to determining the contract delivery price are discussed. The chapter continues with an examination of the features of forward and futures contracts that are designed to offset financial (as opposed to commodity) risk exposures, including interest rate, equity, and currency price movements. Applications and investment strategies involving each of these contract types illustrate this discussion. We conclude with an overview of swap contracting, which we argue are equivalent to portfolios of forward contracts. Examples are provided to show how contracts in this rapidly growing segment of the derivative market can tailored to help investors manage both interest rate and equity price risk in their portfolios.

In Chapter 16, the last chapter of the section, the focus turns to option contracting. The discussion begins with a consideration of how option markets are organized and how both puts and calls—the two basic types of option contracts—are quoted and traded. Several different option-based investment and hedging strategies are described, as well as how these contracts can be used in conjunction with other securities to create customized payoff distributions. The chapter also includes a formal treatment of how option contracts are valued in an efficient market. Starting with the simple two-state option pricing model, which contains the essence of the basic valuation argument, the discussion progresses to include state-of-the-art approaches such as the binomial and Black–Scholes models. In this development, special attention is paid to the role that price volatility plays in the valuation process. We conclude the chapter with a consideration of how option contracts can be structured into other financial arrangements, such as with convertible bonds and credit default swaps.

CHAPTER 14

An Introduction to Derivative Markets and Securities

After you read this chapter, you should be able to answer the following questions:

- What distinguishes a derivative security, such as a forward, futures, or option contract, from more fundamental securities, such as stocks and bonds?
- What are the important characteristics of forward, futures, and option contracts, and in what sense can they be interpreted as insurance policies?
- How are the markets for derivative securities organized, and how do they differ from other security markets?
- What terminology is used to describe derivative market transactions?
- How are prices for derivative securities quoted, and how should this information be interpreted?
- What are the similarities and differences between forward and futures contracts?
- What do the payoff and profit diagrams look like for forward and futures contracts?
- What do the payoff and profit diagrams look like for put and call option contracts?
- How are forward contracts, put options, and call options related to one another?
- How can derivatives be used in conjunction with stock and Treasury bills to replicate the payoffs to other securities and create arbitrage opportunities for an investor?
- How can derivative contracts be used to restructure cash flow patterns and modify the risks in existing investment portfolios?

So far, we have seen several ways in which individuals and institutions can design their investments to take advantage of future market conditions. We have also seen how investors can control the volatility associated with their stock and bond positions—at least in part—by forming well-diversified portfolios of securities to reduce or eliminate a security's unsystematic risk.

In this chapter, we begin our investigation of the role played by **derivative securities** in modern investment portfolios. A derivative instrument is one for which the ultimate payoff to the investor depends directly on the value of another security or commodity. Earlier in the text, we briefly described two basic types of derivatives: (1) forward and futures contracts and (2) option contracts. A call option, for example, gives its owner the right to purchase an underlying security, such as a stock or a bond, at a fixed price within a certain amount of time. So the option's ultimate value can be said to depend on—and thus derive from—that of the other asset. Similarly, a forward contract to sell a bond for a fixed price at a future date will see its value to the investor rise or fall with decreases or increases in the market price of the underlying bond.

The growth of the markets in which derivative securities are created and exchanged has been nothing short of phenomenal. The past few decades have seen the emergence of contracts to trade such fundamental products as agricultural commodities, energy, precious metals, currencies, common stock, and bonds. There are even derivatives to trade hypothetical underlying assets (for example, option and futures contracts on the Standard & Poor's stock indexes) as well as combination derivatives, such as option contracts that allow the investor to decide at a later date to enter into a futures contract involving another security or commodity.

As we will see, investors can use derivative securities in the same way as the underlying assets; an investor who believes that a certain common stock will increase in value can benefit from either a purchase of the stock directly or an option to purchase that stock at a predetermined price. The exact returns will not be equal for these two alternatives, but both will gain from an upward movement in the stock's price. Ultimately, however, the real key to understanding how and why derivatives are used lies in their ability to modify the risk and expected return characteristics of existing investment portfolios. That is, options and futures allow investors to **hedge** (or even increase) the risk of a collection of stocks in ways that go far beyond the diversification concept presented in the preceding chapters. Also, derivative securities allow for the duplication of cash flow patterns that already exist in other forms, creating the possibility of **arbitrage** if two otherwise identical series of cash flows do not carry the same current price.

The balance of this chapter describes the fundamental nature and uses of forward, futures, and option contracts on common stock and bonds. (Subsequent chapters deal with more advanced forms of these products and valuation issues.) First, we describe the basic terminology associated with these markets and explain the payoff structures created by each of these instruments. We then develop the formal relationship between forwards and options, a series of conditions collectively known as **put–call parity**. Finally, we briefly introduce three popular ways in which derivatives can be used to manage the risks in stock and bond portfolios.

14.1 OVERVIEW OF DERIVATIVE MARKETS

Like other financial products, derivative transactions have a specific terminology that must be understood in order to use these instruments effectively. The language used to describe forward, futures, and option contracts is often a confusing blend of jargon drawn from the equity, debt, and insurance markets, with some unique expressions thrown in for good measure. Thus, we begin by summarizing the most important aspects of these products and the markets in which they trade.

It is useful to first consider the basic types of positions that an investor can hold in these markets. Exhibit 14.1 illustrates the possibilities. The chart reinforces the point made earlier that, at the broadest level, there are only two kinds of derivatives available: (1) forward and futures contracts and (2) option contracts. Further, as we will explain shortly, while only one forward contract is needed for any particular maturity date and underlying asset, there must be two types of options—calls and puts—in order to offer investors a full range of choices. Finally, for each of these derivative arrangements (that is, the forward contract, the call option, and the put option), an investor can enter into a transaction as either the long position (the buyer) or the short position (the seller). This leads to the six possible basic positions shown in Exhibit 14.1.

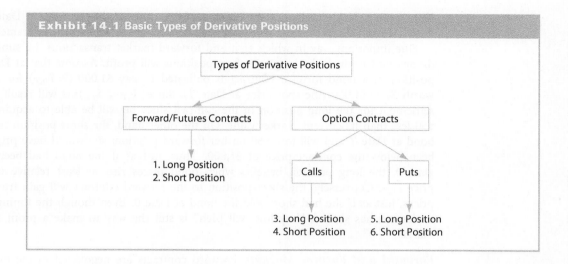

Exhibit 14.1 Basic Types of Derivative Positions

Types of Derivative Positions

Forward/Futures Contracts

Option Contracts

1. Long Position
2. Short Position

Calls

Puts

3. Long Position
4. Short Position

5. Long Position
6. Short Position

Every derivative arrangement that investors might hold in their portfolios can be viewed in terms of one of these six positions or as a combination of these positions. For instance, later in the chapter, we consider how an equity investor can use derivatives to protect himself against general declines in the stock market. Two such strategies involve (1) shorting an equity index forward contract and (2) buying an equity index "collar" agreement. In terms of Exhibit 14.1, we will see that the forward-based strategy represents Position 2, while the collar strategy involves a combination of the purchase of a put option (Position 5) and the sale of a call option (Position 4).

14.1.1 The Language and Structure of Forward and Futures Markets

To most investors, the **forward contract** is the most basic derivative product available. A forward contract gives its holder both the *right and the full obligation* to conduct a transaction involving another security or commodity—the underlying asset—at a predetermined future date and at a predetermined price. The future date on which the transaction is to be consummated is called the contract's *maturity* (or expiration) *date*, while the predetermined price at which the trade takes place is the forward **contract price**. Notice there must always be two parties (sometimes called **counterparties**) to a forward transaction: the eventual buyer (or **long position**), who will pay the contract price and receives the underlying security, and the eventual seller (or **short position**), who delivers the security for the fixed price.

Forward and Spot Markets Forward contracts are not securities in the traditional sense; they are more appropriately viewed as *trade agreements* negotiated directly between two parties for a transaction that is scheduled to take place in the future. Suppose that two investors agree at Date 0 (the present) to transfer a bond from one party to the other at the future Date T. The two parties must agree on which bond and how much of it is to be exchanged, the date and location at which this exchange will take place, and the price at which the bond will be bought and sold. So, the terms that must be considered in forming a forward contract are the same as those necessary for a bond transaction that settled immediately (that is, a *spot market* transaction)—with two exceptions. First, the settlement date agreed to in the contract is purposefully set to be in the future. Second, the contract price—which we will represent as

$F_{0,T}$, meaning a forward price set at Date 0 for a contract that matures at Date T—is usually different from the prevailing spot price (S_0) because of the different time frames involved.

One important way in which spot and forward market transactions are similar is the conditions under which the long and short positions will profit. Assume that at Date T, the long position in a bond forward contract is obligated to pay \$1,000 ($= F_{0,T}$) for a bond that is worth $S_T = \$1,050$ (the spot price at Date T). Since $F_{0,T} < S_T$, this will result in a profitable settlement for the long position in the contract since he will be able to acquire the bond for \$50 less than its current market value. On the other hand, the short position must deliver the bond at Date T and will lose \$50 on her forward position; she would have profited if S_T had been below the contract price of \$1,000. Thus, just as if the bond had been purchased at Date 0, the long position benefits when bond prices rise, at least relative to the contract price $F_{0,T}$. Conversely, the short position to the forward contract will gain from falling bond prices, just as if she had short sold the bond at Date 0. Even though the timing of the trade's settlement has shifted, "buy low, sell high" is still the way to make a profit in the forward market.

Forward and Futures Markets Forward contracts are negotiated in the over-the-counter market. This means that forward contracts are agreements between two private parties—one of which is often a derivatives intermediary, such as a bank—rather than traded through a formal exchange. One advantage of this private arrangement is that the terms of the contract are completely flexible; they can be whatever any two mutually consenting counterparties agree to. Another desirable feature to many counterparties is that these arrangements may not require *collateral*; instead, the long and short positions sometimes trust each other to honor their respective commitments at Date T. This lack of collateral means that forward contracts involve *credit* (or *default*) *risk*, which is one reason why banks are often market makers in these instruments.

One disadvantage of a forward contract is that it is quite often *illiquid*, meaning that it might be difficult or costly for a counterparty to exit the contract before it matures. Illiquidity is really a by-product of the contract's flexibility because the more specifically tailored an agreement is to the needs of a particular individual, the less marketable it will be to someone else. **Futures contracts** try to solve this problem by standardizing the terms of the agreement (expiration date, identity, and amount of the underlying asset) and having both parties trade through a centralized market, called a *futures exchange*. Although the standardization of contracts reduces the ability of the ultimate end users to select the most desirable terms, it does create contract *homogeneity*, whereby the counterparties can always *unwind* a previous commitment prior to expiration by simply trading their existing position back to the exchange at the prevailing market price.

The *futures price* is analogous to the forward contract price and, at any time during the life of a contract, is set at a level such that a brand-new long or short position would not have to pay an initial premium. However, the futures exchange will require both counterparties to post collateral, or *margin*, to protect itself against the possibility of default. (A futures exchange is not a credit-granting institution.) These margin accounts are held by the exchange's *clearinghouse* and are *marked to market* (that is, adjusted for contract price movements) on a daily basis to ensure that both end users always maintain sufficient collateral to guarantee their eventual participation. A list of some popular futures contracts, along with the markets where they trade, is shown in Exhibit 14.2. Although generally quite diverse, all of these underlying assets have two things in common: *volatile price movements* and *strong interest* from both buyers and sellers.

14.1.2 Interpreting Futures Price Quotations: An Example

To illustrate how futures prices are typically quoted in financial markets, consider Exhibit 14.3, which lists spot and futures prices for contracts on the Standard & Poor's 500 Index as of

Exhibit 14.2 Popular Futures Contracts and Exchanges

Underlying Asset	Exchange
A. Physical Commodities	
Corn, soybeans, soybean meal, soybean oil, wheat	CME Group (Chicago Board of Trade)
Cattle-feeder, cattle-live, hogs	CME Group (Chicago Mercantile Exchange)
Lumber	
Dairy	
Ethanol	
Canola, cocoa, coffee, sugar	Intercontinental Exchange
Orange juice	
Cotton, barley	
Crude oil, heating oil, gasoline, natural gas	CME Group
Coal	(New York Mercantile Exchange)
Platinum	
Gold, silver, copper, zinc	CME Group (Comex)
B. Financial Securities	
Yen, Euro, Canadian dollar, Swiss franc, British pound, Mexican peso, Australian dollar, Eurodollar (LIBOR) S&P 500, Nikkei 225, Russell 2000, S&P 500 sector indexes	CME Group
Treasury bonds, Treasury notes, Federal funds, Interest Rate Swap	CME Group (Chicago Board of Trade)
Dow Jones Industrials Average	
British gilt, German bund	Intercontinental Exchange
FT-SE 100, CAC 40 indexes	(NYSE Euronext)
Euro Stoxx 50 index, Euro stock volatility	Eurex
Euro government bonds	
Euroibor	

June 26, 2017. Recall from Chapter 4 that the S&P 500 is a value-weighted index of a broad collection of industrial, financial, utility, and transportation companies representing the U.S. stock market. At the close of trading on this particular day, the index level stood at 2,439.07, which can be considered as the spot price of one "share" of the S&P index (S_0).[1] Exhibit 14.3 gives futures contract prices for 11 different expiration dates falling in the months of March, June, September, and December from September 2017 through June 2019, as well as three others that expire in December of 2019, 2020, and 2021.

Consider the futures contract that expires in September 2017. The settle (or closing) contract price is listed as 2,436.00 $(= F_{0,T})$. This means that an investor taking a long position in this contract would be committing in June to buy a certain number of shares in the S&P 500 Index—250 shares in this case—at a price of $2,436.00 per share on the expiration date in September. Conversely, the short position in this contract would be committing to sell 250 S&P shares under the same conditions. Note that, except for the margin posted with the futures exchange (the Chicago Mercantile Exchange [CME] for this contract), no money changes hands between the long and short positions at the origination of the contract in June.

---

[1] In reality, purchasing a portfolio of the 500 S&P index stocks would cost considerably more than $2,439.07. However, as the eventual profit or loss from a stock index futures contract is determined by the *difference* between the futures contract price and the spot price prevailing at contract expiration, this interpretation is valid. The trading mechanics of these contracts will be described in greater detail in Chapter 15.

Exhibit 14.3 Standard & Poor's 500 Index Futures Contract Price Quotations

Month	Open	High	Low	Last	Change	Settle	Estimated Volume	Prior Day Open Interest
Spot	—	—	—	—	—	2439.07	—	—
Sep 17	2435.50	2447.40	2430.40A	2436.50	+1.10	2436.00	549	39,693
Dec 17	—	2444.70B	2432.10A	2435.20A	+1.00	2434.10	9	243
Mar 18	—	2442.80B	2430.20A	2433.30A	+1.00	2432.20	0	0
Jun 18	—	2441.80B	2429.20A	2432.30A	+1.00	2431.20	0	0
Sep 18	—	2442.80B	2430.20A	2433.30A	+1.00	2432.20	0	0
Dec 18	—	2447.50B	2434.90A	2438.00A	+1.00	2436.90	0	0
Mar 19	—	2451.70B	2439.10A	2442.20A	+1.00	2441.10	0	0
Jun 19	—	2455.90B	2443.30A	2446.40A	+1.00	2445.30	0	0
Dec 19	—	2470.70B	2458.10A	2461.20A	+1.00	2460.10	0	0
Dec 20	—	—	—	—	+1.00	2499.70	0	0
Dec 21	—	—	—	—	+1.00	2553.80	0	0
Total							558	39,936

Sources: CME Group (www.cmegroup/trading/equity-index/us-index/sandp-500_settlements_quotes), June 26, 2017; author calculations.

Exhibit 14.4 summarizes the payoff and net profit for this contract from the long position's point of view, assuming a hypothetical set of S&P index levels on the September expiration date (S_T). The main thing to note is that the payoff to the long position is positive when the S&P index level rises (relative to the contract price of 2,436.00), while a loss is incurred when the S&P falls. For instance, if the expiration date level of the index is 2,475.00, the long position will receive a profit of $39.00 per share ($= 2,475 - 2,436.00$). In that case, the investor profits from being able to buy stock that is worth $2,475.00 for the predetermined price of only $2,436.00. On the other hand, if the September index level turns out to be 2,415, the futures contract still obligates the investor to purchase stock for the contract price, thus resulting in a loss of $21.00. This reinforces the fact that the long position as the buyer benefits when stock prices rise and suffers when prices fall, just as would be the case for an investor purchasing stock directly in the spot market. Of course, the short position as the seller would have exactly the opposite payoffs to those shown in the Exhibit 14.4. Finally, because entering the futures contract required no upfront premium payment, the net profit to the counterparty is the same as the expiration date payoff.

Exhibit 14.4 Contract Payoff and Net Profit at Expiration from a Long Position in an S&P 500 Futures Contract

September S&P 500 Index Level	Futures Payoff at Expiration	Initial Futures Premium	Net Profit
2355.00	(2,355 − 2,436.00) = −81.00	0.00	−81.00
2375.00	(2,375 − 2,436.00) = −61.00	0.00	−61.00
2395.00	(2,395 − 2,436.00) = −41.00	0.00	−41.00
2415.00	(2,415 − 2,436.00) = −21.00	0.00	−21.00
2436.00	(2,436.00 − 2,436.00) = 0.00	0.00	−0.70
2455.00	(2,455 − 2,436.00) = 19.00	0.00	19.00
2475.00	(2,475 − 2,436.00) = 39.00	0.00	39.00
2495.00	(2,495 − 2,436.00) = 59.00	0.00	59.00
2515.00	(2,515 − 2,436.00) = 79.00	0.00	79.00

The data displayed in Exhibit 14.3 contains other information useful to investors as well. First, recognize that the spot index level rose slightly from the previous day, and all of the futures contract prices listed went up as well; this can be seen from the positive entries in the "Change" column. This suggests that although other factors matter as well, the futures contract prices are strongly linked to the prevailing level of the underlying spot index. Second, notice that contract prices decrease between September 2017 and June 2018 but then increase after that point. That is, although all 12 closing prices listed (that is, the spot and the 11 futures contracts) were set on the same day and correspond to the same S&P index share, the cost of that share gets steadily less expensive and then steadily more expensive the further forward in time the delivery date is set. We will see later that this relationship is common for some securities but not for others. Third, Exhibit 14.3 also lists the *open interest* and *trading volume* for each contract. Open interest is the number of outstanding contracts, while trading volume is the number of those contracts that changed hands that day. Thus, it appears in this case that the nearest-term contract (September 2017) is by far the most widely used in practice.

14.1.3 The Language and Structure of Option Markets

An **option contract** gives its holder the right—but not the obligation—to conduct a transaction involving an underlying security or commodity at a predetermined future date and at a predetermined price. Unlike with a forward contract, the option gives the long position the right to decide whether the trade will eventually take place. On the other hand, the seller (or *writer*) of the option must perform on his side of the agreement if the buyer chooses to exercise the option. Thus, the obligation in the option market is inherently one-sided: Buyers can do as they please, but sellers are obligated to the buyers under the terms of the agreement. As a consequence, two different types of options are needed to cover all potential transactions: a **call option**—the right to buy the underlying security—and a **put option**—the right to sell that same asset.

Option Contract Terms Two prices are important in evaluating an option position. The **exercise**, or strike, **price** is the price the call buyer will pay to—or the put buyer will receive from—the option seller if the option is exercised. The exercise price (represented here as X) is to an option what the contract price ($F_{0,T}$) is to a forward agreement. The second price of interest is what the option buyer must pay to the seller at Date 0 to acquire the contract itself. To avoid confusion, this second price is typically referred to as the **option premium**. A basic difference between options and forwards is that an option requires this upfront premium payment from buyer to seller, while the forward ordinarily does not. This is because the forward contract allowed both the long and the short positions to "win" at Date T (depending on where S_T settled, relative to $F_{0,T}$), but the option agreement will only be exercised in the buyer's favor; hence the seller must be compensated at Date 0, or she would never agree to the deal. Notice also that although both puts and calls require premium payments, it is quite likely that these two prices will differ. In the analysis that follows, we will define the Date 0 premium to acquire an option expiring at Date T as $C_{0,T}$ for a call and $P_{0,T}$ for a put. For example, instead of a long position in a bond forward contract, the investor in an earlier example could have paid $20 ($= C_{0,T}$) at Date 0 for a call option that would have given him the right to buy the bond for $1,000 ($= X$) at Date T but would not require him to do so if $S_T < \$1,000$.

Options can be designed to provide a choice of when the contract can be exercised. **European options** can be exercised only at maturity (Date T), while **American options** can be executed any time up to expiration. For a European-style call option, the buyer will exercise only when the expiration date market value of the underlying asset is greater than the exercise price. On the other hand, a European-style put option will only be rationally exercised when the Date T price of the asset is lower than X. (The decision to exercise an American-style contract is more complex and will be considered in Chapter 16.)

Option Valuation Basics The Date 0 option premium can be divided into two components: **intrinsic value** and **time premium**. Intrinsic value represents the value that the buyer could extract from the option if she exercised it immediately. For a call, this is the greater of either zero or the difference between the price of the underlying asset and the exercise price $(\max[0, S_0 - X])$. For a put, intrinsic value would be $\max[0, X - S_0]$, as X would now represent the proceeds generated from the asset's sale. An option with positive intrinsic value is said to be **in the money**, while one with zero intrinsic value is **out of the money**. For the special case where $S_0 = X$, the option is **at the money**. The time premium component is then simply the difference between the whole option premium and the intrinsic component: $(C_{0,T} - \max[0, S_0 - X])$ for a call and $(P_{0,T} - \max[0, X - S_0])$ for a put. The buyer is willing to pay this amount in excess of the option's immediate exercise value because of her ability to complete the transaction at a price of X that will remain in force until Date T. Thus, the time premium is connected to the likelihood that the underlying asset's price will move in the anticipated direction by the contract's maturity.

Chapter 16 provides a more complete discussion of valuing option premia, but several basic relationships can be seen now. First, because the buyer of a call option is never obligated to exercise, the contract should always at least be worth its intrinsic value. (The situation for put option prices or when the underlying asset pays a dividend can be more complicated and will be discussed later.) In any event, neither a call nor a put option can be worth less than zero. Second, for call options having the same maturity and the same underlying asset, the lower the exercise price, the higher the contract's intrinsic value and, hence, the greater its overall premium. Conversely, for the same reason, put options with higher exercise prices are more valuable than those with lower strike prices. Third, increasing the amount of time until any option expires will increase the contract's time premium because it allows the price of the underlying security more opportunity to move in the direction anticipated by the investor (that is, up for a call option, down for a put option). Finally, because they provide investors with more choices about exercising the agreement, American-style options are at least as valuable as otherwise comparable European-style contracts.

Option Trading Markets Like forwards and futures, options trade both in over-the-counter markets and on exchanges. When exchange traded, just the seller of the contract is required to post a margin account because he is the only one obligated to perform on the contract at a later date. Also, options can be based on a wide variety of underlying securities, including futures contracts or other options. Exhibit 14.5 lists the underlying assets and exchanges where a number of popular option contracts trade.

14.1.4 Interpreting Option Price Quotations: An Example

Exhibit 14.6 shows data for a variety of call and put options on the S&P 500 Index as of June 26, 2017. All of the contracts listed expire in September 2017, making them comparable to the S&P 500 futures contracts considered above. However, unlike the futures contracts, for which there is a single contract price for a given expiration month, Exhibit 14.6 indicates that there are several September 2017 options having different exercise prices. The display lists bid and ask premium quotes for both puts and calls having strike prices ranging from 2,395 to 2,485.[2] As noted earlier, calls become more valuable (for example, higher ask premia) as the exercise price declines, with the opposite holding true for put options.

Consider the outcomes of two different investors, one of whom purchases a September S&P call struck at 2,435 (X) and one of whom buys a September 2,435 put. At the origination of the

---

[2]Recall that an investor buys a security from a dealer—in this case, the options exchange—at the ask price and sells securities to the dealer at the bid price. The difference in these prices, the *bid–ask spread*, represents part of the compensation to the exchange for making a market in these contracts.

Exhibit 14.5 Popular Option Contracts and Exchanges	
Underlying Asset	**Exchange**
A. Financial Securities	
Individual equities and ETFs	Chicago Board Options Exchange
S&P 100 index, Dow Jones Industrial Average	
VIX index, S&P 500 volatility index	
Yen, Euro, Canadian dollar, Swiss franc	NASDAQ PHLX
British pound, Australian dollar	
Individual equities and ETFs	
NASDAQ 100, Equity sector indexes	
Euro Stoxx 50, DAX, SMI indexes	Eurex
Euro Stoxx 50 volatility index	
B. Futures Options	
Cattle-feeder, cattle-live, hogs, dairy	CME Group
Yen, Euro, Canadian dollar, Australian dollar,	
British pound	
Eurodollar (LIBOR)	
S&P 500 Index, Nasdaq 100 Index	
Corn, soybeans, soybean meal, wheat	CME Group
Treasury bonds, Treasury notes, Interest rate swaps,	(Chicago Board of Trade)
Federal funds	
Dow Jones Industrial Average	
British gilt	Intercontinental Exchange
Wheat, cotton	
Crude oil, gasoline, natural gas	CME Group
Platinum	(New York Mercantile Exchange)
Copper, gold, silver	CME Group (Comex)

transaction in June, these investors will pay their sellers the ask prices of $43.00\,(C_{0,T})$ and $42.10\,(P_{0,T})$, respectively. In return, the investor holding the call option has the right, but not the obligation, to buy one S&P share for $2,435 at the expiration date in September. Since the current (spot) price of the index is 2439.07, this call option is in the money. Thus, the total call premium of $43.00 can be divided into an intrinsic value component of $4.07 (= 2439.07 − 2435.00) and a time premium of $38.93 (= 43.00 − 4.07). Similarly, the investor holding the put option has the right, but not the obligation, to sell one S&P share for $2,435 at the expiration date in September. The put is out of the money, however, as this exercise price is lower than the current index level. Thus, the put option has no intrinsic value so the entire $42.10 ask price is a time premium.

The expiration date payoffs and net profits to these long option positions are listed in Exhibit 14.7 for a variety of possible S&P index levels. Looking first at the call option payoffs in Panel A, recall that the investor will exercise the contract to buy a share of the S&P index only when the September S&P level is above 2,435; at index levels at or below 2,435, the investor will let the option expire worthless and simply lose his initial investment. However, while the call is in the money at index levels above 2,435, the investor will not realize a net profit until the September index level rises above 2,478.00, an amount equal to the exercise price plus the call premium $(X + C_{0,T})$. For the put option payoffs shown in Panel B, the holder will exercise the contract at September index levels below the exercise price, using the contract to sell for $2,435 an S&P share that is worth less than that. However, Exhibit 14.7 also documents that the put investor will not realize a positive net profit until the index level falls below 2,392.90 $(X − P_{0,T})$. For September S&P values above 2,435, the put option expires out of the money.

Exhibit 14.6 Standard & Poor's 500 Index Option Contract Price Quotations

SPX	↑ **2439.07**	+0.77	⟋⟍⟋⟍	2433.39 / 2442.26
At 15:04 d	O 2443.32	H 2450.42	L 2437.03	Prev 2438.30

SPX Index	95) Actions ▾	97) Settings ▾	Option Monitor

| S&P 500 INDEX | ↑ 2439.07 | .77 | .0316% | 2433.39 / 2442.26 | Hi 2450.42 | Lo 2437.03 | Volm 0 | HV 7.91 |

Center **2442.26** Strikes **5** Exp **30-Jun-17** ☐ ✎ Exch **US Composite** ☐   92) Events Calendar | EVTS »

℻ Calc Mode   As of ‹ 26-Jun-2017 › ☐   ⊕Q

81) Center Strike   82) Calls/Puts   83) Calls   84) Puts   85) Term Structure   87) Moneyness

	Calls					Strike	Puts				
Ticker	Bid	Ask	Last	IVM	Volm		Ticker	Bid	Ask	Last	IVM	Volm
15-Sep-17 (81d); CSize 100; IDiv 1.89; R 1.28; FF 2439.09						19☐	15-Sep-17 (81d); CSize 100; IDiv 1.89; R 1.28; FF 2439.09					
36) SPX 9/15/17 C2395	70.10	72.00	77.07y	10.59		2395	110) SPX 9/15/17 P2395	29.30	30.40	32.25y	10.51	
37) SPX 9/15/17 C2400	66.30	68.30	73.25	10.44	1	2400	111) SPX 9/15/17 P2400	30.50	31.60	31.20	10.35	442
38) SPX 9/15/17 C2405	62.60	63.90	68.40y	10.20		2405	112) SPX 9/15/17 P2405	31.80	32.90	34.05	10.19	4
39) SPX 9/15/17 C2410	59.00	60.30	58.70y	10.04		2410	113) SPX 9/15/17 P2410	33.10	34.20	32.25	10.02	19
40) SPX 9/15/17 C2415	55.40	56.70	58.00y	9.88		2415	114) SPX 9/15/17 P2415	34.50	35.70	35.50	9.87	110
41) SPX 9/15/17 C2420	51.90	53.20	54.00y	9.71		2420	115) SPX 9/15/17 P2420	36.00	37.10	35.55	9.70	61
42) SPX 9/15/17 C2425	48.50	49.80	51.30	9.55	250	2425	116) SPX 9/15/17 P2425	37.50	38.70	37.70	9.53	1009
43) SPX 9/15/17 C2430	45.20	46.30	45.20y	9.38		2430	117) SPX 9/15/17 P2430	39.20	40.30	38.30	9.37	29
44) SPX 9/15/17 C2435	42.00	43.00	43.00	9.22	1097	2435	118) SPX 9/15/17 P2435	40.90	42.10	41.00	9.22	1105
45) SPX 9/15/17 C2440	38.80	40.10	40.30	9.08	4746	2440	119) SPX 9/15/17 P2440	42.70	43.90	42.30	9.05	4745
46) SPX 9/15/17 C2445	35.80	36.80	37.90	8.92	3477	2445	120) SPX 9/15/17 P2445	44.70	45.80	42.60	8.89	3513
47) SPX 9/15/17 C2450	32.90	33.80	34.37	8.75	2933	2450	121) SPX 9/15/17 P2450	46.70	47.90	45.63	8.74	2584
48) SPX 9/15/17 C2455	30.00	31.20	32.80y	8.60		2455	122) SPX 9/15/17 P2455	49.10	50.20	54.00y	8.59	
49) SPX 9/15/17 C2460	27.30	28.40	30.10y	8.44		2460	123) SPX 9/15/17 P2460	51.10	52.40	50.30	8.43	14
50) SPX 9/15/17 C2465	24.80	25.80	26.38	8.29	1	2465	124) SPX 9/15/17 P2465	52.80	54.80		8.20	
51) SPX 9/15/17 C2470	22.30	23.40	23.55	8.15	1	2470	125) SPX 9/15/17 P2470	56.00	57.30	58.21y	8.12	
52) SPX 9/15/17 C2475	20.10	21.10	21.85	8.02	115	2475	126) SPX 9/15/17 P2475	58.70	60.00	59.90	7.98	7
53) SPX 9/15/17 C2480	17.90	18.70	19.15	7.85	1	2480	127) SPX 9/15/17 P2480	60.70	63.20	61.63y	7.79	
54) SPX 9/15/17 C2485	15.90	16.60	17.80y	7.72		2485	128) SPX 9/15/17 P2485	64.50	67.00	85.20y	7.86	

Australia 61 2 9777 8600 Brazil 5511 2395 9000 Europe 44 20 7330 7500 Germany 49 69 9204 1210 Hong Kong 852 2977 6000
Japan 81 3 3201 8900   Singapore 65 6212 1000   U.S. 1 212 318 2000   Copyright 2017 Bloomberg Finance L.P.
                                                                                    SN 335716 CDT GMT−5:00 H698−3396−1 26−Jun−2017 15:19:28

14.2 Investing with Derivative Securities

Although the preceding section highlighted many of the differences between forward and option agreements, the two types of derivatives are quite similar in terms of the benefits they produce for investors. The ultimate difference between forwards and options lies in the way the investor must pay to acquire those benefits. This concept, along with an examination of the basic payoff and net profit structures that exist in these markets, is described below.

14.2.1 The Basic Nature of Derivative Investing

Consider Investor 1 who decides at Date 0 to purchase a share of stock in SAS Corporation six months from now, coinciding with an anticipated receipt of funds. We assume that both SAS stock forward contracts and call options are available with the market prices of $F_{0,T}$ and $C_{0,T}$ (where $T = 0.50$ year) and that the exercise price of the call option, X, is equal to $F_{0,T}$. Thus, if the investor wants to lock in the price now at which the stock purchase will eventually take place, he has two choices: a long position in the forward or the purchase of the call option. Exhibit 14.8 compares the Date 0 and Date T cash flow exchanges for both possibilities.

Exhibit 14.7 Contract Payoff and Net Profit at Expiration from Long Positions in S&P 500 Call and Put Option Contracts

A. Long Call with Exercise Price of 2,435

September S&P 500 Index Level	Call Payoff at Expiration	Initial Call Premium	Net Profit
2355.00	0.00	−43.00	−43.00
2375.00	0.00	−43.00	−43.00
2395.00	0.00	−43.00	−43.00
2415.00	0.00	−43.00	−43.00
2435.00	$(2,435 - 2,435) = 0.00$	−43.00	−43.00
2455.00	$(2,455 - 2,435) = 20.00$	−43.00	−23.00
2478.00	$(2,478 - 2,435) = 43.00$	−43.00	0.00
2495.00	$(2,495 - 2,435) = 60.00$	−43.00	17.00
2515.00	$(2,415 - 2,435) = 80.00$	−43.00	37.00

B. Long Put with Exercise Price of 2,435

September S&P 500 Index Level	Put Payoff at Expiration	Initial Put Premium	Net Profit
2355.00	$(2,435 - 2,355) = 80.00$	−42.10	37.90
2375.00	$(2,435 - 2,475) = 60.00$	−42.10	17.90
2392.90	$(2,435 - 2,392.90) = 42.10$	−42.10	0.00
2415.00	$(2,435 - 2,415) = 20.00$	−42.10	−22.10
2435.00	$(2,435 - 2,435) = 0.00$	−42.10	−42.10
2455.00	0.00	−42.10	−42.10
2475.00	0.00	−42.10	−42.10
2495.00	0.00	−42.10	−42.10
2515.00	0.00	−42.10	−42.10

The clear difference between these strategies is that the forward position requires no initial payment or receipt by either party to the transaction, whereas the investor (the call buyer) must pay a cash premium to the seller of the option. As noted, this front-end option payment releases the investor from the obligation to purchase SAS stock at Date T if the terms of the contract turn out to be unfavorable ($S_T < X$). This is shown in Panel B of Exhibit 14.8. When the expiration date price of SAS stock exceeds the exercise price, the investor will exercise the call and purchase the share of stock. However, this leads to exactly the same exchange as the long forward contract. It is only when the stock price falls below X (and $F_{0,T}$) on Date T that there is a difference between the two positions; under this condition, the right provided by the option *not* to purchase SAS stock is valuable since the investor in the forward contract will be required to execute that position at a loss. Thus, the call option can be viewed as the "good half" of the long forward position because it allows for the future acquisition of SAS stock at a fixed price but doesn't require the transaction to take place.

This is the critical distinction between forward and option contracts. Both the long forward and the long call positions provide the investor with exactly the same amount of "insurance" against the price of SAS stock rising over the next six months. That is, both contracts provide a payoff of $[S_T - X] = [S_T - F_{0,T}]$ whenever S_T exceeds X, which reduces the effective purchase price for the stock back to X. The difference is how the investor is required to pay for that price insurance. With a forward contract, no money is paid up front, but the investor will have to complete the purchase at the expiration date, even if the stock price falls below $F_{0,T}$. Conversely, the call option will never require a future settlement payment, but the investor will have to pay the premium at origination. Thus, for the same Date T benefit, the investor's

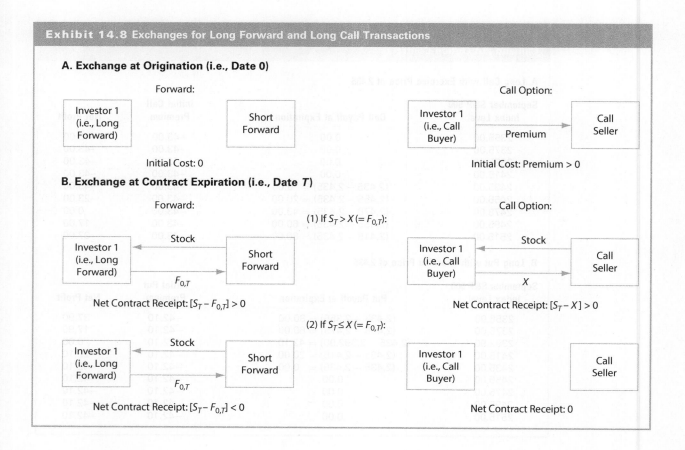

Exhibit 14.8 Exchanges for Long Forward and Long Call Transactions

A. Exchange at Origination (i.e., Date 0)

Forward:

Investor 1 (i.e., Long Forward) → Short Forward

Initial Cost: 0

Call Option:

Investor 1 (i.e., Call Buyer) — Premium → Call Seller

Initial Cost: Premium > 0

B. Exchange at Contract Expiration (i.e., Date T)

(1) If $S_T > X (= F_{0,T})$:

Forward:

Investor 1 (i.e., Long Forward) ← Stock — Short Forward, $F_{0,T}$ →

Net Contract Receipt: $[S_T - F_{0,T}] > 0$

Call Option:

Investor 1 (i.e., Call Buyer) ← Stock — Call Seller, X →

Net Contract Receipt: $[S_T - X] > 0$

(2) If $S_T \leq X (= F_{0,T})$:

Forward:

Investor 1 (i.e., Long Forward) — Stock → Short Forward ← $F_{0,T}$

Net Contract Receipt: $[S_T - F_{0,T}] < 0$

Call Option:

Investor 1 (i.e., Call Buyer)   Call Seller

Net Contract Receipt: 0

decision between these two "insurance policies" comes down to choosing the certainty of a present premium payment (long call) versus the possibility of a future payment (long forward) that could potentially be much larger.

To make this distinction clearer, suppose that Investor 1 plans to buy SAS stock in six months when some of the bonds in his portfolio mature. He is concerned that share values could rise substantially between now and the time he receives his investment funds, and so to hedge that risk he considers two insurance strategies to lock in the eventual purchase price: (1) Pay nothing now to take the long position in a six-month SAS stock forward contract with a contract price of $F_{0,T} = \$45$ or (2) pay a premium of $C_{0,T} = \$3.24$ for a six-month, European-style call option with an exercise price of $X = \$45$. If at the time of his decision the price of SAS stock is $S_0 = \$40$, the call option is out of the money, meaning that its intrinsic value is zero and the entire $3.24 is time premium.

As mentioned earlier, an obvious difference between these two strategies is that the option entails a front-end expense, while the forward position does not. The other difference occurs at the expiration date, depending on whether the SAS stock price is above or below $45. If, for instance, $S_T = \$51$, both the long forward position and the call option will be worth $6 (= 51 - 45) to the investor, reducing his net purchase price for SAS shares to $45 (= 51 - 6). That is, when the stock settled above $45 (the common value for $F_{0,T}$ and X), both the long forward and the long call positions provided the same protection against rising prices. On the other hand, if $S_T = \$40.75$, the forward contract would require the investor to pay $4.25 (= 40.75 - 45) to his counterparty, raising once again the net cost of his shares to $45. With the call option, however, he could have let the contract expire without exercising it and purchased his SAS shares in the market for only $40.75. Thus, in exchange for the option's front-end expense of $3.24, the investor retains the possibility of paying less than $45 for his eventual stock purchase.

The connection between forward contracts and put options can be made in a similar fashion. Suppose a different investor—call her Investor 2—has decided to liquidate a share of SAS stock from her portfolio in six months' time. Rather than risk a falling stock price over that period, she could arrange now to sell the share at that future date for a predetermined fixed price in one of two ways: a short forward position or the purchase of a put option. Exhibit 14.9 illustrates these alternatives. Similar to before, for the same insurance against SAS stock price declines, the choice comes down to the certainty of paying the put option premium versus the possibility of making a potentially larger payment with the forward contract by having to sell her stock for X $(= F_{0,T})$ when the stock's Date T market price is higher. Notice once again that the put option allows the investor to walk away from her obligation under the short forward position to sell her stock on the expiration date under disadvantageous conditions. Thus, in exchange for a front-end premium payment, the put option enables the investor to acquire the "good half" of the short position in a forward contract.

14.2.2 Basic Payoff and Profit Diagrams for Forward Contracts

Exhibit 14.8 and Exhibit 14.9 show that the respective expiration date payoffs for long and short positions in a forward contract are $[S_T - F_{0,T}]$ and $[F_{0,T} - S_T]$ and that these values could be either positive or negative, depending on the spot price prevailing at Date T.

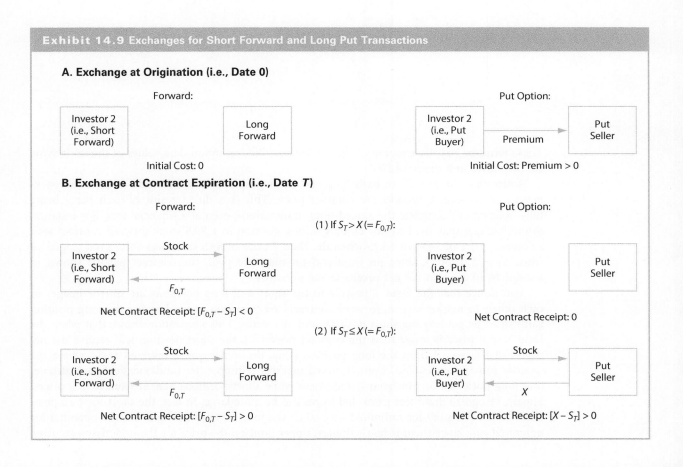

Exhibit 14.9 Exchanges for Short Forward and Long Put Transactions

A. Exchange at Origination (i.e., Date 0)

Forward:

Investor 2 (i.e., Short Forward) → Long Forward

Initial Cost: 0

Put Option:

Investor 2 (i.e., Put Buyer) — Premium → Put Seller

Initial Cost: Premium > 0

B. Exchange at Contract Expiration (i.e., Date T)

Forward:

(1) If $S_T > X (= F_{0,T})$:

Investor 2 (i.e., Short Forward) — Stock → Long Forward ← $F_{0,T}$

Net Contract Receipt: $[F_{0,T} - S_T] < 0$

(2) If $S_T \leq X (= F_{0,T})$:

Investor 2 (i.e., Short Forward) — Stock → Long Forward ← $F_{0,T}$

Net Contract Receipt: $[F_{0,T} - S_T] > 0$

Put Option:

Investor 2 (i.e., Put Buyer)   Put Seller

Net Contract Receipt: 0

Investor 2 (i.e., Put Buyer) — Stock → Put Seller ← X

Net Contract Receipt: $[X - S_T] > 0$

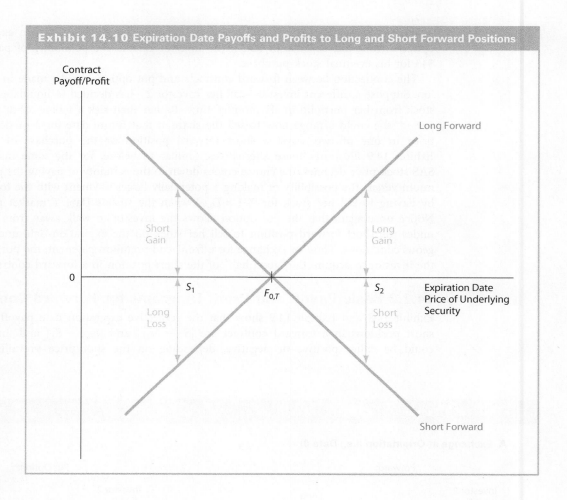

Exhibit 14.10 Expiration Date Payoffs and Profits to Long and Short Forward Positions

These terminal payoffs are plotted against the possible expiration date values of the underlying security price in Exhibit 14.10.

Notice that the payoffs to both long and short positions in the forward contract are *symmetric*, or two-sided, around the contract price. This is a direct result of each party being fully obligated to complete the agreed-upon transaction—even at a financial loss. For instance, in the last example, the investor holding a long position in a SAS stock forward contract with a contract price of $45 lost $4.25 when the Date T price of SAS stock was $40.75 but gained $6 when $S_T = \$51$. Also, since no front-end premia were paid, the contract payoffs shown in Exhibit 14.10 are also the net profits to the investors.

Also notice that the Date T payoffs to the short and long positions are mirror images of each other; in market jargon, forward contracts are *zero-sum games* because the long position gains must be paid by the short position and vice versa. This illustration shows that when the Date T spot price is lower than the contract price (S_1), the short position will receive the net payoff of $[F_{0,T} - S_1]$ from the long position while the settlement is reversed at S_2, where the security price is above $F_{0,T}$. Thus, forward markets reinforce the fundamental financial tenet that long positions benefit from rising prices while short positions benefit from falling prices. Finally, recognize that these gains and losses can be quite large. In fact, the short forward position has the potential for unlimited loss, while the long forward position has the potential for unlimited gain since there is no theoretical upper limit on the price for the underlying security.

Conversely, the loss potential for the long position (and the gain potential for the short position) is limited because the price of the underlying security cannot fall below zero.

14.2.3 Basic Payoff and Profit Diagrams for Call and Put Options

Exhibits 14.8 and 14.9 also show that options differ from forward contracts in two fundamental ways: (1) The expense of purchasing either a put or a call represents a sunk cost to the investor, reducing the upside return relative to the comparable forward position, and (2) the investor receives expiration date payoffs that are decidedly *asymmetric*, or one-sided. Exhibit 14.11 shows the terminal payoffs and net profits to both long and short positions in call options, while Exhibit 14.12 provides a similar illustration for put option traders. This analysis assumes that both options are European style, meaning they cannot be exercised prematurely.

For call option positions, notice again that the buyer of the contract receives a payoff whenever the terminal security price (S_T) exceeds the contract purchase (exercise) price of X. However, given an initial premium of $C_{0,T}$, the position doesn't generate a positive profit until S_T is greater than X by the amount of the premium paid. Put another way, although the call option is in the money (and hence will be exercised) when $S_T > X$, it will not produce a capital gain for the buyer until $S_T > (X + C_{0,T})$.[3] (Recall that this result was shown for the S&P 500 Index option example in Exhibit 14.7.) When $X < S_T < (X + C_{0,T})$, the option is exercised at a loss, but this loss will be less than the full initial cost of the option, which is what the long position would incur if the call were not exercised. In fact, when $S_T < X$, the option is out of the money and the buyer who makes the rational decision to let the contract expire will lose $C_{0,T}$.

The buyer of the call option has unlimited gain potential as the underlying security price could rise indefinitely but his losses are limited to the option premium, no matter how far the security's price falls. On the other hand, the option seller benefits when the terminal price of the underlying asset is lower than X but only to the extent that he gets to keep the full amount of the option premium. When $S_T > X$, the seller of the call has unlimited liability. As with forward contracts, the call option is a zero-sum game between the long and short positions.

For the put option positions shown in Exhibit 14.12, the buyer benefits whenever $X > S_T$ and receives a positive profit when the Date T price of the underlying security falls below the exercise price, less the cost of the option. In this case, the put buyer's maximum capital gain is limited to $X - P_{0,T}$ as the underlying security itself is limited to a minimum price of zero; the best the put holder can hope for is to force the seller of the contract to buy worthless stock for X at the expiration date. As with the call option, the owner of an out-of-the-money put can only lose his initial investment of $P_{0,T}$, which will occur when $S_T > X$. Not surprisingly, the profit and loss opportunities for the put seller are exactly opposite of those for the put buyer. The contract seller will gain when $S_T > (X - P_{0,T})$, but this gain is limited to the amount of the option premium. A short position in a put also has limited loss potential; but, at a maximum of $X - P_{0,T}$, this can still be a large amount.

In summary, when held as investments, options are *directional views* on movements in the price of the underlying security. Call buyers and put sellers count on S_T to rise (or remain) above X, while put buyers and call sellers hope for S_T to fall (or remain) below the exercise price at the expiration date. Importantly, option buyers—whether a put or a call—always have limited liability since they do not have to exercise an out-of-the-money position.

---

[3]The expiration date profits shown in Exhibits 14.11 and 14.12 are somewhat inaccurate in that they show the net of the Date T value of the option and its initial cost, which was paid at Date 0. Thus, although this is an accurate way of portraying capital gains and losses from an accounting standpoint, it ignores the difference in the timing of the two payments.

Exhibit 14.11 Expiration Date Payoffs and Profits to Long and Short Call Positions

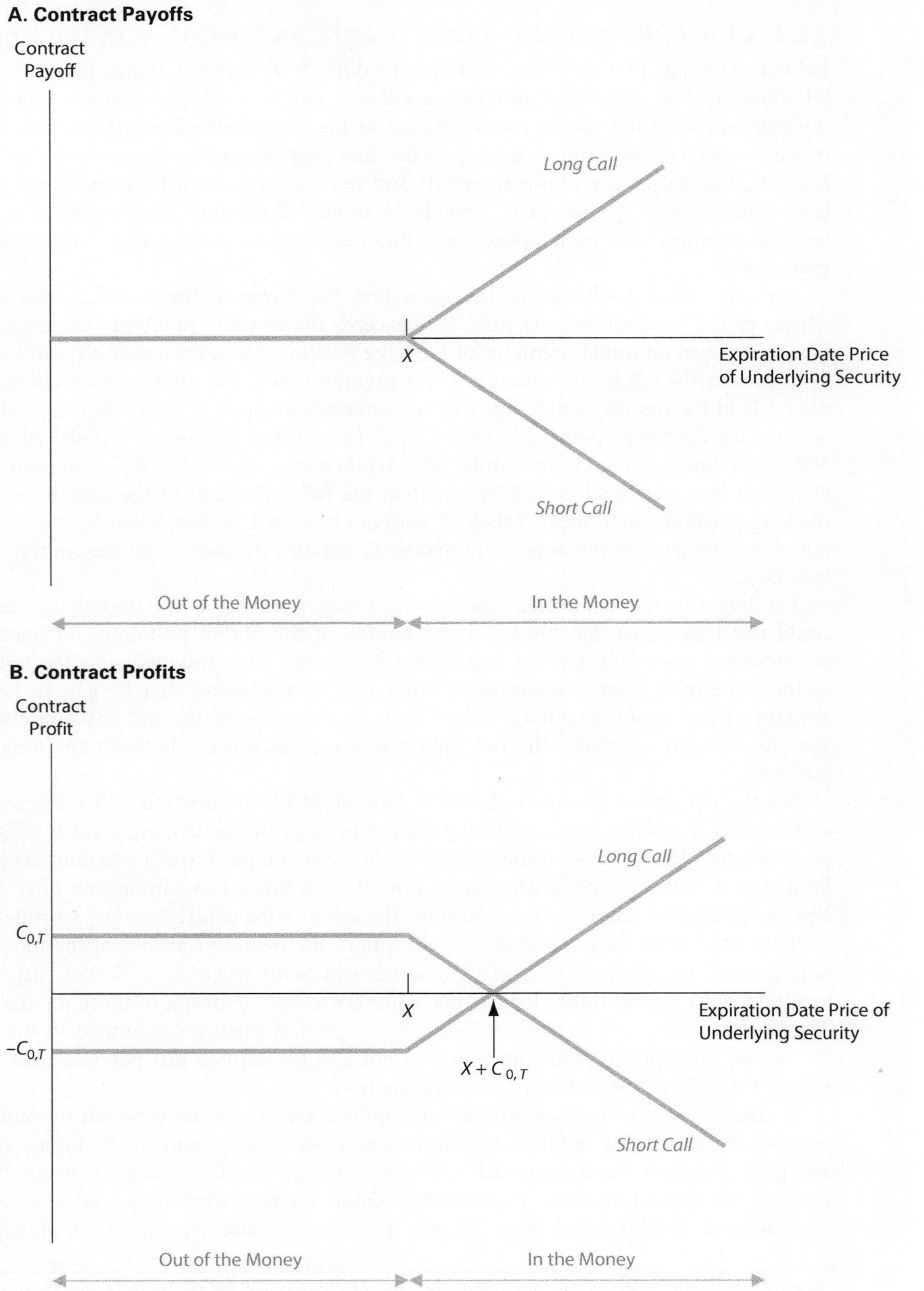

A. Contract Payoffs

Contract
Payoff

Long Call

X

Expiration Date Price
of Underlying Security

Short Call

Out of the Money ⟷ In the Money

B. Contract Profits

Contract
Profit

Long Call

$C_{0,T}$

X

Expiration Date Price of
Underlying Security

$-C_{0,T}$

$X + C_{0,T}$

Short Call

Out of the Money ⟷ In the Money

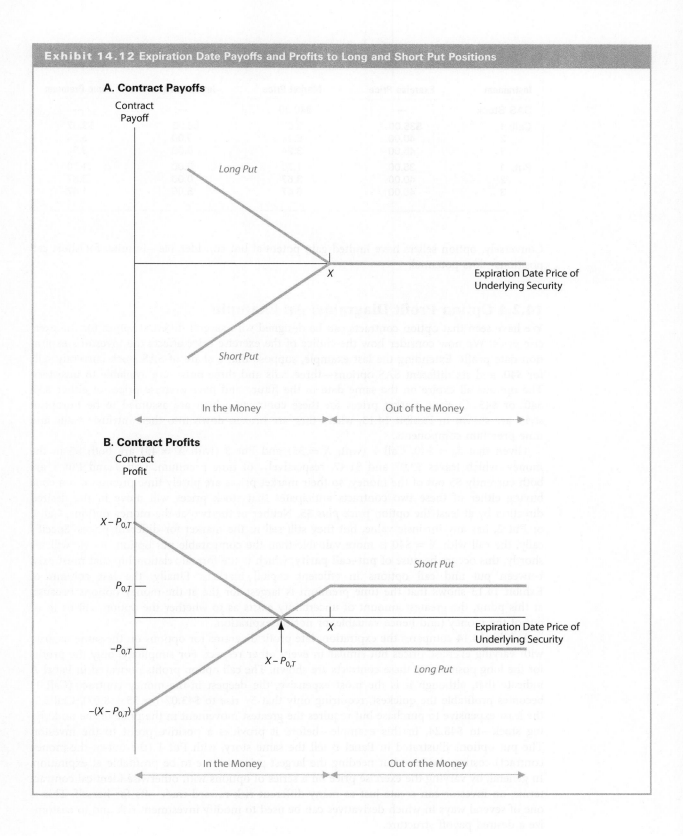

Exhibit 14.12 Expiration Date Payoffs and Profits to Long and Short Put Positions

A. Contract Payoffs

Contract Payoff

Long Put

X

Expiration Date Price of Underlying Security

Short Put

In the Money ⟷ Out of the Money

B. Contract Profits

Contract Profit

$X - P_{0,T}$

Short Put

$P_{0,T}$

X

Expiration Date Price of Underlying Security

$-P_{0,T}$

$X - P_{0,T}$

Long Put

$-(X - P_{0,T})$

In the Money ⟷ Out of the Money

Exhibit 14.13 Hypothetical Stock and Option Prices

Instrument	Exercise Price	Market Price	Intrinsic Value	Time Premium
SAS Stock	—	$40.00	—	—
Call: 1	$35.00	8.07	$5.00	$3.07
2	40.00	5.24	0.00	5.24
3	45.00	3.24	0.00	3.24
Put: 1	35.00	1.70	0.00	1.70
2	40.00	3.67	0.00	3.67
3	45.00	6.47	5.00	1.47

Conversely, option sellers have limited gain potential but considerable—infinite, for short call positions—loss potential.

14.2.4 Option Profit Diagrams: An Example

We have seen that option contracts can be designed with several different values for the exercise price. We now consider how the choice of the exercise price affects the investor's expiration date profit. Extending the last example, suppose that a share of SAS stock currently sells for $40, and six different SAS options—three calls and three puts—are available to investors. The options all expire on the same date in the future and have exercise prices of either $35, $40, or $45. Current market prices for these contracts, which are assumed to be European style, are shown in Exhibit 14.13, where they are broken down into their intrinsic value and time premium components.

Given that $S_0 = \$40$, Call 1 (with $X = 35$) and Put 3 (with $X = 45$) are both $5 in the money, which leaves $3.07 and $1.47, respectively, of time premium. Call 3 and Put 1 are both currently $5 out of the money, so their market prices are purely time premium; someone buying either of these two contracts anticipates that stock prices will move in the desired direction by at least the option price *plus* $5. Neither of the two at-the-money options, Call 2 or Put 2, has any intrinsic value, but they still sell in the market for different prices. Specifically, the call with $X = \$40$ is more valuable than the comparable put option. As we will see shortly, this occurs because of **put–call parity**, which is the formal relationship that must exist between put and call options in efficient capital markets. Finally, the last column of Exhibit 14.13 shows that the time premium is largest for the at-the-money options because, at this point, the greatest amount of uncertainty exists as to whether the option will be in or out of the money (and hence valuable, or not) at expiration.

Exhibit 14.14 compares the expiration date profit diagrams for options on the same security with varying exercise prices but similar in every other respect. For simplicity, only the profits for the long positions in these contracts are shown. The call option profits portrayed in Panel A indicate that, although it is the most expensive, the deepest in-the-money contract (Call 1) becomes profitable the quickest, requiring only that S_T rise to $43.07 ($= 35 + 8.07$). Call 3 is the least expensive to purchase but requires the greatest movement in the price of the underlying stock—to $48.24, in this example—before it provides a positive profit to the investor. The put options illustrated in Panel B tell the same story, with Put 1 (the out-of-the-money contract) costing the least but needing the largest price decline to be profitable at expiration. In general, by varying the exercise price on a series of options with otherwise identical contract terms, an investor can create just as many different risk-reward trade-offs for herself. This is one of several ways in which derivatives can be used to modify investment risk and to customize a desired payoff structure.

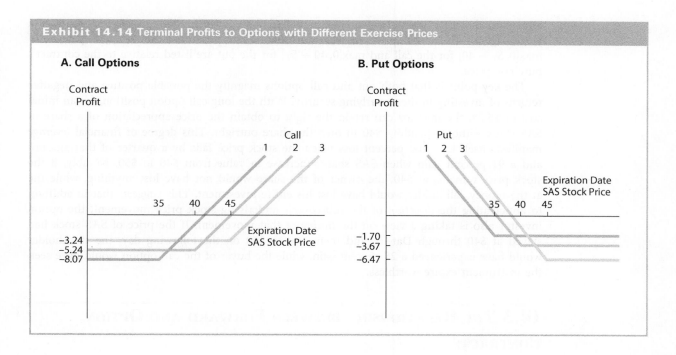

Exhibit 14.14 Terminal Profits to Options with Different Exercise Prices

A. Call Options

Contract Profit

Call 1 2 3

35 40 45

Expiration Date SAS Stock Price

−3.24
−5.24
−8.07

B. Put Options

Contract Profit

Put 1 2 3

35 40 45

Expiration Date SAS Stock Price

−1.70
−3.67
−6.47

Options and Leverage As a final extension of this example, we compare the returns to an investment in either a put or a call option with a direct investment (or short sale) in a share of the underlying SAS stock. We will limit the analysis to Call 2 and Put 2, the two at-the-money contracts. Exhibit 14.15 summarizes the holding period returns for various positions assuming three different expiration date stock prices: $30, $40, and $50. Two different comparisons are made: (1) long stock versus long call and (2) short stock versus long put. In calculating the

Exhibit 14.15 Stock and Option Investment Returns

A. Long Stock versus Long Call

Terminal Stock Price	Long Stock	Long Call
30	$\frac{30}{40} - 1 = -25.0\%$	$\frac{0}{5.24} - 1 = -100.0\%$
40	$\frac{40}{40} - 1 = 0.0\%$	$\frac{0}{5.24} - 1 = -100.0\%$
50	$\frac{50}{40} - 1 = 25.0\%$	$\frac{10}{5.24} - 1 = 90.8\%$

B. Short Stock versus Long Put

Terminal Stock Price	Long Stock	Long Call
30	$1 - \frac{30}{40} = 25.0\%$	$\frac{10}{3.67} - 1 = 172.5\%$
40	$1 - \frac{40}{40} = 0.0\%$	$\frac{0}{3.67} - 1 = -100.0\%$
50	$1 - \frac{50}{40} = -25.0\%$	$\frac{0}{3.67} - 1 = -100.0\%$

returns to the stock positions, we have measured the change in value of the SAS share as a percentage of the initial price of $40. For the option positions, the terminal payoffs of $\max[0, S_T - 40]$ for the call and $\max[0, 40 - S_T]$ for the put are listed relative to the contract's purchase price.

The key point is that both put and call options magnify the possible positive and negative returns of investing in the underlying security. With the long call option position, for an initial cost of $5.24, the investor can retain the right to obtain the price appreciation of a share of SAS stock without spending $40 to own the share outright. This degree of financial *leverage* manifests itself in a 100 percent loss when the stock price falls by a quarter of that amount and a 91 percent gain when SAS shares increase in value from $40 to $50. Notably, if the stock price remains at $40, the owner of the share would not have lost anything, while the at-the-money call holder would have lost his entire investment. This suggests that in addition to anticipating the *direction* of the subsequent underlying stock price movement, the option investor also is taking a view on the *timing* of that movement. If the price of SAS stock had stayed at $40 through Date T and then rose to $50 on the following day, the stockholder would have experienced a 25 percent gain, while the buyer of the call option would have seen the instrument expire worthless.

14.3 THE RELATIONSHIP BETWEEN FORWARD AND OPTION CONTRACTS

The preceding discussion showed that positions in forward and option contracts can lead to similar investment payoffs if the price of the underlying security moves in the anticipated direction. This similarity in payoff structures suggests that these instruments are connected. In fact, we will see that the values of five different securities can be linked: a risk-free bond, an underlying asset, a forward contract for the future purchase or sale of that asset, a call option, and a put option. These relationships, known as put–call parity, specify how the put and call premia should be set relative to one another. Further, these conditions can be expressed in terms of these two option types and either the spot or the forward market price for the underlying asset. They depend on the assumption that financial markets are free from arbitrage opportunities, meaning that securities (or portfolios of securities) offering identical payoffs with identical risks must sell for the same current price. As such, put–call parity represents a crucial first step in understanding how derivatives are valued in an efficient capital market.[4]

14.3.1 Put–Call–Spot Parity

Suppose that at Date 0 an investor forms the following portfolio involving three securities related to Company WYZ:

- Long in a share of WYZ common stock at a purchase price of S_0.
- Long in a put option to deliver one share of WYZ stock at an exercise price of X on the Expiration Date T. This put is purchased for the price of $P_{0,T}$.
- Short in a call option allowing the purchase of one share of WYZ stock at an exercise price of X on the Expiration Date T. This call is sold for the price of $C_{0,T}$.

In this example, both of the WYZ options are European style and have the same expiration date and exercise price. However, the specific values of the expiration date and exercise price

[4]The development of the relationships linking put and call option prices is commonly attributed to Stoll (1969). Others have embellished Stoll's findings in many interesting ways; those subsequent studies include Merton (1973a), Klemkosky and Resnick (1979), Cremers and Weinbaum (2010), and Chen, Chung, and Yuan (2014).

Exhibit 14.16 Put–Call–Spot Parity

A. Net Portfolio Investment at Initiation (Date 0)

Portfolio

Long 1 WYZ stock	S_0
Long 1 put option	$P_{0,T}$
Short 1 call option	$-C_{0,T}$
Net investment:	$S_0 + P_{0,T} - C_{0,T}$

B. Portfolio Value at Option Expiration (Date T)

Portfolio	(1) If $S_T \leq X$:	(2) If $S_T > X$:
Long 1 WYZ stock	S_T	S_T
Long 1 put option	$(X - S_T)$	0
Short 1 call option	0	$-(S_T - X)$
Net position:	X	X

---

do not matter in the analysis that follows. Further, we will assume initially that WYZ stock does not pay a dividend during the life of the options.

Panel A of Exhibit 14.16 lists the Date 0 investment necessary to acquire this portfolio as $(S_0 + P_{0,T} - C_{0,T})$, which is the cost of the long positions in the stock and the put option less the proceeds generated by the sale of the call option.[5] Consider also the value that this portfolio will have at the expiration date of the two options. Given that the stock's value at Date T (S_T) is unknown when the investment is made at Date 0, two general outcomes are possible: (1) $S_T \leq X$ and (2) $S_T > X$. Panel B shows the value of each position as well as the net value of the whole portfolio at Date T.

Whenever the Date T value of WYZ stock is less than the exercise price common to the put and call options, the investor will exercise the long position in the put and sell the WYZ share for X instead of its lower market value. In that case, it will not be rational for the holder of the call to pay X for a share that is worth less so the call will expire out of the money. On the other hand, when S_T exceeds X, the holder of the call will exercise the option to purchase WYZ stock for X, while the put would be out of the money. In either scenario, the net expiration date value of the portfolio is X because the combination of options guarantees that the investor will sell the share of WYZ stock at Date T for the fixed price X. The investor has, in effect, a guaranteed contract to sell the share of stock when the long put and short call positions are held jointly.

The consequence of this result is that when the investor commits $(S_0 + P_{0,T} - C_{0,T})$ to acquire the position at Date 0, he knows that the portfolio will be worth X at Date T. Thus, this particular portfolio has a comparable payoff structure to a U.S. Treasury bill, another risk-free, zero-coupon security that can have a face value of X and a maturity date T. In an arbitrage-free market, this means that the Date 0 value of the portfolio must be equal to that of the T-bill, which is just the face value X discounted to the present using the risk-free rate. This "no arbitrage" condition can be formalized as:

14.1
$$S_0 + P_{0,T} - C_{0,T} = \frac{X}{(1 + \text{RFR})^T}$$

---

[5]In the "arithmetic" of engineering financial portfolios, a plus ($+$) sign can be interpreted as a long position, and a minus ($-$) sign represents a short position. Thus, the portfolio investment represented by $(S_0 + P_{0,T} - C_{0,T})$ can also be expressed as (long stock) + (long put) + (short call). Smith (1989a) explains this approach in more detail.

where:

RFR = annualized risk-free rate

T = time to maturity (expressed in years)

Defining $[X(1 + \text{RFR})^{-T}]$ as the present value of a T-bill, this equation can be expressed on Date 0 in financial arithmetic terms as:

$$(\text{Long Stock}) + (\text{Long Put}) + (\text{Short Call}) = (\text{Long T-Bill})$$

In either form, this condition—known as the *put–call–spot* parity condition—represents the efficient market linkages between prices for stock, T-bills, put options, and call options.

14.3.2 Put–Call Parity: An Example

Suppose that WYZ stock is currently valued at $53 and that call and put options on WYZ stock with an exercise price of $50 sell for $6.74 and $2.51, respectively. If both options can only be exercised in exactly six months, Equation 14.1 suggests that we can create a synthetic T-bill (that is, mimic the cash flows and risk profile of a T-bill) by purchasing the stock, purchasing the put, and selling the call for a net price of $48.77 (= 53.00 + 2.51 − 6.74). On the options' expiration date, this portfolio would have a terminal value of $50. Thus, the risk-free rate implied by this investment can be established by solving the following equation for RFR:

$$48.77 = 50(1 + \text{RFR})^{-0.5}$$

or:

$$\text{RFR} = [(50 \div 48.77)^2 - 1] = 5.11\%$$

If the rate of return on an actual six-month T-bill with a face value of $50 is not 5.11 percent, then an investor could exploit the difference. Suppose, for instance, that the actual T-bill rate is 6.25 percent and that there are no restrictions against using the proceeds from the short sale of any security. An investor wanting a risk-free investment would clearly choose the actual T-bill to lock in the higher return, while someone seeking a loan might attempt to secure a 5.11 percent borrowing rate by short-selling the synthetic T-bill. With a rearrangement of Equation 14.1, such an artificial short position can be obtained as:

$$(\text{Short Stock}) + (\text{Short Put}) + (\text{Long Call}) = (\text{Short T-Bill})$$

With no transaction costs, a financial arbitrage could be constructed by combining a long position in the actual T-bill with a short sale of the synthetic portfolio. Given that the current value of the actual T-bill is $48.51 [= $50(1.0625)^{-0.5}]$, this set of transactions would generate the cash flows shown in Exhibit 14.17 and produce a $0.26 profit per each T-bill pair created. As the arbitrage trade did not require the investor to bear any risk (since both the Date 0 and the Date T values of the net position were known at inception) or commit any capital, there is nothing in this example to prevent the investor from expanding the size of the trade to increasingly larger levels. However, as additional transactions take place, the price discrepancy will disappear. In this case, the purchase of the actual T-bill and sale of the synthetic (short stock, short put, and long call) will continue until rates are equalized. This is how the markets remain efficient through arbitrage trading.

Another way of seeing this trade is:

$$C_{0,T} - P_{0,T} = S_0 - X(1 + \text{RFR})^{-T}$$

Exhibit 14.17 Put–Call Parity Arbitrage Example

A. Net Initial Investment (Date 0)

Transaction	
1. Long actual T-bill at 6.25%	−48.51
2. Short synthetic T-bill at 5.11%:	
Short WYZ stock	53.00
Short put option	2.51
Long call option	−6.74
Net receipt:	0.26

B. Position Value at Option Expiration (Date T)

Transaction	(1) If $S_T \leq 50$:	(2) If $S_T > 50$:
1. Long actual T-bill at 6.25%	50	50
2. Short synthetic T-bill at 5.11%:		
Short WYZ stock	$-S_T$	$-S_T$
Short put option	$-(50 - S_T)$	0
Long call option	0	$(S_T - 50)$
Net position:	0	0

That is, the "no arbitrage" difference between the call and put prices should equal the difference between the stock price and the present value of the joint exercise price. The market-determined risk-free rate of 6.25 percent implies that the correct difference between the two derivatives should be $4.49 ($= 53 − 48.51$), which is $0.26 greater than the $4.23 ($= 6.74 − 2.51$) actual difference. This discrepancy suggests that if you assume the actual T-bill is priced correctly, the call price is undervalued relative to the put option. Not surprisingly, then, the arbitrage transaction requires the purchase of the call option while shorting the put option.

14.3.3 Creating Synthetic Securities Using Put–Call Parity

The preceding example demonstrates that a risk-free portfolio could be created by combining three risky securities: stock, a put option, and a call option. The parity condition developed in the example can be expressed in other useful ways as well. In particular, one of the four assets represented in Equation 14.1 is always *redundant* because it can be defined in terms of the others. Three additional ways of expressing this result are:

14.2
$$P_{0,T} = \frac{X}{(1 + \text{RFR})^T} - S_0 + C_{0,T}$$

14.3
$$C_{0,T} = S_0 + P_{0,T} - \frac{X}{(1 + \text{RFR})^T}$$

14.4
$$S_0 = \frac{X}{(1 + \text{RFR})^T} - P_{0,T} + C_{0,T}$$

Equation 14.2 and Equation 14.3 indicate, respectively, that (1) the payoffs to a long position in a put option can be replicated by a portfolio holding a long position in a T-bill, a short stock position, and the purchase of a call option; and (2) a synthetic call option can be mimicked by a portfolio that is long in the stock and the put option and short in the T-bill. Equation 14.4 indicates that the payoff to the stock itself can be created with its derivative securities and the T-bill.

These results are useful in two ways. First, if actual put or call options do not exist, these equations demonstrate how investors can obtain the desired, but unavailable, pattern of cash

---

Exhibit 14.18 Replicating a Put Option

A. Net Portfolio Investment at Initiation (Date 0)

Portfolio

Long 1 T-bill	$X(1 + \text{RFR})^{-T}$
Short 1 WYZ stock	$-S_0$
Long 1 call option Net position:	$C_{0,T}$
Net investment:	$X(1 + \text{RFR})^{-T} - S_0 + C_{0,T}$

B. Portfolio Value at Option Expiration (Date *T*)

Portfolio	(1) If $S_T \leq X$:	(2) If $S_T > X$:
Long 1 T-bill	X	X
Short 1 WYZ stock	$-S_T$	$-S_T$
Long 1 call option Net position:	0	$(S_T - X)$
Net position:	$X - S_T$	0

---

flows through the appropriate "packaging" of the other three assets. Suppose, for example, that a put option on WYZ stock did not exist but a call option does. Exhibit 14.18 shows the Date 0 and Date T cash flows associated with the portfolio replicating the terminal payoff. Combining both panels of the display, an initial investment of $[X(1 + \text{RFR})^{-T} - S_0 + C_{0,T}]$ leads to a final cash flow that is no less than zero and as large as $X - S_T$ whenever $X > S_T$. Expressed in a more traditional manner, the expiration date payoff to the synthetic put is $\max[0, X - S_T]$.

A second way these alternative put–call parity expressions are used in practice is in identifying arbitrage opportunities. Even when a derivative instrument does exist, if its cash flows and risks can be duplicated, this leads to the possibility that the price of the actual instrument and the net cost of the replicating portfolio will differ. From the previous example, the Date T distribution of $\max[0, 50 - S_T]$ could be acquired through the synthetic strategy at a cost of $\$2.25(= 48.51 - 53 + 6.74)$ or through the purchase of the actual put for $\$2.51$.

This is the same $\$0.26$ price differential we saw earlier when designing an arbitrage transaction involving the actual and synthetic T-bill. The put option arbitrage would be to short the actual put while buying the replicating portfolio (long T-bill, short stock, and long call), which is the same set of transactions we used in the T-bill arbitrage in Exhibit 14.17. This underscores the important point that the put–call parity model only allows us to make *relative*—not absolute—statements about security values. Although we can change our perspective about the misvalued instrument (for example, T-bill versus put option), the real source of the market inefficiency came from examining the *difference* between the put and call prices in relation to the stock and T-bill prices. Consequently, all four securities need to be included in the arbitrage trade.

14.3.4 Adjusting Put–Call–Spot Parity for Dividends

Another extension of the put–call–spot parity model involves the payment of dividends to the shareholders of WYZ stock. Suppose that in the basic portfolio listed in Exhibit 14.16, WYZ stock pays a dividend of D_T immediately prior to the expiration of the options at Date T and that the amount of this distribution is known when the investment is initiated. With this adjustment, the terminal value of the long stock position will be $(S_T + D_T)$, while the terminal payoffs to the put and call options remain $\max[0, X - S_T]$ and $\max[0, S_T - X]$, respectively, as the holders of the two derivative contracts will not participate directly in the payment of dividends to the stockholder.[6] Thus, the net Date T value of the portfolio acquired originally for $(S_0 + P_{0,T} - C_{0,T})$ is $(X + D_T)$.

Since the dividend payment is known at Date 0, the portfolio long in WYZ stock, long in the put, and short in the call once again can be viewed as equivalent to a T-bill, now having a face value of $(X + D_T)$. This allows Equation 14.1 to be adapted as follows:

$$S_0 + P_{0,T} - C_{0,T} = \frac{X + D_T}{(1 + \text{RFR})^T} = \frac{X}{(1 + \text{RFR})^T} + \frac{D_T}{(1 + \text{RFR})^T}$$

which can be interpreted as:

(Long Stock) + (Long Put) + (Short Call) = (Long T-Bill) + (Long Present Value of Dividends).

Alternatively, it is often more useful to rearrange this result as follows:

$$\left\{ S_0 - \frac{D_T}{(1 + \text{RFR})^T} \right\} + P_{0,T} - C_{0,T} = \frac{X}{(1 + \text{RFR})^T}$$

This form of the equation can be compared directly with the no-dividend put–call–spot parity result and shows that the current stock price must be *adjusted downward* by the present value of the dividend. With an initial stock price of $53 and an annualized risk-free rate on a six-month T-bill of 6.25 percent, a $1 dividend paid just before the expiration of a call and a put option with an exercise price of $50 would result in a theoretical price differential of:

$$C_{0,0.5} - P_{0,0.5} = \left\{ 53 - \frac{1}{(1 + 0.0625)^{0.5}} \right\} - \frac{50}{(1 + 0.0625)^{0.5}} = \$3.52.$$

This value differs from the parity differential for options on the non-dividend-paying stock, which was shown earlier to be $4.49. Thus, the payment of the dividend has reduced the price of the call relative to the put by $0.97, which is the discounted amount of the $1 cash distribution.

14.3.5 Put–Call–Forward Parity

Suppose that instead of buying the stock in the spot market at Date 0, we took a long position in a forward contract, allowing us to purchase one share of WYZ stock at Date T. The price of this acquisition, $F_{0,T}$, would be established at Date 0. As before, we assume that this transaction is supplemented by the purchase of a put option and the sale of a call option, each having the same exercise price and expiration date. Exhibit 14.19 summarizes both the initial and the terminal cash flows to this position.

Panel B reveals that this is once again a risk-free portfolio. There are, however, two important differences in its cash flow patterns. First, the net initial investment of $(P_{0,T} - C_{0,T})$ is substantially smaller than when the stock was purchased in the spot market. Second, the riskless terminal payoff of $(X - F_{0,T})$ also is smaller than before as the stock is now purchased at Date T rather than at Date 0. This intuition leads to the *put–call–forward* parity condition:

14.5
$$P_{0,T} - C_{0,T} = \frac{X - F_{0,T}}{(1 + \text{RFR})^T} = \frac{X}{(1 + \text{RFR})^T} - \frac{F_{0,T}}{(1 + \text{RFR})^T}$$

---

[6]The fact that the expiration date payoff to a call option on both a dividend- and a non-dividend-paying stock can be expressed as $\max[0, S_T - X]$ does not mean that the two will generate the same dollar amount of cash flow. This is because the stock's value will be reduced by the payment of the dividend in the former case but not in the latter. Thus, the call on the dividend-paying stock will be less valuable than an otherwise comparable contract on a non-dividend-paying equity. We will explore this topic more fully in Chapter 16.

Exhibit 14.19 Put-Call-Forward Parity

A. Net Portfolio Investment at Initiation (Date 0)

Portfolio	
Long 1 WYZ stock	0
Long 1 put option	$P_{0,T}$
Short 1 call option	$-C_{0,T}$
Net investment:	$P_{0,T} - C_{0,T}$

B. Portfolio Value at Option Expiration (Date T)

Portfolio	(1) If $S_T \leq X$:	(2) If $S_T > X$:
Long 1 WYZ stock	$(S_T - F_{0,T})$	$(S_T - F_{0,T})$
Long 1 put option	$(X - S_T)$	0
Short 1 call option	0	$-(S_T - X)$
Net position:	$(X - F_{0,T})$	$(X - F_{0,T})$

---

which says that for markets to be free from arbitrage, the difference between put and call prices must equal the discounted difference between the joint option exercise price and the forward contract price.

This result implies that the only time that put and call prices should be equal to one another in an efficient market is when $X = F_{0,T}$. That is, although the put–call parity result holds for *any* common exercise price, there is only one value of X for which there would be no net cost to the option combination and that is the prevailing forward price. Recall, for example, that when WYZ stock did not pay a dividend, the theoretically correct difference between $C_{0,0.5}$ and $P_{0,0.5}$ was $4.49(= 53 - 48.51)$. So, an investor long in the call and short in the put with a joint $50 exercise price would have what amounted to a forward contract to buy WYZ stock in six months at a price of $50.[7] However, she would have to pay $4.49 for this arrangement, suggesting that $50 is a below-market forward price. How much below the prevailing forward contract price is $50? By the future value of $4.49, invested at the prevailing risk-free rate of 6.25 percent. Thus, the no-arbitrage forward price under these circumstances should be $54.63[= 50 + 4.49(1 + 0.0625)^{0.5}]$.

Another way to see this result comes from inserting the expression for $(P_{0,T} - C_{0,T})$ from the put–call–forward parity condition into the put–call–spot condition:

$$S_0 + \left\{ \frac{X}{(1 + \text{RFR})^T} - \frac{F_{0,T}}{(1 + \text{RFR})^T} \right\} = \frac{X}{(1 + \text{RFR})^T}$$

which simplifies to:

$$S_0 = \frac{F_{0,T}}{(1 + \text{RFR})^T}.$$

In the absence of dividend payments, notice that the spot price for the share of stock should simply be the discounted value of purchasing the same security in the forward market.

---

[7]This interpretation follows by noting that the long call position will be exercised when $S_T > 50$, and the short put will be exercised against the investor when $S_T \leq 50$. Therefore, the investor's net option position produces an identical result to holding a long position in a forward contract with a contract price of $50. Generalizing this result, any time we have a call and a put option on the same underlying stock with a common exercise price and expiration date, the following is true: (long call at X) + (short put at X) = (long forward at X). Similarly, shorting the call and buying the put produces a synthetic short forward position.

Equivalently, this equation can be rewritten so that $F_{0,T} = S_0(1 - \text{RFR})^T$. In the preceding example, the market-clearing (no net initial cost) contract price for a WYZ stock forward agreement should be $F_{0, 0.5} = (53)(1 + 0.0625)^{0.5} = \$54.63$. Finally, when dividends are paid, the put–call–forward parity condition can be inserted into the dividend-adjusted spot parity condition to produce:

$$\left\{ S_0 - \frac{D_T}{(1 + \text{RFR})^T} \right\} = \frac{F_{0,T}}{(1 + \text{RFR})^T}$$

Thus, if a \$1 dividend were paid just prior to the maturity of the contract in six months, the forward price would be adjusted down to $F_{0, 0.5} = (53)(1 + 0.0625)^{0.5} - 1 = \$53.63$ to account for the payment to the actual shareholders but not the derivative holder.

14.4 AN INTRODUCTION TO THE USE OF DERIVATIVES IN PORTFOLIO MANAGEMENT

Beyond the unique risk–reward profiles they offer as stand-alone investments, derivatives also are used widely to restructure existing portfolios of assets. Typically, the intent of this restructuring is to modify the portfolio's risk. In this section, we review three prominent derivative applications in the management of equity positions: shorting forward contracts, purchasing **protective puts**, and purchasing **equity collars**.

14.4.1 Restructuring Asset Portfolios with Forward Contracts

Suppose the manager of a small corporate pension fund currently has all of her investable funds committed to a well-diversified portfolio of equity securities designed to track the S&P 500 Index. This indexed strategy is based on the manager's belief that she cannot add value by trying to select superior individual securities. She does, however, feel that it is possible to take advantage of perceived trends at a macroeconomic level by switching her funds on a tactical basis between her current equity holding and any of several other portfolios mimicking different asset classes (for example, fixed-income, cash equivalents).

The stock market has increased steadily over the past several months, and the pension fund has a present market value of \$100 million. The manager has now become concerned about the possibility that inflationary pressures will dampen corporate earnings and drive stock prices down. She also feels confident that the uncertainty will be resolved during the coming quarter. So, she would like to shift her allocation from 100 percent equity to 100 percent T-bills for the next three months.

There are two ways she can make this change. The most direct method would be to sell her stock portfolio and buy \$100 million (less the transaction costs) of 90-day T-bills. When the T-bills mature in three months, she could then repurchase her original equity holdings.

The second approach would be to maintain her current stock holdings but convert them into a synthetic risk-free position using a three-month forward contract with \$100 million of the stock index as the underlying asset. This is a classic example of a *hedge position*, wherein the price risk of the underlying asset is offset by a supplementary derivative transaction. The following table captures the basic dynamics of this hedge:

Economic Event	Actual Stock Exposure	Desired Forward Exposure
Stock prices fall	Loss	Gain
Stock prices rise	Gain	Loss

To neutralize the risk of falling stock prices, the fund manager will need to adopt a forward position that benefits from that potential movement. That is, the manager requires a hedge position with payoffs that are *negatively correlated* with the existing exposure. As we saw in Exhibit 14.10, this requires committing to the short side of the contract. This hedging argument is identical to the point we made in the portfolio formation analysis of Chapter 6 that it is always possible to combine two perfectly negatively correlated assets to create a risk-free position.

It is often far quicker and more cost-effective to convert the pension fund's asset allocation using this synthetic approach than the physical transformations demanded by the first solution. For instance, Hill (1993) has shown that when all of the costs of transaction are considered (for example, trading commissions, market impact, taxes), the average expense of actually rebalancing a U.S. equity portfolio is about 42 basis points of the position's value, while the same trade with an equity forward contract would cost just 6 basis points. Trading expenses in other countries, though different in absolute level, reflect this same general trend.

To see how this hedging strategy might work, suppose that the contract price for a S&P 500 forward contract maturing in three months is $F_{0,\,0.25} = \$101$. (For simplicity, this price is expressed relative to the current stock portfolio of $100 million.) The expiration date value of the hedged stock position will be: (1) the value of the unhedged stock portfolio, *plus* (2) the value of the short forward position, *less* (3) the initial cost of the derivative position, which is zero in the case of a forward contract. Exhibit 14.20 indicates terminal values for a range of possible stock portfolio prices.

As shown in the last column of Exhibit 14.20, the short forward-hedged stock portfolio will have an expiration date value of $101 no matter what the actual value of the stock portfolio turns out to be. Thus, the short position in the forward contract has *exactly offset* (that is, completely hedged) all of the market risk in holding the stock portfolio for the next three months. It is as if the manager has invested $100 in a risk-free security at Date 0 that pays back $101 with certainty in three months. This is equivalent to owning a T-bill that pays a return of 1 percent ($= 101/100 - 1$) over the next quarter, or 4 percent on an annual basis.

This synthetic restructuring can also been viewed through the effect that it has had on the systematic risk—or beta—of the portfolio. Assume that the original stock position had a beta of 1.0, matching the volatility of a proxy for the market portfolio. The combination of being long $100 million of stock and short a forward covering $100 million of a stock index converts the systematic portion of the portfolio into a synthetic T-bill, which by definition has a beta of 0.0. Once the contract matures in three months, however, the position will revert to its original risk profile. This is illustrated in Exhibit 14.21. More generally, the short forward position can be designed to allow for intermediate combinations of stock and T-bills as well. To see this, let w_S be the stock allocation so that $(1 - w_S)$ is the allocation to the risk-free asset created

Exhibit 14.20 Expiration Date Value of a Short Forward-Hedged Portfolio

Potential Portfolio Value	Value of Short Forward	Initial Cost of Forward	Net Forward-Hedged Position
60	$(101 - 60) = \quad 41$	0	$(60 + 41) - 0 = 101$
70	$(101 - 70) = \quad 31$	0	$(70 + 31) - 0 = 101$
80	$(101 - 80) = \quad 21$	0	$(80 + 21) - 0 = 101$
90	$(101 - 90) = \quad 11$	0	$(90 + 11) - 0 = 101$
100	$(101 - 100) = \quad 1$	0	$(100 + 1) - 0 = 101$
110	$(101 - 110) = \quad -9$	0	$(110 - 9) - 0 = 101$
120	$(101 - 120) = -19$	0	$(120 - 19) - 0 = 101$
130	$(101 - 130) = -29$	0	$(130 - 29) - 0 = 101$
140	$(101 - 140) = -39$	0	$(140 - 39) - 0 = 101$

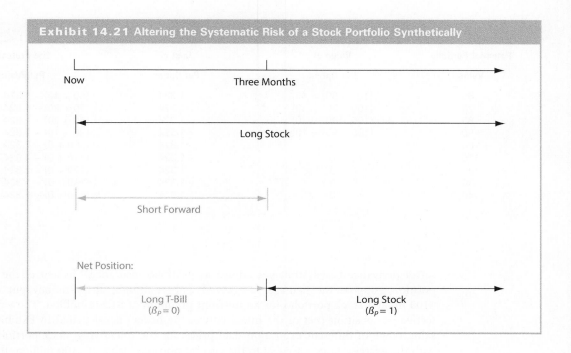

Exhibit 14.21 Altering the Systematic Risk of a Stock Portfolio Synthetically

synthetically. The net beta for the converted portfolio is simply a weighted average of the systematic risks of its equity and T-bill portions or:

14.6
$$\beta_P = (w_S)\beta_S + (1 - w_S)\beta_{\text{RFR}}$$

Thus, if the manager had wished to change the original allocation from 100 percent stock to a "60–40" mix of stock and T-bills, she would have shorted only \$40 million of the index forward to leave her with an unhedged equity position totaling \$60 million ($w_S = 0.60$ and $(1 - w_S) = 0.40$). This in turn would leave her with an adjusted portfolio beta of $[(0.6)(1) + (0.4)(0)] = 0.6$.

14.4.2 Protecting Portfolio Value with Put Options

The manager's concern in the previous example was to protect her stock portfolio against possible share price declines over the next three months. However, by shorting the stock index forward contract, she has effectively committed to "selling" her equity position, even if stock prices rise. That is, by using a derivative with a symmetric payoff structure to hedge her risk, the manager also has surrendered the upside potential of her original holding. Suppose instead that she designed a hedge position correlated to her stock portfolio as follows:

Economic Event	Actual Stock Exposure	Desired Forward Exposure
Stock prices fall	Loss	Gain
Stock prices rise	Gain	*No loss*

In seeking an asymmetric hedge, this manager wants a derivative contract that allows her to sell stock when prices fall but keep her shares when prices rise. As we have seen, she must purchase a put option to obtain this exposure.

The purchase of a put option to hedge the downside risk of an underlying security holding is called a protective put position and is the most straightforward example of a more general

Exhibit 14.22 Expiration Date Value of a Protective Put Position

Potential Portfolio Value	Value of Put Option	Cost of Put Option	Net Protective Put Position
60	(100 − 60) = 40)	−1.324	(60 + 40) − 1.324 = 98.676
70	(100 − 70) = 30)	−1.324	(70 + 30) − 1.324 = 98.676
80	(100 − 80) = 20)	−1.324	(80 + 20) − 1.324 = 98.676
90	(100 − 90) = 10)	−1.324	(90 + 10) − 1.324 = 98.676
100	0	−1.324	(100 + 0) − 1.324 = 98.676
110	0	−1.324	(110 + 0) − 1.324 = 108.676
120	0	−1.324	(120 + 0) − 1.324 = 118.676
130	0	−1.324	(130 + 0) − 1.324 = 128.676
140	0	−1.324	(140 + 0) − 1.324 = 138.676

set of derivative-based strategies known as portfolio insurance.[8] In lieu of the short forward position, suppose the manager purchased a three-month, at-the-money put option on her $100 million stock portfolio for an up-front premium of $1.324 million. The value of the protective put position (net of the initial cost of the hedge) is calculated in Exhibit 14.22 for the same range of different expiration date prices for the underlying stock portfolio. Notice that with the exercise price set equal to the current portfolio value of $100 million, the put contract exactly offsets any expiration date share price decline while allowing the position to increase in value as stock prices increase. Thus, the put provides the manager with insurance against falling prices with no deductible.[9]

The terminal value of the combined stock and put option portfolio shown in the last column of Exhibit 14.22 resembles the payoff diagram of the long call option position illustrated in Exhibit 14.11. This is shown in Exhibit 14.23, which indicates that being long in the stock and long in the put generates the same net payoff as an at-the-money long call option holding "elevated" by $100 million. Given the put–call–spot parity results of the previous section, this should come as no surprise. Indeed, the no-arbitrage equation (Equation 14.1) can be rewritten:

$$S_0 + P_{0,T} = C_{0,T} + \frac{X}{(1 + \text{RFR})^T}$$

This expression says that the protective put position generates the same expiration date payoff as a long position in a call option with equivalent characteristics and a long position in a T-bill with a face value equal to the options' exercise price. This final term provides the elevation to the call payoff diagram in Exhibit 14.23. Thus, the manager has two ways of providing price insurance for her current stock holding: (1) Continue to hold her shares and purchase a put option or (2) sell her shares and buy both a T-bill and a call option. Her choice between them will undoubtedly come down to considerations such as relative option prices and transaction costs.

---

[8]The concept and use of portfolio insurance have received a great deal of scrutiny in the research literature. See, for example, the studies by Rubinstein (1985a), Basak (2002), and Maalej and Prigent (2016).

[9]In general, the deductible portion of the portfolio insurance contract can be defined as $[S_0 - X]$. For instance, with an exercise price of only 95, the manager would not receive compensation from the hedge until the portfolio value fell below $95 million; she would effectively be self-insuring the first $5 million of losses. Naturally, the larger this deductible amount, the lower the cost of the put option.

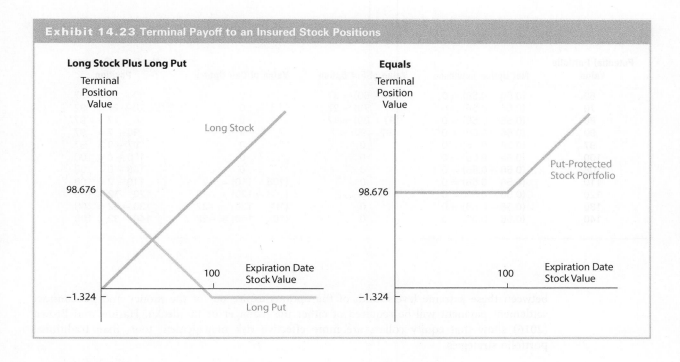

Exhibit 14.23 Terminal Payoff to an Insured Stock Positions

14.4.3 An Alternative Way to Pay for a Protective Put

There is a third alternative for protecting against potential stock price declines, which fits between paying nothing for a hedge but surrendering future stock gains for the next three months (the short forward position) and keeping those potential gains in exchange for a considerable initial payment (the protective put position). Specifically, suppose that the manager makes two simultaneous decisions. First, she decides to purchase a three-month, out-of-the-money protective put option with an exercise price of $97 million and a lower initial cost of $0.560 million. (Notice that in purchasing an out-of-the-money contract, the manager is creating a $3 million deductible compared to her current portfolio value.) Second, she decides not to pay cash for the put option; instead, she sells to the option dealer a call option with a three-month expiration and an exercise price of $108 million that also carries an initial premium of $0.560 million. The simultaneous purchase of an out-of-the-money put and sale of an out-of-the-money call on the same underlying asset and with the same expiration date and market price is a strategy known as a **collar agreement**.

Exhibit 14.24 shows the expiration date outcomes of the manager's equity collar-protected portfolio for several different terminal stock portfolio values. Like the forward contract hedge, there is no initial out-of-pocket expense associated with this derivative combination. Instead, the manager effectively pays for her desired portfolio insurance by surrendering an equivalent amount of the portfolio's future upside potential. That is, in exchange for being compensated for any stock decline below $97 million, she agrees to give up any stock price appreciation beyond $108 million. As with the protective put (and unlike with the short forward position), she does retain some of the benefit of a rising stock market. However, this upside gain potential stops at the exercise price of the call option. As shown in Exhibit 14.25, the manager has placed a collar around her portfolio for the next three months—its net value will not fall below $97 million and will not rise above $108 million. At any terminal value for the stock portfolio

Exhibit 14.24 Expiration Date Value of an Equity Collar-Protected Portfolio

Potential Portfolio Value	Net Option Expense	Value of Put Option	Value of Call Option	Net Collar-Protected Position
60	(0.56 − 0.56) = 0	(97 − 60) = 37	0	60 + 37 = 97
70	(0.56 − 0.56) = 0	(97 − 70) = 27	0	70 + 27 = 97
80	(0.56 − 0.56) = 0	(97 − 80) = 17	0	80 + 17 = 97
90	(0.56 − 0.56) = 0	(97 − 90) = 7	0	90 + 7 = 97
97	(0.56 − 0.56) = 0	0	0	97 + 0 = 97
100	(0.56 − 0.56) = 0	0	0	100 + 0 = 100
108	(0.56 − 0.56) = 0	0	0	108 − 0 = 108
110	(0.56 − 0.56) = 0	0	(108 − 110) = −2	110 − 2 = 108
120	(0.56 − 0.56) = 0	0	(108 − 120) = −12	120 − 12 = 108
130	(0.56 − 0.56) = 0	0	(108 − 130) = −22	130 − 22 = 108
140	(0.56 − 0.56) = 0	0	(108 − 140) = −32	140 − 32 = 108

between these extreme levels, both of the options expire out of the money and no contract settlement payment will be required of either the manager or the dealer. Harlow and Brown (2016) show that equity collars are more effective risk management tools than traditional portfolio strategies.

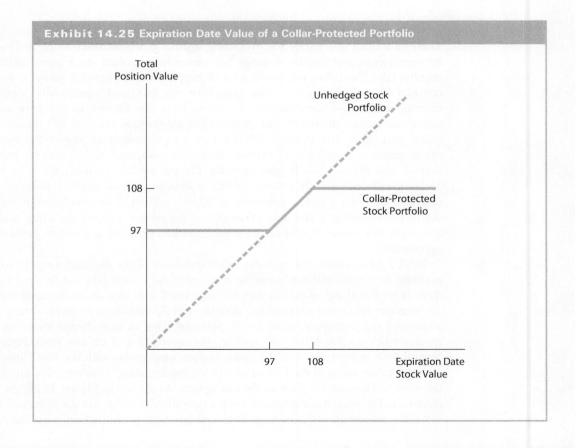

Exhibit 14.25 Expiration Date Value of a Collar-Protected Portfolio

SUMMARY

- As their popularity in financial markets has increased over the past few decades, derivative securities have become an indispensable part of the investment manager's toolkit. Although forward, futures, and option contracts play important roles as stand-alone investments, the real advantage of derivatives is their ability to modify the risk–return characteristics of a collection of existing securities in a cost-effective manner. This use of forwards and options to restructure a portfolio synthetically has two dimensions: (1) It is possible to combine derivatives with the underlying position to replicate the cash flows of another traded instrument, and (2) derivatives can be used with the original portfolio to create a payoff structure that is otherwise unavailable.

- Forward and option contracts can be viewed as insurance policies that an investor can hold against adverse price movements in his underlying position. The basic difference between these contracts lies in how the investor must pay for the desired insurance. Forwards, with symmetrical terminal payoffs, typically do not require any initial payment but do obligate the investor to the possibility of an unfavorable transaction at a future date. Options provide asymmetrical terminal payoffs, but the investor must pay an up-front premium.

- Some well-defined relationships must exist in an efficient capital market between the prices of forward and option contracts. The put-call parity conditions delineate the linkages between five different securities: the underlying asset (for example, stock), T-bills, forward contracts, call options, and put options. One of these securities is always redundant because its cash flow patterns can be replicated by the remaining instruments. This leads to another important use for derivatives: arbitrage investing. Through their ability to help create synthetic replicas of existing securities, derivatives provide investors with the possibility of riskless excess returns when the synthetic and actual instruments sell for different prices.

- There are several issues related to the use and management of derivative securities that remain to be addressed, such as how individual positions in forwards, futures, and options are valued and the adjustments that investors need to make when using derivatives on an underlying asset other than common stock. These topics will be considered in subsequent chapters. For now, though, it is important to appreciate these instruments for their ability to assist investors in repackaging the risks and cash flows of their portfolios.

SUGGESTED READINGS

Bookstaber, Richard M., and Roger G. Clarke. "Options Can Alter Portfolio Return Distributions." *Journal of Portfolio Management* 7, no. 3 (Spring 1981): 63–70.

Brown, David T., Gideon Ozik, and Daniel Scholz. "Rebalancing Revisited: The Role of Derivatives." *Financial Analysts Journal* 63, no. 5 (September/October 2007): 32–44.

Brown, Keith C., ed. *Derivative Strategies for Managing Portfolio Risk*. Charlottesville, VA: AIMR, 1993.

Chance, Don M., and Robert Brooks. *An Introduction to Derivatives and Risk Management*, 10th ed. Boston: Cengage Learning, 2016.

QUESTIONS

1. When comparing futures and forward contracts, it has been said that futures are more liquid but forwards are more flexible. Explain what this statement means and comment on how differences in contract liquidity and design flexibility might influence an investor's preference in choosing one instrument over the other.

2. Compare and contrast the gain and loss potential for investors holding the following positions: long forward, short forward, long call, short call, long put, and short put. Indicate what the terms *symmetric* and *asymmetric* mean in this context.

3. You are the manager of a medium-sized hedge fund, and the recent fluctuations in the capital markets have attracted your attention. In particular, the prices of stocks and bonds have now dropped to what you consider to be unprecedentedly attractive levels. Although you expect the prices of these investments to rise in the near future, your hedge fund is currently cash-constrained due to an unforeseen redemption wave; "fire-selling" the best holdings in your portfolio is not a practical way to generate investable funds. Further, the next round of incoming cash flows from new investor subscriptions and from the existing investments are not expected to occur for approximately three months.
   a. Briefly explain the details of two investment strategies that employ derivative instruments that would allow you to take advantage of the anticipated market rally.
   b. What are the benefits and potential risk factors for undertaking these derivative strategies in lieu of direct cash-oriented investments?

4. As the manager of a large, well-diversified school endowment fund, you are actively considering implementing sophisticated derivative strategies to protect your fund's market value in the event of a substantial decline in the overall level of equity prices. Your colleagues have suggested that you acquire either (1) a short position in an S&P 500 Index futures contract or (2) a long position in an S&P index put option contract. Explain how each of these derivative strategies would affect the risk and return of the resulting augmented endowment portfolio.

5. Explain how call and put options can represent a leveraged way of investing in the stock market and also enable investors to hedge their risk completely. Specifically, under what circumstances will the addition of an option increase the risk of an existing portfolio, and under what circumstances will it decrease portfolio risk?

6. It has been said that, from an investor's perspective, a long position in a call option represents the "good half" of a long position in a forward contract. Explain what is meant by this statement. Also, describe what the "bad half" of the long forward position would have to be for this statement to be true.

7. The put–call–spot parity relationship involves four different securities: the underlying asset, a call option on that asset, a put option, and a T-bill. Explain how it is possible that one of those assets is always redundant (that is, can be expressed in terms of the other three). Discuss the transactions that would be necessary to make the call option in this situation the redundant asset.

8. Explain why the difference between put and call prices depends on whether the underlying security pays a dividend during the life of the contracts.

9. Compare the differences and similarities of three different ways of protecting a stock portfolio against price declines over the next three months: (i) short a three-month forward contract, (ii) buy an at-the-money three-month put option for cash, or (iii) buy an out-of-the-money three-month put option and sell an out-of-the-money three-month call option. Specifically, what are the initial cost and expiration date payoff potential for each strategy?

10. Discuss the difficulties that having options in a security portfolio creates for the measurement of portfolio risk. Specifically, explain why standard deviation is a deficient statistic for capturing the essence of risk in a put-protected portfolio. How could the standard deviation statistic be modified to account for this concern?

PROBLEMS

1. The common stock of Sophia Enterprises serves as the underlying asset for the following derivative securities: (1) forward contracts, (2) European-style call options, and (3) European-style put options.
   a. Assuming that all Sophia derivatives expire at the same date in the future, complete a table similar to the following for each of the following contract positions:

(1) A long position in a forward with a contract price of $50

(2) A long position in a call option with an exercise price of $50 and a front-end premium expense of $5.20

Expiration Date Sophia Stock Price	Expiration Date Derivative Payoff	Initial Derivative Premium	Net Profit
25	_____	_____	_____
30	_____	_____	_____
35	_____	_____	_____
40	_____	_____	_____
45	_____	_____	_____
50	_____	_____	_____
55	_____	_____	_____
60	_____	_____	_____
65	_____	_____	_____
70	_____	_____	_____
75	_____	_____	_____

(3) A short position in a call option with an exercise price of $50 and a front-end premium receipt of $5.20

In calculating net profit, ignore the time differential between the initial derivative expense or receipt and the terminal payoff.

b. Graph the net profit for each of the three derivative positions, using net profit on the vertical axis and Sophia's expiration date stock price on the horizontal axis. Label the breakeven (zero profit) point(s) on each graph.

c. Briefly describe the belief about the expiration date price of Sophia stock that an investor using each of these three positions implicitly holds.

2. Refer once again to the derivative securities using Sophia common stock as an underlying asset discussed in Problem 1.

a. Assuming that all Sophia derivatives expire at the same date in the future, complete a table similar to the following for each of the following contract positions:

(1) A short position in a forward with a contract price of $50

(2) A long position in a put option with an exercise price of $50 and a front-end premium expense of $3.23

(3) A short position in a put option with an exercise price of $50 and a front-end premium receipt of $3.23

Expiration Date Sophia Stock Price	Expiration Date Derivative Payoff	Initial Derivative Premium	Net Profit
25	_____	_____	_____
30	_____	_____	_____
35	_____	_____	_____
40	_____	_____	_____
45	_____	_____	_____
50	_____	_____	_____
55	_____	_____	_____
60	_____	_____	_____
65	_____	_____	_____
70	_____	_____	_____
75	_____	_____	_____

In calculating net profit, ignore the time differential between the initial derivative expense or receipt and the terminal payoff.

b. Graph the net profit for each of the three derivative positions, using net profit on the vertical axis and Sophia's expiration date stock price on the horizontal axis. Label the breakeven (zero profit) point(s) on each graph.

c. Briefly describe the belief about the expiration date price of Sophia stock that an investor using each of these three positions implicitly holds.

3. Suppose that an investor holds a share of Sophia common stock, currently valued at $50. She is concerned that over the next few months the value of her holding might decline, and she would like to hedge that risk by supplementing her holding with one of three different derivative positions, all of which expire at the same point in the future:

   (1) A short position in a forward with a contract price of $50
   (2) A long position in a put option with an exercise price of $50 and a front-end premium expense of $3.23
   (3) A short position in a call option with an exercise price of $50 and a front-end premium receipt of $5.20

   a. Using a table similar to the following, calculate the expiration date value of the investor's combined (stock and derivative) position. In calculating net portfolio value, ignore the time differential between the initial derivative expense or receipt and the terminal payoff.

   b. For each of the three hedge portfolios, graph the expiration date value of her combined position on the vertical axis, with potential expiration date share prices of Sophia stock on the horizontal axis.

   c. Assuming that the options are priced fairly, use the concept of put–call parity to calculate the zero-value contract price ($F_{0,T}$) for a forward agreement on Sophia stock.

   Explain why this value differs from the $50 contract price used in part (a) and part (b).

Expiration Date Sophia Stock Price	Expiration Date Derivative Payoff	Initial Derivative Premium	Combined Terminal Position Value
25	_____	_____	_____
30	_____	_____	_____
35	_____	_____	_____
40	_____	_____	_____
45	_____	_____	_____
50	_____	_____	_____
55	_____	_____	_____
60	_____	_____	_____
65	_____	_____	_____
70	_____	_____	_____
75	_____	_____	_____

4. You strongly believe that the price of Breener Inc. stock will rise substantially from its current level of $137, and you are considering buying shares in the company. You currently have $13,700 to invest. As an alternative to purchasing the stock itself, you are also considering buying call options on Breener stock that expire in three months and have an exercise price of $140. These call options cost $10 each.

   a. Compare and contrast the size of the potential payoff and the risk involved in each of these alternatives.

   b. Calculate the three-month rate of return on both strategies assuming that at the option expiration date Breener's stock price has (1) increased to $155 or (2) decreased to $135.

c. At what stock price level will the person who sells you the Breener call option break even? Can you determine the maximum loss that the call option seller may suffer, assuming that he does not already own Breener stock?

5. The common stock of Company XYZ is currently trading at a price of $42. Both a put and a call option are available for XYZ stock, each having an exercise price of $40 and an expiration date in exactly six months. The current market prices for the put and call are $1.45 and $3.90, respectively. The risk-free holding period return for the next six months is 4 percent, which corresponds to an 8 percent annual rate.

   a. For each possible stock price in the following sequence, calculate the expiration date payoffs (net of the initial purchase price) for the following positions: (1) buy one XYZ call option, and (2) short one XYZ call option:

$$20, 25, 30, 35, 40, 45, 50, 55, 60$$

   Draw a graph of these payoff relationships, using net profit on the vertical axis and potential expiration date stock price on the horizontal axis. Be sure to specify the prices at which these respective positions will break even (produce a net profit of zero).

   b. Using the same potential stock prices as in part (a), calculate the expiration date payoffs and profits (net of the initial purchase price) for the following positions: (1) buy one XYZ put option, and (2) short one XYZ put option. Draw a graph of these relationships, labeling the prices at which these investments will break even.

   c. Determine whether the $2.45 difference in the market prices between the call and put options is consistent with the put–call parity relationship for European-style contracts.

6. Consider Commodity Z, which has both exchange-traded futures and option contracts associated with it. As you look in today's paper, you find the following put and call prices for options that expire exactly six months from now:

Exercise Price	Put Price	Call Price
$40	$0.59	$8.73
45	1.93	—
50	—	2.47

   a. Assuming that the futures price of a six-month contract on Commodity Z is $F_{0, 0.5} = \$48$, what must be the price of a put with an exercise price of $50 in order to avoid arbitrage across markets? Similarly, calculate the "no arbitrage" price of a call with an exercise price of $45. In both calculations, assume that the yield curve is flat and the annual risk-free rate is 6 percent.

   b. What is the "no arbitrage" price differential that should exist between the put and call options having an exercise price of $40? Is this differential satisfied by current market prices? If not, demonstrate an arbitrage trade to take advantage of the mispricing.

7. Dosley Endowment Fund, which supports the activities of the Dosley Charitable Trust, is relatively new and small in terms of assets under management. The trustees of the endowment have adopted a conservative investment strategy: at the current time, all of the $700 million in assets are equally invested in an S&P 500 Index tracking fund and U.S. Treasury bonds. Right now, the annual dividend yield on the S&P 500 Index fund is 3.0 percent, whereas the annual coupon rate is 4.0 percent for the T-bonds. As the fund manager, you expect that over the next three months the market will be very volatile. Given that the priority of the trustees is to preserve the value of the endowment fund, you are required to use various derivative strategies to protect the assets under management. The current level of S&P 500 is 1,000, and the price of U.S. T-bonds is 100. Assume that the current three-month T-bill rate is 1.2 percent.

a. Using the derivative information listed below, discuss the details of two derivative strategies that could be employed to protect the endowment's current asset value.

	Contract Size	Expiration	Current Price	Strike Price
		S&P 500 Index		
Call option	$ 45,000	3 months later	$ 21.00	$1,000
Put option	45,000	3 months later	18.00	1,000
Future	250,000	3 months later	1,007.00	—
		U.S. Treasury Bonds		
Call option	$100,000	3 months later	$ 6.00	$100
Put option	100,000	3 months later	6.50	100
Future	100,000	3 months later	103.00	—

b. Applying the put–call parity relationship, which derivative strategy should you recommend and why? Recall that the put and futures prices are as follows:

$$Put\ Price = Call\ Price - Security\ Price + Present\ Value\ of\ Exercise\ Price$$
$$+ Income\ on\ the\ Underlying\ Security$$
$$Futures\ Price = Underlying\ Security\ Price + (Treasury\ Bill\ Income$$
$$- Income\ on\ the\ Underlying\ Security)$$

8. As an option trader, you are constantly looking for opportunities to make an arbitrage transaction (that is, a trade in which you do not need to commit your own capital or take any risk but can still make a profit). Suppose you observe the following prices for options on DRKC Co. stock: $3.18 for a call with an exercise price of $60, and $3.38 for a put with an exercise price of $60. Both options expire in exactly six months, and the price of a six-month T-bill is $97.00 (for face value of $100).
   a. Using the put–call–spot parity condition, demonstrate graphically how you could synthetically re-create the payoff structure of a share of DRKC stock in six months, using a combination of puts, calls, and T-bills transacted today.
   b. Given the current market prices for the two options and the T-bill, calculate the no-arbitrage price of a share of DRKC stock.
   c. If the actual market price of DRKC stock is $60, demonstrate the arbitrage transaction you could create to take advantage of the discrepancy. Be specific as to the positions you would need to take in each security and the dollar amount of your profit.

9. You are currently managing a stock portfolio worth $55 million, and you are concerned that over the next four months, equity values will be flat and may even fall. Consequently, you are considering two different strategies for hedging against possible stock declines: (1) buying a protective put and (2) selling a *covered call* (selling a call option based on the same underlying stock position you hold). An over-the-counter derivatives dealer has expressed interest in your business and has quoted the following bid and offer prices (in millions) for at-the-money call and put options that expire in four months and match the characteristics of your portfolio:

	Bid	Ask
Call	$2.553	$2.573
Put	1.297	1.317

a. For each of the following expiration date values for the unhedged equity position, calculate the terminal values (net of initial expense) for a protective put strategy.

$$35, 40, 45, 50, 55, 60, 65, 70, 75$$

b. Draw a graph of the protective put net profit structure in part (a) and demonstrate how this position could have been constructed by using call options and T-bills, assuming a risk-free rate of 7 percent.

c. For each of these same expiration date stock values, calculate the terminal net profit values for a covered call strategy.

d. Draw a graph of the covered call net profit structure in Part c, and demonstrate how this position could have been constructed by using put options and T-bills, again assuming a risk-free rate of 7 percent.

10. The common stock of Company XLT and its derivative securities currently trade in the market at the following prices and contract terms:

	Price ($)	Exercise Price ($)
Stock XLT	21.50	—
Call option on Stock XLT	5.50	21.00
Put option on Stock XLT	4.50	21.00

Both of these options will expire 91 days from now, and the annualized yield for the 91-day Treasury bill is 3.0 percent.

a. Briefly explain how to construct a synthetic Treasury bill position.

b. Calculate the annualized yield for the synthetic Treasury bill in part (a) using the market price data provided.

c. Describe the arbitrage strategy implied by the difference in yields for the actual and synthetic T-bill positions. Show the net, riskless cash flow you could generate assuming a transaction involving 21 actual T-bills and 100 synthetic T-bills.

d. What is the net cash flow of this arbitrage strategy at the option expiration date, assuming that Stock XLT trades at $23 at expiration three months from now?

CHAPTER 15

Forward, Futures, and Swap Contracts

After you read this chapter, you should be able to answer the following questions:

- What are the historical differences in the way forward and futures contracts are structured and traded?
- How are the margin accounts on a futures contract adjusted for daily changes in market conditions?
- How can an investor use forward and futures contracts to hedge an existing risk exposure?
- What is a hedge ratio, and how should it be calculated?
- What economic functions do the forward and futures markets serve?
- How are forward and futures contracts valued after origination?
- What is the relationship between futures contract prices and the current and expected spot price for the underlying commodity or security?
- How can an investor use forward and futures contracts to speculate on a particular view about changing market conditions?
- How can forward and futures contracts be designed to hedge interest rate risk?
- What is stock index arbitrage, and how is it related to program trading?
- How can forward and futures contracts be designed to hedge foreign exchange rate risk?
- What is interest rate parity, and how would you construct a covered interest arbitrage transaction?
- What are forward rate agreements and interest rate swaps, and how can they transform the cash flows of a fixed or floating rate security?
- How does the swap market operate, and how are swap contracts quoted and valued?

As we saw in Chapter 14, forward and futures contracts are the most straightforward form of *derivative instrument* because they allow an investor to lock in the price of a transaction that will not be completed until a later date. We now continue our discussion of these contracts along several lines. First, we take a closer look at the contract terms and trading mechanics of forwards and futures. We examine important differences that exist between the two markets and describe the process by which futures contracts are **marked to market** on a daily basis. Further, we discuss how these contracts are used to hedge the price risk inherent in an existing or anticipated position and how **hedge ratios** are computed.

Second, we consider how forward and futures contracts are priced in an efficient capital market. Given how these instruments differ from stocks and bonds, the notion of traditional security valuation is not quite appropriate. Instead, valuation involves specifying the proper relationship between the forward contract price and the spot price for the underlying position. We develop the "no arbitrage" result that the forward contract price should be equal to the spot price plus the cumulative costs of transporting the underlying security or commodity from the present to the future delivery date.

Next, we demonstrate several applications for using forward and futures contracts. We concentrate on a class of contracts—*financial forwards and futures*—that are particularly useful to investors. The underlying securities in financial futures include stock indexes, Treasury bonds, bank deposits, and foreign currencies. The use of these contracts will be illustrated in a series of examples demonstrating the connections between cash and futures markets. Finally, we consider the market for OTC forward contracts, such as forward rate agreements, interest rate swaps, and equity index-linked swaps. These OTC rate agreements represent one of the fastest-growing segments of the derivatives industry over the past 30 years.

15.1 AN OVERVIEW OF FORWARD AND FUTURES TRADING

Forward contracts are agreements negotiated directly between two parties in the OTC (non-exchange-traded) markets. A typical participant in a forward contract is a commercial or investment bank that, serving the role of the market maker, is contacted directly by the customer. Forward contracts can be tailored to the specific needs of the ultimate end user. Futures contracting, on the other hand, is somewhat more complicated. An investor wishing either to buy or to sell in the futures market gives his order to a broker (a futures commission merchant), who then passes it to a trader on the floor of an exchange (the trading pit) or through an electronic trading network. After a trade has been agreed on, details of the deal are passed to the **exchange clearinghouse**, which catalogs the transaction. The ultimate end users in a futures contract never deal with each other directly but transact with the clearinghouse, which is also responsible for overseeing the delivery process, settling daily gains and losses, and guaranteeing the overall transaction. Exhibit 15.1 highlights the differences in how these contracts are created.[1]

As an example, consider the agricultural commodity futures that have been traded for more than 170 years beginning with the creation of the Chicago Board of Trade (CBT), the world's oldest derivatives exchange. Futures contracts based on a wide array of commodities and securities have been created and now trade on more than 100 exchanges worldwide. Exhibit 15.2 lists the leading futures exchanges in the United States and elsewhere in the world, ranked by trading volume. Notice that only 2 of the top 10 exchanges in the world are located in the United States, underscoring that these are truly global products. In addition, Exhibit 15.3 shows price and trade activity data for a representative sample of commodity futures contracts; financial futures will be described in detail later in the chapter. Each of these commodity contracts is standardized in terms of the amount and type of the commodity involved and the available dates on which it can be delivered. As we will see, this standardization can lead to an important source of risk that may not exist in forward contracts.

15.1.1 Futures Contract Mechanics

To interpret Exhibit 15.3, consider the gold futures contract traded on the Commodity Exchange (COMEX), a division of the CME Group, on July 7, 2017. Each contract calls for the long position to buy, and the short position to sell, 100 troy ounces of gold in the appointed months. With commodity futures, it usually is the case that delivery can take place any time during the month at the discretion of the short position. Contracts are available with settlement dates every other month for the next five years, although only the next five contracts are shown. An investor committing on this particular date to a long position in the October 2017 contract (which is highlighted in the display) is obligated to buy 100 ounces of

---

[1]For a more detailed discussion of the historical futures trading process, see Garner (2013).

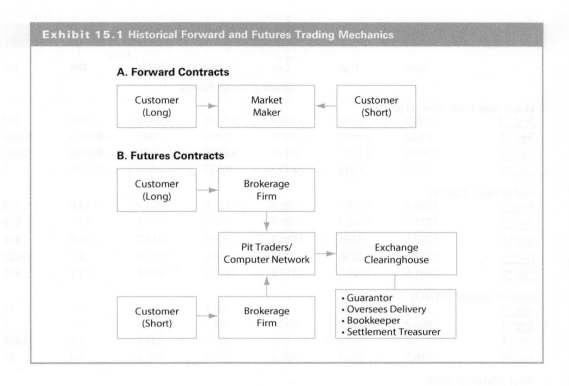

Exhibit 15.1 Historical Forward and Futures Trading Mechanics

A. Forward Contracts

Customer (Long) → Market Maker ← Customer (Short)

B. Futures Contracts

Customer (Long) → Brokerage Firm

Pit Traders/Computer Network ↔ Exchange Clearinghouse

Customer (Short) → Brokerage Firm

Exchange Clearinghouse:
• Guarantor
• Oversees Delivery
• Bookkeeper
• Settlement Treasurer

Exhibit 15.2 Leading Futures Exchanges by Trading Volume (Millions of Contracts)

A. U.S. Futures Exchanges (2016 Annual Data)

Exchange Name & Abbreviation	Trading Volume
CME Group: Chicago Mercantile (CME)	1,939.9
CME Group: Chicago Board of Trade (CBT)	1,273.8
CME Group: New York Mercantile Exchange (NYM)	618.4
ICE Futures U.S. (ICE)	370.2

B. International Futures Exchanges & Groups (2016 Annual Data)

Exchange & Country	Trading Volume
National Stock Exchange, India	2,119.4
Moscow Exchange, Russia	1,950.1
Eurex, Germany	1,727.8
Shanghai Futures Exchange, China	1,680.7
Dalian Commodity Exchange, China	1,537.5
BM&FBovespa, Brazil	1,487.3
ICE Futures Europe	973.9
Zhengzhou Commodity Exchange, China	901.3
Korea Exchange, Korea	693.0
BSE, India	543.1

Source: Futures Industry Association, *FIA 2016 Volume Survey* (March 2017).

Exhibit 15.3 Commodity Futures Quotations

	Open	High	Low	Last	Settle	Chg	Vol	Open Int
			Metals & Energy Futures:					
Copper High Grade (Globex) (COMEX)								
Aug'17	2.6505	2.662	2.6385	2.6445	2.6415	−0.014	367	3576
Sep'17	2.662	2.6695	2.6405	2.649	2.647	−0.0145	53574	139961
Dec'17	2.6775	2.6865	2.659	2.6695	2.6655	−0.0145	5264	70537
Jan'18	2.673	2.673	2.673	2.673	2.672	−0.0145	1	996
Gold (Globex) (COMEX)								
Aug'17	1224.6	1228.1	1206.6	1211.9	1209.7	−13.6	311153	283733
Sep'17	1221.7	1228.9	1209.8	1213	1211.4	−13.6	510	328
Oct'17	1228.5	1231	1210.1	1216	1213.3	−13.6	1944	18441
Dec'17	1232.4	1235	1214	1219.5	1216.9	−13.7	17353	130522
FEb'18	1231.6	1238.3	1217.5	1221.8	1220.4	−13.7	503	12561
Platinum (Globex) (NYMEX)								
Aug'17	905	909	900	905.2	902	−6	15	95
Sep'17	906.7	906.7	906.7	906.7	902.7	−6	2	3
Oct'17	911.8	918.5	901	909.4	904.1	−6.2	16469	68563
Jan'18	916.5	920.5	905.4	908.3	907.6	−5.8	97	3593
Silver (Globex) (COMEX)								
Aug'17	16.1	16.11	15.31	15.55	15.4	−0.557	806	465
Sep'17	16.025	16.14	14.34	15.56	15.425	−0.558	153255	158741
Dec'17	16.175	16.19	14.44	15.675	15.525	−0.56	6135	41651
Mar'18	15.875	16.1	15.225	15.7	15.627	−0.562	355	2370
Brent Crude Last Day (NYMEX)								
Sep'17	47.98	47.99	46.28	46.8	46.71	−1.4	27715	22791
Oct'17	48.17	48.17	46.56	46.97	46.98	−1.41	8353	7505
Nov'17	48.06	48.06	47.16	47.25	47.27	−1.41	7379	6626
Dec'17	48.51	48.51	47.18	47.7	47.57	−1.4	12919	27403
Jan'18	48.1	48.1	47.51	47.6	47.86	−1.4	3974	7452
Heating Oil (Globex) (NYMEX)								
Sep'17	1.4844	1.4854	1.4334	1.4594	1.4541	−0.0339	34477	78521
Oct'17	1.4922	1.4922	1.442	1.4648	1.4611	−0.035	20996	35920
Nov'17	1.4866	1.4895	1.4514	1.4723	1.4693	−0.0356	11350	25856
Dec'17	1.51	1.51	1.4604	1.4817	1.4781	−0.0359	19761	56255
Jan'18	1.509	1.509	1.4695	1.4889	1.4863	−0.0361	3746	24245
Natural Gas (Globex) (NYMEX)								
Aug'17	2.899	2.947	2.847	2.854	2.864	−0.024	151395	280707
Sep'17	2.887	2.938	2.842	2.85	2.857	−0.024	46453	191917
Oct'17	2.912	2.964	2.872	2.885	2.886	−0.022	31599	180280
Nov'17	2.971	3.019	2.934	2.945	2.947	−0.02	12996	74534
Dec'17	3.123	3.169	3.091	3.1	3.104	−0.018	10184	65655
Jan'18	3.218	3.262	3.187	3.197	3.201	−0.016	15001	106533

Exhibit 15.3 Commodity Futures Quotations (*Continued*)

	Open	High	Low	Last	Settle	Chg	Vol	Open Int
				Agriculture & Livestock Futures:				
Coffee (ICE Futures)								
Sep'17	129.45	129.5	126.8	128.9	128.9	−0.2	19133	118475
Dec'17	132.8	132.95	130.4	132.4	132.4	−0.2	6008	50817
Mar'18	136.25	136.4	133.85	135.8	135.8	−0.25	1953	22042
May'18	138.45	138.6	136.15	138.1	138.1	−0.25	1619	14912
Cotton #2 (ICE Futures)								
Oct'17	69.47	69.9	69.47	69.75	69.75	0.28	7	216
Dec'17	68.05	68.92	67.95	68.59	68.59	0.24	15481	162443
Mar'18	67.9	68.43	67.52	68.38	68.38	0.26	4052	30950
Orange Juice (ICE Futures)								
Sep'17	136.75	136.75	131.65	133.75	133.75	−3.05	532	7254
Nov'17	134.1	135.3	132	133.85	133.85	−2.15	87	1765
Jan'18	135.75	135.8	134.05	135.2	135.2	−2.2	48	917
Corn (Globex) (CBOT)								
Sep'17	389 $^4/_8$	397	388 $^2/_8$	392 $^4/_8$	392 $^4/_8$	2	167382	590669
Dec'17	402	409	400 $^2/_8$	404 $^6/_8$	404 $^6/_8$	2	221545	492076
Mar'18	411 $^2/_8$	418	409 $^6/_8$	413 $^6/_8$	413 $^6/_8$	1 $^4/_8$	39643	107010
Soybeans (Globex) (CBOT)								
Aug'17	985	1003 $^4/_8$	983	1001	1001	15 $^2/_8$	52870	106762
Nov'17	999	1017 $^6/_8$	995 $^6/_8$	1015 $^4/_8$	1015 $^4/_8$	16 $^2/_8$	166701	358115
Jan'18	1006 $^4/_8$	1025 $^2/_8$	1003 $^4/_8$	1023 $^2/_8$	1023 $^2/_8$	16 $^4/_8$	18576	48618
Wheat (Globex) (CBOT)								
Sep'17	538	545 $^6/_8$	530	535	535	−4	95454	213010
Dec'17	560 $^6/_8$	567 $^6/_8$	552	557 $^6/_8$	557 $^6/_8$	−3 $^4/_8$	33760	121740
Mar'18	577 $^2/_8$	583 $^4/_8$	568 $^4/_8$	574 $^4/_8$	574 $^4/_8$	−3 $^4/_8$	13937	46156
Lean Hogs (Globex) (CME)								
Aug'17	82.5	83.65	82.5	83.225	83.225	0.575	16721	88222
Oct'17	70.65	71.425	70.425	70.975	70.975	0.25	12553	78866
Dec'17	65	65.5	64.875	65.35	65.35	0.1	5133	43907
Feb'18	68.325	68.9	68.325	68.875	68.875	0.15	3163	20918
Live Cattle (Globex) (CME)								
Aug'17	115.25	115.85	114.35	114.775	114.775	−0.175	25859	144710
Oct'17	114.075	114.5	113.425	113.825	113.825	−0.05	17738	121572
Dec'17	114.575	115.1	114.125	114.6	114.6	0.05	5817	61153
Feb'18	115.3	115.725	114.8	115.3	115.3	0.05	4019	27975

Source: TradingCharts.com (futures.tradingcharts.com); July 7, 2017.

gold three months later for the contract settlement price of $1,213.30 per ounce. Open interest—the total number of outstanding contracts—was 18,441 for this expiration date.[2]

[2]New contracts are created when a new customer comes to the exchange at a time when no existing contract holder wishes to liquidate his position. On the other hand, if an existing customer wants to close out her short position and there is not a new customer to take her place, the contract price will be raised until an existing long position is enticed to sell back his agreement, thereby canceling the contract and reducing open interest by one.

Another important difference between forward and futures contracts is how the two types of agreements account for the possibility that a counterparty will fail to honor its obligation. Forward contracts may not require either counterparty to post collateral, in which case each is exposed to the potential default of the other during the entire life of the contract. In contrast, the futures exchange requires each customer to post an *initial* **margin account** in the form of cash or government securities when the contract is originated. (The futures exchange, as a well-capitalized corporation, does not post collateral to protect customers from its potential default.) This margin account is then adjusted, or marked to market, at the end of each trading day, according to that day's price movements. All outstanding positions are adjusted to the **settlement price**, which is set by the exchange after trading ends to reflect the midpoint of the closing price range.

The marked-to-market process credits or debits each customer's margin account for daily trading gains or losses as if the customer had closed out her position, even though the contract remains open. For example, Exhibit 15.3 indicates that the settlement price of the October 2017 gold contract decreased by $13.60 per ounce from the previous trading day. This price change benefits the holder of a short position by $1,360 (=13.60 per ounce × 100 ounces). Specifically, if she had entered into the contract yesterday, she would have a commitment to sell gold in October for $1,226.90, which she could now buy for $1,213.30. Accordingly, her margin account will be increased by $1,360. Conversely, any party who is long October gold futures will have his margin account reduced by $1,360 per contract. To ensure that the exchange always has enough protection, collateral accounts are not allowed to fall below a predetermined *maintenance level*, typically about 75 percent of the initial level. If this $1,360 adjustment reduced the long position's account beneath the maintenance margin, he would receive a **margin call** and be required to restore the account to its full initial level or face involuntary liquidation.

15.1.2 Comparing Forward and Futures Contracts

To summarize, the main trade-off historically between forward and futures contracts is *design flexibility* versus *credit and liquidity risk*s, as highlighted by the following comparison:

	Futures	Forwards
Design flexibility	Standardized	Can be customized
Credit risk	Clearinghouse risk	Counterparty risk
Liquidity risk	Depends on trading	Negotiated exit

These differences represent extremes; some forward contracts are quite standard and liquid, while some futures contracts now allow for greater flexibility in the terms of the agreement. Also, forwards have historically required less managerial oversight and intervention—especially on a daily basis—because of the lump-sum settlement at delivery (that is, no margin accounts or marked-to-market settlement), a feature that is often important to unsophisticated or infrequent users of these products.

One interesting development that resulted from the global capital market decline in 2008–2009 was the increased scrutiny that OTC derivatives received from regulators. The Dodd-Frank Wall Street Reform and Consumer Protection Act, which was adopted by the U.S. Congress in 2010, contains several provisions that change the nature of the way some OTC derivatives can be created and traded. In particular, the act (1) provides the Security Exchange Commission (SEC) and Commodity Futures Trading Commission (CFTC) with the authority to regulate OTC derivative transactions in an attempt to create more transparency in the financial system and (2) requires central clearing and exchange trading for derivative positions that can be cleared. Thus, under these statutes, forward contracts have begun to look more like futures contracts in form and function.

15.2 HEDGING WITH FORWARDS AND FUTURES

15.2.1 Hedging and the Basis

The goal of a *hedge* transaction is to create a position that will offset the price risk of another, more fundamental holding. The word *offset* is used here rather than *eliminate* because the hedge transaction attempts to neutralize an exposure that remains on the balance sheet. In Chapter 14, we expressed this concept with the following chart, which assumes that the underlying exposure results from a long commodity position:

Economic Event	Actual Commodity Exposure	Desired Hedge Exposure
Commodity prices fall	Loss	Gain
Commodity prices rise	Gain	Loss

In this case, a short position in a forward contract based on the same commodity would provide the desired negative price correlation. By holding a short forward position against the long position in the commodity, the investor has entered into a **short hedge**. A **long hedge** is created by supplementing a short commodity holding with a long forward position.

The basic premise behind any hedge is that as the underlying commodity price changes, so too will the price of a forward contract based on that commodity. For instance, the short hedger in the preceding example is hoping that if the value of her underlying asset falls, the forward contract price also will fall by the same amount to create an offsetting gain on the derivative. Thus, a critical feature that affects the quality of a hedge transaction is how spot and forward prices change over time.

Defining the Basis To understand the relationship between spot and forward price movements, it is useful to develop the concept of the **basis**. At any Date t, the basis is the spot price minus the forward price for a contract maturing at Date T:

15.1
$$B_{t,T} = S_t - F_{t,T}$$

where:

$S_t =$ Date t spot price
$F_{t,T} =$ Date t forward price for a contract maturing at Date T

Potentially, a different level of the basis may exist on each trading Date t. Two facts always are true, however. First, the *initial basis* at Date 0 $(B_{0,T})$ is known since both the current spot and the forward contract prices can be observed. Second, the *maturity basis* at Date T $(B_{T,T})$ always is zero whenever the commodity underlying the forward contract matches the asset held exactly. For this to occur, the forward price must *converge* to the spot price as the contract expires $(F_{T,T} = S_T)$.

Consider again the investor who hedged her long position in a commodity by agreeing to sell it at Date T through a short position in a forward contract. The initial value of the combined position is $(F_{0,T} - S_0)$. If the investor decides to liquidate her entire position (including the hedge) prior to maturity, she will have to (1) sell her commodity position on the open market for S_t and (2) buy back her short forward position for the new contract price of $F_{t,T}$.[3] The profit from the short hedge liquidated at Date t is:

15.2
$$B_{t,T} - B_{0;T} = (S_t - F_{t,T}) - (S_0 - F_{0,T})$$

The term $B_{t,T}$ often is called the *cover basis* because that is when the forward contract is closed out, or covered.

---

[3]The mechanics of liquidating a forward or futures contract prior to maturity are described in the next section.

15.2.2 Understanding Basis Risk

Equation 15.2 highlights an important fact about hedging. Once the hedge position is formed, the investor no longer is exposed to the absolute price movement of the underlying asset alone. Instead, she is exposed to **basis risk** because the terminal value of her combined position is defined as the cover basis minus the initial basis. Notice that only the cover basis is unknown at Date 0, and so her real exposure is to the **correlation** between subsequent changes in the spot and forward contract prices. If these movements are highly correlated, the basis risk will be quite small. It is usually possible to design a forward contract that reduces basis risk to zero, since $F_{T,T} = S_T$. However, basis risk is a possibility when contract terms are standardized, which is most likely to occur in the futures market.

To illustrate the concept of basis risk, suppose the investor wishes in early July to hedge a long position of 75,000 pounds of coffee she is planning to sell in November. Exhibit 15.3 shows that coffee futures contracts do exist, but with delivery months either in September or in December. With each contract requiring the delivery of 37,500 pounds of coffee, she decides to short two of the December contracts, specifically intending to liquidate her position a month early. Suppose that on the date she initiates her short hedge, the spot coffee price is $1.2655 per pound, and the December futures contract price is $1.3240 per pound. This means that her initial basis is −5.85 cents, which she hopes will move toward zero in a smooth and predictable manner. Suppose that when she closes out her combined position in November, coffee prices have declined so that $S_t = \$1.2141$ and $F_{t,T} = \$1.2255$, leaving a cover basis of −1.14 cents. This means the basis has increased in value, or *strengthened*, which is to the short hedger's advantage. The net November selling price for her coffee is $1.3126 per pound, which is equal to the spot price of $1.2141 plus the net futures profit of $0.0985 ($=1.3240 - 1.2255$). Notice that this is lower than the original futures price but considerably higher than the November spot price. Thus, the short hedger has benefited by exchanging pure price risk for basis risk.

Although it is difficult to generalize, substantial indirect evidence exists that minimizing basis risk is the primary goal of most hedgers. Brown and Smith (1995) noted that the phenomenal growth of OTC products to manage interest rate risk—despite the existence of exchange-traded contracts—is a response to the desire to create customized solutions. However, Bali, Hume, and Martell (2007) showed that hedging with futures does not necessarily reduce a firm's rate of return.

15.2.3 Calculating the Optimal Hedge Ratio

In the preceding example, the decision to short two coffee futures contracts was simple because the investor held exactly twice as much of the same commodity as was covered by a single contract. In most cases, calculating the appropriate hedge ratio, or the number of futures contracts per unit of the spot asset, is not that straightforward. The approach suggested by Johnson (1960) and Castelino (2000) is to choose the number of contracts that minimizes the variance of net profit from a hedged commodity position.

Consider the position of a short hedger who is long one unit of a particular commodity and short N forward contracts on that commodity. Rewriting Equation 15.2 accordingly, the net profit (Π_t) of this position at Date t can be written:

$$\Pi_t = (S_t - S_0) - (F_{t;T} - F_{0;T})(N) = (\Delta S) - (\Delta F)(N)$$

The variance of this value is then given as:

$$\sigma_{\Pi}^2 = \sigma_{\Delta S}^2 + (N^2)\sigma_{\Delta F}^2 - 2(N)\text{COV}_{\Delta S, \Delta F}$$

where:

　　COV = covariance of changes in the spot and forward prices

Minimizing this expression and solving for N leaves:

15.3
$$N^* = \frac{COV_{\Delta S, \Delta F}}{\sigma_{\Delta F}^2} = \left(\frac{\sigma_{\Delta S}}{\sigma_{\Delta F}}\right)\rho$$

where:

ρ = correlation coefficient between the spot and forward price changes[4]

The optimal hedge ratio (N^*) is determined by the ratio of total spot and forward price volatilities deflated by ρ to account for the *systematic* relationship between the two. (It is directly comparable to the beta coefficient of a common stock.) So, the best contract to use in hedging an underlying spot position is the one that has the highest value of ρ. What if, for instance, a clothing manufacturer wanted to hedge the eventual purchase of a large quantity of wool, a commodity for which no exchange-traded futures contract exists? The expression for N^* suggests that it may be possible to form an effective **cross hedge** if prices for a contract based on a related commodity (for example, cotton) are highly correlated with wool prices. The expected basis risk of such a cross hedge can be measured as $(1 - \rho^2)$. Finally, the value for N^* also can be calculated as the slope coefficient of a regression using ΔS and ΔF as the dependent and independent variables, respectively.[5] In the regression context, ρ^2 is called the coefficient of determination or, more commonly, R^2.

15.3 FORWARD AND FUTURES CONTRACTS: BASIC VALUATION CONCEPTS

Forward and futures contracts are not securities but *trade agreements* that enable both buyers and sellers of an underlying commodity or security to lock in the eventual price of their transaction. They typically require no front-end payment from either the long or the short position, so the contract's initial market value usually is zero. Once the terms of the agreement are set, however, any change in market conditions will likely increase the value of the contract to one of the participants. For example, an obligation made in May to purchase soybeans in September for $9.85 per bushel is surely quite valuable in July if soybean prices in the spot market are already $10.00 and no additional harvest is anticipated in the next two months. A description of the valuation of these agreements, which is different for futures and forward contracts, follows.

15.3.1 Valuing Forwards and Futures

Suppose that at Date 0 you contracted in the forward market to buy Q ounces of gold at Date T for $F_{0,T}$. At Date t, prior to the maturity Date T, you decide that this long position is no longer necessary for your portfolio, and you want to **unwind** your original obligation. One way to do this is to take a short position in a Date t forward contract designed to offset the terms of the first. That is, at Date t you would agree to sell Q ounces of gold at Date T for the price of $F_{t,T}$. This is shown in Panel A of Exhibit 15.4. Because you now have contracts to buy and sell Q ounces of gold, you have no exposure to gold price movements between Dates t and T. The profit or loss on this pair of forward contracts is $(Q)[F_{t,T} - F_{0,T}]$. However,

---

[4]Given data for spot and forward prices, σ_{Π}^2 is a function of just one variable, N. Differentiating with respect to N leaves, $[d\sigma_{\Pi}^2/dN] = 2(N)\sigma_{\Delta F}^2 - 2COV_{\Delta S, \Delta F}$, which can be set equal to zero and solved for N^*. It is easily confirmed that the second derivative of this function is positive and so N^* is a minimizing value.

[5]Some have questioned whether regression-based hedge ratios are stable enough to be useful in practice. Ferguson and Leistikow (1998) have concluded that they are stationary, although Fan, Li, and Park (2016) suggests that the covariance between spot and forward prices can change over time.

> **Exhibit 15.4 Unwind Values for Forward and Futures Contracts**
>
> | Date 0 | Date t | Date T |
> |---|---|---|
> | (Origination) | (Unwind) | (Maturity) |
>
> **A. Forward Contract**
> - Long Forward ($F_{0,T}$)
>   - Short Forward ($F_{t,T}$)
>   - Contract Unwind Value: $V_{t,T} = (Q)[F_{t,T} - F_{0,T}] \div (1 + i)^{(T-t)}$
>
> **B. Futures Contract**
> - Long Futures ($F^*_{0,T}$)
>   - Short Futures ($F^*_{t,T}$)
>   - Contract Unwind Value: $V^*_{t,T} = (Q)[F^*_{t,T} - F^*_{0,T}]$

this amount would not be exchanged until Date T, meaning that the value of the original long forward position when it is sold on Date t (its unwind value) would be the *present value* of $(Q)[F_{t,T} - F_{0,T}]$, or:

15.4
$$V_{t,T} = (Q)[F_{t,T} - F_{0,T}] \div (1 + i)^{(T-t)}$$

where:

i = appropriate annualized discount rate

Equation 15.4 expresses the Date t value of a long forward contract maturing at Date t. The value $V_{t,T}$ can be positive or negative, depending on whether $F_{t,T}$ is greater or less than the original contract price, $F_{0,T}$. Also, the value of the short side of the same contract is just $(Q)[F_{0,T} - F_{t,T}] \div (1 + i)^{(T-t)}$, reinforcing the fact that forward contracts are *zero-sum games*. For example, if you had originally agreed to a long position in a six-month gold forward at $F_{0,0.5} = \$1,215$, and after three months the new forward contract price is $F_{0.25,0.5} = \$1,230$, the value of your position would be $\$1,464.68 [= (100)(1,230 - 1,215) \div (1.1)^{0.25}]$, assuming a 10 percent discount rate. Conversely, the value of the original short position would then have to be $-\$1,464.68$.

Valuing a futures contract is conceptually similar to valuing a forward contract with one important difference. As we saw earlier, futures contracts are marked to market on a daily basis, and this settlement amount was not discounted to account for the difference between Dates t and T. That is, the Date t value of the futures contract is simply the undiscounted difference between the futures prices at the origination and unwind (or cover) dates, multiplied by the contract quantity, as shown in Panel B of Exhibit 15.4 and:

15.5
$$V^*_{t,T} = (Q)(F^*_{t,T} - F^*_{0,T})$$

where:

* = possibility that forward and futures prices for the same commodity at the same point in time might be different

Cox, Ingersoll, and Ross (1981) showed that $F^*_{0,T}$ and $F_{0,T}$ would be equal if short-term interest rates (i in Equation 15.4) are known but need not be the same under other circumstances.

Typically, for commodities and securities that support both forward and futures markets, differences between $F^*_{0,T}$ and $F_{0,T}$ exist but are often small. Cornell and Reinganum (1981) found few economically meaningful differences between forward and futures prices in the foreign exchange market, while Park and Chen (1985) showed that certain agricultural and precious metal futures prices were significantly higher than the analogous forward prices.

Grinblatt and Jegadeesh (1996) documented that differences in prices for Eurodollar forward and futures contracts are due to a mispricing of the latter, although this mispricing has been eliminated over time.

15.3.2 The Relationship between Spot and Forward Prices

The relationship between the spot and forward prices at any moment in time is often a more challenging question than how the contract is valued. We can understand the intuition for this relationship with an example: You have agreed at Date 0 to deliver 5,000 bushels of corn to your counterparty at Date T. What is a fair price ($F_{0,T}$) to charge? One way to look at this question is to consider how much it will cost you to fulfill your obligation. If you wait until Date T to purchase the corn on the spot market, you have a *speculative* position, since your purchase price (S_T) will be unknown when you commit to a selling price.

Suppose instead you buy the corn now for the current cash price of S_0 per bushel and store it until you have to deliver it at Date T. The forward contract price you would be willing to commit to would have to be high enough to cover (1) the present cost of the corn and (2) the cost of storing the corn until contract maturity. In general, these storage costs, denoted here as $SC_{0,T}$, can involve several things, including commissions paid for the physical warehousing of the commodity ($PC_{0,T}$) and the cost of financing the initial purchase of the underlying asset ($i_{0,T}$) but less any cash flows received ($D_{0,T}$) by owning the asset between Dates 0 and T. Thus, in the absence of arbitrage opportunities, the forward contract price should be equal to the current spot price plus the **cost of carry** necessary to transport the asset to the future delivery date:

15.6
$$F_{0,T} = S_0 + SC_{0,T} = S_0 + (PC_{0,T} + i_{0,T} - D_{0,T})$$

Notice that even if the funds needed to purchase the commodity at Date 0 are not borrowed, $i_{0,T}$ accounts for the opportunity cost of committing one's own financial capital to the transaction.

This cost of carry model is useful in practice because it applies in a wide variety of cases. For some commodities, such as corn or cattle, physical storage is possible but the costs are enormous. Also, neither of these assets pays periodic cash flows. In such situations, it is quite likely that $F_{0,T} > S_0$, and the market is said to be in **contango**. On the other hand, common stock is costless to store but often pays a dividend. This cash flow sometimes makes it possible for the basis to be positive ($F_{0,T} < S_0$), meaning that $SC_{0,T}$ can be negative. There is another reason $SC_{0,T}$ might be less than zero. For certain storable commodities that do not pay a dividend, $F_{0,T} < S_0$ can occur when there is a premium placed on currently owning the commodity. This premium, called a **convenience yield**, results from a small supply of the commodity at Date 0 relative to what is expected at Date T after, say, a crop harvest. (Cotton satisfies this condition in Exhibit 15.3.) Although it is extremely difficult to quantify, the convenience yield can be viewed as a potential negative storage cost component that works in a manner similar to $D_{0,T}$. A futures market in which $F_{0,T} < S_0$ is said to be **backwardated**.

Equation 15.6 implies that there should be a direct relationship between contemporaneous forward and spot prices. A related question involves the relationship between $F_{0,T}$ and the spot price expected to prevail at the time the contract matures ($E(S_T)$). There are three possibilities. First, the *pure expectations* hypothesis holds that, on average, $F_{0,T} = E(S_T)$, so that futures prices serve as unbiased forecasts of future spot prices. When this is true, futures prices serve an important *price discovery* function for participants in the applicable market. Conversely, $F_{0,T}$ could be less than $E(S_T)$, a situation that Keynes (1930) and Hicks (1939) argued would arise whenever short hedgers outnumber long hedgers. In that case, a risk premium in the form of a lower contract price would be necessary to attract a sufficient number of long speculators. This situation is termed *normal backwardation*. Finally, a *normal contango* market occurs when the opposite is true, specifically, when $F_{0,T} > E(S_T)$.

15.4 FINANCIAL FORWARDS AND FUTURES: APPLICATIONS AND STRATEGIES

Originally, forward and futures markets were organized largely around trading agricultural commodities, such as corn and wheat. Although markets for these products remain strong, the most significant recent developments involve the use of financial securities as the asset underlying the contract. Exhibit 15.5 shows that the most heavily traded derivative contracts globally are based on financial securities. In this section, we take a detailed look at three different types of financial forwards and futures: interest rate, equity index, and foreign exchange.

15.4.1 Interest Rate Forwards and Futures

Interest rate forwards and futures were among the first derivatives to specify a financial security as the underlying asset. To understand the nuances of the most popular exchange-traded instruments, it is useful to separate them according to whether they involve long- or short-term rates.

15.4.2 Long-Term Interest Rate Futures

Treasury Bond and Note Contract Mechanics The U.S. Treasury bond and note contracts at the Chicago Board of Trade (CBOT) are among the most popular of all the financial futures contracts. Delivery dates for both note and bond futures fall in March, June, September, and December. Exhibit 15.6 shows a representative set of quotes for these contracts on July 7, 2017.

Both the T-bond and the longer-term T-note contracts traded at the CBOT call for the delivery of $100,000 face value of the respective instruments. For the T-bond contract, any Treasury bond that has between 15 and 25 years to maturity can be used for delivery. Bonds with maturities ranging from 6.5 to 10 years and 4.17 to 5.25 years can be used to satisfy the 10-year and 5-year T-note contracts, respectively. Delivery can take place on any day during the month of maturity, with the last trading day of the contract falling 7 business days prior to the end of the month.

Mechanically, the quotation process for T-bond and T-note contracts works the same way. For example, the settlement price of $151^{21}/_{32}$, for the highlighted September 2017 T-bond contract represents 151.65625 percent of the face amount, or $151,656.25. The contract price went down by 20 ticks from the previous day's settlement, meaning that the long side had its

Exhibit 15.5 Leading Global Derivative Contract Categories Ranked by Trading Volume		
Underlying Asset of Contract	**2016 Volume (millions)**	**2015 Volume (millions)**
Equity Indexes	7,117.5	8,339.6
Individual Equities	4,557.9	4,944.7
Interest Rate	3,514.9	3,251.1
Foreign Currency	3,077.8	2,797.2
Agricultural Commodities	2,214.1	1,410.9
Energy Products	1,931.9	1,639.7
Non-Precious Metals	1,877.3	1,280.9
Precious Metals	312.1	316.7
Other	616.3	820.0

Source: Futures Industry Association, *FIA 2016 Volume Survey* (March 2017).

Exhibit 15.6 Treasury Bond and Note Futures Quotations

	Open	High	Low	Last	Settle	Chg	Vol	Open Int
U.S. T-Bond (Globex) (CBOT)								
Sep'17	$152^{09}/_{32}$	$152^{12}/_{32}$	$151^{18}/_{32}$	$151^{21}/_{32}$	$151^{21}/_{32}$	$-0^{20}/_{32}$	273433	727663
Dec'17	$150^{26}/_{32}$	151	$150^{11}/_{32}$	$150^{13}/_{32}$	$150^{13}/_{32}$	$-0^{21}/_{32}$	40	189
Mar'18	—	$149^{22}/_{32}$	$149^{22}/_{32}$	$149^{22}/_{32}$	$149^{22}/_{32}$	$-0^{21}/_{32}$	0	0
10-Year T-Note (Globex) (CBOT)								
Sep'17	$125^{01}/_{64}$	$125^{07}/_{64}$	$124^{51}/_{64}$	$124^{54}/_{64}$	$124^{54}/_{64}$	$-0^{09}/_{64}$	1454435	3079463
Dec'17	$124^{41}/_{64}$	$124^{45}/_{64}$	$124^{28}/_{64}$	$124^{30}/_{64}$	$124^{30}/_{64}$	$-0^{09}/_{64}$	1256	8986
Treasury Notes 5-Year (Globex) (CBOT)								
Sep'17	$117^{074}/_{128}$	$117^{086}/_{128}$	$117^{060}/_{128}$	$117^{063}/_{128}$	$117^{063}/_{128}$	$-0^{008}/_{128}$	625958	3011110
Dec'17	$117^{035}/_{128}$	$117^{037}/_{128}$	$117^{014}/_{128}$	$117^{014}/_{128}$	$117^{014}/_{128}$	$-0^{009}/_{128}$	391	3179
Mar'18	—	$116^{111}/_{128}$	$116^{111}/_{128}$	$116^{111}/_{128}$	$116^{111}/_{128}$	$-0^{009}/_{128}$	0	0
2-Year Treasury Note (Globex) (CBOT)								
Sep'17	108	$108^{006}/_{128}$	$107^{124}/_{128}$	$107^{126}/_{128}$	$107^{126}/_{128}$	$-0^{001}/_{128}$	276327	1392387
Dec'17	—	$107^{110}/_{128}$	$107^{110}/_{128}$	$107^{110}/_{128}$	$107^{110}/_{128}$	$-0^{001}/_{128}$	0	0

Source: TradingCharts.com (futures.tradingcharts.com); July 7, 2017.

margin account decreased by $^{20}/_{32}$ percent of $100,000—or $625—where each $^{1}/_{32}$ movement in the bond's price equals $31.25 ($=1,000 \div 32$).

Although T-bond and T-note futures contracts are called interest rate futures, what the long and short positions actually agree to is the price of the underlying bond. Once that price is set, however, the yield will be locked in. When a yield is quoted, it is for reference only and historically has assumed a coupon rate of 6 percent and 20 years to maturity. For the September 2017 bond contract, the settlement yield would be 2.654 percent, which can be established by solving for the internal rate of return in the following bond math problem:

$$\$1,516.5625 = \sum_{t=1}^{40} \frac{\$30}{(1 + i/2)^t} + \frac{\$1,000}{(1 + i/2)^{40}}$$

This pricing formula takes into account the fact that Treasury bonds pay semiannual interest. So, a 20-year, 6 percent bond makes 40 coupon payments of 3 percent each. Thus, the long position in this contract has effectively agreed in July to buy a 20-year T-bond in September priced to yield 2.654 percent. If, in September, the actual yield on the 20-year bond is below 2.654 percent (that is, the bond's price is greater than $151,626.25), the long position will have made a wise decision. Thus, the long position in this contract gains as prices rise and rates decrease and loses as increasing rates lead to lower prices.[6]

A Duration-Based Approach to Hedging   In Chapter 13, we stressed that the main benefit of calculating the duration statistic was its ability to link interest rate changes to bond price changes by the formula:

$$\left(\frac{\Delta P}{P}\right) \approx -D\left(\frac{\Delta(1 + i/n)}{(1 + i/n)}\right)$$

---

[6]Because the bond and note futures contracts allow so many different instruments to qualify for delivery, the seller will naturally choose the *cheapest-to-deliver* bond. The CBOT uses **conversion factors** to correct for coupon and maturity differences in the deliverable bonds. See Labuszewski, Kamradt, and Gibbs (2013) for more details.

We also saw that a more convenient way to write this expression is:

$$\left(\frac{\Delta P}{P}\right) \approx - \left(\frac{D}{(1 + i/n)}\right)\Delta(1 + i/n) = -D_{\mathrm{mod}}\Delta(i/n)$$

where:

D_{mod} = bond's modified duration

Earlier in this chapter, we noted that the objective of hedging was to select a hedge ratio (N) such that $\Delta S - \Delta F(N) = 0$, where S is the current spot price of the underlying asset and F is the current futures contract price. Rewriting this leaves:

$$N^* = \frac{\Delta S}{\Delta F}$$

or, with the modified duration relationship:

$$N^* = \frac{\Delta S}{\Delta F} = \frac{\left(\frac{\Delta S}{S}\right)}{\left(\frac{\Delta F}{F}\right)} \times \frac{S}{F} = \frac{-D_{\mathrm{mod}\,S} \times \Delta(i_S/n)}{-D_{\mathrm{mod}\,F} \times \Delta(i_F/n)} \times \frac{S}{F}$$

which leaves:

15.7
$$N^* = \frac{D_{\mathrm{mod}\,S}}{D_{\mathrm{mod}\,F}} \times \beta_i \times \frac{S}{F}$$

where:

β_i = yield beta

The yield beta is also called the ratio of changes in the yields applicable to the two instruments, where n is the number of payment periods per year (for example, $n = 2$ for semiannual coupon bonds). Consider the following fixed-income securities making annual payments ($n = 1$):

Instrument	Coupon (%)	Maturity (yrs)	Yield (%)
A	8%	10	10%
B	10	15	8

How much of Instrument B is necessary to hedge A? This can be answered in three steps. First, using the method shown in Chapter 13, the duration statistics for each position are:

$$D_A = 7.0439, \text{ so } D_{\mathrm{modA}} = (7.0439) \div (1.10) = 6.4036 \text{ years}$$
$$D_B = 8.8569, \text{ so } D_{\mathrm{modB}} = (8.8569) \div (1.08) = 8.2009 \text{ years}$$

Second, suppose that yield beta is unity ($\beta_i = 1$); this is usually calculated by observing historical yield curve movements across the 10- and 15-year maturities. Finally, current prices are easily confirmed to be 87.71 for Security A and 117.12 for Security B, assuming par value of 100. Thus, the duration-based hedge ratio is:

$$N^* = \left(\frac{6.4036}{8.2009}\right)(1)\left(\frac{87.71}{117.12}\right) = 0.5847$$

or 0.5847 unit of B short for every one unit of A held long.

Treasury Futures Application: Hedging a Funding Commitment In late April, the treasurer of a U.S.-based company is arranging a 15-year, $100 million funding. The company will be ready to launch its new debt issue in late June, but he is concerned that, between April and June, interest rates may rise, thereby increasing the company's funding cost. He decides to hedge this exposure in the T-bond futures market with a *short* position in, which will appreciate in value if interest rates increase.

If the bond issue was placed today, the credit standing of the firm would lead to a funding cost of 8.25 percent for the 15-year period. He knows that a June T-bond futures contract is trading at a price of 83–16 to yield 7.62 percent and that bond yields beyond 10 years to maturity tend to move in a parallel fashion, so he is comfortable that a yield beta of 1.0 is appropriate. Further, the treasurer is aware that T-bond futures cannot hedge for changes in the firm's risk premium over the risk-free rate; he will have to live with this source of basis risk.

If he plans to launch his new issue at par value, how many T-bond futures contracts would he need to short today? Assuming semiannual coupons for both the Treasury and the corporate issues, their durations can be calculated using the closed-form equation shown in Chapter 13:

$$D_{\text{corp}} = \frac{1.04125}{0.04125} - \frac{1.04125 + [30(0.04125 - 0.04125)]}{0.04125\left[(1.04125)^{30} - 1\right] + 0.04125} = 17.74 \text{ periods}$$

and:

$$D_{\text{trsy}} = \frac{1.0381}{0.0381} - \frac{1.0381 + [40(0.03 - 0.0381)]}{0.03\left[(1.0381)^{40} - 1\right] + 0.0381} = 22.22 \text{ periods}$$

These statistics are denominated in half years so that the hedge ratio will be expressed in the same terms used to price the bonds. We can calculate the modified durations as follows: $D_{\text{modC}} = 17.04\,(= 17.74 \div 1.04125)$ and $D_{\text{modT}} = 21.40\,(= 22.22 \div 1.0381)$. Finally, since each T-bond futures contract is standardized to a denomination of $100,000, the treasurer can calculate the optimal number of contracts to short as:

$$(\text{Number of Contracts}) = \frac{(17.04)}{(21.40)} \times (1.0) \times \frac{(\$100,000,000)}{(\$83,500)} = 953.6 \text{ or } 954 \text{ Contracts}$$

15.4.3 Short-Term Interest Rate Futures

Short-term interest rate futures have become a rapidly expanding segment of the exchange-traded market. Currently, investors can hedge their exposures to various different money market rates (for example, LIBOR, federal funds rate) denominated in a multitude of currencies (for example, U.S. dollar, Japanese yen, euro). Exhibit 15.7 shows a representative set of quotes

Exhibit 15.7 Eurodollar (LIBOR) and Federal Funds Futures Quotations

	Open	High	Low	Last	Settle	Chg	Vol	Open Int
Eurodollar (Globex) (CME)								
Aug'17	98.67	98.68	98.67	98.68	98.675	0.005	8204	58058
Sep'17	98.64	98.66	98.63	98.655	98.65	0.015	218322	1482699
Dec'17	98.515	98.53	98.505	98.53	98.525	0.015	314399	1808736
Mar'18	98.415	98.425	98.4	98.42	98.415	0.005	189180	1137063
Jun'18	98.33	98.345	98.315	98.335	98.325	—	201173	1081725
Sep'18	98.25	98.26	98.225	98.245	98.24	—	200843	1052215
Dec'18	98.145	98.17	98.125	98.145	98.135	−0.005	261809	1338740
30-Day Fed Funds (Globex) (CBOT)								
Aug'17	98.84	98.845	98.84	98.845	98.845	—	14067	179274
Sep'17	98.83	98.835	98.825	98.835	98.835	0.005	17370	75774
Dec'17	98.73	98.745	98.725	98.74	98.74	0.01	8808	77253
Jan'18	98.685	98.695	98.68	98.695	98.695	0.01	40272	210283

Source: TradingCharts.com (futures.tradingcharts.com); July 7, 2017.

for Eurodollar and federal funds contracts as of July 7, 2017. In the following analysis, we concentrate on Eurodollar futures.

Eurodollar Contract Mechanics The Eurodollar contract traded on the Chicago Mercantile Exchange (CME) has become enormously successful since it was launched in the early 1980s. Delivery dates occur monthly for a brief period before following the March, June, September, December cycle, and they now extend 10 years into the future. The final trading and settlement date is the second London business day before the third Wednesday of the delivery month.

Hypothetically, a Eurodollar contract requires the long position to make a $1,000,000, 90-day bank deposit with the short position at the maturity date. Unlike the Treasury bond futures just described, this contract requires all outstanding obligations to be settled in cash. The underlying interest rate is the 3-month (90-day) LIBOR that is quoted on a 360-day bank add-on basis. The listed settlement price for the September 2017 contract is 98.65, which is not an actual purchase price but merely an index calculated as 100 minus the effective settlement yield of 1.35 percent. Eurodollar futures use this settlement price index because it conveniently preserves the inverse relation between price and yield. Thus, a long position in this contract will benefit when prices rise—and the short position benefits with falling prices—even though it is the opposite movement in the underlying interest rate that matters.

If the price index for this contract moved by one "tick" (that is, 0.015), the contract itself would change by $25 ($=\$1,000,000 \times 0.0001 \times 90/360$), which is called the *basis point value* of the position. Thus, the 1.5-tick increase in the price of the September 2011 contract means that LIBOR decreased by 1.5 basis points from the prior day's settlement. This would benefit a person who acquired a long position at the close of the prior day, inasmuch as he would have a locked-in borrowing cost for the 90-day period from September to December 2017 that is now 1.5 basis points lower than the market level. In fact, all buyers of this contract gained $37.50 per contract ($=\$25$ per tick $\times 1.5$ ticks) in their margin accounts.

Short-Term Interest Rate Future Application: Creating a Synthetic Fixed Rate Funding Suppose that on March 15, a bank loan officer is considering an investment scheme for lending $2,000,000 to a large-cap manufacturing firm. The plan would last for one year and have the payment rate reset on a quarterly basis at LIBOR. At the planning stage, the LIBOR yield curve appears as follows:

$$
\begin{array}{ll}
\text{90-day LIBOR} & 5.00\% \\
\text{180-day LIBOR} & 5.10 \\
\text{270-day LIBOR} & 5.20 \\
\text{360-day LIBOR} & 5.30
\end{array}
$$

Given the debt market convention for floating-rate deal structures, she knows that her loan receipt for the first three months would be based on the prevailing 5.00 percent rate and be receivable in 90 days. Her concern is the level of her receipts in the subsequent three quarters may fall to an unacceptable level. So, she considers using the Eurodollar futures market to hedge her exposure.

Before checking futures contract price quotes, she calculates the forward rates implied by the current yield curve, using the money-market implied forward rate formula shown in the appendix to this chapter:

$$_{180}IFR_{90} = \left[\frac{(0.051)(180) - (0.050)(90)}{(180 - 90)}\right] \left[\frac{1}{1 + \left(\dfrac{(90)(0.050)}{360}\right)}\right] = 5.14\%$$

$$_{270}IFR_{180} = \left[\frac{(0.052)(270) - (0.051)(180)}{(270 - 180)}\right] \left[\frac{1}{1 + \left(\dfrac{(180)(0.51)}{360}\right)}\right] = 5.27\%$$

$$_{360}IFR_{270} = \left[\frac{(0.053)(360) - (0.052)(270)}{(360 - 270)}\right] \left[\frac{1}{1 + \left(\dfrac{(270)(0.052)}{360}\right)}\right] = 5.39\%$$

She checks the quotes on the relevant Eurodollar futures contracts and finds:

Contract Expiration	Settlement Price
June	94.86
September	94.73
December	94.61

The futures settlement prices indicate LIBOR contract rates that are identical to the implied forward rates, suggesting that there is no arbitrage potential between the cash and futures markets.

To lock in her receipts for the $2,000,000 loan, the banker would go long a *strip* of Eurodollar futures contracts by taking long positions in two June contracts, two September contracts, and two December contracts. With these positions, her quarterly interest receipts will be fixed at the following levels:

$$\text{June Receipt} = (\$2,000,000)\left[\frac{(0.0500)(90)}{360}\right] = \$25,000$$

$$\text{September Receipt} = (\$2,000,000)\left[\frac{(0.0514)(90)}{360}\right] = \$25,700$$

$$\text{December Receipt} = (\$2,000,000)\left[\frac{(0.0527)(90)}{360}\right] = \$26,350$$

$$\text{March (Next Year)Receipt} = (\$2,000,000)\left[\frac{(0.0539)(90)}{360}\right] = \$26,950$$

Although these cash inflows are fixed in advance, they clearly differ in amount from quarter to quarter. The banker then asks herself the following question: What quarterly annuity payment does this sequence of receipts imply? This amount is the solution to:

$$\frac{\$25,000}{\left[1 + \dfrac{(0.050)(90)}{360}\right]} + \frac{\$25,700}{\left[1 + \dfrac{(0.051)(180)}{360}\right]} + \frac{\$26,350}{\left[1 + \dfrac{(0.052)(270)}{360}\right]} + \frac{\$26,950}{\left[1 + \dfrac{(0.053)(360)}{360}\right]}$$

$$= \frac{\text{Annuity}}{\left[1 + \dfrac{(0.050)(90)}{360}\right]} + \frac{\text{Annuity}}{\left[1 + \dfrac{(0.051)(180)}{360}\right]} + \frac{\text{Annuity}}{\left[1 + \dfrac{(0.052)(270)}{360}\right]} + \frac{\text{Annuity}}{\left[1 + \dfrac{(0.053)(360)}{360}\right]}$$

Solving this formula for annuity gives a value of $25,989.38. So, when expressed on an annualized percentage basis, the annuity receipt is:

$$\left[\frac{\$25,989.38}{\$2,000,000}\right]\left[\frac{360}{90}\right] = 5.198\%$$

15.4.4 Stock Index Futures

In this section, we consider the basics of stock index futures trading and discuss two applications for these instruments, including a popular form of computer-assisted trading known as stock index arbitrage.

Stock Index Futures Contract Fundamentals Like interest rate futures, stock index futures were originally intended to provide a hedge against movements in an underlying financial asset. As detailed in Chapter 4, the underlying financial asset for a stock index futures contract is a hypothetical creation that does not exist in practice and therefore cannot be delivered to settle a contract. Thus, stock index futures can only be settled in cash, similar to the Eurodollar (LIBOR) contract.

Exhibit 15.8 lists quotes for futures contracts on several stock indexes, including the Dow Jones Industrial Average, Nikkei 225, Standard & Poor's 500, and Russell 1000. Contracts for indexes representing other global markets [for example, FTSE 100 (Great Britain), DAX 30 (Germany), Euro Stoxx 50] are traded actively but not shown in the display. For example, an

Exhibit 15.8 Stock Index Futures Quotations

	Open	High	Low	Last	Settle	Chg	Vol	Open Int
Dow Jones E-mini ($5) (Globex) (CBOT)								
Sep'17	21279	21377	21264	21370	21370	90	106494	129530
Dec'17	21252	21331	21225	21329	21329	89	58	209
Mar'18	—	21294	21294	21294	21294	89	1	10
Nasdaq 100 E-mini (CME)								
Sep'17	5598.5	5676.5	5591.5	5657.25	5655.75	59	266248	290424
Dec'17	5604.5	5681.25	5602.5	5662.5	5662	59	240	921
Mar'18	5667	5686.25	5667	5676	5670.5	59	4	37
Nikkei 225 Yen (CME)								
Aug'17	—	—	—	20180	20010	130	—	2
Sep'17	19885	20055	19825	20020	20020	130	37838	72617
Dec'17	19805	19805	19805	19805	19890	130	1	22
Russell 1000 Index Mini (ICE Futures)								
Sep'17	1337.5	1344	1336.2	1344	1344	10.7	782	8172
Dec'17	1343.6	1343.6	1343.5	1343.5	1343.5	10.7	—	1
Russell 2000 Mini (ICE Futures)								
Sep'17	1400	1417.1	1399.4	1414.2	1414.2	13.9	137268	562719
Dec'17	1403	1415.1	1401	1413.3	1413.3	13.9	12	116
S&P 500 (CME)								
Sep'17	2414.3	2422.6	2412	2422.6	2422.6	14.2	2631	44829
Dec'17	—	2421.9	2421.9	2420.6	2420.6	14.2	30	226
Mar'18	—	2420.3	2420.3	2419	2419	14.2	30	30

Source: TradingCharts.com (futures.tradingcharts.com); July 7, 2017.

investor planning in July to buy stock the following September can hedge against the risk of his eventual purchase price increasing by entering into the long position in the September 2017 S&P 500 contract. Given the settlement price of 2,422.60, he has obligated himself to the theoretical purchase of 250 shares of the S&P 500 on the day before the third Friday of September for $605,650 ($=2,422.60 \times 250$). The minimum contract price movement is 0.10 index points, which equals $25. So, if the actual index level on the contract settlement date turned out to be 2,424.80, the long position would gain $550, or $25 times 22 ticks $[=(2,424.80 - 2,422.60) \div 0.10]$, thereby reducing the net purchase price for his desired equity position. Finally, notice that a "mini" version of the S&P 500 futures contract requiring the hypothetical purchase or sale of only 50 shares is also available.

Stock Index Futures Valuation and Index Arbitrage Stock index futures often are used to convert entire stock portfolios into synthetic riskless positions to exploit an apparent mispricing between stock in the cash and futures markets. This strategy, commonly called **stock index arbitrage**, is the most prominent example of a wider class of computer-assisted trading schemes known as *program trading*. Suppose that at Date 0 an investor (1) purchases a portfolio of stock representing the underlying stock index for S_0 and (2) goes short a stock index future (with an expiration date of T) for $F_{0,T}$. Assume also that the funds for the long position are borrowed at the risk-free rate of RFR. On unwinding this position at Date t, the net profit (Π) is given by:

$$\Pi = (F_{0,T} - F_{t,T}) + (S_t - S_0 - S_0\text{RFR}_t + S_0d_t) = (F_{0,T} - F_{t,T}) + [S_t - S_0(1 + \text{RFR}_t - d_t)]$$

where:

d_t = dividend yield accruing to the stocks comprising the index between Dates 0 and t

The profit you make on this short stock index futures hedge will consist of two components: the net difference in the futures position and the net difference in the underlying index position (after adding borrowing costs and subtracting dividends received from the initial purchase).

Now suppose the long position in the stock portfolio is held until the expiration of the futures contract (Date $t = T$) so that the futures price and index level will converge to $F_{T,T} = S_T$, meaning the short hedge profit (Π) equation is:

$$\Pi = [F_{0,T} - S_0 - S_0 (\text{RFR}_t - d_T)]$$

As before, $\text{RFR}_t - d_T$ is called the net cost of carry.

If the dividend yield is known at Date 0, this position is riskless and requires no initial investment. Thus, buying and selling among arbitrageurs trading in both markets should ensure that $\Pi = 0$. The futures price set at Date 0 will be:

15.8 $$F_{0,T} = S_0 + S_0 (\text{RFR}_t - d_T)$$

As discussed earlier, the futures price could be set below the spot level of the index (a backwardated market) if $(\text{RFR}_t - d_T) < 0$, or whenever the dividends received by holding stock exceed the borrowing cost.

To illustrate this parity relationship, assume that one share of the S&P 500 Index can be purchased for $2,250.00 and that the dividend yield and risk-free rate over the holding period are 1.5 percent and 2.5 percent, respectively. The contract price on a six-month S&P 500 futures should then be:

$$F_{0,0.5} = 2,250 + 2,250 (0.025 - 0.015) = 2,272.50$$

Now suppose that you construct a short hedge position by (1) purchasing the index at 2,250.00 and (2) shorting the futures at 2,272.50. If the position is held to expiration, your profit at

Exhibit 15.9 Stock Index Futures Valuation Example

			S&P at Expiration:		
	2,220	**2,240**	**2,260**	**2,280**	**2,300**
Net futures profit	52.50	32.50	12.50	(7.50)	(27.50)
Net index profit	(30.00)	(10.00)	10.00	30.00	50.00
Dividend	33.75	33.75	33.75	33.75	33.75
Net profit	56.25	56.25	56.25	56.25	56.25

various expiration date levels of the S&P will be as shown in Exhibit 15.9. Notice that your net profit remains constant no matter the level of the index at the expiration date:

$$(56.25) \div (2,250) = 2.5\%$$

which is the assumed cost of borrowing.

Implementing an Index Arbitrage Strategy What if the parity condition between the stock index and the stock index futures price does not hold? Suppose that in the preceding example the actual contract price on a six-month S&P 500 futures was 2,275.50 [that is, $F_{0,T} > S_0 + S_0(RFR_t - d_T)$]. You could then implement the following arbitrage transaction: (1) Short the stock index future at a price of 2,275.50, (2) borrow money at 2.5 percent to purchase the stock index at 2,250.00, and (3) hold the position until maturity, collecting 33.75 in dividends and then selling the stock to repay your loan. Your net profit at maturity would be:

$$2,275.50 - 2,250 - 2,250(0.025 - 0.015) = \$3.00$$

However, since this strategy was riskless (that is, the sales price of the stock and the dividends were known in advance) and none of your own capital was used, it is an arbitrage profit, assuming it covers the cost of your transactions. If the actual level of $F_{0,T} < S_0 + S_0(RFR_t - d_T)$, the previous strategy could be reversed: (1) Buy the stock index future at a price of $F_{0,T}$, (2) lend money at RFR_t and short the stock index at S_0, and (3) cover the position at the expiration date of the futures contract. Indeed, index arbitrage is a popular form of trading.

One important side effect of this trading activity is that stock index futures prices tend to stay close to their theoretical levels. This is because the arbitrage prescription for a futures settlement price that is too low (too high) is to go long (short) in the contract, which, when done in sufficient volume, adjusts the price in the proper direction. Exhibit 15.10 compares the actual and theoretical levels of the nearest-term future contract for several stock indexes throughout the world, including the S&P 500, Dow Jones Industrial, and the Nikkei 225. The pricing errors on this particular day never exceeded 1 percent in any market and averaged less than $1/10$ of 1 percent for all contracts. These values support the notion that the stock index futures market is very efficient.

The empirical evidence tends to support this view, particularly after transaction costs and other trading realities are considered. Cornell (1985) found that stock index futures prices tracked their model values more closely as the market matured, which is consistent with the notion that index arbitrage reduces volatility by stabilizing cash and futures prices. Also, Bohl, Salm, and Schuppli (2011) demonstrate how this connection between spot and futures price facilitates the price discovery process.

A Stock Index Futures Application: Isolating Unsystematic Risk In Chapter 14, we demonstrated how stock index futures could alter the systematic risk of an otherwise

Exhibit 15.10 Actual and Theoretical Global Stock Index Futures Prices

Hit (#) Go to monitor the intra-day spread of cash and futures (basis)

EQUITY INDEX FUTURE ANALYSIS
FAIR VALUE

	Ticker : N	Cash	Future	Theo. Future	Fair Value	Spread Basis	Percent Misprice
1)	**Americas**						
4)	DOW JONES INDUS.	21432.94	21387.00	21370.12	−62.82	−45.94	+.079%
5)	S&P 500 INDEX	2431.00	2428.80	2427.22	−3.78	−2.20	+.065%
6)	NASDAQ 100	5696.55	5702.25	5696.88	.34	5.70	+.094%
7)	S&P 400 MIDCAP	1749.40	1749.70	1748.25	−1.15	.30	+.083%
8)	S&P/TSX COMP	892.45	889.10	889.90	−2.55	−3.35	−.090%
9)	MEXICO BOLSA IDX	50633.96	50765.00	51231.02	597.06	131.04	−.910%
2)	**Europe**						
10)	FTSE 100 INDEX	7370.03	7309.00	7304.92	−65.11	−61.03	+.056%
11)	FTSE EUROTOP 100	N.A.	7309.00	N.A.	N.A.	N.A.	N.A.
12)	CAC 40 INDEX	5165.64	5171.50	5164.94	−.70	5.86	+.127%
13)	DAX INDEX	12445.92	12451.00	12437.86	−8.06	5.08	+.106%
14)	AMSTERDAM EXCHGS	512.05	512.65	511.98	−.07	.60	+.131%
15)	SWISS MARKET IDX	8943.84	8937.00	8931.08	-12.76	−6.84	+.066%
3)	**Asis/Pacific**						
16)	NIKKEI 225 (OSE)	20080.98	20080.00	20067.85	−13.13	−.98	+.061%
17)	NIKKEI 225 (SGX)	20080.98	20075.00	20067.85	−13.13	−5.98	+.036%
18)	TOPIX INDEX	1615.48	1616.00	1614.93	−.55	.52	+.066%
19)	S&P/ASX 200 IDX	5724.44	5683.00	5671.02	−53.41	−41.44	+.211%

Hit <#> <Index> **FVD** Go for detail Fair Value analysis.

Australia 61 2 9777 8600 Brazil 5511 2395 9000 Europe 44 20 7330 7500 Germany 49 69 9204 1210 Hong Kong 852 2977 6000
Japan 81 3 3201 8900   Singapore 65 6212 1000   U.S. 1 212 318 2000   Copyright 2017 Bloomberg Finance L.P.

SN 335716 CDT GMT-5:00 H444-1446-2 10-Jul-2017 13:33:34

well-diversified portfolio. When the holding is an individual stock, this process can isolate the unique attributes of the company. Recall that:

$$\text{Total Stock Risk} = \text{Systematic Risk} + \text{Unsystematic Risk}$$

with the systematic component representing about 25–50 percent of the total risk for the typical firm. Thus, using stock index futures to adjust the stock's beta to zero effectively isolates the unsystematic portion of risk.

To see how this might work, suppose that in early July you own 75,000 shares of Pharmco Inc., a multinational pharmaceutical firm. The current price of Pharmco stock is $41.00, and you calculate the company's beta at 0.99. You like the stock as an investment because of the quality of its management, but you are concerned that over the next few months the aggregate stock market might undergo a sizable correction that could more than offset any firm-specific gains.

To protect yourself, you decide to sell September S&P 500 futures contracts, which are currently trading at a settlement price of 2,422.60. At this price, we have seen that the implied dollar value of a single contract is $605,650. The current value of your Pharmco stock is $3,075,000. Since the stock's beta can be defined as $\rho[\sigma_{\Delta S} \div \sigma_{\Delta F}]$, the optimal hedge ratio formula developed earlier leaves:

$$N^* = \left[\frac{\text{Market Value of Spot Position}}{\text{Value Implied by Futures Contract}} \right] \beta$$

$$= [(\$3,075,000) \div (\$605,650)](0.99) = 5.02$$

so you decide to short five contracts.

Now suppose that by mid-September when your futures position expires, the S&P 500 Index settles at a level of 2,372.60 while the price of Pharmco stock has increased to $41.75. Although you have made a modest profit on your common stock holding ($56,250, or 1.8 percent), you will also benefit from a trading profit on the futures position of $62,500 ($=(5) [2,422.60 - 2,372.60](250)$). Your total return is $118,750, which expressed as a percentage of your original investment is equivalent to an unsystematic appreciation in Pharmco's stock of 3.9 percent. Notice that the difference between this amount and the gross increase of 1.8 percent in Pharmco stock is equal to the 2.1 percent ($=[2,372.6 \div 2,422.6] - 1$) that the stock index futures position fell.

15.4.5 Currency Forwards and Futures

Whether in the spot or forward markets, foreign exchange (FX) transactions often involve a confusing blend of unique terminology and market conventions. We begin our analysis of currency derivatives with a brief overview of some of the fundamental features of these products.

The Mechanics of Currency Transactions   The market for foreign currency is no different than any other market, in that buyer and seller negotiate for the exchange of a certain amount of a predetermined commodity at a fixed cash price. The challenge in FX transactions is that the "commodity" involved is someone else's currency. This means that the transaction can be viewed in two ways. For example, suppose that Company A agrees to pay 100 U.S. dollars to Company B in exchange for 50 British pounds. Is Company A buying sterling (GBP) or selling dollars (USD)?[7] Both are correct, depending on one's point of view.

Because of this dual interpretation, the price for all FX transactions also can be quoted in two ways. Assuming that Company A is a U.S.-based firm, it would probably think of the transaction as the purchase of 50 pounds at a cost of 100 dollars, which would yield the price of USD 2.0000/GBP ($=100/50$). This method of quoting FX prices is called the *direct*, or *American*, convention. Under this convention, the pound (that is, the foreign currency from the U.S. firm's perspective) is treated as the commodity, and its price per unit is expressed in terms of dollars. If Company B is a British corporation, its managers would likely think of prices in terms of the amount of sterling they have to pay to acquire dollars, or GBP 0.5000/USD. Treating the dollar as the commodity yields the *indirect*, or *European*, quotation method. The direct and indirect quotes are just *reciprocals* of one another.

Exhibit 15.11 shows a representative set of FX quotes. Two prices are listed beside each currency. The first column reports the current day's dollar price for trading one unit of that currency (direct quote). For instance, the prevailing price of a New Zealand dollar on that date was USD 0.72850. The next column expresses this same price in indirect terms (for example, NZD 1.37268/USD = 1 ÷ USD 0.72850/NZD). Thus, the terms of a spot FX transaction can be structured to meet the particular needs of the counterparties involved.

Another important aspect of the FX markets is that although many currencies trade in the spot market, relatively few also quote prices for forward transactions. In this list, only the Euro, British, and Japanese currencies have forward contracts. These contracts, which are negotiated in the OTC market with a currency dealer (such as a multinational bank), carry maturities one, three, and six months into the future. For example, an investor wishing to buy euros would pay USD 1.14030 per euro if the transaction were completed immediately, 1.14213 if the transaction were negotiated now but consummated in 30 days, and USD 1.14586 or USD 1.15181 for exchanges completed in 90 or 180 days, respectively.

In the situation where it costs increasingly more dollars to buy the same euro the farther out in the future it is delivered, the dollar is said to be trading at a **forward discount** to the euro. Conversely, the euro is at a **forward premium** to the dollar. This relationship depends on the currencies being compared. In this set of quotes, the U.S. dollar is trading at a forward

---

[7]Currency traders often use three-letter abbreviations to denote a particular currency. Some of the most common abbreviations are USD (U.S. dollars), CAD (Canadian dollars), GBP (British pounds), JPY (Japanese yen), CHF (Swiss franc), and EUR (euro currency). For a more complete listing, see Gastineau and Kritzman (2001).

Exhibit 15.11 Spot and Forward Currency Quotations

Currency	in USD	per USD
Euro	1.14030	0.87696
1-mos forward	1.14213	0.87556
3-mos forward	1.14586	0.87271
6-mos forward	1.15181	0.86820
British pound	1.28950	0.77549
1-mos forward	1.29079	0.77472
3-mos forward	1.29328	0.77323
6-mos forward	1.29697	0.77103
Switzerland franc	1.03788	0.96350
Norway krone	0.11945	8.37150
Japan yen	0.00878	113.93000
1-mos forward	0.00879	113.76670
3-mos forward	0.00881	113.46300
6-mos forward	0.00885	112.93700
Australia dollar	0.76060	1.31475
New Zealand dollar	0.72850	1.37268
Hong Kong dollar	0.12800	7.81270
Canada dollar	0.77646	1.28790
Mexico peso	0.05513	18.13840
Chile peso	0.00150	667.60000

Source: TradingCharts.com (forex.tradingcharts.com), Investing.com (www.investing.com/currencies/), Author calculations; July 7, 2017.

discount to all three currencies with forward markets. We will see that whether a currency trades at a discount or a premium to another depends on the relative level of the investment rates in the two countries.

Exhibit 15.12 lists quotes for a sample of exchange-traded currency futures contracts traded at the CME on July 7, 2017. Each contract involving U.S. dollars follows the convention that the U.S. dollar is the native monetary unit and the foreign currency is the commodity, meaning that all prices are quoted using the direct method. These contracts are also standardized to deliver a set number of units of the foreign currency on a specific date in the future. For instance, the September 2017 euro contract negotiated on that date required the long position to purchase—and the short position to deliver—125,000 euros at the price of USD 1.14445 per euro. By convention, all currency futures on the CME mature on the third Wednesday of the stated delivery month and can be settled with a wire transfer of the foreign currency.

A Currency Futures Application: Covered Interest Arbitrage The term **interest rate parity** specifies the "no arbitrage" relationship between spot and forward FX rates and the level of interest rates in each currency. This connection is best seen through an example. Suppose that an institutional investor has USD 100,000 to invest for 1 year and is considering two different riskless alternatives. The first strategy entails the purchase of a U.S. Treasury bill. Assume the effective U.S. dollar risk-free interest rate is 4.50 percent for a 1-year maturity, so that a direct T-bill investment would return USD 104,500 at the end of the 12 months.

For the second strategy, suppose that the investor also can sell the USD 100,000 in the spot market at the exchange rate of AUD 1.20/USD (or, equivalently, USD 0.8333/AUD) to obtain a total of 120,000 Australian dollars. We assume that amount can then be invested in an Australian risk-free security at a rate of 7.00 percent, returning AUD 128,400 at the end of the year. To make this return comparable to the first strategy, the Australian dollars will have to be converted back into U.S. currency. If this translation is negotiated at the end of the

Exhibit 15.12 Currency Futures Quotations

	Open	High	Low	Last	Settle	Chg	Vol	Open Int
Australian Dollar (Globex) (CME)								
Aug'17	0.7579	0.76	0.7576	0.7598	0.76	0.0019	137	317
Sep'17	0.7577	0.7617	0.7565	0.7599	0.7596	0.0018	74535	96333
Dec'17	0.756	0.759	0.756	0.7583	0.7587	0.0018	14	1457
British Pound (Globex) (CME)								
Aug'17	1.2972	1.2978	1.289	1.2897	1.2897	−0.0091	172	371
Sep'17	1.2999	1.3003	1.2894	1.2908	1.291	−0.0091	98729	192761
Dec'17	1.3032	1.3035	1.2937	1.2948	1.2946	−0.009	80	1578
Mar'18	1.3048	1.3048	1.3048	1.3048	1.2983	−0.0092	4	287
Canadian Dollar (Globex) (CME)								
Aug'17	0.7707	0.778	0.7698	0.77715	0.7769	0.00485	91	195
Sep'17	0.77145	0.7785	0.77045	0.77735	0.77725	0.0048	86655	147778
Dec'17	0.77145	0.7792	0.77145	0.7778	0.7779	0.00475	292	4554
Euro (Globex) (CME)								
Aug'17	1.1442	1.14615	1.1401	1.1421	1.1424	−0.002	674	1573
Sep'17	1.1464	1.1482	1.14215	1.14435	1.14445	−0.002	200596	419291
Dec'17	1.152	1.15365	1.1481	1.14975	1.1501	−0.00205	1297	3953
Mar'18	1.157	1.15795	1.154	1.15435	1.15615	−0.0021	66	721
Japanese Yen (Globex) (CME)								
Aug'17	0.88405	0.88475	0.8777	0.87925	0.8786	−0.0057	415	496
Sep'17	0.8863	0.88675	0.8784	0.8805	0.8799	−0.0057	182104	219991
Dec'17	0.88945	0.88945	0.88275	0.8843	0.88375	−0.0057	52	604
Mexican Peso (Globex) (CME)								
Aug'17	—	—	—	0.05484	0.05499	0.00062	—	64
Sep'17	0.05411	0.05489	0.05401	0.05468	0.05469	0.00062	44065	210382
Dec'17	0.05377	0.05391	0.05377	0.05391	0.05393	0.00062	19	61
Swiss Franc (Globex) (CME)								
Sep'17	1.0454	1.0461	1.0404	1.0416	1.0418	−0.0034	19550	37649
Dec'17	—	1.0506	1.0506	1.0506	1.048	−0.0035	—	250
Mar'18	—	—	—	1.0471	1.0548	−0.0036	—	17

Source: TradingCharts.com (futures.tradingcharts.com); July 7, 2017.

investment, however, the investor will be subjected to foreign exchange risk in that he will not know at Date 0 what the AUD/USD exchange rate will be at Date *T*. So, to make the second strategy riskless, the investor must enter into a forward contract to exchange AUD back into USD at the end of the year. What would the exchange rate in a one-year futures contract have to be at Date 0 to leave the investor indifferent between these two strategies?

These investments are depicted in Exhibit 15.13. The essence of the arbitrage argument is that the one-year forward FX rate must be such that USD 104,500 equals AUD 128,400, implying a forward rate of AUD 1.2287/USD (=128,400 ÷ 104,500) on an indirect basis, or USD 0.8139/AUD quoted directly. This is a breakeven value in the sense that it allows the 4.50 percent investment return in the United States to be equal to the 7.00 percent available in Australia when the two are converted to the same currency. That is, the Australian return must be "deflated" by 250 basis points to leave the investor indifferent between the two

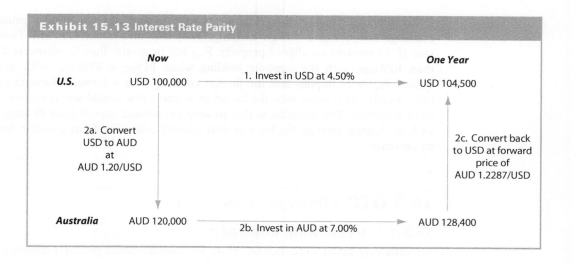

Exhibit 15.13 Interest Rate Parity

strategies. This reduction occurs because, to invest in the AUD-denominated security, the investor buys Australian dollars at a price of USD 0.8333/AUD but must sell them back in the futures market at the lower price of USD 0.8139/AUD.

If the actual one-year futures contract FX rate were *higher* than this breakeven level—say, for instance, AUD 1.25/USD—the currency translation loss would be greater than 250 basis points, leaving the USD-based strategy the most profitable choice so that arbitrage is possible. In this case, an arbitrageur could enter the following transactions:

1. Borrow AUD 120,000 at 7.00 percent; agree to repay AUD 128,400 in one year.
2. Sell the foreign currency on the spot market at AUD 1.20/USD; receive USD 100,000.
3. Invest the USD 100,000 at 4.50 percent; receive USD 104,500 in one year.
4. Sell USD 104,500 forward at AUD 1.25/USD; agree to receive AUD 130,625.
5. Repay the AUD loan; collect net profit of AUD 2,225.

This strategy is known as **covered interest arbitrage** because the arbitrageur will always hold the security denominated in the currency that is the least expensive to deliver in the futures market. The arbitrage position is hedged, or covered, against adverse foreign exchange movements while receiving the largest amount of net interest income. In practice, traders involved in covered interest arbitrage strategies utilize bank rates (for example, LIBOR) for borrowing and lending, which injects a slight amount of credit risk into the scheme.

With exchange rates quoted on an *indirect basis* (foreign currency [FC] per U.S. dollar), the general relationship between the forward and spot rates implied by interest rate parity is:

15.9
$$\frac{F_{0,T}}{S_0} = \left(\frac{1 + (\text{RFR}_{\text{FC}})\left(\frac{T}{365}\right)}{1 + (\text{RFR}_{\text{USD}})\left(\frac{T}{365}\right)} \right)$$

where:

RFR_{USD} = annualized risk-free rate in the United States
RFR_{FC} = annualized risk-free rate in the foreign market
T = number of days from the joint settlement of the futures and cash positions until they mature

In the last example, $T = 365$ so that [AUD 1.2287/USD ÷ AUD 1.20/USD] = (1.07 ÷ 1.045).

Equation 15.9 defines the relationship between four different Date 0 prices: spot foreign exchange rate, forward foreign exchange rate, U.S. investment rate, and foreign investment rate. If the markets are aligned properly, $F_{0,T}$ will be greater than S_0 whenever RFR_{FC} is greater than RFR_{USD}, with the opposite holding when $RFR_{FC} < RFR_{USD}$. With indirect currency quotes, $F_{0,T} > S_0$ implies that the foreign currency is at a forward discount to the dollar. In other words, the country with the lowest investment rate should see its currency trade at a forward premium. The intuition is that to keep investment capital from flowing to the country with the highest returns, the high-interest country will suffer from a weaker forward value for its currency.

15.5 OTC FORWARD CONTRACTS

15.5.1 Interest Rate Contracts

An extremely active OTC market exists for forward-based products designed to manage an investor's or an issuer's interest rate risk.[8]

Forward Rate Agreements The **forward rate agreement (FRA)** is the most basic of the OTC interest rate contracts. Two parties agree today to a future exchange of cash flows based on different interest rates. One cash flow is tied to a yield that is fixed at the deal's origination (the fixed rate); the other is determined at some later date (the floating rate). On the contract's settlement date, the difference between the two interest rates is multiplied by the FRA's **notional principal** and prorated to the length of the holding period. LIBOR is frequently used as the floating rate index, making FRAs the OTC equivalent of Eurodollar futures contracts.

An FRA's settlement date and maturity are defined by its name: A 3 × 6 FRA allows the investor to lock in three-month LIBOR, three months forward; a 12 × 18 FRA locks in six-month LIBOR, one year forward. FRA market makers quote a bid-offer spread on a rate basis. Suppose the FRA rates for three-month LIBOR shown in Exhibit 15.14 prevail in the market at Date 0, with the three-month LIBOR spot rate assumed to be 4.50 percent. This means that on a 3 × 6 FRA, the market maker is prepared to pay a fixed rate of 4.81 percent for receipt of three-month LIBOR and to receive a fixed rate of 4.83 percent for payment of LIBOR. In either case, there will be no payment until LIBOR is revealed in Month 3.

Exhibit 15.14 Indicative Bid–Offer Quotes on Three-Month Forward Rate Agreements

Period	Bid (%)	Offer (%)
3 × 6	4.81	4.83
6 × 9	5.20	5.22
9 × 12	5.64	5.66
12 × 15	6.37	6.39
15 × 18	6.78	6.80
18 × 21	7.10	7.12
21 × 24	7.36	7.38

[8]Some of the discussion in this section is based on work by Brown and Smith (1995).

Settlement can then be made in arrears at Month 6 with the settlement flow adjusted to the actual number of days in the holding period and calculated as:

15.10 $$[\text{LIBOR} - \text{Fixed Rate}] \times [\text{Notional Principal}] \times \left[\frac{\text{Number of Days}}{360}\right]$$

since, in the U.S. market, LIBOR is based on a 360-day year. This settlement occurs on a net basis, with only a single check for the rate differential being written.

To see how FRAs are used, assume that Company Z decides to borrow financial capital for a six-month period, in two three-month installments. Thus, the firm finds itself exposed to rising interest rates over the next three months because the level of its second interest payment will not be established until the end of that period. (The amount of Company Z's first three-month payment would be known at origination.) The firm can acquire a 3 × 6 FRA whereby it pays the dealer's quoted fixed rate of 4.83 percent in exchange for receiving three-month LIBOR at the settlement date. This is illustrated on the right-hand side of Exhibit 15.15.

Once the dealer has committed to the FRA with Company Z, two things occur. First, Company Z is no longer exposed to a rising funding cost because it now has a forward contract that locks in the rate of 4.83 percent. Second, the dealer is now exposed to rising LIBOR because it will be obligated to make the net settlement payment if LIBOR exceeds 4.83 percent three months from now. Company Z has effectively used the FRA to transfer its interest rate exposure to the dealer. That exposure can be hedged by "buying" LIBOR from another counterparty for its bid rate of 4.81 percent. This is shown on the left-hand side of Exhibit 15.15 as a second FRA with Company Y, which is assumed to be an investor in a variable-rate asset who is naturally concerned about falling rates.

Now suppose that three-month LIBOR is 5.00 percent in Month 3 and that the agreements with Companies Y and Z both have notional principal of $10 million. Company Y would be obligated to pay the market maker $4,750, calculated as:

$$[0.0500 - 0.0481] \times [10,000,000] \times \left[\frac{90}{360}\right]$$

assuming that there are 90 days between Months 3 and 6. Similarly, the payment from the dealer to Company Z would be $4,250 [= (0.0500 − 0.0483) × 10,000,000 × (90/360)] in Month 6. By matching the FRAs, the market maker is fully hedged from interest rate risk. Its spread of two basis points, which translates into $500, compensates for the costs (transaction costs, credit risk) of making a market in these contracts.

Interest Rate Swaps Both investors and borrowers are routinely exposed to interest rate movements at regular intervals over an extended period of time, such as with a

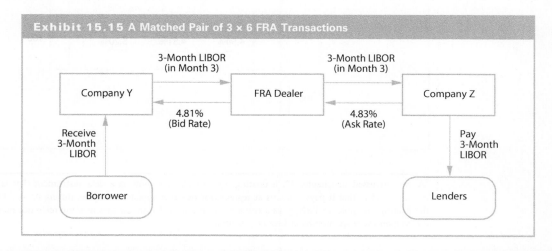

Exhibit 15.15 A Matched Pair of 3 × 6 FRA Transactions

floating-rate note (FRN) that resets its coupon rate twice annually for several years according to movements in six-month LIBOR.[9] In that case, several exposure dates would need to be hedged, which could be accomplished with a series of FRAs. For example, suppose that an investor holding a one-year FRN paying quarterly coupons of three-month LIBOR becomes concerned that rates may fall in the future and reduce the level of her last three coupons. (By convention, her first coupon, payable in three months, is based on current LIBOR, which was assumed to be 4.50 percent.) She offsets this exposure by agreeing to receive the fixed rate on three separate FRA contracts: the 3×6, the 6×9, and the 9×12. From the bid rates in Exhibit 15.5, these positions transform the cash flows on the variable-rate asset, as shown in Exhibit 15.16.

This series of FRAs locks in the coupon levels, but they are at different fixed rates and require three separate contracts. However, the investor might prefer a single contract that covers all the

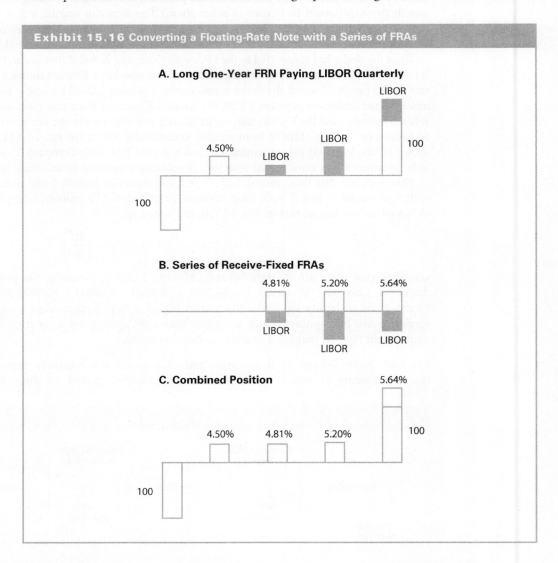

Exhibit 15.16 Converting a Floating-Rate Note with a Series of FRAs

A. Long One-Year FRN Paying LIBOR Quarterly

B. Series of Receive-Fixed FRAs

C. Combined Position

---

[9]As we discussed in Chapter 12, a floating (or variable) rate note is a debt instrument that is similar to a fixed-income bond in that it pays coupons at regular (for example, semiannual) dates during its life. The difference is that the floating-rate note, or FRN, pays a coupon that is adjusted with changes in some reference rate (for example, reset the coupon every six months at LIBOR + 0.50%).

future coupon dates using the same fixed rate. This is exactly what an interest rate swap does—it can be viewed as a prepackaged series of LIBOR forward contracts (that is, FRAs) at the same fixed rate. For the swap and FRA markets to remain efficient, the single fixed rate on the swap would have to be the appropriate average of 4.50 percent, 4.81 percent, 5.20 percent, and 5.64 percent. For simplicity, assume that each quarterly settlement period is exactly 0.25 year. This average can be approximated by solving for the internal rate of return on the hedged FRN:

$$100 = \frac{4.50 \times 0.25}{(1 + \text{IRR})^1} + \frac{4.81 \times 0.25}{(1 + \text{IRR})^2} + \frac{5.20 \times 0.25}{(1 + \text{IRR})^3} + \frac{100 + [5.64 \times 0.25]}{(1 + \text{IRR})^4}$$

or IRR = 1.258 percent. Thus, 5.03 percent($=1.258 \times 4$) would be the fixed rate on a one-year, receive-fixed swap consistent with these forward rate agreements. This IRR calculation is a very accurate approximation for the forward rate annuitization process we saw earlier. A more general way to determine the swap fixed rate (SFR) that represents the appropriate average of this sequence of spot and forward LIBOR would be to solve the following equation:

$$\frac{(4.50)(0.25)(\text{NP})}{\left[1 + \frac{i_{0.3}}{4}\right]^1} + \frac{(4.81)(0.25)(\text{NP})}{\left[1 + \frac{i_{0.6}}{4}\right]^2} + \frac{(5.20)(0.25)(\text{NP})}{\left[1 + \frac{i_{0.9}}{4}\right]^3} + \frac{(5.64)(0.25)(\text{NP})}{\left[1 + \frac{i_{0.12}}{4}\right]^4}$$

$$= \frac{(\text{SFR})(0.25)(\text{NP})}{\left[1 + \frac{i_{0.3}}{4}\right]^1} + \frac{(\text{SFR})(0.25)(\text{NP})}{\left[1 + \frac{i_{0.6}}{4}\right]^2} + \frac{(\text{SFR})(0.25)(\text{NP})}{\left[1 + \frac{i_{0.9}}{4}\right]^3} + \frac{(\text{SFR})(0.25)(\text{NP})}{\left[1 + \frac{i_{0.12}}{4}\right]^4}$$

where NP is the swap's notional principal and $i_{0,t}$ is the spot discount rate for a cash flow received or paid at a date t months in the future. For a given interest rate term structure and contract notional principal, SFR is the only unknown element in this equation and can be solved for accordingly.

The fixed-rate side of an interest rate swap generally is broken down to two components for trading purposes: (1) the yield of a Treasury bond with a maturity comparable to that of the swap and (2) a risk premium term known as the **swap spread**. Exhibit 15.17 lists a representative set of fixed-rate quotes from a recent market period for U.S. dollar swaps, both in absolute and in swap spread terms. Each of the swaps represented in this exhibit assumes semiannual settlement dates with six-month LIBOR as the floating rate. For example, the swap dealer would be willing to receive the fixed rate of 4.720 percent on a five-year contract, a rate that is 65.90 basis points greater than the five-year T-bond yield.

With the fixed rate on the swap linked to a bond (30/360 day count) yield and the floating rate as a money market (actual/360 day count in the U.S. market) yield, the swap settlement cash flows are calculated in a slightly different manner than for FRAs. While the swap is still a net settlement contract, the Date t fixed- and floating-rate payments are determined separately as:

$$(\text{Fixed-Rate Payment})_t = (\text{Swap Fixed Rate}) \times \left(\frac{\text{Number of "30/360" Days}}{360}\right) \times (\text{Notional Principal})$$

and:

$$(\text{Floating-Rate Payment})_t = (\text{Reference Rate})_{t-1} \times \left(\frac{\text{Number of Days}}{360}\right) \times (\text{Notional Principal})$$

In these equations, the fixed rate never changes and the floating-rate reference rate (LIBOR) always is determined at the beginning of a given settlement period.

Assume that Counterparty A is an institutional investor who currently holds a three-year bond paying a semiannual coupon of 4.80 percent. He feels that interest rates are likely to

Exhibit 15.17 Representative Interest Rate Swap and Swap Spread Quotes

U.S. Semi-Annual Fixed (30/360) versus 6-Month LIBOR

Swap Maturity (yrs)	Swap Fixed Rate (%)			Swap Spread (bp)	
	Bid	Ask	Mid	Bid	Ask
1	4.6560	4.6640	4.6600	—	—
2	4.4870	4.4920	4.4895	66.80	67.20
3	4.5310	4.5460	4.5410	70.38	70.70
4	4.6270	4.6320	4.6295	67.50	68.00
5	4.7170	4.7200	4.7185	65.50	65.90
6	4.8040	4.8040	4.8040	66.80	67.20
7	4.8770	4.8770	4.8770	67.10	67.50
8	4.9400	4.9400	4.9400	66.40	66.80
9	4.9940	4.9990	4.9975	64.90	66.00
10	5.0410	5.0460	5.0435	61.63	62.90
15	5.1940	5.1990	5.1975	70.70	71.10
20	5.2690	5.2690	5.2690	70.50	70.90
25	5.2900	5.2960	5.2930	65.60	66.00
30	5.2980	5.3030	5.3005	59.00	59.40

rise in the near term and decides to convert his investment into a synthetic floating-rate note whose coupons will rise with future LIBOR increases. He accomplishes this by agreeing to pay the fixed rate on a three-year interest rate swap contract with Counterparty B (the swap dealer). The terms of this agreement can be summarized as follows:

- Origination date: October 23, Year 0
- Maturity date: October 23, Year 3
- Notional principal: $30 million
- Fixed-rate payer: Counterparty A (the investor)
- Swap fixed rate: 4.546 percent (semiannual, 30/360 bond basis)
- Fixed-rate receiver: Counterparty B (the swap dealer)
- Floating rate: Six-month LIBOR (money market basis)
- Settlement dates: October 23 and April 23

This "fixed-for-floating" transaction—the most basic form of a swap—is often called a *plain vanilla* agreement. Exhibit 15.18 illustrates the approximate effect (ignoring slight day count differentials) of combining the swap with the underlying bond position, while Exhibit 15.19 lists the precise settlement cash flows from the investor's perspective for a hypothetical time series of six-month LIBOR. In this agreement, the fixed-rate payer makes the net settlement payment when the day count-adjusted level of LIBOR is less than 4.546 percent; the fixed-rate receiver makes the settlement payment when LIBOR exceeds 4.546 percent.

Plain vanilla swaps are generally used for the same reason as FRAs: to restructure the cash flows of an interest-sensitive asset or liability. In this example, the investor has reduced the price sensitivity (that is, duration) of his asset by converting the fixed-rate coupon into one that adjusts to shifting market conditions without having to actually sell what might be a highly illiquid bond. The net annualized cash flow he will receive after accounting for the swap position will be (again ignoring day count differentials):

Fixed-Rate Bond Coupon Receipt	= 4.800%	
Swap:	(1) LIBOR Receipt = LIBOR	
	(2) Fixed Payment = (4.546%)	
Net Interest Income:	= LIBOR + 0.254%	

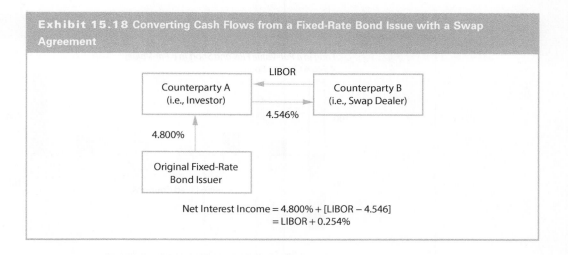

Exhibit 15.18 Converting Cash Flows from a Fixed-Rate Bond Issue with a Swap Agreement

Net Interest Income = 4.800% + [LIBOR − 4.546]
= LIBOR + 0.254%

Thus, the net impact of combining the swap with the fixed-rate bond is to convert that security into a variable-rate asset paying a coupon of LIBOR plus 25.4 basis points.

Counterparty A is effectively paying the fixed-rate coupons he receives from his bond in exchange for receiving floating-rate coupons. That is, the pay-fixed swap position is equivalent to holding a portfolio consisting of (1) a long position in a par-value FRN paying semiannual coupons of LIBOR and (2) a short position in a par-value fixed-rate note paying semiannual coupons of 4.546 percent. This capital market interpretation is illustrated in Exhibit 15.20. By essentially buying and selling two different par-value instruments, no net principal amount exists at origination or maturity; this is what allows the swap's principal to be notional. Thus, all the swap agreement really does is transform the nature of the investor's coupon payments.

Interest rate swaps have been in existence since 1981, and some empirical evidence exists on how they are valued in the marketplace. The available evidence includes Sun, Sundaresan, and Wang (1993), Brown, Harlow, and Smith (1994), Minton (1997), Liu, Longstaff, and Mandell (2006), Bhansali, Schwarzkopf, and Wise (2009), and Park (2015). Although each study examined a different aspect of the swap contracting process, the collective evidence is consistent with the notion that this market works in an efficient manner and seems to be integrated with other affiliated securities, such as Treasury notes and bills and Eurodollar futures contracts.

Exhibit 15.19 Settlement Cash Flows for a Three-Year Plain Vanilla Interest Rate Swap (Fixed-Payer's Perspective)

Settlement Year	Settlement Date	Number of Actual Days	Number of 30/360 Days	Current LIBOR	Fixed-Rate Payment	Floating-Rate Receipt	Net Payment (receipt)
0	October 23	—	—	4.25%	—	—	—
1	April 23	183	180	4.40%	681,900	648,125	33,775
1	October 23	183	180	4.90%	681,900	671,000	10,900
2	April 23	182	180	5.05%	681,900	743,167	(61,267)
2	October 23	183	180	4.60%	681,900	770,125	(88,225)
3	April 23	182	180	4.35%	681,900	697,667	(15,767)
3	October 23	183	180	4.20%	681,900	663,375	18,525

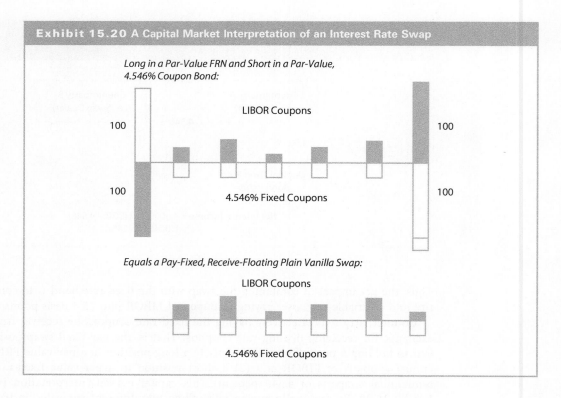

Exhibit 15.20 A Capital Market Interpretation of an Interest Rate Swap

Long in a Par-Value FRN and Short in a Par-Value, 4.546% Coupon Bond:

LIBOR Coupons

100

100

100

4.546% Fixed Coupons

100

Equals a Pay-Fixed, Receive-Floating Plain Vanilla Swap:

LIBOR Coupons

4.546% Fixed Coupons

15.5.2 Equity Index-Linked Swaps

Equity-index-linked swaps, or **equity swaps**, are equivalent to portfolios of forward contracts calling for the exchange of cash flows based on two different investment rates: (1) a variable-debt rate (for example, three-month LIBOR) and (2) the return to an equity index (for example, Standard & Poor's 500). The index-linked payment is based on either the total return (dividends plus capital gain or loss) or just the percentage index change for the settlement period plus a fixed spread adjustment. Equity swaps are traded in the OTC markets and can have maturities out to 10 years or beyond.

In addition to the S&P 500, equity swaps can be structured around foreign indexes, such as TOPIX (Japan), FT-SE 100 (Great Britain), DAX (Germany), and Hang Seng (Hong Kong). The equity-index-based cash flow typically is denominated in the currency of the index's country of origination, but this payment can be automatically hedged into a different currency. Further, these agreements specify a notional principal that is not exchanged at origination but serves the purpose of converting percentage returns into cash flows. This notional principal can be either variable or fixed during the life of the agreement.

As Kat (2001) and Chance (2004) noted, the equity swap market has developed for several reasons. First, these agreements allow investors to take advantage of overall price movements in a specific country's stock market without having to purchase the equity securities directly, thereby reducing both the transaction costs and the tracking error. Second, creating a direct equity investment in a foreign country may be difficult for some investors where prohibited by law or policy. Finally, an investment fund may not be legally permitted to obtain sufficient exchange-traded derivative contracts to hedge a direct equity investment. The equity swap can be structured so that there is no need for separate hedging transactions.

The most common application for an equity swap involves a counterparty that receives the index-based payment in exchange for making the floating-rate payment. Consider a pension fund that currently has a substantial portion of its asset portfolio invested in floating-rate notes paying quarterly coupons based on LIBOR. If the fund manager wants to alter her existing asset allocation by converting some of this debt into equity, she can enter into an equity swap with an initial notional principal equal to the amount of the existing debt holdings she wants to convert. The mechanics of this arrangement are illustrated in Panel A of Exhibit 15.21.

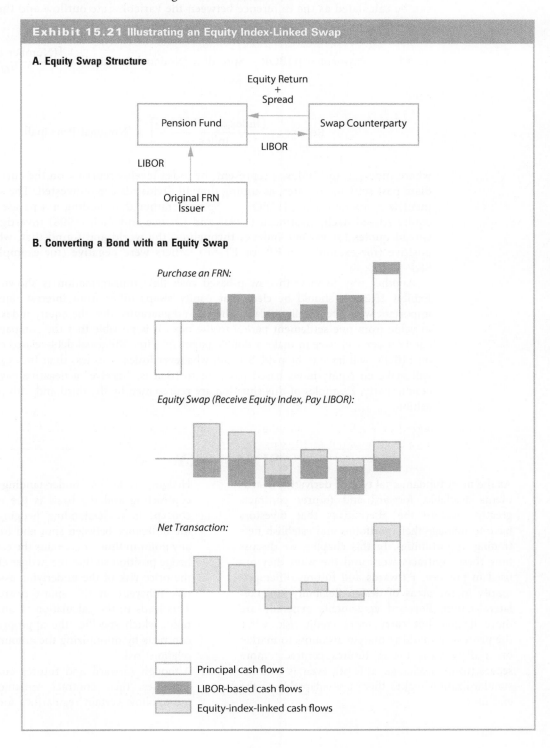

Exhibit 15.21 Illustrating an Equity Index-Linked Swap

A. Equity Swap Structure

Equity Return + Spread

Pension Fund

Swap Counterparty

LIBOR

LIBOR

Original FRN Issuer

B. Converting a Bond with an Equity Swap

Purchase an FRN:

Equity Swap (Receive Equity Index, Pay LIBOR):

Net Transaction:

☐ Principal cash flows
■ LIBOR-based cash flows
▨ Equity-index-linked cash flows

The net return to the fund in this example is simply the return on the equity index plus the spread adjustment. Further, if the FRNs yield more than LIBOR, this would increase the overall net return. Assuming both cash flows are denominated in the same currency, the net settlement payment on the equity swap from the company's standpoint can be calculated as the difference between the variable-rate outflow and the equity-linked inflow:

15.11 $$\text{Payment} = [\text{LIBOR} - \text{Spread}] \times [\text{Notional Principal}] \times \left[\frac{(\text{Number of Days})}{360}\right]$$

and:

$$\text{Receipt} = \left[\frac{\text{Index}_{new} - \text{Index}_{old}}{\text{Index}_{old}}\right] \times [\text{Notional Principal}]$$

where Index_{new} and Index_{old} represent the index levels occurring on the current and immediate past settlement dates, assuming that all dividends are reinvested. The settlement payment is computed using [LIBOR − Spread] rather than adding a separate inflow for the equity spread itself. Gastineau (1993) and Chance and Rich (1998) investigated indicative spread quotes for various indexes throughout the world and found that, while some were positive (for example, 25 BP for FT-SE), others were negative (for example, −10 BP for S&P 500).

Another way to view this swap-based cash flow transformation is shown in Panel B of Exhibit 15.21. It should be clear that equity swaps differ from interest rate swaps in one important way. Specifically, because there is no guarantee that the equity index will appreciate in value from one settlement period to the next, it is possible that the company receiving the equity index will have to make a double payment. First, the usual debt-related cash flow, based on LIBOR, will have to be paid. Second, whenever Index_{new} is less than Index_{old}, the company will make an equity-index-based payment to (that is, "receive" a negative payment from) its counterparty. Examples of this situation are represented by the third and fifth payments in the exhibit.

SUMMARY

- As the most fundamental type of derivative instruments available, forward and futures contracts greatly increase the alternatives that investors have to manage their portfolios and establish new trading opportunities. In this chapter, we discuss how these contracts work and the ways they are used in practice. Forwards and futures differ primarily in the areas of design flexibility and collateralization. Forward agreements generally are more flexible but carry more credit risk, while the process of marking margin accounts to market on a daily basis makes futures contracts more secure (to the exchange, at least), even as contract standardization makes them less adaptable to the end user.

- Hedging is key to understanding forward-based contracting and the basis is the most important concept in understanding hedging. The basis is the difference between spot and forward prices at any point in time. It contains the essence of a short hedge position so that the hedger effectively trades the price risk of the underlying asset for the basis risk inherent in the spot-forward combination. This leads to the calculation of an optimal hedge ratio, which specifies the appropriate number of contracts by minimizing the amount of basis (correlation) risk.

- Although forward and futures contracts are not securities, their contract settlement prices still must follow certain regularities for these markets to remain efficient. The cost of carry model suggests that in order to avoid arbitrage, the forward price should be equal to the spot price plus the cost of transporting the underlying asset to the future delivery date. These carrying costs can include commissions for physical storage, an opportunity cost for the net amount of invested capital, and a premium for the convenience of consuming the asset now.

- These concepts were illustrated with examinations of three types of financial futures contracts: interest rate, equity index, and foreign exchange. In addition to describing the dynamics of each of these markets, we discussed different applications, including those involving hedging, speculation, and arbitrage. These applications produced some useful adaptations of the basic concepts, such as hedge ratios for interest rate and stock index futures as well as interest rate parity for currency futures. OTC derivative products such as FRAs, interest rate swaps, and equity swaps provide another set of useful tools with which investors can manage their interest rate and equity risk exposures.

SUGGESTED READINGS

Beder, Tanya S., and Cara M. Marshall. *Financial Engineering: The Evolution of a Profession*. New York: Wiley, 2011.

Chisholm, Andrew M. *Derivatives Demystified: A Step-by-Step Guide to Forwards, Futures, Swaps and Options*, 2nd ed. London, England: John Wiley, 2010.

McDonald, Robert L. *Derivatives Markets*, 3rd ed. Boston, MA: Pearson, 2013.

Working, Holbrook. "Economic Functions of Futures Markets." In *Selected Writings of Holbrook Working*. Chicago, IL: Chicago Board of Trade, 1977.

QUESTIONS

1. We have futures contracts on Treasury bonds, but we do not have futures contracts on individual corporate bonds. We have cattle and hog futures but no chicken futures. What do you think are the most important characteristics for the success of a new futures contract concept?

2. "Hedgers trade price risk for basis risk." What is meant by this statement? Explain the concept of the basis in a hedge transaction and how forward and futures contracts can be selected to minimize risk.

3. Suppose you are a derivatives trader specializing in creating customized commodity forward contracts for clients and then hedging your position with exchange-traded futures contracts. Your latest position is an agreement to deliver 100,000 gallons of unleaded gasoline to a client in three months.
   a. Explain how you can hedge your position using gasoline futures contracts.
   b. If the only available gasoline futures contracts call for the delivery of 42,000 gallons and mature in either two or four months, describe the nature of the basis risk involved in your hedge.

4. A multinational corporation is about to embark on a major financial restructuring program. One critical stage will be the issuance of 7-year Eurobonds sometime within the next month. The CFO is concerned with recent instability in capital markets and with the particular event that market yields rise prior to issuance, forcing the corporation to pay a higher coupon rate on the bonds. It is decided to hedge that risk by selling 10-year Treasury note futures contracts. Notice that this is a classic cross hedge wherein 10-year Treasury notes are used to manage the risk of 7-year Eurobonds.

Describe the nature of the basis risk in the hedge. In particular, what specific events with respect to the shape of the Treasury yield curve and the Eurobond spread over Treasuries could lead to the hedge failing and make the corporation worse off?

5. You are the chief financial officer of a large multinational company, and 6 months from now you will be receiving a settlement payment of $50 million, which you plan to invest in 10-year U.S. Treasury bonds. Your interest rate forecast indicates that the yield curve will drop dramatically in the next two quarters. You are considering ways that you can guard against the possible decline in interest rates before you have the funds available to invest.

   a. Briefly describe the hedging strategy using the 10-year Treasury note futures contract that would provide the best protection against this possible decline in yields.

   b. Suppose that 6 months after you have entered into a futures contract as suggested in part (a), interest rates increases in the market actually increase substantially due to an unexpected change in monetary policy. Discuss whether you would have been better off (1) with the hedge position or (2) without the hedge position in this situation.

6. You own an equally weighted portfolio of 50 different stocks worth about $5,000,000. The stocks are from several different industries, and the portfolio is reasonably well diversified. Which do you think would provide you with the best overall hedge: a single position in an index futures or 50 different positions in futures contracts on the individual stocks? What are the most important factors to consider in making this decision?

7. Since their introduction, stock index futures contracts have become very popular and are now widely traded by finance professionals. Many factors, including (1) the current price of the underlying stock index, (2) the time to contract maturity, and (3) the dividends paid to the stocks in the underlying index, will affect the settlement price of a stock index futures contract. What is the fourth primary factor involved in stock index futures contract pricing, and how does this factor affect settlement prices?

8. As the risk manager for a large pension fund, you know that the investment staff is considering a move to diversify the portfolio over the next six months by investing $900 million in Japanese government bonds. Although you like the investment profile of these securities, you are concerned that adverse foreign exchange rate fluctuations could reduce or even eliminate the expected returns from owning the bonds. Consequently, you want to consider a hedge against this exposure using currency futures contracts.

   a. Describe how a currency futures contract position could be employed along with the purchase of the bond in this situation to mitigate the risk exposure the risk manager is concerned with.

   b. Explain what would happen to both the currency futures position and the underlying bond holding if the USD/JPY exchange rate moved up unexpectedly after you initiated the FX hedge transaction.

9. Explain why the currency of Country A, whose interest rates are twice as great as those in Country B, must trade at a forward discount. If there were no difference between the spot and forward exchange rates in this interest rate environment, what arbitrage trade could be constructed to take advantage of the situation?

10. Interest rate swap contracts have become very popular among participants in the investment community, particularly in managing portfolios of fixed-income securities.

    a. What is an interest rate swap, and how does it work?

    b. How could a fixed-income portfolio manager use an interest rate swap to enhance portfolio performance or control risk? Briefly describe two examples.

11. Explain how an interest rate swap can be viewed as either a series of forward rate agreements, a pair of bond transactions, or a pair of option agreements. To make your description more precise, take the point of view of the fixed-rate receiver in the swap.

PROBLEMS

1. It is March 9, and you have just entered into a short position in a soybean meal futures contract. The contract expires on July 9 and calls for the delivery of 100 tons of soybean meal. Further, because this is a futures position, it requires the posting of a $3,000 initial margin and a $1,500 maintenance margin; for simplicity, however, assume that the account is marked to market on a monthly basis. Assume the following represent the contract delivery prices (in dollars per ton) that prevail on each settlement date:

March 9 (initiation)	$173.00
April 9	179.75
May 9	189.00
June 9	182.50
July 9 (delivery)	174.25

    a. Calculate the equity value of your margin account on each settlement date, including any additional equity required to meet a margin call. Also compute the amount of cash that will be returned to you on July 9, and the gain or loss on your position, expressed as a percentage of your initial margin commitment.

    b. Now suppose that on March 9 you also entered into a long forward contract for the purchase of 100 tons of soybean meal on July 9. Assume further that the July forward and futures contract prices always are identical to one another at any point in time. Calculate the cash amount of your gain or loss if you unwind both positions in their respective markets on May 9 and June 9, taking into account the prevailing settlement conditions in the two markets.

2. You are a coffee dealer anticipating the purchase of 82,000 pounds of coffee in three months. You are concerned that the price of coffee will rise, so you take a long position in coffee futures. Each contract covers 37,500 pounds, and so, rounding to the nearest contract, you decide to go long in two contracts. The futures price at the time you initiate your hedge is 55.95 cents per pound. Three months later, the actual spot price of coffee turns out to be 58.56 cents per pound and the futures price is 59.20 cents per pound.

    a. Determine the effective price at which you purchased your coffee. How do you account for the difference in amounts for the spot and hedge positions?

    b. Describe the nature of the basis risk in this long hedge.

3. June Klein, CFA, manages a $100 million (market value) U.S. government bond portfolio for an institution. She anticipates a small parallel shift in the yield curve and wants to fully hedge the portfolio against any such change.

    Portfolio and Treasury Bond Futures Contract Characteristics

Security	Modified Duration	Basis Point Value	Conversion Factor for Cheapest to Deliver Bond	Portfolio Value/ Future Contract Price
Portfolio	10 years	$100,000.00	Not Applicable	$100,000,000
U.S. Treasury bond futures contract	8 years	$75.32	1	94–05

    a. Discuss two reasons for using futures rather than selling bonds to hedge a bond portfolio. No calculations required.

    b. Formulate Klein's hedging strategy using only the futures contract shown. Calculate the number of futures contracts to implement the strategy. Show all calculations.

c. Determine how each of the following would change in value if interest rates increase by 10 basis points as anticipated. Show all calculations.

(1) The original portfolio
(2) The Treasury bond futures position
(3) The newly hedged portfolio

d. State three reasons Klein's hedging strategy might not fully protect the portfolio against interest rate risk.

4. A bond speculator currently has positions in two separate corporate bond portfolios: a long holding in Portfolio 1 and a short holding in Portfolio 2. All the bonds have the same credit quality. Other relevant information on these positions includes:

Portfolio	Bond	Market Value ($ millions)	Coupon Rate (%)	Compounding Frequency	Maturity (yrs)	Yield to Maturity (%)
1	A	$6.0	0.0%	Annual	3	7.31%
	B	4.0	0.0	Annual	14	7.31
2	C	11.5	4.6	Annual	9	7.31

Treasury bond futures (based on $100,000 face value of 20-year T-bonds having an 6 percent semi-annual coupon) with a maturity exactly six months from now are currently priced at 104-24 with a corresponding yield to maturity of 5.602 percent. The "yield betas" between the futures contract and Bonds A, B, and C are 1.13, 1.03, and 1.01, respectively. Finally, the modified duration for the T-bond underlying the futures contract is 11.769 years.

a. Calculate the modified duration (expressed in years) for each of the two bond portfolios. What will be the *approximate* percentage change in the value of each if all yields increase by 60 basis points on an annual basis?

b. Assuming that the bond speculator wants to hedge her *net* bond position, what is the optimal number of futures contracts that must be bought or sold? Start by calculating the optimal hedge ratio between the futures contract and the two bond portfolios separately and then combine them.

5. Arshia Hershey, a newly hired bond trader, is eager to exploit what she perceives to be an inefficiency in futures market prices. Specifically, she observes the following information concerning prices in the spot market for bonds and for the bond futures contract maturing three months from now:

Spot price	$102.30
Three-month futures contract price	$112.15
Income from the Treasury bond for three months	$2.20
Finance charge for three months	$1.10

a. Describe the arbitrage transaction that Arshia should undertake to take advantage of these market conditions.

b. Demonstrate the arbitrage profit that she will realize at the expiration date of the futures contract.

c. Does your answer to part (b) depend of the price of the underlying bond at the maturity date of the futures contract? Explain why or why not.

6. As a relationship officer for a money-center commercial bank, one of your corporate accounts has just approached you about a one-year loan for $1,000,000. The customer would pay a quarterly interest expense based on the prevailing level of LIBOR at the

beginning of each three-month period. As is the bank's convention on all such loans, the amount of the interest payment would then be paid at the end of the quarterly cycle when the new rate for the next cycle is determined. You observe the following LIBOR yield curve in the cash market:

90-day LIBOR	4.60%
180-day LIBOR	4.75
270-day LIBOR	5.00
360-day LIBOR	5.30

a. If 90-day LIBOR rises to the levels "predicted" by the implied forward rates, what will the dollar level of the bank's interest receipt be at the end of each quarter during the one-year loan period?

b. If the bank wanted to hedge its exposure to failing LIBOR on this loan commitment, describe the sequence of transactions in the futures markets it could undertake.

c. Assuming the yields inferred from the Eurodollar futures contract prices for the next three settlement periods are equal to the implied forward rates, calculate the annuity value that would leave the bank indifferent between making the floating-rate loan and hedging it in the futures market and making a one-year fixed-rate loan. Express this annuity value in both dollar and annual (360-day) percentage terms.

7. An investment bank engages in stock index arbitrage for its own and customer accounts. On a particular day, the index for the New York Stock Exchange is 602.25 when the index futures contract for delivery in 90 days is 614.75. If the annualized 90-day interest rate is 8.00 percent and the (annualized) dividend yield is 3 percent, would program trading involving stock index arbitrage possibly take place? If so, describe the transactions that should be undertaken, and calculate the profit that would be made per each "share" of the index used in the trade.

8. Alex Andrew, who manages a $95 million large-capitalization U.S. equity portfolio, currently forecasts that equity markets will decline soon. Andrew prefers to avoid the transaction costs of making sales but wants to hedge $15 million of the portfolio's current value using S&P 500 futures.

Because Andrew realizes that his portfolio will not track the S&P 500 Index exactly, he performs a regression analysis on his actual portfolio returns versus the S&P futures returns over the past year. The regression analysis indicates a risk-minimizing beta of 0.88 with a correlation coefficient of 0.96.

Futures Contract Data

S&P 500 futures price	1,000
S&P 500 index	999
S&P 500 index multiplier	250

a. Calculate the number of futures contracts required to hedge $15 million of Andrew's portfolio, using the data shown. State whether the hedge is long or short. Show all calculations.

b. Identify two alternative methods (other than selling securities from the portfolio or using futures) that replicate the strategy in part (a). Contract each of these methods with the futures strategy.

9. The treasurer of a middle market, import-export company has approached you for advice on how to best invest some of the firm's short-term cash balances. The company, which has been a client of the bank that employs you for a few years, has $250,000 that it is able to commit for a one-year holding period. The treasurer is currently considering two

alternatives: (1) invest all the funds in a one-year U.S. Treasury bill offering a bond equivalent yield of 4.25 percent, and (2) invest all the funds in a Swiss government security over the same horizon, locking in the spot and forward currency exchanges in the FX market. A quick call to the bank's FX desk gives you the following two-way currency exchange quotes.

	Swiss Francs per U.S. Dollar	U.S. Dollar per Swiss Franc (CHF)
Spot	1.5035	0.6651
1-year CHF futures	—	0.6586

a. Calculate the one-year bond equivalent yield for the Swiss government security that would support the interest rate parity condition.

b. Assuming the actual yield on a one-year Swiss government bond is 5.50 percent, which strategy would leave the treasurer with the greatest return after one year?

c. Describe the transactions that an arbitrageur could use to take advantage of this apparent mispricing, and calculate what the profit would be for a $250,000 transaction.

10. Bonita Singer is a hedge fund manager specializing in futures arbitrage involving stock index contracts. She is investigating potential trading opportunities in S&P 500 stock index futures to see if there are any inefficiencies that she can exploit. She knows that the S&P 500 stock index is currently trading at 1,100.

a. Assume that the Treasury yield curve is flat at 3.2 percent and the annualized dividend yield on the S&P index is 1.8 percent. Using the cost of carry model, demonstrate what the theoretical contract price should be for a futures position expiring six months from now.

b. Describe the set of transactions that Bonita would have to undertake to take advantage of an actual futures contract price that was (1) substantially higher or (2) substantially lower than the theoretical value you established in part (a).

c. Assuming that total round-trip arbitrage transaction costs are $20 for the set trades described in part (b), calculate the upper and lower bounds for the theoretical contract price such that arbitrage trading would not be profitable.

11. With the interest rate swap quotations shown in Exhibit 15.17, calculate the swap cash flows from the point of view of the fixed-rate receiver on a two-year swap with a notional principal of $22.5 million. You may assume the relevant part of the settlement date pattern and the realized LIBOR path shown in Exhibit 15.19 for the three-year agreement. Also, calculate the fixed-rate payment on a 30/360-day count and the floating-rate payments on an actual/360-day basis.

12. On December 2, the manager of a tactical asset allocation fund that is currently invested entirely in floating-rate debt securities decides to shift a portion of her portfolio to equities. To effect this change, she has chosen to enter into the "receive equity index" side of a one-year equity swap based on movements in the S&P 500 Index plus a spread of 10 basis points. The swap is to have quarterly settlement payments, with the floating-rate side of the agreement pegged to three-month LIBOR denominated in U.S. dollars. At the origination of the swap, the value of the S&P 500 Index was 463.11 and three-month LIBOR was 3.50 percent. The notional principal of the swap is set for the life of the agreement at $50 million, which matches the amount of debt holdings in the fund that she would like to convert to equity.

a. Calculate the net cash receipt or payment—from the fund manager's perspective—on each future settlement date, assuming the value for the S&P 500 index (with all dividends reinvested) and LIBOR are as follows:

Settlement Date	Number of Days	S&P Level	LIBOR Level
December 2 (initial year)	—	463.11	3.50%
March 2 (following year)	90	477.51	3.25
June 2	92	464.74	3.75
September 2	92	480.86	4.00
December 2	91	482.59	—

b. Explain why the fund manager might want the notional principal on this swap to vary over time and what the most logical pattern for this variation would be.

Calculating Money Market Implied Forward Rates

Implied forward rates are an essential factor in understanding how short-term interest rate futures contracts are priced. In Chapter 13, we discussed that implied forward rates represented the sequence of future short-term rates that were built into the yield to maturity of a longer-term security. However, implied forward rates can have another interpretation. Consider an investor who is deciding between the following strategies for making a two-year investment: (1) buy a single two-year, zero coupon bond yielding 6 percent per annum; or (2) buy a one-year, zero coupon bond with a 5 percent yield and replace it at maturity with another one-year instrument. An implied forward rate is the answer to the following question: At what rate must the investor be able to reinvest the interim proceeds from the second strategy to exactly equal the total return from the first investment? In other words, the implied forward rate is a *breakeven* reinvestment rate. In the notation of Chapter 13, we want to solve for $_2r_1$ in the following equation:

$$(1 + 0.06)^2 = (1 + 0.05)(1 +_2r_1)$$

or:

$$_2r_1 = [(1 + 0.06)^2 \div (1 + 0.05)] - 1 = 7\%$$

Implied forward money market rates can be interpreted in the same way as bond yields, but they must be calculated differently because of differences in the quotation methods for the various rates. We have seen that LIBOR is a bank *add-on yield* (AY) that is used to figure out how much money, F, an investor will have at maturity in T days given an initial investment of P (that is, interest is "added on"):

$$F = P + \left[P \times AY \times \frac{T}{360}\right] = P\left[1 \times AY \times \frac{T}{360}\right]$$

LIBOR is based on a presumed 360-day year, the standard U.S. money market practice. Smith (1989b) has shown that the implied forward rate between two money market instruments quoted on an add-on basis (for example, LIBOR) can be calculated as:

15A.1
$$_BAY_A = \left[\frac{(B \times AY_B) - (A \times AY_A)}{B - A}\right]\left[\frac{1}{1 + \left(\dfrac{A \times AY_A}{360}\right)}\right]$$

where AY_A and AY_B are add-on yields for A and B days from settlement to maturity, with $B > A$. The implied forward rate ($_BAY_A$) also is on an add-on basis and has maturity of $(B - A)$ days.

Consider the following short-term yield curve for LIBOR:

Maturity	LIBOR
30 days	4.15%
60 days	4.25
90 days	4.35

What is the implied forward LIBOR between Days 60 and 90? Using $AY_A = 0.0425$, $AY_B = 0.0435$, $A = 60$ days, and $B = 90$ days for LIBOR, we have:

$$_{90}AY_{60} = \left[\frac{(90 \times 0.0435) - (60 \times 0.0425)}{90 - 60} \right] \left[\frac{1}{1 + \left(\dfrac{60 \times 0.0425}{360} \right)} \right] = 4.52\%$$

So, investing in a 60-day bank deposit at 4.25 percent and then a 30-day deposit at 4.52 percent would have the same total return as the 90-day deposit at 4.35 percent.

After you read this chapter, you should be able to answer the following questions:

- How are options traded on exchanges and in OTC markets?
- How are options for stock, stock indexes, ETFs, and foreign currency quoted?
- How can investors use option contracts to hedge an existing risk exposure?
- What are the three steps in establishing the fundamental no-arbitrage value of an option contract?
- What is the binomial (or two-state) option pricing model, and in what way is it an extension of the basic valuation approach?
- What is the Black–Scholes option pricing model, and how does it extend the binomial valuation approach?
- What is the relationship between the Black–Scholes and put-call parity valuation models?
- How do American- and European-style options differ from one another?
- What is implied volatility, and what is its role in the contract valuation process?
- How do investors use options with the underlying security or in combination with one another to create payoff structures tailored to a particular need or view of future market conditions?
- What differentiates a spread from a straddle, a strangle, and a range forward?
- How are options structured into other applications, such as convertible bonds and credit default swaps?

At the most basic level, only two kinds of derivative contracts exist: forwards, which fix the price or rate of an underlying asset, and options, which allow holders to decide at a later date whether such a fixing is in their best interest. This chapter focuses on the trading and valuation of option contracts. We develop the discussion in four parts. First, we consider contract terms and trading mechanics for both call and put options. We concentrate on options that have financial instruments as underlying securities, including options on individual stocks, stock indexes and ETFs, and foreign currency.

The second topic we explore is how option contracts are valued in an efficient capital market. We show that this can be viewed as a simple, three-step process: (1) creating a riskless hedge portfolio combining options with the underlying security, (2) invoking a no-arbitrage assumption about the return that such a portfolio should earn, and (3) solving for the option value consistent with the first two steps. We also discuss how several of the most widely used valuation models, including the *binomial* and *Black–Scholes* models, follow this approach. In this analysis, it is important to keep in mind that we will be *valuing* options and not *pricing* them. Prices are established through the actions of buyers and sellers; investors and analysts use valuation models to estimate what those prices should be.

Third, we consider several extensions in option valuation. We show how the Black–Scholes model for call options on stock can be adapted to value put options. We describe how the payment of dividends affects an option's value and how the model can be adjusted accordingly. We discuss the practical differences between the European and American styles of contracting, and we also examine the role price volatility plays in the valuation process and how investors can estimate it in practice.

Finally, several option-based investment and hedging strategies are examined. After describing protective put and covered call strategies, we demonstrate how options can be used in combination with one another to create risk–reward trade-offs that do not otherwise exist in financial markets. We consider three broad classes of option combination strategies: *straddles*, which involve both puts and calls; *spreads*, in which the investor simultaneously buys one call (or put) while selling another; and *range forwards* (or collars), which require the purchase of a call and the concurrent sale of a put, or vice versa. We conclude by discussing how options can also be embedded or structured in other applications to manage various types of risk.

16.1 AN OVERVIEW OF OPTION MARKETS AND CONTRACTS

In Chapter 15, we discussed the primary difference between forward and futures contracts: Futures are standardized and trade on exchanges, while forward contracts have negotiable terms and therefore must be arranged in the OTC market. Option contracts offer investors similar trading alternatives. The most important features of these contracts are highlighted in the following sections.

16.1.1 Option Market Conventions

Option contracts have been traded for centuries in the form of separate agreements or embedded in other securities. Malkiel (2015), for example, describes how call options were used to speculate on flower prices during the tulip bulb frenzy in 17th-century Holland. Then, and for most of the time until now, options were arranged and executed in private transactions. Collectively, these private transactions represent the OTC market for options, and agreements can be structured around any terms to which two parties can agree. This has been a useful mechanism when the underlying asset is too illiquid to support a widely traded contract. Also, credit risk is a paramount concern in this market if OTC agreements are not collateralized. This credit risk is one-sided with an option agreement because the buyer worries about the seller's ability to honor his obligations, but the seller has received everything he will get up front and is not concerned about the buyer's creditworthiness.

OTC options ultimately are created in response to the needs and desires of the corporations and individual investors who use them. Financial institutions, such as money-center banks and investment banks, serve as market makers by facilitating the arrangement and execution of these deals. Over the years, various trade associations of broker-dealers in OTC options have emerged (and, in some cases, faded), including the Put and Call Brokers and Dealers Association, which helped arrange private stock option transactions, and the International Swaps and Derivatives Association, which monitors the activities of market makers for interest rate and foreign exchange derivatives. These trade groups create a common set of standards and language to govern industry transactions. More recently, the enactment of the Dodd-Frank Act in 2011 created a new level of regulatory oversight for OTC options.

In April 1973, the Chicago Board of Trade opened the Chicago Board Options Exchange (CBOE). Specializing in stock and stock index options, the CBOE has introduced several important aspects of market uniformity. Foremost, contracts offered by the CBOE are standardized in terms of the underlying common stock, the number of shares covered, the delivery dates, and the range of available exercise prices. This standardization helped develop a secondary market for the contracts. The rapid increase in trading volume on the CBOE and other options exchanges suggests that this feature is desirable compared to OTC contracts that must often be held to maturity due to a lack of liquidity.

Centralizing the trading function also required the creation of the **Options Clearing Corporation (OCC)**, which acts as the guarantor of each CBOE-traded contract. Therefore, end users in option transactions ultimately bear the credit risk of the OCC. For this reason, even though the OCC is independent of the exchange, it demands that the option seller post margin to guarantee future performance. The option buyer will not have a margin account because a future obligation to the seller is nonexistent. Finally, this central market structure makes monitoring, regulation, and price reporting much easier than in the decentralized OTC markets.

16.1.2 Price Quotations for Exchange-Traded Options

Equity Options Options on the common stock of individual companies have traded on the CBOE since 1973. Several other markets, including the American (AMEX), Philadelphia (PHLX), and International Securities (ISE) Exchanges, began trading their own contracts soon afterward. As of mid-2017, the CBOE remained the largest exchange in terms of option market volume, with a market share of about 26 percent; PHLX was second largest, at around 16 percent. Options on each of these exchanges are traded similarly, with a typical contract covering 100 shares of stock. Because exchange-traded contracts are not issued by the company whose common stock serves as the underlying asset, they require secondary transactions in the equity if exercised.[1]

Panel A of Exhibit 16.1 displays volume statistics for the 10 most actively traded individual equity options in June 2017. Some of the names represented—Apple (AAPL), Bank of America (BAC), and Microsoft (MSFT)—also rank among the most actively traded stocks. The display lists monthly volume and average daily volume for both calls and puts. For instance, a total of 1.56 million BAC options changed hands during this month, with an average of almost 71,000 contracts trading each day.

Panel B of Exhibit 16.1 provides details for several BAC options with four different expiration dates: August 2017, September 2017, October 2017, and December 2017. To consider a specific transaction in more detail, assume that on this date in July 2017, an investor wants buy the September 2017 BAC 24 call. Based on the last reported price, her contract would cost a total of $131.00, calculated as the stated per-share price of 1.31 multiplied by 100 shares. In exchange for that payment, the holder of this American-style call would then be able to exercise the option at expiration in mid-September—or any time before then—by paying $2,400 ($= 24 \times 100$) and would receive 100 Bank of America shares from the option seller. Such an action will only be rational if the mid-September price of BAC stock is greater than $24. If that price closes below $24, the investor will simply let the call expire without acting on the option. Finally, with the prevailing BAC share price being $24.62 on this day, the investor could immediately recover $0.62 of the $1.31 she paid for the contract. Her time premium of $0.69 ($= 1.31 - 0.62$) preserves her right to buy BAC stock at a price of $24 for the next two months, even if the market value of those shares moves higher.[2]

Consider another investor who sells the August 24 Bank of America put, the details of which are shown on the right side of Panel B of Exhibit 16.1. If this sale took place at the last reported price, in return for an upfront receipt of $48 ($= 0.48 \times 100$), he must stand ready to buy 100 shares of stock in mid-August for $2,400 if the put holder chooses to exercise

---

[1]Call options issued directly by the firm whose common stock is the underlying asset are called *warrants*; see Galai and Schneller (1978) and Howe and Su (2001).

[2]Recall that a call option's value can be divided into two components: the *intrinsic value*, which is the greater of either zero or the stock price minus the exercise price, and the *time premium*. Here, the BAC call is *in the money* because it has positive intrinsic value, whereas an option with no intrinsic value is *out of the money*.

Exhibit 16.1 Stock Option Quotations

A. Most Active Individual Stock Options (June 2017)

Symbol	Name	Call Volume	Put Volume	Total Volume	Days	Tot ADV	Call ADV	Put ADV
AAPL	Apple Inc	1,342,792	917,987	2,260,779	22	102,763	61,036	41,727
BAC	Bank of America Corp	1,145,277	415,160	1,560,437	22	70,929	52,058	18,871
FB	Facebook Inc	754,026	454,847	1,208,873	22	54,949	34,274	20,675
AMD	Advanced Micro Devices Inc	710,266	362,813	1,073,079	22	48,776	32,285	16,492
TSLA	Tesla Inc	528,523	466,097	994,620	22	45,210	24,024	21,186
BABA	Alibaba Group Holding Ltd	682,958	297,883	980,841	22	44,584	31,044	13,540
NVDA	NVIDIA Corp	442,493	370,802	813,295	22	36,968	20,113	16,855
MU	Micron Technology Inc	496,647	231,121	727,768	22	33,080	22,575	10,506
AMZN	Amazon.com Inc	325,361	366,913	692,274	22	31,467	14,789	16,678
MSFT	Microsoft Corp	304,206	197,896	502,102	22	22,823	13,828	8,995

B. Stock Options for Bank of America (BAC)

| | Calls: | | | | | | | Puts: | | | | | |
Strike	Last	Net	Bid	Ask	Vol	Int	Strike	Last	Net	Bid	Ask	Vol	Int
						AUGUST 2017 (EXPIRATION: 08/18)							
BAC1718H23-E	1.87	0.24	1.81	1.87	474	28309	BAC1718T23-E	0.20	−0.04	0.19	0.24	100	80902
BAC1718H24-E	1.12	0.19	1.09	1.12	250	45373	BAC1718T24-E	0.48	−0.02	0.45	0.47	244	34707
BAC1718H25-E	0.56	0.09	0.55	0.57	413	66470	BAC1718T25-E	0.94	−0.08	0.91	0.96	116	12140
BAC1718H26-E	0.23	0.04	0.23	0.25	235	130351	BAC1718T26-E	1.69	0.00	1.59	1.67	0	5074
						SEPTEMBER 2017 (EXPIRATION: 09/15)							
BAC1715I23-E	1.96	0.17	1.95	2.02	1	13030	BAC1715U23-E	0.42	−0.01	0.39	0.41	125	24399
BAC1715I24-E	1.31	0.12	1.26	1.31	73	95868	BAC1715U24-E	0.72	0.05	0.70	0.73	96	8737
BAC1715I25-E	0.76	0.11	0.73	0.79	399	34822	BAC1715U25-E	1.25	0.05	1.18	1.20	110	6297
BAC1715I26-E	0.37	0.02	0.39	0.41	163	25219	BAC1715U26-E	1.92	−0.04	1.79	1.86	1	3106
						OCTOBER 2017 (EXPIRATION: 10/20)							
BAC1720J23-E	2.21	0.13	2.19	2.25	126	488	BAC1720V23-E	0.67	0.00	0.62	0.64	173	2990
BAC1720J24-E	1.48	0.01	1.54	1.59	22	1653	BAC1720V24-E	1.01	−0.03	0.95	0.99	20	708
BAC1720J25-E	1.04	0.09	1.03	1.05	186	13899	BAC1720V25-E	1.53	0.00	1.38	1.48	0	2526
BAC1720J26-E	0.57	0.00	0.64	0.69	0	4003	BAC1720V26-E	1.95	0.00	2.05	2.09	0	75
						DECEMBER 2017 (EXPIRATION: 12/15)							
BAC1715L23-E	2.73	0.00	2.47	2.50	0	5886	BAC1715X23-E	0.97	0.00	0.86	0.95	0	8635
BAC1715L24-E	1.75	−0.15	1.85	1.88	22	8109	BAC1715X24-E	1.33	−0.03	1.31	1.33	20	12321
BAC1715L25-E	1.30	0.02	1.34	1.37	16	36450	BAC1715X25-E	1.81	0.00	1.80	1.82	0	5630
BAC1715L26-E	0.84	0.00	0.93	1.01	0	34404	BAC1715X26-E	2.50	0.00	2.38	2.48	0	782

Source: Data from Chicago Board Options Exchange (www.cboe.com), July 13, 2017. Provided as a courtesy by Chicago Board Options Exchange, Inc.

his option to sell. Of course, the stock price will have to fall from its current level before this will occur. The investor in this case has sold an out-of-the-money contract and hopes that it will stay out of the money through expiration. As we saw earlier, the front-end premium is all that sellers of an option ever receive, and they hope to retain as much of it possible. Like the long position in the call, the short put position benefits from an increase in BAC share prices.

Notice that the options listed in Exhibit 16.1 expire within a few months of the quotation date. The expiration dates available for most exchange-traded contracts are the two nearest term months and up to three additional months from a quarterly cycle beginning in either January, February, or March. For high-volume stocks like BAC, additional expiration months can also be added that extend years into the future; these are called Long-Term Equity Anticipation Securities (LEAPS). Finally, for investors with a very short-term perspective, the CBOE has created *Weeklys*, which are option contracts created on a Thursday morning and expiring on Friday afternoon of the following week.

Stock Index and Index ETF Options As we saw in Chapter 14, options on stock indexes, such as the Standard & Poor's 500, are patterned closely after equity options. However, they differ in one important way: Index options can only be settled in cash. This is because the underlying index is a hypothetical portfolio. First traded on the CBOE in 1983, index options are popular with investors for the same reason as stock index futures: They provide a relatively inexpensive and convenient way to take an investment or hedge position in a broad-based indicator of market performance. Index puts are particularly useful in portfolio insurance applications, such as the protective put strategy described earlier and again at the end of this chapter.

Prices for a representative sample of S&P 500 Index (SPX) options are listed in Panel A of Exhibit 16.2. They are interpreted the same way as individual equity option prices, with each contract specifying the transfer of 100 "shares" of the underlying index. For example, the September 2017 SPX Index call option with an exercise price of 2,450 is out of the money, given that the index level on this day in July 2017 was 2,447.83. This contract could be purchased at the ask price for \$3,250 ($= 32.50 \times 100$) and would only be exercised to acquire \$245,000 worth of the index if the S&P rises above 2,450 by the expiration date.

Chapter 11 discussed using exchange-traded funds (ETFs) as an effective way to make an investment in a stock index. Given the popularity of these products, it is not surprising that the derivatives market now offers options based on them as well. Panel B of Exhibit 16.2 lists a price and volume data for SPDR S&P 500 ETF (SPY) options. Since the underlying ETF is a security (unlike the index itself), these options are designed like regular stock options and permit physical delivery. For example, the September 2017 SPY ETF put option with an exercise price of 245 is in the money, because SPY traded at 244.42. In exchange for an upfront payment of \$414 ($= 4.14 \times 100$), the owner of this put contract would find it advantageous to sell \$24,500 worth of the index ETF, assuming it remained below 245 at the expiration date.

Foreign Currency Options In our analysis of currency futures contracts in Chapter 15, we saw that those agreements are generally designed from the viewpoint of a U.S. dollar–based investor who thinks of the foreign (non–U.S. dollar) currency as the underlying asset in the transaction. Foreign currency options traded on U.S. exchanges are similar in that each contract allows for the sale or purchase of a set amount of currency at a fixed foreign exchange (FX) rate. A currency call option permits, but does not obligate, the contract holder to buy the currency at a later date, while a put allows the holder to sell the foreign currency. FX option contracts exist for several major currencies, including the euro, Australian dollars, Japanese yen, Canadian dollars, British pounds, and Swiss francs. Although most currency options trade in OTC markets, exchange-traded versions have existed since being launched by the PHLX in 1982. Exhibit 16.3 shows the prevailing USD/GBP spot rate as well as quotes for some of the British pound contracts that were available on July 13, 2017.

Consider a U.S. investor who holds British pound–denominated government bonds in her portfolio. It is July, and when the bonds mature next month, she will need to convert the proceeds back into U.S. dollars. This exposes the investor to the risk that the British currency will weaken (that is, will be exchangeable for fewer dollars) by mid-August. To hedge this risk, she buys the August put with an exercise price of USD 130/GBP, which is expressed in U.S. cents per pound. Thus, her initial cost to acquire a put option allowing her to sell 10,000 pounds is USD 141 ($= 0.0141 \times 10,000$), using the ask price (fifth entry under the "Puts—18Aug17" block) and delivery amount associated with the contract. This option would allow the investor to exchange the GBP 10,000 that will come from her maturing British bond in August for USD 13,000 ($= 10,000 \times 1.30$). She will only exercise the contract if the spot USD/GBP rate prevailing in August remains at a level less than 1.30 (or weakens further), which was her original concern. Finally, because the July spot rate at the time the put is acquired is USD 1.2942/GBP, this contract is in the money.

Exhibit 16.2 Index and Index ETF Option Quotations for SPX and SPY

A. Standard & Poor's 500 Index (SPX)

Strike	Last	Net	Bid	Ask	Vol	Int		Strike	Last	Net	Bid	Ask	Vol	Int
			Calls:								**Puts:**			
AUGUST 2017 (EXPIRATION: 08/18)														
SPX1718H2440-E	28.20	2.10	27.30	28.40	701	3126		SPX1718T2440-E	21.10	−2.70	20.50	21.40	2913	2405
SPX1718H2445-E	23.90	1.30	24.00	25.10	82	1358		SPX1718T2445-E	23.00	−3.40	22.10	23.20	100	965
SPX1718H2450-E	21.00	0.65	20.90	21.90	3986	13821		SPX1718T2450-E	24.65	−3.77	24.00	25.10	4520	6277
SPX1718H2455-E	18.40	0.75	18.00	19.00	56	576		SPX1718T2455-E	27.55	−2.10	26.00	27.10	5	228
SEPTEMBER 2017 (EXPIRATION: 09/15)														
SPX1715I2440-E	39.48	1.98	38.80	40.00	6192	16344		SPX1715U2440-E	33.95	−2.80	33.20	34.30	5203	16695
SPX1715I2445-E	35.50	1.33	35.60	36.70	13024	10401		SPX1715U2445-E	35.50	−3.17	34.80	35.80	13033	10044
SPX1715I2450-E	32.50	0.20	32.40	33.60	8710	37408		SPX1715U2450-E	37.55	−1.75	36.80	37.90	7860	16310
SPX1715I2455-E	30.09	3.02	29.50	30.60	4	44		SPX1715U2455-E	39.45	−1.85	38.80	39.90	13	212
DECEMBER 2017 (EXPIRATION: 12/15)														
SPX1715L2400-E	96.22	−0.03	98.80	100.60	8	35055		SPX1715X2400-E	56.60	−2.10	55.60	57.00	62	33980
SPX1715L2425-E	82.50	1.75	81.60	83.40	682	17706		SPX1715X2425-E	64.25	−3.75	63.20	64.70	2814	17030
SPX1715L2450-E	66.60	2.65	65.60	67.40	851	19520		SPX1715X2450-E	73.20	−2.90	72.00	73.60	175	6425
SPX1715L2475-E	52.30	3.20	51.20	52.80	604	17426		SPX1715X2475-E	84.00	−4.00	82.30	84.00	2	848

B. SPDR S&P 500 ETF Trust (SPY)

Strike	Last	Net	Bid	Ask	Vol	Int		Strike	Last	Net	Bid	Ask	Vol	Int
			Calls:								**Puts:**			
AUGUST 2017 (EXPIRATION: 08/18)														
SPY1718H243-E	3.69	0.27	3.52	3.59	61	37187		SPY1718T243-E	1.83	−0.31	1.83	1.88	3869	61109
SPY1718H244-E	2.93	0.20	2.82	2.88	772	131612		SPY1718T244-E	2.16	−0.27	2.13	2.20	1211	131915
SPY1718H245-E	2.30	0.16	2.18	2.24	579	169116		SPY1718T245-E	2.52	−0.22	2.49	2.56	777	113643
SPY1718H246-E	1.71	0.12	1.62	1.67	889	54701		SPY1718T246-E	2.91	−0.36	2.93	3.01	183	27181
SEPTEMBER 2017 (EXPIRATION: 09/15)														
SPY1715I243-E	4.77	0.19	4.68	4.75	26	24196		SPY1715U243-E	3.31	−0.29	3.30	3.37	38	26667
SPY1715I244-E	4.03	0.13	4.00	4.06	438	16127		SPY1715U244-E	3.68	−0.31	3.65	3.72	137	8468
SPY1715I245-E	3.41	0.06	3.35	3.41	391	75231		SPY1715U245-E	4.14	−0.25	4.06	4.14	45	18954
SPY1715I246-E	2.81	0.13	2.76	2.81	60	22886		SPY1715U246-E	4.93	0.00	4.51	4.60	0	3187
DECEMBER 2017 (EXPIRATION: 12/15)														
SPY1715L239-E	9.21	0.00	10.63	10.72	0	7332		SPY1715X239-E	5.78	0.00	5.62	5.68	0	5901
SPY1715L240-E	9.94	0.34	9.89	9.98	12	29641		SPY1715X240-E	5.94	−0.14	5.91	5.97	153	42376
SPY1715L245-E	6.61	0.15	6.55	6.63	247	64511		SPY1715X245-E	7.77	−0.11	7.66	7.73	67	9847
SPY1715L250-E	3.88	0.09	3.81	3.88	160	29241		SPY1715X250-E	10.13	−0.18	10.04	10.13	89	8279

Source: Data from Chicago Board Options Exchange (www.cboe.com), July 13, 2017. Provided as a courtesy by Chicago Board Options Exchange, Inc.

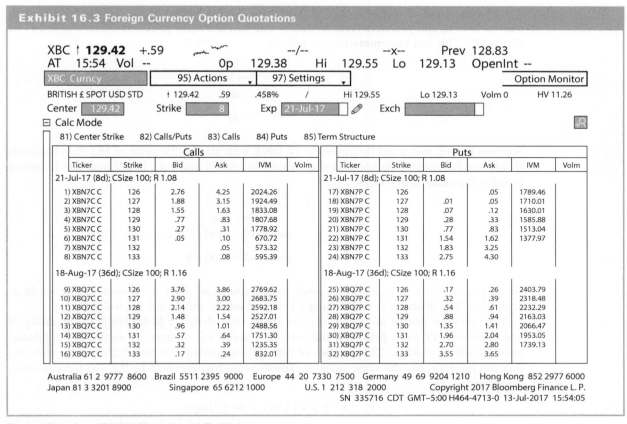

Exhibit 16.3 Foreign Currency Option Quotations

| XBC ↑ **129.42** +.59 | | --/-- | | --x-- | Prev 128.83 |
| AT   15:54 Vol -- | 0p 129.38 | Hi 129.55 | Lo 129.13 | OpenInt -- |

XBC Curncy   95) Actions ▾   97) Settings ▾   Option Monitor

BRITISH £ SPOT USD STD   ↑ 129.42   .59   .458%   /   Hi 129.55   Lo 129.13   Volm 0   HV 11.26

Center 129.42   Strike 8   Exp 21-Jul-17 ✎   Exch

⊟ Calc Mode   🔍

81) Center Strike   82) Calls/Puts   83) Calls   84) Puts   85) Term Structure

		Calls						Puts			
	Ticker	Strike	Bid	Ask	IVM	Volm	Ticker	Strike	Bid	Ask	IVM	Volm
21-Jul-17 (8d); CSize 100; R 1.08							**21-Jul-17 (8d); CSize 100; R 1.08**					
1)	XBN7C C	126	2.76	4.25	2024.26		17) XBN7P C	126		.05	1789.46	
2)	XBN7C C	127	1.88	3.15	1924.49		18) XBN7P C	127	.01	.05	1710.01	
3)	XBN7C C	128	1.55	1.63	1833.08		19) XBN7P C	128	.07	.12	1630.01	
4)	XBN7C C	129	.77	.83	1807.68		20) XBN7P C	129	.28	.33	1585.88	
5)	XBN7C C	130	.27	.31	1778.92		21) XBN7P C	130	.77	.83	1513.04	
6)	XBN7C C	131	.05	.10	670.72		22) XBN7P C	131	1.54	1.62	1377.97	
7)	XBN7C C	132		.05	573.32		23) XBN7P C	132	1.83	3.25		
8)	XBN7C C	133		.08	595.39		24) XBN7P C	133	2.75	4.30		
18-Aug-17 (36d); CSize 100; R 1.16							**18-Aug-17 (36d); CSize 100; R 1.16**					
9)	XBQ7C C	126	3.76	3.86	2769.62		25) XBQ7P C	126	.17	.26	2403.79	
10)	XBQ7C C	127	2.90	3.00	2683.75		26) XBQ7P C	127	.32	.39	2318.48	
11)	XBQ7C C	128	2.14	2.22	2592.18		27) XBQ7P C	128	.54	.61	2232.29	
12)	XBQ7C C	129	1.48	1.54	2527.01		28) XBQ7P C	129	.88	.94	2163.03	
13)	XBQ7C C	130	.96	1.01	2488.56		29) XBQ7P C	130	1.35	1.41	2066.47	
14)	XBQ7C C	131	.57	.64	1751.30		30) XBQ7P C	131	1.96	2.04	1953.05	
15)	XBQ7C C	132	.32	.39	1235.35		31) XBQ7P C	132	2.70	2.80	1739.13	
16)	XBQ7C C	133	.17	.24	832.01		32) XBQ7P C	133	3.55	3.65		

Australia 61 2 9777 8600   Brazil 5511 2395 9000   Europe 44 20 7330 7500   Germany 49 69 9204 1210   Hong Kong 852 2977 6000
Japan 81 3 3201 8900   Singapore 65 6212 1000   U.S. 1 212 318 2000   Copyright 2017 Bloomberg Finance L. P.
SN 335716 CDT GMT−5:00 H464-4713-0 13-Jul-2017 15:54:05

16.2 THE FUNDAMENTALS OF OPTION VALUATION

Although investors can use options to anticipate future security prices, the key to understanding how they are valued is that they also are risk-reduction tools. An option's theoretical value depends on combining it with its underlying security to create a *synthetic risk-free portfolio*. That is, it is theoretically possible to use the option as a perfect *hedge* against value fluctuations in the asset on which it is based.

This was essentially the same approach we used in Chapter 14 to establish the put-call parity relationships. The primary differences between put-call parity and what follows are twofold. First, the hedge portfolio implied by the put-call parity transaction did not require special adjustment; it simply consisted of one stock long, one put long, and one call short held until the expiration date. However, hedging an underlying asset position's risk with a single option position—whether a call or a put—often involves using multiple contracts and frequent changes in the number needed to maintain the riskless portfolio. Second, put-call parity did not demand a forecast of the underlying asset's future price level, whereas the following analysis will. We will see that *forecasting the volatility of future asset prices* is the most important input the investor must provide in determining option values.

16.2.1 The Basic Approach

While the mathematics associated with option valuation can be complex, the fundamental intuition behind the process can be illustrated quite simply. Suppose you have just purchased a share of stock in WYZ Corp. for $50. The stock is not expected to pay a dividend while you plan to hold it, and you have forecast that in one year the stock price will either rise to $65 or fall to $40. This can be summarized as follows:

Suppose further that a call option on WYZ stock with an exercise price of $52.50 is available. If this is a European-style contract that expires in exactly one year, it will have the following possible expiration date values:

$$
C_0 \Big\langle
\begin{array}{l}
\text{max}[0, 65 - 52.5] = 12.50 \\
\text{max}[0, 40 - 52.5] = 0
\end{array}
$$

Given your forecast of future WYZ stock prices, you know what the option will be worth at expiration. The dilemma is establishing what the contract should sell for today (C_0).

This question can be answered in three steps. First, design a *hedge portfolio* consisting of one share of WYZ stock held long and some number of call options (h), so that the combined position will be riskless. The number of call options needed can be established by ensuring that the portfolio has the same value at expiration no matter which of the two forecast stock values occurs, or:

$$65 + (h)(12.50) = 40 + (h)(0)$$

leaving:

$$h = \frac{(65 - 40)}{(0 - 12.5)} = -2.00$$

There are both *direction* and *magnitude* dimensions to this number. The negative sign indicates that, in order to create negative correlation between two assets that are naturally positively correlated, call options must be *sold* to hedge a long stock position. Further, given that the range of possible expiration date option outcomes ($= 12.5 - 0$) is only half as large as the range for WYZ stock ($= 65 - 40$), twice as many options must be sold as there is stock in the hedge portfolio. The value h is known as the *hedge ratio*.[3] Thus, the risk-free hedge portfolio can be created by purchasing one share of stock and selling two call options.

The second step assumes capital markets that are free from arbitrage so that all riskless investments are priced to earn the risk-free rate over the time until expiration. The hedge portfolio costing $[50 - (2)(C_0)]$ today would grow to the certain value of $40 by the following formula:

$$[50 - (2.00)(C_0)](1 + RFR)^T = 40$$

where:

RFR = annualized risk-free rate

T = time to expiration (one year, in this example)

---

[3]In some valuation models (for example, Black–Scholes), the hedge ratio is expressed as the option's potential volatility divided by that of the stock. In this example, that would be $(0 - 12.5) \div (65 - 40) = -0.5$, meaning that the option is half as volatile in dollar terms as the share of stock. Of course, this alternative calculation is just the reciprocal of the value of $h = -2.00$.

Two unknown values exist in this formula: C_0 and *RFR*. Finding a suitable estimate for *RFR* seldom is a problem because the investor can use the yield to maturity on a U.S. Treasury security of appropriate length. For example, if the one-year T-bill yield is 8 percent, the formula for C_0 can be solved as follows:

$$C_0 = \frac{50 - 40/1.08}{2.00} = \$6.48$$

This calculation is the third and final step in establishing the call's fair market value. That is, $6.48 represents the fundamental value of a one-year call option on WYZ stock, given both the prevailing market prices for two other securities (stock and T-bills) and the investor's forecast of future share values, which becomes the critical element in determining if this present value is reasonable. Finally, because the call option is currently out of the money, this amount is purely a time premium.

16.2.2 Improving Forecast Accuracy

Because it is unrealistic to assume only two possible outcomes for future WYZ share prices, the expiration date forecast of stock prices can be expanded to allow for numerous possibilities. To see the consequences of this expansion in the simplest terms possible, consider a revised forecast that includes only one additional potential price falling between the previous values:

Today	One Year
	65.00
50	50.99
	40.00

The three-step riskless hedge approach to calculating C_0 is still conceptually valid, but it must be modified because it is now impossible to calculate a single hedge ratio that simultaneously accounts for all three Date *T* possibilities.

Creating a Stock Price Tree The adjustment involves dividing the time to expiration into as many *subintervals* as necessary so that at any point in time the subsequent price can only move up or down. In this example, only one additional subinterval is needed. Exhibit 16.4 shows how the WYZ stock price forecast might be embellished. This illustration, which is sometimes called a *stock price tree*, indicates that for the stock price to reach, say, $65 in one year, it must first move up to $57.01 in Subperiod S1 before moving up a second time to its final value. Similarly, the lower extreme of $40 can only be reached by two consecutive "down" price changes. There are two different paths to the terminal outcome in the middle: (1) one "up" followed by one "down" or (2) a down movement followed by an up movement.

Exhibit 16.4 Forecasted Stock Price Tree (Three Terminal Outcomes)

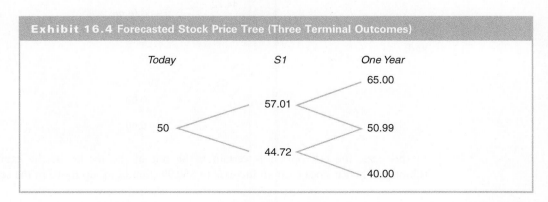

Once the investor fills in this price tree, the call option's value can be solved by working backward on each pair of possible outcomes from the future. If, for instance, an initial up movement left the price of WYZ stock at $57.01, a price change over the remaining subperiod could be characterized as:

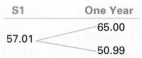

The corresponding change in the value of the call option (C_{11}) is then:

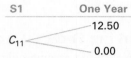

With $X = 52.50$, the call option will be in the money at expiration only if WYZ stock moves up in price again. This suggests a hedge ratio of:

$$h = \frac{(65.00 - 50.99)}{(0.00 - 12.50)} = -1.12$$

so that the riskless hedge portfolio at this point would contain one share of stock long and 1.12 calls short. The intermediate option value is then found by solving:

$$[57.01 - (1.12)(C_{11})](1.08)^{0.5} = [65 - (1.12)(12.50)] = 50.99$$

or:

$$C_{11} = \frac{57.01 - 50.99/1.0392}{1.12} = \$7.09$$

Here the factor $1.0392\ [= (1.08)^{0.5}]$ is roughly one-half the annual risk-free rate (plus one) since the original holding period was divided into two six-month subintervals.

Valuing in Other Subintervals Having established C_{11}, the value for the option corresponding to an S1 share price of $44.72 ($C_{12}$) can be established by the same three-step procedure with the stock and option price trees truncated as follows:

and:

In this case, the call option is certain to be out of the money at the expiration date one subinterval hence since even an increase to $50.99 (that is, an up move in the second subperiod)

would leave the share price below the $52.50 exercise price. Thus, C_{12} must be $0.00 and the concept of forming a riskless hedge portfolio under such circumstances is meaningless.

These intermediate calculations have little importance to the investor who only cares about the current value of the option. However, they are necessary as C_0 cannot be established before determining C_{11} and C_{12}. With these values in hand, the relevant part of the stock price tree is:

Today	S1
	57.01
50.00	
	44.72

with the corresponding call option tree being given by:

Today	S1
	7.09
C_0	
	0.00

Once again applying the three-step process, the initial (Date 0) hedge ratio is:

$$h = \frac{(57.01 - 44.72)}{(0.00 - 7.09)} = -1.73$$

so that the riskless hedge portfolio at inception would short 1.73 calls for every share held long. The current option value is then found by solving:

$$[50.00 - (1.73)(C_0)](1.08)^{0.5} = [44.72 - (1.73)(0.00)] = 44.72$$

or:

$$C_0 = \frac{50.00 - 44.72/1.0392}{1.73} = \$4.02$$

Exhibit 16.5 summarizes these initial, intermediate, and terminal option values.

Two interesting things resulted from this expansion of possible stock price outcomes. First, the addition of a third potential terminal stock price had the effect of reducing the Date 0 option value from $6.48 to $4.02. Although this reduction was a consequence of choosing a third possible stock price ($50.99) that caused the option to be out of the money—selecting a value closer to $65.00 would have increased C_0—it does underscore that the option valuation process critically depends on the investor's stock price forecast. Second, the hedge ratio

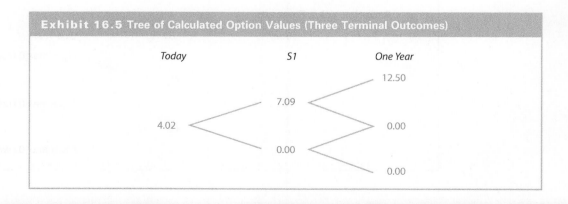

Exhibit 16.5 Tree of Calculated Option Values (Three Terminal Outcomes)

Today	S1	One Year
		12.50
	7.09	
4.02		0.00
	0.00	
		0.00
		0.00

changes with stock price changes prior to the expiration date, meaning the composition of the riskless hedge portfolio must be rebalanced after each share price movement. From the initial position of being short 1.73 calls against one share held long, an upward movement in WYZ stock from $50.00 to $57.01 would require buying back 0.61 ($= 1.73 - 1.12$) options. Thus, replicating a risk-free position with stock and call options is a *dynamic* process.

16.2.3 The Binomial Option Pricing Model

A crucial aspect of this option valuation approach is that future changes in the underlying asset's price always can be reduced to two possibilities: an up movement or a down movement. As shown by Rendleman and Bartter (1979) and Cox, Ross, and Rubinstein (1979), this is part of a more general valuation methodology known as the *two-state option pricing model*. The preceding example required the investor to specify dollar amounts for the future potential stock prices in all the subperiods in the forecast—a daunting task as the number of terminal outcomes grows larger.

Forecasting Price Changes To streamline this process, suppose an investor focuses her estimates on how stock prices *change* between subperiods, rather than on the dollar levels. Beginning with today's known stock price, for the next subperiod she forecasts: (1) one plus the percentage change for an up (u) movement and (2) one plus the percentage change for a down (d) movement. Further, to limit the number of forecasts, suppose she also assumes that the same values for u and d apply to every price change in all subsequent subperiods. With these assumptions, the investor need only forecast three things: u, d, and N (the total number of subperiods).

Exhibit 16.6 shows the effect that these modifications—which represent the essence of the **binomial option pricing model**—have on the forecast stock and option value trees. Like the three-outcome version in the preceding example, this illustration allows for two subperiods ($N = 2$).

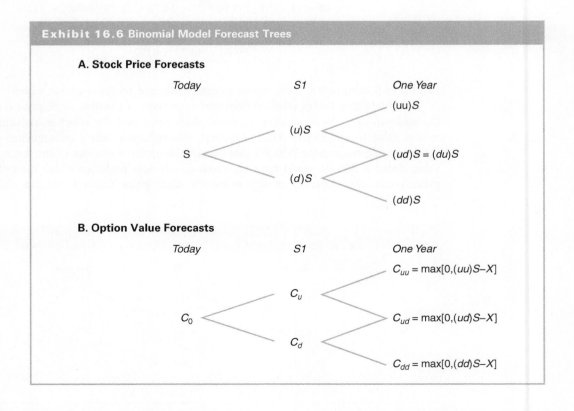

Exhibit 16.6 Binomial Model Forecast Trees

A. Stock Price Forecasts

Today   S1   One Year

$(uu)S$

$(u)S$

S $(ud)S = (du)S$

$(d)S$

$(dd)S$

B. Option Value Forecasts

Today   S1   One Year

$C_{uu} = \max[0, (uu)S - X]$

C_u

C_0 $C_{ud} = \max[0, (ud)S - X]$

C_d

$C_{dd} = \max[0, (dd)S - X]$

The upper panel of the display shows that after an up and a down movement in two consecutive subperiods, the initial stock price of S will have changed to $(ud)S$. The values $(ud)S$ and $(du)S$ are equal, meaning that the forecast does not depend on whether the stock price begins its journey by rising or falling. Once u, d, and N are determined, the expiration date payoffs to the option (C_{uu}, C_{ud}, and C_{dd}) are established.

As before, the initial value for the call, C_0, can be solved by working backward through the tree and solving for each intermediate option value. With the binomial model, however, these intermediate values are much easier to compute. In the jth state in any subperiod, the value of the option is:

16.1
$$C_j = \frac{(p)C_{ju} + (1 - p)C_{jd}}{r}$$

where:

$$p = \frac{r - d}{u - d}$$

and:

r = one plus the risk-free rate over the subperiod

If p is interpreted as the probability of an up movement in the security's price, which would mean that $(1 - p)$ is the probability of a down move, then the formula for C_j has an intuitive interpretation. The option's value at any point is simply its expected value one subperiod hence discounted back to the current time. Further, although p was not an explicit part of the investor's forecast, it is generated by the model. In this sense, p is the *implied probability* of an upward price movement. To ensure that this interpretation holds, the binomial model requires that $d < r < u$, a condition that is quite reasonable in practice.

Generalizing the Model Equation 16.1 can be extended by recognizing that the value for an option in Subperiod t can be inserted into the right-hand side of the formula for Subperiod $t - 1$. Carrying this logic all the way back to Date 0, the binomial option valuation model becomes:

16.2
$$C_0 = \left[\sum_{j=0}^{N} \frac{N!}{(N - j)!\, j!} p^j (1 - p)^{N-j} \max[0, (u^j d^{N-j})S - X] \right] \div r^N$$
$$= \left[\sum_{j=m}^{N} \frac{N!}{(N - j)!\, j!} \; p^j (1 - p)^{N-j} [(u^j d^{N-j})S - X] \right] \div r^N$$

where:

m = smallest number of up moves guaranteeing an in-the-money option at expiration (that is, $(u^m d^{N-m})S > X$)

$N! = [(N)(N - 1)(N - 2) \ldots (2)(1)]$

To interpret Equation 16.2, the ratio $[N! \div (N - j)!\, j!]$ is the "combinatorial" way of stating how many distinct paths lead to a particular terminal outcome, $p^j (1 - p)^{N-j}$ is the probability of getting to that outcome, and $\max[0, (u^j d^{N-j})S - X]$ is the payoff associated with that outcome.

As an example, assume that the investor has gathered data and made forecasts as follows: $S = 50.00$, $X = 52.50$, T = one year, $RFR = 8$ percent (through expiration), $u = 1.14018$, $d = 0.89443$, and $N = 2$. This divides the one-year life of the option into two subperiods and estimates up and down moves during any subperiod as slightly greater than 14.0 percent and 10.5 percent, respectively. The values for r and p implied by these forecasts are

1.0392 $[= (1.08)^{0.5}]$ and 0.589 $[= (1.0392 - 0.89443) \div (1.14018 - 0.89443)]$. By Equation 16.2, the value of a one-year European-style call option with an exercise price of $52.50 is:

$$C_0 = \frac{(1)(0.589)^2(12.50) + (2)(0.589)(0.411)(0) + (1)(0.411)^2(0)}{(1.0392)^2}$$

$$= \frac{(1)(0.589)^2(12.50)}{(1.0392)^2} = \$4.02$$

This is the same value the three-step approach produced in the previous example because the forecast stock price tree in Exhibit 16.4 was generated with these values of u and d (for example, $(uu)S = (1.14018)^2(50) = \$65.00$). So, the tree of forecast option values in Exhibit 16.5 may be replicated for any State j.[4] The hedge ratio for the jth state becomes:

$$h_j = \frac{(u - d)S_j}{(C_{jd} - C_{ju})}$$

meaning a share of stock held long could be hedged initially by shorting 1.73 call options $[= (1.14018 - 0.89443)(50) \div (0.00 - 7.09)]$, a position that would be rebalanced to 1.12 calls after one subperiod if the first price change was positive.

16.2.4 The Black–Scholes Valuation Model

The binomial model is a *discrete* method for valuing options because it allows security price changes to occur in distinct upward or downward movements. Prices can also be assumed to change *continuously* over time. This was the approach taken by Black and Scholes (1973) in developing their method for valuing European-style options. This is not a more realistic assumption because it presumes that security prices change when markets are closed (for example, at night or on weekends). The advantage of the **Black–Scholes model**—identical in spirit to the basic three-step, riskless hedge method outlined earlier—is that it leads to a relatively simple, closed-form equation capable of valuing options accurately under a wide array of circumstances.

The Black–Scholes model assumes that stock price movements can be described by a statistical process known as *geometric Brownian motion*. This process is summarized by a volatility factor, σ, which is analogous to the investor's stock price forecasts in the previous models. Formally, the assumed stock price process is:

$$\frac{\Delta S}{S} = \mu[\Delta T] + \sigma\varepsilon[\Delta T]^{1/2}$$

so that a stock's return ($\Delta S/S$) from the present through any future period T has both an expected component ($\mu[\Delta T]$) and a "noise" component ($\sigma\varepsilon[\Delta T]^{1/2}$), where μ is the mean return and ε is the standard normally distributed random error term.[5]

Assuming that the continuously compounded risk-free rate and the stock's variance (σ^2) remain constant until the expiration date T, Black and Scholes used the riskless hedge intuition to derive the following formula for valuing a call option on a non-dividend-paying security:

16.3 $$C_0 = SN(d_1) - X(e^{-(RFR)T})N(d_2)$$

where $e^{-(RFR)T}$ is the discount function for continuously compounded variables,

$$d_1 = [\ln(S/X) + (RFR + 0.5\sigma^2)[T]] \div (\sigma[T]^{1/2})$$

---

[4]For example, $C_u = [(0.589)(12.50) + (0.411)(0)] \div (1.0392) = \$7.09$.

[5]For a detailed analysis of the mathematics underlying the Black–Scholes model, see Hull (2015).

and:

$$d_2 = d_1 - \sigma[T]^{1/2}$$

with ln($\cdot$) being the natural logarithm function. The variable $N(d)$ represents the cumulative probability of observing a value drawn from the standard normal distribution (that is, one with a mean of zero and a standard deviation of one) equal to or less than d. As the standard normal distribution is symmetric around zero, a value of $d = 0$ would lead to $N(d) = 0.5000$; positive values of d would then have cumulative probabilities greater than 50 percent, with negative values of d leading to cumulative probabilities of less than one-half.

Values for $N(d)$ can be established in two ways. First, an investor can use a table of calculated values for the standard normal distribution, as in Appendix D at the end of the book. For example, if the value of d_1 is 0.65, $N(d_1)$ could be established by finding the entry corresponding to the 0.6 row and the 0.05 column, or 0.7422. This means that 74.22 percent of the observations in the standard normal distribution have a value of 0.65 or less. If d_1 had been -0.65, the value of $N(-d_1) = 1 - N(d_1) = 1 - 0.7422 = 0.2578$.

A second approach to calculating cumulative normal probabilities is approximating them with the following formula, shown by Carr (1988):

$$N(d) \approx \begin{cases} 0.5e^{-(d2)/2-281/(83-351/d)} & \text{if } d < 0 \\ 1 - 0.5e^{-(d2)/2-281(83+351/d)} & \text{if } d \geq 0 \end{cases}$$

For example, with $d = 0.65$, we have an approximate probability of:

$$N(0.65) \approx 1 - 0.5e^{-(0.652)/2-281/(83+351/0.65)} = 0.7422$$

Properties of the Model   The Black–Scholes valuation model shows that the option's value is a function of five variables:

1. Current security price, S
2. Exercise price, X
3. Time to expiration, T
4. Risk-free rate, RFR
5. Security price volatility, σ

or:

$$C = f(S, X, T, RFR, \sigma)$$

The first and fourth factors are observable market prices, and the second and third variables are defined by the contract itself. So, the only variable an investor must provide is the volatility factor, which embeds the investor's forecast of future stock prices.

The value of the call option will rise with increases in each of the five factors *except* the exercise price. Exhibit 16.7 summarizes these relationships. The intuition behind the first three is straightforward: An increase in the underlying asset's price (S) will increase the call's intrinsic value; a larger exercise price (X) will reduce the intrinsic value. Also, the longer the option has until it expires, the more valuable the time premium component. This is because a greater opportunity exists for the contract to finish in the money. On the other hand, the relationships between C, RFR, and σ are less obvious. An increase in RFR will increase the call's value because this reduces the present value of X, which the call holder must pay at expiration to exercise the contract. Similarly, when the volatility of the underlying asset's price increases, the call becomes more valuable since this increases the probability that the option will be deeper in the money at expiration.[6]

---

[6]In more technical terms, these relationships can be summarized as $\delta C/\delta S > 0$, $\delta C/\delta RFR > 0$, $\delta C/\delta T > 0$, $\delta C/\delta \sigma > 0$, and $\delta C/\delta X < 0$.

Exhibit 16.7 Factors Affecting Black-Scholes Option Values

An Increase In:	WILL CAUSE AN INCREASE/DECREASE IN:	
	Call Value	Put Value
Security price (S)	Increase	Decrease
Exercise price (X)	Decrease	Increase
Time to expiration (T)	Increase	Increase or decrease
Risk-free rate (RFR)	Increase	Decrease
Security volatility (σ)	Increase	Increase

The hedge ratio in the Black–Scholes model is simply $N(d_1)$, the partial derivative of the call's value with respect to the stock price ($\delta C/\delta S$). $N(d_1)$ is the change in the option's value given a $1 change in the underlying security's price. For this reason, $N(d_1)$ often is called the option's **delta**, and it indicates the number of stock shares that can be hedged by a single call—exactly the reciprocal of the previous interpretation of the hedge ratio, h. Finally, the Black–Scholes model is actually an extension of the binomial model. As the number of subperiods (that is, N) approaches infinity, the up or down price movements begin to occur on a continuous basis. If the values of u and d are then set equal to $e^{\sigma[\Delta T]12}$ and $e^{\sigma[\Delta T]1/2}$, respectively, the binomial model collapses to become the Black–Scholes formula.

An Example Consider the following values for the five input variables: $S = 40$, $X = 40$, $T =$ one year, $RFR = 9$ percent (or, 0.09), and $\sigma = 0.30$. To calculate the Black–Scholes value of a European-style call option under these conditions, first calculate:

$$d_1 = (\ln(40/40) + (0.09 + 0.5(0.3)^2)[1]) \div (0.3[1]^{\frac{1}{2}}) = 0.45$$

and:

$$d_2 = 0.45 - 0.3[1]^{1/2} = 0.15$$

so that:

$$N(d_1) = 1 - 0.5e^{-(0.45^2)/2 - 281/(83 + 351/0.45)} = 0.6736$$

and:

$$N(d_2) = 1 - 0.5e^{-(0.15^2)/2 - 281/(83 + 351/0.15)} = 0.5596$$

Thus:

$$C_0 = (40)(0.6736) - 40(e^{-.09})(0.5596) = \$6.49$$

$N(d_1)$ says that the call option will change in value by about 67 cents for every dollar of a change in the underlying asset, which suggests a hedge ratio of one-and-a-half calls short for every stock share held long. Exhibit 16.8 shows how both the option's value and $N(d_1)$ change as the security's value changes, with the other factors held constant. Notably, the hedge ratio ranges from 0 to 1 and increases as stock prices increase. Therefore, the deeper in the money the option is, the closer its price movements will come to duplicating those of the stock itself. The relationship between stock prices and call option prices for this example is shown in Exhibit 16.9.

16.2.5 Estimating Volatility

Just as the growth rate of dividends (g) is crucial to establishing the fundamental value of common stock, option valuation depends critically on an accurate forecast of the underlying asset's

Exhibit 16.8 Example of Black-Scholes Valuation

Stock Price ($)	Call Value ($)	Hedge Ratio
25	0.44	0.1321
30	1.51	0.3054
35	3.53	0.5020
40	6.49	0.6736
45	10.19	0.8003
50	14.42	0.8837
55	18.98	0.9347

Note: Assumes $X = 40$, $T = 1$ year, $RFR = 9\%$, and $= 0.30$.

Exhibit 16.9 Black-Scholes Values

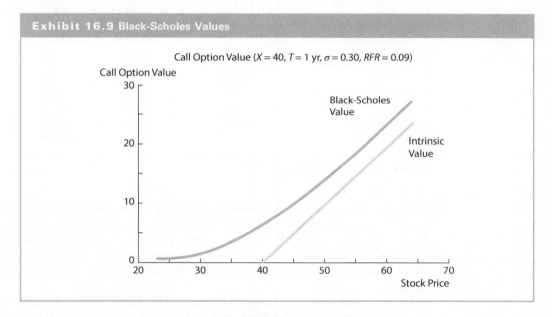

Call Option Value ($X = 40$, $T = 1$ yr, $\sigma = 0.30$, $RFR = 0.09$)

future price level. In the Black–Scholes framework, this means selecting the proper σ, which is equivalent to the standard deviation of returns to the underlying asset. This value can be estimated in two ways. First, it can be calculated in the traditional manner using historical returns. Specifically, calculate the Day t *price relative* as $R_t = \ln(P_t \div P_{t-1})$. If a series of price relatives are calculated for a sequence of N days in the recent past, the mean and standard deviation of this series can be established as:

$$\overline{R} = \left(\frac{1}{N}\right)\sum_{t=1}^{N} R_t \quad \text{and} \quad \sigma^2 = \left(\frac{1}{N-1}\right)\sum_{t=1}^{N} (R_t - \overline{R})^2$$

The factor σ is expressed in terms of daily price movements. To annualize this value, σ can be multiplied by the square root of the number of trading days in the year (usually assumed to be 250). The advantage of historical volatility is that it is easy to compute and requires no assumption about market efficiency; its disadvantage is its presumption that future stock price behavior will continue as it has in the past. Exhibit 16.10 lists annualized 30-day historical volatilities for a representative sample of firms during 2007, 2012, and 2017. These statistics highlight how dramatically stock volatility can vary over time.

A second volatility estimation approach involves the Black–Scholes equation itself. Recall that if we know all five input factors—S, X, T, RFR, and σ—we can solve for the value of the

Exhibit 16.10 Annualized Historical Volatility Estimates

Company	Ticker	30-Day Volatility Estimate (%)		
		July 2007	July 2012	July 2017
Altria	MO	14.84	11.70	11.04
Amazon.com	AMZN	32.12	23.04	21.28
Apple Computer	AAPL	32.04	18.58	21.06
Applied Materials	AMAT	27.70	30.59	33.26
Bank of America	BAC	13.67	48.27	20.69
Cisco Systems	CSCO	21.76	26.88	12.44
Citigroup	C	18.90	45.68	16.36
Coca-Cola	KO	10.78	14.37	8.28
Duke Energy	DUK	22.59	16.10	8.66
eBay	EBAY	24.33	30.90	23.68
General Electric	GE	18.12	25.76	21.71
Halliburton	HAL	23.17	32.90	23.78
Intel	INTC	29.16	27.46	17.92
L3 Technologies	LLL	16.47	21.25	15.23
Merck	MRK	20.99	18.43	14.53
Oracle	ORCL	25.11	28.84	27.47
Pfizer	PFE	15.58	12.58	13.48
Tivo	TIVO	49.92	37.19	31.47
Walmart	WMT	18.90	16.36	20.14
Xerox	XRX	21.41	28.46	19.11

Source: Author calculations.

call option. However, if we know the current price of the option (call it C^*) and the four other variables, we can calculate the level of σ that forces the Black–Scholes value to equal C^*. That is, the volatility implied by current market prices is established by finding σ^* such that $C^* = f(S, X, T, RFR, \sigma^*)$; the value σ^* is known as the **implied volatility**. No simple closed-form solution exists for performing this calculation; it must be done using a search routine.

Implied volatility is advantageous because it calculates the same volatility forecast investors use to set option prices. The disadvantage of implied volatility is its presumption that markets are efficient in that the option price set in the market corresponds directly to the Black–Scholes equation. Beckers (1981) has shown that implied volatilities do a better job than historical volatilities of predicting future stock price movements; however, Figlewski (1989b) and Shiu, Pan, Lin, and Wu (2010) caution that σ^* can be "noisy" as it picks up not only the true level of volatility but also any errors in the valuation or trading process.

The concept of implied volatility is also the foundation of a popular measure of stock market sentiment. Introduced by Whaley (1993), the **Volatility Index (VIX)** is calculated as a weighted average of the implied volatility estimates from options on the Standard & Poor's 500 Index using a wide range of exercise prices. VIX purports to measure investor expectations of near-term (30-day) volatility in the stock market, with higher levels of the index indicating greater investor wariness about future economic conditions. In a typical year, the VIX can range between 10.00 percent and 45.00 percent. Futures and option contracts using the VIX as the underlying asset have traded on the CBOE since 2004 and 2006, respectively, and a S&P 500 VIX ETF began trading in 2010.

16.2.6 Problems with Black–Scholes Valuation

The Black–Scholes option valuation model is popular with investors because it is computationally convenient, and it produces reasonable values under a wide variety of conditions. There are, however, circumstances in which the model is less than desirable. MacBeth and Merville (1979) showed that implied volatilities tended to be overly large when the associated call options were in the money and too small for out-of-the-money contracts. Thus, the Black–Scholes model overvalued out-of-the-money call options and undervalued in-the-money contracts. Interestingly, in two different studies, Rubinstein (1985b, 1994) found evidence that both supported and contradicted these results.

In general, any violation of the assumptions upon which the Black–Scholes model is based could lead to misvaluation of the option contract. Figlewski (1989a) noted that market imperfections (brokerage fees, bid-ask spreads, and inflexible position sizes) can create differences between option values and prices. He cautioned that Black–Scholes values should be viewed as approximations, best suited for comparing prices of different contracts. Black (1989a) observed that other conditions of the model are almost certain to be violated in practice—for example, that the risk-free rate and volatility level remain constant until the expiration date. Cornell (2010) notes that misestimations of future stock price dynamics due to inappropriate historical volatilities can lead to option misvaluations.

16.3 OPTION VALUATION: EXTENSIONS

The preceding discussion has concentrated on the valuation of European-style call options having a non-dividend-paying stock as the underlying asset. Many other situations exist for which options need to be valued.

16.3.1 Valuing European-Style Put Options

The put-call-spot parity model of Chapter 14 held that the value of a European-style put on a non-dividend-paying security should be equivalent to a portfolio short in the security while long in both a call option and a Treasury bill having a face value equal to the joint exercise price X. With continuous discounting for the T-bill, this relationship can be expressed:

$$P_0 = C_0 + X(e^{-(RFT)T}) - S$$

so, if we know the prices of the security, the call option, and the T-bill, we can solve for the value of the put option. Inserting the Black–Scholes value for C into this expression, we have:

$$P_0 = [SN(d_1) - X(e^{-(RFR)T})N(d_2)] + X(e^{-(RFR)T}) - S$$

which can be manipulated to equal:

16.4
$$P_0 = X(e^{-(RFR)T})N(-d_2) - SN(-d_1)$$

where all the notation is the same as before. Equation 16.4 is the Black–Scholes put option valuation model.

As shown in the last column of Exhibit 16.7, the value of the put will increase with higher levels of X but decline with an increase in S because of the effect these movements have on the contract's intrinsic value. Like the call option, the put's value benefits from an increase in σ since this increases the likelihood that the contract will finish in the money. Also, an increase in the risk-free rate reduces the present value of X, which hurts the holder of the put who receives the exercise price if the contract is executed. Finally, the sign of $\delta P/\delta T$ could be either positive or negative, depending on the trade-off between the longer time over which the security price could move down and the reduced present value of the exercise price received by the seller at expiration.

In the preceding valuation example, we had the following inputs: $S = 40$, $X = 40$, $T =$ one year, $RFR = 9$ percent, and $\sigma = 0.30$. With these assumptions, d_1 and d_2 still are

0.45 and 0.15, respectively, but now we need to compute $N(-0.45) = 1 - 0.6736 = 0.3264$ and $N(-0.15) = 1 - 0.5596 = 0.4404$. Thus:

$$P_0 = 40(e^{-0.09})(0.4404) - 40(0.3264) = \$3.04$$

Finally, the hedge ratio for the put option in this model is $[N(d_1) - 1]$, which in this case is -0.3264 and indicates that the put option's value will *decrease* by approximately 33 cents for every dollar *increase* in S.

16.3.2 Valuing Options on Dividend-Bearing Securities

We learned earlier that the put-call parity relationship required an adjustment when the underlying asset paid a dividend because this payment reduces the asset's market value. Other than the tax implications, the underlying asset's owner should not lose any overall net worth with the payment of the dividend. However, the call option owner will not receive the dividend; therefore, the reduction in the present value of the stock will diminish the value of his derivative position. So, dividends become a sixth factor in the option valuation process.

We can modify the original Black–Scholes valuation model to incorporate dividend payments in two ways. The first is to simply reduce the current share price by the present value of the dividends paid during the option's life and then using this amount in place of the actual stock price—that is, replace S in the model with $S' = S - PV(\text{dividends})$. For the one-year, at-the-money call option with an exercise price of $40 that we saw earlier, assume that a dividend payment of $1 is made in six months, with another $1 paid just prior to expiration. The continuously compounded risk-free rate and volatility factors were 9 percent and 30 percent, respectively, so:

$$S' = 40 - (1)e^{-(0.09)(0.5)} - (1)e^{-(0.09)(1.0)} = 38.13$$

When inserted into the formulas for d_1 and d_2, S' generates values of 0.29 and -0.01, respectively.

With these inputs, the Black–Scholes valuation then becomes:

$$C_0 = (38.13)N(0.29) - (40)e^{-0.09}N(-0.01) = (38.13)(0.6141) - (36.56)(0.4960) = \$5.28$$

This amount can be compared to the $6.49 value for an otherwise identical call on a non-dividend-paying share that we estimated earlier. The reduction in option value ($1.21) is not as great as the present value of the dividends ($1.87) because the option might have expired out of the money even without the dividend payment. Also, the hedge ratio in the formula is reduced from its original level of 0.6736 to 0.6141.

The second approach involves modifying the form of the model rather than the stock price input. This requires expressing the dividend in continuous *yield* form, defined as the annual payment divided by the current stock price. Merton (1973b) showed that the Black–Scholes model can then be rewritten as:

16.5
$$C_0 = (e^{-(D)T})SN(d_1) - X(e^{-(RFR)T})N(d_2)$$

with:

$$d_1 = [\ln((e^{-(D)T})S/X) + (RFR + 0.5\sigma^2)[T]] \div (\sigma[T]^{1/2})$$

and:

$$d_2 = d_1 - \sigma[T]^{1/2}$$

where:

$D = $ annualized dividend yield

The yield appears as a "discount" factor to the current stock value in two places in these equations. If we set $S' = (e^{-(D)T})S$, this second dividend adjustment is just a continuous version of the first.

Extending the original example, we now have six factors: $S = 40$, $X = 40$, $T =$ one year, $RFR = 9$ percent, $\sigma = 30$ percent, and $D = (2/40) = 5$ percent. Plugging these into the model, we get values of 0.28 for d_1 and -0.02 for d_2 so that:

$$C_0 = (e^{-0.05})(40)N(0.28) - (e^{-0.09})(40)N(-0.02)$$

$$= (38.05)(0.6103) - (36.56)(0.4920) = \$5.23$$

This amount differs from the first adjustment process because the assumption of a continuous dividend stream does not match t how these payments are actually made.

Garman and Kohlhagen (1983) and Biger and Hull (1983) have shown that the FX options considered earlier can be valued using this dividend-adjusted Black–Scholes model. Recalling that an exchange-traded currency call option is the right to buy the foreign (non-USD) currency with U.S. dollars, the risk-free rates in the foreign and domestic markets can be expressed RFR_f and RFR_d, respectively. Equation 16.5 can then be used to value a currency call option when the exchange rate is quoted on a direct basis (USD/FC) using RFR_f in place of the dividend yield, D.

16.3.3 Valuing American-Style Options

The preceding discussion considered European-style options. If the contract had been American style—that is, with its exercise not limited to the expiration date—how would the valuation process change? The possibility of early exercise makes the derivation of an exact closed-form analog to the Black–Scholes equation an elusive goal. Instead, Roll (1977b), Geske (1979), and Whaley (1981) have designed elaborate approximation procedures for estimating the value of American-style calls. Further, Johnson (1983) and Barone-Adesi and Whaley (1986) have taken different approaches to address the issue of American put valuation.

We consider several fundamental properties of these models. Most important is that an American put or call has to be at least as valuable as its European-style counterpart because, by definition, the American option gives the holder more choices. Letting C_a and C_e represent the values of American and European calls, this relationship can be stated as:

$$S \geq C_a(S, T, X) \geq C_e(S, T, X) \geq \max[0, S - Xe^{-(RFR)T}] \geq \max[0, S - X] \geq 0$$

This expression says that (1) the American call is at least as valuable as the European contract, (2) neither call can be more valuable than the underlying stock, and (3) both contracts are at least as valuable as their intrinsic values, expressed on both a nominal and a discounted basis. For puts, a similar boundary condition would be:

$$X \geq P_a(S, T, X) \geq P_e(S, T, X) \geq \max[0, Xe^{-(RFR)T} - S] \geq 0$$

For a stock that does not pay dividends, C_a and C_e will be equal to one another. Prior to expiration, the preceding relationship shows that $C_a(S, T, X) - \max[0, S - X] > 0$, with $\max[0, S - X]$ being the value the investor would extract from the option's exercise. Therefore, without the reduction in the stock's price caused by the dividend payment, an investor wishing to liquidate his American call position would sell it rather than exercise it so as not to surrender the contract's time premium.[7]

---

[7]For a complete development of these boundary conditions, see Chance and Brooks (2016).

When the stock pays dividends, this situation changes. Suppose an investor holds an American call option on a stock just before a dividend payment. On the ex-dividend date—call it Date t—the value of the stock will decline by about the dividend amount, leaving $S_t = S_{t-1} - (\text{dividend})_t$, assuming that no new information impacted the share's value. The value of the option will decline as well, from $C(S_{t-1})$ to $C(S_t)$. Selling the contract on the day prior to the ex-date will not be possible since rational buyers know what will soon happen. So, the investor must decide on Date $t - 1$ whether to exercise the contract and receive only the intrinsic value of $\max[0, S_{t-1} - X]$. This is the proper choice if the loss of the option's time premium is less than $C(S_{t-1}) - C(S_t)$, which will likely occur when the option is close to maturity and the dividend is large. Because the American option allows the investor this choice when the European contract does not, we must have $C_a > C_e$ for almost all cases.

Deciding to exercise a put prior to maturity does not depend on the presence of dividends. Instead, the relevant issue is the limited liability of the stock itself. Suppose an investor holds an American put on a nearly bankrupt company. The contract has an exercise price of $50, has three months to expiration, and the stock is selling for $1. In this case, the option holder would evaluate the trade-off between exercising the contract today to capture the $49 intrinsic value or waiting three months and hoping the stock becomes worthless, making the put worth $50. Depending on the discount rate, it is likely that she will exercise now.

On the other hand, the European put does not offer the investor this choice. Because the stock's expected return is positive, the price of the non-dividend-paying stock is expected to be higher in three months, thereby reducing the expiration date value of the contract below $49. Without the ability to exercise the put prior to expiration, the European put sometimes can be worth less than its intrinsic value, which is most likely to occur at extremely low values of S and large values of T. The preceding boundary condition shows that P_e must only be greater than the discounted version of the intrinsic value formula, or $\max[0, Xe^{-(RFR)T} - S]$. These relationships are illustrated in Exhibit 16.11.

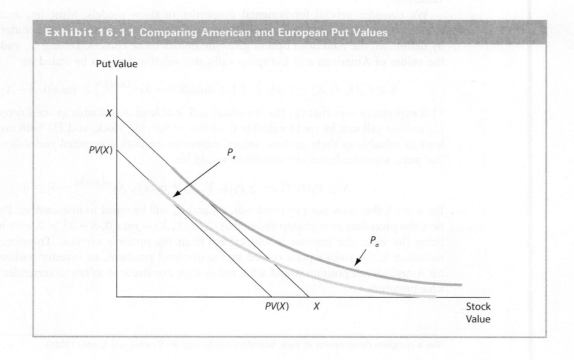

Exhibit 16.11 Comparing American and European Put Values

16.4 OPTION TRADING STRATEGIES

Chapter 14 highlighted two ways in which investors use options. First, the asymmetrical payoff structures they possess as stand-alone positions allow investors to isolate the benefits of an anticipated change in the value of an underlying security while limiting the downside risk of an adverse price movement. Second, we also saw that put options could be used in conjunction with an existing portfolio to limit the portfolio's loss potential. After revisiting this protective put application for individual stock holdings, we will now consider a **covered call** option strategy as another method for modifying the risk or enhancing the return of an existing equity position.

This section also emphasizes a third way in which options are used: in *combination* with one another to create customized payoff distributions that do not exist in more fundamental securities, like stocks or bonds. The equity collar application that concluded Chapter 14 is a good example of this type of option strategy. In designing such combinations, the investor usually attempts to exploit a very specific view about future economic conditions. To develop these strategies, we will return to the hypothetical example of SAS Corporation, which has exchange-traded common stock, as well as call and put options. Prices for SAS stock and six different derivatives having the same expiration date are reproduced in Exhibit 16.12.

16.4.1 Protective Put Options

Although the protective put strategy is most often used to provide insurance for price declines in entire portfolios, Brown and Statman (1987) have noted that the technique can also be employed with individual equity positions. To see how this "insured stock" concept works, consider an investor who holds SAS stock in her portfolio but is concerned that an unexpected downturn in the company's product sales may lead to a decline in the value of her position. To hedge against this exposure, she decides to purchase an at-the-money put option on SAS shares, meaning that she would spend $3.67 to buy Put #2 with an exercise price of $40. If at expiration the price of SAS had declined below $40, the put option would pay her the difference.

The effect of this acquisition is shown in Exhibit 16.13, which lists the expiration date value of the combined protective put position for a range of possible SAS prices. As noted earlier, the primary benefit of the insured stock strategy is that it preserves the investor's upside potential from rising share prices but limits her losses when share prices fall. In this case, the at-the-money put insures her against any losses beyond the $3.67 initial put premium. This is the same outcome the investor would have if, instead of the put-protected SAS shares, she had held an at-the-money SAS call option and a T-bill; the risk-free security provides the safety

Exhibit 16.12 Hypothetical SAS Corporation Stock and Option Prices

Instrument		Exercise Price ($)	Market Price ($)	Intrinsic Value ($)	Time Premium ($)
Stock:		—	40.00	—	—
Call:	#1	35.00	8.07	5.00	3.07
	#2	40.00	5.24	0.00	5.24
	#3	45.00	3.24	0.00	3.24
Put:	#1	35.00	1.70	0.00	1.70
	#2	40.00	3.67	0.00	3.67
	#3	45.00	6.47	5.00	1.47

Exhibit 16.13 Expiration Date Value of a Protective Put Position

Potential SAS Stock Value	Value of Put Option	Cost of Put Option	Net Protective Put Position
20	$(40 - 20) = 20$	-3.67	$(20 + 20) - 3.67 = 36.33$
25	$(40 - 25) = 15$	-3.67	$(25 + 15) - 3.67 = 36.33$
30	$(40 - 30) = 10$	-3.67	$(30 + 10) - 3.67 = 36.33$
35	$(40 - 35) = 5$	-3.67	$(35 + 5) - 3.67 = 36.33$
40	0	-3.67	$(40 + 0) - 3.67 = 36.33$
45	0	-3.67	$(45 + 0) - 3.67 = 41.33$
50	0	-3.67	$(50 + 0) - 3.67 = 46.33$
55	0	-3.67	$(55 + 0) - 3.67 = 51.33$
60	0	-3.67	$(60 + 0) - 3.67 = 56.33$

and the call option provides the potential for price appreciation. Recall from the put-call parity model of Chapter 14 that this result was shown as $S_0 + P_{0,T} = C_{0,T} + PV(X)$, or:

$$(\text{Long Stock}) + (\text{Long Put}) = (\text{Long Call}) + (\text{Long T-bill})$$

To extend the insurance interpretation of the protective put, Exhibit 16.14 shows the expiration date profits (net of the initial $40 purchase price for the investor's SAS shares) for using each of three put options. To interpret this display, if SAS shares are priced at $40 on the expiration date, for Protective Put #2 (the at-the-money contract), the investor's combined position will be worth $36.33, giving her a net loss of $3.67. The main thing about this illustration is the trade-off it shows between the risk and reward potential of the various positions. Put #1 has the smallest front-end expense, but its $35 exercise price forces the investor to bear the

Exhibit 16.14 Terminal Net Profits to Three Protective Put Positions

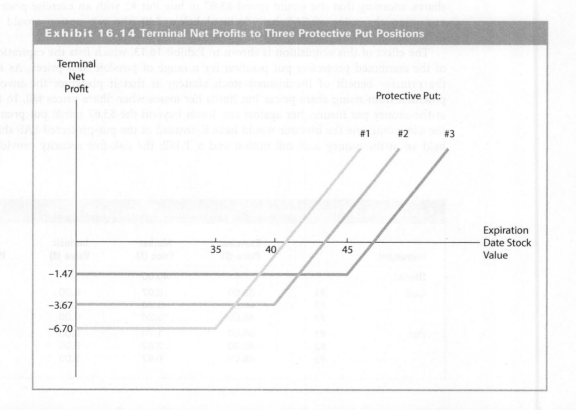

first $5 of SAS stock price declines; this $5 "deductible" leads to the largest potential loss of three positions at $6.70 ($= 1.70 + 5.00$). However, for this degree of self-insuring on the part of the investor, Protective Put #1 has, at $41.70 ($= 35.00 + 6.70$), the smallest breakeven price. Conversely, Put #3, with an exercise price above the current share value, does not break even until SAS prices reach $46.47 but has a maximum possible loss of only $1.47 and therefore provides the best downside protection.

16.4.2 Covered Call Options

Another popular way to alter the payoff structure of an equity position involves the sale of call options. When investors sell call options based on an underlying position they own, they are said to be *writing* covered calls. Usually, the purpose of this strategy is to generate additional income for a stock holding that is not expected to change in value much over the near term. By selling a call, an investor receives the premium from the option contract to bolster an otherwise small (or negative) return. The danger is that the value of the stock position rises above the exercise price by the end of the contract's life, causing the shares to be called away.

Suppose now that our investor believes that over the next few months, the value of her SAS stock will neither rise nor fall appreciably. She decides not to insure her position against losses but, instead, to increase the cash flow of the investment by selling an at-the-money call option (Call #2). In exchange for granting the contract buyer the right to purchase her stock for $40 at the expiration date, she receives an immediate payment of $5.24. The expiration date values for the covered call position are listed in Exhibit 16.15. The construction of the terminal profit diagram—once again net of the current SAS share price—is depicted in Exhibit 16.16.

Both of these displays indicate that the expiration date payoff to the covered call position is comparable in form to that of a short position in a put option. Once again, this can be seen from the put-call parity condition as follows:

$$(\text{Long Stock}) + (\text{Short Call}) = (\text{Long T-bill}) + (\text{Short Put})$$

There are two dimensions to the price risk inherent in this strategy. First, if by the option expiration date SAS stock has risen above $40, the investor will be forced to sell her shares for less than they are actually worth. However, this will represent a lost opportunity only at prices above $45.24, or the exercise price plus the initial call premium. Second, if SAS stock experiences a decline in value, her potential loss is not hedged beyond the $5.24 in premium income that she received for selling the call; after prices fall beyond $31.09 ($= 40 - 5.24 - 3.67$), she would have been better off purchasing the at-the-money protective put option. Thus, to be profitable, the covered call strategy requires that the investor guess correctly that share values remain reasonably close to their present levels.

Exhibit 16.15 Expiration Date Value of a Covered Call Position

Potential SAS Stock Value	Value of Call Option	Proceeds from Call Option	Net Covered Call Position
20	0	5.24	$(20 - \ \ 0) + 5.24 = 25.24$
25	0	5.24	$(25 - \ \ 0) + 5.24 = 30.24$
30	0	5.24	$(30 - \ \ 0) + 5.24 = 35.24$
35	0	5.24	$(35 - \ \ 0) + 5.24 = 40.24$
40	0	5.24	$(40 - \ \ 0) + 5.24 = 45.24$
45	$-(45 - 40) = \ \ -5$	5.24	$(45 - \ \ 5) + 5.24 = 45.24$
50	$-(50 - 40) = -10$	5.24	$(50 - 10) + 5.24 = 45.24$
55	$-(55 - 40) = -15$	5.24	$(55 - 15) + 5.24 = 45.24$
60	$-(60 - 40) = -20$	5.24	$(60 - 20) + 5.24 = 45.24$

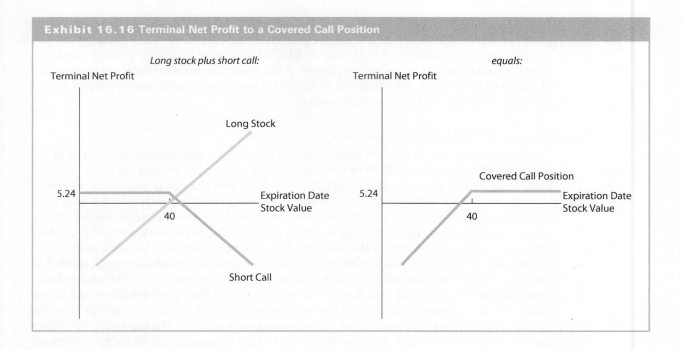

Exhibit 16.16 Terminal Net Profit to a Covered Call Position

16.4.3 Straddles, Strips, and Straps

A **straddle** is the simultaneous purchase (or sale) of a call and a put option with the same underlying asset, exercise price, and expiration date. A long straddle requires the purchase of the put and the call, while a short straddle sells both contracts. The long straddle gives the investor a combination that will appreciate in value whether stock prices rise or fall in the future. Buying two options increases the initial cost, meaning that stock price movements must be more pronounced than if the investor had predicted changes in a single direction. In this sense, a straddle is a *volatility* play—the buyer expects stock prices to move strongly one way or the other, while the seller hopes for lower-than-normal volatility.

Assume that an investor who does not hold SAS stock purchases a put and a call, each with an exercise price of $40. The cost of this purchase will be the combined prices of Call #2 and Put #2, or $8.91 (= 5.24 + 3.67). Because the terminal values of the options are max[0, S_T − 40] and max[0, 40 − S_T], respectively, the potential expiration date profits to the straddle position (net of the initial cost, unadjusted for the time value differential) are shown in Exhibit 16.17. These are illustrated in Exhibit 16.18, which also depicts the profit to the seller of the straddle. The breakeven points on this graph occur at $31.09 (= 40 − 8.91) and $48.91 (= 40 + 8.91).

The expiration date values to the long and short positions are mirror images of each other. The buyer of the straddle is hoping for a dramatic event—such as a company-specific technological breakthrough or the impending judgment in a major lawsuit—that will either increase or decrease the stock price from its present $40 by at least $8.91. Conversely, the best result for the straddle seller is for SAS stock to continue to trade at its current price through the expiration date (that is, no volatility at all) so that both options expire worthless. The seller's position demonstrates that it is possible to make money in the stock market even when prices do not change.

The long straddle position assumes implicitly that the investor has no intuition about the likely direction of future stock price movements. A slight modification is overweighting either the put or the call holding to emphasize a directional belief. A long *strap* position is the purchase of two calls and one put with the same exercise price, suggesting an investor who thinks

Exhibit 16.17 Expiration Date Profits to a Long Straddle Position

SAS Stock Price at Expiration	Value of Calls	Value of Puts	Cost of Options	Net Profit
20.00	0.00	20.00	−8.91	11.09
25.00	0.00	15.00	−8.91	6.09
30.00	0.00	10.00	−8.91	1.09
35.00	0.00	5.00	−8.91	−3.91
40.00	0.00	0.00	−8.91	−8.91
45.00	5.00	0.00	−8.91	−3.09
50.00	10.00	0.00	−8.91	1.09
55.00	15.00	0.00	−8.91	6.09
60.00	20.00	0.00	−8.91	11.09

Exhibit 16.18 The Straddle Illustrated

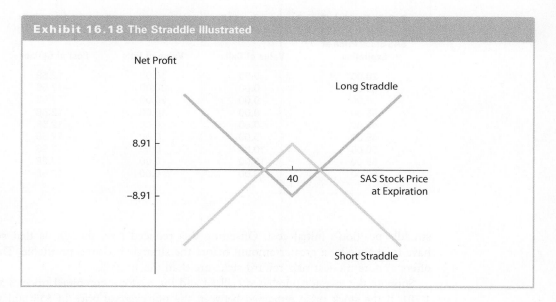

stock prices are more likely to increase. An investor with a more bearish view could create a long *strip* position by purchasing two puts and only one call. The terminal profits to both of these combinations are listed in Exhibit 16.19, again using of the two at-the-money SAS contracts. Panel A of the exhibit shows that for the higher up-front payment of $14.15 [= (2 × 5.24) + 3.67], the strap will accelerate the profit in a rising market relative to the straddle. The settlement payment when SAS stock is above $40 on the expiration date is twice as great because the strap has doubled the investor's number of calls. The gross payoff when the price falls below $40 remains the same; however, the net amount received is considerably lower because the extra contract the investor purchased would then be out of the money. The net terminal value of the strip position tells a similar story, only with the acceleration of the profit generated by falling stock prices.

16.4.4 Strangles

One final variation on the straddle is an option combination known as a **strangle**, which also involves the simultaneous purchase or sale of a call and a put on the same underlying security with the same expiration date. The options used in the strangle do not have the same exercise price. Instead, they are selected so that both are out of the money, which reduces the original

Exhibit 16.19 Expiration Date Profits to Long Strap and Long Strip Positions

A. Strap Position (Two Calls and One Put)

SAS Stock Price at Expiration	Value of Calls	Value of Puts	Cost of Options	Net Profit
20.00	0.00	20.00	−14.15	5.85
25.00	0.00	15.00	−14.15	0.85
30.00	0.00	10.00	−14.15	−4.15
35.00	0.00	5.00	−14.15	−9.15
40.00	0.00	0.00	−14.15	−14.15
45.00	10.00	0.00	−14.15	−4.15
50.00	20.00	0.00	−14.15	5.85
55.00	30.00	0.00	−14.15	15.85
60.00	40.00	0.00	−14.15	25.85

B. Strip Position (Two Puts and One Call)

SAS Stock Price at Expiration	Value of Calls	Value of Puts	Cost of Options	Net Profit
20.00	0.00	40.00	−12.58	27.42
25.00	0.00	30.00	−12.58	17.42
30.00	0.00	20.00	−12.58	7.42
35.00	0.00	10.00	−12.58	−2.58
40.00	0.00	0.00	−12.58	−12.58
45.00	5.00	0.00	−12.58	−7.58
50.00	10.00	0.00	−12.58	−2.58
55.00	15.00	0.00	−12.58	2.42
60.00	20.00	0.00	−12.58	7.42

straddle position's initial cost. Offsetting this reduced cost, though, is that stock prices will have to change by a greater amount before the strangle becomes profitable. Thus, the strangle offers a more modest risk–reward structure than the straddle.

Suppose the investor purchased Call #3 and Put #1 for a combined price of $4.94 (= 3.24 + 1.70). If the stock price remained between the put exercise price of $35 and the call exercise price of $45, both contracts would expire worthless and the investor would lose his entire investment. Prices would have to decline to $30.06 (= 35 − 4.94) or increase to $49.94 (= 45 + 4.94) before the investor would break even on the position. Exhibit 16.20 shows that these breakeven points for the strangle are outside those for the straddle, described earlier. Thus, among the set of "volatility bets," the strangle costs less to implement than the straddle but requires greater stock price movement before it generates a positive return.

16.4.5 Spreads

As described by Black (1975), option **spreads** are the purchase of one contract and the sale of another, where the options are alike except for one distinguishing characteristic. In a *money* spread, the investor would sell an out-of-the-money call and purchase an in-the-money call on the same stock and expiration date. Alternatively, a *calendar* (or time) spread requires the purchase and sale of two calls—or two puts—with the same exercise price but different expiration dates. Option spreads are often used when one contract is thought to be misvalued relative to the other. For instance, if an investor determines that a call option with an exercise price of X_1 and an expiration date T is selling at a price that is too high, he can short it, thereby speculating on an eventual correction. However, if an increase in the overall market

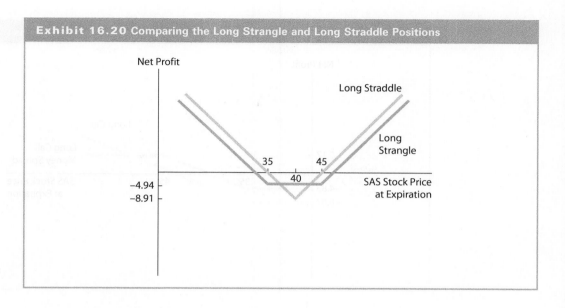

Exhibit 16.20 Comparing the Long Strangle and Long Straddle Positions

occurs before this contract-specific correction, he stands to lose a great deal because the short call position has unlimited liability. Thus, when he sells the first option, he can hedge some or all of the risk by buying a call with an exercise price of X_2 also expiring at T.

Returning to the data for SAS options, assume the investor purchases the in-the-money call (Call #1) and sells the contract that is out of the money (Call #3). This requires a net cash outlay of $4.83 ($= 8.07 - 3.24$). At the common expiration date, three price ranges should be considered. If SAS stock settles below $35, both options will expire worthless. With an SAS price above $45, both contracts will be exercised, meaning that the investor must sell at $45 the share he bought for $35, leaving a $10 gross payoff. Finally, if SAS prices fall between the two exercise prices, the option the investor owns will be in the money while the contract he sold will not. This situation is summarized by the net profit calculations shown in Exhibit 16.21.

This is sometimes called a *bull* money spread because it will be profitable when stock prices rise. With the initial cost of $4.83, the investor's breakeven point occurs when the stock price rises to $39.83 ($= 35 + 4.83$). His benefit stops increasing if SAS shares reach $45, or where the short position in Call #3 becomes a liability. Exhibit 16.22 contrasts this situation with the outright purchase of the in-the-money call. This contract costs $8.07 initially, leading to

Exhibit 16.21 Expiration Date Profits to a Bull Money Spread Position

SAS Stock Price at Expiration	Value of Call #1	Value of Call #3	Cost of Options	Net Profit
20.00	0.00	0.00	−4.83	−4.83
25.00	0.00	0.00	−4.83	−4.83
30.00	0.00	0.00	−4.83	−4.83
35.00	0.00	0.00	−4.83	−4.83
40.00	5.00	0.00	−4.83	0.17
45.00	10.00	0.00	−4.83	5.17
50.00	15.00	−5.00	−4.83	5.17
55.00	20.00	−10.00	−4.83	5.17
60.00	25.00	−15.00	−4.83	5.17

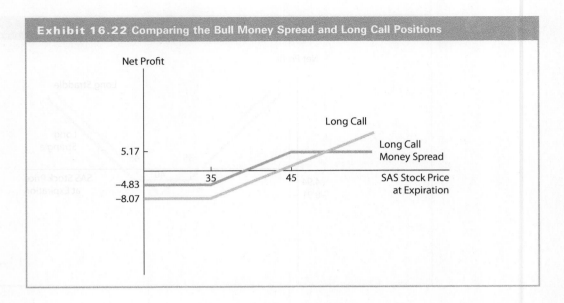

Exhibit 16.22 Comparing the Bull Money Spread and Long Call Positions

the higher breakeven price of $43.07. It would not limit the upside profit potential, however, so once a share price of $48.24 is reached [= 45 + (8.07 − 4.83)], it would become the preferable alternative. Thus, in exchange for a lower initial purchase price, the bull spread investor is giving up the benefits of rising SAS prices after some point—a strategy that makes sense only if he expects the share price to settle within a fairly narrow range.

The profit for a *bear* money spread (the purchase of Call #3 and the sale of Call #1) is the opposite of that for the bull money spread. Consequently, a long bear spread position could be used by an investor who believed stock prices might decline but did not want to be short in the stock. A spread transaction also can be created using put options. For instance, suppose a new investor undertakes the simultaneous purchase of Put #3 and sale of Put #1. Her net cost to acquire the position would be $4.77 (= 6.47 − 1.70), which would then generate the terminal profits displayed in Exhibit 16.23. If SAS stock settled at $45 or higher, both puts would be

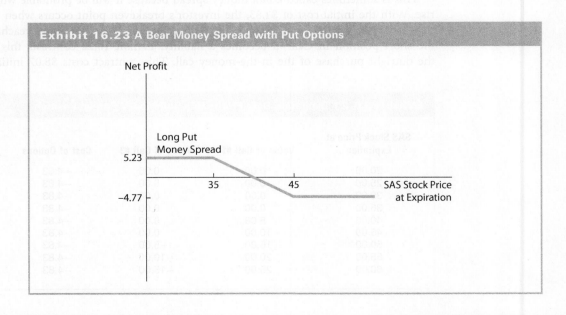

Exhibit 16.23 A Bear Money Spread with Put Options

worthless. If the expiration date share price was $35 or less, both options would be in the money, leaving the investor with a net position of $5.23 ($= 45 - 35 - 4.77$).

16.4.6 Range Forwards

In Chapter 14, we discussed an *equity collar* as a tool for an investor to protect her stock portfolio from adverse movements while allowing for some upside gain potential. We saw that although the equity collar had some of the same attributes as a forward contract (for example, no upfront premium expense), it was actually a combination of two options—the purchase of an out-of-the money put and sale of an out-of-the-money call. Equity collars are an example of a strategy also known as **range** (or flexible) **forwards**.

To see how range forward positions might be used in a different context, assume that the treasurer of a U.S. multinational corporation knows today that he will have a bill for imported goods that must be paid in three months. This bill, requiring payment of 1,000,000 Swiss francs, means the dollar-based company must buy the francs it needs and offers a classic opportunity to use derivatives to hedge the FX exposure.

The treasurer obtains prices for several CHF forward and option contracts, as listed in Exhibit 16.24, which are stated on a direct (USD/CHF) basis. The treasurer could lock in a three-month forward rate of USD 0.67/CHF without cost in two ways. First, he could commit to a long position in the CHF forward with a contract amount of CHF 1,000,000. Second, he could buy the CHF call option struck at USD 0.67/CHF and pay for it by selling the CHF put at the same exercise rate. We saw earlier that buying a call and selling a put with the same exercise rate is equivalent to a long forward position and would generate a zero-cost forward ($C_0 = P_0$) when the joint exercise rate is equal to the prevailing forward rate.

As a third alternative, what if the treasurer (1) bought the 0.70 call for USD $0.004 per franc and (2) sold the 0.64 put for the same price? Once again, this would be a costless combination of options; however, since the two options do not have the same exercise price, this combination is not equivalent to the actual forward—it is a range forward. At the expiration date, one of three things will happen: (1) If the spot FX rate is greater than USD 0.70/CHF, the treasurer will exercise his call and buy francs at that level; (2) if the spot FX rate is less than USD 0.64/ CHF, the dealer to whom the treasurer sold the put will force him to buy francs for USD 0.64 per franc; and (3) if the spot FX rate is between these extremes, both options will finish out of the money and the treasurer will buy the required currency at the regular market price. This payoff scheme is contrasted with the regular forward contract in Exhibit 16.25.

If the treasurer takes a long position in the regular forward contract, he will buy his francs at USD 0.67/CHF, regardless of the prevailing exchange rate in three months. Although he is protected against a weakening dollar, he cannot benefit if the domestic currency strengthens.

Exhibit 16.24 Hypothetical CHF Derivative Prices and Terms

Derivative	Contract/Exercise Price (USD/CHF)	Expiration	CHF Amount	Price (USD/CHF)
Forward:	0.67	3 months	1,000,000	—
Calls:	0.64	3 months	1,000,000	0.034
	0.67	3 months	1,000,000	0.015
	0.70	3 months	1,000,000	0.004
Puts:	0.64	3 months	1,000,000	0.004
	0.67	3 months	1,000,000	0.015
	0.70	3 months	1,000,000	0.034

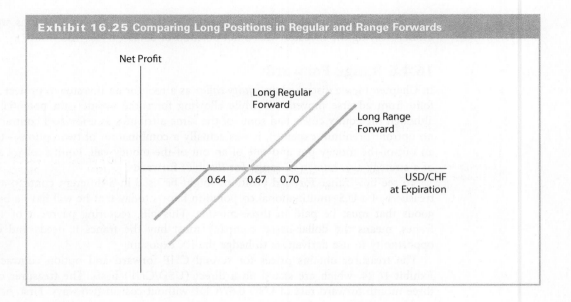

Exhibit 16.25 Comparing Long Positions in Regular and Range Forwards

With a long position in the range forward, though, in exchange for worse FX insurance—namely, a maximum purchase USD 0.70/CHF—he could pay as little as USD 0.64/CHF if the dollar gets stronger. Finally, many zero-cost range forwards could be created. For any desired out-of-the money call option, there will be an out-of-the-money put at some exercise price that has the same premium. In fact, the actual forward contract can be viewed as a zero-cost range forward for which the put and the call options are both struck at USD 0.67/CHF.

16.5 Other Option Applications

Beyond their use as stand-alone contracts, options also appear in myriad additional forms, either embedded into other security structures or in specialized arrangements on their own. In this section, we consider an example of each type of application.

16.5.1 Convertible Bonds

A convertible bond can be viewed as a prepackaged portfolio containing two distinct securities: a regular bond and an option to exchange the bond for a prespecified number of shares of the issuing firm's common stock. It represents a hybrid investment involving elements of both the debt and the equity markets. From the investor's standpoint, there are both advantages and disadvantages to this packaging. The buyer receives equity-like returns with a "guaranteed" terminal payoff equal to the bond's face value, but he must also pay the option premium embedded in the price of the security. Lummer and Riepe (1993) argue that the risk–return dynamics convertible bonds offer are sufficiently unique as to merit their own asset class. Arak and Martin (2005) note that the issuer of a convertible bond increases the company's leverage while providing a potential source of equity financing in the future.

Consider the 2.375 percent coupon convertible bond issued by Dish Network (DISH), the broadcast satellite television provider whose stock trades in the OTC market. Details for this security, which is scheduled to mature in March 2024, are highlighted in Exhibit 16.26. The bond pays interest semiannually on March 15 and September 15 and has a composite default rating of B. The bond issue has $1,000 million outstanding and is convertible until maturity. At the time of this report (July 15, 2017), the listed price of the bond was 108.256 percent of

Exhibit 16.26 Details of Dish Network's Convertible Bond Issue

DISH 2 $\frac{3}{8}$ 03/15/24 $ ↑ **108.256**   +1.76   Yld 1.086
                              As of 14 Jul   Vol 4.0MM   Source TRMT

| DISH 2 $\frac{3}{8}$ 03/15/24 Corp | Settings ▾ | | Page 1/11 | Security Description: Convertible |
| | | 94) Notes ▤ | 95) Buy | 96) Sell |

25) Convertible Bond   26) Underlying Description

Pages	Issuer Information		Identifiers	
11) Bond Info	Name	DISH NETWORK CORP	ID Number	AM8409501
12) Addtl Info	Industry	Cable & Satellite	CUSIP	25470MAC3
13) Convenants			ISIN	US25470MAC38
14) Guarantors	Convertible Information			
15) Bond Ratings	Mkt of Issue Priv Placement Convertible		Bond Ratings	
16) Identifiers	Country	US Currency USD		
17) Exchanges	Rank	Sr Unsecured Series 144A	Moody's	Ba3
18) Inv Parties			S&P	B–
19) Fees, Restrict	Conv Ratio 12.1630 Conv Price 82.2166		Fitch	BB–u
20) Schedules	Stock Tkr DISH US Stock Price 65.6500		Composite	B
21) Coupons	Parity 79.85 Premium 35.5740		Issuance & Trading	
Quick Links	Coupon 2.375000 Init Prem 32.50			
32) ALLQ Pricing	Type Fixed Freq S/A		Amt Issued/Outstanding	
33) QRD Quote Recap			USD	1,000,000.00 (M) /
34) TDH Trade Hist	Calc Type (49)CONVERTIBLE		USD	1,000,000.00 (M)
35) CACS Corp Action	Pricing Date	03/13/2017	Min Piece/Increment	
36) CF Prospectus	1st Coupon Date	09/15/2017		1,000.00 / 1,000.00
37) CN Sec News	Convertible Until	03/14/2024	Par Amount	1,000.00
38) HDS Holders	Maturity	03/15/2024	Book Runner	DB
39) VPRD Underly Info			Reporting	TRACE
40) OVCV Valuation				
66) Send Bond				

Australia 61 2 9777 8600   Brazil 5511 2395 9000   Europe 44 20 7330 7500   Germany 49 69 9204 1210   Hong Kong 852 2977 6000
Japan 81 3 3201 8900   Singapore 65 6212 1000   U.S. 1 212 318 2000   Copyright 2017 Bloomberg Finance L.P.
                                       SN 335716 CDT GMT–5:00 H698-5305-1 17-Jul-2017 09:48:57

par, and the price of DISH common stock was $65.65. This particular issue includes no other embedded option features (for example, call protection for the issuer, put protection for the investor).

As spelled out in the middle of Exhibit 16.26, each $1,000 face value of this bond can be converted into 12.1630 shares of DISH common stock. This statistic is called the instrument's **conversion ratio**. At the listed share price of $65.65, an investor exercising her conversion option would have received $798.50 (= 65.65 × 12.1630) worth of stock, an amount less than the bond's current market value. In fact, the **conversion parity price** (the common stock price at which immediate conversion would make sense) is equal to $89.00, which is the bond price of $1,082.56 divided by the conversion ratio of 12.1630. The prevailing market price of $65.65 is below this parity level, so the conversion option is currently out of the money. If the conversion parity price ever fell below the market price for the common stock, an astute investor could buy the bond and immediately exchange it into stock with a greater market value.

The **payback time**, or **breakeven, time**, measures how long the higher interest income from the convertible bond (compared to the dividend income from the common stock) must persist to make up for the difference between the price of the bond and its conversion value (the conversion premium). The calculation is as follows:

$$\text{Payback} = \frac{\text{Bond Price} - \text{Conversion Value}}{\text{Bond Income} - \text{Income from Equal Investment in Common Stock}}$$

The annual coupon payment on the Dish Network convertible bond is $23.75, while the firm does not pay a dividend to its stockholders. Thus, assuming that you sold the bond for 1,082.56 and used the proceeds to purchase 16.49 shares (= 1082.56/65.65) of DISH stock, the payback period would be:

$$\frac{\$1,082.56 - \$798.50}{\$23.75 - \$0} = 11.96 \text{ years}$$

This implies a point in the future considerably after when the bond matures in less than seven years, suggesting that investors are not likely to make back the conversion premium with the incremental cash flow from the bond alone.

It is also possible to calculate whether investors have properly valued the conversion option embedded in this bond. With a market price of $1,082.56, the DISH convertible's yield-to-maturity can be calculated as 1.086 percent, which is shown in the top line of Exhibit 16.26. Since the indicative yield on a DISH debt issue with no embedded options and the same credit rating (B) and maturity was 4.620 percent, the present value (or, flat price) of a "straight" fixed-income security with the same cash flows can be established by the process described in Chapter 12 for valuing a bond between coupon dates:

(1) *Value on last coupon date (3/15/17):*

$$867.03 = \sum_{t=1}^{14} \frac{11.875}{(1+.0462/2)^t} + \frac{1000}{(1+.0462/2)^{14}}$$

(2) *Total invoice value on 7/15/17:*

$$\$867.03 \times (1+.0462/2)^{(120/180)} = \$880.33$$

(3) *Flat price on 7/15/17:*

$$\$880.33 - [(23.75) \times (120/180)] = \$872.41$$

This means that the investor is actually paying $210.15, or $1,082.56 minus $872.41, for the convertibility feature in the bond. Using the Black–Scholes valuation model in Equation 16.3, a 6.667-year call option to buy *one* share of DISH stock at an exercise price of $89.00 (the conversion parity value) is equal to $12.237.[8] Thus, the fair value of the investor's conversion option must only be $148.83 (= 12.1630 × $12.237). So, it appears on this valuation date, investors are overpaying by $61.32 for the right to convert their bond into DISH stock.

Exhibit 16.27 illustrates the value of a convertible bond in a more general way. Since it cannot sell for more than the company's assets, the value of the firm is an upper bound for the value of a convertible. The "straight" bond value component is relatively flat because, at some point, higher firm values do not benefit bondholders who receive only their promised payments. At fairly low firm values, the value of the bond drops off as bankruptcy becomes more likely. Conversion value rises directly with the value of the firm. The value of the convertible shows that when firm value is low, the convertible will act more like a bond, trading for only a slight premium over the bond value. Alternatively, when firm values are high, the convertible will act more like a stock, selling for only a slight premium over the conversion value. In the middle range—which is where the DISH bond falls—the convertible will trade as a hybrid security that acts somewhat like a bond and somewhat like a stock.

---

[8]This calculation assumes the following input values: $S = 65.65$, $X = 89.00$, $T = 6.667$, $RFR = 0.0214$, $\sigma = 0.2409$, and $D = 0.00$.

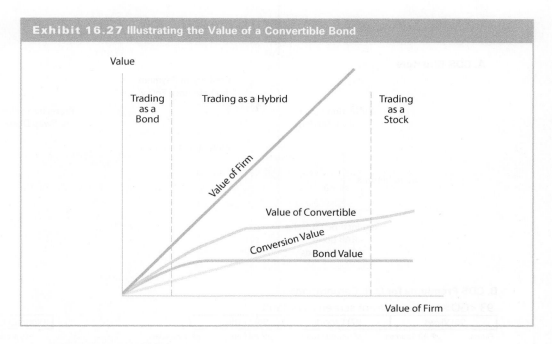

Exhibit 16.27 Illustrating the Value of a Convertible Bond

16.5.2 Credit Default Swaps

In Chapter 15, we introduced interest rate and equity index-linked swaps as arrangements where two counterparties agreed to make periodic future exchanges of cash flows based on different interest rates or stock returns. These agreements were considered forward contracts because (1) neither party paid an upfront premium, and (2) both parties were fully obligated to execute the cash flow exchange on the future settlement dates. Despite having a similar name, a **credit default swap (CDS)** is better regarded as an option-like arrangement because it does require one party to pay an initial premium (or a series of premiums) to the other, and any subsequent settlement payment is not obligatory but contingent on the occurrence of a future event.

To see how and why a CDS agreement is used, consider a fixed income portfolio manager who holds a bond issued by Company BAB, but he is concerned that the firm's financial position might be deteriorate to the point where the company defaults on its loan. In lieu of trying to sell the BAB bond outright, the manager could purchase a CDS on Company BAB from a swap dealer. The important feature of this arrangement is that, in exchange for a premium payment, the swap dealer will pay compensation to the manager in the event that BAB actually experiences an adverse credit event during the life of the CDS. So, the swap dealer has essentially sold default protection to the portfolio manager with the future protection payment being *contingent on the actual occurrence of a credit-related event*. As illustrated in the top panel of Exhibit 16.28, the *protection buyer* (the bond manager) pays a premium in exchange for the *protection seller's* (the swap dealer's) obligation to make a settlement payment if a credit-related event occurs to the *reference entity* (Company BAB) during the life of the agreement. The range of credit-related events covered by a CDS can include bankruptcy, failure to pay in a timely fashion, or a default-rating downgrade resulting from a corporate restructuring.

Suppose the manager holding the BAB bond decides to hedge his credit exposure with a CDS agreement. Assume further that he owns $5 million in par value of a security that matures in five years and that the swap premium is 160 basis points. This means he will pay an annual protection premium to the swap dealer of $80,000 ($= 0.016 \times 5,000,000$), usually in quarterly installments of $20,000. These payments continue until the expiration of the contract—assumed here to match the bond's maturity—or until a credit event occurs. If, for instance, Company BAB does default after two years, the swap dealer will be obligated to

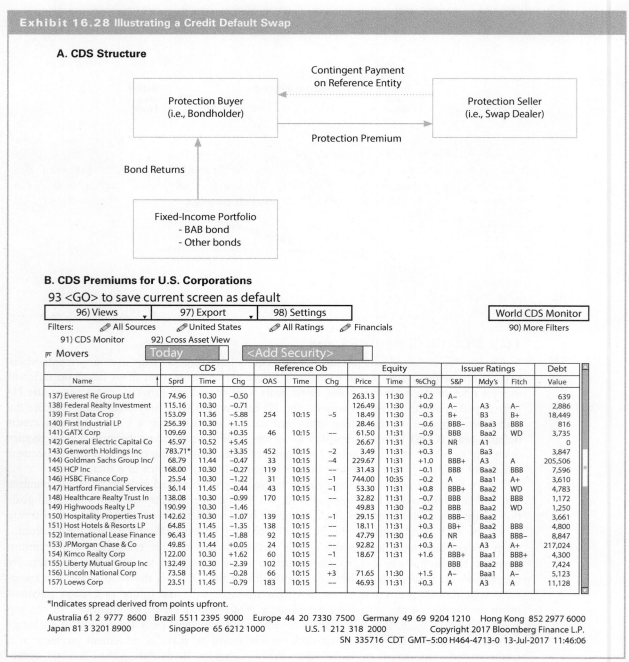

Exhibit 16.28 Illustrating a Credit Default Swap

A. CDS Structure

B. CDS Premiums for U.S. Corporations

93 <GO> to save current screen as default

| | 96) Views ▾ | 97) Export ▾ | 98) Settings | | World CDS Monitor |

Filters: ✎ All Sources ✎ United States ✎ All Ratings ✎ Financials   90) More Filters

91) CDS Monitor   92) Cross Asset View

▥ Movers   Today   <Add Security>

	CDS			Reference Ob			Equity			Issuer Ratings			Debt
Name	Sprd	Time	Chg	OAS	Time	Chg	Price	Time	%Chg	S&P	Mdy's	Fitch	Value
137) Everest Re Group Ltd	74.96	10.30	−0.50				263.13	11:30	+0.2	A−			639
138) Federal Realty Investment	115.16	10.30	−0.71				126.49	11:30	+0.9	A−	A3	A−	2,886
139) First Data Crop	153.09	11.36	−5.88	254	10:15	−5	18.49	11:30	−0.3	B+	B3	B+	18,449
140) First Industrial LP	256.39	10.30	+1.15				28.46	11:31	−0.6	BBB−	Baa3	BBB	816
141) GATX Corp	109.69	10.30	+0.35	46	10:15	─	61.50	11:31	−0.9	BBB	Baa2	WD	3,735
142) General Electric Capital Co	45.97	10.52	+5.45				26.67	11:31	+0.3	NR	A1		0
143) Genworth Holdings Inc	783.71*	10.30	+3.35	452	10:15	−2	3.49	11:31	+0.3	B	Ba3		3,847
144) Goldman Sachs Group Inc/	68.79	11.44	−0.47	33	10:15	−4	229.67	11:31	+1.0	BBB+	A3	A	205,506
145) HCP Inc	168.00	10.30	−0.27	119	10:15	─	31.43	11:31	−0.1	BBB	Baa2	BBB	7,596
146) HSBC Finance Corp	25.54	10.30	−1.22	31	10:15	−1	744.00	10:35	−0.2	A	Baa1	A+	3,610
147) Hartford Financial Services	36.14	11.45	−0.44	43	10:15	−1	53.30	11:31	+0.8	BBB+	Baa2	WD	4,783
148) Healthcare Realty Trust In	138.08	10.30	−0.99	170	10:15	─	32.82	11:31	−0.7	BBB	Baa2	BBB	1,172
149) Highwoods Realty LP	190.99	10.30	−1.46				49.83	11:30	−0.2	BBB	Baa2	WD	1,250
150) Hospitality Properties Trust	142.62	10.30	−1.07	139	10:15	−1	29.15	11:31	+0.2	BBB−	Baa2		3,661
151) Host Hotels & Resorts LP	64.85	11.45	−1.35	138	10:15	─	18.11	11:31	+0.3	BB+	Baa2	BBB	4,800
152) International Lease Finance	96.43	11.45	−1.88	92	10:15	─	47.79	11:30	+0.6	NR	Baa3	BBB−	8,847
153) JPMorgan Chase & Co	49.85	11.44	+0.05	24	10:15	─	92.82	11:31	+0.3	A−	A3	A+	217,024
154) Kimco Realty Corp	122.00	10.30	+1.62	60	10:15	−1	18.67	11:31	+1.6	BBB+	Baa1	BBB+	4,300
155) Liberty Mutual Group Inc	132.49	10.30	−2.39	102	10:15	─				BBB	Baa1	BBB	7,424
156) Lincoln National Corp	73.58	11.45	−0.28	66	10:15	+3	71.65	11:30	+1.5	A−	Baa1	A−	5,123
157) Loews Corp	23.51	11.45	−0.79	183	10:15	─	46.93	11:31	+0.3	A	A3	A	11,128

*Indicates spread derived from points upfront.

Australia 61 2 9777 8600   Brazil 5511 2395 9000   Europe 44 20 7330 7500   Germany 49 69 9204 1210   Hong Kong 852 2977 6000
Japan 81 3 3201 8900   Singapore 65 6212 1000   U.S. 1 212 318 2000   Copyright 2017 Bloomberg Finance L.P.
SN 335716 CDT GMT−5:00 H464-4713-0 13-Jul-2017 11:46:06

either purchase the BAB bond from the portfolio manager at par value or pay him the difference between par value and the post-default market value of the bond, depending on how the CDS contract is structured. If BAB bonds trade at 31 percent of their par value after default, the settlement payment would be $3,450,000 ($= [1.00 - 0.31] \times 5,000,000$). This credit event–contingent payment then cancels the remainder of the agreement. Thus, the bondholder in this example used the CDS contract to hedge his credit exposure to a specific bond by effectively paying the swap dealer to bear that risk for him.

Since we have seen that any risky bond yield can be decomposed into (1) the yield for a risk-free bond with the same maturity and (2) a credit spread (risk premium), it is easy to see that protection payer is using the CDS to transfer just the credit spread to the protection seller. That is, if the BAB bond does not default before maturity, the bond manager's net return on that position should be the risk-free rate. This means that the CDS premium should be approximately equal to the difference between the par yield on the risky bond and the par yield on a Treasury bond with comparable maturity. Hull and White (2003), Benzschawel and Corlu (2011), and Choudhry, Moskovic, and Wong (2014) demonstrate that this amount can be calculated from default probability estimates that allow for the estimation of the value of the cash flows expected to be paid by the risky bond. Panel B of Exhibit 16.28 lists five-year CDS premium prices for a number of U.S. corporations as of July 2017. These data emphasize the wide range of spreads that can occur for firms with credit ratings ranging from A (for example, 23.51 basis points for Loews Corp.) to B (for example, 783.71 basis points for Genworth Holdings). As in other credit markets, CDS spreads often increase dramatically for credit ratings that fall below investment grade status.

SUMMARY

- Along with forwards and futures, options represent another basic form of derivative contracting. Puts and calls are used either as standalone investments or as supplements to an existing collection of assets. They provide investors with a convenient way to restructure the risk–reward trade-off in a portfolio and create unique payoff structures by combining different options in various ways.

- Option straddles, for instance, allow the holder to take advantage of a view on the underlying asset's volatility while remaining neutral about the direction of future price movements. Range forward (or collars) can be viewed as a specifically chosen pair of options. We also demonstrate how option-like structures can be incorporated into other financial products, such as convertible bonds and credit default swaps.

- We consider how option contracts are valued in an efficient market. Each of three models we discuss—the two-state, the binomial, and the Black–Scholes—is based on the same three-step evolution. The first step is combining options with the underlying asset in order to create a riskless position. This usually requires the sale (purchase) of multiple calls (puts) to offset to the full cash exposure of a single share of stock held long. This hedge ratio changes with movements in the underlying asset's price and the passage of time; therefore, the riskless hedge portfolio needs to be rebalanced frequently. Once it is formed, however, the option's value can be established by assuming that the hedge portfolio should earn the risk-free rate and solving for the option value that makes this assumption true.

- The Black–Scholes model is extremely flexible. Although originally formulated for European-style call options on non-dividend-bearing stock, this model extends easily to valuing put options and options on dividend-paying stocks. We also consider how volatility, the only user-provided variable in the valuation model, is either estimated directly from a historical series of asset prices or implied from option prices themselves. Finally, we discuss the process for valuing American-style puts and calls and how this differs from the valuation of their European counterparts.

SUGGESTED READINGS

Black, Fisher. "How We Came Up with the Option Formula," *Journal of Portfolio Management* 15, no. 2 (Winter 1989): 4–8.

Cox, John C., and Mark Rubinstein. *Option Markets*. Englewood Cliffs, NJ: Prentice Hall, 1985.

Hull, John C. *Options, Futures, and Other Derivatives*, 9th ed. Boston, MA: Pearson Education, 2015.

Sincere, Michael. *Understanding Options*, 2nd ed. Columbus, OH: McGraw-Hill Education, 2014.

QUESTIONS

1. Straddles have been described as "volatility plays." Explain what this means for both long and short straddle positions. Given the fact that volatility is a primary factor in how options are priced, under what conditions might an investor who believes that markets are efficient ever want to create a straddle?

2. Put-call-forward parity and range forward positions both involve the purchase of a call option and the sale of a put option (or vice versa) on the same underlying asset. Describe the relationship between these two trading strategies. Is one a special case of the other?

3. Techno-Logical Inc. is a smart-phone manufacturer and has issued a five-year discount note in the amount of 160 million Japanese yen for procurement from its suppliers in Japan. Techno-Logical wants to hedge its currency exposure and the firm's financial director has the following suggestions:
    *   At-the-money Japanese yen call option contracts
    *   Japanese yen forward contracts
    *   Japanese yen futures contracts
    Explain exactly the way in which the company could use any of these products in its hedging strategy, being sure to compare and contrast the advantages and disadvantages of each.

4. In the Black–Scholes option pricing model, six factors affect the value of call options on stocks. Three of these factors are (1) the current price of the underlying stock, (2) the time to maturity for the option contract, and (3) the dividend on the stock. Identify the remaining three factors and explain how they affect the value of call options.

5. "Although options are risky investments, they are valued by virtue of their ability to convert the underlying asset into a synthetic risk-free security." Explain what this statement means, being sure to describe the basic three-step process for valuing option contracts.

6. The covered call option trading strategy combines a long position in the underlying security with the sale of a call option. Under what market conditions involving the future price of the underlying asset are necessary for this strategy to make sense? What is the risk involved with this trading scheme?

7. Describe the condition under which it would be rational to exercise both an American-style put and call stock option before the expiration date. In both cases, comment specifically on the role that dividends play.

8. Explain why a change in the time to expiration (T) can have either a positive or negative impact on the value of a European-style put option. In this explanation, it will be useful to contrast the put's reaction with that of a European-style call, for which an increase in T has an unambiguously positive effect.

9. Currency option traders often speak of "buying low volatility (or *vol*) and selling high vol" rather than buying or selling the option itself. What does this mean exactly? From this perspective, what is the real underlying asset: volatility or the foreign currency?

10. On October 19, 1987, the stock market (as measured by the Dow Jones Industrial Average) lost almost one-quarter of its value in a single day. Nevertheless, some traders made a profit buying call options on the stock index and then liquidating their positions before the market closed. Explain how this is possible, assuming that it was not a case of the traders taking advantage of spurious upward ticks in stock prices.

11. Bonds that are convertible into common stock are said to provide investors with both upside potential and downside protection. Explain how one security can possess both attributes. What implications do these features have for the way a convertible bond is priced?

PROBLEMS

1. You work on a proprietary trading desk of a large investment bank, and you have been asked for a quote on the sale of a call option with a strike price of $50 and one year until expiration. The call option would be written on a stock that does not pay a dividend. From your analysis, you expect that the stock will either increase to $70 or decrease to $35 over the next year. The current price of the underlying stock is $50, and the risk-free interest rate is 4 percent per annum.
   a. Briefly describe the steps involved in applying binomial option pricing model to value the call option in this situation.
   b. What is this fair market value for the call option under these conditions?

2. Joel Franklin is a portfolio manager responsible for derivatives. Franklin observes an American-style option and a European-style option with the same strike price, expiration, and underlying stock. Franklin believes that the European-style option will have a higher premium than the American-style option.
   a. Critique Franklin's belief that the European-style option will have a higher premium.
      Franklin is asked to value a one-year European-style call option for Abaco Ltd. common stock, which last traded at $43.00. He has collected the following information:

Closing stock price	$43.00
Call and put option exercise price	$45.00
One-year put option price	$ 4.00
One-year Treasury bill rate	5.50%
Time to expiration	One year

   b. Calculate, using put-call parity and the information provided, the European-style call option value.
   c. State the effect, if any, of each of the following three variables on the value of a call option: (1) an increase in short-term interest rate, (2) an increase in stock price volatility, and (3) a decrease in time to option expiration.

3. Assuming that a one-year call option with an exercise price of $28 is available for the stock of the DEW Corp., consider the following is a two-period price tree for DEW stock over the next year:

Now	S1	One Year
		36.30
	33.00	
30		29.70
	27.00	
		24.30

   You also know that the risk-free rate is $RFR = 5$ percent per subperiod (or 10.25 percent annualized).
   a. If the sequence of stock prices that DEW stock follows over the year is $30.00, $33.00, and $29.70, describe the composition of the initial riskless portfolio of stock and options you would form and all the subsequent adjustments you would have to make to keep this portfolio riskless.
   b. Given the initial DEW price of $30, what are the probabilities of observing each of the three terminal stock prices in one year? (Hint: In arriving at your answer, it will be useful to consider (1) the number of different ways that a particular terminal price could be achieved and (2) the probability of an up or down movement.)

    c. Use the binomial option model to calculate the present value of this call option.

    d. Calculate the value of a one-year put option on DEW stock having an exercise price of $28; be sure your answer is consistent with the correct response to part (c).

4. Consider the following regarding the pricing of options on the stock of ARB Inc.:

    a. A share of ARB stock sells for $75 and has a standard deviation of returns equal to 20 percent per year. The current risk-free rate is 9 percent and the stock pays two dividends: (1) a $2 dividend just prior to the option's expiration day, which is 91 days from now (exactly one-quarter of a year), and (2) a $2 dividend 182 days from now (exactly one-half year). Calculate the Black–Scholes value for a European-style call option with an exercise price of $70.

    b. What would be the price of a 91-day European-style put option on ARB stock having the same exercise price?

    c. Calculate the change in the call option's value that would occur if ARB's management suddenly decided to suspend dividend payments and this action had no effect on the price of the company's stock.

    d. Briefly describe (without calculations) how your answer in part (a) would differ under the following separate circumstances: (1) the volatility of ARB stock increases to 30 percent, and (2) the risk-free rate decreases to 8 percent.

5. Consider the following data relevant to valuing a European-style call option on a non-dividend-paying stock: $X = 40$, $RFR = 9$ percent, $T = $ six months (that is, 0.5), and $\sigma = 0.25$.

    a. Compute the Black–Scholes option and hedge ratio values for the series of hypothetical current stock price levels shown in Exhibit 16.8.

    b. Explain why the values in part (a) differ from those shown in Exhibit 16.8.

    c. For $S = 40$, calculate the Black–Scholes value for a European-style put option. How much of this value represents time premium?

6. Suppose the current value of a popular stock index is 653.50, and the dividend yield on the index is 2.8 percent. Also, the yield curve is flat at a continuously compounded rate of 5.5 percent.

    a. If you estimate the volatility factor for the index to be 16 percent, use the Black–Scholes model to calculate the value of an index call option with an exercise price of 670 and an expiration date in exactly three months.

    b. If the actual market price of this option is $17.40, explain why the implied volatility coefficient might differ from the historical volatility level.

    c. Besides volatility estimation error, explain why your valuation and the option's traded price might differ from one another.

7. Consider the following price data for TanCo stock in two different subperiods:

Subperiod A: 168.375; 162.875; 162.5; 161.625; 160.75; 157.75; 157.25; 157.75; 161.125; 162.5; 157.5; 156.625; 157.875; 155.375; 150.5; 155.75; 154.25; 155.875; 156; 152.75; 150.5; 150.75

Subperiod B: 122.5; 124.5; 121.875; 120.625; 119.5; 118.125; 117.75; 119.25; 122.25; 121.625; 120; 117.75; 118.375; 115.625; 117.75; 117.5; 118.5; 117.625; 114.625; 110.75

    a. For each subperiod, calculate the annualized historical measure of stock volatility that could be used in pricing an option for TanCo. In your calculations, you may assume that there are 250 trading days in a year.

    b. Suppose now that you decide to gather additional data for each subperiod. Specifically, you obtain information for a call option with a current price of $12.25 and the following characteristics: $X = 115$; $S = 120.625$; time t expiration $= 62$ days; $RFR = 7.42$ percent; and dividend yield $= 3.65$ percent. Here the risk-free rate and dividend yields are stated on an annual basis. Use the volatility measure from Subperiod B and the Black–Scholes model to obtain the "fair value" for this call option. Based on your calculations, is the option currently priced as it should be? Explain.

8. In March, a derivatives dealer offers you the following quotes for June British pound option contracts (expressed in U.S. dollars per GBP):

Contract	Strike Price	MARKET PRICE OF CONTRACT Bid	MARKET PRICE OF CONTRACT Offer
Call	USD 1.40	0.0642	0.0647
Put		0.0255	0.0260
Call	USD 1.44	0.0417	0.0422
Put		0.0422	0.0427
Call	USD 1.48	0.0255	0.0260
Put		0.0642	0.0647

a. Assuming that each of these contracts specifies the delivery of GBP 31,250 and expires in exactly three months, complete a table similar to the following (expressed in dollars) for a portfolio consisting of the following positions:
    (1) Long one 1.44 call
    (2) Short one 1.48 call
    (3) Long one 1.40 put
    (4) Short one 1.44 put

June USD/GBP	Net Initial Cost	Call 1.44 Profit	Call 1.48 Profit	Put 1.40 Profit	Put 1.44 Profit	Net Profit
1.36	——	——	——	——	——	——
1.40	——	——	——	——	——	——
1.44	——	——	——	——	——	——
1.48	——	——	——	——	——	——
1.52	——	——	——	——	——	——

b. Graph the total net profit (cumulative profit less net initial cost, ignoring time value considerations) relationship, using the June USD/GBP rate on the horizontal axis—and be sure to label the breakeven point(s). Also, comment briefly on the nature of the currency speculation represented by this portfolio.

c. If in exactly one month (in April) the spot USD/GBP rate falls to 1.385 and the effective annual risk-free rates in the United States and England are 5 percent and 7 percent, respectively, calculate the equilibrium price differential that should exist between a long 1.44 call and a short 1.44 put position. (Hint: Consider what sort of forward contract this option combination is equivalent to and treat the British interest rate as a dividend yield.)

9. Melissa Simmons is the chief investment officer of a hedge fund specializing in options trading. She is currently back-testing various option trading strategies that will allow her to profit from large fluctuations—either up or down—in a stock's price. An example of such typical trading strategy is straddle strategy that involves the combination of a long call and a long put with an identical strike price and time to maturity. She is considering the following pricing information on securities associated with Friendwork, a new Internet start-up hosting a leading online social network:

Friendwork stock: $100
Call option with an exercise price of $100 expiring in one year: $9
Put option with an exercise price of $100 expiring in one year: $8

a. Use the above information on Friendwork and draw a diagram showing the net profit/ loss position at maturity for the straddle strategy. Clearly label on the graph the breakeven points of the position.

b. Melissa's colleague proposes another lower-cost option strategy that would profit from a large fluctuation in Friendwork's stock price:

Long call option with an exercise price of $110 expiring in one year: $6
Long put option with an exercise price of $90 expiring in one year: $5

Similar to part (a), draw a diagram showing the net profit/loss position for the above alternative option strategy. Clearly label on the graph the breakeven points of the position.

10. In mid-May, there are two outstanding call option contracts available on the stock of ARB Co.:

Call #	Exercise Price	Expiration Date	Market Price
1	$50	August 19	$8.40
2	60	August 19	3.34

a. Assuming that you form a portfolio consisting of *one* Call #1 held long and *two* Calls #2 held short, complete the following table, showing your intermediate steps. In calculating net profit, be sure to include the net initial cost of the options.

Price of ARB Stock at Expiration ($)	Profit on Call #1 Position	Profit on Call #2 Position	Net Profit on Total Position
40	——	——	——
45	——	——	——
50	——	——	——
55	——	——	——
60	——	——	——
65	——	——	——
70	——	——	——
75	——	——	——

b. Graph the net profit relationship in part (a), using stock price on the horizontal axis. What is (are) the breakeven stock price(s)? What is the point of maximum profit?

c. Under what market conditions will this strategy (which is known as a *call ratio spread*) generally make sense? Does the holder of this position have limited or unlimited liability?

11. You are considering the purchase of a convertible bond issued by Bildon Enterprises, a non-investment-grade medical services firm. The issue has seven years to maturity and pays a semiannual coupon rate of 7.625 percent (that is, 3.8125 percent per period). The issue is callable by the company at par and can be converted into 48.852 shares of Bildon common stock. The bond currently sells for $965 (relative to par value of $1,000), and Bildon stock trades at $12.125 a share.

a. Calculate the current conversion value for the bond. Is the conversion option embedded in this bond in the money or out of the money? Explain.

b. Calculate the conversion parity price for Bildon stock that would make conversion of the bond profitable.

c. Bildon does not currently pay its shareholders a dividend, having suspended these distributions six months ago. What is the payback (breakeven time) for this convertible security, and how should it be interpreted?

d. Calculate the convertible's current yield to maturity. If a "straight" Bildon fixed-income issue with the same cash flows would yield 9.25 percent, calculate the net value of the combined options (the issuer's call and the investor's conversion) embedded in the bond.

PART 6

Analysis and Evaluation of Asset Management

Chapter 17
Professional Portfolio Management, Alternative Assets, and Industry Ethics

Chapter 18
Evaluation of Portfolio Performance

This final section of the book contains two chapters: The first deals with professional asset management, and the second is concerned with the evaluation of portfolio performance. The discussions of both of these topics are designed to address the needs of individual and institutional investors alike; both individual and institutional investors periodically need the services of a professional money manager, and both types of investors also need to be aware of how one should evaluate investment performance.

Because many investors employ professional asset managers to manage their assets, Chapter 17 is an important wrap-up to their asset allocation and portfolio construction process. After providing a broad overview of the different ways that professional asset management firms can be organized, the chapter describes how the asset management industry has changed over time and how professional managers are compensated for their expertise. Particular emphasis is paid to the role of *investment companies* (more commonly called *mutual funds*), which manage the majority of assets held by individual investors. The discussion includes a description of the major forms of investment companies and the general types of funds available, such as money market, growth, value, balanced, and bond funds. We argue that almost any investment objective can be met by investing in one or several investment companies. The chapter also provides a detailed examination of how *alternative asset* investments—hedge funds and private equity—are structured and managed. These investments are among the fastest-growing segments of the money management industry.

We wrap up Chapter 17 with a discussion of ethical and regulatory issues that arise when hiring a professional asset manager. We argue that most of these issues arise from the classical *principal-agent problem* that defines many economic relationships. After first examining the myriad regulations that govern the behavior of professional portfolio managers, we describe the set of standards that the industry has adopted voluntarily in an effort to foster an atmosphere of trust and responsibility. The chapter ends with several examples of ethical conflicts that can arise when investors employ professional money managers, including the design of compensation contracts to provide managers with the proper incentives to act in the investor's best interest and the proper use of trading commission fees.

The book concludes with Chapter 18, which deals with the evaluation of portfolio performance. We stress that analyzing investment performance involves addressing two questions: *How* did the manager perform? and *Why* did the manager perform as he or she did? Perhaps the most important concept to understand from this discussion is that any meaningful evaluation of a manager's performance must consider both the return and the riskiness of the portfolio. Thus, after a discussion of what is required of a portfolio manager, we review in detail the major *risk-adjusted* portfolio performance models, including a recent performance attribution model that, in turn, is capable of evaluating a global portfolio that necessarily includes the effect of currency allocation. We also consider how the alternative models relate to each other. This is followed by a demonstration of their use with a sample of mutual funds.

As always, it is important to understand potential problems with a technique or model. Therefore, we discuss *holdings-based* measures, which evaluate a manager's performance by examining the contents of the portfolio rather than relying on a statistical model to measure expected returns (for example, CAPM). We also consider potential problems with the traditional performance measures, including a review of the effect that selecting an inappropriate benchmark can have on these performance models. It is demonstrated that this benchmark problem has become more significant with the growth of global investing. The chapter finishes with a consideration of how investment performance results should be presented so as to be consistent with industry practice.

CHAPTER **17**

Professional Portfolio Management, Alternative Assets, and Industry Ethics

After you read this chapter, you should be able to answer the following questions:

- What are the different ways that professional money management firms can be organized, and how has the structure of the industry changed over time?
- Who manages the portfolios at investment advisory firms and investment companies, and how are those managers compensated?
- How do you compute the net asset value (*NAV*) for investment companies?
- What is the difference between closed-end and open-end investment companies?
- What are load fees, 12b-1 fees, and management fees, and how do they influence investment company performance?
- How are funds classified by investment objective, and which groups have experienced relative growth or decline?
- What are hedge funds, and how do they differ from other professionally managed investment products?
- What investment strategies do hedge funds employ, and what has been the performance of those fund types over time?
- What attributes do private equity investments possess that make them a unique asset class?
- How do venture capital and buyout-oriented private equity investments differ from one another, and what has been their historical performance?
- What are some of the ethical dilemmas involved in the professional money management industry?
- What functions should investors expect professional asset managers to perform?

So far, we have discussed how investors can analyze the aggregate market, different industry sectors, and individual companies when organizing their own investment portfolios. This chapter introduces another possibility to the investor: entrusting one's money to a professional portfolio manager. Using a professional money manager can entail establishing a private account with an investment advisor, purchasing shares of an established mutual fund, or becoming a limited partner in an organization managed by a general partner.

Both individual and institutional (pension plans, endowment funds) investors seek the services of professional managers for several reasons. Chiefly, these managers may possess superior investment skills that will lead to higher returns than investors could obtain on their own. Beyond that, professional managers offer access to asset classes and investment strategies that might otherwise be unavailable and may also provide a cost-effective way to choose among a wide variety of diversified portfolios. However, these relationships also create potential conflicts of interest between the goals of the investor and the manager that need to be considered.

After explaining how asset management firms are typically organized and charge for their services, we explore three different types of professional money management firms: traditional private management firms, investment fund companies, and "alternative asset" companies (hedge funds, private equity firms) created through limited partnerships. We pay particular attention to the contrast between investment companies, which are the most prevalent way in which investors employ professional counsel, and alternative asset vehicles, which represent the most rapidly growing segment of the industry. We conclude with a description of the legal and regulatory environment that governs professional investors.

17.1 THE ASSET MANAGEMENT INDUSTRY: STRUCTURE AND EVOLUTION

There are two basic ways that traditional asset management firms are organized. In the most straightforward structure, investors make contracts directly with a **management and advisory firm** for its services. These services can range from providing standard banking transactions (savings accounts, loans) to advising clients on creating their own portfolios to actually managing the investment funds themselves. Although banking and financial advice were once the main services these firms offered, there has recently been a shift toward the *assets under management* (*AUM*) approach. In that arrangement, the management firm becomes the custodian of the investor's capital, usually with full discretion over how those funds are invested. An important feature of this structure is that each client of the management firm has a *separately managed account*. Even if investors select the firm because of its expertise in a particular niche—say, selecting small-cap growth stocks—the assets of each client will be managed separately, regardless of whether the firm employs a single "model" portfolio. This situation is illustrated in Panel A of Exhibit 17.1.

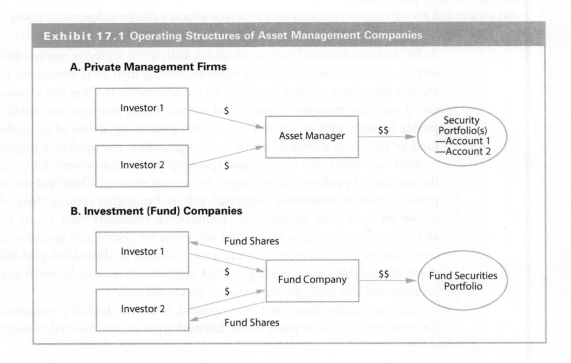

Exhibit 17.1 Operating Structures of Asset Management Companies

A. Private Management Firms

Investor 1 → $ → Asset Manager → $$ → Security Portfolio(s) —Account 1 —Account 2

Investor 2 → $

B. Investment (Fund) Companies

Investor 1 ← Fund Shares / $ → Fund Company → $$ → Fund Securities Portfolio

Investor 2 ← $ / Fund Shares

A second general approach to asset management involves the *commingling* of investment capital from several clients. An **investment company** invests a pool of funds belonging to many individuals in a single portfolio of securities. In exchange for this capital, the investment company issues to each investor new shares representing his or her proportional ownership of the mutually held securities portfolio, which is commonly known as *a fund*. For example, assume an investment company sells 10 million shares to the public at $10 a share, thereby raising $100 million. If the fund's purpose is to emphasize large-cap common stocks, the manager would invest the proceeds of the fund share sale ($100 million less any management fees) in the stock of such companies as Merck, IBM, ExxonMobil, and General Electric. Each investor who bought shares of the investment company would then own a percentage of the overall fund, rather than any portion of the shares held in the portfolio. Panel B of Exhibit 17.1 shows how this structure works.

There are important differences between these two organizational forms. Private management and advisory firms typically develop a personal relationship with their clients, getting to know the specific investment objectives and constraints of each. The assets held in the various separate accounts can then be tailored to these special needs, even if a general blueprint portfolio is used for all clients. Of course, special attention comes at a cost, and for this reason private management firms are used mainly by investors with substantial levels of capital, such as pension fund sponsors and high-net-worth individuals. Conversely, a mutual fund offered by an investment company is formed as a general solution to an investment problem and then marketed to investors who might fit that profile. The primary clients seeking professional asset management through investment companies are individual investors with relatively small pools of capital, who hold 89 percent of all mutual fund shares.[1]

It is not unusual for professional asset management firms to combine these two structures by offering private advisory services as well as publicly traded funds. For instance, consider T. Rowe Price Associates, a multi-asset, independent advisory firm located in Baltimore, Maryland. Founded in 1937, T. Rowe Price has seen its business grow to the point where it managed over $800 billion by the end of 2016, compared with less than $54 billion AUM just over 20 years earlier. The majority of this capital is invested in the firm's various public mutual fund portfolios, but T. Rowe Price also has several hundred private clients, including corporate retirement funds, public funds and unions, foundations and endowments, and individual investors.[2]

The AUM growth that T. Rowe Price has experienced during the past few years has been typical for the entire industry. Exhibit 17.2 charts the top 50 asset management companies as of the end of 1994 and 2016. A striking feature of these lists is the rapid increase in the number of large asset management firms, defined as those organizations with AUM of more than $100 billion. In 1994, there were only 10 such firms; by 2016, all 50 firms listed on the left side of Exhibit 17.2 managed that much. Much of this asset growth can be explained by the strong performance of global equity markets during this period, but another important contributing factor was the consolidation trend that marked the industry. Typical of this phenomenon was the merger of the asset management groups Union Bank of Switzerland and Brinson Partners (ranked 36th and 39th on the 1994 list, respectively) to become UBS Global Asset Management (ranked 25th on the 2016 list). This consolidation trend is likely to continue because the competition among existing asset management firms for the flow of new investment capital is expected to increase significantly.[3]

---

[1]See Chapter 6 of *2017 Investment Company Fact Book* (Washington, DC: Investment Company Institute).

[2]This information is available from T. Rowe Price's public home page, at www.troweprice.com.

[3]Good economic analysis of the professional asset management business can be found in Brinson (2005) and CFA Institute (2017).

Exhibit 17.2 Assets Under Management (AUM) for Leading Firms

	DECEMBER 31, 2016		DECEMBER 31, 1994	
Rank	Firm	AUM ($ millions)	Firm	AUM ($ millions)
1	BlackRock	5,147,852	Fidelity Management & Research	314,543
2	Vanguard Group	3,965,018	Bankers Trust Company	186,797
3	State Street Global	2,468,456	Merrill Lynch Asset Management Group	163,822
4	Fidelity Investments	2,130,798	Capital Group	162,634
5	J.P. Morgan Asset & Wealth	1,770,867	Wells Fargo/BMZ	158,392
6	BNY Mellon	1,647,990	State Street Global Advisors	140,413
7	Capital Group	1,478,523	Alliance Capital Management	121,290
8	Goldman Sachs Group	1,379,000	Franklin/Templeton Group	114,100
9	Prudential Financial	1,263,765	J.P. Morgan Investment Management	111,983
10	Amundi	1,141,286	American Express Financial/IDS	102,128
11	Legal & General Investment	1,104,873	Putnam Investments	95,182
12	PIMCO	1,092,276	INVESCO	94,066
13	Wellington Mgmt.	979,210	Scudder Stevens & Clark	91,253
14	Northern Trust Asset Mgmt.	942,452	The Northern Trust Company	82,353
15	Nuveen	881,748	Wellington Management Company	81,970
16	Invesco	812,918	The Vanguard Group	81,743
17	T. Rowe Price	810,800	Citibank Global Asset Management	73,999
18	MetLife	800,806	Pacific Investment Management	72,175
19	Morgan Stanley	778,003	Company (PIMCO) Smith Barney Capital	69,114
20	AXA Investment	756,401	Kemper Financial Services	62,748
21	Deutsche Asset Mgmt.	746,050	Dreyfus Corp.	62,055
22	Franklin Templeton	719,989	New England Investment Cos.	56,609
23	Legg Mason	710,387	PNC Asset Management Group	56,422
24	Manulife/John Hancock	663,575	T. Rowe Price Associates	53,705
25	UBS Asset Mgmt.	644,958	Dean Witter InterCapital	51,197
26	Allianz Global Investors	506,422	Federated Investors	50,743
27	New York Life Investments	504,649	Van Kampen American Capital	46,699
28	AllianceBernstein	480,201	John Nuveen Co.	46,497
29	Schroders	476,976	Chase Manhattan Corp.	44,839
30	BNP Paribas Investment	463,545	Bank of New York	42,599
31	Dimensional Fund Advisors	460,010	TCW Group	41,981
32	Columbia Threadneedle	456,319	SunTrust Banks	41,811
33	Asset Management One	455,854	Chemical Bank Portfolio Group	41,725
34	Aviva Investors	425,704	Bank of America Investment Mgmt Services	41,328
35	MFS Investment	425,602	NationsBank	40,771
36	HSBC Global Asset	413,413	Union Bank of Switzerland	38,685
37	Principal Global Investors	411,129	GE Investments	38,230
38	Nomura Asset Mgmt.	397,862	Goldman Sachs Asset Management	37,400
39	Aberdeen Asset Mgmt.	373,969	Brinson Partners	36,540
40	Federated Investors	365,908	Boatmen's Trust Co.	36,420
41	Macquarie Asset Mgmt.	362,101	Morgan Stanley Asset Management	35,678
42	Aegon Asset Mgmt.	349,550	National Bank of Detroit	35,590
43	Wells Capital Mgmt.	348,339	Mitchell Hutchins Asset Management	34,394
44	Standard Life Investments	343,423	Harris Bankcorp.	33,827
45	MassMutual Financial	325,663	Massachusetts Financial Services	33,432
46	Credit Suisse Asset Mgmt.	314,389	U.S. Trust Company of New York	33,032
47	Charles Schwab Investment	302,550	Mellon Capital Management	31,910
48	RBC Global Asset Mgmt.	292,628	Banc One Investment Corp.	31,537
49	Dodge & Cox	275,917	HSBC Asset Management	30,488
50	Barings	271,463	Fiduciary Trust Co. Int'l	29,903

Sources: Goldman Sachs, *Pensions & Investments*.

17.2 PRIVATE MANAGEMENT AND ADVISORY FIRMS

While larger management companies offer a broader range of services and products, the majority of private management and advisory firms are still much smaller and more narrowly focused on a particular niche of the market. To examine one typical organization in greater detail, consider Prudent Capital Management (PCM),[4] a growth-oriented equity and fixed-income manager located in California. PCM utilizes a "bottom-up" security selection process, with its portfolio managers looking for companies that have exceptional profitability, market share, return on equity, and earnings growth. PCM's clients include both institutional investors and high-net-worth individuals (with between $2 million and $5 million in assets) in both separate and commingled accounts. The firm offers management of both taxed and non-taxed products. Exhibit 17.3 shows the myriad investment products that PCM offers, along with the minimum investment accepted in each.

Like the industry as a whole, PCM saw its AUM increase steadily over the past several years. Panel A of Exhibit 17.4 reports that over a recent five-year period, the firm's assets grew by almost 80 percent, from $11.8 billion to $21.2 billion. During this period, the median separate account size jumped from $24.8 million to over $39 million. This suggests that PCM's clients tend to be institutional investors, which the client profile in Panel B of Exhibit 17.4 confirms. The company offers services to more than 350 clients, but the majority of these are institutional investors. Because of the minimum investment restrictions, relatively few of the clients are individual investors, who represent slightly less than 3 percent (535 ÷ 21,165) of PCM's business.

Panel C of Exhibit 17.4 shows fee schedules representative of both the equity and fixed-income management services that PCM offers. Typical of the entire industry, these fees are not flat amounts but are expressed as percentages of invested capital on an annual basis.

Exhibit 17.3 Representative Private Management Firm Investment Products			
	Large-Cap	**Mid-Cap**	**Small-Cap**
Equity:	$5 million $2 million Commingled fund (Delaware Business Trust) $2 million for sponsored program affiliates	$5 million $5 million Commingled fund (Delaware Business Trust) $2 million for sponsored program affiliates	$10 million Commingled fund (closed)
Balanced:	$5 million $2 million for sponsored program affiliates		
Concentrated:	$5 million $2 million for sponsored program affiliates		
Tax-Sensitive Management:	$5 million Equity, balanced, fixed $2 million for sponsored program affiliates		
Active Fixed Income:	$5 million Separately managed $2 million for sponsored program affiliates		

[4]Prudent Capital Management is a pseudonym for a real firm whose name has been changed by request. However, the subsequent information reported is real.

Exhibit 17.4 Representative Private Management Firm: AUM, Clients, and Fees

A. AUM

Date	Assets Managed ($ millions)	No. of Institutional Clients	ACCOUNT SIZE	
			Average ($ millions)	Median ($ millions)
Year 5	21,165.0	207	97.5	39.3
Year 4	18,441.0	206	85.1	34.9
Year 3	17,608.0	226	74.2	30.6
Year 2	17,808.0	233	72.3	30.4
Year 1	14,578.0	237	61.5	27.8
Year 0	11,833.0	230	51.4	24.8

B. Clients

	No. of Clients	Assets ($ millions)
Corporate retirement funds	126	7,937.0
Public funds	35	3,881.0
Unions (Taft-Hartley)	18	1,442.0
Foundations, endowments, associations	66	1,656.0
Commingled funds	4	1,682.0
General insurance accounts	N/A	N/A
Limited partnership	N/A	N/A
Mutual funds	18	3,411.0
Individuals: IRAs and other	75	535.0
Other	5	186.0
Taxable corporate	17	435.0

C. Fee Schedule

Large-Cap Growth Equity Accounts	Fixed-Income Accounts
• 1.00% on the first $10,000,000	• 0.375% on the first $25,000,000
• 0.75% on the next $10,000,000	• 0.30% over $25,000,000
• 0.50% above $20,000,000	

Source: Data adapted from *Nelson's Directory of Investment Managers.*

They are also graduated on a declining scale so that the more capital an investor commits, the lower his or her average cost would be. An individual with $15 million invested would pay annual fees of $137,500 (10,000,000 × 0.01 + 5,000,000 × 0.0075), or 0.92 percent of total invested capital. On the other hand, the fee paid by a pension fund with $115 million under management would be $650,000 (10,000,000 × 0.01 + 10,000,000 × 0.0075 + 95,000,000 × 0.005), or 0.57 percent. One advantage to the investor of having the fee schedule tied directly to AUM is that, as the management firm performs better for the client, its fees will increase. This reward system helps to align the incentives of the investor and the manager.

17.2.1 Investment Strategy at a Private Money Management Firm

The representation of a private money management firm shown in Panel A of Exhibit 17.1 indicated that each client's assets were held in a separate account. It was also noted that the security portfolios formed for each client are likely to be guided by the firm's overall investment philosophy. It is this investment philosophy—along with the returns it produces—that attracts clients to a particular money manager in the first place. Exhibit 17.5 reproduces the

---

Exhibit 17.5 Investment Strategy at a Representative Private Management Firm

A. Large-Cap Growth Equity Portfolio

Investment Approach:

Our focused, fundamental research process is primarily based on the ideas from our in-house analysts. Our analysts operate as specialists. They direct their expertise on specific industries and sectors covering seven key growth sectors: technology/components, technology/systems, telecom, health care, retail, consumer, and finance.

Our investment process seeks out companies that have at least one or more catalysts for growth. The catalysts may be identified as new products, exploitation of demographic trends, proprietary products, gaining market share, and/or changing cost structure, in order to attain or maintain very strong earnings per share growth.

We search for companies that have significant management ownership, well-thought-out management goals and growth plans supported by stringent controls, and a commitment to enhancing shareholder value. We also seek out companies with a proven track record (at least three to five years) of superior revenue and earnings growth, strong pretax margins, low levels of debt, exceptional profitability, market share, high return on equity, high reinvestment rates, and attractive valuations relative to their industry and the market in general.

Largest Holdings:			
1. Microsoft		6. Oracle
2. Nokia		7. Facebook
3. Cisco Systems		8. Juniper Networks
4. Qualcomm		9. Amgen
5. Genentech		10. Adobe Systems

Benchmark Used: Russell 1000 Growth Index

B. Active Fixed Income

Investment Approach:

We believe that superior risk-adjusted returns can be achieved by capturing changes in relative value through active yield curve management, sector rotation, and prudent security selection. We follow a disciplined process designed to add incremental value over long periods of time by taking advantage of relative value opportunities without accepting excessive interest rate risk. Our process is not dependent on forecasts of future interest rates or economic events. Rather, our decisions are based on current conditions, analyzed in the context of historical relationships. Our performance record has been built employing this process. We expect that in the future market conditions will offer similar opportunities. While markets will change, our process will not.

Largest Holdings:	
1. A- to Baa-rated corporates (56.9%)
2. Treasury/agencies (33.6%)
3. Aaa- to Aa-rated corporates (9.5%)

Benchmark Used: Barclays Government/Corporate Index

Source: Data adapted from *Nelson's Directory of Investment Managers.*

---

investment strategy and major holdings for two of PCM's model portfolios, one in equities and one in fixed-income securities.

The investment approach expressed in Panel A of Exhibit 17.5 makes it clear that PCM's large-cap growth stock product will invest client money primarily in technology companies. While the specific stock allocations might vary from one client to another, the same fundamental orientation toward stock selection will be applied to all accounts. Similarly, a client choosing to invest in PCM's core fixed-income product will end up holding a portfolio of bonds split between government and investment-grade corporate names. The stated investment process at PCM requires extensive interaction between the firm's 11 equity portfolio managers, 10 equity analysts, 3 equity traders, and 6 additional manager/analysts.

17.3 ORGANIZATION AND MANAGEMENT OF INVESTMENT COMPANIES

An investment company typically is a corporation that has as its major assets the portfolio of marketable securities referred to as a fund. The management of the portfolio of securities and most of the other administrative duties are handled by a separate **investment management company** hired by the board of directors of the investment company. This legal description oversimplifies the typical arrangement. The actual management usually begins with an investment advisory firm that starts an investment company and selects a board of directors for the fund. Subsequently, this board of directors hires the investment advisory firm as the fund's portfolio manager.

The contract between the investment company (the portfolio of securities) and the investment management company details the duties and compensation of the latter. The major duties of the investment management company include investment research, the management of the portfolio, and administrative duties, such as issuing securities and handling redemptions and dividends. The management fee is generally stated as a percentage of the total value of the fund and typically ranges from 25 to 75 basis points, with a sliding scale as the size of the fund increases.

To achieve economies of scale, many management companies launch numerous funds with different characteristics. The variety of funds allows the management group to appeal to many investors with different risk–return preferences. In addition, it allows investors to switch among funds as economic or personal conditions change. This "family of funds" promotes flexibility and increases the total capital managed by the investment firm.

17.3.1 Valuing Investment Company Shares

When clients have their invested capital held in separate accounts, the value of any given account can be calculated by simply totaling the market value of the securities held in the portfolio, less fees. When the securities are held jointly, as they are in an investment company, the appropriate way to value a client's investment is to multiply the number of shares in the fund owned by the per-share value of the entire security fund. This per-share value is known as the **net asset value (*NAV*)** of the investment company. It equals the total market value of all the firm's assets divided by the total number of fund shares outstanding, or:

17.1 $$\text{Fund } NAV = \frac{(\text{Total Market Value of Fund Portfolio}) - (\text{Fund Expenses})}{(\text{Total Fund Shares Outstanding})}$$

The *NAV* for an investment company is analogous to the share price of a corporation's common stock; like common stock, the *NAV* of the fund shares will increase as the value of the underlying assets increases.

Earlier we saw that an investment company with a $100 million large-cap stock portfolio and 10 million outstanding shares would have a *NAV* of $10. What would happen if during a holding period the value of the stock portfolio increased to $112.5 million while the fund incurred $0.1 million in trading and management fees? If no new shares were sold during the period, the net value of the total investment company is $112.4 million, which leaves a net asset value for each existing fund share of $11.24 ([112,500,000 − 100,000] ÷ 10,000,000). Thus, the *NAV* provides an immediate reflection of the investment company's market value net of operating expenses. Had the investment company made any capital gain or dividend distributions to its investors, these would reduce the value of the fund portfolio. For publicly traded funds, *NAV*s are calculated and reported on a daily basis.

17.3.2 Closed-End versus Open-End Investment Companies

Investment companies begin like any other company, selling common stock to a group of investors. However, an investment company uses the proceeds to purchase the securities of other publicly held companies rather than buildings and equipment. An open-end investment company (often referred to as a **mutual fund**) differs from a closed-end investment company (typically referred to as a *closed-end fund*) in the way each operates *after* the initial public offering.

A **closed-end investment company** functions like any other public firm. Its stock trades on a regular secondary market, and the market price of its shares is determined by supply and demand conditions. So, if you want to buy or sell shares in a closed-end fund, you must do so in the market where its shares are listed (for example, NYSE). No new investment dollars are available unless the company makes another public sale of securities and no funds can be withdrawn unless it decides to repurchase stock, which is quite unusual. Exhibit 17.6 lists the number of closed-end funds traded on U.S. exchanges, broken down by investment objective

Exhibit 17.6 Closed-End Funds: Categories and AUM

STATISTIC			VALUE
Total Number of Closed-End Funds:			608
Total Assets ($ millions):			$205,396.1

ASSETS BY CLASSIFICATION

Classifications	Code	Funds	Assets ($ millions)
CA Muni Debt Funds	CAG	19	7,429.80
Convertible Sec Funds	CV	14	6,175.00
Core Funds	CE	19	9,499.70
Corp Debt BBB Leveraged	BBBL	7	4,083.90
Corp Debt BBB Rated Fds	BBB	7	1,709.90
Developed Market Funds	DM	15	2,920.90
Emerging Markets Funds	EM	22	5,364.30
Emg Mkts HC Debt Funds	EMD	7	2,960.00
Energy MLP Funds	EMP	25	7,182.70
Gen & Ins Leveraged	GML	61	37,872.70
Gen & Ins Unleveraged	GIM	7	1,458.80
General Bond Funds	GB	40	13,323.80
Global Funds	GL	23	7,521.10
Global Income Funds	GLI	14	9,317.10
Growth Funds	GE	2	144.00
Hi Yld Muni Debt Funds	HM	11	3,695.60
High Yield Fds Leveraged	HYL	36	16,015.00
High Yield Funds	HY	13	3,355.00
Income & Pref Stock Fds	PS	32	15,813.80
Intmdt Muni Debt Funds	IMD	11	2,173.30
Loan Participation Funds	LP	42	12,578.30
Natural Resources Funds	NR	11	3,100.40
NJ Muni Debt Funds	NJ	8	1,645.10
NY Muni Debt Funds	NY	19	4,372.20
Opt Arbitrage/Opt Strat	OS	31	20,380.00
Other States Muni Debt	OTH	26	3,546.30
PA Muni Debt Funds	PA	6	1,216.60
Pacific Ex Japan Funds	XJ	5	500.50
Real Estate Funds	RE	32	7,352.60
Sector Equity Funds	SE	18	7,315.80
US Mortgage Funds	USM	7	1,506.80
Utility Funds	UT	11	6,439.40
Value Funds	VE	7	6,959.40

Note: Assets are net assets after deductions of all operating costs, expressed in $ millions.

Source: Closed-End Fund Association, August 3, 2017. Reprinted with permission.

and AUM. More than 600 funds are represented in more than 30 categories, including general domestic equity and bond funds, global equity funds, loan participation funds, flexible income funds, national municipal bond funds, and single-state municipal bond funds.

The closed-end investment company's *NAV* is computed throughout the day based on prevailing market prices for the portfolio securities, but the *market price* of the shares is determined by how they trade on the exchange. When buying or selling shares of a closed-end fund, investors pay or receive this market adjusted, for a trading fee. The *NAV* and the market price of a closed-end fund are almost never the same. Over the long run, the market price of these shares has historically been from 5 to 20 percent below the *NAV*, meaning that closed-end funds typically sell at a discount to *NAV*.

This relationship has prompted questions from investors: Why do these funds sell at a discount? Why do the discounts differ between funds? What are the returns available to investors from funds that sell at large discounts? This final question arises because an investor who acquires a portfolio at a price below market value (below NAV) expects an above-average dividend yield. Still, the total return on the fund depends on what happens to the discount during the holding period. If the discount relative to the NAV declines, the investment should generate positive excess returns. If the discount increases, the investor will likely experience negative excess returns. The analysis of these discounts remains a major question in modern finance.[5]

Open-end investment companies, or mutual funds, continue to sell and repurchase shares after their initial public offerings. They stand ready to sell additional shares of the fund at the *NAV*, with or without sales charge, or to buy back (redeem) shares of the fund at the *NAV*, with or without redemption fees. Open-end investment companies have enjoyed substantial growth (in both number of funds and AUM) since World War II, as shown by the figures in Exhibit 17.7.

Load versus No-Load Open-End Funds One distinction of open-end funds is that some charge a share sales fee. The offering price for a share of a *load fund* equals the *NAV* of the share plus a sales charge, which can be as large as 5.5 percent of the *NAV*. A fund with a 5 percent sales charge (load) would give an individual who invested $1,000 in the fund shares that

---

Exhibit 17.7 Open-End Investment Companies: Number and Value of Assets: 1945–2016

	Number of Reporting Funds	Assets ($ billions)		Number of Reporting Funds	Assets ($ billions)
1945	73	1.3	2005	7,977	8,891.4
1950	98	2.5	2006	8,123	10,398.2
1955	125	7.8	2007	8,041	12,000.2
1960	161	17.0	2008	8,040	9,620.6
1965	170	35.2	2009	7,666	11,112.6
1970	361	47.6	2010	7,556	11,833.5
1975	426	45.6	2011	7,590	11,632.6
1980	564	134.8	2012	7,590	13,054.5
1985	1,528	495.4	2013	7,715	15,049.0
1990	3,079	1,065.2	2014	7,927	15,873.4
1995	5,725	2,811.3	2015	8,115	15,650.5
2000	8,155	6,964.6	2016	8,066	16,343.7

Note: Does not include money market and short-term bond funds.

Source: Adapted from data in Investment Company Institute, *2017 Investment Company Fact Book.*

---

[5]Research studies over the years include Lee, Shleifer, and Thaler (1991), Berk and Stanton (2007), and Ramadorai (2012).

are worth only $950. Such funds generally charge no redemption fee, which means the shares can be redeemed at their *NAV*. These funds typically are quoted with an *NAV* and an offering price. The *NAV* price is the redemption (bid) price, and the offering (ask) price equals the *NAV* divided by 1.0 minus the percent load. For example, if the *NAV* of a fund with a 5 percent load is $8.50 a share, the offering price would be $8.95 ($8.50/0.95). The 45-cent differential is really 5.3 percent of the *NAV*. The load percentage typically declines with the size of the order.

A **no-load fund** imposes no initial sales charge, so it sells shares at their *NAV*. Some of these funds charge a small redemption fee of about 0.5 percent. In the financial press, quotes for these no-load funds list bid prices as the *NAV* with the designation "NL" (no load) for the offering price—that is, the bid and offer are the same. The number of no-load funds has increased substantially in recent years. In fact, by 2003 the number of no-load equity funds exceeded the number of load funds for the first time.

Between the full-load and pure no-load funds, several important variations exist. The first is the **low-load fund**, which imposes a front-end sales charge when the fund is bought, but typically in the 1 to 2 percent range. Generally, low-load funds are used for bond funds or equity funds offered by management companies that also offer no-load funds. Also, some funds previously charging full loads have reduced their loads.

The second major innovation is the **12b-1 plan**, named after a 1980 SEC ruling. This plan permits funds to deduct as much as 0.75 percent of average net assets *per year* to cover distribution costs, such as advertising, brokers' commissions, and general marketing expenses. A large and growing number of no-load funds are adopting these plans, as are a few low-load funds. Finally, some funds have instituted **contingent, deferred sales loads**, in which a sales fee is charged when the fund is sold if it is held for less than some time period, perhaps three or four years.

17.3.3 Fund Management Fees

In addition to selling charges (loads or 12b-1 charges), all investment firms charge annual **management fees** to compensate the fund's managers. Similar to the compensation structure for private management firms, such a fee typically is a percentage of a fund's average net assets and varies from about 0.25 to 1.00 percent. Most management fees are on sliding scales that decline with fund size. A fund with assets under $1 billion might charge 1 percent, funds with assets between $1 billion and $5 billion might charge 0.50 percent, and those over $5 billion might charge 0.25 percent.

These management fees are a major factor driving the creation of new funds. More assets under management generate more fees, but management costs do not increase at the same rate because substantial economies of scale exist in managing financial assets. Once the research staff and management structure are established, the incremental costs do not rise in line with the assets under management. The cost of managing $1 billion of assets is *not* twice the cost of managing $500 million. Finally, one consequence of the industry consolidation we discussed earlier is that mutual fund fees have been declining. The Investment Company Institute (2017) reported that between 1980 and 2016, total shareholder costs to equity fund investors decreased by almost 75 percent, from 2.32 to 0.63 percent of average fund AUM.

17.3.4 Investment Company Portfolio Objectives

A mutual fund can be created around any portfolio of assets. However, mutual funds tend to exist for only the more liquid asset classes, such as stocks and bonds. There are four broad (Level 2) fund objective categories recognized by the Investment Company Institute: common stock funds, bond funds, hybrid funds, and money market funds. Each of these strategies is described briefly here, and Exhibit 17.8 provides a more detailed list of many of the more popular subcategories (Levels 4 and 5) within these objective classes.

Exhibit 17.8 Mutual Fund Objective Definitions

Level 1: Long-Term Funds
Level 2: Equity
Level 3: Domestic Equity

- **Capital appreciation** funds seek growth of capital; dividends are not a primary consideration. (Level 4)
- **Growth** funds invest primarily in common stock of growth companies, which are those that exhibit signs of above-average growth, even if the share price is high relative to earnings/intrinsic value. (Level 5)
- **Sector** funds seek capital appreciation by investing in companies in related fields or specific industries. (Level 5)
- **Alternative strategy** funds seek to provide capital appreciation while minimizing risk by employing long/short, market neutral, leveraged, or inverse strategies. (Level 5)
- **Total return** funds seek a combination of current income and capital appreciation by investing in equity securities. (Level 4)
- **Value** funds invest primarily in common stock of value companies, which are those that are out of favor with investors, appear underpriced by the market relative to their earnings/intrinsic value, or have high dividend yields. (Level 5)
- **Blend** funds invest primarily in common stock of both growth and value companies or are not limited to the types of companies in which they can invest. (Level 5)

Level 3: World Equity

- **World equity** funds invest primarily in stocks of foreign companies. (Level 4)
- **Emerging market** funds invest primarily in companies based in less-developed countries. (Level 5)
- **Global equity** funds invest primarily in equity securities traded worldwide, including equity securities of U.S. companies. (Level 5)
- **International equity** funds must invest in equity securities of companies located outside the United States, and cannot invest in U.S. companies' stocks. (Level 5)
- **Regional equity** funds invest in companies that are based in a specific part of the world. (Level 5)
- **Alternative strategies: world equity** funds invest in companies traded worldwide, including companies based in the United States, specific regions, or emerging markets, while employing long/short, market neutral, leveraged, or inverse strategies. (Level 5)

Level 2: Hybrid
Level 3: Hybrid

- **Hybrid** funds invest in a mix of equity and debt securities. (Level 4)
- **Asset allocation** funds seek high total return by investing in a mix of equities, fixed-income securities, and money market instruments. Unlike flexible portfolio funds (defined below), this type of fund is required to strictly maintain a precisely defined weighting of its asset classes. (Level 5)
- **Balanced** funds invest in a specific mix of equity securities and bonds with the three-part objective of conserving principal, providing income, and achieving long-term growth of both principal and income. (Level 5)
- **Flexible portfolio** funds are designed to provide high total return by investing in common stock, bonds and other debt securities, and money market securities. The portfolio may hold up to 100 percent of any one of these types of securities and may easily change, depending on market conditions. (Level 5)
- **Income-mixed** funds invest in a variety of income producing securities, including equities and fixed-income securities. They seek a high level of current income for shareholders. Capital appreciation is not a primary objective. (Level 5)
- **Hybrid: alternative strategies** funds seek to provide capital appreciation while minimizing risk by investing in a mix of equity and fixed-income securities while employing long/short, market neutral, leverage, inverse, or commodity strategies. (Level 5)

Level 2: Bond
Level 3: Taxable Bond

- **Investment grade** funds seek current income by investing primarily in investment grade debt securities. (Level 4)
- **Investment grade: multi-term** funds seek a high level of income by investing two-thirds or more of their portfolios in investment grade debt with no explicit restrictions on average maturity or duration. (Level 5)
- **Investment grade: long-term** funds seek a high level of income by investing two-thirds or more of their portfolios in investment grade debt with an average maturity or duration of more than 10 years. (Level 5)
- **Investment grade: intermediate-term** funds seek a high level of income with two-thirds or more of their portfolios at all times in investment grade debt with an average maturity or duration of 5 to 10 years. (Level 5)

Exhibit 17.8 Mutual Fund Objective Definitions (Continued)

- **Investment grade: short-term** funds seek a high level of current income by investing two-thirds or more of their portfolios at all times in investment grade debt with an average maturity or duration of one to five years. (Level 5)
- **Investment grade: ultrashort-term** funds seek a high level of current income by investing two-thirds or more of their portfolios at all times in investment grade debt with an average maturity or duration of less than one year. (Level 5)
- **Inflation protected** funds invest in inflation-protected or inflation-indexed securities other than TIPS. (Level 5)
- **High yield** funds seek current income by investing two-thirds or more of their portfolios in lower-rated corporate bonds (Baa or lower by Moody's and BBB or lower by Standard and Poor's rating services). (Level 5)
- **Government bond** funds pursue an objective of high current income by investing in taxable bonds issued, or backed, by the U.S. government. (Level 4)
- **Government bond: multi-term** funds invest at least two-thirds of their portfolios in U.S. government securities with no stated average maturity or duration. (Level 5)
- **Government bond: long-term** funds invest at least two-thirds of their portfolios in U.S. government securities that have an average maturity or duration of more than 10 years. (Level 5)
- **Government bond: intermediate-term** funds invest at least two-thirds of their portfolios in U.S. government securities that have an average maturity or duration of 5 to 10 years. (Level 5)
- **Government bond: short-term** funds invest at least two-thirds of their portfolios in U.S. government securities that have an average maturity or duration of one to five years. (Level 4)
- **Mortgage-backed** funds invest at least two-thirds of their portfolios in pooled mortgage-backed securities. (Level 5)
- **Multisector bond** funds seek to provide high current income for their shareholders by investing predominantly in a combination of domestic fixed-income securities, including mortgage-backed securities and high yield bonds, and may invest up to 25 percent in bonds issued by foreign companies and governments. (Level 5)
- **Multisector: multi-term** funds invest at least two-thirds of their portfolios in U.S. fixed-income securities with no stated average maturity or duration. (Level 5)
- **Multisector: long/intermediate-term** funds invest at least two-thirds of their portfolios in U.S. fixed-income securities with average maturity or duration of more than five years. (Level 4)
- **Multisector: short-term** funds invest at least two-thirds of their portfolios in U.S. fixed-income securities with average maturity or duration of one to five years. (Level 5)
- **Multisector: alternative strategies** funds seek to provide high capital appreciation and/or current income while minimizing risk by investing in U.S. fixed-income securities while employing long/short, market neutral, leverage, or inverse strategies. (Level 5)
- **World bond** funds seek current income by investing in the debt securities of foreign companies and governments. (Level 4)
- **Global bond: multi-term** funds invest in worldwide debt securities, with no stated average maturity/duration or an average maturity/duration of more than five years. These funds may invest in debt securities of U.S. companies. (Level 5)
- **Global bond: short-term** funds invest in worldwide debt securities, with an average maturity or duration of one to five years. These funds may invest in debt securities of U.S. companies. (Level 5)
- **International bond** funds invest at least two-thirds of their portfolios in a combination of foreign government and corporate debt. (Level 5)

Level 3: Municipal Bond

- **State municipal bond** funds invest primarily in municipal bonds of a single state. The bonds are exempt from federal income tax as well as state taxes for residents of that state. (Level 5)
- **National municipal bond** funds invest in a national mix of municipal bonds with the objective of providing high after-tax yields. (Level 4)
- **National municipal bond: multi-term** funds invest predominantly in municipal bonds with an average maturity or duration of more than five years or no specific stated maturity. The bonds are usually exempt from federal income tax, but may be taxed under state and local laws. (Level 5)
- **National municipal bond: short-term** funds invest predominantly in municipal bonds with an average maturity or duration of one to five years. The bonds are usually exempt from federal income tax, but may be taxed under state and local laws. (Level 5)

Level 1: Money Market
Level 2: Money Market
Level 3: Taxable Money Market

- **Taxable money market** funds seek to maintain a stable net asset value by investing in short-term, high-grade securities sold in the money market. The average maturity of their portfolios is limited to 60 days or less. (Level 4)

(Continued)

Exhibit 17.8 Mutual Fund Objective Definitions (*Continued*)

- **Treasury and repo money market** funds invest in securities issued by the U.S. Treasury, including repurchase agreements collateralized fully by U.S. Treasury securities. (Level 5)
- **Treasury and agency money market** funds invest in securities issued or guaranteed by the U.S. government or its agencies and repurchase agreements for those securities. (Level 5)
- **Prime money market** funds invest in a variety of money market instruments, including certificates of deposit of large banks, commercial paper, and banker's acceptances. (Level 5)

Level 3: Tax-Exempt Money Market

- **Tax-exempt money market** funds seek income that is not taxed by the federal government, and in some cases states and municipalities, by investing in municipal securities with relatively short maturities. The average maturity of their portfolios is limited to 60 days or less. (Level 4)
- **National tax-exempt money market** funds seek income that is not taxed by the federal government by investing in municipal securities with relatively short maturities. (Level 5)
- **State tax-exempt money market** funds predominantly invest in short-term municipal bonds of a single state, which are exempt from federal income tax as well as state taxes for residents of the state included in the fund issue. (Level 5)

Source: Adapted from Investment Company Institute, *Mutual Fund Investment Objective Definitions*, November 2016.

Equity funds invest almost exclusively in common stocks. Within that broad mission, however, substantial differences can be found, including funds that focus on specific industries, a collection of industries (sectors), security characteristics (for example, growth or value), or even geographic areas. With several thousand to choose from, any investor should find an existing equity fund that matches his or her desired investment strategy.

Bond funds concentrate on various types of bonds to generate high current income with minimal risk. They are similar to common stock funds; however, their investment policies differ. Some funds concentrate on U.S. government or high-grade corporate bonds, others hold a mixture of investment-grade bonds, and some concentrate on high-yield (junk) bonds. Management strategies also can differ, ranging from buy and hold to extensive trading of the portfolio bonds.

In addition to government, mortgage, and corporate bond funds, a change in the tax law in 1976 caused the creation of numerous municipal bond funds. These funds provide investors with monthly interest payments that are exempt from federal income taxes. Some municipal bond funds concentrate on bonds from specific states, such as the New York Municipal Bond Fund, which allows New York residents to avoid most state taxes on the interest income.

Balanced funds diversify outside a single market by combining common stock with fixed-income securities, including government and corporate bonds, convertible bonds, or preferred stock. The ratio of stocks to fixed-income securities will vary by fund. **Flexible portfolio** (or *asset allocation*) **funds** seek high total returns by investing in a mix of stocks, bonds, and money-market securities. Target date (or life cycle) funds adjust the asset allocation weights in the portfolio to match the needs of an investor who is aging toward retirement.

Money market funds were initiated during 1973 when short-term interest rates were at record high levels. These funds attempt to provide current income, safety of principal, and liquidity by investing in diversified portfolios of Treasury bills, banker certificates of deposit, bank acceptances, and commercial paper. Exhibit 17.9 documents the growth pattern of these funds over time, which often depends on investor attitudes toward the stock market as well as the level of short-term yields. When investors are bullish on stocks, they withdraw funds from their money market accounts; when they are uncertain, they shift from stocks to the money funds.

17.3.5 Breakdown by Fund Characteristics

Exhibit 17.10 groups funds by their method of sale and by investment objectives for two recent years. The two major means of distribution are (1) by a sales force or investment professional

Exhibit 17.9 Money Market Funds: 1975–2016

| | Number of Funds | | Total Net Assets |
	Taxable	Tax Exempt	($ billions)
1975	36	—	3.7
1980	96	10	76.4
1985	350	110	243.8
1990	505	236	498.3
1995	676	321	753.0
2000	704	335	1,845.2
2005	593	277	2,026.8
2010	442	210	2,803.5
2015	336	145	2,754.7
2016	319	102	2,728.1

Note: Data for funds that invest primarily in other mutual funds were excluded from the series.

Source: Adapted from data in Investment Company Institute, *2017 Investment Company Fact Book.*

Exhibit 17.10 Total Net Assets by Fund Characteristics

| | | 2016 | | 2010 | |
		Dollars ($ billions)	Percentage	Dollars ($ billions)	Percentage
Total net assets		$16,343.72	100.0%	$11,120.70	100.0%
Method of Sale:					
Sales force/professionals		—	66.0%	—	64.0%
Direct marketing		—	34.0%	—	36.0%
Investment Objective:					
Equity funds	Capital appreciation	1,779.39	10.9%	2215.44	19.9%
	world	2,162.53	13.2%	1274.42	11.5%
	Total return	4,635.47	28.4%	1467.72	13.2%
Bond funds	Investment grade	1,641.24	10.0%	357.42	3.2%
	High yield	373.19	2.3%	187.55	1.7%
	World	420.41	2.6%	124.15	1.1%
	Government	280.96	1.7%	271.1	2.4%
	Multisector	320.03	2.0%	808.84	7.3%
	State muni	160.86	1.0%	158.96	1.4%
	National muni	452.84	2.8%	298.18	2.7%
Hybrid funds		1,388.66	8.5%	640.75	5.8%
Money market funds	Taxable	2,597.87	15.9%	2918.72	26.2%
	Tax exempt	130.27	0.8%	397.45	3.6%

Sources: Adapted from data in Investment Company Institute, *Investment Company Fact Book* (2017 and 2011) and *Profile of Mutual Fund Shareholders* (2016 and 2010).

and (2) by direct purchase from the fund or direct marketing. Sales forces would include brokers, such as Morgan Stanley; commission-based financial planners; or dedicated sales forces, such as Ameriprise Financial Advisors. Mutual funds acquired from these companies will often charge sales loads from which salespeople are compensated.

Investors typically purchase shares of directly marketed funds through online accounts or at an office of the fund. These direct sales funds usually impose a low sales charge or none at all.

In the past, because they had no sales fee, they had to be sold directly because a broker had no incentive to sell a no-load fund. This has changed recently because some brokerage firms, such as Charles Schwab & Co., have developed agreements with specific no-load funds whereby they will sell these funds to their clients and collect a fee from the fund. As of 2017, Schwab had a list of hundreds of no-load funds it sells through its OneSource service. As seen in Exhibit 17.10, the division between these two major distribution channels is currently about two-to-one in favor of the sales force method.

The breakdown by investment objective indicates the investment companies' response to a shift in investor emphasis toward equity and bond funds and reflects not only overall industry growth but also the evolving demands of investors. Total return funds have continued to grow and have generally increased their percentages. Finally, the growing desire for international diversification is reflected in the ongoing popularity of world equity funds, a trend discussed below.

17.3.6 Global Investment Companies

As described throughout this text, investors must give serious thought to global diversification of their investment portfolios. Funds that invest in non-U.S. securities are generally called either *international funds* or *global funds*. International funds often hold only non-U.S. stocks, while global funds contain both U.S. and non-U.S. securities. Both international and global funds fall into familiar categories: money funds, government and corporate bond funds, and equity funds. In turn, an international equity fund might limit its focus to a segment of the non-U.S. market, such as the European Fund, or to a single country. Given the need to invest in a diversified portfolio of emerging markets, an emerging market mutual fund with exposure to a number of countries is an ideal vehicle for this allocation. Most global or international funds are open-end funds (either load or no load), but a significant number are closed-end funds to minimize trading of illiquid foreign securities.

A final alternative that all investors—particularly those in the United States—should appreciate is the large number of non-U.S. investment companies that offer both domestic and global products in their local markets. In fact, the Investment Company Institute (2017) reported that of $40.4 trillion invested worldwide in open-end investment companies at the end of 2016, about 53 percent of these assets were controlled by firms located outside the United States. In order, the largest AUM concentrations occurred in Luxembourg, Korea, France, Japan, and Brazil. Further, of the 110,271 investment companies in operation during 2016, only about 9,800 were domiciled in the United States. From these statistics, it appears that no single region of the world has a monopoly on investment management skill.

17.3.7 Mutual Fund Organization and Strategy: An Example

The Dreyfus Corporation, established in 1951 and headquartered in New York City, is a leading mutual fund company in the United States. As part of BNY Mellon Financial Corporation, it helped in the management of over $260 billion as of June 2016.[6] The Dreyfus Appreciation Fund (DGAGX) is a one of several equity-oriented portfolios that the company offers to its institutional and retail investors. The Appreciation Fund, which follows a large-cap blend investment style, is different from other funds in the Dreyfus family in that it is not managed directly by in-house portfolio managers. Rather, DGAGX is managed by Fayez Sarofim, a Houston-based professional who has run his own private management firm since 1958 and serves Dreyfus as a subinvestment advisor. A description of DGAGX is shown in Exhibit 17.11. Notice that the portfolio holds just under $2.0 billion (Panel A) of assets and is a no-load fund that also does not charge a 12b-1 fee. However, investors do pay an annual

---

[6]Much of the information contained in this example is available from Dreyfus Corporation's Web site, at www.dreyfus.com.

Exhibit 17.11 Description of Dreyfus Appreciation Fund (DGAGX)

A. Overview

DGAGX US **$ NAV** **35.94** –0.05 Purch Prc 35.94
----- On 03 Aug

DGAGX US Equity	Report	Page 1/4	Security Description

1) Profile   2) Performance   3) Holdings   4) Organizational

DREYFUS APPRECIATION-INV   Objective   Growth Large Cap

Dreyfus Appreciation Fund Inc is an open-end fund incorporated in the USA. The Fund seeks long-term capital growth consistent with the preservation of capital, and its secondary goal is current income. The Fund invests in the common stock of U.S. and foreign blue-chip companies of market capitalization of more than $5 billion. [FIGI BBG000BBW0L3]

6) Comparative Returns | COMP »

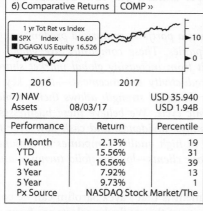

1 yr Tot Ret vs Index
■ SPX Index 16.60
■ DGAGX US Equity 16.526

2016   2017

7) NAV   USD 35.940
Assets   08/03/17   USD 1.94B

Bloomberg Classification

Fund Type	Open-End Fund
Asset Class	Equity
Market Cap	Large-cap
Strategy	Growth
Geo. Focus Country	U.S.

Performance	Return	Percentile
1 Month	2.13%	19
YTD	15.56%	31
1 Year	16.56%	39
3 Year	7.92%	13
5 Year	9.73%	1
Px Source	NASDAQ Stock Market/The	

Fund Info			Fees	
Inception Date	01/18/1984		Front Load	.00%
Share Class	Retail		Back Load	.00%
Min Investment	USD 2.50k		Early Withdrawal	.00%
Min Subsequent	USD 1.00k		Current Mgmt Fee	.55%
Min IRA	USD 750		Performance Fee	N.A.
Expense Ratio	.94%		12b1 Fee	.00%

Australia 61 2 9777 8600   Brazil 5511 2395 9000   Europe 44 20 7330 7500   Germany 49 69 9204 1210   Hong Kong 852 2977 6000
Japan 81 3 3201 8900   Singapore 65 6212 1000   U.S. 1 212 318 2000   Copyright 2017 Bloomberg Finance L.P.
SN 335716 CDT GMT–5:00 H443-1130-0 04-Aug-2017 12:49:38

B. Portfolio Composition

DGAGX US **$ NAV** **35.94** –0.05 Purch Prc 35.94
----- On 03 Aug

DGAGX US Equity	Report	Page 3/4	Security Description

1) Profile   2) Performance   3) Holdings   4) Organizational

Holdings As Of   06/30/2017   Portfolio Stats As Of   06/30/2017   Alloc As Of   06/30/2017

6) Top Holdings | MHD »

Name	Position	% Net	Value
10) Philip Morris International In	1.11M	6.744%	130.15M
11) Apple Inc	720.58K	5.378%	103.78M
12) Facebook Inc	583.03K	4.561%	88.03M
13) Microsoft Corp	1.21M	4.333%	83.62M
14) Altria Group Inc	892.95K	3.446%	66.50M
15) Alphabet Inc	70.68K	3.328%	64.23M
16) JPMorgan Chase & Co	668.59K	3.167%	61.11M
17) Chubb Ltd	401.79K	3.027%	58.41M
18) Coca-Cola Co/The	1.29M	2.987%	57.65M
19) Exxon Mobil Corp	708.45K	2.964%	57.19M

Top Asset Allocation

Equity	98.94%
Cash and Other	1.06%

Top Ind. Group Allocation

Agriculture	10.19%
Internet	8.63%
Oil&Gas	7.66%
Pharmaceutic...	7.54%
Diversified Fin...	7.43%
Beverages	6.70%

7) Holdings Analysis | PORT »

Top 10 Hldings % Port	39.93	Average P/C	16.12
Median Mkt Cap	182.42B	Average P/S	3.28
Avg Wtd Mkt Cap	232.54B	Average P/E	22.37
Avg Div Yield	2.11	Average P/B	3.87

Top Geo. Allocation

U.S.	83.25%
Switzerland	8.67%
Denmark	1.67%
Canada	1.52%

Australia 61 2 9777 8600   Brazil 5511 2395 9000   Europe 44 20 7330 7500   Germany 49 69 9204 1210   Hong Kong 852 2977 6000
Japan 81 3 3201 8900   Singapore 65 6212 1000   U.S. 1 212 318 2000   Copyright 2017 Bloomberg Finance L.P.
SN 335716 CDT GMT–5:00 H443-1130-0 04-Aug-2017 12:52:41

management fee of 0.55 percent of the portfolio's assets, which is the largest component of the fund's overall expense ratio. For DGAGX, this expense ratio is listed as 0.94 percent of AUM, which accounts for the total cost of running the fund.

One of the reasons Dreyfus chose to enter into this arrangement was to allow investors who would not otherwise have sufficient capital to gain access to a private manager with a noteworthy long-term performance record. Fayez Sarofim's investment philosophy is somewhat unique among mutual fund managers in that he preaches a patient approach to portfolio formation that seeks to keep turnover below 15 percent per annum. The firm describes its investment approach as follows:

> *Our investment philosophy leads us to construct a portfolio comprised predominantly of large capitalization, US-based, multinational companies. These companies are global leaders in structurally attractive industries. They benefit from increasing global market share, ongoing product introduction or innovation, and productivity enhancements—three key drivers of long-term earnings growth. In addition, their financial strength allows them to make profitable investments at any point in the economic cycle. We believe these businesses are most capable of generating superior growth in earnings, dividends, and cash flow over time, leading to greater capital appreciation. Investing in high quality companies at reasonable prices also produces two additional advantages for our clients—low portfolio turnover and a higher likelihood of preservation of capital.[7]*

One interesting concept implied in this statement is that Fayez Sarofim can be considered a global portfolio manager, even though the majority of the stocks he selects are from companies domiciled in the United States. The equity holdings of DGAGX are designed to mimic the portfolios that Sarofim assembles for his own private clients and thus follows the same philosophy. Panel B of Exhibit 17.11 shows the top 10 holdings of the fund as of August 2017. Not surprisingly, all of these stocks (for example, Philip Morris, Apple, Coca-Cola) fit the profile of being large companies with dominant global franchises and are mostly located in the United States (83.3 percent). Also, although not shown in the display, the DGAGX portfolio has a lower level of systematic risk than the market, with a beta coefficient of 0.86.

17.4 INVESTING IN ALTERNATIVE ASSET CLASSES

The investment structures just described—private management firms and investment companies—offer efficient ways for investors to gain access to a number of different asset classes and strategies. This is particularly true when the desired asset class investments are in liquid markets, such as with stocks, bonds, or money market securities. Recently, many investors have also become interested in committing their financial capital in nontraditional asset classes. These **alternative asset** classes can include a wide variety of investment opportunities, the most notable of which are hedge funds, private equity, real estate, or natural resources and commodities. In this section, we will take a detailed look at hedge funds and private equity investments.

Alternative asset investing can take place either through the creation of separate accounts for each investor or through the commingling of investor capital into a single pool of assets. Thus, these structures can appear as either Panel A or Panel B in Exhibit 17.1. Most often, though, an alternative asset investment is structured as a commingled collection of assets (Panel B), with the important difference that it is usually formed as a **limited partnership** rather than as a mutual fund. In a limited partnership, one or more *general partners* are responsible for running the organization and assuming its legal obligations, while the remaining *limited partners* are liable only to the extent of their investments. For example, in a hedge fund or private equity partnership, the general partner develops, implements, and maintains

---

[7]The complete statement of the Fayez Sarofim investment philosophy can be found on the firm's Website, www .sarofim.com.

the investment portfolio around an initial strategy, while the limited partners (high-net-worth individuals, pension funds, endowment funds) provide most of the capital but have no direct involvement in the actual investment process.

One of the reasons that investors consider hiring professional asset managers is the belief that they will be able to deliver superior performance relative to simple indexed investments. That is, investors feel that professional managers can consistently add *alpha*, or the difference between a fund's actual and expected (CAPM or benchmark) returns. In fact, the impressive recent development of the alternative assets market is due to the growing belief that they are better able to produce superior returns than traditional investment funds. This argument is summarized in Exhibit 17.12, which illustrates a security market line (SML) for several different asset classes. Notice that standard "long only" positions in U.S. stocks and bonds plot virtually on the SML—indicating very little possibility for adding alpha—while the alternative asset classes (hedge funds, private equity) have substantially more potential in that area.

17.4.1 Hedge Funds

One of the most significant developments in the professional asset management industry over the past 25 years has been the emergence of the global market for hedge fund investing. Exhibit 17.13 shows that the increase in both the number of hedge funds and the assets under management in those funds has been remarkable. There were about 600 funds at the start of the 1990s, controlling less than $40 billion in assets; by 2016, there were almost 10,000 active funds, controlling an estimated $3 trillion in assets. This represents AUM expansion of about 18 percent per annum over the past several years, even after accounting for the industry contraction that occurred as a result of the economic downturn in 2008.

Despite this recent surge in growth, hedge fund investing is not new. In fact, Lhabitant (2006) notes that use of the term *hedge fund* originated in 1949, when Alfred Winslow Jones

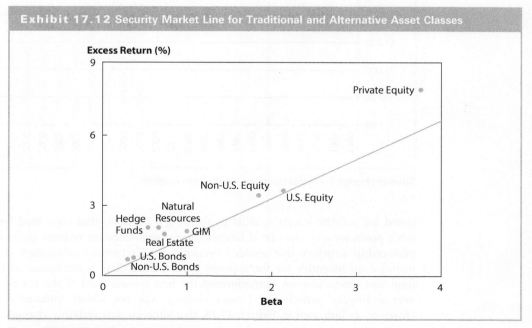

Exhibit 17.12 Security Market Line for Traditional and Alternative Asset Classes

Note: GIM = Global Investment Market

Source: Brian D. Singer, Renato Staub, and Kevin Terhaar, "Determining the Appropriate Allocation to Alternative Investments," *Hedge Fund Management* (Charlottesville, VA: CFA Institute, 2002), 10. Copyright © 2002 CFA Institute. Reproduced and republished from *Financial Analysts Journal* with permission from the CFA Institute. All rights reserved.

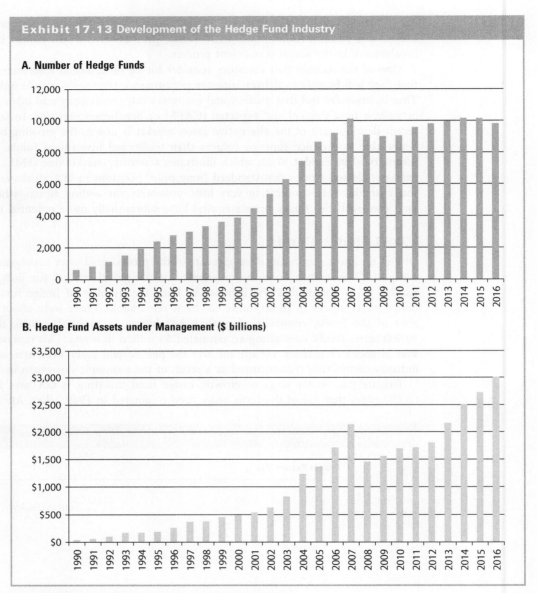

Exhibit 17.13 Development of the Hedge Fund Industry

A. Number of Hedge Funds

B. Hedge Fund Assets under Management ($ billions)

Sources: Hedge Fund Research Inc.; author calculations.

tested his security selection skills by forming a portfolio that combined both long and short stock positions with the use of financial leverage to enhance returns. Jones did this by using a partnership structure that avoided Security and Exchange Commission restrictions and also included an incentive fee for superior performance. The performance of this original hedge fund was spectacular—it outperformed the best mutual fund of the era by almost 90 percent over a 10-year period—but Jones's strategy was not widely imitated for several decades. However, as indicated in Exhibit 17.13, that situation has certainly changed.

17.4.2 Characteristics of a Hedge Fund

There are several immediate consequences to creating a hedge fund as a limited partnership. Most notably, hedge fund investments are far less liquid than mutual fund shares; there are severe limitations on how often investment capital can be contributed to or removed from a partnership. However, as a private partnership, hedge funds are generally less restricted in how and where they can make investments, which is perhaps the biggest reason investors believe that these vehicles have the ability to deliver abnormally large returns. They also tend to be less correlated with traditional asset class investments, providing investors with additional diversification benefits.

Exhibit 17.14 highlights several important features related to the way hedge funds are structured. The average hedge fund permits investors to enter or exit only a few times a year (monthly and quarterly, respectively) compared to the daily ownership adjustments allowed by mutual funds. Also, most hedge funds allow managers to use leverage (71 percent), short sell (82 percent), and derivatives (69 percent). By contrast, Almazan et al. (2004) document that the vast majority of mutual fund managers cannot employ these investment tools. Further, as Fung and Hsieh (2006) note, it is typical for hedge fund managers to receive their compensation in two components: a regular management fee (for example, 1 percent of AUM) and a performance allocation fee, which normally amounts to 20 percent of the fund's profits beyond a certain return level (hurdle rate). In calculating this performance fee, investors usually require that any past losses be recouped before managers receive the additional payout; this arrangement is known as a *high-water mark*.

17.4.3 Hedge Fund Strategies

Several investment strategies are often included under the hedge fund designation, and they vary greatly in the risk and expected return profiles they imply. Within a given strategic category, there can be as many interpretations of how the portfolio should be designed as there are

Exhibit 17.14 Characteristics of Hedge Fund Investments

	Mean	Median	Mode
Fund size	$83 million	$26.5 million	$20 million
Fund age	6.8 years	6.2 years	8.0 years
Minimum investment required	$649,000	$250,000	$1,000,000
Number of entry dates per year	22	12	12
Number of exit dates per year	17	4	4
Management fee	1.4%	1.0%	1.0%
Performance allocation ("fee")	17.2%	20.0%	20.0%

	YES
Fund has hurdle rate (of those with a performance allocation)	14%
Fund has high-water mark	93%
Fund has audited financial statements or audited performance	95%
Manager has $500,000 of own money in fund	78%
Fund can handle "hot issues"	56%
Fund is diversified	44%
Fund can short sell	82%
Fund can use leverage	71%
Fund uses derivatives for hedging only, or none	69%

Level of Turnover	Low (0–25%) = 17%	Medium (26–75%) = 26%	High (>75%) = 58%	
Capitalization of underlying investments	Small ($1–$500 million) = 12%	Medium ($500–$1,000 million) = 4%	Large (>$1,000 million) = 10%	Mixed = 73%

Source: © 2004 Greenwich Alternative Investments, LLC.

fund managers. Nevertheless, some common features define the more popular hedge fund strategies:[8]

I. *Equity-Based Strategies*

- *Long–short equity:* The original and perhaps the most basic form of hedge fund investing. Managers attempt to identify misvalued stocks and take long positions in the undervalued ones and short positions in the overvalued ones. Since investors participate in both the long and the short side of the market, one major advantage of the long–short strategy is the ability to generate "double alpha" (that is, profit from price corrections in both directions), unlike long-only mutual funds. The 130/30 funds discussed in Chapter 11 can be considered as a variation of this strategy.

- *Equity market neutral:* Like the long–short strategy, returns are generated by exploiting pricing inefficiencies between securities. However, equity market neutral strategies also attempt to limit the fund's overall volatility exposure by taking offsetting risk positions on the long and short side, which might involve derivative positions. Absent leverage, these portfolios are expected to produce returns of 2 to 4 percent above the risk-free rate, which has led some investors to refer to them as *absolute return* strategies.

II. *Arbitrage-Based Strategies*

- *Fixed-income arbitrage:* Returns are generated by taking advantage of bond pricing disparities caused by changing market events or investor preferences. Because the valuation disparities between related instruments (for example, coupon-bearing Treasury bonds and zero-coupon Treasury strips) are typically small, managers usually employ leverage to enhance their overall returns. The ability to generate alpha is driven largely by the manager's skill at building quantitative models, as well as structuring and managing fixed-income portfolios.

- *Convertible arbitrage:* Seeks to profit from disparities in the relationship between prices for convertible bonds and the underlying common stock. A typical position involves purchasing the convertible bond and short selling the underlying stock, thereby isolating the conversion option. Returns are generated through interest income on the convertible bonds, interest on the proceeds of related equity short sales, and the price appreciation of the convertible bonds as they gradually assume the value of the underlying equity. Like fixed-income arbitrage, convertible arbitrage positions often utilize leverage to enhance returns.

- *Merger (risk) arbitrage:* Returns are dependent upon the magnitude of the spread on merger transactions, which are directly related to the likelihood of the deal not being completed due to regulatory, financial, or company-specific reasons. As the probability of the merger improves, the spread narrows, generating profits for the position. Merger arbitrage investors essentially bet that their subjective assessment of the proposed deal being completed is superior to that of the other investors in the market.

III. *Opportunistic Strategies*

- *High yield and distressed:* One advantage that bond investors enjoy relative to stock investors is that, if the issuer does not default, a bond's price will return to par at maturity. When companies are distressed, their securities can be purchased at deep discounts. If and when the turnaround materializes, security prices will approach their intrinsic value, generating profits for the distressed manager. *Emerging market* investing can be viewed as a global application of this strategy using sovereign securities.

---

[8]This list of hedge fund strategies, which draws from the discussion in Nicholas (2005), is intended to be representative rather than exhaustive. An alternative list of strategies can be found at www.barclayhedge.com.

- *Global macro:* This broad class of strategies seeks to profit from changes in global economies, typically brought about by shifts in government policy that impact interest rates, in turn affecting currency, stock, and bond markets. Fund managers typically use a "top-down" global approach to identifying opportunities and often participate in all major markets—equities, bonds, currencies, and commodities—though not always at the same time. The strategy uses leverage and derivatives to enhance returns, but also might hedge exposures on a situational basis.

- *Managed futures:* This strategy uses long and short positions in futures contracts, both to take "directional" positions on certain economic or company-specific events and to exploit pricing discrepancies between various contracts. The assets underlying these futures positions may involve commodities, equities, interest rates, or foreign currencies. These strategies frequently employ a substantial degree of financial leverage.

- *Special situations:* Special situation returns occur due to the outcomes of significant events that happen during the normal life cycle of a corporation. These strategies may involve investing in companies around the time of bankruptcies, financial restructurings or recapitalizations, spin-offs, or carve-outs. Given the underlying reason for the investment, positions are usually directional and not fully hedged. *Event-driven* returns are realized when the catalyst necessary to generate the position's intrinsic value (for example, spin-off of an operating division) takes place.

IV. *Multiple Strategies*

- *Fund of funds:* Although not formally a separate category, this investment vehicle acts like a mutual fund of hedge funds, giving investors access to managers otherwise unavailable. The fund of funds position is often a convenient method for achieving a well-diversified hedge fund allocation. It can offer a concentration in a particular strategy (for example, long–short equity) and then either diversify across different hedge fund managers—this is a *multiple manager* approach—or diversify across strategies, which is the *multiple strategy* approach. The primary disadvantage is that there is an extra layer of fees necessary to compensate the fund of funds manager.

17.4.4 Risk Arbitrage Investing: A Closer Look

A popular hedge fund strategy involves taking equity positions in companies that are the target of a merger or takeover attempt. These risk arbitrage investments require managers to compare their own subjective judgment about the ultimate success of the proposed takeover with that implied by the market price of the target firm's stock following the announcement of the prospective deal. If the manager thinks the takeover is more likely to occur than the market does, she will buy shares in the target firm. Conversely, the manager might short sell the target firm shares if she thinks the proposed deal is less likely to be completed.

Consider the following hypothetical example. Suppose the shareholders of Company XYZ receive an unsolicited cash tender offer of $30 per share. At the time of the offer, XYZ's shares traded for $20. Shortly after the takeover announcement—which still must be approved by regulatory authorities—the price of XYZ's shares rises to $28. Brown and Raymond (1986) showed that a simple estimate of the market's *implied probability* that the takeover bid will ultimately be successful is $(28 - 20) \div (30 - 20)$, or 80 percent. In this situation, the risk arbitrage hedge fund manager must think the deal has better than a four-in-five chance of being completed in order to justify purchasing XYZ stock for $28 in the hope of selling at the tender offer price of $30; if the deal falls apart, the manager can assume that XYZ's shares will return to $20. Exhibit 17.15 compares the implied probabilities for a sample of proposed takeovers that were successfully completed (both competing and noncompeting) to a sample of deals that failed. Investors in the market are very good at discriminating between "good" and "bad" deals as far as three months prior to the final resolution.

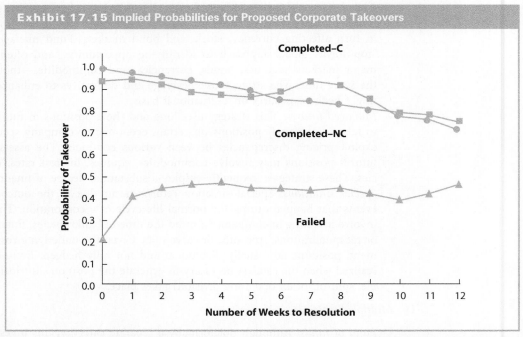

Source: Keith C. Brown and Michael V. Raymond, "Risk Arbitrage and the Prediction of Successful Corporate Takeovers," *Financial Management* 15, no. 3 (August 1986), 54–63.

Panel A of Exhibit 17.16 summarizes JPMorgan Chase (JPM) Bank's takeover of Hambrecht & Quist (HQ), a San Francisco–based investment bank. JPM made a tender offer of $50 per share for all of the outstanding shares of HQ, which at the time of the announcement were trading for $39.28. This represents a tender premium of $10.72, and capturing as much of this premium as possible is the goal of the risk arbitrage investor. However, Panel B indicates that within a day of the announcement, HQ shares were already trading for $48.69. This means that the market had already assessed the probability of this friendly takeover attempt to be 88 percent [= (48.69 − 39.28) ÷ (50 − 39.28)]. Thus, a hedge fund manager who did not already own HQ stock would have to be extremely confident that this deal would be completed to purchase shares at that point.

17.4.5 Hedge Fund Performance

Ibbotson, Chen, and Zhu (2011) have studied hedge fund performance and concluded that, on average, these strategies do produce significant risk-adjusted returns over time. This general conclusion is illustrated in Exhibit 17.17, which plots a capital market line (CML) comparing total risk and return characteristics over the period from 1990 to 2016. During this time, almost all of the indicated strategies plotted above the CML, demonstrating the ability of hedge fund managers to add a positive alpha to their investors over and above the returns produced by traditional products like T-bills and the S&P 500 index. There is also tremendous variation in the risk levels of the myriad strategies; arbitrage-based strategies and those that take both long and short positions (for example, equity market neutral) tend to exhibit far less volatility than those that adopt directional positions (for example, macro and event-driven strategies).

While these CML results are encouraging for potential hedge fund investors, keep in mind that they represent comparisons based on long-term averages. Returns to these strategies show a high degree of variability on a year-to-year basis, in both an absolute and a relative sense. Exhibit 17.18, which lists the annual returns and rankings for 10 different broad hedge fund

Exhibit 17.16 JPMorgan Chase's Takeover of Hambrecht & Quist

A. Tender Offer Details

<HELP> for explanation.
<MENU> to return

N090 **Equity CACS**

More Deal Info ▾	Target Info ▾	Acquirer Info ▾	Acquisition Detail
Target: JP Morgan H&Q	HQ US		Price:
Industry: Finance–Invest Bnkr/Brkr			SIC Code: SEC BROKER/DLR
Country: United States			

Acquirer: JPMorgan Chase & Co	JPM US	Price:	39.28 USD
Industry: Money Center Banks		SIC Code: NATL COML BANK	
Country: United States			

Announced Date: 9/28/99		
Completion Date: 12/10/99	% owned:	
Status: Completed	% acquired: 100.00	

Currency: USD	
Annd tot. value: 1222.2290 Mln	Announced premium: 22.35%
Final tot. val: 1222.2290 Mln	
Paym't Type: Cash	Arbitrage profit:
Cash Terms: 50.000 /Sh.	Cash Value:
Stock Terms:	Acct'g meth:
Net Debt:	
Nature of Bid: Friendly	Action ID: 4845653

TENDER OFFER EFF: 12/08/99 (94.5%). ACQ'R N/C FROM HAMBRECHT & QUIST GROUP UPON COMPLETION.

B. HQ Share Price Movements

HQ US $ Acquired
Screen Printed

Equity GP

Trade Line HQ US Equity   1/4
Range 8/ 1/99 – 12/ 9/99   Period D Daily   Base Currency: USD
Upper Chart: 3 Trade Line   Moving Averages
Lower Chart: V Volume Histogram   Moving Average 15   1) News

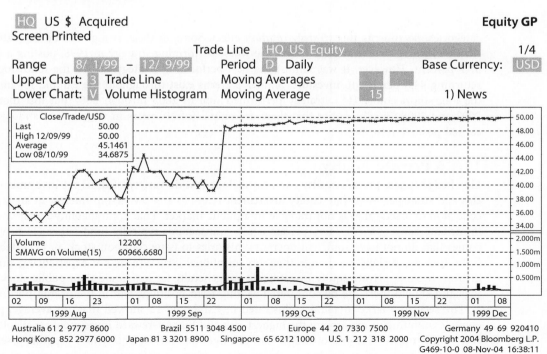

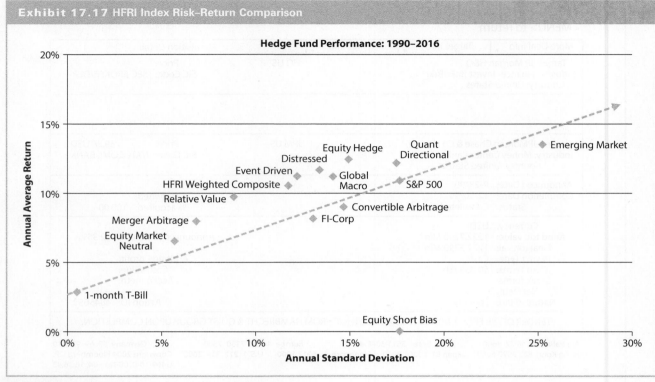

Exhibit 17.17 HFRI Index Risk–Return Comparison

Sources: Hedge Fund Research, Inc.; author calculations.

categories, documents this *strategy rotation* effect. Some of these swings can be dramatic. For example, emerging markets (EM) was the worst-performing strategy in 1998, posting a loss of 37.7 percent. However, it was almost the best-performing strategy during the following year, returning 44.8 percent to investors. Similar patterns exist throughout the exhibit; for instance, the long–short equity (LS) strategy performed well in 2003 through 2007 but lost money in 2002 and 2008. Finally, notice that there are only 2 (of 20) years in which every strategy class earned positive returns.

17.4.6 Private Equity

Like hedge funds, **private equity** can also include a wide variety of different investment vehicles and strategies. A private equity investment refers to any ownership interest in an asset (or collection of assets) that is not tradable in a public market. This nontradability feature has two immediate consequences. First, private equity transactions typically fund either (1) new companies that do not have sufficient operating histories to issue common stock, or (2) established firms that are seeking to change their organizational structure or are experiencing financial distress. Second, private equity investments are generally far less liquid than public stock holdings and should therefore be considered as long-term positions within the overall portfolio.

The security market dynamics illustrated in Exhibit 17.12 showed that, on average, private equity commitments are among the highest-risk and highest-reward investments available. This risk–return trade-off is one of things that distinguishes private equity as a separate asset class from other forms of ownership in the public markets. Another important aspect of private equity that defines it as a unique investment category is that it is not perfectly correlated with the other traditional asset classes (U.S. and non-U.S. stocks, U.S. bonds) or alternative asset

Exhibit 17.18 Hedge Fund Strategy Return Performance: 1997–2016

1997	1998	1999	2000	2001	2002	2003	2004	2005	2006	2007	2008	2009	2010	2011	2012	2013	2014	2015	2016
GM 37.1%	MF 20.6%	LS 47.2%	CA 25.6%	ED 20.0%	MF 18.3%	EM 28.8%	ED 15.6%	EM 17.4%	EM 20.5%	EM 20.3%	MF 18.3%	CA 47.4%	GM 13.5%	GM 6.4%	ED 11.8%	LS 17.7%	MF 18.4%	LS 3.6%	CA 6.6%
EM 26.6%	LS 17.2%	EM 44.8%	DS 15.8%	GM 18.4%	DS 18.1%	ED 25.1%	EM 12.5%	DS 17.0%	ED 15.7%	GM 17.4%	DS 14.9%	EM 30.0%	FI 12.5%	FI 4.7%	FI 11.0%	ED 16.0%	LS 5.6%	DS 2.4%	ED 6.4%
LS 21.5%	MN 13.3%	ED 22.2%	MN 15.0%	CA 14.6%	GM 14.7%	GM 18.0%	LS 11.6%	ED 11.7%	LS 14.4%	LS 13.7%	RA -3.3%	FI 27.4%	MF 12.2%	MN 4.5%	EM 10.3%	MN 9.3%	FI 4.4%	MN 1.7%	RA 5.9%
ED 20.7%	RA 5.6%	CA 16.0%	RA 14.7%	MN 9.3%	MN 7.4%	LS 17.3%	GM 8.5%	LS 9.7%	CA 14.3%	MN 9.3%	GM -4.6%	ED 21.0%	EM 11.3%	DS 3.9%	LS 8.2%	EM 8.8%	GM 3.1%	CA 0.8%	EM 4.5%
MN 14.8%	ED -1.7%	MN 15.3%	GM 11.7%	FI 8.0%	EM 7.4%	MF 14.1%	FI 6.9%	GM 9.3%	GM 13.5%	RA 8.8%	LS -19.8%	LS 19.5%	CA 11.0%	CA 1.1%	CA 7.8%	CA 6.0%	ED 2.6%	FI 0.6%	FI 4.3%
CA 14.5%	GM -3.6%	RA 13.2%	FI 6.3%	EM 5.8%	FI 5.8%	CA 12.9%	MN 6.5%	MN 6.1%	MN 11.2%	ED 8.4%	ED -20.5%	RA 12.0%	ED 10.3%	RA 0.8%	GM 4.6%	RA 4.9%	EM 1.5%	RA 0.4%	GM 3.6%
RA 9.8%	CA -4.4%	FI 12.1%	MF 4.2%	RA 5.7%	CA 4.1%	RA 9.0%	MF 6.0%	RA 3.1%	FI 8.7%	DS 6.0%	FI -28.8%	GM 11.6%	LS 9.3%	MF -4.2%	RA 2.8%	GM 4.3%	MN -1.2%	GM 0.2%	LS -3.4%
FI 9.3%	DS -6.0%	GM 5.8%	LS 2.1%	MF 1.9%	ED -0.7%	FI 8.0%	RA 5.5%	FI 0.6%	RA 8.2%	MF 6.0%	EM -30.4%	MN 4.1%	RA 3.2%	ED -4.2%	MN 0.9%	FI 3.8%	RA -1.3%	EM -0.2%	MN -4.6%
MF 3.1%	FI -8.2%	MF -4.7%	ED 2.0%	DS -3.6%	LS -1.6%	MN 7.1%	CA 2.0%	MF -0.1%	MF 8.1%	CA 5.2%	CA -31.6%	MF -6.6%	MN -0.9%	EM -6.7%	MF -2.9%	MF -2.6%	CA -1.7%	MF -0.9%	MF -6.8%
DS 0.4%	EM -37.7%	DS -14.2%	EM -5.5%	LS -3.7%	RA -3.5%	DS -32.6%	DS -7.7%	CA -2.6%	DS -6.6%	FI 3.8%	MN -40.3%	DS -25.0%	DS -22.5%	LS -7.3%	DS -20.4%	DS -24.9%	DS -5.6%	ED -5.3%	DS -16.9%

Legend:
- **CA** = Convertible Arbitrage
- **DS** = Dedicated Short Bias
- **ED** = Event Driven-Distressed
- **EM** = Emerging Markets
- **FI** = Fixed-Income Arbitrage
- **GM** = Global Macroeconomic
- **LS** = Long/Short Equity
- **MF** = Managed Futures
- **MN** = Equity Market Neutral
- **RA** = Event Driven-Risk Arbitrage

Exhibit 17.19 Asset Class Return, Risk, and Correlations Statistics

Asset Class	Expected Return	Standard Deviation	Correlations:					
			U.S. Equity	Non-U.S. Equity	U.S. Bonds	Hedge Funds	Real Estate	Private Equity
U.S. stock	8.9%	16.4%	1.00					
Non-U.S. stock	8.9	17.5	0.67	1.00				
U.S. bonds	5.2	5.3	0.05	−0.13	1.00			
Hedge funds	6.9	6.5	0.51	0.48	0.06	1.00		
Real estate	7.9	13.6	0.53	0.47	−0.12	0.37	1.00	
Private equity	*13.1*	*30.1*	*0.50*	*0.45*	*0.05*	*0.40*	*0.15*	*1.00*

Source: University of Texas Investment Management Company, *Asset Allocation Review.*

classes (hedge funds, real estate). This is shown in Exhibit 17.19, which lists expected return, standard deviation, and correlation statistics for several different asset classes based on data from a recent 10-year period. While the private and public equity markets in the United States are highly correlated (a correlation coefficient of 0.50), the same is not as true for private equity with U.S. bonds (0.05) or real estate (0.15). Thus, in addition to their potential to deliver high returns, private equity investments also serve as an important source of diversification.

This combination of higher risk and less liquidity often prevents small investors from participating in the private equity market. It is not unusual for private equity funds to require minimum initial investment levels of several million dollars as well as capital "lock ups" (minimum time commitments) of one year or longer. Further, cash distributions from a fund may occur sporadically and only after an extended period of time. Thus, private equity deals are designed for investors who can afford to have the funds committed for a lengthy period of time and who are able to absorb considerable risk. This best describes institutional investors, such as pension funds or endowments, and high-net-worth individual investors.

Development and Organization of the Private Equity Market As Hsu and Kenney (2005) discuss, organized private equity investing began in the United States with the creation of the American Research & Development Corporation (ARD) in 1946. The ARD was formed after World War II as a means of providing investment capital for new business ventures created by and for returning soldiers. The overriding premise of ARD that helped shape the modern private equity industry was the belief that combining a pool of investment capital with skilled management could benefit start-up companies and produce superior returns for investors. Although ultimately disbanded, ARD did manage to raise about $7.5 million in capital and fund at least one highly profitable firm (Digital Equipment Company). It also served as the model for the limited partnership format employed by most private equity funds today, which separates the sources of the investment capital and the source of the investment expertise (for example, the company serving as general partner). By the late 1950s, various agencies of the government had joined the effort to help start-up companies by sponsoring Small Business Investment Companies (SBIC), in which private equity partnerships augment their capital by borrowing federal funds.

While private equity investments can be defined to include any nonpublic ownership interest, these transactions are typically classified into three subcategories:[9]

I. *Venture capital:* Focuses on investments in start-up firms, early-stage businesses, and new products and services created by established businesses. For the past two decades, venture

---

[9]These descriptions of the various types of private equity investments mirror those in Voya Investment Management (2017), which also provides an excellent overview of the industry.

investments have often been concentrated in the technology and health care industries. Venture capital funds tend to specialize by stage of investing, as determined by the time frame in a company's development:

- *Seed:* An entrepreneur has a new idea or product, but no established organization or operations. Investors at this stage (who are sometimes called "angels") provide limited financial capital and other physical resources to help the entrepreneur develop a coherent business plan.
- *Early stage:* The business organization has moved beyond the planning stage and has now been formed. It has employees and products that are in the developmental stage. Early-stage investors commit capital once companies complete the business plan and have at least part of the management team in place.
- *Later stage:* The firm now has an established infrastructure in place, as well as a viable product that is either ready for the market or already producing revenues. Later-stage investors usually provide financing for the expansion of a company that is already producing and shipping a product and increasing its sales volume.

II. *Buyouts:* Involves the acquisition of a product line, set of assets, or entire business from an established company. The company that is being acquired can be either a public or a private firm of virtually any size, and payment for the transaction can involve both debt and equity. (A transaction that involves the use of debt to fund the acquisition of a company is called a *leveraged buyout* [*LBO*].) In an LBO, the assets of the acquired firm are used as collateral for the debt, which is then paid off using either the cash flow generated by the company or the sale of some of the assets. A change in ownership control is almost always a feature of a buyout transaction, which can also include recapitalizations, spin-offs, carveouts, consolidations, and roll-ups. Firms seek buyout financing for several reasons, including a desire to expand their operations, divest themselves of a business unit that no longer fits strategically, or to change management or ownership. When a public firm is taken private, there also may be less scrutiny of its operations by outside parties (regulators, financial analysts), as Brown and Wiles (2015) note.

III. *Special situations:* Includes investments in distressed companies or firms with unique opportunities that may be available on a one-time basis (for example, an investment subsidy resulting from a new governmental regulation). Two important classes in this category are:

- *Distressed debt:* Investors acquire multiple classes of the debt or equity of a publicly traded firm that is in or near bankruptcy. The goal of distressed investors is to create new value in the firm through an infusion of capital and a reorganization of its operations. In a reorganization, distressed investors often forgive the debt obligations of the company in exchange for equity. However, these funds can also profit by liquidating a firm, which is why they are sometimes called "vulture capitalists."
- *Mezzanine financing:* Investors provide a middle level of funding that is subordinated to senior debt but ranks above the existing equity. A typical mezzanine investment includes a subordinated loan to the company along with the receipt of some form of equity participation (warrants, common stock, preferred stock).

Not all of these categories will produce investments with the same risk–return trade-offs. Venture capital commitments are generally considered to be the riskiest private equity transactions because they are often made before the company has a viable source of revenue. Buyout investments can also involve a considerable amount of risk—especially when a large amount of leverage is used—but they do involve companies with established product markets, which typically makes them somewhat more predictable deals. Finally, special situation investments such as mezzanine transactions fall on the safer end of the private equity spectrum because they involve a commitment of capital with a senior claim on the firm's resources.

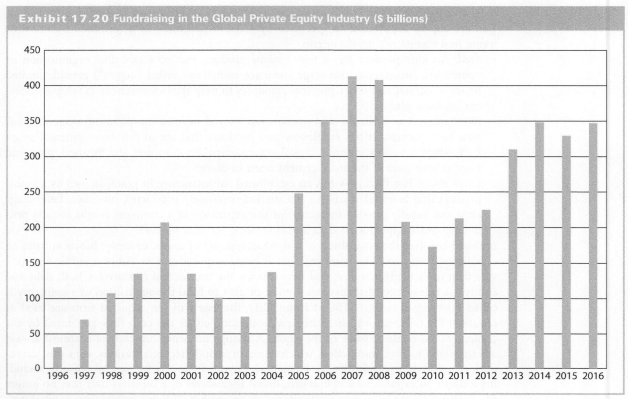

Exhibit 17.20 Fundraising in the Global Private Equity Industry ($ billions)

Source: *2017 Preqin Global Private Equity & Venture Capital Report.*

Exhibit 17.20 illustrates the extent of global private equity investing, in terms of the dollars committed. Generally, there has been a significant increase in private equity investments over the past 20 years, although this market did become depressed following the 2008 financial crisis. As Acharya, Franks, and Servaes (2007) point out, this overall trend reflects the simultaneous impact of several factors in place during this period: (1) the influx of substantial new investment capital as institutional investors shifted their strategic allocation policies toward alternative assets, (2) the availability of relatively inexpensive credit, and (3) relatively high valuations in the equity market.

The Private Equity Investment Process To better understand the dynamics of private equity investing, consider the progression followed by the hypothetical company illustrated in Exhibit 17.21. Bob and Susan, two entrepreneurs who recently graduated from college, have developed a more cost-effective way to search the Internet. After exhausting their personal savings and bank loans to develop the business—which is sometimes called *zero-stage capital*—they turn to a venture capital firm to provide the additional seed and early stage funding they need to advance their idea to the next level. After an evaluation of Bob and Susan's business plan, Venture Partners Fund agrees to provide financial capital and operating expertise to help launch the Internet Search Engine Company (step 1a). In exchange for these resources, Venture Partners receives an equity stake in the new company.

Venture capital investing is extremely risky because the enterprise in question is unlikely to have an established stream of revenues or profits. So, investors like Venture Partners Fund must evaluate firms like Internet Search Engine Company on the basis of their *potential* for future success. Typically, only 2 or 3 out of 10 first-stage ventures become profitable, and

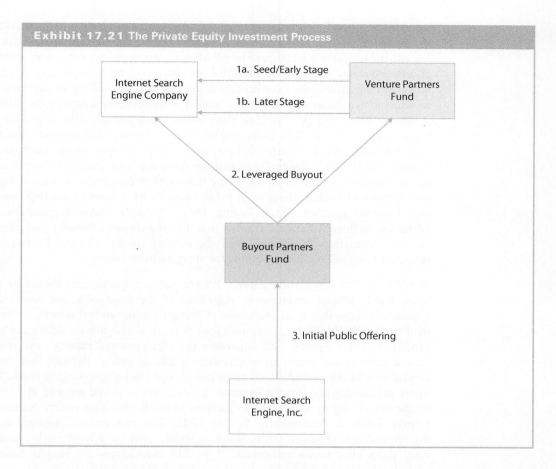

Exhibit 17.21 The Private Equity Investment Process

only 1 in 10 becomes a huge success (for example, Apple, Genentech, FedEx). Venture capital firms usually mitigate their risk by diversifying their investments across a portfolio of start-up companies and limit their exposure to a given start-up by providing funding in stages as the company demonstrates its capacity for success. Thus, Venture Partners Fund will only provide later-stage equity capital to help Internet Search Engine Company expand its operations once the firm has established a viable product (step 1b).

While venture capital funds help companies develop and grow, they will eventually want to sell their equity holdings to create a return on their investment and provide capital to finance new ventures. A typical holding period for successful investments is between three and seven years. Generally, there are two ways that a venture fund can "exit" a company in their investment portfolio: (1) a buyout arranged with another private equity investor or (2) an initial public offering (IPO) of common stock to the public equity market. Assuming that Internet Search Engine Company has developed a solid support base for its product, now suppose that it has attracted the interest of Buyout Partners Fund, a firm specializing in doing leveraged buyouts of privately held companies. Using both debt and its own capital, Buyout Partners Fund purchases all of the existing equity from both Bob and Susan (the original entrepreneurs) and Venture Partners Fund (step 2). Like the venture capitalists, buyout funds attempt to diversify their collection of investments across as many as two or three dozen companies.

Of course, a primary goal of all equity investors is to sell their holdings for more than they paid for them. Given the risk of private transactions compared to the public stock market, buyout capitalists typically attempt to receive an average return of two to three times their initial cost. To achieve this outcome, which can take 10 years or longer, these investors must be able to increase the value of their holdings in any of three ways. First, buyout funds provide a considerable amount of expertise in how a particular business can be run more effectively. Second, buyout firms can also unlock value in a company by adjusting its capital structure to a more optimal combination of debt and equity financing. Finally, value can also be created by expanding the cash flow multiple (price–earnings, enterprise value–EBITDA) that the market is willing to pay for a firm, which can be achieved by expanding growth opportunities or reducing the company's level of risk.

Buyout funds can also liquidate their investments through either a private sale to another buyout investor or an IPO in the public market. Assume that Internet Search Engine Company has continued to expand its operations under the new management team from Buyout Partners Fund. After continuing to run the company with a combination of debt and private equity funds for a number of years, the buyout firm now feels the time is right to sell additional shares of stock to the general public (step 3). As a result of the IPO event, the company now becomes Internet Search Engine, Inc., a publicly traded corporation. An immediate advantage to Buyout Partners Fund is that the IPO creates a broader and more liquid market for their ownership shares. However, the existing owners (Buyout Partners) are frequently restricted from selling their positions for six months or more.

Returns to Private Equity Funds Private equity commitments should be viewed as long-term, highly illiquid investments, regardless of the stage of a company's development in which the partnership fund specializes. Although average annual returns for these investments tend to be quite high over time, the initial years of a new private equity commitment usually produce negative returns. This is because the organizational expenses incurred by the fund's general partner are drawn from invested capital, as well as the fact that the less-successful investments in the portfolio tend to be recognized quickly and written down. However, as the better-performing investments increase in value over time and are sold at a profit, the returns to the private equity fund tend to increase dramatically. This return pattern, known as the **J-curve effect**, is illustrated in Exhibit 17.22. The performance measure in this exhibit is the internal rate of return (IRR), which is widely used for private market investments. In the early years of a fund's operations, these IRR calculations are usually based on valuation

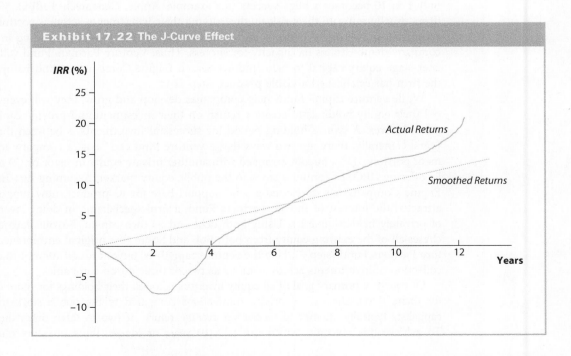

Exhibit 17.22 The J-Curve Effect

	U.S. Equity		Non-U.S.	Fixed Income		Private
Quartile Break	Large Cap	Small Cap	Equity	U.S.	Non-U.S.	Equity
25th	9.87%	14.35%	11.79%	6.82%	7.45%	23.33%
Median	9.14	13.38	9.95	6.05	6.16	13.78
75th	8.61	11.21	8.03	5.88	5.30	11.95
Interquartile range	1.26%	3.14%	3.76%	0.94%	2.15%	11.38%

Exhibit 17.23 Dispersion of Asset Class Investment Returns

Source: Data from a report to the Board of Trustees at Texas Teachers Retirement System.

estimates, since the portfolio companies are themselves illiquid assets that trade infrequently. As these assets are sold over time, the IRR statistics become based on the actual cash distributions to the investors.

Beyond the historical data summarized in Exhibit 17.12 and Exhibit 17.19, another way to think about the performance of private equity investments relative to other asset classes is to compare the *dispersion* of outcomes that investors experience over time. Exhibit 17.23 lists returns for several asset class categories when the investment was made with (1) a "good" fund manager (a manager with performance in the top quartile of all available managers), (2) an "average" manager (the median performer), and (3) a "bad" manager (a bottom-quartile performer). The data reflect historical performance over a recent 10-year period. The last row of the exhibit lists the *interquartile range* for each asset class, which is the difference in the returns between the top- and bottom-quartile managers. This statistic serves as a measure of the dispersion in returns for a given asset category because it reflects the opportunity cost of placing capital with a low-performing manager instead of a top performer. For instance, in large-cap U.S. public equities, the difference between the performance of a good and bad manager is only 1.26 percent. However, in private equity, this difference is 11.38 percent—almost 10 times as large! Thus, in addition to its higher overall risk level, investors also need to realize that the selection of the right private equity fund manager is critical to the success of the investment.

17.5 Ethics and Regulation in the Professional Asset Management Industry

The issue of ethical behavior arises any time one person is hired to look after the interests of another. Economists often refer to this potential conflict as the *principal–agent problem*, which is summarized as follows: A principal (owner of the assets) hires an agent (manager) to manage her assets. She rightfully expects the manager to make decisions that are in her best interest. Although he is being paid to protect the owner's assets, the manager also has the incentive to take actions in his best interest instead. For instance, the manager might misuse the owner's assets in both subtle ways (generating unnecessary expenses for first-class travel or office furnishings) and more blatant ways (expropriation of resources).

This **agency conflict** occurs frequently in financial relationships. Stockholders of a corporation (principals) are the owners of the firm's assets, but they usually hire professional managers (agents) to run the company. Thus, the stockholders face the constant challenge of how they can keep the managers' incentives aligned with theirs. This is particularly important for the investment management business because the entire industry is based on handling someone else's money, meaning that agency issues are always present. In this section, we consider how the industry addresses these conflicts, from both a legal (regulatory) and an ethical standpoint.

17.5.1 Regulation in the Asset Management Industry

Professional portfolio managers are entrusted with the management of trillions of dollars. It is therefore not surprising that the investment industry is highly regulated to ensure a minimum level of acceptable practice. These regulations, which often involve a complex interaction between state and federal laws, are designed so that portfolio managers will act in the best interests of their investors. At their most basic level, regulations are written to promote adequate disclosure of information related to the investment process and to provide various antifraud protections. Exhibit 17.24 describes eight principal securities laws that govern the investment management industry: the Securities Act of 1933 (primary regulatory target: security issuers), the Securities Exchange Act of 1934 (security brokers), the Investment Company Act of 1940 (mutual funds), the Investment Advisers Act of 1940 (advisors and private managers), the Employee Retirement Income Security Act of 1974 (retirement asset managers and fiduciaries), the Sarbanes-Oxley Act of 2002 (corporate managers), the Pension Protection Act

Exhibit 17.24 Principal Securities Laws for the Asset Management Industry

The **Securities Act of 1933** requires federal registration of all public offerings of securities, including investment company shares or units. The 1933 Act also requires that all investors receive a current prospectus describing the fund.

The **Securities Exchange Act of 1934** regulates broker-dealers, including investment company principal underwriters and other entities that sell mutual fund shares, and requires them to register with the SEC. Among other things, the 1934 act requires registered broker-dealers to maintain extensive books and records, segregate customer securities in adequate custodial accounts, and file detailed annual financial reports.

The **Investment Company Act of 1940** regulates the structure and operations of investment companies by imposing restrictions on investments and requiring investment companies, among other things, to maintain detailed books and records, safeguard their portfolio securities, and file semiannual reports with the U.S. Securities and Exchange Commission (SEC).

The **Investment Advisers Act of 1940** requires federal registration of all investment advisers, including those to mutual funds and other investment companies. The Advisers Act contains provisions requiring fund advisers to meet recordkeeping, custodial, reporting, and other regulatory responsibilities.

The **Employee Retirement Income Security Act of 1974** requires minimum standards for the organization, management, and disclosure of employee benefit plans, such as pension plans in private industry. ERISA also establishes standards of conduct for employee benefit plan fiduciaries and created the Individual Retirement Account (IRA) investment vehicle.

The **Sarbanes-Oxley Act of 2002** mandates a number of reforms to enhance corporate responsibility, enhance financial disclosures, and combat corporate and accounting fraud, and created the Public Company Accounting Oversight Board (PCAOB) to oversee the activities of the auditing profession.

The **Pension Protection Act of 2006** requires pension plan sponsors to more accurately calculate their plan obligations and gives employees greater control over how their accounts are invested. The Act also reforms regulations regarding the management and payout provisions for private foundations.

The **Dodd-Frank Wall Street Reform and Consumer Protection Act of 2010** provides for comprehensive regulation of financial markets including increased transparency of derivative securities. The act also provides for significantly enhanced consumer and investor protection reforms.

Source: Adapted in part from data in Investment Company Institute, *2017 Investment Company Fact Book*, and www.sec.gov.

of 2006 (pension fund sponsors and managers), and the Dodd-Frank Wall Street Reform and Consumer Protection Act of 2010 (investor protection).

A main intention of these regulations is to guarantee that investment professionals keep accurate and detailed transaction records and that account information is reported to investors in a fair and timely manner. As the Investment Company Institute notes, the U.S. Securities and Exchange Commission (SEC) is the main federal agency responsible for regulating professional asset management activities in the United States. In addition to monitoring compliance with existing statutes, the SEC performs the following functions:

- Maintains strict standards on the use of leverage so that funds do not take undue risk
- Ensures that funds maintain effective governance systems
- Requires understandable reporting and full disclosure to investors and works to eliminate fraud and abuse
- Reviews required filings of investment companies
- Develops and revises rules to adapt regulations to new circumstances

Other regulatory agencies that help to govern behavior in the investment industry include the Department of Labor (protection of pension plans, including 401(k) plans), the Financial Industry Regulatory Authority (FINRA; the largest independent regulator for all securities firms doing business in the United States), the Commodity Futures Trading Commission (monitoring of futures, swaps, and commodities trading activities), and the Internal Revenue Service (setting and enforcing of tax policies).

The main federal regulation governing private pension funds is the Employee Retirement Income Security Act (ERISA), which was enacted in 1974 and primarily impacts the activities of private management companies as well as mutual funds. ERISA clearly states that pension funds are to be managed to the needs of the plan participants and their beneficiaries—as opposed to the corporation sponsoring the plan—and that managers should diversify plan assets so as to minimize the risk of large losses. As Del Guercio (1996) discusses, a key feature of ERISA is the *prudent man* statute, which outlines the level of fiduciary care that the manager must provide to the investor. This definition of the manager's required level of "care, skill, prudence, and diligence" was the first legal recognition of prudence involving the entire portfolio, rather than the individual securities on a case-by-case basis.

One of the advantages that the hedge fund industry has enjoyed historically is being relatively free from regulatory prohibitions that might impede the investment process. These funds tended to adopt a limited liability format (limited partnership) purposely to avoid having to register with the SEC. This freedom allowed hedge funds to employ strategic tools (leverage, short selling) that were not available to traditional managers. However, the Dodd-Frank Reform Act of 2010 made registration mandatory for hedge fund advisers with more than $150 million in regulatory AUM. A hedge fund qualifies for an exemption from the Investment Company Act if it has fewer than 100 investors, while hedge fund managers are exempt from the Investment Advisors Act if they manage less than $25 million in assets. On the other hand, if a quarter of a hedge fund's assets consist of retirement plan assets, the fund must comply with the restrictions set forth under ERISA.

17.5.2 Standards for Ethical Behavior

Many developed economies like that in the United States are founded on the notion of financial market discipline. In such a system, government intervention is necessary to remedy situations when market forces fail to adequately protect investor interests. Unfortunately, as Boatright (2008) points out, such failures do occur. Investors are well aware of the securities scandals of the 1980s that made Ivan Boesky and Michael Milken household names. Further, the market timing trading scandals that tainted the mutual fund industry in 2003 as well as the subprime loan crisis of 2008 proved that lapses in ethical judgment could take place at the company level as well. The financial rescue of Long Term Capital Management in the 1990s created considerable interest in increasing governmental oversight of the hedge fund industry.

Transgressions of this nature underscore that although regulations can punish those violating the law, they cannot prevent all such abuses from occurring, as noted by Statman (2009). Absolute prevention requires self-regulation on the part of the asset manager in the form of a strict set of personal ethical standards. Prentice (2007) stressed that the desire of individuals and firms in investment management to maintain their reputation with clients is a major motivating factor in the practice of self-regulation. Avera (1994) outlines four general principles for conduct in the profession: (1) Managers conduct themselves with integrity and act in an ethical manner, (2) they perform financial analysis in a professional and ethical manner, (3) they act with competence and strive to improve, and (4) they always use proper care and exercise independent professional judgment.

The CFA (Chartered Financial Analysts) Institute has developed for its worldwide membership of security analysts and money managers a rigorous *Code of Ethics* and *Standards of Professional Conduct* based on these principles. (These are available online at www.cfainstitute.org and in Appendix B at the back of this book.) The *Code of Ethics* expands on the four themes listed previously:

Members of the CFA Institute must:

- *Act with integrity, competence, diligence, respect, and in an ethical manner with the public, clients, prospective clients, employers, employees, colleagues in the investment profession, and other participants in the global capital markets.*
- *Place the integrity of the investment profession and the interests of clients above their own personal interests.*
- *Use reasonable care and exercise independent professional judgment when conducting investment analysis, making investment recommendations, taking investment actions, and engaging in other professional activities.*
- *Practice and encourage others to practice in a professional and ethical manner that will reflect credit on themselves and the profession.*
- *Promote the integrity of, and uphold the rules governing, capital markets.*
- *Maintain and improve their professional competence and strive to maintain and improve the competence of other investment professionals.* (CFA Institute, 2014)

The specific standards of practice suggested by these ethical mandates provide asset managers with precisely defined conduct and actions that are acceptable (or, more to the point, unacceptable) in daily practice. For example, the general principle that managers should use proper care becomes a specific requirement that they must be able to justify the suitability of any investment decision made on behalf of a particular client. The CFA Institute expects all of its members, which includes everyone holding the CFA designation, to uphold these standards. Violations deemed severe enough can result in the loss of a manager's charter.

In recognition of the unique place of trust that portfolio managers enjoy, a recent initiative of the CFA Institute has been the creation of a comprehensive *Asset Manager Code*. This code sets forth minimum standards for providing asset management services to clients, based on the following general principles:

Managers have the following responsibilities to their clients. Managers must:

1. *Act in a professional and ethical manner at all times.*
2. *Act for the benefit of clients.*
3. *Act with independence and objectivity.*

4. *Act with skill, competence, and diligence.*

5. *Communicate with clients in a timely and accurate manner.*

6. *Uphold the applicable rules governing capital markets.* (CFA Institute, 2014)

Many firms already have such standards in place, but others (including traditional and hedge fund managers) do not, and this is the niche the Code attempts to fill.

17.5.3 Examples of Ethical Conflicts

Many ethical breaches, such as plagiarizing research reports or falsifying performance statements, are unambiguously wrong. Other lapses are not as clear-cut. We conclude this section with a discussion of three examples of how possible conflicts between the manager and the investor can arise from accepted business practices.

Incentive Compensation Schemes We saw earlier in the chapter that traditional asset management companies—both public and private—typically receive fees based on AUM. Further, hedge fund and private equity managers also receive a performance allocation fee that is tied directly to the portfolio's performance. The managers at these companies, in turn, are often compensated with a base salary and bonus that depends on the performance of their fund relative to those of their peers. Brown, Harlow, and Starks (1996) argued that this arrangement is analogous to a golf or tennis tournament where the players with the best relative performance at the end of the competition receive the largest payoffs. They documented that mutual fund managers with the worst relative performance midway through a compensation period were more likely to increase the risk of the portfolio in an effort to increase their final standing. Of course, altering fund risk to enhance their own compensation suggests that some managers may not always act in their clients' best interests.

Soft Dollar Arrangements A second potential ethical dilemma for professional asset managers involves the use of **soft dollars**. Soft dollars are generated when a manager commits the investor to paying a brokerage commission that is higher than the simple cost of executing a security trade in exchange for the manager receiving additional bundled services from the broker. A typical example of this practice would be for a manager to route her equity trades through a nondiscount broker in order to receive security research reports that the brokerage firm produces. It may not be hard for the manager to justify how this additional research benefits the investor—who ultimately pays for the service—but the story is quite different if, instead of research, the manager receives from the broker "perks," such as office equipment, secretarial services, or even payment for personal travel. Bogle (2009) argues that this practice can result in a misallocation of resources or an expropriation of investor wealth by the manager, although Horan and Johnsen (2000) document that the use of soft dollars is actually a cost-effective way for investors to monitor a manager's behavior.

Marketing Investment Management Services How and when should money managers advertise their services? Conventional wisdom holds that it is in the investors' best interests for managers to build a steady awareness over time of their relative merits. However, in their survey of the mutual fund market, Capon, Fitzsimons, and Prince (1996) documented that the main factor determining which fund to invest in was the immediate past return of the portfolio. Zweig (2000) observed that this tendency causes mutual funds to time their advertisements around relative peaks in their performance. Further, firms that run a family of funds can choose which portfolio or manager they want to promote on a situational basis, while still maintaining continuous brand awareness for the entire operation. Despite the usual disclaimers that "past returns are not an indication of future performance," the decision to always promote the "hot hand" is likely to be effective, but it is also likely to result in a misallocation of investor capital.

In summary, investors should recognize that potential ethical conflicts will exist any time they hire professional investment managers. Investors are protected by regulations that oversee the security industry as well as the strict standards imposed by trade associations such as CFA Institute. Perhaps the best protection that investors have is the vast majority of investment advisors and managers throughout the world who are unwilling to do anything that would jeopardize their reputations.

17.6 WHAT DO YOU WANT FROM A PROFESSIONAL ASSET MANAGER?

What functions do you want your portfolio manager to perform for you? The list probably includes the following items:

1. Help determine your investment objectives and constraints (return goals, risk tolerance), and develop a portfolio that is consistent with them.
2. Maintain your portfolio diversification within your desired risk class, while allowing flexibility so that you can shift between alternative investment instruments as desired.
3. Attempt to achieve a risk-adjusted performance level that is superior to that of your relevant benchmark; some investors may be willing to sacrifice diversification for superior returns in limited segments of their portfolios.
4. Administer the account, keep records of costs and transactions, provide timely information for tax purposes, and reinvest dividends if desired.
5. Maintain ethical standards of behavior at all times.

Not all of the types of asset management organizations we have discussed in this chapter address each of these goals. For instance, mutual funds do not determine your risk preference for you, while alternative asset investments are seldom well diversified. However, once you determine your risk–return preferences, you can choose a mutual fund designed to achieve almost any investment goal. In general, these types of managers are proficient in meeting their stated goals for investment strategies and risk. Private asset management companies are oriented toward providing similar services (including investment policy development) for clients who have larger amounts of investable capital.

The second function your portfolio manager might perform for you is to maintain the diversification of your portfolio within your desired risk class. Both types of traditional asset manager (private management companies and mutual funds) generally maintain the stability of their correlation with the market over time because few managers change the makeup of reasonably well-diversified portfolios very much. Mutual funds also meet the desire for flexibility to change investment instruments by creating numerous funds within a given management company. Typically, investment groups—such as Vanguard or Fidelity Investments—will allow you to shift between portfolios in their family of funds without a charge. By their nature, private management companies, hedge funds, and private equity firms tend to restrict an investor's ability to make these sorts of changes; accordingly, these management types are considered to be less liquid than mutual funds.

The third function of your portfolio manager is to provide risk-adjusted performance that is superior to your benchmark, which implies that it is superior to a naive buy-and-hold investment policy. The rapid development of the alternative asset industry over the past several years suggests two things. First, investors increasingly view these managers as being better suited to produce positive alphas than traditional managers. Second, it is increasingly difficult for most traditional managers to generate superior risk-adjusted returns because of the many constraints imposed on their investment process (for example, short sale prohibitions, leverage restrictions).

The fourth function of a portfolio manager is account administration. All managers provide this service to some degree. However, private management companies are the most likely to see substantially all of a client's assets, and so these firms are in the best position to administer the account most effectively. Most mutual funds also provide many valuable administrative services. For instance, they allow automatic reinvestment of dividends and supply annual statements of distribution activity that can be used to prepare tax returns. Given their partnership format, hedge funds and private equity funds also provide investors with necessary tax information, as well as periodic accounting of investment activity.

The final function that you should expect from your portfolio manager is ethical behavior that follows the prevailing regulations and standards of conduct in the industry. For all investors, this is—and should be—a nonnegotiable requirement, regardless of the organizational form of the company. As we have seen, professional asset management is a fiduciary business, and managers whose conduct violates the trust of those whose wealth they protect and grow will not last long and, in extreme cases, may even suffer legal consequences.

Typically, no single manager is equipped to provide all of the services that you may require. Therefore, it is quite common for investors to form a "portfolio" of managers with different capabilities (for example, a hedge fund manager to provide superior risk-adjusted returns, an index mutual fund manager to provide diversification for the majority of your assets). Given what we know about the value of diversifying financial capital across different asset classes and securities, it should come as no surprise that the same principle holds for portfolio management skills as well.

SUMMARY

- There are two primary types of professional asset management companies. Management and advisory firms hold the assets of individual and institutional investors in separate accounts. Investment companies are pools of assets that are managed collectively. Investors in these funds receive shares representing their proportional ownership in the underlying portfolio of securities. These fund shares can be either traded in the secondary market (closed-end) or sold directly back to the investment company (mutual fund) at the prevailing net asset value. A wide variety of funds are available, so you can find one to match almost any investment objective or combination of objectives.

- In recent years, the professional asset management industry has undergone considerable structural change. Among traditional "long-only" asset management firms, there has been a trend toward consolidating assets under management (AUM) in large, multiproduct companies. This has reduced management fees, which are usually charged on a declining percentage of AUM. Investment companies also often charge fees for marketing their shares, in the form of front-end fees, annual 12b-1 fees, or back-end load fees. Publicly available information exists on mutual fund investment practices and performance, to help investors make decisions that are appropriate for their circumstances.

- A second trend that has marked the professional asset management industry in recent years has been the rapid development of vehicles to invest in alternative asset classes, such as hedge funds and private equity. One of the main advantages that these funds enjoy is that they are generally less restricted in what strategies they can follow and investment techniques they can employ, such as the use of both leverage and short selling. Many investors regard alternative asset managers as being in a unique position to produce superior risk-adjusted returns.

- Issues of ethical behavior arise any time one person is hired to perform a service for another. The professional asset management industry protects investors through a series of government regulations and voluntary standards of practice. The primary purpose of these regulations and standards is to ensure that managers deal with all investors fairly and equitably and that information about investment performance is accurately reported. Two areas of concern in the investment community involve manager compensation arrangements and soft dollars.

SUGGESTED READINGS

Bailey, Jeffrey V., Jesse L. Phillips, and Thomas M. Richards. *A Primer for Investment Trustees.* Charlottesville, VA: Research Foundation of the CFA Institute, 2011.

CFA Institute. *Standards of Practice Handbook,* 11th ed. Charlottesville, VA: CFA Institute, 2014.

Pozen, Robert, and Theresa Hamacher. *The Fund Industry: How Your Money Is Managed,* 2nd ed. Hoboken, NJ: Wiley, 2015.

Zask, Ezra. *All About Hedge Funds,* 2nd ed. Columbus, OH: McGraw-Hill Education, 2013.

Zeisberger, Claudia, Michael Prahl, and Bowen White. *Mastering Private Equity.* West Sussex, England: John Wiley & Sons, 2017.

QUESTIONS

1. What are the differences between a management and advisory firm and an investment company? Describe the approach toward portfolio management adopted by each organization.

2. It has been suggested that the professional asset management community is rapidly becoming dominated by a fairly small number of huge, multiproduct firms. Discuss whether the data presented in Exhibit 17.2 support that view.

3. Closed-end funds generally invest in securities and financial instruments that are relatively illiquid, whereas most mutual funds invest in widely traded stocks and bonds. Explain the difference between closed-end and open-end funds and why this liquidity distinction matters.

4. What is the difference between a load fund and a no-load fund?

5. Should you care about how well a mutual fund is diversified? Why or why not?

6. As an investigator evaluating how well mutual fund managers select undervalued stocks or forecast market returns, discuss whether net or gross (before fund expenses) returns are more relevant.

7. Many investors in private equity transactions do so through participation in limited partnership arrangements. Explain how limited partnership structures are organized and illustrate your answer with a flowchart diagram showing how client investments are structured in this form of asset management organization.

8. Catherine Marco is a portfolio manager with Mouton Investments, Inc., a regional money management firm. She is considering investments in alternative assets and decides to research the following three questions about long-short strategies and hedge funds:

   (1) How can the alpha generated from a long-short hedge fund strategy in one asset class be transported to another asset class?

   (2) What are the *three* major quantifiable sources of risk that a fund of hedge funds manager must consider in risk monitoring?

   (3) For a fund of hedge funds, how does risk-based leverage differ from accounting-based leverage?

   a. Formulate *one* correct response to *each* of Marco's three questions.

   Marco decides to explore various hedge fund investment strategies and reviews the following three strategy components:

   i. Buy stocks after positive earnings surprise announcements, anticipating that the stock price will rise in the short term.

   ii. Establish appropriate long and short positions in stocks of companies that have announced a merger or acquisition or are rumored to be considering such a transaction.

   iii. Use neural networks to detect patterns in historical data.

   b. Identify the hedge fund investment strategy that is best characterized by *each* of the three strategy components reviewed by Marco.

Following her research, Marco applies her findings to the situation of an individual client. This client currently holds only traditional equity and fixed income investments and is willing to consider investing in alternative assets to lower the risk of his portfolio.

Marco forms the following five conclusions about investing in alternative assets for this client:

i. Investing in a fund of hedge funds is likely to increase the client's portfolio diversification and allow the client's portfolio to have exposure to a wide variety of hedge funds that may not otherwise be available to the client.

ii. A lack of transparency and the fund manager's inability to add value through portfolio construction are both disadvantages of investing in a fund of hedge funds.

iii. Because a directional hedge fund is expected to exhibit a lower dispersion of returns than a nondirectional hedge fund, a directional hedge fund is a more appropriate investment for this client.

iv. One appropriate hedge fund investment strategy for this client is a macro hedge fund, which is likely to provide increased returns with a relatively low standard deviation of returns.

v. Another approach that is consistent with the client's objectives is to use an equitized long-short strategy, which can be expected to neutralize market risk.

c. Judge whether *each* of Marco's five conclusions is correct or incorrect. If incorrect, give *one* reason why the conclusion is incorrect.

9. Most money managers have a portion of their compensation tied to the performance of the portfolios they manage. Explain how this arrangement can create an ethical dilemma for the manager.

10. What are soft dollar arrangements? Describe one potential way they can be used to transfer wealth from the investor to the manager.

PROBLEMS

1. Suppose ABC Mutual Fund had no liabilities and owned only four stocks, as follows:

Stock	Shares	Price	Market Value
W	1,000	$12	$12,000
X	1,200	15	18,000
Y	1,500	22	33,000
Z	800	16	12,800
			$75,800

The fund began by selling $50,000 of stock at $8.00 per share. What is its *NAV*?

2. Suppose you are considering investing $1,000 in a load fund that charges a fee of 8 percent, and you expect your investment to earn 15 percent over the next year. Alternatively, you could invest in a no-load fund with similar risk that charges a 1 percent redemption fee. You estimate that this no-load fund will earn 12 percent. Given your expectations, which is the better investment and by how much?

3. Consider the recent performance of the Closed Fund, a closed-end fund devoted to finding undervalued, thinly traded stocks:

Period	NAV	Premium/Discount
0	$10.00	0.0%
1	11.25	−5.0
2	9.85	+2.3
3	10.50	−3.2
4	12.30	−7.0

Here, price premiums and discounts are indicated by pluses and minuses, respectively, and Period 0 represents Closed Fund's initiation date.

a. Calculate the average return per period for an investor who bought 100 shares of the Closed Fund at the initiation and then sold her position at the end of Period 4.

b. What was the average periodic growth rate in *NAV* over that same period?

c. Calculate the periodic return for another investor who bought 100 shares of Closed Fund at the end of Period 1 and sold his position at the end of Period 2.

d. What was the periodic growth rate in *NAV* between Periods 1 and 2?

4. CMD Asset Management has the following fee structure for clients in its equity fund:

1.00% of first $5 million invested

0.75% of next $5 million invested

0.60% of next $10 million invested

0.40% above $20 million

a. Calculate the annual dollar fees paid by Client 1, who has $27 million under management, and Client 2, who has $97 million under management.

b. Calculate the fees paid by both clients as a percentage of their assets under management.

c. What is the economic rationale for a fee schedule that declines (in percentage terms) with increases in assets under management?

5. Describe a potential conflict of interest in each of the following four situations:

a. An investment advisor whose compensation is based on commissions from client trades

b. An investment manager's use of client brokerage ("soft dollars") to purchase research or other services

c. A portfolio manager of a mutual fund who purchases, for the fund, a substantial amount of stock in a small-capitalization company whose warrants the manager owns

d. A research analyst who accepts reimbursement for food, lodging, and air transportation expenses for a site visit from the company on which she is writing a research report

> Note: In formulating your answers, you should consider CFA Institute's *Code of Ethics and Standards of Professional Conduct* located in Appendix B in the back of this book.

6. Suppose that at the start of the year, a no-load mutual fund has a net asset value of $27.15 per share. During the year, it pays its shareholders a capital gain and dividend distribution of $1.12 per share and finishes the year with an *NAV* of $30.34.

a. What is the return to an investor who holds 257.876 shares of this fund in his (nontaxable) retirement account?

b. What is the after-tax return for the same investor if these shares were held in an ordinary savings account? Assume that the investor is in the 30 percent tax bracket.

c. If the investment company allowed the investor to automatically reinvest his cash distribution in additional fund shares, how many additional shares could the investor acquire? Assume that the distribution occurred at year end and that the proceeds from the distribution can be reinvested at the year-end *NAV*.

7. The Focus Fund is a mutual fund that holds long-term positions in a small number of non-dividend-paying stocks. Its holdings at the end of two recent years are as follows:

Stock	YEAR 1		YEAR 2	
	Shares	Price	Shares	Price
A	100,000	$45.25	100,000	$48.75
B	225,000	25.38	225,000	24.75
C	375,000	14.50	375,000	12.38
D	115,000	87.13	115,000	98.50
E	154,000	56.50	154,000	62.50
F	175,000	63.00	175,000	77.00
G	212,000	32.00	212,000	38.63
H	275,000	15.25	275,000	8.75
I	450,000	9.63	450,000	27.45
J	90,000	71.25	90,000	75.38
K	87,000	42.13	87,000	49.63
L	137,000	19.88	0	27.88
M	0	17.75	150,000	19.75
Cash		$3,542,000		$2,873,000
Expenses		$ 730,000		$ 830,000

At the end of both years, Focus Fund had 5,430,000 shares outstanding.

a. Calculate the net asset value for a share of the Focus Fund at the end of Year 1, being sure to include the cash position in the net total portfolio value.

b. Immediately after calculating its Year 1 *NAV*, Focus Fund sold its position in Stock L and purchased its position in Stock M (both transactions were done at Year 1 prices). Calculate the Year 2 *NAV* for Focus Fund, and compute the growth rate in the fund share value on a percentage basis.

c. At the end of Year 2, how many fund shares of the Focus Fund could the manager redeem without having to liquidate her stock positions (that is, using only the cash account)?

d. If immediately after calculating the Year 2 *NAV* the manager received investor redemption requests for 500,000 shares, how many shares of each stock would she have to sell in order to maintain the same proportional ownership position in each stock? Assume that she liquidates the entire cash position before she sells any stock holdings.

8. Mutual funds can effectively charge sales fees in one of three ways: front-end load fees, 12b-1 (annual) fees, or deferred (back-end) load fees. Assume that the SAS Fund offers its investors the choice of the following sales fee arrangements: (1) a 3 percent front-end load, (2) a 0.50 percent annual deduction, or (3) a 2 percent back-end load, paid at the liquidation of the investor's position. Also, assume that SAS Fund averages *NAV* growth of 12 percent per year.

a. If you start with $100,000 in investment capital, calculate what an investment in SAS would be worth in three years under each of the proposed sales fee schemes. Which scheme would you choose?

b. If your investment horizon were 10 years, would your answer in part (a) change? Demonstrate.

c. Explain the relationship between the timing of the sales charge and your investment horizon. In general, if you intend to hold your position for a long time, which fee arrangement would you prefer?

9. Clark & Kerns (C&K), a U.S. pension fund manager for more than 20 years, plans to establish offices in a European and a Pacific Rim country in order to manage pension funds located in those countries and invest in their local stock markets. Tony Clark, CFA, managing partner, learns that investment organizations and their affiliates in the European country perform three functions:

- Consult with corporate pension sponsors on how the pension fund should be managed and by whom
- Manage their portfolios
- Execute securities transactions as a broker for the funds

Common practice in this country is to withhold disclosure of the ownership of business organizations. Clark believes that C&K must provide all three functions to compete effectively. He therefore decides to establish offices in Europe to offer all three services to prospective pension fund clients, through local organizations owned by C&K. The pension consulting organization will be Europension Group; the portfolio management firm will be C&K International; and the broker-dealer operation will be Alps Securities.

a. Briefly describe two CFA Institute Standards of Professional Conduct that apply to Clark, if C&K provides all three functions on a combined basis. Describe the specific duty Clark is required to perform to comply with these standards.

Clark learns that a customary practice in the European country is to allocate at least 80 percent of pension fund assets to fixed-income securities.

b. Identify and briefly explain two CFA Institute Standards of Professional Conduct that apply to this situation.

Clark observes that portfolio managers in the Pacific Rim country frequently use insider information in their investment decisions. Because the pension fund management industry is performance oriented, Clark decides to adopt local investment practices as the only way to attract and retain local corporate clients in that country.

c. Identify and briefly explain two CFA Institute Standards of Professional Conduct that apply to this situation.

10. Peter and Andrea Mueller have built up their $600,000 investment portfolio over many years through regular purchases of mutual funds holding only U.S. securities. Each purchase was based on personal research but without consideration of their other holdings. They would now like advice on their total portfolio, which follows:

	Type	Market Sector	Beta	Percent of Total
Andrea's company stock	Stock	Small-cap growth	1.40	35
Blue-chip growth fund	Stock	Large-cap growth	1.20	20
Super-beta fund	Stock	Small-cap growth	1.60	10
Conservative fund	Stock	Large-cap value	1.05	2
Index fund	Stock	Large-cap index	1.00	3
No-dividend fund	Stock	Large-cap growth	1.25	25
Long-term zero-coupon fund	Bond	Government	—	5

Evaluate the Muellers' portfolio in terms of the following criteria:
a. Preference for "minimal volatility"
b. Equity diversification
c. Asset allocation (including cash flow needs)

11. You are running an arbitrage-based hedge fund focusing on merger transactions. Company XYZ has just received a tender offer for $45 per share from the management of AcquisiCorp. For the past two weeks, XYZ's shares traded at around $30, but immediately after the tender

offer the market price of those shares rose to their current level of $42. On the other hand, AcquisiCorp's share price fell from $83 to $79 right after the announcement of the proposed takeover. Further, interest rates in the economy have recently risen from 2.7 percent to 3.3 percent based on renewed fears of inflation.

a. Calculate the market's implied probability that the takeover will ultimately be successful.

b. Explain how you can use this information to decide whether you should take a long position or a short position in the stock of Company XYZ.

CHAPTER 18

Evaluation of Portfolio Performance

After you read this chapter, you should be able to answer the following questions:

- What are the two main questions of performance measurement?
- What are the peer group comparison and portfolio drawdown methods of evaluating an investor's performance?
- What are the Sharpe and Treynor portfolio performance measures?
- What is the Jensen portfolio performance measure, and how can it be adapted to include multifactor models of risk and expected return?
- What are the information ratio and the Sortino ratio, and how are they related to the other performance measures?
- When evaluating a sample of portfolios, how do you determine how well diversified they are?
- How can investment performance be measured by analyzing the security holdings of a portfolio?
- What is attribution analysis, and how can it be used to distinguish between a portfolio manager's market timing and security selection skills?
- What are customized benchmarks, and what are the important characteristics that any benchmark should possess?
- What are time-weighted and dollar-weighted returns, and which should be reported under the CFA Institute's Global Investment Performance Standards?

This chapter outlines the theory and practice of evaluating the performance of an investment portfolio. The first thing about this process to recognize is that it is always *ex post* in nature. That is, unlike the portfolio formation and management endeavors themselves, which the investor does in anticipation of producing great return outcomes in the future, the exercise of evaluating those outcomes occurs at the back end of the investor's horizon. So, portfolio performance evaluation looks in the "rearview mirror" to see if the investor has achieved his or her expected investment goals.

We begin by considering what investors hope to accomplish in measuring the performance of their portfolios, as well as the two questions framing the entire process. To answer these questions, which represent the *how* and the *why* of performance evaluation, we discuss the development a number of techniques that define the basic performance measurement toolkit. Some of these tools are quite simple in that they compare realized returns without taking risk into account. Many others, though, are *risk-adjusted measures* that do consider some aspect of the volatility investors encountered. In fact, we will see that a central tenet of modern performance measurement is that it is impossible to make a thorough evaluation of an investment without explicitly controlling for the risk of the portfolio.

Given the complexity of the topic, it comes as no surprise that there is not a single universally accepted procedure for risk-adjusting portfolio returns. Although some redundancy exists among the measures we examine, each of them provides a unique perspective, so they are best viewed as a complementary set. We also demonstrate how an investor can evaluate a manager's performance by looking at the underlying security holdings of the portfolio and we examine attribution analysis, a measurement technique designed to establish the source of a portfolio manager's skill.

The chapter concludes with a discussion of a number of factors to consider when applying these various measures, including the selection of the proper benchmark to use in the risk-adjustment process and the characteristics of a good benchmark. Finally, we examine industry standards for calculating returns and reporting portfolio performance to investors.

18.1 THE TWO QUESTIONS OF PERFORMANCE MEASUREMENT

In our discussion of passive and active portfolio management in Chapter 11, we saw that the actual return a manager produces over an investment horizon can be split into (1) the return she should have earned given her capital commitment and the amount of risk in the portfolio (the expected return) and (2) any incremental return due to her superior investment skills (alpha). This was expressed as:

$$\text{Total Actual Return} = [\text{Expected Return}] + [\text{Alpha}]$$
$$= [\text{Risk-Free Rate} + \text{Risk Premium}] + [\text{Alpha}]$$

This becomes relevant once again as we consider the notion of how to measure the quality of a manager's investment performance. Generally speaking, we will see that assessing the performance of an investment portfolio is an exercise in comparing the return that the fund *actually produced* to a measure of the returns that the fund *should have produced*. So, the manager is ultimately judged on her ability to deliver on expectations and produce an additional alpha component.

Clearly, an essential aspect of assessing investment performance properly is specifying the expected return the manager should produce. As we have seen, investors can only expect to be rewarded, on average, for their systematic risk exposures, so the ability to maintain a diversified portfolio is often a critical skill for a manager to demonstrate. Further, an important concept that underlies the performance measurement process is that the expected return can be thought of as the **opportunity cost** for investing in the managed portfolio. That is, the expected return becomes the answer to the following question: If an investor did not hold her actual portfolio, what would be the return be to her *next best alternative*?

In practice, there are three ways that investors can estimate expected returns:

1. The average contemporaneous return to a **peer group** of comparably managed portfolios
2. The contemporaneous return to an index (or index fund) serving as a **benchmark** for the managed portfolio
3. The return estimated by a **risk factor model**, such as the CAPM or multifactor model

Each of these approaches has advantages and disadvantages. Peer groups and benchmarks are easily observable and often represent viable alternative investment vehicles—thus making them a genuine opportunity cost—but they do not control explicitly for the risk incurred by the actual portfolio. Conversely, factor models can estimate systematic risk exposures very precisely but are generally not investible alternatives; it is difficult to "buy" the return from a theoretical model. Consequently, in making a full assessment of a given manager's performance, it is frequently the case that multiple sources of expected returns are used.

> **Exhibit 18.1** Taxonomy of Popular Portfolio Performance Measures
>
> 1. *How* **did the portfolio manager actually perform?**
>   - Simple performance measures
>   - Peer group comparison
>   - Portfolio drawdown
>   - Risk-adjusted performance measures
>   - Sharpe ratio
>   - Treynor ratio
>   - Jensen's alpha
>   - Information ratio
>   - Sortino ratio
>   - Holdings-based performance measures
>   - Grinblatt-Titman measure
>   - Characteristic selectivity measure
> 2. *Why* **did the portfolio manager perform as he or she did?**
>   - Decomposition of portfolio returns
>   - Attribution analysis
>   - Fama selectivity measure

There are two main questions that an investor attempts to answer when assessing the performance of an investment manager:

First, *how did the portfolio manager actually perform?*
Second, *why did the portfolio manager perform as he or she did?*

The first of these questions is likely to be the most important one the investor asks because this is where the manager's actual return will be compared to the expected return. For many investors, the answer to this question represents the "bottom line" as to whether the manager they hired possesses genuine investment skill. With the second question, the investor then attempts to move beyond the issue of whether the manager was able to satisfy expectations to investigate the *source* of the actual performance. That is, given all of the things a manager can do in an attempt to produce positive alpha (for example, superior security selection, market timing), which decisions were effective and which were ineffective?

The performance measurement process comprises a number of conceptual and statistical tools designed to answer these two questions. Exhibit 18.1 provides a taxonomy of the most popular techniques used in practice, categorized by the question they were designed to address. Notice that most of these performance measures are aimed at answering the first question. They differ according to whether they either do (risk-adjusted measures) or do not (simple measures) explicitly assess the portfolio's risk exposure, as well as how that risk is defined and how returns are adjusted to account for risk. We will also see that a manager's decision-making skills can be assessed *indirectly* by looking at the returns the portfolio produces or *directly* by looking at changes in the fund's holdings. In the rest of the chapter, we discuss each of these measures in more detail.

18.2 SIMPLE PERFORMANCE MEASUREMENT TECHNIQUES

At one time, investors evaluated portfolio performance almost entirely on the basis of returns. Developments in portfolio theory in the early 1960s showed investors how to quantify risk in terms of the variability of returns. Still, because no single measure combined both return and risk, the two factors had to be considered separately, as Friend, Blume, and Crockett (1970) did by grouping portfolios into similar risk classes based on return variance and then comparing the rates of return for alternative portfolios directly within these risk classes.

18.2.1 Peer Group Comparisons

A **peer group comparison**, which Kritzman (1990) describes as the most common manner of evaluating portfolio managers, collects the returns produced by a representative set of investors over a specific period of time and displays them in a simple boxplot format. The universe is typically divided into percentiles, showing the relative ranking of a given investor. For instance, a manager who produced a one-year return of 12.4 percent would be in the 10th percentile if only 9 other portfolios in a universe of 100 produced a higher return. Although these comparisons can get quite detailed, it is common for the boxplot graphic to include the maximum and minimum returns, as well as the returns falling at the 25th, 50th (the median), and 75th percentiles.

Exhibit 18.2 shows the returns from periods of varying length for a representative investor—labeled here as "U.S. Equity with Cash"—relative to its peer universe of other U.S. domestic equity managers.[1] Also included in the comparison are the periodic returns to three indexes of the overall market: Standard & Poor's 500, Russell 1000, and Russell 3000. The display shows return quartiles for investment periods ranging from 5 to 10 years. The investor in question (indicated by the large dot) performed well, finishing above the median in each of the comparison periods. The manager of this portfolio produced the largest 9-year return (16.5 percent), well above the median return of 13.0 percent. Notice that the investor's 10-year average return exceeds the 9-year level (16.6 percent) but falls below the fifth percentile and is no longer the best.

There are several potential problems with the peer group comparison method of evaluating an investor's performance. First, the boxplots shown in Exhibit 18.2 do not make any explicit adjustment for the risk level of the portfolios in the universe. Investment risk is only *implicitly* considered to the extent that all portfolios in the universe have essentially the same level of volatility. This is not likely to be the case for any sizable peer group, particularly if the universe mixes portfolios with different investment styles. Second, it is almost impossible to form a truly comparable peer group that is large enough to make the percentile rankings meaningful. Finally, by just focusing on relative returns, the comparison loses sight of whether the investor in question has accomplished his individual objectives and satisfied his investment expectations.

18.2.2 Portfolio Drawdown

One way to gauge the job a portfolio manager has done is to consider how well he has protected the investor against losses over time. If we look at a time series illustration of the portfolio's market value during the investment horizon, what is the largest downturn the fund experienced? This is what **portfolio drawdown** measures. Specifically, *maximum drawdown* calculates the largest percentage decline in value—from peak to trough—wherever during the horizon that occurs. Although there is no explicit risk analysis made in the calculation, the drawdown statistic itself can be viewed as a measure of how much downside risk the investor has been exposed to when holding a particular portfolio. The underlying assumption is that for two managers following the same investment style, the one with the smaller drawdown percentage has been more successful in protecting the investor against adverse movements in the market.

Exhibit 18.3 demonstrates this measure over a recent investment period for two actual equity portfolio managers, each of whom has a large-cap growth-oriented style mandate. Both managers increased the value of their portfolios substantially over this horizon; Manager A grew each initial dollar to $2.14, while Manager B's terminal value was $2.10 per initial dollar invested. However, Manager A also appears to have exposed the investor to a somewhat more volatile investment path. In particular, the point of the maximum drawdown—which occurred at Month 23 for both managers—saw Manager A's portfolio decline from its previous peak by almost 19 percent, whereas the comparable decline for Manager B was only 15.4 percent. In this sense, Manager B would be considered to have done at least a slightly better job of

---

[1]This example comes from Singer (1996) and was based on data from the Frank Russell Company.

Exhibit 18.2 An Illustrative Peer Group Comparison

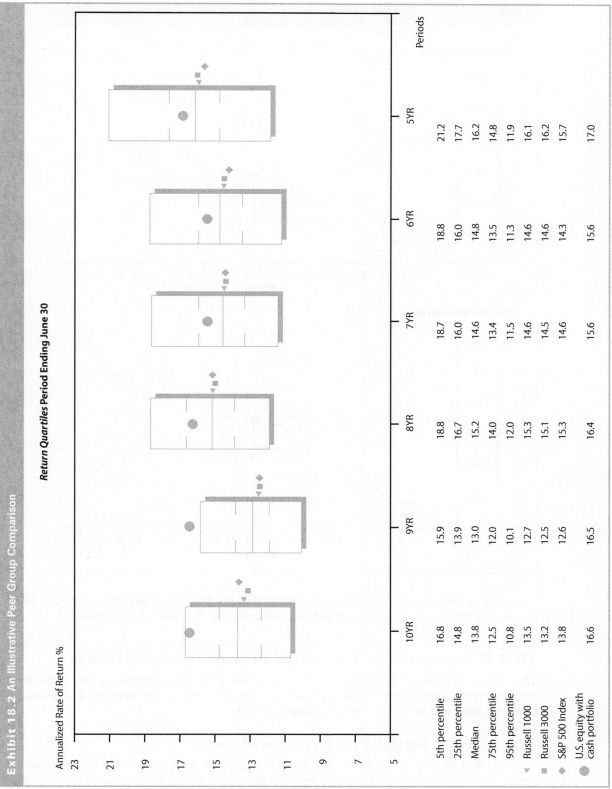

Return Quartiles Period Ending June 30

Annualized Rate of Return %

	10YR	9YR	8YR	7YR	6YR	5YR
5th percentile	16.8	15.9	18.8	18.7	18.8	21.2
25th percentile	14.8	13.9	16.7	16.0	16.0	17.7
Median	13.8	13.0	15.2	14.6	14.8	16.2
75th percentile	12.5	12.0	14.0	13.4	13.5	14.8
95th percentile	10.8	10.1	12.0	11.5	11.3	11.9
▼ Russell 1000	13.5	12.7	15.3	14.6	14.6	16.1
■ Russell 3000	13.2	12.5	15.1	14.5	14.6	16.2
◆ S&P 500 Index	13.8	12.6	15.3	14.6	14.3	15.7
● U.S. equity with cash portfolio	16.6	16.5	16.4	15.6	15.6	17.0

Periods

Source: Brian Singer, "Valuation of Portfolio Performance: Aggregate Return and Risk Analysis," *The Journal of Performance Measurement*, 1, no.1 (Fall 1996): 6–16.

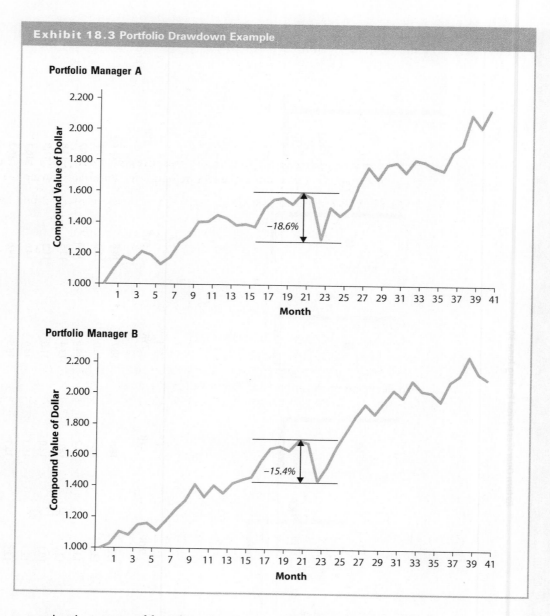

Exhibit 18.3 Portfolio Drawdown Example

preserving investor wealth. Sekine (2006) argued that the fund management process can be improved when investors consider drawdown constraints as they form their portfolio.

18.3 RISK-ADJUSTED PORTFOLIO PERFORMANCE MEASURES

This section describes in detail the five major portfolio performance measures that combine risk and return performance into a single statistic. We also compare the measures and discuss how they differ and why they rank portfolios differently.

18.3.1 Sharpe Portfolio Performance Measure

Sharpe (1966) developed one of the first composite portfolio performance that included risk. The measure followed closely his earlier work on the capital market theory dealing specifically with the capital market line (CML). The **Sharpe measure** of portfolio performance (designated S) is stated as follows:

18.1
$$S_i = \frac{\overline{R}_i - \overline{RFR}}{\sigma_i}$$

where:

$\overline{R}_M$ = average rate of return for Portfolio i during a specified time period
$\overline{RFR}$ = average rate of return on a risk-free investment during the same time period
σ_i = standard deviation of the rate of return for Portfolio i during the time period

This performance measure seeks to measure the total risk of the portfolio by using the standard deviation of returns. Because the numerator of this ratio $(\overline{R}_i - \overline{RFR})$ is the *risk premium* and the denominator is a measure of risk, the total expression indicates the portfolio's *risk premium return per unit of risk*. Also, the standard deviation in S_i can be calculated using either (1) total portfolio returns or (2) portfolio returns in excess of the risk-free rate.[2] Amenc, Goltz, and Lioui (2011) document that the Sharpe ratio the most frequently used performance statistic by many investors.

Demonstration of Comparative Sharpe Measures Suppose that during the most recent 10-year period, the average annual total rate of return (including dividends) on an aggregate market portfolio, such as the S&P 500, was 14 percent $(\overline{R}_M = 0.14)$ and the average nominal rate of return on government T-bills was 8 percent $(\overline{RFR} = 0.08)$. You are told that the standard deviation of the annual rate of return for the market portfolio over the past 10 years was 20 percent $(\sigma_M = 0.20)$. You want to examine the risk-adjusted performance of the following portfolios:

Portfolio	Average Annual Rate of Return	Standard Deviation of Return
D	0.13	0.18
E	0.17	0.22
F	0.16	0.23

The Sharpe measures for each of these funds are as follows:

$$S_M = \frac{0.14 - 0.08}{0.20} = 0.300$$

$$S_D = \frac{0.13 - 0.08}{0.18} = 0.278$$

$$S_E = \frac{0.17 - 0.08}{0.22} = 0.409$$

$$S_F = \frac{0.16 - 0.08}{0.23} = 0.348$$

Portfolio D had the lowest risk premium return per unit of total risk, failing to perform as well as the market portfolio. In contrast, Portfolios E and F performed better than the aggregate market: Portfolio E did better than Portfolio F.

---

[2]The Sharpe measure was formulated using the total risk (σ) of a portfolio, but recently Sharpe (1994, 2007) and Lo (2002) have suggested using the standard deviation of the *excess* portfolio return (σ_{ER}) instead. With this adjustment, the measure becomes $S_i = [\overline{R}_i - \overline{RFR}] \div \sigma_{ER}$. The advantage of this approach will be clear shortly when we discuss the *information ratio* performance measure.

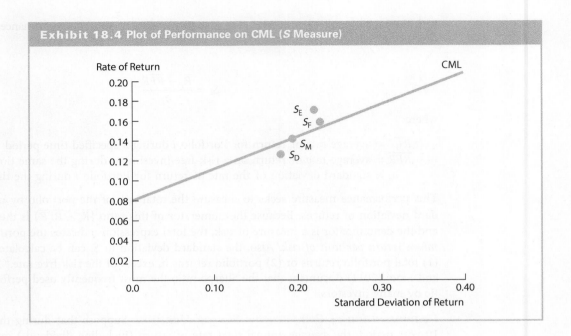

Exhibit 18.4 Plot of Performance on CML (S Measure)

Given the market portfolio performance, it is possible to draw the CML. If we plot the results for Portfolios D, E, and F on this graph, as shown in Exhibit 18.4, we see that Portfolio D plots below the line, whereas the E and F portfolios are above the line, indicating superior risk-adjusted performance.

18.3.2 Treynor Portfolio Performance Measure

Treynor (1965) likewise conceived of a composite measure to evaluate the performance of mutual funds. He postulated two components of risk: (1) risk produced by general market fluctuations and (2) risk resulting from unique fluctuations in the portfolio securities. To identify risk due to market fluctuations, he introduced the *characteristic line*, which defines the relationship between the returns to a managed portfolio and the market portfolio. As we know from Chapter 7, the slope of this line is the portfolio's beta coefficient.

Treynor was interested in a measure of performance that would apply to all investors, regardless of their risk preferences. Building on capital market theory, he introduced a risk-free asset that could be combined with different portfolios to form a portfolio possibility line. He showed that rational investors would always prefer the portfolio line with the largest slope. The slope of this portfolio possibility line (designated T) is:[3]

18.2
$$T_i = \frac{\overline{R}_i - \overline{RFR}}{\beta_i}$$

where in addition to the earlier notation:

β_i = slope of the fund's characteristic line during that time period

As noted, a larger T value indicates a better portfolio for all investors. The risk variable beta measures systematic risk and tells us nothing about the diversification of the portfolio. It *implicitly assumes* a completely diversified portfolio.

---

[3]The terms used in the formula differ from those used by Treynor but are consistent with our earlier discussion.

Comparing a portfolio's T value to a similar measure for the market portfolio indicates whether the portfolio would plot above the security market line (SML). Calculate the T value for the aggregate market as follows:

$$T_M = \frac{\overline{R_M} - \overline{RFR}}{\beta_M}$$

In this expression, β_M equals 1.0 (the market's beta), and T_M indicates the slope of the SML. Therefore, a portfolio with a higher T value than the market portfolio plots above the SML, indicating superior risk-adjusted performance.

Demonstration of Comparative Treynor Measures Assume again that $\overline{R_M} = 0.14$ and $\overline{RFR} = 0.08$. You are deciding between three different portfolio managers, based on their past performance:

Investment Manager	Average Annual Rate of Return	Beta
W	0.12	0.90
X	0.16	1.05
Y	0.18	1.20

You compute T values for the market portfolio and for each of the individual portfolio managers as follows:

$$T_M = \frac{0.14 - 0.08}{1.00} = 0.060$$

$$T_W = \frac{0.12 - 0.08}{0.90} = 0.044$$

$$T_X = \frac{0.16 - 0.08}{1.05} = 0.076$$

$$T_Y = \frac{0.18 - 0.08}{1.20} = 0.083$$

These results indicate that Investment Manager W not only ranked the lowest of the three managers but did not perform as well as the aggregate market on a risk-adjusted basis. In contrast, both Manager X and Manager Y beat the market portfolio, and Manager Y performed somewhat better than Manager X. Both of their portfolios plotted above the SML, as shown in Exhibit 18.5.

Very good performance with very low risk may yield negative T values. A portfolio with a *negative* beta and an average rate of return above the risk-free rate of return would likewise have a negative T value. In this case, however, it indicates exemplary performance. Suppose Portfolio Manager G invested heavily in gold mining stocks during a period of great political and economic uncertainty. Because gold often has a negative correlation with most stocks, this portfolio had a beta of -0.20 and yet experienced an average rate of return of 10 percent. The T value for this portfolio would then be:

$$T_G = \frac{0.10 - 0.08}{-0.20} = -0.100$$

Although the T value is negative, it would indicate a position substantially above the SML in Exhibit 18.5.

Because negative betas can yield T values that give confusing results, it is preferable either to plot the portfolio on an SML graph or to compute the expected return for this portfolio

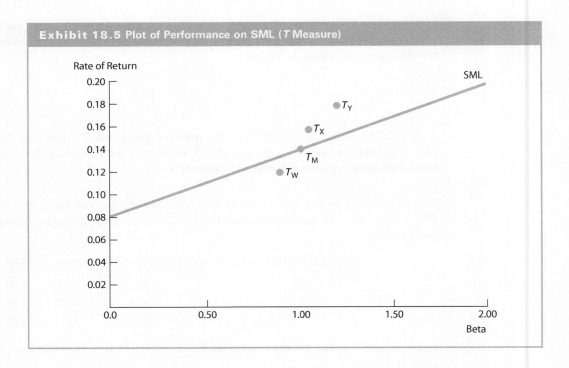

Exhibit 18.5 Plot of Performance on SML (T Measure)

using the SML equation and then compare this expected return to the actual return. For Portfolio G, the expected return would be:

$$E(R_G) = RFR + \beta_i(R_M - RFR) = 0.08 + (-0.20)(0.06) = 0.068$$

Comparing this expected return of 6.8 percent to the actual return of 10 percent shows that Portfolio Manager G has done a superior job.

18.3.3 Jensen Portfolio Performance Measure

Like the T measure, the **Jensen measure** (Jensen, 1968) was originally based on the capital asset pricing model (CAPM), which calculates the expected one-period return on any security or portfolio by the following expression:

18.3 $$E(R_j) = RFR + \beta_j[E(R_M) - RFR]$$

where:

$E(R_j)$ = expected return on security or Portfolio j
RFR = one-period risk-free interest rate
β_j = systematic risk (beta) for security or Portfolio j
$E(R_M)$ = expected return on the market portfolio of risky assets

We can express Equation 18.3 in terms of *realized* rates of return as follows:

$$R_{jt} = RFR_t + \beta_j[R_{mt} - RFR_t] + e_{jt}$$

This equation states that the realized rate of return on a security or portfolio during a given time period should be a linear function of the risk-free rate of return during the period, plus a risk premium that depends on the systematic risk of the security or portfolio during the period plus a random error term (e_{jt}). Subtracting the risk-free return from both sides, we have:

$$R_{jt} - RFR_t = \beta_j[R_{mt} - RFR_t] + e_{jt}$$

so that the risk premium earned on the jth portfolio is equal to β_j times a market risk premium plus a random error term. An intercept for the regression is not expected if all assets and portfolios are in equilibrium.

Alternatively, superior portfolio managers who forecast market turns or consistently select undervalued securities earn higher risk premiums over time than those implied by this model. Such managers produce actual returns for their portfolios that exceed their expected returns. To detect this superior performance, you must allow for an intercept (a nonzero constant) that measures any positive or negative difference from the model. Consistent positive differences cause a positive intercept, whereas consistent negative differences (inferior performance) cause a negative intercept. With an intercept included, the relationship becomes:

18.4
$$R_{jt} - RFR_t = \alpha_j + \beta_j[R_{mt} - RFR_t] + e_{jt}$$

In Equation 18.4, the α_j value indicates whether the portfolio manager is superior or inferior in her investment ability. A superior manager has a significant positive α (alpha) value, while an inferior manager's returns consistently fall short of expectations based on the CAPM, leading to a significant negative α.

The performance of a portfolio manager with no forecasting ability should equal that of a passive buy-and-hold policy. Because returns on such a portfolio typically match the returns you expect, the residual returns generally are randomly positive and negative. This gives a constant term that differs insignificantly from zero, indicating that the portfolio manager basically matched the market on a risk-adjusted basis. Therefore, α represents how much of the managed portfolio's return is attributable to the manager's ability to derive above-average returns adjusted for risk. Ferson (2010) has called α the most famous performance measure because of its frequent use in both theory and practice.

Applying the Jensen Measure The Jensen alpha measure of performance requires using a different RFR for each time interval during the sample period. To examine the performance of a fund manager over a 10-year period using yearly intervals, you must examine the fund's annual returns less the return on risk-free assets for each year and relate this to the annual return on the market portfolio less the same risk-free rate. This contrasts with the Treynor and Sharpe measures, which examine the *average* returns for the total period for the portfolio, the market, and the risk-free asset.

Also, like the Treynor measure, the Jensen measure does not directly consider the portfolio manager's ability to diversify because it calculates risk premiums in terms of systematic risk. When evaluating the performance of a group of well-diversified portfolios such as mutual funds, this is likely to be a reasonable assumption. Finally, the Jensen performance measure is flexible enough to allow for alternative models of risk and expected return than the CAPM. Specifically, risk-adjusted performance (α) can be computed relative to any multifactor model:

18.5
$$R_{jt} - RFR_t = \alpha_j + [b_{j1}F_{1t} + b_{j2}F_{2t} + \cdots + b_{jk}F_{kt}] + e_{jt}$$

where:

$F_{kt} =$ Period t return to the kth common risk factor

18.3.4 Information Ratio Performance Measure

Closely related to the statistics just presented is a fourth widely used performance measure: the **information ratio**. This statistic measures a portfolio's average return in excess of that for a **benchmark portfolio** divided by the standard deviation of this excess return. Formally, the information ratio (*IR*) for portfolio j is calculated as:

18.6
$$IR_j = \frac{\overline{R}_j - \overline{R}_b}{\sigma_{ER}} = \frac{\overline{ER}_j}{\sigma_{ER}}$$

where:

$$\overline{R}_b = \text{average return for the benchmark portfolio during the period}$$
$$\sigma_{ER} = \text{standard deviation of the excess return during the period}$$

To interpret IR, the mean return differential in the numerator represents the investor's ability to use her talent and information to generate a portfolio return that differs from the benchmark against which her performance is being measured (for example, the Standard & Poor's 500 Index). In fact, $\overline{ER}_j$ can be considered the investor's average alpha if the average return to the benchmark is taken to be the expected return. The denominator of the IR statistic measures the amount of residual (unsystematic) risk that the investor incurred in pursuit of those incremental returns. As we saw in Chapter 11, the coefficient σ_{ER} is called the *tracking error* of the investor's portfolio, and it is a "cost" of active management in that fluctuations in the periodic ER_j values represent random noise that could hurt performance. So, the IR can be viewed as a benefit-to-cost ratio that assesses the quality of the investor's information deflated by unsystematic risk generated by the investment process.

To see how IR can be computed and interpreted, consider the returns produced by an active portfolio manager over the past eight quarters, along with the returns to her benchmark index:

Quarter	Active Portfolio Returns	Benchmark Returns	Difference
1	2.3%	2.7%	−0.4%
2	−3.6	−4.6	1.0
3	11.2	10.1	1.1
4	1.2	2.2	−1.0
5	1.5	0.4	1.1
6	3.2	2.8	0.4
7	8.9	8.1	0.8
8	−0.8	0.6	−1.4
Average:	3.0%	2.8%	0.2%
Std Dev. (*TE*):	—	—	1.0%

In this case, the manager outperformed her benchmark by an average of 20 basis points per quarter, but she did so with a periodic tracking error of 1.0 percent. Thus, her quarterly information ratio is 0.20 (=0.2% ÷ 1.0%). This represents the manager's average alpha (relative to the index) per unit of incremental risk. Notice that IR will be positive only when the investor outperforms her benchmark.

Goodwin (1998) noted that the Sharpe ratio is a special case of the IR where the risk-free asset is the benchmark portfolio, although this interpretation violates the spirit of a statistic that should have a value of zero for any passively managed portfolio. He also showed that an information ratio based on periodic returns measured T times per year could be annualized as follows:

$$\text{Annualized } IR = \frac{(T)\alpha_j}{\sqrt{T}\sigma_e} = \sqrt{T}(IR)$$

For instance, the investor from the preceding example that generated a quarterly ratio of 0.200 would have an annualized IR of 0.40 = ($\sqrt{4} \times 0.20$).

Grinold and Kahn (2000) argued that reasonable information ratio levels should range from 0.50 to 1.00, with an investor having an IR of 0.50 being good, and one with an IR of 1.00 being exceptional. These are difficult hurdles to clear. Goodwin (1998) studied the performance of more than 200 professional equity and fixed-income portfolio managers with various investment styles over a 10-year period. He found that the IR of the median manager in each style group was positive but never exceeded 0.50. Thus, while the average manager added value to investors—α (and hence IR) is greater than zero—she doesn't qualify as "good." Further, no style group had more than 3 percent of its managers deliver an IR in excess of 1.00. Information ratio histograms summarizing this research are shown in Exhibit 18.6.

Exhibit 18.6 Information Ratios for Six Investment Styles

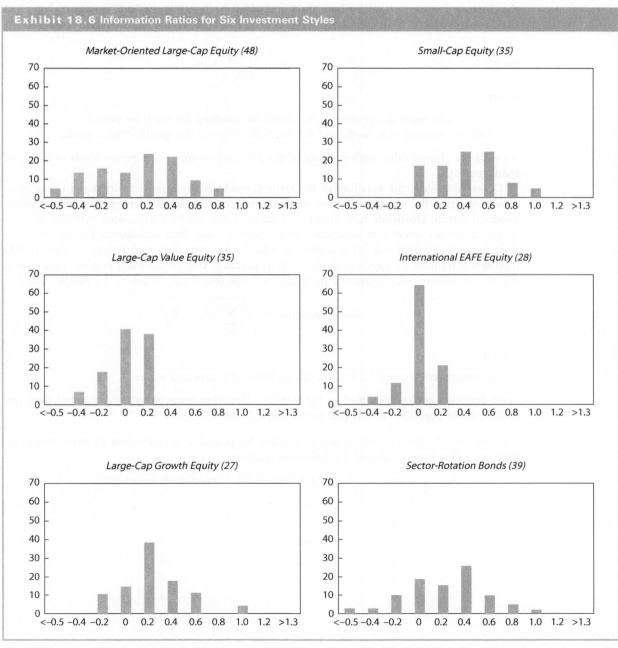

Note: Midpoints of ranges. Information ratios are on the x-axes; relative frequencies, in percentages, are on the y-axes. Data from 1986:Q1 to 1995:Q4.

Source: Thomas H. Goodwin, "The Information Ratio." *Financial Analysts Journal* 54, no. 4 (July–August 1998): 34–43.

18.3.5 Sortino Performance Measure

The **Sortino measure** is a risk-adjusted performance statistic that differs from the Sharpe ratio in two ways. First, the Sortino ratio measures the portfolio's average return in excess of a user-selected *minimum acceptable return threshold*, which is often the risk-free rate used in the S statistic although it need not be. Second, the Sharpe measure focuses on total risk—effectively penalizing the manager for returns that are both too low *and* too high—while the Sortino ratio captures just the **downside risk** (DR) in the portfolio. Sortino and Price (1994) calculate this measure as follows:

18.7
$$ST_i = \frac{\overline{R}_i - \tau}{DR_i}$$

where:

τ = minimum acceptable return threshold specified for the time period
DR_i = downside risk coefficient for Portfolio i during the specified time period

As with the Sharpe ratio, higher values of the ST measure indicate superior levels of portfolio management.

Downside risk is the volatility of the returns produced by a portfolio that *fall below some hurdle rate* that the investor chooses, such as zero (that is, negative returns) or the portfolio's expected return. Downside risk attempts to measure the volatility associated with the *shortfall* that occurs if an investment produces a return that is lower than anticipated. DR comes closer than measures of total risk (σ) to capturing what investors truly consider risky. Harlow (1991) discusses a number of ways to calculate DR in practice. One of the most popular measures is the *semi-deviation*, which uses the portfolio's average (expected) return as the hurdle rate:

$$Semi\text{-}Deviation = \sqrt{\frac{1}{n}\sum_{R<\overline{R}}(R_{it} - \overline{R}_i)^2}$$

where:

n = number of portfolio returns falling below the expected return

Semi-deviation is closely related to the standard deviation measure of total risk, but does not include those portfolio returns that exceed expectations.

Comparing the Sharpe and Sortino Ratios Suppose that over the past 10 years, two portfolio managers have produced the following returns:

Year	Portfolio A Return (%)	Portfolio B Return (%)
1	−5	−1
2	−3	−1
3	−2	−1
4	3	−1
5	3	0
6	6	4
7	7	4
8	8	7
9	10	13
10	13	16
Average:	4	4
Std. Dev.:	5.60	5.92

Both portfolios had an average annual return of 4 percent over this horizon, meaning that how their risk is measured will determine which manager performed the best.

Based on the standard deviation coefficients, Portfolio A is the less volatile portfolio. However, a substantial amount of the variation for Portfolio B came from two large positive returns, which are included in the computation of total risk. If the average risk-free rate during this period was 2 percent, the Sharpe ratio calculations confirm that Portfolio A outperformed Portfolio B:

$$S_A = 0.357 \; (= [4-2]/5.60)$$

and:

$$S_B = 0.338 \; (= [4-2]/5.92)$$

The story changes when just the downside risk of the portfolios is considered. In addition to more extreme positive values, Portfolio B also had losses that were limited to 1 percent in any given year, perhaps as a result of a portfolio insurance strategy. Using semi-deviation to compute DR for both portfolios leaves:

$$DR_A = \sqrt{[(-5-4)^2 + (-3-4)^2 + (-2-4)^2 + (3-4)^2 + (3-4)^2] \div 5} = 5.80$$

and:

$$DR_B = \sqrt{[(-1-4)^2 + (-1-4)^2 + (-1-4)^2 + (-1-4)^2 + (0-4)^2] \div 5} = 4.82$$

Thus, when only the possibility of receiving a less-than-expected return is considered, Portfolio A now appears to be the riskier alternative due to the fact it has more extreme negative returns than Portfolio B. Assuming a minimum return threshold of 2 percent to match the Sharpe measure, the Sortino ratios for both portfolios indicate that, by limiting the extent of his downside risk, the manager for Portfolio B was actually the superior performer:

$$ST_A = 0.345 \; (= [4-2]/5.80)$$

and:

$$ST_B = 0.415 \; (= [4-2]/4.82)$$

18.3.6 Summarizing the Risk-Adjusted Performance Measures

Each of the risk-adjusted performance statistics just described is widely used in practice and has strengths and weaknesses. The primary advantages and disadvantages of the T, S, α, IR, and ST measures are listed in Exhibit 18.7. The important thing to recognize is that none of these measures dominates the others, and they all provide at least slightly different information useful in the assessment of a portfolio's performance. Consequently, it is generally advisable to compute all of them to provide a complete performance picture.

The Sharpe ratio is the simplest measure to compute, requiring just a few straightforward calculations based on the portfolio returns. In its original form, S uses the standard deviation of total returns, whereas the Treynor ratio uses the portfolio's systematic risk (beta) coefficient. As we saw in Chapter 7, beta can also be calculated directly from the returns to the portfolio and the market index, but that is a somewhat more involved process. For a completely diversified portfolio, T and S give identical performance rankings because total risk and systematic risk are the same. However, a poorly diversified portfolio could have a high ranking based on the Treynor ratio, which ignores unsystematic risk, but a much lower ranking with the Sharpe measure, which does not. Any difference in rankings produced by T and S comes directly from a difference in portfolio diversification levels.

A disadvantage of the Treynor and Sharpe measures is that they only produce *relative*, not absolute, performance rankings. For example, the Sharpe values for Portfolios E and F in

Exhibit 18.7 Comparing the Risk-Adjusted Performance Measures

Performance Measure	Risk-Adjustment Measure	Advantages	Disadvantages
Treynor ratio (T)	Portfolio beta relative to market index proxy	• Simple and intuitive "benefit–cost" comparison of the risk–return trade-off • Linked conceptually to the SML and capital market theory • Relatively simple to calculate and widely used in practice	• Permits only relative assessments of performance for different portfolios • Difficult to interpret and assess statistical significance • Ignores unsystematic risk in a portfolio
Sharpe ratio (S)	(1) Standard deviation of total portfolio return; or (2) Standard deviation of portfolio return in excess of risk-free rate	• Simple and intuitive "benefit–cost" comparison of the risk–return trade-off • Linked conceptually to the CML and capital market theory • Simplest to calculate and widely used in practice	• Permits only relative assessments of performance for different portfolios • Difficult to interpret and assess statistical significance • Ignores diversification potential of portfolio
Jensen's alpha (α)	(1) Portfolio beta relative to market index *proxy*; or (2) Portfolio betas relative to multiple risk factors	• Most rigorous risk-adjustment process separating systematic and unsystematic risk components • Can be adapted to either CAPM or multifactor models of the risk–return trade-off • Intuitive interpretation of measure that permits statistical significance assessment	• More difficult computation requiring formal regression analysis • Diversification of portfolio assessed in separate measure from performance • Alpha level and significance can vary greatly depending on specification of return-generating model
Information ratio (IR)	Standard deviation of portfolio return in excess of return to style-class benchmark index (i.e., tracking error)	• Direct comparison of portfolio performance compared to benchmark in investment style class • Simple and intuitive measure of the "benefit–cost" trade-off involved with active management • Flexible design permitting multiple benchmark comparisons	• Permits only relative assessments of performance for different portfolios in a style class • Difficult to interpret and assess statistical significance • Implicitly assumes that portfolio and benchmark have similar levels of systematic risk
Sortino ratio (ST)	Downside risk measure (e.g., semi-deviation of portfolio returns)	• Straightforward and intuitive "benefit–cost" comparison of the risk–return trade-off • Conceptually valid risk measure focusing on left-hand side of return distribution • Allows for investor input as to the appropriate risk threshold level	• Can be difficult to produce relative assessments of performance for portfolios with different risk thresholds • Difficult to interpret and assess statistical significance • Somewhat more difficult to calculate necessary inputs

Exhibit 18.4 show that both managers generated risk-adjusted returns above the market. Further, E's risk-adjusted performance measure (0.409) is larger than F's (0.348). We cannot say with certainty, however, that this difference is statistically significant. The same dilemma exists when comparing the performance of Portfolio X and Y using the Treynor measure illustrated in Exhibit 18.5.

The Jensen's alpha measure is typically the most difficult to compute because it requires a formal regression analysis. Offsetting that drawback are three substantial advantages relative to the T and S measures. First, it is easier to understand: An alpha value of 0.02 indicates that the manager generated a return of 2 percent per period more than what was expected given the portfolio's risk level. On the other hand, a Sharpe ratio of 0.409 means that the portfolio manager generated *0.409 units of excess return per unit of total risk*, which is more challenging language to interpret. Second, because α is estimated from a formal statistical process, it is possible to make statements about the statistical significance of the manager's skill level, or the difference in skill between two different managers. Third, Jensen's alpha can be computed relative to *any* risk–return model, in contrast to S, which focuses only on total risk, and T, which is locked into beta as the specific estimate of systematic risk.

Because the information ratio is similar in form to T and S, it shares many of the same strengths and weakness. The primary advantage that differentiates IR is that it provides a direct comparison between the return performance of the portfolio manager and that of the specific benchmark index against which she is competing. Since investors can often own this benchmark portfolio directly—either through index mutual funds or exchange-traded funds— the IR measure calculates the risk-adjusted value added by the active portfolio manager relative to a passive investment alternative. However, Baker, Bradley, and Wurgler (2011) note that tying performance to a single benchmark could lead to missed investment opportunities.

Finally, the Sortino ratio is distinctive in that it takes into account the downside risk exposure in the portfolio, which could be very important for funds that do not produce symmetric return distributions (for example, managers that use portfolio insurance strategies to reduce the potential for negative return outcomes) Also, ST allows investors to specify their own risk thresholds. However, this design flexibility also makes the measure more difficult to calculate and apply in a consistent manner across portfolios that may involve different thresholds and different ways to calculate downside risk.

18.4 Application of Portfolio Performance Measures

To demonstrate several of these risk-adjusted measures, we selected 30 open-end mutual funds from the nine investment-style classes described in Chapter 11 and used monthly return data for a five-year period from June 2012 to May 2017. Exhibit 18.8 displays the returns for one of these funds—Fidelity Magellan (FMAGX)—and the S&P 500 index. The total return for each month is computed as follows:

$$R_{it} = \frac{EP_{it} + Div_{it} + Cap.Dist._{it} - BP_{it}}{BP_{it}}$$

where:

$$R_{it} = \text{total return on Fund } i \text{ during month } t$$
$$EP_{it} = \text{ending price for Fund } i \text{ during month } t$$
$$Div_{it} = \text{dividend payments made by Fund } i \text{ during month } t$$
$$Cap.Dist._{it} = \text{capital gain distributions made by Fund } i \text{ during month } t$$
$$BP_{it} = \text{beginning price for Fund } i \text{ during month } t$$

These return computations do not take into account any sales charges by the funds.

The arithmetic average annual return for FMAGX was 15.06 percent versus 14.24 percent for the market, and the fund's beta was slightly larger than 1.00 (1.046). Using the average annual T-bill rate of 0.10 percent as $\overline{RFR}$, the Treynor measure for FMAGX, T_i, was slightly bigger than the comparable measure for the market, T_M: 0.143 versus 0.141. However, the annualized standard deviation of returns of the Magellan fund was also larger than the market's (10.48 percent versus 9.61 percent), so the Sharpe measure for the fund, S_i, while positive, was slightly smaller than the market, S_M: 1.427 versus 1.471.

Finally, a one-factor regression of the fund's monthly risk premium $(R_{it} - RFR_t)$ and the market's monthly risk premium $(R_m - RFR_t)$ indicated a positive alpha (intercept) value of

Exhibit 18.8 Example of Computing Portfolio Evaluation Measures Using Fidelity Magellan (FMAGX) Fund

	R_{it}	R_{mt}	RFR_t	$R_{it} - RFR_t$	$R_{mt} - RFR_t$
June 2012	3.37	4.12	0.00	3.37	4.12
July 2012	1.17	1.26	0.00	1.17	1.26
August 2012	3.34	1.98	0.01	3.33	1.97
September 2012	3.21	2.42	0.01	3.20	2.41
October 2012	−2.58	−1.98	0.01	−2.59	−1.99
November 2012	0.96	0.28	0.01	0.95	0.27
December 2012	0.77	0.71	0.01	0.76	0.70
January 2013	5.08	5.04	0.00	5.08	5.04
February 2013	0.69	1.11	0.00	0.69	1.11
March 2013	3.15	3.60	0.00	3.15	3.60
April 2013	0.99	1.81	0.00	0.99	1.81
May 2013	3.58	2.08	0.00	3.58	2.08
⋮	⋮	⋮	⋮	⋮	⋮
June 2016	−1.84	0.26	0.02	−1.86	0.24
July 2016	3.80	3.68	0.02	3.78	3.66
August 2016	0.51	0.14	0.02	0.49	0.12
September 2016	0.30	0.02	0.02	0.28	0.00
October 2016	−1.96	−1.82	0.02	−1.98	−1.84
November 2016	2.97	3.70	0.01	2.96	3.69
December 2016	1.09	1.97	0.03	1.06	1.94
January 2017	2.41	1.90	0.04	2.37	1.86
February 2017	3.93	3.70	0.04	3.89	3.66
March 2017	−0.02	0.12	0.03	−0.05	0.09
April 2017	1.32	1.03	0.05	1.27	0.98
May 2017	2.17	1.41	0.06	2.11	1.35
Average (annual)	15.06	14.24	0.10	14.96	14.14
Standard deviation	10.48	9.61	0.05	10.48	9.61
Beta	1.046				
S_i	1.427				
S_m	1.471				
T_i	0.143				
T_m	0.141				
Jensen alpha (1 factor)	0.014				
R_{im}^2	0.919				

0.014 but was not statistically significant. Therefore, it appears that FMAGX generated returns in line with its risk-adjusted expectations over this period.

Total Sample Results The overall results in Exhibit 18.9 indicate that, on average, active fund managers performed somewhat below expectations. A primary factor for this outcome was the relatively strong performance of the index during the sample period. Also, our sample was rather casually selected because we intended it for demonstration purposes only. The mean annual return for all the funds was below the market return (13.74 percent versus 14.24 percent). Considering their returns only, fewer than half (14 of the 30) of these funds outperformed the market.

The R^2 statistic comparing a portfolio with the market can serve as a measure of diversification. The closer the R^2 is to 1.00, the more completely diversified the portfolio. The average R^2 for our sample was fairly high, at 0.741, but the range was quite wide, from 0.353 to 0.966. Many of the funds were reasonably well diversified, with 21 of the 30 portfolios having R^2 values greater than 0.70. (Recall that a typical individual stock would have an R^2 value of around 20 to 40 percent.)

Exhibit 18.9 Performance Measures for 30 Selected Mutual Funds

Fund	Ticker	Style Class	Average Annual Rate of Return	Standard Deviation	Beta	R^2	Sharpe	Treynor	Jensen (1 Factor)
AllianceBerstein Growth	AGRYX	Large Growth	14.17	10.57	0.956	0.756	1.331 (8)	0.147 (7)	0.046 (7)
American Century Sm Val	ASVIX	Small Value	13.52	13.44	1.127	0.649	0.998 (24)	0.119 (20)	−0.210 (21)
Buffalo Small Cap	BUFSX	Small Growth	11.88	14.24	1.138	0.591	0.828 (28)	0.104 (27)	−0.359 (28)
Ariel Appreciation	CAAPX	Mid Blend	15.18	13.66	1.280	0.810	1.104 (19)	0.118 (22)	−0.251 (24)
Dreyfus Appreciation	DGAGX	Large Blend	10.86	9.95	0.981	0.900	1.082 (21)	0.110 (25)	−0.260[a] (25)
DFA Tax–Managed Value	DTMMX	Large Value	16.08	11.11	1.082	0.876	1.438 (3)	0.148 (6)	0.056 (6)
Fidelity Magellan	FMAGX	Large Growth	15.06	10.48	1.046	0.919	1.427 (5)	0.143 (11)	0.014 (11)
Goldman Sachs Mid Value	GCMAX	Mid Value	11.95	10.65	1.002	0.816	1.112 (18)	0.118 (21)	−0.193 (20)
Hartford Growth Opp	HGOYX	Large Growth	16.94	11.88	1.039	0.707	1.419 (6)	0.162 (1)	0.180 (1)
Heartland Value	HRTVX	Small Blend	9.61	13.64	0.998	0.495	0.697 (29)	0.095 (30)	−0.384 (29)
Hotchkis & Wiley Lrg Val	HWLIX	Large Value	15.63	12.46	1.156	0.795	1.246 (13)	0.134 (14)	−0.068 (14)
Janus Forty Fund	JACCX	Large Growth	15.07	11.50	1.031	0.743	1.302 (11)	0.145 (9)	0.032 (9)
Dodge & Cox Stock Fund	DODGX	Large Value	16.71	11.57	1.105	0.842	1.436 (4)	0.150 (4)	0.082 (4)
Columbia Acorn	LACAX	Mid Growth	11.59	11.95	1.051	0.715	0.962 (25)	0.109 (26)	−0.280 (26)
Scout Mid Cap Fund	UMBMX	Mid Blend	14.16	10.68	0.960	0.746	1.317 (9)	0.147 (8)	0.041 (8)
Munder Mid Cap Select	MGOYX	Mid Growth	12.71	10.94	1.023	0.809	1.153 (17)	0.123 (18)	−0.155 (17)
MFS Mid Cap Value	MVCAX	Mid Value	14.30	10.37	0.986	0.835	1.369 (7)	0.144 (10)	0.022 (10)
Neuberger Berman Partners	NPRTX	Large Value	14.12	11.93	1.054	0.722	1.176 (15)	0.133 (15)	−0.074 (15)
Wells Fargo Small Cap Op	NVSOX	Small Blend	14.39	11.19	0.962	0.682	1.277 (12)	0.149 (5)	0.058 (5)
JPMorgan Small Growth	PGSGX	Small Growth	15.11	16.39	1.274	0.559	0.917 (26)	0.118 (23)	−0.250 (23)
T. Rowe Price Dividend Gr	PRDGX	Large Blend	14.40	8.99	0.919	0.966	1.591 (1)	0.156 (3)	0.108 (3)
Putnam Small Cap Value	PSLAX	Small Value	13.92	12.53	0.989	0.575	1.103 (20)	0.140 (13)	−0.014 (13)
RS Partners	RSPFX	Small Blend	12.46	12.02	1.029	0.677	1.028 (23)	0.120 (19)	−0.183 (19)
Royce Premier	RYPRX	Small Blend	11.36	13.11	1.091	0.640	0.859 (27)	0.103 (28)	−0.347 (27)
Schneider Small Cap Value	SCMVX	Small Value	14.70	23.09	1.427	0.353	0.632 (30)	0.102 (29)	−0.465 (30)
Jensen Quality Growth Funds	JENRX	Large Growth	14.59	9.40	0.915	0.875	1.542 (2)	0.158 (2)	0.130 (2)
TCW Diversified Value	TGDVX	Large Value	13.99	11.56	1.124	0.873	1.201 (14)	0.124 (17)	−0.167 (18)
Tweedy, Browne American	TWEBX	Large Value	10.20	8.72	0.814	0.806	1.158 (16)	0.124 (16)	−0.118 (16)
Vanguard Selected Value	VASVX	Mid Value	14.62	11.13	1.021	0.778	1.305 (10)	0.142 (12)	0.007 (12)
Invesco Van Kampen Mid Gr	VGRAX	Mid Growth	12.92	12.28	1.089	0.727	1.044 (22)	0.118 (24)	−0.215 (22)
Average Fund			13.74	12.05	1.056	0.741	1.168	0.130	−0.107
S&P 500			14.24	9.61	1.000	1.000	1.471	0.141	0.000
90-day T-bill rate			0.10	0.05					

[a]Significant at the 0.05 level.

The two risk measures (standard deviation and beta) also show a wide degree of dispersion but generally are consistent with expectations. Specifically, 27 of the 30 funds had larger standard deviations than the market, and the mean standard deviation was also larger (12.05 versus 9.61). Only 10 of the funds had a beta of less than 1.00; the average beta was 1.056.

The various performance measures ranked the performance of individual funds quite consistently. (These rankings are listed in parentheses beside each measure.) Only 12 out of 30 funds had a higher Treynor ratio than the index; only 2 funds had a higher Sharpe as well, which resulted from exceptionally low market volatility over this horizon. Also, just 12 of the 30 Jensen's alpha values using the single-index model were positive, with none of them being statistically significant. One of the funds with a negative alpha was statistically significant. The mean Jensen's alpha value of −0.107 indicates that the average manager in the sample produced a monthly return of about 11 basis points lower than what would have been expected given the risk level of the fund. The mean values for the Sharpe and Treynor measures were both lower than the aggregate market figure. These results confirm that, overall, this sample of funds produced somewhat worse risk-adjusted performance than the market during this time period.

Exhibit 18.10 reports information ratios for these 30 funds. To interpret the display, consider that the Hartford Growth Opportunity Fund had a monthly IR value of 0.087, calculated

Exhibit 18.10 Information Ratios for 30 Funds

Fund	Alpha	Tracking Error	IR	Annualized IR	Rank
AllianceBerstein Growth	−0.104	1.156	−0.090	−0.312	(20)
American Century Sm Val	−0.022	1.076	−0.020	−0.070	(11)
Buffalo Small Cap	−0.218	1.351	−0.162	−0.560	(25)
Ariel Appreciation	0.041	1.538	0.026	0.091	(6)
Dreyfus Appreciation	−0.340	0.994	−0.343	−1.187	(30)
DFA Tax−Managed Value	0.167	0.746	0.224	0.777	(1)
Fidelity Magellan	−0.030	0.801	−0.038	−0.130	(14)
Goldman Sachs Mid Value	−0.265	0.786	−0.337	−1.167	(29)
Hartford Growth Opp	0.127	1.463	0.087	0.301	(4)
Heartland Value	−0.378	1.722	−0.220	−0.761	(27)
Hotchkis & Wiley Lrg Val	0.130	1.381	0.094	0.326	(3)
Janus Forty Fund	−0.030	1.138	−0.026	−0.090	(12)
Dodge & Cox Stock Fund	0.220	1.174	0.187	0.649	(2)
Columbia Acorn	−0.220	1.199	−0.184	−0.636	(26)
Scout Mid Cap Fund	−0.044	1.078	−0.041	−0.143	(15)
Munder Mid Cap Select	−0.127	0.846	−0.150	−0.521	(24)
MFS Mid Cap Value	−0.069	0.701	−0.098	−0.339	(21)
Neuberger Berman Partners	0.004	1.440	0.003	0.010	(9)
Wells Fargo Small Cap Op	−0.061	1.287	−0.047	−0.164	(16)
JPMorgan Small Growth	0.051	1.369	0.037	0.129	(5)
T. Rowe Price Dividend Gr	−0.045	0.545	−0.083	−0.289	(18)
Putnam Small Cap Value	0.012	0.880	0.013	0.047	(8)
RS Partners	−0.141	1.684	−0.084	−0.290	(19)
Royce Premier	−0.299	2.144	−0.140	−0.483	(23)
Schneider Small Cap Value	0.077	4.321	0.018	0.062	(7)
Jensen Quality Growth Funds	−0.069	1.178	−0.059	−0.203	(17)
TCW Diversified Value	−0.007	1.002	−0.007	−0.023	(10)
Tweedy, Browne American	−0.323	1.313	−0.246	−0.851	(28)
Vanguard Selected Value	−0.042	1.211	−0.035	−0.120	(13)
Invesco Van Kampen Mid Gr	−0.110	1.013	−0.108	−0.375	(22)
Mean	−0.071	1.285	−0.061	−0.211	
Median	−0.045	1.176	−0.044	−0.153	

as its alpha (0.127)—computed as the average of the return difference between the fund and its large-cap growth benchmark—divided by its tracking error (1.463). This statistic is then annualized to 0.301 by multiplying the monthly *IR* by the square root of 12. Notice that only 9 of the 30 funds had positive *IR* levels, which is fairly consistent with the number of funds that also had a positive Jensen's alpha. The mean annualized *IR* for the sample was −0.211, which is negative and falls far below the Grinold-Kahn standard for "good" performance of 0.500. Thus, even before accounting for tracking error costs, the average fund in this sample failed to add value to its investors.

Measuring Performance with Multiple Risk Factors Exhibit 18.11 shows Jensen measures calculated for the 30 mutual funds using two different versions of the Fama–French model (discussed in Chapter 7) to estimate expected returns:

$$R_{jt} - RFR_t = \alpha_j + \{[b_{j1}(R_{mt} - RFR_t) + b_{j2}SMB_t + b_{j3}HML_t] + b_{j4}MOM_t\} + e_{jt}$$

Specifically, alphas are computed relative to (1) a three-factor model, including the market ($R_m - RFR$), firm size (*SMB*), and relative valuation (*HML*) variables; and (2) a four-factor model that also includes the return momentum (*MOM*) variable.

Exhibit 18.11 Performance Measures for 30 Funds Using Multifactor Models

Fund	Style Class	$R_m - RFR$	SMB	HML	MOM	Jensen Alpha (3-factor)	Rank	Jensen Alpha (4-factor)	Rank
		Factor Betas							
AGRYX	Large Growth	0.942	0.126	−0.363	0.022	0.106	(6)	0.097	(8)
ASVIX	Small Value	1.032	0.785	0.408	0.035	−0.100	(19)	−0.116	(22)
BUFSX	Small Growth	1.006	0.966	−0.305	0.009	−0.148	(23)	−0.152	(27)
CAAPX	Mid Blend	1.172	0.456	0.058	−0.171	−0.181	(26)	−0.107	(20)
DGAGX	Large Blend	0.990	−0.187	−0.073	−0.062	−0.291[a]	(29)	−0.265[a]	(30)
DTMMX	Large Value	1.054	0.217	0.305	−0.003	0.067	(11)	0.069	(10)
FMAGX	Large Growth	1.030	0.151	−0.123	0.020	0.056	(12)	0.047	(12)
GCMAX	Mid Value	0.954	0.300	0.124	−0.027	−0.150	(25)	−0.139	(25)
HGOYX	Large Growth	0.979	0.303	−0.549	−0.052	0.287	(1)	0.309	(1)
HRTVX	Small Blend	0.832	0.970	0.275	−0.133	−0.237	(27)	−0.179	(28)
HWLIX	Large Value	1.110	0.197	0.363	−0.084	−0.072	(16)	−0.035	(16)
JACCX	Large Growth	1.002	0.128	−0.460	−0.030	0.099	(7)	0.112	(4)
DODGX	Large Value	1.070	0.140	0.261	−0.067	0.079	(9)	0.108	(5)
LACAX	Mid Growth	0.957	0.679	−0.076	0.001	−0.145	(22)	−0.146	(26)
UMBMX	Mid Blend	0.947	0.371	0.124	0.139	0.107	(5)	0.047	(13)
MGOYX	Mid Growth	0.956	0.374	−0.087	−0.058	−0.080	(17)	−0.054	(17)
MVCAX	Mid Value	0.939	0.329	0.154	−0.010	0.068	(10)	0.072	(9)
NPRTX	Large Value	0.965	0.261	0.278	−0.208	−0.065	(15)	0.025	(14)
NVSOX	Small Blend	0.892	0.731	0.152	0.111	0.187	(2)	0.139	(2)
PGSGX	Small Growth	1.117	1.194	−0.357	0.034	0.010	(14)	−0.004	(15)
PRDGX	Large Blend	0.927	0.043	−0.008	0.050	0.120	(4)	0.099	(7)
PSLAX	Small Value	0.900	0.824	0.502	0.075	0.096	(8)	0.064	(11)
RSPFX	Small Blend	0.946	0.560	0.323	−0.033	−0.111	(20)	−0.097	(19)
RYPRX	Small Blend	0.973	0.673	0.201	−0.103	−0.247	(28)	−0.202	(29)
SCMVX	Small Value	1.131	1.088	0.802	−0.578	−0.374	(30)	−0.123	(23)
JENRX	Large Growth	0.918	0.008	−0.067	0.017	0.139	(3)	0.132	(3)
TGDVX	Large Value	1.073	0.244	0.199	−0.071	−0.145	(21)	−0.114	(21)
TWEBX	Large Value	0.821	−0.106	0.110	−0.030	−0.150	(24)	−0.137	(24)
VASVX	Mid Value	0.940	0.373	0.173	−0.119	0.053	(13)	0.104	(6)
VGRAX	Mid Growth	0.998	0.499	−0.376	−0.076	−0.090	(18)	−0.057	(18)
	Mean	0.986	0.423	0.065	−0.047	−0.037		−0.017	

[a]Significant at the 0.05 level.

Although the information ratio results in Exhibit 18.10 take into account the performance of a fund's investment style-specific benchmark, the single-factor model findings in Exhibit 18.9 do not. So, it is possible that some of the measured performance was an illusion because the S&P 500 Index was not the appropriate benchmark for many of the portfolios. The advantage of evaluating a fund's alpha using a multifactor approach is that it is designed to control for market (R_m), style (*SMB* and *HML*), and momentum (*MOM*) risk.

Although not listed in Exhibit 18.11, the average monthly returns (risk premia) for the *SMB*, *HML*, and *MOM* factors were −0.03 percent, 0.09 percent, and 0.06 percent, respectively. This indicates that in the stock market as a whole over this investment period, large stocks slightly outperformed small stocks (negative mean *SMB* return), value stocks outperformed growth stocks (positive mean *HML* return), and high-momentum stocks outperformed low-momentum stocks (positive mean *MOM* return). For this particular collection of 30 funds, the mean factor betas—0.986 for the market factor, 0.423 for the *SMB* factor, 0.065 for the *HML* factor, and −0.047 for the *MOM* factor—indicate that the average fund has slightly less systematic market risk than average and is oriented toward holding smaller, more value-oriented stocks that exhibit negative return momentum.

The Jensen's alpha results from both the three-factor and the four-factor models are generally comparable to the findings from the one-factor model with some notable differences. In particular, the mean value for alpha is still slightly negative in each case (−0.037 and −0.017, respectively) but less so than before. Also, 14 (rather than 12) of the funds had positive alpha values (none statistically significant) in both the three-factor and four-factor models. Conversely, one fund (DGAGX) continued to exhibit statistically significant underperformance when measured against both multifactor specifications. For instance, PGSGX, a small-cap growth fund, had a large negative alpha of −0.250 when its performance was measured relative to a large-cap blend index (S&P 500), but relative to models that take investment style and momentum into account, its alpha increased to virtually zero (0.010 for three-factor, −0.004 for four-factor). This highlights the fact that the one-factor and multifactor Jensen measures produce similar but distinct performance rankings and should therefore be considered to be different from one another.

Relationship among Performance Measures Exhibit 18.12 contains the matrix of rank correlation coefficients among the Sharpe, Treynor, Jensen (one-factor, three-factor, and four-factor), and information ratio measures. The striking feature of the display is that all of these statistics are positively correlated with one another—but not perfectly so. (The Sharpe, Treynor, and one-factor Jensen statistics produced virtually identical rankings for this fund sample.) This suggests that although the measures provide a generally consistent assessment of portfolio

Exhibit 18.12 Correlations between Alternative Portfolio Performance Measures

	Sharpe	Treynor	Jensen (1-factor)	Jensen (3-factor)	Jensen (4-factor)	Information Ratio
Sharpe	—					
Treynor	0.936	—				
Jensen (1-factor)	0.936	0.996	—			
Jensen (3-factor)	0.780	0.912	0.917	—		
Jensen (4-factor)	0.801	0.908	0.907	0.935	—	
Information ratio	0.321	0.410	0.373	0.391	0.520	—

performance when taken as a whole, they remain distinct at an individual level. The exhibit reinforces our earlier point that it is best to consider these measures collectively and that the user must understand what each means.

18.5 HOLDINGS-BASED PORTFOLIO PERFORMANCE MEASURES

Each of the conventional performance measures just discussed uses the returns produced by the investment portfolios being compared. There are two advantages to assessing performance with investment returns. First, returns are usually easy for the investor to observe on a frequent (for example, daily) basis. Second, they represent the investor actually benefits from the manager's investing prowess. However, *returns-based* measures are indirect indications of the manager's decision-making ability that do not reveal the underlying reasons the portfolio produced the returns it did.

It is also possible to view investment performance in terms of which securities the manager buys or sells from the portfolio. By looking at how the portfolio's holdings change over time, the investor is able to establish precisely which stock or bond positions were responsible for creating that performance. Thus, using a **holdings-based measure** can provide additional insights about the quality of the portfolio manager. Two of the most popular holdings-based performance measures are described below.

18.5.1 Grinblatt–Titman Performance Measure

Assuming that an investor knows the exact investment proportions of each security position in her portfolio on two consecutive reporting dates (for example, quarterly reports for mutual funds), Grinblatt and Titman (1993) showed that the manager's security selection ability can be established by how he adjusted these weights. For a particular reporting period t, their performance measure (GT) is:

18.8
$$GT_t = \sum_j (w_{jt} - w_{jt-1})R_{jt}$$

(w_{jt}, w_{jt-1}) = portfolio weights for the jth security at the beginning of Period t and Period $t - 1$, respectively

R_{jt} = return to the jth security during Period t, which begins on Date $t - 1$ and ends on Date t

A series of GT_t statistics for a manager can be averaged over several periods to create a better indication of his overall decision-making ability:

$$\text{Average } GT = \frac{\sum_t GT_t}{T}$$

where:

T = total number of investment periods used in the evaluation

Exhibit 18.13 illustrates the GT performance measure for two different portfolios: (1) a passive value-weighted index of all the stocks in the market and (2) an active portfolio manager. Panel A shows the share prices for five stocks representing the investable universe on six different dates relative to the current Date 0. No dividends are paid, and the returns to each stock are also shown for the four full holding periods starting at Date 0 (where Period 1 begins at Date 0 and ends at Date 1).

Exhibit 18.13 Holdings-Based Performance Measurement with the GT Method

A. Stock Market Data

Stock	Share Price ($)						Return (%)			
	Date −1	Date 0	Date 1	Date 2	Date 3	Date 4	Period 1	Period 2	Period 3	Period 4
A	10	10	14	13	13	14	40.00	−7.14	0.00	7.69
B	10	10	8	8	8	6	−20.00	0.00	0.00	−25.00
C	10	10	8	8	7	6	−20.00	0.00	−12.50	−14.29
D	10	10	10	11	12	12	0.00	10.00	9.09	0.00
E	10	10	10	10	10	10	0.00	0.00	0.00	0.00

B. Value-Weighted Index Holding Data

Stock	Shares Outstanding on						Index Weight (w_{it}) At Beginning of				
	Date −1	Date 0	Date 1	Date 2	Date 3	Date 4	Period 0	Period 1	Period 2	Period 3	Period 4
A	200	200	200	200	200	200	0.200	0.200	0.280	0.260	0.260
B	200	200	200	200	200	200	0.200	0.200	0.160	0.160	0.160
C	200	200	200	200	200	200	0.200	0.200	0.160	0.160	0.140
D	200	200	200	200	200	200	0.200	0.200	0.200	0.220	0.240
E	200	200	200	200	200	200	0.200	0.200	0.200	0.200	0.200

C. Active Manager Holding Data

Stock	Shares Held on						Portfolio Weight (w_{it}) At Beginning of				
	Date −1	Date 0	Date 1	Date 2	Date 3	Date 4	Period 0	Period 1	Period 2	Period 3	Period 4
A	0	10	10	10	10	14	0.000	0.250	0.333	0.310	0.310
B	10	5	5	0	0	6	0.250	0.125	0.095	0.000	0.000
C	10	5	5	10	10	6	0.250	0.125	0.095	0.190	0.167
D	10	10	10	10	10	12	0.250	0.250	0.238	0.262	0.286
E	10	10	10	10	10	10	0.250	0.250	0.238	0.238	0.238

D. Calculation of GT Measure

Index

Stock	$(w_1 − w_0) × R_1$	$(w_2 − w_1) × R_2$	$(w_3 − w_2) × R_3$	$(w_4 − w_3) × R_4$
A	0.00	−0.57	0.00	0.00
B	0.00	0.00	0.00	0.00
C	0.00	0.00	0.00	0.29
D	0.00	0.00	0.18	0.00
E	0.00	0.00	0.00	0.00
GT_t:	0.00%	−0.57%	0.18%	0.29%

Average GT: −0.03%

Active Manager

Stock	$(w_1 − w_0) × R_1$	$(w_2 − w_1) × R_2$	$(w_3 − w_2) × R_3$	$(w_4 − w_3) × R_4$
A	10.00	−0.59	0.00	0.00
B	2.50	0.00	0.00	0.00
C	2.50	0.00	−1.19	0.34
D	0.00	−0.12	0.22	0.00
E	0.00	0.00	0.00	0.00
GT_t:	15.00%	−0.71%	−0.97%	0.34%

Average GT: 3.41%

Panel B shows the total shares outstanding for each stock on Date −1, Date 0, Date 1, Date 2, and Date 3, which are the beginning dates for Period 0, Period 1, Period 2, Period 3, and Period 4, respectively. Alongside the shares outstanding, which do not change, Panel B lists the corresponding index weights that would apply at the beginning of each investment period. For instance, the index weight shown for Stock A at the beginning of Period 2 (w_2) is 28.0 percent, which is calculated by multiplying the share price at Date 1 (that is, $14) by the shares outstanding at Date 1 (that is, 200) and then dividing that product by the total market value of all five stocks at Date 1 ($[200 \times 14] + \cdots + [200 \times 10] = \$10,000$). As the share prices change over time, the value-based index weights will also change, even though the number of shares outstanding does not.

Panel C provides similar data for a hypothetical active portfolio manager. This manager has made two explicit adjustments to his portfolio holdings. First, on Date 0 (the beginning of Period 1), he has sold half of his share positions in Stocks B and C in order to buy 10 shares of Stock A. Second, on Date 2 (the beginning of Period 3), he sells the remainder of his Stock B holding to repurchase five shares of Stock C. The portfolio weights of this active manager change because of both explicit stock trades and implicit adjustments due to changing market prices.

The last panel of Exhibit 18.13 calculates the GT measure for both the stock index and the active manager. For the index, the average GT across the four investment periods is virtually zero (-0.03 percent $= [0.00 - 0.57 + 0.18 + 0.29]/4$). This should be the case for any passive buy-and-hold portfolio, assuming that the stock returns are not correlated from one period to the next. That is, while index weights will vary with stock prices (for example, $w_2 - w_1 = 0.280 - 0.200 = 0.080$, for Stock A), the product of these weight changes with the subsequent stock returns should net out over time if there is no momentum effect present in the returns. This is consistent with viewing the GT measure as the return to a zero-cost hedge portfolio that is long at the current investment weights and short at the previous weights.

In contrast, the GT measure for an active portfolio manager will likely not be zero. Here, the manager's average GT value is 3.41 percent $[= (15.00 - 0.71 - 0.97 + 0.34)/4]$, indicating that he added a substantial amount of value through his stock-picking prowess. In Period 1, the decision to buy Stock A at Date 0, whose price subsequently rose, contributed 10.00 percent $[= (0.250 - 0.000) \times 40\%]$, whereas the decisions to sell some of Stocks B and C contributed 2.50 percent each $[= (0.125 - 0.250) \times -20\%]$ since both stocks declined in value during Period 1. On the other hand, the decision to repurchase Stock C on Date 2 subtracted 1.19 percent of value $[= (0.190 - 0.095) \times -12.5\%]$ since the price of these shares fell from $8 to $7 during Period 3.

An advantage of the *GT* statistic is that it can be computed without reference to any specific benchmark, which was not true for returns-based measures such as the information ratio. However, the *GT* measure fails to reward or penalize the manager for portfolio adjustments where the share price change actually occurs in a later period. For instance, the manager received no credit in Period 3 for the decision to sell Stock B because the subsequent share price decline from $8 to $6 did not occur until Period 4. This deficiency can be overcome by calculating portfolio weight adjustments over longer holding periods (for example, annual versus quarterly).

18.5.2 Characteristic Selectivity Performance Measure

A limitation of the *GT* measure is that it does not control directly for changes in either risk or investment style that result when a manager revises his portfolio holdings. If a manager sells a risky stock in order to buy a more risky one, he should be rewarded with higher gross returns over time but not necessarily higher risk-adjusted returns. Similarly, *GT* does not distinguish between stocks that perform well because of security-specific factors and those that merely benefit from broader trends, such as price momentum effects. Daniel et al. (1997) developed an alternative holdings-based measure that compares the returns of each stock held in an actively managed portfolio to the return of a benchmark portfolio that has the same aggregate investment characteristics. Their *characteristic selectivity* (CS) performance statistic is given by:

18.9
$$CS_t = \sum_j w_{jt}(R_{jt} - R_{Bjt})$$

where:

R_{Bjt} = Period t (that is, from Date $t-1$ to Date t) return to a passive portfolio whose investment characteristics are matched at the beginning of Period t with those of Stock j

As with GT, a series of CS_t values can be averaged to indicate the manager's ability to pick stocks within the context of a larger style mandate:

$$\text{Average } CS = \frac{\sum_t CS_t}{T}$$

The CS measure credits the active manager whenever he holds a stock that outperforms a style-matched index investment and penalizes him when the opposite is true. The implicit assumption is that, in lieu of hiring the active manager, investors could always purchase an indexed product with equivalent investment characteristics. Thus, the true test of the active manager's skill is whether he can pick specific stocks that outperform portfolios that investors could have formed for themselves.

The major obstacle to implementing CS is identifying a set of benchmark portfolios to match the risk and style characteristics of every stock that an active manager might want to hold. Daniel et al. (1997) proposed forming 125 different passive portfolios, based on three investment characteristics: (1) market capitalization (size), (2) book-to-market ratio, and (3) stock price momentum. They created their benchmarks by sorting every stock listed on the NYSE, AMEX, and NASDAQ exchanges into quintiles based first on size, then on book-to-market ratios, and finally on price momentum. The benchmark returns (R_{Bjt}) were calculated as value-weighted averages of all of the stocks contained in that particular portfolio. The appropriate characteristic-matched benchmark for any given stock position is simply the one that contains that stock.

Exhibit 18.14 summarizes a performance evaluation of almost 2,000 mutual funds with a diverse set of investment objectives from 1975 to 1994. Four different measures are compared:

Exhibit 18.14 Comparison of *GT, CS,* and Jensen Performance Measures

Investment Period	Number of Funds	Gross Return (%)	*GT* Measure (%)	*CS* Measure (%)	1-Factor Jensen (%)	4-Factor Jensen (%)
1975–1979	214	21.33	2.06[a]	1.58[b]	2.78[b]	1.44
1980–1984	508	16.31	2.10[b]	0.79	0.62	0.98
1984–1989	786	20.07	1.79[b]	0.33	−0.80	0.83
1990–1994	1,973	10.26	1.86[b]	0.45	−0.16	−0.36
1975–1994	—	16.99	1.94[a]	0.79[b]	0.60	0.39

[a]Significant at the 0.01 level.

[b]Significant at the 0.05 level.

Source: Kent Daniel, Mark Grinblatt, Sheridan Titman, and Russ Wermers, "Measuring Mutual Fund Performance with Characteristic Benchmarks," *Journal of Finance,* 52, no. 3 (July 1997). Data from Blackwell Publishing.

(1) *GT*, (2) *CS*, (3) one-factor Jensen, and (4) four-factor Jensen. The *GT* measure, which captures the net benefit of the broad range of active trading strategies, shows that the average fund added 1.94 percent of value per year over the 20-year horizon. However, the *CS* measure—which controls for momentum, size, and value-growth effects—shows that the benefit provided by just the manager's security selection skills accounted for less than half of this amount (0.79 percent per year). Both of the Jensen performance measures were also positive, but statistically insignificant.

18.6 THE DECOMPOSITION OF PORTFOLIO RETURNS

The preceding risk-adjusted and holding-based measures were designed to answer the first question of performance measures: namely, *how* did the portfolio manager actually perform? The answer to the second question—*why* did the manager perform as he or she did?—requires an additional decomposition of portfolio returns.

18.6.1 Performance Attribution Analysis

Portfolio managers can add value for their investors in two ways: selecting superior securities or demonstrating superior timing skills by allocating funds to different asset or sector classes. **Attribution analysis** attempts to distinguish the source of the portfolio's overall performance. This method compares the manager's total return to the return for a predetermined benchmark policy portfolio and decomposes the difference into an *allocation effect* and a *selection effect*. The most straightforward way to measure these two effects is:

18.10
$$\text{Allocation Effect} = \Sigma_i[(w_{pi} - w_{bi}) \times (R_{bi} - R_b)]$$
$$\text{Selection Effect} = \Sigma_i[(w_{pi}) \times (R_{pi} - R_{bi})]$$

where:

w_{pi}, w_{bi} = investment proportions of the ith *market segment* (asset class, industry group) in the active manager's portfolio and the benchmark policy portfolio's respectively

R_{pi}, R_{bi} = investment return to the ith market segment in the active manager's portfolio and the benchmark portfolio, respectively

R_b = total return to the benchmark portfolio

The allocation effect measures the manager's decision to over- or underweight a particular market segment ($[w_{pi} - w_{bi}]$) in terms of that segment's return performance relative to the overall return to the benchmark ($[R_{bi} - R_b]$). Good timing skill is therefore a matter of investing more money in those market segments that end up producing greater-than-average returns. The selection effect measures the manager's ability to create specific market segment portfolios that generate superior returns relative to how those market segments are defined in the benchmark ($[R_{pi} - R_{bi}]$), weighted by the manager's actual investment proportions. The manager's total value-added performance is the sum of the allocation and selection effects.[4]

An Example   Consider an investor whose top-down portfolio strategy consists of two dimensions. First, he decides on a broad allocation across three asset classes: U.S. stocks, U.S. long-term bonds, and cash equivalents, such as Treasury bills. The investor's second general

---

[4]Bailey, Richards, and Tierney (2007) argue that a better way to measure the selection effect is to multiply the market segment return differential by the benchmark segment weight, or $\Sigma_i[(w_{bi}) \times (R_{pi} - R_{bi})]$. A drawback of this approach is that the allocation and selection effects no longer sum to the total value-added return. To balance this, they calculate an *interaction effect* as $\Sigma_i[(w_{pi} - w_{bi}) \times (R_{pi} - R_{bi})]$ to measure residual performance. Hsu, Kalesnik, and Myers (2010) also developed an alternative framework that measures a manager's *dynamic* allocation skills.

decision is choosing which specific stocks, bonds, and cash instruments to buy. As a policy benchmark, he selects a hypothetical portfolio with a 60 percent allocation to the Standard & Poor's 500 Index, a 30 percent investment in the Barclays Aggregate Bond Index, and a 10 percent allocation to three-month T-bills.

Suppose that at the start of the investment period, the investor believes equity values are inflated relative to the fixed-income market. Compared to the benchmark, he decides to underweight stocks and overweight bonds and cash with 50 percent in equity, 38 percent in bonds, and 12 percent in cash. Further, he decides to concentrate on equities in the interest rate–sensitive sectors, such as utilities and financial companies, while deemphasizing the technology and consumer durables sectors. Finally, he resolves to buy shorter-duration bonds of a higher credit quality than are contained in the benchmark bond index, and to buy commercial paper rather than Treasury bills.

The manager has made active investment decisions involving both the allocation of assets and the selection of individual securities. To determine if either (or both) of these decisions proved to be wise, at the end of the investment period, he can calculate his overall and segment-specific performance. Exhibit 18.15 summarizes these returns for the investor's actual and benchmark asset class portfolios, as well as the investment weightings for each. The overall returns can be computed as:

$$\text{Overall manager return} = (0.50 \times 0.097) + (0.38 \times 0.091) + (0.12 \times 0.056)$$
$$= 8.98\%$$

and:

$$\text{Overall benchmark return} = (0.60 \times 0.086) + (0.30 \times 0.092) + (0.10 \times 0.054)$$
$$= 8.46\%$$

So, the manager beat the policy benchmark by 52 basis points $(= 0.0898 - 0.0846)$ over this particular investment horizon.

The goal of attribution analysis is to isolate the reason for this value-added performance. The manager's allocation effect can be computed by multiplying the excess asset class weight by that class's relative investment performance:

$$[-0.10 \times (0.086 - 0.0846)] + [0.08 \times (0.092 - 0.0846)] + [0.02 \times (0.054 - 0.0846)] = -0.02\%$$

If the investor had made just his market timing decisions and not picked different securities than those in the benchmark, his performance would have lagged behind the policy return by two basis points. This total allocation effect can be broken down further into an equity allocation return of -2 basis points $[= -0.10 \times (0.086 - 0.0846)]$, a bond allocation return of 6 basis points $[= 0.08 \times (0.092 - 0.0846)]$, and a cash allocation return of -6 basis points $[= 0.02 \times (0.054 - 0.0846)]$. Therefore, the decision to underweight stock and overweight cash resulted in diminished performance that more than offset the benefit of overweighting bonds.

Exhibit 18.15 Asset Class Performance Attribution Analysis

Asset Class	INVESTMENT WEIGHTS			RETURNS		
	Actual	Benchmark	Excess	Actual	Benchmark	Excess
Stock	0.50	0.60	−0.10	9.70%	8.60%	1.10%
Bonds	0.38	0.30	0.08	9.10	9.20	−0.10
Cash	0.12	0.10	0.02	5.60	5.40	0.20

Since the investor knows that he outperformed the benchmark overall, a negative allocation effect must mean that he exhibited positive security selection skills. His selection effect can be computed as:

$$[0.50 \times (0.097 - 0.086)] - [0.38 \times (0.091 - 0.092)] + [0.12 \times (0.056 - 0.054)] = 0.54\%$$

The investor formed superior stock and cash portfolios, although his bond selections did not perform quite as well as the Barclays index. One important caveat is that because the returns are not risk adjusted, it is possible that the asset class portfolios formed by the investor are riskier than their benchmark counterparts. This is almost certainly true for a cash portfolio that holds short-term corporate debt instead of T-bills, so the investor should expect a higher return that has nothing to do with his skill. The investor's total incremental return of 52 basis points can be decomposed as:

$$\text{Total Value Added} = \text{Allocation Effect} + \text{Selection Effect}$$
$$= -0.02\% + 0.54\% = 0.52\%$$

Using a similar procedure, Brinson, Hood, and Beebower (1986) examined the performance of a group of 91 large U.S. pension plans from 1974 to 1983. The mean annual return for this sample was 9.01 percent, compared to 10.11 percent for the benchmark. Thus, active management cost the average plan 110 basis points of return per year. This "value-subtracted" return increment consisted of a −77-basis-point allocation effect and a −33-basis-point selection effect. They concluded that a plan's initial strategic asset allocation choice, rather than its active management decisions, was the primary determinant of portfolio performance. In a follow-up study, Brinson, Singer, and Beebower (1991) reached a similar conclusion for a different group of 82 pension plans over the 1977–1987 period.

A Performance Attribution Extension The attribution methodology can also be used to distinguish security selection skills from other decisions that an investor might make. For instance, the manager of an all-equity portfolio must decide which economic sectors (for example, basic materials, consumer nondurables, transportation) to under- and overweight before selecting her preferred companies in those sectors. Exhibit 18.16 summarizes the performance of the growth-oriented stock portfolio managed by The MBA Investment Fund, LLC, a privately funded investment management company run by a group of graduate students at the University of Texas. Because the Fund's investment mandate was to beat the return on the Standard & Poor's 500, the managers had two basic decisions to make: which sectors to emphasize and which individual stocks to buy within those sectors.

During the year shown here, the overall returns to the S&P 500 and the MBA Investment Fund were 29.63 percent and 29.54 percent, respectively. The second and third columns of

Exhibit 18.16 MBA Investment Fund Sector Performance Attribution Analysis

S&P 500 Sector	INVESTMENT WEIGHTS			EXCESS RETURNS
	Actual	S&P 500	Excess	S&P Sector—Overall S&P
Basic materials	0.0331	0.0670	−0.0339	−15.15%
Capital equipment and technology	0.2544	0.1841	0.0703	−3.31
Consumer services	0.0208	0.0692	−0.0484	6.95
Consumer durables	0.0588	0.0353	0.0235	−21.34
Consumer nondurables	0.2752	0.2851	−0.0099	5.85
Energy	0.1170	0.0935	0.0235	−7.08
Financial	0.1619	0.1249	0.0370	7.15
Transportation	0.0199	0.0172	0.0027	−1.72
Utilities	0.0590	0.1000	−0.0410	1.91
Miscellaneous	0.0000	0.0242	−0.0242	−13.15

Exhibit 18.16 document the actual and benchmark weights for the 10 economic sectors comprising the S&P 500 Index, with the fund's excess weightings (that is, $[w_{pi} - w_{bi}]$) listed in the fourth column. The last column shows the benchmark sector return relative to the overall S&P return (that is, $[R_{bi} - R_b]$). The sector allocation effect can be calculated by summing the product of the entries in the last two columns:

$$(-0.0339 \times -0.1515) + (0.0703 \times -0.0331) + \cdots + (-0.0242 \times -0.1315) = -0.28\%$$

With an overall return difference of -9 basis points ($= 0.2954 - 0.2963$), this means that the fund's managers generated a security selection effect of 19 basis points $[= (-0.0009) - (-0.0028)]$. Consequently, while the student managers virtually matched the strong performance of the entire stock market, it appears they were better at picking stocks than forecasting broader economic trends.

Measuring Market Timing Skills As we saw in Chapter 11, tactical asset allocation (TAA) attempts to produce active value-added returns solely by adjusting their asset class exposures based on perceived changes in the relative valuations of those classes. Thus, the relevant performance measurement criterion for a TAA manager is how well he is able to time broad market movements. There are two reasons why attribution analysis is ill-suited for this task. First, by design, a TAA manager indexes his actual asset class investments, and so the selection effect is not relevant. Second, TAA might entail dozens of changes to asset class weightings during an investment period, which could render meaningless an attribution effect computed on the average holdings. Because of these problems, many analysts consider a regression-based method for measuring timing skills to be a superior approach.

Weigel (1991) tested the market timing skills of a group of 17 U.S.-based TAA managers. His methodology was motivated by the work of Merton (1981) and Hendriksson and Merton (1981) and assumed that perfect market timing ability was equivalent to owning a lookback call option that pays at expiration the return to the best-performing asset class among stocks, bonds, and cash. That is, in Period t, a manager with perfect market timing skills would have a return (R_{pt}) equal to:

$$R_{pt} = RFR_t + \max[R_{st} - RFR_t, R_{bt} - RFR_t, 0]$$

where:

R_{st} and R_{bt} = Period t returns to the stock and bond benchmark portfolios, respectively

Controlling for stock and bond price movements in a manner comparable to Jensen's method, the following regression equation can be calculated:

$$(R_{pt} - RFR_t) = \alpha + \beta_b(R_{bt} - RFR_t) + \beta_s(R_{st} - RFR_t) + \gamma\{\max[R_{st} - RFR_t, R_{bt} - RFR_t, 0]\} + e_t$$

The average value for γ, which measures the proportion of the perfect timing option that the TAA managers were able to capture, was 0.30. This value was statistically significant, meaning that these managers had reliable, although not perfect, market timing skills. Also, the average alpha was -0.5 percent per quarter, indicating that these same managers had negative nonmarket timing skills (for example, hedging strategies). Other studies that have examined market timing ability include Kon (1983), Coggin, Fabozzi, and Rahman (1993), and Fulkerson (2013).

18.6.2 Fama Selectivity Performance Measure

Fama (1972) suggested that *overall performance* in a portfolio, in excess of the risk-free rate, can be decomposed into measures of risk-taking and security selection skill:

Overall Performance = Excess Return = Portfolio Risk + Selectivity

The *selectivity* component represents the portion of the portfolio's actual return beyond that of an unmanaged portfolio with identical systematic risk. This component is used to assess the manager's investment prowess.

Evaluating Selectivity Formally, you can measure the return due to selectivity as:

$$\text{Selectivity} = R_a - R_x(\beta_a)$$

where:

R_a = actual return on the portfolio being evaluated

$R_x(\beta_a)$ = return on the combination of the riskless asset and the market portfolio M that has risk β_x equal to β_a, the risk of the portfolio being evaluated

As shown in Exhibit 18.17, selectivity measures the vertical distance between the actual return and the *ex post* market line and is quite similar to Treynor's measure.

Overall performance can be written:

18.11
$$\text{Overall Performance} = \text{Selectivity} + \text{Risk}$$
$$[R_a - RFR] = [R_a - R_x(\beta_a)] + [R_x(\beta_a) - RFR]$$

Exhibit 18.17 shows that overall performance is the total return above the risk-free return and includes the return that *should* have been received for accepting the portfolio risk (β_a), which is equal to $[R_x(\beta_a) - RFR]$. Any excess over this expected return is due to selectivity.

Evaluating Diversification The selectivity component in Equation 18.11 can also be broken down into two parts. If a portfolio manager attempts to select undervalued stocks and in the process gives up some diversification, it is possible to measure the added return necessary to justify this decision. The portfolio's *gross selectivity* is made up of *net selectivity* plus *diversification*:

$$\begin{matrix} \text{Selectivity} & & \text{Diversification} \\ R_a - R_x(\beta_a) = \text{Net Selectivity} + & [R_x(\sigma(R_a)) - R_x(\beta_a)] \end{matrix}$$

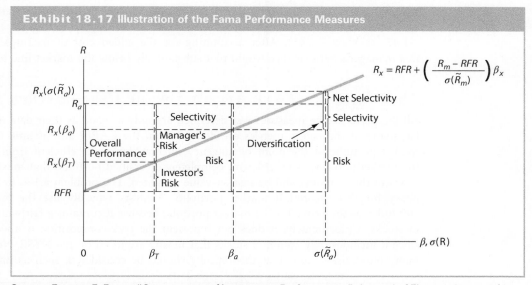

Exhibit 18.17 Illustration of the Fama Performance Measures

or:

18.12
$$\text{Net Selectivity} = R_a - R_x(\beta_a) - [R_x(\sigma(R_a)) - R_x(\beta_a)]$$
$$= R_a - R_x(\sigma(R_a))$$

where:

$R_x(\sigma(R_a))$ = return on the combination of the riskless asset and the market portfolio that has return volatility equivalent to that of the portfolio being evaluated

The diversification measure in Equation 18.12 indicates the added return required to justify any loss of diversification in the portfolio. If the portfolio is completely diversified so that total risk (σ) is equal to systematic risk (β), then the $R_x(\sigma(R_a))$ would be the same as $R_x(\beta_a)$, and the diversification term would equal zero. Because the diversification measure always is non-negative, net selectivity will always be equal to or less than gross selectivity.[5]

Example of Fama Performance Measure   Suppose that over a recent five-year investment period, you observed that the average annual return on the market portfolio and the risk-free security were 22.96 percent and 5.28 percent, respectively. Thus, an investment portfolio with a beta of 0.815 would be expected to deliver a return of 19.69 percent [$=5.28 + 0.815$ $(22.96 - 5.28)$]. Suppose further that this portfolio actually returned 19.67 percent per annum. The return for *selectivity* is the difference between the actual excess performance $(19.67 - 5.28 = 14.39)$ and the required excess return for risk of 14.41 ($=19.69 - 5.28$), or -0.02, indicating the manager fell slightly short of matching expectations consistent with the actual risk level of the portfolio.

What if the manager also did not fully diversify the portfolio? Assume that the standard deviations on the market and the manager's portfolio were 14.95 percent and 13.41 percent, respectively. The ratio of total risk in the portfolio per unit of market total risk is 0.897 ($=13.41/14.95$), but since the manager's beta (0.815) is less than this, it appears that the portfolio contained elements of unsystematic risk. Thus, the selectivity measure of -0.02 understates the true performance shortfall.

To adjust the selectivity measure for the lack of complete diversification, notice that the fund's required return given its standard deviation is 21.14 [$=5.28 + 0.897(22.96 - 5.28)$]. The difference of 1.45 ($=21.14 - 19.69$) between the required returns using total versus systematic risk is the added return required because of less-than-perfect diversification. This is subtracted from the selectivity measure to create the manager's *net selectivity* performance of -1.47 ($=-0.02 - 1.45$). After accounting for the added cost of incomplete diversification, this manager's performance would plot substantially below the market line in Exhibit 18.17.

18.7 FACTORS THAT AFFECT USE OF PERFORMANCE MEASURES

All the performance measures just described are only as good as their data inputs. In particular, many of the equity metrics are derived from the CAPM and assume the existence of a market portfolio at the point of tangency on the Markowitz efficient frontier. Theoretically, the market portfolio is an efficient, completely diversified portfolio that must contain all risky assets in the economy and be market-value weighted. The problem arises in finding a realistic proxy for this theoretical market portfolio. Analysts typically use the Standard & Poor's 500 Index as the proxy for the market portfolio because it contains a fairly diversified portfolio of stocks. Unfortunately, it does not represent the true composition of the market portfolio since it includes only common stocks that mostly are listed on the NYSE. Notably, it excludes many other risky assets that theoretically should be considered, such as numerous domestic

---

[5]Modigliani and Modigliani (1997) present a performance measure (dubbed M^2) that is a variation of both the Sharpe measure and Fama's $R_x[\sigma(R_a)]$ component.

stocks, foreign stocks, foreign and domestic bonds, real estate, alternative assets, and collectibles.

This lack of completeness was highlighted in several articles by Roll (1977a, 1978, 1980, 1981), who detailed the problem with the market proxy and pointed out its implications for measuring portfolio performance. He refers to this as the **benchmark error** problem. He showed that if the proxy for the market portfolio is not a truly efficient portfolio, then the SML using this proxy may not be the true SML. In such a case, a portfolio plotted above the SML and derived using a poor benchmark could actually plot below the SML that uses the true market portfolio.

Another problem is that the beta could differ from that computed using the true market portfolio. For example, if the true beta were larger than the beta computed using the proxy, the true position of the portfolio would shift to the right. In an empirical test, Brown and Brown (1987) documented a considerable amount of ranking reversal when the definition of the market portfolio was changed in a Jensen's alpha analysis of a sample of well-established mutual funds. Terhaar (2001) also showed how the benchmark error problem can affect attribution analysis.

18.7.1 Demonstration of the Global Benchmark Problem

As an illustration of the benchmark problem in global capital markets, consider how individual measures of risk change when the world equity market is employed as the market portfolio proxy. Exhibit 18.18 contains beta estimates for the 30 stocks in the Dow Jones Industrial Average (DJIA) using the S&P 500, the typical proxy for U.S.-domiciled stocks, and the Morgan Stanley Capital International (MSCI) World Stock Index, a market-value-weighted index of stocks from around the globe. These findings were calculated using weekly returns from two different three-year periods: 2005–2007 and 2014–2016. The percentage difference between the U.S. beta and the World beta is also shown, using the higher of the two risk estimates as the base.

There are two major differences in the various beta statistics. First, for many stocks, the beta estimates change a great deal over time. For example, Boeing's U.S. and world betas during 2005–2007 were 0.87 and 0.78, respectively. However, during 2014–2016, both of these values substantially increased (to 1.07 and 1.19, respectively). Second, although the mean and median values for the U.S. and world beta estimates appear to be somewhat similar during both time periods, the "% Diff" columns show that there are some substantial differences in betas estimated for the same stock over the same time period when two different definitions of the benchmark portfolio are employed. For instance, the U.S. and world beta estimates for Wal-Mart differed by almost 17 percent in 2005–2007 and then by about 17 percent again in 2014–2016. Overall, the median size of this discrepancy itself changed over time—from 12.0 percent to 4.2 percent—indicating that the specification of the proper benchmark remains a critical issue in the performance evaluation process.

Reilly and Akhtar (1995) examined the effect of the choice of a benchmark on global performance measurement by plotting SMLs for six different indexes over three time horizons: 1983–1988, 1989–1994, and 1983–1994. Their results show that using alternative market proxies for different countries generates SMLs that differ substantially during a given time period and are very unstable over time. For instance, the Japanese SML had the largest risk premium during 1983–1988 but a negative risk premium during 1989–1994, which clearly is contrary to capital market theory. The S&P 500 provided investors with the biggest performance hurdle over the whole sample period, due to the high-risk premiums in the United States during 1989–1994.

18.7.2 Implications of the Benchmark Problems

The problems noted by Roll, which are increased with global investing, do not negate the value of the CAPM as a *normative* model of equilibrium pricing; the theory may still be viable.

Exhibit 18.18 Beta Estimates for Dow Jones Industrials Stocks Using Domestic and World Stock Market Indexes: 2005–2007 and 2014–2016

Stock	Ticker	2005–2007			2014–2016		
		Beta—U.S.	Beta—World	% Diff	Beta—U.S.	Beta—World	% Diff
3M Company	MMM	0.83	0.73	12.0%	0.99	0.97	2.0%
American Express	AXP	1.30	1.05	19.2	1.04	1.06	1.9
Apple	AAPL	1.65	1.55	6.1	1.19	1.14	4.2
Boeing	BA	0.87	0.78	10.3	1.07	1.19	10.1
Caterpillar	CAT	1.70	1.67	1.8	1.34	1.39	3.6
Chevron	CVX	1.14	1.11	2.6	1.19	1.20	0.8
Cisco Systems	CSCO	1.03	0.82	20.4	1.20	1.15	4.2
Coca-Cola	KO	0.61	0.49	19.7	0.63	0.61	3.2
Du Pont	DD	1.24	1.09	12.1	0.82	0.83	1.2
ExxonMobil	XOM	1.27	1.23	3.1	0.90	0.87	3.3
General Electric	GE	0.67	0.52	22.4	1.12	1.10	1.8
Goldman Sachs	GS	1.60	1.42	11.3	1.35	1.31	3.0
Home Depot	HD	1.29	1.10	14.7	1.06	0.98	7.5
Intel	INTC	1.31	1.16	11.5	1.23	1.17	4.9
Intl Business Machines	IBM	0.90	0.74	17.8	0.84	0.91	7.7
Johnson & Johnson	JNJ	0.47	0.40	14.9	0.76	0.74	2.6
JPMorgan	JPM	1.23	0.99	19.5	1.29	1.23	4.7
McDonald's	MCD	0.92	0.81	12.0	0.56	0.49	12.5
Merck	MRK	0.71	0.67	5.6	0.82	0.79	3.7
Microsoft	MSFT	0.86	0.79	8.1	1.22	1.10	9.8
Nike	NKE	0.61	0.54	11.5	0.93	0.85	8.6
Pfizer	PFE	1.04	1.00	3.8	0.84	0.80	4.8
Procter & Gamble	PG	0.43	0.33	23.3	0.55	0.52	5.5
Travelers	TRV	0.98	0.80	18.4	0.83	0.77	7.2
United Technologies	UTX	0.99	0.96	3.0	1.07	1.07	0.0
United Health	UNH	0.45	0.31	31.1	0.88	0.87	1.5
Verizon	VZ	0.93	0.78	16.1	0.69	0.68	1.4
Visa	V	—	—	—	1.00	0.95	5.0
Wal-Mart Stores	WMT	0.85	0.71	16.5	0.58	0.48	17.2
Walt Disney	DIS	0.81	0.76	6.2	1.08	1.03	4.6
Mean:		0.99	0.87	12.9%	0.97	0.94	4.9%
Median:		0.93	0.80	12.0%	1.00	0.96	4.2%

The problem is one of *measurement* when using the theory to evaluate portfolio performance. You need to find a better proxy for the market portfolio or to adjust measured performance for benchmark errors. Roll (1981) and Grinold (1992) have made several suggestions to help overcome this problem.

Alternatively, the analyst might consider giving greater weight to the Sharpe and Sortino portfolio performance measures which do not depend on the market portfolio. Although the evaluation process based on these statistics generally uses a benchmark portfolio as an example of an unmanaged portfolio for comparison purposes, the risk measure for the portfolio being evaluated does not directly depend on a market proxy. Also, recall that the portfolio rank from the Sharpe measure typically correlates highly with the ranks derived from alternative performance measures.

18.7.3 Required Characteristics of Benchmarks

Bailey, Richards, and Tierney (2007) consider the issue of the appropriate definition for **normal portfolios**, which are customized benchmarks that reflect the specific styles of alternative managers. They contend that any useful benchmark should have the following characteristics:

- *Unambiguous.* The names and weights of securities comprising the benchmark are clearly delineated.
- *Investable.* The option is available to forgo active management and simply hold the benchmark.
- *Measurable.* It is possible to calculate the return on the benchmark on a reasonably frequent basis.
- *Appropriate.* The benchmark is consistent with the manager's investment style or biases.
- *Reflective of current investment opinions.* The manager has current investment knowledge (be it positive, negative, or neutral) of the securities that make up the benchmark.
- *Specified in advance.* The benchmark is constructed prior to the start of an evaluation period.
- *Owned.* The manager should accept accountability for benchmark performance.

If a benchmark does not possess all of these properties, it is considered an ineffective management tool. One example of a flawed benchmark is using the median manager from a broad universe in a peer group comparison.

18.8 REPORTING INVESTMENT PERFORMANCE

The performance measures described in this chapter represent the essential elements of how any investor's performance should be evaluated. However, before the various statistics can be calculated, a more fundamental issue must be addressed: How should the returns used in the evaluation process be reported to the investor? We conclude our discussion by exploring two dimensions of this problem. First, we consider the issue of how returns should be computed for a portfolio that experiences infusions and withdrawals of cash during the investment period. Second, we will briefly summarize the **performance presentation standards** created by the CFA Institute, an international organization of more than 128,000 investment practitioners and educators in almost 150 countries.

18.8.1 Time-Weighted and Money-Weighted Returns

As we saw in Chapter 1, the holding period yield (*HPY*) for any investment position was determined by that position's market value at the end of the period divided by its initial value:

$$HPY = \frac{\text{Ending Value of Investment}}{\text{Beginning Value of Investment}} - 1$$

For any security or portfolio, there are two reasons why the ending and beginning values could differ: the receipt of cash payments (dividends) or a change in price (capital gains) during the period. So, for most investment positions, calculating returns during a given time frame is a reasonably straightforward matter.

For professional money managers and management companies, however, the beginning and ending values of a portfolio can differ for a reason that has nothing to do with the manager's investment prowess. If the investor either withdraws or adds to her initial investment capital during the period, the ending value of the position will reflect these changes. Of course, it would be unfair to credit the manager with having produced high returns that were due to additional capital commitments or penalize him for reductions in the ending value of the investment caused by the investor removing funds from her account. Consequently, an evaluation of the manager's true performance must take these contributions and withdrawals into account.

Consider two portfolio managers (A and B) who have exactly identical investment styles and stock-picking skill. We will assume that over a two-period investment horizon, they produce *exactly* the same returns with the investment capital entrusted to them: 25 percent in Period 1, and 5 percent in Period 2. Further, suppose that each manager receives from his respective investor $500,000 to invest. The difference is that Manager A receives all of these funds immediately, but Manager B's investor commits only $250,000 initially and the other $250,000 at the end of the first period.

This investment timing difference can be seen by calculating the terminal (Period 2) value of each portfolio:

$$\text{Portfolio A: } 500,000[(1 + 0.25)(1 + 0.05)] = \$656,250$$

and:

$$\text{Portfolio B: } 250,000[(1 + 0.25)(1 + 0.05)] + 250,000(1 + 0.05) = \$590,625$$

Obviously, Manager B's portfolio is worth less than Manager A's, but this is a result of the way the investment funds were committed rather than any difference in the performance of the two managers. The managers' performance evaluation should not be affected by the investors' decisions concerning the timing of their capital commitments. In other words, Manager B should not be held accountable for the fact that Investor B did not have all of her funds invested during the high-return environment of the first period.

One common method of computing average returns that we have seen is to use a discounted cash flow approach to calculate an investment's internal rate of return. For the two managers in this example, these calculations generate the following returns:

$$\text{Manager A: } 500,000 = \frac{656,250}{(1 + r_{dA})^2}, \text{ or } r_{dA} = 14.56\%$$

and:

$$\text{Manager B: } 250,000 = \frac{-250,000}{(1 + r_{dB})^1} = \frac{590,625}{(1 + r_{dB})^2}, \text{ or } r_{dB} = 11.63\%$$

These returns (r_{dA} and r_{dB}) are sometimes called **money-weighted returns** because they are the discount rates that set the present value of future cash flows (including future investment contributions and withdrawals) equal to the level of the initial investment. In this case, money-weighted returns give an inaccurate impression of Manager B's ability; he did not actually perform 2.93 percent ($= 0.1456 - 0.1163$) worse than Manager A. Thus, while this internal rate of return method gives an accurate assessment of *Investor* B's return, it is a misleading measure of *Manager* B's talent.

A better way of evaluating a manager's performance considers how well he did regardless of the timing of the funds involved. For both managers, the **time-weighted return** is simply the geometric average of (one plus) the periodic returns:

$$r_{tA} = r_{tB} = \sqrt[2]{(1 + 0.25)(1 + 0.05)} - 1 = 14.56\%$$

Money-weighted and time-weighted returns are only the same when there are no interim investment contributions within the evaluation period, as for Manager A. For Manager B, the money-weighted return understates the true (time-weighted) performance because of how the funds were deployed. When there are contributions, Dietz and Kirschman (1990) suggested a method for adjusting holding period yields:

$$\text{Adjusted } HPY = \frac{\text{Ending Value of Investment} - (1 - DW)(\text{Contribution})}{\text{Beginning Value of Investment} + (DW)(\text{Contribution})} - 1$$

where the contribution can be either positive (a new commitment) or negative (a withdrawal). This adjustment process alters the initial and terminal values of the portfolios by the weighted amount of the contribution made during the holding period. The day-weight (*DW*) factor represents the portion of the period that the contribution is actually held in the account. For example, if a contribution were placed in the portfolio halfway through a 30-day month, *DW* would be 0.5 [= (30 − 15)/30].

18.8.2 Performance Presentation Standards

The preceding example underscores the fact that there may not always be a straightforward answer to a seemingly simple question. Although Portfolio B had a money-weighted return of 11.63 percent, its manager generated an average return of 14.56 percent. Which should be reported to the investor? The Securities and Exchange Commission has established regulations to guard against the publication of outright fraudulent claims, but Lawton and Remington (2007) point out that several questionable reporting practices have been historically permissible, including presenting returns only for the best-performing portfolios, selecting the most favorable measurement period, and choosing a benchmark the manager has outperformed by the greatest margin. Largely as a result of such abuses, the investment community has recently begun to demand the adoption of a more rigorous set of reporting guidelines.

In an effort to fulfill the call for uniform, accurate, and consistent performance reporting, the CFA Institute has developed a comprehensive Performance Presentation Standards (PPS). Introduced in 1987 and formally adopted in 1993, the PPS quickly became the accepted practice within the investment management community. However, early versions of these standards tended to have country-specific elements that made them difficult to translate to a fully global platform. Consequently, in 1999 the CFA Institute also adopted the companion **Global Investment Performance Standards (GIPS)**, which were intended to accomplish the following goals:

- To establish investment industry best practices for calculating and presenting investment performance that promote investor interests and instill investor confidence
- To obtain worldwide acceptance of a single standard for the calculation and presentation of investment performance based on the principles of fair representation and full disclosure
- To promote the use of accurate and consistent investment performance data
- To encourage fair, global competition among investment firms without creating barriers to entry
- To foster the notion of industry "self-regulation" on a global basis[6]

By 2010, the GIPS had been adopted by 32 countries throughout North America, Europe, Africa, and the Asia Pacific region. GIPS is now considered the definitive set of standards for reporting investment performance.

A detailed analysis of these standards (which are revised frequently) is beyond our current scope, but several of the underlying fundamental principles include:

- Total return, including realized and unrealized gains plus income, must be used when calculating investment performance.
- Time-weighted rates of return must be used.
- Portfolios must be valued at least monthly, and periodic returns must be geometrically linked.
- If composite return performance is presented, this composite must contain all actual fee-paying accounts, including all terminated accounts for periods up through the last full

---

[6]See *Global Investment Performance Standards (GIPS) Handbook*, 3rd ed. Charlottesville, VA: CFA Institute, 2012.

reporting period the account was under management. Composite results may not link simulated or model portfolios with actual performance.

- Performance must be calculated after the deduction of actual trading expenses (broker commissions and SEC fees), if any.
- For taxable clients, taxes on income and realized capital gains must be recognized in the same period they were incurred and must be subtracted from results, regardless of whether taxes are paid from assets outside the account.
- Annual returns for all years must be presented. Performance of less than one year must not be annualized. A 10-year performance record (or a record for the period since firm inception if less than 10 years) must be presented.
- Performance presentation must disclose whether performance results are calculated gross or net of investment management fees and what the firm's fee schedule is. Presentation should also disclose any use of leverage (including derivatives) and any material change in personnel responsible for investment management.

In addition to these requirements, the CFA Institute also encourages managers to disclose the volatility of the composite return and to identify benchmarks that parallel the risk or investment style the composite tracks. Exhibit 18.19 shows a sample performance presentation that is in compliance with the standards.

Exhibit 18.19 A Sample Performance Presentation

SAMPLE 1
INVESTMENT FIRM
BALANCED GROWTH COMPOSITE
1 JANUARY 2002 THROUGH 31 DECEMBER 2011

Year	Composite Gross Return (%)	Composite Net Return (%)	Custom Benchmark Return (%)	Composite 3-Yr St Dev (%)	Benchmark 3-Yr St Dev (%)	Number of Portfolios	Internal Dispersion (%)	Composite Assets ($ M)	Firm Assets ($ M)
2002	−10.5	−11.4	−11.8			31	4.5	165	236
2003	16.3	15.1	13.2			34	2.0	235	346
2004	7.5	6.4	8.9			38	5.7	344	529
2005	1.8	0.8	0.3			45	2.8	445	695
2006	11.2	10.1	12.2			48	3.1	520	839
2007	6.1	5.0	7.1			49	2.8	505	1,014
2008	−21.3	−22.1	−24.9			44	2.9	475	964
2009	16.5	15.3	14.7			47	3.1	493	983
2010	10.6	9.5	13.0			51	3.5	549	1,114
2011	2.7	1.7	0.4	7.1	7.4	54	2.5	575	1,236

Sample 1 Investment Firm claims compliance with the Global Investment Performance Standards (GIPS®) and has prepared and presented this report in compliance with the GIPS standards. Sample 1 Investment Firm has been independently verified for the periods 1 January 2000 through 31 December 2010. The verification report is available upon request. Verification assesses whether (1) the firm has complied with all the composite construction requirements of the GIPS standards on a firm-wide basis and (2) the firm's policies and procedures are designed to calculate and present performance in compliance with the GIPS standards. Verification does not ensure the accuracy of any specific composite presentation.

Notes:

1. Sample 1 Investment Firm is a balanced portfolio investment manager that invests solely in U.S.-based securities. Sample 1 Investment Firm is defined as an independent investment management firm that is not affiliated with any parent organization. Policies for valuing portfolios, Calculating performance, and preparing compliant presentations are available upon request.

> **Exhibit 18.19 A Sample Performance Presentation (*Continued*)**
>
> 2. The Balanced Growth Composite includes all institutional balanced portfolios that invest in large-cap U.S. equities and investment-grade bonds with the goal of providing long-term capital growth and steady income from a well-diversified strategy. Although the strategy allows for equity exposure ranging between 50–70%, the typical allocation is between 55–65%. The account minimum for the composite is $5 million.
> 3. The custom benchmark is 60% YYY U.S. Equity Index and 40% ZZZ U.S. Aggregate Bond Index. The benchmark is rebalanced monthly.
> 4. Valuations are computed and performance is reported in U.S. dollars.
> 5. Gross-of-fees returns are presented before management and custodial fees but after all trading expenses. Composite and benchmark returns are presented net of non-reclaimable withholding taxes. Net-of-fees returns are calculated by deducting the highest fee if 0.83% from the monthly gross composite return. The management fee schedule is as follows: 1.00% on the first $25 million; 0.60% thereafter.
> 6. This composite was created in February 2000. A complete list of composite descriptions is available upon request.
> 7. Internal dispersion is calculated using the equal-weighted standard deviation of annual gross returns of those portfolios that were included in the composite for the entire year.
> 8. The three-year annualized standard deviation measures the variability of the composite and the benchmark returns over the preceding 36-month period. The standard deviation is not presented for 2002 through 2010 because monthly composite and benchmark returns were not available and is not required for periods prior to 2011.

Source: Copyright 2012, CFA Institute. Reproduced and republished from *Global Investment Performance Standards (GIPS) Handbook*, 3rd ed., 2012, with permission of the CFA Institute. All rights reserved.

SUMMARY

- The primary goal of active portfolio management is to produce returns over time exceeding those expected on a passively managed investment fund with a similar level of risk. The goal of the investment performance evaluation process, which attempts to provide an historical assessment of that effort, is twofold. First, was the manager actually able to beat the investor's expectations? Second, what decisions that the manager made (security selection, market timing) were ultimately responsible for the realized performance?

- Several techniques have been derived to help answer both of those questions. Simple performance measures, such as peer group comparisons and portfolio drawdown measures, analyze just the returns a given portfolio produces relative to those of otherwise comparable funds. On the other hand, risk-adjusted measures are designed make explicit adjustments to a portfolio's returns that account for the volatility incurred in the investment process. These measures form the basic toolkit for performance managers and include statistics such as the Sharpe ratio, Treynor ratio, Jensen's alpha, Information ratio, and Sortino ratio. Risk-adjusted statistics differ from one another in terms of how risk is measured, how

returns are adjusted for that risk, or both. No single measure provides a complete picture of a manager's performance and so they are usually considered jointly.

- Beyond performance measures that focus on portfolio returns, it is also possible to evaluate a manager's skill by looking directly at the investment decisions he or she makes. Holdings-based evaluation tools, such as the Grinblatt–Titman statistic, credit managers for purchasing securities in advance of a price increase or selling positions before a price decline. Finally, to address the issue of why managers produced the performance they did, several techniques attempt to decompose returns to discover their ultimate source. For instance, attribution analysis seeks to establish whether market timing or security selection skills are responsible for a manager's observed performance.

- There are several outstanding issues regarding the performance measurement process. There have been challenges to the validity of techniques assuming a market portfolio that theoretically includes all risky assets but which then use a proxy such as the S&P 500 that is limited to U.S. common stocks. This criticism does not invalidate the asset pricing model itself, but only its application because of measurement problems related to the proxy for the market portfolio. This potential for measurement error is increased in an environment where global investing is the norm.

SUGGESTED READINGS

Amenc, Noel, and Veronique LeSourd. *Portfolio Theory and Performance Analysis.* West Sussex, England: Wiley, 2003.

Bacon, Carl. *Practical Risk-Adjusted Performance Measurement and Attribution.* West Sussex, England: John Wiley & Sons, 2013.

Christopherson, Jon A., David R. Carino, and Wayne E. Ferson. *Portfolio Performance Measurement and Benchmarking.* Columbus, OH: McGraw-Hill, 2009.

Lawton, Philip, and Todd Jankowski, eds. *Investment Performance Measurement: Evaluating and Presenting Results.* Charlottesville, VA: CFA Institute, 2009.

Spaulding, David. *Investment Performance Attribution.* New York: McGraw-Hill, 2003.

QUESTIONS

1. Describe the two questions that an investor should consider when evaluating the investment performance of a portfolio manager. What tools are available to help the investor answer these questions and what is the most important feature that these tools should possess?

2. Consider the five different measures of risk-adjusted portfolio performance we have examined: Sharpe ratio, Treynor ratio, Jensen alpha, information ratio, and Sortino ratio.
   a. Describe how each of these measures defines the risk that investors face.
   b. Describe how each of these measures adjusts a portfolio's return performance for the level of that risk.

3. The Sharpe and Treynor performance measures both calculate a portfolio's average excess return per unit of risk. Under what circumstances would it make sense to use both measures to compare the performance of a given set of portfolios? What additional information is provided by a comparison of the rankings achieved using the two measures?

4. Describe how the Jensen measure of performance is calculated. Under what conditions should it give a similar set of portfolio rankings as the Sharpe and Treynor measures? Is it possible to adjust the Jensen measure so that a portfolio's alpha value is measured relative to an empirical form of the arbitrage pricing theory rather than the CAPM? Explain.

5. The information ratio (*IR*) has been described as a benefit-cost ratio. Explain how the *IR* measures portfolio performance and whether this analogy is appropriate.

6. Assessing the performance of an investment portfolio can be accomplished with either *returns-based* measures or *holdings-based* measures. What are the major advantages and major disadvantages of each approach to performance measurement?

7. Performance attribution analysis is an attempt to divide a manager's "active" residual return into an allocation effect and a selection effect. Explain how these two effects are measured and why their sum must equal the total value-added return for the manager. Is this analysis valid if the actual portfolio in question is riskier than the benchmark portfolio to which it is being compared?

8. During the annual review of Acme's pension plan, several trustees questioned Lucy Graham, a pension consultant, about various aspects of performance measurement and risk assessment. In particular, one trustee asked about the appropriateness of using each of the following benchmarks:
   - Market index
   - Benchmark normal portfolio
   - Median of the manager universe

a. Explain *two* different weaknesses of using each of the three benchmarks to measure the performance of a portfolio.

Another trustee asked how to distinguish among the following performance measures:
- Sharpe ratio
- Treynor ratio
- Jensen's alpha
- Information ratio
- Sortino ratio

b. (1) Describe how *each* of the five performance measures is calculated.

(2) State whether *each* measure assumes that the relevant risk is systematic, unsystematic, total, or something else. Explain how each measure relates excess return and the relevant risk.

9. Richard Roll, in an article on using the capital asset pricing model (CAPM) to evaluate portfolio performance, indicated that it may not be possible to evaluate portfolio management ability if there is error in the benchmark used.

a. In evaluating portfolio performance, describe the general procedure, with emphasis on the benchmark employed.

b. Explain what Roll meant by the benchmark error, and identify the specific problem with this benchmark.

c. Draw a graph that shows how a portfolio that has been judged as superior relative to a "measured" security market line (SML) can be inferior to the "true" SML.

d. Assume that you are informed that a given portfolio manager has been evaluated as superior when compared to the DJIA, the S&P 500, and the NYSE Composite Index. Explain whether this consensus would make you feel more comfortable regarding the portfolio manager's true ability.

e. While conceding the possible problem with benchmark errors as set forth by Roll, some contend this does not mean the CAPM is incorrect but only that there is a measurement problem when implementing the theory. Others contend that because of benchmark errors, the whole technique should be scrapped. Take and defend one of these positions.

10. Many investors contend that it is not possible to evaluate a manager's investment performance properly without taking portfolio risk into account in some fashion. Nevertheless, simple (not risk-adjusted) measures, such as peer group comparisons and portfolio drawdown, remain popular evaluation tools. Explain what information these simple performance measures offer to investors in the absence of an explicit consideration of investment risk.

PROBLEMS

1. The following portfolios are being considered for investment. During the period under consideration, $RFR = 0.07$.

Portfolio	Return	Beta	σ_i
P	0.15	1.0	0.05
Q	0.20	1.5	0.10
R	0.10	0.6	0.03
S	0.17	1.1	0.06
Market	0.13	1.0	0.04

a. Compute the Sharpe measure for each portfolio and the market portfolio.

b. Compute the Treynor measure for each portfolio and the market portfolio.

c. Rank the portfolios using each measure, explaining the cause for any differences you find in the rankings.

2. An analyst wants to evaluate Portfolio X, consisting entirely of U.S. common stocks, using both the Treynor and Sharpe measures of portfolio performance. The following table provides the average annual rate of return for Portfolio X, the market portfolio (as measured by the Standard & Poor's 500 Index), and U.S. Treasury bills (T-bills) during the past eight years.

	Annual Average Rate of Return	Standard Deviation of Return	Beta
Portfolio X	10%	18%	0.60
S&P 500	12	13	1.00
T-bills	6	n/a	n/a

n/a = not applicable

a. Calculate both the Treynor measure and the Sharpe measure for both Portfolio X and the S&P 500. Briefly explain whether Portfolio X underperformed, equaled, or outperformed the S&P 500 on a risk-adjusted basis using both the Treynor measure and the Sharpe measure.

b. Based on the performance of Portfolio X relative to the S&P 500 calculated in part (a), briefly explain the reason for the conflicting results when using the Treynor measure versus the Sharpe measure.

3. You have been assigned the task of comparing the investment performance of five different pension fund managers. After gathering 60 months of excess returns (returns in excess of the monthly risk-free rate) on each fund as well as the monthly excess returns on the entire stock market, you perform the regressions of the form:

$$(R_{fund} - RFR)_t = \alpha + \beta(R_{mkt} - RFR)_t + e_t$$

You have prepared the following summary of the data, with the standard errors for each of the coefficients listed in parentheses.

	REGRESSION DATA			$(R_{FUND} - RFR)$	
Portfolio	α	β	R^2	Mean	σ
ABC	0.192	1.048	94.1%	1.022%	1.193%
	(0.11)	(0.10)			
DEF	−0.053	0.662	91.6	0.473	0.764
	(0.19)	(0.09)			
GHI	0.463	0.594	68.6	0.935	0.793
	(0.19)	(0.07)			
JKL	0.355	0.757	64.1	0.955	1.044
	(0.22)	(0.08)			
(MNO)	0.296	0.785	94.8	0.890	0.890
	(0.14)	(0.12)			

a. Which fund had the highest degree of diversification over the sample period? How is diversification measured in this statistical framework?

b. Rank these funds' performance according to the Sharpe, Treynor, and Jensen measures.

c. Since you know that according to the CAPM the intercept of these regressions (alpha) should be zero, this coefficient can be used as a measure of the value added provided by the investment manager. Which funds have statistically outperformed and underperformed the market using a two-sided 95% confidence interval? (Note: The relevant t-statistic using 60 observations is 2.00.)

4. Consider the following historical performance data for two different portfolios, the Standard & Poor's 500, and the 90-day T-bill.

Investment Vehicle	Average Rate of Return	Standard Deviation	Beta	R^2
Fund 1	26.40%	20.67%	1.351	0.751
Fund 2	13.22	14.20	0.905	0.713
S&P 500	15.71	13.25		
90-day T-bill	6.20	0.50		

a. Calculate the Fama overall performance measure for both funds.
b. What is the return to risk for both funds?
c. For both funds, compute the measures of (1) selectivity, (2) diversification, and (3) net selectivity.
d. Explain the meaning of the net selectivity measure and how it helps you evaluate investor performance. Which fund had the best performance?

5. You are evaluating the performance of two portfolio managers, and you have gathered annual return data for the past decade:

Year	Manager X Return (%)	Manager Y Return (%)
1	−1.5	−6.5
2	−1.5	−3.5
3	−1.5	−1.5
4	−1.0	3.5
5	0.0	4.5
6	4.5	6.5
7	6.5	7.5
8	8.5	8.5
9	13.5	12.5
10	17.5	13.5

a. For each manager, calculate (1) the average annual return, (2) the standard deviation of returns, and (3) the semi-deviation of returns.
b. Assuming that the average annual risk-free rate during the 10-year sample period was 1.5 percent, calculate the Sharpe ratio for each portfolio. Based on these computations, which manager appears to have performed the best?
c. Calculate the Sortino ratio for each portfolio, using the average risk-free rate as the minimum acceptable return threshold. Based on these computations, which manager appears to have performed the best?
d. When would you expect the Sharpe and Sortino measures to provide (1) the same performance ranking or (2) different performance rankings? Explain.

6. Consider the following performance data for two portfolio managers (A and B) and a common benchmark portfolio:

	BENCHMARK		MANAGER A		MANAGER B	
	Weight	Return	Weight	Return	Weight	Return
Stock	0.6	−5.0%	0.5	−4.0%	0.3	−5.0%
Bonds	0.3	−3.5	0.2	−2.5	0.4	−3.5
Cash	0.1	0.3	0.3	0.3	0.3	0.3

a. Calculate (1) the overall return to the benchmark portfolio, (2) the overall return to Manager A's actual portfolio, and (3) the overall return to Manager B's actual portfolio. Briefly comment on whether these managers have under- or outperformed the benchmark fund.

b. Using attribution analysis, calculate (1) the *selection effect* for Manager A, and (3) the *allocation effect* for Manager B. Using these numbers in conjunction with your results from part (a), comment on whether these managers have added value through their selection skills, their allocation skills, or both.

7. A U.S. pension plan hired two offshore firms to manage the non-U.S. equity portion of its total portfolio. Each firm was free to own stocks in any country market included in Morgan Stanley/Capital International's Europe, Australia, and Far East Index (EAFE), and free to use any form of dollar and/or non-dollar cash or bonds as an equity substitute or reserve. After three years had elapsed, the records of the managers and the EAFE Index were as follows:

SUMMARY: CONTRIBUTIONS TO RETURN

	Currency	Country Selection	Stock Selection	Cash/Bond Allocation	Total Return Recorded
Manager A	(9.0%)	19.7%	3.1%	0.6%	14.4%
Manager B	(7.4)	14.2	6.0	2.81	5.6
Composite of A & B	(8.2)	16.9	4.5	1.71	5.0
EAFE Index	(12.9)	19.9	—	—	7.0

You are a member of the plan sponsor's pension committee, which will soon meet with the plan's consultant to review manager performance. In preparation for this meeting, you go through the following analysis:

a. Briefly describe the strengths and weaknesses of each manager, relative to the EAFE Index data.

b. Briefly explain the meaning of the data in the "Currency" column.

8. To illustrate for the pension committee of the profit-sharing plan to which you are a consultant on some of the issues that arise in measuring performance, you have identified three U.S. fixed-income management firms whose investment approaches are representative of general practice. Each firm's approach follows.

Firm A: An enhanced index fund manager that seeks to add value by superior security selection while maintaining portfolio duration and sector weights equal to the overall bond market.

Firm B: An active duration manager investing only in the government and corporate bond sectors. The firm uses futures to manage portfolio duration.

Firm C: An active manager seeking to add value by correctly anticipating changes in the shape of the yield curve, while maintaining portfolio duration and sector weights roughly equal to the overall bond market.

You have provided the pension committee with the following additional information about these firms, derived from a consultant's database.

ANNUALIZED TOTAL RETURN DATA (PAST FIVE YEARS)

	Firm A	Firm B	Firm C
Reported Returns	9.2%	9.3%	9.0%

	INDEX SECTORS				
	Aggregate Index	Governments	Corporates	Government/ Corporate	Mortgages
Index Return	8.7%	9.0%	9.8%	9.5%	8.3%

	CONSULTANT'S MANAGER UNIVERSE		
	All Managers	Managers Using the Aggregate Index as Their Benchmark	Managers Using the Govt./Corp. Sector as Their Benchmark
Return 5th percentile	6.0%	7.7%	8.4%
25th percentile	7.1	8.1	8.9
50th percentile	8.0	8.6	9.4
75th percentile	8.6	9.1	9.9
95th percentile	9.3	13.1	13.9

Evaluate the performance of each of these three firms relative to its appropriate index and to the manager universe. Use only the data from the descriptions and the preceding table, even though other information would be required for a more complete and accurate appraisal.

9. For each of the past six quarters, Managers L and M have provided you with the total dollar value of the funds they manage, along with the quarterly contributions or withdrawals made by their clients. (Note: Contributions are indicated by positive numbers, withdrawals by negative numbers.)

	MANAGER L		**MANAGER M**	
Quarter	Total Funds under Management	Contributions/ Withdrawals	Total Funds under Management	Contributions/ Withdrawals
Initial	$500,000	—	$700,000	—
1	527,000	12,000	692,000	−35,000
2	530,000	7,500	663,000	−35,000
3	555,000	13,500	621,000	−35,000
4	580,000	6,500	612,000	−35,000
5	625,000	10,000	625,000	−35,000

For each manager, calculate:
a. Her money-weighted return
b. Her time-weighted return
c. Estimates of her quarterly performance returns using the Dietz approximation method, assuming that contributions/withdrawals are made exactly halfway through the quarter

10. You work for a private wealth management firm that follows an "external investment" model, whereby it decides which outside managers it should recommend to clients. One mutual fund that is a candidate for inclusion on your Premier Recommended List of approved managers is Active Fund (AFNDX), an actively managed stock portfolio benchmarked to the Standard & Poor's 500 (SPX) Index. You have been asked to perform an evaluation of AFNDX's past investment performance, using a sample of monthly returns on the following positions: (1) AFNDX portfolio, (2) SPX Index, (3) U.S. Treasury bills, and (4) the three primary Fama–French risk factors (excess market, SMB, and HML). These data are listed in Exhibit 18.20

Exhibit 18.20 Monthly Return Data for AFNDX, SPX, T-Bill, and Fama–French Factors

| | % RETURNS TO: | | | F-F FACTOR % RETURNS: | | |
| | | | | Excess | | |
Month	AFNDX	SPX Index	T-Bill (RF)	Mkt	SMB	HML
1	9.254	2.757	0.420	0.970	−4.030	4.620
2	7.576	7.552	0.410	6.160	−3.460	0.090
3	−2.106	−1.981	0.460	−1.600	3.140	1.080
4	5.085	6.244	0.450	4.850	−1.580	−2.540
5	−1.745	0.785	0.390	−0.480	−2.540	4.830
6	−5.031	−4.101	0.430	−4.870	−0.320	3.850
7	4.064	5.965	0.430	3.820	−5.140	−1.200
8	8.062	6.084	0.490	6.640	4.620	−4.090
9	3.394	4.478	0.370	4.050	1.360	0.830
10	6.900	7.955	0.430	7.200	−2.370	−0.690
11	0.292	−5.597	0.410	−4.060	7.440	0.900
12	3.074	5.476	0.440	5.360	2.580	−0.380
13	−1.616	−3.336	0.420	−3.830	−0.930	2.530
14	−2.932	4.625	0.390	2.720	−5.050	1.050
15	0.445	1.716	0.480	1.320	−2.330	3.600
16	−1.064	1.105	0.430	0.010	−1.010	−1.670
17	8.570	7.208	0.390	6.890	0.290	−1.230
18	3.807	5.117	0.390	4.750	−1.450	1.920
19	0.732	1.006	0.430	0.660	0.410	0.220
20	−2.555	−1.717	0.400	−2.950	−3.620	4.290
21	4.641	4.059	0.410	2.860	−3.400	−1.540
22	−1.793	−1.062	0.400	−2.720	−4.510	−1.790
23	−17.065	−14.443	0.430	−16.110	−5.920	5.690
24	15.715	6.407	0.460	5.950	0.020	−3.760
25	−3.536	8.127	0.320	7.110	−3.360	−2.850
26	3.582	6.058	0.310	5.860	1.360	−3.680
27	10.010	5.759	0.380	5.940	−0.310	−4.950
28	6.630	4.180	0.350	3.470	1.150	−6.160
29	−4.205	−3.103	0.350	−4.150	−5.590	1.660
30	5.430	3.999	0.430	3.320	−3.820	−3.040
31	0.803	3.873	0.370	4.470	2.890	2.800
32	−3.520	−2.358	0.340	−2.390	3.460	3.080
33	4.740	5.545	0.400	4.720	3.420	−4.330
34	−0.759	−3.115	0.380	−3.450	2.010	0.700
35	−1.875	−0.498	0.390	−1.350	−1.160	−1.260
36	−1.187	−2.738	0.390	−2.680	3.230	−3.180
37	7.071	6.326	0.390	5.800	−6.530	−3.190
38	2.434	2.033	0.360	3.200	7.710	−8.090
39	10.059	5.886	0.440	7.830	6.980	−9.050
40	−3.845	−5.024	0.410	−4.430	4.080	−0.160
41	5.785	−1.891	0.430	2.550	21.490	−12.030

a. For both AFNDX and SPX, calculate the series of monthly risk premia (stated returns in excess of the risk-free rate) for the 41-month sample period. Use these excess return data to compute the Sharpe ratio for both AFNDX and SPX.

b. Based on a regression of the excess returns to AFNDX on the excess returns to SPX, use regression analysis to calculate the active manager's (1) one-factor Jensen's alpha coefficient, (2) beta coefficient, and (3) R-squared measure. Briefly explain what each of these statistics tells you about how AFNDX has been managed.

c. Using your work in parts (a) and (b), calculate the Treynor ratio performance measures for both AFNDX and SPX, assuming a beta coefficient of 1.00 for the latter.

d. Compare what the Sharpe and Treynor measures indicate about the ability of AFNFX's manager to beat the market on a risk-adjusted basis. If the two measures give contradictory indications, reconcile that discrepancy.

e. Calculate the tracking error (*TE*) for AFNDX relative to the SPX benchmark, on both a monthly and an annualized basis. What does this *TE* error measure suggests about the consistency of the active manager's investment style and whether *TE* is at an appropriate level for a mutual fund manager?

f. Using the excess returns from part (a), compute the information ratio (*IR*) for AFNDX relative to the SPX benchmark on both a monthly basis and an annualized basis. Briefly explain what this *IR* suggests about the manager's investment prowess relative to the general equity market.

g. Estimate a regression of AFNDX's excess returns on the three Fama–French risk factors. Interpret each of the following components of your regression output: (1) the intercept coefficient, (2) the beta coefficients for each of the three independent variables, and (3) the *R*-squared measure. Explain what each of these statistics tells you about the manager's investment style and the ability for AFNDX to outperform market expectations.

h. Based on all of the preceding analysis, would you advise the senior management to include AFNDX on its Premier Recommended List of approved managers? Justify your decision.

The CFA® Charter

Demonstrate your mastery of the investment analysis and decision-making skills most needed for a competitive career in the global investment management profession.

The Chartered Financial Analyst® (CFA) credential is the professional standard of choice for more than 31,000 investment firms worldwide. When hiring leading firms demand investment professionals with real-world analytical skills, technical competence, and the highest professional standards, often requiring the CFA credential for consideration.

BENEFITS OF EARNING THE CFA CHARTER

- **REAL-WORLD EXPERTISE.** Demonstrate your fluency with an advanced investment management and analysis curriculum that leverages current best practices and the experience of practitioners around the world to bridge real-world practices and theoretical knowledge.
- **CAREER RECOGNITION.** Stand out in the competitive global industry and gain instant credibility with peers, employers, and clients who know the hard work, intelligence, and profound commitment it takes to earn the charter.
- **ETHICAL GROUNDING.** Learn to apply ethical principles and gain a foundation in the skills needed to demonstrate a commitment to high standards of accountability and integrity that build a trusted reputation.
- **GLOBAL COMMUNITY.** Join a vast professional network of more than 135,000 charterholders worldwide and gain unmatched career resources, important relationships, and lifelong insights.
- **EMPLOYER DEMAND.** The top 11 global employers of charterholders include JPMorgan Chase, Bank of America, Merrill Lynch, UBS, RBC, HSBC, Wells Fargo, Credit Suisse, Morgan Stanley, Smith Barney, BlackRock, and Citigroup.

WHAT JOBS DOES IT PREPARE YOU FOR?

Top CFA Charterholder Occupations

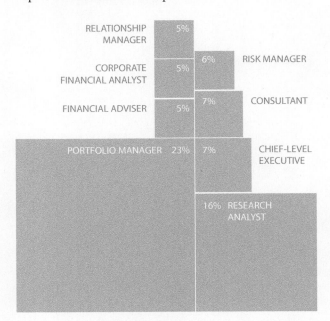

WHAT YOU WILL LEARN

The CFA Program is offered in a self-study format and is divided into three levels of exams.

The curriculum is organized into ten general topic areas that provide a framework for making investment decisions:

I. ETHICAL AND PROFESSIONAL STANDARDS
II. QUANTITATIVE METHODS
III. ECONOMICS
IV. FINANCIAL REPORTING AND ANALYSIS
V. CORPORATE FINANCE
VI. EQUITY INVESTMENTS
VII. FIXED-INCOME INVESTMENTS
VIII. DERIVATIVES
IX. ALTERNATIVE INVESTMENTS
X. PORTFOLIO MANAGEMENT AND WEALTH PLANNING

HOW TO EARN THE CHARTER

1. Become a CFA candidate and enroll in the CFA Program. To do so, you must
   - meet one of the following criteria:
     - Have a bachelor's (or equivalent) degree,
     - Be in the final year of a bachelor's degree program,
     - Have four years of professional work experience, or
     - Have a combination of professional work and university experience that totals at least four years.
   - be prepared to take the exams in English.
   - have a valid international passport.
   - meet the professional conduct admission criteria.
2. Pass the level I Exam (June or December).
3. Pass the level II Exam (June).
4. Pass the level III Exam (June).
5. Have four years of professional work experience in the investment decision-making process (accrued before, during, or after participation in the CFA Program).
6. Join CFA Institute as a regular member.

APPENDIX B
Code of Ethics and Standards of Professional Conduct

PREAMBLE

The CFA Institute Code of Ethics and Standards of Professional Conduct are fundamental to the values of CFA Institute and essential to achieving its mission to lead the investment profession globally by promoting the highest standards of ethics, education, and professional excellence for the ultimate benefit of society. High ethical standards are critical to maintaining the public's trust in financial markets and in the investment profession. Since their creation in the 1960s, the Code and Standards have promoted the Integrity of CFA Institute members and served as a model for measuring the ethics of investment professionals globally, regardless of job function, cultural differences, or local laws and regulations. All CFA Institute members (including holders of the Chartered Financial Analyst® [CFA®] designation) and CFA candidates must abide by the Code and Standards and are encouraged to notify their employer of this responsibility. Violations may result in disciplinary sanctions by CFA Institute. Sanctions can include revocation of membership, revocation of candidacy in the CFA Program, and revocation of the right to use the CFA designation.

THE CODE OF ETHICS

Members of CFA Institute (including CFA charterholders) and candidates for the CFA designation ("Members and Candidates") must:

- Act with integrity, competence, diligence, respect and in an ethical manner with the public, clients, prospective clients, employers, employees, colleagues in the investment profession, and other participants in the global capital markets.
- Place the integrity of the investment profession and the interests of clients above their own personal interests.
- Use reasonable care and exercise independent professional judgment when conducting investment analysis, making investment recommendations, taking investment actions, and engaging in other professional activites.
- Practice and encourage others to practice in a professional and ethical manner that will reflect credit on themselves and the profession.
- Promote the integrity and viability of the global capital markets for the ultimate benefit of society.
- Maintain and improve their professional competence and strive to maintain and improve the competence of other investment professionals.

STANDARDS OF PROFESSIONAL CONDUCT

I. PROFESSIONALISM

A. Knowledge of the Law. Members and Candidates must understand and comply with all applicable laws, rules, and regulations (including the CFA Institute Code of Ethics and Standards of Professional Conduct) of any government, regulatory organization, licensing agency, or professional association governing their professional activities. In the event of conflict, Members and Candidates must comply with the more strict law, rule, or regulation. Members and Candidates must not knowingly participate or assist in and must dissociate from any violation of such laws, rules, or regulations.

B. Independence and Objectivity. Members and Candidates must use reasonable care and judgment to achieve and maintain independence and objectivity in their professional activities. Members and Candidates must not offer, solicit, or accept any gift, benefit, compensation, or consideration that reasonably could be expected to compromise their own or another's independence, and objectivity.

C. Misrepresentation. Members and Candidates must not knowingly make any misrepresentations relating to investment analysis, recommendations, actions, or other professional activities.

D. Misconduct. Members and Candidates must not engage in any professional conduct involving dishonesty, fraud, or deceit or commit any act that reflects adversely on their professional reputation, integrity, or competence.

II. INTEGRITY OF CAPITAL MARKETS

A. Material Nonpublic Information. Members and Candidates who possess material nonpublic information that could affect the value of an investment must not act or cause others to act on the information.

B. Market Manipulation. Members and Candidates must not engage in practices that distort prices or artificially inflate trading volume with the intent to mislead market participants.

III. DUTIES TO CLIENTS

A. **Loyalty, Prudence, and Care.** Members and Candidates have a duty of loyalty to their clients and must act with reasonable care and exercise prudent judgment. Members and Candidates must act for the benefit of their clients and place their clients' interests before their employer's or their own interests.

B. **Fair Dealing.** Members and Candidates must deal fairly and objectively with all clients when providing investment analysis, making investment recommendations, taking investment action, or engaging in other professional activities.

C. **Suitability.**
   1. When Members and Candidates are in an advisory relationship with a client, they must:
   a. Make a reasonable inquiry into a client's or prospective client's investment experience, risk and return objectives, and financial constraints prior to making any investment recommendation or taking investment action and must reassess and update this information regularly.
   b. Determine that an investment is suitable to the client's financial situation and consistent with the client's written objectives, mandates, and constraints before making an investment recommendation or taking investment action.
   c. Judge the suitability of investments in the context of the client's total portfolio.
   2. When Members and Candidates are responsible for managing a portfolio to a specific mandate, strategy, or style, they must make only investment recommendations or take only investment actions that are consistent with the stated objectives and constraints of the portfolio.

D. **Performance Presentation.** When communicating investment performance information, Members and Candidates must make reasonable efforts to ensure that it is fair, accurate, and complete.

E. **Preservation of Confidentiality.** Members and Candidates must keep information about current, former, and prospective clients confidential unless:
   1. The information concerns illegal activities on the part of the client or prospective client,
   2. Disclosure is required by law, or
   3. The client or prospective client permits disclosure of the information.

IV. DUTIES TO EMPLOYERS

A. **Loyalty.** In matters related to their employment, Members and Candidates must act for the benefit of their employer and not deprive their employer of the advantage of their skills and abilities, divulge confidential information, or otherwise cause harm to their employer.

B. **Additional Compensation Arrangements.** Members and Candidates must not accept gifts, benefits, compensation, or consideration that competes with or might reasonably be expected to create a conflict of interest with their employer's interest unless they obtain written consent from all parties involved.

C. **Responsibilities of Supervisors.** Members and Candidates must make reasonable efforts to ensure that anyone subject to their supervision or authority complies with applicable laws, rules, regulations, and the Code and Standards.

V. INVESTMENT ANALYSIS, RECOMMENDATIONS, AND ACTIONS

A. **Diligence and Reasonable Basis.** Members and Candidates must:
   1. Exercise diligence, independence, and thoroughness in analyzing investments, making investment recommendations, and taking investment actions.
   2. Have a reasonable and adequate basis, supported by appropriate research and investigation, for any investment analysis, recommendation, or action.

B. **Communication with Clients and Prospective Clients.** Members and Candidates must:
   1. Disclose to clients and prospective clients the basic format and general principles of the investment processes they use to analyze investments, select securities, and construct portfolios and must promptly disclose any changes that might materially affect those processes.
   2. Disclose to clients and prospective clients significant limitations and risks associated with the investment process.
   3. Use reasonable judgment in identifying which factors are important to their investment analyses, recommendations, or actions and include those factors in communications with clients and prospective clients.
   4. Distinguish between fact and opinion in the presentation of investment analysis and recommendations.

C. **Record Retention.** Members and Candidates must develop and maintain appropriate records to support their investment analyses, recommendations, actions, and other investment-related communications with clients and prospective clients.

VI. CONFLICTS OF INTEREST

A. **Disclosure of Conflicts.** Members and Candidates must make full and fair disclosure of all matters that could reasonably be expected to impair their independence and objectivity or interfere with respective duties to their clients, prospective clients, and employer. Members and Candidates must ensure that such disclosures are prominent, are delivered in plain language, and communicate the relevant information effectively.

B. **Priority of Transactions.** Investment transactions for clients and employers must have priority over investment transactions in which a Member or Candidate is the beneficial owner.

C. **Referral Fees.** Members and Candidates must disclose to their employer, clients, and prospective clients, as appropriate, any compensation, consideration, or benefit received from or paid to others for the recommendation of products or services.

VII. RESPONSIBILITIES AS A CFA INSTITUTE MEMBER OR CFA CANDIDATE

A. **Conduct as Participants in CFA Institute Programs.** Members and Candidates must not engage in any conduct that compromises the reputation or integrity of CFA Institute or the CFA designation or the integrity, validity, or security of the CFA Institute programs.

B. **Reference to CFA Institute, the CFA Designation, and the CFA Program.** When referring to CFA Institute, CFA Institute membership, the CFA designation, or candidacy in the CFA Program, Members and Candidates must not misrepresent or exaggerate the meaning or implications of membership in CFA Institute, holding the CFA designation, or candidacy in the CFA program.

APPENDIX C

Interest Tables

TABLE C.1   Present Value of $1: PVIF $= 1/(1 + k)^t$

Period	1%	2%	3%	4%	5%	6%	7%	8%	9%	10%	12%	14%	15%	16%	18%	20%	24%	28%	32%	36%
1	.9901	.9804	.9709	.9615	.9524	.9434	.9346	.9259	.9174	.9091	.8929	.8772	.8696	.8621	.8475	.8333	.8065	.7813	.7576	.7353
2	.9803	.9612	.9426	.9246	.9070	.8900	.8734	.8573	.8417	.8264	.7972	.7695	.7561	.7432	.7182	.6944	.6504	.6104	.5739	.5407
3	.9706	.9423	.9151	.8890	.8638	.8396	.8163	.7938	.7722	.7513	.7118	.6750	.6575	.6407	.6086	.5787	.5245	.4768	.4348	.3975
4	.9610	.9238	.8885	.8548	.8227	.7921	.7629	.7350	.7084	.6830	.6355	.5921	.5718	.5523	.5158	.4823	.4230	.3725	.3294	.2923
5	.9515	.9057	.8626	.8219	.7835	.7473	.7130	.6806	.6499	.6209	.5674	.5194	.4972	.4761	.4371	.4019	.3411	.2910	.2495	.2149
6	.9420	.8880	.8375	.7903	.7462	.7050	.6663	.6302	.5963	.5645	.5066	.4556	.4323	.4104	.3704	.3349	.2751	.2274	.1890	.1580
7	.9327	.8706	.8131	.7599	.7107	.6651	.6227	.5835	.5470	.5132	.4523	.3996	.3759	.3538	.3139	.2791	.2218	.1776	.1432	.1162
8	.9235	.8535	.7894	.7307	.6768	.6274	.5820	.5403	.5019	.4665	.4039	.3506	.3269	.3050	.2660	.2326	.1789	.1388	.1085	.0854
9	.9143	.8368	.7664	.7026	.6446	.5919	.5439	.5002	.4604	.4241	.3606	.3075	.2843	.2630	.2255	.1938	.1443	.1084	.0822	.0628
10	.9053	.8203	.7441	.6756	.6139	.5584	.5083	.4632	.4224	.3855	.3220	.2697	.2472	.2267	.1911	.1615	.1164	.0847	.0623	.0462
11	.8963	.8043	.7224	.6496	.5847	.5268	.4751	.4289	.3875	.3505	.2875	.2366	.2149	.1954	.1619	.1346	.0938	.0662	.0472	.0340
12	.8874	.7885	.7014	.6246	.5568	.4970	.4440	.3971	.3555	.3186	.2567	.2076	.1869	.1685	.1372	.1122	.0757	.0517	.0357	.0250
13	.8787	.7730	.6810	.6006	.5303	.4688	.4150	.3677	.3262	.2897	.2292	.1821	.1625	.1452	.1163	.0935	.0610	.0404	.0271	.0184
14	.8700	.7579	.6611	.5775	.5051	.4423	.3878	.3405	.2992	.2633	.2046	.1597	.1413	.1252	.0985	.0779	.0492	.0316	.0205	.0135
15	.8613	.7430	.6419	.5553	.4810	.4173	.3624	.3152	.2745	.2394	.1827	.1401	.1229	.1079	.0835	.0649	.0397	.0247	.0155	.0099
16	.8528	.7284	.6232	.5339	.4581	.3936	.3387	.2919	.2519	.2176	.1631	.1229	.1069	.0930	.0708	.0541	.0320	.0193	.0118	.0073
17	.8444	.7142	.6050	.5134	.4363	.3714	.3166	.2703	.2311	.1978	.1456	.1078	.0929	.0802	.0600	.0451	.0258	.0150	.0089	.0054
18	.8360	.7002	.5874	.4936	.4155	.3503	.2959	.2502	.2120	.1799	.1300	.0946	.0808	.0691	.0508	.0376	.0208	.0118	.0068	.0039
19	.8277	.6864	.5703	.4746	.3957	.3305	.2765	.2317	.1945	.1635	.1161	.0829	.0703	.0596	.0431	.0313	.0168	.0092	.0051	.0029
20	.8195	.6730	.5537	.4564	.3769	.3118	.2584	.2145	.1784	.1486	.1037	.0728	.0611	.0514	.0365	.0261	.0135	.0072	.0039	.0021
25	.7798	.6095	.4776	.3751	.2953	.2330	.1842	.1460	.1160	.0923	.0588	.0378	.0304	.0245	.0160	.0105	.0046	.0021	.0010	.0005
30	.7419	.5521	.4120	.3083	.2314	.1741	.1314	.0994	.0754	.0573	.0334	.0196	.0151	.0116	.0070	.0042	.0016	.0006	.0002	.0001
40	.6717	.4529	.3066	.2083	.1420	.0972	.0668	.0460	.0318	.0221	.0107	.0053	.0037	.0026	.0013	.0007	.0002	.0001	•	•
50	.6080	.3715	.2281	.1407	.0872	.0543	.0339	.0213	.0134	.0085	.0035	.0014	.0009	.0006	.0003	.0001	•	•	•	•
60	.5504	.3048	.1697	.0951	.0535	.0303	.0173	.0099	.0057	.0033	.0011	.0004	.0002	.0001	•	•	•	•	•	•

*The factor is zero to four decimal places.

TABLE C.2

Present Value of an Annuity of \$1 Per Period for *n* Periods:

$$PVIFA = \sum_{t=1}^{n} \frac{1}{(1+k)^t} = \frac{1 - \dfrac{1}{(1+k)^n}}{k}$$

Number of Payments	1%	2%	3%	4%	5%	6%	7%	8%	9%	10%	12%	14%	15%	16%	18%	20%	24%	28%	32%
1	0.9901	0.9804	0.9709	0.9615	0.9524	0.9434	0.9346	0.9259	0.9174	0.9091	0.8929	0.8772	0.8696	0.8621	0.8475	0.8333	0.8065	0.7813	0.7576
2	1.9704	1.9416	1.9135	1.8861	1.8594	1.8334	1.8080	1.7833	1.7591	1.7355	1.6901	1.6467	1.6257	1.6052	1.5656	1.5278	1.4568	1.3916	1.3315
3	2.9410	2.8839	2.8286	2.7751	2.7232	2.6730	2.6243	2.5771	2.5313	2.4869	2.4018	2.3216	2.2832	2.2459	2.1743	2.1065	1.9813	1.8684	1.7663
4	3.9020	3.8077	3.7171	3.6299	3.5460	3.4651	3.3872	3.3121	3.2397	3.1699	3.0373	2.9137	2.8550	2.7982	2.6901	2.5887	2.4043	2.2410	2.0957
5	4.8534	4.7135	4.5797	4.4518	4.3295	4.2124	4.1002	3.9927	3.8897	3.7908	3.6048	3.4331	3.3522	3.2743	3.1272	2.9906	2.7454	2.5320	2.3452
6	5.7955	5.6014	5.4172	5.2421	5.0757	4.9173	4.7665	4.6229	4.4859	4.3553	4.1114	3.8887	3.7845	3.6847	3.4976	3.3255	3.0205	2.7594	2.5342
7	6.7282	6.4720	6.2303	6.0021	5.7864	5.5824	5.3893	5.2064	5.0330	4.8684	4.5638	4.2883	4.1604	4.0386	3.8115	3.6046	3.2423	2.9370	2.6775
8	7.6517	7.3255	7.0197	6.7327	6.4632	6.2098	5.9713	5.7466	5.5348	5.3349	4.9676	4.6389	4.4873	4.3436	4.0776	3.8372	3.4212	3.0758	2.7860
9	8.5660	8.1622	7.7861	7.4353	7.1078	6.8017	6.5152	6.2469	5.9952	5.7590	5.3282	4.9464	4.7716	4.6065	4.3030	4.0310	3.5655	3.1842	2.8681
10	9.4713	8.9826	8.5302	8.1109	7.7217	7.3601	7.0236	6.7101	6.4177	6.1446	5.6502	5.2161	5.0188	4.8332	4.4941	4.1925	3.6819	3.2689	2.9304
11	10.3676	9.7868	9.2526	8.7605	8.3064	7.8869	7.4987	7.1390	6.8052	6.4951	5.9377	5.4527	5.2337	5.0286	4.6560	4.3271	3.7757	3.3351	2.9776
12	11.2551	10.5753	9.9540	9.3851	8.8633	8.3838	7.9427	7.5361	7.1607	6.8137	6.1944	5.6603	5.4206	5.1971	4.7932	4.4392	3.8514	3.3868	3.0133
13	12.1337	11.3484	10.6350	9.9856	9.3936	8.8527	8.3577	7.9038	7.4869	7.1034	6.4235	5.8424	5.5831	5.3423	4.9095	4.5327	3.9124	3.4272	3.0404
14	13.0037	12.1062	11.2961	10.5631	9.8986	9.2950	8.7455	8.2442	7.7862	7.3667	6.6282	6.0021	5.7245	5.4675	5.0081	4.6106	3.9616	3.4587	3.0609
15	13.8651	12.8493	11.9379	11.1184	10.3797	9.7122	9.1079	8.5595	8.0607	7.6061	6.8109	6.1422	5.8474	5.5755	5.0916	4.6755	4.0013	3.4834	3.0764
16	14.7179	13.5777	12.5611	11.6523	10.8378	10.1059	9.4466	8.8514	8.3126	7.8237	6.9740	6.2651	5.9542	5.6685	5.1624	4.7296	4.0333	3.5026	3.0882
17	15.5623	14.2919	13.1661	12.1657	11.2741	10.4773	9.7632	9.1216	8.5436	8.0216	7.1196	6.3729	6.0472	5.7487	5.2223	4.7746	4.0591	3.5177	3.0971
18	16.3983	14.9920	13.7535	12.6593	11.6896	10.8276	10.0591	9.3719	8.7556	8.2014	7.2497	6.4674	6.1280	5.8178	5.2732	4.8122	4.0799	3.5294	3.1039
19	17.2260	15.6785	14.3238	13.1339	12.0853	11.1581	10.3356	9.6036	8.9501	8.3649	7.3658	6.5504	6.1982	5.8775	5.3162	4.8435	4.0967	3.5386	3.1090
20	18.0456	16.3514	14.8775	13.5903	12.4622	11.4699	10.5940	9.8181	9.1285	8.5136	7.4694	6.6231	6.2593	5.9288	5.3527	4.8696	4.1103	3.5458	3.1129
25	22.0232	19.5235	17.4131	15.6221	14.0939	12.7834	11.6536	10.6748	9.8226	9.0770	7.8431	6.8729	6.4641	6.0971	5.4669	4.9476	4.1474	3.5640	3.1220
30	25.8077	22.3965	19.6004	17.2920	15.3725	13.7648	12.4090	11.2578	10.2737	9.4269	8.0552	7.0027	6.5660	6.1772	5.5168	4.9789	4.1601	3.5693	3.1242
40	32.8347	27.3555	23.1148	19.7928	17.1591	15.0463	13.3317	11.9246	10.7574	9.7791	8.2438	7.1050	6.6418	6.2335	5.5482	4.9966	4.1659	3.5712	3.1250
50	39.1961	31.4236	25.7298	21.4822	18.2559	15.7619	13.8007	12.2335	10.9617	9.9148	8.3045	7.1327	6.6605	6.2463	5.5541	4.9995	4.1666	3.5714	3.1250
60	44.9550	34.7609	27.6756	22.6235	18.9293	16.1614	14.0392	12.3766	11.0480	9.9672	8.3240	7.1401	6.6651	6.2402	5.5553	4.9999	4.1667	3.5714	3.1250

TABLE C.3   Future Value of $1 at the End of n Periods: $FVIF_{k,n} = (1 + k)^n$

Period	1%	2%	3%	4%	5%	6%	7%	8%	9%	10%	12%	14%	15%	16%	18%	20%	24%	28%	32%	36%
1	1.0100	1.0200	1.0300	1.0400	1.0500	1.0600	1.0700	1.0800	1.0900	1.1000	1.1200	1.1400	1.1500	1.1600	1.1800	1.2000	1.2400	1.2800	1.3200	1.3600
2	1.0201	1.0404	1.0609	1.0816	1.1025	1.1236	1.1449	1.1664	1.1881	1.2100	1.2544	1.2996	1.3225	1.3456	1.3924	1.4400	1.5376	1.6384	1.7424	1.8496
3	1.0303	1.0612	1.0927	1.1249	1.1576	1.1910	1.2250	1.2597	1.2950	1.3310	1.4049	1.4815	1.5209	1.5609	1.6430	1.7280	1.9066	2.0972	2.3000	2.5155
4	1.0406	1.0824	1.1255	1.1699	1.2155	1.2625	1.3108	1.3605	1.4116	1.4641	1.5735	1.6890	1.7490	1.8106	1.9388	2.0736	2.3642	2.6844	3.0360	3.4210
5	1.0510	1.1041	1.1593	1.2167	1.2763	1.3382	1.4026	1.4693	1.5386	1.6105	1.7623	1.9254	2.0114	2.1003	2.2878	2.4883	2.9316	3.4360	4.0075	4.6526
6	1.0615	1.1262	1.1941	1.2653	1.3401	1.4185	1.5007	1.5869	1.6771	1.7716	1.9738	2.1950	2.3131	2.4364	2.6996	2.9860	3.6352	4.3980	5.2899	6.3275
7	1.0721	1.1487	1.2299	1.3159	1.4071	1.5036	1.6058	1.7138	1.8280	1.9487	2.2107	2.5023	2.6600	2.8262	3.1855	3.5832	4.5077	5.6295	6.9826	8.6054
8	1.0829	1.1717	1.2668	1.3686	1.4775	1.5938	1.7182	1.8509	1.9926	2.1436	2.4760	2.8526	3.0590	3.2784	3.7589	4.2998	5.5895	7.2058	9.2170	11.703
9	1.0937	1.1951	1.3048	1.4233	1.5513	1.6895	1.8385	1.9990	2.1719	2.3579	2.7731	3.2519	3.5179	3.8030	4.4355	5.1598	6.9310	9.2234	12.166	15.916
10	1.1046	1.2190	1.3439	1.4802	1.6289	1.7908	1.9672	2.1589	2.3674	2.5937	3.1058	3.7072	4.0456	4.4114	5.2338	6.1917	8.5944	11.805	16.059	21.646
11	1.1157	1.2434	1.3842	1.5395	1.7103	1.8983	2.1049	2.3316	2.5804	2.8531	3.4785	4.2262	4.6524	5.1173	6.1759	7.4301	10.657	15.111	21.198	29.439
12	1.1268	1.2682	1.4258	1.6010	1.7959	2.0122	2.2522	2.5182	2.8127	3.1384	3.8960	4.8179	5.3502	5.9360	7.2876	8.9161	13.214	19.342	27.982	40.037
13	1.1381	1.2936	1.4685	1.6651	1.8856	2.1329	2.4098	2.7196	3.0658	3.4523	4.3635	5.4924	6.1528	6.8858	8.5994	10.699	16.386	24.758	36.937	54.451
14	1.1495	1.3195	1.5126	1.7317	1.9799	2.2609	2.5785	2.9372	3.3417	3.7975	4.8871	6.2613	7.0757	7.9875	10.147	12.839	20.319	31.691	48.756	74.053
15	1.1610	1.3459	1.5580	1.8009	2.0789	2.3966	2.7590	3.1722	3.6425	4.1772	5.4736	7.1379	8.1371	9.2655	11.973	15.407	25.195	40.564	64.358	100.71
16	1.1726	1.3728	1.6047	1.8730	2.1829	2.5404	2.9522	3.4259	3.9703	4.5950	6.1304	8.1372	9.3576	10.748	14.129	18.488	31.242	51.923	84.953	136.96
17	1.1843	1.4002	1.6528	1.9479	2.2920	2.6928	3.1588	3.7000	4.3276	5.0545	6.8660	9.2765	10.761	12.467	16.672	22.186	38.740	66.461	112.13	186.27
18	1.1961	1.4282	1.7024	2.0258	2.4066	2.8543	3.3799	3.9960	4.7171	5.5599	7.6900	10.575	12.375	14.462	19.673	26.623	48.038	85.070	148.02	253.33
19	1.2081	1.4568	1.7535	2.1068	2.5270	3.0256	3.6165	4.3157	5.1417	6.1159	8.6128	12.055	14.231	16.776	23.214	31.948	59.567	108.89	195.39	344.53
20	1.2202	1.4859	1.8061	2.1911	2.6533	3.2071	3.8697	4.6610	5.6044	6.7275	9.6463	13.743	16.366	19.460	27.393	38.337	73.864	139.37	257.91	468.57
21	1.2324	1.5157	1.8603	2.2788	2.7860	3.3996	4.1406	5.0338	6.1088	7.4002	10.803	15.667	18.821	22.574	32.323	46.005	91.591	178.40	340.44	637.26
22	1.2447	1.5460	1.9161	2.3699	2.9253	3.6035	4.4304	5.4365	6.6586	8.1403	12.100	17.861	21.644	26.186	38.142	55.206	113.57	228.35	449.39	866.67
23	1.2572	1.5769	1.9736	2.4647	3.0715	3.8197	4.7405	5.8715	7.2579	8.9543	13.552	20.361	24.891	30.376	45.007	66.247	140.83	292.30	593.19	1178.6
24	1.2697	1.6084	2.0328	2.5633	3.2251	4.0489	5.0724	6.3412	7.9111	9.8497	15.178	23.212	28.625	35.236	53.108	79.496	174.63	374.14	783.02	1602.9
25	1.2824	1.6406	2.0938	2.6658	3.3864	4.2919	5.4274	6.8485	8.6231	10.834	17.000	26.461	32.918	40.874	62.668	95.396	216.54	478.90	1033.5	2180.0
26	1.2953	1.6734	2.1566	2.7725	3.5557	4.5494	5.8074	7.3964	9.3992	11.918	19.040	30.166	37.856	47.414	73.948	114.47	268.51	612.99	1364.3	2964.9
27	1.3082	1.7069	2.2213	2.8834	3.7335	4.8223	6.2139	7.9881	10.245	13.110	21.324	34.389	43.535	55.000	87.259	137.37	332.95	784.63	1800.9	4032.2
28	1.3213	1.7410	2.2879	2.9987	3.9201	5.1117	6.6488	8.6271	11.167	14.421	23.883	39.204	50.065	63.800	102.96	164.84	412.86	1004.3	2377.2	5483.8
29	1.3345	1.7758	2.3566	3.1187	4.1161	5.4184	7.1143	9.3173	12.172	15.863	26.749	44.693	57.575	74.008	121.50	197.81	511.95	1285.5	3137.9	7458.0
30	1.3478	1.8114	2.4273	3.2434	4.3219	5.7435	7.6123	10.062	13.267	17.449	29.959	50.950	66.211	85.849	143.37	237.37	634.81	1645.5	4142.0	10143.
40	1.4889	2.2080	3.2620	4.8010	7.0400	10.285	14.974	21.724	31.409	45.259	93.050	188.88	267.86	378.72	750.37	1469.7	5455.9	19426.	66520.	•
50	1.6446	2.6916	4.3839	7.1067	11.467	18.420	29.457	46.901	74.357	117.39	289.00	700.23	1083.6	1670.7	3927.3	9100.4	46890.	•	•	•
60	1.8167	3.2810	5.8916	10.519	18.679	32.987	57.946	101.25	176.03	304.48	897.59	2595.9	4383.9	7370.1	20555.	56347.	•	•	•	•

*FVIFA > 99,999

TABLE C.4

Sum of an Annuity of $1 Per Period for n Periods:

$$FVIFA_{k,n} = \sum_{t=1}^{n}(1+k)^{t-1} = \frac{(1+k)^{n}-1}{k}$$

Number of Periods	1%	2%	3%	4%	5%	6%	7%	8%	9%	10%	12%	14%	15%	16%	18%	20%	24%	28%	32%	36%
1	1.0000	1.0000	1.0000	1.0000	1.0000	1.0000	1.0000	1.0000	1.0000	1.0000	1.0000	1.0000	1.0000	1.0000	1.0000	1.0000	1.0000	1.0000	1.0000	1.0000
2	2.0100	2.0200	2.0300	2.0400	2.0500	2.0600	2.0700	2.0800	2.0900	2.1000	2.1200	2.1400	2.1500	2.1600	2.1800	2.2000	2.2400	2.2800	2.3200	2.3600
3	3.0301	3.0604	3.0909	3.1216	3.1525	3.1836	3.2149	3.2464	3.2781	3.3100	3.3744	3.4396	3.4725	3.5056	3.5724	3.6400	3.7776	3.9184	4.0624	4.2096
4	4.0604	4.1216	4.1836	4.2465	4.3101	4.3746	4.4399	4.5061	4.5731	4.6410	4.7793	4.9211	4.9934	5.0665	5.2154	5.3680	5.6842	6.0156	6.3624	6.7251
5	5.1010	5.2040	5.3091	5.4163	5.5256	5.6371	5.7507	5.8666	5.9847	6.1051	6.3528	6.6101	6.7424	6.8771	7.1542	7.4416	8.0484	8.6999	9.3983	10.146
6	6.1520	6.3081	6.4684	6.6330	6.8019	6.9753	7.1533	7.3359	7.5233	7.7156	8.1152	8.5355	8.7537	8.9775	9.4420	9.9299	10.980	12.135	13.405	14.798
7	7.2135	7.4343	7.6625	7.8983	8.1420	8.3938	8.6540	8.9228	9.2004	9.4872	10.089	10.730	11.066	11.413	12.141	12.915	14.615	16.533	18.695	21.126
8	8.2857	8.5830	8.8923	9.2142	9.5491	9.8975	10.259	10.636	11.028	11.435	12.299	13.232	13.726	14.240	15.327	16.499	19.122	22.163	25.678	29.731
9	9.3685	9.7546	10.159	10.582	11.026	11.491	11.978	12.487	13.021	13.579	14.775	16.085	16.785	17.518	19.085	20.798	24.712	29.369	34.895	41.435
10	10.462	10.949	11.463	12.006	12.577	13.180	13.816	14.486	15.192	15.937	17.548	19.337	20.303	21.321	23.521	25.958	31.643	38.592	47.061	57.351
11	11.566	12.168	12.807	13.486	14.206	14.971	15.783	16.645	17.560	18.531	20.654	23.044	24.349	25.732	28.755	32.150	40.237	50.398	63.121	78.998
12	12.682	13.412	14.192	15.025	15.917	16.869	17.888	18.977	20.140	21.384	24.133	27.270	29.001	30.850	34.931	39.580	50.894	65.510	84.320	108.43
13	13.809	14.680	15.617	16.626	17.713	18.882	20.140	21.495	22.953	24.522	28.029	32.088	34.351	36.786	42.218	48.496	64.109	84.852	112.30	148.47
14	14.947	15.973	17.086	18.291	19.598	21.015	22.550	24.214	26.019	27.975	32.392	37.581	40.504	43.672	50.818	59.195	80.496	109.61	149.23	202.92
15	16.096	17.293	18.598	20.023	21.578	23.276	25.129	27.152	29.360	31.772	37.279	43.842	47.580	51.659	60.965	72.035	100.81	141.30	197.99	276.97
16	17.257	18.639	20.156	21.824	23.657	25.672	27.888	30.324	33.003	35.949	42.753	50.980	55.717	60.925	72.939	87.442	126.01	181.86	262.35	377.69
17	18.430	20.012	21.761	23.697	25.840	28.212	30.840	33.750	36.973	40.544	48.883	59.117	65.075	71.673	87.068	105.93	157.25	233.79	347.30	514.66
18	19.614	21.412	23.414	25.645	28.132	30.905	33.999	37.450	41.301	45.599	55.749	68.394	75.836	84.140	103.74	128.11	195.99	300.25	459.44	700.93
19	20.810	22.840	25.116	27.671	30.539	33.760	37.379	41.446	46.018	51.159	63.439	78.969	88.211	98.603	123.41	154.74	244.03	385.32	607.47	954.27
20	22.019	24.297	26.870	29.778	33.066	36.785	40.995	45.762	51.160	57.275	72.052	91.024	102.44	115.37	146.62	186.68	303.60	494.21	802.86	1298.8
21	23.239	25.783	28.676	31.969	35.719	39.992	44.865	50.422	56.764	64.002	81.698	104.76	118.81	134.84	174.02	225.02	377.46	633.59	1060.7	1767.3
22	24.471	27.299	30.536	34.248	38.505	43.392	49.005	55.456	62.873	71.402	92.502	120.43	137.63	157.41	206.34	271.03	469.05	811.99	1401.2	2404.6
23	25.716	28.845	32.452	36.617	41.430	46.995	53.436	60.893	69.531	79.543	104.60	138.29	159.27	183.60	244.48	326.23	582.62	1040.3	1850.6	3271.3
24	26.973	30.421	34.426	39.082	44.502	50.815	58.176	66.764	76.789	88.497	118.15	158.65	184.16	213.97	289.49	392.48	723.46	1332.6	2443.8	4449.9
25	28.243	32.030	36.459	41.645	47.727	54.864	63.249	73.105	84.700	98.347	133.33	181.87	212.79	249.21	342.60	471.98	898.09	1706.8	3226.8	6052.9
26	29.525	33.670	38.553	44.311	51.113	59.156	68.676	79.954	93.323	109.18	150.33	208.33	245.71	290.08	405.27	567.37	1114.6	2185.7	4260.4	8233.0
27	30.820	35.344	40.709	47.084	54.669	63.705	74.483	87.350	102.72	121.09	169.37	238.49	283.56	337.50	479.22	681.85	1383.1	2798.7	5624.7	11197.9
28	32.129	37.051	42.930	49.967	58.402	68.528	80.697	95.338	112.96	134.20	190.69	272.88	327.10	392.50	566.48	819.22	1716.0	3583.3	7425.6	15230.2
29	33.450	38.792	45.218	52.966	62.322	73.639	87.346	103.96	124.13	148.63	214.58	312.09	377.16	456.30	669.44	984.06	2128.9	4587.6	9802.9	20714.1
30	34.784	40.568	47.575	56.084	66.438	79.058	94.460	113.28	136.30	164.49	241.33	356.78	434.74	530.31	790.94	1181.8	2640.9	5873.2	12940.	28172.2
40	48.886	60.402	75.401	95.025	120.79	154.76	199.63	259.05	337.88	442.59	767.09	1342.0	1779.0	2360.7	4163.2	7343.8	22728.	69377.	*	*
50	64.463	84.579	112.79	152.66	209.34	290.33	406.52	573.76	815.08	1163.9	2400.0	4994.5	7217.7	10435.	21813.	45497.	*	*	*	*
60	81.669	114.05	163.05	237.99	353.58	533.12	813.52	1253.2	1944.7	3034.8	7471.6	18535.	29219.	46057.	*	*	*	*	*	*

*FVIF > 99.999

APPENDIX D
Standard Normal Probabilities

z	0.00	0.01	0.02	0.03	0.04	0.05	0.06	0.07	0.08	0.09
0.0	.5000	.5040	.5080	.5120	.5160	.5199	.5239	.5279	.5219	.5359
0.1	.5398	.5438	.5478	.5517	.5557	.5596	.5636	.5675	.5714	.5753
0.2	.5793	.5832	.5871	.5910	.5948	.5987	.6026	.6064	.6103	.6141
0.3	.6179	.6217	.6255	.6293	.6331	.6368	.6406	.6443	.6480	.6517
0.4	.6554	.6591	.6628	.6664	.6700	.6736	.6772	.6808	.6844	.6879
0.5	.6915	.6950	.6985	.7019	.7054	.7088	.7123	.7157	.7190	.7224
0.6	.7257	.7291	.7324	.7357	.7389	.7422	.7454	.7486	.7517	.7549
0.7	.7580	.7611	.7642	.7673	.7704	.7734	.7764	.7794	.7823	.7852
0.8	.7881	.7910	.7939	.7967	.7995	.8023	.8051	.8078	.8106	.8133
0.9	.8159	.8186	.8212	.8238	.8264	.8289	.8315	.8340	.8365	.8389
1.0	.8413	.8438	.8461	.8485	.8508	.8531	.8554	.8577	.8599	.8621
1.1	.8643	.8665	.8686	.8708	.8729	.8749	.8770	.8790	.8810	.8830
1.2	.8849	.8860	.8888	.8907	.8925	.8943	.8962	.8980	.8997	.9015
1.3	.9032	.9049	.9066	.9082	.9099	.9115	.9131	.9147	.9162	.9177
1.4	.9192	.9207	.9222	.9236	.9251	.9265	.9279	.9292	.9306	.9319
1.5	.9332	.9345	.9357	.9370	.9382	.9394	.9406	.9418	.9429	.9441
1.6	.9452	.9463	.9474	.9484	.9495	.9505	.9515	.9525	.9535	.9545
1.7	.9554	.9564	.9573	.9582	.9591	.9599	.9608	.9616	.9625	.9633
1.8	.9641	.9649	.9656	.9664	.9671	.9678	.9686	.9693	.9699	.9706
1.9	.9713	.9719	.9726	.9732	.9738	.9744	.9750	.9756	.9761	.9767
2.0	.9772	.9778	.9783	.9788	.9793	.9798	.9803	.9808	.9812	.9817
2.1	.9821	.9826	.9830	.9834	.9838	.9842	.9846	.9850	.9854	.9857
2.2	.9861	.9864	.9868	.9871	.9875	.9878	.9881	.9884	.9887	.9890
2.3	.9893	.9896	.9898	.9901	.9904	.9906	.9909	.9911	.9913	.9916
2.4	.9918	.9920	.9922	.9925	.9927	.9929	.9931	.9932	.9934	.9936
2.5	.9938	.9940	.9941	.9943	.9945	.9946	.9948	.9949	.9951	.9952
2.6	.9953	.9955	.9956	.9957	.9959	.9960	.9961	.9962	.9963	.9964
2.7	.9965	.9966	.9967	.9968	.9969	.9970	.9971	.9972	.9973	.9974
2.8	.9974	.9975	.9976	.9977	.9977	.9978	.9979	.9979	.9980	.9981
2.9	.9981	.9982	.9982	.9983	.9984	.9984	.9985	.9985	.9986	.9986
3.0	.9987	.9987	.9987	.9988	.9988	.9989	.9989	.9989	.9990	.9990

Comprehensive References List

Acharya, Viral A., Julian Franks, and Henri Servaes. 2007. "Private Equity: Boom or Bust?" *Journal of Applied Corporate Finance* 19, no. 4 (Fall): 44–53.

Alexeev, Vitali, and Francis Tapon. 2014. "The Number of Stocks in Your Portfolio Should Be Larger Than You Think: Diversification Evidence from Five Developed Markets." *Journal of Investment Strategies* 4, no. 1 (December): 43–82.

Alford, A., R. Jones, and K. Winkelmann. 2003. "A Spectrum Approach to Active Risk Budgeting." *Journal of Portfolio Management* 30: 49–60.

Almazan, Andres, Keith C. Brown, Murray Carlson, and David A. Chapman. 2004. "Why Constrain Your Mutual Fund Manager?" *Journal of Financial Economics* 73, no. 2 (August): 289–321.

Altman, Edward I., and Scott A. Nammacher. 1987. *Investing in Junk Bonds: Inside the High Yield Debt Market*. Hoboken, NJ: John Wiley & Sons.

Amenc, Noel, Felix Goltz, and Abraham Lioui. 2011. "Practitioner Portfolio Construction and Performance Measurement: Evidence from Europe." *Financial Analysts Journal* 67, no. 3 (May/June): 39–50.

Ammann, Manuel, and Heinz Zimmermann. 2001. "Tracking Error and Tactical Asset Allocation." *Financial Analysts Journal* 57, no. 2 (March/April): 32–43.

Ang, Andrew. 2014. *Asset Management: A Systematic Approach to Factor Investing*. New York: Oxford University Press.

Ang, Andrew, Robert J. Hodrick, Yuhang Xing, and Xiaoyan Zhang. 2006. "The Cross-Section of Volatility and Expected Returns." *Journal of Finance* 61, no. 1 (February): 259–299.

Arak, Marcelle, and L. Ann Martin. 2005. "Convertible Bonds: How Much Equity, How Much Debt?" *Financial Analysts Journal* 61, no. 2 (March/April): 44–50.

Arbel, Avner, and Paul Strebel. 1983. "Pay Attention to Neglected Firms!" *Journal of Portfolio Management* 9, no. 2 (Winter): 37–42.

Arnott, Robert D., Jason C. Hsu, and John M. West. 2008. *The Fundamental Index*. New York: Wiley.

Asness, Clifford S. 2012. "An Old Friend: The Stock Market's Shiller P/E." *AQR Capital Management* (November).

Asness, Clifford S., Tobias J. Moskowitz, and Lasse Heje Pedersen. 2013. "Value and Momentum Everywhere." *Journal of Finance* 68, no. 3 (June): 929–985.

Avera, William F. 1994. "Definition of Industry Ethics and Development of a Code." In *Good Ethics: The Essential Element of a Firm's Success*, ed. K. Baker. Charlottesville, VA: AIMR.

Bailey, Jeffrey V., Thomas M. Richards, and David E. Tierney. 2007. "Evaluating Portfolio Performance." In *Managing Investment Portfolio: A Dynamic Process*, 3rd ed., eds. John L. Maginn, Donald L. Tuttle, Jerald E. Pinto, and Dennis W. McLeavey. Hoboken, NJ: Wiley.

Baker, Malcolm, Brendan Bradley, and Jeffrey Wurgler. 2011. "Performance Attribution: Measuring Dynamic Allocation Skill." *Financial Analysts Journal* 67, no. 1 (January–February): 40–54.

Bali, Turan G., Susan R. Hume, and Terrence F. Martell. 2007. "A New Look at Hedging with Derivatives: Will Firms Reduce Market Risk Exposure?" *Journal of Futures Markets* 27, no. 11 (November): 1053–1083.

Banz, R. W. 1981. "The Relationship between Return and Market Value of Common Stocks." *Journal of Financial Economics* 9, no. 1 (March): 3–18.

Barber, Brad, and Terrance Odean. 1999. "The Courage of Misguided Convictions: The Trading Behavior of Individual Investors." *Financial Analysts Journal* 55, no. 6 (November–December): 41–55.

Barber, Brad, and Terrance Odean. 2000. "Trading Is Hazardous to Your Wealth: The Common Stock Investment Performance of Individual Investors." *Journal of Finance* 55, no. 2 (April): 773–806.

Barber, Brad, and Terrance Odean. 2001. "Boys Will Be Boys: Gender, Overconfidence, and Common Stock Investment." *Quarterly Journal of Economics* 116, no. 1 (February): 261–292.

Barberis, Nicholas, and Richard Thaler. 2003. "A Survey of Behavioral Finance." *Handbook of the Economics of Finance*, eds. G. M. Constantianides, M. Harris, and Rene Stulz. New York: Elsevier Science.

Barone-Adesi, Giovanni, and Robert E. Whaley. 1986. "The Valuation of American Call Options and the Expected Ex-Dividend Stock Price Declines." *Journal of Financial Economics* 17, no. 1 (September): 91–112.

Baruch, Lev. 1989. "On the Usefulness of Earnings and Earnings Research: Lessons and Directions from Two Decades of Empirical Research." *Journal of Accounting Research* 27 (Supplement).

Basak, Suleyman. 2002. "A Comparative Study of Portfolio Insurance." *Journal of Economic Dynamics and Control* 26, no. 7–8 (July): 1217–1241.

Basu, Senjoy. 1977. "Investment Performance of Common Stocks in Relation to Their Price-Earnings Ratios: A Test of the Efficient Market Hypothesis." *Journal of Finance* 32, no. 3 (June): 663–682.

Basu, Senjoy. 1983. "The Relationship between Earnings, Yield, Market Value, and Return for NYSE Common Stocks." *Journal of Financial Economics* 12, no. 1 (June): 129–156.

Beard, Allison. 2001. "Short Selling Goes from Strength to Strength." *Financial Times*, March 16, p. 29.

Beard, Craig, and Richard Sias. 1997. "Is There a Neglected-Firm Effect?" *Financial Analysts Journal* 53, no. 5 (September–October): 19–23.

Beckers, Stan. 1981. "Standard Deviations Implied in Option Prices as Predictors of Future Stock Price Variability." *Journal of Banking and Finance* 5, no. 3 (September): 363–381.

Benesh, Gary A., and Pamela P. Peterson. 1986. "On the Relation between Earning Changes, Analysts' Forecasts and Stock Price Fluctuations." *Financial Analysts Journal* 42, no. 6 (November/December): 29–39.

Benzschawel, Terry, and Alper Corlu. 2011. "Credit Default Swaps: A Cash Flow Analysis." *Journal of Fixed Income* 20, no. 3 (Winter): 40–55.

Berk, Jonathan B., and Richard Stanton. 2007. "Managerial Ability, Compensation, and the Closed-End Fund Discount." *Journal of Finance* 62, no. 2 (April): 529–556.

Berkshire Hathaway. 1993. *Annual Report*, March 1, p. 3.

Bernard, Victor L., and Jacob K. Thomas. 1989. "Post-Earnings-Announcements Drift: Delayed Price Response or Risk Premium?" *Journal of Accounting Research* 27 (Supplement).

Bernard, Victor L., and Jacob K. Thomas. 1990. "Evidence That Stock Prices Do Not Fully Reflect the Implications of Current Earnings for Future Earnings." *Journal of Accounting and Economics* (December): 305–341.

Bhandari, Laxmi Chand. 1988. "Debt/Equity Ratio and Expected Common Stock Returns: Empirical Evidence." *Journal of Finance* 43, no. 2 (June): 507–528.

Bhansali, Vineer, Yonathan Schwarzkopf, and Mark B. Wise. 2009. "Modeling Swap Spreads in Normal and Stressed Environments." *Journal of Fixed Income* 18, no. 4 (Spring): 5–23.

Bierwag, G. O., and George G. Kaufman. 1977. "Coping with the Risk of Interest Rate Fluctuations: A Note." *Journal of Business* 50, no. 3 (July): 364–370.

"The Big Squeeze." 2017. *The Economist*, May 13.

Biger, Nahum, and John Hull. 1983. "The Valuation of Currency Options." *Financial Management* 12, no. 1 (Spring): 24–28.

Billingsley, Randall S., R. Lamy, M. Marr, and T. Thompson. 1985. "Split Ratings and Bond Reoffering Yields." *Financial Management* 14, no. 2 (Summer): 59–65.

Black, Fischer. 1972. "Capital Market Equilibrium with Restricted Borrowing." *Journal of Business* 45, no. 3 (July): 444–455.

Black, Fischer. 1975. "Fact and Fantasy in the Use of Options." *Financial Analysts Journal* 31, no. 4 (July–August): 36–41, 61–72.

Black, Fischer. 1989. "How to Use the Holes in Black–Scholes." *Journal of Applied Corporate Finance* 1, no. 4 (Winter): 67–73.

Black, Fischer, Michael Jensen, and Myron Scholes. 1972. "The Capital Asset Pricing Model: Some Empirical Tests." In *Studies in the Theory of Capital Markets*, ed. Michael Jensen. New York: Praeger.

Black, Fischer, and Myron Scholes. 1973. "The Pricing of Options and Corporate Liabilities." *Journal of Political Economy* 81, no. 2 (May–June): 637–654.

Black, Fischer, and Myron Scholes. 1979. "The Effects of Dividend Yield and Dividend Policy on Common Stock Prices and Returns." *Journal of Financial Economics* 1, no. 1 (March): 1–22.

Blitz, David. 2015. "Factor Investing Revisited." *Journal of Index Investing* 6, no. 2 (Fall): 7–17.

Blitz, David, Matthias X. Hanauer, Milan Vidojevic, and Pim Van Vliet. 2016. "Five Concerns with the Five-Factor Model." Working Paper, Robeco Asset Management.

Boatright, John R. 2008. *Ethics in Finance*, 2nd ed. Malden, MA: Blackwell Publishing.

Bogle, John C. 2009. "The End of 'Soft Dollars'?" *Financial Analysts Journal* 65, no. 2 (March–April): 48–53.

Bohl, Martin T., Christian A. Salm, and Michael Schuppli. 2011. "Price Discovery and Investor Structure." *Journal of Futures Markets* 31, no. 3 (March): 282–306.

Booth, Laurence, Dimitrios Gounopoulos, and Frank Skinner. 2014. "The Choice Between Callable and Noncallable Debt." *Journal of Financial Research* 37, no. 4 (Winter): 435–459.

Boyd, Naomi E., and Jeffrey M. Mercer. 2010. "Gains from Active Bond Portfolio Management Strategies." *Journal of Fixed Income* 19, no. 4 (Spring): 73–83.

Branch, Ben. 1977. "A Tax Loss Trading Rule." *Journal of Business* 50, no. 2 (April): 198–207.

Branch, Ben, and Kyun Chun Chang. 1985. "Tax-Loss Trading—Is the Game Over or Have the Rules Changed?" *Financial Review* 20, no. 1 (February): 55–69.

Brealey, Richard A., and Stewart C. Myers. 2010. *Principles of Corporate Finance*, 10th ed. New York: McGraw-Hill.

Brigham, Eugene. 2010. *Fundamentals of Financial Management*, 12th ed. Mason, OH: South-Western.

Brinson, Gary P. 2005. "The Future of Investment Management." *Financial Analysts Journal* 61, no. 4 (July/August): 24–28.

Brinson, Gary P., L. Randolph Hood, and Gilbert L. Beebower. 1986. "Determinants of Portfolio Performance." *Financial Analysts Journal* 42, no. 4 (July–August): 39–44.

Brinson, Gary P., Brian D. Singer, and Gilbert L. Beebower. 1991. "Determinants of Portfolio Performance II: An Update." *Financial Analysts Journal* 47, no. 3 (May–June): 40–48.

Brown, Gregory. 1999. "Volatility, Sentiment, and Noise Traders." *Financial Analysts Journal* 55, no. 2 (March–April): 82–90.

Brown, Keith C., and Gregory D. Brown. 1987. "Does the Composition of the Market Portfolio Really Matter?" *Journal of Portfolio Management* 13, no. 2 (Winter): 26–32.

Brown, Keith C., Lorenzo Garlappi, and Cristian Tiu. 2010. "Asset Allocation and Portfolio Performance: Evidence from University Endowment Funds." *Journal of Financial Markets* 13, no. 2 (May): 268–294.

Brown, Keith C., W. V. Harlow, and Donald J. Smith. 1994. "An Empirical Analysis of Interest Rate Swap Spreads." *Journal of Fixed Income* 3, no. 3 (March): 61–78.

Brown, Keith C., W. V. Harlow, and Laura T. Starks. 1996. "Of Tournaments and Temptations: An Analysis of Managerial Incentives in the Mutual Fund Industry." *Journal of Finance* 51, no. 1 (March): 85–110.

Brown, Keith C., and Michael V. Raymond. 1986. "Risk Arbitrage and the Prediction of Successful Corporate Takeovers." *Financial Management* 15, no. 3 (August): 54–63.

Brown, Keith C., and Donald J. Smith. 1995. *Interest Rate and Currency Swaps: A Tutorial.* Charlottesville, VA: Research Foundation of Institute of Chartered Financial Analysts.

Brown, Keith C., and Meir Statman. 1987. "The Benefits of Insured Stocks for Corporate Cash Management." *Advances in Futures and Options Research* 2: 243–261.

Brown, Keith C., and Kenneth W. Wiles. 2015. "In Search of Unicorns: Private IPOs and the Changing Markets for Private Equity Investments and Corporate Control." *Journal of Applied Corporate Finance* 27, no. 3 (Summer): 34–48.

Brown, Ken. 2000. "Fund Diversification Dies a Not Very Slow Death." *The Wall Street Journal,* February 7: R1, R5.

Brown, Lawrence. D., Andrew C. Call, Michael B. Clement, M. B., and Nathan Y. Sharp. 2016. "The Activities of Buy-Side Analysts and the Determinants of the Stock Recommendations." *Journal of Accounting and Economics* 62, no. 1 (August): 139–156.

Brown, Stephen J., and William Goetzmann. 1995. "Performance Persistence." *Journal of Finance* 50, no. 3 (June): 679–698.

Brown, Stephen J., and Mark I. Weinstein. 1983. "A New Approach to Testing Asset Pricing Models: The Bilinear Paradigm." *Journal of Finance* 38, no. 3 (June): 711–743.

Brynjolfsson, John B. 2012. "Inflation-Linked Bonds." In *The Handbook of Fixed Income Securities,* 8th ed., eds. F. Fabozzi and S. Mann. New York: McGraw-Hill.

Burmeister, Edwin, Richard Roll, and Stephen A. Ross. 1994. "A Practitioner's Guide to Arbitrage Pricing Theory." In *A Practitioner's Guide to Factor Models,* ed. John Peavy. Charlottesville, VA: Research Foundation of the Institute of Chartered Financial Analysts.

Cabana, Mark O., and Frank J. Fabozzi. 2012. "Agency Debt Securities." In *The Handbook of Fixed Income Securities,* 8th ed. eds. Frank J. Fabozzi and Steven V. Mann. New York: McGraw-Hill.

Cagan, Phillip. 1969. *Essays on Interest Rates.* New York: Columbia University Press for the National Bureau of Economic Research.

Callahan, Dan, and Michael J. Mauboussin. 2014. "Capital Allocation: Evidence, Analytical Methods, and Assessment Guidance." *Journal of Applied Corporate Finance* 26, no. 4 (Fall).

Campbell, John Y., Martin Lettau, Burton G. Malkiel, and Yexiao Xu. 2001. "Have Individual Stocks Become More Volatile? An Empirical Exploration of Idiosyncratic Risk." *Journal of Finance* 56, no. 1 (February): 1–43.

Capon, N., G. Fitzsimons, and R. Prince. 1996. "An Individual Level Analysis of the Mutual Fund Investment Decision." *Journal of Financial Services Research* 10: 59–82.

Carhart, Mark M. 1997. "On Persistence in Mutual Fund Performance." *Journal of Finance* 52, no. 1 (March): 57–82.

Carr, Peter. 1988. "A Calculator Program for Option Values and Implied Standard Deviations." *Journal of Financial Education* 17, no. 1 (Fall): 89–93.

Carter, Richard B., Frederick Dark, and Asah Singh. 1998. "Underwriter Reputation, Initial Returns, and the Long-Run Performance of IPO Stocks." *Journal of Finance* 53, no. 1 (February): 285–311.

Case, Carl, and Robert Shiller. 1987. "Price of Single Family Homes since 1970: New Indexes for Four Cities." Working Paper no. 2393. New York: National Bureau of Economic Research.

Castelino, Mark G. 2000. "Hedging Effectiveness: Basis Risk and Minimum Variance Hedging." *Journal of Futures Markets* 20, no. 1 (January): 89–103.

Cavaglia, Stefano, Christopher Brightman, and Michael Aked. 2000. "The Increasing Importance of Industry Factors." *Financial Analysts Journal* 56, no. 5 (September–October): 41–54.

CFA Institute. 2012. *Global Investment Performance Standards (GIPS) Handbook,* 3rd ed. Charlottesville, VA: CFA Institute.

CFA Institute. 2014. *Standards of Practice Handbook,* 11th ed. Charlottesville, VA: CFA Institute.

CFA Institute. 2017. *Future State of the Investment Profession.* Charlottesville, VA: CFA Institute.

Chan, Louis, Narasimhan Jegadeesh, and Josef Lakonishok. 1999. "The Profitability of Momentum Strategies." *Financial Analysts Journal* 55, no. 6 (November/December): 80–90.

Chan, Louis, and Josef Lakonishok. 2004. "Value and Growth Investing: Review and Update." *Financial Analysts Journal* 60, no. 1 (January/ February): 71–86.

Chan, Wesley. 2003. "Stock Price Reaction to News and No-News: Drift and Reversal after Headlines." *Journal of Financial Economics* 70, no. 2 (November): 223–260.

Chance, Don M. 2004. "Equity Swaps and Equity Investing." *Journal of Alternative Investing* 7 (Summer): 75–97.

Chance, Don M., and Robert Brooks. 2016. *An Introduction to Derivatives and Risk Management,* 10th ed. Boston: Cengage Learning.

Chance, Don M., and Don Rich. 1998. "The Pricing of Equity Swaps and Swaptions." *Journal of Derivatives* 5, no. 2 (Summer): 19–31.

Chemmanur, Thomas, and An Yan. 2004. "A Theory of Corporate Spinoffs." *Journal of Financial Economics* 72, no. 2 (May): 259–290.

Chen, Chin-Ho, Huimin Chung, and Shu-Fang Yuan. 2014. "Deviations from Put–Call Parity and Volatility Prediction: Evidence from the Taiwan Index Option Market." *Journal of Futures Market* 34, no. 12 (December): 1122–1145.

Chen, H. L., N. Jegadeesh, and R. Wermers. 2000. "An Examination of the Stockholdings and Trades of Mutual Fund Managers." *Journal of Financial and Quantitative Analysis* 35 (September): 343–368.

Chen, Nai-fu. 1983. "Some Empirical Tests of the Theory of Arbitrage Pricing." *Journal of Finance* 38, no. 5 (December): 1393–1414.

Chen, Nai-fu, Richard Roll, and Stephen A. Ross. 1986. "Economic Forces and the Stock Market." *Journal of Business* 59, no. 3 (April): 383–404.

Cherney, Elena, and Thom Beal. 2000. "As NYSE Plans for Global Market, Nasdaq Gets Left Out in the Cold." *The Wall Street Journal,* June 8, p. C1.

Cho, Chinhyung D., Edwin J. Elton, and Martin J. Gruber. 1984. "On the Robustness of the Roll and Ross Arbitrage Pricing Theory." *Journal of Financial and Quantitative Analysis* 19, no. 1 (March): 1–10.

Choudhry, Moorad, David Moskovic, and Max Wong. 2014. *Fixed Income Markets: Management, Trading and Hedging,* 2nd ed. Singapore: John Wiley & Sons.

Chowdhury, M., J. S. Howe, and J. C. Lin. 1993. "The Relation between Aggregate Insider Transactions and Stock Market Returns." *Journal of Financial and Quantitative Analysis* 28, no. 3 (September): 431–437.

Christie, William. 1990. "Dividend Yield and Expected Returns." *Journal of Financial Economics* 28, no. 1 (November–December): 95–125.

Christie, William G., and Paul H. Schultz. 1994. "Why Do NASDAQ Market Makers Avoid Odd-Eighth Quotes?" *Journal of Finance* 49, no. 5 (December): 1813–1840.

Christopherson, Jon A., and C. Nola Williams. 1995. "Equity Style: What It Is and Why It Matters." In *The Handbook of Equity Style Management*, eds. T. Daniel Coggin and Frank J. Fabozzi. New Hope, PA: Frank J. Fabozzi Associates.

Clarke, Roger G., and Meir Statman. 1998. "Bullish or Bearish." *Financial Analysts Journal* 54, no. 3 (May–June): 63–72.

Clayman, Michelle. 1987. "In Search of Excellence: The Investor's Viewpoint." *Financial Analysts Journal* 43, no. 3 (May–June): 54–63.

Clements, Jonathan. 1997a. "Retirement Honing: How Much Should You Have Saved for a Comfortable Life?" *The Wall Street Journal*, January 28, p. C1.

Clements, Jonathan. 1997b. "Squeezing the Right Amount from a Retirement Stash." *The Wall Street Journal*, February 25, p. C1.

Clements, Jonathan. 1997c. "Jam Today or Jam Tomorrow? Roth IRA Will Show Many Investors It Pays to Wait." *The Wall Street Journal*, September 16, p. C1.

Coggin, Daniel T., Frank J. Fabozzi, and Shafiqur Rahman. 1993. "The Investment Performance of U.S. Equity Pension Fund Managers: An Empirical Investigation." *Journal of Finance* 48, no. 3 (July): 1039–1055.

Cohen, Abby J. 1996. "Economic Forecasts and the Asset Allocation Decision." In *Economic Analysis for Investment Professionals*. Charlottesville, VA: AIMR, November.

Cohn, D'Vera, and Andrea Caumont. 2016. *10 Demographic Trends That Are Shaping the U.S. and the World*. Pew Research Center.

Connor, Gregory, and Robert A. Korajczyk. 1993. "A Test for the Number of Factors in an Approximate Factor Model." *Journal of Finance* 48, no. 4 (September): 1263–1291.

Cornell, Bradford. 1985. "Taxes and the Pricing of Stock Index Futures: Empirical Results." *Journal of Futures Markets* 5, no. 1: 89–101.

Cornell, Bradford. 2010. "Warren Buffett, Black-Scholes, and the Valuation of Long-Dated Options." *Journal of Portfolio Management* 36, no. 4 (Summer): 107–111.

Cornell, Bradford, and Marc R. Reinganum. 1981. "Forward and Futures Prices: Evidence from Foreign Exchange Markets." *Journal of Finance* 36, no. 5 (December): 1035–1045.

Cox, John C., Jonathan Ingersoll, and Stephen Ross. 1981. "The Relation between Forward Prices and Futures Prices." *Journal of Financial Economics* 9, no. 4 (December): 321–346.

Cox, John C., Stephen A. Ross, and Mark Rubinstein. 1979. "Option Pricing: A Simplified Approach." *Journal of Financial Economics* 7, no. 3 (September): 229–264.

Crawford, Alexander. 2012. "Agency Collateralized Mortgage Obligations." In *The Handbook of Fixed Income Securities*, 8th ed., eds. F. Fabozzi and S. Mann. New York: McGraw-Hill.

Cremers, Martijn K. J., and Antti Petajisto. 2009. "How Active Is Your Fund Manager? A New Measure That Predicts Performance." *Review of Financial Studies* 22, no. 9 (September): 3329–3365.

Cremers, Martijn, and David Weinbaum. 2010. "Deviations from Put-Call Parity and Stock Return Predictability." *Journal of Financial and Quantitative Analysis* 45, no. 2 (April): 335–367.

Daniel, Kent, Mark Grinblatt, Sheridan Titman, and Russ Wermers. 1997. "Measuring Mutual Fund Performance with Characteristics-Based Portfolios." *Journal of Finance* 52, no. 3 (July): 1035–1058.

Davidson, Steve. 2001. "Core Plus Bond Strategies: The Investor Search for Higher Returns." *Community Banker* 2, no. 7 (July).

DeBondt, Werner F. M., and Richard Thaler. 1985. "Does the Stock Market Overreact?" *Journal of Finance* 40, no. 3 (July): 793–805.

Dechev, I., J. Graham, C. R. Harvey, and S. Rajgopal. 2016. "The Misrepresentation of Earnings." *Financial Analysts Journal* 72(1): 22–35.

DeFusco, Richard A., Dennis W. McLeavey, Jerald E. Pinto, and David E. Runkle. 2004. *Quantitative Methods for Investment Analysis*, 2nd ed. Charlottesville, VA: CFA Institute.

Degennaro, Ramon P., and Cesare Robotti. 2007. "Financial Market Frictions." *Economic Review* 92, no. 3 (Third Quarter): 1–16.

Del Guercio, Diane. 1996. "The Distorting Effect of the Prudent-Man Laws on Institutional Equity Investments." *Journal of Financial Economics* 40, no. 1 (January): 31–62.

Desai, H., and P. Jain. 1999. "Firm Performance and Focus: Long-Run Stock Market Performance Following Spin-offs." *Journal of Financial Economics* 54, no. 1 (February): 75–102.

Dhrymes, Phoebus J., Irwin Friend, and N. Bulent Gultekin. 1984. "A Critical Re-examination of the Empirical Evidence on the Arbitrage Pricing Theory." *Journal of Finance* 39, no. 2 (June): 323–346.

Dialynas, Chris P., and Alfred Murata. 2006. "The Active Decisions in the Selection of Passive Management and Performance Bogeys." In *Active Bond Portfolio Management*, eds. Frank J. Fabozzi, Lionel Martellini, and Philippe Priaulet. Hoboken, NJ: John Wiley.

Dietz, Peter O., and Jeannette R. Kirschman. 1990. "Evaluating Portfolio Performance." In *Managing Investment Portfolios*, 2nd ed., eds. J. Maginn and D. Tuttle. Boston: Warren, Gorham, & Lamont.

Doole, S., L. Renelleau, and A. Sevilla. 2009. "The Equity Risk Premium and the Risks of Equity Investing." *Journal of Investment Strategy* 4, no. 1 (November).

DuBois, Charles H. 1992. "Tactical Asset Allocation: A Review of Current Techniques." In *Active Asset Allocation*, eds. R. Arnott and F. Fabozzi. Chicago: Probus.

Eckbo, B. Espen, Ronald W. Masulis, and Oyvind Norli. 2007. "Security Offerings." In *Handbook of Corporate Finance: Empirical Corporate Finance*, Vol. 1, ed. B. E. Eckbo. New York: Elsevier/North-Holland Handbook of Finance Series.

Eichholtz, A. 1996. "Does International Diversification Work Better for Real Estate Than for Stocks and Bonds?" *Financial Analysts Journal* 52, no. 1 (January–February): 56–62.

Elton, Edwin J., Martin J. Gruber, and Christopher R. Blake. 1996. "The Persistence of Risk-Adjusted Mutual Fund Performance." *Journal of Business* 69, no. 2 (April): 133–157.

Elton, Edwin J., Martin J. Gruber, and Joel Rentzler. 1983. "A Single Examination of the Empirical Relationship between Dividend Yields and Deviations from the CAPM." *Journal of Banking and Finance* 7, no. 1 (March): 135–146.

Evans, John, and Stephen Archer. 1968. "Diversification and the Reduction of Dispersion: An Empirical Analysis." *Journal of Finance* 23, no. 5 (December): 761–767.

Ewing, Terzah, and Silvia Ascarelli. 2000. "One World, How Many Stock Exchanges?" *The Wall Street Journal*, (May 15): C1.

Fabozzi, Frank J., ed. 1990. *The Japanese Bond Markets* Chicago: Probus.

Fabozzi, Frank J. 2012a. "Bond Immunization: An Asset/Liability Optimization Strategy." In *The Handbook of Fixed Income Securities*, 8th ed., eds. F. J. Fabozzi and S. V. Mann. New York: McGraw-Hill.

Fabozzi, Frank J. 2012b. "Dedicated Bond Portfolios." In *The Handbook of Fixed Income Securities*, 8th ed., eds. F. J. Fabozzi and S. V. Mann. New York: McGraw-Hill.

Fabozzi, Frank J., Gerald W. Buetow, Robert R. Johnson, and Brian J. Henderson. 2012. "Measuring Interest-Rate Risk." In *The Handbook of Fixed Income Securities*, 8th ed., eds. F. Fabozzi and S. Mann. New York: McGraw-Hill.

Fabozzi, Frank J., Andrew Kalotay, and Michael Dorigan. 2012. "Valuation of Bonds with Embedded Options." In *The Handbook of Fixed Income Securities*, 8th ed., eds. F. Fabozzi and S. Mann. New York: McGraw-Hill.

Fabozzi, Frank J., and Christopher K. Ma. 1988. "The Over-the-Counter Market and New York Stock Exchange Trading Halts." *Financial Review* 23, no. 4 (November): 427–437.

Fabozzi, Frank J., and Steven V. Mann. 2012. *The Handbook of Fixed Income Securities*, 8th ed. New York: McGraw-Hill.

Fama, Eugene F. 1970. "Efficient Capital Markets: A Review of Theory and Empirical Work." *Journal of Finance* 25, no. 2 (May): 383–417.

Fama, Eugene F. 1972. "Components of Investment Performance." *Journal of Finance* 27, no. 3 (June): 551–567.

Fama, Eugene F. 1991. "Stock Returns, Real Activity, Inflation and Money." *American Economic Review* 71, no. 2 (June): 545–565.

Fama, Eugene F., L. Fisher, M. Jensen, and R. Roll. 1969. "The Adjustment of Stock Prices to New Information." *International Economic Review* 10, no. 1 (February): 1–21.

Fama, Eugene F., and Kenneth French. 1992. "The Cross Section of Expected Stock Returns." *Journal of Finance* 47, no. 2 (June): 427–465.

Fama, Eugene F., and Kenneth French. 1995. "Size and Book-to-Market Factors in Earnings and Returns." *Journal of Finance* 50, no. 1 (March): 131–155.

Fama, Eugene F., and Kenneth R. French. 1993. "Common Risk Factors in the Returns on Stocks and Bonds." *Journal of Financial Economics* 33, no. 1 (January): 3–56.

Fama, Eugene F., and Kenneth R. French. 2015. "A Five-Factor Asset Pricing Model." *Journal of Financial Economics* 116, no. 1 (April): 1–22.

Fan, Rui, Haiqi Li, and Sung Y. Park. 2016. "Estimation and Hedging Effectiveness of Time-Varying Hedge Ratio: Nonparametric Approaches." *Journal of Futures Markets* 36, no. 10 (October): 968–991.

Feldstein, Sylvan G., Frank J. Fabozzi, Alexander Grant, and David Ratner. 2012. "Municipal Bonds." In *The Handbook of Fixed Income Securities*, 8th ed., eds. F. Fabozzi and S. Mann. New York: McGraw-Hill.

Ferguson, Robert, and Dean Leistikow. 1998. "Are Regression Approach Futures Hedge Ratios Stationary?" *Journal of Futures Markets* 18, no. 7 (October): 851–866.

Fernández, Pablo. 2006. "Equity Premium: Historical, Expected, Required and Implied." Working Paper 661, University of Navarra.

Fernholz, Robert, Robert Garvy, and John Hannon. 1998. "Diversity-Weighted Indexing." *Journal of Portfolio Management* 24, no. 2 (Winter): 74–82.

Ferson, Wayne E. 2010. "Investment Performance Evaluation." *Annual Review of Financial Economics* 2: 207–234.

Figlewski, Stephen. 1989a. "Options Arbitrage in Imperfect Markets." *Journal of Finance* 44, no. 5 (December): 1289–1311.

Figlewski, Stephen. 1989b. "What Does an Option Pricing Model Tell Us about Option Prices?" *Financial Analysts Journal* 45, no. 5 (September–October): 12–15.

Finnerty, John D. 1983. "Evaluating the Economics of Refunding High- Coupon Sinking-Fund Debt." *Financial Management* 12, no. 1 (Spring): 5–10.

Fisher, Lawrence, and Roman L. Weil. 1971. "Coping with the Risk of Interest-Rate Fluctuations: Returns to Bondholders from Naive and Optimal Strategies." *Journal of Business* 44, no. 4 (October): 408–431.

Fogler, H. Russell. 1993. "A Modern Theory of Security Analysis." *Journal of Portfolio Management* 19, no. 3 (Spring): 6–14.

Foster, F. D., and S. Viswanathan. 1993. "The Effects of Public Information and Competition on Trading Volume and Price Volatility." *Review of Financial Studies* 6, no. 1 (Spring): 23–56.

Fox, Merritt B., Lawrence R. Glosten, and Gabriel V. Rauterberg. 2015. "The New Stock Market: Sense and Nonsense." *Duke Law Journal* 65, no. 2 (November): 193–277.

Fridson, Martin S. 1994. "The State of the High-Yield Bond Market: Overshooting or Return to Normalcy." *Journal of Applied Corporate Finance* 7, no. 1 (Spring): 85–97.

Fridson, Martin, Frank J. Fabozzi, and Adam B. Cohen. 2012. "Credit Analysis for Corporate Bonds." In *The Handbook of Fixed Income Securities*, 8th ed., eds. F. Fabozzi and S. Mann. New York: McGraw-Hill.

Friedman, Milton, and Leonard J. Savage. 1948. "The Utility Analysis of Choices Involving Risk." *Journal of Political Economy* 56, no. 3 (August): 279–304.

Friend, Irwin, Marshall Blume, and Jean Crockett. 1970. *Mutual Funds and Other Institutional Investors.* New York: McGraw-Hill.

Fulkerson, Jon A. 2013. "Is Timing Everything? The Value of Mutual Fund Manager Trades." *Financial Management* 42, no. 2 (Summer): 243–261.

Fung, William, and David A. Hsieh. 2006. "Hedge Funds: An Industry in Its Adolescence." *Economic Review* 91, no. 4 (Fourth Quarter): 1–33.

Galai, Dan, and Meir I. Schneller. 1978. "Pricing Warrants and the Value of the Firm." *Journal of Finance* 33, no. 5 (December): 1333–1342.

Garman, Mark B., and Steven W. Kohlhagen. 1983. "Foreign Currency Option Values." *Journal of International Money and Finance* 2, no. 3 (December): 231–237.

Garner, Carley. 2013. *A Trader's First Book on Commodities*, 2nd ed. Upper Saddle River, NJ: Pearson Education.

Gastineau, Gary. 1993. "Using Swaps in Equity Portfolios." In *Derivative Strategies for Managing Portfolio Risk*, ed. K. Brown. Charlottesville, VA: AIMR.

Gastineau, Gary. 2001. "Exchange-Traded Funds: An Introduction." *Journal of Portfolio Management* 27, no. 3 (Spring): 88–96.

Gastineau, Gary L., and Mark P. Kritzman. 2001. *Dictionary of Financial Risk Management*, 3rd ed. New York: Wiley.

Gentry, James A., David T. Whitford, and Paul Newbold. 1988. "Predicting Industrial Bond Ratings with a Profit Model and Funds Flow Components." *Financial Review* 23, no. 3 (August): 269–286.

Gervais, S., and T. Odean. 2001. "Learning to Be Overconfident." *Review of Financial Studies* 14, no. 1: 1–27.

Geske, Robert. 1979. "A Note on an Analytical Valuation Formula for Unprotected American Call Options on Stocks with Known Dividends." *Journal of Financial Economics* 7, no. 4 (June): 375–380.

Geweke, John, and Guofu Zhou. 1996. "Measuring the Price of the Arbitrage Pricing Theory." *Review of Financial Studies* 9, no. 2 (Summer): 557–587.

Gibbons, Michael. 1982. "Multivariate Tests of Financial Models: A New Approach." *Journal of Financial Economics* 10, no. 1 (March): 3–28.

Glickstein, David A., and Rolf E. Wubbels. 1983. "Dow Theory Is Alive and Well." *Journal of Portfolio Management* 9, no. 3 (Spring): 28–32.

Goetzmann, William N., and Roger G. Ibbotson. 1990. "The Performance of Real Estate as an Asset Class." *Journal of Applied Corporate Finance* 3, no. 1 (Spring): 65–76.

Goodwin, Thomas H. 1998. "The Information Ratio." *Financial Analysts Journal* 54, no. 4 (July–August): 34–43.

Gressle, Mark, and Stephen F. O'Byrne. 2013. "How 'Competitive Pay' Undermines Pay for Performance (and What Companies Can Do to Avoid That)." *Journal of Applied Corporate Finance* 25, no. 2 (Spring).

Grinblatt, Mark, and Narasimhan Jegadeesh. 1996. "Relative Pricing of Eurodollar Futures and Forward Contracts." *Journal of Finance* 51, no. 4 (September): 1499–1522.

Grinblatt, Mark, and Sheridan Titman. 1993. "Performance Measurement without Benchmarks: An Examination of Mutual Fund Returns." *Journal of Business* 66, no. 1 (January): 47–68.

Grinold, Richard C. 1992. "Are Benchmark Portfolios Efficient?" *Journal of Performance Management* 19, no. 1 (Fall): 34–40.

Grinold, Richard C., and Ronald N. Kahn. 1994. "Multiple-Factor Models for Portfolio Risk." In *A Practitioner's Guide to Factor Models*, ed. John Peavy. Charlottesville, VA: Research Foundation of the Institute of Chartered Financial Analysts.

Grinold, Richard C., and Ronald N. Kahn. 2000. *Active Portfolio Management*, 2nd ed. New York: McGraw-Hill.

Gultekin, Mustofa N., and N. Bulent Gultekin. 1987. "Stock Return Anomalies and the Tests of APT." *Journal of Finance* 42, no. 5 (December): 1213–1224.

Hagstrom, Robert G. 2001. *The Essential Buffett.* New York: Wiley.

Handa, Puneet, and Robert A. Schwartz. 1996. "How Best to Supply Liquidity to a Securities Market." *Journal of Portfolio Management* 22, no. 2 (Winter): 44–51.

Hanks, Sara. 1990. "SEC Ruling Creates a New Market." *The Wall Street Journal*, May 16, p. A12.

Harding, Matthew C. 2008. "Explaining the Single Factor Bias of Arbitrage Pricing Models in Finite Samples." *Economic Letters* 99, no. 1 (April): 85–88.

Harlow, W. V. 1991. "Asset Allocation in a Downside Risk Framework." *Financial Analysts Journal* 47, no. 5 (September/October): 28–40.

Harlow, W. V., and Keith C. Brown. 2006. "The Right Answer to the Wrong Question: Identifying Superior Active Portfolio Management." *Journal of Investment Management* 4, no. 4 (Fourth Quarter): 15–40.

Harlow, W. V., and Keith C. Brown. 2016. "Improving the Outlook for a Successful Retirement: A Case for Using Downside Hedging." *Journal of Retirement* 3, no. 3 (Winter): 35–50.

Harris, Larry. 2015. *Trading and Electronic Markets: What Investment Professionals Need to Know.* Charlottesville, VA: CFA Institute.

Hawthorne, Fran. 1986. "The Battle of the Bond Indexes." *Institutional Investor* 20, no. 4 (April).

Hendriksson, Roy D., and Robert C. Merton. 1981. "On Market Timing and Investment Performance: Statistical Procedures for Evaluating Forecasting Skills." *Journal of Business* 54, no. 4 (October): 513–534.

Hersey, Brian E. 2001. "Core-Plus: Prospects and Implications." In *CorePlus Bond Management*, Association for Investment Management and Research. Charlottesville, VA: 11–20.

Hicks, John. 1939. *Value and Capital.* Oxford, UK: Clarendon Press.

Hill, Joanne M. 1993. "Adding Value with Equity Derivatives: Part II." In *Derivative Strategies for Managing Portfolio Risk*, ed. K. Brown. Charlottesville, VA: Association for Investment Management and Research: 62–73.

Hirschleifer, David. 2001. "Investor Psychology and Asset Pricing." *Journal of Finance* 56, no. 4 (August): 1533–1597.

Hopewell, Michael H., and Arthur L. Schwartz, Jr. 1978. "Temporary Trading Suspensions in Individual NYSE Securities." *Journal of Finance* 33, no. 5 (December): 1355–1373.

Hopewell, Michael H., and George Kaufman. 1973. "Bond Price Volatility and Term to Maturity: A Generalized Respecification." *American Economic Review* 63, no. 4 (September): 749–753.

Horan, Stephen M., and David Adler. 2009. "Tax-Aware Investment Management Practice." *Journal of Wealth Management* 12, no. 2 (Fall): 71–88.

Horan, Stephen M., and D. Bruce Johnsen. 2000. *The Welfare Effects of Soft Dollar Brokerage: Law and Economics.* Charlottesville, VA: Research Foundation of the Institute of Chartered Financial Analysts.

Horowitz, Jed, and Kate Kelly. 2005. "NASD Completes Its Sale of Amex to Member Group." *The Wall Street Journal*, January 4, p. C3.

Howe, John S., and Tie Su. 2001. "Discretionary Reductions in Warrant Exercise Prices." *Journal of Financial Economics* 61, no. 2 (August): 227–252.

Hsu, David H., and Martin Kenney. 2005. "Organizing Venture Capital: The Rise and Demise of American Research & Development Corporation, 1946–1973." *Industrial and Corporate Change* 14, no. 4 (August): 579–616.

Hsu, Jason C., Vitali Kalesnik, and Brett W. Myers. 2010. "Performance Attribution: Measuring Dynamic Allocation Skill." *Financial Analysts Journal* 66, no. 6 (November–December): 17–26.

Hull, John C. 2015. *Options, Futures, and Other Derivatives*, 9th ed. Boston: Pearson Education.

Hull, John C., and Alan D. White. 2003. "The Valuation of Credit Default Options." *Journal of Fixed Income* 10, no. 3 (Spring): 40–50.

Ibbotson, Roger G., and Gary P. Brinson. 1993. *Global Investing.* New York: McGraw-Hill.

Ibbotson, Roger G., Peng Chen, and Kevin X. Zhu. 2011. "The ABCs of Hedge Funds: Alphas, Betas, and Costs." *Financial Analysts Journal* 67, no. 1 (January–February): 15–25.

Ibbotson, Roger G., and Paul D. Kaplan. 2000. "Does Asset Allocation Policy Explain 40, 90, or 100 Percent of Performance?" *Financial Analysts Journal* 56, no. 1 (January–February): 26–33.

Ibbotson, Roger G., Jody L. Sindelar, and Jay R. Ritter. 1994. "The Market Problems with the Pricing of Initial Public Offerings." *Journal of Applied Corporate Finance* 7, no. 1 (Spring): 66–74.

Ineichen, Alexander M. 2000. "Twentieth Century Volatility." *Journal of Portfolio Management* 27, no. 1 (Fall): 93–101.

Investment Company Institute. 2017. *Investment Company Fact Book*, 57th ed. Washington DC: Investment Company Institute.

Ip, Greg. 1998. "What's Behind the Trailing Performance of the Dow Industrials vs. the S&P 500?" *The Wall Street Journal*, August 20, pp. C1, C17.

Ivkovic, A., and N. Jegadeesh. 2004. "The Timing and Value of Forecast and Recommendation Revisions." *Journal of Financial Economics* 73, no. 3 (September): 433–463.

Jacobs, Bruce I., and Kenneth N. Levy. 2007. "20 Myths about Enhanced Active 120–20 Strategies." *Financial Analysts Journal* 63, no. 4 (July–August): 19–26.

Jaffe, Jeffrey F., and Gershon Mandelker. 1976. "The 'Fisher Effect' for Risky Assets: An Empirical Analysis." *Journal of Finance* 31, no. 2 (May): 447–458.

Jagannathan, Ravi, and Zhenyu Wang. 1996. "The Conditional CAPM and the Cross Section of Expected Returns." *Journal of Finance* 51, no. 1 (March): 3–53.

Jain, Prem C. 1988. "Response of Hourly Stock Prices and Trading Volume to Economic News." *Journal of Business* 61, no. 2 (April): 219–231.

James, Christopher, and Robert Edmister. 1983. "The Relation between Common Stock Returns, Trading Activity, and Market Value." *Journal of Finance* 38, no. 4 (September): 1075–1086.

Jegadeesh, Narasimhan, J. Kim, S. Krische, and C. M. Lee. 2004. "Analyzing the Analysts: When Do Recommendations Add Value?" *Journal of Finance* 59, no. 3 (June): 1083–1124.

Jensen, Gerald R., Robert R. Johnson, and Jeffrey M. Mercer. 1997. "New Evidence on Size and Price-to-Book Effects in Stock Returns." *Financial Analysts Journal* 53, no. 6 (November–December): 34–42.

Jensen, Michael C. 1968. "The Performance of Mutual Funds in the Period 1945-1964." *Journal of Finance* 23, no. 2 (May): 389–416.

Jensen, Michael C., and Clifford W. Smith, Jr., eds. 1986. "Symposium on Investment Banking and the Capital Acquisition Process." *Journal of Financial Economics* 15, no. 1/2 (January–February): 3–29.

Jensen, Michael C., and Jerald B. Warner. 1988. "The Distribution of Power among Corporate Managers, Shareholders, and Directors." *Journal of Financial Economics* 20, no. 1–2 (January–March): 3–24.

Johnson, H. E. 1983. "An Analytic Approximation for the American Put Price." *Journal of Financial and Quantitative Analysis* 18, no. 1 (March): 143–151.

Johnson, Leland L. 1960. "The Theory of Hedging and Speculation in Commodity Futures." *Review of Economic Studies* 27: 139–160.

Jones, C. N., G. Kaul, and M. L. Lipson. 1994. "Information, Trading and Volatility." *Journal of Financial Economics* 36, no. 1 (August): 127–154.

Jones, C. P., R. J. Rendleman, Jr., and H. A. Latané. 1985. "Earnings Announcements: Pre- and Post-Responses." *Journal of Portfolio Management* 11, no. 3 (Spring): 28–32.

Jones, Christopher S. 2001. "Extracting Factors From Heteroskedastic Asset Returns." *Journal of Financial Economics* 62, no. 2 (November): 293–325.

Jorion, Philippe. 1991. "The Pricing of Exchange Rate Risk in the Stock Market." *Journal of Financial and Quantitative Analysis* 26, no. 3 (September): 363–376.

Jost, Kathryn Dixon, ed. 2001. *Best Execution and Portfolio Performance.* Charlottesville, VA: AIMR.

Kahneman, Daniel, and Amos Tversky. 1979. "Prospect Theory: An Analysis of Decision under Risk." *Econometrica* 47, no. 2 (March): 263–291,

Kalotay, A. J. 1981. "On the Management of Sinking Funds." *Financial Management* 10, no. 2 (Summer): 34–40.

Kalotay, A. J. 1982a. "On the Structure and Valuation of Debt Refundings." *Financial Management* 11, no. 1 (Spring): 41–42.

Kalotay, A. J. 1982b. "Sinking Funds and the Realized Cost of Debt." *Financial Management* 11, no. 1 (Spring): 43–54

Kaplan, Stephen N. 2013. "CEO Pay and Corporate Governance in the U.S.: Perceptions, Facts, and Challenges." *Journal of Applied Corporate Finance* 25, no. 2 (Spring).

Kat, Harry M. 2001. *Structured Equity Derivatives: The Definitive Guide to Exotic Options and Structured Notes.* London: Wiley.

Keim, Donald B. 1983. "Size-Related Anomalies and Stock Return Seasonality." *Journal of Financial Economics* 12, no. 1 (June): 13–32.

Keynes, John Maynard. 1930. *A Treatise on Money.* London: Macmillan.

Khorana, Ajay, Edward Nelling, and Jeffrey Trester. 1998. "The Emergence of Country Index Funds." *Journal of Portfolio Management* 24, no. 4 (Summer): 78–84.

Klemkosky, Robert C., and Bruce G. Resnick. 1979. "Put-Call Parity and Market Efficiency." *Journal of Finance* 34, no. 5 (December): 1141–1155.

Knewston, Heather S., Richard W. Sias, and David A. Whidbee. 2010. "Style Timing with Insiders." *Financial Analysts Journal* 66, no. 4 (July/August): 46–66.

Koenig, Evan, and Kenneth Emery. 1991. "Misleading Indicators? Using the Composite Leading Indicators to Predict Cyclical Turning Points." Federal Reserve Bank of Dallas. *Economic Review* (July): 1–14.

Koh, Kevin, Dawn A. Matsumoto, and Shivaram Rajgopal. 2008. "Meeting or Beating Analyst Expectations in the Post-Scandals World: Changes in Stock Market Rewards and Managerial Actions." *Contemporary Accounting Research* 25, no. 4 (Winter): 1067–1098.

Kon, Stanley J. 1983. "The Market-Timing Performance of Mutual Fund Managers." *Journal of Business* 56, no. 3 (July): 323–347.

Kostovetsky, Leonard. 2003. "Index Mutual Funds and Exchange-Traded Funds." *Journal of Portfolio Management* 29, no. 4 (Summer): 80–92.

Kothari, S. P., and Jay Shanken. 2004. "Asset Allocation with Inflation- Protected Bonds." *Financial Analysts Journal* 60, no. 1 (January/ February): 54–70.

Kothari, S. P., Jay Shanken, and Richard G. Sloan. 1995. "Another Look at the Cross Section of Expected Stock Returns." *Journal of Finance* 50, no. 2 (March): 185–224.

Kramer, Charles. 1994. "Macroeconomic Seasonality and the January Effect." *Journal of Finance* 49, no. 5 (December): 1883–1891.

Kritzman, Mark P. 1990. "Quantitative Methods in Performance Measurement." In *Quantitative Methods for Financial Analysis*, 2nd ed., eds. S. Brown and M. P. Kritzman. Homewood, IL: Dow Jones-Irwin.

Kritzman, Mark. 1992. "What Investors Need to Know about Duration and Convexity." *Financial Analysts Journal* 48, no. 6 (November– December): 17–20.

Labuszewski, John. W., Michael Kamradt, and David Gibbs. 2013. "Understanding Treasury Futures." CME Group Working Paper.

Lawton, Philip, and W. Bruce Remington. 2016. "Global Investment Performance Standards." In *Managing Investment Portfolio: A Dynamic Process*, 3rd ed., eds. John L. Maginn, Donald L. Tuttle, Jerald E. Pinto, and Dennis W. McLeavey. Hoboken, NJ: Wiley.

Layard-Liesching, Ronald. 2001. "Exploiting Opportunities in Global Bond Markets." In *Core–Plus Bond Management*. Charlottesville, VA: Association for Investment Management and Research, 30–38.

Lee, Charles. 2003. "Fusion Investing." In *Equity Valuation in a Global Context*. Charlottesville, VA: AIMR.

Lee, Charles, Andrei Shleifer, and Richard Thaler. 1991. "Investor Sentiment and the Closed-End Fund Puzzle." *Journal of Finance* 46, no. 1 (March): 76–110.

Leibowitz, Martin L. 1986a. "The Dedicated Bond Portfolio in Pension Funds—Part I: Motivations and Basics." *Financial Analysts Journal* 42, no. 1 (January–February): 68–75.

Leibowitz, Martin L. 1986b. "The Dedicated Bond Portfolio in Pension Funds—Part II: Immunization, Horizon Matching, and Contingent Procedures." *Financial Analysts Journal* 42, no. 2 (March–April): 47–57.

Leibowitz, Martin L., and Alfred Weinberger. 1982. "Contingent Immunization—Part I: Risk Control Procedures." *Financial Analysts Journal* 38, no. 6 (November–December): 17–32.

Leibowitz, Martin L., and Alfred Weinberger. 1983. "Contingent Immunization—Part II: Problem Areas." *Financial Analysts Journal* 39, no. 1 (January–February): 35–50.

Leibowitz, Martin L., and Sidney Homer. 2013. *Inside the Yield Book*, 3rd ed., Hoboken, NJ: John Wiley & Sons.

Leibowitz, Martin L., Thomas E. Klaffky, Steven Mandel, and Alfred Weinberger. 1983. *Horizon Matching: A New Generalized Approach for Developing Minimum–Cost Dedicated Portfolios*. New York: Salomon Brothers.

Lewis, Michael. 2014. *Flash Boys: A Wall Street Revolt*. New York: W. W. Norton.

Lhabitant, François-Serge. 2006. *The Handbook of Hedge Funds*. West Sussex, England: John Wiley.

Lightner, Renee, and Theo Francis. 2016. "How Much Do Top CEOs Make?" *The Wall Street Journal*, March 17.

Lintner, John. 1965. "Security Prices, Risk and Maximal Gains from Diversification." *Journal of Finance* 20, no. 4 (December): 587–615.

Litzenberger, Robert, and K. Ramaswamy. 1979. "The Effect of Personal Taxes and Dividends on Capital Asset Prices: Theory and Empirical Evidence." *Journal of Financial Economics* 7, no. 2 (June): 163–196.

Liu, Jun, Francis A. Longstaff, and Ravit E. Mandell. 2006. "The Market Price of Risk in Interest Rate Swaps: The Roles of Default Risk and Liquidity Risks." *Journal of Business* 79, no. 5 (September): 2337–2359.

Liu, P., and W. T. Moore. 1987. "The Impact of Split Bond Ratings on Risk Premia." *The Financial Review* 22, no. 1 (February): 71–85.

Lo, Andrew W. 2002. "The Statistics of Sharpe Ratios." *Financial Analysts Journal* 58, no. 4 (July–August): 36–52.

Loughran, Timothy, and Jay Ritter. 1995. "The New Issues Puzzle." *Journal of Finance* 50, no. 1 (March): 23–51.

Ludvigson, Sydney C., and Serena Ng, 2007, "The Empirical Risk–Return Relation: A Factor Analysis Approach." *Journal of Financial Economics* 83, no. 1 (January): 171–222.

Lummer, Scott L., and Mark W. Riepe. 1993. "Convertible Bonds as an Asset Class: 1957–1992." *Journal of Fixed Income* 3, no. 2 (September): 47–56.

Lyandres, Evgeny, Le Sun, and Lu Zhang. 2008. "The New Issues Puzzle: Testing the Investment-Based Explanation." *The Review of Financial Studies* 21, no. 6 (November): 2825–2855.

Lynch, Peter. 1989. *One up on Wall Street*. New York: Simon & Schuster.

Maalej, Hela, and Jean-Luc Prigent. 2016. "On the Stochastic Dominance of Portfolio Insurance Strategies." *Journal of Mathematical Finance* 6, no. 1 (February): 14–27.

Macaulay, Frederick R. 1938. *Some Theoretical Problems Suggested by the Movements of Interest Rates, Bond Yields, and Stock Prices in the United States since 1856*. New York: National Bureau of Economic Research.

MacBeth, James D., and Larry J. Merville. 1979. "An Empirical Examination of the Black–Scholes Call Option Pricing Model." *Journal of Finance* 34, no. 5 (December): 1173–1186.

Maginn, John L., Donald L. Tuttle, Jerald E. Pinto, and Dennis W. McLeavey., eds., 2016. *Managing Investment Portfolios: A Dynamic Process*, 3rd ed. Sponsored by CFA Institute. Hoboken, NJ: Wiley.

Malkiel, Burton G. 2015. *A Random Walk Down Wall Street*. New York: W.W. Norton & Co.

Malkiel, Burton G. 2017. "Index Funds Still Beat 'Active' Portfolio Management." *The Wall Street Journal*, June 6.

Malkiel, Burton G., and John G. Cragg. 1970. "Expectations and the Structure of Share Prices." *American Economic Review* 60, no. 4 (September): 601–617.

Malvey, Jack. 2012. "Global Credit Bond Portfolio Management." In *The Handbook of Fixed Income Securities*, 8th ed., eds. F. Fabozzi and S. Mann. New York: McGraw-Hill.

Markowitz, Harry. 1952. "Portfolio Selection." *Journal of Finance* 7, no. 1 (March): 77–91.

Markowitz, Harry. 1959. *Portfolio Selection—Efficient Diversification of Investments*. New York: Wiley.

Marshall, William, and Jess B. Yawitz. 1980. "Optimal Terms of the Call Provision on a Corporate Bond." *Journal of Financial Research* 3, no. 3 (Fall): 203–211.

Mathis, J., J. McAndrews, and J. C. Rochet. 2009. "Rating the Raters: Are Reputation Concerns Powerful Enough to Discipline Rating Agencies?" *Journal of Monetary Economics* 56, no. 5 (July): 657–674.

Mauboussin, Michael J. and Dan Callahan. 2014. "Capital Allocation: Evidence, Analytical Methods, and Assessment

Guidance." *Journal of Applied Corporate Finance* 26, no. 4 (Fall): 48–74.

May, Anthony D. 2010. "The Impact of Bond Rating Changes on Corporate Bond Prices: New Evidence for the Over-the-Counter Market." *Journal of Banking and Finance* 34, no. 11 (November): 2822–2836.

McConnell, John J., and Gary Sanger. 1989. "A Trading Strategy for New Listings on the NYSE." *Financial Analysts Journal* 40, no. 1 (January– February): 38–39.

McCulloch, Huston J. 1975. "An Estimate of the Liquidity Premium." *Journal of Political Economy* 83, no. 1 (January–February): 95–119.

Merjos, Anne. 1990. "How's the Market Doing?" *Barron's*, August 20, 18–20, 27, 28.

Merton, Robert C. 1973a. "The Relationship between Put and Call Option Prices: Comment." *Journal of Finance* 28, no. 1 (March): 183–184.

Merton, Robert C. 1973b. "Theory of Rational Option Pricing." *Bell Journal of Economics and Management* 4, no. 1 (Spring): 141–183.

Merton, Robert C. 1981. "On Market Timing and Investment Performance: An Equilibrium Theory of Value for Market Forecasts." *Journal of Business* 54, no. 3 (July): 363–406.

Meyers, Stephen L. 1973. "A Reexamination of Market and Industry Factors in Stock Price Behavior." *Journal of Finance* 28, no. 3 (June): 695–705.

Miller, Merton H. 1991. *Financial Innovations and Market Volatility.* Cambridge, MA: Blackwell.

Miller, Merton H., and Franco Modigliani. 1961. "Dividend Policy, Growth, and the Valuation of Shares." *Journal of Business* 34, no. 4 (October): 411–433.

Miller, Merton H., and Myron Scholes. 1982. "Dividends and Taxes: Some Empirical Evidence." *Journal of Political Economy* 90, no. 4 (December): 1118–1141.

Miller, Robert E., and Frank K. Reilly. 1987. "Examination of Mispricing, Returns, and Uncertainty for Initial Public Offerings." *Financial Management* 16, no. 2 (January): 33–38.

Milligan, John W. 1990. "Two Cheers for 144A." *Institutional Investor* 24, no. 9 (July): 117–119.

Minton, Bernadette A. 1997. "An Empirical Examination of Basic Valuation Models for Plain Vanilla U.S. Interest Rate Swaps." *Journal of Financial Economics* 44, no. 2 (May): 251–277.

Mishel, Lawrence, and Alyssa Davis. 2015. "CEO Pay Has Grown 90 Times Faster than Typical Worker Pay Since 1978." Retrieved from http://www.epi.org/publication/ceo-pay-has-grown-90-times-faster-than-typical-worker-pay-since-1978/

Modigliani, Franco, and Leah Modigliani. 1997. "Risk-Adjusted Performance." *Journal of Portfolio Management* 23, no. 2 (Winter): 45–54.

Mody, Ashoka, and Mark P. Taylor. 2003. "The High-Yield Spread as a Predictor of Real Economic Activity: Evidence of a Financial Accelerator for the United States." *IMF Staff Papers* 50, no. 3: 373–402.

Moore, Geoffrey, and John P. Cullity. 1988. "Security Markets and Business Cycles." In *The Financial Analyst's Handbook*, 2nd ed., ed. Sumner N. Levine. Homewood, IL: Dow Jones-Irwin.

Mossavar-Rahmani, Sharmin. 1988. "Customized Benchmarks in Structured Management." *Journal of Portfolio Management* 13, no. 4 (Summer): 65–68.

Mossavar-Rahmani, Sharmin. 1991. *Bond Index Funds.* Chicago: Probus.

Mossavar-Rahmani, Sharmin. 2005. "Indexing Fixed-Income Assets." In *The Handbook of Fixed-Income Securities*, 7th ed., ed. Frank J. Fabozzi. New York: McGraw-Hill.

Mossin, J. 1966. "Equilibrium in a Capital Asset Market." *Econometrica* 34, no. 4 (October): 768–783.

Mull, S. R., and L. A. Socnen. 1997. "U.S. REITs as an Asset Class in International Investment Portfolios." *Financial Analysts Journal* 53, no. 2 (March–April): 55–61.

Myers, S. L. 1973. "A Re-examination of Market and Industry Factors in Stock Price Behavior." *Journal of Finance* 28, no. 3 (June), 695–705.

Nemerever, Bill. 2010. "New World Bond Management: A Practical Framework for Decision Making." GMO White Paper (August).

Ng, Serena, and Thomas Gryta. 2017. "New Wall Street Conflict: Analysts Say 'Buy' to Win Special Access for Their Clients." *The Wall Street Journal*, January 19.

Nicholas, Joseph G. 2005. *Investing in Hedge Funds.* Princeton, NJ: Bloomberg Press.

O'Hara, Maureen, and Mao Ye. 2011. "Is Market Fragmentation Harming Market Quality?" *Journal of Financial Economics* 100, no. 3 (June): 459–474.

Odean, Terrance. 1998. "Are Investors Reluctant to Realize Their Losses?" *Journal of Finance* 53, no. 5 (October): 1775–1798.

Odean, Terrance. 1999. "Do Investors Trade Too Much?" *American Economic Review* 89 (December): 1279–1298.

Olsen, Robert A. 1998. "Behavioral Finance and Its Implications for Stock-Price Volatility." *Financial Analysts Journal* 54, no. 2 (March/April): 10–18.

Orwall, Bruce, and Joann S. Lublin. 1997. "Eisner Fires Back at Investors Who Criticize Disney's Board." *The Wall Street Journal*, February 24.

Ou, J., and S. Penman. 1989. "Financial Statement Analysis and the Prediction of Stock Returns." *Journal of Accounting and Economics*, no. 4 (November).

Palepu, Krishna, Paul Healy, and Victor Bernard. 2012. *Business Analysis and Valuation*, 5th ed. Cincinnati, OH: South-Western Publishing.

Park, H. Y., and Andrew H. Chen. 1985. "Differences between Forward and Futures Prices: A Further Investigation of Marking to Market Effects." *Journal of Futures Markets* 5, no. 7 (February): 77–88.

Park, Hail. 2015. "Dislocations in the Currency Swap and Interest Rate Swap Markets: The Case of Korea." *Journal of Futures Markets* 35, no. 5 (May): 455–475.

Pastor, Lubos, Robert F. Stambaugh, and Lucian A. Tayor. 2015. "Scale and Skill in Active Management." *Journal of Financial Economics* 116, no. 1 (April): 23–45.

Peavy, John W., III, and David A. Goodman. 1983. "The Significance of P/Es for Portfolio Returns." *Journal of Portfolio Management* 9, no. 2 (Winter): 43–47.

Perry, Kevin J., and Robert A. Taggart, Jr. 1988. "The Growing Role of Junk Bonds in Corporate Finance." *Journal of Applied Corporate Finance* 1, no. 1 (Spring): 37–45.

Petajisto, Antti. 2013. "Active Share and Mutual Fund Performance." *Financial Analysts Journal* 69, no. 4 (July–August): 73–93.

Peters, Donald J. 1991. "Valuing a Growth Stock." *Journal of Portfolio Management* 17, no. 3 (Spring): 49–51.

Pettit, R. R., and P. C. Venkatesh. 1995. "Insider Trading and Long-Run Return Performance." *Financial Management* 24, no. 2 (Summer): 88–103.

Pierce, Douglas, and Vance Roley. 1985. "Stock Prices and Economic News." *Journal of Business* 59, no. 1 (Summer): 49–67.

Porter, Michael E. 1980a. *Competitive Strategy: Techniques for Analyzing Industries and Competitors.* New York: Free Press.

Porter, Michael E. 1985. *Competitive Advantage: Creating and Sustaining Superior Performance.* New York: Free Press.

Prentice, Robert A. 2007. "Ethical Decision Making: More Needed Than Good Intentions." *Financial Analysts Journal* 63, no. 6 (November/ December): 17–30.

Ptak, Jeffrey. 2002. "Morningstar's Tax Cost Ratio Tool." Working Paper, November 21.

Quan, D. C., and S. Titman. 1997. "Commercial Real Estate Prices and Stock Market Returns: An International Analysis." *Financial Analysts Journal* 53, no. 3 (May–June): 21–34.

Ramadorai, Tarun. 2012. "The Secondary Market for Hedge Funds and the Closed Hedge Fund Premium." *Journal of Finance* 67, no. 2 (April): 479–572.

Ramanathan, Karthik. 2012. "International Bond Markets and Instruments." In *The Handbook of Fixed-Income Securities*, 8th ed., ed. Frank J. Fabozzi. New York: McGraw-Hill.

Ramnath, Sundaresh, Steve Rock, and Philip B. Shane. 2008. "The Financial Analyst Forecasting Literature: A Taxonomy with Suggestions for Further Research." *International Journal of Forecasting* 24.

Redington, F. M. 1952. "Review of the Principles of Life—Office Valuations." *Journal of the Institute of Actuaries* 78: 286–340.

Reichenstein, William. 2006. "Trends and Issues: Tax-Efficient Saving and Investing." TIAA–CREF Institute Monograph, February.

Reilly, Frank K. 1992. "Risk and Return for Art and Antiquities." University of Notre Dame Working Paper.

Reilly, Frank K., and Rashid A. Akhtar. 1995. "The Benchmark Error Problem with Global Capital Markets." *Journal of Portfolio Management* 22, no. 1 (Fall): 33–52.

Reilly, Frank K., Wenchi Kao, and David J. Wright. 1992. "Alternative Bond Market Indexes." *Financial Analysts Journal* 48, no. 3 (May–June): 44–58.

Reilly, Frank K., and Dominic R. Marshall. 1999. "Using P/E/ Growth Ratios to Select Stocks." Paper presented at Financial Management Association Meeting, Seattle, October.

Reilly, Frank K., and David J. Wright. 1988. "A Comparison of Published Betas." *Journal of Portfolio Management* 14, no. 3 (Spring): 64–69.

Reilly, Frank K., and David J. Wright. 1994. "An Analysis of High-Yield Bond Benchmarks." *Journal of Fixed Income* 3, no. 4 (March): 6–25.

Reilly, Frank K., and David J. Wright. 1997. "Introducing a Comprehensive U.S. Treasury Bond Market Benchmark." In *Yield Curve Dynamics*, ed. Ronald J. Ryan. Chicago: Glen Lake.

Reilly, Frank K., and David J. Wright. 2002. "Alternative Small-Cap Stock Benchmarks." *The Journal of Portfolio Management* 28, no. 3 (Spring): 82–95.

Reilly, Frank K., and David J. Wright. 2004. "Analysis of Risk-Adjusted Performance for Global Market Assets." *Journal of Portfolio Management* 30, no. 3 (Spring): 63–77.

Reilly, Frank K., and David J. Wright. 2012. "Bond Market Indexes." In *The Handbook of Fixed Income Securities*, 8th ed., eds. F. Fabozzi and S. Mann. New York: McGraw-Hill.

Reilly, Frank K., David J. Wright, and Kam C. Chan. 2000. "Bond Market Volatility Compared to Stock Market Volatility." *Journal of Portfolio Management* 27, no. 1 (Fall): 82–92.

Reilly, Frank A., David J. Wright, and James A. Gentry. 2009. "Historic Changes in the High Yield Market." *Journal of Applied Corporate Finance* 21, no. 3 (Summer): 65–79.

Reinganum, Marc R. 1981. "The Arbitrage Pricing Theory: Some Empirical Results." *Journal of Finance* 36, no. 2 (May): 313–321.

Reinganum, Marc R. 1983. "Portfolio Strategies Based on Market Capitalization." *Journal of Portfolio Management* 9, no. 2 (Winter).

Reinganum, Marc R. 1992. "A Revival of the Small-Firm Effect." *Journal of Portfolio Management* 18, no. 3 (Spring): 55–62.

Rendleman, Richard J., Jr., and Brit J. Bartter. 1979. "Two-State Option Pricing." *Journal of Finance* 34, no. 5 (December): 1093–1110.

Rendleman, Richard J., Jr., Charles P. Jones, and Henry A. Latané. 1982. "Empirical Anomalies Based on Unexpected Earnings and the Importance of Risk Adjustments." *Journal of Financial Economics* 10, no. 3 (November): 269–287.

Ritter, Jay R. 1991. "The Long-Run Performance of Initial Public Offerings." *Journal of Finance* 46, no. 1 (March): 3–27.

Ritter, Jay. R. 2011. "Equilibrium in the Initial Public Offering Market." *Annual Review of Financial Economics* 3.

Rogowski, Robert J., and Eric H. Sorensen. 1985. "Deregulation in Investment Banking: Shelf Registration, Structure and Performance." *Financial Management* 14, no. 1 (Spring): 5–15.

Roll, Richard. 1977a. "A Critique of the Asset Pricing Theory's Tests." *Journal of Financial Economics* 4, no. 4 (March): 129–176.

Roll, Richard. 1977b. "An Analytic Valuation Formula for Unprotected American Call Options on Stocks with Known Dividends." *Journal of Financial Economics* 5, no. 2 (November): 251–258.

Roll, Richard. 1978. "Ambiguity When Performance Is Measured by the Securities Market Line." *Journal of Finance* 33. no. 4 (September): 1051–1069.

Roll, Richard. 1980. "Performance Evaluation and Benchmark Error I." *Journal of Portfolio Management* 6, no. 4 (Summer): 5–12.

Roll, Richard. 1981. "Performance Evaluation and Benchmark Error II." *Journal of Portfolio Management* 7, no. 2 (Winter): 17–22.

Roll, Richard, and Stephen A. Ross. 1980. "An Empirical Investigation of the Arbitrage Pricing Theory." *Journal of Finance* 35, no. 5 (December): 1073–1103.

Roll, Richard, and Stephen A. Ross. 1984. "A Critical Re-examination of the Empirical Evidence on the Arbitrage Pricing Theory." *Journal of Finance* 39, no. 2 (June): 347–350.

Rosenberg, Barr, Kenneth Reid, and Ronald Lanstein. 1985. "Persuasive Evidence of Market Inefficiency." *Journal of Portfolio Management* 11, no. 3 (Spring): 9–17.

Ross, Stephen. 1976. "The Arbitrage Theory of Capital Asset Pricing." *Journal of Economic Theory* 13, no. 2 (December): 341–360.

Ross, Stephen. 1977. "Return, Risk, and Arbitrage." In *Risk and Return in Finance*, eds. I. Friend and J. Bicksler: 189–218. Cambridge, MA: Ballinger.

Rubinstein, Mark. 1985a. "Alternative Paths to Portfolio Insurance." *Financial Analysts Journal* 41, no. 4 (July–August): 42–52.

Rubinstein, Mark. 1985b. "Nonparametric Tests of Alternative Options Pricing Models Using All Reported Trades and Quotes on the 30 Most Active CBOE Options Classes from August 23, 1976, through August 31, 1978." *Journal of Finance* 40, no. 2 (June): 455–80.

Rubinstein, Mark. 1994. "Implied Binomial Trees." *Journal of Finance* 49, no. 3 (July): 771–818.

Ruffenach, Glenn. 2001. "Fewer Americans Save for Their Retirement." *The Wall Street Journal*, May 10, p. A2.

Schwert, G. William. 1989. "Why Does Stock Market Volatility Change over Time?" *Journal of Finance* 44, no. 5 (December): 1115–1153.

Scott, J., M. Stumpp, and P. Xu. 1999. "Behavioral Bias Valuation and Active Management." *Financial Analysts Journal* 55, no. 4 (July–August): 49–57.

Securities and Exchange Commission. 2011. "Work Plan for the Consideration of Incorporating International Financial Reporting Standards into the Financial Reporting System for U.S. Issuers." Staff Paper.

Sekine, Jun. 2006. "A Note on Long-Term Optimal Portfolios under Drawdown Constraints." *Advances in Applied Probability* 38, no. 3 (September): 673–692.

Shanken, Jay. 1982. "The Arbitrage Pricing Theory: Is It Testable?" *Journal of Finance* 37, no. 5 (December): 1129–1140.

Shanken, Jay. 1985. "Multivariate Tests of the Zero Beta CAPM." *Journal of Financial Economics* 14, no. 3 (September): 327–348.

Sharpe, William F. 1964. "Capital Asset Prices: A Theory of Market Equilibrium under Conditions of Risk." *Journal of Finance* 19, no. 3 (September): 425–442.

Sharpe, William F. 1966. "Mutual Fund Performance." *Journal of Business* 39, no. 1, part 2 (January): 119–138.

Sharpe, William F. 1987. "Integrated Asset Allocation." *Financial Analysts Journal* 43, no. 5 (September/October): 25–32.

Sharpe, William F. 1990. "Asset Allocation." In *Managing Investment Portfolios: A Dynamic Process*, 2nd ed., eds. John L. Maginn and Donald L. Tuttle. Boston: Warren, Gorham, & Lamont.

Sharpe, William F. 1992. "Asset Allocation: Management Style and Performance Measurement." *Journal of Portfolio Management* 18, no. 2 (Winter): 7–19.

Sharpe, William F. 1994. "The Sharpe Ratio." *Journal of Portfolio Management* 21, no. 1 (Fall): 49–59.

Sharpe, William F. 2007. *Investors and Markets: Portfolio Choices, Asset Prices, and Investment Advice*. Princeton, NJ: Princeton University Press.

Sharpe, William F., and Guy M. Cooper. 1972. "Risk–Return Classes of New York Stock Exchange Common Stocks: 1931–1967." *Financial Analysts Journal* 28, no. 2 (March–April): 46–54.

Sharpe, William. 1991. "The Arithmetic of Active Management." *Financial Analysts Journal* 47, no. 1 (January–February): 7–9.

Shefrin, Hersh, and Meir Statman. 1995. "Making Sense of Beta, Size, and Book-to-Market." *Journal of Portfolio Management* 21, no. 2 (Winter): 26–34.

Shefrin, Hersh. 1999. *Beyond Greed and Fear: Understanding Behavioral Finance and the Psychology of Investing*. Boston: Harvard Business School Press.

Shefrin, Hersh. 2001. "Behavioral Corporate Finance." *Journal of Applied Corporate Finance* 14, no. 3 (Fall): 113–124.

Shen, Pu. 1998. "Features and Risks of Treasury Inflation Protection Securities." Federal Reserve Bank of Kansas City *Economic Review* (First Quarter): 23–38.

Shiller, Robert J. 1984. "Stock Prices and Social Dynamics." *Brookings Papers on Economic Activity*, 2: 457–498. Washington, DC.

Shiu, Yung-Ming, Ging-Ginq Pan, Shu-Hui Lin, and Tu-Cheng Wu. 2010. "Impact of Net Buying Pressure on Changes in Implied Volatility: Before and after the Onset of the Subprime Crisis." *Journal of Derivatives* 17, no. 4 (Summer): 54–66.

Siegel, Jeremy J. 1991. "Does It Pay Stock Investors to Forecast the Business Cycle?" *Journal of Portfolio Management* 18, no. 1 (Fall): 27–34.

Singer, Brian. 1996. "Valuation of Portfolio Performance: Aggregate Return and Risk Analysis." *Journal of Performance Measurement* 1, no. 1 (Fall): 6–16.

Singer, Brian D., Renato Staub, and Kevin Terhaar. 2002. "Determining the Appropriate Allocation to Alternative Investments." In *Hedge Fund Management*, Charlottesville, VA: AIMR.

Skreta, V., and L. Veldkamp. 2009. "Ratings Shopping and Asset Complexity: A Theory of Ratings Inflation." *Journal of Monetary Economics* 56, no. 2.

Smith, Clifford W., Jr. 1986. "Investment Banking and the Capital Acquisition Process." *Journal of Financial Economics* 15, no. 1–2 (January–February): 3–29.

Smith, Donald J. 1989a. "The Arithmetic of Financial Engineering." *Journal of Applied Corporate Finance* 1, no. 4 (Winter): 49–58.

Smith, Donald J. 1989b. "The Calculation and Use of Money Market Implied Forward Rates." *Journal of Cash Management* 98, no. 5 (September/October): 46–49.

Smith, Donald J. 2011. *Bond Math*. Hoboken, NJ: John Wiley.

Solomon, Ezra. 1963. *The Theory of Financial Management*. New York: Columbia University Press.

Solt, Michael, and Meir Statman. 1989. "Good Companies, Bad Stocks." *Journal of Portfolio Management* 15, no. 4 (Summer): 39–44.

Sondhi, Ashwinpaul C., ed. 1995. *Credit Analysis of Nontraditional Debt Securities*. Charlottesville, VA: AIMR.

Sorensen, Eric H., Keith L. Miller, and Vele Samak. 1998. "Allocating between Active and Passive Management." *Financial Analysts Journal* 54, no. 4 (September/October): 18–31.

Sortino, Frank A., and Lee N. Price. 1994. "Performance Measurement in a Downside Risk Framework." *Journal of Investing* 3, no. 3 (Fall): 59–65.

Stambaugh, Robert. 1982. "On the Exclusion of Assets from Tests of the Two-Parameter Model: A Sensitivity Analysis." *Journal of Financial Economics* 10, no. 4 (November): 237–268.

Statman, Meir. 1987. "How Many Stocks Make a Diversified Portfolio?" *Journal of Financial and Quantitative Analysis* 22, no. 3 (September): 353–363.

Statman, Meir. 2009. "Regulating Financial Markets: Protecting Us from Ourselves and Others." *Financial Analysts Journal* 65, no. 3 (May/June): 22–31.

Stickney, Clyde P., Paul Brown, and James Wahlen. 2007. *Financial Reporting and Statement Analysis*, 6th ed. Mason, OH: South-Western.

Stoll, Hans R. 1969. "The Relationship between Put and Call Option Prices." *Journal of Finance* 24, no. 5 (December): 801–824.

Stoll, Hans R., and Robert E. Whaley. 1983. "Transaction Costs and the Small Firm Effect." *Journal of Financial Economics* 12 no. 1: 57–79.

Sun, Tong-sheng, Suresh Sundaresan, and Ching Wang. 1993. "Interest Rate Swaps: An Empirical Investigation." *Journal of Financial Economics* 34, no. 1 (August): 77–99.

Sundaresan, Suresh. 2009. *Fixed-Income Markets and Their Derivatives*, 3rd ed. San Diego, CA: Academic Press.

Terhaar, Kevin. 2001. "Return, Risk, and Performance Attribution." In *Benchmarks and Attribution Analysis*, ed. Katrina Sherrerd. Charlottesville, VA: AIMR.

Thompson, Donald J., II. 1976. "Sources of Systematic Risk in Common Stocks." *Journal of Business* 49, no. 2 (April): 173–188.

Tobin, James. 1958. "Liquidity Preference as Behavior towards Risk." *Review of Economic Studies* 25, no. 2 (February): 65–85.

Tole, Thomas. 1982. "You Can't Diversify without Diversifying." *Journal of Portfolio Management* 8, no. 2 (Winter): 5–11.

Treynor, Jack L. 1965. "How to Rate Management of Investment Funds." *Harvard Business Review* 43, no. 1 (January–February): 63–75.

Van Horne, James C. 2001. *Financial Market Rates and Flows*, 6th ed. Englewood Cliffs, NJ: Prentice Hall.

Vine, Allen A. 2001. "High-Yield Analysis of Emerging Markets Debt." In *The Handbook of Fixed-Income Securities*, 6th ed., ed. Frank J. Fabozzi. New York: McGraw-Hill.

Volpert, Kenneth E. 2012. "Introduction to Bond Portfolio Management." In *The Handbook of Fixed Income Securities*, 8th ed., eds. F. Fabozzi and S. Mann. New York: McGraw-Hill.

Voya Investment Management. 2017. *An Overview of Private Equity Investing*. New York: Voya Investments Distributor LLC.

Weigel, Eric J. 1991. "The Performance of Tactical Asset Allocation." *Financial Analysts Journal* 47, no. 5 (September–October): 63–70.

Whaley, Robert E. 1981. "On the Valuation of American Call Options on Stocks with Known Dividends." *Journal of Financial Economics* 9, no. 2 (June): 207–212.

Whaley, Robert E. 1993. "Derivatives on Market Volatility: Hedging Tools Long Overdue." *Journal of Derivatives* 1 (Fall): 71–84.

Womack, Kent L. 1996. "Do Brokerage Analysts' Recommendations Have Investment Value?" *Journal of Finance* 51, no. 1 (March): 137–167.

Wommack, William. W. 1979. "The Board's Most Important Function." *Harvard Business Review* 57 (September): 48–55.

Wood, Arnold S., ed. 2010. *Behavioral Finance and Investment Management*. Charlottesville, VA: Research Foundation of CFA Institute.

Xiong, James X., Roger G. Ibbotson, Thomas M. Idzorek, and Peng Chen. 2010. "The Equal Importance of Asset Allocation and Active Management." *Financial Analysts Journal* 66, no. 2 (March/April): 22–30.

Zhang, Chu. 2009. "Testing the APT with the Maximum Sharpe Ratio of Extracted Factors." *Management Science* 55, no. 7 (July): 1255–1266.

Zweig, Jason. 2017. "Put a Fork in Stock Pickers." *The Wall Street Journal*, May 13–14.

Zweig, Martin E. 1987. *Understanding Technical Forecasting*. New York: Dow Jones.

Zweig, Martin E. 2000. "You Get the Clients You Deserve." In *Ethical Issues for Today's Firm*. Charlottesville, VA: AIMR.

Glossary

A

Abnormal rate of return The amount by which a security's actual return differs from its expected rate of return, which is based on the market's rate of return and the security's relationship with the market.

Accrued interest The interest that has accumulated on a bond since the last coupon payment date.

Accumulation phase Phase in the investment life cycle during which individuals in the early to middle years of their working career attempt to accumulate assets to satisfy short-term needs and longer term goals.

Active share A statistical measure that establishes the degree of active management in an investment portfolio.

Agency conflict An ethical problem that can arise any time one person (i.e., agent) is hired to perform a service or act in the interest of another (i.e., principal).

Algorithmic trading Trading carried out based upon computer programs (algorithms) that specify trading instructions determined by either fundamental events (e.g., earning announcements or earning revisions) or technical signals (momentum patterns or other technical rules). Trades implemented using the computer algorithms can react significantly faster than human traders—the algorithmic traders can be in and out of a stock in micro-seconds. The result is higher trading volume but also the potential for greater volatility (see "Flash Crash").

Alpha A term commonly used to describe a manager's abnormal rate of return, which is the difference between the return the portfolio actually produced and the expected return given its risk level.

Alternative asset A nontraditional (i.e., not common stocks or bonds) asset class investment, including hedge funds, private equity, real estate, and commodities.

Alternative trading system (ATS) A nontraditional, computerized trading system that competes with or supplements dealer markets and traditional stock exchanges. They are typically crossing networks in which buy and sell orders are matched and executed at a single price. While they facilitate trading in shares, they do not provide listing services.

American Depository Receipts (ADRs) Certificates of ownership issued by a U.S. bank that represent indirect ownership of a certain number of shares of a specific foreign firm. Shares are held on deposit in a bank in the firm's home country.

American options An option contract that can be exercised at any time until its expiration date.

Anomalies Security price relationships that appear to contradict a well-regarded hypothesis—in this case, the efficient market hypothesis.

Arbitrage A trading strategy designed to generate a guaranteed profit from a transaction that requires no capital commitment or risk bearing on the part of the trader. A simple example of an arbitrage trade would be the simultaneous purchase and sale of the same security in different markets at different prices.

Arbitrage pricing theory (APT) A theory that posits that the expected return to a financial asset can be described by its relationship with several common risk factors. The multifactor APT can be contrasted with the single-factor CAPM.

Arithmetic mean (AM) A measure of mean annual rates of return equal to the sum of annual holding period rates of return divided by the number of years.

Asset allocation The process of deciding how to distribute an investor's wealth among different asset classes for investment purposes.

Asset-backed securities (ABS) Securitized debt that can be backed by a range of assets beyond the traditional mortgage assets. The other assets include car loans, credit card debt, student loans, or home equity loans.

Asset class Securities that have similar characteristics, attributes, and risk/return relationships.

Asset-liability management A matched-funding approach to portfolio management where the characteristics (e.g., cash flow amount, duration) of the assets are coordinated with those of the liabilities that the investor faces.

Assets under management (AUM) The total market value of the assets managed by an investment firm.

At the money A special case of an option where the exercise price and the price of the underlying asset are identical.

Attribution analysis An assessment technique designed to establish whether a manager's performance relative to a benchmark resulted from market timing or security selection skills.

Autocorrelation tests A test of the efficient market hypothesis that compares security price changes over time to check for predictable correlation patterns.

B

Backwardated A situation in a futures market where the current contract price is less than the current spot price for the underlying asset.

Balanced funds A mutual fund with, generally, a three-part investment objective: (1) to conserve the investor's principal, (2) to pay current income, and (3) to increase both principal and income. The fund aims to achieve this by owning a mixture of bonds, preferred stocks, and common stocks.

Basis The difference between the spot price of the underlying asset and the futures contract price at any point in time (e.g., the *initial* basis at the time of contract origination, the *cover* basis at the time of contract termination).

Basis point value (BPV) A measure of the dollar change in the price of a bond induced by a one basis point change (for example, from 5.00 percent to 4.99 percent) in the yield to a maturity.

Basis risk The residual exposure to the price volatility of an underlying asset that results from a cross hedge transaction.

Bearer bond An unregistered bond for which ownership is determined by possession. The holder receives interest payments by clipping coupons attached to the security and sending them to the issuer for payment.

Behavioral finance Involves the analysis of various psychological traits of individuals and how these traits affect how they act as investors, analysts, and portfolio managers.

Benchmark error Situation where an inappropriate or incorrect benchmark is used to compare and assess portfolio returns and management.

Benchmark portfolio A comparison standard of risk and assets included in the policy statement and similar to the investor's risk preference and investment needs, which can be used to evaluate the investment performance of the portfolio manager.

Best efforts offering An initial public offering that only commits the investment bank to use its best effort to find investors for the new shares.

Beta A standardized measure of systematic risk based upon an asset's covariance with the market portfolio.

Binomial option pricing model A valuation equation that assumes the price of the underlying asset changes through a series of discrete upward or downward movements.

Black-Scholes model A valuation equation that assumes the price of the underlying asset changes continuously through the option's expiration date by a statistical process known as *geometric Brownian motion.*

Bond ladder A strategy for managing a fixed-income portfolio where the investment funds are divided evenly among bonds that mature at regular intervals surrounding the desired time horizon.

Bond swap An active bond portfolio management strategy that exchanges one position for another to take advantage of some difference between them.

Bottom-up approach An approach to security analysis that starts at the company level, in contrast to top-down analysis that starts at the aggregate market level.

Breakeven time It measures how long the higher interest income from the convertible bond must persist to make up for the difference between the price of the bond and its conversion value.

Business cycle The period of time from which an economy's output of goods and services peaks, contracts, recovers to reach the prior peak (recovery), and then grows further (expansion).

Business risk The variability of operating income arising from the characteristics of the firm's industry. Two sources of business risk are sales variability and operating leverage.

Buy-and-hold A passive portfolio management strategy in which securities (bonds or stocks) are bought and held to maturity.

Buy-side Firms that assist individuals and institutions to invest their capital. Examples include mutual funds, hedge funds, trust companies, pension funds, and endowments.

C

Call markets A market in which trading for individual stocks only takes place at specified times. All the bids and asks available at the time are combined and the market administrators specify a single price that will possibly clear the market at that time.

Call option Option to buy an asset within a certain period at a specified price called the *exercise price.*

Call premium Amount above par that an issuer must pay to a bondholder for retiring the bond before its stated maturity.

Capital allocation How a firm's management uses resources to create value for shareholders, including mergers and acquisitions, investing in new projects, paying dividends, and repurchasing shares.

Capital appreciation A return objective in which the investor seeks to increase the portfolio value, primarily through capital gains, over time to meet a future need rather than dividend yield.

Capital asset pricing model (CAPM) A theory concerned with deriving the expected or required rates of return on risky assets based on the assets' systematic risk relative to a single market-wide portfolio.

Capital market line (CML) The line from the intercept point that represents the risk-free rate tangent to the original efficient frontier; it becomes the new efficient frontier since investments on this line dominate all the portfolios on the original Markowitz efficient frontier.

Capital preservation A return objective in which the investor seeks to minimize the risk of loss; generally a goal of the risk-averse investor.

Certificates of deposit (CDs) Instruments issued by banks and S&Ls that require minimum deposits for specified terms and that pay higher rates of interest than deposit accounts.

Characteristic line Regression line that indicates the systematic risk (beta) of a risky asset.

Closed-end investment company An investment company that issues only a limited number of shares, which it does not redeem (buy back). Instead, shares of a closed-end fund are traded in securities markets at prices determined by supply and demand.

Coefficient of variation (CV) A measure of relative variability that indicates risk per unit of return. It is equal to: standard deviation divided by the mean value. When used in investments, it is equal to: standard deviation of returns divided by the expected rate of return.

Collar agreement A hedging arrangement where an underlying asset is protected against decreases in value by the simultaneous purchase of a put option and sale of a call option.

Collateralized debt obligations (CDOs)   Considered part of the asset-backed securities (ABSs) market because they are backed by the cash flows from a portfolio of securities. In contrast to the specific securities such as mortgages, credit card debt, and auto loans, CDOs are unique because they will generally include a variety of debt with a diversity of credit ratings. Finally, there are typically several tranches with different credit ratings from AAA to non-investment grade.

Collateralized mortgage obligations (CMOs)   A debt security based on a pool of mortgage loans that provides a relatively predictable term by paying of tranches in specified order.

Commission brokers   Employees of a member firm who buy or sell securities for the customers of the firm.

Common stock   An equity investment that represents ownership of a firm, with full participation in its success or failure. The firm's directors must approve dividend payments.

Competitive bid   An underwriting alternative wherein an issuing entity (governmental body or a corporation) specifies the type of security to be offered (bonds or stocks) and the general characteristics of the issue, and the issuer solicits bids from competing investment banking firms with the understanding that the issuer will accept the highest bid from the bankers.

Completely diversified portfolio   A portfolio in which all unsystematic risk has been eliminated by diversification.

Completeness funds   A specialized index used to form the basis of a passive portfolio whose purpose is to provide diversification to a client's total portfolio by excluding those segments in which the client's active managers invest.

Consolidation phase   Phase in the investment life cycle during which individuals who are typically past the midpoint of their career have earnings that exceed expenses and invest them for future retirement or estate planning needs.

Constant growth model   An approach to valuing stocks that assumes cash flows will grow at a constant rate. Also known as the Gordon Growth Model, this formula represents a growing perpetuity.

Contango   A situation in a futures market where the current contract price is greater than the current spot price for the underlying asset.

Contingent, deferred sales loads   A mutual fund that imposes a sales charge when the investor sells or redeems shares; also referred to as *rear-end loads* or *redemption charges*.

Continuous market   A market where stocks are priced and traded continuously by an auction process or by dealers when the market is open.

Contract price   The transaction price specified in a forward or futures contract.

Contrarian   An investment strategy that attempts to buy (or sell) securities on which the majority of other investors are bearish (or bullish).

Convenience yield   An adjustment made to the theoretical forward or futures contract delivery price to account for the preference that consumers have for holding spot positions in the underlying asset.

Conversion factors   The adjustments made to Treasury bond futures contract terms to allow for the delivery of an instrument other than the standardized underlying asset.

Conversion premium   The excess of the market value of the convertible security over its equity value if immediately converted into common stock. Typically expressed as a percentage of the equity value.

Conversion parity price   The price at which common stock can be obtained by surrendering the convertible instrument at par value.

Conversion ratio   The number of shares of common stock for which a convertible security may be exchanged.

Convertible bonds   A bond with the added feature that the bondholder has the option to turn the bond back to the firm in exchange for a specified number of common shares of the firm.

Convexity   A measure of the degree to which a bond's price-yield curve departs from a straight line. This characteristic affects estimates of a bond's price volatility for a given change in yields.

Core-plus   Bond portfolio management that places a significant part of the available funds in a passively managed portfolio of highgrade securities that broadly reflects the overall bond market; this is the "core" of the strategy.

Corporate governance   The rules, policies, and procedures that are used to direct and control a company.

Correlation coefficient   A standardized measure of the relationship between two variables that ranges from −1.00 to +1.00.

Cost of carry   The net amount that would be required to store a commodity or security for future delivery, usually calculated as physical storage costs plus financial capital costs less dividends paid to the underlying asset.

Counterparties   The participants to a derivative transaction.

Country risk   Uncertainty due to the possibility of major political or economic change in the country where an investment is located; also called *political risk*.

Coupon   Indicates the interest payment on a debt security. It is the coupon rate times the par value that indicates the interest payments on a debt security.

Coupon reinvestment risk   The component of interest rate risk due to the uncertainty of the rate at which coupon payments will be reinvested.

Covariance   A measure of the degree to which two variables, such as rates of return for investment assets, move together over time relative to their individual mean returns.

Covered call   A trading strategy in which a call option is sold as a supplement to a long position in an underlying asset or portfolio of assets.

Covered interest arbitrage   A trading strategy involving borrowing money in one country and lending it to another designed to exploit price deviations from the interest rate parity model.

Credit analysis   An active bond portfolio management strategy designed to identify bonds that are expected to experience changes in rating. This strategy is critical when investing in high-yield bonds.

Credit default swap (CDS)   An agreement in which the protection buyer makes periodic premium payments in exchange for the protection seller's obligation to make a settlement payment that is contingent on the occurrence of a credit-related event to a predetermined reference entity, usually a specific bond or bond index.

Cross hedge A trading strategy in which the price volatility of a commodity or security position is hedged with a forward or futures contract based on a different underlying asset or different settlement terms.

Crossover price The price at which the yield to maturity equals the yield to call. Above this price, yield to call is the appropriate yield measure; below this price, yield to maturity is the appropriate yield measure.

Current income A return objective in which the investor seeks to generate income rather than capital gains. This is generally a goal of an investor who wants to supplement earnings with income to meet living expenses.

Current yield A bond's yield as measured by its current income (coupon) as a percentage of its market price.

Cyclical company A firm whose earnings rise and fall with general economic activity.

Cyclical stock A stock with a high beta; its gains typically exceed those of a rising market and its losses typically exceed those of a falling market.

D

Date of record The date on which you must be listed as the owner of a stock share in order to receive the dividend payment.

Dealer market A market where individual dealers provide liquidity for investors by buying and selling the shares of stock for themselves.

Declaration date The date that a dividend is announced by the board of directors.

Dedication A portfolio management technique in which the portfolio's cash flows are used to retire a set of liabilities over time.

Dedication with reinvestment A dedication strategy in which portfolio cash flows may precede their corresponding liabilities. Such cash flows can be reinvested to earn a return until the date the liability is due to be paid.

Default risk The possibility that a bond issuer will not be able to fulfill its obligation to make required coupon or principal payments.

Defensive companies Firms whose future earnings are likely to withstand an economic downturn.

Defensive stock A stock whose return is not expected to decline as much as that of the overall market during a bear market (a beta less than one).

Delta The change in the price of the option with respect to a one dollar change in the price of the underlying asset; this is the option's *hedge ratio,* or the number of units of the underlying asset that can be hedged by a single option contract.

Demographics The statistical characteristics of a group of people that describe factors such as age, ethnic mix, and income.

Derivative security An instrument whose market value ultimately depends upon, or derives from, the value of a more fundamental investment vehicle called the underlying asset or security.

Disclosure statute Securities laws where the SEC simply ensures that the issuing firm has disclosed all necessary information so that an investor can fairly make an informed decision.

Discount A bond selling at a price below par value due to capital market conditions.

Discounted cash flow analysis A method of valuing a security in which future cash flows are estimated and then discounted at the appropriate cost of capital to reach today's value.

Diversification An investment technique that reduces risk by allocating investments among a wide variety of financial instruments, sectors, or factor characteristics.

Dividend discount model (DDM) A technique for estimating the value of a stock issue as the present value of all future dividends.

Downside risk The volatility in a portfolio based on returns that fall below a minimum acceptable threshold level, which is specified by the investor.

Duration A measure of the interest rate sensitivity of a bond's market price taking into consideration its coupon and term to maturity; the percent change in price for 100-basis point change in yield.

E

Earnings momentum A strategy in which portfolios are constructed of stocks of firms with rising earnings.

Earnings surprise A company announcement of earnings that differ from analysts' prevailing expectations.

EBITDA Earnings before interest, taxes, depreciation, and amortization.

Effective duration Direct measure of the interest rate sensitivity of a bond (or any financial instrument) based upon price changes derived from a pricing model.

Efficient capital market A market in which security prices rapidly reflect all information about securities.

Efficient frontier The set of portfolios that has the maximum rate of return for every given level of risk, or the minimum risk for every potential rate of return.

Electronic Communication Network (ECN) A computerized trading system that matches buy and sell orders, usually for retail and small institutional trading. ECNs act for customers as a broker— they do not buy or sell from their own accounts. Put another way, they are electronic order books without designated market makers.

Enhanced indexing A portfolio management strategy that attempts to outperform a designated benchmark on a risk-adjusted basis by combining passive (i.e., indexed) and active management approaches.

Environmental, social, and governance (ESG) Factors that a socially conscious investor may consider prior to making an investment.

Equity collar An option-based hedging strategy that protects a stock position from price declines by purchasing a put option that is paid for by the sale of a call option.

Equity multiples A tool used to value the equity of a company; the multiple is used to describe how many times earnings or book value must be multiplied in order to calculate the value of the equity.

Equity swap   A derivative transaction in which one cash flow is tied to the return to an equity portfolio position, often an index such as the Standard and Poor's 500, while the other is based on a floating-rate index.

Estimated rate of return   The rate of return an investor anticipates earning from a specific investment over a particular future holding period.

Eurobonds   Bonds denominated in a currency not native to the country in which they are issued.

European option   An option contract that can only be exercised on its expiration date.

Ex-dividend date   The day on which the stock starts trading without the right to the dividend.

Exchange clearinghouse   The functional unit attached to a futures exchange that guarantees contract performance, oversees delivery, serves as a bookkeeper, and calculates settlement transactions.

Exchange rate risk   Uncertainty due to the denomination of an investment in a currency other than that of the investor's own country.

Exchange traded fund (ETF)   A tradable depository receipt that gives investors a pro rata claim to the returns associated with a portfolio of securities (often designed to mimic an index, such as the Standard and Poor's 500) held in trust by a financial institution.

Exercise price   The transaction price specified in an option contract; also known as the *strike price*.

Expected rate of return   The return that analysts' calculations suggest a security should provide, based on the market's rate of return during the period and the security's relationship to the market.

Expense ratio   The percentage of a fund's assets deducted annually for expenses, including management fees, administrative fees, and operating costs, but not including security trading fees.

F

Factor investing   An investment strategy that forms portfolios to emphasize security charateristics (relative value, market capitalization, systematic risk, momentum) instead of traditional asset class definitions.

Fiduciary   A person who supervises or oversees the investment portfolio of a third party, such as in a trust account, and makes investment decisions in accordance with the owner's wishes.

Financial risk   The variability of future income arising from the firm's fixed financing costs, for example, interest payments. The effect of fixed financial costs is to magnify the effect of changes in operating profit on net income or earnings per share.

Firm commitment   An agreement between an investment bank and a company issuing shares in which the bank commits to purchasing the shares at an agreed upon price and has the risk of reselling the shares to investors.

Flash crash   A major decline in stock prices that occurred on May 6, 2010, caused by a group of sell transactions imbedded in an algorithmic trading program. The sudden decline caused several other trading programs to withdraw from the market that resulted in significant illiquidity and the crash.

Flat price   The difference between the total invoice price of a bond and the amount of the accrued interest.

Flexible portfolio   Mutual fund that allows managers to shift assets between stocks, bonds, and cash according to changing market conditions; also known as *asset allocation* fund.

Floating-rate note (FRN)   Short- to intermediate-term bonds with regularly scheduled coupon payments linked to a variable interest rate, most often LIBOR.

Forward contract   An agreement between two counterparties that requires the exchange of a commodity or security at a fixed time in the future at a predetermined price.

Forward discount   A situation where, from the perspective of the domestic country, the spot exchange rate is smaller than the forward exchange rate with a foreign country.

Forward multiple   A measure for estimating the value of the equity or enterprise value based on next year's earnings or EBITDA or other metric, as opposed to last year's earnings or EBITDA or other metric.

Forward rate   A short-term yield for a future holding period implied by the spot rates of two securities with different maturities.

Forward premium   A situation where, from the perspective of the domestic country, the spot exchange rate is larger than the forward exchange rate with a foreign country.

Forward rate agreement (FRA)   A transaction in which two counterparties agree to a single exchange of cash flows based on a fixed and floating rate, respectively.

Free cash flow to equity (FCFE)   This cash flow measure equals cash flow from operations minus capital expenditures and debt payments.

Free cash flow to the firm (FCFF)   Cash flow that remains after running a business, reinvesting in the long-term assets or the business and the net working capital; this remaining cash flow can be distributed to the providers of capital.

Full replication   A technique for constructing a passive index portfolio in which all securities in an index are purchased in proportion to their weights in the index.

Fundamental multiples   A measure used to value the equity of firm value that is based on underlying fundamental factors such as growth, profit margins, and return on equity.

Futures contracts   An agreement that provides for the future exchange of a particular asset at a specified delivery date in exchange for a specified payment at the time of delivery.

G

General obligation bonds (GOs)   A municipal issue serviced from and guaranteed by the issuer's full taxing authority.

Geometric mean (GM)   The nth root of the product of the annual holding period returns for *n* years minus 1.

Gifting phase   Phase in the investment life cycle during which individuals use excess assets to financially assist relatives or friends, establish charitable trusts, or construct trusts to minimize estate taxes.

Global Investment Performance Standards (GIPS)   A definitive set of standards for reporting investment performance.

Government sponsored enterprises (GSEs)   Entities set up by the government to provide support for specific segments of the economy considered important by the government. Examples are the Federal National Mortgage Association (Fannie Mae) and Federal Home Loan Corporation (Freddie Mac).

Gross spread   Compensation received by the underwriting in an IPO that is equal to the price per share that new investors pay for stock minus the amount per share that the issuing company receives; also known as the underwriting spread.

Growth companies   Firms with the management ability and opportunities to consistently make investments that yield returns that are greater than the firm's required cost of capital.

Growth duration model   A way to calculate how much longer a company must grow at a particular rate to justify paying a higher multiple than the investor would pay for a slower growing company or market index.

Growth stock   A stock issue that generates a higher rate of return than other stocks in the market with similar risk characteristics.

H

Hedge   A trading strategy in which derivative securities are used to reduce or completely offset a counterparty's risk exposure to an underlying asset.

Hedge fund   An investment vehicle designed to manage a private, unregistered portfolio of assets according to any of several strategies. The investment strategy often employs arbitrage trading and significant financial leverage (e.g., short selling, borrowing, derivatives), while the compensation arrangement for the manager typically specifies considerable profit participation.

Hedge ratio   The number of derivative contracts that must be transacted to offset the price volatility of an underlying commodity or security position.

High Frequency Trading (HFT)   Numerous short term trades by firms or institutions that are initiated and determined by computer algorithms as discussed under "algorithmic trading." The result can be thousands of daily trades with round trip transactions completed in microseconds.

High-yield bonds   A bond rated below investment grade; also referred to as *speculative-grade bonds* or *junk bonds*.

Holding period return (HPR)   The total return from an investment, including all sources of income, for a given period of time. A value of 1.0 indicates no gain or loss. Equal to ending wealth/beginning wealth.

Holding period yield (HPY)   The total return from an investment for a given period of time stated as a percentage; equal to HPR-1.

Holdings-based measure   A performance measure based on how a manager changes the portfolio's security holdings over time, often in comparison to a benchmark portfolio.

Horizon yield   The expected rate of return of a bond that you anticipate selling prior to its maturity.

I

Immunization   A bond portfolio management technique of matching modified duration to the investment horizon of the portfolio to eliminate interest rate risk.

Implied forward rate   An estimate of the future interest rate over a maturity of N years that is based on the relationship between current interest rates for maturities of T and T+N years.

Implied volatility   The standard deviation of changes in the price of the underlying asset that can be inferred from an option's market price in relation to a specific valuation model.

In the money   An option that has positive intrinsic value.

Index funds   An investment portfolio designed to mimic the exact composition of an underlying index, such as the S&P 500.

Indexing   A passive bond portfolio management strategy that seeks to match the composition, and therefore the performance, of a selected market index.

Indications of interest   The state of telling the underwriter how many shares he or she is willing to purchase at particular prices.

Informationally efficient market   A more technical term for an efficient capital market that emphasizes the role of information in setting the market price.

Information ratio   Statistic used to measure a portfolio's average return in excess of a comparison, benchmark portfolio divided by the standard deviation of this excess return.

Initial public offerings (IPOs)   A new issue by a firm that has no existing public market.

Interest rate anticipation   An active bond portfolio management strategy designed to preserve capital or take advantage of capital gains opportunities by predicting interest rates and their effects on bond prices.

Interest rate parity   The relationship that must exist in an efficient market between the spot and forward foreign exchange rates between two countries and the interest rates in those countries.

Interest rate risk   The uncertainty of returns on an investment due to possible changes in interest rates over time.

Interest rate swap   An agreement calling for the periodic exchange of cash flows, one based on an interest rate that remains fixed for the life of the contract and the other that is linked to a variable-rate index.

Intermarket Trading System (ITS)   A computerized system that connects competing exchanges and dealers who trade stocks listed on an exchange. Its purpose is to help customers find the best market for these stocks at a point in time.

Internal rate of return (IRR)   The discount rate at which cash outflows of an investment equal cash inflows.

Intrinsic value   The portion of a call option's total value equal to the greater of either zero or the difference between the current value of the underlying asset and the exercise price; for a put option, intrinsic value is the greater of either zero or the exercise price less the underlying asset price; for a stock, it is the value derived from fundamental analysis of the stock's expected returns or cash flows.

Investment   The current commitment of dollars for a period of time in order to derive future payments that will compensate the investor for the time the funds are committed, the expected rate of inflation, and the uncertainty of future payments.

Investment company   A firm that sells shares of the company and uses the proceeds to buy portfolios of stock, bonds, or other financial instruments.

Investment horizon The time period used for planning and forecasting purposes or the future time at which the investor requires the invested funds.

Investment management company A company separate from the investment company that manages the portfolio and performs administrative functions.

Investment strategy A decision by a portfolio manager regarding how he or she will manage the portfolio to meet the goals and objectives of the client. This will include either active or passive management and, if active, what style in terms of top-down or bottom-up or fundamental versus technical.

J

J-curve effect The tendency for the returns to private equity funds to be negative initially and then positive in later years as the more profitable investments are realized.

January effect A frequent empirical anomaly where risk-adjusted stock returns in the month of January are significantly larger than those occurring in any other month of the year.

Jensen measure An absolute measure of a portfolio's risk-adjusted performance, computed as the intercept in a regression equation where the excess returns to a manager's portfolio and the market index are, respectively, the dependent and independent variables.

L

Limit order An order that lasts for a specified time to buy or sell a security when and if it trades at a specified price.

Limited partnership A business organization with one or more general partners who manage the business and assume legal debts and obligations, and one or more limited partners who are liable only to the extent of their investments.

Liquidity Term used to describe an asset that can be quickly converted to cash at a price close to fair market value.

Liquidity risk Uncertainty due to the ability to buy or sell an investment in the secondary market.

Long hedge A long position in a forward or futures contract used to offset the price volatility of a short position in the underlying asset.

Long position The buyer of a commodity or security or, for a forward contract, the counterparty who will be the eventual buyer of the underlying asset.

Low-load fund A mutual fund that imposes a moderate front-end sales charge when the investor buys the fund, typically 3 to 4 percent.

M

Macaulay duration A measure of the time flow of cash from a bond where cash flows are weighted by present values discounted by the yield to maturity.

Maintenance margin The required proportion that the investor's equity value must be to the total market value of the stock. If the proportion drops below this percent, the investor will receive a margin call.

Management and advisory firm A firm that provides a range of services from standard banking transactions (savings accounts, personal loans) to advising individual and institutional investors on structuring their portfolios and managing investment funds.

Management fee The compensation an investment company pays to the investment management company for its services. The average annual fee is about 0.5 percent of fund assets.

Margin The percent of the total cost a buyer pays in cash for a security, borrowing the balance from the broker. This introduces leverage, which increases the risk of the transaction.

Margin account The collateral posted with the futures exchange clearinghouse by an outside counterparty to insure its eventual performance; the *initial* margin is the deposit required at contract origination while the *maintenance* margin is the minimum collateral necessary at all times.

Margin call A request by an investor's broker for additional capital for a security bought on margin if the investor's equity value declines below the required maintenance margin.

Marked to market The settlement process used to adjust the margin account of a futures contract for daily changes in the price of the underlying asset.

Market The means through which buyers and sellers are brought together to aid in the transfer of goods and/or services.

Market order An order to buy or sell a security immediately at the best price available.

Market portfolio The portfolio that includes all risky assets with relative weights equal to their proportional market values.

Market risk premium The amount of return above the risk-free rate that investors expect from the market in general as compensation for systematic risk.

Mean rates of return The average of an investment's returns over an extended period of time.

Mean-variance optimization An approach to forming portfolios in which the investor seeks to minimize portfolio risk for a given expected (mean) return goal.

Modified duration A measure of Macaulay duration divided by one plus the bond's periodic yield used to approximate the bond's price volatility.

Money market The market for short-term debt securities with maturities of less than one year.

Money market fund A fund that invests in short-term securities sold in the money market. (Large companies, banks, and other institutions also invest their surplus cash in the money market for short periods of time.) In the entire investment spectrum, these are generally the safest, most stable securities available. They include Treasury bills, certificates of deposit of large banks, and commercial paper (short-term IOUs of large corporations).

Money-weighted return The discount rate that sets the present value of a future set of cash flows equal to the investment's current value; also known as the *internal rate of return*.

Moving average The continually recalculating average of security prices for a period, often 200 days, to serve as an indication of the general trend of prices and also as a benchmark price.

Multifactor model An empirical version of the APT where the investor chooses the exact number and identity of the common risk factors used to describe an asset's risk-return relationship. Risk factors are often designated as *macroeconomic* variables (e.g., inflation, changes in gross domestic product) or *microeconomic* variables (e.g., security-specific characteristics like firm size or book-to-market ratios).

Mutual fund An investment company that pools money from shareholders and invests in a variety of securities, including stocks, bonds, and money market securities. A mutual fund ordinarily stands ready to buy back (redeem) its shares at their current net asset value, which depends on the market value of the fund's portfolio of securities at the time. Mutual funds generally continuously offer new shares to investors.

N

National Association of Securities Dealers Automated Quotation (Nasdaq) system An electronic system for providing bid-ask quotes on OTC securities.

Negotiated sales An underwriting arrangement wherein the sale of a security issue by an issuing entity (governmental body or a corporation) is done using an investment banking firm that maintains an ongoing relationship with the issuer. The characteristics of the security issue are determined by the issuer in consultation with the investment banker.

Net asset value (*NAV*) The market value of an investment company's assets (securities, cash, and any accrued earnings) after deducting liabilities, divided by the number of shares outstanding.

Net present value (NPV) A measure of the excess cash flows expected from an investment proposal. It is equal to the present value of the cash *inflows* from an investment proposal, discounted at the required rate of return for the investment, minus the present value of the cash *outflows* required by the investment, also discounted at the investment's required rate of return. If the derived net present value is a positive value (i.e., there is an excess net present value), the investment should be acquired since it will provide a rate of return above its required returns.

New issue Common stocks or bonds offered by companies for public sale.

No-load fund A mutual fund that sells its shares at net asset value without adding sales charges.

Normal portfolio A specialized or customized benchmark constructed to evaluate a specific manager's investment style or philosophy.

Notional principal The principal value of a swap transaction, which is not exchanged but is used as a scale factor to translate interest rate differentials into cash settlement payments.

O

Objectives The investor's goals expressed in terms of risk and return and included in the policy statement.

130/30 strategy An active equity portfolio management approach that allows short positions up to a certain percentage (e.g., 30) of capital and an equal percentage of leveraged long positions.

Open-end investment company The more formal name for a mutual fund, which derives from the fact that it continuously offers new shares to investors and redeems them (buys them back) on demand.

Opportunity cost The expected return on the next best alternative to the investment that was actually made.

Optimal portfolio The portfolio on the efficient frontier that has the highest utility for a given investor. It lies at the point of tangency between the efficient frontier and the curve with the investor's highest possible utility.

Option-adjusted spread (OAS) A type of yield spread that considers changes in the term structure and alternative estimates of the volatility of interest rates. It is spread after adjusting for embedded options.

Option contract An agreement that grants the owner the right, but not the obligation, to make a future transaction in an underlying commodity or security at a fixed price and within a predetermined time in the future.

Option premium The initial price that the option buyer must pay to the option seller to acquire the contract.

Options Clearing Corporation (OCC) A company designed to guarantee, monitor margin accounts, and settle exchange-traded option transactions.

Out of the money An option that has no intrinsic value.

Overallotment option Also known as the "Green Shoe" option, this is a stipulation in an underwriting agreement that allows the investment bank to purchase 15% more shares within thirty days.

Overweighted A condition in which a portfolio, for whatever reason, includes more of a class of securities than the relative market value alone would justify.

Overvalued When a security is trading at a price above its intrinsic value; the result is that the market price does not offer the investor an adequate amount of compensation for the risk that he is taking.

P

Par value The face value of the principal amount that a bond investor receives at maturity.

Payback period The time required for the added income from the convertible security relative to the stock to offset the conversion premium.

Peak The culmination of a bull market when prices stop rising and begin declining.

Peer group comparison A method of measuring portfolio performance by collecting the returns produced by a representative universe of investors over a specific period of time.

Performance presentation standards A comprehensive set of reporting guidelines created by the Association for Investment Management and Research (AIMR) (now the CFA Institute), in an effort to fulfill the call for uniform, accurate, and consistent performance reporting.

Policy statement A statement in which the investor specifies investment goals, constraints, and risk preferences.

Portfolio Any collection of assets held by an investor in one place at the same time.

Portfolio drawdown A performance measure that assesses a manager's ability to protect a portfolio from declines in value during an investment period.

Portfolio turnover The total dollar value of securities sold from a portfolio in a year divided by the average assets under management for the fund during the same period.

Preferred stock An equity investment that stipulates the dividend payment either as a coupon or a stated dollar amount. The firm's directors may withhold dividend payments.

Preliminary prospectus Also known as the "red herring," this is a prospectus that may be distributed to potential investors prior to the SEC's declaration that the registration statement is effective.

Premium A bond selling at a price above par value due to capital market conditions.

Present value of the growth opportunity (PVGO) The portion of a stock's intrinsic value that is attributable to the company's future growth opportunities.

Price The amount that an investor in the market currently must pay for a security.

Price continuity A feature of a liquid market in which there are small price changes from one transaction to the next due to the depth of the market.

Price-earnings (P/E) ratios The number by which expected earnings per share is multiplied to estimate a stock's value; also called the *earnings multiplier.*

Price momentum A portfolio strategy in which you acquire stocks that have enjoyed above-market stock price increases.

Price risk The component of interest rate risk due to the uncertainty of the market price of a bond caused by changes in market interest rates.

Price-weighted index An index calculated as an arithmetic mean of the current prices of the sampled securities.

Primary market The market in which newly issued securities are sold by their issuers, who receive the proceeds.

Principal The original value of the debt underlying a bond that is payable at maturity.

Principal-agent conflict The conflict that occurs when the management may not act in the best interest of shareholders.

Private equity An ownership interest in a company or collection of assets that is not publicly traded on an exchange or in the over-the-counter market.

Private placement A new issue sold directly to a small group of investors, usually institutions.

Prospectus A document that contains information about the business, a discussion of past performance and management's plans, financial information, how the company will use the proceeds from the offering, the dividend policy, management compensation, and critical accounting issues.

Protective put A trading strategy in which a put option is purchased as a supplement to a long position in an underlying asset or portfolio of assets; the most straightforward form of *portfolio insurance.*

Public bond A long-term, fixed-obligation debt security in a convenient, affordable denomination for sale to individuals and financial institutions.

Pure auction market A trading system in which interested buyers and sellers submit bid and ask prices for given stocks to a central location where the orders are matched by a broker who does not own the stock but acts as a facilitating agent. In the

current environment the facilitator can be a computer as well as an individual.

Pure cash-matched dedicated portfolio A conservative dedicated portfolio management technique aimed at developing a bond portfolio that will provide cash payments that exactly match the specified liability schedules.

Put-call parity The relationship that must exist in an efficient market between the prices for put and call options having the same underlying asset, exercise price, and expiration date.

Put option Options to sell a security (stock or bond) within a certain period at a specified price.

Q

Quadratic optimization A technique that relies on historical correlations in order to construct a portfolio that seeks to minimize tracking error with an index.

R

Range forward A trading strategy based on a variation of the putcall parity model where, for the same underlying asset but different exercise prices, a call option is purchased and a put option is sold (or vice versa).

Rate anticipation effect The difference in return because of changing the duration of the portfolio during a period as compared with the portfolio's long-term policy duration.

Real estate investment trusts (REITs) Investment funds that hold portfolios of real estate investments.

Real risk-free rate (RRFR) The basic interest rate with no accommodation for inflation or uncertainty; the pure time value of money.

Realized yield The expected compounded yield on a bond that is sold before it matures assuming the reinvestment of all cash flows at an explicit rate. Also called *horizon yield* for the yield realized during an investment horizon period.

Refunding issue Bonds that provide funds to prematurely retire another bond issue. These bonds can be either a junior or senior issue.

Registered bonds A bond for which ownership is registered with the issuer. The holder receives interest payments by check directly from the issuer.

Registration statement The disclosure document filed with the SEC that is required in order to take a company public; also known as Form S-1.

Reinvestment rate risk The risk that cash flows received prior to maturity will be reinvested at a rate lower than the original investment's yield to maturity.

Relative valuation A method of valuing a security by comparing its value to a comparable company or to use fundamental factors to compare it to an index.

Relative-strength (RS) ratios The ratio of a stock price or an industry index value to a market indicator series, indicating the stock's or the industry's performance relative to the overall market.

Required rate of return The return that compensates investors for their time, the expected rate of inflation, and the uncertainty of the return.

Resistance level A price at which a technician would expect a substantial increase in the supply of a stock to reverse a rising trend.

Revenue bond A bond that is serviced by the income generated from specific revenue-producing projects of the municipality such as toll roads or athletic stadiums.

Risk The uncertainty that an investment will earn its expected rate of return.

Risk averse The assumption about investors that they will choose the least risky alternative, all else being equal.

Risk factor model A model such as the CAPM or multifactor model used to estimate expected returns.

Risk premium (RP) The increase over the nominal risk-free rate that investors demand as compensation for an investment's uncertainty.

Risky asset An asset with uncertain future returns.

Road show A term used to refer to the process when after filing the S-1, the underwriter takes the issuing company's management to the large money centers around the country (and possibly around the world) to meet with potential investors.

Runs test A test of the weak-form efficient market hypothesis that checks for trends that persist longer in terms of positive or negative price changes than one would expect for a random series.

S

S-1 The disclosure document filed with the SEC that is required in order to take a company public; also known as the registration statement.

Sampling A technique for constructing a passive index portfolio in which the portfolio manager buys a representative sample of stocks that comprise the benchmark index.

Seasoned equity issues New equity shares offered by firms that already have stock outstanding.

Secondary markets The market in which outstanding securities are bought and sold by owners other than the issuers. Purpose is to provide liquidity for investors.

Sector rotation A sector is a group of similar industries; sector rotation involves the attempt to overweight sectors (such as technology or consumer staples) that you expect to perform well and to underweight sectors that you expect to perform poorly.

Secured (senior) bonds A bond backed by a legal claim on specified assets of the issuer.

Security market index An index created as a statistical measure of the performance of an entire market or segment of a market based on a sample of securities from the market or segment of a market.

Security market line (SML) The line that reflects the combination of risk and return of alternative investments. In CAPM, risk is measured by systematic risk (beta).

Sell-side A term that refers to firms that assist corporations in selling securities to raise capital; examples include investment banks and brokerage firms.

Semistrong-form EMH The belief that security prices fully reflect all publicly available information, including information from security transactions and company, economic, and political news.

Separation theorem The proposition that the investment decision, which involves investing in the market portfolio on the capital market line, is separate from the financing decision, which targets a specific point on the CML based on the investor's risk preference.

Serial obligation bond A bond issue that has a series of maturity dates. Typical for municipal bonds.

Settlement price The price determined by the exchange clearinghouse with which futures contract margin accounts are marked to market.

Sharpe measure A relative measure of a portfolio's benefit-to-risk ratio, calculated as its average return in excess of the risk-free rate divided by the standard deviation of portfolio returns.

Short hedge A short position in a forward or futures contract used to offset the price volatility of a long position in the underlying asset.

Short position The seller of a commodity or security or, for a forward contract, the counterparty who will be the eventual seller of the underlying asset.

Short sale The sale of borrowed securities with the intention of repurchasing them later at a lower price and earning the difference.

Signaling effect The interpretation that an outside party gives to the actions of an agent; for example, repurchasing shares may be seen as a signal that management believes shares are priced too low.

Sinking fund Bond provision that requires the issuer to redeem some or all of the bond systematically over the term of the bond rather than in full at maturity.

Small-firm effect A frequent empirical anomaly where risk-adjusted stock returns for companies with low market capitalization (i.e., share price multiplied by number of outstanding shares) are significantly larger than those generated by high market capitalization (large cap) firms.

Smart beta The approach to investing when adjustment of systematic risk exposures as market conditions fluctuate and makes factor investing an active portfolio strategy.

Soft dollars A form of compensation to a money manager generated when the manager commits the investor to paying higher brokerage fees in exchange for the manager receiving additional services (e.g., stock research) from the broker.

Sortino measure A relative measure of a portfolio's performance, calculated as its average return in excess of minimum acceptable return threshold, divided by its downside risk coefficient.

Special dividend A dividend payment in which the company is signaling that the payment is a one-time occurrence and will not repeat on a regular basis.

Speculative company A firm with a great degree of business and/ or financial risk, with commensurate high earnings potential.

Speculative stock A stock that appears to be highly overpriced compared to its intrinsic valuation.

Spending phase Phase in the investment life cycle during which individuals' earning years end as they retire. They pay for expenses with income from social security and returns from prior investments and invest to protect against inflation.

Spot yield The yield on a zero-coupon bond of a given maturity.

Spread   A trading strategy where long and short positions in two call (or two put) option contracts having the same underlying asset but different exercise prices or expiration dates are combined to create a customized return distribution.

Standard deviation   A measure of variability equal to the square root of the variance.

Stock index arbitrage   A trading strategy involving a long position in a stock portfolio and a short position in a stock index futures contract (or vice versa) designed to exploit a mispricing in the futures contract relative to the underlying index.

Stock pitch   A written or oral argument designed to provide background about a stock as well as the reasons why the stock should be purchased or shorted.

Straddle   A trading strategy requiring the simultaneous purchase of a call option and a put option having the same exercise price, underlying asset, and expiration date. Variations of this theme include *strips, straps, strangles,* and *chooser options.*

Strangle   An option combination which involves the simultaneous purchase or sale of a call and a put on the same underlying security with the same expiration date.

Strong-form EMH   The belief that security prices fully reflect all information from both public and private sources.

Style analysis   An attempt to explain the variability in the observed returns to a security portfolio in terms of the movements in the returns to a series of benchmark portfolios designed to capture the essence of a particular security characteristic such as size, value, and growth.

Style grid   A graph used to classify and display the investment style that best defines the nature of a security portfolio.

Subordinate (junior) debentures   Debentures that, in case of default, entitle holders to claims on the issuer's assets only after the claims of holders of senior debentures and mortgage bonds are satisfied.

Support level   A price at which a technician would expect a substantial increase in price and volume for a stock to reverse a declining trend that was due to profit taking.

Sustainable growth rate equation   The equation states growth equals return on equity multiplied by retention rate.

Swap spread   A measure of the risk premium for an interest rate swap, calculated as the difference between the agreement's fixed rate and the yield on a Treasury bond with the same maturity.

SWOT analysis   An examination of a firm's Strengths, Weaknesses, Opportunities, and Threats. This analysis helps an analyst evaluate a firm's strategies to exploit its competitive advantages or defend against its weaknesses.

Systematic risk   The variability of returns that is due to macroeconomic factors that affect all risky assets. Because it affects all risky assets, it cannot be eliminated by diversification.

T

Tactical asset allocation   An investment strategy that adjusts the investor's mix of stocks and bonds by increasing the allocation to the asset class that is relatively undervalued.

Tax cost ratio   Based on the ratio of the portfolio's tax-adjusted and pretax returns, the measure indicates the average annual

percentage of a taxable investor's assets that have been consumed by taxes over the measurement period.

Tax efficiency   The extent to which the investor controls the tax consequences of the security trades in a portfolio by balancing capital gains and capital losses.

Technical analysis   Estimation of future security price movements based on past price and volume movements.

Term bond   A bond that has a single maturity date.

Term structure of interest rates   The relationship between term to maturity and yield to maturity for a sample of comparable bonds at a given time. Popularly known as the *yield curve.*

Term to maturity   Specifies the date or the number of years before a bond matures or expires.

Time premium   The difference between an option's total market value and its intrinsic value.

Time-series analysis   An examination of a firm's performance data over a period of time.

Time-weighted return   The geometric average of (one plus) the *holding period yields* to an investment portfolio.

Total invoice price   The total amount that investor would be to acquire a bond between coupon dates; this includes the present value of the remaining cash flows ("flat" price) plus accrued interest.

Total return   A return objective in which the investor wants to increase the portfolio value to meet a future need by both capital gains and current income reinvestment.

Tracking error   The standard deviation of the difference in returns between an active investment portfolio and its benchmark portfolio; also called *tracking error volatility.*

Trailing multiples   A way of estimating the value of the equity or enterprise value based on the past year's earnings or EBITDA or other metric, as opposed to next year's earnings or EBITDA or other metric.

Transaction cost   The cost of executing a trade. Low costs characterize an operationally efficient market.

Treasury bill   A negotiable U.S. government security with a maturity of less than one year that pays no periodic interest but yields the difference between its par value and its discounted purchase price.

Treasury bond   A U.S. government security with a maturity of more than 10 years that pays interest periodically.

Treasury note   A U.S. government security with maturities of 1 to 10 years that pays interest periodically.

Treynor measure   A relative measure of a portfolio's performance calculated as its average return in excess of the risk-free rate divided by its beta coefficient.

Trough   The culmination of a bear market at which prices stop declining and begin rising.

12b-1 plan   A fee charged by some funds, named after the SEC rule that permits it. Such fees pay for distribution costs, such as advertising, or for brokers' commissions. The fund's prospectus details any 12b-1 charges that apply.

U

Underpricing   The difference between the IPO price and the closing price at the end of the first day of trading, assuming that the stock closed higher than the IPO price.

Undervalued   When a security is trading at a price below its intrinsic value; the result is that the market price offers the investor an amount of compensation that is greater than required for the risk that he is taking.

Underweighted   A condition in which a portfolio, for whatever reason, includes less of a class of securities than the relative market value alone would justify.

Underwriting spread   Compensation received by the underwriting in an IPO that is equal to the price per share that new investors pay for stock minus the amount per share that the issuing company receives; also known as the gross spread.

Unsecured bonds (debentures)   Bonds that promise payments of interest and principal but pledge no specific assets. Holders have first claim on the issuer's income and unpledged assets. Also known as *debentures*.

Unsystematic risk   Risk that is unique to an asset, derived from its particular characteristics. It can be eliminated in a diversified portfolio.

Unweighted index   An indicator series affected equally by the performance of each security in the sample regardless of price or market value. Also referred to as an *equal-weighted series*.

Unwind   The negotiated termination of a forward or futures position before contract maturity.

V

Valuation   The process by which investors determine whether a stock is fairly priced, overpriced, or underpriced.

Value stocks   Stocks that appear to be undervalued for reasons besides earnings growth potential. These stocks are usually identified based on high dividend yields, low *P/E* ratios, or low price-to-book ratios.

Value-weighted index   An index calculated as the total market value of the securities in the sample. Market value is equal to the number of shares or bonds outstanding times the market price of the security.

Variable-rate notes   A debt security for which the interest rate changes to follow some specified short-term rate, for example, the T-bill rate; see *Floating rate note*.

Variance   A measure of variability equal to the sum of the squares of a return's deviation from the mean, divided by the total number of returns.

Volatility Index (VIX)   A measure of investor expectations of near-term volatility in the stock market calculated as a weighted average of the implied volatilities estimated from Standard and Poor's 500 option contracts.

W

Warrant   An instrument that allows the holder to purchase a specified number of shares of the firm's common stock from the firm at a specified price for a given period of time.

Weak-form EMH   The belief that security prices fully reflect all security market information.

Winner's curse   The idea that anyone who wins an auction must have bid too much (greater than the intrinsic value).

Y

Yankee bond   Bonds sold in the United States and denominated in U.S. dollars but issued by a foreign firm or government.

Yield   The promised rate of return on an investment under certain assumptions.

Yield spread   The difference between the promised yields of alternative bond issues or market segments at a given time relative to yields on Treasury issues of equal maturity.

Yield to call (YTC)   The return on a bond that is called by the issuer before the maturity date.

Yield to worst   Given a bond with multiple potential maturity dates and prices due to embedded call options, the practice is to calculate a yield to maturity for each of the call dates and prices and select the lowest yield (the most conservative possible yield) as yield to worst.

Z

Zero-coupon bond   A bond that pays its par value at maturity but no periodic interest payments. Its yield is determined by the difference between its par value and its discounted purchase price. Also called *original issue discount (OID) bonds*.

Index